Fifth Canadian Edition

Management
Accounting

Charles T. Horngren
Stanford University

Gary L. Sundem
University of Washington—
Seattle

William O. Stratton
Pepperdine University

Howard D. Teall
Late Professor, Wilfrid Laurier
University

George A. Gekas
Ryerson University

PEARSON
Prentice
Hall

Toronto

To Joan, Chelsea, Erik, Marissa, Liz, Garth, Jens, Reed, Grant, Norma, Gina, Adam, Nisha, and Tiana
—Charles T. Horngren, Gary L. Sundem, William O. Stratton

To my past, present, and future students. Also, to Andrew, Michael, and Krystalia, the special people in my life who keep me going and make everything possible.
—George A. Gekas

Library and Archives Canada Cataloguing in Publication

Management accounting/Charles T. Horngren ... [et al.].—5th Canadian ed.
First Canadian ed. by Charles T. Horngren, Gary L. Sundem, Howard D. Teall with Frank H. Selto.
Includes index.

ISBN 0-13-192268-8

1. Managerial accounting—Textbooks. I. Horngren, Charles T., 1926–
HF5657.4.M349 2007   658.15'11   C2005-906491-9

Vice President, Editorial Director: Michael J. Young
Editor-in-Chief: Gary Bennett
Executive Marketing Manager: Cas Shields
Executive Editor: Samantha Scully
Developmental Editor: Pamela Voves
Production Editor: Marisa D'Andrea
Copy Editor: Jennifer Therriault
Proofreader: Lu Cormier
Production Coordinator: Andrea Falkenberg
Indexer: Belle Wong
Page Layout: Gerry Dunn
Art Director: Julia Hall
Interior and Cover Design: David Cheung
Cover Image: Getty Images/Ryan McVay

1 2 3 4 5   11 10 09 08 07

Printed and bound in the United States.

Charles T. Horngren is the Edmund W. Littlefield Professor of Accounting at Stanford University. A graduate of Marquette University, he received his MBA from Harvard and his PhD from the University of Chicago. He is also the recipient of honorary doctorates from Marquette as well as De Paul University.

A Certified Public Accountant, Horngren has served on the Accounting Principles Board, the Financial Accounting Standards Board Advisory Council, the Council of the American Institute of Certified Public Accountants, and as a trustee of the Financial Accounting Foundation.

A member of the American Accounting Association, Horngren has been its President and its Director of Research. He received the Outstanding Accounting Educator Award in 1973. The California Certified Public Accountants Foundation gave Horngren its Faculty Excellence Award in 1975 and its Distinguished Professor Award in 1983. In 1985, the AICPA presented its first Outstanding Accounting Educator to Horngren. In 1990, he was elected to the Accounting Hall of Fame.

Professor Horngren is also a member of the Institute of Management Accountants. He is a member of its Board of Regents, which administers the CMA examinations.

Horngren is the co-author of four other books published by Pearson Education: *Cost Accounting: A Managerial Emphasis*, Eleventh Edition, 2003 (with Srikant Datar and George Foster); *Introduction to Financial Accounting*, Eighth Edition, 2002 (with Gary L. Sundem and John A. Elliott); *Accounting*, Sixth Edition, 2005 (with Walter T. Harrison, Jr. and Linda Smith Bamber), and *Financial Accounting*, Fifth Edition, 2004 (also with Harrison). In addition, he is the Consulting Editor for the Prentice Hall Series in Accounting.

Gary L. Sundem is the Julius A. Roller Professor of Accounting at the University of Washington, Seattle. He received his BA degree from Carleton College and his MBA and PhD degrees from Stanford University.

Professor Sundem was the 1992–93 President of the American Accounting Association. He had served as Editor of *The Accounting Review*, 1982–86.

A member of the Institute of Management Accountants, Sundem is past president of the Seattle chapter. He has served on IMA's national Board of Directors, the Committee on Academic Relations, and the Research Committee.

Professor Sundem has numerous publications in accounting and finance journals, including *Issues in Accounting Education, The Accounting Review, Journal of Accounting Research*, and *The Journal of Finance*. He received an award for the most notable contribution to accounting literature in 1978; that same year he was selected Outstanding Accounting Educator by the Washington Society of CPAs. He has made more than 200 presentations at universities in the United States and abroad.

William O. Stratton is Professor of Accounting at Pepperdine University. He received BS degrees from Florida State University and Pennsylvania State University, his MBA from Boston University, and his PhD from the Claremont Graduate University.

A Certified Management Accountant, Stratton has lectured extensively at management accounting conferences in North America, South America, and Europe. He has developed and delivered workshops on activity-based management to manufacturing and service organizations throughout the United States and South America. In 1993, Professor Stratton was awarded the Boeing Competition prize for classroom innovation.

Stratton has numerous publications in accounting and international business journals, including *Management Accounting, Decision Sciences, IIE Transaction*, and *Synergie*.

Howard D. Teall (1954–2004) was a Professor in the School of Business and Economics at Wilfrid Laurier University, where he previously held the positions of Acting Dean, Associate Dean of Business, and Accounting Area Head. He received HBA, MBA, and PhD degrees from the Ivey School of Business Administration at the University of Western Ontario. He obtained a CA designation while employed with Price Waterhouse and was awarded an FCA by the Institute of Chartered Accountants of Ontario.

Previous university positions were held at the Graduate School of Business, Marseille, France; the Helsinki School of Economics and Business Administration; INSEAD (The European Institute of Business Administration); the International University of Japan; and the University of Western Ontario.

Professor Teall was also a consultant and provided management training programs for IBM Canada Ltd., Equifax Canada, Rockwell Automation Canada Ltd., Tiger Brand Knitting Factory Co., Woodbridge Limited, Lear Corporation Canada Ltd., Centra Gas Corporation, Challenger Motor Freight Inc., Ontario Hydro, B.F. Goodrich Canada Limited, Petro-Canada, General Motors of Canada Limited, General Motors Corporation, the Federal Business Development Bank, the Canadian Department of Industry, Science and Technology Canada, The Liquor Control Board of Ontario, The Banff Centre for Management, Polysar Rubber Corporation, and Royal Bank of Trinidad and Tobago, as well as professional qualification programs for Pricewaterhouse-Coopers, Deloitte & Touche, the Chartered Accountants Students' Association of Ontario, the Institute of Chartered Accountants of Ontario, the Atlantic Provinces Association of Chartered Accountants, and CMA Canada.

Howard taught many accounting students throughout the years and was fondly known as the "Seinfeld of accounting" by his students.

George A. Gekas is an Associate Professor of Management Accounting at the School of Business Management of Ryerson University in Toronto. Prior to his appointment to Ryerson, Dr. Gekas taught for more than 20 years at several different universities in Canada, the United States, and Europe. His academic career includes appointments with the University College of Cape Breton, Algoma University College, University of Maryland, American College of Greece (Deree), and the University of Western Ontario.

Dr. Gekas holds several degrees and designations. He received his first honours BA degree from the Athens University of Economics in Greece. He has also earned a Master in Economics from Lakehead University, honours Bachelor of Commerce and MBA degrees from the University of Windsor in Canada, and a PhD from Hull University in England. Professor Gekas is a CMA and an active member of the Society of Management Accountants where he held a number of important positions. Recently, he was awarded the prestigious FCMA designation.

Dr. Gekas' active research program includes several research projects, grants, and a number of articles on a wide variety of business topics. He has also authored many teaching aids and manuals. His expertise covers the entire financial management spectrum with a special emphasis on management accounting.

In terms of civic duty and social service, he has been involved in a number of organizations in a variety of capacities and is fully immersed in the issues facing publicly funded organizations, including universities. Dr. Gekas has a genuine interest in issues of community and social development.

TESTIMONIALS

In light of the need for accuracy in accounting textbooks, all solutions have been checked.

As requested, we have read the proof copy of the text, consisting of Chapters 1 to 15, and have checked the arithmetic and logic in all of the worked examples and exhibits in that proof, as well as ensured that references to those examples and exhibits within the text were accurate.

Ian Farmer, CA
Michelle Hodgson, CGA

Brief Contents

Contents

2   COST BEHAVIOUR AND COST-VOLUME RELATIONSHIPS   41

3   MEASUREMENT OF COST BEHAVIOUR   88

4   COST MANAGEMENT SYSTEMS   135

PART TWO   PRODUCT COSTING

5   COST ALLOCATION AND ACTIVITY-BASED COSTING SYSTEMS   184

6   JOB-ORDER COSTING AND ACCOUNTING FOR OVERHEAD   256

9 RELEVANT INFORMATION AND DECISION MAKING: PRODUCTION DECISIONS 409

PART FIVE FINANCIAL STATEMENT ANALYSIS

Preface

Managers need to understand how their decisions affect costs. Knowledge of management accounting is an essential tool that enhances both a manager's and an accountant's ability to make effective decisions. Managers of all organizations—manufacturing, wholesale, service, e-commerce, not-for-profit, government—make decisions in an increasingly complex and changing environment. Information is used by managers to assess the relative merits of alternative courses of action for any given decision. Management accounting generates and uses some of this information.

Management Accounting, Fifth Canadian Edition, describes both theory and common practices to help students understand how to produce information that is useful in daily decision making. Because understanding concepts is more important than memorizing techniques, students are encouraged to think about, evaluate, and apply the various practices companies use.

Management Accounting deals with the wholesale, retail, service, not-for-profit, and manufacturing business sectors. It focuses on planning and control, and not on product or service costing. More emphasis is placed on the role of management rather than on accounting for product costing and income determination.

Our Philosophy

The main philosophy behind *Management Accounting*, Fifth Canadian Edition, is to introduce management accounting and strategic management concepts as effectively as possible. Where appropriate, we address them to build on acquired knowledge and provide students with further understanding. In each stage of the process, we strive to provide real company examples to enhance learning and balance concepts and practice. Well-known companies appear throughout the text material so that students can better understand management accounting concepts in a real company context.

Just as management accounting builds on financial accounting, the concepts of management accounting build on one another. Students often have an easier time relating how financial accounting topics connect for eventual income determination; it is a greater challenge to interrelate management accounting topics in order to achieve better decision making. Our objectives are to relate relevant subject matter and better present the relationship among certain management accounting concepts that form the body of management accounting knowledge.

Text Organization

Based on valuable feedback from students and faculty, we have restructured the organization of chapters for *Management Accounting*, Fifth Canadian Edition.

Part One, Management Accounting, Focus on Information and Cost Measuring (Chapters 1–4), describes how managers make decisions. The relationship between management accounting and other business fields is discussed to help students understand the subject within the context of the field of management education. Part One also deals with the generation of management accounting information and covers various cost concepts, classifications, and cost systems that managers use to produce information. A common objective of this information is to indicate the effect of managerial decisions on the organization's profits and goals.

Part Two, Product Costing (Chapters 5–7), describes product costing systems. Special emphasis is given to job-order costing, process costing, activity-based costing, and cost allocation.

Part Three, Focus on Decision Making (Chapters 8–10), centres on decision making that maximizes shareholder value. It considers the typical marketing and production decisions faced by modern organizations. It fully examines such topics as the impact of pricing decisions and alternative courses of action, adding or deleting products or departments, deciding whether to make or buy, and deciding whether to sell or process further. In addition, this part considers capital budget decisions that have long-term strategic implications on a firm and that require significant capital investments.

Part Four, Management Accounting for Planning and Control (Chapters 11–14), recognizes that goal congruence, as desirable as it might be, does not always exist in organizations. Conflict often exists among managers and also between management and shareholders. To assess the performance of an organization and its managers, planning and control systems are needed to establish plans and goals and to reward successful performance.

Part Five, Financial Statement Analysis (Chapter 15), considers the use of financial information reported to external users. This part does not deal with the preparation of this information, but rather its use by such decision makers as analysts, creditors, and investors. This part can be beneficial to students who may need a financial accounting review. It may also be specially suited to MBA courses where students take a term course in management accounting.

This book has been used successfully as either an introductory or advanced course in management accounting at undergraduate, graduate, and MBA levels. Advanced courses that are case oriented may use the Managerial Decision Cases as assigned material. Given its focus on decision making, this book is also appropriate for executive development programs.

Features of the Fifth Canadian Edition

Some of the features of the fourth edition have been updated, and a number of new elements have been added to this edition:

- The definitions of key terms have been reworked and updated to reflect contemporary terminology.
- A new section called "Variable Costing, Segmented Reporting, and Performance Evaluation" has been added to Chapter 4.
- The fourth edition's Chapters 10 and 11 on capital budgeting decisions

have been merged into a new Chapter 10, making this a 15-chapter text-book that is better suited for a one-term undergraduate course or an MBA course.

- **Making Managerial Decisions** boxes have been added throughout the chapters. They enable students to take what they have learned, apply the material to a real business situation, and then plot a course of action.
- **Excel Application Exercises** appear near the end of each chapter. They help students to solve problems using Microsoft Excel.
- A **Glossary** at the end of the text will aid students in their review of key terms used throughout the text.

The fifth edition retains and updates the elements of the previous edition:

- **Strategic Insights and Company Practices** boxes (previously called "Company Strategies") provide insights into operations at well-known corporations.
- **Highlights to Remember** emphasize the main points covered in each chapter.
- **Questions** address conceptual and discussion-oriented material and are generally used to engage the student to understand the issues in the context of managerial decisions.

- **Problems** involve assignments that are primarily quantitative and have directed requirements. Spreadsheets are available for problems flagged with a spreadsheet logo (see the Companion Website, **www.pearsoned.ca/horngren**, for further details).

- **Managerial Decision Cases** (previously called "Cases") require critical-thinking skills. They may be open-ended or may require specific answers. In both instances, they provide students with the opportunity to apply concepts in practical situations. Many of these cases are provided by such organizations as the Certified Management Accountants of Canada (CMA), the Institute of Chartered Accountants of Ontario (CICA), and the Certified General Accountants of Canada (CGA), and are identified by a filefolder logo in the margin.
- **Collaborative Learning Exercises** encourage team building and group learning skills.

Alternative Ways of Using This Book

Instructors are not unanimous on the subject of appropriate topic sequence in a management accounting course. Criticisms of any sequence in a management accounting textbook are inevitable. Consequently, this book provides a **modular approach** that permits skipping back and forth with minimal inconvenience. Our rationale is to provide a loosely constrained sequence to ease diverse approaches to teaching. Content is of primary importance; sequence is secondary.

As the authors, we prefer to assign the chapters in the sequence provided in the book. But you need not feel constrained by this sequence. We have used a variety of sequences, depending on the readers' backgrounds. Teaching is highly personal and is heavily influenced by the backgrounds and interests of assorted students in various settings. To satisfy this audience, a book must be a pliable tool, not a straitjacket.

Part One, "Management Accounting, Focus on Information and Cost Measuring," provides a bedrock introduction, so we assign it in its entirety. Part

Two, "Product Costing," is introduced in the first half of the text (as is done in most management accounting texts). Part Three, "Focus on Decision Making," can be covered at any stage during the course. If there is time in the course for students to become more familiar with budgeting and standard costing, Chapters 10 and 11 can be assigned immediately after Chapter 5. Furthermore, there is a logical appeal to studying capital budgeting (Chapter 10) immediately after Part Four's chapters on planning and control (Chapters 11 through 14). Capital budgeting is often covered in finance courses, but in order to reinforce capital budgeting knowledge, we believe in covering it as well.

Chapter 15 introduces students to the fundamentals of financial statement analysis. This chapter covers basic statement analysis in capsule form with heavy emphasis on the interpretation of financial statements. Little attention is paid to the accumulation of the information included in the financial statements.

Chapter 15 may be skipped entirely or may be used in different ways:

1. To quickly review financial statement analysis for students who already have some background in this area.
2. To teach the fundamentals of financial statement analysis to students with no prior background.
3. To demonstrate how to interpret financial statements for students who have no accounting background but where the main emphasis is on management rather than financial accounting.

Supplementary Material

The following supplements have been carefully prepared to aid instructors and students in using this edition:

Instructor's Resource CD-ROM (0-13-174552-2): This resource CD includes the following instructor supplements:

- **Instructor's Solutions Manual**—includes solutions to all questions, problems, and cases in the text. All solutions were technically reviewed by a professional accountant.
- **Instructor's Resource Manual**—provides insightful and useful tips on how to best manage course content when using this text in class. Chapter-by-chapter explanations and pedagogical philosophies are clearly delineated and oriented to greatly aid the teaching process.
- **PowerPoints**—highlight key points and examples from the text, providing a framework for in-class or online lectures.
- **TestGen**—a computerized testbank consisting of more than 1,600 questions. Each question is accompanied by the correct answer, page reference in the textbook, learning objective, and difficulty level. TestGen is a testing software that enables instructors to view and edit existing questions, add questions, generate tests, and distribute the tests in a variety of formats. Powerful search and sort functions make it easy to locate questions and arrange them in any order desired. TestGen also enables instructors to administer tests on a local area network, have the tests graded electronically, and have the results prepared in electronic or printed reports. TestGen is compatible with Windows and Macintosh operating systems, and can be downloaded from the TestGen website located at www.pearsoned.com/testgen. Contact your local sales representative for details and access.

Companion Website (at **www.pearsoned.ca/horngren**): This site includes a comprehensive online study guide that presents students with numerous review exercises and research tools. There is a detailed review of key concepts for every chapter and practice tests with true/false and multiple-choice questions, completion exercises, and accounting problems. Students obtain instant feedback for questions and exercises, and they may view full solutions to problems. A page reference to the text is supplied with every answer. The Companion Website also provides Excel templates for all problems flagged in the text with the spreadsheet disk icon, as well as a syllabus builder for instructors.

Acknowledgments

We have received assistance from many people who have contributed to this book, and we are grateful for the assistance and support provided by Ryerson University.

Our appreciation is also extended to the Canadian Institute of Chartered Accountants (CICA), the Institute of Chartered Accountants of Ontario (ICAO), the Society of Management Accountants of Canada (SMAC), the Certified General Accountants Association of Canada (CGAC), and to the other sources as indicated for their generous permission to use or adapt problems from their publications.

We would like to thank the following reviewers of this text for their insights and suggestions:

Tashia Batstone, Memorial University of Newfoundland
Philip Beaulieu, University of Calgary
Robert J. Collier, University of Ottawa
K. Suzanne Coombs, Kwantlen University College
Patricia Corkum, Acadia University
Dr. Hemantha Herath, Brock University
Mary Oxner, St. Francis Xavier University
Pamela Quon, Athabasca University
Doug Ringrose, Grant MacEwan College

Special thanks are due to Bruce A. La Rochelle, University of Ottawa, for his thorough examination of the manuscript and his research and contributions to the material throughout.

Many people at Pearson Education Canada also earn our deepest thanks for their thoughtful contributions. Special thanks go to Pamela Voves, Senior Developmental Editor; Meaghan Eley, Developmental Editor; Gary Bennett, Editor-in-Chief; Gilaine Waterbury, Sales Representative; Samantha Scully, Executive Editor; Marisa D'Andrea, Production Editor; Jennifer Therriault, Copyeditor; Gerry Dunn, Compositor; Patricia Ciardullo and Andrea Falkenberg, Production Coordinators; and Ian Farmer and Michelle Hodgson, Technical Reviewers.

A Great Way to Learn and Instruct Online

The Pearson Education Canada Companion Website is easy to navigate and is organized to correspond to the chapters in this textbook. Whether you are a student in the classroom or a distance learner you will discover helpful resources for in-depth study and research that empower you in your quest for greater knowledge and maximize your potential for success in the course.

[www.pearsoned.ca/horngren]

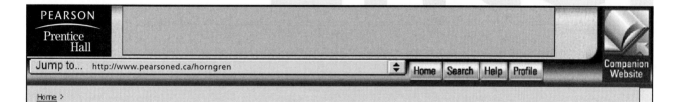

PEARSON
Prentice
Hall

Jump to...   http://www.pearsoned.ca/horngren   [▲▼]   Home | Search | Help | Profile

Companion
Website

Home >

Companion Website

Management Accounting, Fifth Canadian Edition, by Horngren, Sundem, Stratton, Teall, and Gekas

Student Resources

The modules in this section provide students with tools for learning course material. These modules include:

- Chapter Objectives
- Review of Key Concepts
- Quizzes (Multiple-Choice, True/False, Completion, and Essay Questions)
- Excel Spreadsheets
- Glossary

In the quiz modules, students can send answers to the grader and receive instant feedback on their progress through the Results Reporter. Coaching comments and references to the textbook may be available to ensure that students take advantage of all available resources to enhance their learning experience.

Instructor Resources

A link to this book on the Pearson Education Canada online catalogue (vig.pearsoned.ca) provides instructors with these additional teaching tools: downloadable PowerPoint Presentations, Instructor's Resource Manual, Instructor's Solutions Manual, and TestGen test bank. To get a password, simply contact your Pearson Education Canada Representative or call Faculty Sales and Services at 1-800-850-5813.

Introduction to Managerial Accounting

LEARNING OBJECTIVES

After studying this chapter, you will be able to

1. Describe the role of management accounting in today's organizations and explain the role of the management accountant.

2. Understand that management accounting also applies to service and not-for-profit organizations.

3. Explain the role of management accountants in an organization's value-chain functions.

4. Identify the staff authority and role of the accounting department in the organization.

5. Describe the two major philosophies of this book: cost-benefit and behavioural implications.

6. Identify the major similarities and differences between management accounting and financial accounting.

7. Identify the most important areas of ethical conduct by management accountants.

MANAGEMENT ACCOUNTING FOR MANAGERS

Management accounting exists because managers require financial and other information to make decisions; therefore, *management accounting is user-driven not data-driven*. The subject of management accounting goes far beyond the issues of generating and disseminating facts and, while these tasks may be part of management accounting, they are not the essence of management accounting. There is a subtle but important difference between the word "data" and the word "information." Information is data that have been used to generate records of facts that may be used in a future decision. Once the data have been used they become information. For example, keeping records on business tax rates of European countries produces data. Using this data to decide in what European country to establish a branch operation is information. It is important for students of management accounting to appreciate the fact that an integral part of the subject deals with information systems and not data systems. In other words, *accounting information systems are the data used (means) to reach better decisions (ends)*.

The management accounting information system provides information to numerous user groups for a variety of purposes. Some of these user groups are external to the organization. The focus of management accounting is on the needs of users within the organization. For example, information is required for technical and operating decisions such as those concerning quality control and scheduling. Also, managers in an organization's human resources department require pay rate information to make decisions during labour negotiations with employee groups. The generation of financial statements for external investors and creditors is another primary requirement of the information system. Some have argued that meeting external reporting needs has inappropriately become the dominant use of accounting information systems. Finally, the management accounting information system must also provide the information required for product costing, pricing, and evaluation of segment profitability. In summary, management accounting does not exist to generate data, but it exists because managers require information for decisions.

In any organization, whether it is profit-oriented, not-for-profit, manufacturing, service, or government, numerous decisions are made each day. Because of the variety of decisions made in any one day, management accounting is diverse, dealing with a number of sometimes loosely related topics. This diversity makes it more difficult for students to organize the subject of management accounting than the subject of financial accounting that has the single objective to produce accurate financial statements. To help make this diversity comprehensive, the study of management accounting has been organized into frameworks—two of which are presented here.

The first framework focuses on the types of decisions that must be made and categorizes those decisions into "operational control," "management control," and "strategic planning."[1] Operational control decisions ensure that specific tasks are carried out effectively and efficiently. Management control decisions make sure that the resources are used effectively and efficiently by the managers of the organization. Strategic planning decisions focus on the objectives of the organization and the manner in which resources are acquired and employed.

---

[1] R.N. Anthony, *Planning and Control Systems: A Framework for Analysis*, Boston: Graduate School of Business Administration, Harvard University, 1965.

The second framework focuses on the characteristics of decisions.[2] It places decisions on a continuum between structured and unstructured.

Structured decisions are those that are routine and normal, where the information requirements and decision processes are relatively well understood. Unstructured decisions are unique and uncommon and thus the information and decision processes need to be developed for that decision. Exhibit 1-1 provides examples of decisions that have been classified within the two, in this case, complementary frameworks.

EXHIBIT 1-1		OPERATIONAL CONTROL	MANAGEMENT CONTROL	STRATEGIC PLANNING
Frameworks for Management Accounting[3]	**Structured**	Accounts receivable	Budget analysis	Tanker fleet mix
		Order entry	Short-term forecasting	Warehouse and factory location
		Inventory reordering	Engineered costs	
		Inventory control	Variance analysis	Mergers and acquisitions
	Semi-Structured	Production scheduling	Overall budget	Capital acquisition analysis
		Bond trading	Budget preparation	New product planning
		Cash management		
	Unstructured	PERT COST systems	Sales and production	R and D planning

A MANAGEMENT DECISION PROCESS

The two management accounting frameworks provide an initial basis for students to organize the subject of management accounting. These two frameworks also highlight another important point: to practise management accounting it is necessary to make decisions and to understand the role of information in the decision-making process and the decisions that can be made with the information provided. Making good decisions requires a process that is logical and rational. The decision process depicted in Exhibit 1-2 is sufficiently generic to be useful in most situations, but is not the only effective decision process.

As Exhibit 1-2 shows, the first step is to clearly identify the problem or issue. Then, ask the following two questions: What information do I need to develop a solution to the problem? What analysis will provide the information that I require?

The answers to these questions will result in a list of possible analyses that will often address both quantitative and qualitative issues (second step). It is important not to limit your analysis to only the numerical aspects of the problem in order to avoid missing important qualitative dimensions of the issue. After conducting the necessary analysis, the third step is to identify alternative solutions to

---

[2] H.A. Simon, *The New Science of Management Decision,* New York: Harper and Row, 1960.
[3] Reprinted from "A Framework for Management Information Systems," by G.A. Garry and M.S. Scott Morton, *Sloan Management Review,* Fall, 1970, p. 62. Copyright 1993 by the Sloan Management Review Association. All Rights Reserved.

EXHIBIT 1-2

A Management
Decision Process

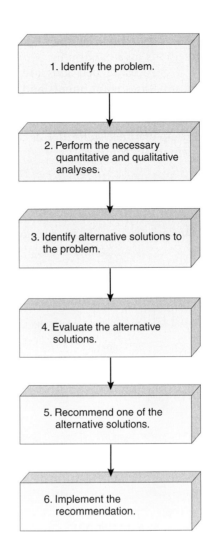

1. Identify the problem.

2. Perform the necessary quantitative and qualitative analyses.

3. Identify alternative solutions to the problem.

4. Evaluate the alternative solutions.

5. Recommend one of the alternative solutions.

6. Implement the recommendation.

the problem. Alternative solutions must exist because if there were only one correct solution, a decision was not required in the first place. Each alternative solution must have the potential to resolve the identified problem. The fourth step is to analyze each alternative solution in terms of its advantages/disadvantages, costs/benefits, and pros/cons. After a thorough analysis of the possible courses, a decision can be recommended (fifth step). The rationale for the decision should focus on its advantages and should explain why the disadvantages are not significant or describe how they can be managed. The implementation of the recommendation (final step) may be the most difficult step as it may depend on the ability of the manager to effectively change the way an organization operates.

Managers must adopt a decision process that is both flexible and effective. The decision process must be flexible because it has to adapt to the numerous situations that a manager faces and effective because it has to enable the manager to reach a decision.

THE MANAGEMENT ACCOUNTANT'S ROLE

Management Accounting.
The process of identifying, measuring, accumulating, analyzing, preparing, interpreting, and communicating information that helps managers fulfill organizational objectives.

Management accounting can be described as the process of identification, measurement, accumulation, analysis, preparation, interpretation, and communication of information that assists managers in making decisions. The management accountant ensures that this process is effective. The management accountant's role involves scorekeeping, attention-directing, and problem-solving as described in Exhibit 1-3. While descriptions of the tasks do overlap or merge, it is necessary to recognize the importance of planning and controlling in the management accountant's role.

The Nature of Planning and Controlling

Exhibit 1-4 demonstrates the division of management accounting into the two processes of planning and controlling.

Planning (the top box in Exhibit 1-4) means setting objectives and outlining the means for their attainment. Planning provides the answers to three questions: What is desired? When and how is it to be accomplished? How is success to be evaluated? Controlling (the two boxes labelled "Action" and "Evaluation") entails implementing plans and using feedback to attain objectives. The feedback loop is the central facet of control, and timely, systematic measurement is the chief means of providing useful feedback. Planning and controlling are so intertwined that it is difficult to separate them; yet at times it is useful to concentrate on one or the other.

EXHIBIT 1-3

Management Accountant's Role

Problem-solving.
Aspect of accounting that quantifies the likely results of possible courses of action and often recommends the best course of action to follow.

Attention-directing.
Reporting and interpreting of information that helps managers focus on operating problems, imperfections, inefficiencies, and opportunities.

Scorekeeping.
The accumulation and classification of data.

1. **Problem-solving.** This aspect of accounting involves the concise quantification of the relative merits of possible courses of action, often with recommendations as to the best procedure. Problem-solving is commonly associated with nonrecurring decisions—situations that require special accounting analyses or reports.

2. **Attention-directing.** The reporting and interpreting of information that helps managers focus on operating problems, imperfections, inefficiencies, and opportunities. This aspect of accounting helps managers to concentrate on important aspects of operations promptly enough for effective action. Attention-directing is commonly associated with current planning and control and with the analysis and investigation of recurring routine internal accounting reports.

3. **Scorekeeping.** The accumulation of information. This aspect of accounting enables both internal and external parties to evaluate organizational performance and position.

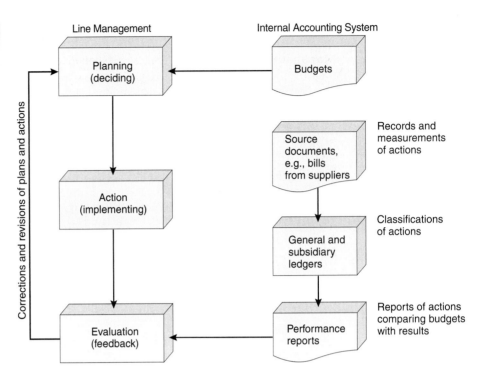

EXHIBIT 1-4

Management
Accounting for
Planning and Control

Line Management

Planning (deciding) → Action (implementing) → Evaluation (feedback)

Corrections and revisions of plans and actions

Internal Accounting System

Budgets

Source documents, e.g., bills from suppliers — Records and measurements of actions

General and subsidiary ledgers — Classifications of actions

Performance reports — Reports of actions comparing budgets with results

Management by Exception

Budget. A quantitative expression of a plan of action as an aid to coordinating and implementing the plan.

Performance Reports. Feedback provided by comparing results with plans and by highlighting variances.

Management by Exception. Concentrating on areas that deserve attention and ignoring areas that are presumed to be running smoothly.

The right side of Exhibit 1-4 shows that accounting formalizes plans by expressing them in the language of figures as budgets. A **budget** quantitatively expresses a plan of action and aids the coordination and implementation of that plan.

Accounting formalizes control as **performance reports** (the last box in Exhibit 1-4), which provide feedback by comparing results with plans and by highlighting variances (i.e., deviations from plans). The accounting system records, measures, and classifies actions in order to produce performance reports.

Exhibit 1-5 shows a simple performance report form for a law firm. Such reports spur investigation of exceptions—when actual amounts differ significantly from budgeted amounts. Operations are then brought into conformity with the plans, or the plans are revised. This is an example of management by exception. **Management by exception** is the practice of concentrating on areas that deviate from the plan and ignoring areas that are presumed to be running smoothly. Management should not ordinarily be concerned with results that conform closely to plans. However, well-conceived plans should incorporate enough discretion or flexibility so that the manager feels free to pursue any unforeseen opportunities. In other words, the definition of control does not mean that managers should blindly cling to a pre-existing plan when unfolding events call for actions that were not specifically authorized in the original plan.

EXHIBIT 1-5

Performance Report

	BUDGETED AMOUNTS	ACTUAL AMOUNTS	DEVIATIONS OR VARIANCES	EXPLANATION
Revenue from fees	xxx	xxx	xx	—
Various expenses	xxx	xxx	xx	—
Net income	xxx	xxx	xx	—

Illustration of the Budget and the Performance Report

An assembly department constructs microwave ovens. After the assembly and installation of all parts, each unit is inspected before being transferred to the painting department. In light of the present sales forecast, a production schedule of 4,000 0.8-cubic-foot and 6,000 1-cubic-foot microwave ovens is planned for the coming month. The Assembly Department Budget in Exhibit 1-6 shows cost classifications.

The operating plan, in the form of a department budget for the coming month, is prepared in meetings attended by the department manager, the manager's supervisor, and an accountant. Each of the costs subject to the manager's control is scrutinized. Its average amount for the past few months is often used as a guide, especially if past performance has been reasonably efficient. However, the budget is a *forecast* of costs. Each cost is projected in light of trends, price changes, alterations in product mix, specifications, labour methods, and changes in production volume from month to month. The budget is then formulated, and it becomes the manager's target for the month.

As actual factory costs are incurred during the month, the accounting system collects them and classifies them by department. At the end of the month (or perhaps weekly, or even daily for such key items as materials or assembly labour), the accounting department prepares an Assembly Department Performance Report (Exhibit 1-7). In practice, this report may be very detailed and contain explanations of variances from the budget.

Department heads and their superiors use this report to help appraise performance. The spotlight is cast on the **variance**—the deviations from the budget. When managers investigate these variances, they may discover better

Variance. Deviations from plans.

EXHIBIT 1-6

Assembly Department
Budget for the Month
Ended March 31, 2007

Material (detailed by type: metal stampings, plastic, etc.)	$ 68,000
Assembly labour (detailed by job classification, number of workers, etc.)	43,000
Other labour (managers, inspectors)	12,000
Utilities, maintenance, etc.	7,500
Supplies (small tools, lubricants, etc.)	2,500
Total	$133,000

EXHIBIT 1-7

Assembly Department
Performance Report for
the Month Ended
March 31, 2007

	BUDGET	ACTUAL	VARIANCE
Material (detailed by type: metal stampings, plastic, etc.)	$ 68,000	$ 69,000	$1,000 U
Assembly labour (detailed by job classification, number of workers, etc.)	43,000	44,300	1,300 U
Other labour (managers, inspectors)	12,000	11,200	800 F
Utilities, maintenance, etc.	7,500	7,400	100 F
Supplies (small tools, lubricants, etc.)	2,500	2,600	100 U
Total	$133,000	$134,500	$1,500 U

U = Unfavourable
F = Favourable

New Tools—New Mindsets for Management Accountants

Mastering the new role of finance requires more than learning a new skill or computer program. It will entail a change in mindset, away from the traditional control and transaction orientation to one that focuses on active participation in a company's ongoing pursuit of competitive excellence.

In becoming business partners, management accountants must build the culture of continuous improvement and value creation into the very fibre of new financial systems and methods. The key to these efforts is the development of dynamic, flexible accounting and decision-support systems that can aid managers throughout the organization in understanding, creating, and using reliable and relevant financial information.

Management accounting in this millennium is embedded in the cycle of learning created by the continuous improvement paradigm (see figure below). This paradigm, and the tools it has created or recreated, are at the heart of the race to gain and sustain a global competitive advantage.

These new tools, and others like them, are the means by which management accountants can understand—hence know—what needs to be done to meet ongoing organizational and competitive challenges. The knowing—or art of management accounting—is understanding what tool should be used, when it should be used, and why, as well as being able to implement this knowledge, first hand, or through others.

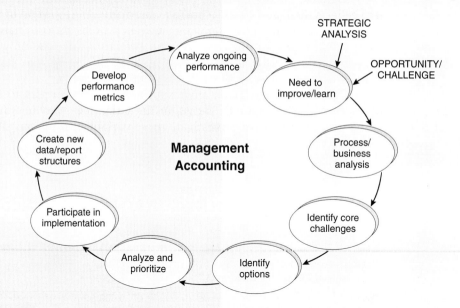

Source: Reprinted from an article appearing in *CMA Management* by C.J. McNair, February 1997, with permission of the Society of Management Accountants of Canada.

Accounting System. A formal mechanism for gathering, organizing, and communicating information about an organization's activities.

ways of doing things. The budget is the tool that aids planning; the performance report is the tool that aids controlling. The **accounting system** thus helps to direct managerial attention to the exceptions. Exhibit 1-4 shows that accounting does not do the controlling. Controlling consists of actions performed by the managers and their subordinates and of the evaluation that follows their actions. Accounting assists the managerial control function by

Managers use accounting information for many different types of decisions. Accountants must make sure that they produce information that is useful for these various decisions. What type of information—scorekeeping, attention-directing, or problem-solving—would managers use for each of the following decisions? Why?

1. Deciding whether to replace a traditional assembly line with a fully automated robotic process.
2. Evaluating the performance of a particular division for the preceding year.
3. Identifying which products exceeded their budgeted profitability and which ones fell short of budget.

ANSWERS

1. Problem-solving. This is a one-time decision for which managers need information targeted at the specific alternatives under consideration.
2. Scorekeeping. This is a routine evaluation of an organizational unit for which managers want systematic data on a regular basis.
3. Attention-directing. Managers want information that highlights deviations from the budget to make them aware of products that need attention.

providing prompt measurements of actions and by systematically pinpointing trouble spots. This management-by-exception approach frees managers from needless concern with those phases of operations that are adhering to plans.

MANAGEMENT ACCOUNTING AND SERVICE ORGANIZATIONS

OBJECTIVE 2

Understand that management accounting also applies to service and not-for-profit organizations.

The basic ideas of management accounting were developed in manufacturing organizations. However, these ideas have evolved so that they are applicable to all types of organizations, including service organizations. Service organizations or industries are defined in various ways. For our purposes, they are organizations that do not make or sell tangible goods. Examples are public accounting firms, law firms, management consultants, real estate firms, transportation companies, banks, insurance companies, and hotels. Almost all non-profit organizations are service industries. Examples are hospitals, schools, libraries, museums, and government departments.

The characteristics of service organizations include the following:

1. *Labour is intensive.* For example, the highest proportion of expenses in schools and law firms are wages, salaries, and payroll-related costs, not costs relating to the use of machinery, equipment, and extensive physical facilities.
2. *Output is usually difficult to define.* For example, the output of a university might be defined as the number of degrees granted, but many critics would maintain that the real output is "what is contained in the students' brains." The output of schools and hospitals is often idealized; attempts to measure output are normally considered impossible.
3. *Major inputs and outputs cannot be stored.* For example, although raw materials and retail merchandise may be stored, a hotel's available labour force and rooms are either used or unused as each day occurs.

4. *Products are diversified.* For example, a hospital provides many related services from essentially the same capacity and therefore management of the portfolio of products is very important.

The economies of developed nations (Canada, the U.S., western Europe, and Japan) have changed from manufacturing-based industries to those whose primary components are knowledge and innovation. Manufacturing jobs as a proportion of total jobs are in decline while jobs in the service industry are on the rise. In the post-industrial society the growth industries can be found in the service sector. For example, in terms of the number of employees, the U.S. motion picture industry is larger than the automotive parts industry and the travel service industry is larger than the petroleum and steel industries combined.

Management Accounting and Not-for-Profit Organizations

This book is aimed at a variety of readers, including students who aspire to become managers or professional accountants for not-for-profit organizations. The book's focus is on profit-seeking organizations, although the fundamental ideas for profit-seeking organizations also apply to not-for-profit organizations.

Managers and accountants in various settings such as hospitals, universities, and government agencies have much in common with their counterparts in profit-seeking organizations. Money must be raised and spent. Budgets must be prepared, and control systems must be designed and implemented. There is an obligation to use resources wisely. If used intelligently, accounting contributes to efficient operations.

Government administrators and politicians are much better equipped to deal with problems inside and outside their organizations if they understand accounting. For example, a knowledge of accounting is crucial for decisions regarding research contracts, government contracts, and loan guarantees.

Key Success Factors

Key Success Factors. The factors that must be managed successfully to achieve organizational success.

While management accounting is relevant to all organizations, whether manufacturing-oriented, service-oriented, or not-for-profit, the factors that must be managed effectively if the organization is to be successful vary. Managers are required to make many decisions that vary in their degree of importance. Errors in decisions of lesser importance, while not desirable, are not critical to the success of the organization. However, errors in some key decisions are critical to the organization's success. Factors that must be managed successfully are called **key success factors**. While this term has also been used to refer to industry factors, the reference here is to organization-specific factors. Management accountants should be aware of the key success factors of their organization, as these factors must remain the focus of their decisions. Some management accountants are overwhelmed with developing the perfect information system. It is, however, much more efficient and effective to concentrate on servicing the requirements of the key success factors when developing the information system. This perspective will assist the management accountant in maintaining a balance between the demand for complexity and the need for simplicity.

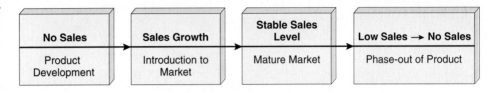

EXHIBIT 1-8

Typical Product
Life Cycle

No Sales	Sales Growth	Stable Sales Level	Low Sales → No Sales
Product Development	Introduction to Market	Mature Market	Phase-out of Product

PLANNING AND CONTROL FOR PRODUCT LIFE CYCLES AND THE VALUE CHAIN

Product Life Cycle. The various stages through which a product passes, from conception and development through introduction into the market through maturation and, finally, withdrawal from the market.

Many management decisions relate to a single good or service, or to a group of related products. To effectively plan for and control production of such goods or services, accountants and other managers must consider the product's life cycle. **Product life cycle** refers to the various stages through which a product passes, from conception and development through introduction into the market through maturation and, finally, withdrawal from the market. At each stage, managers face differing costs and potential returns. Exhibit 1-8 shows a typical product life cycle.

Product life cycles range from a few months (for fashion clothing or faddish goods) to many years (for automobiles or refrigerators). Some products, such as many computer software packages, have long development stages and relatively short market lives. Others, such as Boeing 777 airplanes, have market lives many times longer than their development stage.[4]

In the planning process, managers must identify revenues and costs over the entire life cycle—however long or short. Accounting needs to track actual costs and revenues throughout the life cycle, too. Periodic comparisons between *planned* costs and revenues and *actual* costs and revenues allow managers to assess the current profitability of a product, determine its current product life-cycle stage, and make any needed changes in strategy.

Value Chain. A set of business functions that add value to the product or service of an organization.

For example, suppose a pharmaceutical company is developing a new drug to reduce high blood pressure. The budget for the product should plan for costs without revenues in the product development stage. Most of the revenues come in the introduction and mature-market stages, and a pricing strategy should recognize the need for revenues to cover both development and phase-out costs, as well as the direct costs of producing the drug. During phase-out, costs of producing the drug must be balanced with both the revenue generated and the need to keep the drug on the market for those who have come to rely on it.

The Value Chain

OBJECTIVE 3

Explain the role of management accountants in an organization's value-chain functions.

How does a company actually create the goods or services that it sells? Whether making donuts in a donut shop or making $50 million airplanes, all organizations try to create goods or services that are valued by their customers. The **value chain** is the set of business functions that add value to the products or services of an organization. As shown in Exhibit 1-9, these functions are as follows:

- Research and development—the generation of, and experimentation with, ideas related to new products, services, or processes.

---

[4] To assess this long-term market life, see www.boeing.com/commercial/777family.

EXHIBIT 1-9

The Value Chain of
Business Functions

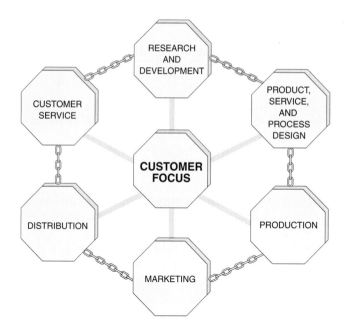

• Design of products, services, or processes—the detailed engineering of products.
• Production—the coordination and assembly of resources to produce a product or deliver a service.
• Marketing—the manner by which individuals or groups learn about the value and features of products or services.
• Distribution—the mechanism by which products or services are delivered to the customer.
• Customer service—the support activities provided to the customer.

Not all of these functions are equally important to the success of a company. Senior management must decide which of these functions enables the company to gain and maintain a competitive edge. For example, Dell Computers considers the *design* function a key success factor. The features designed into Dell's computers create higher quality. In addition, the design of efficient processes used to make and deliver computers lowers costs and speeds up delivery to customers. Of course, Dell also performs the other value-chain functions, but it concentrates on being the best process designer in the computer market.

Management accountants play a key role in all value-chain functions. Providing estimated revenue and cost data during the research and development and design stages (especially the design stage) of the value chain enables managers and engineers to reduce the life-cycle costs of products or services more than in any other value-chain function. Using computer-based planning software, accountants can give managers rapid feedback on ideas for costs reduction long before a commitment must be made to purchase expensive equipment. Then, during the production stage, management accountants help track the effects of continuous improvement programs. Management accountants also play a central role in cost planning and control through the use of budgets and performance reporting as described in the previous section. Marketing decisions have a significant impact on sales but the cost of promotional programs is also significant. The tradeoff between increased costs and revenues is analyzed by accountants. Distributing products or services to customers is a complex function. Should a company sell its products directly to a chain of retail stores, or should it sell to a wholesaler? What transportation system should be used—trucks or trains? What are the costs of each alternative? Finally, accountants provide cost data for customer service activities, such as warranty and repair costs and the costs of goods returned. As you can see, cost management is very important throughout the value chain, as is the role of accounting.

Note that customer focus is at the centre of Exhibit 1-9. Successful businesses never lose sight of the importance of maintaining a focus on the needs of customers. For example, consider the comments of the following business leader:

> Customers, by the choices they make, grant companies a future or condemn them to extinction. We will continuously strive to achieve total customer satisfaction. . . . We will seek to truly understand the complexity of our customers' needs, not push our own ideas or technology.
>
> PHILIP CONDIT, FORMER CHAIRMAN AND CHIEF EXECUTIVE OFFICER, BOEING COMPANY

MAKING MANAGERIAL DECISIONS

Measuring costs at various stages of the value chain is important to Starbucks (see company profile at www.starbucks.com/aboutus/overview.asp). Suppose that you are a Starbucks manager or accountant. For each of the following activities, indicate the value-chain function that is being performed and what accounting information might be helpful to managers in the function.

1. Process engineers investigate methods to reduce the time to roast coffee beans and to better preserve their flavour.
2. A direct-to-your-home mail-order system is established to sell custom-blended coffees.
3. Arabica coffee beans are purchased and transported to company processing plants.
4. Focus groups investigate the feasibility of a new line of Frappuccino drinks.
5. A telephone hotline is established for mail-order customers to call with comments on the quality and speed of delivery.
6. Each company-owned retail store undertakes a campaign to provide information to customers about the processes used to make its coffee products.

ANSWERS

1. Design. Both the design of products and, as here, design of production processes are part of the entire design function. Managers need the costs of various possible production processes to decide among the alternatives.

2. Distribution. This provides an additional way to deliver products to customers. Managers need information on the costs of a mail-order system to compare to the added revenue from mail-order sales.

3. Production. The purchase price of beans and transportation (or freight-in) costs are part of product costs incurred during the production function. Starbucks purchases only premium beans, but the company is still concerned about the price paid and the added costs of transportation.

4. Research and development. These costs (mostly wages) are incurred prior to management's final decision to design and produce a new product. Predicted revenues and costs from the Frappuccino market can help managers design a drink that is both marketable and profitable.

5. Customer service. These costs include all expenditures made after Starbucks has delivered the product to the customer; in this case, Starbucks obtains feedback on the quality and speed of delivery. Managers will trade off the cost of the hotline and the value of the information generated from the calls.

6. Marketing. These costs are for activities that enhance the existing or potential customers' awareness and opinion of the product. Like many advertising expenses, it is easy to estimate the costs of such a program but hard to quantify the benefits.

THE ROLE OF THE ACCOUNTANT IN THE ORGANIZATION

Line and Staff Authority

OBJECTIVE 4

Identify the staff
authority and role of
the accounting
department in the
organization.

The organization chart in Exhibit 1-10 shows a typical manufacturing company divided into subunits. The distinction between line and staff authority needs special consideration. Most organizations specify certain activities as their basic mission, such as the production and sale of goods or services. All subunits of the organization that are *directly* responsible for conducting these basic activities are called *line* departments. The others are called *staff* departments because their principal task is to support or service the line departments. Thus, *staff* activities are

EXHIBIT 1-10

Partial Organization
Chart of a
Manufacturing
Company

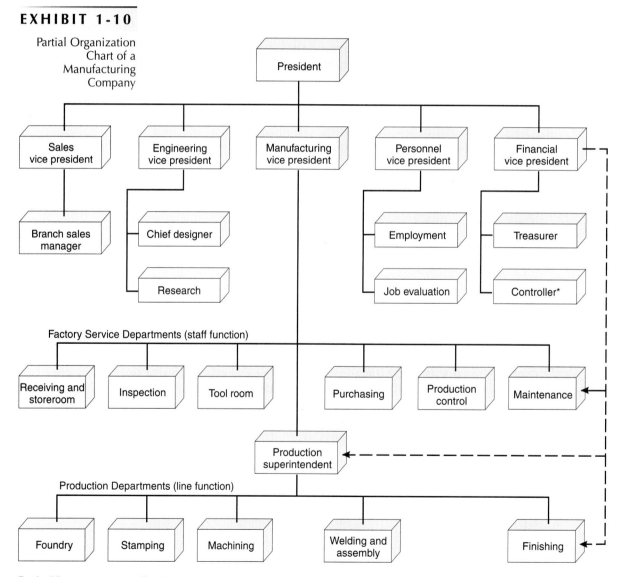

Dashed line represents staff authority.

*For detailed organization of a controller's department, see Exhibit 1-11.

indirectly related to the basic activities of the organization. For instance, Exhibit 1-10 shows a series of factory-service departments that perform the staff functions of supporting the line functions carried out by the production departments. **Line authority** is exerted downward over subordinates. **Staff authority** is the authority to advise but not to command; it may be exerted downward, laterally, or upward.

Line Authority. Authority exerted downward over subordinates.

Staff Authority. Authority to advise but not command. It may be exerted downward, laterally, or upward.

The accounting department is responsible for providing other managers with specialized services, including advice and help in budgeting, analyzing variances, pricing, and making special decisions. The accounting department does not exercise direct authority over line departments; its authority to prescribe uniform accounting and reporting methods is delegated to the controller by top-line management. The uniform accounting procedure is authorized by the company president and is implemented by the controller. The controller fills a staff role, in contrast to the line roles of sales and production executives. When the controller prescribes the line department's role in supplying accounting information, the controller is not speaking as a staff person, but is speaking for top-line management.

Exhibit 1-11 shows how a controller's department may be organized. In particular, note the distinctions among the scorekeeping, attention-directing, and problem-solving roles. Unless some internal accountants are given the last two roles as their primary responsibilities, the scorekeeping tasks tend to dominate, making the system less helpful in management's decision making.

EXHIBIT 1-11

Organization Chart of a Controller's Department

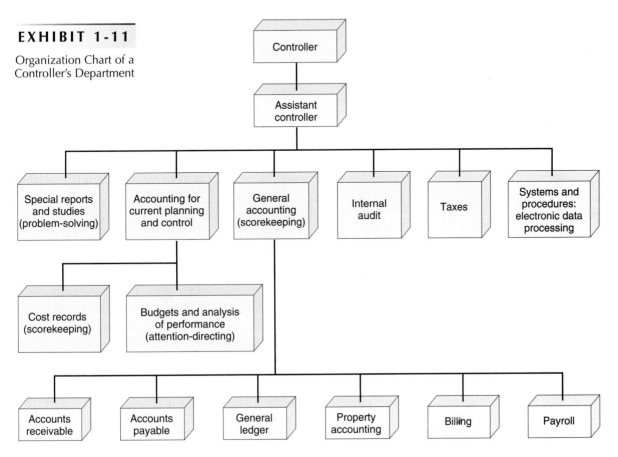

The Controller

Controller (Comptroller). The top accounting officer of an organization.

The controller position varies in stature and duties from company to company. In some firms the controller is little more than a bookkeeper who compiles data, primarily for external reporting purposes. In other companies the controller is a key executive who aids managerial planning and control across the company's subdivisions. In most firms, controllers fall somewhere between these two extremes. For example, their opinions on the tax implications of certain management decisions may be carefully weighed, yet their opinions on other aspects of these decisions (such as human resource or marketing issues) may not be sought. In this book, **controller** (sometimes called **comptroller**, derived from the French *compte*, for "account") refers to the financial executive who has primary responsibility for both management accounting and financial accounting. We have already seen that the modern controller does not do any controlling in terms of line authority except over his or her own department. Yet the modern concept of controllership maintains that, in a special sense, the *controller does control*: by reporting and interpreting relevant data, the controller exerts a force or influence, or projects an attitude, that impels management toward logical decisions that are consistent with the company's financial objectives.

Distinctions between Controller and Treasurer

Many people confuse the roles of controller and treasurer. The Financial Executives Institute, an association of corporate treasurers and controllers, distinguishes the functions as follows:

Controllership	Treasurership
1. Planning for control	1. Provision of capital
2. Reporting and interpreting	2. Investor relations
3. Evaluating and consulting	3. Short-term financing
4. Tax administration	4. Banking and custody
5. Government reporting	5. Credits and collections
6. Protection of assets	6. Investments
7. Economic appraisal	7. Insurance

Note that management accounting is the controller's primary *means* of implementing the first three functions of controllership.

We shall not dwell at length on the treasurer's functions. As the seven points indicate, the treasurer is concerned mainly with financial rather than operating problems. The exact division of various accounting and financial duties obviously varies from company to company.

The controller has been compared to the ship's navigator. The navigator, with the help of his or her specialized training, assists the captain (president of the company). Without the navigator, the ship may flounder on reefs or miss its destination entirely, but the captain exerts his or her right to command. The navigator guides and informs the captain on how well the ship is being steered. The navigator's role is especially evident in the first three points listed for controllership.

TWO MAJOR MANAGEMENT ACCOUNTING PHILOSOPHIES

OBJECTIVE 5

Describe the two major philosophies of this book: cost-benefit and behavioural implications.

This book emphasizes two major philosophies regarding the design of management accounting systems: (1) cost-benefit and (2) behavioural implications. Both themes are briefly described.

Cost-Benefit Philosophy

Accounting systems and methods are economic goods that are available at various costs. Which system does a manager want to buy? A simple file drawer for amassing receipts and cancelled cheques? An elaborate budgeting system based on computerized descriptive models of the organization and its subunits? Or something in between?

The answer depends on the buyer's perceptions of the expected incremental (additional) benefits in relation to the incremental costs. For example, a hospital administrator may contemplate the installation of a computerized system for controlling hospital operations. Such a system uses a single document of original entry for automatic accumulation of data for financial records, medical records, costs by departments, nurse staffing requirements, drug administration, billings for patients, revenue generated by physicians, and so forth. This system leads to higher efficiency, less waste, and fewer errors, but costs $14 million. Thus, the system is not good or bad by itself. It must meet the economic test where its value must exceed its cost. This is the **cost-benefit philosophy** that permeates this book. The primary criterion for choosing among accounting systems and methods is how well they achieve management goals in relation to their costs.

Cost-Benefit Philosophy. The primary consideration in choosing among accounting systems and methods: how well they achieve management goals in relation to their costs.

A particular accounting system may be a wise investment in the eyes of the buyer if it generates a sufficiently better set of decisions to justify its added cost. However, an existing *accounting system is only one source of information* for decision making. It may be more economical to gather information by one-shot special efforts than by a system that repetitively gathers rarely used information.

The cost-benefit theme has a general appeal. Managers have been employing the cost-benefit test for years, sometimes in a crude form of pros and cons. But the cost-benefit theme has an exceedingly rich underlying theory of information economics. It is a good theory that can supply the missing rationale for many management practices.

Behavioural Philosophy

Financial accounting is often regarded as a cold, objective discipline because it is perceived to represent only the reporting of financial information. In contrast, management accounting is greatly affected by behavioural considerations and philosophies and is also related to other disciplines, such as production and operations management, economics, and finance.[5] A management accountant considering the purchase of a new accounting system should be concerned with how

---

[5] See, for example, the discussion of behavioural research and management accounting at the School of Accountancy, University of Waterloo, www.accounting.uwaterloo.ca/phd/behavioral scienceresearch.html.

it will affect the decisions and behaviour of the affected employees. Earlier, we saw how budgets and performance reports may play a key role in modifying management behaviour to comply with budget controls, avoid unfavourable variances, and motivate excellence. Budgets are the chief devices for compelling and disciplining management planning. Without budgets, planning may not get the front-and-centre attention that it usually deserves.

Performance reports are widely used to judge decisions, subunits, and managers and have enormous influence on the behaviour of the affected individuals. Performance reports not only provide feedback for improving future economic decisions but may also provide desirable or undesirable motivation. The choices of the content, format, timing, and distribution of performance reports are heavily influenced by their probable impact on motivation.

MANAGEMENT ACCOUNTING AND FINANCIAL ACCOUNTING

Freedom of Choice

Financial accounting emphasizes the preparation of reports of an organization for external users such as banks and the investing public. Management accounting emphasizes the preparation of reports of an organization for its internal users such as company presidents, university deans, and chief physicians. Therefore, financial accounting could be labelled as external accounting and management accounting as internal accounting.

The same basic accounting system compiles the fundamental data for both financial accounting and management accounting. Furthermore, external forces (e.g., income tax authorities and regulatory bodies, such as the Ontario Securities Commission and the National Energy Board) often limit management's choices of accounting methods. Organizations frequently limp along with a system that has been developed in response to the legal requirements imposed by external parties. In short, many existing systems are externally oriented and neglect the needs of internal users.

Generally accepted accounting standards or principles affect both internal and external accounting. However, change in internal accounting is not inhibited by generally accepted financial accounting standards. Managers can create any kind of internal accounting system they want—as long as they are willing to pay the price. For instance, for its own management purposes, a hospital, a manufacturer, or a university can account for its assets on the basis of *current values*, as measured by estimates of replacement costs. No outside agency can prohibit such accounting. There are no "generally accepted management accounting principles" that forbid particular measurements. Indeed, the cost-benefit philosophy refrains from stating that any given accounting is good or bad. *Instead, the philosophy suggests that any accounting system or method is desirable as long as it brings incremental benefits in excess of incremental costs.*

Satisfying both internal demands for data as well as external demands means that organizations may have to keep more than one set of records. In North America, there is nothing immoral or unethical about having many sets of books for different users—but they are expensive. The cost-benefit test says that their perceived increases in benefits must exceed their perceived increases in costs. Ultimately, benefits are measured by whether decisions result in increased net cost savings or profit or, in the case of many not-for-profit institutions, increased quality or quantity of service rendered for each dollar spent.

	MANAGEMENT ACCOUNTING	FINANCIAL ACCOUNTING
1. Primary users	Organization managers at various levels.	Outside parties such as investors, creditors, suppliers, and government agencies (but also organization managers).
2. Freedom of choice	No constraints other than costs in relation to benefits of improved management decisions.	Constrained by generally accepted accounting principles (GAAP).
3. Behavioural implications	Concern about how measurements and reports will influence managers' daily behaviour.	Concern about how to measure accurately and communicate economic results. Behavioural impact is secondary.
4. Time focus	Future orientation: formal use of budgets (future). But also historical records. Past budgets versus actual performance.	Past orientation: historical evaluation. Example: actual financial or operational results of year one versus actual performance of year two.
5. Time span	Flexible, varying from hourly to 10 or 15 years.	Less flexible. Usually one year or one quarter.
6. Reports	Detailed reports: concern about parts of the entity, products, departments, territories, etc.	Summary reports: concern primarily with entity as a whole.
7. Delineation of activities	Field is less sharply defined. Heavier use of economics, decision sciences, and behavioural sciences.	Field is more sharply defined. Lighter use of related disciplines.

The major differences between management accounting and financial accounting are briefly discussed in Exhibit 1-12. These points will become clearer in succeeding chapters.

Career Opportunities

Certified Management
Accountants of Canada
www.cma-canada.org

Canadian Institute of
Chartered Accountants
www.cica.ca

Certified General
Accountants Association
of Canada
www.cga-canada.org

**Society of Management
Accountants of Canada
(SMAC).** An organization of
professional accountants,
Certified Management
Accountants whose primary
interest is in management
accounting.

Accounting deals with all facets of a complex organization and provides an excellent opportunity for gaining a broad range of knowledge. Senior accountants or controllers in a corporation are sometimes chosen as production or marketing executives. Why? Because they may have impressed other executives as having acquired the necessary general management skills. Accounting must embrace all management functions, including purchasing, manufacturing, wholesaling, retailing, and a variety of marketing and transportation activities. A number of recent surveys have indicated that more chief executive officers began their careers in an accounting position than in any other area.

In Canada, there are three professional accounting organizations. The **Society of Management Accountants of Canada (SMAC)**, also known as CMA Canada, confers the **CMA (Certified Management Accountant)** designation; its education program focuses on management accounting and strategic decision making. The **Canadian Institute of Chartered Accountants (CICA)** confers the **CA (Chartered Accountant)** designation. The CA education program focuses on external financial reports and, in particular, the auditing function. The **Certified General Accountants Association of Canada (CGAAC)** confers the **CGA (Certified General Accountant)** designation, and provides a broad-based education program in accounting and financial management.

Certified Management Accountant (CMA). A professional accountant who is a member of the Society of Management Accountants of Canada.

Education is a provincial jurisdiction, so accounting students wishing to pursue one of the said accounting designations need to register with the provincial organization. They may qualify for admission and be awarded a designation from any one of the three accounting bodies through passing a national examination. While management accounting is a component of each of the three education programs, the extent of coverage of the subject varies.

ADAPTING TO CHANGE

Canadian Institute of Chartered Accountants (CICA). An organization of professional accountants, Chartered Accountants.

Chartered Accountant (CA). A professional accountant who is a member of the CICA.

Certified General Accountants Association of Canada (CGAAC). An organization of professional accountants, Certified General Accountants.

Certified General Accountant (CGA). A professional accountant who is a member of the CGAAC.

The growing interest in management accounting also stems from its ability to help managers adapt to change. Indeed, the one constant in the world of business is change. Accountants must adapt their systems to the changes in management practices and technology. A system that produces valuable information in one setting may be valueless in another. Information that was relevant for management decisions yesterday may be out-of-date tomorrow or even today.

Accountants have not always been responsive to the need for change. A decade ago many managers complained about the irrelevance of accounting information. Why? Because their decision environment had changed but accounting systems had not. However, most progressive companies have changed their accounting systems to recognize the realities of today's complex, technical, and global business environment. Instead of being irrelevant, accountants in such companies are adding more value than ever. By working with managers to produce the information considered relevant for their decisions, accountants can be regarded as "business partners" instead of a "financial police department." Modern accountants do not merely point out problems and preach frugality and efficiencies, but are also part of the team that produces solutions to current problems and plans the success and prosperity of the organizations they serve.

Current Trends

Three major factors are causing changes in management accounting today:

1. The major shift from a manufacturing based to a service-based economy.
2. Globalization and increased global competition.
3. Technological advances.

Each of these factors will affect your study of management accounting.

The service sector now accounts for an increasing proportion of total employment. Service industries are becoming increasingly competitive, and their need for and use of accounting information is growing. Basic accounting principles are applied to service organizations throughout this book.

Global competition has increased in recent years as many international barriers to trade, such as tariffs and duties, have been lowered or eliminated. In addition, there has been a worldwide trend toward deregulation and trade partnerships (for example, NAFTA and the European Union). The result has been a shift in the balance of economic power in the world. To regain a competitive edge, many companies are redesigning accounting systems to provide more accurate and timely information about the cost of activities, products, or services. To be competitive, managers must understand the effects of their decisions on costs and accountants must help managers predict such effects.

By far, the most dominant influence on management accounting over the past decade has been technological change. This change has affected both the production and use of accounting information. The increasing capabilities and lower cost of computers have changed how accountants gather, store, manipulate, and report data. Frequently, the result is faster information at a lower cost. Most accounting systems, even small ones, are automated. In addition, computers enable managers to access data directly and to generate their own reports and analyses with up-to-the-minute information. By using spreadsheet software and graphics packages, managers can use accounting information directly in their decision process. All managers need a better understanding of accounting information than they may have needed in the past, and accountants need to create databases that can be readily understood by managers.

Technological change has also dramatically altered the manufacturing environment for many companies, causing changes in how accounting information is used. Manufacturing processes are increasingly automated and automated manufacturing processes make extensive use of robots and other computer-controlled equipment and less use of human labour for direct production activities. Many early accounting systems were designed primarily to measure and report the cost of labour because human labour was the largest cost in producing many products and services. Clearly, such systems are not appropriate in automated environments. Accountants in such settings have had to change their systems to produce information for decisions about how to acquire and efficiently use materials and automated equipment.

Just-in-Time Philosophy and Computer-Integrated Manufacturing

Just-in-Time (JIT) Philosophy.
A philosophy to eliminate waste by reducing the time products spend in the production process and eliminating the time that products spend in activities that do not add value.

Standard Aero
www.standardaero.ca

Changes in management philosophy have accompanied technological change. The most important recent change leading to increased efficiency in factories has been the adoption of a **just-in-time (JIT) philosophy**. The essence of the philosophy is to eliminate waste. Managers try to (1) reduce the time that employees spend in the production process and (2) eliminate the time that employees spend on activities that do not add value (such as inspection and waiting time). For instance, Standard Aero of Winnipeg, Manitoba, a company dedicated to repairing and overhauling airplane engines, once sought to cut down overhaul time from two months to 15 days by eliminating inefficient activities and waiting time.[6]

Originally, JIT referred only to an inventory system that minimized inventories by arranging for materials and subcomponents to arrive just as they were needed and for goods to be made just in time to be shipped to customers—no sooner and no later. But JIT has become the cornerstone of a broad management philosophy. It originated in Japanese companies such as Toyota and Kawasaki, and has been adopted by many large companies, including Hewlett-Packard and Xerox. Many small firms have also embraced JIT.

Process time can be reduced by redesigning and simplifying the production process. Companies can use *computer-aided design (CAD)* to design products that can be manufactured efficiently. Even small changes in design often lead to large manufacturing cost savings. Companies can also use *computer-aided manufacturing (CAM)*, in which computers direct and control production equipment. CAM often leads to a smoother, more efficient flow of production with fewer delays.

---

[6] "World class productivity at Standard Aero," *CMA Management*, April 1991, p. 7.

Computer-Integrated
Manufacturing (CIM)
Systems.
Systems that use com-
puter-aided design and
computer-aided manufac-
turing together with
robots and computer-
controlled machines.

Systems that use CAD and CAM together with robots and computer-
controlled machines are called **computer-integrated manufacturing (CIM)
systems**. Companies that install full CIM systems use very little labour. Robots
and computer-controlled machines perform the routine jobs previously done by
assembly-line workers. In addition, well-designed systems provide greater flexibility because design changes only require alterations in computer programs, not
the retraining of an entire workforce.

Time spent on activities that do not add value to the product can be eliminated or reduced by focusing on quality, improving plant layout, and cross-
training workers. Achieving zero production defects ("doing it right the first
time") reduces inspection time and eliminates rework time. One factory saved
more time by redesigning its plant layout so that the distance products travelled
from one operation to the next during production was reduced from 422 metres
to 107 metres. Another company reduced setup time on a machine from 45 minutes to one minute by storing the required tools nearby and training the machine
operator to do the setup. A third company reduced the time required to manufacture a vacuum pump from three weeks to six minutes by switching from long
assembly lines to manufacturing cells that allowed accomplishment of the entire
task in quick succession.

Implications for the Study of Management Accounting

As you read this book, remember that accounting systems change as the world
changes. The techniques presented here are being applied in organizations
today. But tomorrow may be different. To adapt to changes, you must understand why the techniques are being used, not just how they are used. We urge
you to resist the temptation to simply memorize rules and techniques. Instead,
develop your understanding of the underlying concepts and principles. These
will continue to be useful in developing and understanding new techniques for
changing environments.

Professional Ethics

OBJECTIVE 7

Identify the most
important areas of
ethical conduct by
management
accountants.

Accountants have consistently ranked highly in terms of professional ethics in
public-opinion surveys. Professional accountants adhere to codes of conduct
regarding competence, confidentiality, integrity, and objectivity. Exhibit 1-13
contains the Code of Professional Ethics for Management Accountants published
by the Society of Management Accountants of Ontario. Professional accounting
organizations have procedures for reviewing alleged behaviour that is not consistent with the Code.

External and internal financial reports are primarily the responsibility of
line managers. However, management accountants are also responsible for these
reports. Accounting systems, procedures, and compilations should be reliable and
free of manipulation.

Ethical Dilemmas

What makes an action by an accountant unethical? An unethical act is one that
violates the ethical standards of the profession. However, the standards leave

Suppose you are a manager of a chemical plant. The plant has just undertaken a business process reengineering project and, as a result, has substantially changed its production process. It is much more automated, with newly acquired equipment replacing labour-intensive operations. The plant is also making more use of electronic commerce and moving toward a just-in-time inventory policy. You have a meeting with your accountant to discuss possible changes in your accounting system. What types of accounting-system changes might be warranted?

ANSWER

Major changes in production processes generally lead to different information needs. The old accounting system may have focused on accounting for labour; the new system should carefully monitor and report on the use of the automated equipment. This will direct attention to the most important costs in the process and make sure that they are not out of control. Problem-solving needs will also be different. Initially, the plant's managers will probably want comparative data on the costs of the new process versus the old. In the future, they will need information about how best to use a capacity that the plant owns (the equipment) rather than how much labour to use for the planned level of production.

much room for individual interpretation and judgment. When one action is clearly unethical and another alternative is clearly ethical, managers and accountants should have no difficulty choosing between them. Unfortunately, most ethical dilemmas are not clear-cut. The most difficult situations arise when there is strong pressure to take an action that is "borderline" or when two ethical standards conflict.

Here is an ethical scenario: Suppose you are an accountant who has been asked to supply the company's banker with a profit forecast for the coming year. A badly needed bank loan rides on the prediction. The company president is

EXHIBIT 1-13

Code of Professional Ethics for Management Accountants

All Members shall adhere to the following "Code of Professional Ethics" of the Society:

(a) A Member shall act at all times with

    (i) responsibility for and fidelity to public needs;

    (ii) fairness and loyalty to his associates, clients and employers; and

    (iii) competence through devotion to high ideals of personal honour and professional integrity;

(b) A Member shall

    (i) maintain at all times independence of thought and action;

    (ii) not express his opinion on financial statements without first assessing his relationship with his client to determine whether he might expect his opinion to be considered independent, objective and unbiased by one who has knowledge of all the facts; and

    (iii) when preparing financial statements or expressing an opinion on financial statements which are intended to inform management only, disclose all material facts known to him in order not to make such financial statements misleading, acquire sufficient information to warrant an expression of opinion and report all material misstatements or departures from generally accepted accounting principles;

Society of Management
Accountants of Ontario
www.cma-ontario.org

(c) A Member shall

   (i) not disclose or use any confidential information concerning the affairs of his employer or client unless acting in the course of his duties or except when such information is required to be disclosed in the course of any defence of himself or any associate or employee in any lawsuit or other legal proceeding or against alleged professional mis-conduct by order of lawful authority or the Board or any committee of the Society in the proper exercise of their duties but only to the extent necessary for such purpose;

   (ii) inform his employer or client of any business connections or interests of which his employer or client would reasonably expect to be informed;

   (iii) not, in the course of exercising his duties on behalf of his employer or client, hold, receive, bargain for or acquire any fee, remuneration or benefit without his employer's or client's knowledge and consent; and

   (iv) take all reasonable steps, in arranging any engagement as a consultant, to establish a clear understanding of the scope and objectives of the work before it is commenced and shall furnish the client with an estimate of cost, preferably before the engagement is commenced, but in any event as soon as possible thereafter.

(d) A Member shall

   (i) conduct himself toward other Members with courtesy and good faith;

   (ii) not commit an act discreditable to the profession;

   (iii) not engage in or counsel any business or occupation which, in the opinion of the Society, is incompatible with the professional ethics of a management accountant;

   (iv) not accept any engagement to review the work of another Member for the same employer except with the knowledge of that Member, or except where the connection of that Member with the work has been terminated, unless the Member reviews the work of others as a normal part of his responsibilities;

   (v) not attempt to gain an advantage over other Members by paying or accepting a commission in securing management accounting work;

   (vi) uphold the principle of adequate compensation for management accounting work; and

   (vii) not act maliciously or in any other way which may adversely reflect on the public or professional reputation or business of another Member.

(e) A Member shall

   (i) at all times maintain the standards of competence expressed by the academic and experience requirements for admission to the Society and for continuation as a Member;

   (ii) disseminate the knowledge upon which the profession of management accounting is based to others within the profession and generally promote the advancement of the profession;

   (iii) undertake only such work as he is competent to perform by virtue of his training and experience and shall, where it would be in the best interests of an employer or client, engage, or advise the employer or client to engage, other specialists;

   (iv) expose before the proper tribunals of the Society any incompetent, unethical, illegal or unfair conduct or practice of a Member which involves the reputation, dignity or honour of the Society; and

   (v) endeavour to ensure that a professional partnership or company, with which he is associated as a partner, principal, director or officer abides by the Code of Professional Ethics and the rules of professional conduct established by the Society.

Source: Management Accounting Handbook: Bylaw 20 (The Society of Management Accountants of Ontario).

Ethics, Accounting, and Whistle-Blowers

Companies often rely on accountants to safeguard company ethics. Accountants have a special responsibility to make sure that managers act with integrity and that information disclosed to customers, suppliers, regulators, and the public is accurate. If accountants do not take this responsibility seriously, or if the company ignores the accountants' reports, dire consequences can follow. Just ask WorldCom or Enron. In both companies, an accountant decided to be a *whistle-blower*, one who reports wrongdoings to his or her supervisor. The WorldCom and Enron whistle-blowers became two of the three 2002 Persons of the Year in *Time* magazine.

In June 2002, Cynthia Cooper, vice president of internal audit for WorldCom, told the company's board of directors that fraudulent accounting entries had turned a U.S. $662 million loss into a U.S. $2.4 billion profit in 2001. This disclosure led to additional discoveries totalling U.S. $9 billion in erroneous accounting entries—the largest accounting fraud in history. Cooper was proud of WorldCom and highly committed to its success. Nevertheless, when she and her internal audit team discovered the unethical actions of superiors she admired, she did not hesitate to do the right thing. She saw no joy when CEO Bernie Ebbers and CFO Scott Sullivan were handcuffed and led away. She simply applied what she had learned when she sat in the middle of the front row of seats in her accounting classes at Mississippi State University. Accountants ask hard questions, find the answers, and act with integrity. Being a whistle-blower has not been easy for Cooper. She is a hero to some, a villain to others. But regardless of the reaction of others, Cooper knows that she did what any good accountant should do—no matter how painful it is to tell the truth.

At Enron, Sherron Watkins had a different experience. An accounting major at the University of Texas at Austin who started her career at Arthur Andersen, Watkins moved out of accounting when she took a position at Enron in 1993. But in the spring of 2001 she moved back into the financial arena, working directly for CFO Andrew Fastow. As she became more familiar with the accounting at Enron, she discovered the off-the-books liabilities that have now become famous. In August, she wrote a memo to CEO Kenneth Lay and met with him personally, explaining to him "an elaborate accounting hoax." Later she discovered that, rather than the hoax being investigated, her report had generated a memo from Enron's legal counsel titled "Confidential Employee Matter" that included the following: ". . . how to manage the case with the employee who made the sensitive report. . . . Texas law does not currently protect corporate whistle-blowers. . . ." In addition, her boss confiscated her hard drive, and she was demoted. She now regrets that she did not take the matter to higher levels, but she thought that Lay would take her allegations seriously. In the end, Watkins proved to be right. While many at Enron knew what was happening, they ignored it. Watkins's accounting background made her both able to spot the irregularities and impelled to report them. Another Enron employee, Lynn Brewer, said that "hundreds, perhaps thousands, of people inside the company knew what was going on, and chose to look the other way." Watkins made the ethical decision and did not look the other way. In Canada, as of September 2004, it is now a general offence under s. 425.1 of the *Criminal Code* for an employer to discipline or otherwise act against an employee who provides information in relation to the violation of any federal or provincial law. This provision of the *Criminal Code* was enacted in part in response to whistle-blower treatment at Enron. The provision reads as follows:

> No employer or person acting on behalf of an employer or in a position of authority in respect of an employee of the employer shall take a disciplinary measure against, demote, terminate or otherwise adversely affect the employment of such an employee, or threaten to do so,
> (a) with the intent to compel the employee to abstain from providing information to a person whose duties include the enforcement of federal or provincial law, respecting an offence that the employee believes has been or is being committed contrary to this or any other federal or provincial Act or regulation by the employer or an officer or employee of the employer or, if the employer is a corporation, by one or more of its directors; or
> (b) with the intent to retaliate against the employee because the employee has provided information referred to in paragraph (a).

Sources: "The Party Crasher," *Time*, December 30, 2002–January 6, 2003, pp. 52–56; "The Night Detective," *Time*, December 30, 2002–January 6, 2003, pp. 45–50; M. Flynn, "Enron Insider Shares Her Insights," *Puget Sound Business Journal*, March 7–13, 2003, p. 50.

absolutely convinced that profits will be at least $500,000. Anything less than that and the loan is not likely to be approved. Your analysis shows that if the planned introduction of a new product goes extraordinarily well, profits will exceed $500,000. If the product fails, the company stands to lose $600,000. But the most likely outcome is for a modestly successful introduction and a $100,000 profit. Without the loan, the new product cannot be taken to the market, and there is no way the company can avoid a loss for the year.

Bankruptcy is even a possibility. What forecast would you make? There is no easy answer. A forecast of less than $500,000 seems to guarantee financial problems, perhaps even bankruptcy. Shareholders, management, employees, suppliers, and customers may all be hurt. But a forecast of $500,000 may not be fair and objective. The bank may be misled by it. Still, the president apparently thinks a $500,000 forecast is reasonable, and you know that there is some chance it will be achieved. Perhaps the potential benefit to the company of an overly optimistic forecast is greater than the possible cost to the bank. There is no right answer to this dilemma. The important thing is to recognize the ethical dimensions and weigh them when forming your judgment.

Professional Ethics Resources
www.ethicsweb.ca/
institutes.html

The tone set by top management can have a great influence on managers' ethics. Complete integrity and outspoken support for ethical standards by senior managers is the single greatest motivator of ethical behaviour throughout an organization. But in the final analysis, ethical standards are personal and depend on the values of the individual.

SUMMARY

Accounting information is useful to managers for making short-term planning and control decisions, making nonroutine decisions, and formulating overall policies and long-range plans. Management accounting focuses on information for internal decision makers (managers) and financial accounting focuses on information for external parties.

Initially, many management accounting techniques were developed in manufacturing companies because of a greater need for sophisticated accounting information. Today, however, there is increasing application of management accounting in service and not-for-profit organizations.

Management accounting systems exist for the benefit of managers and better decision making. These systems should be judged by a cost-benefit criterion—the benefits derived from better decisions should exceed the cost of developing and running the system. The benefit of a system will be affected by behavioural factors—how the system affects managers and their decisions. The future worth of an accounting system will be affected by how easily the system can adapt to change. A changing business environment may require the accounting system to collect and report new data and discontinue reporting information that is no longer needed. Changes affecting accounting systems include growth in the service sector of the economy, increased global competition, and advances in technology. Organizations that adopt a just-in-time philosophy or use computer-aided design and manufacturing systems have different needs for information than do more traditional firms.

An essential tool for performance evaluation is a budget. A performance report compares actual results to the budget. To appropriately interpret accounting information about a particular product, it is often important to recognize the product's competitive strengths and weaknesses.

Accountants are staff employees who provide information and advice for line managers. The head of accounting is often called the controller. Unlike the treasurer, who is concerned primarily with financial matters, the controller measures and reports on operating performance.

Finally, both external and internal accountants are expected to adhere to standards of ethical conduct. However, many ethical dilemmas require value judgments, not a simple application of standards.

HIGHLIGHTS TO REMEMBER

1. **Describe the major users and uses of accounting information.** Internal managers use accounting information for making short-term planning and control decisions, for making nonroutine decisions, and for formulating overall policies and long-range plans. External users such as investors and regulators use published financial statements to make investment decisions, regulatory rulings, and many other decisions. Managers use accounting information to answer scorekeeping, attention-directing, and problem-solving questions.

2. **Explain why ethics is important to management accountants.** Integrity is essential to accountants because they provide information that users must trust to be right. Users cannot directly assess the quality of accounting data, and if they cannot rely on accountants to produce unbiased information, the information will have little value to the users.

3. **Describe the cost-benefit and behavioural issues involved in designing an accounting system.** Companies design management accounting information systems for the benefit of managers. These systems should be judged by a cost-benefit criterion—the benefits of better decisions should exceed the cost of the system. Behavioural factors—how the system affects managers and their decisions—greatly affect the benefit of a system.

4. **Explain the role of budgets and performance reports in planning and control.** Budgets and performance reports are essential tools for planning and control. Budgets result from the planning process. Managers use them to translate the organization's goals into action. A performance report compares actual results to the budget. Managers use these reports to monitor, evaluate, and reward performance and, thus, exercise control.

5. **Discuss the role accountants play in the company's value-chain functions.** Accountants play a key role in planning and control. Throughout the company's value chain, accountants gather and report cost and revenue information for decision makers.

6. **Contrast the functions of controllers and treasurers.** Accountants are staff employees who provide information and advice for line managers. The head of accounting is often called the controller. Unlike the treasurer, who is concerned mainly with financial matters such as raising capital and investing excess funds, the controller measures and reports on operating performance.

7. **Explain why accounting is important in a variety of career paths.** Accounting skills are useful in many functional areas of an organization. Management accountants often work with managers throughout the

company and learn much from them. This exposure makes management accountants prime candidates for promotions to operating and executive positions.

8. **Identify current trends in management accounting.** Many factors have caused changes in accounting systems in recent years. Most significant are globalization, technology, and changed business processes. Without continuous adaptation and improvement, accounting systems would become obsolete.

9. **Appreciate the importance of a code of ethical conduct to professional accountants.** Users of accounting information expect both external and internal accountants to adhere to high standards of ethical conduct. Many ethical dilemmas, however, require value judgments, not the simple application of standards.

DEMONSTRATION PROBLEMS FOR YOUR REVIEW

Try to solve these problems before examining the solutions that follow.

Problem One

The scorekeeping, attention-directing, and problem-solving duties of the accountant were described in this chapter. The accountant's usefulness to management is said to be directly influenced by how good an attention director and problem solver he or she is.

Evaluate this contention by specifically relating the accountant's duties to the duties of operating management.

Solution

Operating managers may have to be good scorekeepers, but their major duties are to concentrate on the day-to-day problems that most need attention, to make longer-range plans, and to arrive at special decisions. Accordingly, because managers are concerned mainly with attention-directing and problem-solving, they will obtain the most benefit from the alert internal accountant who is a useful attention director and problem solver.

Problem Two

Using the organization charts in this chapter (Exhibits 1-10 and 1-11), answer the following questions.

1. Which of the following have line authority over the machining manager: maintenance manager, manufacturing vice president, production superintendent, purchasing agent, storekeeper, personnel vice president, president, chief budgetary accountant, chief internal auditor?

2. What is the general role of service departments in an organization? How are they distinguished from operating or production departments?

3. Does the controller have line or staff authority over the cost accountants? Over the accounts receivable clerks?

4. What is probably the major duty (scorekeeping, attention-directing, or problem-solving) of the following:

Payroll clerk	Cost analyst
Accounts receivable clerk	Head of internal auditing
Cost record clerk	Head of special reports and studies
Head of general accounting	Head of accounting for planning and
Head of taxes	control
Budgetary accountant	Controller

Solution

1. The only executives that have line authority over the machining manager are the president, the manufacturing vice president, and the production superintendent.
2. A typical company's major purpose is to produce and sell goods or services. Unless a department is directly concerned with producing or selling, it is called a service or staff department. Service departments exist only to help the production and sales departments with their most important functions: the efficient production and sale of goods or services.
3. The controller has line authority over all members of his or her own department—all those shown in the controller's organization chart (Exhibit 1-11).
4. The major duty of the first five in column 1—through to the head of taxes—is typically scorekeeping. Attention-directing is probably the major responsibility of the next three. Problem-solving is probably the primary duty of the head of special reports and studies. The head of accounting for planning and control and the controller should be concerned with all three duties: scorekeeping, attention-directing, and problem-solving. However, there is a perpetual danger that day-to-day pressures will emphasize scorekeeping. Therefore, accountants and managers should ensure that attention-directing and problem-solving are also stressed. Otherwise the major management benefits of an accounting system may be lost.

Problem Three

Yang Electronics Company (YEC) developed a high-speed, low-cost copying machine. It marketed the machine primarily for home use. However, as YEC customers learned how easy and inexpensive it was to make copies with the YEC machine, its use by small businesses grew. Sales soared as some businesses ordered large numbers of the copiers. However, the heavier use of these companies caused a certain component of the equipment to break down. The copiers were warranted for two years, regardless of the amount of usage. Consequently, YEC experienced high costs for replacing the damaged components.

As the quarterly meeting of the Board of Directors of YEC approached, Mark Chua, assistant controller, was asked to prepare a report on the situation. Unfortunately, it was hard to predict the exact effects. However, it seemed that many business customers were starting to switch to more expensive copiers sold by competitors. And it was clear that the increased maintenance costs would significantly affect YEC's profitability. Chua summarized the situation the best he could for the Board.

Alice Martinez, the controller of YEC, was concerned about the impact of the report on the Board. She did not disagree with the analysis, but thought it made management look bad and might even have led the Board to discontinue the product. She was convinced from conversations with the head of engineering that the copier could be slightly redesigned to meet the needs of high-volume users, so discontinuing it might have passed up a potentially profitable opportunity.

Martinez called Chua into her office and asked him to delete the part of his report dealing with the component failures. She said it was all right to mention this orally to the Board, noting that engineering is nearing a solution to the problem. However, Chua felt strongly that such a revision in his report would mislead the Board about a potentially significant negative impact on the company's earnings.

Explain why Martinez's request to Chua is unethical. How should Chua resolve this situation?

Solution

According to the standards of Ethical Conduct for Management Accountants in Exhibit 1-13, Martinez's request violates requirements for competence, fairness, and independence. It violates competence because she is asking Chua to prepare a report that is not complete and clear—one that omits potentially relevant information. Therefore, the Board will not have all the information it should to make a decision about the component failure problem.

The request violates the fairness requirement because the revised report may subvert the attainment of the organization's objectives in order to achieve Martinez's objectives. Management accountants are specifically responsible for communicating unfavourable as well as favourable information.

Finally, the revised report would not be independent. It would not disclose all relevant information that could be expected to influence the Board's understanding of operations and, therefore, decisions.

Chua's responsibility is to discuss this issue with increasingly higher levels of authority within YEC. First, he should let Martinez know about his misgivings. Possibly the issue can be resolved by her withdrawing the request. If not, he should inform her that he intends to take up the matter with her superior and then approach higher levels of authority, even to the Board, if necessary, until the issue is resolved. So that Chua does not violate the standard of confidentiality, he should not discuss the matter with persons outside of YEC.

KEY TERMS

Vocabulary is an essential and often troublesome phase of the learning process. A fuzzy understanding of terms hampers the learning of concepts and the ability to solve accounting problems.

Before proceeding to the assignment material or to the next chapter, be sure you understand the listed words or terms. Their meanings are explained in the margin notes in the chapter.

accounting system *p. 8*
attention-directing *p. 5*
budget *p. 6*
Canadian Institute of Chartered
   Accountants (CICA) *p. 20*
Certified General Accountant (CGA)
   p. 20
Certified General Accountants
   Association of Canada (CGAAC)
   p. 20
Certified Management Accountant
   (CMA) *p. 20*
Chartered Accountant (CA) *p. 20*
comptroller *p. 16*
computer-integrated manufacturing
   (CIM) systems *p. 22*
controller *p. 16*

cost-benefit philosophy *p. 17*
financial accounting *p. 18*
just-in-time (JIT) philosophy *p. 21*
key success factors *p. 10*
line authority *p. 15*
management accounting *p. 5*
management by exception *p. 6*
performance reports *p. 6*
problem-solving *p. 5*
product life cycle *p. 11*
scorekeeping *p. 5*
Society of Management Accountants of
   Canada (SMAC) *p. 19*
staff authority *p. 15*
value chain *p. 11*
variance *p. 7*

ASSIGNMENT MATERIAL

The assignment material for each chapter is divided into five sections: *questions, problems, cases, Excel exercises,* and *collaborative exercises.* The questions are intended to clarify concepts and definitions. The problems require students to exhibit an understanding of the issues that need further thought and analysis. Cases are selected that require students to apply a decision process in recommending a solution to the problem, which may or may not be explicitly stated in the case.

QUESTIONS

Q1-1   What two major philosophies will be emphasized in succeeding chapters?

Q1-2   What are the three broad purposes of an accounting system?

Q1-3   "The emphases of financial accounting and management accounting differ." Explain.

Q1-4   Distinguish among scorekeeping, attention-directing, and problem-solving.

Q1-5   Give examples of special nonrecurring decisions and of long-range planning.

Q1-6   "Planning is much more vital than control." Do you agree? Explain.

Q1-7   Distinguish among a budget, a performance report, and a variance.

Q1-8   "Management by exception means abdicating management responsibility for planning and control." Do you agree? Explain.

Q1-9 "Good accounting provides automatic control of operations." Do you agree? Explain.

Q1-10 Explain the term "key success factors" and why it is important to identify them for a company.

Q1-11 Name the six business functions that comprise the value chain.

Q1-12 "The controller does control in a special sense." Explain.

Q1-13 Give three examples of service organizations. What distinguishes them from other types of organizations?

Q1-14 "The accounting system is intertwined with operating management. Business operations would be a hopeless tangle without the paperwork that is so often regarded with disdain." Do you agree? Explain, giving examples.

Q1-15 What is the essence of the JIT philosophy?

Q1-16 Why is it important for management accountants to abide by a code of ethics?

PROBLEMS

P1-1   MANAGEMENT AND FINANCIAL ACCOUNTING.   Jan Harvi, an able mechanical engineer, was informed that she would be promoted to assistant factory manager. Jan was pleased but uncomfortable. She knew little about accounting and had taken only one course in "financial" accounting.

Jan planned to enrol in a management accounting course as soon as possible. Meanwhile she asked Harland Young, a cost accountant, to state three or four of the principal distinctions between financial and management accounting.

Prepare Harland's written response to Jan.

P1-2   MANAGEMENT ACCOUNTING IN UNIVERSITIES.   Historically, Canadian universities were funded primarily on a per student basis in the form of tuitions and government grants. More recently there has been increased use of program-specific grants, and ceilings have been placed on the number of students that the government will fund at any one university.

How might these changes alter the management accounting practices of universities? Relate your answer to the decisions of senior university administrators.

P1-3   SCOREKEEPING, ATTENTION-DIRECTING, AND PROBLEM-SOLVING.   For each of the activities listed below, identify the major function (scorekeeping, attention-directing, or problem-solving). Also state whether the departments mentioned are production or service departments.

1. Analyzing, for a Ford production superintendent, the impact on costs of new drill presses.
2. Preparing a scrap report for the finishing department of a Honda parts factory.
3. Preparing the budget for the maintenance department of St. Jude's Hospital.
4. Interpreting why a Springfield foundry did not adhere to its production schedule.
5. Explaining the stamping department's performance report.
6. Preparing a monthly statement of European sales for the Ford marketing vice president.

7. Preparing, for the manager of production control of a Dofasco plant, a cost comparison of two computerized manufacturing control systems.
8. Interpreting variances on the University of Alberta purchasing department's performance report.
9. Analyzing, for a Honda international manufacturing manager, the desirability of having some auto parts made in Korea.
10. Preparing a schedule of amortization for forklift trucks in the receiving department of a General Electric factory in Scotland.

P1-4 **MANAGEMENT BY EXCEPTION.** A fraternity held a homecoming party. The fraternity expected attendance of 80 persons and prepared the following budget:

Room rental	$150
Food	800
Entertainment	600
Decorations	220
Total	$1,770

After all bills for the party were paid, the total cost came to $1,948, $178 over budget. Details are $150 for room rental; $1,013 for food; $600 for entertainment; and $185 for decorations. Ninety-five persons attended the party.

1. Prepare a performance report for the party that shows how actual costs differed from the budget. That is, include in your report the budget amounts, actual amounts, and variances.
2. Suppose the fraternity uses a management-by-exception rule. Which costs deserve further examination? Why?

P1-5 **ACCOUNTING'S POSITION IN ORGANIZATION: CONTROLLER AND TREASURER.** For each of the following activities, indicate whether it is most likely to be performed by the controller (C) or treasurer (T). Explain each answer.

1. Prepare credit checks on customers
2. Help managers prepare budgets
3. Advise which alternative action is least costly
4. Prepare divisional financial statements
5. Arrange short-term financing
6. Prepare tax returns
7. Arrange insurance coverage
8. Meet with financial analysts

P1-6 **COSTS AND BENEFITS.** Marks & Spencer, a huge retailer in the United Kingdom, was troubled by its paper bureaucracy. Looked at in isolation, each form seemed reasonable, but overall a researcher reported that there was substantial effort in each department to verify the information. Basically, the effort seemed out of proportion to any value received, and, eventually, many of the documents were simplified or eliminated.
Describe the rationale that should govern systems design.

P1-7 **FOCUS ON FINANCIAL DATA.**   A news story reported:

John Anderson, a veteran of Rockwell's automotive operations, recalls that when he sat in on meetings at the company's North American Aircraft Operations 20 years ago, "there'd be 60 or 70 guys talking technical problems, with never a word on profits." Such inattention to financial management helped Rockwell lose the F-15 fighter to McDonnell Douglas, Pentagon sources say. Anderson brought in profit-oriented executives, and he has now transformed North American's staff meetings to the point that "you seldom hear talk of technical problems any more," he says. "It's all financial."

What is your reaction to Anderson's comments? Are his comments related to management accounting?

P1-8 **CHANGES IN ACCOUNTING SYSTEMS.**   In the early 1990s, the Boeing Company undertook a large-scale study of its accounting system. The study led to several significant changes. None of these changes was required for reporting to external parties. However, management thought that the new system gave more accurate costs of the airplanes and other products.

1. Boeing had been a very successful company using their old accounting system. What might have motivated it to change the system?
2. When Boeing changed its system, what criteria might its managers have used to decide whether to invest in the new system?
3. Is a change to a system that provides more accurate product costs always a good change? Why or why not?

P1-9 **VALUE CHAIN.** Nike is an Oregon-based company that focuses on the design, development, and worldwide marketing of high-quality footwear, apparel, equipment, and accessory products. Nike is the largest seller of athletic footwear and athletic apparel in the world. The company sells its products to approximately 19,700 retail accounts in the United States and, through a mix of independent distributors, licensees, and subsidiaries, in approximately 110 countries around the world. Virtually all of the company's products are manufactured by independent contractors. Most footwear products are produced outside North America, while apparel products are produced both in North America and abroad.

1. Identify one decision that Nike managers make in each of the six value-chain functions.
2. For each decision in the above question, identify one piece of accounting information that would aid the manager's decision.

P1-10 **ROLE OF CONTROLLER.**   Juanita Palencia, newly hired controller of Braxton Industries, had been lured away from a competitor to revitalize the controller's department. Her first day on the job proved to be an eye-opener. One of her first interviews was with Bill Belton, production supervisor in the Alberta factory. Belton commented: "I really don't want to talk to anyone from the controller's office. The only time we see those accountants is when our costs go over their budget. They wave what they call a 'performance report,' but it's actually just a bunch of numbers they make up. It has nothing to do with what happens on the shop floor. Besides, my staff can't afford the time to fill out all the paperwork those accountants want, so I just plug in some numbers and send it back. Now, if you'll let me go back to important matters . . . ." Palencia left quickly, but she was already planning for her next visit with Belton.

1. Identify some of the problems in the relationship between the controller's department and the production departments (assuming that the Alberta factory is representative of the production departments).
2. What should Juanita Palencia do next?

P1-11 **LINE AND STAFF AUTHORITY** (CMA ADAPTED). Electronic Equipment Leasing Company (EEL) leases office equipment to a variety of customers. The company's organization chart follows.

The four positions indicated in the chart are described below:

- Ralph Biddle, assistant controller, special projects. Biddle works on projects assigned to him by the controller. The most recent project was to design a new accounts payable system.
- Betty Kelly, leasing contracts manager. Kelly coordinates and implements leasing transactions. Her department handles everything after the sales department gets a signed contract. This includes requisitioning equipment from the purchasing department, maintaining appropriate insurance, delivering equipment, issuing billing statements, and seeking renewal of leases.
- Larry Dukes, chief accountant. Dukes supervises all the accounting functions. He produces reports for the four supervisors in the functional areas.

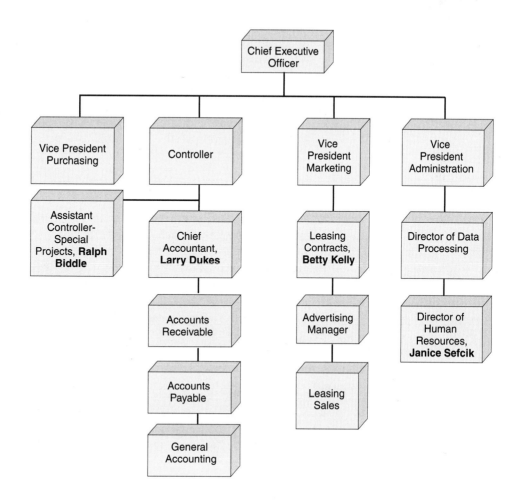

- Janice Sefcik, director of human resources. Sefcik works with all departments of EEL in hiring personnel. Her department advertises all positions and screens candidates, but the individual departments conduct interviews and make hiring decisions. Sefcik also coordinates employee evaluations and administers the company's salary schedule and employee-benefit program.

1. Distinguish between line and staff positions in an organization and discuss why conflicts might arise between line and staff managers.
2. For each of the four managers described, identify whether their position is a line or staff position and explain why you classified it that way. Also, indicate any potential conflicts that might arise with other managers in the organization.

P1-12 **ETHICAL ISSUES.** Suppose you are controller of a medium-sized oil exploration company in Calgary. You adhere to the standards of ethical conduct for management accountants. How would those standards affect your behaviour in each of the following situations:

1. Late one Friday afternoon you receive a geologist's report on a newly purchased property. It indicates a much higher probability of oil than had previously been expected. You are the only one to read the report that day. At a party on Saturday night, a friend asks about the prospects for the property.
2. An oil industry stock analyst invites you and your spouse to spend a week in Hawaii free of charge. All she wants in return is to be the first to know about any financial information your company is about to announce to the public.
3. It is time to make a forecast of the company's annual earnings. You know that some additional losses will be recognized before the final statements are prepared. The company's president has asked you to ignore these losses in making your prediction because a lower-than-expected earnings forecast could adversely affect the chances of obtaining a loan that is being negotiated and will be completed before actual earnings are announced.
4. You do not know whether a particular expense is deductible for income tax purposes. You are debating whether to research the tax laws or to simply assume that the item is deductible. After all, if you are not audited, no one will ever know the difference. And, if you are audited, you can plead ignorance of the law.

MANAGERIAL DECISION CASES

C1-1 **PROFESSIONAL ETHICS AND TOXIC WASTE.** Yukon Mining Company extracts and processes a variety of ores and minerals. One of its operations is a coal-cleaning plant that produces toxic wastes. For many years the wastes have been properly disposed of through National Disposal, a company experienced in disposing of such items. However, disposal of the toxic waste was becoming an economic hardship because increasing government regulations had caused the cost of such disposal to quadruple in the last six years.

Rebecca Long, director of financial reporting for Yukon Mining, was preparing the company's financial statements for the year ended June 30, 2006. In researching the material needed for preparing a footnote on environmental contingencies, Rebecca found the following note scribbled in pencil at the bottom of a memo to the general manager of the coal-cleaning plant. The body of the memo gave details on the increases in the cost of toxic waste disposals:

Ralph—We've got to keep these costs down or we won't meet budget. Can we mix more of these wastes with the shipments of refuse to the Oak Hill landfill? Nobody seems to notice the coal-cleaning fluids when we mix them in well.

Rebecca was bothered by the note. She considered ignoring it, pretending that she had not seen it. But, after a couple of hours, her conscience would not let her do it. Therefore, she pondered the following three alternative courses of action:

- Seek the advice of her boss, the vice president, finance of Yukon.
- Anonymously release the information to the local newspaper.
- Give the information to an outside member of the board of directors of Yukon whom she knows because he lives in her neighbourhood.

Required:
1. Discuss why Rebecca Long has an ethical responsibility to take some action about her suspicion of illegal dumping of toxic wastes.
2. For each of the three alternative courses of action, explain whether the action is appropriate.
3. Assume that Rebecca sought the advice of the vice president, finance and discovered that he knew about and approved of the dumping of toxic wastes. What steps should she take to resolve the conflict in this situation?

C1-2 **ETHICS AND ACCOUNTING PERSONNEL.** Mercury Shoe Company has an equal employment opportunity policy. This policy has the full support of the company's president, Beverly Watson, and is included in all advertisements for open positions.

Hiring in the accounting department is done by the controller, Dwight Laughton. The assistant controller, Jack Smith, also interviews candidates, but Laughton makes all decisions. In the last year, the department hired five new persons. There were 175 applications for the open positions. From this set, 13 had been interviewed, including four minority candidates. The five people who were hired included three sons of close friends of Laughton and no minorities. Smith felt that at least two of the minority candidates were very well qualified and that the three sons of friends were definitely not among the most qualified.

When Smith questioned Laughton concerning his reservations about the hiring practices, he was told that these decisions were Laughton's and not his, so he should not question them.

Required:
1. Explain why Laughton's hiring practices were unethical.
2. What should Smith do about this situation?

C1-3 **CASE ON KEY SUCCESS FACTORS** (CICA).[7] Earthstone Clays Ltd. began as a small pottery studio, selling pottery made by the owners and by other local craftspeople. Gradually, other kinds of crafts and supplies were added, until the company became both a retailer of finished crafts and a supplier to the craftspeople. For example, the company sells the raw clay, the glaze materials, and the wheels and kilns used to make pottery, as well as finished pottery.

Over the years, the company has expanded to become a major regional supplier of raw materials and equipment. Although the retail business has grown, most of Earthstone's revenue comes from wholesale sales to craftspeople. The company now has four outlets, each of which has combined wholesale and retail operations. The company mixes most of its clay and glazes and performs other manufacturing and assembly work in a shop attached to its central warehouse.

In the past, all the retail sales and a large portion of the wholesale sales were for cash. Therefore, the company had low receivables. Recently, however, the company has tried to maintain its sales level by allowing more credit to wholesale customers.

Wholesale inventories have always been high in dollar value, particularly for larger pieces of equipment, and have been slow to turn over. Due to the nature of the crafts business, it is necessary to carry a wide variety of inventory items.

Retail merchandise quantities are maintained at a high level. Most of this merchandise is held on consignment, and the remainder consists of items purchased from a few well-established craftspeople or produced in the company's shop.

Much of the wholesale inventory is imported from the United States and Japan. The company's margins have been severely squeezed because of recent currency fluctuations. Crafts are considered a luxury good, so the company's retail sales and those to its wholesale customers have been hard-hit. In spite of significant price reductions, sales volume has generally fallen.

Recently, cash flow has been a problem. The company exceeded its credit limit and the bank expressed concern about the company's financial state and inability to determine its cash requirements. In an effort to alleviate the problem, several cost-cutting measures were implemented and advertising expenditures were increased to try to encourage sales. However, the company's position continued to deteriorate. The president then considered the following courses of action: the reduction of inventory levels; the elimination of product lines; the shift of emphasis from wholesale to retail sales; and further price reductions. However, the president was unable to evaluate any of these possibilities since the accounting system did not generate the necessary information.

Required:

1. Identify the key success factors for Earthstone Clays Ltd. and identify how they have changed since the company's initial operation.
2. What information is required by the president to manage Earthstone Clays successfully?

---

[7] Reprinted, with permission, from Uniform Final Examination, Paper III, Q#2, 1983, © 1993, The Canadian Institute of Chartered Accountants, Toronto Canada. Any changes to the original material are the sole responsibility of the authors and have not been reviewed or endorsed by the CICA.

E1-1 BUDGETS AND PERFORMANCE EVALUATION

Goal: Create an Excel spreadsheet to prepare a performance report, and use the results to answer questions about your findings.

Scenario: Beta Gamma Sigma, the business honourary fraternity, has asked you to prepare a performance report about a homecoming party that they recently held. The background data for Beta Gamma Sigma's performance report appears in Problem P1-4.

When you have completed your spreadsheet, answer the following questions:

1. Based on the formatting option used in the exercise, do the negative (red) variances represent amounts that are over or under budget?

2. Which cost/costs changed because the number of attendees increased?

3. Did the fraternity stay within the budgeted amount for food on a per person basis?

Step by Step:

1. Open a new Excel spreadsheet.

2. In column A, create a bold-faced heading that contains the following:
   Row 1: Chapter 1 Decision Guideline
   Row 2: Beta Gamma Sigma Homecoming Party
   Row 3: Performance Report
   Row 4: Today's Date

3. Merge and centre the date across columns A through D.

4. In row 7, create the following bold-faced, right-justified column headings:
   Column B: Budget
   Column C: Actual
   Column D: Variance

5. In column A, create the following row headings:
   Row 8: Room Rental
   Row 9: Food
   Row 10: Entertainment
   Row 11: Decorations
   Row 12: Total Costs
   Skip a row
   Row 14: Attendees
   Skip a row
   Row 16: Food per Person

6. Use the data from Problem P1-4 and enter the budget and actual amounts for room, food, entertainment, decorations, and attendees.

7. Use budget minus actual formulas to generate variances for each of the cost categories.

8. Use the SUM function to generate total costs for the budget, actual, and variance columns.

9. Use a formula to generate the "per person" food amount for the budget and actual columns.

10. Format all amounts as:
    Number tab:

	Category:	Currency
	Decimal places:	0
	Symbol:	None
	Negative numbers:	Red with parentheses

COLLABORATIVE LEARNING EXERCISE

CL1-1   **THE FUTURE MANAGEMENT ACCOUNTANT**

Students should gather in groups of four to six each. Half of each group should read the first of the following articles and half should read the second article. (Alternatively, you can do this exercise as a whole class, with half of the class reading one article and half reading the other.)

- Kulesza, C., and G. Siegel, "It's Not Your Father's Management Accounting," *Management Accounting*, May 1997, pp. 56–59.

- Russell, K., G. Siegel, and C. Kulesza, "Counting More, Counting Less: Transformations in the Management Accounting Profession," *Strategic Finance*, September 1999, pp. 39–44.

1. Individually, write down the three most important lessons you learned from the article you read.
2. As a group, list all the lessons identified in requirement 1. Combine those that are the same.
3. Prioritize the list you developed in requirement 2 in terms of importance to someone considering a career in management accounting.
4. Discuss whether this exercise has changed your impression of management accounting and, if so, how.

Cost Behaviour and Cost-Volume Relationships

After studying this chapter, you will be able to

1. Explain how cost drivers affect cost behaviour.

2. Do a comparison of variable and fixed costs and understand the relevant range in which they are formulated.

3. Calculate break-even sales volume in total dollars and total units and construct a cost-volume-profit graph.

4. Identify the limiting assumptions that underlie cost-volume-profit analysis.

5. Calculate sales volume in total dollars and total units to reach a target profit.

6. Explain the effects of sales mix on profits.

7. Compute cost-volume-profit relationships on an after-tax basis.

8. Distinguish between contribution margin and gross margin.

How do the costs and revenues of a hospital change as one more patient is admitted for a four-day stay? How are the costs and revenues of an airline affected when one more passenger is boarded at the last moment, or when another flight is added to the schedule? How should the budget request by a university be affected by the addition of a new program? These questions have a common theme: What will happen to financial results if a specified level of activity or volume fluctuates? Answering this question is the first step in analyzing **cost behaviour**—how the activities of an organization affect its costs. A knowledge of patterns of cost behaviour offers valuable insights in planning and controlling short- and long-run operations. In this chapter, however, our goal is to provide perspective rather than to impart an intimate knowledge of the complexities of cost behaviour.

Cost Behaviour. How the activities of an organization affect its costs.

COST DRIVERS

Cost Drivers. Activities that affect (drive) costs.

Activities that affect (drive) costs are often called **cost drivers**. An organization may have many cost drivers. Consider the costs of running a warehouse that receives and stores material and supplies. The costs of operating the warehouse may be driven by the total dollar value of items handled, the weight of the items handled, the number of different orders received, the number of different items handled, the number of different suppliers, the fragility of the items handled, and possibly several other cost drivers. A major task in specifying cost behaviour is to identify the cost drivers—that is, to determine the activities that cause costs to be incurred.

An organization has many cost drivers across its value chain. Exhibit 2-1 lists examples of costs and potential cost drivers for each of the value-chain functions. How well the accountant does at identifying the most appropriate cost drivers determines how well managers understand cost behaviour and how well costs are controlled.

EXHIBIT 2-1

Examples of Value-Chain Functions, Costs, and Cost Drivers

VALUE-CHAIN FUNCTION AND EXAMPLE COSTS	EXAMPLE COST DRIVERS
Research and development	
• Salaries of marketing-research personnel, costs of market surveys	Number of new product proposals
• Salaries of product and process engineers	Complexity of proposed products
Design of products, services, and processes	
• Salaries of product and process engineers	Number of engineering hours
• Cost of computer-aided design equipment, cost to develop prototype of product for testing	Number of parts per product
Production	
• Labour wages	Labour hours
• Supervisory salaries	Number of people supervised
• Maintenance wages	Number of mechanic hours
• Amortization of plant and machinery, supplies	Number of machine hours
• Energy	Kilowatt hours
Marketing	
• Cost of advertisements	Number of advertisements
• Salaries of marketing personnel, travel costs, entertainment costs	Sales dollars
Distribution	
• Wages of shipping personnel	Labour hours
• Transportation costs including amortization of vehicles and fuel	Weight of items delivered
Customer service	
• Salaries of service personnel	Hours spent servicing products
• Costs of supplies, travel	Number of service calls

This chapter will focus on *volume-related cost drivers* without examining other cost drivers in detail. Later chapters will introduce cost drivers that are not related to volume. Volume-related cost drivers include the number of orders processed, the number of items billed in a billing department, the number of admissions to a theatre, the number of kilograms handled in a warehouse, the hours of labour worked in an assembly department, the number of rides in an amusement park, the seat-miles on an airline, and the dollar sales in a retail business. All of these cost drivers can serve either directly or indirectly as a measure of the volume of output of goods or services. Of course, when only one product is being produced, the unit of production is the most obvious volume-related cost driver for production-related costs.

Utopia Fabricating Ltd. of Winnipeg, Manitoba, converted old oil into reusable replacement diesel fuel. Traditional oil recovery processes required large volumes of old oil to be trucked to large refineries. While trucking distances and capital costs were significant cost drivers, traditional cost systems focused on the volumes of old oil being processed. By focusing on the more significant cost drivers of trucking distances and capital costs, Utopia's process used a small refinery that required substantially smaller volumes. By reducing the trucking expenses, the capital costs of a number of small refineries were justified.[1]

COMPARISON OF VARIABLE AND FIXED COSTS

Variable Cost. A cost that changes in direct proportion to changes in the level (volume) of economic activity.

Fixed Cost. A cost that is not immediately affected by changes in the cost driver.

A key to understanding cost behaviour is distinguishing *variable costs* from *fixed costs*. Costs are classified as variable or fixed depending on how much they change as the level of a particular cost driver changes. A **variable cost** is a cost that changes in direct proportion to changes in the level (volume) of economic activity. In contrast, a **fixed cost** remains unchanged as the level of economic activity changes.

Some examples may help clarify the differences between fixed and variable costs. The costs of most merchandise, materials, parts, supplies, commissions, and many types of labour are variable with respect to volume of economic activity. For example, the higher the volume of sales the higher the costs of units sold, materials, parts and supplies used, and commissions and labour costs paid. On the other hand, real estate taxes, real estate insurance, many executive salaries, and space rentals tend to be fixed with respect to any volume of economic activity. For example, a firm pays the same property tax, premium on fire insurance, rent on rental property, and executive salaries no matter how high or low the volume of economic activity (sales).

Consider some variable costs. Suppose Watkins Products pays its door-to-door sales personnel a 40 percent straight commission. The total cost of sales commissions to Watkins is 40 percent of sales dollars. Thus sales commissions is a variable cost with respect to sales revenues. Suppose Dan's Bait Shop buys bags of fish bait for $4 each. The total cost of fish bait is $4 times the number of bags purchased. Thus fish bait is a variable cost with respect to units (number of bags) purchased. Notice that variable costs are the same *per unit*, but that the *total* fluctuates in direct proportion to the cost-driver activity. Exhibit 2-2 graphically depicts these relationships between cost and cost-driver activity.

Now consider a fixed cost. Suppose Sony rents a factory to produce picture tubes for colour television sets for $500,000 per year. The *total cost* of $500,000 is

Sony
www.sony.ca

---

[1] "Utopia finds small solution for used oil," *The Globe and Mail*, March 25, 1992.

EXHIBIT 2-2

Variable-Cost Behaviour

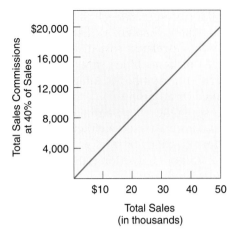

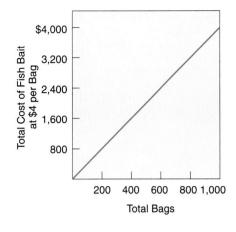

not affected by the number of picture tubes produced. However, the *unit cost* of rent applicable to each tube does depend on the total number of tubes produced. If 100,000 tubes are produced, the unit cost will be $500,000 ÷ 100,000 = $5. If 50,000 tubes are produced, the unit cost will be $500,000 ÷ 50,000 = $10. Therefore, a fixed cost does not change *in total*, but it becomes progressively smaller on a *per unit* basis as the volume increases. So, fixed cost per unit is, in a way, variable while variable cost per unit is, in a way, fixed!

It is important to note from these examples that the "variable" or "fixed" characteristic of a cost relates to its *total dollar amount* and not to its per unit amount. The following table summarizes these relationships.

| TYPE OF COST | IF COST-DRIVER ACTIVITY LEVEL INCREASES (OR DECREASES): | |
	TOTAL COST	COST PER UNIT*
Fixed costs	No change	Decrease (or increase)
Variable costs	Increase (or decrease)	No change

* Per-unit activity volume, for example, product units, passenger-miles, sales dollars.

When predicting costs, two rules of thumb are useful:

1. Think of fixed costs as a *total*. Total fixed costs remain unchanged regardless of changes in cost-driver activity.
2. Think of variable costs on a *per unit* basis. The per unit variable cost remains unchanged regardless of changes in cost-driver activity.

Relevant Range

Although we have just described fixed costs as unchanging regardless of cost-driver activity, this rule of thumb holds true only within reasonable limits. For example, rent costs will rise beyond $500,000 if increased production requires Sony to rent a larger or additional building—or if the landlord decides to raise the rent. Conversely, rent costs may go down if decreased production causes the

Relevant Range. The limits of cost-driver activity within which a specific relationship between costs and the cost driver is valid.

company to move to a smaller plant. The **relevant range** is the limits of cost-driver activity within which a specific relationship between costs and the cost driver (volume) is valid. Remember that within the relevant range, a fixed cost remains fixed only over a given time period—usually the budget period. Fixed costs may change from budget year to budget year solely because of changes in insurance and property tax rates, executive salary levels, or rent levels. But these items are unlikely to change within a given year.

For example, assume that a General Electric plant has a relevant range of between 40,000 and 85,000 cases of light bulbs per month and that total monthly fixed costs within the relevant range is $100,000. Within the relevant range, fixed costs will remain the same. If production falls below 40,000 cases, changes in personnel and salaries would reduce fixed costs to $60,000. If operations rise above 85,000 cases, increases in personnel and salaries would boost fixed costs to $115,000.

These assumptions—a given time period and a given activity range—are shown graphically at the top of Exhibit 2-3. However, it is highly unusual for monthly operations to be outside the relevant range. Therefore, the three-level refinement at the top of Exhibit 2-3 is usually not graphed. Instead, a single horizontal line is typically extended through the plotted activity levels, as at the bottom of the exhibit. A dashed line is often used outside the relevant range.

EXHIBIT 2-3

Fixed Costs and the Relevant Range

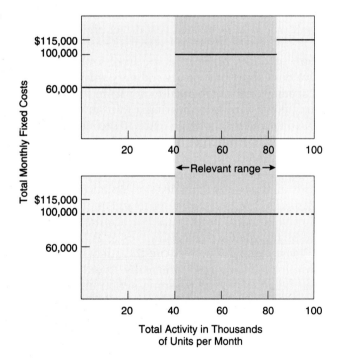

The basic idea of a relevant range also applies to variable costs. That is, outside a relevant range, some variable costs, per unit, may be different at different levels of activity. For example, fuel consumed or kilometres per litre of gas consumed may be different for short distances within the city than for long distances in highway travel.

Difficulties in Classifying Costs

As you may suspect, it is often difficult to classify a cost as exactly variable or exactly fixed. Many complications arise, including the possibility of costs behaving in some nonlinear way (i.e., not behaving as a straight line). For example, as tax preparers learn to process the new year's tax forms, their productivity rises and they complete more tax returns in a given period of time. This means that total costs may actually behave like this:

Moreover, costs may simultaneously be affected by more than one cost driver. For example, shipping labour costs may be affected by *both* the weight and the number of units handled. We shall investigate various facets of this problem in succeeding chapters; for now, we shall assume that any cost may be classified as either variable or fixed. We assume also that a given variable cost is associated with *only one* volume-related cost driver and that the relationship is *linear*.

Finally, in the real world, classifying costs as fixed or variable depends on the decision situation. More costs are fixed and fewer are variable when decisions involve very short time spans and very small increases in activities. Suppose an Air Canada plane is scheduled to depart in two minutes. A potential passenger is running down a corridor bearing a transferable ticket from a competing airline. Unless the plane is held for an extra 30 seconds, the passenger will miss the departure and will not switch to Air Canada for the planned trip. What are the variable costs to Air Canada of delaying the departure and placing one more passenger in an otherwise empty seat? Variable costs (for example, fuel costs) are negligible. Virtually all the costs in that decision situation are fixed. Now in contrast, suppose Air Canada's decision is whether to add another flight, acquire another gate, add another destination to its routes, or acquire another airplane. Many more costs would be regarded as variable and fewer as fixed.

These examples underscore the importance of the need for analysis of cost behaviour. Whether costs are really "fixed" depends heavily on the relevant range, the length of the planning period in question, and the specific situation under which a decision is made.

COST-VOLUME-PROFIT ANALYSIS

Managers often classify costs as fixed or variable when making decisions that affect the volume of output. The managers want to know how such decisions will affect costs and revenues. They realize that many factors, in addition to the volume of output, will affect costs. Yet, a useful starting point in their decision process is to specify the relationship between the volume of output and the costs and revenues.

The managers of profit-seeking organizations usually study the effects of output volume on revenue (sales), expenses (costs), and net profit. This study is

Cost-Volume-Profit (CVP) Analysis. The study of the effects of output volume on revenue (sales), expenses (costs), and net profit.

commonly called **cost-volume-profit (CVP) analysis**. The managers of not-for-profit organizations also benefit from the study of cost-volume-profit relationships. Why? No organization has unlimited resources, and knowledge of how costs fluctuate as volume changes helps managers understand how to control costs. For example, administrators of not-for-profit hospitals are constantly concerned about the behaviour of costs as the volume of patients fluctuates.

To apply CVP analysis, managers resort to some simplifying assumptions. A major assumption is to classify costs as either variable or fixed with respect to a single measure of the volume (activity level).

MAKING MANAGERIAL DECISIONS

A key factor in helping managers understand cost behaviour is distinguishing between variable and fixed costs. Test your understanding by answering the following questions.

1. A producer of premium ice cream uses "litres of ice cream produced" as a cost driver for dairy ingredients. Is the cost of dairy ingredients a variable or a fixed cost?

2. The same company uses "square metres occupied" as a cost driver for occupancy costs such as building amortization and insurance. Is occupancy cost variable or fixed?

ANSWERS

The best way to determine whether the cost of a resource is fixed or variable is to ask the question, "If the level of the cost driver changes, what will happen to the cost?" If the company increases (decreases) its production of ice cream, then the cost of dairy ingredients will also increase (decrease). Thus, the cost of dairy ingredients is variable. If the square metres occupied by a particular unit in an organization increases (decreases), the building amortization and insurance on the building will not change. Thus, building occupancy costs such as amortization and insurance are fixed costs.

CVP Scenario

Amy Winston, the manager of food services for a university's food services department, is trying to decide whether to rent a line of food vending machines. Although individual snack items have various acquisition costs and selling prices, Winston has decided that an average selling price of $0.50 per unit and an average acquisition price of $0.40 per unit will suffice for purposes of this analysis. She predicts the following revenue and expense relationships:

	PER UNIT	PERCENT OF SALES
Selling price	$ 0.50	100%
Variable cost of each item	0.40	80%
Selling price less variable cost	$ 0.10	20%
Monthly fixed expenses		
Rent	$1,000	
Wages for replenishing and servicing	4,500	
Other fixed expenses	500	
Total fixed expenses per month	$6,000	

We will next use these data to illustrate several applications of cost-volume-profit analysis.

Break-Even Point—Contribution Margin and Income Statement Equation Approaches

OBJECTIVE 3

Calculate break-even sales volume in total dollars and total units and construct a cost-volume-profit graph.

Break-Even Point. The level of sales at which revenue equals expenses, and income is zero.

Break-Even Analysis. The study of cost-volume-profit relationships.

Margin of Safety. Equal to the planned unit sales less the breakeven unit sales; it shows how far sales can fall below the planned level before losses occur.

A basic CVP analysis computes the monthly break-even point in number of units and in dollar sales. The **break-even point** is the level of sales at which revenue equals expenses and, therefore, net income is zero.

The study of cost-volume-profit relationships is often called **break-even analysis**. This term may be misleading, because finding the break-even point is just one aspect of CVP analysis. Managers need to go beyond the break-even point and consider how the decision will affect sales, costs, and net income.

However, one direct use of the break-even point is to assess possible risks. By comparing planned sales with the break-even point, managers can determine a **margin of safety**.

$$\text{margin of safety} = \text{planned unit sales} - \text{break-even unit sales}$$

The margin of safety shows how far sales can fall below the planned level before losses occur. The higher the planned unit sales are above the break-even unit sales, the greater the margin of safety.

There are two basic techniques for computing a break-even point: the contribution margin approach and the income statement equation approach.

Contribution-Margin Approach

Contribution Margin. The sales price minus all the variable expenses.

Consider the following commonsense arithmetic approach. Every unit sold generates a **contribution margin**, which is the sales price minus the variable costs per unit. For the vending machine snack items the contribution margin is

Unit sales price	$0.50
Unit variable cost	0.40
Unit contribution margin to fixed costs and net income	$0.10

When enough units have been sold to generate a total contribution margin equal to the total fixed costs, the break-even point is reached. Divide the $6,000 in fixed costs by the $0.10 unit contribution margin. The number of units that must be sold to break even is

Break-even in units:
fixed expenses ÷ contribution margin per unit = $6,000 ÷ $0.10 = 60,000 units

The sales revenue at the break-even point is 60,000 units × $0.50 per unit, or $30,000.

Think about the contribution margin of the snack items. Each unit purchased and sold generates *extra* revenue of $0.50 and *extra* cost of $0.40. Fixed costs are unaffected. Therefore, profit increases by $0.10 for each unit purchased and sold. If zero units were sold, a loss equal to the fixed cost of $6,000 would be incurred. Each unit reduces the loss by $0.10 until sales reach the break-even point of 60,000 units. After that point, each unit adds (or *contributes*) $0.10 to profit.

The condensed income statement at the break-even point is

		PER UNIT	PERCENTAGE
Units	60,000		
Sales 60,000 x $0.50	$30,000	$0.50	100%
Variable costs 60,000 x $0.40	24,000	0.40	80%
Contribution margin	$6,000	$0.10	20%
Fixed costs	6,000		
Net income	$0		

Sometimes the unit price and unit variable costs are not known. In such cases, you must work with total sales and total variable costs and calculate variable costs as a *percentage of each sales dollar*.

Consider our vending machine example:

Sales price	100%
Variable expenses as a percentage of dollar sales	80%
Contribution-margin percentage	20%

Therefore, 20 percent of each sales dollar is available for the recovery of fixed expenses and the making of net income:

Break-even in dollars:
fixed expenses ÷ contribution margin ratio = $6,000 ÷ 20% = $30,000 sales

The contribution margin percentage you can compute is based on dollar sales without determining the break-even point in units.

The Income Statement Equation Approach

The income statement equation approach is a more general form of analysis. You are familiar with a typical income statement. Any income statement can be expressed in equation form, as follows:

$$\text{sales} - \text{variable expenses} - \text{fixed expenses} = \text{net income} \qquad (1)$$

That is

$$\left(\begin{array}{c}\text{unit} \\ \text{sales} \\ \text{price}\end{array} \times \begin{array}{c}\text{number} \\ \text{of} \\ \text{units}\end{array}\right) - \left(\begin{array}{c}\text{unit} \\ \text{variable} \\ \text{cost}\end{array} \times \begin{array}{c}\text{number} \\ \text{of} \\ \text{units}\end{array}\right) - \begin{array}{c}\text{fixed} \\ \text{expenses}\end{array} = \begin{array}{c}\text{net} \\ \text{income}\end{array}$$

At the break-even point net income is zero:

$$\text{sales} - \text{variable expenses} - \text{fixed expenses} = 0$$

Let N = number of units to be sold to break even. Then

Procter & Gamble Canada Inc.: The Scope Example

Procter & Gamble
www.pg.com/canada

Procter & Gamble was founded over 150 years ago when soapmaker James Gamble and candlemaker William Procter decided to join forces in Cincinnati, Ohio. The company concentrated on the consumer products market, focusing its effort on quality and consumer satisfaction. One of P&G's historic strengths is its ability to develop truly innovative products to meet consumers' needs. Today, Procter & Gamble is one of the most successful consumer goods companies in the world and its products can be found in nine out of ten Canadian homes. It operates in 54 countries and had sales of more than $27 billion and net earnings of $1.8 billion in 1991. The Canadian subsidiary contributed $1.3 billion in sales and $54 million in net earnings in 1991. This subsidiary has been recognized as the leader in the Canadian packaged goods industry, and its consumer brands lead in most of the categories in which the company operates.

One such brand is Scope, which is part of Procter & Gamble's Health Care Division. Scope was launched in the mid-1960s as the first brand that provided both effective protection against bad breath and a better taste than other mouthwashes. Advertising lines included, "Scope fights bad breath" and "Don't let the good taste fool you." Very quickly it became the market leader.

The following analysis indicates the difference between contribution margin and gross margin and provides a break-even volume calculation for the Scope brand. (The numbers are fictitious to protect the confidentiality of P&G's actual cost data.)

	$ Thousands	$ Product cost/case	$ Variable cost/case
Net Sales	$16,860	$38.32	$38.32
Expenses:			
Ingredients	3,337	7.58	7.58
Packaging	2,088	4.74	4.74
Manufacturing	2,861	6.50	3.25
Delivery	1,081	2.46	2.46
Miscellaneous	467	1.06	0.78
Cost of goods sold	9,834	22.34	
Variable costs			18.81
Gross Margin	$ 7,026	$15.98	
Contribution Margin			$19.51

Break-even volume = Fixed costs of $1,554,000 ÷ Contribution margin of $19.51= 79,651 cases

Source: Adapted from a case "Gwen Hearst's Dilemma." Written by Franklin Ramsoomair, Wilfrid Laurier University, and David LeNeveau, Mike Wingert, and Colleen Jay, Procter & Gamble Canada. www.pg.com/en_CA/product_card/hw_scope.jhtml.

$$\$0.50N - \$0.40N - \$6,000 = 0$$
$$\$0.10N = \$6,000$$
$$N = \frac{\$6,000}{\$0.10}$$
$$N = 60,000 \text{ units}$$

To find the *dollar* sales, multiply 60,000 *units* by $0.50, which would yield the break-even dollar sales of $30,000.

You can also solve the equation for sales dollars without computing the unit break-even point by using the relationship of variable costs and profits as a *percentage* of sales:

$$\text{variable-cost ratio or percentage} = \frac{\text{variable cost per unit}}{\text{sales price per unit}}$$

$$= \frac{\$0.40}{\$0.50}$$

$$= 0.80 \text{ or } 80\%$$

Let S = sales in dollars needed to break even. Then

$$S - 0.80S - \$6,000 = 0$$
$$0.20S = \$6,000$$
$$S = \frac{\$6,000}{0.20}$$
$$S = \$30,000$$

Relationship between the Two Break-Even Approaches

You may have noticed that the contribution-margin approach is merely a shortcut of the income statement equation technique. Look at the last three lines in the two solutions given for Equation 1. They read

BREAK-EVEN VOLUME	
In Units	**In Dollars**
$0.10N = \$6,000$	$0.20S = \$6,000$
$N = \dfrac{\$6,000}{\$0.10}$	$S = \dfrac{\$6,000}{0.20}$
$N = 60,000 \text{ units}$	$S = \$30,000$

From these equations we can derive the general shortcut formulas:

$$\frac{\text{break-even volume}}{\text{in units}} = \frac{\text{fixed costs}}{\text{contribution margin per unit}} = \frac{FC}{CM} \quad (2)$$

$$\frac{\text{break-even volume}}{\text{in dollars}} = \frac{\text{fixed costs}}{\text{contribution margin ratio}} = \frac{FC}{CM\%} \quad (3)$$

You may use either the equation or the contribution-margin technique. The choice is a matter of personal preference or convenience for each particular case.

CVP/Break-Even Point—Graph

Exhibit 2-4 shows the cost-volume-profit relationships in our vending machine example. Study the graph as you read the procedure for constructing it.

Step 1: Draw the axes. The horizontal axis represents the sales units, and the vertical axis sales and cost.

Step 2: Plot sales volume. Select a convenient sales volume, say, 100,000 units, and plot point A for total sales dollars at that volume: 100,000 × $0.50 = $50,000. Draw the revenue (i.e., sales) line from point A to the origin, point 0.

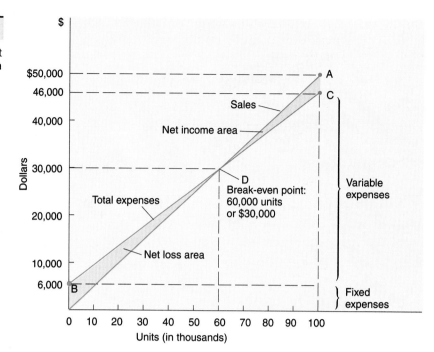

EXHIBIT 2-4

Cost-Volume-Profit Graph

Step 3: Plot fixed expenses. Draw the line showing the $6,000 fixed portion of expenses. It should be a horizontal line intersecting the vertical axis at $6,000, point B.

Step 4: Determine the variable portion of expenses at a convenient level of activity: 100,000 units × $0.40 = $40,000. Add this to the fixed expenses ($40,000 + $6,000 = $46,000). Plot point C for 100,000 units and $46,000. Then draw a line between this point and point B. This is the total expenses line.

Step 5: Locate the break-even point. The break-even point is where the total expenses line crosses the sales line, 60,000 units or $30,000, namely, where total sales revenues exactly equal total costs, point D.

The break-even point is only one facet of this cost-volume-profit graph. More generally, the graph shows the profit or loss at *any* rate of activity. At any given volume, the vertical distance between the sales line and the total expenses line measures the net income or net loss.

Managers often use break-even graphs because they show potential profits over a wide range of volume more easily than numerical exhibits. Whether graphs or other types of exhibits are used depends largely on management's preference.

Note that the concept of a relevant range applies to the entire break-even graph. Almost all break-even graphs show revenue and cost lines extending back to the vertical axis as shown in Exhibit 2-5(A). This approach is misleading because the relationships depicted in such graphs are valid only within the relevant range that underlies the construction of the graph. Exhibit 2-5(B), a modification of the conventional break-even graph, partially demonstrates the multitude of assumptions that must be made in constructing the typical break-even graph. Some of these assumptions follow.

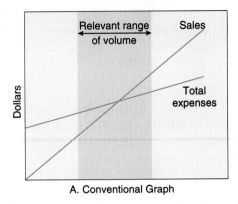

EXHIBIT 2-5

Conventional and Modified Break-Even Graphs

A. Conventional Graph

B. Modified Graph

Break-Even Point Assumptions

OBJECTIVE 4

Identify the limiting assumptions that underlie cost-volume-profit analysis.

1. Expenses may be classified into variable and fixed categories. (This may not always be true!) Total variable expenses vary directly with volume. Total fixed expenses do not change with volume.
2. The behaviour of revenues and expenses is accurately portrayed and is linear over the relevant range. (This is not always true!) The principal differences between the accountant's break-even chart and the economist's chart are that (a) the accountant's sales line is drawn on the assumption that selling prices do not change with production or sales, and the economist assumes that reduced selling prices are normally associated with increased sales volume; (b) the accountant usually assumes a constant variable expense per unit, and the economist assumes that the variable expense per unit changes with production levels. Within the relevant range, the accountant's and the economist's sales and expense lines are usually close to one another, although the lines may diverge greatly outside the range.
3. Efficiency and productivity will remain unchanged. (This is not always true!)
4. Sales mix of different products sold will be constant. (This is rarely true!) The **sales mix** is the relative proportions or combinations of quantities of products that comprise total sales. For example, 30% of the total units sold are product A and 70% are product B.
5. The difference in inventory levels at the beginning and at the end of a period is insignificant. Otherwise the number of units sold will be significantly different from the number of units produced. This is not always true as inventories fluctuate, sometimes widely.

Sales Mix. The relative proportions or combinations of quantities of products that comprise total sales.

Changes in Fixed Expenses

Changes in fixed expenses cause changes in the break-even point. For example, if the $1,000 monthly rent for the vending machines were doubled, what would the monthly break-even point be in number of units and in dollar sales?

The fixed expenses would increase from $6,000 to $7,000, so

Chapter 2   Cost Behaviour and Cost-Volume Relationships   **53**

$$\text{break-even volume in units} = \frac{\text{fixed expenses}}{\text{contribution margin per unit}} = \frac{\$7,000}{\$0.10} = 70,000 \text{ units} \quad (2)$$

$$\text{break-even volume in dollars} = \frac{\text{fixed expenses}}{\text{contribution margin ratio}} = \frac{\$7,000}{0.20} = \$35,000 \quad (3)$$

Note that a one-sixth increase in fixed expenses altered the break-even point by one-sixth: from 60,000 to 70,000 units and from $30,000 to $35,000. This type of relationship always exists between fixed expenses and the break-even point, if everything else remains constant.

Companies frequently lower their break-even points by reducing their total fixed costs. For example, closing or selling buildings decreases property taxes, insurance, amortization, and managers' salaries. Further, it is, of course, also possible to reduce a break-even point by reducing variable costs per unit or by increasing the selling price per unit.

Changes in Contribution Margin per Unit

Companies reduce their break-even points by increasing their contribution margins per unit of product through either increases in sales prices or decreases in unit-variable costs, or both. For example, assume that the fixed rent is still $1,000. (1) If the owner is paid $0.01 rental per unit in addition to the fixed rent, find the monthly break-even point in number of units and in dollar sales. (2) If the selling price falls from $0.50 to $0.45 per unit, and the original variable expenses per unit are unchanged, find the monthly break-even point in number of units and in dollar sales.

1. The variable expenses would increase from $0.40 to $0.41, the unit contribution margin would decline from $0.10 to $0.09, and the contribution-margin ratio would become 0.18 ($0.09 ÷ $0.50).

MAKING MANAGERIAL DECISIONS

Managers use CVP analysis to predict effects of changes in sales or costs. Using shortcut formulas (2) and (3), answer the following questions. Remember that the contribution margin per unit equals the sales price per unit minus the variable costs per unit.

1. What would be the effect on the unit and dollar break-even level if fixed costs increase (and there are no other changes)?

2. What would be the effect on the unit and dollar break-even level if variable cost per unit decreases (and there are no other changes)?

3. What would be the effect on the unit and dollar break-even level if sales volume increases (and there are no other changes)?

ANSWERS

1. The break-even level in both units and sales dollars would increase if fixed costs increase.

2. The break-even level in both units and sales dollars would decrease if variable cost per unit decreases.

3. Think before answering this question. The actual (or even planned) volume of sales in units has nothing to do with determining the break-even point. This is why unit volume does not appear in either equation (2) or (3).

The original fixed expenses of $6,000 would be unaffected, but the denominators would change from those previously used. Thus,

$$\text{break-even point in units} = \frac{\$6,000}{\$0.09} = 66,667 \text{ units} \qquad (2)$$

$$\text{break-even point in dollars} = \frac{\$6,000}{0.18} = \$33,333 \qquad (3)$$

2. If the selling price fell from $0.50 to $0.45, and the original variable expenses were unchanged, the unit contribution would be reduced from $0.10 to $0.05 (i.e., $0.45 – $0.40) and the break-even point would soar to 120,000 units ($6,000 ÷ $0.05). The break-even point, in dollars, would be $54,000 (120,000 units × $0.45) or, using the formula:

$$\text{break-even point in units} = \frac{\$6,000}{\$0.05} = 120,000 \text{ units} \qquad (2)$$

$$\text{break-even point in dollars} = \frac{\$6,000}{0.1111^*} = \$54,000 \qquad (3)$$

* $0.05 ÷ $0.45

Target Net Profit

OBJECTIVE 5

Calculate sales volume in total dollars and total units to reach a target profit.

Managers can also use CVP analysis to determine the total sales and/or units needed to reach a target profit. For example, in our vending machine example, suppose Winston considers $480 per month the minimum acceptable net income. How many units will have to be sold to justify the adoption of the vending machine plan? How does this figure "translate" into dollar sales?

The method for computing desired or target sales volume in units and the desired or target net income is the same as we used in our earlier break-even computations. However, now the targets are expressed in the following equations:

target sales – variable expenses – fixed expenses = target net income

$$\text{target sales in units} = \frac{\text{fixed expenses + target net income}}{\text{contribution margin per unit}} \qquad (4)$$

$$= \frac{\$6,000 + \$480}{\$0.10}$$

$$= 64,800 \text{ units} \qquad (5)$$

Incremental Approach. The change in results (such as revenue, expenses, or income) given a change in one of the determinants of this result.

Another way of getting the same answer is to use your knowledge of the break-even point and adopt an **incremental approach**. The term incremental is widely used in accounting. It refers to the change in final results (such as revenue, expenses, or income) given a change in one of the determinants of this result.

In this instance, the given condition is assumed to be the 60,000 unit break-even point. All expenses would be recovered at that volume. Therefore the *change* or *increment* in net income for every unit *beyond* 60,000 would be equal to the contribution margin of $0.50 – $0.40 = $0.10. If $480 were the target net profit, $480 ÷ $0.10 would show that the target volume must exceed the break-even volume by 4,800 units; it would therefore be 60,000 + 4,800 =

64,800 units. To find the answer in terms of *dollar* sales, multiply 64,800 units by $0.50 or use the formula:

$$\text{target sales volume in dollars} = \frac{\text{fixed expenses} + \text{target net income}}{\text{contribution margin ratio}} \quad (6)$$

$$= \frac{\$6,000 + \$480}{0.20} = \$32,400$$

To solve directly for sales dollars with the alternative incremental approach, we would start at the break-even point in dollar sales of $30,000. Every sales dollar beyond that point contributes $0.20 to net profit. Divide $480 by 0.20. Dollar sales must exceed the break-even volume by $2,400 to produce a net profit of $480; thus the total dollar sales would be $30,000 + $2,400 = $32,400.

The following table summarizes these assumptions:

	BREAK-EVEN POINT	INCREMENT	NEW CONDITION
Volume in units	60,000	4,800	64,800
Sales	$30,000	$2,400	$32,400
Variable expenses	24,000	1,920	25,920
Contribution margin	6,000	480	6,480
Fixed expenses	6,000	—	6,000
Net Income	$ 0	$ 480	$ 480

Multiple Changes in the Key Factors

So far we have seen changes in one CVP factor at a time. In the real world, managers often must make decisions about the probable effects of multiple factor changes. For instance, suppose that after the vending machines have been in place for a while, Winston is considering locking them from 6:00 p.m. to 6:00 a.m., which she estimates will save $820 in wages monthly. The cutback from 24-hour service would hurt volume because many nighttime employees use the machines. Should the machines remain available 24 hours per day? Assume that monthly sales would decline by 10,000 units from current sales.

We will perform the analysis using two different levels of current sales volume: (a) 62,000 units and (b) 90,000 units.

Consider two approaches. One approach is to construct and solve equations for conditions that prevail under each alternative and select the volume level that yields the highest net income.

Regardless of the current volume level, be it 62,000 or 90,000 units, if we accept the prediction that sales will decline by 10,000 units as accurate, closing from 6:00 p.m. to 6:00 a.m. will decrease net income by $180:

	DECLINE FROM 62,000 TO 52,000 UNITS		DECLINE FROM 90,000 TO 80,000 UNITS	
Units	62,000	52,000	90,000	80,000
Sales	$31,000	$26,000	$45,000	$40,000
Variable expenses	24,800	20,800	36,000	32,000
Contribution margin	6,200	5,200	9,000	8,000
Fixed expenses	6,000	5,180	6,000	5,180
Net Income	$ 200	$ 20	$ 3,000	$ 2,820
Change in net income	($180)		($180)	

A second approach—an incremental approach—is quicker and simpler. Simplicity is important to managers because it keeps the analysis from being cluttered by irrelevant and potentially confusing data.

What does the insightful manager see in this situation? First, whether 62,000 or 90,000 units are being sold is irrelevant to the decision at hand. The issue is the decline in volume, which would be 10,000 units in either case. The essence of this decision is whether the prospective savings in cost exceed the prospective loss in total contribution margin dollars:

Lost total contribution margin, 10,000 units @ $0.10	$1,000
Savings in fixed expenses	820
Prospective decline in net income	$ 180

Locking the vending machines from 6:00 p.m. to 6:00 a.m. would cause a $180 decrease in monthly net income. Whichever way you analyze it, locking the machines is not a sound financial decision. The quality of the overall working conditions for the employees should the vending machines stay locked at night is also a consideration. Could employees find food elsewhere in the premises or would they have to go out for food? This could be costly as some might be late returning to work. Considering that the profit change of $180 is not substantial, it may not be wise to lock the machines. The moral of the story is that non-quantitative factors and qualitative considerations may be the deciding factors when costs or profits differ little between alternatives.

CVP Analysis in the Computer Age

As we have seen, cost-volume-profit analysis is based on a mathematical model, the equation

$$\text{sales} - \text{variable expenses} - \text{fixed expenses} = \text{net income}$$

The CVP model is widely used in planning. Managers in a variety of organizations use a personal computer and a CVP modelling program to study combinations of changes in selling prices, unit variable costs, fixed costs, and desired profits. Many not-for-profit organizations also use computerized CVP modelling. For example, some universities have models that help measure how decisions such as raising tuition, adding programs, and decreases in government grants will affect financial results. The computer quickly calculates the results of changes.

In addition to speed and convenience, computers allow a more sophisticated approach to CVP analysis than the one illustrated in this chapter. Computer models can include multiple cost drivers, nonlinear relationships between costs and cost drivers, varying sales mixes, and analyses that need not be restricted to a relevant range.

Use of computer models is a cost/benefit issue. Sometimes the costs of modelling are exceeded by the value of better decisions made using the models. However, the reliability of these models depends on the accuracy of their underlying assumptions about how revenues and costs will actually be affected. Moreover, in small organizations, simplified CVP models are often accurate enough that more sophisticated modelling is unwarranted.

SALES MIX ANALYSIS

To emphasize fundamental ideas, the cost-volume-profit analysis in this chapter has focused on a single product. But nearly all companies sell more than one product. Sales mix is defined as the relative proportions or combinations of quantities of different products that comprise total sales. If the proportions of the mix change, the cost-volume-profit relationships also change.

Suppose Ramos Retail Company sells two products, wallets (W) and key cases (K). The income budget follows:

	WALLETS (W)	KEY CASES (K)	TOTAL
Sales in units	300,000	75,000	375,000
Sales @ $30 and $5	$9,000,000	$375,000	$9,375,000
Variable expenses @ $14 and $3	4,200,000	225,000	4,425,000
Contribution margins @ $16 and $2	$4,800,000	$150,000	$4,950,000
Fixed expenses			198,000
Net income			$4,752,000

For simplicity, ignore income taxes. What would be the break-even point? The typical answer assumes a constant mix of four units of W for every unit of K. The ratio of W to K is 4 to 1.

$$K = \text{number of units of product K to break even}$$
$$4K = \text{number of units of product W to break even}$$
$$\text{sales} - \text{variable expenses} - \text{fixed expenses} = \text{zero net income}$$
$$\$30(4K) + \$5(K) - \$14(4K) - \$3(K) - \$198,000 = 0$$
$$\$120K + \$5K - \$56K - \$3K - \$198,000 = 0$$
$$\$66K = \$198,000$$
$$K = 3,000$$
$$W = 4K = 12,000$$

The break-even point is 3,000K + 12,000W = 15,000 units.

This is only the break-even point for a sales mix of four wallets for every key case. Clearly, there are other break-even points for other sales mixes. For instance, suppose only key cases were sold, fixed expenses being unchanged:

$$\text{break-even point} = \frac{\text{fixed expenses}}{\text{contribution margin per unit}}$$

$$= \frac{\$198,000}{\$2}$$

$$= 99,000 \text{ key cases}$$

If only wallets were sold:

$$\text{break-even point} = \frac{\$198,000}{\$16}$$

$$= 12,375 \text{ wallets}$$

Managers are not primarily interested in the break-even point for its own sake. Instead, they want to know how changes in a planned sales mix will affect net income. When the sales mix changes, the break-even point and the expected net income at various sales levels are altered. For example, suppose overall actual total sales were equal to the budget of 375,000 units. However, if only 50,000 key cases and 325,000 wallets were sold:

	WALLETS (W)	KEY CASES (K)	TOTAL
Sales in units	325,000	50,000	375,000
Sales @ $30 and $5	$9,750,000	$250,000	$10,000,000
Variable expenses @ $14 and $3	4,550,000	150,000	4,700,000
Contribution margins @ $16 and $2	$5,200,000	$100,000	$ 5,300,000
Fixed expenses			198,000
Net income			$ 5,102,000

The change in sales mix has resulted in a $5,102,000 actual net income rather than the $4,752,000 budgeted net income—a favourable difference of $350,000. The budgeted and actual sales in number of units were identical, but the proportion of sales of the product bearing the higher unit contribution margin (wallets) increased.

Different advertising strategies may also affect the sales mix. Normally, the higher the advertising budget the higher the sales of the advertised product. Clearly, if a sales budget is not actually attained, the budgeted net income will be affected by the individual sales volumes of each product. The fewer the units sold, the lower the profit, and vice versa. All other things being equal, the higher the proportion of the more profitable products, the higher the profit. For any given level of total sales, the greater the proportion of the wallets, in our example, the greater the total profit.

Managers usually want to maximize the sales of all their products. However, faced with limited resources and time, executives prefer to generate the most profitable sales mix achievable. For example, consider the explanation provided in a recent annual report of Deere & Co., a manufacturer of farm equipment. "The increase in the ratio of cost of goods sold to net sales resulted from higher production costs, a less favourable mix of products sold, and sales incentive programs."

Profitability of a given product helps guide executives who must decide to emphasize or de-emphasize particular products. For example, given limited production facilities or limited time of sales personnel, should we emphasize brand A or brand B production? These decisions may be affected by other factors

Deere & Co.
www.deere.com

beyond the contribution margin per unit of product. Chapter 8 explores some of these factors, including the importance of the amount of contribution per *unit of time* rather than per *unit of product*.

IMPACT OF INCOME TAXES

OBJECTIVE 7

Compute cost-volume-profit relationships on an after-tax basis.

Thus far we have (as so many people would like to) ignored income taxes. However, in most nations, private enterprises are subject to income taxes. Reconsider the vending machine example. In Objective 5, as part of our CVP analysis, we discussed the sales necessary to achieve a target income before income taxes of $480. If an income tax were levied at 40 percent, the new results would be:

Income before income tax	$480	100%
Income tax	192	40%
Net income	$288	60%

Note that:

net income = income before income taxes − 0.40 (income before income taxes)
net income = 0.60 (income before income taxes)

$$\text{income before income taxes} = \frac{\text{net income}}{0.60}$$

$$\text{target income before income taxes} = \frac{\text{target after-tax net income}}{1 - \text{tax rate}}$$

$$\text{target income before income taxes} = \frac{\$288}{1 - 0.40} = \frac{\$288}{0.60} = \$480$$

Suppose the target net income after taxes was $288. The only change in the general equation approach would be on the right-hand side of the following equation:

$$\text{target sales} - \text{variable expenses} - \text{fixed expenses} = \frac{\text{target after-tax net income}}{1 - \text{tax rate}}$$

Thus, letting N be the number of units to be sold at $0.50 each with a variable cost of $0.40 each and total fixed costs of $6,000:

$$\$0.50N - \$0.40N - \$6,000 = \frac{\$288}{1 - 0.40}$$

$$\$0.10N = \$6,000 + \frac{\$288}{0.60}$$

$$\$0.06N = \$3,600 + \$288$$

$$N = \$3,888 \div \$0.06$$

$$N = 64,800 \text{ units}$$

Sales of 64,800 units produce an *after-tax profit* of $288 as shown here and a *before-tax profit* of $480.

Suppose the target net income after taxes was $480. The volume needed would rise to 68,000 units as follows:

$$\$0.50N - \$0.40N - \$6,000 = \frac{\$480}{1 - 0.40}$$

$$\$0.10N = \$6,000 + \frac{\$480}{0.60}$$

$$\$0.06N = \$3,600 + \$480$$

$$N = \$4,080 \div \$0.06$$

$$N = 68,000 \text{ units}$$

As a shortcut to computing the effects of volume on the change in after-tax income, use the formula:

$$\begin{array}{l}\text{change in} \\ \text{net income}\end{array} = \left(\begin{array}{c}\text{change in volume} \\ \text{in units}\end{array}\right) \times \left(\begin{array}{c}\text{contribution margin} \\ \text{per unit}\end{array}\right) \times (1 - \text{tax rate})$$

In our example, suppose operations were at a level of 64,800 units and $288 after-tax net income. The manager is wondering how much after-tax net income would increase if sales became 68,000 units:

$$\begin{aligned}\text{change in net income} &= (68,000 - 64,800) \times \$0.10 \times (1 - 0.4) \\ &= 3,200 \times \$0.10 \times 0.60 = 3,200 \times \$0.06 \\ &= \$192\end{aligned}$$

In brief, each unit beyond the break-even point adds to after-tax net profit at the unit contribution margin multiplied by (1 − income tax rate).

Throughout our illustration, the break-even point itself does not change. Why? *Because there is no income tax at a level of zero profits.*

USES AND LIMITATIONS OF COST-VOLUME ANALYSIS

Best Combination of Fixed and Variable Costs

Managers try to obtain the most profitable combination of variable- and fixed-cost factors. For example, one Canadian bread manufacturer handles and distributes its products to grocery stores by using independent commissioned agents. Agents are assigned a territory and are responsible for delivering the product. This bread manufacturer has shifted a substantially fixed cost of salaries otherwise paid to sales and distribution staff employed by the company to a substantially variable cost in commissions paid to outside agents.

Generally, companies that spend heavily for advertising (fixed costs) are willing to do so because they have high contribution-margin percentages (airline, cigarette, and cosmetic companies). Conversely, companies with low contribution-margin percentages usually spend less for advertising and promotion (manufacturers of industrial equipment). Obviously, two companies with the same unit sales volumes at the same unit prices could have different attitudes toward risking a fixed cost advertising outlay. Assume the following:

	PERFUME COMPANY	JANITORIAL SERVICE
Unit sales volume	100,000 bottles	100,000 square metres
Dollar sales at $20 per unit	$2,000,000	$2,000,000
Variable costs	200,000	1,700,000
Contribution margin	$1,800,000	$ 300,000
Contribution-margin percentage	90%	15%

Suppose each company wants to increase sales volume by 10 percent:

	PERFUME COMPANY	JANITORIAL SERVICE
Increase in sales volume, 10,000 × $20	$200,000	$200,000
Increase in contribution margin (90%, 15%)	$180,000	$ 30,000

The perfume company would be inclined to increase advertising considerably to boost the contribution margin by $180,000. In contrast, it would be riskier for the janitorial service to spend large amounts to increase the contribution margin by $30,000.

Note that when the contribution-margin percentage of sales is low, great increases in volume are necessary before significant increases in net profits can occur. As sales exceed the break-even point, a high contribution-margin percentage increases profits faster than does a small contribution-margin percentage.

Operating Leverage

Operating Leverage. A firm's ratio of fixed and variable costs.

In addition to weighing the varied effects of changes in fixed and variable costs, managers need to consider their firms' ratio of fixed and variable costs, called **operating leverage**. In highly leveraged companies—those with high fixed costs and low variable costs—small changes in sales volume result in large changes in net income. Companies with less leverage (that is, lower fixed costs and higher variable costs) are not affected as much by changes in sales volume.

Exhibit 2-6 shows cost behaviour relationships at two firms—one highly leveraged and one with low leverage. The firm with higher leverage has fixed costs of $14,000 and variable cost per unit of $0.10. The firm with lower leverage has fixed costs of only $2,000 but variable costs of $0.25 per unit. Expected sales at both companies are 80,000 units at $0.30 per unit. At this sales level, both firms would have net incomes of $2,000. If sales fall short of 80,000 units, profits *drop* more sharply for the highly leveraged business. But if sales exceed 80,000 units, profits *increase* more sharply for the highly leveraged concern.

The highly leveraged alternative is more risky. Why? Because it provides the higher possible net income, and the higher possible losses. In other words, net income is highly variable, depending on the actual level of sales. The low-leverage alternative is less risky because variations in sales lead to only small variability in net income. At sales of 90,000 units, net income is $4,000 for the higher-leveraged firm but only $2,500 for the lower-leveraged firm.

Tech Firms Lower Break-Even Points

In late 2002 and early 2003, many high-technology companies reported on their attempts to achieve profitability in spite of declining sales. They often focused on how their efforts to control costs reduced their break-even points. If a company faces rapidly falling sales, it must restructure its costs to be able to break even at a lower volume.

The early twenty-first century was hard on technology companies. After the bursting of the stock-price bubble of the 1990s, demand for most technology products plummeted. Nearly all technology companies experienced declines in sales. Most lost money in 2001 and 2002, but because of restructured operations, most predicted a return to profitability in 2003.

Consider Alcatel, the French telecommunications company. CEO Serge Tchuruk indicated that the company cut its break-even point, which was Euro 6 billion in the fourth quarter of 2001, to Euro 4.1 billion by the last quarter of 2002. It planned to further cut its quarterly break-even point to Euro 3 billion by the end of 2003. This focus on reducing break-even points, among other strategies, has resulted in a turnaround for Alcatel. Alcatel's 2004 net income was €281 million, compared to a 2003 loss of nearly €2 billion. Its performance has continued to improve, with 2005 net income reported at €930 million. For 2004 and 2005, Alcatel's operating profit was €978 million and €1.2 billion, respectively.

Lucent Technologies, a U.S. telecom company, faced a similar situation. Sales in 2002 were only 43% of those in 2000, and Lucent lost nearly U.S. $12 billion in 2002. CEO Patricia Russo indicated that the company "intends to lower its break-even point on a quarterly revenue basis to between $2.5 billion and $3 billion," and cited a need to possibly reduce Lucent's break-even point even further because its anticipated quarterly sales were only U.S. $2.5 to U.S. $3 billion, leaving little margin for error. For its later fiscal years, Lucent was able to reduce its loss from continuing operations from U.S. $11.2 billion in 2002 to a loss of U.S. $770 million in 2003. As of 2004, Lucent had returned to profitability, with income from continuing operations of U.S. $2 billion.

Sources: www.alcatel.com; www.lucent.com.

Like Lucent, Nortel, the Canadian telecom company, had sales in 2002 that were less than half of those at its peak. By mid-2002 it had reduced its quarterly break-even point to about $2.6 billion, but since third-quarter 2002 sales were only $2.36 billion, the company sought a further reduction of its break-even by $200 million.

Shareholders responded to these efforts to lower the break-even point. In early 2003, stock prices for Alcatel, Lucent, and Nortel doubled, tripled, and quadrupled, respectively. The media attributed this to two factors: "First, each company announced staff reductions that promise to lower their quarterly break-even rates. Second, demand for telecom equipment no longer appears to be plunging at a neck-snapping rate."

The need to cut break-even points was not confined to telecom companies. Sun Microsystems, the developer of products and services for network computing, said it would "bring the group's quarterly break-even point to [U.S.] $3.2 billion–$3.3 billion." With quarterly sales running under U.S. $3 billion, even that goal would not bring automatic profitability. And Hector de Jesus Ruiz, president and chief executive officer of chip-maker Advanced Micro Devices (AMD), "reaffirmed his goal of reducing expenses to a break-even point of $775 million by the end of the second quarter of 2003." With 2002 sales down 30% and averaging U.S. $675 million a quarter, the expense reduction will have to be combined with a sales increase of about $100 million a quarter before AMD breaks even.

A look at many other cases would reveal the same picture. Technology companies of all types had net losses in 2001 and 2002, and profitability in 2003 would depend on reducing their break-even point to a level consistent with realistic sales expectations.

Sources: "Alcatel Plans to Lower Break-Even Point to Euro 3 Billion," *Europe Information Service,* January 30, 2003; "Russo Sees Lower Lucent Break-Even," *Financial Post,* September 19, 2002; "Nortel to Slash Costs by $1.25B," *Edmonton Journal,* October 12, 2002; "AMD Firing 2,000," *San Francisco Chronicle,* November 15, 2002; 2002 annual reports for Alcatel, Lucent, Nortel, Sun Microsystems, and Advanced Micro Devices.

EXHIBIT 2-6

High versus Low
Leverage

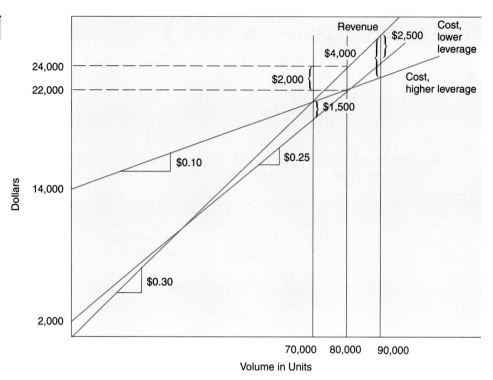

Contribution Margin and Gross Margin

OBJECTIVE 8

Distinguish between
contribution margin
and gross margin.

**Variable-Cost Ratio
(Variable-Cost
Percentage)**. All variable
costs divided by sales.

**Gross Margin (Gross
Profit)**. The excess of
sales over the total cost
of goods sold.

Cost of Goods Sold. The
cost of the merchandise
that is acquired or manu-
factured and resold.

Contribution margin may be expressed as a *total* absolute amount, a *unit* absolute amount, a *ratio*, and a *percentage*. The **variable-cost ratio** or **variable-cost percentage** is defined as all variable costs divided by sales. Thus a contribution-margin ratio of 20 percent means that the variable-cost ratio is 80 percent.

Too often people confuse the terms contribution margin and gross margin. **Gross margin** (which is also called **gross profit**) is the excess of sales over the **cost of goods sold** (that is, the cost of the merchandise that is acquired or manufactured and resold). It is a widely used concept, particularly in the retailing industry.

Compare the gross margin with the contribution margin:

$$\text{gross margin} = \text{sales price} - \text{cost of goods sold}$$
$$\text{contribution margin} = \text{sales price} - \text{all variable expenses}$$

The following comparisons show the similarities and differences between the contribution margin and the gross margin in a retail store:

	CONTRIBUTION MARGIN	GROSS MARGIN
Sales		$0.50	$0.50
Acquisition cost of unit sold	$0.40		0.40
Variable commission	0.01		
Total variable expense		0.41	
Contribution margin		$0.09	
Gross margin			$0.10

Did Blockbuster Violate Disney Contract?
Accounting Disagreement or Ethical Issue?

In early 2003, the Walt Disney Company sued Blockbuster, claiming that Blockbuster had violated a 1997 agreement between the two companies. Prior to the agreement, Blockbuster purchased videos from Disney for about U.S. $65 each and kept all the rental revenue. Under the pact, Blockbuster agreed to purchase movies from Disney for U.S. $7 a copy and then pay the studio a portion of the revenue from each rental.

Walt Disney Company
www.disney.com
Blockbuster
www.blockbuster.com

The contract allowed Blockbuster to buy more copies of each video, which led to the guarantee that customers could rely on Blockbuster to have a copy of any movie they wanted or else the rental was free. With this policy, Blockbuster increased its share of the video rental market from 28 to 40 percent. Essentially, Blockbuster turned a fixed cost, U.S. $65 per tape, into primarily a variable cost, with a small U.S. $7 fixed-cost portion and a larger variable-cost portion that depended on how much revenue Blockbuster generated from its rentals.

The arrangement was similar to that between the owners of shopping malls and many of their retail store tenants. Each store pays a monthly rental fee plus a percentage of its sales. Just as shopping mall owners rely on their tenants to truthfully report their sales, Disney relied on Blockbuster to correctly account for its video rentals.

In addition, Blockbuster and Disney also agreed on when Blockbuster could sell old rental tapes. Since these were so inexpensive for Blockbuster, selling them could be a lucrative business. But Disney did not want these low-cost tapes competing with its own videotape sales. Thus, it placed restrictions on when Blockbuster could sell them.

In the suit, Disney claimed that Blockbuster improperly deducted "promotional" credits from its gross rental fees, failed to account for "hundreds of thousands" of missing videos, and sold videos prematurely. Disney had to rely on Blockbuster to correctly account for its rental revenues and inventory of tapes. Blockbuster claimed that its accounting was in accordance with the original agreement.

This is an example where good ethics and good accounting are both important. The original agreement promised benefits to both companies—more rental income for Disney on hit movies and more cost-structure flexibility for Blockbuster. But such a contract will not work if each party cannot trust the other. It's not clear who is right in this case, but both companies were hurt by the allegations. At a minimum, both will need to include better monitoring provisions in future contracts because other companies will suspect Disney of trying to get more than it deserves and Blockbuster of playing accounting tricks to minimize its payment.

Sources: "Disney Sues Blockbuster over Contract," *New York Times,* January 4, 2003; "Disney Sues Top Video Chain," *Los Angeles Times,* January 3, 2003.

As the preceding tabulation indicates, contribution margin and gross margin are not the same concepts. Contribution margin focuses on sales in relation to *all variable* costs, whereas gross margin focuses on sales in relation to cost of goods sold.

NOT-FOR-PROFIT APPLICATION

Consider how cost-volume-profit relationships apply to not-for-profit organizations. Suppose a city has a $100,000 lump-sum budget appropriation from a government agency to conduct a counselling program for drug addicts. The variable costs for drug prescriptions are $400 per patient per year. Fixed costs are $60,000 in the relevant range of 50 to 150 patients. If all of the budget appropriation is spent, how many patients can be served in a year? We can use the break-even equation to solve this problem.

Let N be the number of patients.

revenue – variable expenses – fixed expenses = 0 if budget is completely spent

$100,000 lump sum – $400N – $60,000 = 0

$400N = $100,000 – $60,000

N = $40,000 ÷ $400

N = 100 patients

Suppose the total budget to the not-for-profit for the following year is cut 10 percent by the granting agency. Fixed costs will be unaffected, but service will decline. How many patients can be served now with the reduced budget?

revenue – variable expenses – fixed expenses = 0

$90,000 – $400N – $60,000 = 0

$400N = $90,000 – $60,000

N = $30,000 ÷ 400

N = 75 patients

The percentage reduction in service is more than the 10 percent reduction in the budget. Unless the city restructured its operations, the service volume must be reduced 25 percent (from 100 to 75 patients) to stay within budget. Exhibit 2-7 presents an illustration of this example. Please note that lump-sum revenue is a horizontal line on the graph.

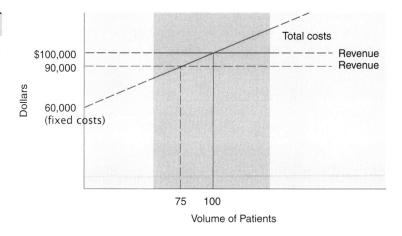

EXHIBIT 2-7

Break-Even Graph

HIGHLIGHTS TO REMEMBER

1. **Explain how cost drivers affect cost behaviour.** A cost driver is an output measure that causes the use of costly resources. When the level of an activity changes, the level of the cost driver or output measure will also change, causing changes in costs.

2. **Show how changes in cost-driver activity levels affect variable and fixed costs.** Different types of costs behave in different ways. If the cost of the resource used changes in proportion to changes in the cost-driver level, the resource is a variable-cost resource (its costs are variable). If the cost of the resource used does not change because of

cost-driver level changes, the resource is a fixed-cost resource (its costs are fixed).

3. **Calculate break-even sales volume in total dollars and total units.** We can approach CVP analysis (sometimes called break-even analysis) graphically or with equations. To calculate the break-even point in total units, divide the fixed costs by the unit contribution margin. To calculate the break-even point in total dollars (sales dollars), divide the fixed costs by the contribution-margin ratio.

4. **Create a cost-volume-profit graph and understand the assumptions behind it.** We can create a cost-volume-profit graph by drawing revenue and total cost lines as functions of the cost-driver level. Be sure to recognize the limitations of CVP analysis and that it assumes constant efficiency, sales mix, and inventory levels.

5. **Calculate sales volume in total dollars and total units to reach a target profit.** Managers use CVP analysis to compute the sales needed to achieve a target profit or to examine the effects on profit of changes in factors such as fixed costs, variable costs, or cost-driver volume.

6. **Differentiate between contribution margin and gross margin.** The contribution margin—the difference between sales price and variable costs—is an important concept. Do not confuse it with gross margin, the difference between sales price and cost of goods sold.

DEMONSTRATION PROBLEMS FOR YOUR REVIEW

Problem One

The budgeted income statement of Port Williams Gift Shop is summarized as follows:

Net revenue	$800,000
Less: expenses, including $400,000 of fixed expenses	880,000
Net loss	$ (80,000)

The manager believes that an increase of $200,000 in advertising outlays will increase sales substantially.

1. At what sales volume will the store break even after spending $200,000 in advertising?
2. What sales volume will result in a net profit of $40,000?

Solution

1. Note that all data are expressed in dollars. No unit data are given. Most companies have many products, so the overall break-even analysis deals with dollar sales units. The variable expenses are $880,000 – $400,000, or $480,000. The variable expense ratio is $480,000 ÷ $800,000, or 0.60. Therefore, the contribution margin is 0.40.

Let S = break-even sales in dollars, then

$$S - \text{variable expenses} - \text{fixed expenses} = \text{net profit}$$
$$S - 0.60S - (\$400,000 + \$200,000) = 0$$
$$0.40S = \$600,000$$
$$S = \frac{\$600,000}{0.40} = \frac{\text{fixed expenses}}{\text{contribution-margin ratio}}$$
$$S = \$1,500,000$$

2.
$$\text{required sales} = \frac{\text{fixed expenses} + \text{target net profit}}{\text{contribution-margin ratio}}$$
$$\text{required sales} = \frac{\$600,000 + \$40,000}{0.40} = \frac{\$640,000}{0.40}$$
$$\text{required sales} = \$1,600,000$$

Alternatively, we can use an incremental approach and reason that all dollar sales beyond the $1.5 million break-even point will result in a 40 percent contribution to net profit. Divide $40,000 by 0.40. Sales must therefore be $100,000 beyond the $1.5 million break-even point to produce a net profit of $40,000.

Problem Two

Hospitals measure their volume in terms of patient-days, which are defined as the number of patients multiplied by the number of days that the patients are hospitalized. Suppose a large hospital has fixed costs of $48 million per year and variable costs of $600 per patient-day. Daily revenues vary among classes of patients. For simplicity, assume that there are two classes: (1) private-plan patients (P) who are the responsibility of insurance companies and who pay an average of $1,000 per day and (2) government-plan patients (G) who are the responsibility of government agencies and who pay an average of $800 per day. Twenty percent of the patients are private-plan.

Required:

1. Compute the break-even point in patient-days, assuming that the planned mix of patients is maintained.
2. Suppose that 200,000 patient-days were achieved but that 25% of the patient-days were private-plan (instead of 20%). Compute the net income. Compute the break-even point.

Solution

1. Let P = number of private-plan patients (P)
   4P = number of government-plan patients (G)
   $$\$1,000P + \$800(4P) - \$600P - \$600(4P) - \$48,000,000 = 0$$
   $$\$1,000P + \$3,200P - \$600P - \$2,400P = \$48,000,000$$
   $$\$1,200P = \$48,000,000$$
   $$P = 40,000$$
   $$4P = 160,000 = G$$

The break-even point is 40,000 private-plan patient-days plus 40,000 × 4 = 160,000 government-plan patient-days, a grand total of 200,000 patient-days.

2. Contribution Margins:

$$P = \$1,000 - \$600 = \$400 \text{ per patient-day}$$
$$G = \$\ 800 - \$600 = \$200 \text{ per patient-day}$$

Patient-days:

$$P = 0.25 \times 200,000 = 50,000$$
$$G = 0.75 \times 200,000 = 150,000$$

Net income $= 50,000(\$400) + 150,000(\$200) - \$48,000,000$
$= \$20,000,000 + \$30,000,000 - \$48,000,000 = \$2,000,000$

Let P = number of private-plan patients (P)
  3P = number of government-plan patients (G)

$$\$1,000P + \$800(3P) - \$600P - \$600(3P) - \$48,000,000 = 0$$
$$\$1,000P + \$2,400P - \$600P - \$1,800P = \$48,000,000$$
$$\$1,000P = \$48,000,000$$
$$P = 48,000$$
$$3P = 144,000 = G$$

The break-even point is now lower (192,000 patient-days instead of 200,000 patient-days). The more profitable mix produces a net income of $2,000,000 at the 200,000 patient-day level.

KEY TERMS

break-even analysis *p. 48*

break-even point *p. 48*

contribution margin *p. 48*

cost behaviour *p. 42*

cost drivers *p. 42*

cost of goods sold *p. 64*

cost-volume-profit (CVP) analysis *p. 47*

fixed cost *p. 43*

gross margin *p. 64*

gross profit *p. 64*

incremental approach *p. 55*

margin of safety *p. 48*

operating leverage *p. 62*

relevant range *p. 45*

sales mix *p. 53*

variable cost *p. 43*

variable-cost percentage *p. 64*

variable-cost ratio *p. 64*

ASSIGNMENT MATERIAL

QUESTIONS

Q2-1 "Cost behaviour is simply identification of cost drivers and their relationships to costs." Comment.

Q2-2 Give three examples of variable costs and fixed costs.

Q2-3 "Fixed costs decline as volume increases." Do you agree? Explain.

Q2-4 "It is confusing to think of fixed costs on a per-unit basis." Do you agree? Why or why not?

Q2-5 "All costs are either fixed or variable. The only difficulty in cost analysis is determining which of the two categories each cost belongs to." Do you agree? Explain.

Q2-6 "The relevant range pertains to fixed costs, not variable costs." Do you agree? Explain.

Q2-7 Identify two simplifying assumptions that underlie CVP analysis.

Q2-8 "Classification of costs into variable and fixed categories depends on the decision situation." Explain.

Q2-9 "Contribution margin is the excess of sales over fixed costs." Do you agree? Explain.

Q2-10 Why is "break-even analysis" a misnomer?

Q2-11 "Companies in the same industry generally have about the same break-even point." Do you agree? Explain.

Q2-12 "It is essential to choose the right CVP technique—equation, contribution margin, or graphical. If you pick the wrong one, your analysis will be faulty." Do you agree? Explain.

Q2-13 Describe three ways of lowering a break-even point.

Q2-14 "Incremental analysis is quicker, but it has no other advantage over an analysis of all costs and revenues associated with each alternative." Do you agree? Why or why not?

Q2-15 Explain operating leverage and why a highly leveraged company is risky.

Q2-16 "The contribution margin and gross margin are always equal." Do you agree? Explain.

Q2-17 "CVP relationships are unimportant in not-for-profit organizations." Do you agree? Explain.

Q2-18 "Two products were sold. Total budgeted and total actual sales of both products combined in number of units were identical. Unit variable costs and sales prices were the same. Actual contribution margin was lower." What could be the reason for the lower contribution margin?

Q2-19 Present the CVP formula for computing the target income before income taxes.

Q2-20 Present the CVP formula for computing the effects of a change in volume on after-tax income.

PROBLEMS

P2-1 **NATURE OF VARIABLE AND FIXED COSTS.** "As I understand it, costs such as the salary of the vice president of transportation operations are variable because the more traffic you handle, the less your unit cost. In contrast, costs such as fuel are fixed because each tonne-kilometre should entail consumption of the same amount of fuel and hence bear the same unit cost." Do you agree? Explain.

P2-2 **BASIC REVIEW EXERCISES.** Fill in the blanks for each of the following independent cases (ignore income taxes):

	SALES	VARIABLE EXPENSES	CONTRIBUTION MARGIN	FIXED EXPENSES	NET INCOME
1.	$900,000	$500,000	—	$350,000	—
2.	800,000	—	$350,000	—	$80,000
3.	—	600,000	340,000	250,000	—

P2-3 BASIC REVIEW EXERCISES.   Fill in the blanks for each of the following independent cases:

CASE	(A) SELLING PRICE PER UNIT	(B) VARIABLE COST PER UNIT	(C) TOTAL UNITS SOLD	(D) TOTAL CONTRIBUTION MARGIN	(E) TOTAL FIXED COSTS	(F) NET INCOME
1.	$30	—	120,000	$720,000	$640,000	—
2.	10	$ 6	100,000		320,000	—
3.	20	15	—	100,000	—	$15,000
4.	30	20	70,000	—	—	12,000
5.	—	9	80,000	160,000	120,000	—

P2-4 HOSPITAL COSTS AND PRICING.   A hospital has overall variable costs of 20 percent of total revenue and fixed costs of $40 million per year.

     1. Compute the break-even point expressed in total revenue.
     2. A patient-day is often used to measure the volume of a hospital. Suppose there are going to be 40,000 patient-days next year. Compute the average daily revenue per patient necessary to break even.

P2-5 MOTEL RENTALS.   The Holiday Motel has annual fixed costs applicable to its rooms of $1.6 million for its 200-room motel, average daily room rents of $50, and average variable costs of $10 for each room rented. It operates 365 days per year.

     1. How much net income on rooms will be generated (a) if the motel is completely full throughout the entire year? and (b) if the motel is half full?
     2. Compute the break-even point in number of rooms rented. What percentage occupancy for the year is needed to break even?

P2-6 BASIC RELATIONSHIPS, HOTEL.   The Pippin Hotel in Vancouver has 400 rooms, with a fixed cost of $350,000 per month during the peak season. Room rates average $65 per day with variable costs of $15 per rented room per day. Assume a 30-day month.

     1. How many rooms must be occupied per day to break even?
     2. How many rooms must be occupied per month to make a monthly profit of $120,000?
     3. Assume that the Pippin Hotel has these average contribution margins per month from use of space in its hotel:

Leased shops in hotel	$70,000
Meals served, conventions	40,000
Dining room and coffee shop	32,400
Bar and cocktail lounge	30,000

Also assume that the Pippin Hotel averages 80 percent occupancy per day. What average rate per day per rented room must the hotel charge to make a profit of $120,000 per month?

P2-7 SALES MIX ANALYSIS.   Nakata Farms produces strawberries and raspberries. Annual fixed costs are $14,400. The cost driver for variable costs is litre of fruit produced. The variable cost is $0.65 per litre of strawberries and $0.85 per litre of raspberries.

Strawberries sell for $1.00 per litre, raspberries for $1.35 per litre. Two litres of strawberries are produced for every litre of raspberries.

1. Compute the number of litres of strawberries and the number of litres of raspberries produced and sold at the break-even point.
2. Suppose only strawberries are produced and sold. Compute the break-even point in litres.
3. Suppose only raspberries are produced and sold. Compute the break-even point in litres.

P2-8 **COST-VOLUME-PROFIT RELATIONSHIPS.** The Global United Moving Company specializes in hauling heavy goods over long distances. The company's revenues and expenses depend on revenue kilometres, a measure that combines both weights and distance travelled. Summarized budget data for next year are based on predicted total revenue kilometres of 800,000.

	Per Revenue Kilometre
Average selling price (revenue)	$1.50
Average variable expenses	1.30
Fixed expenses, $120,000	

1. Compute the budgeted net income. Ignore income taxes.
2. Management is trying to decide how various possible conditions or decisions might affect net income. Compute the new net income for each of the following changes. Consider each case independently.
   a. A 10% increase in revenue kilometres
   b. A 10% increase in sales price
   c. A 10% increase in variable expenses
   d. A 10% increase in fixed expenses
   e. An average decrease in selling price of $0.3 per kilometre and a 5% increase in revenue kilometres. Refer to the original data.
   f. An average increase in selling price of 5% and a 10% decrease in revenue kilometres
   g. A 10% increase in fixed expenses in the form of more advertising and a 5% increase in revenue kilometres

P2-9 **BASIC COST-VOLUME-PROFIT ANALYSIS.** Carmen Guerrero opened Carmen's Corner, a small daycare facility, just over two years ago. After a rocky start, Carmen's has been thriving. Guerrero is now preparing a budget for November 2006.
Monthly fixed costs for Carmen's are

Rent	$ 800
Salaries	1,500
Other fixed costs	100
Total fixed costs	$2,400

The salary is for Ann Penilla, the only employee, who works with Carmen in caring for the children. Guerrero does not pay herself a salary, but she receives the excess of revenues over costs each month.

The cost driver for variable costs is "child-days." One child-day is one day in daycare for one child, and the variable cost is $10 per child-day. The facility is open 6:00 a.m. to 6:00 p.m. weekdays (that is, Monday through Friday), and there are 22 weekdays in November 2006. An average day has eight children attending Carmen's Corner. Provincial law prohibits Carmen's from having more than 14 children, a limit it has never reached. Guerrero charges $30 per day per child, regardless of how long the child is at the facility.

1. Suppose attendance for November 2006 is equal to the average, resulting in 22 × 8 = 176 child-days. What amount will Guerrero have left after paying all her expenses?

2. Suppose both costs and attendance are difficult to predict. Compute the amount Guerrero will have left after paying all her expenses for each of the following situations. Consider each case independently.

    a. Average attendance is 9 children per day instead of 8, generating 198 child-days

    b. Variable costs increase to $11 per child-day

    c. Rent is increased by $200 per month

    d. Guerrero spends $300 on advertising (a fixed cost) in November, which increases average daily attendance to 9.5 children

    e. Guerrero begins charging $33 per day on November 1, and average daily attendance slips to 7 children

P2-10 **INCOME TAXES AND COST-VOLUME-PROFIT ANALYSIS.** Suppose Merla Security Company has a 40 percent income tax rate, a contribution-margin ratio of 30 percent, and fixed costs of $440,000. How many sales are necessary to achieve an after-tax income of $42,000?

P2-11 **FIXED COSTS AND RELEVANT RANGE.** Boulder Systems Group (BSG) has a substantial year-to-year fluctuation in billings to clients. Top management has the following policy regarding the employment of key personnel:

IF GROSS ANNUAL BILLINGS ARE	NUMBER OF PERSONS TO BE EMPLOYED	ANNUAL SALARIES AND RELATED EXPENSES
$2,000,000 or less	10	$1,200,000
$2,000,001 – 2,400,000	11	1,320,000
$2,400,001 – 2,800,000	12	1,440,000

Top management believes that at least 10 individuals should be retained for a year or more even if billings drop below $2 million.

For the past five years, gross annual billings for BSG have fluctuated between $2,020,000 and $2,380,000. Expectations for next year are that gross billings will be between $2,100,000 and $2,300,000. What amount should be budgeted for key professional personnel? Graph the relationships on an annual basis, using the two approaches illustrated in Exhibit 2-3. Indicate the relevant range on each graph. You need not use graph paper; simply approximate the graphical relationships.

P2-12 **MOVIE MANAGER.** Malia Mertz is the manager of Lakehead's traditional Sunday Flicks. Each Sunday a film has two showings. The admission price is deliberately set at a very low $3. A maximum of 500 tickets is sold for each showing. The rental of the auditorium is $330 and labour is $400, including $90 for Mertz. Mertz must pay the film distributor a guarantee, ranging from $300 to $900 or 50 percent of gross admission receipts, whichever is higher.

Before and during the show, refreshments are sold; these sales average 12 percent of gross admission receipts, and yield a contribution margin of 40 percent.

1. On June 3, Mertz showed *Canadian Bacon*. The film grossed $2,250. The guarantee to the distributor was $750, or 50 percent of gross admission receipts, whichever is higher. What operating income was produced for the Students Association, which sponsored the showings?
2. Recompute the results if the film grossed $1,350.
3. The "four-wall" concept is increasingly being adopted by movie producers. In this situation the movie's producer pays a fixed rental to the theatre owner for, say, a week's showing of a movie. As a theatre owner, how would you evaluate a "four-wall" offer?

P2-13 **BASIC RELATIONSHIPS, RESTAURANT.** Genevieve Giraud owns and operates a restaurant. Her fixed costs are $21,000 per month. Lunches and dinners are served. The average total bill (excluding tax and tip) is $18 per customer. Giraud's present variable costs average $9.60 per meal.

1. How many meals must be served to attain a profit before taxes of $8,400 per month?
2. What is the break-even point in number of meals served per month?
3. Giraud's rent and other fixed costs rise to a total of $29,400 per month. Assume that variable costs also rise to $11.50 per meal. If Giraud increases her average price to $22, how many meals must she now serve to make $8,400 profit per month?
4. Giraud's accountant tells her she may lose 10 percent of her customers if she increases her prices to a $22 average price. If this happens, what would be Giraud's profit per month? Assume that the restaurant had been serving 3,500 customers per month.
5. To help offset the anticipated 10 percent loss of customers, Giraud hires a pianist to perform for four hours each night for $2,000 per month. Assume that this would increase the total monthly meals from 3,150 to 3,450. Would Giraud's total profit change? By how much?

P2-14 **COST-VOLUME-PROFIT ANALYSIS AND BARBERING.** Andre's Hair Styling in Singapore has five barbers. (Andre is not one of them.) Each barber is paid $9.90 per hour and works a 40-hour week and a 50-week year. Rent and other fixed expenses are $1,750 per month. Assume that cutting hair is the only service performed and has a unit price of $12.

1. Find the contribution margin per haircut. Assume that the barbers' compensation is a fixed cost.
2. Determine the annual break-even point, in number of haircuts.
3. What will the operating income be if 20,000 haircuts are sold?
4. Suppose Andre revises the compensation method. The barbers will receive $4 per hour plus $6 for each haircut. What is the new contribution margin per haircut? What is the annual break-even point (in number of haircuts)?
5. Ignore requirements 3 and 4 and assume that the barbers cease to be paid by the hour but receive $7 for each haircut. What is the new contribution margin per haircut? What is the annual break-even point (in number of haircuts)?
6. Refer to requirement 5. What would be the operating income if

20,000 haircuts are sold? Compare your answer with the answer in requirement 3.

7. Refer to requirement 5. If 20,000 haircuts are sold, at what rate of commission would Andre earn the same operating income as he earned in requirement 3?

P2-15 **BINGO AND LEVERAGE.** An Ontario law permits a game of chance called bingo when it is offered by specific not-for-profit institutions, including churches. Reverend Matthew Pappas, the priest of a new parish in suburban Mississauga, is investigating the desirability of conducting weekly bingo nights. The parish has no hall, but a local hotel would be willing to commit its hall for a lump-sum rental of $800 per night. The rent would include cleaning, setting up and taking down the tables and chairs, and so on.

1. Bingo cards would be provided by a local printer in return for free advertising therein. Door prizes would be donated by local merchants. The services of clerks, callers, a security force, and others would be donated by volunteers. Admission would be $4.00 per person, entitling the player to one card; extra cards would be $1.50 each. Reverend Pappas learns that many people buy extra cards, so there would be an average of four cards played per person. What is the maximum in total cash prizes that the church may award and still break even if 200 persons attend each weekly session?

2. Suppose the total cash prizes are $900. What will be the church's operating income if 100 persons attend? If 200 persons attend? If 300 persons attend? Briefly explain the effects of the cost behaviour on income.

3. After operating for 10 months, Reverend Pappas is considering negotiating a different rental arrangement but keeping the prize money unchanged at $900. Suppose the rent is $400 weekly plus $2 per person. Compute the operating income for attendance of 100, 200, and 300 persons, respectively. Explain why the results differ from those in requirement 2.

P2-16 **PROMOTION OF A ROCK CONCERT.** NLR Productions, Ltd., is promoting a rock concert in London. The bands will receive a flat fee of £8 million in cash. The concert will be shown worldwide on closed-circuit television. NLR will collect 100 percent of the receipts and will return 30 percent to the individual local closed-circuit theatre managers. NLR expects to sell 1.1 million seats at a net average price of £13 each. NLR will also receive £300,000 from the London arena (which has sold out its 19,500 seats, ranging from £150 for box seats to £25 for general admission, for a gross revenue of £1.25 million); NLR will not share the £300,000 with the local promoters.

1. The general manager of NLR Productions is trying to decide what amount to spend for advertising. What is the most NLR could spend and still break even on overall operations, assuming sales of 1.1 million tickets?

2. If NLR desired an operating income of £500,000, how many seats would have to be sold? Assume that the average price was £13 and the total fixed costs were £9 million.

P2-17 **ADDING A PRODUCT.** Andy's Ale House, a pub located in a university community, serves as a gathering place for the university's more social scholars. Andy sells draft beer and all brands of bottled beer at a contribution margin of $0.60 a beer.

Andy is considering also selling hamburgers during selected hours. His reasons are twofold. First, hamburgers would attract daytime customers. A hamburger and a beer are a quick lunch. Second, he has to compete with other local bars, some of which provide more extensive menus.

Andy analyzed the costs as follows:

Monthly fixed expenses:	
Wages of part-time cook	$1,200
Other	360
Total	$1,560

Variable expenses per hamburger	
Rolls	$0.12
Meat @ $2.80 per kilogram	
(7 hamburgers per kilogram)	0.40
Other	0.18
Total	$0.70

Andy planned a selling price of $1.10 per hamburger to lure many customers. For all questions, assume a 30-day month.

1. What are the monthly and daily break-even points, in number of hamburgers?
2. What are the monthly and daily break-even points, in dollar sales?
3. At the end of two months, Andy finds he has sold 3,600 hamburgers. What is the operating profit per month on hamburgers?
4. Andy thinks that at least 60 extra beers are sold per day because he sells hamburgers. This means that 60 extra people come to the bar or that 60 buy an extra beer because they are attracted by the hamburgers. How does this affect Andy's monthly operating income?
5. Refer to requirement 3. How many extra beers would have to be sold per day so that the overall effects of the hamburger sales on monthly operating income would be zero?

P2-18 **COST-VOLUME-PROFIT RELATIONSHIPS AND A RACE TRACK.** The Lakehead Race Track, in Thunder Bay, Ontario, is a horse-racing track. Its revenue is derived mainly from attendance and a fixed percentage of the betting. Its expenses for a 90-day season are

Wages of cashiers and ticket takers	$160,000
Commissioner's salary	20,000
Maintenance (repairs, etc.)	20,000
Utilities	30,000
Other expenses (amortization, insurance, advertising, etc.)	90,000
Purses: Total prizes paid to winning racers	810,000

The track made a contract with A.P. Inc. to park cars. A.P. charged the track $6 per car. A survey revealed that on the average, three people arrived in each car and half the attendees arrived by private automobiles. The others arrived by taxi and public buses.

The track's sources of revenue are

Rights for concession and vending	$50,000
Admission charge (deliberately low)	$1 per person
Percentage of the amount of bets placed	10%

1. Assuming that each person bets $27 a night:
   a. How many persons have to be admitted for the track to break even for the season?
   b. What is the total contribution margin at the break-even point?
   c. If the desired operating profit for the year is $270,000, how many people would have to attend?
2. If a policy of free admission brought a 20 percent increase in attendance, what would be the new level of operating profit? Assume that the previous level of attendance was 600,000 people.
3. If the purses were doubled in an attempt to attract better horses and thus increase attendance, what would be the new break-even point? Refer to the original data and assume that each person bets $27 a night.

P2-19 **COST-VOLUME-PROFITS AND VENDING MACHINES.** Cola Food Services operates and services soft-drink vending machines located in restaurants, gas stations, factories, etc. The machines are rented from the manufacturer. In addition, Cola must rent the space occupied by its machines. The following expense and revenue relationships pertain to a contemplated expansion program of 20 machines.

Machine rental: 20 machines @ $43.50	$870
Space rental: 20 locations @ $28.80	576
Part-time wages to service the additional 20 machines	1,454
Other fixed costs	100
Total monthly fixed costs	$3,000

Other data follows:

	PER UNIT	PER $100 OF SALES
Selling price	$1.00	100%
Cost	0.80	80%
Contribution margin	$0.20	20%

These questions relate to the above data unless otherwise noted. **Consider each question independently**.

1. What is the monthly break-even point in number of units? In dollar sales?
2. If 18,000 units were sold, what would be the company's net income?
3. If the space rental cost were doubled, what would be the monthly break-even point in number of units? In dollar sales?
4. If, in addition to the fixed rent, Cola Food Services Company paid the vending machine manufacturer $0.01 per unit sold, what would be the monthly break-even point in number of units? In dollar sales? Refer to the original data.
5. If, in addition to the fixed rent, Cola paid the machine manufacturer $0.02 for each unit sold in excess of the break-even point, what would be the new net income if 18,000 units were sold? Refer to the original data.

P2-20 **TRAVELLING EXPENSES.** Yuko Takase is a travelling inspector for Environment Canada. She uses her own car and the department reimburses her at $0.23 per kilometre. Yuko claims she needs $0.27 per kilometre just to break even. Shaun McHale, the district manager, looks into the matter and compiles the following information about Yuko's expenses:

Oil change every 3,000 kilometres	$ 30
Maintenance (other than oil) every 6,000 kilometres	240
Yearly insurance	700
Auto cost $13,500 with an average cash trade-in value of $6,000; has a useful life of three years	
Gasoline is approximately $0.60 per litre and Yuko averages 6 kilometres per litre	

When Yuko is on the road, she averages 120 kilometres a day. McHale knows that Yuko does not work Saturdays or Sundays, has 10 working days' vacation and six holidays, and spends approximately 15 working days in the office.

1. How many kilometres per year would Yuko have to travel to break even at the current rate of reimbursement?
2. What would be an equitable per-kilometre rate?

P2-21 **GOVERNMENTAL ORGANIZATION.** A social welfare agency has a government budget appropriation for 2006 of $900,000. The agency's major mission is to help disabled persons who are unable to hold jobs. On the average, the agency supplements each person's other income by $5,000 annually. The agency's fixed costs are $290,000. There are no other costs.

1. How many people are helped during 2006?
2. For 2007, the agency's budget appropriation has been reduced by 15 percent. If the agency continues the same level of monetary support per person, how many people will be helped in 2007? Compute the percentage decline in the number of persons helped.
3. Assume a budget reduction of 15 percent, as in requirement 2. The manager of the agency has discretion as to how much to supplement each person's income. She does not want to reduce the number of people served. On the average, what is the amount of the supplement that can be given to each person? Compute the percentage decline in the annual supplement.

P2-22 **CVP AND FINANCIAL STATEMENTS.** Canadian Foods, Inc. produces food products under various brand names. In 2007, the company's sales increased by 10 percent and its 2007 income statement showed the following (in millions):

Net sales	$24,002
Cost of goods sold	20,442
Selling, administrative, and general expense	2,265
Interest expense	277
Operating income (before tax)	$ 1,018

Suppose that the cost of goods sold is the only variable cost; selling, administrative, general, and interest expenses are fixed with respect to sales. Assume that Canadian Foods had another 10 percent increase in sales in 2008 and that there was no change in costs except for increases associated with the higher volume of sales. Compute the predicted 2008 operating profit for Canadian Foods and the percentage increase in operating profit. Explain why the percentage increase in profit differs from the percentage increase in sales.

P2-23 **GROSS MARGIN AND CONTRIBUTION MARGIN.** Photography, Inc. produces and sells cameras, film, and other imaging products. A condensed 2006 income statement follows (in millions):

Sales	$15,968
Cost of goods sold	8,326
Gross margin	7,642
Other operating expenses	6,086
Operating income	$ 1,556

Assume that $1,800 million of the cost of goods sold is a fixed cost representing amortization and other production costs that do not change with the volume of production. In addition, $4,000 million of the other operating expenses is fixed.

1. Compute the total contribution margin for 2006 and the contribution margin percentage. Explain why the contribution margin differs from the gross margin.
2. Suppose that sales for Photography, Inc. were predicted to increase by 10 percent in 2007 and that the cost behaviour was expected to continue in 2007 as it had been in 2006. Compute the predicted operating income for 2007. By what percentage did this predicted 2007 operating income exceed the 2006 operating income?
3. What assumptions were necessary to compute the predicted 2007 operating income in requirement 2?

P2-24 **CHOOSING EQUIPMENT FOR DIFFERENT VOLUMES.** Multiplex Cinema owns and operates a nationwide chain of movie theatres. The 500 properties in the Multiplex chain vary from low-volume, small-town, single-screen theatres to high-volume, big-city, multiscreen theatres.

The management is considering installing machines that will make popcorn on the premises. These machines would allow the theatres to sell popcorn that would be freshly popped daily rather than the prepopped corn that is currently purchased in large bags. This proposed feature would be properly advertised and is intended to increase patronage at the company's theatres.

The machines can be purchased in several different sizes. The annual rental costs and the operating costs vary with the size of the machines. The machine capacities and costs are

	POPPER MODEL		
	Economy	**Regular**	**Super**
Annual capacity	50,000 boxes	120,000 boxes	300,000 boxes
Costs:			
Annual machine rental	$8,000	$11,200	$20,200
Popcorn cost per box	0.14	0.14	0.14
Cost of each box	0.09	0.09	0.09
Other variable costs per box	0.22	0.14	0.05

1. Calculate the volume level in boxes at which the Economy Popper and Regular Popper would earn the same operating profit (loss).
2. The management can estimate the number of boxes to be sold at each of its theatres. Present a decision rule that would enable Multiplex's management to select the most profitable machine without having to make a separate cost calculation for each theatre. That is, at what anticipated range of unit sales should the Economy model be used? The Regular model? The Super model?

3. Could the management use the average number of boxes sold per seat for the entire chain and the capacity of each theatre to develop this decision rule? Explain your answer.

P2-25 **SALES-MIX ANALYSIS.** The Atlantic Catering Company specializes in preparing tasty main courses that are frozen and shipped to the finer restaurants in the Halifax area. When a diner orders the item, the restaurant heats and serves it. The budget data for 2006 are

	PRODUCT	
	Chicken Cordon Bleu	Veal Marsala
Selling price to restaurants	$7	$9
Variable expenses	$4	$5
Contribution margin	$3	$4
Number of units	250,000	125,000

The items are prepared in the same kitchens, delivered in the same trucks, and so forth. Therefore, the fixed costs of $1,320,000 are unaffected by the specific products.

1. Compute the planned net income for 2006.
2. Compute the break-even point in units, assuming that the planned sales mix is maintained.
3. Compute the break-even point in units if only veal marsala were sold or if only chicken cordon bleu were sold.
4. Suppose 99,000 units of veal marsala and 297,000 units of chicken were sold. Compute the net income. Compute the new break-even point if these relationships persisted in 2006. What is the major lesson of this problem?

P2-26 **INCOME TAXES ON HOTELS.** The Grove Hotel has annual fixed costs applicable to rooms of $10 million for its 600-room hotel, average daily room rates of $105, and average variable costs of $25 for each room rented. It operates 365 days per year. The hotel is subject to an income tax rate of 40 percent.

1. How many rooms must the hotel rent to earn a net income after taxes of $720,000? of $360,000?
2. Compute the break-even point in number of rooms rented. What percentage occupancy for the year is needed to break even?
3. Assume that the volume level of rooms sold is 150,000. The manager is wondering how much income could be generated by adding sales of 15,000 rooms. Compute the additional net income after taxes.

P2-27 **HOSPITAL COSTS.** The Metropolitan City Hospital is unionized. In 2006, nurses received an average annual salary of $45,000. The hospital administrator is considering how the contract with nurses should be changed for 2007. In turn, charging nursing costs to each department might also be changed.

Each department is accountable for its financial performance. Revenues and expenses are allocated to departments. Consider the expenses of the obstetrics department in 2006:

Variable expenses (based on 2006 patient-days) are

Meals	$ 510,000
Laundry	260,000
Laboratory	900,000
Pharmacy	800,000
Maintenance	150,000
Other	530,000
Total	$3,150,000

Fixed expenses (based on number of beds) are

Rent	$3,000,000
General administrative services	2,100,000
Janitorial	200,000
Maintenance	150,000
Other	450,000
Total	$5,900,000

Nurses are assigned to departments on the basis of annual patient-days, as follows:

VOLUME LEVEL INPATIENT-DAYS	NUMBER OF NURSES
10,000 – 12,000	30
12,001 – 16,000	35

Total patient-days are the number of patients multiplied by the number of days they are hospitalized. Each department is charged for the salaries of the nurses assigned to it.

During 2006 the obstetrics department had a capacity of 60 beds, billed insurance and government agencies an average of $800 per day for each patient, and had revenues of $12 million.

1. Compute the 2006 volume of activity in patient-days.
2. Compute the 2006 patient-days that would have been necessary for the obstetrics department to recoup all fixed expenses except nursing expenses.
3. Compute the 2006 patient-days that would have been necessary for the obstetrics department to break even, including nurses' salaries as a fixed cost.
4. Suppose obstetrics must pay $200 per patient-day for nursing services. This plan would replace the two-level fixed-cost system employed in 2006. Compute what the break-even point in patient-days would have been in 2006 under this plan.

P2-28 **MULTIPRODUCT BREAK-EVEN IN A RESTAURANT.** La Brasserie, a French restaurant in Moncton, New Brunswick, prepared a simplified version of its income statement as follows:

Revenues	$2,098,400
Cost of sales, all variable	1,246,500
Gross profit	$ 851,900
Operating expenses	
Variable	222,380
Fixed	170,700
Administrative expenses, all fixed	451,500
Net income	$ 7,320

The average dinner tab at La Brasserie is $40, and the average lunch tab is $20.

Assume that the variable cost of preparing and serving dinner is also twice that of a lunch. The restaurant serves twice as many lunches as dinners. Assume that the restaurant is open 305 days a year.

1. Compute the daily break-even volume in lunches and dinners for La Brasserie. Compare this to the actual volume reflected in the income statement.
2. Suppose that an extra annual advertising expenditure of $15,000 would increase the average daily volume by three dinners and six lunches, and that there is plenty of capacity to accommodate the extra business. Prepare an analysis for the management of La Brasserie explaining whether this would be desirable.
3. La Brasserie uses only premium food, and the cost of food makes up 25 percent of the restaurant's total variable costs. Use of average rather than premium ingredients could cut the food cost by 20 percent. Assume that La Brasserie uses average-quality ingredients and does not change its prices. How much of a drop-off in volume could it endure and still maintain the same net income? What factors in addition to revenue and costs would influence the decision about the quality of food to use?

P2-29 **CVP AND PREDICTION OF INCOME.** According to an article in *Business Week*, T.J. Izzo had a great idea after a bad back almost forced him to give up golf. His problem was carrying a golf bag, not swinging a club. So he designed a harness-like golf bag strap that distributed the weight equally on both shoulders. In April 1992, he formed Izzo Systems Inc. In 1993, Izzo made an operating income of $12,000 on revenue of $1 million from selling 75,000 straps. In 1994, Izzo expected to sell 92,000 straps for $1.7 million.

1. Suppose that variable costs per strap are $10. Compute total fixed and total variable costs for 1993.
2. Suppose the cost behaviour in 1994 was the same as in 1993. Estimate Izzo's operating income for 1994 (a) with sales at the predicted 92,000, (b) with sales 10 percent above the predicted level, and (c) with sales 10 percent below the predicted level.
3. Explain why the predicted 1994 operating income was so much greater than the 1993 operating income.

P2-30 **CVP IN A MODERN MANUFACTURING ENVIRONMENT.** A division of a computer company changed its production operations from one where a large labour force assembled electronic components to an automated production facility dominated by computer-controlled robots. The change was necessary because of fierce competitive pressures. Improvements in quality, reliability, and flexibility of production schedules were necessary just to match the competition. As a result of the change, variable costs fell and fixed costs increased, as shown in the following assumed budgets:

	OLD PRODUCTION OPERATION	NEW PRODUCTION OPERATION
Unit variable cost		
Material	$0.88	$0.88
Labour	1.22	0.22
Total per unit	$2.10	$1.10
Monthly fixed costs		
Rent and amortization	$450,000	$ 875,000
Supervisory labour	85,000	175,000
Other	50,000	90,000
Total per month	$585,000	$1,140,000

Expected volume is 600,000 units per month, with each unit selling for $3.10. Capacity is 800,000 units.

1. Compute the budgeted profit at the expected volume of 600,000 units under both the old and the new production environments.
2. Compute the budgeted break-even point under both the old and the new production environments.
3. Discuss the effect on profits if volume falls to 500,000 units under both the old and the new production environments.
4. Discuss the effect on profits if volume increases to 700,000 units under both the old and the new production environments.
5. Comment on the riskiness of the new operation versus the old operation.

P2-31 AIRLINE CVP. Airline companies regularly provide operating statistics with their financial statements. In 2006 North America Airlines reported that it had approximately 61,000 million seat-kilometres available, of which 68.1 percent were filled. (A seat-kilometre is one seat travelling one kilometre. For example, if an airplane with 100 seats travelled 400 kilometres, capacity would be 100 × 400 = 40,000 seat-kilometres.) The average revenue was $0.1310 per revenue-passenger-kilometre, where a revenue-passenger-kilometre is one seat occupied by a passenger travelling one kilometre. In 2005, approximately the same number of seat-kilometres were available, but only 65.6 percent of them were filled at an average revenue of $0.1251 per filled seat-kilometre. North America calls the percentage of seat-kilometres available that are filled with passengers their load factor.

1. Compute North America's passenger revenue for 2006 and 2005.
2. Assume that North America's variable costs were $0.05 per revenue-passenger-kilometre in both 2005 and 2006 and that fixed costs are $3,000 million per year each year.
   a. Compute North America's break-even point at the 2005 level of revenue per passenger-kilometre. Express it in both revenue-passenger-kilometres and as a load factor (that is, as a percentage of available capacity used).
   b. Compute North America's break-even point at the 2006 level of revenue per passenger-kilometre. Express it in both revenue-passenger-kilometres and as a load factor (that is, as a percentage of available capacity used).
3. Suppose North America maintained the same level of seat-kilometres available in 2007, had revenue of $0.13 per revenue-passenger-kilometre, and maintained the same level of fixed and variable costs as in the previous two years. Compute the load factor necessary to achieve an operating income of $400 million.

P2-32 BOEING BREAKS EVEN. Boeing is the largest commercial airplane manufacturer in the world. In 1996 it began development of the 757-300, a 240-plus passenger plane with a range over 6,000 kilometres. First deliveries took place in 1999 at a price of $70 million per plane.

Assume that Boeing's annual fixed costs for the 757-300 are $950 million, and its variable cost per airplane is $45 million.

1. Compute Boeing's break-even point in number of 757-300 airplanes and in dollars of sales.

2. Suppose Boeing plans to sell forty-two 757-300 airplanes in 2005. Compute Boeing's projected operating profit.
3. Suppose Boeing increased its fixed costs by $84 million and reduced variable costs per airplane by $2 million. Compute its operating profit if forty-two 757-300 airplanes are sold. Compute the break-even point. Comment on your results.
4. Ignore requirement 3. Suppose fixed costs do not change but variable costs increase by 10 percent before deliveries of 757-300 airplanes begin in 2006. Compute the new break-even point. What strategies might Boeing use to help assure profitable operations in light of increases in variable cost?

MANAGERIAL DECISION CASE

C2-1 **EFFECTS OF CHANGES IN COSTS, INCLUDING TAX EFFECTS.** Friendly Candy Company is a wholesale distributor of candy. The company services grocery, convenience, and drug stores in a large metropolitan area.

Small but steady growth in sales has been achieved by the company over the past few years while candy prices have been increasing. The company is formulating its plans for the coming fiscal year. Presented below are the data used to project the current year's after-tax net income of $138,000.

Average selling price per box	$ 5.00
Average variable costs per box:	
Cost of candy	$ 2.50
Selling expenses	0.50
Total	$ 3.00
Annual fixed costs	
Selling	$ 200,000
Administrative	350,000
Total	$ 550,000
Expected annual sales volume	
(390,000 boxes)	$1,950,000
Tax rate	40%

Manufacturers of candy have announced that they will increase prices of their products an average of 15 percent in the coming year, owing to increases in raw material (sugar, cocoa, peanuts, etc.) and labour costs. Friendly Candy Company expects that all other costs will remain at the same rates or levels as in the current year.

Required:
1. What is Friendly Candy Company's break-even point in boxes of candy for the current year?
2. What selling price per box must Friendly charge to cover the 15 percent increase in the cost of candy and still maintain the current contribution-margin ratio?
3. What volume of sales in dollars must Friendly achieve in the coming year to maintain the same net income after taxes as projected for the current year if the selling price of candy remains at $5 per box and the cost of candy increases 15 percent?
4. What strategies might Friendly use to maintain the same net income after taxes as projected for the current year?

E2-1 CVP AND BREAK-EVEN

Goal: Create an Excel spreadsheet to perform CVP analysis and show the relationship between price, costs, and break-even points in terms of units and dollars. Use the results to answer questions about your findings.

Scenario: Phonetronix, Inc., is a small manufacturer of telephone and communications devices. Recently, company management decided to investigate the profitability of cellular phone production. They have three different proposals to evaluate. Under all of the proposals, the fixed costs for the new phone would be $110,000. Under proposal A, the selling price of the new phone would be $99 and the variable cost per unit would be $55. Under proposal B, the selling price of the phone would be $129 and the variable cost would remain the same. Under proposal C, the selling price would be $99 and the variable cost would be $49.

When you have completed your spreadsheet, answer the following questions:

1. What are the break-even points in units and dollars under proposal A?

2. How did the increased selling price under proposal B impact the break-even points in units and dollars compared to the break-even points calculated under proposal A?

3. Why did the change in variable cost under proposal C not impact the break-even points in units and dollars as significantly as proposal B did?

Step by Step:

1. Open a new Excel spreadsheet.

2. In column A, create a bold-faced heading that contains the following:
   Row 1: Chapter 2 Decision Guideline
   Row 2: Phonetronix, Inc.
   Row 3: Cost-Volume-Profit (CVP) Analysis
   Row 4: Today's Date

3. Merge and centre the four heading rows across columns A through D.

4. In row 7, create the following bold-faced, right-justified column headings:
   Column B: Proposal A
   Column C: Proposal B
   Column D: Proposal C

   Note: Adjust cell widths when necessary as you work.

5. In Column A, create the following row headings:
   Row 8: Selling price
   Row 9: Variable cost

Row 10: Contribution margin
Row 11: Contribution margin ratio
Skip a row
Row 13: Fixed cost
Skip a row
Row 15: Break-even in units
Skip a row
Row 17: Break-even in dollars

6. Use the scenario data to fill in the selling price, variable cost, and fixed cost amounts for the three proposals.

7. Use the appropriate formulas from Chapter 2 to calculate contribution margin, contribution margin ratio, break-even in units, and break-even in dollars.

8. Format all amounts as

Number tab:	Category:	Currency
	Decimal places:	0
	Symbol:	None
	Negative numbers:	Red with parentheses

9. Change the format of the selling price, contribution margin, fixed cost, and break-even in dollar amounts to display a dollar symbol.

10. Change the format of both contribution margin headings to display as indented.

Alignment tab:	Horizontal:	Left (indent)
	Indent:	1

11. Change the format of the contribution margin amount cells to display a top border, using the default line style.

Border tab:	Icon:	Top Border

12. Change the format of the contribution margin ratio amounts to display as a percentage with two decimal places.

Number tab:	Category:	Percentage
	Decimal places:	2

13. Change the format of all break-even headings and amounts to display as boldfaced.

14. Activate the ability to use heading names in formulas under Tools > Options.

Calculation tab:	Check the box:	Accept labels in formulas

15. Replace the cell-based formulas with "word-based" equivalents for each formula used in Proposal A.

Example: Contribution margin for Proposal B would be
= ('Selling price' 'Proposal B') – ('Variable cost' 'Proposal B')

Note: The tic marks used in the example help avoid naming errors caused by data having similar titles, i.e., "contribution margin" and "contribution margin ratio." The parentheses help clarify groupings.

Help: Ask the Answer Wizard about "Name cells in a workbook."

Select "Learn about labels and names in formulas" from the right-hand panel.

16. Save your work to a disk, and print a copy for your files.

COLLABORATIVE LEARNING EXERCISE

CL2-1 CVP FOR A SMALL BUSINESS

Form into groups of two to six students. Each group should select a very simple business, one with a single product or one with approximately the same contribution margin percentage for all products. Some possibilities are

A child's lemonade stand
A retail video rental store
An espresso cart
A retail store selling compact discs
An athletic shoe store
A cookie stand in a mall

However, you are encouraged to use your imagination rather than just select one of these examples.

The following tasks might be split up among the group members:

1. Make a list of all fixed costs associated with running the business you selected. Estimate the amount of each fixed cost per month (or per day or per year, if one of them is more appropriate for your business).

2. Make a list of all variable costs associated with making or obtaining the product or service your company is selling. Estimate the cost per unit for each variable cost.

3. Given the fixed and variable costs you have identified, compute the break-even point for your business in either units or dollar sales.

4. Assess the prospects of your business making a profit.

3

Measurement of Cost Behaviour

After studying this chapter, you will be able to

1. Explain step- and mixed-cost behaviour.

2. Explain management's influence on cost behaviour.

3. Measure and mathematically express cost functions and use them to predict costs.

4. Describe the importance of activity analysis for measuring cost functions.

5. Measure cost behaviour using the engineering analysis, account analysis, high-low, visual fit, and least squares regression methods.

Chapter 2 demonstrates the importance of understanding cost volume profit relationships. This chapter focuses on *measuring cost behaviour*, which means understanding and *quantifying* how activities of an organization affect levels of costs. Recall that the activities that affect costs are called *cost drivers*. Understanding relationships between costs and their cost drivers allows managers in all types of organizations—profit-seeking, not-for-profit, and government—to

- Evaluate new manufacturing methods or service practices (Chapter 5)
- Design accurate and useful product costing systems (Chapters 5, 6, 7)
- Make proper short-run decisions (Chapters 8 and 9)
- Make proper long-run decisions (Chapters 10 and 11)
- Plan or budget the effects of future activities (Chapters 12 and 13)
- Design effective management control systems (Chapters 14 and 15)

As you can see, understanding cost behaviour is fundamental to management accounting. There are numerous real-world cases where managers have made poor decisions to drop product lines, close manufacturing plants, or bid too high or too low on projects because they used erroneous cost-behaviour information. This chapter, therefore, deserves careful study.

COST DRIVERS AND COST BEHAVIOUR

Linear-Cost Behaviour.
Activity that can be graphed with a straight line when a cost changes proportionately with changes in a cost driver.

Accountants and managers usually assume that cost behaviour is *linear* over some *relevant range* of activities or cost drivers. When a cost changes proportionately with changes in a cost driver it can be illustrated with a straight line; this is known as a **linear-cost behaviour**. Recall that a linear or other cost behaviour is valued only within the limits of the relevant range. Managers usually define the relevant range based on their previous experience with different levels of activity and cost.

Costs are influenced by many activities or cost drivers, but for some costs, *volume* of a product produced or service provided is the primary driver. These costs are easy to identify with or trace to products or services. Examples of volume-driven costs include the costs of printing labour, paper, ink, and binding to produce this textbook. We could *trace* the use of these resources to the copies of the text printed. Schedules, payroll records, and other documents show how much of each was used to produce the copies of this text.

However, some other costs are more affected by activities *not* directly related to volume and often have *multiple* cost drivers. Such costs are not easy to identify with or trace to outputs. Examples of costs that are difficult to trace include the wages and salaries of the editorial staff of the publisher of this textbook. These editorial personnel produce many different textbooks, and it would be difficult to determine exactly what portion of their salaries went into a specific book, such as this one.

Understanding and measuring costs that are difficult to trace to outputs can be especially challenging. In practice, many organizations use single cost drivers to describe each cost even though many costs have multiple causes. This approach is easier and less expensive than using nonlinear relationships and/or multiple cost drivers. *Careful* use of linear-cost behaviour with a single cost driver often provides cost estimates that are accurate enough for most decisions. Linear-cost behaviour with a simple cost driver may not accurately depict reality, but it may be easier to understand and less costly to alter the "true" cost behaviour.

For ease of communication and understanding, accountants usually describe cost behaviour in visual or graphical terms. Exhibit 3-1 shows linear-cost behaviour, the relevant range, and a cost driver.

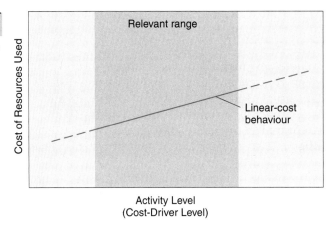

Types of Cost Behaviour

Chapter 2 describes two patterns of cost behaviour: *variable* and *fixed* costs. Recall that a purely variable cost varies in proportion to the selected cost driver, while a purely fixed cost is not affected by the cost-driver activity. In addition to these pure versions of cost, there are *mixed* and *step* costs that combine characteristics of both fixed- and variable-cost behaviour.

Step Costs

Step costs change at intervals of activity or steps because their costs are incurred in indivisible batches or chunks. An example of step costs could be the wage of a chambermaid who is supposed to clean 15 rooms per shift in a local hotel. If 1 to 15 rooms are occupied, 1 chambermaid is needed. If between 16 and 30 rooms are occupied, 2 chambermaids are needed. That is, the cleaning costs, as far as the chambermaid wages are concerned, do not change on a per-room basis but, instead, per batches of 15 rooms. If the individual chunks of cost are relatively large and apply to a specific, broad range of activity, the cost is considered a fixed cost over that range of activity. Exhibit 3-2 (panel A) shows the cost of leasing oil and gas drilling equipment. When oil and gas exploration activity reaches a certain level in a given region, an additional rig must be leased. However, one level of oil and gas rig leasing will support all volumes of exploration activity within a relevant range of drilling. Within each relevant range, this step cost behaves as a *fixed cost*. The amount of fixed cost appropriate for a given range of activity is the total step cost.

In contrast, accountants describe step costs as variable when the individual chunks of cost are relatively small and apply to a narrow range of activity. Exhibit 3-2 (panel B) shows the wage cost of cashiers at a supermarket. Suppose 1 cashier can serve an average of 20 shoppers per hour and that, within the relevant range of shopping activity, the number of shoppers can range from 40 to 440 per hour. The corresponding number of cashiers would range between 2 and 22. Because the steps are relatively small, this step cost behaves much like a variable cost, and could be used as such for planning with little loss of accuracy.

EXHIBIT 3-2

Step-Cost Behaviour

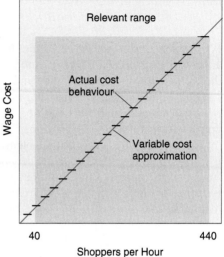

Panel A: Lease Cost

Panel B: Supermarket Checker Wage Cost

Mixed Costs

Mixed Costs. Costs that contain elements of both fixed and variable costs.

Mixed costs contain elements of both fixed and variable costs. As with step costs, the fixed element is determined by the planned *range* of activity level. In a mixed cost, the variable cost is incurred in addition to the fixed cost: the total mixed cost is the sum of the fixed cost plus the variable cost. The variable-cost element of the mixed cost is a purely variable cost that varies proportionately with activity within the single relevant range.

Many costs are mixed costs. For example, consider the monthly facilities maintenance department cost at St. Michael's Hospital, shown in Exhibit 3-3. Salaries of the maintenance personnel and costs of equipment are fixed at $10,000 per month. In addition, cleaning supplies and repair materials may vary at a rate of $5 per patient-day delivered by the hospital.

EXHIBIT 3-3

Mixed-Cost Behaviour

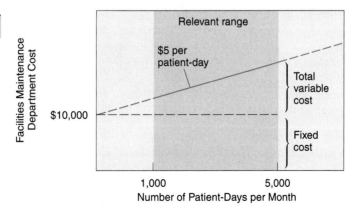

Understanding Cost Behaviour in the PVC Industry

Brampton, Ontario–based AT Plastics Inc. and Waterloo, Ontario–based Noveon Canada Inc. produce and sell polyvinyl chloride (PVC) resins and compounds. PVC resin is the second-largest volume thermoplastic sold in the world. In North America, the market approximates 5 billion kilograms and Canada is slightly less than 10 percent of this total. Traditional applications for vinyl have included construction products (such as pipe and house siding), wire-and-cable covering, and window frames. In recent years, the market has expanded to include appliance parts and business machine components, among other applications.

The PVC industry is very capital-intensive and is becoming more so; the traditional applications for vinyl that use large volumes of PVC resins are very price-competitive and are marketed as "commodities." Typically, North American purchasers of PVC resin buy by the truckload or railcar. Off-shore orders are usually for volumes in the range of millions of kilograms. In many instances, an order is won or lost based on pricing of a mere one-tenth of a cent.

As a result of the commodity nature of the PVC resin market and the desire on the part of producers to keep their plants running at capacity (shutdowns are extremely costly and do not result in any ability to reduce fixed costs in the short term), prices tend to drift downward in weak markets—eventually settling out at the variable cost of the incremental producer.

It is therefore critical that participants in the PVC industry understand cost structures in detail, such as through precisely identifying variable selling and manufacturing costs. Additionally, to the extent that costs are variable within a particular volume range, the variable component may be segregated from the fixed component for greater precision in decision making. (See also Gooderich, Ontario–based Jokey Plastics North America Inc., at www.jokey.com.)

	A	B
Net Unit Selling Price	26.0¢	20.5¢
Variable Selling & Manufacturing Costs		
Freight	2.1	–
Duty	0.6	–
Raw materials	17.1	17.1
Utilities	3.5	3.5
Packaging (material and labour)	–	1.1
Export allowance	(1.5)	(2.5)
Selling	0.6	0.1
Total Variable Costs	22.4	19.3
Incremental Contribution (per kilogram)	3.6	1.2
Fixed Costs (per unit)		
Manufacturing - overhead	3.2	3.2
- amortization	1.8	1.8
Selling and administration	1.6	0.5
Total Fixed Costs	6.6	5.5
Operating Income/(Loss)	(3.0)¢	(4.3)¢

The major focus on large export orders (where the pricing will not have any negative impacts on domestic pricing) is "Incremental Contribution per kilogram." In many cases, orders will be accepted with Incremental Contributions of one cent per kilogram or less. Raw material suppliers for these export orders will be approached to determine their desire to provide an "Export Allowance" in order to obtain an order; these approaches will usually result in negotiation as to the amount of the Export Allowance required to obtain the order and the willingness of the supplier to accept it.

A typical analysis of the profitability of two proposed sales is demonstrated in the table on the adjacent page. Note that variable costs are clearly separated from fixed costs. With a positive "Incremental Contribution," the order will be accepted rather than rejected even though it will result in an operating loss. The contribution to fixed costs is a better result than the alternative of a greater total operating loss.

Source: Adapted from material written by Stuart J. Macdonnell, former Corporate Controller & Chief Administrative Officer, B.F. Goodrich Canada Inc.

AT Plastics Inc.
www.atplas.com

Noveon canada Inc.
www.noveon.com

An administrator at St. Michael's Hospital could use knowledge of the facilities maintenance department cost behaviour to

1. Plan costs. Suppose the hospital expects to service 4,000 patient-days[1] next month. The month's predicted facilities maintenance department costs are $10,000 fixed plus the variable cost that equals 4,000 patient-days times $5 per patient-day, for a total of $30,000.
2. Provide feedback to managers. Suppose actual facilities maintenance costs were $35,000 in a month when 4,000 patient-days were serviced as planned. Managers would want to know why the hospital overspent by $5,000 ($35,000 less the planned $30,000) so that they could take corrective action.
3. Make decisions about the most efficient use of resources. For example, managers might weigh the long-run tradeoffs of increased fixed costs of highly automated floor-cleaning equipment against the variable costs of extra hours needed to clean floors manually.

MANAGEMENT'S INFLUENCE ON COST FUNCTIONS

OBJECTIVE 2

Explain management's influence on cost behaviour.

Managers can influence cost behaviour through decisions about such factors as *product* or *service attributes, capacity, size, technology employed*, and policies implemented to create *incentives to control costs.*

Product and Service Decisions

Budget Rent-a-Car
www.budgetcanada.com

Perhaps the greatest influences on product and service costs are a manager's choices of product mix, design, performance, quality, features, distribution, and so on. Each of these decisions contributes to the organization's performance and should be made in a cost-benefit analysis. For example, Budget Rent-a-Car would add a feature to its services only if the cost of the feature (for example, free mileage) could be justified (more than recovered by increased business).

---

[1] A patient-day is one patient spending one day in the hospital—one patient spending five days is five patient-days of service.

Capacity Decisions

Capacity Costs. The fixed costs associated with a desired level of production or a desired level of service, while maintaining the chosen product or service attributes.

Strategic decisions about the scale and scope of an organization's activities generally result in fixed levels of *capacity costs*. **Capacity costs** are the fixed costs associated with a desired level of production or a desired level of service, while maintaining the chosen product or service attributes. Companies in industries with long-term variations in demand must exercise caution when making capacity decisions. Fixed-capacity costs cannot be recovered when demand falls during an economic downturn.

Consider the dilemma facing an auto manufacturer operating at full capacity. To meet demand, workers may work overtime and the company may outsource some of its production. The auto company has to choose between building new plants and assembly lines or continuing to pay premiums for overtime and outside production. Building new plants would enable the company to produce cars at a lower cost but at higher fixed-capacity costs. Overtime and outsourcing production may be expensive, but the auto company could control these variable costs much more easily during any business downturn.

Faced with the strategic decision concerning scale and scope of operations, a company may choose to forego sales and market share by controlling overtime and outsourcing costs and keeping the same capacity. Alternatively, if the company is convinced that demand over capacity is to continue in the long run, adding fixed costs by increasing capacity makes sense.

Committed Fixed Costs

Committed Fixed Costs. Costs arising from the possession of facilities, equipment, and a basic organization; large, indivisible chunks of costs that are largely unavoidable.

Every organization has some costs to which it is committed perhaps for quite a few years. **Committed fixed costs** usually arise from the possession of facilities, equipment, and a basic organization. These are large, indivisible chunks of cost that are largely unavoidable. Committed fixed costs include mortgage or lease payments, interest payments on long-term debt, property taxes, insurance, and salaries of key personnel. Only major changes in the philosophy, scale, or scope of operations could change these committed fixed costs in future periods. Recall the example of the facilities maintenance department for the St. Michael's Hospital. The capacity of the department was a management decision and, in this case, that decision determined the magnitude of the equipment cost. Suppose St. Michael's Hospital were to increase permanently its patient-days per month beyond the relevant range of 5,000 patient-days. Because more capacity would be needed, the committed equipment cost would rise to a new level.

Discretionary Fixed Costs

Discretionary Fixed Costs. Costs determined by management as part of the periodic planning process in order to meet the organization's goals.

Some costs are fixed at certain levels only because management decided that these costs should be incurred in order to meet the organization's goals. These **discretionary fixed costs** have no obvious relationship to levels of output activity, but are determined as part of the periodic planning process. During each planning period, management will determine how much to spend on discretionary items such as advertising and promotion costs, public relations, research and development costs, charitable donations, employee training programs, and purchased management consulting services.

Unlike committed fixed costs, managers can alter discretionary fixed costs easily—up or down—even within a budget period, if they decide that different levels of spending are desirable. Conceivably, managers could reduce such discretionary costs almost entirely for a given year in dire times, whereas they could not reduce committed costs. Discretionary fixed costs may be essential to the long-run achievement of the organization's goals, but managers can vary spending levels broadly in the short run.

Sometimes managers plan discretionary fixed costs, such as advertising or research and development, as a percentage of planned sales revenue. This does not mean that advertising or research and development should depend on current revenues. Rather, this planning is needed if the organization is to be able to pay for discretionary fixed costs.

Consider Marietta Corporation, which is experiencing financial difficulties. Sales for its major products are down, and Marietta's management is considering cutting back on costs *temporarily*. Marietta's management must determine which of the following fixed costs to reduce or eliminate, and how much money each would save:

COSTS	PLANNED AMOUNTS
Advertising and Promotion	$ 30,000
Amortization	400,000
Employee Training	100,000
Management Salaries	800,000
Mortgage Payment	250,000
Property Taxes	600,000
Research and Development	1,500,000
Total	$3,680,000

Can Marietta reduce or eliminate any of these fixed costs? The answer depends on Marietta's long-run outlook. Marietta could reduce costs, but also greatly reduce its ability to compete in the future, if it cuts carelessly. Rearranging these costs by categories of committed and discretionary costs yields the following analysis:

FIXED COSTS	PLANNED AMOUNTS
Committed:	
Amortization	$ 400,000
Mortgage Payment	250,000
Property Taxes	600,000
Total Committed	$1,250,000
Discretionary (Potential Savings):	
Advertising and Promotion	30,000
Employee Training	100,000
Management Salaries	800,000
Research and Development	1,500,000
Total Discretionary	$2,430,000
Total Committed and Discretionary	$3,680,000

Eliminating all discretionary fixed costs would save Marietta $2,430,000 per year. As is clear from Chapter 2, reducing fixed costs lowers the break-even point or increases the profit at a given level of sales, which might benefit Marietta at this time. Distinguishing committed and discretionary fixed costs would be the company's first step to identifying where costs *could* be reduced. It would be unwise to arbitrarily reduce or eliminate any of the fixed costs.

Technology Decisions

One of the most critical decisions that managers make is the type of technology that the organization will use to produce its products and/or deliver its services. Choice of technology (for example, traditional teller banking services versus automatic tellers) positions the organization to meet its current goals and to respond to changes in the environment (for example, changes in customer needs or actions by competitors). Not surprisingly, technology may have a great impact on the costs of products and services.

Cost Control Incentives

Finally, future costs may be affected by the *incentives* that management creates for employees to control costs. Managers use their knowledge of cost behaviour to set cost expectations, and employees may receive compensation or other rewards that are tied to meeting these expectations. For example, the administrator of St. Michael's Hospital may give the supervisor of the facilities maintenance department a favourable evaluation if the supervisor maintained quality of service *and* kept department costs below the expected amount for the level of patient-days serviced. This strong form of feedback could cause the supervisor to carefully watch department costs and to find ways to reduce costs without reducing quality of service.

MEASURING COST BEHAVIOUR

OBJECTIVE 3

Measure and mathematically express cost functions and use them to predict costs.

The decision-making, planning, and control activities of management accounting require accurate and useful estimates of future fixed and variable costs. It is usually easy to measure costs that are obviously linked with a volume-related cost driver. Why? Because you can trace such costs to particular cost drivers, and measurement simply requires a system for identifying the costs. For example, payroll systems that use labour records or time cards may detail the amount of time each employee spends on a particular product or service and measure labour costs.

In contrast, it is usually difficult to measure costs without obvious links to cost drivers or those with multiple cost drivers. *Assumed* relationships between costs and cost drivers often are used because a link is not obvious or observable.

Cost Functions

Measuring Cost Behaviour (Cost Measurement). Understanding and quantifying how activities of an organization affect level of cost.

Cost Function. An algebraic equation used by managers to describe the relationship between a cost and its cost driver(s).

The first step in estimating or predicting costs is **measuring cost behaviour (cost measurement)** as a function of appropriate cost drivers. The second step is to use these cost measures to estimate future costs at expected future levels of cost-driver activity.

In order to describe the relationship between a cost and its cost driver(s), managers often use an algebraic equation called a **cost function**. When there is only one cost driver, the cost function is similar to the algebraic CVP relationships discussed in Chapter 2. Consider the mixed cost graphed in Exhibit 3-3 on page 91, facilities maintenance department cost:

$$\begin{aligned}
\text{total facilities maintenance} &= \text{total fixed} + \text{total variable}\\
\text{department cost} &\quad \text{maintenance cost} \quad \text{maintenance cost}
\end{aligned}$$

$$= \text{fixed maintenance cost per month} + \left(\text{variable cost per patient-day} \times \text{number of patient-days} \right)$$

Let

$$\begin{aligned}
Y &= \text{total (facilities maintenance department) cost}\\
F &= \text{fixed maintenance cost per month}\\
V &= \text{the variable cost (per patient-day)}\\
X &= \text{the cost driver (number of patient-days)}
\end{aligned}$$

We can rewrite the mixed-cost function as

$$Y = F + VX, \text{ or}$$
$$Y = \$10{,}000 + \$5X$$

This mixed-cost function has the familiar form of a straight line—it is called a *linear*-cost function. When graphing a cost function, F is the *intercept*, the point on the vertical axis where the cost function begins. In Exhibit 3-3 the intercept is the $10,000 fixed cost per month. V, the variable cost per unit of activity, is the *slope* of the cost function. In Exhibit 3-3 the cost function slopes upwards at the rate of $5 for each additional patient-day.

Criteria for Choosing Functions

Managers should apply two criteria to obtain accurate and useful cost functions: plausibility and reliability. Managers must use both criteria together to determine an accurate cost function.

1. The cost function must be plausible or believable. Personal observation of costs and activities, when it is possible, provides the best evidence of a plausible relationship between a cost and its driver. Some cost relationships, by nature, are not directly observable, so the cost analyst must be confident that the proposed relationship is sound. Many costs may move together with a number of cost drivers, but no cause-effect relationships may exist. A cause-effect relationship (that is, X causes Y) is necessary for cost functions to be accurate and useful.
2. In addition to being plausible, a cost function's estimates of costs at actual levels of activity must reliably conform to actually observed costs. Reliability can be assessed in terms of "goodness of fit"—how well the cost function explains past cost behaviour. If the fit is good and conditions do not change, the cost function should be a reliable predictor of future costs.

Knowledge of operations and how costs are recorded is helpful in choosing a plausible and reliable cost function that links cause and effect. For example, maintenance is often performed when output is low, because that is when machines can be taken out of service. However, lower output does not *cause* increased maintenance costs, nor does increased output *cause* lower maintenance costs. The timing of maintenance is somewhat discretionary. A more plausible explanation is that, over a longer period of time, increased output causes higher maintenance costs, but daily or weekly recording of maintenance costs may make it appear otherwise. Understanding the nature of maintenance costs should lead to a reliable, long-run cost function.

Choosing Cost Drivers: Activity Analysis

OBJECTIVE 4

Describe the importance of activity analysis for measuring cost functions.

Activity Analysis. The process of identifying appropriate cost drivers for each individual activity and their effects on the costs of making a product or providing a service.

Incorrect assumptions about cost behaviour may cause incorrect decisions. The remedy is a careful examination of cost behaviour. To aid such an examination, managers apply **activity analysis**, which identifies appropriate cost drivers for each individual activity and their effects on the costs of making a product or providing a service. The final product or service may have a number of cost drivers because a number of separate activities may be involved. The greatest benefit of activity analysis is that it directs management accountants to the appropriate cost drivers for each cost.

Activity analysis is especially important for measuring and predicting costs for which cost drivers are not obvious. Earlier in this chapter we said that a cost is fixed or variable *with respect to a specific cost driver*. A cost that appears fixed in relation to one cost driver could, in fact, be variable in relation to another. For example, suppose an automobile plant uses automated painting equipment. The cost of adjusting this equipment for different colours and types of finishes may be fixed with regard to the total *number* of automobiles produced; that is, there is no discernible cost relationship between these support costs and the number of automobiles produced. However, this same cost may vary dramatically with the number of different *colours* and *types of finishes* of automobiles produced. Activity analysis examines various potential cost drivers for plausibility and reliability. As always, the expected benefits of improved decision making from using more accurate cost behaviour should exceed the expected costs of the cost-driver search.

Identifying the appropriate cost drivers is the most critical aspect of any method for measuring cost behaviour. For many years, most organizations used only one cost driver: the amount of labour used. In essence, they assumed that the only activity affecting costs was the use of labour. But in the past decade we have learned that previously "hidden" activities greatly influence cost behaviour. Often analysts in both manufacturing and service companies find that activities related to the complexity of performing tasks affect costs more directly than labour usage or other cost drivers that are related to the volume of output activity.

Northern Computers Inc.
www.nci1.com

Consider Northern Computers Inc., which makes two products for personal computers: a plug-in music board ("Mozart-Plus") and a hard disk drive ("Powerdrive"). Many years ago when most of the work was done by hand, most costs, other than the cost of materials, were related to (driven by) labour cost. However, the use of computer-controlled assembly equipment has increased the costs of support activities and has reduced labour cost. Labour cost is now only 5 percent of the total costs. Furthermore, activity analysis has shown that the majority of today's support costs are driven by the number of components added to products (a measure of product complexity), not by labour cost.

On average, support costs were twice as much as labour costs. Suppose the company wants to assess how much support cost is incurred in producing one Mozart-Plus and in one Powerdrive. Using the old cost driver, labour cost and support costs would be

	MOZART-PLUS	POWERDRIVE
Labour Cost	$ 8.50	$130.00
Support Cost		
2 × Direct Labour Cost	$17.00	$260.00

Using the more appropriate cost driver, the *number of components added to products*, the support costs are

	MOZART-PLUS	POWERDRIVE
Support Cost		
at $20 per component		
$20 × 5 components	$100.00	
$20 × 9 components		$180.00
Difference in Support Cost		
	$ 83.00	$ 80.00
	higher	lower

By using an appropriate cost driver, the company can measure its support costs on a much more meaningful basis. Managers will make better decisions with this revised information. For example, prices charged for products can be more closely related to the costs of production.

METHODS OF MEASURING COST FUNCTIONS

OBJECTIVE 5

Measure cost behaviour using the engineering analysis, account analysis, high-low, visual fit, and least squares regression methods.

Once managers have determined the most plausible drivers behind different costs, they can choose from a broad selection of methods of approximating cost functions, including (1) engineering analysis, (2) account analysis, (3) high-low method, (4) visual fit analysis, and (5) least squares regression analysis. These methods are not mutually exclusive; managers frequently use two or more together to avoid major errors in measuring cost behaviour. The first two methods may rely only on logical analysis, while the last three involve analysis of past costs.

Engineering Analysis

Engineering Analysis. The systematic review of materials, supplies, labour, support services, and facilities needed for products and services; measuring cost behaviour according to what cost should be, not by what costs have been.

The first method, **engineering analysis**, measures cost behaviour according to what costs *should be*, not by what costs *have been*. It entails a systematic review of materials, supplies, labour, support services, and facilities needed for products and services. Measures can be based on information from personnel who are directly involved with the product or service. Analysts can even use engineering analysis successfully for new products and services. Analysts learn about new costs from experiments with prototypes, accounting and industrial engineering literature, the experience of competitors, and the advice of management consultants. From this information, cost analysts determine what future costs should be. If the cost analysts are experienced and understand the activities of the organization, their engineering cost predictions may be quite reliable and useful for decision making. The disadvantages of engineering cost analysis are that the efforts are costly and often not timely.

A Not-for-Profit Example

Manufacturing companies were the first organizations to use activity analysis. However, its use has spread to many service industries and not-for-profit organizations. A recent article described how a health-care organization undertook an activity analysis to better understand its costs.

The Hospice is a medical care facility providing services to the terminally ill. In addition to seeing to the medical needs of its patients, the Hospice has social workers, home health aides, volunteers, and chaplains. It also provides an 18-month bereavement program for families of patients.

Many of the Hospice's costs were related directly to patients, and understanding these costs posed no problems. However, support costs were large, and the Hospice had little information about what caused these costs. Before undertaking an activity analysis, the Hospice simply assumed that the patient-day was the only cost driver for all support costs. All that the Hospice knew about support costs was that they were $35.53 per patient-day.

Because the Hospice felt the squeeze of increasing costs while reimbursements from provincial health plans remained constant, management at the Hospice wanted better cost information to make various decisions. To do this, the organization undertook an activity analysis to determine the appropriate cost drivers for support costs. This consisted of two basic tasks: (1) identify the activities being performed and (2) select a cost driver for each activity.

To identify the activities and the costs related to each activity, the Hospice formed a cross-functional team. Identifying the activities takes a thorough understanding of all the operations of the Hospice, so a team of only finance or accounting professionals would not be knowledgeable enough for this task. The team included the director of operations, the bereavement coordinator, the billing coordinator, a nurse, and a representative of the community service program. Among them they knew all aspects of the Hospice's operations.

The team identified 14 activities. The next step was to select a cost driver for each activity. Here are some of the activities and their related cost drivers:

Activity	Cost Driver
Referral	Number of (indexed) referrals
Admission	Number of admissions
Bereavement	Number of deaths
Accounting/finance	Number of (indexed) patient-days
Billing	Number of billings
Volunteer services	Number of volunteers

Using the cost information from the activity analysis, management was able to learn how much each different activity cost and could recognize that patients requiring use of expensive activities were more expensive to treat. Management could then try to reduce the costs of activities that were not worth the amount being spent for them, and they could better negotiate contracts so that the provincial health plan would provide more support for patients that required the most expensive activities.

Source: Adapted from Sidney J. Baxendale and Victoria Dornbusch, "Activity-Based Costing for a Hospice," *Strategic Finance*, March 2000, pp. 65–70, published by the Institute of Management Accountants (accessible at www.imanet.org, under "publications").

Weyerhaeuser
www.weyerhaeuser.com

Weyerhaeuser Company, producer of wood products, used engineering analysis to determine the cost functions for its 14 corporate service departments. These cost functions are used to measure the cost of corporate services used by three main business groups. For example, accounts payable costs for each division are a function of three cost drivers: the number of hours spent on each division, the number of documents, and the number of invoices. This approach to measuring cost behaviour could also be used by nearly any service organization.

At St. Michael's Hospital, an assistant to the hospital administrator interviewed facilities maintenance personnel and observed their activities on several random days for a month. From data she collected, she confirmed that the most plausible cost driver for facilities maintenance cost is the number of patient-days. She also estimated from current department salaries and equipment charges that monthly fixed costs approximate $10,000 per month. From interviews and supplies usage during the month, she estimated that variable costs are $5 per patient-day. She communicated this information to the hospital administrator, but cautioned that her cost measures may be in error because

1. The month she observed may be abnormal.
2. The facilities maintenance personnel may have altered their normal work habits because she was observing them.
3. The facilities maintenance personnel may not have told the complete truth about their activities because of concerns about the use of the information.

If we assume the observed and estimated information is correct, facilities maintenance cost in any month could be predicted by first forecasting that month's expected patient-days and then entering that figure into the following algebraic, mixed-cost function:

$$Y = \$10,000 \text{ per month} + \$5 \times \text{patient-days}$$

For example, if the administrator expects 4,000 patient-days next month, she will predict facilities maintenance costs to be

$$Y = \$10,000 + \$5 \times 4,000 \text{ patient-days} = \underline{\$30,000}$$

MAKING MANAGERIAL DECISIONS

A cost function is a mathematical expression of the components of a particular cost. However, an intuitive understanding of cost functions is just as important as being able to write the mathematical formula. Suppose you have been using a cost function to predict total order-processing activity costs. The cost function is total costs = $25,000 + $89 × (number of orders processed). This formula is based on data that are in the range of 500 to 700 orders processed. Now, you need to predict the total cost for 680 orders. You have a few questions to answer before you are comfortable using the cost function in this situation. Why is it important to know the relevant range? What does it mean when a cost function is linear? Why do managers want to know whether a cost is linear?

ANSWER
As long as the operating conditions that existed when the data were collected have not changed significantly, then knowing that the number of orders processed is within the relevant range—500 to 700, in this case—gives you confidence in the predicted total cost. A linear mixed-cost function means that there are two parts to the cost. One part is fixed—that is, it's independent of the cost driver. The other part varies in proportion to the cost driver—that is, if the cost driver increases by X%, this part of the cost also increases by X%. Knowing that a cost is linear allows a manager to separate the cost into fixed and variable components—a simplification that helps understand how decisions will affect costs. Incidentally, the predicted total cost for 680 orders is $25,000 + $89 × 680 = $85,520.

Account Analysis

Account Analysis. Selecting a volume-related cost driver and classifying each account as a variable cost or as a fixed cost.

In contrast to engineering analysis, users of **account analysis** look to the accounting system for information about cost behaviour. The simplest method of *account analysis* selects a volume-related cost driver and classifies each account as a variable cost or as a fixed cost. The cost analyst then looks at each cost account balance and estimates either the variable cost per unit of cost-driver activity or the periodic fixed cost.

To illustrate this approach let's use the same example of St. Michael's Hospital for 2006. The most plausible driver for these costs is the number of patient-days serviced per month. The table below shows costs recorded in a month with 3,700 patient-days:

COST	JANUARY 2006 AMOUNT
Supervisor's salary and benefits	$ 3,800
Hourly workers' wages and benefits	14,674
Equipment amortization and rentals	5,873
Equipment repairs	5,604
Cleaning supplies	7,472
Total facilities maintenance cost	$37,423

Next, the analyst determines how much of each cost may be fixed and how much may be variable. Assume that the analyst has made the following judgments:

COST	JANUARY 2006 AMOUNT	FIXED/ MONTH	VARIABLE
Supervisor's salary and benefits	$ 3,800	$3,800	
Hourly workers' wages and benefits	14,674		$14,674
Equipment amortization and rentals	5,873	5,873	
Equipment repairs	5,604		5,604
Cleaning supplies	7,472		7,472
Totals	$37,423	$9,673	$27,750

Measuring total facilities maintenance cost behaviour, then, requires only simple arithmetic. Add all the fixed costs to get the total fixed cost per month. Divide the total variable costs by the units of cost-driver activity to get the variable cost per unit of cost driver.

$$\text{fixed cost per month} = \$9,673$$
$$\text{variable cost per patient-day} = \$27,750 \div 3,700 \text{ patient-days}$$
$$= \$7.50 \text{ per patient-day}$$

The algebraic, mixed-cost function, measured by account analysis is

$$Y = \$9,673 \text{ per month} + \$7.50 \times (\text{patient-days})$$

Account analysis methods are less expensive to conduct than engineering analysis, but they require recording of relevant cost accounts and cost drivers. In addition, account analysis is subjective because the analyst decides whether each cost is variable or fixed based on judgment.

High-Low, Visual Fit, and Least Squares Regression Methods

When enough cost data are available, we can use historical data to measure the cost function mathematically. Three popular historical-cost methods are the high-low, visual fit, and least squares methods.

These three methods are more objective than the engineering analysis method because each is based on hard evidence as well as on judgment. They can also be more objective than account analysis because they use more than one period's cost and activity information. However, because these methods require more past cost data, account analysis—and especially engineering analysis—probably will remain primary methods of measuring cost behaviour. Products, services, technologies, and organizations are changing rapidly in response to increased global competition. *In some cases, by the time enough historical data are collected to support these analyses, the data are obsolete*—the organization has changed, the production process has changed, or the product has changed. The cost analyst must be careful using historical data from the past that may or may not resemble the future environment for which costs are being predicted. This can be particularly troublesome if data are collected on a monthly basis and they do not capture the operations they are being used to model. Another concern is that historical data may hide past inefficiencies that no longer exist. Furthermore, one must ensure that the high and low points are representative of the full set of points and do not significantly change the analysis if, for example, they are excluded and the second highest and lowest points are selected.

Data for Illustration

In discussing the high-low, visual fit, and least squares regression methods, we will use the St. Michael's Hospital facilities maintenance department costs. The table below shows monthly data collected on the facilities maintenance department costs and on the number of patient-days serviced in the year 2006:

MONTH	FACILITIES MAINTENANCE DEPARTMENT COST (Y)	NUMBER OF PATIENT-DAYS (X)
January	$37,000	3,700
February	23,000	1,600
March	37,000	4,100
April	47,000	4,900
May	33,000	3,300
June	39,000	4,400
July	32,000	3,500
August	33,000	4,000
September	17,000	1,200
October	18,000	1,300
November	22,000	1,800
December	20,000	1,600

High-Low Method

When sufficient cost data are available, the cost analyst may use historical data to measure the cost function mathematically. A simple method to measure a linear cost function from past cost data is the **high-low method**. Using simple observation and arithmetic, one can determine the high and low as follows:

High-Low Method. A simple method for measuring a linear cost function from past cost data, focusing on the highest-activity and lowest-activity points and fitting a line through these two points.

MONTH	FACILITIES MAINTENANCE DEPARTMENT COST (Y)	NUMBER OF PATIENT-DAYS (X)
High: April	$47,000	4,900
Low: September	17,000	1,200
Difference	$30,000	3,700

Variable cost per patient-day,

$$V = \frac{\text{change in costs}}{\text{change in activity}} = \frac{\$47,000 - \$17,000}{4,900 - 1,200 \text{ patient-days}}$$

$$V = \frac{\$30,000}{3,700} = \underline{\$8.108} \text{ per patient-day}$$

Fixed cost per month, F = total mixed cost less total variable cost

$$
\begin{aligned}
\text{at X (high):} \quad F &= \$47,000 - \$8.108(4,900) \\
&= \$47,000 - \$39,730 \\
&= \underline{\$7,270} \text{ per month}
\end{aligned}
$$

$$
\begin{aligned}
\text{at X (low):} \quad F &= \$17,000 - \$8.108(1,200) \\
&= \$17,000 - \$9,730 \\
&= \underline{\$7,270} \text{ per month}
\end{aligned}
$$

Therefore, the facilities maintenance department algebraic, total mixed-cost function, measured by the high-low method, is

$$Y = \$7,270 \text{ per month} + \$8.108 \times \text{(patient-days)}$$

The high-low method is easy to use and illustrates mathematically how a change in a cost driver can change total cost. The cost function that resulted in this case is *plausible*. However, it depends entirely upon the selected high and low points. Without further information—for example, whether either of the points represents a typical month—this method may be *unreliable*. The high-low method is not often used in practice because of its unreliability and because it makes inefficient use of information, using only two (top and bottom) periods. However, it is a quick method for a rough approximation of what the cost function might be.

Graphically, the high-low method requires plotting the historical data on a graph as shown in Exhibit 3-4. This visual display helps the analyst see whether there are obvious errors in the data. Even though many points are plotted, the high-low method focuses on the highest-activity and lowest-activity points. Normally, the next step is for the analyst to fit a line through these two points. However, if one of these points is an "outlier" that seems in error or nonrepresen-

EXHIBIT 3-4

High-Low Method

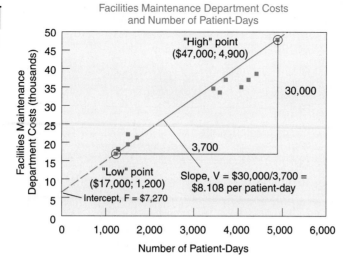

Facilities Maintenance Department Costs and Number of Patient-Days

tative of normal operations, the analyst will use the next-highest or next-lowest activity point. For example, you should not use a point from a time period with abnormally low activity caused by a labour strike or fire. Why? Because that point is not representative of a normal relationship between the cost and the cost driver.

After selecting the representative high and low points, the analyst can draw a line between them, extending the line to the vertical (Y) axis of the graph. Note that this extension in Exhibit 3-4 is a dashed line as a reminder that costs may not be linear outside the relevant range. Also, managers usually are concerned with how costs behave within the relevant range, not with how they behave either at zero activity or at impossibly high activity (given current capacity). Measurements of costs within the relevant range probably are not reliable measures or predictors of costs *outside* the relevant range.

The point at which the line intersects the Y-axis is the intercept, F, or estimate of fixed cost. The slope of the line measures the variable cost, V, per patient-day.

Visual Fit Method

Visual Fit Method. A method in which the cost analysis visually fits a straight line through a plot for all the available data, not just between the high and low points, making it more reliable than the high-low method.

The **visual fit method** is more reliable than the high-low method because it can use all the available data instead of just two points. In the visual fit method, the cost analyst visually fits a straight line through a plot of all the available data, not just between the high point and the low point. If the cost function for the data is linear, it is possible to visualize a straight line through the scattered points that comes reasonably close to most of them and thus captures the general tendency of the data. The analyst extends that line back until it intersects the vertical axis of the graph.

Exhibit 3-5 shows this method applied to the facilities maintenance department cost data for the past 12 months. By measuring where the line intersects the cost axis, the analyst can estimate the monthly fixed cost—in this case, about $10,000 per month. To find the variable cost per patient-day, select any activity level (say 1,000 patient-days) and find the total cost at the activity level ($17,000). Then divide the variable cost (which is the total cost less the fixed cost) by the units of activity:

$$\text{variable cost per patient-day} = (\$17,000 - \$10,000) \div 1,000$$
$$= \$7 \text{ per patient-day}$$

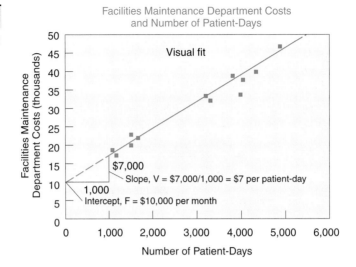

EXHIBIT 3-5

Visual Fit Method

Facilities Maintenance Department Costs
and Number of Patient-Days

The linear cost function measured by the visual fit method is:

$$Y = \$10,000 \text{ per month} + \$7 \times \text{(patient-days)}$$

Although the visual fit method can use all the data, the placement of the line and the measurement of the fixed and variable costs are subjective. The method is somewhat unreliable because it depends on the skill of an analyst who must "eyeball" a straight line by visually "averaging" the fit through the data. This subjectivity is the primary reason why the visual fit method is now rarely used in practice, even though using computers to plot data and draw lines has made the method easier to implement. This method is a good introduction to what least squares regression accomplishes with statistics.

Least Squares Regression Method

Least squares regression measures a cost function more objectively. Least squares regression analysis (or simply, **regression analysis**) uses statistics to fit a cost function to all the data. Regression analysis that uses one cost driver to measure a cost function is called simple regression. The use of multiple cost drivers for a single cost is called multiple regression. Only a basic discussion of simple regression analysis is presented in this section. Some statistical properties of regression and using computer regression software are discussed in the next section.

Regression analysis usually measures cost behaviour more reliably than other cost measurement methods. In addition, regression analysis yields important statistical information about the reliability of cost estimates, so analysts can assess confidence in the cost measures and select the best cost driver. One such measure of reliability, or goodness of fit, is the **coefficient of determination**, R^2 (or R-squared), which measures how much of the fluctuation of a cost is explained by changes in the cost driver.

Exhibit 3-6 shows the linear, mixed-cost function for the facilities maintenance costs as measured by simple regression analysis.

Least Squares Regression (Regression Analysis). Measuring a cost function objectively by using statistics to fit a cost function to all the data.

Coefficient of Determination. A measurement of how much of the fluctuation of a cost is explained by changes in the cost driver.

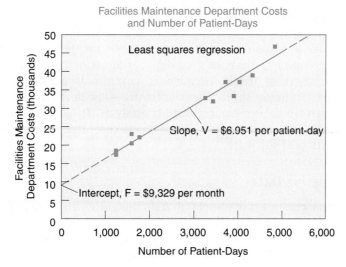

EXHIBIT 3-6

Least Squares
Regression Method

Facilities Maintenance Department Costs
and Number of Patient-Days

LEAST SQUARES REGRESSION ANALYSIS

Regression analysis of historical cost data can be accomplished with no more than a simple calculator. It would be unusual, however, to find cost analysts doing regression analysis by hand—computers are much faster and less prone to error. Therefore, we focus on using a computer to perform regression analysis and on interpretation of the results.

This presentation should not be considered a substitute for a good statistics class or for self-taught statistics. More properly, this analysis should be seen as a motivator for studying statistics so that analysts can provide and managers can interpret top-quality variable and fixed cost estimates.

Assume that there are two potential cost drivers for the costs of the facilities maintenance department at St. Michael's Hospital: (1) number of patient-days and (2) total value of hospital room charges. Regression analysis helps to determine which activity is the better cost driver. The following table shows the past 12 months' cost and cost-driver data for the facilities maintenance department.

MONTH	FACILITIES MAINTENANCE COST (Y)	NUMBER OF PATIENT-DAYS (X_1)	VALUE OF ROOM CHARGES (X_2)
January	$37,000	3,700	$2,983,000
February	23,000	1,600	3,535,000
March	37,000	4,100	3,766,000
April	47,000	4,900	3,646,000
May	33,000	3,300	3,767,000
June	39,000	4,400	3,780,000
July	32,000	3,500	3,823,000
August	33,000	4,000	3,152,000
September	17,000	1,200	2,625,000
October	18,000	1,300	2,315,000
November	22,000	1,800	2,347,000
December	20,000	1,600	2,917,000

Most spreadsheet software available for personal computers offers basic regression analysis in the "data" analysis or "tools" commands. We illustrate elements of these spreadsheet commands because many readers may be familiar with spreadsheet software—*not* because spreadsheets are the best software to use for regression analysis. In general, sophisticated regression analysis, beyond what spreadsheets can offer, is easier with more specialized statistical software.

Entering Data

First, create a spreadsheet with the historical cost data in rows and columns. Each row should be data from one time period. Each column should be a cost category or a cost driver. For ease of analysis, all the potential cost drivers should be in adjacent columns. Each row and column should be complete (no missing data) and without errors.

Plotting Data

There are two main reasons why the first step in regression analysis should be to plot the cost against each of the potential cost drivers: (1) Plots may show obvious nonlinear trends in the data; if so, linear regression analysis may not be appropriate for the entire range of the data. (2) Plots help identify "outliers"—costs that are in error or are otherwise obviously inappropriate. There is little agreement about what to do with any outliers that are not the result of data entry errors or nonrepresentative cost and activity levels (e.g., periods of labour strikes, natural catastrophes). Some analysts might recommend removing outliers from the data set. Leaving these outliers in the data makes regression analysis statistically less appealing, since, by definition, outliers are far removed from the rest of the data set and will not fit the line well. The most conservative action is to leave all data in the data set unless uncorrectable errors are detected or unless the data are known to be nonrepresentative of the process.

Plotting with spreadsheets uses "graph" commands on the columns of cost and cost-driver data. These graph commands typically offer many optional graph types (such as bar charts and pie charts). The most useful plot for regression analysis is usually called the XY graph. This graph is the type shown earlier in this chapter—the X-axis is the cost driver, and the Y-axis is the cost.

Regression Output

The regression output is generated by commands that are unique to each software package but they identify the cost to be explained ("dependent variable") and the cost driver(s) ("independent variable[s]").

Producing regression output with spreadsheets is simple: select the "regression" command, specify (or "highlight") the X-dimension (the cost driver) and specify the Y-dimension or "series" (the cost). Next specify a blank area on the spreadsheet where the output will be displayed, and select "ok." Following is a regression analysis of the facilities maintenance department costs using one of the two possible cost drivers, number of patient-days, X_1, or value of hospital room charges, X_2.

**FACILITIES MAINTENANCE DEPARTMENT COSTS
EXPLAINED BY NUMBER OF PATIENT-DAYS**

REGRESSION OUTPUT:

Constant	$9,328.849028
Standard Error of Y Estimate	$1,542.85447
R-Squared	0.9546625
No. of Observations	12
Degrees of Freedom	11
X Coefficient(s)	$6.9506726
Standard Error of Coefficient	0.478995

Interpreting Regression Output

The fixed cost measure (labelled "Constant" or "Intercept") is $9,328.849028 per month. The variable cost measure (labelled "X Coefficient[s]" or something similar) is $6.9506726 per patient-day. The linear cost function (after rounding) is:

$$Y = \$9,329 \text{ per month} + \$6.951 \times (\text{patient-days})$$

Typically, the computer output gives a number of statistical measures that indicate how well each cost driver explains the cost and how reliable the cost predictions are likely to be. One of the most important statistics, the coefficient of determination or R^2 (or *R-squared*), is very important to assessing the goodness of fit of the cost function to the actual cost data.

In general, the better a cost driver is at explaining a cost, the closer the data points will lie on the line, and the higher the R^2. R^2 varies between 0 and 1. An R^2 of 0 would mean that the cost driver does not explain the cost at all, while an R^2 of 1 means that the cost driver explains the cost perfectly. The R^2 is 0.955, which is quite high and, as a function of patient-days, explains the facilities maintenance department costs extremely well. It can be interpreted as meaning that the number of patient-days explains 95.5 percent of the facilities maintenance department costs in the past 12 months.

In contrast, performing a regression analysis on the relationship between the facilities maintenance department costs and value of hospital room charges produces the following results:

**FACILITIES MAINTENANCE DEPARTMENT COSTS
EXPLAINED BY VALUE OF HOSPITAL ROOM CHARGES**

REGRESSION OUTPUT:

Constant	$ –8,627.01
Standard Error of Y Estimate	$ 12,063.458
R-Squared	0.511284
No. of Observations	12
Degrees of Freedom	11
X Coefficient(s)	0.011939
Standard Error of Coefficient	0.003691

The R^2 value, 0.511, indicates that the facilities maintenance department cost as a function of hospital room charges is not as good as the cost function using number of patient-days.

To fully use the information generated by regression analysis, an analyst must understand the meaning of the statistics and must be able to determine whether the statistical assumptions of regression are satisfied by the cost data. With this understanding, analysts can provide organizations with top-quality estimates of cost behaviour.

Compare the cost measures produced by each of the five approaches:

METHOD	FIXED COST PER MONTH	VARIABLE COST PER PATIENT-DAY
Engineering Analysis	$10,000	$5.000
Account Analysis	9,673	7.500
High-Low	7,270	8.108
Visual Fit	10,000	7.000
Regression	9,329	6.951

To see the differences in results between methods, we will use account analysis and regression analysis measures to predict the total facilities maintenance department costs at 1,000 and 5,000 patient-days, the approximate limits of the relevant range.

	ACCOUNT ANALYSIS	REGRESSION ANALYSIS	DIFFERENCE
Lower level of activity 1,000 Patient-days:			
Fixed Cost	$ 9,673	$ 9,329	$ 344
Variable Costs			
$7.500 (1,000)	7,500		
$6.951 (1,000)		6,951	549
Predicted Total Cost	$17,173	$16,280	$ 893
Higher level of activity 5,000 Patient-days:			
Fixed Cost	$ 9,673	$ 9,329	$ 344
Variable Costs			
$7.500 (5,000)	37,500		
$6.951 (5,000)		34,755	2,745
Predicted Total Cost	$47,173	$44,084	$3,089

At lower levels of patient-day activity, both methods yield similar cost predictions. At higher levels of patient-day activity, however, the account analysis cost function predicts much higher facilities maintenance department costs. The difference between the predicted total costs is primarily due to the higher variable cost per patient-day (approximately $0.55 more) measured by account analysis, which increases the difference in predicted total variable costs proportionately as the number of planned patient-days increases. Because of their grounding in statistical analysis, the regression cost measures are probably more reliable than are the other methods. Managers would feel more confidence in cost predictions from the regression cost function.

Manual Regression Calculation

MONTH	FACILITIES MAINTENANCE COST (Y)	NUMBER OF PATIENT-DAYS (X_1)	(X_1^2)	(X_1Y)	VALUE OF ROOM CHARGES (X_2)
January	$37,000	3,700	13,690,000	136,900,000	$2,983,000
February	23,000	1,600	2,560,000	36,800,000	3,535,000
March	37,000	4,100	16,810,000	151,700,000	3,766,000
April	47,000	4,900	24,010,000	230,300,000	3,646,000
May	33,000	3,300	10,890,000	108,900,000	3,767,000
June	39,000	4,400	19,360,000	171,600,000	3,780,000
July	32,000	3,500	12,250,000	112,000,000	3,823,000
August	33,000	4,000	16,000,000	132,000,000	3,152,000
September	17,000	1,200	1,440,000	20,400,000	2,625,000
October	18,000	1,300	1,690,000	23,400,000	2,315,000
November	22,000	1,800	3,240,000	39,600,000	2,347,000
December	20,000	1,600	2,560,000	32,000,000	2,917,000
	$\Sigma y = 358,000$	$\Sigma X_1 = 35,400$	$\Sigma x^2 = 124,500,000$	$\Sigma x_1 y = 1,195,600,000$	

The equations to compute the a (fixed) and b (variable) values are

$$b = \frac{n(\Sigma xy) - (\Sigma x)(\Sigma y)}{n(\Sigma x^2) - (\Sigma x)^2}$$

$$a = \frac{(\Sigma y)(\Sigma x^2) - (\Sigma x)(\Sigma xy)}{n(\Sigma x^2) - (\Sigma x)^2}$$

The b value is calculated first since it is used to compute a. Substituting the appropriate amounts into the above formulas we get

$b = \$6.951$
$a = \$9,329$

Thus the cost formula under the least squares regression is

G = $9,329 per month + $6.951 × patient-days

HIGHLIGHTS TO REMEMBER

1. **Explain step- and mixed-cost behaviour.** Cost behaviour refers to how costs change as levels of an organization's activities change. Costs can behave as fixed, variable, step, or mixed. Step and mixed costs both combine aspects of variable- and fixed-cost behaviour. Step costs form graphs that look like steps. Costs will remain fixed within a given range of activity or cost-driver level, but then will rise or fall abruptly when the cost-driver level is outside this range. Mixed costs involve a fixed element and a variable element of cost behaviour. Unlike step costs, mixed costs have a single fixed cost at all levels of activity and, in addition, have a variable cost element that increases proportionately with activity.

2. **Explain management influences on cost behaviour.** Managers can affect the costs and cost behaviour patterns of their companies through the decisions they make. Decisions on product and service features, capacity, technology, and cost-control incentives, for example, can affect cost behaviour.

3. **Measure and mathematically express cost functions and use them to predict costs.** The first step in estimating or predicting costs is measuring cost behaviour. This is done by finding a cost function. This is an algebraic equation that describes the relationship between a cost and its cost driver(s). To be useful for decision-making purposes, cost functions should be plausible and reliable.

4. **Describe the importance of activity analysis for measuring cost functions.** Activity analysis is the process of identifying the best cost drivers to use for cost estimation and prediction and determining how they affect the costs of making a product or service. This is an essential step in understanding and predicting costs.

5. **Measure cost behaviour using the engineering analysis, account analysis, high-low, visual fit, and least squares regression methods.** Once analysts have identified cost drivers, they can use one of several methods to determine the cost function. Engineering analysis focuses on what costs should be by systematically reviewing the materials, supplies, labour, support services, and facilities needed for a given level of production. Account analysis involves examining all accounts in terms of an appropriate cost driver and classifying each account as either fixed or variable with respect to the driver. The cost function consists of the variable cost per cost-driver unit multiplied by the amount of the cost driver plus the total fixed cost. The high-low, visual fit, and least squares methods use historical costs to determine cost functions. Of these three methods, high-low is the easiest and least squares is the most reliable.

DEMONSTRATION PROBLEMS FOR YOUR REVIEW

Problem One

The Reetz Company has its own photocopying department. Reetz's photocopying costs include costs of copy machines, operators, paper, toner, utilities, and so on. We have the following cost and activity data:

MONTH	TOTAL PHOTOCOPYING COST	NUMBER OF COPIES
1	$25,000	320,000
2	29,000	390,000
3	24,000	300,000
4	23,000	310,000
5	28,000	400,000

1. Use the high-low method to measure the cost behaviour of the photocopy department in formula form.
2. What are the advantages and disadvantages of using the high-low method for measuring cost behaviour?

Solution

1. The lowest and highest activity levels are in months 3 (300,000 copies) and 5 (400,000 copies).

$$\text{variable cost per copy} = \frac{\text{change in cost}}{\text{change in activity}} = \frac{\$28,000 - \$24,000}{400,000 - 300,000}$$

$$= \frac{\$4,000}{\$100,000} = \underline{\$0.04} \text{ per copy}$$

fixed cost per month = total cost less variable cost
at 400,000 copies: $28,000 − $0.04(400,000) = $12,000 per month

at 300,000 copies: $24,000 − $0.04(300,000) = $12,000 per month

Therefore, the photocopy cost function is:

Y (total cost) = $12,000 per month + $0.04 × (number of copies)

2. The benefits of using the high-low method are as follows:

- The method is easy to use.
- Not many data are needed.

The disadvantages of using the high-low method are below:

- The choice of the high and low points is subjective.
- The method does not use all available data.
- The method may not be reliable.

Problem Two

The Reliable Insurance Company processes a variety of insurance claims for losses, accidents, thefts, and so on. Account analysis has estimated the variable cost of processing each claim at 0.5 percent (.005) of the dollar value of the claim. This estimate seemed reasonable since higher claims often involve more analysis before settlement. To better control processing costs, however, Reliable Insurance conducted an activity analysis of claims processing. The analysis suggested that more appropriate cost drivers and behaviour for automobile accident claims are

- 0.2 percent of Reliable Insurance policyholders' property claims
- 0.6 percent of other parties' property claims
- 0.8 percent of total personal injury claims

Below are data from two recent automobile accident claims.

	AUTOMOBILE CLAIM #607788	AUTOMOBILE CLAIM #607991
Policyholder Claim	$ 4,500	$23,600
Other Party Claim	0	3,400
Personal Injury Claim	12,400	0
Total Claim Amount	$16,900	$27,000

1. Estimate the cost of processing each claim using data from the account analysis and the activity analysis.
2. How would you recommend that Reliable Insurance estimate the cost of processing claims?

Solution

1.

	AUTOMOBILE CLAIM #607788	AUTOMOBILE CLAIM #607991
Using account analysis:		
Total claim amount	$ 16,900.00	$ 27,000.00
Estimated processing cost at 0.5 percent	$ 84.50	$135.00
Using activity analysis:		
Policyholder claim	$ 4,500.00	$ 23,600.00
Estimated processing cost at 0.2 percent	9.00	47.20
Other party claim	0	3,400.00
Estimated processing cost at 0.6 percent	0	20.40
Personal injury claim	$ 12,400.00	0
Estimated processing cost at 0.8 percent	99.20	0
Total estimated processing cost	$ 108.20	$ 67.60

2. The activity analysis estimates of processing costs are considerably different from those using cost account analysis. If the activity analyses are reliable, then automobile claims that include personal injury losses are considerably more costly to process than property damage claims. If these estimates are relatively inexpensive to keep current and to use, then it seems reasonable to adopt the activity analysis approach. Reliable Insurance will have more accurate cost estimates and will be better able to plan its claims processing activities. However, Reliable Insurance processes many different types of claims. Extending activity analysis to all types of claims would result in a complicated system for predicting costs—much more complex (and costly) than simply using the total dollar value of claims. Whether to adopt the activity approach overall depends on cost-benefit considerations that may be estimated by first adopting activity analysis for one type of claim and assessing the usefulness and cost of the more accurate information.

Problem Three

Contell, Inc. makes computer peripherals (disk drives, tape drives, and printers). Until recently, production scheduling and control (PSC) costs were predicted to vary in proportion to labour costs according to the following cost function:

PSC costs, Y = 2 × (labour cost) (or 200 percent of labour)

Because PSC costs have been growing at the same time that labour costs have been shrinking, Contell is concerned that its cost estimates are neither plausible nor reliable. Contell's controller has just completed activity analysis to determine the most appropriate drivers of PSC costs. She obtained two cost functions using different cost drivers:

$$Y = 2 \times (\text{labour cost})$$
$$R^2 = 0.233$$

and

$$Y = \$10,000/\text{month} + \$11 \times (\text{number of components used})$$
$$R^2 = 0.782$$

1. What would be good tests for determining which cost function better predicts PSC costs?
2. During a subsequent month, labour costs were $12,000 and 2,000 product components were used. Actual PSC costs were $31,460. Using each of the above cost functions, prepare reports that show predicted and actual PSC costs and the difference or variance between the two.
3. What is the meaning and importance of each cost variance?

Solution

1. A statistical test of which function better explains past PSC costs compares the R^2 of each function. The second function, using the number of components used, has a considerably higher R^2, so it better explains the past PSC costs. If the environment is essentially unchanged in the future, the second function will probably predict future PSC costs better than the first, too.

   A useful predictive test would be to compare the cost predictions of each cost function with actual costs for several months that were not used to measure the cost functions. The function that more closely predicted actual costs is probably the more reliable function.

2. Note that more actual cost data would be desirable for a better test, but the procedure would be the same.

   PSC cost predicted on the basis of

	predicted cost	actual cost	variance
labour cost	2($12,000) = $24,000	$31,460	$7,460 underestimate
components	$10,000 + $11(2,000) = $32,000	$31,460	$540 overestimate

3. The cost function that relies on labour cost underestimated PSC cost by $7,460. The cost function that uses number of components closely predicted actual PSC costs (off by $540). Planning and control decisions would have been based on more accurate information using this prediction than using the labour cost-based prediction. An issue is whether the benefits of collecting data on the number of components used exceed the added cost of so doing.

KEY TERMS

account analysis *p. 102*
activity analysis *p. 98*
capacity costs *p. 94*
coefficient of determination *p. 106*
committed fixed costs *p. 94*
cost function *p. 96*
discretionary fixed costs *p. 94*
engineering analysis *p. 99*
high-low method *p. 104*

least squares regression *p. 106*
linear-cost behaviour *p. 89*
measuring cost behaviour
(cost measurement) *p. 96*
mixed costs *p. 91*
regression analysis *p. 106*
step costs *p. 90*
visual fit method *p. 105*

ASSIGNMENT MATERIAL

QUESTIONS

Q3-1 What is a cost driver? Give three examples of costs and their possible cost drivers.

Q3-2 What is the "relevant range"? Why is it important?

Q3-3 Explain linear-cost behaviour.

Q3-4 "Variable costs should fluctuate directly in proportion to sales." Do you agree? Explain.

Q3-5 Why are fixed costs also called capacity costs?

Q3-6 "Step costs can be fixed or variable depending on your perspective." Explain.

Q3-7 Explain how mixed costs are related to both fixed and variable costs.

Q3-8 What are the benefits of using "cost functions" to describe cost behaviour?

Q3-9 How do management's product and service choices affect cost behaviour?

Q3-10 How do committed fixed costs differ from discretionary fixed costs?

Q3-11 Why are committed fixed costs the most difficult to change of the fixed costs?

Q3-12 What are the primary determinants of the level of committed costs? Discretionary costs?

Q3-13 "Planning is far more important than day-to-day control of discretionary costs." Do you agree? Explain.

Q3-14 How can a company's choice of technology affect its costs?

Q3-15 Explain the use of incentives to control cost.

Q3-16 Describe the methods for measuring cost functions using past cost data.

Q3-17 Explain "plausibility" and "reliability" of cost functions. Which is preferred? Explain.

Q3-18 What is activity analysis?

Q3-19 What is engineering analysis? Account analysis?

Q3-20 How could account analysis be combined with engineering analysis?

Q3-21 Explain the strengths and weaknesses of the high-low method and the visual fit method.

Q3-22 Why is regression analysis usually preferred to the high-low method?

Q3-23 "You never know how good your fixed and variable cost measures are if you use account analysis or if you visually fit a line on a data plot. That's why I like least squares regression analysis." Explain.

Q3-24 At a conference, a consultant stated, "Before you can control, you must measure." An executive complained, "Why bother to measure when work rules and guaranteed employment provisions in labour contracts prevent discharging workers, using part-time employees, and using overtime?" Evaluate these comments. Summarize your personal attitudes toward the usefulness of engineering analysis.

PROBLEMS

P3-1 **VARIOUS COST-BEHAVIOUR PATTERNS.** In practice, there is often a tendency to simplify approximations of cost behaviour patterns, even though the "true" underlying behaviour is not simple. Choose from the accompanying graphs A through H (below) the one that matches the numbered items. Indicate by letter which graph best fits each of the situations described. Next to each number-letter pair, identify a likely cost driver for that cost.

The vertical axes of the graphs represent total dollars of costs incurred, and the horizontal axes represent levels of cost driver activity *during a particular time period*. The graphs may be used more than once.

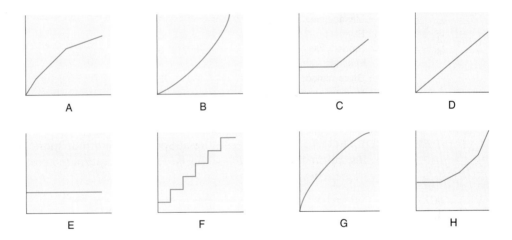

1. Availability of quantity discounts, where the cost per unit falls as each price break is reached.
2. Price of an increasingly scarce raw material as the quantity used increases.
3. Guaranteed annual wage plan, whereby workers get paid for 40 hours of work per week even at zero or low levels of production that require working only a few hours weekly.
4. Water bill, which entails a flat fee for the first 10,000 litres used and then an increasing unit cost for every additional 10,000 litres used.
5. Cost of machining labour that tends to decrease as workers gain experience.
6. Amortization of office equipment.
7. Cost of sheet steel for a manufacturer of farm implements.
8. Salaries of supervisors, where one supervisor is added for every 12 phone solicitors.
9. Natural gas bill consisting of a fixed component, plus a constant variable cost per thousand cubic metres after a specified number of cubic metres are used.

P3-2 **PREDICTING COSTS.** Given the following cost behaviours and expected levels of cost driver activity, predict total costs:

1. Fuel costs of driving vehicles, $0.20 per kilometre driven; at 15,000 kilometres per month.
2. Equipment rental cost, $6,000 per piece of equipment per month; at seven pieces for three months.
3. Ambulance personnel cost for a soccer tournament, $1,100 for each 250 tournament participants; the tournament is expecting 2,400 participants.
4. Purchasing department cost, $7,500 per month plus $4 per material order processed; at 4,000 orders in one month.

P3-3 **IDENTIFYING DISCRETIONARY AND COMMITTED FIXED COSTS.** Identify and compute total monthly discretionary and total committed fixed costs from the following list prepared by the accounting supervisor for Nicholas Inc.:

Advertising	$20,000
Amortization	47,000
Company health insurance	15,000
Management salaries	85,000
Payment on long-term debt	50,000
Property tax	32,000
Grounds maintenance	9,000
Office remodelling	21,000
Research and development	36,000

P3-4 **COST EFFECTS OF TECHNOLOGY.** Recreational Sports, an outdoor sports retailer, is considering automating its order-taking process. The estimated costs of two alternative approaches are below:

	ALTERNATIVE 1	ALTERNATIVE 2
Annual fixed cost	$200,000	$400,000
Variable cost per order	$8.00	$4.00
Expected number of orders	70,000	70,000

At the expected level of orders, which automated approach is preferred? What is the "break-even" level of orders? What is the meaning of this level of orders?

P3-5 **MIXED-COST, CHOOSING COST DRIVERS, HIGH-LOW AND VISUAL FIT METHODS.** Wheatown Implement Company produces farm implements for various large vehicles used for farming. Wheatown is in the process of measuring its manufacturing costs and is particularly interested in the costs of the manufacturing maintenance activity since maintenance is a significant mixed cost. Activity analysis indicates that maintenance activity consists primarily of maintenance labour setting up machines using certain supplies. A setup consists of preparing the necessary machines for a particular production run of a product. During setup, machines must still be running, which consumes energy. Thus, the costs associated with maintenance include labour, supplies, and energy. Unfortunately, Wheatown's cost accounting system does not trace these costs to maintenance activity separately. Wheatown employs two full-time maintenance mechanics. The annual salary of a maintenance mechanic is $25,000 and is considered a fixed cost. Two plausible cost drivers have been suggested: units produced and number of setups.

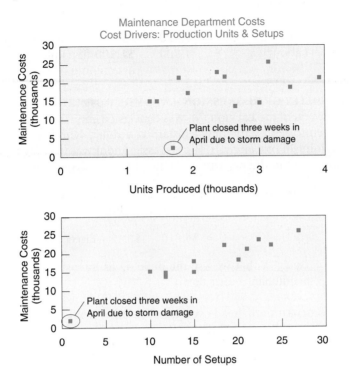

Data had been collected for 12 months and a plot made for the cost driver—units of production. The maintenance cost figures collected include estimates for labour, supplies, and energy. Sue Hatcher, controller at Wheatown, recently attended an activity-based costing seminar where she learned that some types of activities are performed each time a batch of goods is produced rather than each time a unit is produced. Based on this concept, she has gathered data on the number of setups performed over the past 12 months. The plot of monthly maintenance costs versus the two potential cost drivers is shown above.

1. Find the monthly fixed maintenance cost and the variable maintenance cost per driver unit using the visual fit method based on each potential cost driver. Explain how you treated the April data.
2. Find the monthly fixed maintenance cost and the variable maintenance cost per driver unit using the high-low method based on each potential cost driver.
3. Which cost driver best meets the criteria for choosing cost functions? Explain.

P3-6 **ACCOUNT ANALYSIS.** From the following costs of a recent month, compute the total cost function and total cost for the month. Genial Computers, Inc. is a company started by two university students to market and assemble personal computers for faculty and students. The company operates out of the garage of one of the student's homes.

Phone	$ 50	fixed
Utilities	260	25 percent attributable to the garage, 75 percent to the house
Advertising	75	fixed
Insurance	80	fixed
Materials	7,500	variable, for five computers
Labour	1,800	$1,300 fixed plus $500 for hourly help for assembling five computers

P3-7 ECONOMIC PLAUSIBILITY OF REGRESSION ANALYSIS RESULTS.   The head of the Warehousing Division of the Lackton Co. was concerned about some cost-behaviour information given to her by the new assistant controller, who was hired because of his recent training in cost analysis. His first assignment was to apply regression analysis to various costs in the department. One of the results was presented as follows:

A regression on monthly data was run to explain building maintenance cost as a function of direct labour hours as the cost driver. The results are

$$Y = \$6,810 - \$0.47 \times \text{direct labour hours}$$

I suggest that we use the building as intensively as possible to keep the maintenance costs down.

The department head was puzzled. How could increased use cause decreased maintenance cost? Explain this counter-intuitive result to the department head. What step(s) did the assistant controller probably omit in applying and interpreting the regression analysis?

P3-8 LINEAR COST FUNCTIONS.   Let Y = total costs, X_1 = production volume, and X_2 = number of setups. Which of the following are linear cost functions? Which are mixed cost functions?

a. $Y = \$1,000$
b. $Y = \$8X_1$
c. $Y = \$5,000 + \$4X_1$
d. $Y = \$3,000 + \$6X_1 + \$30X_2$
e. $Y = \$9,000 + \$3X_1 \times \$2X_2$
f. $Y = \$8,000 + \$1.50X_1^2$

P3-9 HIGH-LOW METHOD.   Southampton Foundry produced 45,000 tonnes in March at a cost of £1,100,000. In April, 35,000 tonnes were produced at a cost of £900,000. Using only these two data points, determine the cost function for Southampton.

P3-10 TYPES OF COST BEHAVIOUR.   Identify the following planned costs as (a) purely variable costs, (b) discretionary fixed costs, (c) committed fixed costs, (d) mixed costs, or (e) step costs. For purely variable costs and mixed costs, indicate the most likely cost driver.

1. Total repairs and maintenance of a school building.
2. Sales commission based on revenue dollars. Payments to be made to advertising salespersons employed by a radio station.
3. Jet fuel costs of Air Canada.
4. Total costs of renting trucks by the city of Vancouver. Charge is a lump sum of $300 per month plus $0.20 per kilometre.

5. Straight-line amortization on desks in the office of an attorney.
6. Advertising costs, a lump sum planned by ABC, Inc.
7. Rental payment by the federal government on a five-year lease for office space in a private office building.
8. Advertising allowance granted to wholesalers by Pepsi Bottling on a per-case basis.
9. Compensation of lawyers employed internally by Microsoft.
10. Crew supervisor in a Lands' End, Inc. mail-order house. A new supervisor is added for every 12 workers employed.
11. Public relations employee compensation to be paid by Imperial Oil.

P3-11 **ACTIVITY ANALYSIS.** Evergreen Signs makes customized signs for businesses and residences. These signs are made of wood, which the owner glues and carves by hand or with power tools. After carving the signs, he paints them or applies a natural finish. He has a good sense of his labour and materials cost behaviour, but he is concerned that he does not have good measures of other support costs. Currently, he predicts support costs to be 60 percent of the cost of materials. Close investigation of the business reveals that $40 times the number of power tool operations is a more plausible and reliable support cost relationship.

Consider estimated support costs of the following two signs that Evergreen is making:

	SIGN A	SIGN B
Material cost	$300	$150
Number of power tool operations	3	6
Support cost	?	?

1. Prepare a report showing the support costs of both signs using each cost driver and showing the differences between the two.
2. What advice would you give Evergreen Signs about predicting support costs?

P3-12 **ACTIVITY ANALYSIS.** NewWave Technology, a manufacturer of printed circuit boards, has always costed its circuit boards with a 100 percent "markup" over its material costs to cover its manufacturing support costs (which include labour). An activity analysis suggests that support costs are driven primarily by the number of manual operations performed on each board, estimated at $4 per manual operation. Compute the estimated support costs of the two typical circuit boards below using the traditional markup and the activity analysis results:

	BOARD Z15	BOARD Q52
Material cost	$30	$55
Manual operations	16	7

Why are the cost estimates different?

P3-13 **DIVISION OF MIXED COSTS INTO VARIABLE AND FIXED COMPONENTS.** The president and the controller of Monterrey Transformer Company (Mexico) have agreed that refinement of the company's cost measurements will aid planning and control decisions. They have asked you to measure the function for mixed-cost behaviour of repairs and maintenance from the following sparse data. Currency is the Mexican peso (P).

MONTHLY ACTIVITY IN MACHINE HOURS	MONTHLY REPAIR AND MAINTENANCE COST
8,000	P190,000,000
12,000	P260,000,000

P3-14 CONTROLLING RISK, CAPACITY DECISIONS, TECHNOLOGY DECISIONS.   Ford Motor Co. had been outsourcing production to Mazda and using overtime for as much as 20 percent of production—Ford's plants and assembly lines were running at 100 percent of capacity and demand was sufficient for an additional 20 percent. Ford had considered building new highly automated assembly lines and plants to earn more profits since overtime premiums and outsourcing were costly. However, the investment in high technology and capacity expansion was rejected.

Assume that all material and labour costs are variable with respect to the level of production and that all overhead costs are fixed. Consider one of the plants that makes Ford Probes. The cost to convert the plant to use fully automated assembly lines is $20 million. The resulting labour costs would be significantly reduced. The costs, in millions of dollars, of the build option and the outsource/overtime option are given in the table below.

	BUILD OPTION		
Percent of capacity	60%	100%	120%
Material costs	$18	$30	$36
Labour costs	6	10	12
Overhead costs	40	40	40
Total costs	$64	$80	$88

	OUTSOURCE/OVERTIME OPTION		
Percent of capacity	60%	100%	120%
Material costs	$18	$30	$ 36
Labour costs	18	30	44
Overhead costs	20	20	20
Total costs	$56	$80	$100

1. Prepare a line-graph showing total costs for the two options: build new assembly lines, and continue to use overtime and outsource production of Probes. Give an explanation of the cost behaviour of the two options.
2. Which option enables Ford management to control risk better? Explain. Assess the cost/benefit associated with each option.
3. A solid understanding of cost behaviour is an important prerequisite to effective managerial control of costs. Suppose you are an executive at Ford and currently the production (and sales) level is approaching the 100 percent level of capacity and the economy is expected to remain strong for at least one year. While sales and profits are good now, you are aware of the cyclical nature of the automobile business. Would you recommend committing Ford to building automated assembly lines in

order to service potential near-term increases in demand or would you recommend against building, looking to the likely future downturn in business? Discuss your reasoning.

P3-15 **ACTIVITY ANALYSIS.** Violet Blossom Technology develops and markets computer software for the agriculture industry. Since support costs comprise a large portion of the cost of software development, the director of cost operations of Violet Blossom, Shirley Donko, is especially concerned with understanding the effects of support cost behaviour. Donko has completed a preliminary activity analysis of one of its primary software products: Ferti Mix (software to manage fertilizer mixing). This product is a software "template" that is customized for specific customers, who are charged for the basic product plus customizing costs. The activity analysis is based on the number of customized lines of Ferti Mix code. Currently, support cost estimates are based on a fixed rate of 50 percent of the basic cost. Data are shown below for two recent customers:

	CUSTOMER	
	WEST ACRES PLANT	BEAUTIFUL BLOOM
Basic cost of Ferti Mix	$12,000	$12,000
Lines of customized code	490	180
Estimated cost per line of customized code	$ 23	$ 23

1. Compute the support cost of customizing Ferti Mix for each customer using each cost estimating approach.
2. If the activity analysis is reliable, what are the pros and cons of adopting it for all of Violet Blossom's software products?

P3-16 **SEPARATION OF DRUG-TESTING LABORATORY MIXED COSTS INTO VARIABLE AND FIXED COMPONENTS.** A staff meeting has been called at Sports Lab, a drug-testing facility retained by several professional and university sport leagues and associations. The chief of testing, Dr. Levendis, has demanded an across-the-board increase in prices for a particular test due to the increased testing and precision that is now required.

The administrator of the laboratory has asked you to measure the mixed-cost behaviour of this particular testing department and to prepare a short report that she can present to Dr. Levendis. Consider the limited data below:

	AVERAGE TEST PROCEDURES PER MONTH	AVERAGE MONTHLY COST OF TEST PROCEDURES
Monthly averages, 2004	500	$ 60,000
Monthly averages, 2005	600	70,000
Monthly averages, 2006	700	144,000

P3-17 **HIGH-LOW, REGRESSION ANALYSIS.** On November 15, 2006, Sandra Pery, a newly hired cost analyst at Demgren Company, was asked to predict overhead costs for the company's operations in 2007, when 500 units are expected to be produced. She collected the following quarterly data:

QUARTER	PRODUCTION IN UNITS	OVERHEAD COSTS
1/2003	76	$ 721
2/2003	79	715
3/2003	72	655
4/2003	136	1,131
1/2004	125	1,001
2/2004	128	1,111
3/2004	125	1,119
4/2004	133	1,042
1/2005	124	997
2/2005	129	1,066
3/2005	115	996
4/2005	84	957
1/2006	84	835
2/2006	122	1,050
3/2006	90	991

1. Using the high-low method to estimate costs, prepare a prediction of overhead costs for 2007.
2. Sandra ran a regression analysis using the data she collected. The result was:

$$Y = \$337 + \$5.75X$$

Using this cost function, predict costs for 2007.
3. Which prediction do you prefer? Why?

P3-18 **INTERPRETATION OF REGRESSION ANALYSES.** Elliott Bay Tarp and Tent (EBTT) Company has difficulty controlling its use of supplies. The company has traditionally regarded supplies as a purely variable cost. But nearly every time production was above average, EBTT spent less than predicted for supplies; when production was below average, EBTT spent more than predicted. This pattern suggested to Kosta Kane, the new controller, that part of the supplies cost was probably not related to production volume, or was fixed.

He decided to use regression analysis to explore this issue. After consulting with production personnel, he considered two cost drivers for supplies cost: (1) number of tents and tarps produced, and (2) square metres of material used. He obtained the following results based on monthly data:

	COST DRIVER	
	NUMBER OF TENTS AND TARPS	SQUARE METRES OF MATERIAL USED
Constant	2,200	1,900
Variable Coefficient	0.033	0.072
R^2	0.220	0.686

1. Which is the preferred cost function? Explain.
2. What percentage of supplies cost depends on square metres of materials? Do fluctuations in supplies cost depend on anything other than square metres of materials? What proportion of the fluctuations are not explained by square metres of materials?

P3-19 STEP COSTS. Atlantic Jail requires a staff of at least one guard for every four prisoners. The jail will hold 48 prisoners. Atlantic has a beach that attracts numerous tourists and transients in the spring and summer. However, the region is rather sedate in the fall and winter. The fall/winter population of the jail is generally between 12 and 16 prisoners. The numbers in the spring and summer can fluctuate from 12 to 48, depending on the weather, among other factors (including phases of the moon, according to some longtime residents).

Atlantic has four permanent guards hired on a year-round basis at an annual salary of $36,000 each. When additional guards are needed, they are hired on a weekly basis at a rate of $600 per week. (For simplicity, assume that each month has exactly four weeks.)

1. Prepare a graph with the weekly planned cost of jail guards on the vertical axis and the number of prisoners on the horizontal axis.
2. What would be the amount planned for jail guards for the month of January? Would this be a fixed cost or a variable cost?
3. Suppose the jail population of each of the four weeks in July was 25, 38, 26, and 43, respectively. The actual amount paid for jail guards in June was $19,800. Prepare a report comparing the actual amount paid for jail guards with the amount that would be expected with efficient scheduling and hiring.
4. Suppose Atlantic treated jail-guard salaries for nonpermanent guards as a variable expense of $150 per week per prisoner. This variable cost was applied to the number of prisoners in excess of 16. Therefore, the weekly cost function was

   weekly jail-guard cost = $3,000 + $150 × (total prisoners − 16)

   Explain how this cost function was determined.
5. Prepare a report similar to that in step 3 above except that the cost function in step 4 should be used to calculate the expected amount of jail-guard salaries. Which report, this one or the one in step 3, is more accurate? Is accuracy the only concern?

P3-20 REGRESSION ANALYSIS. Liao, Inc., a manufacturer of fine china and stoneware, is troubled by fluctuations in productivity and wants to compute how much manufacturing support costs are related to the various sizes of batches of output. The following data show the results of a random sample of ten batches of one pattern of stoneware:

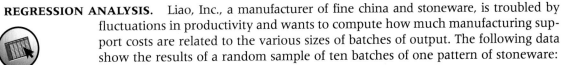

SAMPLE	BATCH SIZE, X	SUPPORT COSTS, Y
1	15	$180
2	12	140
3	20	230
4	17	190
5	12	160
6	25	300
7	22	270
8	9	110
9	18	240
10	30	320

1. Plot support costs versus batch size.
2. Using regression analysis, measure the cost function of support costs and batch size.

3. Predict the support costs for a batch size of 30.

4. Using the high-low method, repeat steps 2 and 3 above. Should the manager use the high-low method or the regression method? Explain.

P3-21 **DIVISION OF MIXED-COSTS INTO VARIABLE AND FIXED COMPONENTS.** Martina Fernandez, the president of Fernandez Tool Co., has asked for information about the cost behaviour of manufacturing support costs. Specifically, she wants to know how much support cost is fixed and how much is variable. The following data are the only records available:

MONTH	MACHINE HOURS	SUPPORT COSTS
May	850	$ 9,000
June	1,400	12,500
July	1,000	7,900
August	1,250	11,000
September	1,750	13,500

1. Find the monthly fixed support cost and the variable support cost per machine hour by the high-low method.

2. A least squares regression analysis gave the following output:

$$\text{Regression equation: } Y = \$1,500 + 6.80X$$

What recommendations would you give the president based on this analysis?

MANAGERIAL DECISION CASES

C3-1 **ACTIVITY ANALYSIS.** The costs of the Systems Support (SS) department (and other service departments) of Northwest Wood Products have always been charged to the three business divisions (Forest Resources, Lumber Products, and Paper Products) based on the *number of employees* in each division. This measure is easy to obtain and update, and until recently none of the divisions has complained about the charges. The Paper Products division has recently automated many of its operations and has reduced its number of employees. At the same time, however, in order to monitor its new process, Paper Products has increased its requests for various reports provided by the SS department. The other divisions have begun to complain that they are being charged more than their fair share of SS department costs. Based on activity analysis of possible cost drivers, cost analysts have suggested using the number of reports prepared as a means of charging for SS costs and have gathered the following information:

	FOREST RESOURCES	LUMBER PRODUCTS	PAPER PRODUCTS
2006 Number of Employees	762	457	502
2006 Number of Reports	410	445	377
2006 SS Costs: $300,000			
2007 Number of Employees	751	413	131
2007 Number of Reports	412	432	712
2007 SS Costs: $385,000			

Required:

1. Discuss the *plausibility* and probable *reliability* of each of the cost drivers—number of employees or number of reports.
2. What are the 2006 and 2007 SS costs per unit of cost driver for each division using each cost driver? Do the Forest Resources and Lumber Products divisions have legitimate complaints? Explain.
3. What are the *incentives* that are implied by each cost driver?
4. Which cost driver should Northwest Wood Products use to charge its divisions for SS services? For other services? Why?

C3-2 CHOICE OF COST DRIVER. Hassan Gurdezi, the director of cost operations of Micro Devices Company, wishes to develop the most accurate cost function to explain and predict support costs in the company's printed circuit board assembly operation. Mr. Gurdezi has read about activity-based costing and is concerned that the cost function that he currently uses—based on direct labour costs—is not accurate enough for proper planning and control of support costs. Mr. Gurdezi directed one of his financial analysts to obtain a random sample of 25 weeks of support costs and three possible cost drivers in the circuit board assembly department: direct labour cost, number of boards assembled, and average cycle time of boards assembled. Average cycle time is the average time between the start and the certified completion after quality testing of boards assembled during a week. Much of the effort in this assembly operation is devoted to testing for quality and reworking defective boards, all of which increase the average cycle time in any period. Therefore, Mr. Gurdezi believes that average cycle time will be the best support cost driver. Mr. Gurdezi wants his analyst to use regression analysis to demonstrate which cost driver best explains support costs.

SAMPLE NUMBER	CIRCUIT BOARD ASSEMBLY SUPPORT COSTS	DIRECT LABOUR HOURS	NUMBER OF BOARDS ASSEMBLED	AVERAGE CYCLE TIME (HOURS)
1	$66,402	7,619	2,983	186.44
2	56,943	7,678	2,830	139.14
3	60,337	7,816	2,413	151.13
4	50,096	7,659	2,221	138.39
5	64,241	7,646	2,701	158.63
6	60,846	7,765	2,656	148.71
7	43,119	7,685	2,495	105.85
8	63,412	7,962	2,128	174.02
9	59,283	7,793	2,127	155.30
10	60,070	7,732	2,127	162.20
11	53,345	7,771	2,338	142.97
12	65,027	7,842	2,685	176.08
13	58,220	7,940	2,602	150.19
14	65,406	7,750	2,029	194.06
15	35,268	7,954	2,136	100.51
16	46,394	7,768	2,046	137.47
17	71,877	7,764	2,786	197.44
18	61,903	7,635	2,822	164.69
19	50,009	7,849	2,178	141.95
20	49,327	7,869	2,244	123.37
21	44,703	7,576	2,195	128.25
22	45,582	7,557	2,370	106.16
23	43,818	7,569	2,016	131.41
24	62,122	7,672	2,515	154.88
25	52,403	7,653	2,942	140.07

1. Plot support costs versus each of the possible cost drivers.
2. Use regression analysis to measure cost functions using each of the cost drivers.
3. Interpret the economic meaning of the best cost function.
4. According to the criteria of plausibility and reliability, which is the best cost driver for support costs in the circuit board assembly department?

C3-3 **USE OF COST FUNCTIONS FOR PRICING.** Read the previous case. If you worked through this case, use your measured cost functions. If you did not work the previous problem, assume the following measured cost functions:

$$Y = \$9,000/wk + \$6 \times (\text{direct labour hours}); R^2 = 0.10$$
$$Y = \$20,000/wk + \$14 \times (\text{number of boards assembled}); R^2 = 0.40$$
$$Y = \$5,000/wk + \$350 \times (\text{average cycle time}); R^2 = 0.80$$

Required:

1. Which of the above cost functions would you expect to be the most reliable for explaining and predicting support costs? Why?
2. Micro Devices prices its products by adding a percentage markup to its product costs. Product costs include assembly labour, components, and support costs. Using each of the cost functions, compute the circuit board portion of the support cost of an order that used the following resources:
   a. Effectively utilized the capacity of the assembly department for three weeks.
   b. Assembly labour hours: 20,000
   c. Number of boards: 6,000 hours
   d. Average cycle time: 180
3. Which cost would you recommend that Micro Devices use? Why?
4. Assume that the market for this product is extremely cost-competitive. What do you think of Micro Devices' pricing method?

C3-4 **IDENTIFYING RELEVANT DATA.** Super Byte Company manufactures palm-sized portable computers. Because these very small computers compete with larger portable computers that have more functions and flexibility, understanding and using cost behaviour is critical to Super Byte's profitability. Super Byte's controller, Kelly Hudsa, has kept meticulous files on various cost categories and possible cost drivers for most of the important functions and activities of Super Byte. Because most of the manufacturing at Super Byte is automated, labour cost is relatively fixed. Other support costs comprise most of Super Byte's costs. On the next page are partial data that Hudsa has collected on one of these support costs, logistics operations (materials purchasing, receiving, warehousing, and shipping), over the past 25 weeks.

Required:

1. Plot logistics cost versus number of orders. What cost behaviour is evident? What do you think happened in week 14?
2. What is your recommendation to Kelly Hudsa regarding the relevance of the past 25 weeks of logistics cost and number of orders data for measuring logistics cost behaviour?
3. Hudsa remarks that one of the improvements that Super Byte made in the past several months was to negotiate just-in-time deliveries from its suppliers. This was made possible by substituting an automated ordering system for the previous manual (labour-intensive) system. Though fixed costs increased, the variable cost of placing an order was expected to drop greatly. Do the data support this expectation? Do you believe that the change to the automated ordering system was justified? Why or why not?

WEEK	LOGISTICS COST	NUMBER OF ORDERS
1	$23,907	1,357
2	18,265	1,077
3	24,208	1,383
4	23,578	1,486
5	22,211	1,292
6	22,862	1,425
7	23,303	1,306
8	24,507	1,373
9	17,878	1,031
10	18,306	1,020
11	20,807	1,097
12	19,707	1,069
13	23,020	1,444
14	20,407	733
15	20,370	413
16	20,678	633
17	21,145	711
18	20,775	228
19	20,532	488
20	20,659	655
21	20,430	722
22	20,713	373
23	20,256	391
24	21,196	734
25	20,406	256

C3-5 **REGRESSION ANALYSIS.** (CGAC) 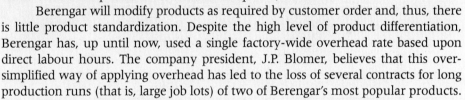 Berengar Ltd. is a small manufacturing company that produces a variety of products using a number of different processes in different-sized job lots. For example, some products will be ordered in lots of ten or less, while others are produced in batches of up to 1,000 units.

Berengar will modify products as required by customer order and, thus, there is little product standardization. Despite the high level of product differentiation, Berengar has, up until now, used a single factory-wide overhead rate based upon direct labour hours. The company president, J.P. Blomer, believes that this over-simplified way of applying overhead has led to the loss of several contracts for long production runs (that is, large job lots) of two of Berengar's most popular products.

Blomer has consulted with the operations staff in the machining department to see whether they have any suggestions for alternate overhead bases (other than direct labour hours for their department). Because of the recent addition of five numerically controlled machines, the supervisor of scheduling has noticed that direct labour hours in the department have declined considerably. The chief production engineer for machining believes that, with the new machine environment, production overhead probably varies more with machine hours per batch and setup time than it does with the current overhead application base, direct labour hours.

Blomer asked the controller to run four regressions to assist in predicting overhead cost in the machining department. The four regressions were based on

1. direct labour hours
2. machine hours
3. setup hours
4. machine hours and setup hours

One problem that the controller had to deal with was that approximately 35 percent of departmental overhead consisted of various lump-sum monthly charges
for central services such as personnel and power. The controller decided that
these charges were justifiably an expense of running the machining department
and left them in for the regression analyses.

   The results of the regressions (using the most recent 24 weeks of data,
shown below) are given in Exhibit 3A-1.

BERENGAR LTD.
MACHINE DEPARTMENT
DATA FOR REGRESSION ANALYSIS
MOST RECENT 24 WEEKS

WEEK	OVERHEAD COST (OH COST)	DIRECT LABOUR HOURS (DL HRS)	MACHINE HOURS (MACH HRS)	SETUP HOURS (SETUP HRS)
1	$72,892	2,036	379	98
2	76,451	2,125	385	101
3	75,930	2,012	378	110
4	78,591	1,900	390	112
5	77,870	1,934	401	108
6	75,420	2,095	376	110
7	73,529	1,966	365	95
8	78,210	1,924	387	103
9	85,620	1,865	464	130
10	84,322	1,912	451	110
11	89,621	1,901	496	125
12	79,739	1,864	401	101
13	81,221	1,850	425	95
14	85,130	1,812	456	102
15	83,550	1,800	446	110
16	79,985	1,712	398	114
17	87,870	1,718	485	135
18	90,565	1,741	502	129
19	89,032	1,622	491	142
20	87,979	1,639	487	110
21	86,646	1,641	479	124
22	90,772	1,628	516	99
23	85,542	1,598	472	125
24	90,159	1,597	508	160

Required:

a. From the results of the regression output of overhead cost with machine hours
and setup hours (Exhibit 3A-1, regression 4), identify the following:
i) the independent variables
ii) the marginal cost of an additional setup hour
iii) the regression equation

b. Using the information provided in Exhibit 3A-1, evaluate the results of the regressions, based upon the coefficient of determination (R^2).

Regression 1
Regression Output: Overhead cost with direct labour hours

Constant		135479.2
Standard Error of Y Estimate		8417.705
R-Squared		0.642200
No. of Observations		24
Degrees of Freedom		23
X Coefficient(s)	−28.8174	
Standard Error of Coefficient.	4.585940	
t-statistic	−6.28387	

Regression 2
Regression Output: Overhead cost with machine hours

Constant		33310.56
Standard Error of Y Estimate		1848.054
R-Squared		0.970568
No. of Observations		24
Degrees of Freedom		23
X Coefficient(s)	112.6582	
Standard Error of Coefficient	4.182588	
t-statistic	26.93505	

Regression 3
Regression Output: Overhead cost with setup hours

Constant		56802.56
Standard Error of Y Estimate		6705.380
R-Squared		0.410114
No. of Observations		24
Degrees of Freedom		23
X Coefficient(s)	226.8502	
Standard Error of Coefficient	58.00416	
t-statistic	3.910930	

Regression 4
Regression Output: Overhead cost with machine hours and setup hours

Constant		33060.920
Standard Error of Y Estimate		1922.676
R-Squared		0.97105226
No. of Observations		24
Degrees of Freedom		22
X Coefficient(s)−Machine Hours	110.6029	
Standard Error of Coefficient	5.482857	
t-statistic	20.17249	
X Coefficient(s)−Setup hours	10.0620	
Standard Error of Coefficient	16.984198	
t-statistic	0.592	

E3-1   FIXED AND VARIABLE COST DATA

Goal: Create an Excel spreadsheet to calculate fixed and variable cost data for evaluating alternative approaches. Use the results to answer questions about your findings.

Scenario: Recreational Sports, Inc. has asked you to evaluate two alternative cost approaches for their new Web site. They would like you to calculate fixed and variable costs at different numbers of orders.

The estimated costs of the two alternative approaches are as follows:

	Alternative 1	Alternative 2
Annual fixed cost	$200,000	$400,000
Variable cost per order	$8	$4
Expected number of orders	70,000	70,000

When you have completed your spreadsheet, answer the following questions:

1. At what number of orders are the total costs for the two approaches the same? What does this mean?

2. Which alternative should be selected if the expected number of orders is less than the break-even level of orders? If the expected number of orders is greater than the break-even level of orders?

3. What conclusion regarding cost predictions can be drawn from your analysis?

Step by Step:

1. Open a new Excel spreadsheet.

2. In column A, create a bold-faced heading that contains the following:
   Row 1: Chapter 3 Decision Guideline
   Row 2: Recreational Sports, Inc.
   Row 3: Analysis of Alternative Cost Approaches
   Row 4: Today's Date

3. Merge and centre the four heading rows across columns A through K.

4. In row 7, create the following bold-faced, right-justified column headings:
   Column A: Number of Orders
   Column B: Alternative 1
   Column C: Alternative 2

   Note: Adjust column widths as necessary.

5. In column A, rows 8 through 12, enter order levels from 40,000 to 80,000 in 10,000-unit increments.

6. Use the scenario data to create formulas in columns B and C for calculating the total costs (fixed plus variable costs) for each alternative at the order level in column A.

7. Format all amounts as

Number tab:	Category:	Number
	Decimal places:	0
	Use 1000 Separator (,):	Checked

8. Modify the Page Setup by selecting File, Page Setup.

Page tab:	Orientation:	Landscape
Margins tab:	Top:	.5
	Bottom:	.5

9. Select the data in columns A through C, rows 7 through 12, and start the Chart Wizard either by inserting a chart (Insert, Chart) or by clicking the Chart Wizard icon on the toolbar.

Step 1 of 4—Chart Type
a. Custom Types tab:
b. Chart Type: Smooth Lines
c. Click "Next >" button

Note: List is alphabetical.

Step 2 of 4—Chart Source Data
d. Data Range tab:
e. Modify Data range to: =SheetName!$B$7:$C$12
f. Series in: Columns
g. Series tab:
h. Category (X) axis labels: =SheetName!$A$8:$A$12
i. Click "Next >" button

Step 3 of 4—Chart Options
j. Titles tab:
k. Chart Title: Analysis of Alternative Cost Approaches
l. Category (X) axis: Number of Orders
m.Value (Y) axis: Total Costs
n. Gridlines tab:
o. Category (X) axis: Major Gridlines (checked)
p. Value (Y) axis: Major Gridlines (checked)
q. Click "Next >" button

Step 4 of 4—Chart Location
r. As object in SheetName   Checked
s. Click "Finish" button

10. Move the chart so the upper-left corner is on the left margin, row 14. Left-mouse click the upper-left handle and drag it to the designated location.

11. Resize the chart so the lower-right corner fills cell K37. Left-mouse click the lower-right handle and drag it to the designated location.

12. Format the Y-axis amounts (Total Costs) to display a dollar symbol by doing the following:

Double-click any cost amount on the Y-axis to open the Format Axis dialog box.

Scale tab: Minimum: 300,000

Number tab: Category: Currency

                              Decimal Places: 0

                                  Symbol: $

13. Save your work to disk, and print a copy for your files.

Note: Select cell A8 before printing if you want both the data and the chart to print. If you want only the chart to print, ignore the "Select cell A8" instruction.

Print your spreadsheet using landscape in order to ensure that all columns appear on one page.

COLLABORATIVE LEARNING EXERCISE

CL3-1 **COST BEHAVIOUR EXAMPLES.** Select about ten students to participate in a "cost-behaviour bee." The game proceeds like a spelling bee—when a participant is unable to come up with a correct answer, he or she is eliminated from the game. The last one in the game is the winner.

The object of the game is to identify a type of cost that fits a particular cost-behaviour pattern. The first player rolls a die.[2] If a 1 or a 6 comes up, the die passes to the next player (and the roller makes it to the next round). If a 2, 3, 4, or 5 comes up, the player has to identify one of the following types of costs:

If a 2 is rolled, identify a variable cost.
If a 3 is rolled, identify a fixed cost.
If a 4 is rolled, identify a mixed cost.
If a 5 is rolled, identify a step cost.

A scribe should label four columns on the board, one for each type of cost, and list the costs that are mentioned for each category. Once a particular cost has been used, it cannot be used again.

Each player has a time limit of 10 seconds to produce an example. (For a tougher game, make the time limit 5 seconds.) The instructor is the referee, judging if a particular example is acceptable. It is legitimate for the referee to ask a player to explain why he or she thinks the cost mentioned fits the category before making a judgment.

After each player has had a turn, a second round begins with the remaining players taking a turn in the same order as in the first round. The game continues through additional rounds until all but one player has failed to give an acceptable answer within the time limit. The remaining player is the winner.

---

[2] Instead of rolling a die, players could draw one of the four cost categories out of a hat (or similar container) or from a deck of four 3 × 5 cards. This eliminates the chance element that can let some players proceed to a later round without having to give an example of a particular cost behaviour. However, the chance element can add to the enjoyment of the game.

Cost Management Systems

LEARNING OBJECTIVES

After studying this chapter, you will be able to

1. Define and differentiate among the following terms: cost, cost object, cost accumulation, cost allocation, direct costs, indirect costs, product costs, and period costs.

2. Define and identify examples of the three major categories of manufacturing costs, prime costs, and conversion costs.

3. Explain how the financial statements of merchandisers and manufacturers differ.

4. Compare income statements of a manufacturing company in both the absorption and contribution formats.

5. Identify the basic features that distinguish the variable costing approach from the absorption costing approach and the pros and cons of using one or the other.

6. Construct an income statement using the variable costing approach and the absorption costing approach.

Managers rely on accountants to measure the cost of the goods or services the company produces. Consider the case of Mark Controls Company, a valve manufacturer that relies on strict financial controls to protect its profit margins. The company had been relying on broad averages of product costs to make manufacturing and pricing decisions. According to one report, "The company set up a computerized costing system that calculated the precise cost and profit margin for each of the 15,000 products the company sold. Since then, about 15 percent of those products have been dropped from the company's line because they were insufficiently profitable." Similarly, Sears has installed a cost system capable of judging the profitability (or unprofitability) of the products it sells. Likewise not-for-profit organizations such as hospitals and universities are finding it necessary to develop accurate costs for the different types of services they provide.

All kinds of organizations—manufacturing firms, service companies, and not-for-profit organizations—need some form of **cost accounting**, that part of the accounting system that determines the costs of making a product or performing a service. Because cost accounting in a manufacturing setting is the most general case and embraces production, marketing, and general administration functions, we will focus on it. Bear in mind, though, that you can apply this framework to any organization, including services and not-for-profit entities.

This chapter introduces the concepts of cost and management accounting appropriate to any manufacturing company. Manufacturing companies are in the midst of great changes. The need to compete in global markets has changed the types of information useful to managers. At the same time technology has changed both the manufacturing processes and information processing capabilities. While the basic concepts of management accounting have not changed, their *application* is significantly different in many companies than it was a decade ago. Management accountants today must be able to develop systems to support globally oriented, technology-intensive companies, often called *world-class manufacturing companies*.

CLASSIFICATION OF COSTS

Costs may be classified in many ways. We have already seen costs classified by their behaviour into fixed, variable, step, and mixed costs. This section concentrates on how costs arc accumulated and classified.

Cost Objects

Cost Accounting. That part of the accounting system that determines the costs of making a product or performing a service.

Cost. The monetary value of what is given up to acquire a current or future benefit (product or service) for the organization.

A **cost** may be defined as the monetary value of what is given up to acquire a current or a future benefit (product or service) for the organization. Costs are frequently measured by the monetary units (e.g., dollars) that must be paid for goods and services. Costs are initially recorded in elementary form (e.g., repairs or advertising). These costs are then grouped in different ways to help managers make decisions, such as evaluating subordinates and subunits of the organization, expanding or dropping products, and replacing equipment.

Cost Object. Any activity for which a separate measurement of costs is desired.

To aid decision making, managers want to know the cost of something. This "something" is called a **cost object**, defined as any activity for which a separate measurement of costs is desired. Examples of cost objects include departments, products, territories, kilometres driven, patients seen, students taught, and tax bills sent. Costs are then assigned or allocated to one or more cost objects.

EXHIBIT 4-1

Cost Accumulation and
Assignment

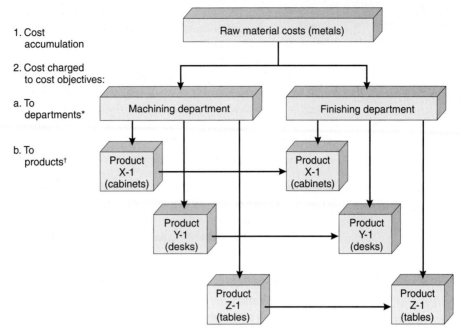

1. Cost
   accumulation

2. Cost charged
   to cost objectives:

a. To
   departments*

b. To
   products†

* Purpose: to evaluate performance of manufacturing departments.
† Purpose: to obtain costs of various products for valuing inventory, determining income, and judging product profitability.

OBJECTIVE 1

Define and differentiate among the following terms: cost, cost object, cost accumulation, cost allocation, direct costs, indirect costs, product costs, and period costs.

Exhibit 4-1 illustrates the process of cost accumulation and assignment. In it, the costs of all raw materials are *accumulated*. They are then *charged* to the departments that use them and further to the specific products made by the departments. The total raw materials cost of a particular product is the sum of the raw materials costs charged to it by the various departments.

To make intelligent decisions, managers want reliable measurements. When A&P ran into profit difficulties, it began retrenching by closing many stores. Management's lack of adequate cost information about individual store operations made the closing program a hit-or-miss affair. A news story reported the following:

> Because of the absence of detailed profit-and-loss statements, and a cost-allocation system that did not reflect true costs, A&P's strategists could not be sure whether an individual store was really unprofitable. For example, distribution costs were shared equally among all the stores in a marketing area without regard to such factors as a store's distance from the warehouse. One close observer of the company said: "When they wanted to close a store, they had to wing it. They could not make rational decisions, because they did not have a fact basis."

Direct and Indirect Costs

A major feature of costs in both manufacturing and nonmanufacturing activities is whether the costs have a direct or an indirect relationship to a particular cost

Direct Costs. Costs that are easily, clearly, and economically identified and traced exclusively to a cost object.

Indirect Costs. Costs that cannot be identified and specifically traced to a particular cost object.

object. **Direct costs** can be easily, clearly, and economically identified and traced exclusively to a cost object. Thus, direct costs can be assigned specifically to a cost object. **Indirect costs**, in contrast, cannot be identified and specifically traced to a particular cost object. Thus, indirect costs can only be charged to a cost object by means of allocating the costs on some basis.

Terms for assigning costs or allocating costs to a cost object tend to be interchangeable. However, students may find it helpful to think of direct costs being *assigned* to a cost object and indirect costs being *allocated* to a cost object. This distinction will become clearer as we proceed through the study of cost systems.

Managers prefer to classify costs as direct rather than indirect. In this way, managers have greater confidence in the reported costs of products and services. But managers do not want cost accounting to be too expensive in relation to expected benefits. For example, it may be economically feasible to trace the exact cost of steel and fabric (direct costs) to a specific lot of desk chairs, but it may not be economically feasible to trace the exact cost of rivets or thread (indirect costs) to the chairs.

Other factors also influence whether a cost is considered direct or indirect. The key is the particular cost object. For example, consider a supervisor's salary in a maintenance department of a telephone company. If the cost object is the department, the supervisor's salary is a direct cost. In contrast, if the cost object is a service (the "product" of the company) such as a telephone call, the supervisor's salary is an indirect cost. In general, many more costs are direct when a department is the cost object than when a service (a telephone call) or a physical product (a razor blade) is the cost object.

Managers want to know both the costs of running departments and the costs of products and services; costs are inevitably charged to more than one cost object. Thus, a particular cost may simultaneously be direct and indirect. As you have just seen, a supervisor's salary can be both direct (with respect to his or her department) and indirect (with respect to the department's individual products or services).

Classifications of Labour-Related Costs

Indirect Labour. All factory labour wages, other than those for direct labour and managers' salaries.

All factory labour wages, other than those for direct labour and managers' salaries, are usually classified as **indirect labour** costs—a major component of factory overhead. Factory overhead may include the following indirect labour-related costs:

Forklift truck operators (internal handling of materials)
Maintenance
Production setup
Expediting (overseeing special and rush orders)
Janitors
Plant guards
Rework labour (time spent by direct labourers redoing defective work)
Overtime premium paid to all factory workers
Idle time
Managers' salaries
Employee benefit costs (e.g., health-care premiums, pension costs)

The term *indirect labour* is usually divided into many subsidiary classifications. For example, the wages of forklift truck operators are generally not combined with janitors' salaries, although both are regarded as indirect labour.

Costs are classified in a detailed fashion primarily to associate a specific cost with its specific cost driver. Two classes of indirect labour deserve special mention: overtime premium and idle time.

Overtime premium paid to all factory workers is usually considered a part of overhead. If a lathe operator earns $18 per hour for straight time and time and a half for overtime, the premium is $9 per overtime hour. If the operator works 44 hours, including four overtime hours, in one week, the gross earnings are classified as follows:

Direct labour: 44 hours x $18	$792
Overtime premium (factory overhead): 4 hours x $9	36
Total earnings for 44 hours	$828

Why is overtime premium considered an indirect cost rather than a direct cost? After all, it can usually be traced to specific batches of work. Overtime is not considered a direct charge because the scheduling of production jobs is generally random. That is, a job requiring 10 hours to be completed, done during regular working hours, would cost 18×10 hours = $180. The same job done during the overtime period would cost 27×10 hours = $270. The timing of the job should not determine the cost charged for the job. Suppose that you and a friend bring your automobiles to a shop for repair. Through random scheduling, your auto is repaired when the mechanics receive overtime pay, while your friend's car is repaired during the mechanics' regular pay. When you pick up your car, the entire overtime premium appears on your bill. You probably would not be overjoyed to find out that you were charged a direct per-hour cost of $27, not $18.

Thus, in most companies, the overtime premium is not allocated to any specific job. Instead, the overtime premium is considered to be attributable to the heavy overall volume of work, and its cost is thus regarded as part of the indirect manufacturing costs because it happened to be worked on during the overtime hours.

Another subsidiary classification of indirect labour costs is **idle time**. This cost typically represents wages paid for unproductive time caused by machine breakdowns, material shortages, sloppy production scheduling, and the like. For example, if the same lathe operator's machine broke down for three hours during the week, the operator's earnings would be classified as follows:

Direct labour: 41 hours x $18	$738
Overtime premium (factory overhead): 4 hours x $9	36
Idle time (factory overhead): 3 hours x $18	54
Total earnings for 44 hours	$828

Managers' salaries usually are not classified as a part of indirect labour. Instead, the compensation of supervisors, department heads, and all others who are regarded as part of manufacturing management are placed in a separate classification of factory overhead.

A type of labour cost growing in importance is **employee benefit costs** (e.g., employer contributions to employee benefits such as Canada/Quebec Pension Plan, employment insurance, life insurance, health insurance, and pensions).

Historically, these costs were referred to as fringe benefits; but today, for most organizations, these costs are too substantial to be referred to as "fringe" costs. Most companies classify these as factory overhead. In some companies, however, employee benefits related to direct labour are charged as an additional direct-labour cost. For instance, a direct labourer, such as a lathe operator or an auto mechanic whose gross wages are computed on the basis of $20 an hour, may enjoy fringe benefits totalling $4 per hour. Most companies classify the $20 as direct-labour cost and the $4 as factory overhead. Other companies classify the entire $24 as direct-labour cost. The latter approach is conceptually preferable because these costs are a fundamental part of acquiring labour services.

Accountants and managers need to pinpoint exactly what direct labour includes and excludes. Such clarity may avoid disputes regarding cost reimbursement contracts, income tax payments, and labour union matters. For example, some governments offer substantial income tax savings to companies that locate factories in their countries. To qualify, "direct labour" in that country must equal a specified percentage of the total manufacturing costs of products. Disputes have arisen regarding how to calculate the direct-labour percentage in order to qualify for such tax relief. For instance, are employee benefits on direct labour an integral part of direct labour, or are they a part of factory overhead? Depending on how companies classify costs, two firms may show different percentages of total manufacturing costs. Consider a company with $10,000 of employee benefit costs (figures are assumed):

CLASSIFICATION A			CLASSIFICATION B		
Direct materials	$ 80,000	40%	Direct materials	$ 80,000	40%
Direct labour	40,000	20%	Direct labour	50,000	25%
Factory overhead	80,000	40%	Factory overhead	70,000	35%
Total manufacturing costs	$200,000	100%	Total manufacturing costs	$200,000	100%

Classification A assumes that employee benefit costs are part of factory overhead. In contrast, Classification B assumes that employee benefit costs are part of direct labour.

Product Costs and Period Costs

Product Costs. Costs identified with goods produced or purchased for resale.

Period Costs. The costs of resources consumed during the current period that are deducted as expenses without going through an inventory stage.

When preparing income statements and balance sheets, accountants frequently distinguish between product costs and period costs. **Product costs** are costs identified with goods produced or purchased for resale. Product costs are initially identified as part of the inventory on hand. These product costs (inventoriable costs) become expenses (in the form of cost of goods sold) only when the inventory is sold. **Period costs** are the costs of resources consumed during the current period in order to support various activities of the company. They are deducted from revenues as expenses during the current period without being inventoried.

For example, look at the top half of Exhibit 4-2. A merchandising company (retailer or wholesaler) acquires goods for resale without changing their basic form. The only product cost is the purchase of the merchandise. Unsold goods are held as merchandise inventory cost and are shown as an asset on a balance sheet. As the goods are sold, their costs become expenses in the form of "cost of goods sold."

EXHIBIT 4-2

Relationship of Product Costs and Period Costs

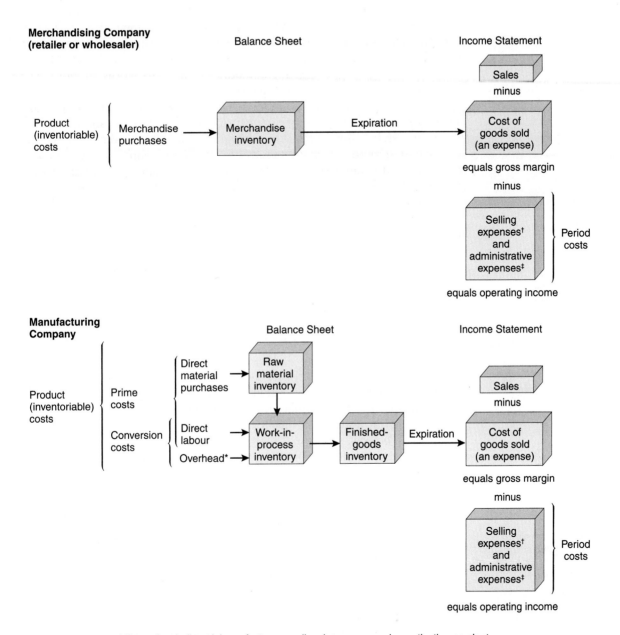

*Examples: indirect labour, factory supplies, insurance, and amortization on plant.

† Examples: insurance on salespersons' cars, amortization on salespersons' cars, salespersons' salaries and commissions.

‡ Examples: insurance on corporate headquarters building, amortization on office equipment, clerical salaries.

Note particularly that where insurance and amortization relate to the manufacturing function, they are inventoriable, but where they relate to selling and administration, they are not inventoriable.

A merchandising company also has a variety of selling and administrative expenses. These costs are considered period costs because they are deducted from revenue as expenses without ever being part of inventory.

The bottom half of Exhibit 4-2 illustrates product and period costs in a manufacturing firm. Note that direct materials are transformed into saleable form with the help of direct labour and factory overhead. All these costs are product costs because they are allocated to inventory until the goods are sold. As in merchandising accounting, the selling and administrative expenses are not regarded as product costs but are treated as period costs.

Be sure you are clear on the differences between merchandising accounting and manufacturing accounting for such costs as insurance, amortization, and wages. In merchandising accounting, all such items are period costs (expenses of the current period). In manufacturing accounting, many of these items are related to production activities and thus factory insurance, factory amortization, and factory wages, as factory overhead, are product costs. They become expenses in the form of cost of goods sold as the inventory is sold.

In both merchandising and manufacturing accounting, selling and general administrative costs are period costs. Thus, the inventory costs of a manufactured product exclude sales salaries, sales commissions, advertising, legal, public relations, and the president's salary. Manufacturing overhead is traditionally regarded as a part of finished-goods inventory cost, whereas selling expenses and general administrative expenses are not.

Manufacturing Costs

OBJECTIVE 2

Define and identify examples of the three major categories of manufacturing costs, prime costs, and conversion costs.

Any raw material, labour, or other input used by an organization could, in theory, be identified as a direct or indirect cost, depending on the cost object. In manufacturing, the transformation of raw materials and other inputs, through the use of labour and factory facilities to finished products, makes the finished products cost objects. As a result, manufacturing costs are most often divided into three categories: (1) direct materials, (2) direct labour, and (3) factory overhead.

Direct-Materials Costs. The acquisition costs of all materials that are physically identified as a part of manufactured goods and that may be traced to manufactured goods in an economically feasible way.

Direct-Labour Costs. The wages of all labour that can be traced specifically and exclusively to manufactured goods in an economically feasible way.

1. **Direct-materials costs** include the acquisition costs of all materials that are physically identified as a part of the manufactured goods and that may be traced to the manufactured goods in an economically feasible way. Examples are iron castings, lumber, aluminum sheets, and subassemblies. Direct materials often do not include minor items such as tacks or glue because the costs of tracing these items are greater than the possible benefits of obtaining more precise product costs. Such items are usually called *supplies* or *indirect materials* and are classified as a part of the factory overhead described in this list.

2. **Direct-labour costs** include the wages of all labour that can be traced specifically and exclusively to the manufactured goods in an economically feasible way. Examples are the wages of machine operators and assemblers. Much labour, such as that of janitors, forklift truck operators, plant guards, and storeroom clerks, is considered indirect labour because it is impossible or economically infeasible to trace such activity to specific products. Such indirect labour is generally classified as a part of factory overhead. In highly automated factories there may be no direct labour costs. Why? Because it may not be economically feasible to physically trace any labour cost directly to specific products.

Factory Overhead Costs (Manufacturing Overhead, Indirect Manufacturing Costs). All costs other than direct material or direct labour that are associated with the manufacturing process.

3. **Factory overhead costs** include all costs other than direct material or direct labour that are associated with the manufacturing process. Other terms that are used to describe this category are **manufacturing overhead** and **indirect manufacturing costs**. Examples are power, supplies, indirect labour, supervisory salaries, property taxes, rent, insurance, and amortization.

In traditional accounting systems, all manufacturing overhead costs are considered to be indirect. However, computers have allowed modern systems to physically trace many overhead costs to products in an economically feasible manner. For example, meters wired to computers can monitor the electricity used to produce each product, and the costs of setting up a batch production run can be traced to the items produced in the run. In general, the more overhead costs that can be traced directly to products, the more complete and accurate the product cost.

Prime Costs, Conversion Costs, and Direct-Labour Category

Prime Costs. Direct-labour costs plus direct-materials costs.

Conversion Costs. Direct-labour costs plus factory-overhead costs.

Exhibit 4-3 shows that direct labour is sometimes combined with one of the other types of manufacturing costs. The combined categories are **prime costs**—direct labour plus direct materials—and **conversion costs**—direct labour plus factory overhead.

The twofold categorization—direct materials and conversion costs—has replaced the threefold categorization (direct materials, direct labour, and factory overhead) in many modern automated manufacturing companies. Why? Because direct labour is increasingly a small part of costs and not worth tracing directly to the products. In fact, some companies call their two categories direct materials and factory overhead and simply include direct labour costs in the factory overhead category.

Why so many different systems? As mentioned earlier, accountants and managers weigh the costs and benefits of additional categories when they design their cost accounting systems. Where the costs of any single category or item

EXHIBIT 4-3

Relationships of Key Categories of Manufacturing Costs for Product-Costing Purposes

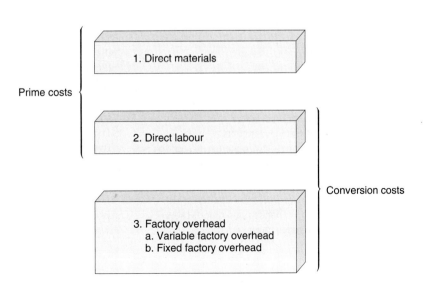

become relatively insignificant, separate tracking may no longer be desirable. For example, in highly automated factories, direct labour may be less than five percent of total manufacturing costs. In such cases, it may make economic sense to combine direct-labour costs with one of the other major cost categories. For example in a Canadian automotive parts manufacturer, automation on some lines eliminated the need for almost all of the direct labour.

To recap, the three major categories for manufacturing product costs are direct materials, direct labour, and factory overhead. However, some companies have only two categories: direct materials and conversion costs.

In addition to direct-materials, direct-labour, and factory-overhead costs, all manufacturing companies also incur selling and administrative costs. These costs are accumulated by departments such as research and development, advertising, and sales. As you will see later in this chapter, most firm's financial statements do not allocate these costs to the physical units produced. In short, these costs do not become a part of the inventory cost of the manufactured products. However, to aid in making decisions, managers may want to know all the costs associated with each product line. Therefore, management reports sometimes include such costs as product costs.

Balance Sheet for a Manufacturing Company

OBJECTIVE 3

Explain how the financial statements of merchandisers and manufacturers differ.

The balance sheets of manufacturers and merchandisers differ with respect to inventories. In a manufacturing company, the "inventory account" is segmented into three inventory classes that help managers trace all product costs through the production process to the time of sales. These classes are

- *Direct-materials inventory:* Materials on hand and awaiting use in the production process (raw materials and supplies).
- *Work-in-process inventory:* Goods undergoing the production process but not yet fully completed. Costs include appropriate amounts of the three major manufacturing costs (direct materials, direct labour, and factory overhead).
- *Finished-goods inventory:* Goods fully completed but not yet sold.

Current Asset Sections of Balance Sheets ($ millions)

	LABRADOR CORPORATION MARCH 31, 2006		CARLETON COMPANIES LIMITED JANUARY 2, 2006
Cash	$1,226,550		$ 672
Accounts receivable	1,169,982		345
Short-term investments	541,747		0
Inventories – raw materials & supplies	110,943	– merchandise	1,141
– work in process	101,239		
– finished goods	523,247		
Prepaid expenses and other assets	699,479		84
Taxes recoverable	–		7
	$4,373,187		$2,249

The only difference between the structure of the balance sheet of a manufacturer and that of a retailer or wholesaler would appear in their respective current asset sections.

Unit Cost for Product Costing

Reporting cost of goods sold or inventory values requires costs to be assigned to units of product. Assume the following:

Total cost of goods manufactured	$40,000,000
Total units manufactured	10,000,000
Unit cost of product for inventory	
purposes ($40,000,000 ÷ 10,000,000)	$4

If some of the 10 million units manufactured are still unsold at the end of the period, a part of the $40 million cost of goods manufactured will be "held back" as a cost of the ending inventory of finished goods (and shown as an asset on a balance sheet). The remainder becomes "cost of goods sold" for the current period and is shown as an expense on the income statement.

Income Statements for a Manufacturing Company

The detailed reporting of selling and administrative expenses as they appear in the income statements is typically the same for manufacturing and merchandising organizations. However, the cost of goods sold is different.

Consider the *additional assumed* details as they are presented in the model income statement of a manufacturing company in Exhibit 4-4. The $40 million cost of goods manufactured is subdivided into the major components of direct materials, direct labour, and factory overhead. In contrast, a wholesale or retail company would replace the entire "cost of goods manufactured" section with a single line, "cost of goods purchased."

The terms "costs" and "expenses" are often used loosely by accountants and managers. "Expenses" denote all costs deducted from (matched against) revenue in a given period. On the other hand, "costs" is a much broader term and is used, for example, to describe both an asset (the cost of inventory) and an expense (the cost of goods sold). Thus, manufacturing costs are funnelled into an income statement as an expense (in the form of cost of goods sold) via the multistep inventory procedure shown earlier in Exhibit 4-2. In contrast, selling and general administrative costs are commonly deemed expenses immediately as they are incurred.

The Three Manufacturing Inventory Accounts

The three manufacturing inventory accounts are affected by the following transactions:

- *Direct-Materials Inventory*
  Increased by purchases of direct materials
  Decreased by use of direct materials

EXHIBIT 4-4

Model Income
Statement,
Manufacturing
Company

Sales (8,000,000 units @ $10)			$80,000,000
Cost of goods manufactured and sold:			
Beginning finished-goods inventory		$ —0—	
Cost of goods manufactured:			
Direct materials used	$20,000,000		
Direct labour	12,000,000		
Factory overhead	8,000,000	40,000,000	
Cost of goods available for sale		$40,000,000	
Ending finished-goods inventory			
2,000,000 units @ $4		8,000,000	
Cost of goods sold			32,000,000
Gross margin or gross profit			$48,000,000
Less: Other expenses			
Selling expenses		$30,000,000	
General and administrative expenses		$ 8,000,000	$38,000,000
Operating income*			$10,000,000

* Also net income in this example since interest and income taxes are ignored here for simplicity.
Manufacturer: Manufacturing cost of goods produced and then sold, usually composed of three major categories of cost: direct materials, direct labour, and factory overhead.
Retailer or Wholesaler: Merchandise cost of goods sold, usually composed of the purchase cost of items, including freight in, that are acquired and then resold.

- *Work-in-Process Inventory*
  Increased by use of direct materials, direct labour, or factory overhead
  Decreased by transfers to finished-goods inventory

- *Finished-Goods Inventory*
  Increased by transfers of finished goods from work-in-process inventory
  Decreased by amount of cost of goods sold at time of sale

Direct labour and factory overhead are used at the same time they are acquired. Therefore, they are entered directly into work-in-process inventory and have no separate inventory account. In contrast, direct materials are often purchased in advance of their use and held in inventory for some time.

Exhibit 4-5 traces the effects of these transactions. It uses the dollar amounts from Exhibit 4-4, with one exception. Purchases of direct materials totalled $30 million, with $20 million used in production (as shown in Exhibit 4-4) and $10 million left in inventory at the end of the period. As the bottom of Exhibit 4-5 indicates, the ending balance sheet amounts would be:

Direct-materials inventory	$10,000,000
Work-in-process inventory	0
Finished-goods inventory	8,000,000
Total inventories	$18,000,000

EXHIBIT 4-5

Inventory Transactions
($ millions)

TRANSACTION	DIRECT-MATERIALS INVENTORY ($ MILLIONS)	WORK-IN-PROCESS INVENTORY ($ MILLIONS)	FINISHED-GOODS INVENTORY ($ MILLIONS)
Beginning balance	$ 0	$ 0	$ 0
Purchase direct materials	+30	–	–
Use direct materials	–20	+20	–
Acquire and use direct labour	–	+12	–
Acquire and use factory overhead	–	+8	–
Complete production	–	–40	+40
Sell goods and record cost of goods sold	–	–	–32
Ending balance	$ 10	$ 0	$ 8

Absorption and Contribution Approach to Income Statements

OBJECTIVE 4

Compare income
statements of a
manufacturing
company in both the
absorption and
contribution formats.

In addition to differences between manufacturing and merchandising firms in their external financial reporting, manufacturers differ among themselves in accounting for internal decision making. Some companies favour an absorption approach and others a contribution approach to income statements. To highlight the different effects of these approaches, we will assume that, in 2006, the Samson Company has direct-materials costs of $7 million and direct-labour costs of $4 million. Assume also that the company incurred the factory overhead illustrated in Exhibit 4-6 and the selling and administrative expenses illustrated in Exhibit 4-7. Total sales were $20 million. Finally, assume that the units produced are equal to the units sold. That is, there is no change in inventory levels.

Note that Exhibits 4-6 and 4-7 subdivide costs as variable or fixed. Many companies do not make such subdivisions in their income statements. Furthermore, when these subdivisions are made, sometimes arbitrary decisions are necessary as to whether a given cost is variable, fixed, or partially fixed (e.g., repairs). Nevertheless, to aid decision making, many companies are attempting to report the extent to which their costs are approximately variable or fixed.

EXHIBIT 4-6

SAMSON COMPANY
Schedules of
Manufacturing
Overhead (which are
product costs) for the
Year Ended
December 31, 2006
(in thousands of
dollars)

SCHEDULE 1: VARIABLE COSTS

Supplies (lubricants, expendable tools, coolants, sandpaper)	$ 150	
Material-handling labour (forklift operators)	700	
Repairs	100	
Power	50	$1,000

SCHEDULE 2: FIXED COSTS

Managers salaries	$ 200	
Employee training	90	
Factory picnic and holiday party	10	
Supervisory salaries, except supervisor's salaries	700	
Amortization, plant and equipment	1,800	
Property taxes	150	
Insurance	50	3,000
Total manufacturing overhead		$4,000

EXHIBIT 4-7

SAMSON COMPANY
Schedules of Selling
and Administrative
Expenses (which are
period costs) for the
Year Ended
December 31, 2006
(in thousands of dollars)

SCHEDULE 3: SELLING EXPENSES

Variable:		
Sales commissions	$ 700	
Shipping expenses for products sold	300	$1,000
Fixed:		
Advertising	$ 700	
Sales salaries	1,000	
Other	300	2,000
Total selling expenses		$3,000

SCHEDULE 4: ADMINISTRATIVE EXPENSES

Variable:		
Some clerical wages	$ 80	
Computer time rented	20	$ 100
Fixed:		
Office salaries	$ 100	
Other salaries	200	
Amortization on office facilities	100	
Public-accounting fees	40	
Legal fees	100	
Other	360	900
Total administrative expenses		$1,000

Absorption Approach

Absorption Approach. A costing approach that considers all factory overhead (both variable and fixed) to be product (inventoriable) costs that become an expense in the form of manufacturing cost of goods sold only as sales occur.

Exhibit 4-8 presents Samson's income statement using the **absorption approach** (absorption costing)—the approach used by most companies. Firms that take this approach consider all factory overhead (both variable and fixed) to be product (inventoriable) costs that become an expense in the form of manufacturing cost of goods sold only as sales occur.

Take a moment to compare Exhibits 4-4 and 4-8. Note that gross profit or gross margin is the difference between sales and the *manufacturing* cost of goods sold. Note, too, that the *primary classifications* of costs on the income statement are by three major management *functions*: manufacturing, selling, and administrative.

EXHIBIT 4-8

SAMSON COMPANY
Absorption Income
Statement for the Year
Ended December 31,
2006 (in thousands
of dollars)

Sales		$20,000
Less: Manufacturing costs of goods sold:		
Direct material	$7,000	
Direct labour	4,000	
Factory overhead (Schedules 1 and 2)	4,000	15,000
Gross margin or gross profit		$ 5,000
Selling expenses (Schedule 3)	$3,000	
Administrative expenses (Schedule 4)	1,000	
Total selling and administrative expenses		4,000
Operating income		$1,000

Note: Schedules 1 and 2 are in Exhibit 4-6. Schedules 3 and 4 are in Exhibit 4-7.

Contribution Approach

Contribution Approach. A method of internal (management accounting) reporting that emphasizes the distinction between variable and fixed costs for the purpose of better decision making.

In contrast, Exhibit 4-9 uses the **contribution approach** (variable costing) to present Samson's income statement. The contribution approach is generally not allowed for external financial reporting. However, many companies use this approach for internal (management accounting) purposes and an absorption format for external purposes, because they expect the benefits of making better decisions to exceed the extra costs of using different reporting systems simultaneously.

For decision purposes, the major difference between the contribution approach and the absorption approach is that the former emphasizes the distinction between variable and fixed costs. Its primary classifications of costs are by variable and fixed *cost behaviour patterns*, not by *business functions*.

The contribution income statement provides a *contribution margin*, which is computed after deducting all variable costs, including variable selling and administrative costs. This approach makes it easier to see the impact of changes in sales demand on operating income. It also dovetails neatly with the cost-volume-profit analysis illustrated in Chapter 2.

The contribution approach stresses the lump-sum amount of fixed costs to be recouped before net income emerges. This highlighting of total fixed costs focuses management attention on fixed-cost behaviour and control in making both short-run and long-run plans. Keep in mind that advocates of the contribution approach do not maintain that fixed costs are unimportant or irrelevant.

The difference between the gross margin (from the absorption approach) and the contribution margin (from the contribution approach) is striking in manufacturing companies. Why? Because fixed manufacturing costs are regarded as a part of cost of goods sold, and these fixed costs reduce the gross margin accordingly. However, *fixed* manufacturing costs do not reduce the contribution margin, which is affected solely by revenues and *variable* costs.

EXHIBIT 4-9

SAMSON COMPANY
Contribution Income Statement for the Year Ended December 31, 2006 (in thousands of dollars)

Sales		$20,000
Less: Variable expenses:		
Direct material	$ 7,000	
Direct labour	4,000	
Variable manufacturing overhead costs (Schedule 1)	1,000	
Total variable manufacturing cost of goods sold	12,000	
Variable selling expenses (Schedule 3)	1,000	
Variable administrative expenses (Schedule 4)	100	
Total variable expenses		13,100
Contribution margin		$ 6,900
Less: Fixed expenses:		
Manufacturing overhead (Schedule 2)	$ 3,000	
Selling (Schedule 3)	2,000	
Administrative (Schedule 4)	900	5,900
Operating income		$ 1,000

Note: Schedules 1 and 2 are in Exhibit 4-6. Schedules 3 and 4 are in Exhibit 4-7.

Variable Versus Absorption Costing: A Company President's Perspective

Arriscraft International Income Fund, an income trust comprising the assets of Arriscraft International, is based in Cambridge, Ontario, with additional manufacturing facilities in St-Étienne-des-Grès, Quebec, and Fort Valley, Georgia. It also owns a limestone quarry on the Bruce Peninsula in southwestern Ontario. Arriscraft International's main business is the production and sale of natural stone, manufactured stone, and brick. It commenced operations in 1949. For its fiscal year ended December 31, 2004, Arriscraft had slightly over $2 million in gross sales, yet had nearly $130 million in assets. Randy White, CA, president and chief executive officer, spoke about variable versus absorption costing:

Arriscraft
www.arriscraft.com

> To properly understand the difference between variable cost accounting and absorption cost accounting to today's manufacturers, the individual must understand that the environment in which the manufacturer operates and the concerns of the manager of such an operation have changed with time.

Priorities are now product quality, which includes all aspects of design, service, and price. A common definition of quality is "that which the customer wants, at a competitive price."

The accounting system must provide the correct data to make informed decisions about these quality issues. The absorption-costing system was developed by accountants whose objective was to match revenue and expenses for financial statement presentation. It was developed during times of high setup costs and long runs of identical products. There is no mention in these objectives of customer or quality.

Consider the environment in which decisions are presently being made:

- *Global Market.* The whole world is the market and the whole world is the competitor. This market cares only about product quality. Competitors are interested only in what they can do better than the competition. Manufacturers must ensure that no such opportunity exists or they will lose competitive position.
- *Niche Marketing.* Specific products are aimed at particular markets or market segments. Customer needs do vary, which means the manufacturer must be in a position to continually make decisions as to the costs associated with making the changes requested and required by the individual customer.
- *Flexible Manufacturing.* Companies must be capable of setting up quickly and changing or modifying products quickly to meet the demands of the niche market.
- *Continuous Improvement.* Everyone in the operation, from the president to the floor sweeper, must continually strive to find better methods to do what they do. If they do not, they can be assured that a competitor somewhere will be doing so, and the organization will lose competitive advantage.

None of the above refers to short-term profit presentation, financial statement ratios, or current share prices—the issues around which absorption costing was developed.

Since managers are now looking at numerous customized orders and specialized markets, their decisions in this environment cannot be made on the basis of an arbitrary allocation of overhead costs. Rather, the managers must know what costs will vary with any particular decision and how the costs will vary with volume. The manager must look at the price that can be obtained for the product in question and at the contribution margin generated by that product during the plant time absorbed to produce the product. The manager must investigate the overheads to ensure that in fact these will not vary as a result of taking a particular order (or entering a particular market). The manager must compare the value of that order against other possible orders that cannot be accepted because they would require the same production time slot.

The manager can then consider all aspects of an order (or market segment) and its effect on the overall marketing plans of the organization, including such subjective items as corporate image and market share and the long-term effect on customers and markets.

A manager who follows this procedure will be in a position to truly maximize real profits. Real profits are the cash generated over time, not the short-term results reported in audited financial statements in any particular year.

Variable costs are important not only to managers but to all levels of the manufacturing organization. The people on the floor are involved in making recommendations and improvements in the organization. As such, they have access to and are using costs to calculate the return on investment of proposed improvements. Such decisions must be made on the basis of cash flow, not financial statement profit and loss. Only variable costing systems provide the correct information.

Absorption costing is meant to match revenue with costs. If used by managers to make operating decisions about quality or competitive position, it will distort the decisions. These are the decisions that affect the customers and the markets. It must be understood that the key to the success of the manufacturer is the customer; it is not an accountant's view of profit and loss.

The absorption costing system adds nothing of value to the manager's operating decisions, therefore, nothing of value to the product or the customer. If the important decisions within the company are being based upon variable costs, does it not follow that eventually the outside investor will want to make their decisions on a similar basis? Perhaps absorption costing will go the way of the large, inflexible manufacturer and the dinosaur.

Sources: Randy White, CA, President and Chief Executive Officer, Arriscraft International Income Fund; Arriscraft International Income Fund 2004 Annual Report.

MAKING MANAGERIAL DECISIONS

When making decisions, it is important for managers to distinguish between gross margin and contribution margin. List the ways in which these two margins differ.

ANSWER
Among the differences are the following:

- Gross margin appears in an absorption-costing income statement; contribution margin is in a variable-costing income statement.

- Gross margin is revenue less manufacturing costs; contribution margin is revenue less all variable costs.

- Gross margin is based on a categorization of costs by function; contribution margin divides costs by cost behaviour.

- Gross margin is required for financial reporting; contribution margin is most useful for short-term management decisions.

VARIABLE VERSUS ABSORPTION COSTING

Accounting for Fixed Manufacturing Overhead

OBJECTIVE 5

Identify the basic features that distinguish the variable costing approach from the absorption costing approach and the pros and cons of using one or the other.

Two major methods of product costing are compared in this chapter: *variable costing* (the contribution approach) and *absorption costing* (the functional, full-costing, or traditional approach). These methods differ in one primary conceptual respect: fixed manufacturing overhead is excluded from the cost of products under *variable costing* but is included in the cost of products under *absorption costing*. In other words, variable costing signifies that fixed factory overhead is not inventoried. In contrast, absorption costing indicates that inventory values include fixed factory overhead.

As Exhibit 4-10 shows, a variable costing system treats fixed manufacturing overhead (fixed factory overhead) as an expired cost to be immediately charged against sales—not as an unexpired cost to be held back as inventory and charged against sales later as part of cost of goods sold.

EXHIBIT 4-10

Comparison of Flow of Costs

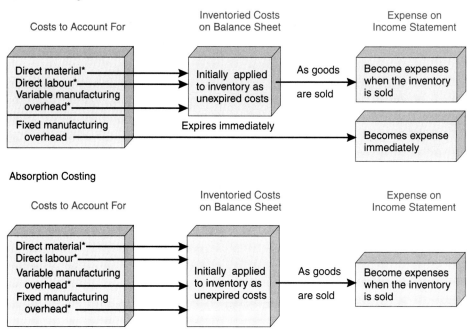

*As goods are manufactured, the costs are "applied" to inventory, usually via the use of unit costs.

Variable costing is also called *direct costing*. However, this is a misnomer because the inventorying of costs is not confined to only "direct" materials and labour; it also includes an "indirect" cost—the *variable* manufacturing overhead. Such confusion is unfortunate but apparently unavoidable in a field such as management accounting, where new analytical ideas or approaches arise in isolated fashion. Newly coined terms, which may not be accurately descriptive, often become embedded too deeply to be supplanted later.

Consider Exhibit 4-10. Note that the primary difference between variable and absorption costing is the accounting for fixed manufacturing overhead.

Absorption costing is more widely used than variable costing. However, the growing use of the contribution approach in performance measurement and cost analysis has led to the increasing use of variable costing for internal reporting purposes. Many major firms use variable costing for some internal reporting, and nearly 25 percent of firms use it as the primary internal format.

For external purposes, the use of variable costing is much more restricted. The *CICA Handbook* states that cost of inventories should include "the laid-down cost of material plus the cost of direct labour applied to the product and the applicable share of overhead expense properly chargeable to production."[1] Thus, the *CICA Handbook* advocates absorption costing. However, Canada Revenue Agency's position is somewhat more flexible as noted in the following:

> In the case of inventories of work-in-process and finished goods, cost means the laid-down cost of materials plus the cost of direct labour applied to the product and the applicable share of overhead expense properly chargeable to production. Either direct costing, which allocates variable overheads to inventory, or absorption costing, which allocates

Canada Revenue Agency
(CRA)
http://www.cra-arc.gc.ca/

---

[1] *CICA Handbook*, section 3030, paragraph .06.

both variable and fixed overheads to inventory, is acceptable as a method of costing inventory.... In some manufacturing organizations only standard costs are developed. In such cases, "standard cost" is an acceptable basis for inventory valuation provided that there is no significant variation between the aggregate standard costs and the aggregate actual costs properly applicable to the inventory.[2]

Use of variable costing for internal reporting traditionally has been expensive. It requires information to be processed two ways—one for external reporting and one for internal reporting. The increasing use and decreasing cost of computers has reduced the added cost of a variable costing system. Most managers no longer face the question of whether to invest in a separate variable costing *system*. Rather, they simply choose a variable-costing or absorption-costing *format* for reports. Many well-designed accounting systems used today can produce either format.

An Illustration of Variable and Absorption Costing

To make these ideas more concrete, consider the following example. In 2006 and 2007, the Greenberg Company had the following costs for production of its single product:

BASIC PRODUCTION DATA AT STANDARD COST	
Direct material	$1.30
Direct labour	1.50
Variable manufacturing overhead	.20
Variable costs per unit	$3.00

Fixed manufacturing overhead (fixed factory overhead) was budgeted at $150,000. Expected (or budgeted) production in each year is 150,000 units, and the sales price is $5 per unit. For simplicity, we will assume that there is a $0.20 per unit variable manufacturing overhead and that both budgeted and actual selling and administrative expenses are fixed at $65,000 yearly, except for sales commissions at 5 percent of dollar sales. Actual product quantities are:

	2006	2007
In units:		
Opening inventory	–	30,000
Production	170,000	140,000
Sales	140,000	160,000
Ending inventory	30,000	10,000

We will also assume that the standard variable manufacturing costs and fixed manufacturing overhead were incurred as budgeted.

Based on this information, we can

1. Prepare income statements for 2006 and 2007 under variable costing.
2. Prepare income statements for 2006 and 2007 under absorption costing.

---

[2] Canada Revenue Agency, Interpretation Bulletin IT-473R (December 1998), "Inventory Valuation," paragraphs 12 and 14. Reproduced with permission of the Minister of Public Works and Government Services Canada, 2006.

3. Show a reconciliation of the difference in operating income for 2006, 2007, and the two years as a whole.

Variable Costing Method Illustration

We begin by preparing income statements under variable costing. The variable costing statement shown in Exhibit 4-11 has the same format that was introduced earlier. The only new characteristic of Exhibit 4-11 is the presence of a detailed calculation of cost of goods sold, which is affected by changes in the beginning and ending inventories.

The costs of the product are accounted for by applying all *variable* manufacturing costs to the goods produced at a rate of $3 per unit; thus inventories are valued at the total variable costs. In contrast, fixed manufacturing costs are not applied to any products but are regarded as expenses in the period they are incurred.

Before reading on, be sure to trace the facts from the illustrative problem to the presentation in Exhibit 4-11, step by step. Note that both variable cost of goods sold and variable selling and administrative expense are deducted in computing the contribution margin. However, variable selling and administrative expense is not inventoriable. It is affected only by the level of sales, not by changes in inventory.

Absorption Costing Method Illustration

Fixed Overhead Rate. The amount of fixed manufacturing overhead applied to each unit of production. It is determined by dividing the budgeted fixed overhead by the expected volume of production for the budget period.

Exhibit 4-12 shows the absorption-costing framework. As you can see, it differs from the variable costing format in three ways.

First, the unit product cost used for computing cost of goods sold is $4, not $3. Why? Because fixed manufacturing overhead of $1 is added to the $3 variable manufacturing cost. The $1 of fixed manufacturing overhead applied to each unit is the **fixed overhead rate**. It is determined by dividing the budgeted fixed overhead by the expected volume of production for the budget period:

$$\text{fixed overhead rate} = \frac{\text{budgeted fixed manufacturing overhead}}{\text{expected volume of production}} = \frac{\$150,000}{150,000 \text{ units}} = \$1$$

EXHIBIT 4-11

Variable Costing
GREENBERG COMPANY
Comparative Income Statements for the Years 2006 and 2007 (in thousands of dollars)

		2006		2007	
Sales, 140,000 and 160,000 units, respectively (1)			$700		$800
Variable expenses:					
Variable manufacturing cost of goods sold					
Opening inventory, at standard variable cost of $3	$ –			$ 90	
Add: Variable cost of goods manufactured at standard, 170,000 and 140,000 units, respectively	510			420	
Available for sale, 170,000 units in each year	$510			$510	
Deduct: Ending inventory, at standard variable cost of $3	90*			30†	
Variable manufacturing cost of goods sold	$420			$480	
Variable selling expenses, at 5% of dollar sales	35			40	
Total variable expenses (2)			455		520
Contribution margin (3) = (1) − (2)			$245		$280
Fixed expenses:					
Fixed factory overhead	150			150	
Fixed selling and administrative expenses	65			65	
Total fixed expenses (4)			215		215
Operating income (3) − (4)			$ 30		$ 65

* 30,000 units × $3 = $90,000.
† 10,000 units × $3 = $30,000.

EXHIBIT 4-12

Absorption Costing
**GREENBERG
COMPANY**
Comparative Income
Statements for the Years
2006 and 2007 (in
thousands of dollars)

	2006	2007
Sales	$700	$800
Cost of goods sold:		
Opening inventory, at absorption cost of $4*	$ –	$120
Cost of goods manufactured at $4	680	560
Available for sale	680	680
Deduct: Ending inventory at absorption cost of $4*	120	40
Cost of goods sold	560	640
Gross profit	$140	$160
Production volume variance†	20 F	10 U
Gross margin or gross profit, at "actual"	160	150
Selling and administrative expenses	100	105
Operating income	$60	$45

* Variable cost	$3
Fixed cost ($150,000 ÷ 150,000)	1
Absorption cost	$4

† Computation of production volume variance based on expected volume of production of 150,000 units:

2006	$20,000 F	(170,000 – 150,000) × $1
2007	10,000 U	(140,000 – 150,000) × $1
Two years together	$10,000 F	(310,000 – 300,000) × $1

U = Unfavourable; F = Favourable.

Second, fixed factory overhead does not appear as a separate line in an absorption costing income statement. Instead, the fixed factory overhead is included in two places: as part of the cost of goods sold and as a *production volume variance*. A **production volume variance** (which is explained in more detail later) appears whenever actual production deviates from the expected volume of production used in computing the fixed overhead rate:

production volume variance = (actual volume – expected volume) × fixed-overhead rate

Finally, the format for an absorption costing income statement separates costs into the major categories of *manufacturing* and *nonmanufacturing*. In contrast, a variable costing income statement separates costs into the major categories of *fixed* and *variable*. In an absorption costing statement, revenue less *manufacturing* cost (both fixed and variable) is *gross profit* or *gross margin*. In a variable costing statement, revenue less all *variable* costs (both manufacturing and nonmanufacturing) is the *contribution margin*. This difference is illustrated by a condensed comparison of 2007 income statements (in thousands of dollars):

Production Volume Variance. A variance that appears whenever actual production deviates from the expected volume of production used in computing the fixed-overhead rate. It is calculated as (actual volume – expected volume) × fixed-overhead rate.

VARIABLE COSTING		ABSORPTION COSTING	
Revenue	$800	Revenue	$800
All variable costs	520	All manufacturing costs*	650
Contribution margin	280	Gross margin	150
All fixed costs	215	All nonmanufacturing costs	105
Operating income	$ 65	Operating income	$ 45

* Absorption cost of goods sold plus production volume variance.

Despite the importance of such differences in most industries, more and more firms are not concerned with the choice between variable and absorption costing. Why? Because they have implemented just-in-time production methods

Some accountants claim that the production-volume variance is a good measure of how well a company uses its capacity: Favourable (unfavourable) variances imply effective (ineffective) use of capacity. As a manager, be careful not to fall into that trap. Why?

ANSWER

The production volume variance tells you one thing and only one thing—whether actual production was above or below the predicted volume used in setting the fixed-overhead rate. If a manager can avoid an unfavourable production-volume variance by lowering the price enough to use up the idle capacity but the result is a decline in contribution margin (i.e., the new price is less than the variable cost), this would not be an effective use of the capacity. If a favourable production-volume variance occurs because excess production is being forced through, despite quality declines or other inefficiencies caused by overburdened production facilities, the "favourable" variance is certainly not desirable.

and sharply reduced inventory levels. There is no difference between variable costing and absorption costing income if the inventory level does not change, and companies with little inventory generally experience only insignificant changes in inventory.

Reconciliation of Variable Costing and Absorption Costing

Exhibit 4-13 reconciles the operating incomes shown in Exhibits 4-11 and 4-12. The difference in those two earlier exhibits is explained by multiplying the fixed-overhead product-costing rate by the *change* in the total units in the beginning and ending inventories. Consider 2007: the change in units was 20,000, so the difference in net income would be 20,000 units multiplied by $1 = $20,000.

The difference in income also equals the difference in the total amount of fixed manufacturing overhead charged as expense during a given year. (See Exhibits 4-14 and 4-15.) The $150,000 fixed manufacturing overhead incurred in 2007 is automatically the amount recognized as an expense on a variable costing income statement.

EXHIBIT 4-13		2006	2007	TOGETHER
Reconciliation of Operating Income Under Variable Costing and Absorption Costing	Operating income under			
	Absorption costing (see Exhibit 4-12)	$60,000	$ 45,000	$105,000
	Variable costing (see Exhibit 4-11)	−30,000	−65,000	−95,000
	Difference to be explained	$30,000	$ −20,000	$ 10,000
	The difference can be reconciled by multiplying the fixed-overhead rate by the change in the total inventory units:			
	Fixed-overhead rate	$1	$1	$1
	Change in inventory units:			
	Opening inventory	–	30,000	–
	Ending inventory	30,000	10,000	10,000
	Change	30,000	−20,000	10,000
	Difference in operating income explained	$30,000	$ −20,000	$ 10,000

EXHIBIT 4-14

Flow of Fixed Manufacturing Costs During 2007 (Format Derived from Exhibit 4-10)

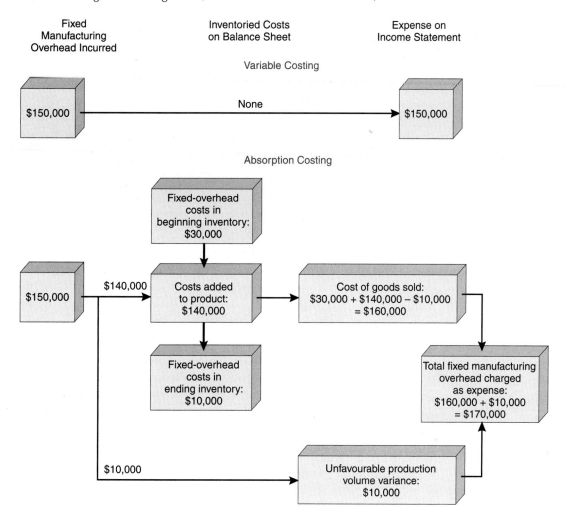

Under absorption costing, fixed manufacturing overhead appears in two places: cost of goods sold and production volume variance. Note that $30,000 of these fixed costs were incurred before 2007 and held over in the beginning inventory. During 2007, $140,000 of fixed manufacturing overhead was added to inventory, and $10,000 was still lodged in the ending inventory of 2007. Thus, the fixed manufacturing overhead included in cost of goods sold for 2007 was $30,000 + $140,000 − $10,000 = $160,000. In addition, the production-volume variance is $10,000 unfavourable. The total fixed manufacturing overhead charged as expenses under absorption costing is $170,000, or $20,000 more than the $150,000 charged under variable costing. Therefore, 2007 variable-costing income is higher by $20,000.

Remember that it is the relationship between sales and production that determines the difference between variable costing and absorption costing income. Whenever sales exceed production, that is, when inventory decreases, variable costing income is greater than absorption costing income. When production exceeds sales and inventory increases, variable costing income is less than absorption costing income.

Chapter 4   Cost Management Systems **157**

EXHIBIT 4-15

VARIABLE COSTING

No fixed overhead carried over from 2006

Fixed overhead actually incurred in 2007	$150,000	──────────────→	$150,000

ABSORPTION COSTING

		UNITS	DOLLARS
Fixed overhead in beginning inventory	$ 30,000	30,000	$ 30,000
Fixed overhead incurred in 2007	150,000		
To account for:	$180,000		
Applied to product, 140,000 @ $1		140,000	140,000
Available for sale		170,000	$170,000
Contained in cost of goods sold	$160,000	160,000	160,000 → $160,000
In ending inventory	10,000	10,000	$ 10,000
Not applied, so becomes unfavourable			
production volume variance		10,000	──────→ 10,000
Fixed factory overhead charged			
against 2007 operations			$170,000
Accounted for, as above	$180,000		
Difference in operating income			
occurs because $170,000 expires			
rather than $150,000			$ 20,000

Why Use Variable Costing?

Why do many companies use variable costing for internal statements? One reason is that absorption costing operating income is affected by production volume, while variable costing income is not. Consider the 2007 absorption costing statement in Exhibit 4-12 that shows operating income of $45,000. Suppose a manager decides to produce 10,000 additional units in December 2007 even though they will remain unsold. Will this affect operating income? First, note that the gross profit will not change. Why? Because it is based on sales, not production. However, the production volume variance will change:

$$\text{If production} = 140,000 \text{ units}$$
$$\text{Production volume variance} = (150,000 - 140,000) \times \$1 = \$10,000 \text{ U}$$
$$\text{If production} = 150,000 \text{ units}$$
$$\text{Production volume variance} = (150,000 - 150,000) \times \$1 = 0$$

Because there is no production volume variance when 150,000 units are produced, the new operating income equals gross profit less selling and administrative expenses, $160,000 − $105,000 = $55,000. Therefore, increasing *production* by 10,000 units without any increase in *sales* increases absorption costing operating income by $10,000, from $45,000 to $55,000.

How will such an increase in production affect the variable costing statement in Exhibit 4-11? Nothing will change. Production does not affect operating income under variable costing.

Suppose the evaluation of a manager's performance is based heavily on operating income. If the company uses the absorption costing approach, a manager might be tempted to produce unneeded units just to increase reported operating income as the increase in inventory would absorb some of the overhead costs rather than being expensed. No such temptation exists with variable costing.

Companies also choose variable or absorption costing based on which system they believe gives a better signal about performance. A sales-oriented company may prefer variable costing because its income is affected primarily by the level of sales. In contrast, a production-oriented company (e.g., a company that can easily sell all the units it produces) might prefer absorption costing. Why? Because additional production increases the operating income with absorption costing but not with variable costing.

Variable Costing, Segmented Reporting, and Performance Evaluation

Variable costing is a useful tool in evaluating management's performance and a business division's (segment's) performance. Reporting the contribution of a business unit or segment to the organization is called segmented reporting. A segment can be considered as any business unit that is important enough to warrant a segmented reporting.

Variable costing is better suited than absorption costing to evaluate a business unit. Variable costing allows us to evaluate the contributions to the company's profitability of various product lines, divisions, departments, or business units. Decisions such as to drop or keep a product line and to continue operating or leave a specific market may depend on accurate segmented reporting. Knowing how profitable a business unit really is allows managers to focus on divisions with problematic profitability, to eliminate units that have been unprofitable, and to concentrate on more profitable business divisions. This may lead to an overall greater profitability for the entire firm.

Evaluation of divisional managers should be based on their managerial ability. Profitability of a business segment is often used as evidence of managerial ability. However, income and profitability are not always due to managerial effort. Favourable market conditions such as customer demand, lack of substitute products, and inferior competition may augment a division's profits. However, when managers work to increase their units' sales while keeping costs in line, profits usually rise.

Variable costing establishes an association between divisional sales and the contribution of the division to the firm. The product cost under variable costing is equal to a cost that varies according to the volume of sales. Variable costs are controllable by the divisional manager. Yet, divisional managers should not be held accountable for fixed costs that they cannot control. This is why variable costing is a good method to evaluate managerial and segmented performance.

In absorption costing, the product cost includes a fixed cost component allocated on the basis of the predetermined overhead rate. This fixed cost component is not under the control of a divisional manager and does not create a cause-effect relationship between the skills of the manager and the fixed cost component. Therefore, absorption costing that includes a fixed component in the product cost and determines net income after fixed costs are taken into account is not an appropriate method to evaluate managers.

Under variable costing an effort can be made to identify what portion of the total fixed company costs are attributable to each division. Fixed costs that owe their existence to more than one division are allocated to an overall corporate account.

We can see in Exhibit 4-16 that the variable-costing method is superior to absorption costing with regards to segmented reporting. The contribution margins

EXHIBIT 4-16

VIDEO ARTS LIMITED
Segmented Reporting
for 2006

	AUDIO DIVISION	VIDEO DIVISION	TOTAL
Sales	$550,000	$450,000	$1,000,000
Less variable expenses			
Variable costs of goods sold	300,000	350,000	650,000
Variable selling & administrative expenses	50,000	25,000	75,000
Contribution margin	200,000	75,000	275,000
Less traceable/allocated fixed expenses			
Fixed overhead	$20,000	$30,000	$50,000
Selling & administrative expenses	20,000	50,000	70,000
Segment margin	$160,000	$(5,000)	$155,000
Less common unallocated fixed expenses			
Common overhead costs			$40,000
Common selling & administrative expenses			15,000
Net income			$100,000

indicate that the audio and video divisions positively contribute toward the firm's fixed costs $200,000 and $75,000, respectively. However, after the allocation of traceable expenses to divisions' fixed costs, the audio division remains profitable with a $160,000 segment margin while the video division is losing $5,000. That means that the audio division helps to recover the common costs of the company to the tune of $160,000. However, the video division is $5,000 short when covering its allocated fixed costs and, as a result, drags down the company profits by the same amount. The allocation of the common costs to the corporate account further reduces the corporate profits to $100,000.

The segment margin loss makes the video division a candidate to be dropped. The overall profitability of the company would increase by $5,000 assuming that the dropping of the video division would have no negative impact on the sales of the audio division. The segment margin is the true measure of evaluating the performance of the two divisions.

HIGHLIGHTS TO REMEMBER

1. **Describe the purposes of cost management systems.** Cost management systems provide cost information for external financial reporting, for strategic decision making, and for operational cost control.

2. **Explain the relationship among cost, cost object, cost accumulation, and cost assignment.** Cost accounting systems provide cost information about various types of objectives—products, customers, activities, and so on. To do this, a system first accumulates resource costs by natural classifications such as materials, labour, and energy. Then it assigns these costs to cost objects, either tracing them directly or assigning them indirectly through allocation.

3. **Distinguish among direct, indirect, and unallocated costs.** Accountants can specifically and exclusively identify direct costs with a cost object in an economically feasible way. When this is not possible, accountants may allocate costs to cost objects using a cost driver. Such costs are called indirect costs. The greater the proportion of direct costs,

the greater the accuracy of the cost system. When the proportion of indirect costs is significant, accountants must take care to find the most appropriate cost drivers. Some costs are unallocated because the accountants can determine no plausible and reliable relationship between resources costs and cost objects.

4. **Explain how the financial statements of merchandisers and manufacturers differ because of the types of goods they sell.** The primary difference between the financial statements of a merchandiser and a manufacturer is the reporting of inventories. A merchandiser has only one type of inventory whereas a manufacturer has three types of inventory—raw materials, work-in-process, and finished goods.

5. **Construct an income statement using the variable-costing approach.** Two major methods of product costing are variable (contribution approach) and absorption costing. The variable-costing method emphasizes the effects of cost behaviour on income. This method excludes fixed manufacturing overhead from the cost of products and expenses it immediately.

6. **Construct an income statement using the absorption-costing approach.** The absorption or traditional approach ignores cost behaviour distinctions. As a result, all costs incurred in the production of goods becomes part of the inventory cost. Thus, we add fixed manufacturing overhead to inventory and it appears on the income statement only when the company sells the goods.

7. **Explain why a company might prefer to use a variable-costing approach.** Companies that use operating income to measure results usually prefer variable costing. This is because changes in production volume affect absorption-costing income but not variable-costing income. A company that wants to focus managers' energies on sales would prefer to use variable costing, since the level of sales is the primary driver of variable-costing income.

DEMONSTRATION PROBLEMS FOR YOUR REVIEW

Problem One

1. Review the illustrations in Exhibits 4-6 through 4-9. Suppose that all variable costs fluctuate in direct proportion to units produced and sold and that all fixed costs are unaffected over a wide range of production and sales. What would operating income have been if sales (at normal selling prices) had been $20.9 million instead of $20.0 million? Which statement—the absorption income statement or the contribution income statement—did you use as a framework for your answer? Why?

2. Suppose employee training (Exhibit 4-6) was regarded as a variable rather than a fixed cost at a rate of $90,000 per 1,000,000 units, or $0.09 per unit. How would your answer in part 1 change?

Solution

1. Operating income would increase from $1,000,000 to $1,310,500, computed as follows:

Increase in revenue			$ 900,000
Ratio in total contribution income statement			
(Exhibit 4-9) is $6,900,000 ÷ $20,000,000 = 0.345			
Ratio times revenue increase is 0.345 × $900,000			$ 310,500
Increase in fixed expenses			0
Operating income before increase			1,000,000
New operating income			$1,310,500

Computations are easily made by using data from the contribution income statement. In contrast, the traditional absorption costing income statement must be analyzed and divided into variable and fixed categories before the effect on operating income can be estimated.

2. The contribution-margin ratio would be lower because the variable costs would be higher by $0.09 per unit:

$$(\$6,900,000 - \$90,000) \div \$20,000,000 = 0.3405$$

	GIVEN LEVEL	HIGHER LEVEL	DIFFERENCE
Revenue	$20,000,000	$20,900,000	$900,000
Variable expenses ($13,100,000 + $90,000)	13,190,000	13,783,550	593,550
Contribution margin at 0.3405	$ 6,810,000	$ 7,116,450	$306,450
Fixed expenses ($5,900,000 − $90,000)	5,810,000	5,810,000	–
Operating income	$ 1,000,000	$ 1,306,450	$306,450

Problem Two

1. Reconsider Exhibits 4-11 and 4-12. Suppose production in 2007 was 145,000 units instead of 140,000 units, but sales were 160,000 units. Assume that the net variances for all variable-manufacturing costs were $37,000, unfavourable. Regard these variances as adjustments to the cost of goods sold. Also assume that actual fixed costs were $157,000. Prepare income statements for 2007 under variable costing and under absorption costing.
2. Explain why operating income was different under variable costing and absorption costing. Show your calculations.
3. Without regard to requirement 1, would variable costing or absorption costing give a manager more leeway in influencing short-run operating income through production-scheduling decisions? Why?

Solution

1. See Exhibits 4-17 and 4-18 on the next page. Note that the ending inventory will be 15,000 units instead of 10,000 units.
2. Decline in inventory levels is 30,000 – 15,000, or 15,000 units. The fixed-overhead rate per unit in absorption costing is $1. Therefore, $15,000 more fixed overhead was charged against operations under absorption costing than under variable costing. The variable costing statement shows fixed factory overhead of $157,000, whereas the absorption costing statement includes fixed factory overhead in three places: $160,000

EXHIBIT 4-17

GREENBERG
COMPANY
Income Statement
(Variable Costing) for
the Year 2007
(in thousands of dollars)

Sales		$800
Opening inventory, at variable cost of $3	$ 90	
Add: Variable cost of goods manufactured	435	
Available for sale	$525	
Deduct: Ending inventory, at variable cost of $3	45	
Variable cost of goods sold		$480
Net variances for all variable costs, unfavourable		37
Variable cost of goods sold, at actual		$517
Variable selling expenses, at 5% of dollar sales		40
Total variable costs charged against sales		557
Contribution margin		$243
Fixed factory overhead		$157*
Fixed selling and administrative expenses		65
Total fixed expenses		222
Operating income		$ 21†

* This could be shown in two lines, $150,000 budget plus $7,000 variance.
† The difference between this and the $65,000 operating income in Exhibit 4-11 occurs because of the $37,000 unfavourable variable-cost variances and the $7,000 unfavourable fixed-cost variance.

EXHIBIT 4-18

GREENBERG
COMPANY
Income Statement
(Absorption Costing)
for the Year 2007
(in thousands of dollars)

Sales		$800
Opening inventory, at cost of $4	$120	
Cost of goods manufactured	580	
Available for sale	$700	
Deduct: Ending inventory	60	
Cost of goods sold	$640	
Net flexible-budget variances for all variable manufacturing costs, unfavourable	$37	
Fixed factory overhead flexible-budget variance, unfavourable	7	
Production volume variance, unfavourable	5*	
Total variances	49	
Cost of goods sold, at actual		689
Gross profit, at actual		$111
Selling and administrative expenses:		
Variable	40	
Fixed	65	105
Operating income		$ 6†

* Production volume variance is $1 × (150,000 denominator volume − 145,000 actual production).
† The difference between this and the $45,000 operating income in Exhibit 4-12 occurs because of the $37,000 unfavourable variable-cost variances, the $7,000 unfavourable fixed-cost variance, and the $5,000 favourable difference in (lower) production-volume variance.

in cost of goods sold, $7,000 U in fixed factory overhead flexible-budget variances, and $5,000 U as a production volume variance, for a total of $172,000. Generally, when inventories decline, absorption costing will show less income than variable costing; when inventories rise, absorption costing will show more income than variable costing.

3. Some versions of absorption costing will give a manager more leeway in influencing operating income via production scheduling. Operating income will fluctuate in harmony with changes in net sales under variable costing, but it is influenced by both production and sales under absorption costing. For example, compare variable costing in Exhibits 4-11 and 4-17. As the second note to Exhibit 4-17 indicates, the operating income may be affected by assorted variances (but not the production-volume variance) under variable costing, but production scheduling *per se* will have no effect on operating income.

As the note to Exhibit 4-18 explains, production scheduling and sales influence operating income. Production was 145,000 rather than 140,000 units. So, $5,000 of fixed overhead became a part of ending inventory (an asset) instead of part of the production volume variance (an expense)—that is, the production volume variance is $5,000 lower and the ending inventory contains $5,000 more fixed overhead. The manager adds $1 to 2007 operating income with each unit of production under absorption costing, even if the unit is not sold.

KEY TERMS

absorption approach *p. 148*	fixed overhead rate *p. 154*
contribution approach *p. 149*	idle time *p. 139*
conversion costs *p. 143*	indirect costs *p. 138*
cost *p. 136*	indirect labour *p. 138*
cost accounting *p. 136*	indirect manufacturing costs *p. 143*
cost object *p. 136*	manufacturing overhead *p. 143*
direct costs *p. 138*	overtime premium *p. 139*
direct-labour costs *p. 142*	period costs *p. 140*
direct-materials costs *p. 142*	prime costs *p. 143*
employee benefit costs *p. 139*	product costs *p. 140*
factory overhead costs *p. 143*	production volume variance *p. 155*

ASSIGNMENT MATERIAL

QUESTIONS

Q4-1 Name four cost objects.

Q4-2 What is the major purpose of detailed cost accounting systems?

Q4-3 "Departments are not cost objects or objects of costing." Do you agree? Explain.

Q4-4 "The same cost can be direct and indirect." Do you agree? Explain.

Q4-5 "Economic feasibility is an important guideline in designing cost accounting systems." Do you agree? Explain.

Q4-6 How does the idea of economic feasibility relate to the distinction between direct and indirect costs?

Q4-7 "The typical accounting system does not allocate selling and administrative costs to units produced." Do you agree? Explain.

Q4-8 Distinguish between prime costs and conversion costs.

Q4-9 "For a furniture manufacturer, glue and tacks become an integral part of the finished product, so they would be direct material." Do you agree? Explain.

Q4-10 Many cost accounting systems have a twofold instead of a threefold category of manufacturing costs. What is a common name for the second item in the twofold category?

Q4-11 "Amortization is an expense for financial statement purposes." Do you agree? Explain.

Q4-12 Distinguish between "costs" and "expenses."

Q4-13 "Unexpired costs are always inventory costs." Do you agree? Explain.

Q4-14 Why is there no direct labour inventory account on a manufacturing company's balance sheet?

Q4-15 What is the advantage of the contribution approach compared with the absorption approach?

Q4-16 Distinguish between manufacturing and merchandising.

Q4-17 "The primary classifications of costs are by variable- and fixed-cost behaviour patterns, not by business functions." Name three commonly used terms that describe this type of income statement.

Q4-18 "With variable costing, only direct material and direct labour are inventoried." Do you agree? Why?

Q4-19 "Absorption costing regards more categories of costs as product costs." Explain. Be specific.

Q4-20 "An increasing number of companies should not be using variable costing in their corporate annual reports." Do you agree? Explain.

Q4-21 Why is variable costing used only for internal reporting and not for external financial reporting?

Q4-22 Compare the contribution margin with the gross margin.

Q4-23 How is fixed overhead applied to products?

Q4-24 Name the three ways that an absorption-costing format differs from a variable costing format.

Q4-25 "Variable costing is consistent with cost-volume-profit analysis." Explain.

PROBLEMS

P4-1 **MEANING OF TECHNICAL TERMS.** Refer to Exhibit 4-4. Give the amounts of the following with respect to the cost of goods available for sale: (1) prime costs, (2) conversion costs, (3) factory overhead, and (4) indirect manufacturing costs.

P4-2 **PRESENCE OF ENDING WORK-IN-PROCESS.** Refer to Exhibits 4-4 and 4-5. Suppose manufacturing costs were the same, but there was an ending work-in-process inventory of $3 million. The cost of the completed goods would therefore be $37 million instead of $40 million. Suppose also that the cost of goods sold is unchanged.

1. Recast the income statement of Exhibit 4-4.
2. What lines and ending balances would change in Exhibit 4-5 and by how much?

P4-3 **RELATING COSTS TO COST OBJECTS.** A company uses an absorption cost system. Prepare headings for two columns: (1) assembly department costs, and (2) products assembled. Fill in the two columns for each of the costs below. If a specific cost is direct to the department but indirect to the product, place a D in column 1 and an I in column 2. The costs are materials used, supplies used, assembly labour, material-handling labour (transporting materials between and within departments), amortization (building), assembly supervisor's salary, and the building and grounds supervisor's salary.

P4-4 **CLASSIFICATION OF MANUFACTURING COSTS.** Classify each of the following as direct or indirect (D or I) with respect to traceability to product and as variable or fixed (V or F) with respect to whether the cost fluctuates in total as activity or volume changes over wide ranges of activity. You will have two answers, D or I and V or F, for each of the 10 items.

1. Supervisor training program
2. Abrasives (sandpaper, etc.)
3. Cutting bits in a machinery department
4. Food for a factory cafeteria
5. Factory rent
6. Salary of a factory storeroom clerk
7. Workers' compensation insurance in a factory
8. Cement for a roadbuilder
9. Steel scrap for a blast furnace
10. Paper towels for a factory washroom

P4-5 **INVENTORY TRANSACTIONS.** Review Exhibit 4-5. Assume that the Slider Company had no beginning inventories. The following transactions occurred in 2006 (in thousands):

1. Purchase of direct materials	$350
2. Direct materials used	300
3. Acquire direct labour	160
4. Acquire factory overhead	200
5. Complete all goods that were started	?
6. Cost of goods sold (half of the goods completed were sold)	?

Prepare an analysis similar to Exhibit 4-5. What are the ending balances of direct materials, work-in-process, and finished goods inventory?

P4-6 **INVENTORY TRANSACTIONS.** Refer to the preceding problem. Suppose some goods were still in process that cost $100,000. Half the goods completed were sold. What are the balances of all the accounts in the ending balance sheet?

P4-7 **STRAIGHTFORWARD ABSORPTION STATEMENT.** The Pierce Company had the following data (in thousands) for a given period:

Sales	$700
Direct materials	210
Direct labour	150
Indirect manufacturing costs	170
Selling and administrative expenses	150

There were no beginning or ending inventories. Compute the (1) manufacturing cost of goods sold, (2) gross profit, (3) operating income, (4) prime cost, and (5) conversion cost.

P4-8 STRAIGHTFORWARD CONTRIBUTION INCOME STATEMENT. Yoko Trucks Ltd. had the following data (in millions of yen) for a given period:

Sales	¥770
Direct materials	290
Direct labour	140
Variable factory overhead	60
Variable selling and administrative expenses	100
Fixed factory overhead	120
Fixed selling and administrative expenses	45

There were no beginning or ending inventories. Compute the (1) variable manufacturing cost of goods sold, (2) contribution margin, and (3) operating income.

P4-9 STRAIGHTFORWARD ABSORPTION AND CONTRIBUTION STATEMENT.
Anzola Company had the following data (in millions of dollars) for a recent period. Fill in the blanks. There were no beginning or ending inventories.

a.	Sales	$920
b.	Direct materials used	350
c.	Direct labour	210
	Factory overhead:	
d.	Variable	100
e.	Fixed	50
f.	Variable manufacturing cost of goods sold	–
g.	Manufacturing cost of goods sold	–
	Selling and administrative expenses:	
h.	Variable	90
i.	Fixed	80
j.	Gross profit	–
k.	Contribution margin	–
l.	Prime costs	–
m.	Conversion costs	–
n.	Operating income	–

P4-10 ABSORPTION STATEMENT. Raynard's Jewellery had the following data (in thousands) for a given period. Assume there are no inventories. Fill in the blanks.

Sales	$ –
Direct materials	370
Direct labour	–
Factory overhead	–
Manufacturing cost of goods sold	780
Gross margin	120
Selling and administrative expense	–
Operating income	20
Conversion costs	–
Prime costs	600

P4-11 **CONTRIBUTION INCOME STATEMENT.** Marlinski had the following data (in thousands) for a given period. Assume there are no inventories.

Direct labour	$170
Direct materials	210
Variable factory overhead	110
Contribution margin	200
Fixed selling and administrative expenses	100
Operating income	10
Sales	970

Compute the (1) variable manufacturing cost of goods sold, (2) variable selling and administrative expenses, and (3) fixed factory overhead.

P4-12 **FINANCIAL STATEMENTS FOR MANUFACTURING AND MERCHANDISING COMPANIES.** Outdoor Equipment Company (OEC) and Mountain Supplies Inc. (MSI) sell tents. OEC purchases its tents from a manufacturer for $90 each and sells them for $120. It purchased 10,000 tents in 2006.

MSI produces its own tents. In 2006 MSI produced 10,000 tents. Costs were

Direct materials purchased		$ 535,000
Direct materials used		$ 520,000
Direct labour		260,000
Factory overhead:		
Amortization	$40,000	
Indirect labour	50,000	
Other	30,000	120,000
Total cost of production		$ 900,000

Assume that MSI had no beginning inventory of direct materials. There was no beginning inventory of finished tents, but ending inventory consisted of 1,000 finished tents. Ending work-in-process inventory was negligible.

Each company sold 9,000 tents for $1,080,000 in 2006 and incurred the following selling and administrative costs:

Sales salaries and commissions	$ 90,000
Amortization on retail store	30,000
Advertising	20,000
Other	10,000
Total selling and administrative cost	$150,000

1. Prepare the inventories section of the balance sheet for December 31, 2006, for OEC.
2. Prepare the inventories section of the balance sheet for December 31, 2006, for MSI.
3. Using Exhibit 4-4 as a model, prepare an income statement for the year 2006, for OEC.
4. Using Exhibit 4-4 as a model, prepare an income statement for the year 2006, for MSI.

5. Summarize the differences among the financial statements of OEC, a merchandiser, and MSI, a manufacturer.

P4-13 VARIABLE COSTS AND FIXED COSTS; MANUFACTURING AND OTHER COSTS. For each of the numbered items, choose the appropriate classifications for a manufacturing company. If in doubt about whether the cost behaviour is basically variable or fixed, decide on the basis of whether the total cost will fluctuate substantially over a wide range of volume. Most items have two answers among the following possibilities with respect to the cost of a particular job:

a. Selling cost
b. Manufacturing costs, direct
c. Manufacturing costs, indirect
d. General and administrative cost
e. Fixed cost
f. Variable cost
g. Other (specify)

Sample answers are

Direct material	b,f
President's salary	d,e
Bond interest expense	e,g (financial expense)

Items for your consideration:

1. Factory power for machines
2. Salespersons' commissions
3. Salespersons' salaries
4. Welding supplies
5. Fire loss
6. Sandpaper
7. Supervisory salaries, production control
8. Supervisory salaries, assembly department
9. Supervisory salaries, factory storeroom
10. Company picnic costs
11. Overtime premium, punch press
12. Idle time, assembly
13. Freight out
14. Property taxes
15. Paint for finished products
16. Heating and air conditioning, factory
17. Material-handling labour
18. Straight-line amortization, salespersons' automobiles

P4-14 CONTRIBUTION AND ABSORPTION INCOME STATEMENTS. The following information is taken from the records of the Kingland Company for the year ending December 31, 2006. There were no beginning or ending inventories.

Sales	$ 10,000,000	Long-term rent, factory	$ 100,000
Sales commissions	500,000	Factory superintendent's	
Advertising	200,000	salary	30,000
Shipping expenses	300,000	Supervisors' salaries	100,000
Administrative executive		Direct material used	4,000,000
salaries	100,000	Direct labour	2,000,000
Administrative clerical		Cutting bits used	60,000
salaries (variable)	400,000	Factory methods research	40,000
Fire insurance on		Abrasives for machining	100,000
factory equipment	2,000	Indirect labour	800,000
Property taxes on		Amortization on	
factory equipment	10,000	equipment	300,000

1. Prepare a contribution income statement and an absorption income statement. If you are in doubt about any cost-behaviour pattern, decide on the basis of whether the total cost in question will fluctuate substantially over a wide range of volume. Prepare a separate support schedule of indirect manufacturing costs subdivided between variable and fixed costs.

2. Suppose that all variable costs fluctuate directly in proportion to sales, and that fixed costs are unaffected over a wide range of sales. What would operating income have been if sales had been $10.5 million instead of $10.0 million? Which income statement did you use to help get your answer? Why?

P4-15 **SIMPLE COMPARISON OF VARIABLE AND ABSORPTION COSTING.** Ithalid Company began business on January 1, 2006, with assets of $150,000 cash and equity of $150,000 capital shares. In 2006 it manufactured some inventory at a cost of $60,000, including $12,000 for factory rent and other fixed factory overhead. In 2007 it manufactured nothing and sold half of its inventory for $42,000 cash. In 2008 it manufactured nothing and sold the remaining half for another $42,000 cash. It had no fixed expenses in 2007 or 2008. There are no other transactions of any kind. Ignore income taxes.

Prepare an ending balance sheet plus an income statement for 2006, 2007, and 2008 under (1) absorption costing and (2) variable costing.

P4-16 **COMPARISONS OVER FOUR YEARS.** The Balakrishnan Corporation began business on January 1, 2005, to produce and sell a single product. Reported operating income figures under both absorption and variable costing for the first four years of operation are

YEAR	VARIABLE COSTING	ABSORPTION COSTING
2005	$70,000	$50,000
2006	70,000	60,000
2007	50,000	50,000
2008	40,000	70,000

Standard production costs per unit, sales prices, application (absorption) rates, and expected-volume levels were the same each year. There were no cost variances in any year. All nonmanufacturing expenses were fixed, and there were no nonmanufacturing cost variances in any year.

1. In what year(s) did "units produced" equal "units sold"?
2. In what year(s) did "units produced" exceed "units sold"?
3. What is the dollar amount of the December 31, 2008, finished-goods inventory? (Give absorption costing value.)
4. What is the difference between "units produced" and "units sold" in 2008, if you know that the absorption-costing fixed-manufacturing-overhead application rate is $3 per unit? (Give answer in units.)

P4-17 VARIABLE AND ABSORPTION COSTING. Chan Company data for 2006 are as follows:

Sales: 12,000 units at $17 each	
Actual production	15,000 units
Expected volume of production	18,000 units
Manufacturing costs incurred:	
Variable	$105,000
Fixed	63,000
Nonmanufacturing costs incurred:	
Variable	$ 24,000
Fixed	18,000

1. Determine operating income for 2006, assuming the firm uses the variable costing approach to product costing. (Do not prepare a statement.)
2. Assume that there is no January 1, 2006, inventory; no variances are allocated to inventory; and the firm uses a "full absorption" approach to product costing. Compute (a) the cost assigned to December 31, 2006, inventory; and (b) operating income for the year ended December 31, 2006. (Do not prepare a statement.)

P4-18 COMPUTE PRODUCTION VOLUME VARIANCE. Osaka Manufacturing Company budgeted its 2006 variable overhead at ¥14,100,000 and its fixed overhead at ¥25,620,000. Expected 2006 volume was 6,100 units. Actual costs for production of 5,800 units during 2006 were

Variable overhead	¥14,160,000
Fixed overhead	25,620,000
Total overhead	¥39,780,000

Compute the production volume variance. Be sure to label it favourable or unfavourable.

P4-19 RECONCILING VARIABLE COSTING AND ABSORPTION COSTING OPERATING INCOME. Blackstone Tools produced 12,000 electric drills during 2006, although expected production was only 10,500 drills. The company's fixed overhead rate is $7 per drill. Absorption-costing operating income for the year is $18,000, based on sales of 11,000 drills.

1. Compute: (a) Budgeted fixed overhead
   (b) Production volume variance
   (c) Variable-costing operating income
2. Reconcile absorption costing operating income and variable-costing operating income. Include the amount of the difference between the two and an explanation for the difference.

P4-20 **COMPARING VARIABLE COSTING AND ABSORPTION COSTING.** Simple numbers are used in this problem to highlight the concepts covered in the chapter.

Assume that the Canberra Company produces one product—a bath mat—that sells for $10. Canberra uses a standard-cost system. Total standard variable costs of production are $4 per mat, fixed manufacturing costs are $1,500 per year, and selling and administrative expenses are $300 per year, all fixed. Expected production volume is 500 mats per year.

1. For each of the following nine combinations of actual sales and production (in units) for 2006, prepare condensed income statements under variable costing and under absorption costing.

	(1)	(2)	(3)	(4)	(5)	(6)	(7)	(8)	(9)
Sales units	300	400	500	400	500	600	500	600	700
Production units	400	400	400	500	500	500	600	600	600

Use the following formats:

VARIABLE COSTING		ABSORPTION COSTING	
Revenue	$ aa	Revenue	$ aa
Cost of goods sold	(bb)	Cost of goods sold	(uu)
Contribution margin	$ cc	Gross profit at standard	$ vv
Fixed manufacturing costs	(dd)	Favourable (unfavourable)	
Fixed selling and adminis-		production-volume variance	ww
trative expenses	(ee)	Gross profit at actual	$ xx
		Selling and administrative	
		expenses	(yy)
Operating income	$ ff	Operating income	$ zz

2. **a.** In which of the nine combinations is variable-costing income greater than absorption-costing income? In which is it lower? The same?
   b. In which of the nine combinations is the production volume variance unfavourable? Favourable?
   c. How much profit is added by selling one more unit under variable costing? Under absorption costing?
   d. How much profit is added by producing one more unit under variable costing? Under absorption costing?
   e. Suppose sales, rather than production, is the critical factor in determining the success of Canberra Company. Which format, variable costing or absorption costing, provides the better measure of performance?

P4-21 **ALL-FIXED COSTS.** The Marple Company has built a massive water-desalting factory next to an ocean. The factory is completely automated. It has its own source of power, light, heat, and so on. The salt water costs nothing. All producing and other operating costs are fixed; they do not vary with output because the volume is governed by adjusting a few dials on a control panel. The employees have flat annual salaries.

The desalted water is not sold to household consumers. It has a special taste that appeals to local breweries, distilleries, and soft-drink manufacturers. The price, $0.50 per litre, is expected to remain unchanged for quite some time.

The following are data regarding the first two years of operations:

	IN LITRES		COSTS (ALL FIXED)	
	SALES	PRODUCTION	MANUFACTURING	OTHER
2006	1,500,000	3,000,000	$600,000	$200,000
2007	1,500,000	0	600,000	200,000

Orders can be processed in four hours, so management decided, in early 2007, to gear production strictly to sales.

1. Prepare three-column income statements for 2006, for 2007, and for the two years together using (a) variable costing and (b) absorption costing.
2. What is the break-even point under (a) variable costing and (b) absorption costing?
3. What inventory costs would be carried on the balance sheets on December 31, 2006 and 2007, under each method?
4. Comment on your answers in requirements 1 and 2. Which costing method appears more useful?

P4-22 SEMIFIXED COSTS. The Carley Company differs from the Marple Company (described in Problem 4-21) in only one respect: it has both variable and fixed manufacturing costs. Its variable costs are $0.14 per litre and its fixed *manufacturing* costs are $390,000 per year.

1. Using the same data as in the preceding problem, except for the change in production-cost behaviour, prepare three-column income statements for 2006, for 2007 and for the two years together using (a) variable costing and (b) absorption costing.
2. What inventory costs would be carried on the balance sheets on December 31, 2006 and 2007, under each method?

P4-23 ABSORPTION AND VARIABLE COSTING. The Trapani Company had the following actual data for 2006 and 2007:

	2006	2007
Units of finished goods:		
Opening inventory	–	2,000
Production	15,000	13,000
Sales	13,000	14,000
Ending inventory	2,000	1,000

The basic production data at standard unit costs for the two years were

Direct materials	$22
Direct labour	18
Variable factory overhead	4
Standard variable costs per unit	$44

Fixed factory overhead was budgeted at $98,000 per year. The expected volume of production was 14,000 units, so the fixed overhead rate was $98,000 ÷ 14,000 = $7 per unit.

Budgeted sales price was $75 per unit. Selling and administrative expenses were budgeted at variable, *$9 per unit sold*, and fixed, $80,000 per year.

Assume that there were absolutely no variances from any standard variable costs, budgeted selling prices, or budgeted fixed costs in 2006.

There were no beginning or ending inventories of work-in-process.

1. For 2006, prepare income statements based on variable costing and absorption costing. (The next problem deals with 2007.)
2. Explain why operating income differs between variable costing and absorption costing. Be specific.

P4-24 **ABSORPTION AND VARIABLE COSTING.** Assume the same facts as in the preceding problem. In addition, consider the following actual data for 2007:

Direct materials	$285,000
Direct labour	174,200
Variable factory overhead	36,000
Fixed factory overhead	95,000
Selling and administrative costs:	
Variable	118,400
Fixed	80,000
Sales	1,068,000

1. For 2007, prepare income statements based on variable costing and absorption costing. Arrange your income statements in the following general format:
   Sales (at budgeted prices)
   Cost of goods sold
   Gross profit
   Selling and administrative costs
   Operating income before variances
   Variances (list in detail)
   Operating income
2. Explain why operating income differs between variable costing and absorption costing. Be specific.

P4-25 **EMPLOYEE BENEFIT COSTS.** Direct labour is often accounted for at the gross wage rate, and the related "benefit costs" such as employer payroll taxes and employer contributions to health care plans are accounted for as part of overhead. Suppose Amy O'Keefe, a direct labourer, works 40 hours during a particular week as an auditor for a public accounting firm. She receives $18 gross pay per hour plus related benefit costs of $10 per hour.

1. What would be the cost of O'Keefe's direct labour? Of related general overhead?
2. Suppose O'Keefe works 30 hours for Client A and 10 hours for Client B, and the firm allocates costs to each client. What would be the cost of O'Keefe's direct labour on the Client A job? The Client B job?
3. How would you allocate general overhead to the Client A job? The Client B job?
4. Suppose O'Keefe works a total of 50 hours (30 for A and 20 for B), 10 of which are paid on the basis of time-and-a-half. What would be the cost of O'Keefe's "direct labour" on the Client A job? The Client B job? The addition to general overhead?

P4-26 REVIEW OF CHAPTERS 2 THROUGH 4. The Gumey Hosiery Company provides you with the following miscellaneous data regarding operations in 2006.

Gross profit	$ 20,000
Net profit (loss)	(5,000)
Sales	100,000
Direct material used	35,000
Direct labour	25,000
Fixed manufacturing overhead	15,000
Fixed selling and administrative expenses	10,000

There are no beginning or ending inventories.
Compute the (1) variable selling and administrative expenses, (2) contribution margin in dollars, (3) variable manufacturing overhead, (4) break-even point in sales dollars, and (5) manufacturing cost of goods sold.

P4-27 REVIEW OF CHAPTERS 2 THROUGH 4. Stephenson Corporation provides you with the following miscellaneous data regarding operations for 2006:

Break-even point (in sales dollars)	$ 66,667
Direct materials used	24,000
Gross profit	25,000
Contribution margin	30,000
Direct labour	28,000
Sales	100,000
Variable manufacturing overhead	5,000

There are no beginning or ending inventories.
Compute the (1) fixed manufacturing overhead, (2) variable selling and administrative expenses, and (3) fixed selling and administrative expenses.

P4-28 REVIEW OF CHAPTERS 2 THROUGH 4. U. Grant Company manufactured and sold 1,000 sabres during November. Selected data for November follow:

Sales	$100,000
Direct materials used	26,000
Direct labour	16,000
Variable manufacturing overhead	13,000
Fixed manufacturing overhead	14,000
Variable selling and administrative expenses	?
Fixed selling and administrative expenses	?
Contribution margin	40,000
Operating income	22,000

There were no beginning or ending inventories.
1. What were the variable selling and administrative expenses for November?
2. What were the fixed selling and administrative expenses for November?
3. What was the cost of goods sold during November (using absorption costing)?

4. Without prejudice to your earlier answers, assume that the fixed selling and administrative expenses for November amounted to $14,000.
   a. What was the break-even point in units for November?
   b. How many units must be sold to earn a target operating income of $12,000?
   c. What would the selling price per unit have to be if the company wanted to earn an operating income of $17,000 on the sale of 900 units?

MANAGERIAL DECISION CASES

C4-1 **ANALYSIS WITH CONTRIBUTION INCOME STATEMENT.** The following data have been condensed from Chateau Corporation's report of 2006 operations (in millions of Euros [EUR]):

	VARIABLE	FIXED	TOTAL
Manufacturing cost of goods sold	EUR64.00	EUR30.50	EUR94.50
Selling and administrative expenses	23.00	11.00	33.50
Sales			145.00

Required:
1. Prepare the 2006 income statement in contribution form, ignoring income taxes.
2. Chauteau's operations have been fairly stable from year to year. In planning for the future, top management is considering several options for changing the annual pattern of operations. You are asked to perform an analysis of their estimated effects. Use your contribution income statement as a framework to compute the estimated operating income (in millions) under each of the following separate and unrelated assumptions:
   a. Assume that a 10 percent reduction in selling prices would cause a 30 percent increase in the physical volume of goods manufactured and sold.
   b. Assume that an annual expenditure of EUR4,570,000 for a special sales promotion campaign would enable the company to increase its physical volume by 10 percent with no change in selling prices.
   c. Assume that a basic redesign of manufacturing operations would increase annual fixed manufacturing costs by EUR12,200,000 and decrease variable manufacturing costs by 15 percent per product unit, but with no effect on physical volume or selling prices.
   d. Assume that a basic redesign of selling and administrative operations would double the annual fixed expenses for selling and administration and increase variable selling and administrative expenses by 25 percent per product unit. Physical volume would also increase by 20 percent. Selling prices would be increased by 5 percent.
   e. Would you prefer to use the absorption form of income statement for the above analyses? Explain.
3. Discuss the desirability of alternatives a through d in requirement 2. If only one alternative could be selected, which would you choose? Explain.

C4-2 **CANADIAN OIL SPILL.** (CICA) Two years ago, a ship owned by a foreign company ran aground during a severe storm and sank at the entrance of a Canadian harbour. The vessel blocked the entrance to the harbour and spilled considerable amounts of oil. Under federal legislation, the Canadian government is required to clean up an oil spill immediately and render the harbour's entrance safe for other vessels. The legislation states that costs are to be compiled in accordance with "accepted Canadian financial and cost accounting practices," and that they are to be charged to the shipping company and/or its insurers.

Neal & Co., Chartered Accountants, has been approached by a federal government department and asked for assistance in supporting its claim against the shipping company. The partner considering acceptance of this engagement has asked you, CA, to prepare a memorandum for him in which you discuss the issues that must be addressed in determining whether the Cost Schedule has been prepared in accordance with "accepted Canadian financial and cost accounting practices."

Currently, there is a lack of agreement between the shipping company and the government. Therefore, the report will also be filed with the court if a lawsuit by the federal government becomes essential. No amount has been paid by the shipping company, although the first invoice was rendered one year ago. Government policy is to charge 10 percent interest on all unpaid amounts.

In the discussion of these issues, CA has been asked to indicate what arguments Neal & Co. can provide in testimony in court. These arguments should include:

1. A defence of the logic of the procedures that were applied in the preparation of the Cost Schedule; and
2. A rebuttal of possible objections to the procedures used in the preparation of the Cost Schedule that might be raised by accountants and lawyers for the shipping company.

Your review of the Cost Schedule and discussions with government employees provided the following information:

1. $14.5 million is made up of the following cost categories:

Direct contract costs	$ 6,200,000
Government ships and helicopters assigned to clean up and salvage	4,500,000
Government supervisory ships assigned to general duty	2,000,000
Shore facilities—to support ships and helicopters	950,000
Administration—government departments involved in clean-up and salvage	850,000
	$14,500,000

2. The "direct contract costs" represent the costs charged by various companies and government groups contracted by the government department for clean-up and salvage. Invoices are available to support the $6.2 million and have been signed by government officials to indicate that the services were provided. Included in the $6.2 million are invoices for $800,000, representing one-half of the $1.6 million billed by one supplier. The other half, $800,000, was charged to a government account and represented improvements to the harbour entrance.
3. The "government ships and helicopters" charge of $4.5 million represents the cost of ships and helicopters specifically assigned to the clean-up. They would normally be performing defence and limited commercial duties elsewhere. The ships and helicopter were taken from specific assignments to perform the clean-up and salvage quickly. The $4.5 million is made up of

Wages and benefits of crews	$2,500,000*
Fuel for ships and helicopters	1,050,000
Supplies for ships and helicopters	500,000
Direct maintenance of ships during clean-up period	150,000
Amortization of ships during clean-up period	300,000
	$4,500,000

* Includes pension costs of $250,000 and personal life insurance costs of $90,000. All crew members were employed by the armed forces of Canada.

4. The "government supervisory ships" charge of $2 million represents the cost of ships that were needed to coordinate the clean-up and direct commercial ships safely through the harbour. They also served to keep sightseeing vessels and other groups away from the wreck. These ships would have been assigned to general civilian rescue and coast guard duties if they had not been at the location of the clean-up and salvage. The $2 million is made up of

Wages and benefits of crews	$1,200,000*
Fuel for ship	270,000
Crew meals and related supplies	80,000
Overtime pay to crews for clean-up period	300,000
Direct maintenance of ships during clean-up period	50,000
Amortization of ships during clean-up	100,000
	$2,000,000

* Includes vacation pay of $80,000, pension costs of $70,000, and insurance and other fringe benefits of $50,000. All crew members are government employees.

5. The "shore facilities" cost of $950,000 is primarily for the refuelling of ships and aircraft:

Fuel used by direct-contract ships (not included in the $6,200,000)	$600,000
Labour to service direct-contract ships	175,000
Labour to fuel government ships and helicopters	75,000
Supplies used by government ships	100,000
	$950,000

6. "Administration" costs of $850,000 include

Armed forces personnel taken from other duties and assigned to shore duties related to the clean-up	$475,000*
Estimated cost of telecommunications equipment used for clean-up—(at commercial rates)	225,000
Cost of assembling the cost data, for invoicing to the shipping company; estimated, using commercial rates for accounting services	100,000
Legal advice on invoicing the shipping company	50,000
	$850,000

* Includes accrued vacation pay of $30,000, pension costs of $45,000, and other fringe benefits of $40,000. These personnel would otherwise have been assigned to general duties.

Required: Prepare the memorandum to the partner by discussing the relevance of each of these costs. In your memorandum, determine an amount that you think should be claimed against the shipping company.

EXCEL APPLICATION EXERCISE

E4-1 OPTIMAL PRODUCT MIX TO MAXIMIZE TOTAL CONTRIBUTION MARGIN DOLLARS

Goal: Create an Excel spreadsheet to determine the optimal product mix for a company that wants to maximize total contribution margin dollars. Use the results to answer questions about your findings.

Scenario: The Ibunez Tool Company has two products: a plain circular saw and a professional circular saw. The plain saw sells for $66 and has a variable cost of $50. The professional circular saw sells for $100 and has a variable cost of $70. The company has only 20,000 machine-hours of manufacturing capacity available. Two plain saws can be produced in the same average time (1 hour) needed to produce one professional saw.

When you have completed your spreadsheet, answer the following questions:

1. What are the contribution margin and contribution margin ratio per unit for the plain circular saw? For the professional circular saw?

2. What is the potential total contribution margin for the plain circular saw if you assume that it is the only saw manufactured by Ibunez? For the professional circular saw?

3. What general conclusion can you draw from the data illustrated by the Excel problem?

Step by Step:

1. Open a new Excel spreadsheet.

2. In column A, create a bold-faced heading that contains the following:
Row 1: Chapter 5 Decision Guideline
Row 2: Ibunez Tool Company
Row 3: Product Mix Analysis
Row 4: Today's Date

3. Merge and centre the four heading rows across columns A through E.

4. Adjust column widths as follows:
Column A: 17
Column B: 15
Column C: 10
Column D: 15
Column E: 10

5. In row 7, create the following bold-faced column heading:
Column B: Products

6. Merge and centre the Products heading across columns B through E.

7. In row 8, create the following bold-faced column headings:
Column B: Plain Circular Saw
Column D: Professional Circular Saw

8. Merge and centre the Plain Circular Saw heading across columns B and C.

9. Merge and centre the Professional Circular Saw heading across columns D and E.

10. In column A, create the following row headings:
Row 9: Selling Price
Row 10: Variable Cost
Row 11: Contribution Margin
Skip 2 rows
Row 14: Available Machine Hours
Row 15: Saws Manufactured per Machine Hour
Row 16: Manufacturing Capacity
Skip 1 row
Row 18: Potential Total Contribution Margin

11. Merge the headings in rows 14 through 18 across columns A and B, then right-justify.
Alignment tab: Horizontal: Right

12. Enter the selling price and variable cost for plain and professional saws in columns B and D respectively.

13. Enter the available machine hours and the number of saws manufactured per machine hour for plain and professional saws in columns C and E respectively.

14. In row 11, create formulas to calculate the contribution margin for each type of saw in columns B and D respectively.

15. In row 11, create formulas to calculate the contribution margin percent for each type of saw in columns C and E respectively.

16. In row 16, create formulas to calculate the manufacturing capacity for each type of saw in columns C and E, respectively.

17. In row 18, create formulas to calculate potential total contribution margin for each type of saw in columns C and E, respectively.

18. Format all amounts in columns B and D as
Number tab: Category: Accounting ($ sign is left-justified)
                     Decimal places: 2
                     Symbol: $

19. Modify the format of the variable cost amounts to exclude the dollar ($) sign.
Number tab: Symbol: None

20. Modify the format of the contribution margin amounts to display a top border, using the default Line Style.
Border tab: Icon: Top Border

21. Format the contribution margin percent in columns C and E as

    Number tab: Category: Percentage
                       Decimal places: 0
    Alignment tab: Horizontal: Centre

22. Format amounts in rows 14 through 16 as

    Number tab: Category: Number
                       Decimal places: 0
            Use 1000 Separator (,): Checked
    Alignment tab: Horizontal: Centre

23. Format potential total contribution margin amounts as

    Number tab: Category: Accounting
                       Decimal places: 0
                             Symbol: $

24. Save your work to disk, and print a copy for your files.

COLLABORATIVE LEARNING EXERCISES

CL4-1 INTERNET RESEARCH AND COST MANAGEMENT SYSTEM. Form groups of three to five persons each. Each member of the group should pick one of the following industry types:

- Manufacturing
- Insurance
- Health care
- Government
- Service

Each person should explore the Internet for an example of an organization that has changed its cost management practices. Prepare and give a briefing for your group. Do this by completing the following:

1. Describe the company and its business.
2. What was the scope of the cost systems project?
3. What were the goals for the cost systems project?
4. Summarize the results of the project.

After each person has briefed the group on his/her company, discuss within your group the commonalities between the cost management systems.

CL4-2 VARIABLE AND ABSORPTION COSTING. Form groups of four persons each. Each person should select one of the following four roles (if groups have between four and eight persons, two persons can play any of the roles in the exercise):

Bernard Schwartz, President
Ramona Sanchez, Controller
Leonard Swanson, Marketing Manager
Kate Cheung, Treasurer

Each of the four should prepare a justification for the type of financial statements, variable or absorption costing, that he or she favours. The setting is explained in the case "Boylston Company" that follows.

Bernard Schwartz took over as president of Boylston Company in mid-May, 2006. The company's operating income for May was $4,000, and Schwartz was determined that June would be a better month. But when he received the following income statements for May and June, he was shocked:

	MAY	JUNE
Sales	$280,000	$340,000
Cost of sales	150,000	180,000
Gross margin	130,000	160,000
Variances:		
Labour	6,000F	4,000F
Material	5,000U	3,000U
Overhead:		
Volume	1,000F	27,000U
Spending	2,000U	1,000U
Selling & administrative	126,000	136,000
Operating income (loss)	$ 4,000	$ (3,000)

He called Ramona Sanchez, the company's controller, and asked, "Sales were up by $60,000 in June. How could operating income possibly have decreased by $7,000? There must be something wrong with your numbers."

Sanchez replied, "The numbers are right. I agree with you they don't make sense, but since our production was down in June, operating income suffered." Schwartz wasn't satisfied with that explanation. "If your accounting numbers don't give a good signal about performance, what good are they?"

Sanchez had anticipated this reaction. She suggested charging the fixed manufacturing costs as a period cost instead of including them in the product cost. Her reworked income statement was as follows:

	MAY	JUNE
Sales	$280,000	$340,000
Cost of sales	102,000	125,000
Gross margin	178,000	215,000
Fixed overhead	66,000	67,000
Variances:		
Labour	6,000F	4,000F
Material	5,000U	3,000U
Overhead spending	2,000U	1,000U
Selling & administrative	126,000	136,000
Operating income (loss)	$ (15,000)	$ 12,000

Sanchez also called on Leonard Swanson, the marketing manager, to support her new statements. Swanson pointed out that the current accounting system did not provide the right incentives to his sales force. For example, he pointed to two products, A and B, with the following prices and costs:

PRODUCT	PRICE	COST OF SALES	MARGIN	% OF SALES
A	$1.90	$1.10	$0.80	42.1
B	2.30	1.30	1.00	43.5

The sales force would be inclined to focus on Product B because of its higher margin as a percent of sales. However, he believed the following figures, based on the controller's new product costs, was a better measure of the relative profitability of the products:

PRODUCT	PRICE	COST OF SALES	MARGIN	% OF SALES
A	$1.90	$0.50	$1.40	73.7
B	2.30	1.00	1.30	56.5

After some discussion, Schwartz brought in Kate Cheung, corporate treasurer, who was sceptical about the new system. She maintained that "the sales force will start cutting prices if we leave fixed costs out of our product costs. They will try for the same margin over the reduced costs, and we will not be able to cover our fixed costs. Further, it's lack of control of long-run costs, not short-run variable costs that can destroy a company. In the short run, things constantly change and we don't make much of a commitment. But if long-run costs get out of control, there isn't much we can do about it."

Cheung was not finished. "And what about taxes? The government won't let us use your new system. And what about the balance sheet? Inventories that we now show at about $520,000 would have to be shown at about $365,000 if the fixed costs are not considered product costs. That sure doesn't make us look better to investors."

Although Schwartz liked the June profit shown by the revised statements, he thought there was some truth in all of the comments made. He wasn't sure how to proceed.

5

Cost Allocation and Activity-Based Costing Systems

After studying this chapter, you will be able to

1. Explain the major attributes of cost allocation and the relationship among activities, costs, and cost drivers.

2. Use recommended guidelines to charge the variable and fixed costs of service departments to other organizational units.

3. Identify methods for allocating the central costs of an organization and use the direct, step-down, and reciprocal allocation methods to allocate service department costs to user departments.

4. Allocate costs to products or services and use the physical units, relative sales value, and net realizable value methods to allocate joint costs.

5. Use activity-based costing to allocate costs to products or services and identify the four steps involved in the design and implementation of activity-based costing systems.

6. Explain why activity-based management systems are being adopted.

7. Explain how just-in-time systems can reduce non-value-added activities.

A university's computer is used for teaching and government-funded research. How much of its cost should be assigned to each task? A police force creates a special police unit to investigate a series of cold case, unresolved murders. What is the total cost of the special cold case police unit? A company uses a machine to make two different products. How much of the cost of the machine belongs to each product? These are all problems of cost allocation, the subject of this chapter. University presidents, police force managers, corporate executives, and others all face problems of cost allocation.

This is the first of three chapters on **cost accounting systems**—the techniques used to determine the cost of a product or service. A cost accounting system collects and classifies costs and assigns them to cost objects. The goal of a cost accounting system is to measure the cost of designing, developing, producing (or purchasing), selling, distributing, and servicing particular products or services. Cost allocation is at the heart of most cost accounting systems.

The first part of this chapter describes general approaches to and methods of cost allocation. The last part of this chapter focuses on activity-based costing as an attempt to improve on the cost allocation methods.

Cost Accounting System. The techniques used to determine the cost of a product or service by collecting and classifying costs and assigning them to cost objects.

COST ALLOCATION INTRODUCTION

Cost allocation is fundamentally a problem of linking (1) some cost or groups of costs with (2) one or more *cost objects*, such as products, departments, and divisions. Ideally, costs should be assigned to the cost object that *caused* it.

Linking costs with cost object is accomplished by selecting cost drivers. When used for allocating costs, a cost driver is often called a **cost-allocation base**. Major costs, such as newsprint for a newspaper and direct professional labour for a law firm, may each be allocated to departments, jobs, and projects on an item-by-item basis, using obvious cost drivers such as tonnes of newsprint consumed or direct-labour hours used.

Cost-Allocation Base. A cost driver when it is used for allocating costs.

Other costs may not be allocated on an item-by-item basis, but more efficiently in cost pools. All costs in a given cost pool should be caused by the same factor, or cost driver. These costs are *pooled* and then allocated together. A **cost pool** is a group of individual costs that is allocated to *cost objects* using a single cost driver. For example, building rent, utilities cost, and janitorial services may be in the same cost pool because all are allocated on the basis of square metres of space occupied. Or a university could pool all the operating costs of its registrar's office and allocate them to its colleges on the basis of the number of students in each faculty.

Cost Pool. A group of individual costs that is allocated to cost objects using a single cost driver.

Many different terms are used by companies to describe cost allocation in practice. Terms such as *cost allocation, cost tracing, cost assignments, cost distributions,* and *cost apportionment* are used interchangeably to describe the allocation of costs to cost object.

Cost Allocation Purposes

Managers within an organizational unit should be aware of all the consequences of their decisions, even consequences that spill over outside of their unit. Examples are the addition of a new course in a university that causes additional work in the registrar's office, the addition of a new flight or an additional passenger on an airline that requires reservation and booking services, and the addition of a new specialty in a medical clinic that produces more work for the medical records department. In each of these situations, it is important to *assign* the *direct* incremental costs of each decision to the organizational unit. Managers often assign direct costs without using allocated costs. However, allocation of costs is necessary when the linkage is between actual costs and the decision or project that brought them about.

A cost allocation base has been described as *incorrigible*, since it is impossible to objectively determine which base perfectly describes the link between the cost and the cost object. Given this subjectivity in the selection of a cost-allocation base, it has always been difficult for managers to determine "When should costs be allocated?" and "On what basis should costs be allocated?" The answers to these questions depend on the principal purpose or purposes of the cost allocation.

Costs are allocated for three main purposes:

1. *To obtain desired employee motivation.* Cost allocations are sometimes made to influence management behaviour and thus promote goal congruence and managerial effort. For example, in some organizations there is no cost allocation for internal auditing services or in-house management development seminars because top management wants to encourage their use. Other organizations do allocate costs for such items to make sure the benefits of the specified services exceed the costs. In this case, managers of departments who feel that such internal programs are of little or no benefit, yet have to assume part of the cost through cost allocation, may ask for their discontinuation.

2. *To better compute income and asset valuations.* Costs are allocated to products and projects to better measure inventory costs, cost of goods sold, and, therefore, departmental income. The results of cost allocation are also used by managers in planning, performance evaluation, and motivating managers, as described above.

3. *To promote fair pricing or obtain reimbursement.* Sometimes prices are based directly on costs so including or excluding allocated costs can make a difference in bidding on a project or contract. Government contracts often specify a price that includes reimbursement for costs plus some profit margin. In these instances, cost allocations become substitutes for the usual marketplace prices.

Moreover, different allocations of costs to products may be made for various purposes. Thus, full costs may guide pricing decisions, manufacturing costs may be appropriate for asset valuations, and some "in-between" costs may be negotiated for a government contract.

Ideally, all three purposes would be served simultaneously by a single cost allocation. But thousands of managers and accountants would testify that for most costs, this ideal is rarely achieved. Instead, cost allocations are often a source of discontent and confusion for the affected parties. Allocating fixed costs usually causes the greatest problems. When all three purposes cannot be attained simultaneously, the manager and the accountant should try to identify which of the purposes should dominate the particular situation.

Often, cost allocation for inventory-costing purposes (because they are externally imposed) is given greater prominence. In decision making and performance evaluation, managers should consider excluding allocated costs from total cost, understanding that cost allocations were used to satisfy inventory-costing purposes. Often, the added benefit of using separate costs for planning and control and inventory-costing purposes is much greater than the added cost.

Types of Allocations

As Exhibit 5-1 shows, there are three types of cost allocations:

1. *Allocation of joint costs to the appropriate responsibility centres.* Costs that are used jointly by more than one unit are allocated based on cost-driver activity in the units. Examples are allocating rent costs to various departments based on floor space occupied and allocating general administrative expenses based on total direct cost.

2. *Allocation of service department to production department costs.* When one unit provides products or services to another, the costs are transferred along with the products or services. Some units, called **service departments**, exist only to support other departments, and their costs are totally reallocated. Service department examples include personnel departments, laundry departments in hospitals, and security departments in commercial firms. These service department costs are passed on to the **revenue-producing departments** that are profit centres.

3. *Allocation of costs of a particular organizational unit to its outputs of products or services.* The pediatrics department of a medical clinic allocates its costs to patient visits, the assembly department of a manufacturing firm to units assembled, and the tax department of an accounting firm to clients served. The costs allocated to products or services include those allocated to the organizational unit in allocation types 1 and 2.

Service Departments. Units that exist only to serve other departments.

Revenue-Producing Departments. Organizational units that are profit centres.

All three types of allocations are fundamentally similar. Let us look first at how service department costs are allocated to production departments.

EXHIBIT 5-1

Three Types of Cost Allocations

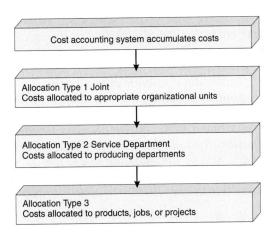

ALLOCATION OF SERVICE DEPARTMENT COSTS

Organizations incur costs to produce goods and services and to provide the support services required for that production. Essentially, production costs, patient costs, and personnel costs are caused by the very same activities that are chosen as cost objects, such as products produced, patients seen, and personnel records processed. To perform activities, resources are required. These resources have costs. Some costs vary in direct proportion to the consumption of resources. Examples include materials, labour, energy, and supplies. Other costs do not directly vary (in the short run) with resource usage. Examples of indirect costs could be amortization, supervisory salaries, and rent. So we say that activities consume resources and the costs of these resources follow various behavioural patterns. Therefore, the manager and the accountant should search for some cost driver that establishes a convincing relationship between the cause (activity being performed) and the effect (consumption of resources and related costs) and that permits *reliable predictions* of how costs will be affected by decisions regarding the activities.

To illustrate this important principle, we will consider the allocation of service department costs. Service departments typically provide a service to a broad range of functions and products within an organization, and thus the allocation of costs becomes more difficult. The preferred guidelines for allocating service department costs are:

1. *Evaluate performance of a service department by comparing actual costs with budgeted costs* regardless of how the costs are later allocated. From the budget, variable-cost pools and fixed-cost pools can be identified.
2. *Charge variable- and fixed-cost pools separately* (sometimes called the dual method of allocation). Note that one service department (such as a computer department) can contain multiple cost pools if more than one cost driver causes the department's costs. At a minimum, there should be a variable-cost pool and a fixed-cost pool.
3. *Establish the rules of the game regarding cost allocation in advance* of rendering the service, rather than after the fact so that all departments can plan appropriately.

Consider a simplified example of a computer department of a university that serves two major users: the School of Business and the School of Engineering. The computer mainframe was acquired on a five-year lease that is not cancellable unless prohibitive cost penalties are paid. How should costs be charged to the user departments? Suppose there are two major purposes for the information: (1) predicting economic effects of the use of the computer and (2) motivating departments and individuals to use its capabilities more fully.

To apply the first of the above guidelines, we need to analyze the costs of the computer department in detail. The primary activity performed is computer processing. Resources consumed include processing time, operator time, consulting time, energy, materials, and building space. Suppose cost behaviour analysis has been performed and the budget formula for the forthcoming fiscal year is $100,000 monthly fixed costs plus $200 variable costs per hour of computer time used.

Variable-Cost Pool

The cost driver for the variable-cost pool is *hours of computer time used*. Therefore, variable costs should be assigned as follows:

budgeted unit rate × actual hours of computer time used

The cause-and-effect relationship is direct and clear: the heavier the usage, the higher the total costs. In this example, the rate used would be the budgeted rate of $200 per hour.

OBJECTIVE 2

Use recommended guidelines to charge the variable and fixed costs of service departments to other organizational units.

The use of *budgeted* cost rates rather than *actual* cost rates for allocating variable costs of service departments protects the user departments from intervening price fluctuations and also protects them from inefficiencies in the service departments. When an organization allocates *actual* total service department cost, it holds user-department managers responsible for costs beyond their control and provides less incentive for service departments to be efficient. Because service departments are sure to pass on any inefficiencies and their costs to the user departments, both effects are undesirable. Consider the charging of *variable* costs to a department that uses 600 hours of computer time. Suppose inefficiencies in the computer department caused the variable costs to be $140,000 instead of the 600 hours times $200, or $120,000 budgeted. A good cost-accounting scheme would charge only the $120,000 to the consuming departments and would let the $20,000 remain as an unfavourable budget variance of the computer department. This scheme holds computer department managers responsible for the $20,000 variance and reduces the resentment of user managers. User-department managers sometimes complain more vigorously about uncertainty over allocations and the poor management of a service department than about the choice of a cost driver (such as direct-labour dollars or number of employees). Such complaints are less likely if the service department managers have budget responsibility and the user departments are protected from short-run price fluctuations and inefficiencies.

Most consumers prefer to know the total price of their purchases in advance. For example, they become nervous when automobile mechanics undertake fixing a car without specifying prices. As a minimum, they like to know the hourly rates that they must bear. Therefore, predetermined unit prices (at least) should be used. Imagine your reaction if you were told after having your car repaired, "Normally your repair would have taken five hours, but we had a new employee work on it, and the job took ten hours. Therefore, we must charge you for ten hours of labour time." Where feasible, predetermined total prices should be used for various kinds of work based on budgets and standards, not actual measurements.

Fixed-Cost Pool

Consider again our example of the university computer department. Suppose the dean had originally predicted the following long-run average monthly usage: Business, 210 hours, and Engineering, 490 hours, for a total of 700 hours. The fixed-cost pool would be allocated as follows:

	BUSINESS	ENGINEERING
Fixed costs per month:		
210/700, or 30% of $100,000	$30,000	
490/700, or 70% of $100,000		$70,000

The cost driver for the fixed-cost pool is the amount of capacity required when the computer facilities were acquired. Therefore, fixed costs could be allocated as follows:

budgeted fraction of capacity available for use × total budgeted fixed costs

This predetermined lump-sum approach is based on the long-run capacity *available* to the user, regardless of actual usage from month to month. The reasoning is that the level of fixed costs is affected by long-range planning regarding the overall level of service and the *relative expected* usage, not by *short-run* fluctuations in service levels and relative *actual* usage.

A major strength of using capacity *available* rather than capacity used when allocating *budgeted* fixed costs is that short-run allocations to user departments are not affected by the *actual* usage by departments. Such a budgeted lump-sum approach is more likely to have the desired motivational effects with respect to the ordering of services in both the short run and the long run.

In practice, fixed-cost pools are often inappropriately allocated on the basis of capacity used, not capacity available. Suppose the computer department allocated the total actual costs after the fact. At the end of the month, total *actual* would be allocated in proportion to the *actual* hours used by the consuming departments. Compare the costs borne by the two schools when Business uses 200 hours and Engineering 400 hours:

Total costs incurred, $100,000 + 600($200) = $220,000	
Business: 200/600 × $220,000 =	$ 73,333
Engineering: 400/600 × $220,000 =	146,667
Total cost allocated	$220,000

What happens if Business uses only 100 hours during the following month while Engineering still uses 400 hours?

Total costs incurred, $100,000 + 500($200) = $200,000	
Business: 100/500 × $200,000 =	$ 40,000
Engineering: 400/500 × $200,000 =	160,000
Total cost allocated	$200,000

Engineering has done nothing differently, but it must bear higher costs of $13,333, an increase of 9 percent. Its short-run costs depend on what *other* consumers have used, not solely on its own actions. This phenomenon is caused by a faulty allocation method for the *fixed* portion of the total costs, a method whereby the allocations are highly sensitive to fluctuations in the actual volumes used by the various consuming departments. This weakness is avoided by using a predetermined lump-sum allocation of fixed costs, based on budgeted usage.

Consider the automobile repair shop example introduced earlier. You would not be happy if you came to get your car and were told, "Our daily fixed overhead is $1,000. Yours was the only car in our shop today, so we are charging you the full $1,000. If we had processed 100 cars today, your charge would have been only $10."

If fixed costs are allocated on the basis of long-range plans, there is a natural tendency on the part of consumers to underestimate their planned usage and thus obtain a smaller fraction of the cost allocation. This is certainly a weakness of allocating fixed costs on long-range plans. Top management can counteract this weakness by monitoring predictions and by using feedback to keep future predictions more honest.

In some organizations there are even rewards in the form of salary increases for managers who make accurate predictions. Moreover, some cost-allocation methods penalize for underpredictions. For example, suppose a manager predicts usage of 210 hours and then demands 300 hours. The manager either doesn't get the hours or pays a price for every hour beyond 210.

Allocating Central Costs

Identify methods for allocating the central costs of an organization and use the direct, step-down, and reciprocal allocation methods to allocate service department costs to user departments.

J. C. Penney
www.jcpenney.com

Business Week Online
www.businessweek.com

The need to allocate central costs is a manifestation of a widespread, deep-seated belief that all costs must somehow be fully allocated to the revenue-producing (operating) parts of the organization. Such allocations are neither necessary from an accounting viewpoint nor useful as management information. However, most managers accept them as a fact of life—as long as all managers are treated alike.

Whenever possible, the preferred cost driver for central services is usage, either actual or estimated. Data processing, advertising, and operations research are the most likely departments to choose usage as a cost driver. However, the costs of such services as public relations, top corporate-management overhead, real estate departments, and corporate-planning departments are the least likely to be allocated on the basis of usage.

Companies that allocate central costs by usage tend to generate less resentment. Consider the experience of J. C. Penney Co. as reported in *Business Week*:

> The controller's office wanted subsidiaries such as Thrift Drug Co. and the insurance operations to base their share of corporate personnel, legal, and auditing costs on their revenues. The subsidiaries contended that they maintained their own personnel and legal departments, and should be assessed far less.
>
> The subcommittee addressed the issue by asking the corporate departments to approximate the time and costs involved in servicing the subsidiaries. The final allocation plan, based on these studies, cost the divisions less than they were initially assessed but more than they had wanted to pay. Nonetheless, the plan was implemented easily.

Usage is not always an economically viable way to allocate central costs. Many central costs, such as the president's salary and related expenses, public relations, legal services, income tax planning, company-wide advertising, and basic research, are difficult to allocate on the basis of cause and effect. As a result, some companies use cost drivers such as the revenue of each division, the cost of goods sold by each division, the total assets of each division, or the total costs of each division (before allocation of the central costs) to allocate central costs.

The use of the foregoing cost drivers might provide a *rough* indication of the cause-and-effect relationship. Basically, they represent an "ability to bear" philosophy of cost allocation. For example, the costs of company-wide advertising, such as the goodwill sponsorship of a program on a non-commercial television station, might be allocated to all products and divisions on the basis of the dollar sales in each. But such costs precede sales. They are discretionary costs as determined by management policies, not by sales results. Although 60 percent of the companies in a large survey treat sales revenue as a cost driver for cost allocation purposes, it is not truly a cost driver in the sense of being an activity that *causes* the costs.

If the costs of central services are to be allocated based on sales even though the costs do not vary in proportion to sales, the use of *budgeted* sales is preferable to the use of *actual* sales. At least this method means that the short-run costs of a given consuming department will not be affected by the fortunes of other consuming departments.

For example, suppose $100 of fixed central advertising costs were allocated on the basis of potential sales in two territories:

| | TERRITORIES | | | |
	A	B	TOTAL	PERCENT
Budgeted sales	$500	$500	$1,000	100%
Central advertising allocated	$ 50	$ 50	$ 100	10%

Consider the possible differences in allocations when actual sales become known:

| | TERRITORIES | |
	A	B
Actual sales	$300	$600
Central advertising:		
1. Allocated on basis of budgeted sales	$ 50	$ 50
or		
2. Allocated on basis of actual sales	$ 33	$ 67

Compare allocation 1 with 2. Allocation 1 is preferable. It indicates a low ratio of sales to advertising in territory A. It directs attention where it is deserved. In contrast, allocation 2 soaks territory B with more advertising cost because of the *achieved* results and relieves territory A despite its lower success. This is another example of the analytical confusion that can arise when cost allocations to one consuming department depend on the activity of other consuming departments.

Cost Allocation Methods

There are three popular methods for allocating service department costs: the direct method, the step-down method, and the reciprocal allocation method.

Consider a hotel company with two producing departments—restaurants and accommodation—and two service departments, facilities management (maintenance, heat, light, janitorial services, etc.) and personnel. All costs in a given service department are assumed to be caused by, and therefore vary in proportion to, a single cost driver. The company has decided that the best cost driver for facilities management costs is square metres occupied and the best cost driver for personnel is the number of employees. Exhibit 5-2 shows the direct costs, square metres occupied, and number of employees for each department. Note that facilities manage-

EXHIBIT 5-2

Cost Drivers

| | SERVICE DEPARTMENTS | | PRODUCTION DEPARTMENTS | |
	FACILITIES MANAGEMENT	PERSONNEL	RESTAURANTS	ACCOMMODATION
Direct department costs	$126,000	$24,000	$100,000	$160,000
Square metres	3,000	9,000	15,000	3,000
Number of employees	20	30	80	320
Direct labour hours			2,100	10,000
Customer receipts issued			30,000	5,400

ment provides services for the personnel department in addition to providing services for the producing departments, and that personnel aids employees in facilities management as well as those in production departments.

Direct Method

As its name implies, the **direct method** ignores other service departments when any given service department's costs are allocated to the revenue-producing (operating) departments. In other words, the fact that facilities management provides services for personnel is ignored, as is the support that personnel provides to facilities management. Facilities management costs are allocated based on the relative square metres *occupied by the production departments only*:

- Total square metres in production departments: 15,000 + 3,000 = 18,000
- Facilities management cost allocated to restaurants: (15,000 ÷ 18,000) × $126,000 = $105,000
- Facilities management cost allocated to accommodation: (3,000 ÷ 18,000) × $126,000 = $21,000

Likewise, personnel department costs are allocated *only to the production departments* on the basis of the relative number of employees in the production departments:

- Total employees in production departments: 80 + 320 = 400
- Personnel costs allocated to restaurants: (80 ÷ 400) × $24,000 = $4,800
- Personnel costs allocated to accommodation: (320 ÷ 400) × $24,000 = $19,200

Step-Down Method

The **step-down method** recognizes that some service departments support the activities in other service departments as well as those in production departments. A sequence of allocations is chosen, usually by starting with the service department that renders the greatest service (as measured by costs) to the greatest number of other service departments. The last service department in the sequence is the one that renders the least service to the least number of other service departments. Once a department's costs are allocated to other departments, no subsequent service department costs are allocated back to it.

In our example, facilities management costs are allocated first. Why? Because facilities management renders more support to personnel than personnel provides for facilities management.[1] Examine Exhibit 5-3. After facilities management costs are allocated, no costs are allocated back to facilities management (one-way street), even though personnel does provide some services for facilities management. The personnel costs to be allocated to the production departments include the amount allocated to personnel from facilities management ($42,000) in addition to the direct personnel department costs of $24,000.

---

[1] How should we determine which of the two service departments provides more service than the other? One way is to carry out step one of the step-down method with facilities management allocated first, and then repeat it assuming personnel is allocated first. With facilities management allocated first, $42,000 is allocated to personnel, as shown in Exhibit 5-3. If personnel had been allocated first, (20/420) × $24,000 = $1,143 would have been allocated to facilities management. Because $1,143 is smaller than $42,000, facilities management is allocated first.

EXHIBIT 5-3

Step-Down Allocation

	FACILITIES MANAGEMENT	PERSONNEL	RESTAURANTS	ACCOMMODATION	TOTAL
Direct department costs before allocation	$126,000	$24,000	$100,000	$160,000	$410,000
Step 1:					
Facilities management	$(126,000)	(9 ÷ 27) × $126,000 = $42,000	(15 ÷ 27) × $126,000 = $70,000	(3 ÷ 27) × $126,000 = $14,000	0
Step 2:					
Personnel		$(66,000)	(80 ÷ 400) × $66,000 = $13,200	(320 ÷ 400) × $66,000 = $52,800	0
Total cost after allocation	$ 0	$ 0	$183,200	$226,800	$410,000

EXHIBIT 5-4

Reciprocal Allocation Method

	FACILITIES MANAGEMENT	PERSONNEL	RESTAURANTS	ACCOMMODATION	TOTAL
Direct department costs before allocation	$126,000	$24,000	$100,000	$160,000	$410,000
Allocation of facilities management	$(129,220)	(9 ÷ 27) × $129,220 = $43,073	(15 ÷ 27) × $129,220 = $71,789	(3 ÷ 27) × $129,220 = $14,358	0
Allocation of personnel	(20 ÷ 420) × $67,030 = $3,192	$(67,030)	(80 ÷ 420) × $67,030 = $12,768	(320 ÷ 420) × $67,030 = $51,070	0
Total cost after allocation	$ (28)*	$ 43*	$184,557	$225,428	$410,000

* Due to rounding.

EXHIBIT 5-5

Comparison of Direct, Step-Down, and Reciprocal Methods

	RESTAURANTS			ACCOMMODATION		
	DIRECT	STEP-DOWN	RECIPROCAL	DIRECT	STEP-DOWN	RECIPROCAL
Direct department costs	$100,000	$100,000	$100,000	$160,000	$160,000	$160,000
Allocated from facilities management	105,000	70,000	71,789	21,000	14,000	14,358
Allocated from personnel	4,800	13,200	12,768	19,200	52,800	51,070
Total costs	$209,800	$183,200	$184,557	$200,200	$226,800	$225,428

Examine the last column of Exhibit 5-3. Before allocation, the four departments incurred costs of $410,000. In step 1, $126,000 was deducted from facilities management and added to the other three departments. There was no net effect on the total cost. In step 2, $66,000 was deducted from personnel and added to the remaining two departments. Again, total cost was unaffected. After allocation, all $410,000 remains, but it is all in restaurants and accommodation. None was left in facilities management or personnel.

Reciprocal Allocation Method

Reciprocal Allocation Method. Allocates costs by recognizing that the service departments provide services to each other as well as to the production departments.

Service departments often support other service departments as well as revenue-producing departments. The **reciprocal allocation method** allocates costs by recognizing that the service departments provide services to each other as well as to the production departments. This method is generally viewed as being the most theoretically correct as it enables us to cost the interdepartmental relationships fully into the service department cost allocations. In our example, the facilities management cost is allocated to the personnel department and the personnel cost is allocated to the facilities management department before the costs of the service departments are allocated to the production departments.

First, we must allocate the costs of the services provided between the two service departments. We do this using the following two equations in which the facilities management costs are defined as FM and the personnel costs as P.

$$FM = \$126,000 + 20/420\ P = \$126,000 + 0.048\ P$$

$$P = \$24,000 + 9/27\ FM = \$24,000 + 0.333\ FM$$

Then we solve the two simultaneous equations to determine the total amount of costs for each service department.

$$FM = \$126,000 + (0.048\ [\$24,000 + 0.333\ FM])$$

$$FM = \$126,000 + \$1,152 + 0.016\ FM$$

$$0.984\ FM = \$127,152$$

$$FM = \$129,220$$

$$P = \$24,000 + 0.333\ (\$129,220)$$

$$P = \$24,000 + \$43,030$$

$$P = \$67,030$$

Thus, the total cost to be allocated for facilities management is $129,220 and for personnel is $67,030. Exhibit 5-4 provides the details of the allocations of the costs for these two service departments to the two production departments. Note that the total of the costs allocated is still $410,000 (after minor adjustments due to rounding errors).

Compare the costs of the production departments under direct, step-down and reciprocal allocation methods as shown in Exhibit 5-5.

Note that the method of allocation can greatly affect the costs. The restaurants department appears to be a much more expensive operation to a manager using the direct method than to one using the step-down or reciprocal allocation

Suppose you are on a cross-functional team that discussed how to allocate the costs of a purchasing department. One team member suggested that "number of purchase orders issued" is the best cost driver. However, a scatter graph of total costs versus number of purchase orders issued showed the following:

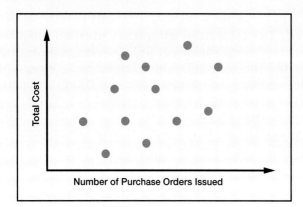

Because the data clearly indicate that the single cost driver, "number of purchase orders issued," is not a reliable measure of the work done in the department (because there is too much scatter in the data), the team investigated. It discovered that a significant amount of work of the purchasing department was certifying new vendors in addition to issuing purchase orders. What alternative method of allocation would you recommend?

ANSWER

Because a large percentage of the work of the purchasing department is not related to the single cost driver, "number of purchase orders," a second cost pool should be used with another cost driver, such as "number of new vendors."

method. Conversely, accommodation seems more expensive to a manager using the non-direct methods.

Which of the three methods is best? It is sometimes difficult to say. The reciprocal method appears to be more accurate since it takes into account the reciprocal (two-way) relationships that exist among service and producing departments as opposed to the step-down method, which is a one-way street, with cost traffic from the service department providing the most support to the service department providing the least support.

In our example, the direct method assumes if the cost of facilities management is caused by the space used, then the space used by personnel causes $42,000 of facilities management costs. If the space used in personnel is caused by the number of production-department employees supported, then the number of production-department employees, not the square metres, causes $42,000 of the facilities management cost. The producing department with the most employees, not the one with the most square metres, should bear this cost.

The greatest virtue of the direct method is its simplicity. An advantage of the step-down method is that it recognizes the effects of the most significant support provided by service departments to other service departments. If the three methods do not produce significantly different results, many companies opt for the direct method because it is easier for managers to understand.

ALLOCATING COSTS TO OUTPUTS

Cost Application. The allocation of total departmental costs to the revenue-producing products or services.

Up to this point, we have concentrated on cost allocation to divisions, departments, and similar segments of a company. Cost allocation is often carried one step further—to the outputs of these departments, however defined. Examples are *products*, such as automobiles, furniture, and newspapers, and *services*, such as banking, health care, and education. Sometimes the allocation of total departmental costs to the revenue-producing products or services is called **cost application** or *cost attribution*.

General Approach

OBJECTIVE 4

Allocate costs to products or services and use the physical units, relative sales value, and net realizable value to allocate joint costs.

The general approach to allocating costs to final products or services is as follows:

1. Allocate production-related costs to production or revenue-producing departments. This includes allocating service department costs to the production departments. The production departments then contain all the costs: their direct department costs and the service department costs.
2. Select one or more cost drivers in each production department. Historically, most companies have used only one cost driver per department. Recently, a large number of companies have started using multiple cost drivers within a department. For example, a portion of the departmental costs may be allocated on the basis of direct-labour hours, another portion on the basis of machine hours, and the remainder on the basis of the number of clients served.
3. Allocate the total costs accumulated in step 1 to products or services that are the outputs of the operating departments using the cost drivers specified in step 2. If only one cost driver is used, two cost pools should be maintained, one for variable costs and one for fixed costs. Variable costs should be assigned on the basis of actual cost driver activity. Fixed costs should either remain unallocated or be allocated on the basis of budgeted cost driver activity.

Consider our service industry hotel example, and assume that the step-down method was used to allocate service department costs. Exhibit 5-3 shows total costs of $183,200 accumulated in restaurants and $226,800 in accommodation. Note that all $410,000 total costs reside in the production departments. To allocate these costs to the products produced, cost drivers must be selected for each department. We will use a single cost driver for each department and assume that all costs are caused by that cost driver. Suppose customer receipts issued is the best measure of what causes costs in the restaurants department, and direct-labour hours measures causation in accommodation. Exhibit 5-2 showed 30,000 total customer receipts issued in restaurants and 10,000 labour hours in accommodation. Therefore, costs are allocated to products as follows:

Restaurants: $183,200 ÷ 30,000 customer receipts = $6.11 per customer receipts issued

Accommodation: $226,800 ÷ 10,000 direct-labour hours = $22.68 per direct-labour hours

A customer who ate breakfast four times at the restaurant and took two direct-labour hours in accommodation would have a cost of

$$(4 \times \$6.11) + (2 \times \$22.68) = \$24.44 + \$45.36 = \$69.80$$

JOINT COSTS ALLOCATION AND BY-PRODUCT COSTS

Joint Costs

Joint costs relate to the production of more than one product through the same process at the same time, and the cost of each product cannot be separately identified. So far we have assumed that cost drivers can be identified with an individual product. For example, if costs are being allocated to products or services on the basis of machine hours, we have assumed that each machine hour is used on a single final product or service. However, sometimes inputs are added to the production process before individual products are separately identifiable (that is, before the *split-off point*). Such costs are called **joint costs**. Joint costs include all inputs of material, labour, and overhead costs that are incurred before the split-off point.

Joint Costs. Costs of inputs added to a process before individual products are separated.

Suppose a department has more than one product and some costs are joint costs. How should such joint costs be allocated to the products? Allocation of joint costs should not affect decisions about the individual products. Nevertheless, joint product costs are routinely allocated to products for purposes of *inventory valuation* and *income determination*.

Dow Chemical
www.dow.ca

Assume a department in Dow Chemical Company produces two chemicals, X and Y. The joint cost is $100,000, and production is 1,000,000 litres of X and 500,000 litres of Y. Product X can be sold for $0.09 per litre and Y for $0.06 per litre. Ordinarily, some part of the $100,000 joint cost will be allocated to the inventory of X and the rest to the inventory of Y. Such allocations are useful for inventory purposes only. Joint costs allocations should be ignored for decisions such as selling a joint product or processing it further.

Three conventional ways of allocating joint costs to products are widely used: *physical units*, *relative sales value*, and *net realizable value*.

Physical Units—Joint Costs Allocation Method

If physical units were used, the joint costs would be allocated as follows:

	LITRES	WEIGHTING	ALLOCATION OF JOINT COSTS	SALES VALUE AT SPLIT-OFF
X	1,000,000	10/15 × $100,000	$ 66,667	$ 90,000
Y	500,000	5/15 × $100,000	33,333	30,000
	1,500,000		$100,000	$120,000

This approach shows that the $33,333 joint cost of producing Y exceeds its $30,000 sales value at split-off, which seems to indicate that Y should not be produced. However, such an allocation is not helpful in making production decisions. Neither of the two products could be produced separately.

A decision to produce Y must be a decision to produce X *and* Y. Because total revenue of $120,000 exceeds the total joint cost of $100,000, both will be produced. The allocation was not useful for this decision.

Relative Sales Value—Joint Costs Allocation Method

The physical units method requires a common physical unit (litres in our example) for measuring the output of each product. However, sometimes such a common denominator is lacking. Consider the production of meat and hides in a slaughterhouse. Meat output is measured in kilograms but hides are not. You might use kilograms as a common denominator, but it is not a good measure of the output of hides. As an alternative, many companies use the relative-sales-value method for allocating joint costs. The following allocation results from applying the relative-sales-value method to the Dow Chemical example:

	RELATIVE SALES VALUE AT SPLIT-OFF	WEIGHTING	ALLOCATION OF JOINT COSTS	PRODUCTION COST PER UNIT
X	$ 90,000	90/120 × $100,000	$ 75,000	$0.075
Y	30,000	30/120 × $100,000	25,000	0.050
	$120,000		$100,000	

The weighting is based on the sales values of the individual products. Because the sales value of X at split-off is $90,000 and total sales value at split-off is $120,000, X is allocated 90/120 of the joint cost.

Now each product would be assigned a joint cost portion that is less than its sales value at split-off. Note how the allocation of a cost to a particular product such as Y depends not only on the sales value of Y but also on the sales value of X. For example, suppose you were the product manager for Y. You planned to sell your 500,000 litres for $30,000, achieving a profit of $30,000 − $25,000 = $5,000. Everything went as expected except that the price of X fell to $0.07 per litre for revenue of $70,000 rather than $90,000. Instead of 30/120 of the joint cost, Y received 30/100 × $100,000 = $30,000 and had a profit of $0. Despite the fact that Y operations were exactly as planned, the cost-allocation method caused the profit on Y to be $5,000 below plan.

Estimated Net Realizable Value (NRV)—Joint Costs Allocation Method

The estimated net realizable value method allocates joint costs on the basis of the relative net realizable value defined as expected final sales value less the expected separable production and marketing costs. To apply the method, we approximate the sales value at split-off as follows:

sales value at split-off = final sales value − separate costs

For example, suppose the 500,000 litres of Y requires $10,000 of processing beyond the split-off point, after which it can be sold for $0.10 per litre. The NRV at split-off would be $0.10 × 500,000 − $10,000 = $50,000 − $10,000 = $40,000, net realizable value. Also suppose that the 1,000,000 litres of X requires $40,000 of processing beyond the split-off point, after which it can be sold for $0.15 per litre. The NRV at the split-off point would be:

$0.15 × 1,000,000 − $40,000 = $150,000 − $40,000 = $110,000

Production cost per unit:

	NRV	WEIGHTING	ALLOCATION OF JOINT COSTS
X	$110,000	110/150 × 100,000 =	$73,333
Y	40,000	40/150 × 100,000 =	26,667
	$150,000		$100,000

X: $73,333 + $40,000 separable cost = $113,333
$113,333 ÷ 1,000,000 litres = 0.11333

Y: $26,667 + $10,000 = $36,667
$36,667 ÷ 500,000 litres = 0.07333

By-Product Costs

By-Product. A product that, like a joint product, is not individually identifiable until manufacturing reaches a split-off point, but has a relatively insignificant total sales value.

A **by-product** is a product that, like a joint product, is not individually identifiable until manufacturing reaches a split-off point. By-products differ from joint products because they have relatively insignificant total sales values in comparison with the other products emerging at split-off. Joint products have relatively significant total sales values at split-off. Examples of by-products are glycerine from soap making and sawdust/wood chips from lumber mill operations.

If an item is accounted for as a by-product, only separable costs are assigned to it. All joint costs are allocated to main products. Any net profits from by-products (revenue less separable costs) are deducted from the cost of the main products.

Consider a lumber company that sells sawdust generated in the production of lumber to companies making particle board. Suppose the company regards the sawdust as a by-product. In 2006, sales of sawdust totalled $30,000, and the cost of loading and shipping the sawdust (that is, costs incurred beyond the split-off point) was $20,000. The inventory cost of the sawdust would consist of only the $20,000 separable cost. None of the joint cost of producing lumber and sawdust would be allocated to the sawdust. The difference between the revenue and separable cost, $30,000 − $20,000 = $10,000, would be used to reduce the cost of the lumber produced.

ACTIVITY-BASED COSTING (ABC)

OBJECTIVE 5

Use activity-based costing to allocate costs to products or services and identify the four steps involved in the design and implementation of ABC systems.

In the past, the vast majority of departments used direct labour hours as the only cost driver for applying costs to products and services. But direct labour hours is not a good measure of the cause of costs in modern, highly automated organizations. Labour-related costs in an automated system may be only a small percentage of the total costs and often are not related to the causes of most overhead costs. Therefore, many companies are beginning to use machine hours or other cost-allocation bases. However, some managers in modern manufacturing firms and automated service companies believe it is inappropriate to allocate all costs based on measures of volume. Using direct labour hours or cost—or even machine hours—as the only cost driver seldom meets the cause/effect criterion desired in cost allocation. If many costs are caused by non-volume-based cost drivers, *activity-based costing (ABC)* should be considered.

Activity-Based Costing

Activity-based costing (ABC) systems first accumulate overhead costs for each of the activities of an organization, and then assign the costs of activities to the products, services, or other cost objects that caused that activity. To establish a cause-effect relationship between an activity and a cost object, cost drivers are identified for each activity. Consider the following activities and *cost drivers* for the Belmont manufacturing plant department of a major appliance producer:

ACTIVITY	COST DRIVER
Production setup	Number of production runs
Production control	Number of production process changes
Engineering	Number of engineering change orders
Maintenance	Number of machine hours
Power	Number of kilowatt hours

Cost-driver activity is measured by the number of transactions involved in the activity. For example, in this case, engineering costs are caused by change orders (a document detailing a production change that requires the attention of the engineering department). Therefore, engineering costs are assigned to products in proportion to the number of engineering change orders issued for each product. If the production of microwave ovens caused 18 percent of the engineering change orders, then the ovens should bear 18 percent of the costs of engineering.

Consider the Belmont manufacturing plant example just mentioned. Exhibit 5-6 contrasts the traditional costing system with an ABC system. In the traditional cost system, the portion of total overhead allocated to a product depends on the proportion of total direct labour hours consumed in making the product. In the ABC system, significant overhead activities (e.g., machining, assembly, quality inspection) and related resources are separately identified and traced to products using cost drivers—machine hours, number of parts, and number of inspections. In the ABC system, the amount of overhead costs allocated to a product depends on the proportion of, for example, total machine hours, total parts, and total inspections, consumed in making the product. One large overhead cost pool has been broken into several pools, each associated with a key activity. We now consider a more in-depth illustration of the design of an ABC system.

EXHIBIT 5-6

Traditional and Activity-Based Cost Systems

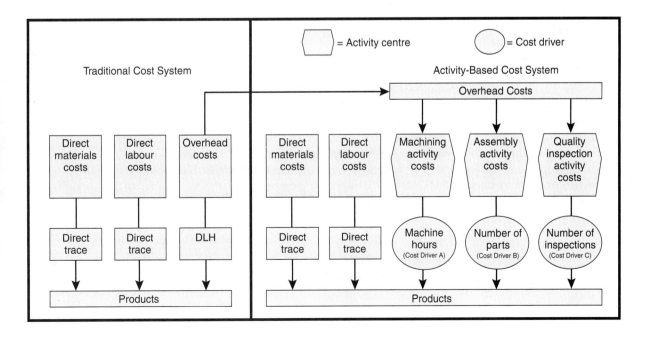

Activity-Based Costing at Schneider Foods

J. M. Schneider
www.schneiderfoods.ca

Kitchener-based Schneider Foods, a subsidiary of Maple Leaf Foods Inc., is one of Canada's largest producers of premium-quality food products. The company's mission statement, which provides a common focus for all activities within the corporation, reads as follows:

> To generate profitable growth in targeted market segments as a customer-focused, innovative provider of quality food products, while being a financially secure, well-managed, ethical company.

In the absence of significant market growth opportunities, concerning red meat consumption and related food processing activities, Schneider launched an initiative in the early 1990s to internally generate efficiencies and cost reductions in order to improve profit margins. The vehicle chosen to drive these improvements was the implementation of a broadly based continuous improvement program.[2]

This program, in order to be successful, required the support of a more up-to-date and relevant cost system. Up until this time, Schneider had used a standard cost system to meet the requirements of measuring the success of its labour and materials yield productivity program. This program measured productivity gains by comparing actual results to costs in the standard cost system.[3]

There were a number of shortcomings with the company's conventional standard cost system, however:

1. The focus was on minimizing costs within each department. Consequently, actions would be taken in one department that would reduce their costs, but would create additional costs in downstream departments.

2. Targets were limited to material yield and direct labour productivity. Opportunities to better control and manage a number of other manufacturing costs and overheads were not measured.

3. Comparisons were made to standards that incorporated allowances for waste and non-value-added activity. Although meeting the standard costs satisfied management, it resulted in "satisfactory" costs rather than "minimum" costs.

Management at Schneider Foods realized that the primary emphasis of its cost system should be to provide relevant and reliable information for management decision making rather than focusing only on financial reporting requirements.

Under continuous improvement, the focus on minimizing costs broadened from control of yields and direct labour productivity to better understanding and managing the entire business cycle. Continuous improvement initiatives were launched to address just-in-time, productive maintenance, total quality control, quick changeover techniques, cycle time, and identification and elimination of non-value-added activities. The standard cost system was unable to accurately measure and report the true costs of these activities, and was in need of an overhaul.

In order to better measure and understand production cost behaviour, management at Schneider Foods decided to implement activity-based costing (ABC). ABC systems are designed on the premise that products require "activities" and that these activities, in turn, consume "resources" (i.e., incur costs). Non-value-added activities and waste are more clearly highlighted and therefore better managed. Non-financial measures have also been recognized as key yardsticks in measuring operational performance (e.g., tonnage throughput, machine downtime hours, process cycle time).

The information generated by this updated management accounting system was intended to be supportive of the firm's continuous improvement and cost reduction programs, providing relevant and reliable decision-making information.

---

[2] Dodds, Douglas W., "MAKING IT BETTER . . . and better," *CMA Magazine*, February 1992, pp. 16–21.

[3] For a more complete discussion of the standard cost system, see H. M. Armitage and A. A. Atkinson, *The Choice of Productivity Measures in Organizations: A Field Study of Practice in Seven Canadian Firms*. Mississauga: Society of Management Accountants of Canada,1990.

Source: Written by John Carney, Manager Accounting Services, and Larry Wozniak, Senior Cost Analyst, J. M. Schneider Inc.

STRATEGIC INSIGHTS & COMPANY PRACTICES

Outsourcing

PrincewaterhouseCoopers Canada
www.pwcglobal.com/ca

Most organizations are now realizing that to succeed they must focus on a few core competencies, things they uniquely do very well. For example, Compaq[4] defines itself as a "platform integrator" developing and marketing products whose components are largely manufactured by others. Such organizations realize that they should not seek to do activities for which they do not have competitive advantage.

Traditionally, outsourcing started with narrow, low-risk activities such as payroll processing, data centre management, and catering. Now much more strategic activities are starting to be outsourced, including financial management, human resources management, supply chain management, and even customer management processes. Also, the scope of the outsourcing relationships is much broader; for example, outsourcing of accounting used to consist primarily of accounts receivable collection and payroll. Now, organizations are outsourcing their entire financial transaction processing, recognizing that their own competencies are in the use of financial information, not its creation.

An important change in the outsourcing environment is the rapid emergence of e-business, which is making it far more possible, and necessary, for organizations to implement new business models, with extensive outsourcing of processes to third parties. Organizations such as Cisco have demonstrated that they can dominate the value chain while outsourcing many processes, including manufacturing, to other organizations.

FUTURE OUTLOOK

The outsourcing market will change quite dramatically over the next few years toward a new relationship characterized by the following factors:
- a broadening of the scope of outsourcing relationships;
- significant investment by the service provider, particularly in information technology infrastructure to support service delivery;
- use of e-business to implement new and highly innovative outsourcing relationships; and
- sharing of risks and rewards associated with the outsourcing.

The outsourcing market move toward highly strategic partnering arrangements addresses such broad processes as financial transaction processing; human resources administration; supply chain management; document and print management; and customer service.

Several of the most progressive global organizations will seek outsourcing partnerships that focus on enhancing shareholder value and enabling organizations to be more focused and flexible.

GLOBAL RESEARCH FINDINGS

PricewaterhouseCoopers commissioned a study of outsourcing trends among 300 of the largest global companies, including 26 large Canadian organizations. The research, conducted by an independent market research organization, highlighted some interesting issues and trends among the Canadian participants:
- Seventy-three percent of the organizations have outsourced at least one activity or process. The main reasons for outsourcing are to enable a focus on core competencies; enhance profitability and shareholder value; and avoid the investment in technology required to enhance efficiency.
- The most commonly outsourced activities and those most likely to be outsourced in the near future are benefits administration; payroll processing; logistics; real estate management; and internal audit.
- About half of the respondents believe outsourcing to be more important to their organizations than it was three years ago, 95 percent were somewhat or very satisfied with their outsourcing to date, while 63 percent achieved the cost savings expected from outsourcing.

[4] In May of 2002, Compaq was acquired by Hewlett Packard. See Ashlee Vance, "It's official: HP acquires Compaq," May 1, 2002, accessible at www.pcworld.com.

Source: John Simke, "Emerging Trends in Outsourcing," *CMA Management*, February 2000, pp. 26–27.

Illustration of Activity-Based Costing[5]

Consider the billing department at Pacific Power Company (PPC), an electric utility. The billing department (BD) at PPC provides account inquiry and bill printing services for two major classes of customers—residential and commercial. Currently, the BD services 120,000 residential and 20,000 commercial customer accounts.

Two factors are having a significant impact on PPC's profitability. First, deregulation of the power industry has led to increased competition and lower rates, so PPC must find ways of reducing its operating costs. Second, the demand for power in PPC's area will increase due to the addition of a large housing development and a shopping centre. The marketing department estimates that residential demand will increase by almost 50 percent and commercial demand will increase by 10 percent during the next year. Since the BD is currently operating at full capacity, it needs to find ways to create capacity to service the expected increase in demand. A local service bureau has offered to take over the BD functions at an attractive lower cost (compared to the current cost). The service bureau's proposal is to provide all the functions of the BD at $3.50 per residential account and $8.50 per commercial account.

Exhibit 5-7 depicts the residential and commercial customer classes (cost objects) and the resources used to support the BD. The costs associated with the BD

MAKING MANAGERIAL DECISIONS

Suppose you have been asked to attend a meeting of top management. When the meeting begins, you are asked to explain, in general terms, the main differences and similarities between traditional and ABC costing systems. You have only Exhibit 5-6 as a guide, so you quickly draw this exhibit on a white board and, after taking a deep breath, begin to talk. List as many differences as you can between the two systems, based on Exhibit 5-6.

ANSWER

1. Traditional costing systems are much simpler than ABC systems and are usually less costly to maintain.

2. Traditional systems and ABC systems both have all three types of costs: direct, indirect, and unallocated.

3. ABC systems unbundle indirect resources into many subgroups, each being assigned to consuming activities.

4. ABC systems assign indirect resource costs to cost objects in two stages of allocation, whereas traditional systems normally assign indirect resource costs in just one stage.

5. Both traditional and ABC systems use average prices and consumption rates for product lines. Prices and costs within each product line do not vary significantly, so the accuracy of product and customer costs is maintained.

6. ABC systems accumulate and report activity costs in several activity-cost pools.

7. ABC systems require many more cost drivers than do traditional systems. When these cost drivers are both plausible and reliable, the overall accuracy of product, service, or customer cost is improved. In addition, more operational information is provided, which can be used to improve operational control.

---

[5] Much of the discussion in this section is based on an illustration used in Implementing Activity-Based Costing—The Model Approach, a workshop sponsored by the Institute of Management Accounting and Sapling Corporation.

EXHIBIT 5-7

Pacific Power
Company—Billing
Department

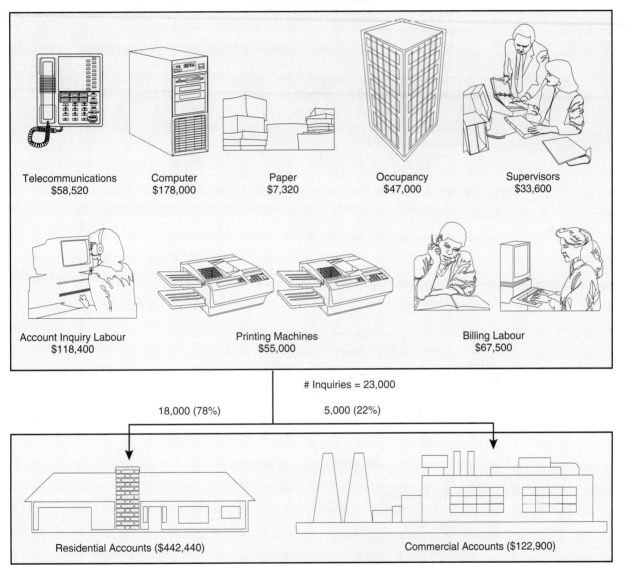

Current Costing Based on One Overall Rate
Total Indirect Cost: $565,340

Telecommunications $58,520

Computer $178,000

Paper $7,320

Occupancy $47,000

Supervisors $33,600

Account Inquiry Labour $118,400

Printing Machines $55,000

Billing Labour $67,500

Inquiries = 23,000

18,000 (78%)   5,000 (22%)

Residential Accounts ($442,440)

Commercial Accounts ($122,900)

	Cost/Inquiry $565,340/23,000 (1)	Number of Inquiries (2)	Number of Accounts (3)	Cost/Account (1) × (2)/(3)
Residential	$24.58	18,000	120,000	$3.69
Commercial	$24.58	5,000	20,000	$6.15

are all indirect—they cannot be identified specifically and exclusively with either customer class in an economically feasible way. The BD used a traditional costing system that allocated all support costs based on the number of account inquiries of the two customer classes. Exhibit 5-7 shows that the cost of the resources used in the BD last month was $565,340. PPC received 23,000 account inquiries during the month, so the indirect cost per inquiry was $565,340 ÷ 23,000 = $24.58. There were 18,000 residential account inquiries, about 78 percent of the total. Thus, residential accounts were charged with 78 percent of the support costs while commercial accounts were charged with 22 percent. The resulting cost per account is $3.69 and $6.15 for residential and commercial accounts, respectively.

Based on the costs provided by the traditional cost system, the BD management would be motivated to accept the service bureau's proposal to service all residential accounts because of the apparent savings of $0.19 ($3.69 − $3.50) per account. The BD would continue to service its commercial accounts because its costs are $2.35 ($8.50 − $6.15), less than the service bureau's bid.

However, management believed that the actual consumption of support resources was much greater than 22 percent for commercial accounts because of their complexity. For example, commercial accounts average 50 lines per bill compared with only 12 for residential accounts. Management was also concerned about activities such as correspondence (and supporting labour) resulting from customer inquiries because these activities are costly but do not add value to PPC's services from the customer's perspective. However, management wanted a more thorough understanding of key BD activities and their interrelationships before making important decisions that would affect PPC's profitability. The company decided to perform a study of the BD, using activity-based costing. The following is a description of the study and its results.

The activity-based costing study was performed by a team of managers from the BD and the chief financial officer from PPC. The team followed a four-step procedure to conduct the study.

Step 1. Determine cost objects, key activities centres, resources, and related cost drivers. In this example, management had set the objective for the study—determine the BD cost per account for each customer class. The team identified the following activities, resources, and related cost drivers for the BD through interviews with appropriate personnel.

ACTIVITY CENTRES	COST DRIVERS
Account Billing	Number of Lines on Bills
Account Verification	Number of Accounts Verified
Account Inquiry	Number of Labour Hours
Correspondence	Number of Letters Written

The four key BD activity centres are account billing, account verification, account inquiry, and correspondence. The resources shown in Exhibit 5-7 support these major activity centres. Cost drivers were selected based on two criteria.

1. There had to be a reasonable assumption of a cause-effect relationship between the driver unit and the consumption of resources and/or the occurrence of supporting activities.

Suppose PPC's management believes that a more plausible and reliable cost driver is "number of printed lines." Each residential bill averages 12 lines and each commercial bill averages 50 lines. What would be the new cost per account for residential and commercial customers based on number of lines per bill? How would this new cost accounting information affect the outsourcing decision?

ANSWER

The total costs would be the same, but the allocation of the total cost to each customer class would change.

Instead of allocating 78% of total costs to residential customers, we would allocate only $(12 \times 120,000) \div (12 \times 120,000 + 50 \times 20,000) = 59\%$ of total costs to residential customers and the other 41% to commercial accounts. The cost per account for residential customers would then be $(59\% \times \$565,340) \div 120,000 = \$2.78$, and the cost per commercial account would be $(41\% \times \$565,340) \div 20,000 = \$11.59$. The outsourcing decision would likely change. We would outsource commercial accounts but not residential accounts. A key issue is how much confidence management has in the costs it uses for decision making. Poor cost data can lead to poor decisions.

2. Data on the cost-driver units had to be available.

Step 2. Develop a process-based map representing the flow of activities, resources, and their interrelationships. An important phase of any activity-based analysis is identifying the interrelationships between key activities and the resources consumed. This is typically done by interviewing key personnel. Once the linkage between activities and resources is identified, a process map is drawn that provides a visual representation of the operations of the BD.

Exhibit 5-8 is a process map that depicts the flow of activities and resources at the BD.[6] Note that there are no costs on Exhibit 5-8. BD first focused on understanding business processes. Costs were not considered until Step 3, after the key interrelationships of the business were understood.

Consider residential accounts. Three key activities support these accounts—account billing, account inquiry, and correspondence. Bill-printing activity consumes printing machine time, paper, computer transaction time, billing labour time, and supervisory time. This activity also takes up significant occupancy space. Account inquiry activity consumes labour time and requires correspondence for some inquiries. Account inquiry labour, in turn, uses the telecommunication, computer, and supervisory resources, and also occupies a significant amount of occupancy space. Finally, the correspondence activity requires supervision and inquiry labour. The costs of each of the resources consumed were determined during Step 3—data collection.

Step 3. Collect relevant data concerning costs and the physical flow of cost-driver units among resources and activities. Using the process map as a guide, BD accountants collected the required cost and operational data by further interviews with relevant personnel. Sources of data include the accounting records, special studies, and sometimes "best estimates of managers."

---

[6] This example illustrates the process-based modelling approach to activity-based costing. For a more detailed description of the process modelling approach, see Raef A. Lawson, "Beyond ABC: Process-Based Costing," *Journal of Cost Management*, Volume 8, No. 3 (Fall 1994), pp. 33–43. Also, for a discussion of how one major firm used process-based costing to implement ABC in its billing centre, see T. Hobdy, J. Thomson, and P. Sharman, "Activity-Based Management at AT&T," *Management Accounting* (April 1994), pp. 35–39.

EXHIBIT 5-8

Process Map of Billing Department Activities

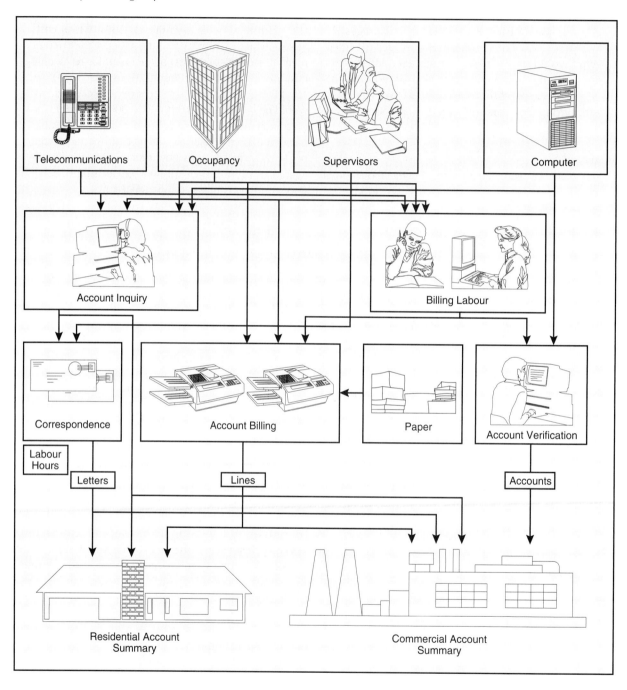

Exhibit 5-9 is a graphical representation of the data collected for the four activity centres identified in Step 1. For each activity centre, data collected included traceable costs and the physical flow of cost-driver units. For example, Exhibit 5-9 shows traceable costs of $235,777 for the account billing activity. Traceable costs include the costs of the printing machines ($55,000 from Exhibit

Confirm your understanding of traditional and ABC allocation by computing the allocation of overhead costs to the deluxe type speaker for the Louder Is Better Company. The company makes two types of speakers, a standard (S) and a deluxe (D) model. The diagrams below show how allocation would be done under ABC versus traditional allocation systems. The production department has overhead costs of $36,000. How would ABC versus traditional allocation to the deluxe product differ?

ANSWER

In the traditional system, the deluxe product receives only 25% of the overhead costs because it uses only 25% of the machine hours. But in the ABC system, it receives 69% of the overhead because it uses 63% of the parts and 83% of the setups.

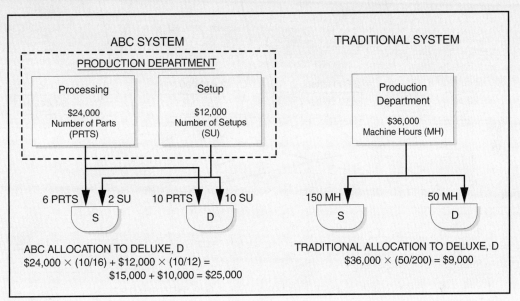

5-7) plus portions of the costs of all other resources that support the billing activity (paper, occupancy, computer, and billing labour). Notice that the total traceable costs of $205,332 + $35,384 + $235,777 + $88,847 = $565,340 in Exhibit 5-9 equals the total indirect costs in Exhibit 5-7. Next, the physical flow of cost-driver units was determined for each activity or cost object. For each activity centre, the traceable costs were divided by the sum of the physical flows to establish a cost per cost-driver unit.

Step 4. *Calculate and interpret the new activity-based information.* The activity-based cost per account for each customer class can be determined from the data in Step 3. Exhibit 5-10 shows the computations.

Examine the last two items in Exhibit 5-10. Notice that traditional costing indicated higher costs for the high-volume residential accounts and substantially lower costs for the low-volume commercial accounts. The ABC cost per account for residential accounts is $2.28, which is $1.41 less than the $3.69 cost generated by the traditional costing system. The cost per account for commercial accounts is $14.57, which is $8.42 more than the $6.15 cost from the traditional cost system. Management's belief that traditional costing was undercosting commercial accounts was supported. PPC's management

EXHIBIT 5-9

ABC System

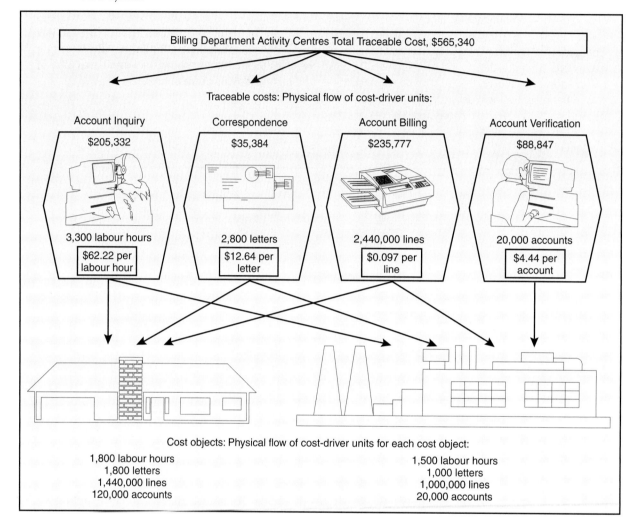

Billing Department Activity Centres Total Traceable Cost, $565,340

Traceable costs: Physical flow of cost-driver units:

Account Inquiry — $205,332 — 3,300 labour hours — $62.22 per labour hour

Correspondence — $35,384 — 2,800 letters — $12.64 per letter

Account Billing — $235,777 — 2,440,000 lines — $0.097 per line

Account Verification — $88,847 — 20,000 accounts — $4.44 per account

Cost objects: Physical flow of cost-driver units for each cost object:

1,800 labour hours
1,800 letters
1,440,000 lines
120,000 accounts

1,500 labour hours
1,000 letters
1,000,000 lines
20,000 accounts

now has the cost information that they think is preferred for planning and decision-making purposes.

These results are common when companies perform activity-based costing studies—high-volume cost objects with simple processes are overcosted when only one volume-based cost driver is used. In the BD, this volume-based cost-driver was the number of inquiries. Which system makes more sense—the traditional allocation system that "spreads" all support costs to customer classes based solely on the number of inquiries, or the activity-based costing system that identifies key activities and assigns costs based on the consumption of units of cost drivers chosen for each key activity? For PPC, the probable benefits of the new activity-based costing system may outweigh the costs of implementing and maintaining the new cost system. However, the cost-benefit balance must be assessed on a case-by-case basis.

EXHIBIT 5-10

Key Results of Activity-Based Costing Study

DRIVER COSTS

Activity/Resource (Driver Units)	Traceable Costs (From Exhibit 5-9) (1)	Total Physical Flow of Driver Units (From Exhibit 5-9) (2)	Cost per Driver Unit (1)÷(2)
Account Inquiry (Labour Hours)	$205,332	3,300 hours	$62.22
Correspondence (Letters)	$ 35,384	2,800 letters	$12.64
Account Billing (Lines)	$235,777	2,440,000 lines	$ 0.097
Account Verification (Accounts)	$ 88,847	20,000 accounts	$ 4.44

COST PER CUSTOMER CLASS

	Cost Per Driver Unit	Residential Physical Flow of Driver Units	Residential Cost	Commercial Physical Flow of Driver Units	Commercial Cost
Account Inquiry	$62.22	1,800 hours	$111,999	1,500 hours	$ 93,333
Correspondence	$12.64	1,800 letters	$ 22,747	1,000 letters	$ 12,638
Account Billing	$ 0.097	1,440,000 lines	$139,147	1,000,000 lines	$ 96,629
Account Verification	$ 4.44	0	$ 0	20,000 accounts	$ 88,847
Total Cost			$273,893		$291,447
Number of Accounts			120,000		20,000
Cost per Account			$ 2.28		$ 14.57
Cost per Account (Traditional System)			$ 3.69		$ 6.15

Note: Some differences may exist due to rounding.

STRATEGIC INSIGHTS & COMPANY PRACTICES

Dow Chemical Uses ABC to Improve Its Allocation of Service Costs

Dow Canada is a wholly owned subsidiary of the Dow Chemical Company. Dow Canada, based in Calgary, has manufacturing operations in Alberta, Manitoba, Ontario, and Quebec. Management of the parent company believes that its ABC allocation system is the foundation of its cost management system. Dow, with annual revenues of more than $40 billion, is the largest chemical company in the United States. The company has three major business segments: plastics, chemicals, and agricultural products. Dow switched from a traditional allocation system to ABC in the mid-1990s as part of a major shift in its total strategy. It sold its pharmaceutical, energy, and consumer products businesses and set a goal to be the number one company in chemicals, plastics, and agroscience. Dow believed that to accomplish its goal, it needed to improve the quality and accuracy of its costing system, including the costs of internal services such as those provided by the human resources and maintenance departments.

Service providers such as human resources and maintenance identified the major activities performed, determined the appropriate cost drivers for each activity, and computed costs for each activity and service provided to user departments. The focus on activities has led to a better understanding of costs and better cost control. One technique Dow's managers use to improve cost control is benchmarking. Service providers benchmark their costs against outside providers to ensure that the service or activity cost is competitive. Another advantage of the ABC system is improved resource planning and utilization. By focusing on activities and their related cost drivers, Dow's maintenance department managers can more effectively plan maintenance resource needs and availability. Overall, since the company integrated ABC into its cost management system, it has realized significant benefits.

Sources: J. Damitio, G. Hayes, and P. Kintzele, "Integrating ABC and ABM at Dow Chemical," *Management Accounting Quarterly*, Winter 2000, pp. 22–26 (published by the Institute of Management Accountants: www.imanet.org, under "publications"); Dow Chemical Company, *2004 Annual Report.*

Activity-Based Management

OBJECTIVE 6

Explain why activity-based management systems are being adopted.

Cost Management System. Identifies how management's decisions affect costs, by first measuring the resources used in performing the organization's activities and then assessing the effects on costs of changes in those activities.

Activity-Based Management (ABM). The use of an activity-based costing system to improve the operations of an organization.

To better support managers' decisions, accountants go beyond simply determining the cost of products and services. They develop cost management systems. A **cost management system** identifies how management's decisions affect costs. To do so, it first measures the resources used in performing the organization's activities and then assesses the effects on costs of changes in those activities.

Recall that managers' day-to-day focus is on managing activities, not costs. So, because ABC systems also focus on activities, they are very useful in cost management. Using an activity-based costing system to improve the operations of an organization is called **activity-based management (ABM)**. In the broadest terms, activity-based management aims to improve the value received by customers and to improve profits by providing this value.

The cornerstone of ABM is distinguishing between value-added costs and non-value-added costs. A **value-added cost** is the cost of an activity that cannot be eliminated without affecting a product's value to the customer. Value-added costs are necessary (as long as the activity that drives such costs is performed efficiently). In contrast, companies try to minimize **non-value-added costs**—costs that can be eliminated without affecting a product's value to the customer. Activities such as handling and storing inventories, transporting partly finished products from one part of the plant to another, and changing the setup of production line operations to produce a different model of the product are all non-value-added activities that can be reduced, if not eliminated, by careful redesign of the plant layout and the production process.

Let us return now to Pacific Power Company to see how the billing department could use the ABC system to improve its operation. Recall that the BD needed to find a way to increase its capacity to handle accounts due to an expected large increase in demand from a new housing development and shopping centre. BD managers also were interested (as always is the case) in reducing the operating costs of the department while not impairing the quality of the service provided to its customers. To do so, they used the ABC information from Exhibit 5-10 to identify non-value-added activities that had significant costs. Account inquiry and account verification activities are non-value-added and costly, so management asked for ideas for cost reductions. The new information provided by the ABC system generated the following ideas for improvement:

- Use the service bureau for commercial accounts because of the significant cost savings. The service bureau's bid is for $8.50 per account compared to the BD's activity-based cost of $14.57 (from Exhibit 5-10), a difference of more than $6 per account! The freed-up capacity can be used to meet the expected increase in residential demand. Account verification, a non-value-added activity, would also be eliminated because only commercial accounts are verified.
- Exhibit 5-10 indicates that account inquiry activity is very costly, accounting for a significant portion of total BD costs. One idea is to make bills more descriptive in order to reduce the number of inquiries. Doing so would add lines to each bill, resulting in higher billing-activity costs, but the number of inquiries would be reduced, thus reducing a significant non-value-added cost. Whether this idea would result in a net cost reduction needs to be evaluated by the accountants with the help of the new ABC system.

Summary of Activity-Based Costing

Activity-based accounting systems can turn many indirect overhead costs into direct costs by identifying each overhead cost/activity separately and using different cost drivers to trace certain costs directly to each activity—costs identified specifically with given cost objects. Appropriate selection of activities and cost drivers allows managers to trace many manufacturing overhead costs to cost objects just as specifically as they have traced direct material and direct-labour costs. Because activity-based accounting systems classify more costs as direct than do traditional systems, managers have greater confidence in the costs of products and services reported by activity-based systems.

Because activity-based accounting systems are more complex and costly than traditional systems, not all companies use them. But more and more organizations in both manufacturing and non-manufacturing industries are adopting activity-based systems for a variety of reasons:

- Globalization and fierce competitive pressure has resulted in shrinking margins. Companies may know their overall margin, but they often do not believe in the accuracy of the margins for *individual* products or services.
- Business complexity has increased, which results in greater diversity in the types of products and services as well as customer classes. Therefore, the consumption of a company's shared resources also varies substantially across different products and customers.

- New production techniques have increased the proportion of indirect costs—that is, indirect costs are far more important in today's world-class business environment. Indirect costs are sometimes over 50 percent of total cost, and activity-based costing assists by turning a good part of them into direct costs.
- The rapid pace of technology change has shortened product life cycles. Hence, companies do not have time to make price or cost adjustments once errors are discovered.
- Computer technology has reduced the costs of developing and operating activity-based cost systems that track many activities.

Just-in-Time (JIT) Systems

OBJECTIVE 7

Explain how JIT systems can reduce non-value-added activities.

Just-in-Time (JIT) Production System. A system in which an organization purchases materials and parts and produces components just when they are needed in the production process, the goal being to have zero or near zero inventory, because holding inventory is a non-value-added activity.

Production Cycle Time. The time from initiating production to delivering the goods to the customer.

Attempts to minimize non-value-added costs have led many organizations to adopt just-in-time systems to eliminate waste and improve quality. In a **just-in-time (JIT) production system**, an organization purchases materials and parts and produces components just when they are needed in the production process. Goods are not produced until it is time for them to be shipped to a customer. The goal is to have zero or near zero inventory, because holding inventory is a non-value-added activity.

JIT companies are customer-oriented because customer orders drive the production process. An order triggers the immediate delivery of materials, followed by production and delivery of the goods. Instead of producing inventory and hoping an order will come, a JIT system produces products directly for received orders. Several factors are crucial to the success of JIT systems:

1. Focus on quality. JIT companies try to involve all employees in controlling quality. While any system can seek quality improvements, JIT systems emphasize *total quality control (TQC)* and *continuous improvement in quality*. If all employees strive for zero defects, non-value-added activities such as inspection and rework of defective items are minimized.

2. Short **production cycle time** is defined as the time from initiating production to delivery of goods to the customer. Keeping production cycle times short allows timely response to customer orders and reduces the level of inventories. Many JIT companies have achieved remarkable reductions in production cycle times. For example, applying JIT methods in one IBM division in Bromont, Quebec, cut process lead times on a ceramic substrate product from 30 to 40 days to seven days.

3. Smooth flow of production. Fluctuations in production rates inevitably lead to delays in delivery to customers and excess inventories. To achieve smooth production flow, JIT companies simplify the production process to reduce the possibilities of delay. Companies develop close relationships with suppliers to assure timely delivery and high quality of purchased materials, and perform routine maintenance on equipment to prevent costly breakdowns. For example, Omark, a chainsaw manufacturer in Guelph, Ontario, reduced production flow distance from 806 to 53 metres.

4. Flexible production operations. Two dimensions are important: facilities flexibility and employee flexibility. Facilities should be able to produce a variety of components and products to provide extra capacity when a particular product is in high demand and to avoid shutdown when a unique facility breaks down. Facilities should also require short setup times—the time it takes to switch from producing one product to another. Cross-

Billing department managers debated whether they should allocate the "other activities" cost pool to the two customer classes or leave it unallocated. Although the plausibility and reliability of the cost driver—number of printed pages—was not as high as normally desired, management accepted it because they wanted to allocate all costs to the two customer classes in order to compare full unit costs to the costs bid by the local service bureau. What would be the impact on the costs per account if the billing department did not allocate the "other activities" cost pool?

ANSWER

The costs per account would be less if the billing department did not allocate the other activities cost pool. This may lead to a bad decision by management to reject the service bureau's offer. The unallocated costs will not go away simply because management does not allocate them to customer classes. This is a common managerial issue—the tradeoff between the need for comparability of cost data and the need for plausible and reliable cost drivers used to generate the cost data.

training employees—training employees to do a variety of jobs—provides further flexibility. Multiskilled workers can fill in when a particular operation is overloaded, and can reduce setup time. One company reported a reduction in setup time from 45 minutes to one minute by training production workers to perform the setup operations.

Many companies help achieve these objectives by improving the physical layout of their plants. In conventional manufacturing, similar machines (e.g., lathes, moulding machines, drilling machines) are grouped together. Workers specialize on only one machine operation (operating either the moulding or the drilling machine). There are at least two negative effects of such a layout. First, products must be moved from one area of the plant to another for required processing. This increases material handling costs and results in work-in-process inventories that can be substantial. These are non-value-added activities and costs. Second, the specialized labour resource is often idle—waiting for work-in-process. This wasted resource—labour time—is also non-value-added.

Cellular Manufacturing. In a JIT production system, the process of organizing machines into cells according to the specific requirements of the product family.

In a JIT production system, machines are often organized in cells according to the specific requirements of a product family. This process is called **cellular manufacturing**. Only the machines that are needed for the product family are in the cell, and these machines are located as close to each other as possible. Workers are trained to use all the cellular machines. Each cell (often shaped in the form of a "U") is a mini-factory or focused factory. Both of the problems associated with the conventional production layout are eliminated in cellular manufacturing. Work-in-process inventories are reduced or eliminated because there is no need for moving and storing inventory. Idle time is reduced or eliminated because workers are capable of moving from idle machine activity to needed activities. As a result, cycle times are reduced.

Accounting for a JIT system is often simpler than for other systems. Most cost accounting systems focus on determining product costs for inventory valuation. But JIT systems have minimal inventories, so there is less benefit from an elaborate inventory costing system. In JIT systems, materials, labour, and overhead costs could potentially be charged directly to cost of goods sold because inventories are small enough to be ignored. All costs of production are assumed to apply to products that have already been sold.

HIGHLIGHTS TO REMEMBER

1. **Explain the major reasons for allocating costs.** The three main purposes of cost allocation are to motivate managers and employees, to better compute income and asset valuation, and to justify costs for pricing or reimbursement.

2. **Allocate the variable and fixed costs of service departments to other organizational units.** The dual method of allocation is used for service department costs. Variable costs should be allocated using budgeted cost rates times the actual cost-driver level. Fixed costs should be allocated using budgeted percent of capacity available for use times the total budgeted fixed costs.

3. **Use the direct and step-down methods to allocate service department costs to user departments.** When service departments support other service departments in addition to producing departments, there are three methods for allocation. The direct method ignores other service departments when allocating costs. The step-down method and the reciprocal allocation method recognize other service departments' use of services.

4. **Integrate service department allocation systems with traditional and ABC systems to allocate total systems costs to final cost objects.** When the cost object is the products or services provided by a company, service department allocations must be integrated with the allocation system used to cost final cost objects. Two approaches that are frequently used are the traditional and ABC approaches. The ABC approach provides more accurate estimates of product or service costs than the traditional approach but is more costly to maintain.

5. **Allocate the central corporate costs of an organization.** Central costs include public relations, top corporate management overhead, legal, data processing, controller's department, and company-wide planning. Often, it is best to allocate only those central costs of an organization for which measures of usage by departments are available.

6. **Allocate joint costs to products using the physical-units, relative-sales-value, and net-realizable-value methods.** Joint costs are often allocated to products for inventory valuation and income determination using the physical-units, relative-sales-value or net-realizable-value method. However, such allocations should not affect decisions.

7. **Understand the main differences between traditional and activity-based costing systems and why ABC systems provide value to managers.** Traditional systems usually allocate only the indirect costs of the production function. ABC systems allocate many (and sometimes all) of the costs of the value-chain functions. Traditional costing accumulates costs using categories such as direct material, direct labour, and production overhead. ABC systems accumulate costs by activities required to produce a product or service. The key value of ABC systems is in their increased costing accuracy and better information provided that can lead to process improvements.

8. **Design a cost accounting system that includes activity-based costing.** Designing and implementing an activity-based costing system involves four steps. First, managers determine the cost objects, key activities, and resources used, and they identify cost drivers (output measures) for each resource and activity. Second, they determine the relationship among cost objects, activities, and resources. The third step is collecting cost and operating data. The last step is to calculate and interpret the new activity-based information. Often, this last step requires the use of a computer due to the complexity of many ABC systems.

9. **Use activity-based cost information to make strategic and operational control decisions.** Activity-based management is using ABC information to improve operations. A key advantage of an activity-based costing system is its ability to aid managers in decision making. ABC improves the accuracy of cost estimates, including product and customer costs and the costs of value-added versus non-value-added activities. ABC also improves managers' understanding of operations. Managers can focus their attention on making strategic decisions, such as product mix, pricing, and process improvements.

DEMONSTRATION PROBLEMS FOR YOUR REVIEW

Problem One

Nonmanufacturing organizations often find it useful to trace costs to final products or services. Consider a hospital. The output of a hospital is not as easy to define as the output of a factory. Assume the following measures of output in three revenue-producing departments:

DEPARTMENT	MEASURES OF OUTPUT*
Radiology	X-ray films processed
Laboratory	Tests administered
Daily Patient Services**	Patient-days of care (that is, the number of patients multiplied by the number of days of each patient's stay)

* These become the "product" cost objects, the various revenue-producing activities of a hospital.
** There would be many of these departments, such as obstetrics, paediatrics, and orthopedics. Moreover, there may be both in-patient and out-patient care.

Budgeted output for 2006 is 60,000 X-ray films processed in Radiology, 50,000 tests administered in the Laboratory, and 30,000 patient-days in Daily Patient Services.

In addition to the revenue-producing departments, the hospital has three main service departments: Administrative and Fiscal Services, Plant Operations and Maintenance, and Laundry. (Of course, real hospitals have more than three revenue-producing departments and more than three service departments. This problem is simplified to keep the data manageable.)

The hospital has decided that the cost driver for Administrative and Fiscal Services costs is the direct department costs of the other departments. The cost driver for Plant Operations and Maintenance is square metres occupied and for Laundry, kilograms of laundry. The pertinent budget data for 2006 are as follows:

	DIRECT DEPARTMENT COSTS	SQUARE METRES OCCUPIED	KILOGRAMS OF LAUNDRY
Administrative and Fiscal Services	$1,000,000	1,000	–
Plant Operations and Maintenance	800,000	2,000	–
Laundry	200,000	5,000	–
Radiology	1,000,000	12,000	80,000
Laboratory	400,000	3,000	20,000
Daily Patient Services	1,600,000	80,000	300,000
Total	$5,000,000	103,000	400,000

1. Allocate service department costs using the direct method.
2. Allocate service department costs using the step-down method. Allocate Administrative and Fiscal Services first, Plant Operations and Maintenance second, and Laundry third.
3. Compute the cost per unit of output in each of the revenue-producing departments using the costs determined using (a) the direct method for allocating service department costs (requirement 1) and (b) the costs determined using the step-down method for allocating service department costs (requirement 2).

Solution

1. The solutions to all three requirements are shown in Exhibit 5-11. The direct method is presented first. Note that no service department costs are allocated to another cost driver in the revenue-producing department. For example, in allocating Plant Operations and Maintenance, square metres occupied by the service departments is ignored. The cost driver is the 95,000 square metres occupied by the revenue-producing departments.

    Note that the total cost of the revenue-producing departments after allocation, $1,474,386 + $568,596 + $2,957,018 = $5,000,000, is equal to the total of the direct department costs in all six departments before allocation.

2. The step-down method is shown in the lower half of Exhibit 5-11. The costs of Administrative and Fiscal Services are allocated to all five other departments. Because a department's own costs are not allocated to itself, the cost driver consists of the $4,000,000 direct department costs in the five departments excluding Administrative and Fiscal Services.

EXHIBIT 5-11

Allocation of Service-Department Costs: Two Methods

	ADMINISTRATIVE AND FISCAL SERVICES	PLANT OPERATIONS AND MAINTENANCE	LAUNDRY	RADIOLOGY	LABORATORY	DAILY PATIENT SERVICES
Allocation base	Accumulated costs	Square metres	Kilograms			
1. Direct Method						
Direct department costs						
before allocation	$1,000,000	$ 800,000	$200,000	$1,000,000	$400,000	$1,600,000
Administrative and fiscal services	(1,000,000)	–	–	333,333*	133,333	533,334
Plant operations and maintenance		(800,000)	–	101,053†	25,263	673,684
Laundry			(200,000)	40,000††	10,000	150,000
Total costs after allocation	0	0	0	$1,474,386	$568,596	$2,957,018
Product output in x-ray films, tests, and patient-days, respectively				60,000	50,000	30,000
3a. Cost per unit of output				$ 24.573	$ 11.372	$ 98.567
2. Step-Down Method						
Direct department costs before allocation	$1,000,000	$ 800,000	$200,000	1,000,000	$400,000	$1,600,000
Administrative and fiscal services	(1,000,000)	200,000§	50,000	250,000	100,000	400,000
Plant operations and maintenance		(1,000,000)	50,000¶	120,000	30,000	800,000
Laundry			(300,000)	60,000#	15,000	225,000
Total costs after allocation	0	0	0	$1,430,000	$545,000	$3,025,000
Product output in x-ray films, tests, and patient-days, respectively				60,000	50,000	30,000
3b. Cost per unit of output				$ 23.833	$ 10.900	$ 100.833

* $1,000,000 ÷ ($1,000,000 + $400,000 + $1,600,000) = 33 1/3%; 33 1/3% × $1,000,000 = $333,333; etc.
† $800,000 ÷ (12,000 + 3,000 + 80,000) = $8.4210526; $8.4210526 × 12,000 square metres = $101,053; etc.
†† $200,000 ÷ (80,000 + 20,000 + 300,000) = $0.50; $0.50 × 80,000 = $40,000; etc.
§ $1,000,000 ÷ ($800,000 + $200,000 + $1,000,000 + $400,000 + $1,600,000) = $0.25; $0.25 × $800,000 = $200,000; etc.
¶ $1,000,000 ÷ (5,000 + 12,000 + 3,000 + 80,000) = $10.00; $10.00 × 5,000 square metres = $50,000; etc.
# $300,000 ÷ (80,000 + 20,000 + 300,000) = $0.75; $0.75 × 80,000 = $60,000; etc.

Plant Operations and Maintenance is allocated second on the basis of square metres occupied. No cost will be allocated to itself or back to Administrative and Fiscal Services. Therefore, the square metres used for allocation is the 100,000 square metres occupied by the other four departments.

Laundry is allocated third. No cost would be allocated back to the first two departments, even if they had used laundry services.

As in the direct method, note that the total costs of the revenue-producing departments after allocation, $1,430,000 + $545,000 + $3,025,000 = $5,000,000, equal the total of the direct department costs before allocation.

3. The solutions are labelled 3a and 3b in Exhibit 5-11. Compare the unit costs derived from the direct method with those of the step-down method. In many instances, the final product costs may not differ

enough to warrant investing in a cost-allocation method that is any fancier than the direct method. But sometimes even small differences may be significant; for example, to a government agency or anybody paying for a large volume of services based on costs. In Exhibit 5-11, the "cost" of an "average" laboratory test is either $11.37 or $10.90. This may be significant for the fiscal committee of the hospital's board of trustees, who must make budgeting and resource-allocation decisions. Thus cost allocation is often a technique that helps answer the vital question, "Who should pay for what, and how much?"

Problem Two

Last year, TCY Company's demand for product H17 was 14,000 units. At a recent meeting, the sales manager asked the controller about the expected cost for the sales-order activity for the current year. A new ABC system had been installed, and the controller had provided a sketch of the order-processing activity to the sales manager (see Exhibit 5-12). The sales manager wanted to know how the order-processing activity affects costs. The average sales order is for 20 units. The order-processing activity shown in Exhibit 5-12 requires a computer, processing labour, and telecommunications. The computer is leased at a cost of $2,000 per period. Salaries are $7,000, and telecommunication charges are $1.60 per minute.

1. How many labour hours does it take to process each order? How much telecommunication time does each order take?
2. What is the total cost formula for the order-processing activity? What is the total and unit cost for demand of 14,000 units?
3. The sales manager calculated the cost per order to be $32.06 based on the expected demand of 14,000 units of H17. Because she believed that this year's demand for H17 may be only 12,000 units, she then calculated the total cost of processing 600 orders as $19,236 = 600 × $32.06. Comment on the validity of the sales manager's analysis.

Solution

1. It takes 0.1 hour or 6 minutes of labour time and 12 minutes of telecommunications time to process an order.
2. The total cost formula for order processing activity is:

$$\text{Total Cost} = \text{Fixed Costs} + \text{Variable Costs}$$
$$= \text{Lease Cost} + \text{Labour Cost} + \text{Telecom.}$$
$$\text{cost/min.} \times \text{min./order} \times \text{no. of orders}$$
$$= \$2,000 + \$7,000 + \$1.60 \times 12 \times \text{Number of Orders}$$
$$= \$9,000 + \$19.20 \times \text{Number of Orders}$$

For 14,000 units, there will be 700 orders processed. The total cost to process these orders is:

$$\text{Total Cost} = \$9,000 + (\$19.20 \times 700) = \$22,440 \text{ and the unit cost is}$$
$$\$32.06 \ (22,440/700)$$

3. The sales manager has fallen into the trap of ignoring cost behaviour. Her calculation assumes that unit fixed costs will not change with

EXHIBIT 5-12

TCY's Order-Processing
Activity

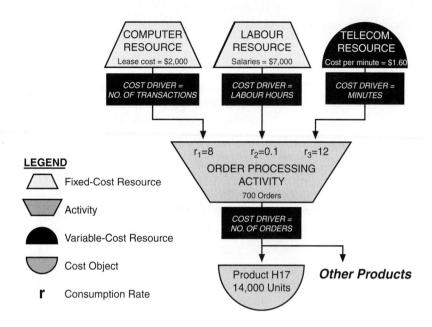

changes in demand or the cost driver. The correct prediction of total cost for a demand of 12,000 units (or 600 orders) is:

$$\text{Total Cost} = \$9,000 + \$19.20 \times 600 = \$20,520$$

This problem illustrates why it is important to take cost behaviour into consideration when using any costing system for planning purposes.

KEY TERMS

activity-based costing (ABC) *p. 200*
activity-based management (ABM)
     p. 212
by-product *p. 200*
cellular manufacturing *p. 215*
cost accounting system *p. 185*
cost-allocation base *p. 185*
cost application *p. 197*
cost management system *p. 212*
cost pool *p. 185*

direct method *p. 193*
joint costs *p. 198*
just-in-time production system *p. 214*
non-value-added costs *p. 212*
production cycle time *p. 214*
reciprocal allocation method *p. 195*
revenue-producing departments *p. 187*
service departments *p. 187*
step-down method *p. 193*
value-added costs *p. 212*

ASSIGNMENT MATERIAL

QUESTIONS

Q5-1 What is the purpose of a cost accounting system?

Q5-2 "A cost pool is a group of costs that is physically traced to the appropriate cost object." Do you agree? Explain.

Q5-3 Give five terms that are sometimes used as substitutes for the term "allocate."

Q5-4 What are the three purposes of cost allocation?

Q5-5 What are the three types of allocations?

Q5-6 Give three guides for the allocation of service department costs.

Q5-7 Why should budgeted-cost rates, rather than actual-cost rates, be used for assigning the variable costs of service departments?

Q5-8 Why do many companies allocate fixed costs separately from variable costs?

Q5-9 "We used a lump-sum allocation method for fixed costs a few years ago, but we gave it up because managers always predicted usage below what they actually used." Is this a common problem? How might it be prevented?

Q5-10 "A commonly misused basis for allocation is dollar sales." Explain.

Q5-11 How could national advertising costs be allocated to territories?

Q5-12 Briefly describe the three popular methods for allocating service-department costs.

Q5-13 "The step-down method allocates more costs to the producing departments than does the direct method." Do you agree? Explain.

Q5-14 How does the term *cost application* differ from *cost allocation*?

Q5-15 What is a non-volume-related cost driver? Give two examples.

Q5-16 How are costs of various overhead resources allocated to products, services, or customers in an ABC system?

Q5-17 Briefly explain each of the three conventional ways of allocating joint costs to products.

Q5-18 What are by-products and how do we account for them?

Q5-19 Give four examples of activities and related cost drivers that can be used in an ABC system to allocate costs to products, services, or customers.

Q5-20 "Activity-based costing is useful for product costing but not for planning and control." Do you agree? Explain.

Q5-21 Refer to Exhibit 5-6. Suppose the appliance maker has two plants—the Salem plant and the Youngstown plant. The Youngstown plant produces only three appliances that are very similar in material and production requirements. The Salem plant produces a wide variety of appliances with diverse material and production requirements. Which type of costing system would you recommend for each plant (traditional or ABC)? Explain.

Q5-22 Name four steps in the design and implementation of an activity-based costing system.

Q5-23 Refer to the Pacific Power illustration. Which resource costs depicted in Exhibit 5-7 could have variable cost behaviour?

Q5-24 Why do organizations adopt activity-based costing systems?

Q5-25 Why do managers want to distinguish between value-added activities and non-value-added activities?

Q5-26 Name four factors crucial to the success of just-in-time production systems.

Q5-27 "ABC and JIT are alternative techniques for achieving competitiveness." Do you agree?

PROBLEMS

P5-1 FIXED- AND VARIABLE-COST POOLS. The city of Castle Rock signed a lease for a photocopy machine at $2,500 per month and $0.02 per copy. Operating costs for toner, paper, operator salary, etc. are all variable at $0.03 per copy. Departments had projected a need for 100,000 copies a month. The City Planning Department predicted its usage at 36,000 copies a month. It made 42,000 copies in August.

1. Suppose one predetermined rate per copy was used for all photocopy costs. What rate would be used and how much cost would be allocated to the City Planning Department in August?
2. Suppose fixed- and variable-cost pools were charged separately. Specify how each pool should be charged. Compute the cost charged to the City Planning Department in August.
3. Which method, the one in requirement 1 or the one in requirement 2, do you prefer? Explain.

P5-2 SALES-BASED ALLOCATIONS. Pioneer Markets has three grocery stores in a metropolitan area. Central costs are allocated using sales as the cost driver. The following are budgeted and actual sales during November:

	SUNNYVILLE	YORKVILLE	DISCOUNTVILLE
Budgeted sales	$600,000	$1,000,000	$400,000
Actual sales	$600,000	$700,000	$500,000

Central costs of $200,000 are to be allocated in November.

1. Compute the central costs allocated to each store with *budgeted* sales as the cost driver.
2. Compute the central costs allocated to each store with *actual* sales as the cost driver.
3. What advantages are there to using budgeted rather than actual sales for allocating the central costs?

P5-3 DIRECT AND STEP-DOWN ALLOCATIONS. Zenith Home Products has two producing departments, machining and assembly, and two service departments, personnel and custodial. The company's budget for April 2006 is

	SERVICE DEPARTMENTS		PRODUCTION DEPARTMENTS	
	PERSONNEL	CUSTODIAL	MACHINING	ASSEMBLY
Direct department costs	$32,000	$70,000	$600,000	$800,000
Square metres	2,000	1,000	10,000	25,000
Number of employees	15	30	200	250

Zenith allocates personnel costs on the basis of number of employees and custodial costs on the basis of square metres.

1. Allocate personnel and custodial costs to the producing departments using the direct method.
2. Allocate personnel and custodial costs to the producing departments using the step-down method. Allocate personnel costs first.

P5-4 **JOINT COSTS.** Lisbon Company's production process for two of its solvents can be diagrammed as follows:

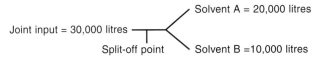

Joint input = 30,000 litres —⟨ Solvent A = 20,000 litres

Split-off point — Solvent B =10,000 litres

The cost of the joint inputs, including processing costs before the split-off point, is $400,000. Solvent A can be sold at split-off for $10 per litre and Solvent B for $30 per litre.

1. Allocate the $400,000 joint cost to Solvents A and B by the physical-units method.
2. Allocate the $400,000 joint cost to Solvents A and B by the relative-sales-value method.

P5-5 **JOINT PRODUCTS.** Kumar Milling buys oats at $0.60 per kilogram and produces Oat Flour, Oat Flakes, and Oat Bran. The process of separating the oats into oat flour and oat bran costs $0.30 per kilogram. The oat flour can be sold for $1.50 per kilogram, the oat bran for $2.00 per kilogram. Each kilogram of oats has 0.2 kilograms of oat bran and 0.8 kilograms of oat flour. A kilogram of oat flour can be made into oat flakes for a fixed cost of $240,000 plus a variable cost of $0.60 per kilogram. Kumar Milling plans to process 1 million kilograms of oats in 2006, at a purchase price of $600,000.

1. Allocate all the joint costs to oat flour and oat bran using the physical-units method.
2. Allocate all the joint costs to oat flour and oat bran using the relative-sales-value method.
3. Suppose there was no market for oat flour. Instead, it must be made into oat flakes to be sold. Oat flakes sell for $2.90 per kilogram. Allocate the joint cost to oat bran and oat flakes using the relative-sales-value method.

P5-6 **BY-PRODUCT COSTING.** The Wenatchee Company buys apples from local orchards and presses them to produce apple juice. The pulp that remains after pressing is sold to farmers as livestock food. This livestock food is accounted for as a by-product.

During the 2006 fiscal year, the company paid $1,000,000 to purchase 8 million kilograms of apples. After processing, 1 million kilograms of pulp remained. Wenatchee spent $35,000 to package and ship the pulp, which was sold for $50,000.

1. How much of the joint cost of the apples is allocated to the pulp?
2. Compute the total inventory cost (and therefore the cost of goods sold) for the pulp.
3. Assume that $130,000 was spent to press the apples and $150,000 was spent to filter, pasteurize, and pack the apple juice. Compute the total inventory cost of the apple juice produced.

P5-7 JIT AND NON-VALUE-ADDED ACTIVITIES. A motorcycle manufacturer was concerned with declining market share because of foreign competition. To become more efficient, the company was considering changing to a just-in-time (JIT) production system. As a first step in analyzing the feasibility of the change, the company identified its major activities. Among the 120 activities were the following:

> Materials receiving and inspection
>
> Production scheduling
>
> Production setup
>
> Rear-wheel assembly
>
> Moving engine from fabrication to assembly building
>
> Assembling handlebars
>
> Paint inspection
>
> Reworking defective brake assemblies
>
> Installing speedometers
>
> Putting completed motorcycle in finished goods storage

> 1. From the list of ten activities given above, prepare two lists—one of value-added activities and one of non-value-added activities.
> 2. For each non-value-added activity, explain how a JIT production system might eliminate, or at least reduce, the cost of the activity.

P5-8 COST ASSIGNMENT AND ALLOCATION. Hwang Management Consulting Company has two departments—accounting services and consulting services. For a given period, the following costs were incurred by the company as a whole: direct materials, $120,000; direct labour, $60,000; and consulting services overhead, $78,000. The total costs were $258,000.

The accounting services department incurred 80 percent of the direct-materials costs, but only 20 percent of the direct-labour costs. Overhead incurred by each department was allocated to projects in proportion to the direct-labour costs of projects within the departments.

Three projects were produced:

PROJECTS	DIRECT MATERIALS	DIRECT LABOUR
X-1	50%	33⅓%
Y-1	25	33⅓
Z-1	25	33⅓
Total for the accounting services department	100%	100%
X-1	33⅓%	40%
Y-1	33⅓	40
Z-1	33⅓	20
Total added by consulting services department	100%	100%

The overhead incurred by the accounting services department and allocated to all projects therein amounted to the following: accounting services, $36,000; consulting services, $42,000.

1. Compute the total costs incurred by the accounting services department and added by the consulting services department.
2. Compute the total costs of each project if all projects were completed.

P5-9 **COST ALLOCATION AND ACTIVITY-BASED ACCOUNTING.**   The cordless phone manufacturing division of a consumer electronics company uses activity-based accounting. For simplicity, assume that its accountants have identified only the following three activities and related cost drivers for manufacturing overhead:

ACTIVITY	COST DRIVER
Materials handling	Direct materials cost
Engineering	Engineering change orders
Power	Kilowatt hours

Three types of cordless phones are produced: SA2, SA5, and SA9. Direct costs and cost-driver activity for each product for a recent month are

	SA2	SA5	SA9
Direct materials cost	$25,000 (12.5%)	$50,000 (25%)	$125,000 (62.5%)
Direct labour cost	$4,000 (50%)	$1,000 (12.5%)	$3,000 (37.5%)
Kilowatt hours	50,000 (12.5%)	200,000 (50%)	150,000 (37.5%)
Engineering change orders	13 (65%)	5 (25%)	2 (10%)

Manufacturing overhead for the month was

Materials handling	$ 8,000
Engineering	20,000
Power	16,000
Total manufacturing overhead	$44,000

1. Compute the manufacturing overhead allocated to each product with the activity-based accounting system.
2. Suppose all manufacturing overhead costs have been allocated to products in proportion to their direct labour costs. Compute the manufacturing overhead allocated to each product.
3. In which product costs—those in requirement 1 or those in requirement 2—do you have the most confidence? Why?

P5-10 **HOSPITAL ALLOCATION BASE.**   Jade Soon, the administrator of General Hospital, is interested in obtaining more accurate cost allocations on the basis of cause and effect. The $180,000 of laundry costs has been allocated on the basis of 600,000 kilograms processed for all departments, or $0.30 per kilogram.

Soon is concerned that government health-care officials will require weighted statistics to be used for cost allocation. She asks you, "Please develop a revised base for allocating laundry costs. It should be better than our present base, but should not be overly complex either."

You study the situation and find that the laundry processes a large volume of uniforms for student nurses and physicians, and for dietary, housekeeping, and other personnel. In particular, the coats or jackets worn by personnel in the radiology department require unusual handwork.

A special study of laundry for radiology revealed that 7,500 of the 15,000 kilograms were jackets and coats that were five times more expensive to process than regular laundry items. A number of reasons explained the difference, but it was principally because of handwork involved.

Ignore the special requirements of the departments other than radiology. Revise the cost-allocation base and compute the new cost-allocation rate. Compute the total cost charged to radiology using kilograms and using the new base.

P5-11 COST OF PASSENGER TRAFFIC. Northern Pacific Railroad (NP) has a commuter operation that services passengers along a route between Vancouver and Whistler. Problems of cost allocation were highlighted in a news story about NP's application to the Public Utilities Commission (PUC) for a rate increase. The PUC staff claimed that the "avoidable annual cost" of running the operation was $700,000, in contrast to NP officials' claim of a loss of $9 million. PUC's estimate was based on what NP would be able to save if it shut down the commuter operations.

The NP loss estimate was based on a "full allocation of costs" method, which allocates a share of common maintenance and overhead costs to the passenger service.

If the PUC accepted its own estimate, a 25 percent fare increase would have been justified, whereas NP sought a 96 percent fare increase.

The PUC stressed that commuter costs represent less than 1 percent of the systemwide costs of NP and that 57 percent of the commuter costs are derived from some type of allocation method—sharing the costs of other operations.

NP's representative stated that "avoidable cost" is not an appropriate way to allocate costs for calculating rates. He said that "it is not fair to include just so-called above-the-rail costs" because there are other real costs associated with commuter service. Examples are maintaining smoother connections and making more frequent track inspections.

1. As Public Utilities Commissioner, what approach toward cost allocation would you favour for making decisions regarding fares? Explain.
2. How would fluctuations in freight traffic affect commuter costs under the NP method?

P5-12 ALLOCATING AUTOMOBILE COSTS. The motor pool of Megalopolis provides automobiles for the use of various city departments. Currently, the motor pool has 50 autos. A recent study showed that it costs $3,600 of annual fixed cost per automobile plus $0.10 per kilometre variable cost to own, operate, and maintain autos such as those provided by the motor pool.

Each month, the costs of the motor pool are charged to the user departments on the basis of kilometres driven. On average, each auto is driven 24,000 kilometres annually, although wide month-to-month variations occur. In April 2006, the 50 autos were driven a total of 50,000 kilometres. The motor pool's total costs for April were $24,000.

The chief planner for the city always seemed concerned about her auto costs. She was especially upset in April when she was charged $7,200 for the 15,000 kilometres driven in the department's five autos. This is the normal monthly mileage in the department. Her memo to the head of the motor pool stated, "I can certainly get autos at less than the $0.48 per kilometre you charged in April." The response was, "I am under instructions to allocate the motor-pool costs to the user departments. Your department was responsible for 30 percent of the April usage (15,000 kilometres ÷ 50,000 kilometres), so I allocated 30 percent of the motor pool's April costs to you (0.30 × $24,000). That just seems fair."

1. Calculate the city's average annual cost per kilometre for owning, maintaining, and operating an auto.
2. Explain why the allocated cost in April ($0.48 per kilometre) exceeds the average in requirement 1 above.
3. Describe any undesirable behavioural effects of the cost-allocation method used.
4. How would you improve the cost-allocation method?

P5-13 **ALLOCATION OF COSTS.** The Pegasus Trucking Company has one service department and two regional operating departments. The budgeted cost behaviour pattern of the service department is $750,000 monthly in fixed costs plus $0.80 per 1,000 tonne-kilometres operated in the East and West regions. (Tonne-kilometres are the number of metric tonnes carried times the number of kilometres travelled.) The actual monthly costs of the service department are allocated using tonne-kilometres operated as the cost driver.

1. Pegasus processed 500 million tonne-kilometres of traffic in April, half for each operating region. The actual costs of the services department were exactly equal to those predicted by the budget for 500 million tonne-kilometres. Compute the costs that would be allocated to each operation region.
2. Suppose the East region was plagued by strikes, so that the freight handled was much lower than originally anticipated. East moved only 150 million tonne-kilometres of traffic. The West region handled 250 million tonne-kilometres. The actual costs were exactly as budgeted for this lower level of activity. Compute the costs that would be allocated to East and West. Note that the total costs will be lower.
3. Refer to the facts in requirement 1 above. Various inefficiencies caused the service department to incur costs of $1,275,000. Compute the costs to be allocated to East and West. Are the allocations justified? If not, what improvement do you suggest?
4. Refer to the facts in requirement 2 above. Assume that assorted investment outlays for equipment and space in the service department were made to provide a basic maximum capacity to serve the East region at a level of 360 million tonne-kilometres and the West region at a level of 240 million tonne-kilometres. Suppose fixed costs are allocated on the basis of this capacity to serve. Variable costs are assigned by using a predetermined standard rate of $0.80 per 1,000 tonne-kilometres. Compute the costs to be allocated to each department. What are the advantages of this method over other methods?

P5-14 **HOSPITAL EQUIPMENT.** Many provinces have a hospital regulatory board that must approve the acquisition of specified medical equipment before the hospitals in the province can qualify for cost-based reimbursement related to that equipment. That is, hospitals cannot bill government agencies for the later use of the equipment unless the board originally authorized the acquisition.

Two hospitals in one such province proposed the acquisition and sharing of some expensive X-ray equipment to be used for unusual cases. The amortization and related fixed costs of operating the equipment were predicted at $12,000 per month. The variable costs were predicted at $30 per patient procedure.

The board asked each hospital to predict its usage of the equipment over its expected useful life of five years. Premier Hospital predicted an average usage of 75 X-rays per month, and St. Mary's Hospital predicted 50 X-rays per month. The commission regarded this information as critical to the size and degree of sophistication that would be justified. That is, if the number of X-rays exceeded a certain quantity per month, a different configuration of space, equipment, and personnel would be required, which would mean higher fixed costs per month.

1. Suppose fixed costs are allocated on the basis of the hospitals' predicted average use per month. Variable costs are assigned on the basis of $30 per X-ray, the budgeted variable-cost rate for the current fiscal year. In October, Premier Hospital had 50 X-rays and St. Mary's Hospital had 50 X-rays. Compute the total costs allocated to Premier Hospital and St. Mary's Hospital.

2. Suppose the manager of the equipment had various operating inefficiencies so that the total October costs were $16,500. Would you change your answers in requirement 1? Why?

3. A traditional method of cost allocation does not use the method in requirement 1. Instead, an allocation rate depends on the actual costs and actual volume encountered. The actual costs are totalled for the month and divided by the actual number of X-rays during the month. Suppose the actual costs agreed exactly with the budget for a total of 100 actual X-rays. Compute the total costs allocated to Premier Hospital and St. Mary's Hospital. Compare the results with those in requirement 1. What is the major weakness in this traditional method? What are some of its possible behavioural effects?

4. Describe any undesirable behavioural effects of the method described in requirement 1. How would you counteract any tendencies toward deliberate false predictions of long-run usage?

P5-15 **DIRECT METHOD FOR SERVICE DEPARTMENT ALLOCATION.** Wheelock Controls Company has two producing departments, Mechanical Instruments and Electronic Instruments. In addition, there are two service departments, Building Services and Materials Receiving and Handling. The company purchases a variety of component parts from which the departments assemble instruments for sale in domestic and international markets.

The Electronic Instruments division is highly automated. The manufacturing costs depend primarily on the number of subcomponents in each instrument. In contrast, the Mechanical Instruments division relies primarily on a large labour force to hand-assemble instruments. Its costs depend on direct labour hours.

The cost of Building Services depends primarily on the square metres occupied. The costs of Materials Receiving and Handling depend primarily on the total number of components handled.

Instruments M1 and M2 are produced in the Mechanical Instruments department, and E1 and E2 are produced in the Electronic Instruments department. Information about these products is as follows:

	DIRECT MATERIALS COST	NUMBER OF COMPONENTS	DIRECT LABOUR HOURS
M1	$74	25	4.0
M2	86	21	8.0
E1	63	10	1.5
E2	91	15	1.0

Budget figures for 2007 include

	BUILDING SERVICES	MATERIALS RECEIVING AND HANDLING	MECHANICAL INSTRUMENTS	ELECTRONIC INSTRUMENTS
Direct department costs (excluding direct materials cost)	$150,000	$120,000	$680,000	$548,000
Square metres occupied		5,000	50,000	25,000
Number of final instruments produced			8,000	10,000
Average number of components per instrument			10	16
Direct labour hours			30,000	8,000

1. Allocate the costs of the service departments using the direct method.
2. Using the results of requirement 1, compute the cost per direct labour hour in the Mechanical Instruments department and the cost per component in the Electronic Instruments department.
3. Using the results of requirement 2, compute the cost per unit of product for instruments M1, M2, E1, and E2.

P5-16 **STEP-DOWN METHOD FOR SERVICE DEPARTMENT ALLOCATION.** Refer to the data in Problem 5-15.

1. Allocate the costs of the service departments using the step-down method.
2. Using the results of requirement 1, compute the cost per direct-labour hour in the Mechanical Instruments department and the cost per component in the Electronic Instruments department.
3. Using the results of requirement 2, compute the cost per unit of product for instruments M1, M2, E1, and E2.

P5-17 **ACTIVITY-BASED COSTING.** Reliable Machining Products (RMP) is an automotive component supplier. RMP has been approached by Chrysler with a proposal to significantly increase production of Part T151A to a total annual quantity of 100,000. Chrysler believes that, by increasing the volume of production of Part T151A, RMP should realize the benefits of economies of scale and hence should accept a lower price than the current $6 per unit. Currently, RMP's gross margin on Part T151A is 3.3 percent, computed as follows:

	TOTAL	PER UNIT ($\div$100,000)
Direct materials	$150,000	$1.50
Direct labour	86,000	0.86
Factory overhead (400% $\times$ direct labour)	344,000	3.44
Total cost	$580,000	$5.80
Sales price		6.00
Gross margin		$0.20
Gross margin percentage		3.3%

The 400 percent overhead allocation rate is based on $3,300,000 annual factory overhead divided by $825,000 annual direct labour.

Part T151A seems to be a marginal profit product. If additional volume of production of Part T151A is to be added, RMP management believes that the sales price must be increased, not reduced as requested by Chrysler. The management of RMP sees this quoting situation as an excellent opportunity to examine the effectiveness of their traditional costing system versus an activity-based costing system. Data have been collected by a team consisting of accounting and engineering analysts.

ACTIVITY CENTRE	TRACEABLE FACTOR OVERHEAD COSTS (ANNUAL)
Quality	$800,000
Production scheduling	50,000
Setup	600,000
Shipping	300,000
Shipping administration	50,000
Production	1,500,000
Total costs	$3,300,000

ACTIVITY CENTRE: COST DRIVERS	ANNUAL COST DRIVER QUANTITY
Quality: No. of pieces scrapped	10,000
Production scheduling and setup:	
No. of setups	500
Shipping: No. of containers shipped	60,000
Shipping administration: No. of shipments	1,000
Production: No. of machine hours	10,000

The accounting and engineering team has provided the following cost-driver consumption estimates for the production of 100,000 units of Part T151A:

COST DRIVER	COST-DRIVER CONSUMPTION
Pieces scrapped	1,000
Setups	12
Containers shipped	500
Shipments	100
Machine hours	500

1. Prepare a schedule calculating the unit cost and gross margin of Part T151A using the activity-based costing approach.
2. Based on the ABC results, what course of action would you recommend regarding the proposal by Chrysler? List the benefits and costs associated with implementing an activity-based costing system at RMP.

P5-18 DIRECT AND STEP-DOWN METHODS OF ALLOCATION.   General Textiles Company has prepared departmental overhead budgets for normal activity levels before reapportionments, as follows:

Building and grounds	$ 20,000
Personnel	1,200
General factory administration*	28,020
Cafeteria operating loss	1,430
Storeroom	2,750
Machining	35,100
Assembly	56,500
	$145,000

* To be reapportioned before cafeteria.

Management has decided that the most sensible product costs are achieved by using departmental overhead rates. These rates are developed after appropriate service department costs are allocated to production departments.

Cost drivers for allocation are to be selected from the following data:

DEPARTMENT	DIRECT LABOUR HOURS	NUMBER OF EMPLOYEES	SQUARE METRES OF FLOOR SPACE OCCUPIED	TOTAL LABOUR HOURS	NUMBER OF REQUISITIONS
Building and grounds	–	–	–	–	–
Personnel*	–	–	2,000	–	–
General factory administration	–	35	7,000	–	–
Cafeteria operating loss	–	10	4,000	1,000	–
Storeroom	–	5	7,000	1,000	–
Machining	5,000	50	30,000	8,000	3,000
Assembly	15,000	100	50,000	17,000	1,500
	20,000	200	100,000	27,000	4,500

* Basis used is number of employees.

1. Allocate service-department costs by the step-down method. Develop overhead rates per direct labour hour for machining and assembly.
2. Same as requirement 1, using the direct method.
3. What would be the blanket plant-wide factory-overhead application rate, assuming that direct labour hours are used as a cost driver?
4. Using the following information about Job K10 and Job K11, prepare three different total overhead costs for each job, using rates developed in requirements 1, 2, and 3.

	Direct Labour Hours	
	MACHINING	ASSEMBLY
Job K10	19	2
Job K11	3	18

P5-19 JOINT COSTS AND DECISIONS. A chemical company has a batch process that takes 1,000 litres of a raw material and transforms it into 80 kilograms of X-1 and 400 kilograms of X-2. Although the joint costs of their production are $1,200, both products are worthless at their split-off point. Additional separable costs of $350 are necessary to give X-1 a sales value of $1,000 as Product A. Similarly, additional separable costs of $200 are necessary to give X-2 a sales value of $1,000 as Product B.

You are in charge of the batch process and the marketing of both products. (Show your computations for each answer.)

1. **a.** Assuming that you believe in assigning joint costs on a physical basis, allocate the total profit of $250 per batch to Products A and B.
   b. Would you stop processing one of the products? Why?
2. **a.** Assuming that you believe in assigning joint costs on a net-realizable-value basis, allocate the total operating profit of $250 per batch to Products A and B. If there is no market for X-1 and X-2 at their split-off point, a net realizable value is usually imputed by taking the ultimate sales value at the point of sale and working backward to obtain approximated "synthetic" relative sales values at the split-off point. These synthetic values are then used as weights for allocating the joint costs to the products.
   b. You have internal product-profitability reports in which joint costs are assigned on a net-realizable-value basis. Your chief engineer says that, after seeing these reports, she has developed a method of obtaining more of Product B and correspondingly less of Product A from each batch, without changing the per-kilogram cost factors. Would you approve this new method? Why? What would the overall operating profit be if 40 kilograms more of B were produced and 40 kilograms less of A?

P5-20 ALLOCATION, DEPARTMENT RATES, AND DIRECT LABOUR HOURS VERSUS MACHINE HOURS. The Olympia Manufacturing Company has two producing departments, machining and assembly. Olympia recently automated the machining department. The installation of a computer-aided manufacturing (CAM) system, together with robotic workstations, drastically reduced the amount of direct labour required. Meanwhile the assembly department remained labour-intensive.

The company had always used one firmwide rate based on direct labour hours as the cost driver for applying all costs (except direct materials) to the final products. Olympia was considering two alternatives: (1) continue using direct labour hours as the only cost driver, but use different rates in machining and assembly, and (2) use machine hours as the cost driver in the machining department while continuing with direct labour hours in assembly.

Budgeted data for 2006 are

	MACHINING	ASSEMBLY	TOTAL
Total cost (except direct materials), after allocating service department costs	$630,000	$450,000	$1,080,000
Machine hours	105,000	*	105,000
Direct labour hours	15,000	30,000	45,000

* Not applicable.

1. Suppose Olympia continued to use one firmwide rate based on direct labour hours to apply all manufacturing costs (except direct materials) to the final products. Compute the cost-application rate that would be used.
2. Suppose Olympia continued to use direct labour hours as the only cost driver but used different rates on machining and assembly:
   a. Compute the cost-application rate for machining.
   b. Compute the cost-application rate for assembly.
3. Suppose Olympia changed the cost accounting system to use machine hours as the cost driver in machining and direct labour hours in assembly:
   a. Compute the cost-application rate for machining.
   b. Compute the cost-application rate for assembly.
4. Three products use the following machine hours and direct labour hours:

	MACHINE HOURS OF MACHINING	DIRECT LABOUR HOURS IN MACHINING	DIRECT LABOUR HOURS IN ASSEMBLY
Product A	10.0	1.0	14.0
Product B	17.0	1.5	3.0
Product C	14.0	1.3	8.0

   a. Compute the manufacturing cost of each product (excluding direct materials) using one firmwide rate based on direct labour hours.
   b. Compute the manufacturing cost of each product (excluding direct materials) using direct labour hours as the cost driver, but with different cost-application rates in machining and assembly.
   c. Compute the manufacturing cost of each product (excluding direct materials) using a cost-application rate based on direct labour hours in assembly and machine hours in machining.
   d. Compare and explain the result in requirements 4a, 4b, and 4c.

P5-21 **MULTIPLE ALLOCATION BASES.** The Glasgow Electronics Company produces three types of circuit boards: L, M, and N. The cost accounting system used by Glasgow until 2005 applied all costs except direct materials to the products using direct labour hours as the only cost driver. In 2005 the company undertook a cost study. The study determined that there were six main factors causing costs to be incurred.

A new system was designed with a separate cost pool for each of the six factors. The factors and the costs associated with each are as follows:

1. Direct labour hours—direct labour cost and related fringe benefits and payroll taxes.
2. Machine hours—amortization and repairs and maintenance costs.
3. Kilograms of materials—materials receiving, handling, and storage costs.
4. Number of production setups—labour used to change machinery and computer configurations for a new production batch.
5. Number of production orders—costs of production scheduling and order processing.
6. Number of orders shipped—all packaging and shipping expenses.

The company is now preparing a budget for 2007. The budget includes the following predictions:

	BOARD L	BOARD M	BOARD N
Units to be produced	10,000	800	5,000
Direct material cost	£66/unit	£88/unit	£45/unit
Direct labour hours	4/unit	18/unit	9/unit
Machine hours	7/unit	15/unit	7/unit
Kilograms of materials	3/unit	4/unit	2/unit
Number of production setups	100	50	50
Number of production orders	300	200	70
Number of orders shipped	1,000	800	2,000

The total budgeted cost for 2007 is £3,712,250, of which £955,400 is direct materials cost, and the amount in each of the six pools defined above is

COST POOL	COST
1	£1,391,600
2	936,000
3	129,600
4	160,000
5	25,650
6	114,000
Total	£2,756,850

1. Prepare a budget that shows the total budgeted cost and the unit cost for each circuit board. Use the new system with six cost pools (plus a separate direct application of direct materials cost).
2. Compute the budgeted total and unit costs of each circuit board if the old direct labour hour-based system had been used.
3. How would you judge whether the new system is better than the old one?

P5-22 **ALLOCATING CENTRAL COSTS.** The National Railroad allocates all central corporate overhead costs to its divisions. Some costs, such as specified internal auditing and legal costs, are identified on the basis of time spent. However, other costs are harder to allocate, so the revenue achieved by each division is used as an allocation base. Examples of such costs are executive salaries, travel, secretarial, utilities, rent, amortization, donations, corporate planning, and general marketing costs.

Allocations on the basis of revenue for 2007 were (in millions)

DIVISION	REVENUE	ALLOCATED COSTS
Northern	$120	$ 7
Central	240	14
Southern	240	14
Total	$600	$35

In 2008, Northern's revenue remained unchanged. However, Southern's revenue soared to $280 million because of unusually bountiful crops. The latter are troublesome to forecast because unpredictable weather has a pronounced influence on volume. Central had expected a sharp rise in revenue, but severe competitive conditions resulted in a decline to $200 million. The total cost allocated on the basis of revenue was again $35 million, despite rises in other costs. The president was pleased that central costs did not rise for the year.

1. Compute the allocations of costs to each division for 2008.
2. How would each division manager probably feel about the cost allocation in 2008 compared with 2007? What are the weaknesses of using revenue as a basis for cost allocation? What other allocative bases could be used?
3. Suppose the budgeted revenues for 2008 were $120 million, $240 million, and $280 million, respectively, and the budgeted revenues were used as a cost driver for allocation. Compute the allocations of costs to each division for 2008. Do you prefer this method to the one used in requirement 1? Why?
4. Many accountants and managers oppose allocating any central costs. Why?

P5-23   **ALLOCATION OF SERVICE-DEPARTMENT COSTS.**   Chief Cleaning, Inc. provides cleaning services for a variety of clients. The company has two producing divisions, Residential and Commercial, and two service departments, Personnel and Administrative. The company has decided to allocate all service-department costs to the producing departments: Personnel, on the basis of number of employees, and Administrative, on the basis of direct department costs. The budget for 2006 shows the following:

	PERSONNEL	ADMINISTRATIVE	RESIDENTIAL	COMMERCIAL
Direct department costs	$70,000	$90,000	$ 240,000	$ 400,000
Number of employees	3	5	12	18
Direct labour hours			24,000	36,000
Square metres cleaned			4,500,000	9,970,000

1. Allocate service-department costs using the direct method.
2. Allocate service-department costs using the step-down method. The Personnel Department costs should be allocated first.
3. Suppose the company prices by the hour in the Residential Department and by the square metre cleaned in Commercial. Using the results of the step-down allocations in requirement 2,

a. Compute the cost of providing one direct labour hour of service in the Residential Department.

b. Compute the cost of cleaning one square metre of space in the Commercial Department.

P5-24 **ACTIVITY-BASED COSTING.** Yamaguchi Company makes printed circuit boards in a suburb of Kyoto. The production process is automated with computer-controlled robotic machines assembling each circuit board from a supply of parts. Yamaguchi has identified four activities:

ACTIVITY	COST DRIVER	RATE
Materials handling	Cost of direct materials	5% of materials cost
Assembly	Number of parts used	¥50 per part
Soldering	Number of circuit boards	¥1,500 per board
Quality assurance	Minutes of testing	¥400 per minute

Yamaguchi makes three types of circuit boards: Model A, Model B, and Model C. Requirements for production of each circuit board are as follows:

	MODEL A	MODEL B	MODEL C
Direct materials cost	¥4,000	¥6,000	¥8,000
Number of parts used	60	40	20
Minutes of testing	5	3	2

1. Compute the cost of production of 100 of the three types of circuit boards and the cost per circuit board for each type.
2. Suppose the design of Model A could be simplified so that it required only 30 parts (instead of 60) and took only three minutes of testing time (instead of five). Compute the cost of 100 Model A circuit boards and the cost per circuit board.

P5-25 **ACTIVITY-BASED COSTING.** The Maori Novelty company makes a variety of souvenirs for visitors to New Zealand. The Otago division manufactures stuffed kiwi birds using a highly automated operation. A recently installed activity-based costing system has four activities:

ACTIVITY	COST DRIVER	RATE*
Materials receiving and handling	Kilograms of materials	$1.20 per kilogram
Production setup	Number of setups	$60 per setup
Cutting, sewing, and assembly	Number of units	$0.40 per unit
Packing and shipping	Number of orders	$10 per order

* In New Zealand dollars.

Two products are called "Standard Kiwi" and "Giant Kiwi." They require 0.20 and 0.40 kilograms of materials, respectively, at a materials cost of $1.30 for Standard Kiwis and $2.20 for Giant Kiwis. One computer-controlled assembly line makes all products. When a production run of a different product is started, a setup procedure is required to reprogram the computers and make other changes in the process. Normally, 600 Standard Kiwis are produced per setup, but only 240 Giant Kiwis. Products are packed and shipped separately, so a request from a customer for, say, three different products is considered three different orders.

Ausiland Waterfront Market just placed an order for 100 Standard Kiwis and 50 Giant Kiwis.

1. Compute the cost of products shipped to Ausiland Waterfront Market.
2. Suppose the products made for Ausiland Waterfront required "AWM" to be printed on each kiwi. Because of the automated process, printing the initials takes no extra time or materials, but it requires a special production setup for each product. Compute the cost of products shipped to the Ausiland Waterfront Market.
3. Explain how the activity-based costing system helps Maori Novelty to measure costs of individual products or orders better than a traditional system that allocates all non-material costs based on direct labour.

P5-26   **ACTIVITY-BASED ALLOCATIONS.**   Winnipeg Wholesaler Distributors uses an activity-based costing system to determine the cost of handling its products. One important activity is the receiving of shipments in the warehouse. Three resources support that activity: recording and record-keeping; labour; and inspection.

Recording and record-keeping is cost driven by number of shipments received. The cost per shipment is $16.50.

Labour is driven by kilograms of merchandise received. Because labour is hired in shifts, it is fixed for large ranges of volume. Currently, labour costs are running at $23,000 per month for handling 460,000 kilograms. This same cost would apply to all volumes between 300,000 kilograms and 550,000 kilograms.

Finally, inspection is cost driven by the number of boxes received. Inspection costs are $2.75 per box.

One product distributed by Winnipeg Wholesale Distributors is candy. There is a wide variety of types of candy, so many different shipments are handled in the warehouse. In July the warehouse received 550 shipments, consisting of 4,000 boxes weighing a total of 80,000 kilograms.

1. Compute the cost of receiving candy shipments in July.
2. Management is considering elimination of brands of candy that have small levels of sales. This would reduce the warehouse volume to 220 shipments, consisting of 2,500 boxes weighting a total of 60,000 kilograms. Compute the cost savings from eliminating the small-sales-level brands.
3. Suppose receiving costs were estimated on a per-kilogram basis. What was the total receiving cost per kilogram of candy received in July? If management had used this cost to estimate the effect of eliminating the 20,000 kilograms of candy, what mistake might be made?

MANAGERIAL DECISION CASES

C5-1   **IDENTIFYING ACTIVITIES, RESOURCES, AND COST DRIVERS IN MANUFACTURING.**   Extrusion Plastics is a multinational, diversified organization. One of its manufacturing divisions, northeast plastics division, has become less profitable due to increased competition. The division produces three major lines of plastic products within its single plant. Product Line A is high-volume, simple pieces produced in large batches.

Product Line B is medium-volume, more complex pieces. Product Line C is low-volume, small-order, highly complex pieces.

Currently, the division allocates indirect manufacturing costs based on direct labour. The VP manufacturing is uncomfortable using the traditional cost-figures. He thinks the company is underpricing the more complex products. He decides to conduct an activity-based costing analysis of the business.

Interviews were conducted with the key managers in order to identify activities, resources, cost drivers, and their interrelationships.

Interviewee: production manager

Q1: What activities are carried out in your area?

A1: *All products are manufactured using three similar, complex, and expensive moulding machines. Each moulding machine can be used in the production of the three product lines. Each setup takes about the same time irrespective of the product.*

Q2: Who works in your area?

A2: *Last year, we employed 30 machine operators, two maintenance mechanics, and two supervisors.*

Q3: How are the operators used in the moulding process?

A3: *It requires nine operators to support a machine during the actual production process.*

Q4: What do the maintenance mechanics do?

A4: *Their primary function is to perform machine setups. However, they are also required to provide machine maintenance during the moulding process.*

Q5: Where do the supervisors spend their time?

A5: *They provide supervision for the machine operators and the maintenance mechanics. For the most part, the supervisors appear to spend the same amount of time with each of the employees that they supervise.*

Q6: What other resources are used to support manufacturing?

A6: *The moulding machines use energy during the moulding process and during the setups. We put meters on the moulding machines to get a better understanding of their energy consumption. We discovered that for each hour that a machine runs, it uses 6.3 kilowatts of energy. The machines also require consumable shop supplies (e.g., lubricants, hoses). We have found a direct correlation between the amount of supplies used and the actual processing time.*

Q7: How is the building used, and what costs are associated with it?

A7: *We have a 100,000 square metre building. The total rent and insurance costs for the year were $675,000. These costs are allocated to production, sales, and administration based on square metres.*

Required:
1. Identify the activities/resources and cost drivers for the division.
2. For each resource identified in requirement 1, indicate its cost behaviour with respect to the activities it supports (assume a planning period of 1 month).

C5-2 **ALLOCATION OF DATA-PROCESSING COSTS.** (CMA, adapted) Independent Outside Underwriters Co. (IOU) established a Systems Department two years ago to implement and operate its own data-processing systems. IOU believed that its own system would be more cost effective than the service bureau it had been using.

IOU's three departments—Claims, Records, and Finance—have different requirements with respect to hardware and other capacity-related resources and operating resources. The system was designed to recognize these differing needs. In addition, the system was designed to meet IOU's long-term capacity needs. The excess capacity designed into the system would be sold to outside users until needed by IOU. The estimated resource requirements used to design and implement the system are shown in the following schedule.

DEPARTMENT	HARDWARE AND OTHER CAPACITY- RELATED RESOURCES	OPERATING RESOURCES
Records	25%	60%
Claims	50	15
Finance	20	20
Expansion (outside use)	5	5
Total	100%	100%

IOU currently sells the equivalent of its expansion capacity to a few outside clients. At the time the system became operational, management decided to redistribute total expenses of the Systems Department to the user departments based on actual computer time used. The actual costs for the first quarter of the current fiscal year were distributed to the user departments as follows:

DEPARTMENT	PERCENTAGE UTILIZATION	AMOUNT
Records	60%	$330,000
Claims	15	82,500
Finance	20	110,000
Outside	5	27,500
Total	100%	$550,000

The three user departments have complained about the cost distribution method since the Systems Department was established. The Records Department's monthly costs have been as much as three times the costs experienced with the service bureau. The Finance Department is concerned about the costs distributed to the outside-user category because these allocated costs form the basis for the fees billed to the outside clients.

Jerry Owens, IOU's controller, decided to review the cost-allocation method. The additional information he gathered for his review is reported in Exhibits 5A-1, 5A-2, and 5A-3.

Owens has concluded that the method of cost allocation should be changed. He believes that the hardware and capacity-related costs should be allocated to the user departments in proportion to the planned long-term needs. Any difference between actual and budgeted hardware costs would not be allocated to the departments but remain with the Systems Department.

The costs for software development and operations would be charged to the user departments based on actual hours used. A predetermined hourly rate based on the annual budget data would be used. The hourly rates that would be used for the current fiscal year are as follows:

FUNCTION	HOURLY RATE
Software development	$ 30
Operations:	
Computer related	200
Input/output related	10

Systems-Department Costs and Activity Levels

| | ANNUAL BUDGET | | FIRST QUARTER | | | |
| | | | BUDGET | | ACTUAL | |
	HOURS	DOLLARS	HOURS	DOLLARS	HOURS	DOLLARS
Hardware and other capacity-related costs	–	$ 600,000	–	$150,000	–	$155,000
Software development	18,750	562,500	4,725	141,750	4,250	130,000
Operations:						
Computer related	3,750	750,000	945	189,000	920	187,000
Input/output related	30,000	300,000	7,560	75,600	7,900	78,000
		$2,212,500		$556,350		$550,000

EXHIBIT 5A-2

Historical Usage

| DEPARTMENT | HARDWARE AND OTHER CAPACITY NEEDS | DEVELOPMENT | | OPERATIONS | | | |
| | | | | COMPUTER | | INPUT/OUTPUT | |
		RANGE	AVERAGE	RANGE	AVERAGE	RANGE	AVERAGE
Records	25%	0–30%	15%	55–65%	60%	10–30%	15%
Claims	50	15–60	40	10–25	15	60–80	75
Finance	20	25–75	40	10–25	20	3–10	5
Outside	5	0–25	5	3–8	5	3–10	5
	100%		100%		100%		100%

EXHIBIT 5A-3

Usage of Systems Department's Services First Quarter (in hours)

	SOFTWARE DEVELOPMENT	OPERATIONS COMPUTER RELATED	INPUT/OUTPUT
Records	450	540	1,540
Claims	1,800	194	5,540
Finance	1,600	126	410
Outside	400	60	410
Total	4,250	920	7,900

Owens plans to use first-quarter activity and cost data to illustrate his recommendations. The recommendations will be presented to the Systems Department and the user departments for their comments and reaction. He then expects to present his recommendations to management for approval.

Required:

1. Calculate the amount of data-processing costs that would be included in the Claims Department's first-quarter budget according to the method Jerry Owens has recommended.

2. Prepare a schedule to show how the actual first-quarter costs of the Systems Department would be charged to the users if Owens' recommended method were adopted.

3. Explain whether Owens' recommended system for charging costs to the user departments will
   a. Improve cost control in the Systems Department, or
   b. Improve planning and cost control in the user departments.

C5-3 **COST DRIVERS AND PRICING DECISIONS.**   (SMAC) The Eastclock Corporation (EC) manufactures timing devices that are used in industrial settings. Recently, profits have fallen and management is seeking your advice as an outside consultant on changes that should be made.

During its 60-year history, EC has developed a strong and loyal customer base due largely to its reputation for quality timing devices. Significant investments in new computer-designed products and automated tooling have reduced operating costs and enabled EC to maintain its competitive edge. However, during the past three years, sales of its two major products have declined or have become stagnant. Had it not been for increased sales of its "custom" timing devices, EC would have incurred losses.

EC's basic product line consists of the "standard" model and the "deluxe" model. The "standard" model requires $8 in direct materials and requires one hour of direct labour (0.4 hours of machining and 0.6 hours of assembly). The "deluxe" model requires an additional $4 worth of direct materials and requires a total of 1.5 hours of direct labour (0.5 hours of machining and one hour of assembly). The standard labour rate is $12 per hour.

In addition to the basic product line, the company manufactures custom timing devices. The average direct material and direct labour costs for a custom timing device are approximately $20 and $30 per unit, respectively. Each custom unit requires 2.5 hours of direct labour (0.8 hours of machining and 1.7 hours of assembly).

Indirect manufacturing overhead costs are significant and totalled $1,700,000 in 2006. Variable overhead costs include small tools, lubricants, and indirect labour charges. Fixed overhead costs consist of the following: engineering (design and estimating) $80,000; quality control (setup time and materials) $130,000; amortization on buildings and equipment $690,000; and other costs such as property taxes, maintenance and supervisory salaries of $200,000. A complete income statement for 2006 is shown in Exhibit 5B-1 of this case.

As an outside consultant, you begin your analysis of the current situation by meeting with the controller, Jack Downie, in early January 2007. Jack, who has no formal training in accounting, is nonetheless proud of the internal accounting system and the changes that he has introduced during the past five years. "We've spent a lot of time converting to the contribution format. We've carefully analyzed the variable and fixed costs using our microcomputer and some pretty powerful software. I'm really confident that we've got an accurate handle on how costs behave as volume rises and falls in the various product lines. Because the volume of 'custom' orders has increased during the past three years, we have charged relatively more overhead to this line on each of the semi-annual statements. The 5 percent sales commission is tacked on to the analysis of each of the product lines and I would like to charge out the fixed selling and administrative expenses based on the volume of orders processed (currently based on volume of units sold)."

	STANDARD	DELUXE	CUSTOM	TOTAL
Volume (units)	50,000	25,000	5,000	80,000
Revenue	$2,100,000	$1,575,000	$525,000	$4,200,000
Variable Costs:				
Material	400,000	300,000	100,000	800,000
Labour	600,000	450,000	150,000	1,200,000
Overhead[1]	300,000	225,000	75,000	600,000
Commission	105,000	78,750	26,250	210,000
Total variable costs	1,405,000	1,053,750	351,250	2,810,000
Contribution margin	695,000	521,250	173,750	1,390,000
Fixed Costs:				
Engineering[2]	40,000	30,000	10,000	80,000
Quality control[2]	65,000	48,750	16,250	130,000
Amortization[2]	345,000	258,750	86,250	690,000
Other manufacturing[3]	125,000	62,500	12,500	200,000
Selling & administrative[3]	78,125	39,063	7,812	125,000
Total fixed costs	653,125	439,063	132,812	1,225,000
Net income	$ 41,875	$ 82,187	$ 40,938	$ 165,000

[1] It has been reliably determined that variable overhead is a function of direct labour dollars.

[2] Fixed manufacturing overhead (Engineering, Quality Control, and Amortization) is allocated to products based on relative proportion of total direct labour dollars.

[3] Other fixed manufacturing overhead and fixed selling and administrative expenses are allocated to products based on the relative volume of units sold.

Further discussions took place with the production people, including representatives of engineering, quality control, and the machining and assembly departments. Interviews also took place with representatives of the marketing and administrative departments. A summary of the highlights of these discussions follows:

Karl Bechtold (Engineering Department): "Our new computer-assisted design system has really changed the way we do things around here. When an order comes in, it is tagged as being either standard, deluxe, or custom. I'd guess that 75 percent of our time is spent on the custom orders, as they usually require significant adaptations. I've pointed this out to the accounting people on several occasions, but they seem pretty tied up lately with their new computer. The standard model requires our attention from time to time but I'd guess that it's only about 5 percent. Revisions to the deluxe model are a little more complicated and take up the remainder of our efforts during the average month. If we were to return to more normal levels of production for the three products, I'd guess that we would spend about half of our time on the custom orders and split the remaining hours between the other two lines."

Harvey Ramsoomair (Quality Control): "Nothing leaves this plant that isn't strictly to our customers' specifications. It may not be what they wanted but it's guaranteed to be what they ordered. This sort of quality assurance is only possible by carefully monitoring the quality of our raw materials and the production process. We check the output of the work centres when they begin each job and monitor outputs randomly. Given that the standard and deluxe models are produced in large batches, I'd guess that they each currently take about 20 percent of our time on a monthly basis. I couldn't be much more accurate than that because we only get official information on production volumes twice a year. If the volume of standard sales returned to its normal level, I'm sure that the amount of time for the two basic products would increase to about 30 percent per product. Whatever happens, the remaining time goes to the custom work, which really keeps us on our toes."

Fran Sprocket (Supervisor Machining & Assembly): "This new computer-aided manufacturing equipment has really changed our manufacturing procedures. I can remember just a few years ago how we had to carefully monitor each operation. Now, once we get the thing set up, all we have to do is monitor the output. This machinery is very expensive. The annual amortization on the machinery is $230,000 for each of the product lines. I've never understood why the accounting system charges so little amortization to the custom line given that we invested a lot in the machinery to accommodate these special orders for customers. The costs that are labelled as 'other manufacturing' in the accounting reports seem to relate mostly to the volume of goods produced and sold. My biggest problem is scheduling the assembling hours. The physical layout of the plant restricts the amount of assembly space and, therefore, the number of hours that I can schedule. The maximum number of assembly hours is 70,000 and nothing can be done to increase this in the next 12 months."

Steve Wong (Marketing): "I don't feel that there is any problem with the costing system as far as marketing expenses are concerned. The amount of time, energy, and expense devoted to each of the product lines seems to depend on the volume of orders sold. The big problem I hear about from the salespeople centres around our prices. We're running about $5 above our competitors on the standard model and this is really cutting into our volume. If we could justify a more competitive price, I expect sales would jump to a more normal level of 74,000 units per year. We currently base all of our prices on a 50 percent markup over variable costs and then round off to the nearest dollar.

"My people are glad to see those custom orders rolling in. It's hard to find out what our competitors are charging for similar work but there is some evidence to suggest that our prices are way out of line compared to our competition. The strategy of the company is to market the standard and deluxe models and offer the custom model as a service to regular customers at a premium price. As a result, we would normally sell about 1,000 custom units per year, which is the level we operated at several years ago. With respect to the deluxe model, I feel that the current price is more or less correct and, thus, we expect that volume will remain at current levels for the foreseeable future."

Toni Anderson (Vice President): "We've got to turn this situation around or we'll have to sell out. The boss says he's been getting some pretty attractive offers from some American tool-and-die firms. I'd hate to see us sell out without a fight because I think we've got a responsibility to our employees—some of whom have been with us since high school. The bottom line is each product should cover its own costs and earn at least a profit margin of 10 percent before taxes this year."

Required: | Assume the role of the outside consultant. Prepare a report addressed to the management of Eastclock Corporation that clearly identifies and analyzes the issues it faces, and make specific recommendations for improvement. Also include a pro forma income statement for 2007 that incorporates your recommendations.

C5-4 COST ALLOCATION AND CONTRIBUTION MARGIN. (R. Anderson, adapted) An analogy helps to understand the treatment of costs incident to various types of operations. Consider the following conversation between a restaurant owner (Joe) and his Accountant-Efficiency-Expert (Eff Ex) about adding a rack of peanuts to the counter in an effort to pick up additional profit in the usual course of business. Some people may consider this conversation an oversimplification, but the analogy highlights some central issues in cost allocation.

Eff Ex: Joe, you said you put in these peanuts because some people ask for them, but do you realize what this rack of peanuts is *costing* you?

Joe: It isn't going to cost. It's going to make me a profit. Sure, I had to pay $250 for a fancy rack to hold the bags, but the peanuts cost $0.60 a bag and I will sell them for $1. I figure if I sell 50 bags a week to start, I will be making $20 profit a week, and it'll take 12 1/2 weeks to cover the cost of the rack. After that I am going to clear a profit of $0.40 a bag. The more I sell, the more I make.

Eff Ex: That is an antiquated and completely unrealistic approach, Joe. Fortunately, modern accounting procedures permit a more accurate picture, which reveals the complexities involved.

Joe: Huh?

Eff Ex: To be precise, those peanuts must be integrated into your entire operation and be allocated their appropriate share of business overhead. They must share a proportionate part of your expenditure for rent, heat, light, equipment amortization, decorating, salaries for your waitresses, cook . . .

Joe: The *cook*? What does he have to do with the peanuts? He doesn't even know I sell them!

Eff Ex: Look Joe, the cook is in the kitchen, the kitchen prepares the food, the food is what brings people in here, and the people ask to buy peanuts. That's why you must charge a portion of the cook's wages as well as part of your own salary to peanut sales. This sheet contains a carefully calculated cost analysis, which indicates that the peanut operation should pay exactly $12,780 per year toward these general overhead costs.

Joe: The peanuts? $12,780 a year for overhead? The nuts?

Eff Ex: It's really a little more than that. You also spend money each week to have the windows washed, have the place swept out in the mornings, and keep soap in the washrooms. That raises the total overhead applied to peanuts to $13,130 per year.

Joe: [Thoughtfully] But the peanut salesman said that I would make money . . . put them on the end of the counter, he said . . . and get $0.40 a bag profit . . .

Eff Ex: [With a sniff] He's not an accountant. Do you actually know what the portion of the counter occupied by the peanut rack is worth to you?

Joe: It's not worth anything . . . there is no stool there . . . just a dead spot at the end.

Eff Ex:	The modern cost picture permits no dead spots. Your counter contains 20 square metres and your counter business grosses $150,000 a year. Consequently each square metre of the counter generates $7,300 year, and the 1/3 square metres of space occupied by the peanut rack is worth $2,500 per year. Since you have taken that area away from general counter use, you must charge the value of the space to the occupant.
Joe:	You mean I have to add $2,500 a year more to the peanuts?
Eff Ex:	Right. That raises their share of the general operating costs to a grand total of $15,630 per year. Now then, if you sell 50 bags of peanuts per week for 52 weeks, you would sell 2,600 bags of peanuts a year. Each bag then should be allocated approximately $6 of the general operating costs.
Joe:	*What?*
Eff Ex:	Obviously, to that must be added your purchase price of $0.60 per bag, which brings the total to $6.60. So you see by selling peanuts at $1 per bag, you are losing $5.60 on every sale.
Joe:	Something is crazy!
Eff Ex:	Not at all! Here are the *figures*. They *prove* your peanuts operation cannot stand on its own feet.
Joe:	[Brightening] Suppose I sell *lots* of peanuts . . . say a thousand bags a week instead of fifty.
Eff Ex:	[Tolerantly] Joe, you don't understand the problem. If the volume of peanut sales increases, your operating costs will go up . . . you'll have to handle more bags with more time, more amortization, more everything. The basic principle of accounting is firm on that subject: "The bigger the operation, the more general overhead costs that must be allocated." No, increasing the volume of sales won't help.
Joe:	Okay, if you're so smart, *you* tell *me* what I have to do.
Eff Ex:	[Condescendingly] Well . . . you could first reduce operating costs.
Joe:	How?
Eff Ex:	Move to a building with cheaper rent. Cut salaries. Wash the windows bi-weekly. Have the floor swept only once a week. Remove the soap from the washrooms. Decrease the square-metre value of your counter. For example, if you can cut your costs by 50 percent, that will reduce the amount allocated to peanuts from $15,630 to $7,815 per year, reducing the cost to $3.60 per bag.
Joe:	[Slowly] That's better?
Eff Ex:	Much, much better. However, even then you would lose $2.60 per bag if you charge only $1. Therefore, you must also raise your selling price. If you want an income of $0.40 per bag you would have to charge $4.00.

Joe: [Flabbergasted] You mean even after I cut operating costs by 50 percent I still have to charge $4 to make $0.40? Nobody's that nuts about nuts! Who would buy them?

Eff Ex: That's a secondary consideration. The point is, at $4 you'd be selling at a price based upon a true and proper evaluation of your then reduced costs.

Joe: [Eagerly] Look! I have a better idea. Why don't I just throw the nuts out?

Eff Ex: Can you afford it?

Joe: Sure. All I have is about 50 bags of peanuts . . . which cost about $30 . . . and I would lose $250 on the rack, but I would be out of this nut business with no more grief.

Eff Ex: [Shaking head] Joe, it isn't that simple. You are in the peanut business! The minute you throw those peanuts out you are adding $15,630 of annual overhead to the rest of your operation. Joe . . . be realistic . . . *can you afford to do that?*

Joe: [Completely crushed] It's unbelievable! Last week I was making money. Now I'm in trouble . . . just because I think peanuts on the counter is going to bring in some extra profit . . . just because I believe 50 bags of peanuts a week is easy.

Eff Ex: [With raised eyebrow] That is the object of modern cost studies, Joe . . . to dispel those false illusions.

Required:

1. Is Joe losing $5.60 on every sale of peanuts? Explain.
2. Do you agree that if the volume of peanut sales is increased, operating losses will increase? Explain.
3. Do you agree with the Efficiency Expert that, in order to make the peanut operation profitable, the operating costs in the restaurant should be decreased and the selling price of the peanuts should be increased? Give reasons.
4. Do you think that Joe can afford to get out of the peanut business? Give reasons.
5. Do you think that Joe should eliminate his peanut operations? Why or why not?

E5-1 TRADITIONAL COSTING VERSUS ACTIVITY-BASED COSTING

Goal: Create an Excel spreadsheet to compare traditional costing versus activity-based costing. Use the results to answer questions about your findings.

Scenario: CompCirc Inc. supplies circuit boards to computer manufacturers. CompCirc currently uses traditional costing for making business decisions. At the urging of one of its major customers, however, management of CompCirc has decided to move to activity-based costing for circuit board production related to products LP-7310 and PC-33. As one of the company's accountants, you have been asked to prepare a spreadsheet comparing the two costing methods for the next company board meeting. Your supervisor has given you the following quarterly data:

TOTAL INDIRECT COSTS FOR THE QUARTER:

Assembly	$630,000
Soldering	$270,000
Inspection	$160,000

	LP-7310	PC-33
Direct costs (materials, labour)	$162,400	$178,240
Machine hours (assembly)	480	1,080
Number of units produced (soldering)	6,000	4,000
Testing hours (inspection)	6,000	8,000

When you have completed your spreadsheet, answer the following questions:

1. What is the total manufacturing cost per unit using traditional costing for LP-7310? For PC-33?

2. What is the total manufacturing cost per unit using activity-based costing for LP-7310? For PC-33?

3. What conclusions can be drawn from your spreadsheet results?

Step by Step:

1. Open a new Excel spreadsheet.

2. In column A, create a bold-faced heading that contains the following:
    Row 1: Chapter 4 Decision Guideline
    Row 2: CompCirc Inc.
    Row 3: Traditional vs. Activity-Based Costing
    Row 4: Today's Date

    Note: Adjust column widths as follows: column A (41.57), columns B, C, and D (21.0). Column D is for check figures only. The column widths have been designed to ensure that column D will not print on the final version of the spreadsheet if only page 1 is printed.

3. Merge and centre the four heading rows across columns A through C.

4. In Column A, create the following row headings:
   Row 7: Raw Data
   Row 8: Indirect Costs for the Quarter:
   Row 9: Assembly
   Row 10: Soldering
   Row 11: Inspection
   Row 12: Total Indirect Costs
   Skip 2 rows
   Row 15: Direct Costs (materials, labour)
   Row 16: Machine Hours (assembly)
   Row 17: Number of Units Produced (soldering)
   Row 18: Testing Hours (inspection)
   Skip 2 rows
   Row 21: Traditional Costing System
   Row 22: Indirect Cost Driver (machine hours)
   Row 23: Allocated Indirect Costs
   Skip a row
   Row 25: Cost per Product
   Row 26: Direct Costs
   Row 27: Manufacturing Overhead
   Row 28: Total Manufacturing Costs per Product
   Skip a row
   Row 30: Number of Units
   Row 31: Total Manufacturing Costs per Unit
   Skip 2 rows
   Row 34: Activity-Based Costing System
   Row 35: Assembly Cost Driver (machine hours)
   Row 36: Allocated Assembly Cost
   Row 37: Soldering Cost Driver (units)
   Row 38: Allocated Soldering Cost
   Row 39: Inspection Cost Driver (testing hours)
   Row 40: Allocated Inspection Cost
   Skip a row
   Row 42: Cost per Product
   Row 43: Direct Costs
   Row 44: Manufacturing Overhead
   Row 45: Assembly
   Row 46: Soldering
   Row 47: Inspection
   Row 48: Total Manufacturing Costs per Product
   Skip a row
   Row 50: Number of Units
   Row 51: Total Manufacturing Costs per Unit

5. Change the format of Raw Data (row 7), Traditional Costing System (row 21), and Activity-Based Costing System (row 34) to bold-faced headings.

   Hint: Use the control key for highlighting multiple cells or rows when making changes.

6. Change the format of Cost per Product (rows 25 and 42) to underlined headings.

7. In rows 14, 21, 25, 34, and 42 create the following bold-faced, right-justified column headings:
   Column B: LP-7310
   Column C: PC-33

8. In rows 21 and 34 create the following bold-faced, right-justified column headings:
   Column D: Total

9. Use the scenario data to fill in the Raw Data section.
   Use the SUM function to calculate Total Indirect Costs (row 12).

10. Traditional costing system:
    Fill in rows 26 and 30 with information from the Raw Data section.
    Use appropriate formulas from Chapter 4 to calculate the cost driver and allocated costs.
    Use the SUM function to calculate the Total column for Manufacturing Overhead Costs.
    Complete the remainder of the Cost per Product data using formulas and calculations.
    Calculate the Total Manufacturing Costs per Product.

11. Activity-based costing system:
    Fill in rows 43 and 50 with information from the Raw Data section.
    Use appropriate formulas from Chapter 4 to calculate the cost drivers and allocated costs.
    Use the SUM function to calculate the Total columns for all allocated costs.
    Complete the remainder of the Cost per Product data using formulas and calculations.
    Calculate the Total Manufacturing Costs per Product.

    Hint: If using the SUM function to calculate Total Manufacturing Costs, verify the range.

12. Format all amounts as:
    Number tab: Category: Currency
                 Decimal places: 2
                       Symbol: None
            Negative numbers: Red with parentheses

13. Change the format of hours and units in rows 16–18, 30, and 50 to display no decimal places.

14. Change the format of the amounts in rows 9, 12, 15, 23, 26, 28, 31, 36, 38, 40, 43, 48, and 51 to display a dollar symbol.

15. Change the format of the row headings in rows 9–11, 15–18, 23, 36, 38, 40, and 45–47 to display as indented.
                 Alignment tab: Horizontal: Left (Indent)
                                  Indent: 1

16. Change the format of the amounts in rows 12, 28, and 48 to display a top border, using the default Line Style.

    Border tab: Icon: Top Border

17. Change the format of the cost driver calculations in rows 22, 35, 37, and 39 to display as left-justified percentages with two decimal places.

    Number tab: Category: Percentage
                       Decimal places: 2
                       Alignment tab: Horizontal: Left (Indent)
                       Indent: 0

18. Accentuate the Cost per Product information for each costing method by applying cell shading to columns A, B, and C of rows 25–31 and 42–51.

    Patterns tab: Colour: Lightest grey

19. Save your work to disk, and print a copy for your files.

    Note: The final version of the spreadsheet will be on page 1. You do not need to print page 2, as it should contain only the check figures.

E5-2 ALLOCATING COSTS USING DIRECT AND STEP-DOWN METHODS

Goal: Create an Excel spreadsheet to allocate costs using the direct method and the step-down method. Use the results to answer questions about your findings.

Scenario: Niagara Cleaning, Inc., provides cleaning services for a variety of clients. The company has two producing departments, residential and commercial, and two service departments, personnel and administrative. The company has decided to allocate all service department costs to the producing departments—personnel on the basis of number of employees and administrative on the basis of direct department costs. The budget for 2006 shows:

	Personnel	Administrative	Residential	Commercial
Direct department costs	$70,000	$90,000	$240,000	$400,000
Number of employees	3	5	12	18
Direct-labour hours			24,000	36,000
Square metres cleaned			4,500,000	9,970,000

Exhibit 5-3 illustrates the types of calculations that are used for allocating costs using the direct method and the step-down method. Niagara Cleaning, Inc., has asked you to help them determine the best method for allocating costs from their service departments to their producing departments.

When you have completed your spreadsheet, answer the following questions:

1. What are the total costs for the residential department using the direct method?

   What are the total costs for the commercial department using the direct method?

2. What are the total costs for the residential department using the step-down method?

3. What are the total costs for the commercial department using the step-down method?

4. Which method would you recommend that Niagara Cleaning, Inc., use to allocate their service departments' costs to their producing departments? Why?

Step by Step:

1. Open a new Excel spreadsheet.

2. In column A, create a bold-faced heading that contains the following:
   Row 1: Chapter 12 Decision Guideline
   Row 2: Niagara Cleaning, Inc.
   Row 3: Cost Allocations from Service Departments to Producing Departments
   Row 4: Today's Date

3. Merge and centre the four heading rows across columns A through H.

4. In row 7, create the following bold-faced, centre-justified column headings:
   Column B: Personnel
   Column C: Administrative
   Column D: Residential
   Column E: Commercial
   Column F: Total Rcs/Comm
   Column G: Total Admin/Res/Comm
   Column H: Grand Total

5. Change the format of the column headings in row 7 to permit the titles to be displayed on multiple lines within a single cell.
   Alignment tab: Wrap Text: Checked

   Note: Adjust column widths so that headings use only two lines. Adjust row height to ensure that row is same height as adjusted headings.

6. In column A, create the following row headings:
   Row 8: Direct Department Costs
   Row 9: Number of Employees
   Skip 2 rows

   Note: Adjust the width of column A to 27.14.

7. In column A, create the following bold-faced, underlined row heading:
   Row 12: Direct Method:

8. In column A, create the following row headings:
   Row 13: Direct Department Costs
   Row 14: Personnel Allocation
   Row 15: Administrative Allocation
   Row 16: Total Costs
   Skip 2 rows

9. In column A, create the following bold-faced, underlined row heading:
   Row 19: Step-Down Method:

10. In column A, create the following row headings:
    Row 20: Direct Department Costs
    Row 21: Step 1–Personnel Allocation
    Row 22: Step 2–Administrative Allocation
    Row 23: Total Costs

11. Use data from above to enter the amounts in columns B through E for rows 8, 9, 13, and 20.

12. Use the appropriate calculations to do the totals in row 8 for columns F and H.
    Use the appropriate calculations to do the totals in row 9 for columns F and G.

13. Use the appropriate formulas to allocate the costs from the service departments to the producing departments using each of the methods.

14. Use the appropriate calculations to do the totals in columns B through E and in column H, rows 16 and 23.

15. Format amounts in columns B through H, rows 8, 13, 16, 20 and 23 as

Number tab:	Category:	Accounting
	Decimal:	0
	Symbol:	$

16. Format the amount in columns B through E, rows 14, 15, 21, and 22 as

Number tab:	Category:	Accounting
	Decimal:	0
	Symbol:	None

17. Change the format of the total costs amounts in columns B through E, rows 16 and 23, to display a top border, using the default line style.

Border tab:	Icon:	Top Border

18. Change the format of the amounts in row 9, columns B through G to centre justified.

19. Save your work to disk, and print a copy for your files.

Note: Print your spreadsheet using landscape in order to ensure that all columns appear on one page.

COLLABORATIVE LEARNING EXERCISES

CL5-1 **INTERNET RESEARCH, ABC, AND ABM.** Form groups of three to five people each. Each member of the group should pick one of the following industries:

- Manufacturing
- Insurance
- Health care
- Government
- Service

Each person should explore the Internet for an example of a company that implemented activity-based costing and activity-based management. One way to do this is to go to the Web site www.hyperion.com and choose one company from the industry chosen. Prepare and give a briefing for your group. Do this by completing the following:

1. Describe the company and its business.
2. What was the scope of the ABC/ABM project?
3. What were the goals for the ABC/ABM project?
4. Summarize the results of the project.

After each person has briefed the group on his or her company, discuss within your group the commonalities between the ABC/ABM applications.

CL5-2 **LIBRARY RESEARCH ON ABC.** Form into groups of three to six students. Each student should choose a different article about activity-based costing (ABC) or activity-based management (ABM) from the current literature. The article should include information about at least one company's application of ABC. Such articles are available in a variety of sources. You might try bibliographic searches for "activity-based costing" or "activity-based management." Journals that will have articles on ABC and ABM include

CMA Management (Canada)
CGA Magazine (Canada)
Strategic Finance (USA)
Management Accounting (United Kingdom)
Journal of Cost Management
Management Accounting Quarterly

1. After reading the article, note the following (if given in the article) for one company:
   a. The benefits of ABC or ABM
   b. The problems encountered in implementing ABC or ABM
   c. Suggestions by the author(s) about employing ABC or ABM

2. As a group, using the collective wisdom garnered from the articles, respond to the following:
   a. What kinds of companies can benefit from ABC or ABM?
   b. What kinds of companies have little to gain from ABC or ABM?
   c. What steps should be taken to ensure successful implementation of ABC or ABM?
   d. What potential pitfalls are there to avoid in implementing ABC or ABM?

6

Job-Order Costing and Accounting for Overhead

After studying this chapter, you will be able to

1. Distinguish between job-order costing and process-costing systems.

2. Prepare summary journal entries for the typical transactions of a job-costing system.

3. Compute budgeted factory-overhead rates and apply them to production, using appropriate cost drivers.

4. Identify the meaning and purpose of normalized overhead rates.

5. Use an activity-based costing system in a job-order environment.

6. Show how job costing is used in service organizations.

Accountants compute product and service costs for both decision-making and financial-reporting purposes. They supply these costs to managers for setting prices and evaluating product lines. For example, Ford managers need to know the cost of each kind of car being produced to set prices, to determine marketing and production strategies for various models, and to evaluate production operations. At the same time, product costs appear as cost of goods sold in income statements and as finished-goods inventory values in balance sheets. Although it would be possible to have two product-costing systems, one for management decision making and one for financial reporting, seldom do the benefits of two systems exceed the costs. Therefore, both decision-making and financial-reporting needs influence the design of product-costing systems.

In this chapter, we will focus on one type of product-costing system, the job-order-costing system, and will look at the elements of such a system and how it tracks the flow of costs. This system focuses on costs involved in the *production* of goods and services. Selling, administrative, distribution, and other nonmanufacturing costs are period costs, not *product* costs, for inventory valuation and other external reporting purposes.

DISTINCTION BETWEEN JOB COSTING AND PROCESS COSTING

OBJECTIVE 1

Distinguish between job-order costing and process-costing systems.

Job-Order Costing (Job Costing). The method of allocating costs to products that are readily identified by individual units or batches, each of which receives varying degrees of attention and skill.

Process Costing. The method of allocating costs to products by averaging costs over large numbers of nearly identical products.

Two fundamental types of product costing are *job-order costing* and *process costing*. **Job-order costing** (or simply **job costing**) allocates costs to products that are readily identified by individual units or batches, each of which receives varying degrees of attention and skill. Job-order methods are used by a variety of industries including construction, printing, aircraft, furniture, special-purpose machinery, and any manufacturer of tailor-made goods.

Process costing averages costs over large numbers of nearly identical products. It is most often found in such industries as chemicals, oil, textiles, plastics, paints, flour, canneries, rubber, lumber, food processing, glass, mining, cement, and meat packing. These industries involve mass production of like units, which usually pass in continuous fashion through a series of uniform production steps called *productions* or *processors*.

The distinction between the job-cost and the process-cost methods centres largely on how product costing is accomplished. Job costing applies costs to specific jobs that may consist of either a single physical unit (such as a custom sofa) or a few like units (such as a dozen tables) in a distinct batch or job lot. In contrast, process costing deals with great masses of like units and broad averages of unit costs.

The most important point is that product costing is an *averaging* process. The unit cost used for inventory purposes is the result of taking some accumulated cost that has been allocated to production departments and dividing it by some measure of production. The basic distinction between job-order costing and process costing is the breadth of the denominator: in job-order costing, it is small (e.g., one painting, 100 advertising circulars, or one special packaging machine) but in process costing, it is large (e.g., thousands of kilograms, litres, or board feet).

Job costing and process costing are extremes along a continuum of potential costing systems. Some companies use hybrid costing systems, which are blends of ideas from both job costing and process costing as each company designs its own accounting system to fit its underlying production activities. Chapter 7 describes process costing and hybrid costing.

ILLUSTRATION OF JOB-ORDER COSTING

First we will examine the basic records used in a job-costing system.

Basic Records

Job-Cost Record (Job-Cost Sheet, Job Order). A document that shows all costs for a particular product, service, or batch of products.

The centrepiece of a job-order costing system is the **job-cost record, job-cost sheet**, or **job order**, shown in Exhibit 6-1. All costs for a particular product, service, or batch of products are recorded on the job-cost record. A file of job-cost records for partially completed jobs provides supporting details for the work-in-process-inventory account, often simply called work-in-process (WIP). A file of completed job-cost records comprises the finished-goods-inventory account.

As Exhibit 6-1 shows, the job-cost record summarizes information contained on source documents such as *materials requisitions* and *labour time tickets*.

EXHIBIT 6-1

Completed Job-Cost Record and Sample Source Documents

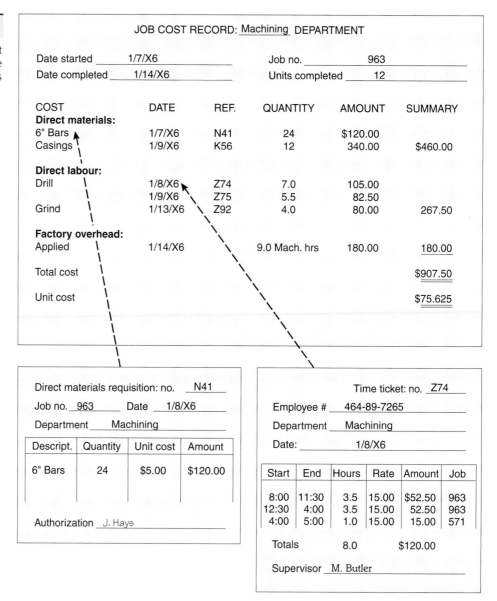

Materials requisitions are records of materials issued to particular jobs. **Labour time tickets** (or *time cards*) record the time a particular direct labourer spends on each job.

Today job-order cost records and source documents are likely to be computer files, not paper records. In fact, with online data entry, bar coding, and optical scanning, much of the information needed for such records enters the computer without ever being written on paper. Nevertheless, whether records are on paper or in computer files, the accounting system must collect and maintain the same basic information.

As each job begins, a job-order cost record is prepared. As units are worked on, entries are made on the job-cost record. Three classes of costs are applied to the units as they pass through the departments: material requisitions are the source of direct material costs, time tickets provide direct labour costs, and budgeted overhead rates are used to apply factory overhead to products. The computation of these budgeted rates will be described later in this chapter.

Explanation of Transactions

OBJECTIVE 2

Prepare summary journal entries for the typical transactions of a job-costing system.

To illustrate the functioning of a job-order costing system, we will use a job-costing system, including the basic records and journal entries, of the Martinez Electronics Company. On December 31, 2006, the firm had the following inventories:

Direct materials (12 types)	$110,000
Work-in-process	–
Finished goods (unsold units from two jobs)	12,000

The following transaction-by-transaction summary analysis will explain how product costing is achieved. Entries are usually made as transactions occur. However, to obtain a sweeping overview, our illustration uses a summary for the entire year 2007.

---

1. Transaction: Direct materials purchased, $1,900,000
   Analysis: The asset Direct Materials Inventory is increased. The liability Accounts Payable is increased.
   Entry: Direct materials inventory $1,900,000
   Accounts payable $1,900,000

2. Transaction: Direct materials requisitioned, $1,890,000
   Analysis: The asset Work-in-Process (Inventory) is increased. The asset Direct Materials Inventory is decreased.
   Entry: Work in process $1,890,000
   Direct materials inventory $1,890,000

3. Transaction: Direct labour cost incurred, $390,000
   Analysis: The asset Work-in-Process (Inventory) is increased. The liability Accrued Payroll is increased.
   Entry: Work-in-process $390,000
   Accrued payroll $390,000

4a. Transaction: Factory overhead incurred, $392,000

    Analysis: These actual costs are first charged to departmental overhead accounts, which may be regarded as assets until their amounts are later "cleared" or transferred to other accounts. Each department has detailed overhead accounts such as indirect labour, utilities, repairs, amortization, insurance, and property taxes. These details support a summary factory department overhead control account. The managers are responsible for regulating these costs, item by item. As these costs are charged to the depart- ments, the other accounts affected will be assorted assets and liabilities. Examples include cash, accounts payable, accrued payables, and accumulated amortization.

    Entry: Factory department overhead $392,000

           Cash, accounts payable, and various

               other balance sheet accounts $392,000

4b. Transaction: Factory overhead applied, $95,000 + $280,000 = $375,000

    Analysis: The asset Work-in-Process (Inventory) is increased. The asset Factory Department Overhead Control is decreased. (A fuller explanation occurs later in this chapter.)

    Entry: Work-in-process $375,000

           Factory department overhead $375,000

5. Transaction: Cost of goods completed, $2,500,000

    Analysis: The asset Finished Goods (Inventory) is increased. The asset Work-in- Process (Inventory) is decreased.

    Entry: Finished goods $2,500,000

           Work-in-process $2,500,000

6a. Transaction: Sales on account, $4,000,000

    Analysis: The asset Accounts Receivable is increased. The revenue account Sales is increased.

    Entry: Accounts receivable $4,000,000

           Sales $4,000,000

6b. Transaction: Cost of goods sold, $2,480,000

    Analysis: The expense Cost of Goods Sold is increased. The asset Finished Goods is decreased.

    Entry: Cost of goods sold $2,480,000

           Finished goods $2,480,000

The following is a summary of pertinent transactions for 2007:

	MACHINING	ASSEMBLY	TOTAL
1. Direct materials purchased on account	–	–	$1,900,000
2. Direct materials requisitioned for manufacturing	$1,000,000	$890,000	1,890,000
3. Direct labour costs incurred	200,000	190,000	390,000
4a. Factory overhead incurred	290,000	102,000	392,000
4b. Factory overhead applied	280,000	95,000	375,000
5. Cost of goods completed and transferred to finished-goods inventory	–	–	2,500,000
6a. Sales on account	–	–	4,000,000
6b. Cost of goods sold	–	–	2,480,000

Exhibit 6-2 is an overview of the general flow of costs through the Martinez Electronics Company's job-order-costing system. The exhibit summarizes the effects of transactions on the key manufacturing accounts in the firm's books. As

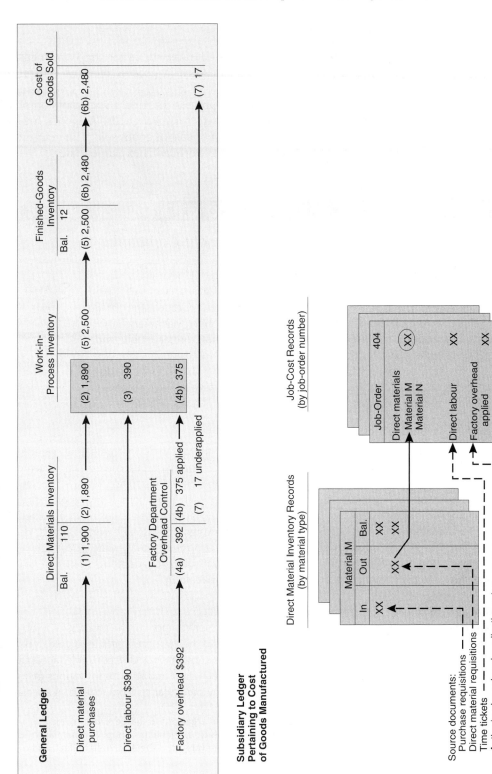

EXHIBIT 6-2

Job-Order Costing, General Flow of Costs (in thousands)

you proceed through the detailed explanation of transactions, keep checking each explanation against the overview in Exhibit 6-2.

Summary of Transactions

Exhibit 6-2 summarizes the Martinez transactions for the year, focusing on the cost flow and inventory accounts. Work-in-process receives central attention. The costs of direct material used, direct labour, and factory overhead applied to products are brought into work-in-process. In turn, the cost of completed goods is transferred from work-in-process to finished goods. As goods are sold, their costs become an expense in the form of cost of goods sold. The year-end accounting for the $17,000 of underapplied overhead is explained later.

STRATEGIC INSIGHTS COMPANY PRACTICES

Job Costing at RMS Equipment Company

Kitchener-based RMS Equipment Company is a former division of Uniroyal Goodrich Canada Inc., now known as Michelin North America (Canada) Inc.[1] RMS Equipment Company is part of the Pettibone Tire Equipment Group. The RMS Equipment Company was founded in 1917 in Kitchener as the Rubber Machinery Shop. Today, RMS Equipment Company is a provider of rubber extrusion, tire assembly, and specialty equipment to the rubber industry worldwide. It can also customize standard machines or develop completely new ones for the rubber industry. Its products are distinguished on the basis of accuracy, quality, and productivity levels. The company's products are used in the rubber, automotive, paper, metals, and plastics industries.

RMS Equipment Company
www.rms-ca.com

Michelin
www.michelin.ca

SALES ORDERS
It is very important to understand the time lag from the time of the quote, to the order, engineering drawings, letting out of purchase orders, to production and final shipping of a product. In some cases final settlements are contingent on the successful installation of the equipment at the customer's plant. Thus, jobs may linger on accounting records for months past the shipping date. Due to each job's complexity, a project engineer is assigned to monitor and be responsible for the project—acting as liaison with the customer and the job floor.

In general, the machinery manufactured is very intricate in design and usually weighs a great deal, so it is very important that the engineering drawings produced for the shop floor be accurate. If parts are incorrectly machined, a new casting or further machining may be required, resulting in additional costs and valuable time lost, which may result in not meeting the customer's delivery expectation.

JOB-COST TRACKING SYSTEM
In order to provide a vehicle for the project engineer and management to monitor the progress of a job, as well as to identify whether it is on schedule to meet financial estimates and the customer's promised date, a detailed job-cost tracking system is mandatory to capture and report data on a very timely and dependable (accurate) basis.

A detailed estimate is entered on the job-cost system for the job-master and subjobs for various major stages of the project. Sequence numbers further break down the subjobs by particular subcomponents. A specialized pur-

---

[1] The Uniroyal Goodrich Tire Company was formed in 1986 by the merger of U.S.-based Uniroyal and B.F. Goodrich. In 1990, the Uniroyal Goodrich Tire Company was acquired by France-based Michelin Group. In Canada, there are three Michelin manufacturing plants, all in Nova Scotia (Pictou County, Bridgewater, and the Annapolis Valley), and one Uniroyal Goodrich plant in Kitchener, Ontario.

chasing group uses the information to issue purchase orders for material or the subcontracting of parts. This also provides manufacturing with a map for machining and assembly scheduling, given the material arrival schedule.

APPLICATION OF BURDEN
Two cost drivers are currently in use for developing applied burden rates:

A. Direct labour dollars
B. Material and outside contracts.

A single rate for each cost driver is used for machining and assembly. The two cost drivers are used to assign burden to jobs, which by their nature or by management's decision may have a high content of outside labour (subcontracts) versus utilization of inside staff.

Over/underapplied burden is treated as a period cost to operations and not allocated to every job. The objective is to keep this amount in check by changing the cost-driver rates if business conditions change favourably or unfavourably, keeping in mind that normal monthly fluctuations do occur and are offset by year-end.

The primary objective is to assign a commensurate amount of burden to each and every job, enabling management to track profitability of a job during the work-in-process stage and at completion.

PROGRESS BILLINGS
Issuing progress billings by its nature causes unique accounting complications in the assignment of costs (material, labour, and burden) to the cost of sales for that particular job resulting in an "anticipated" profit margin. Normal conservatism rules apply to this rate, which is usually worked out from the estimate/quote for the project. Accounting personnel need to monitor jobs closely in order not to be embarrassed by over- or underestimated profit once jobs are completed. Keeping track of this type of activity becomes very important and requires knowledgeable experience about the operation and constant contact with all team members.

Source: Adapted from materials written by Nick Mask, Accounting Manager, Jack O'Donnell, General Manager, and Pat Bandura, Accounting, RMS Machinery Division (as it was then), Uniroyal Goodrich Canada Inc.

ACCOUNTING FOR FACTORY OVERHEAD

OBJECTIVE 3

Compute budgeted factory-overhead rates and apply them to production, using appropriate cost drivers.

In the Martinez Company example, factory overhead of $375,000 was applied to the work-in-process account. This section describes how to determine the amount of applied factory overhead.

Few companies wait until the actual factory overhead is known at the end of the accounting period to compute the costs of products. Most managers want a close approximation of the costs of various products continuously, not just at the end of a year. Managers desire to know these costs for various ongoing uses, including making more accurate pricing decisions, producing interim financial statements, and better managing inventories. Thus, they compute a budgeted (predetermined) overhead rate at the beginning of a fiscal year and use it to apply overhead costs as products are manufactured.

Budgeted Overhead Application Rates

The following steps summarize how to account for factory overhead:

1. Select one or more cost drivers to serve as a base for applying overhead costs. Examples include direct labour hours, direct labour costs, machine hours, production setups, and so on. The cost driver should be an activity that is the common denominator for systematically

relating factory overhead costs with products. The cost driver or drivers should be the best available measure of the cause-and-effect relationships between overhead costs and production volume.

Budgeted Factory Overhead Rate. The budgeted total overhead divided by the budgeted cost-driver activity.

2. Prepare a factory-overhead budget for the planning period, ordinarily a year. The two key items are (a) budgeted overhead and (b) budgeted volume of the cost driver.
3. Compute the **budgeted factory overhead rate** by dividing the budgeted total overhead by the budgeted cost driver. There could be a separate budgeted overhead rate for each cost component of the total overhead.
4. Obtain actual cost-driver data as the year unfolds.
5. Apply the budgeted overhead to the jobs by multiplying the budgeted rate times the actual cost-driver data.
6. At the end of the year, account for any differences between the actual overhead incurred and overhead applied to products.

Illustration of Overhead Application

To understand how to apply factory overhead to jobs, consider the Martinez illustration again.

The following manufacturing overhead budget was prepared for the year 2007:

	MACHINING	ASSEMBLY
Indirect labour	$ 75,600	$ 36,800
Supplies	8,400	2,400
Utilities	20,000	7,000
Repairs	10,000	3,000
Factory rent	10,000	6,800
Supervision	42,600	35,400
Amortization on equipment	104,000	9,400
Insurance, property taxes, etc.	7,200	2,400
	$277,800	$103,200

MAKING MANAGERIAL DECISIONS

Suppose you are a manager of a manufacturing department. Confirm your understanding of product costing in a job-order environment by indicating the transactions that occurred for each of the following journal entries. Which of these transactions records actual costs versus cost estimates?

1. WIP Inventory   XXX
     Accrued Payroll   XXX

2. WIP Inventory   XXX
     Factory Department Overhead Control XXX

3. Cost of Goods Sold   XXX
     Finished Goods   XXX

ANSWER

The first entry records the actual cost of direct labour that the accounting system traces to the specific order being costed. We make the second entry when the order is completed to record the application of factory overhead. This is an estimate of the costs of indirect resources used to complete the order. The last entry records the cost of goods sold when the company ships the order. This cost is a mix of actual costs (direct material and direct labour) and estimated costs (applied factory overhead).

As products are worked on, Martinez applies the factory overhead to the jobs. A budgeted overhead rate is used, computed as follows:

$$\text{budgeted overhead application rate} = \frac{\text{total budgeted factory overhead}}{\text{total budgeted amount of cost driver}}$$

Suppose machine hours are chosen as the only cost driver in the machining department and direct labour cost is chosen in the assembly department. The overhead rates are as follows:

	YEAR 2007	
	MACHINING	ASSEMBLY
Budgeted manufacturing overhead	$277,800	$103,200
Budgeted machine hours	69,450	
Budgeted direct labour cost		206,400
Budgeted overhead rate, per machine hour: $277,800 ÷ 69,450 =	$4	
Budgeted overhead rate, per direct labour dollar: $103,200 ÷ $206,400 =		$0.50

Note that the overhead rates are budgeted; they are estimates. These rates are then used to apply overhead based on *actual* events. That is, the total overhead applied in our illustration is the result of multiplying *actual* machine hours or labour cost by the *budgeted* overhead rates:

Machining: Actual machine hours of 70,000 × $4 =	$280,000
Assembly: Actual direct labour of $190,000 × 0.50 =	95,000
Total factory overhead applied	$375,000

The summary journal entry for the application (entry 4b) is:

4b. Work-in-process	$375,000	
Factory department overhead		$375,000

Choosing Cost Drivers

Factory overhead, unlike direct material or direct labour, is a conglomeration of manufacturing costs that cannot conveniently be applied on an individual job basis. But such overhead is an integral part of a product's total cost. Therefore, it is applied indirectly, using as a base a cost driver that is common to all jobs worked on and is the best available index of the product's relative use of, or benefits from, the overhead items. In other words, there should be a strong cause-and-effect relationship between the factory overhead incurred (the effect) and the cost driver chosen for its application.

As we have noted earlier in this text, no one cost driver is right for all situations. The goal is to find the driver that best links cause and effect. In the Martinez machining department, two or more machines can often be operated simultaneously by a single direct labourer. Use of machines causes the most overhead cost in the machining department, for example, amortization and repairs. Therefore, machine hours is the cost driver and the appropriate base for applying overhead costs. Thus Martinez must keep track of the machine hours used for each job, creating an added data-collection cost. That is, both direct labour costs and machine hours must be accumulated for each job.

In contrast, direct labour is a principal cost driver in the Martinez assembly department. It is an accurate reflection of the relative attention and effort devoted to various jobs. The workers are paid equal hourly rates. Therefore, all that is needed is to apply the 50 percent overhead rate to the cost of direct labour already entered on the job-cost records. No separate job records have to be kept of the labour hours. If the hourly labour rates differ greatly for individuals performing identical tasks, the hours of labour, rather than the dollars spent for labour, might be used as a base. Otherwise a $9-per-hour worker would cause more overhead applied than an $8-per-hour worker, even though the same time would probably be taken and the same facilities used by each employee for the same work.

Sometimes direct labour cost is the best overhead cost driver even if wage rates vary within a department. Survey after survey has indicated that over 90 percent of the companies use direct labour cost or direct labour hours as their single cost driver for overhead application. For example, higher-skilled labour may use more costly equipment and have more indirect labour support. Moreover, many factory-overhead costs include costly employee benefit costs such as pensions and payroll taxes. The latter are often more closely driven by direct labour cost than by direct labour hours.

If a department identifies more than one cost driver for overhead costs, these costs ideally should be put into as many cost pools as there are cost drivers. In practice, such a system is too costly for many organizations. Instead, these organizations select a small number of cost drivers (often only one) to serve as a basis for allocating overhead costs.

The selected cost driver (or drivers) should be the one that causes most of the overhead costs. For example, suppose machine hours cause 70 percent of the overhead costs in a particular department, number of component parts cause 20 percent, and five assorted cost drivers cause the other 10 percent. Instead of using seven cost pools allocated on the basis of the seven cost drivers, most managers would use one cost driver—machine hours—to allocate all overhead costs. Others would assign all costs to two cost pools, one allocated on the basis of machine hours and one on the basis of number of component parts.

No matter which cost drivers are chosen, the overhead rates are applied day after day throughout the year to cost the various jobs worked on by each department. All overhead is applied to all jobs worked on during the year on the appropriate basis of machine hours or direct labour costs of each job. Suppose management predictions coincide exactly with actual amounts (an extremely unlikely situation). Then the total overhead applied to the year's jobs via these budgeted rates would be equal to the total overhead costs actually incurred.

Normalized Overhead Rates

During the year and at year-end, the actual overhead amount incurred will rarely equal the amount applied. This variance between incurred and applied can be analyzed. The most common—and most important—contributor to this vari-

OBJECTIVE 4

Identify the meaning
and purpose of
normalized
overhead rates.

ance is operating at a different level of volume than the level used as a denominator in calculating the budgeted overhead rate (e.g., using 100,000 budgeted direct labour hours as the denominator and then actually working only 80,000 hours). Other frequent contributory causes include poor forecasting, inefficient use of overhead items, price changes in individual overhead items, erratic behaviour of individual overhead items (e.g., repairs made only during slack time), and calendar variations (e.g., 20 work days in one month, 22 in the next).

All these peculiarities of overhead are mingled in an *annual* overhead pool. Thus, an annual rate is budgeted and used regardless of the month-to-month peculiarities of specific overhead costs. Such an approach is more defensible than applying the actual overhead for *each month*. Why? Because a *normal* product cost is more useful for decisions, and more representative for inventory-costing purposes, than an "actual" product cost that is distorted by month-to-month fluctuations in production volume and by the erratic behaviour of many overhead costs. Our Martinez illustration in the previous pages demonstrated the normal costing approach. An annual average overhead rate is used consistently throughout the year for product costing, *without altering it from day to day and from month to month*. The resultant "normal" product costs include an average or **normalized overhead rate**. Consider the employees of a gypsum plant using an "actual" product cost system that had the privilege of buying company-made items "at cost." Employees joked about the benefits of buying "at cost" during high-volume months when unit costs were lower because volume was higher.

Normalized Overhead Rate.
An annual average overhead rate used consistently throughout the year without altering it from month to month.

	ACTUAL OVERHEAD			DIRECT LABOUR HOURS	ACTUAL OVERHEAD APPLICATION RATE* PER DIRECT LABOUR HOUR
	VARIABLE	FIXED	TOTAL		
Peak-volume month	$60,000	$40,000	$100,000	100,000	$1.00
Low-volume month	30,000	40,000	70,000	50,000	$1.40

* Divide total overhead by direct labour hours. Note that the presence of fixed overhead causes the fluctuation in unit costs from $1.00 to $1.40. The variable component is $0.60 an hour in both months, but the fixed component is $0.40 in the peak-volume month ($40,000 ÷ 100,000), and $0.80 in the low-volume month ($40,000 ÷ 50,000).

Disposition of Underapplied and Overapplied Overhead

Our Martinez illustration contained the following data:

Transaction		
4a.	Factory overhead incurred	$392,000
4b.	Factory overhead applied	375,000
	Underapplied factory overhead	$ 17,000

The total actual costs of $392,000 must eventually be expensed in some way. The $375,000 of applied overhead will be expensed to the cost of goods sold when the products to which it is applied are sold. The remaining $17,000 must also be expensed by some method.

Overapplied Overhead. The excess of overhead applied to products over actual overhead incurred.

Underapplied Overhead. The excess of actual overhead over the overhead applied to products.

The difference between incurred and applied overhead is typically allowed to accumulate during the year. At the year-end, when the amount applied to product *exceeds* the amount incurred by the departments, the difference is called **overapplied overhead**; when the amount applied is *less than* incurred, the difference is called **underapplied overhead**. At year-end, the difference ($17,000 in our illustration) is disposed of through either a write-off or proration.

Immediate Write-Off

Under this method, the $17,000 underapplied overhead is added to the cost of goods sold, and the income is reduced by the same amount. The same logic is followed for overapplied overhead. Overapplied overhead is subtracted from the cost of goods sold and as a result income is increased by the same amount.

The theory underlying the direct write-off is that most of the goods worked on have been sold, and ending inventories are low, carrying a small fraction of the total underapplied overhead costs. A more elaborate method of disposition of the under- or overapplied overhead costs between goods sold and goods in ending inventories is not worth the extra trouble. Another justification is that the extra overhead costs represented by underapplied overhead do not qualify as part of ending inventory costs because they do not represent assets. They should be written off because they largely represent inefficiency or the underutilization of available facilities in the current period.

The immediate write-off eliminates the $17,000 difference with a simple journal entry, labelled as transaction 7 in Exhibit 6-2:

7. Cost of goods sold (or a separate charge against revenue) $17,000	
Factory department overhead	$17,000
To close the ending underapplied overhead directly to cost of goods sold	

Proration among Inventories

This method prorates over- or underapplied overhead among work-in-process, finished goods, and cost of goods sold. Theoretically, if the objective is to obtain as accurate a cost allocation as possible, all the overhead costs of the individual jobs worked on should be recomputed, using the actual rather than the budgeted rates. This approach is rarely feasible, so a practical attack is to prorate on the basis of the ending balances in each of three accounts (work-in-process, $155,000; finished goods, $32,000; and cost of goods sold, $2,480,000).

	(1) UNADJUSTED BALANCE, END OF 2007	(2) PRORATION OF UNDERAPPLIED OVERHEAD	(3) ADJUSTED BALANCE, END OF 2007
Work-in-process	$ 155,000	155/2,667 × 17,000 = $ 988	$ 155,988
Finished goods	32,000	32/2,667 × 17,000 = 204	32,204
Cost of goods sold	2,480,000	2,480/2,667 × 17,000 = 15,808	2,495,808
	$2,667,000	$17,000	$2,684,000

The journal entry for the proration follows:

Work-in-process	988	
Finished goods	204	
Cost of goods sold.	$15,808	
Factory department overhead		$17,000
To prorate the ending underapplied overhead		
among three accounts.		

The amounts prorated to inventories here are not significant. In actual practice, prorating is done only when inventory valuations would be materially affected. Exhibit 6-3 provides a schematic comparison of the two major methods of disposing of underapplied (or overapplied) factory overhead.

EXHIBIT 6-3

Year-End Disposition of Underapplied Factory Overhead

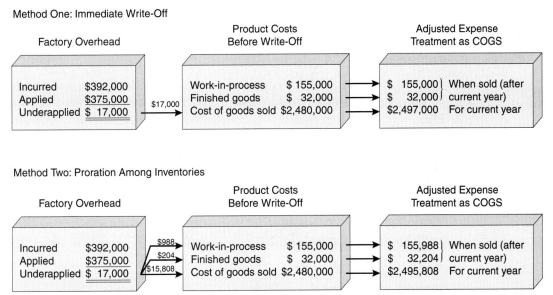

The Use of Variable and Fixed Application Rates

As we have seen, overhead application is the most troublesome aspect of product costing. The presence of fixed costs is a major reason for the costing difficulties. Most companies make no distinction between variable- and fixed-cost behaviour in the design of accounting systems. For instance, the machining department at Martinez Electronics Company developed the following rate:

$$\text{budgeted overhead application rate} = \frac{\text{budgeted total overhead}}{\text{budgeted machine hours}}$$
$$= \frac{\$277,800}{69,450} = \$4 \text{ per machine hour}$$

Some companies distinguish between variable overhead and fixed overhead for product costing as well as for control purposes. If the machining department had made this distinction, then rent, supervision, amortization, and insurance would have been considered the fixed portion of the total manufacturing overhead, and two rates would have been developed:

$$\text{budgeted variable-overhead application rate} = \frac{\text{budgeted total variable overhead}}{\text{budgeted machine hours}}$$
$$= \frac{\$114,000}{69,450}$$
$$= \$1.64 \text{ per machine hour}$$
$$\text{budgeted fixed-overhead application rate} = \frac{\text{budgeted total fixed overhead}}{\text{budgeted machine hours}}$$
$$= \frac{\$163,800}{69,450}$$
$$= \$2.36 \text{ per machine hour}$$

Such rates can be used for product costing. Distinctions between variable and fixed overhead can also be made for control purposes.

Actual Costing versus Normal Costing

Normal Costing System.
The cost system in which overhead is applied on an average or normalized basis in order to get representative or normal inventory valuations.

In an *actual costing system* every effort is made to trace the *actual* costs, as incurred, to the physical units produced. However, it is only partly an actual system because overhead, by definition, cannot be traced to physical products. Instead, overhead is applied on an average or normalized basis, in order to get representative or normal inventory valuations. Hence we shall label the system a **normal costing system**. The cost of the manufactured product comprises *actual* direct material, *actual* direct labour, and *normal* applied overhead.

The two job-order costing approaches may be compared as follows:

	ACTUAL COSTING	NORMAL COSTING
Direct materials	Actual	Actual
Direct labour	Actual	Actual
Manufacturing overhead	Actual	Budgeted rates*

* Actual inputs (such as direct labour hours or direct labour costs) multiplied by budgeted overhead rates (computed by dividing total budgeted manufacturing overhead by a budgeted cost driver such as direct labour hours).

In a true actual costing system, overhead is not applied as jobs are worked on but only after all overhead costs for the year are known. Then, using an "actual" average rate(s) instead of a budgeted rate(s), costs are applied to all jobs that were worked on throughout the year. All costs incurred are exactly offset by costs applied to the work-in-process inventory. However, increased accuracy is obtained at the sacrifice of timeliness in using costs for measuring operating efficiency, determining selling prices, and producing interim financial statements.

Normal costing has replaced actual costing in many organizations precisely because the latter approach fails to provide costs of products as they are worked on during the year. It is possible to use a normal-costing system plus year-end

Overhead Allocation at Harley-Davidson

In August 2003, Milwaukee-based Harley-Davidson, the motorcycle manufacturer, celebrated its 100th birthday. As happy as everyone at Harley is today, it is a bit surprising to some how far the company has come over the past several decades. From near collapse, Harley turned its business around during the 1980s and 1990s, and in 1999 captured the number-one market position from Honda for the first time in three decades. Harley-Davidson (2004 sales of more than $5 billion) is the only major U.S.-based motorcycle producer. One of the keys to the company's return to competitiveness was the adoption of a just-in-time (JIT) philosophy. It is not unusual for a company to discover that a change in an important component of operations requires a corresponding change in the company's accounting system. The main focus of the accounting system was direct labour, which not only made up a part of product cost, but also functioned as an all-purpose base for allocating overhead. However, direct labour was only 10% of total product cost. It certainly did not generate a majority of the overhead costs. Although Harley-Davidson's production process had changed, the accounting system remained static.

Harley-Davidson
www.harley-davidson.com

The JIT system served to emphasize that detailed information on direct-labour costs was not useful to managers. It was costly to have each direct labourer record the time spent on each product or part and then enter the information from the time cards into the accounting system. For example, if each of 500 direct labourers works on 20 products per day, the system must record 10,000 entries per day, which is 200,000 entries per month. The time spent by direct labourers to record the time, by clerks to enter the data into the system, and by accountants to check the data's accuracy, is enormous—and all to produce product cost information that was used for financial reporting but was useless to managers.

The JIT system forced manufacturing managers to focus on satisfying customers and minimizing non-value-added activities. Gradually, accountants began to focus on the same objectives. Accounting's customers were the managers who used the accounting information, and effort put into activities that did not help managers was deemed counterproductive (non-value-added). Therefore, eliminating the costly, time-consuming recording of detailed labour costs became a priority. Direct labour was eliminated as a direct cost, and consequently it could not be used for overhead allocation. After considering process hours, flow-through time, materials value, and individual cost per unit as possible cost drivers for allocating overhead, the company selected process hours. Direct labour and overhead were combined to form conversion costs, which were applied to products on the basis of total process hours. This did not result in costs significantly different from the old system, but the new system was much simpler and less costly. Only direct material was traced directly to the product. Conversion costs were applied at completion of production based on a simple measure of process time.

Accounting systems should generate benefits greater than their costs. More sophisticated systems are not necessarily better systems. Harley-Davidson's main objective in changing its accounting system was simplification—elimination of unnecessary tasks and the streamlining of others. These changes resulted in a revitalized accounting system.

Sources: Adapted from W. T. Turk, "Management Accounting Revitalized: The Harley-Davidson Experience," in B. J. Brinker, ed., *Emerging Practices in Cost Management* (Boston: Warren, Gorham & Lamont, 1990), pp. 155–166; K. Barron, "Hog Wild," *Forbes*, May 15, 2000; Harley-Davidson *2004 Annual Report*.

adjustments to produce final results that closely approximate the results under actual costing. To do so in our illustration, the underapplied overhead is prorated among work-in-process, finished goods, and cost of goods sold, as shown in Exhibit 6-3.

ACTIVITY-BASED COSTING IN A JOB-ORDER ENVIRONMENT

OBJECTIVE 5

Use an activity-based costing system in a job-order environment.

Regardless of the nature of a company's production system, there will always be resources that are shared among different products. The costs of these shared resources are part of overhead and must be accounted for in the company's cost accounting system. In most cases, the magnitude of overhead is large enough to justify investing in a cost system that provides accurate cost information. Whether this cost information is being used for inventory reporting, to cost jobs, or for cost planning and control, most often the benefits of more accurate costs exceed the costs of installing and maintaining the cost system. As we have seen, activity-based costing usually increases costing accuracy because it focuses on the cause-effect relationship between work performed (activities) and the consumption of resources (costs).

Illustration of Activity-Based Costing in a Job-Order Environment

Dell Computer
Corporation
www.dell.com

We illustrate an activity-based costing (ABC) system in a job-order environment by considering Dell Computer Corporation. What motivated Dell to adopt activity-based costing? Company managers cite two reasons: (1) the aggressive cost reduction targets set by top management and (2) the need to understand product-line profitability. As is the case with any business, understanding profitability means understanding the cost structure of the entire business. One of the key advantages of an ABC system is its focus on understanding how work (activities) is related to the consumption of resources (costs). So, an ABC system was a logical choice for Dell. Of course, once Dell's managers understood the company's cost structure, cost reduction through activity-based management was much easier.

Dell began developing its ABC system by viewing its business from a value chain perspective. Exhibit 6-4 shows the functions (or core processes) that add value to the company's products and how the costs of these functions are assigned to an individual job under the current ABC system.

To understand product-line profitability, Dell managers first identified key activities for the research and development, product design, and production functions. Then they used appropriate cost drivers to allocate activity costs to the assembly mods that produced product lines. While each of the functions shown in Exhibit 6-4 is important, we will focus on the product design and production functions. Product design is one of Dell's most important value-adding functions. The role of design is to provide a defect-free computer product that is easy to manufacture and reliable to the customer. Engineering costs (primarily salaries and CAD equipment amortization) account for most of the design costs. These costs are indirect and, thus, must be allocated to assembly mods using a cost driver.

The production costs include direct material, direct labour, and factory overhead. Factory overhead consists of six activity centres and related cost pools: receiving, preparation, assembly, testing, packaging, and shipping. Facility costs (plant amortization, insurance, taxes) are considered part of the production

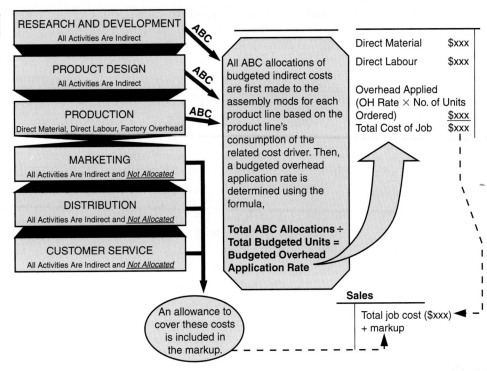

EXHIBIT 6-4

Dell Computer
Corporation's Value
Chain and ABC System

RESEARCH AND DEVELOPMENT
All Activities Are Indirect

ABC

PRODUCT DESIGN
All Activities Are Indirect

ABC

PRODUCTION
Direct Material, Direct Labour, Factory Overhead

ABC

MARKETING
All Activities Are Indirect and *Not Allocated*

DISTRIBUTION
All Activities Are Indirect and *Not Allocated*

CUSTOMER SERVICE
All Activities Are Indirect and *Not Allocated*

All ABC allocations of budgeted indirect costs are first made to the assembly mods for each product line based on the product line's consumption of the related cost driver. Then, a budgeted overhead application rate is determined using the formula,

Total ABC Allocations ÷ Total Budgeted Units = Budgeted Overhead Application Rate

An allowance to cover these costs is included in the markup.

Direct Material	$xxx
Direct Labour	$xxx
Overhead Applied (OH Rate × No. of Units Ordered)	$xxx
Total Cost of Job	$xxx

Sales

Total job cost ($xxx)
+ markup

Refer to Exhibit 6-4. One of the primary purposes of an ABC system is to increase the accuracy of product costs so that managers have a high level of confidence in cost-based decisions. Assume that you are a manager at Dell and that you have to determine prices for computers by adding a markup to the cost accumulated by the costing system. For example, if the accumulated total job cost is $1,200, a markup sufficient to "cover" all unallocated costs and provide a reasonable profit is added. Using the table below, determine whether the percentage markup under the ABC system is higher or lower than under the previous system. Which system gives you a higher degree of confidence that the price for a com-

puter is adequate to cover all costs and provide a reasonable profit? Why?

ANSWER
Under the previous costing system, Dell determined prices by marking up only the cost of production. Thus, the markup was high so that the company would cover all the unallocated costs and also achieve a reasonable profit. Managers had a low level of confidence in this cost system. The ABC system provided estimates of major value-chain costs. The size of the markup was low, and the confidence level in the costs provided was high.

| Value-Chain Function | ABC or Unallocated | |
	Previous Costing System	ABC Costing System
Research and Development	Unallocated	ABC Allocations
Design	Unallocated	ABC Allocations
Production	Traditional Allocation	ABC Allocations
Marketing	Unallocated	Unallocated
Distribution	Unallocated	Unallocated
Customer Service	Unallocated	Unallocated

function and are allocated to each activity centre based on the square metres occupied by the function.

At Dell, there is a different assembly mod for each product line. Thus, the total annual budgeted indirect cost allocated to an assembly mod is divided by the total budgeted units produced to find a budgeted overhead rate. This rate, which is adjusted periodically to reflect changes in the budget, is used to cost individual jobs.

Notice in Exhibit 6-4 that the costs of the marketing, distribution, and customer-service functions are not allocated to the assembly mod. How does Dell account for the indirect costs of marketing, distribution, and customer-service functions? The costs of these functions are estimated during the budgeting process and included in the markup used to price a job. That is, Dell uses cost plus pricing based on total assembly mod costs. The markup includes an allowance for all unallocated costs and the desired profits. As Dell expands its ABC system, these functions will also be broken down by activities, increasing the overall accuracy of the job-costing system.

PRODUCT COSTING IN SERVICE AND NOT-FOR-PROFIT ORGANIZATIONS

This chapter has concentrated on how to apply costs to manufactured products. However, the job-costing approach is used in nonmanufacturing situations too. For example, universities have research "projects," airlines have repair and overhaul "jobs," and public accountants have audit "engagements." In such situations, the focus shifts from the costs of products to the costs of services.

In not-for-profit organizations, the "product" is usually not called a "job order." Instead, it may be called a program or service cost. A "program" is an identifiable group of activities that frequently produces outputs in the form of services rather than goods. Examples include a safety program, an education program, or a family-counselling program. Costs or revenues may be traced to individual hospital patients, individual university research projects and individual social welfare cases. However, departments often work simultaneously on many programs, so the "job-order" costing challenge is to "apply" the various department costs to the various programs. Only then can managers make decisions regarding the allocation of limited resources among competing programs.

In service industries—such as repairing, consulting, legal, and accounting services—each customer order is a different job with a special account or order number. Sometimes only costs are traced directly to the job, sometimes only revenue is traced, and sometimes both. For example, automobile repair shops typically have a repair order for each car worked on, with space for allocating materials and labour costs. Customers are permitted to see only a copy showing the retail prices of the materials, parts, and labour billed to their orders. If the repair manager wants cost data, a system may be designed so that the "actual" parts and labour costs of each order are traced to a duplicate copy of the repair order. That is why you often see auto mechanics "punching in" and "punching out" their starting and stopping times on "time tickets" as each new order is worked on.

Budgets and Control of Engagements

In many service organizations, job orders are used primarily for product costing but also for planning and control purposes. For example, a public accounting firm might have a condensed budget for 2006 as follows:

Revenue	$10,000,000	100%
Direct labour (for professional hours charged to engagements)	2,500,000	25
Contribution to overhead and operating income	$ 7,500,000	75
Overhead (all other costs)	6,500,000	65
Operating income	$ 1,000,000	10%

In this illustration:

$$\text{budgeted overhead rate} = \frac{\text{budgeted overhead}}{\text{budgeted direct labour}}$$
$$= \frac{\$6,500,000}{\$2,500,000} = 260\%$$

As each engagement is budgeted, the partner in charge of the audit predicts the expected number of necessary direct professional hours. Direct professional hours are those worked by partners, managers, and subordinate auditors to complete the engagement. The budgeted direct labour cost is the pertinent hourly labour costs multiplied by the budgeted hours. Partners' time is charged to the engagement at much higher rates than subordinates' time.

How is overhead applied? Accounting firms usually use either direct labour cost or direct labour hours as the cost driver for overhead application. In our example, the firm uses direct labour cost. Such a practice implies that partners require proportionately more overhead support for each of their hours charged.

The budgeted total cost of an engagement is the direct labour cost plus applied overhead (260 percent of direct labour cost in this illustration) plus any other direct costs.

The engagement partner uses a budget for a specific audit that includes detailed scope and steps. For instance, the budget for auditing cash or receivables would specify the exact work to be done, the number of hours, and the necessary hours of partner time, manager time, and subordinate time. The partner monitors progress by comparing the hours logged to date with the original budget and with the estimated hours remaining on the engagement. Obviously, if a fixed audit fee has been quoted, the profitability of an engagement depends on whether the audit can be accomplished within the budgeted time limits.

Accuracy of Costs of Engagements

Suppose the accounting firm has costs on an auditing engagement as follows:

Direct professional labour	$ 50,000
Applied overhead, 260%	130,000
Total costs excluding travel costs	$180,000
Travel costs	14,000
Total costs of engagement	$194,000

Two direct costs—professional labour and travel costs—are traced to the jobs. But only direct professional labour is a cost driver for overhead. (Note that costs reimbursed by the client—such as travel costs—do not add to overhead costs and normally would not be subject to any markups in the setting of fees.)

Managers of service firms, such as auditing and consulting firms, frequently use either the budgeted or "actual" costs of engagements as guides to pricing and to allocating effort among particular services or customers. Hence the accuracy of costs of various engagements may affect decisions.

Activity-Based Costing in Service and Not-For-Profit Organizations

Our accounting firm example described a widely used, relatively simple job-costing system. Only two direct cost items (direct professional labour and travel costs) are used and only a single overhead application rate is used.

In recent years, to obtain more accurate costs, many professional service firms such as manufacturing firms have refined their data-processing systems and adopted activity-based costing. Computers help accumulate information that is far more detailed than was feasible a few years ago. As noted in earlier chapters, firms that use activity-based costing generally shift costs from being classified as overhead to being classified as direct costs. Using our previously assumed numbers for direct labour ($50,000) and travel ($14,000), we recast the costs of our audit engagement as follows:

Direct professional labour	$ 50,000
Direct support labour, such as secretarial costs	10,000
Employee benefits for all direct labour*	24,000
Telephone calls	1,000
Photocopying	2,000
Computer time	7,000
Total direct costs	$ 94,000
Applied overhead**	103,400
Total costs excluding travel costs	$197,400
Travel costs	14,000
Total costs of engagement	$211,400

* 40% assumed rate multiplied by ($50,000 + $10,000) = $24,000.
** 110% assumed rate multiplied by total direct costs of $94,000 = $103,400.

In an ABC system, costs such as direct support labour, telephone calls, photocopying, computer time, and travel costs are applied by directly measuring their usage on each engagement. The remaining costs to be allocated are assigned to cost pools based on their cause. The cost driver for employee benefits is labour cost and for other overhead is total direct costs.

The more detailed approach of activity-based costing will nearly always produce total costs that differ from the total costs in the general approach shown earlier: $211,400 compared with $194,000. Of course, any positive or negative difference is attributable to having more types of costs traced directly to the engagement.

Effects of Classifications on Overhead Rates

There are two reasons why the activity-based costing approach also has a lower overhead application rate, assumed at 110 percent of total direct costs instead of the 260 percent of direct labour used in the first example. First, there are fewer overhead costs because more costs are traced directly. Second, the application base is broader, including all direct costs rather than only direct labour.

Even with activity-based costing, some firms may prefer to continue to apply their overhead based on direct labour costs rather than total direct costs. Why? Because the partners believe that overhead is much more affected by the amount of direct labour costs than other direct costs such as telephone calls. But at least the activity-based costing firm has made an explicit decision that direct labour costs are the best cost driver.

Deciding whether the overhead cost driver should be total direct costs, direct professional labour costs or hours, or some other cost driver is a problem for many firms, including most professional service firms. Ideally, activity analysis should uncover the principal cost drivers and they should all be used for overhead application. In practice, only one or two cost drivers are used.

HIGHLIGHTS TO REMEMBER

1. **Compute budgeted factory-overhead rates and apply factory overhead to production.** Accountants usually apply indirect manufacturing costs (factory overhead) to products using budgeted overhead rates. They compute the rates by dividing total budgeted overhead by a measure of cost-driver activity such as expected machine hours.

2. **Determine and use appropriate cost drivers for overhead application.** There should be a strong cause-and-effect relationship between cost drivers and the overhead costs that are allocated using these drivers.

3. **Identify the meaning and purpose of normalized overhead rates.** Budgeted overhead rates are usually annual averages. The resulting product costs are normal costs, consisting of actual direct materials plus actual direct labour plus applied overhead using the budgeted rates. Normal product costs are often more useful than true actual costs for decision-making and inventory-costing purposes.

4. **Distinguish between job-order costing and process costing.** Product costing is an averaging process. Process costing deals with broad averages and great masses of like units. Job-order costing deals with narrow averages and unique units or a small batch of like units.

5. **Prepare summary journal entries for the typical transactions of a job-costing system.** The focus of journal entries in a job-order-costing system is on inventory accounts. The WIP inventory account receives central attention. Direct materials used, direct labour, and factory overhead applied are accumulated in WIP. In turn, the cost of completed goods is transferred from WIP to finished goods.

6. **Use an activity-based-costing system in a job-order environment.** Activity-based costing can be used for any type of business that has significant levels of shared resources. In a job-order system, ABC helps managers understand the cost structure of the business on a job-by-job basis. Overhead costs are assigned to activity centres and then to jobs based on appropriate cost drivers. Activity-based management uses ABC information and the increased understanding of the organization's cost structure to control and reduce overhead costs.

7. **Show how service organizations use job costing.** The job-costing approach is used in nonmanufacturing as well as in manufacturing. Examples include costs of services such as auto repair, consulting, and

auditing. For example, the job order is a key device for planning and controlling an audit engagement by a public accounting firm.

DEMONSTRATION PROBLEM FOR YOUR REVIEW

Problem

Review the Martinez illustration, especially Exhibits 6-2 and 6-3. Prepare an income statement for 2006 through the gross-profit line. Use the immediate write-off method for overapplied overhead.

Solution

Exhibit 6-5 recapitulates the final effect of the Martinez illustration on the financial statements. Note how the immediate write-off means that the $17,000 is added to the cost of goods sold. As you study Exhibit 6-5, trace the three major elements of cost (direct material, direct labour, and factory overhead) through the accounts.

EXHIBIT 6-5

Relation of Costs of Financial Statements

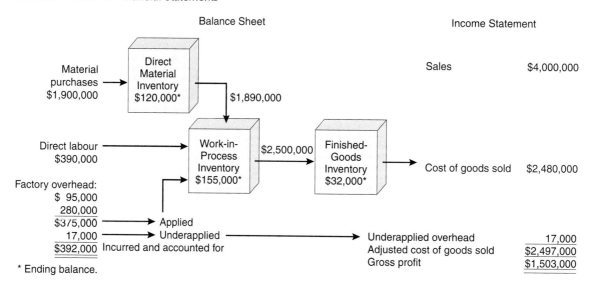

* Ending balance.

KEY TERMS

budgeted factory overhead rate *p. 264*
job costing *p. 257*
job-cost record *p. 258*
job-cost sheet *p. 258*
job order *p. 258*
job-order costing *p. 257*
labour time tickets *p. 259*

materials requisitions *p. 259*
normal costing system *p. 270*
normalized overhead rate *p. 267*
overapplied overhead *p. 268*
process costing *p. 257*
underapplied overhead *p. 268*

ASSIGNMENT MATERIAL

QUESTIONS

Q6-1 "There are different product costs for different purposes." Name at least two purposes.

Q6-2 "Job costs are accumulated for purposes of inventory valuation and income determination." State two other purposes.

Q6-3 Distinguish between job costing and process costing.

Q6-4 "The basic distinction between job-order costing and process costing is the breadth of the denominator." Explain.

Q6-5 How does hybrid costing relate to job costing and process costing?

Q6-6 Describe the supporting details for work-in-process in a job-cost system.

Q6-7 What types of source documents provide information for a job-cost record?

Q6-8 Suppose a company uses machine hours as a cost driver for factory overhead. How does the company compute a budgeted overhead application rate? How does it compute the amount of factory overhead applied to a particular job?

Q6-9 Explain the role of the factory department overhead control account in a job-cost system.

Q6-10 "Each department must choose one cost driver to be used for cost application." Do you agree? Explain.

Q6-11 "There should be a strong relationship between the factory overhead incurred and the cost driver chosen for its application." Why?

Q6-12 "Sometimes direct labour cost is the best cost driver for overhead allocation even if wage rates vary within a department." Do you agree? Explain.

Q6-13 Identify four cost drivers that a manufacturing company might use to apply factory overhead costs to jobs.

Q6-14 What are some reasons for differences between the amounts of *incurred* and *applied* overhead?

Q6-15 "Under actual overhead application, unit costs soar as volume increases, and vice versa." Do you agree? Explain.

Q6-16 Define *normal* costing.

Q6-17 What is the best theoretical method of allocating underapplied or over-applied overhead, assuming that the objective is to obtain as accurate a cost application as possible?

Q6-18 State three examples of service industries that use the job-costing approach.

Q6-19 "Service firms trace only direct labour costs to jobs. All other costs are applied as a percentage of direct labour cost." Do you agree? Explain.

Q6-20 "As data processing becomes more economical, more costs than just direct material and direct labour will be classified as direct costs wherever feasible." Give three examples of such costs.

PROBLEMS

P6-1 **DIRECT MATERIALS.** For each of the following independent cases, fill in the blanks (in millions of dollars):

	1	2	3	4
Direct materials inventory, Dec. 31, 2006	8	8	5	?
Purchased	5	9	?	8
Used	7	?	7	3
Direct materials inventory, Dec. 31, 2007	?	6	8	7

P6-2 DIRECT MATERIALS. Genesis Athletic Shoes had an ending inventory of direct materials of $9 million. During the year the company had acquired $15 million of additional direct materials and had used $12 million. Compute the beginning inventory.

P6-3 USING THE WORK-IN-PROCESS INVENTORY ACCOUNT. September production resulted in the following activity in a key account of Colebury Costing Company (in thousands):

WORK-IN-PROCESS INVENTORY

September 1 balance	$12
Direct material used	50
Direct labour charged to jobs	25
Factory overhead applied to jobs	55

Job Order 13N and 37Q, with total costs of $70,000 and $54,000, respectively, were completed in September.

1. Journalize the completed production for September.
2. Compute the balance in work-in-process inventory, September 30, after recording the completed production.
3. Journalize the credit sale of Job 13N for $101,000.

P6-4 JOB-COST RECORD. East University uses job-cost records for various research projects. A major reason for such records is to justify requests for reimbursement for costs on projects sponsored by the federal government.

Consider the following summarized data regarding Project No. 76 conducted by a group of physicists:

- Jan. 5   Direct materials, various metals, $925
- Jan. 7   Direct materials, various chemicals, $780
- Jan. 5–12   Direct labour, research associates, 120 hours
- Jan. 7–12   Direct labour, research assistants, 180 hours

Research associates receive $32 per hour; assistants, $19. The overhead rate is 70 percent of direct labour cost.

Sketch a job-cost record. Post all the data to the project-cost record. Compute the total cost of the project through January 12.

P6-5 ANALYZING JOB-COST DATA. Job-cost records for Naomi's Remodelling Ltd. contained the following data:

	DATES			TOTAL COST OF JOB
JOB NO.	STARTED	FINISHED	SOLD	AT MAY 31
1	April 19	May 14	May 15	$3,200
2	April 26	May 22	May 25	8,800
3	May 2	June 6	June 8	6,500
4	May 9	May 29	June 5	8,100
5	May 14	June 14	June 16	3,900

Compute Naomi's (1) work-in-process inventory at May 31, (2) finished-goods inventory at May 31, and (3) cost of goods sold for May.

P6-6 **ANALYZING JOB-COST DATA.** The Cortez Construction Company constructs houses on specu-
lation. That is, the houses are begun before any buyer is known. Even if the
buyer agrees to purchase a house under construction, no sales are recorded until
the house is completed and accepted for delivery. The job-cost records contained
the following (in thousands):

| JOB NO. | DATES | | | TOTAL COST OF JOB AT SEPT. 30 | TOTAL CONSTRUCTION COST ADDED IN OCT. |
	STARTED	FINISHED	SOLD		
43	4/26	9/7	9/8	$180	
51	5/17	9/14	9/17	170	
52	5/20	9/30	10/4	150	
53	5/28	10/14	10/18	200	$50
61	6/3	10/20	11/24	115	20
62	6/9	10/21	10/27	180	25
71	7/7	11/6	11/22	118	36
81	8/7	11/24	12/24	106	48

1. Compute Cortez's cost of (a) construction-in-process inventory at
September 30 and October 31, (b) finished-houses inventory at
September 30 and October 31, and (c) cost of houses sold for September
and October.
2. Prepare summary journal entries for the transfer of completed houses
from construction-in-process to finished houses for September and
October.
3. Record the cash sale and cost of house sold of Job 53 for $345,000.

P6-7 **BASIC JOURNAL ENTRIES.** The following data (in thousands) summarize the factory operations
of the Lewis Manufacturing Co. for the year 2006, its first year in business:

a.	Direct materials purchased for cash	$450
b.	Direct materials issued and used	420
c.	Labour used directly on production	125
d1.	Indirect labour	80
d2.	Amortization of plant and equipment	55
d3.	Miscellaneous factory overhead	
	(ordinarily would be detailed)	40
e.	Overhead applied: 180% of direct labour	?
f.	Cost of production completed	705
g.	Cost of goods sold	460

1. Prepare summary journal entries. Omit explanations. For purposes of
this problem, combine the items in *d* as "overhead incurred."
2. Show the T-accounts for all inventories, cost of goods sold, and factory
department overhead. Compute the ending balances of the inventories.
Do not adjust for underapplied or overapplied factory overhead.

P6-8 FINDING UNKNOWNS. DeMond Chemicals has the following balances at December 31, 2006. All amounts are in millions:

Factory overhead applied	$200
Cost of goods sold	500
Factory overhead incurred	210
Direct materials inventory	30
Finished-goods inventory	160
Work-in-process inventory	120

The cost of goods completed was $420 (in millions). The cost of direct materials requisitioned for production during 2006 was $210. The cost of direct materials purchased was $225. Factory overhead was applied to production at a rate of 160 percent of direct labour cost.

Compute the beginning inventory balances of direct materials, work-in-process, and finished goods. Make these computations before considering any possible adjustments for overapplied or underapplied overhead.

P6-9 FINDING UNKNOWNS. The Chickadee Company has the following balances (in millions) as of December 31, 2007:

Work-in-process inventory	$ 14
Finished-goods inventory	205
Direct materials inventory	65
Factory overhead incurred	180
Factory overhead applied at 150%	
of direct labour cost	150
Cost of goods sold	350

The cost of direct materials purchased during 2007 was $305. The cost of direct materials requisitioned for production during 2007 was $265. The cost of goods completed was $523, all in millions.

Before considering any year-end adjustments for overapplied or underapplied overhead, compute the beginning inventory balances of direct materials, work-in-process, and finished goods.

P6-10 JOURNAL ENTRIES FOR OVERHEAD. Consider the following summarized data regarding 2007:

	BUDGET	**ACTUAL**
Indirect labour	$ 290,000	$ 305,000
Supplies	35,000	30,000
Repairs	80,000	75,000
Utilities	130,000	123,000
Factory rent	125,000	125,000
Supervision	60,000	75,000
Amortization, equipment	220,000	220,000
Insurance, property taxes, etc.	40,000	42,000
a. Total factory overhead	$ 980,000	$ 995,000
b. Direct materials used	$1,650,000	$1,605,000
c. Direct labour	$1,225,000	$1,200,000

Omit explanations for journal entries.

1. Prepare a summary journal entry for the actual overhead incurred for 2007.
2. Prepare summary journal entries for direct materials used and direct labour.
3. Factory overhead was applied by using a budgeted rate based on budgeted direct labour costs. Compute the rate. Prepare a summary journal entry for the application of overhead to products.
4. Post the journal entries to the T-accounts for work-in-process and factory department overhead.
5. Suppose overapplied or underapplied factory overhead is written off as an adjustment to cost of goods sold. Prepare the journal entry. Post the entry to the overhead T-account.

P6-11 **RELATIONSHIPS AMONG OVERHEAD ITEMS.** Fill in the unknowns:

	CASE A	CASE B	CASE C
Budgeted factory overhead	$3,400,000	?	$1,750,000
Budgeted cost drivers:			
Direct labour cost	$2,000,000		
Direct labour hours		450,000	
Machine hours			250,000
Overhead application rate	?	$5	?

P6-12 **RELATIONSHIP AMONG OVERHEAD ITEMS.** Fill in the unknowns:

	CASE 1	CASE 2
a. Budgeted factory overhead	$750,000	$420,000
b. Cost driver, budgeted		
direct labour cost	500,000	$50,000
c. Budgeted factory overhead rate	?/150%	120%
d. Direct labour cost incurred	570,000	?325,000
e. Factory overhead incurred	825,000	415,000
f. Factory overhead applied	(c*d) ?855,000	390,000
g. Underapplied (overapplied)		
factory overhead	(30,000)	25,000

P6-13 **UNDERAPPLIED AND OVERAPPLIED OVERHEAD.** Wosepka Welding Company applied factory overhead at a rate of $8.50 per direct labour hour. Selected data for 2006 operations are (in thousands)

	CASE 1	CASE 2
Direct labour hours	30	36
Direct labour cost	$220	$245
Indirect labour cost	32	40
Sales commissions	20	15
Amortization, manufacturing equipment	22	32
Direct material cost	230	250
Factory fuel costs	35	47
Amortization, finished-goods warehouse	5	17
Cost of goods sold	420	510
All other factory costs	138	214

Compute for both cases:

1. Factory overhead applied.
2. Total factory overhead incurred.
3. Amount of underapplied or overapplied factory overhead.

P6-14 **DISPOSITION OF OVERHEAD.** Assume the following at the end of 2007 (in thousands):

Cost of goods sold	$300
Direct materials inventory	70
Work-in-process	50
Finished goods	150
Factory department overhead control	60 cr.

1. Assume that the underapplied or overapplied overhead is regarded as an adjustment to cost of goods sold. Prepare the journal entry.
2. Assume that the underapplied or overapplied overhead is prorated among the appropriate accounts in proportion to their ending unadjusted balances. Show computations and prepare the journal entry.
3. Which adjustment, the one in requirement 1 or 2, would result in the higher gross profit? Explain, indicating the amount of the difference.

P6-15 **DISPOSITION OF OVERHEAD.** A Paris manufacturer uses a job-order system. At the end of 2007 the following balances exist (in millions of Euros [EUR]):

Cost of goods sold	EUR22.86
Finished goods	18.29
Work-in-process	4.57
Factory overhead (actual)	10.67
Factory overhead (applied)	9.14

1. Prepare journal entries for two different ways to dispose of the underapplied overhead.
2. Gross profit, before considering the effects of requirement 1, was EUR6.5 million. What is the adjusted gross profit under the two methods demonstrated?

P6-16 **DISPOSITION OF YEAR-END OVERAPPLIED OVERHEAD.** Gloria Cosmetics uses a normal cost system and has the following balances at the end of its first year's operations:

Work-in-process inventory	$200,000
Finished-goods inventory	200,000
Cost of goods sold	400,000
Actual factory overhead	409,000
Factory overhead applied	457,000

Prepare journal entries for two different ways to dispose of the year-end overhead balances. By how much would gross profit differ?

P6-17 **RELATIONSHIPS OF MANUFACTURING COSTS.** Selected data concerning the past fiscal year's operations of the Mistry Manufacturing Company are as follows (in thousands):

	INVENTORIES	
	BEGINNING	ENDING
Raw materials	$55	$ 75
Work-in-process	75	35
Finished goods	90	110
Other data:		
Raw materials used		$455
Total manufacturing costs charged to production during the year (includes raw materials, direct labour, and factory overhead applied at a rate of 80% of direct labour cost)		851
Cost of goods available for sale		1,026
Selling and general expenses		50

1. Compute the cost of raw materials purchased during the year.
2. Compute the direct labour costs charged to production during the year.
3. Compute the cost of goods manufactured during the year.
4. Compute the cost of goods sold during the year.

P6-18 BASIC JOURNAL ENTRIES. Consider the following data for Words Printing Company (in thousands):

Inventories, December 31, 2007	
Direct materials	£18
Work-in-process	25
Finished goods	100

Summarized transactions for 2008:

a. Purchase of direct materials	£112
b. Direct materials used	98
c. Direct labour	105
d. Factory overhead incurred	90
e. Factory overhead applied, 80% of direct labour	?
f. Cost of goods completed and transferred to finished goods	280
g. Cost of goods sold	350
h. Sales on account	600

1. Prepare summary journal entries for 2008 transactions. Omit explanations.
2. Show the T-accounts for all inventories, cost of goods sold, and factory department overhead control. Compute the ending balances of the inventories. Do not adjust for underapplied or overapplied factory overhead.

P6-19 DISPOSITION OF OVERHEAD. MacLachlan Mfg. Co. had overapplied overhead of $20,000 in 2007. Before adjusting for overapplied or underapplied overhead, the ending inventories for direct materials, WIP, and finished goods were $75,000, $100,000, and $150,000, respectively. Unadjusted cost of goods sold was $250,000.

1. Assume that the $20,000 was written off solely as an adjustment to cost of goods sold. Prepare the journal entry.
2. Management has decided to prorate the $20,000 to the appropriate accounts (using the unadjusted ending balances) instead of writing it off solely as an adjustment of cost of goods sold. Prepare the journal entry. Would gross profit be higher or lower than in requirement 1? By how much?

P6-20 **APPLICATION OF OVERHEAD USING BUDGETED RATES.** The Bellevue Clinic computes the cost of treating each patient. It allocates costs to departments and then applies departmental overhead costs to individual patients using a different budgeted overhead rate in each department. Consider the following predicted 2006 data for two of Bellevue's departments:

	PHARMACY	MEDICAL RECORDS
Department overhead cost	$225,000	$300,000
Number of prescriptions filled	90,000	
Number of patient visits		60,000

The cost driver for overhead in pharmacy is *number of prescriptions filled*; in medical records it is *number of patient visits*.

In June 2006, David Li paid two visits to the clinic and had four prescriptions filled at the pharmacy.

1. Compute departmental overhead rates for the two departments.
2. Compute the overhead costs applied to the patient David Li in June 2006.
3. At the end of 2006, actual overhead costs were:

Pharmacy	$217,000
Medical records	$325,000

The pharmacy filled 85,000 prescriptions, and the clinic had 63,000 patient visits during 2006. Compute the overapplied or underapplied overhead in each department.

P6-21 **RELATIONSHIP OF SUBSIDIARY AND GENERAL LEDGERS, JOURNAL ENTRIES.** The following summarized data are available on three job-cost records of Weeks Company, a manufacturer of packaging equipment:

	412		413		414
	APRIL	MAY	APRIL	MAY	MAY
Direct materials	$9,000	$2,500	$12,000	–	$13,000
Direct labour	4,000	1,500	5,000	2,500	2,000
Factory overhead applied	8,000	?	10,000	?	?

The company's fiscal year ends on May 31. Factory overhead is applied as a percentage of direct-labour costs. The balances in selected accounts on April 30 were direct materials inventory, $19,000; and finished-goods inventory, $18,000.

Job 412 was completed during May and transferred to finished goods. Job 413 was still in process at the end of May as was Job 414, which had begun on May 24. These were the only jobs worked on during April and May.

Job 412 was sold along with other finished goods by May 30. The total cost of goods sold during May was $33,000. The balance in cost of goods sold on April 30 was $450,000.

1. Prepare a schedule showing the balance of the work-in-process inventory, April 30. This schedule should show the total costs of each job record. Taken together, the job-cost records are the subsidiary ledger supporting the general-ledger balance of work-in-process.
2. What is the overhead application rate?

3. Prepare summary general-journal entries for all costs added to work-in-process during May. Also prepare entries for all costs transferred from work-in-process to finished goods and from finished goods to cost of goods sold. Post to the appropriate T-accounts.
4. Prepare a schedule showing the balance of the work-in-process inventory, May 31.

P6-22 **STRAIGHTFORWARD JOB COSTING.** The Decoste Furniture Company has two departments. Data for 2007 include the following:

Direct materials (30 types)	$65,000
Work-in-process (in assembly)	50,000
Finished goods	40,000

Manufacturing overhead budget for 2008:

	MACHINING	ASSEMBLY
Indirect labour	$250,000	$ 410,000
Supplies	45,000	40,000
Utilities	110,000	75,000
Repairs	140,000	110,000
Supervision	130,000	215,000
Factory rent	95,000	75,000
Amortization on equipment	160,000	105,000
Insurance, property taxes, etc.	60,000	70,000
	$990,000	$1,100,000

Budgeted machine hours were 90,000; budgeted direct labour cost in assembly was $2,200,000. Manufacturing overhead was applied using budgeted rates on the basis of machine hours in machining and on the basis of direct labour cost in assembly.

Following is a summary of actual events for the year:

	MACHINING	ASSEMBLY	TOTAL
a. Direct materials purchased			$ 1,900,000
b. Direct materials requisitioned	$ 1,100,000	$ 750,000	1,850,000
c. Direct labour costs incurred	900,000	2,800,000	3,700,000
d1. Factory overhead incurred	1,100,000	1,100,000	2,200,000
d2. Factory overhead applied	880,000	?	?
e. Cost of goods completed	–	–	7,820,000
f1. Sales	–	–	13,000,000
f2. Cost of goods sold	–	–	7,800,000

The ending work-in-process (all in assembly) was $60,000.

1. Compute the budgeted overhead rates.
2. Compute the amount of the machine hours actually worked.
3. Compute the amount of factory overhead applied in the assembly department.
4. Prepare general journal entries for transactions *a* through *f*. Work solely with the total amounts, not the details for machining and assembly.

Explanations are not required. Show data in thousands of dollars. Present T-accounts, including ending inventory balances, for direct materials, work-in-process, and finished goods.

5. Prepare a partial income statement similar to the one illustrated in Exhibit 6-5. Overapplied or underapplied overhead is written off as an adjustment of current cost of goods sold.

P6-23   **NOT-FOR-PROFIT JOB COSTING.**   Job-order costing is usually identified with manufacturing companies. However, service industries and not-for-profit organizations also use the method. Suppose a social service agency has a cost accounting system that tracks cost by department (for example, family counselling, general welfare, and foster children) and by case. In this way, the manager of the agency is better able to determine how its limited resources (mostly professional social workers) should be allocated. Furthermore, the manager's interactions with superiors and various politicians are more fruitful when she can cite the costs of various types of cases.

The condensed line-item budget for the general welfare department of the agency for 2007 showed

Professional salaries:		
Level 12	5 @ $35,000 = $175,000	
Level 10	21 @ $26,000 = 546,000	
Level 8	34 @ $18,000 = 612,000	$1,333,000
Other costs		533,200
Total costs		$1,866,200

For costing various cases, the manager favoured using a single overhead application rate based on the ratio of total overhead to direct labour. The latter was defined as those professional salaries assigned to specific cases.

The professional workers filled out a weekly "case time" report, which approximated the hours spent for each case.

The instructions on the report were: "Indicate how much time (in hours) you spent on each case. Unassigned time should be listed separately." About 20 percent of available time was unassigned to specific cases. It was used for professional development (for example, continuing-education programs). "Unassigned time" became a part of "overhead," as distinguished from the direct labour.

1. Compute the "overhead rate" as a percentage of direct labour (that is, the assignable professional salaries).
2. Suppose that last week a welfare case, Client No. 273, required two hours of Level-12 time, four hours of Level-10 time, and nine hours of Level-8 time. How much job cost should be allocated to Client No. 273 for the week? Assume that all professional employees work an 1,800-hour year.

P6-24   **JOB COSTING IN A CONSULTING FIRM.**   Link Engineering Consultants is a firm of professional civil engineers. It mostly has surveying jobs for the heavy-construction industry throughout Western Canada. The firm obtains its jobs by giving fixed-price quotations, so profitability depends on the ability to predict the time required for the various subtasks on the job. (This situation is similar to that in the auditing profession, where time is budgeted for such audit steps as reconciling cash and confirming accounts receivable.)

A client may be served by various professional staff, who hold positions in the hierarchy from partners to managers and senior engineers to assistants. In addition, there are secretaries and other employees.

Link Engineering has the following budget for 2007:

Compensation of professional staff	$3,600,000
Other costs	1,449,000
Total budgeted costs	$5,049,000

Each professional staff member must submit a weekly time report, which is used for charging hours to a client job-order record. The time report has seven columns, one for each day of the week. Its rows are as follows:

- Chargeable hours:
  Client 156
  Client 183
  Etc.

- Nonchargeable hours:
  Attending seminar on new equipment
  Unassigned time
  Etc.

In turn, these time reports are used for charging hours and costs to the client job-order records. The managing partner regards these job records as absolutely essential for measuring the profitability of various jobs and for providing an "experience base for improving predictions on future jobs."

1. This firm applies overhead to jobs at a budgeted percentage of the professional compensation charged directly to the job ("direct labour"). For all categories of professional personnel, chargeable hours average 85 percent of available hours. Nonchargeable hours are regarded as additional overhead. What is the overhead rate as a percentage of "direct labour," the chargeable professional compensation cost?
2. A senior engineer works 48 weeks per year, 40 hours per week. His compensation is $60,000. He has worked on two jobs during the past week, devoting 10 hours to Job 156 and 30 hours to Job 183. How much cost should be charged to Job 156 because of his work there?

P6-25 **CHOOSING COST DRIVERS IN AN ACCOUNTING FIRM.** The managing partner of Singh Accounting is considering the desirability of tracing more costs to jobs than just direct labour. In this way, the firm will be better able to justify billings to clients.

Last year's costs were

Direct professional labour	$ 5,000,000
Overhead	10,000,000
Total costs	$15,000,000

The following costs were included in overhead:

Computer time	$ 750,000
Secretarial costs	700,000
Photocopying	250,000
Employee benefit costs for direct labour	800,000
Phone call time with clients (estimated but not tabulated)	500,000
Total	$3,000,000

The firm's data-processing techniques now make it feasible to document and trace these costs to individual jobs.

As an experiment in December, Amrinder Singh arranged to trace these costs to six audit engagements. Two job records showed the following:

	ENGAGEMENT	
	EAGLEDALE COMPANY	FIRST VALLEY BANK
Direct professional labour	$15,000	$15,000
Employee benefit costs for direct labour	3,000	3,000
Phone call time with clients	1,500	500
Computer time	3,000	700
Secretarial costs	2,000	1,500
Photocopying	500	300
Total direct costs	$25,000	$21,000

1. Compute the overhead application rate based on last year's costs.
2. Suppose last year's costs were reclassified so that $3 million would be regarded as direct costs instead of overhead. Compute the overhead application rate as a percentage of direct labour and as a percentage of total direct costs.
3. Using the three rates computed in requirements 1 and 2, compute the total costs of engagements for Eagledale Company and First Valley Bank.
4. Suppose that client billing was based on a 30 percent markup of total job costs. Compute the billings that would be forthcoming in requirement 3.
5. Which method of job costing and overhead application do you favour? Explain.

P6-26 **RECONSTRUCTION OF TRANSACTIONS.** You are asked to bring the following incomplete accounts of a printing plant acquired in a merger up to date through January 31, 2006. Also consider the data that appear following the T-accounts.

Direct Materials Inventory		Accrued Factory Payroll	
12/31/05 Balance 20,000			1/31/06 Balance 5,000

Work-in-Process		Factory Department Overhead Control	
		Total January charges 55,000	

Finished Goods		Cost of Goods Sold	
12/31/05 Balance 25,000			

Additional information:

a. The overhead is applied using a budgeted rate that is set every December by forecasting the following year's overhead and relating it to forecast direct labour costs. The budget for 2006 called for $640,000 of direct labour and $800,000 of factory overhead.

b. The only job unfinished on January 31, 2006, was No. 419, on which total labour charges were $3,000 (200 direct labour hours). Total direct material charges were $21,000.

c. Total materials placed into production during January totalled $140,000.

d. Cost of goods completed during January was $260,000.

e. January 31 balances of direct materials totalled $27,000.

f. Finished-goods inventory as of January 31 was $35,000.

g. All factory workers earn the same rate of pay. Direct labour hours for January totalled 3,000. Indirect labour and supervision totalled $12,000.

h. The gross factory payroll paid on January paydays totalled $55,000. Ignore withholdings.

i. All "actual" factory overhead incurred during January has been posted.

Compute:

1. Direct materials purchased during January.

2. Cost of goods sold during January.

3. Direct labour costs incurred during January.

4. Overhead applied during January.

5. Balance, accrued factory payroll, December 31, 2005.

6. Balance, work-in-process, December 31, 2005.

7. Balance, work-in-process, January 31, 2006.

8. Overapplied or underapplied overhead of January.

P6-27 ACCOUNTING FOR OVERHEAD, BUDGETED RATES. Advanced Aeronautics Co. uses a budgeted overhead rate in applying overhead to individual job orders on a *machine-hour* basis for Department A and on a *direct-labour-hour* basis for Department B. At the beginning of 2006, the company's management made the following budget predictions:

	DEPT. A	DEPT. B
Direct labour cost	$1,500,000	$1,200,000
Factory overhead	2,170,000	1,000,000
Direct labour hours	90,000	125,000
Machine hours	350,000	20,000

Cost records of recent months show the following accumulations for Job Order No. M89:

	DEPT. A	DEPT. B
Material placed in production	12,000	32,000
Direct labour cost	$10,800	$10,000
Direct labour hours	900	1,250
Machine hours	3,500	150

1. What is the budgeted overhead rate that should be applied in Department A? In Department B?

2. What is the *total overhead cost* of Job Order No. M89?

3. If Job Order No. M89 consists of 200 units of product, what is the unit cost of this job?

4. At the end of 2006, actual results for the year's operations were as follows:

	DEPT. A	DEPT. B
Actual overhead costs incurred	$1,600,000	$1,200,000
Actual direct labour hours	80,000	120,000
Actual machine hours	300,000	25,000

Find the underapplied or overapplied overhead for each department and for the factory as a whole.

P6-28 JOB COSTING AT DELL COMPUTER.   Dell Computer Company's manufacturing process consists of assembly, functional testing, and quality control of the company's computer systems. The company's build-to-order manufacturing process is designed to allow the company to quickly produce customized computer systems. For example, the company contracts with various suppliers to manufacture unconfigured base Latitude notebook computers and then custom configures these systems for shipment to customers. Quality control is maintained through the testing of components, parts, and subassemblies at various stages in the manufacturing process.

Describe how Dell might set up a job-costing system to determine the costs of its computers. What is a "job" to Dell? How might the costs of components, assembly, testing, and quality control be allocated to each "job"?

MANAGERIAL DECISION CASES

C6-1 MULTIPLE OVERHEAD RATES AND ACTIVITY-BASED COSTING.   A division of Hewlett-Packard assembles and tests printed circuit (PC) boards. The division has many different products. Some are high volume, others are low volume. For years, manufacturing overhead was applied to products using a single overhead rate based on direct labour dollars. However, direct labour had shrunk to 6 percent of total manufacturing costs.

Managers decided to refine the division's product-costing system. Without using a direct labour category, they included all manufacturing labour as a part of factory overhead. They also identified several activities and the appropriate cost driver for each. The cost driver for the first activity, the start station, was the number of raw PC boards. The application rate was computed as follows:

$$\text{application rate for start station activity} = \frac{\text{budgeted total factory overhead at the activity}}{\text{budgeted raw PC boards for the year}}$$

$$= \frac{\$150,000}{125,000} = \$1.20$$

Each time a raw PC board passes through the start station activity, $1.20 is added to the cost of a product. The product cost is the sum of costs directly traced to the product plus the indirect costs (factory overhead) accumulated at each of the manufacturing activities undergone.

Using assumed numbers, consider the following data regarding PC Board 37:

Direct materials	$55.00
Factory overhead applied	?
Total manufacturing product cost	?

The activities involved in the production of PC Board 37 and the related cost drivers chosen were

ACTIVITY	COST DRIVER	FACTORY-OVERHEAD COSTS APPLIED FOR EACH ACTIVITY
1. Start station	No. of raw PC boards	1 × $1.20 = $1.20
2. Axial insertion	No. of axial insertions	39 × 0.07 = ?
3. Dip insertion	No. of dip insertions	? × 0.20 = 5.60
4. Manual insertion	No. of manual insertions	15 × ? = 6.00
5. Wave solder	No. of boards soldered	1 × 3.20 = 3.20
6. Backload	No. of backload insertions	8 × 0.60 = 4.80
7. Test	Standard time board is in test activity	0.15 × 80.00 = ?
8. Defect analysis	Standard time for defect analysis and repair	0.05 × ? = $4.50
Total		$?

Required:

1. Fill in the blanks.
2. How is direct labour identified with products under this product-costing system?
3. As a manager, what would be your assessment of the multiple-overhead rate, activity-costing system compared to the older system?

C6-2 **ONE OR TWO COST DRIVERS.** The Matterhorn Instruments Co. in Geneva, Switzerland, has the following 2007 budget for its two departments, in Swiss francs (SF):

	MACHINING	FINISHING	TOTAL
Direct labour	SF300,000	SF800,000	SF1,100,000
Factory overhead	SF960,000	SF800,000	SF1,760,000
Machine hours	60,000	20,000	80,000

In the past, the company has used a single plant-wide overhead application rate based on direct labour cost. However, as its product line has expanded and as competition has intensified, Hans Volkert, the company president, has questioned the accuracy of the profits or losses shown on various products. Matterhorn makes custom tools on special orders from customers. To be competitive and still make a reasonable profit, it is essential that the firm measure the cost of each customer order. Volkert has focused on overhead allocation as a potential problem. He knows that changes in costs are more heavily affected by machine hours in the first department and by direct labour costs in the second department. As company controller, you have gathered the following data regarding two typical customer orders:

	ORDER NUMBER	
	K102	K156
Machining		
Direct materials	SF4,000	SF4,000
Direct labour	SF3,000	SF1,500
Machine hours	1,200	100
Finishing		
Direct labour	SF1,500	SF3,000
Machine hours	120	120

Required:

1. Compute six factory overhead application rates, three based on direct-labour cost and three based on machine hours for machining, finishing, and for the plant as a whole.
2. Use the application rates to compute the total costs of orders K102 and K156 as follows: (a) plant-wide rate based on direct-labour cost and (b) machining based on machine hours and finishing based on direct-labour cost.
3. Evaluate your answers in requirement 2. Which set of job costs do you prefer? Why?

C6-3 **JOB-COSTING SYSTEM ANALYSIS.** (SMAC) Susan Andrews, the president and major share-holder of Walnut Furniture Limited, was reviewing the 2006 and 2007 comparative income statements (Exhibit 6A-1) and was wondering why, despite all her efforts, profits had not improved. Walnut manufactured and installed fitted furniture and fixtures in new buildings on a contract basis.

Walnut's operations were organized into three departments: fabricating, finishing, and installing. Each department was treated as a cost centre. The total hourly operating costs, including labour of each department, were determined each month and charged to each job on the basis of the hours it was in process in each department (Exhibit 6A-2). The departmental operating costs per hour were compared to those of the previous year for cost control. Andrews attempted to keep her workers employed on a steady full-time basis, which sometimes required workers to be transferred from one department to another. Therefore, she regarded labour costs as being fixed.

EXHIBIT 6A-1

Walnut Furniture Limited Income Statement for the Years Ended December 31

	2007	2006
Sales	$940,000	$925,000
Cost of sales:		
Materials	127,800	123,000
Labour	493,000	486,000
Amortization	36,000	36,000
Heat, light, and power	25,800	21,400
Maintenance	24,200	20,200
Rejects – departmental	17,150	37,000
– corporate	72,050	50,200
Total cost of sales	796,000	773,800
Gross profit	144,000	151,200
Selling and administration expenses	49,000	46,500
Net income before taxes	95,000	104,700
Income taxes	23,800	26,200
Net income	$ 71,200	$ 78,500

Andrews has been very satisfied with the cost accounting system since its introduction, and felt it gave her good cost control and a basis for submitting bids for contracts. However, she had two recurring problems: winning contracts to fill capacity, and controlling rejects. Bids were based on estimates of processing time required in each department costed at the most recent month's departmental processing costs per hour. Andrews and the estimator discussed how much should be added for profit for each bid; normally, the target profit rate of 10 percent of total estimated costs was used as a starting point in deciding the final bid amount to submit.

	FABRICATING	FINISHING	INSTALLING	TOTAL
Labour	$24,000	$4,500	$11,250	$39,750
Amortization	1,900	600	500	3,000
Heat, light, and power[1]	1,200	750	150	2,100
Maintenance[1]	1,400	550	100	2,050
Material	8,575	900	300	9,775
Processing costs	37,075	7,300	12,300	56,675
Rejects – Departmental[2]	556	110	734	1,400
Total processing costs	$37,631	$7,410	$13,034	$58,075
Operating hours[3]	160	100	150	
Processing cost per hour: 2007	$ 235	$ 74	$ 87	
2006	$ 225	$ 72	$ 85	
Number of persons at $15/hour	10	3	5	

[1] About 90% of these costs are fixed.
[2] A majority of the reject costs charged to the fabricating and finishing departments are directly attributable to the regularly scheduled 5% overproduction for standard contracts. A majority of the reject costs charged to the installing department are directly attributable to customized contracts.
[3] Operating hours include reprocessing time as well as normal processing time.

Walnut competed for contracts in two distinct market segments, both involving the manufacture of furniture and fixtures in the plant, and then installation on site. The first segment involved large contracts for standard units to be installed in multiunit apartment buildings and franchised, fast-food outlets. Andrews devoted a great deal of time to pursuing this type of contract since the large quantities involved would fill capacity. She had succeeded in increasing the number of bids won in this segment, but not to the extent she had hoped. The second segment involved smaller contracts for luxury apartments requiring high-quality work and material, often customized for each apartment. Most of Walnut's contracts had been won in the second segment. Andrews had asked her estimator to prepare a schedule of data on two recent bids (Exhibit 6A-3) and a summary of bids submitted and won in 2006 and 2007 (Exhibit 6A-4).

Her second cost-control problem was difficult to analyze. Rejects might be identified either during production or at final inspection by the contractor-customer. In either event, an attempt was made to charge the responsible department with the cost of the reprocessing work. If the responsibility could not be identified, the reprocessing cost was charged to the corporate reject-reprocessing account. In processing large-volume contracts, rejects were normally not a major problem, and production scheduling provided for 5 percent overproduction to replace rejects. In processing the high-priced, low-volume customized contracts, it was not economically feasible to overproduce, so supervisors were urged to emphasize quality work; nevertheless, the reject rate at the final inspection by customers was over 15 percent. Rejects found after installation usually required replacement. Since Andrews had made a point of severely reprimanding each supervisor for any rejects on his or her monthly operating statements, departmental reject charges had significantly declined for each department except the installing department. Much bitterness resulted from attempting to identify responsibility for rejects. Meanwhile, the total reject expense increased slightly.

Andrews was not overly concerned about the reject problem since the cost was incorporated into Walnut's bids. The corporate reject cost percentage of the total processing cost was determined and added to the bids as part of the corporate overhead charge. However, she wondered whether the answer to the reject problem might not be to subcontract installation. She would have liked to spend more time on the reject problem, but felt that this time was better spent on the road soliciting orders.

	BID #SX5-19 100 STD. APTMTS. BATHROOM FIXTS.		BID #CX5-4 40 CUSTOMIZED APTMTS. BUILT-IN CUPBOARDS		
	EST. HOURS	BID AMOUNTS	EST. HOURS	ACTUAL HOURS	BID AMOUNTS
Processing costs:					
Fabricating ($235/hrs.)	120	$28,200	78	80	$18,330
Finishing ($74/hr.)	60	4,440	62	70	4,588
Installing ($87/hr.)	100	8,700	100	110	8,700
		41,340			31,618
Corporate overhead (17%)[1]		7,028			5,375
Total processing costs		48,368			36,993
Profit (10%)		4,837			3,699
Estimated bid amount		$53,205			$40,692
Actual bid amount		$53,000			$41,000
Won/lost		Lost			Won
Successful bid amount		$49,000			$41,000
Next lowest bid		n/a			$45,000

[1] A standard adjustment of 7% to cover head-office expenses and an adjustment of 10% to cover reject costs (not including identified departmental reject costs) are added to total costs.

Other information: the actual hours on standard contracts were usually close to the estimated hours.

	STANDARD				CUSTOMIZED			
	2007		2006		2007		2006	
$	#	(000)	#	(000)	#	(000)	#	(000)
Submitted	90	$3,950	80	$4,410	29	$1,135	35	$1,200
Won	7	350	4	210	15	590	21	715
% Won	8%		5%		52%		60%	

Upon reviewing the 2007 financial statements with Andrews, Walnut's banker was also concerned that profits had not improved and, therefore, requested that a budget be prepared for 2008. She argued that budgets simply were not feasible in this business because production and sales were a function of bids won and could not be predicted accurately.

On her banker's advice, Andrews engaged a management-accounting consultant to study the operations and problems of Walnut, and to submit a report on the findings. She asked the consultant to include an analysis of the following in the report:

Required:

1. Walnut's management-accounting system.
2. The feasibility of budgeting for Walnut.
3. Control of rejects.
4. The bidding process.

As the management-accounting consultant engaged by Susan Andrews, prepare the requested report on Walnut's operations and problems.

E6-1 COMPUTING BUDGETED FACTORY OVERHEAD

Goal: create an Excel spreadsheet to compute budgeted factory overhead rates and apply factory overhead to production. Use the results to answer questions about your findings.

Scenario: Donald Aeronautics Company has asked you to determine their budgeted factory overhead rates. They would also like you to apply the appropriate factory overhead amounts to actual production and determine any variances.

Donald Aeronautics Company uses a budgeted overhead rate in applying overhead to products on a machine-hour basis for Department A and on a direct-labour-hour basis for Department B. At the beginning of 2007, the company's management made the following budget predictions:

	DEPARTMENT A	DEPARTMENT B
Direct-labour cost	$1,500,000	$1,200,000
Factory overhead	$2,170,000	$1,000,000
Direct-labour hours	90,000	125,000
Machine hours	350,000	20,000

When you have completed your spreadsheet, answer the following questions:

1. What was the budgeted factory overhead rate for Department A? Department B?

2. What overhead amount was distributed to Department A? Was the overhead over- or underapplied? By what amount?

3. What overhead amount was distributed to Department B? Was the overhead over- or underapplied? By what amount?

Step by Step:

1. Open a new Excel spreadsheet.

2. In column A, create a bold-faced heading that contains the following:
   Row 1: Chapter 6 Decision Guideline
   Row 2: Donald Aeronautics Company
   Row 3: Overhead Allocations Using Budgeted Rates
   Row 4: Today's Date

3. Merge and centre the four heading rows across columns A through G.

4. In row 7, create the following column headings:
   Column B: 2007 Budget
   Column D: 2007 Actual
   Column F: Variances

5. Merge and centre the 2007 Budget heading across columns B through C.

6. Merge and centre the 2007 Actual heading across columns D through E.

7. Merge and centre the Variances heading across columns F through G.

8. In row 8, create the following centre-justified column headings:
   Columns B, D, and F: Dept. A
   Columns C, E, and G: Dept. B

9. In column A, create the following row headings:
   Row 9: Factory Overhead
   Row 10: Direct Labour Hours
   Row 11: Machine Hours
   Skip a row
   Row 13: Overhead Rate
   Row 14: Distributed Overhead
   Row 15: Over/(Under)Applied

   Note: Recommended column widths: column A = 18, columns B through G = 12.

10. Use data from above to enter the amounts for the Departments A and B 2007 budget predictions and 2007 actual results.

11. Use the appropriate formulas to calculate the following amounts:
2007 budgeted overhead rates for Depts. A and B	Row 13, columns B and C
2007 distributed overhead for Depts. A and B	Row 14, columns D and E
2007 over/underapplied overhead	Row 15, columns D and E
Flexible budget variances for Depts. A and B	Row 9, columns F and G
Activity budget variance for Dept. B	Row 10, column G
Activity budget variance for Dept. A	Row 11, column F
Total variances for Depts. A and B	Row 15, columns F and G

12. Format amounts in rows 10 and 11 as
    Number tab: Category: Accounting
                    Decimal: 0
                    Symbol: None

13. Format amounts in rows 9, 14, and 15 as
    Number tab: Category: Accounting
                    Decimal: 0
                    Symbol: $

14. Format amounts in row 13 as
    Number tab: Category: Accounting
                    Decimal: 2
                    Symbol: $

15. Modify the format of the total variances in row 15, columns F and G to display a top border using the default Line Style.
    Border tab: Icon: Top Border

16. Save your work to disk, and print a copy for your files.

    Note: Print your spreadsheet using landscape in order to ensure that all columns appear on one page.

Cost records of recent months show the following accumulations for product M89:

	DEPARTMENT A	DEPARTMENT B
Material placed in production	$12,000	$32,000
Direct-labour cost	$10,800	$10,000
Direct-labour hours	900	1,250
Machine hours	3,500	150

1. What is the budgeted overhead rate that should be applied in Department A? In Department B?

2. At the end of 2007, actual results for the year's operations were as follows:

	DEPARTMENT A	DEPARTMENT B
Actual overhead costs incurred	$1,600,000	$1,200,000
Actual direct-labour hours	80,000	120,000
Actual machine hours	300,000	25,000

Find the underapplied or overapplied overhead for each department and for the factory as a whole.

COLLABORATIVE LEARNING EXERCISE

CL6-1 ACCOUNTING FOR OVERHEAD. Form groups of four to six persons. Each group should identify a cost accountant at a local company to interview. The interviewee could be the top financial officer of a small company, but a division controller or cost analyst might be more appropriate for a large company. The essential factor is that the person chosen understands how overhead costs are allocated to products or services in the company.

Set up an interview with the cost accountant, and explore the following issues. Be prepared with followup questions in case your question receives a superficial answer. Your goal should be to get as much operational detail as possible about the procedures used for allocating overhead costs at the company. If the company is large, you may want to focus on one department, one product line, or some other subdivision of the company.

The issues to explore are

1. What types of costs are included in overhead? How large is overhead compared with direct materials and labour costs?

2. What types of overhead cost pools exist? Are there different pools by department? By activity? By cost driver? By fixed or variable cost? Be prepared to explain what you mean by these terms, because terminology varies widely.

3. How is overhead applied to final products or services? What cost drivers are used?

After the interview, draw a diagram of the cost allocation system in as much detail as possible. Be prepared to share this with the entire class, using it to explain the overhead cost allocation system at the company your group studied.

7

Process-Costing Systems

After studying this chapter, you will be able to

1. Explain the basic ideas underlying process costing and how those ideas differ from job costing.

2. Compute output in terms of equivalent units.

3. Compute costs and prepare a production cost report for the process-costing system.

4. Demonstrate the computations of unit costs under the weighted-average method.

5. Demonstrate the computation of unit costs under the first-in, first-out method.

6. Use backflush costing with a just-in-time production system.

7. Generate costs using an operation-costing system (Chapter Appendix).

Cost accounting systems fulfil two major purposes: they allocate costs (1) to departments for *planning and control* and (2) to product units for *product costing*. This chapter concentrates on a basic type of product costing called process costing and discusses an adaptation of process costing called *backflush costing*. The Appendix to this chapter (beginning on page 320) describes hybrid-costing systems by illustrating operation costing.

The first part of this chapter presents the basic ideas of process costing. The second part introduces the complications arising from consideration of beginning inventories, which is important in applying process costing. The last part discusses backflush costing, a simplified version of process costing used by many companies that have adopted a just-in-time inventory system.

INTRODUCTION TO PROCESS COSTING

As noted in Chapter 6, all product-costing methods use averaging to determine costs per unit of production. The average unit cost may be calculated on a relatively narrow basis of an order, as in the production of a particular printing order in job-order costing. In contrast, the average may be based on a broad basis of hundreds or thousands of units produced simultaneously, as in process costing, for example, in the production of beverages. *Process-costing systems* apply costs to like products that are usually mass-produced in continuous fashion through a series of production processes. These processes are often organized as separate departments, although a single department sometimes contains more than one process.

Process Costing Compared to Job Costing

OBJECTIVE 1

Explain the basic ideas underlying process costing and how those ideas differ from job costing.

Job-order costing and process costing are used for different types of products. Firms in industries such as printing, construction, and furniture manufacturing, where each unit or batch (job) of product is unique and easily identifiable, use job-order costing. Process costing is used where there is mass production through a sequence of several processes, such as mixing and cooking. Examples include the mass production of chemicals, flour, glass, wine, oil, fuel, and toothpaste.

Exhibit 7-1 shows the major differences between job-order costing and process costing. Process costing requires several work-in-process accounts, one for each process or department. As goods move from process to process, their costs are transferred accordingly. Process manufacturing systems vary in design. The design shown in panel B of Exhibit 7-1 is *sequential*—units pass from Process A to Process B and so on until the product is finished. Many other designs are found in practice—each tailored to meet specific product requirements. For example, processes can be operated in parallel, in which case Process A and Process B might occur simultaneously to produce different parts of the finished product. Then they can be transferred to Process C or the final assembly. Whatever the specific layout, the basic principles of process costing are the same.

The process-costing approach does not distinguish among individual units of product. Instead, accumulated costs for a period are divided by quantities produced during that period to get broad, average unit costs. Process costing is also applied to nonmanufacturing activities. Examples of nonmanufacturing activities include provincial automobile driver's licence tests and post office mail sorting departments. The overall annual cost of giving provincial automobile driver's licence tests

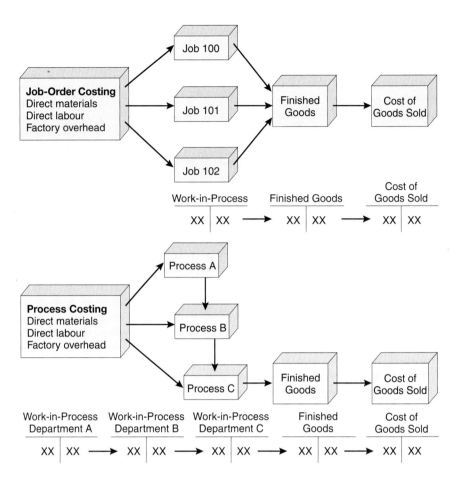

EXHIBIT 7-1

Comparison of Job-Order and Process Costing

is divided by the number of tests given and the post office sorting department cost is divided by the number of items sorted to calculate the overall unit cost.

Process-costing systems are usually simpler and less expensive to operate than job-order costing. Individual jobs do not exist. There are no job-cost records. The unit cost for inventory purposes is calculated by accumulating the costs of each processing department and dividing the total cost by an appropriate measure of output.

To get a feel for process costing, consider Magneta Midget Frozen Vegetables. It quick-cooks tiny carrots, beans, and so on before freezing them. As the following T-accounts show, its cooking costs (in millions of dollars)—divided by the kilograms of vegetables processed—are transferred to the freezing department:

Work-in-Process—Cooking		
Direct materials $14	Transfer cost of	
Direct labour 4	goods completed	
Factory overhead 8	to next	
$26	department	24 →
Ending inventory $ 2		

Work-in-Process—Freezing		
Cost	Transfer cost	
transferred	of goods	
in from	completed to	
cooking $24	finished	
Direct labour 1	goods	$25
Factory overhead 2		
$27		
Ending inventory $ 2		

The journal entries for process-costing systems are similar to those for the job-order costing system. That is, direct materials, direct labour, and factory overhead are accounted for as before. However, now there is more than one single work-in-process account for units being processed. There are two work-in-process accounts, one for cooking and one for freezing: that is, one work-in-process account for each processing department. The foregoing data would be journalized as follows:

1. Work-in-process—Cooking	$14	
Direct-materials inventory		$14
To record direct materials used		
2. Work-in-process—Cooking	$4	
Accrued payroll		$4
To record direct labour		
3. Work-in-process—Cooking	$8	
Factory overhead		$8
To record factory overhead applied to product		
4. Work-in-process—Freezing	$24	
Work-in-process—Cooking		$24
To transfer goods from the cooking process		
5. Work-in-process—Freezing	$3	
Accrued payroll		$1
Factory overhead		$2
To record direct labour and factory overhead applied to product		
6. Finished goods	$25	
Work-in-process—Freezing		$25
To transfer goods from the freezing process		

The central product-costing problem is how each department should compute the cost of goods transferred out and the cost of goods still in the production process remaining in the department. If the units in the work-in-process inventory are each partially completed, the product-costing system must distinguish between the costs of fully completed units transferred out and the costs of partially completed units not yet transferred. Process costing must account for partially completed units still in the production process.

APPLYING PROCESS COSTING

Consider another illustration. Suppose Oreo Wooden Toys Inc. buys wood as a direct material for its Forming Department. The department processes only one type of toy: marionettes. The marionettes are transferred to the Finishing Department, where hand shaping, strings, paint, and clothing are added.

The Forming Department manufactured 25,000 identical units during April, and its costs that month were as follows:

Direct materials		$ 70,000
Conversion costs		
Direct labour	$10,625	
Factory overhead	31,875	42,500
Costs to account for		$112,500

The unit cost of goods completed would simply be $112,500 ÷ 25,000 = $4.50. An itemization would show:

Direct materials, $70,000 ÷ 25,000	$2.80
Conversion costs, $42,500 ÷ 25,000	1.70
Unit cost of a whole completed marionette	$4.50

But what if not all 25,000 marionettes were completed during April? For example, assume that 5,000 were still in process at the end of April—only 20,000 were started and fully completed. All direct materials had been placed in process, but, on average, only 25 percent of the conversion costs had been applied to the 5,000 marionettes. How should the Forming Department calculate the cost of goods transferred and the cost of goods remaining in the ending work-in-process inventory? The answer lies in the following five key steps, known by the acronym, *PECUA*:

- **Step 1:** Calculate the number of *physical* units.
- **Step 2:** Calculate output in terms of *equivalent* units.
- **Step 3:** Calculate total *costs*.
- **Step 4:** Calculate *unit* costs.
- **Step 5:** *Apply* unit costs to units completed and to units in the ending work-in-process inventory.

Physical and Equivalent Units (Steps 1 and 2)

Equivalent Units. The number of completed units that partially completed units amount to.

Step 1, as the first column in Exhibit 7-2 shows, tracks the physical units of production. How should the output for April be measured? Not as 25,000 units. Instead, the output was 20,000 fully completed units and 5,000 partially completed units. A partially completed unit is not the same as a fully completed unit. To add 5,000 partially completed units to 20,000 fully completed units is like adding apples and oranges. Accordingly, partially completed units are usually stated in *equivalent units*, not physical units.

Equivalent units are the number of completed units that partially completed units amount to. For example, two half-completed units amount to one equivalent unit. So, equivalent units are determined by multiplying physical units by the percentage of completion.

EXHIBIT 7-2

Forming Department Output in Equivalent Units for the Month Ended April 30, 2006

	(STEP 1)	(STEP 2) EQUIVALENT UNITS	
FLOW OF PRODUCTION	**PHYSICAL UNITS**	**DIRECT MATERIALS**	**CONVERSION COSTS**
Started and completed	20,000	20,000	20,000
Work-in-process, ending inventory	5,000	5,000	1,250*
Units accounted for	25,000		
Work done to date		25,000	21,250

* 5,000 physical units × 0.25 degree of completion of conversion costs.

In our example, as Step 2 in Exhibit 7-2 shows, in terms of direct materials, the output would be measured as 25,000 equivalent units. However, in terms of conversion costs, the equivalent units are only 21,250. *Conversion costs* include all manufacturing costs (labour and overhead) other than direct materials. Why are there only 21,250 equivalent units in terms of conversion costs but 25,000 in terms of direct-material cost? Direct materials had been added to all 25,000 units, including the 5,000 units, which are 25 percent partially completed. On the other hand, in terms of conversion costs, the 5,000 25-percent partially completed units are equal to only 1,250 equivalents units (5,000 × 25%).

Of course, to compute equivalent units you need to estimate how much of a given resource was applied to units in process, which is not always an easy task. Some estimates are easier to make than others. For example, estimating the amount of direct materials used is fairly easy. However, how do you measure how much energy, maintenance labour, or supervision was used on a given unit or how much effort has been put into the units in process so far? Conversion costs can involve a number of these hard-to-measure resources. Coming up with accurate estimates is further complicated in industries such as textiles, which often have a large work-in-process inventory. To simplify estimation, some companies have decided that all work-in-process must be deemed either one-third, one-half, or two-thirds complete. In cases where continuous processing leaves roughly the same amount in process at the end of every month, work-in-process is ignored altogether and monthly production costs are assigned only to units completed and transferred out.

Measures in equivalent units are not confined to manufacturing situations. Equivalent units are a popular way of expressing workloads in terms of a common denominator. For example, universities use full-time equivalent (FTE) as a measure of enrollment. Five semester courses make up one FTE. That is, five part-time students taking one semester course each make one FTE (equivalent unit). Alternatively, three part-time students taking one, two, and two semester courses each correspondingly make one FTE. Radiology departments measure their output in terms of weight unit. Various X-ray procedures are ranked in terms of the time, supplies, and related costs devoted to each. A simple chest X-ray may receive a weight of three because it uses three times the resources (for example, technicians' time) as a procedure with a weight of one. Each procedure is measured by equivalent (weight) units.

Calculation of Costs, Unit Costs, and Cost Application (Steps 3, 4, and 5)

Production-Cost Report. The report showing the calculation of total costs and unit costs, and their application to finished goods and WIP-ending inventory as part of the process-costing method.

Exhibit 7-3 is a **production-cost report**. A production report shows Steps 3, 4, and 5 of process costing. Step 3 summarizes the total costs to account for (that is, the total costs in, or debits to, work-in-process—Forming). Step 4 obtains unit costs by dividing total costs by the appropriate measures of equivalent units. The unit cost of a completed unit—material costs plus conversion costs—is $2.80 + $2.00 = $4.80.[1] Step 5 then uses these unit costs to apply costs to products.

From Exhibit 7-3, determine how the costs are applied to obtain an ending work-in-process of $16,500. The 5,000 physical units in process are fully completed in terms of direct materials. Therefore, the direct materials applied to work-in-process are 5,000 equivalent units times $2.80, or $14,000.

---

[1] Why is the unit cost $4.80 instead of the $4.50 calculated earlier in this chapter? Because the $42,500 conversion cost is spread over 21,250 units instead of 25,000 units.

EXHIBIT 7-3

Forming Department
Production-Cost Report
for the Month Ended
April 30, 2006

		TOTAL COSTS	DETAILS	
			DIRECT MATERIALS	CONVERSION COSTS
(Step 3)	Costs to account for	$112,500	$70,000	$42,500
(Step 4)	Divide by equivalent units		÷ 25,000	÷ 21,250
	Unit costs	$ 4.80	$ 2.80	$ 2.00
(Step 5)	Cost application:			
	To units completed and transferred to the Finishing Department, 20,000 units ($4.80)	$ 96,000		
	To units not completed and still in process, April 30, 5,000 units:			
	Direct materials	$ 14,000	5,000 ($2.80)	
	Conversion costs	2,500		1,250 ($2.00)
	Work-in-process, April 30	$ 16,500		
	Total costs accounted for	$112,500		

In contrast, the 5,000 physical units are 25 percent completed in terms of conversion costs. Therefore, the conversion costs applied to work-in-process are 1,250 equivalent units (25 percent of 5,000 physical units) times $2 or $2,500. The entire effort of process costing aims at pricing the finished goods ($96,000) and the work-in-process ending inventory ($16,500). The first four steps of the PECUA process are intermediary steps that allow us to reach our ultimate objective of pricing the two inventories of finished goods and work-in-process.

Journal entries for the data in our illustration are as follows:

1.	Work-in-process—Forming	$70,000	
	Direct materials inventory		$70,000
	Materials added to production in April		
2.	Work-in-process—Forming	$10,625	
	Accrued payroll		$10,625
	Direct labour in April		
3.	Work-in-process—Forming	$31,875	
	Factory overhead		$31,875
	Factory overhead applied in April		
4.	Work-in-process—Finishing	$96,000	
	Work-in-process—Forming		$96,000
	Cost of goods completed and transferred in April from Forming to Finishing		

The $112,500 added to the work-in-process—Forming account less the $96,000 transferred out leaves an ending balance of $16,500.

Work-in-Process—Forming			
1. Direct materials	$ 70,000	4. Transferred out to finishing	$96,000
2. Direct labour	10,625		
3. Factory overhead	31,875		
Costs to account for	$112,500		
Balance April 30	$ 16,500		

Process-Costing Systems: A Look at Molson Breweries

Molson* uses a hybrid cost accounting system, which has evolved from the many business pressures facing its management today, as well as certain unique aspects of Molson's operations.

Molson Breweries
www.molson.com

Following is an outline of certain aspects of Molson's cost accounting system and certain complexities that arise as a result of business issues and aspects unique to Molson and/or the brewing industry in Canada.

INVENTORY VALUATION

Molson uses a weighted-average inventory valuation.

In practice, operating costs can often experience unusual fluctuations due to accounting corrections or operating abnormalities. To smooth out these peaks and valleys, Molson actually uses a three-month moving average. To accommodate time pressures, we apply the three-month moving average one month in arrears. For example, the January inventory will be valued at the weighted average of production costs for the months of October, November, and December.

EQUIVALENT UNITS

The concept of equivalent units is not practical for Molson's cost accounting system.

In the packaging department, hundreds of units are completed, from start to finish, each minute. Thus, the cost difference between a fully complete unit and a partially complete unit, extended by the small number of partially complete units at any point in time, is not material enough to warrant the cost of accounting for equivalent units.

In the brewing department, most materials are added at (or near) the beginning of the brewing process and most of the brewing process (in terms of time) involves fermentation and storage with little labour being applied. Thus, it is not considered a material misstatement to value the physical inventory rather than equivalent units.

Though the concept of equivalent units is not significant to the Molson cost accounting system, the critical role of the monthly inventory reconciliation must be stressed. Central to Molson's cost accounting system is a tremendously detailed inventory reconciliation that starts at the first dip measurement in the brewing department and tracks every inventory movement until the beer reaches the customer. This inventory reconciliation includes several physical verifications throughout the production and distribution stages and accounts for every unit along the way. This is considered the single most important aspect of Molson's cost accounting system, and the month-end cycle would stall if this reconciliation could not be accurately completed.

FACTORY OVERHEAD

Brewery overhead (excluding administration) is inventoried in Molson's finished goods and WIP; however, this is not done as part of the monthly cost accounting system.

Year-over-year inventory levels and overhead costs are either stable or predictable. Thus, except for manageable variations, the overhead in inventory is relatively consistent from year to year and overhead costs expensed approximate overhead costs incurred. In addition, management finds it easier to monitor and control overhead costs when they're reported as period items in the P&L. Thus, Molson finds it more efficient to calculate overheads in inventory once a year (though forecasted inventory levels and overhead rates are monitored so there are no surprises).

* As of February 2005, Molson Inc. and the Adolf Coors Company completed their merger.

ADDED COMPLEXITIES

One complexity results from having multiple plants that supply a single finished goods inventory and market in certain provinces. This results in having to apply a weighted-average inventory value that averages the costs of multiple plants as well as multiple production periods (as discussed above).

Another complexity results from Molson's substantial export business. Export brands often have a significantly different cost structure and, thus, an inventory value that averages domestic and export production can yield significant misstatements. Thus, Molson maintains separate cost accounting systems for domestic and export beer.

In addition, substantially different cost structures for the three packaging types (i.e., bottles, cans, and kegs) require separate cost accounting systems.

Molson maintains separate profit and loss reports for each division. Often beer is produced in one division for sale in another. Thus, the cost accounting system of each division is designed to accommodate the inventoried value and cost of sales of imported beer.

Source: Written by Hugh Atkin, former Vice President, Operations/Business Systems, Molson Breweries.

EFFECTS OF BEGINNING INVENTORIES

OBJECTIVE 4

Demonstrate the computations of unit costs under the weighted-average method.

When beginning inventories are present, product costing becomes more complicated. Suppose Oreo Wooden Toys Inc. had 3,000 marionettes in work-in-process in its forming department on March 31. All direct materials had been placed in process, but, on average, only 40 percent of the conversion costs had been applied to the 3,000 units. Because 25,000 units were worked on during April (20,000 units completed plus 5,000 still in process at the end of the month), and because there were 3,000 units in beginning inventory, 22,000 units must have been started in production during April.

The following table presents the data used in our illustrations:

Units:
  Work-in-process, March 31, 3,000 units, 100% completed for
    materials but only 40% completed for conversion costs
  Units started in April, 22,000
  Units completed in April, 20,000
  Work-in-process, April 30, 5,000 units, 100% completed for
    materials but only 25% completed for conversion costs

Costs:		
Work-in-process, March 31:		
Direct materials	$7,500	
Conversion costs	2,125	$ 9,625
Direct materials added during April		70,000
Conversion costs added during April		
($10,625 + $31,875)		42,500
Total costs to account for		$122,125

Note that the $122,125 total costs to account for include the $9,625 of beginning inventory in addition to the $112,500 added during April.

In the next section, we discuss common inventory methods: the weighted-average method and the first-in, first-out method. The five-step approach is recommended for both methods.

Weighted-Average Method

Weighted-Average (WA) Process-Costing Method.
A process costing method that adds the cost of (1) all work done in the current period to (2) the work done in the preceding period on the current period's work-in-process beginning inventory and divides the total by the equivalent units of work done to date.

The **weighted-average (WA) process-costing method** determines total costs by adding the cost of (1) all work done in the current period to (2) the work done in the preceding period on the current period's beginning work-in-process inventory. This total is divided by the equivalent units of work done to date, whether that work was done in the current period or previously.

Why is the term *weighted-average* used to describe this method? Primarily because the unit costs used for applying costs to products are affected by both costs incurred during and before the current period.

Exhibit 7-4 shows the first two steps in this method—the computation of physical units and equivalent units. Note that this illustration differs from the previous illustration in only one major respect: the presence of work-in-process beginning inventory.

EXHIBIT 7-4

Forming Department Output in Equivalent Units for the Month Ended April 30, 2006 (Weighted-Average Method)

| | (STEP 1) | (STEP 2) EQUIVALENT UNITS | |
FLOW OF PRODUCTION	PHYSICAL UNITS	DIRECT MATERIALS	CONVERSION COSTS
Work-in-process, March 31	3,000 (40%)*		
Started in April	22,000		
To account for	25,000		
Completed and transferred out during current period	20,000	20,000	20,000
Work-in-process, April 30	5,000 (25%)	5,000	1,250†
Units accounted for	25,000		
Work done to date		25,000	21,250

* Degrees of completion for conversion costs at the dates of inventories.
† 0.25 × 5,000 = 1,250.

The computation of equivalent units ignores whether all 25,000 units to account for came from beginning work-in-process, or were started in April, or some combination thereof. Exhibits 7-2 and 7-4 show the total work done to date, 25,000 equivalent units of direct materials and 21,250 units of conversion costs. The equivalent units for work done to date, which is the divisor for unit costs, is unaffected by whether all work was done in April or some before April on the March 31 inventory of work-in-process.

Exhibit 7-5 presents a production-cost report. Its pattern is similar to that in Exhibit 7-3. That is, the report summarizes Steps 3, 4, and 5 regarding computations of product costs.

The unit costs in Exhibit 7-5 are higher than those in Exhibit 7-3. Why? Because although the equivalent units are the same, the total costs include the costs incurred before April on the units in beginning inventory as well as those costs added during April.

The following list summarizes the Oreo Wooden Toys Inc. unit cost conclusion:

1. In the first simple example, we assumed no beginning or ending inventories of work-in-process. Thus, when the $112,500 of costs incurred during April were applied to the 25,000 units worked on and fully completed during April, the unit cost was $2.80 + $1.70 = $4.50.

2. In the next example, we assumed that some of the units were not fully completed by the end of the month. This reduced the equivalent units and thus increased the unit cost to $2.80 + $2.00 = $4.80 (Exhibit 7-3).

3. Then, in the last example, we assumed that some of the units had also been worked on before April. The costs of that work are carried in work-in-process inventory, March 31. The addition of these costs (with no change in the equivalent units) increased the unit cost of work completed in April to $3.10 + $2.10 = $5.20 (Exhibit 7-3).

				DETAILS	
			TOTALS	DIRECT MATERIALS	CONVERSION COSTS
(Step 3)		Work-in-process, March 31	$ 9,625	$ 7,500	$ 2,125
		Costs added currently	112,500	70,000	42,500
		Total costs to account for	$122,125	$77,500	$44,625
(Step 4)		Divisor, equivalent units for work done to date		÷ 25,000	÷ 21,250
		Unit costs (weighted averages)	$ 5.20	$ 3.10	$ 2.10
(Step 5)		Application of costs:			
		Completed and transferred, 20,000 units ($5.20)	$104,000		
		Work-in-process, April 30, 5,000 units:			
		Direct materials	$ 15,500	5,000 ($3.10)	
		Conversion costs	2,625		1,250* ($2.10)
		Total work-in-process	$ 18,125		
		Total costs accounted for	$122,125		

EXHIBIT 7-5

Forming Department Production-Cost Report for the Month Ended April 30, 2006 (Weighted-Average Method)

* Equivalent units of work done. For more details, see Exhibit 7-4.

First-In, First-Out Method (FIFO)

OBJECTIVE 5

Demonstrate the computation of unit costs under the first-in, first-out method.

First-In, First-Out (FIFO) Process-Costing Method. A process-costing method that sharply distinguishes the current work done from the previous work done on the work-in-process beginning inventory.

The **first-in, first-out (FIFO) process-costing method** makes a sharp distinction between the current work done and the previous work done on the work-in-process beginning inventory. The calculation of equivalent units is confined to the work done in the current period (April in this illustration).

Exhibit 7-6 presents Steps 1 and 2. The easiest way to compute equivalent units under the FIFO method is, first, to compute the costs associated with work done to date. Exhibit 7-6 shows these computations, which are exactly the same as in Exhibit 7-4. Second, deduct the work done *before* the current period. The remainder is the work done *during* the current period, which is the key to computing the unit costs by the FIFO method.

Exhibit 7-7 is the production-cost report. It presents Steps 3, 4, and 5. The $9,439 beginning inventory balance is kept separate from current costs. The calculations of equivalent unit costs are confined to costs added in April only. The bottom half of Exhibit 7-7 shows two ways to compute the cost of goods completed and transferred out. The first and fastest way is to compute the $18,600 ending work-in-process and then deduct it from the $122,125 total cost. The "plug in" missing amount of $103,525 is the cost of finished units. To check for accuracy and to verify this amount ($103,525), it is advisable to compute the cost of goods transferred in the detailed manner displayed in the verification footnote of Exhibit 7-7.

EXHIBIT 7-6

Forming Department Output in Equivalent Units for the Month Ended April 30, 2006 (FIFO Method)

SAME AS EXHIBIT 7-4 FLOW OF PRODUCTION	(STEP 1) PHYSICAL UNITS	(STEP 2) EQUIVALENT UNITS	
		DIRECT MATERIALS	CONVERSION COSTS
Work-in-process, March 31	3,000 (40%)		
Started in April	22,000		
To account for	25,000		
Completed and transferred out	20,000	20,000	20,000
Work-in-process, April 30	5,000 (25%)*	5,000	1,250†
Units accounted for	25,000		
Work done to date		25,000	21,250
Less: Equivalent units of work from previous periods included in beginning inventory		3,000††	1,200§
Work done in current period only		22,000	20,050

* Degrees of completion for conversion costs at the dates of inventories.
† 5,000 × 0.25 = 1,250.
†† 3,000 × 1.00 = 3,000.
§ 3,000 × 0.40 = 1,200.

EXHIBIT 7-7

Forming Department Production-Cost Report for the Month Ended April 30, 2006 (FIFO Method)

		TOTALS	DETAILS	
			DIRECT MATERIALS	CONVERSION COSTS
(Step 3)	Work-in-process, March 31	$ 9,439	(work done before April)	
	Costs added currently	112,686	$70,180	$42,506
	Total costs to account for	$122,125		
(Step 4)	Divisor, equivalent units of work done in April only		22,000*	20,050*
	Unit costs (for FIFO basis)	$ 5.31	$ 3.19	$ 2.12
(Step 5)	Application of costs:			
	Work-in-process, April 30:			
	Direct materials	$ 15,950	5,000 ($3.19)	
	Conversion costs	2,650		1,250*($2.12)
	Total work-in-process	18,600		
	(5,000 units)			
	Completed and transferred out			
	(20,000 units),			
	$122,125 − $18,600	103,525†		
	Total costs accounted for	$122,125		

* Equivalent units of work done. See Exhibit 7-6 for more details.

† Verification: work-in-process, March 31	$ 9,439
Additional costs to complete, conversion costs of 60% of 3,000 × $2.12 =	3,816
Started and completed, 22,000 − 5,000 = 17,000; 17,000 × $5.31 =	90,270
Total cost transferred	$103,525

Unit cost transferred, $103,525 ÷ 20,000 = $5.17625

Differences between FIFO and Weighted-Average Methods

The key difference between FIFO and weighted-average methods is the calculation of equivalent units:

- FIFO—Equivalent units are based on the work done in the current period only.
- Weighted-average—Equivalent units are based on the work done to date, including the earlier work done on the current period's work-in-process beginning inventory.

These differences in equivalent units lead to differences in unit costs. Accordingly, there are differences in costs applied to goods completed and still in process. In our example, the FIFO method results in a larger work-in-process inventory on April 30, and a smaller April cost of goods transferred out:

	WEIGHTED AVERAGE*	FIFO†
Cost of goods transferred out	$104,000	$103,525
Ending work-in-process	18,125	18,600
Total costs accounted for	$122,125	$122,125

* From Exhibit 7-5.
† From Exhibit 7-7.

Differences in unit costs between FIFO and weighted-average methods are normally insignificant because (a) changes in prices of material, labour wage rates, and other manufacturing costs from month to month tend to be small, and (b) changes in the volume of production and inventory levels also tend to be small.

The FIFO method involves more detailed computations than the weighted-average method. That is why FIFO is almost never used in practice in process costing *for product-costing purposes*. However, the FIFO *equivalent units* for current work done are essential *for planning and control purposes*. Why? Because they isolate the output produced in each particular period. Consider our example. The FIFO computations of equivalent units help managers to measure the efficiency of April's performance independently from March's performance. Thus budgets or standards for each month's departmental costs can be compared against actual results in light of the actual work done during any given month.

Transferred-In Costs

Transferred-In Costs. The costs of the items a department receives from another department.

Many companies that use process costing have sequential production processes. For example, Oreo Wooden Toys Inc. transfers the items completed in its forming department to the finishing department. The finishing department would call the costs of the items it receives **transferred-in costs**—costs incurred in a previous department for items that have been received by a subsequent department. They are similar to, but not identical to, additional direct materials costs. Because transferred-in costs are a combination of all types of costs (direct materials and conversion costs) incurred in previous departments, they should not be called a direct material cost in a subsequent department.

We account for transferred-in costs in the same manner as we account for direct materials, although they are kept separate from the direct materials added in the department. Therefore, reports such as Exhibits 7-5 and 7-7 will include three columns of costs instead of two: transferred-in costs, direct materials costs, and conversion costs. The total unit cost will be the sum of all three types of unit costs.

STRATEGIC INSIGHTS & COMPANY PRACTICES

Activity-Based Costing and Process Map: Snack Peanuts

One of the leading brands of snack peanuts is Planters. In Canada, as of the mid-1990s, the rights to the Planters brand have been owned by Toronto-based Johnvince Foods. Typical Planters peanut products include regular roasted, dry roasted, salted, and unsalted peanuts. Processing a peanut snack food involves several activities; most snack peanuts are blanched (i.e., skins are removed) before roasting. Peanuts can be oil roasted or dry roasted before being packaged and shipped.

Johnvince Foods
www.johnvince.com

What would an activity-based costing system look like for snack peanut products? First, let's look at the big picture. The major activities in the processing of peanuts are shown in Figure 1. Note that in an ABC system, attention is focused on the operating relationships between major activities without regard to "departmental boundaries." In a traditional system, we would typically have a few operating departments, such as the "blanching and frying department" and the "packing and shipping department." The receiving, moving, and storing activities would be part of the "support service department" within a traditional system. While these departments still exist in a company using an ABC system, the focus is on understanding the interrelationships between the activities without regard to departments. This focus translates into designing the cost accounting system to report costs by key activities.

Now, let's take a closer look at the blanching, frying, and moving activities, plus the related resources, as illustrated in Figure 2. To keep our presentation manageable, such resources as indirect materials and supervision have been omitted. From this diagram, we can describe the blanching activity as follows: Blanching involves operating labour putting raw peanuts into a blancher machine. Gas is used to power the blanching activity, and maintenance labour is also needed. The blanching machines occupy space, so a portion of the occupancy costs are allocated to these machines.

Note that cost behaviour is also depicted in this process map. For the blanching activity, raw peanuts and gas are variable cost resources, while the blancher, maintenance labour, operating labour, and occupancy are all fixed-cost resources.

FIGURE 1

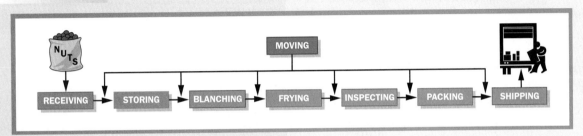

FIGURE 2

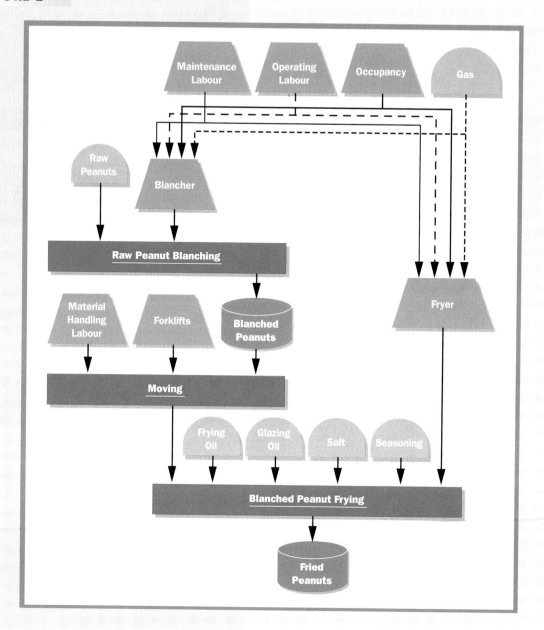

PROCESS COSTING IN A JUST-IN-TIME SYSTEM: BACKFLUSH COSTING

Tracking costs through various stages of inventory—raw materials, work-in-process, and finished goods inventory—makes accounting systems complex. If there were no inventories, all costs would be charged directly to cost of goods sold, and accounting systems would be much simpler. Organizations using just-in-time production systems usually have very small inventories, and they may not want to bear the expense of a system that traces costs through all the inventory accounts. Such firms can use **backflush costing**, an accounting system that applies costs to products only when the production is complete.

Principles of Backflush Costing

Backflush costing has only two categories of costs: materials and conversion costs. Its unique feature is an absence of a work-in-process account. Actual material costs are entered into a *material inventory account*, and actual labour and overhead costs are entered into a *conversion costs account*. Costs are transferred from these two temporary accounts directly into finished goods inventories. Some backflush systems even eliminate the finished goods inventory account and transfer costs directly to cost of goods sold, if goods are not kept in inventory but are shipped immediately upon completion. Backflush systems assume that production follows so soon after the application of conversion activities that balances in the conversion costs accounts always should remain near zero. Thus, costs are transferred out almost immediately after being initially recorded.

Example of Backflush Costing

Speaker Technology Inc. (STI) produces speakers for automobile stereo systems. STI recently introduced a just-in-time production system and backflush costing. Consider the July production for speaker model AX27. The standard material cost per unit of AX27 is $14, and the standard unit conversion cost is $21. During July, STI purchased materials for $5,600, incurred conversion costs of $8,400 (which included all labour costs and manufacturing overhead), and completed and sold 400 units of AX27.

Backflush costing is accomplished in three steps:

1. Record actual materials and conversion costs. For simplicity, we assume for now that actual materials and conversion costs were identical to the standard costs. As materials are purchased, backflush systems add their cost to the materials inventory account:

Materials inventory	$5,600	
Accounts payable (or cash)		$5,600
To record material purchases		

If actual costs do not equal the standard costs that are transferred from the finished goods inventory, the resulting variances are treated as overapplied or underapplied overhead. Similarly, as direct labour and manufacturing overhead costs are incurred, they are added to the conversion costs account.

Conversion costs	$8,400	
Accrued wages and other accounts		$8,400
To record conversion costs incurred		

2. Apply costs to completed units. When production is complete, costs from materials inventory and conversion costs accounts are transferred directly to finished goods based on the number of units completed and the standard cost of each unit:

```
Finished goods inventory (400 x $35) . . . . . . . . .   $14,000
     Materials inventory (400 x $14). . . . . . . . . . . .                $5,600
     Conversion costs (400 x $21) . . . . . . . . . . . . .                 8,400
To record costs of completed production
```

Because of short production cycle times, there is little lag between additions to the conversion costs account and transfers to finished goods. The conversion costs account, therefore, remains near zero.

3. Record cost of goods sold during the period. The standard cost of the items sold is transferred from finished goods inventory to cost of goods sold:

```
Cost of goods sold  . . . . . . . . . . . . . . . . . . . . .   $14,000
     Finished goods inventory  . . . . . . . . . . . . . .                $14,000
To record cost of 400 units sold @ $35 per unit
```

Suppose completed units are delivered immediately to customers, so that finished goods inventories are negligible. Steps 2 and 3 can then be combined and the finished goods inventory account eliminated:

```
Cost of goods sold  . . . . . . . . . . . . . . . . . . . . .   $14,000
     Material inventories  . . . . . . . . . . . . . . . . .                $5,600
     Conversion costs  . . . . . . . . . . . . . . . . . . . .                 8,400
```

Backflush systems assume that conversion costs account balances should be approximately zero at all times. Any remaining balance in the account at the end of an accounting period is charged to cost of goods sold. Suppose actual conversion costs for July had been $8,600 and the amount transferred to finished goods (that is, applied to the product) was $8,400. The $200 balance in the conversion costs account at the end of the month would be written off to cost of goods sold:

```
Cost of goods sold  . . . . . . . . . . . . . . . . . . . . .   $200
     Conversion costs  . . . . . . . . . . . . . . . . . . . .                 $200
To recognize underapplied conversion costs
```

HIGHLIGHTS TO REMEMBER

1. **Explain the basic ideas underlying process costing and how they differ from job costing.** Process costing is used for inventory costing when there is continuous mass production of like units. Process-cost systems accumulate costs by department (or process); each department has its own work-in-process account. Job-order-cost systems differ because costs are accumulated and tracked by the individual job order.

2. **Compute output in terms of equivalent units.** The key concept in process costing is that of equivalent units, the number of fully completed units that could have been produced from the inputs applied.

3. **Compute costs and prepare journal entries for the principal transactions in a process-costing system.** There are five basic steps to process costing:
   1. Summarize the flow of physical units.
   2. Calculate output in terms of equivalent units.
   3. Summarize the total costs to account for.
   4. Calculate unit costs (Step 3 ÷ Step 2).
   5. Apply costs to units completed and to units in the ending work in process.

   Steps 3 and 5 provide the data for journal entries. These entries all involve the work-in-process accounts for the various departments (processes) producing products.

4. **Demonstrate how the presence of beginning inventories affects the computation of unit costs under the weighted-average method and the first-in, first-out (FIFO) method.** Process costing is complicated by the presence of beginning inventories. The weighted-average method and the first-in, first-out (FIFO) method include the work done in previous periods on the current period's beginning inventory with work done in the current period to compute unit costs.

5. **Use backflush costing with a JIT production system.** Many companies with JIT production systems use backflush costing. Such systems have no work-in-process inventory account and apply costs to products once the production process is complete.

DEMONSTRATION PROBLEMS FOR YOUR REVIEW

Problem One

Titan Plastics makes a variety of plastic products. Its Extruding Department had the following output and costs:

> Units:
>   Started and completed, 30,000 units
>   Started and still in process, 10,000 units, 100% completed for direct materials
>   but 60% completed for conversion costs
> Costs applied:
>   Total, $81,600; direct materials of $60,000 plus conversion costs of $21,600

Compute the cost of work completed and the cost of the ending inventory of work-in-process.

Solution

| | (STEP 1) | (STEP 2) EQUIVALENT UNITS | |
FLOW OF PRODUCTION	PHYSICAL UNITS	DIRECT MATERIALS	CONVERSION
Started and completed	30,000	30,000	30,000
Ending work-in-process	10,000	10,000*	6,000*
Units accounted for	40,000		
Work done to date		40,000	36,000

* 10,000 × 100% = 10,000; 10,000 × 60% = 6,000.

		TOTAL COSTS	DETAILS DIRECT MATERIALS	CONVERSION COSTS
(Step 3)	Costs to account for	$81,600	$60,000	$21,600
(Step 4)	Divide by equivalent units		÷ 40,000	÷ 36,000
	Unit costs	$ 2.10*	$ 1.50	$ 0.60
(Step 5)	Application costs:			
	To units completed and transferred,			
	30,000 units ($2.10)	$63,000		
	To ending work-in-process,			
	10,000 units			
	Direct materials	$15,000	10,000($1.50)	
	Conversion costs	3,600		6,000($0.60)
	Work-in-process, ending			
	inventory	$18,600		
	Total costs accounted for	$81,600		

* Unit cost ($2.10) = direct materials costs ($1.50) + conversion costs ($0.60).

Problem Two

Consider the Cooking Department of Middleton Foods, a Brtish food-processing company. Compute the cost of work completed and the cost of the ending inventory of work-in-process, using (1) the weighted-average (WA) method and (2) the FIFO method.

Units:
  Beginning work-in-process, 5,000 units, 100% completed for materials, 40% completed for
    conversion costs.
  Started during month, 28,000 units
  Completed during month, 31,000 units
  Ending work-in-process, 2,000 units, 100% completed for materials, 50% for conversion costs.

Costs:
Beginning work-in-process:		
Direct materials	£8,060	
Conversion costs	1,300	£ 9,360
Direct materials added in current month		41,440
Conversion costs added in current month		14,700
Total cost to account for		£65,500

FLOW OF PRODUCTION	(STEP 1) PHYSICAL UNITS	(STEP 2) EQUIVALENT UNITS MATERIAL	CONVERSION COSTS
Completed and transferred out	31,000	31,000	31,000
Ending work-in-process	2,000	2,000*	1,000*
1. Equivalent units, WA	33,000	33,000	32,000
Less: beginning work-in-process	5,000	5,000†	2,000†
2. Equivalent units, FIFO	28,000	28,000	30,000

* 2,000 × 100% = 2,000; 2,000 × 50% = 1,000.
† 5,000 × 100% = 5,000; 5,000 × 40% = 2,000.

Solution

1.

WEIGHTED-AVERAGE METHOD	TOTAL COST	DIRECT MATERIALS	CONVERSION COSTS
Beginning work-in-process	£ 9,360	£ 8,060	£ 1,300
Costs added currently	56,140	41,440	14,700
Total cost to account for	£65,500	£49,500	£16,000
Equivalent units		÷ 33,000	÷ 32,000
Unit costs	£ 2.00	£ 1.50	£ 0.50
Cost application			
Transferred out, 31,000 × £2.00	£62,000		
Ending work-in-process:			
Direct materials	£ 3,000	2,000(£1.50)	
Conversion cost	500		1,000(£0.50)
Total work-in-process	£ 3,500		
Total costs accounted for	£65,500		

2.

FIFO METHOD	TOTAL COST	DIRECT MATERIALS	CONVERSION COSTS
Beginning work-in-process	£ 9,360	(work done before month)	
Costs added currently	56,140	£41,440	£14,700
Total costs to account for	£65,500		
Equivalent units		÷ 28,000	÷ 30,000
Unit costs	£ 1.97	£ 1.48	£ 0.49
Cost application			
Ending work-in-process:			
Direct materials	£ 2,960	2,000(£1.48)	
Conversion cost	490		1,000(£0.49)
Total work-in-process	£ 3,450		
Transferred out, £65,500 − £3,450	62,050*		
Total costs accounted for	£65,500		

* Verification:

Beginning work-in-process	£ 9,360
Costs to complete, 60% × 5,000 × £0.49	1,470
Started and completed,	
(31,000 − 5,000)(£1.48 + £.49)	51,220
Total cost transferred	£62,050

Unit cost transferred, £62,050 ÷ 31,000 = £2.00161

Problem Three

The most extreme (and simplest) version of backflush costing makes product costing entries at only one point. Suppose Speaker Technology Inc. (STI) had no materials inventory account (in addition to no work-in-process inventory account). Materials are not "purchased" until they are needed for production. Therefore, STI enters both materials and conversion costs directly into its finished goods inventory account.

Prepare journal entries and T-accounts for July's production of 400 units. Material purchases totalled $5,600, and conversion costs were $8,400.

Solution

In one step, material and conversion costs are applied to finished goods inventories:

Finished goods inventories	$14,000	
Accounts payable		$5,600
Wages payable and other accounts		8,400

Finished Goods Inventories		Accounts Payable, Wages Payable, and Other Accounts	
Materials	$5,600		$5,600
Conversion costs	8,400		8,400

Why might a company use this system of backflush costing? This extreme back-flush costing version illustrates a system that is simple and inexpensive. It also provides reasonably accurate product costs if (1) material inventories are low (most likely because of just-in-time delivery schedules), and (2) production cycle times are short so that at any time only inconsequential amounts of material costs or conversion costs have been incurred for products that are not yet complete.

APPENDIX: HYBRID SYSTEMS—OPERATION COSTING

Hybrid-Costing System.
An accounting system that is a blend of ideas from job costing and process costing.

Job costing and process costing are extremes along a continuum of potential costing systems. Each company designs its own accounting system to fit its underlying production activities. Many companies use **hybrid-costing systems**, which are blends of ideas from both job costing and process costing. This appendix discusses one of many possible hybrid costing systems, *operation costing*.

Nature of Operation Costing

OBJECTIVE 7

Generate costs using an operation-costing system.

Operation Costing. A hybrid-costing system often used in the batch or group manufacturing of goods that have some common characteristics plus some individual characteristics.

Operation costing is a hybrid-costing system often used in batch or group manufacturing of goods that have some common characteristics plus some individual characteristics. Examples of such goods include personal computers, clothing, and semiconductors. Such products are specifically identified by work orders. The goods are often variations of a single design but require a varying sequence of standardized operations. For instance, men's suits may differ, requiring various materials and hand operations. Similarly, a textile manufacturer may apply special chemical treatments (such as waterproofing) to some fabrics but not to others.

Operation costing may entail mass production, but there is sufficient product variety to have products scheduled in different batches or groups, each requiring a particular sequence of operations.

An *operation* is a standardized method or technique that is repetitively performed, regardless of the distinguishing features of the finished product. Examples include cutting, planing, sanding, painting, and chemical treating. Products proceed through the various operations in groups as specified by work orders or production orders. These work orders list the necessary direct materials and the step-by-step operations required to make the finished product.

Suppose a clothing manufacturer produces two lines of blazers. The wool blazers use better materials and undergo more operations than the polyester blazers, as follows:

	WORK ORDER A	WORK ORDER B
Direct materials	Wool	Polyester
	Satin lining	Rayon lining
	Bone buttons	Plastic buttons
Operations	1. Cutting cloth	1. Cutting cloth
	2. Checking edges	2. —
	3. Sewing body	3. Sewing body
	4. Checking seams	4. —
	5. —	5. Sewing collars and lapels by machine
	6. Sewing collars and lapels by hand	6. —

The costs of the blazers are compiled by a work order. As in job costing, the direct materials—different for each work order—are specifically identified with the appropriate order. Conversion costs—direct labour plus factory overhead—are initially compiled for each operation. A cost driver, such as the number of units processed or minutes or seconds used, is identified for each operation, and a conversion cost per unit of cost-driver activity is computed. Then conversion costs are applied to products in a manner similar to the application of factory overhead in a job-cost system.

Example of Operation Costing

Suppose our manufacturer has two work orders, one for 100 wool blazers and the other for 200 polyester blazers as follows:

	WORK ORDER A (WOOL)	WORK ORDER B (POLYESTER)
Number of blazers	100	200
Direct materials	$2,500	$3,100
Conversion costs:		
1. Cutting cloth $30 x (20, 40)	600	1,200
2. Checking edges	300	–
3. Sewing body	500	1,000
4. Checking seams	600	–
5. Sewing collars and lapels by machine	–	800
6. Sewing collars and lapels by hand	700	–
Total manufacturing costs	$5,200	$6,100

Direct labour and factory overhead vanish as separate classifications in an operation-costing system. The sum of these costs is most frequently called conversion cost. The conversion costs are applied to products based on the company's budgeted rate for performing each operation. For example, suppose the conversion costs of Operation 1, cutting cloth, are driven by machine hours and are budgeted for the year as follows:

$$\text{budgeted rate for applying conversion costs for cutting cloth to product} = \frac{\text{company's budgeted conversion cost for cutting cloth for the year (direct labour plus power, repairs, supplies, other factory overhead of this operation)}}{\text{budgeted machine hours for the year for cutting cloth}}$$

$$\text{rate per machine hour} = \frac{\$150,000 + \$450,000}{20,000 \text{ hours}} = \$30 \text{ per machine hour}$$

As goods are manufactured, conversion costs are applied to the work orders by multiplying the $30 hourly rate times the number of machine hours used for cutting cloth.

If 20 machine hours are needed to cut the cloth for the 100 wool blazers, then the conversion cost involved is $600 (20 hours × $30 per hour). For the 200 polyester blazers, the conversion cost for cutting the cloth is twice as much, $1,200 (40 hours × $30), because each blazer takes the same cutting time and there are twice as many polyester blazers.

Summary journal entries for applying costs to the polyester blazers follow. (Entries for the wool blazers would be similar.)

The journal entry for the requisition of direct materials for the 200 polyester blazers is as follows:

Work-in-process inventory (polyester blazers) . . .	$3,100	
Direct materials inventory		$3,100

Direct labour and factory overhead are subparts of a conversion costs account in an operation-costing system. Suppose actual conversion costs of $3,150 were entered into the conversion costs account:

Conversion costs	$3,150	
Accrued payroll, accumulated amortization,		
accounts payable, etc.		$3,150

The application of conversion costs to products in operation costing is similar to the application of factory overhead in job-order costing. A budgeted rate per unit of cost-driver activity is used. To apply conversion costs to the 200 polyester blazers, the following summary entry is made for Operations 1, 3, and 5 (cutting cloth, sewing body, and sewing collars and lapels by machine):

Work-in-process inventory (polyester blazers) . . .	$3,000	
Conversion costs, cutting cloth		$1,200
Conversion costs, sewing body		1,000
Conversion costs, sewing collars and lapels		
by machine		800

After posting, work-in-process inventory has the following debit balance:

Work-in-Process Inventory (polyester blazers)		
Direct materials	$3,100	
Conversion costs applied	3,000	
Balance	$6,100	

As the blazers are completed, their cost is transferred to finished-goods inventory in the usual manner.

Any overapplication or underapplication of conversion costs is disposed of at the end of the year in the same manner as overapplied or underapplied overhead in a job-order costing system. In this case, conversion costs have been debited for the actual cost of $3,150 and credited for costs applied of $3,000. The debit balance of $150 indicates that conversion costs are underapplied.

KEY TERMS

backflush costing *p. 315*
equivalent units *p. 304*
first-in, first-out (FIFO) process-
   costing method *p. 310*
hybrid-costing systems *p. 320*

operation costing *p. 320*
production-cost report *p. 305*
transferred-in costs *p. 312*
weighted-average(WA) process-
   costing method *p. 309*

ASSIGNMENT MATERIAL

QUESTIONS

Q7-1 Give three examples of industries where process-costing systems are probably used.

Q7-2 Give three examples of not-for-profit organizations where process-costing systems are probably used.

Q7-3 What is the central product-costing problem in process costing?

Q7-4 "There are five key steps in process-cost accounting." What are they?

Q7-5 Identify the major distinction between the first two and the final three steps of the five major steps in accounting for process costs.

Q7-6 Suppose a university has 10,000 full-time students and 5,000 half-time students. Using the concept of equivalent units, compute the number of "full-time equivalent" students.

Q7-7 "Equivalent units are the work done to date." What method of process costing is being described?

Q7-8 Present an equation that describes the physical flow in process costing, where there are beginning inventories in work-in-process.

Q7-9 "The beginning inventory is regarded as if it were a batch of goods separate *and* distinct from the goods started and completed by a process during the current period." What method of process costing is being described?

Q7-10 Why is "work done in the current period only" a key measurement of equivalent units?

Q7-11 "The total conversion costs are divided by the equivalent units for the work done to date." Does this quotation describe the weighted-average method or does it describe FIFO?

Q7-12 "Ordinarily, the differences in unit costs under FIFO and weighted-average methods are insignificant." Do you agree? Explain.

Q7-13 "FIFO process costing is helpful for planning and control even if it is not used for product costing." Do you agree? Explain.

Q7-14 How are transferred-in costs similar to direct materials costs? How are they different?

Q7-15 "Backflush costing systems only work for companies using a just-in-time production system." Do you agree? Explain.

Q7-16 Explain what happens in a backflush costing system when the amount of actual conversion cost in a period exceeds the amount applied to the products completed that period.

Q7-17 Give three examples of industries that probably use operation costing.

Q7-18 "In operation costing or activity costing, average conversion costs are applied to products in a manner similar to the application of factory overhead in a job-cost system." Do you agree? Explain.

PROBLEMS

P7-1 **BASIC PROCESS COSTING.** A department of Calcutta Textiles produces cotton fabric. All direct materials are introduced at the start of the process. Conversion costs are incurred uniformly throughout the process.

In April there was no beginning inventory. Units started, completed, and transferred were 650,000. Units in process, April 30, were 220,000. Each unit in ending work-in-process was 60 percent converted. Costs incurred during April were as follows: direct materials, $3,741,000; conversion costs, $860,200.

1. Compute the total work done in equivalent units and the unit cost for April.
2. Compute the cost of units completed and transferred. Also compute the cost of units in ending work-in-process.

P7-2 **UNEVEN FLOW.** One department of Wamego Technology Company manufactures basic hand-held calculators. Various materials are added at different stages of the process. The outer front sheet and the carrying case, which represent 10 percent of the total material cost, are added at the final step of the assembly process. All other materials are considered to be "in process" by the time the calculator reaches a 50 percent stage of completion.

During 2006, 74,000 calculators were started in production. At year-end, 6,000 calculators were in various stages of completion, but all of them were beyond the 50 percent stage and on the average they were regarded as being 70 percent completed.

The following costs were incurred during the year: direct materials, $205,520; conversion costs, $397,100.

1. Prepare a schedule of physical units and equivalent units.
2. Tabulate the unit costs, cost of goods completed, and cost of ending work-in-process.

P7-3 BASIC PROCESS COSTING. Celltel Ltd. produces cellular phones in large quantities. For simplicity, assume that the company has two departments, Assembly and Testing. The manufacturing costs in the Assembly Department during February were

Direct materials added		$ 57,000
Conversion costs		
Direct labour	$50,000	
Factory overhead	40,000	90,000
Assembly costs to account for		$147,000

There was no beginning inventory of work-in-process. Suppose work on 19,000 phones was begun in the Assembly Department during February, but only 17,000 phones were fully completed and transferred to the Testing Department. All the parts had been made or placed in process, but only half the labour had been completed for each of the phones still in process.

   1. Compute the equivalent units and unit costs for February.
   2. Compute the costs of units completed and transferred to the Testing Department. Also compute the cost of the ending work-in-process.
   3. Prepare summary journal entries for the use of direct materials, direct labour, and factory overhead applied. Also prepare a journal entry for the transfer of goods completed and transferred. Show the postings to the work-in-process account.

P7-4 BASIC PROCESS COSTING. Hasoon Company produces digital watches in large quantities. The manufacturing costs of the Assembly Department were

Direct materials added		$1,620,000
Conversion costs		
Direct labour	$475,000	
Factory overhead	275,000	750,000
Assembly costs to account for		$2,370,000

For simplicity, assume that this is a two-department company—Assembly and Finishing. There was no beginning work-in-process.

    Suppose 900,000 units were begun in the Assembly Department. There were 600,000 units completed and transferred to the Finishing Department. The 300,000 units in ending work-in-process were fully completed regarding direct materials but half completed regarding conversion costs.

   1. Compute the equivalent units and unit costs in the Assembly Department.
   2. Compute the costs of units completed and transferred to the Finishing Department. Also compute the cost of the ending work-in-process in the Assembly Department.
   3. Prepare summary journal entries for the use of direct materials, direct labour, and factory overhead applied. Also prepare a journal entry for the transfer of goods completed and transferred. Show the postings to the work-in-process—Assembly Department account.

P7-5 PHYSICAL UNITS. Fill in the unknowns in physical units:

	CASE	
FLOW OF PRODUCTION	A	B
Work-in-process, beginning inventory	1,500	4,000
Started	6,500	7,800
Completed and transferred	6,800	8,000
Work-in-process, ending inventory	2,000	3,300

P7-6 FLOW OF PRODUCTION, FIFO. Fill in the unknowns in physical or equivalent units:

		EQUIVALENT UNITS	
FLOW OF PRODUCTION	PHYSICAL UNITS	DIRECT MATERIALS	CONVERSION COSTS
Beginning work-in-process	1,000 (50%)		
Started	?		
To account for	36,000		
Completed and transferred out	33,000	33,000	33,000
Ending work-in-process	? (40%)*	?	?
Units accounted for	?		
Work done to date		?	?
Equivalent units in beginning inventory		?	?
Work done in current period only		?	?

* Degree of completion of conversion costs at dates of inventory. Assume that all materials are added at the beginning of the process.

P7-7 EQUIVALENT UNITS. The production department of Garcia Paints Inc. had the following flow of litres of latex paint for the month of April:

Litres completed:	
From work-in-process on April 1	5,000
From April production	25,000
	30,000

Direct materials are added at the beginning of the process. Units of work-in-process at April 30 were 10,000. The work-in-process at April 1 was 30 percent complete regarding conversion costs, and the work-in-process at April 30 was 50 percent complete regarding conversion costs. What are the equivalent units (litres) of production for (a) direct materials and (b) conversion costs for the month of April using the FIFO method?

P7-8 **EQUIVALENT UNITS.** Fill in the unknowns.

	(STEP 1)	(STEP 2) EQUIVALENT UNITS	
FLOW OF PRODUCTION IN UNITS	PHYSICAL UNITS	DIRECT MATERIALS	CONVERSION COSTS
Work-in-process, beginning inventory	20,000*		
Started	45,000		
To account for	65,000		
Completed and transferred out	?	?	?
Work-in-process, ending inventory	2,000†	?	?
Units accounted for	65,000		
Work done to date		?	?
Less: equivalent units of work from previous periods included in beginning inventory		?	?
Work done in current period only (FIFO method)		?	?

* Degree of completion: direct materials, 80%; conversion costs 40%.
† Degree of completion: direct materials, 40%; conversion costs, 10%.

P7-9 **COMPUTE EQUIVALENT UNITS.** Consider the following data for 2007:

	PHYSICAL UNITS
Started in 2007	80,000
Completed in 2007	90,000
Ending inventory, work-in-process	10,000
Beginning inventory, work-in-process	20,000

The beginning inventory was 80 percent complete regarding direct materials and 40 percent complete regarding conversion costs. The ending inventory was 20 percent complete regarding direct materials and 30 percent complete regarding conversion costs.

Prepare a schedule of equivalent units for the work done to date and the work done during 2007 only, using the FIFO method.

P7-10 **FIFO AND UNIT DIRECT MATERIAL COSTS.** The Fujita Company uses the FIFO process-cost method. Consider the following for July:

- Beginning inventory, 15,000 units, 70 percent completed regarding direct materials, which cost ¥89,250,000.
- Units completed, 80,000.
- Cost of materials placed in process during July, ¥580,000,000.
- Ending inventory, 5,000 units, 60 percent completed regarding materials.

Compute the direct material cost per equivalent unit for the work done in July only.

P7-11 **FIFO METHOD, CONVERSION COST.** Given the following information, compute the unit conversion cost for the month of February for the Michael-Michael Company, using the FIFO process-cost method. Show details of your calculations.

- Units completed, 45,000.
- Conversion cost in beginning inventory, $30,000.

- Beginning inventory, 10,000 units with 75 percent of conversion cost.
- Ending inventory, 15,000 units with 30 percent of conversion cost.
- Conversion costs put into production in February, $222,600.

P7-12 WEIGHTED-AVERAGE PROCESS-COSTING METHOD.   The Rainbow Paint Co. uses a process-cost system. Materials are added at the beginning of a particular process, and conversion costs are incurred uniformly. Work-in-process at the beginning of the month is 40 percent complete; at the end, 20 percent. One litre of material makes one litre of product. Data are as follows:

Beginning inventory	550 litres
Direct material added	7,150 litres
Ending inventory	400 litres
Conversion costs incurred	$34,986
Cost of direct materials added	$65,340
Conversion costs, beginning inventory	$ 1,914
Cost of direct materials, beginning inventory	$ 3,190

1. Use the weighted-average method. Prepare a schedule of output in equivalent units and a schedule of application of costs to products. Show the cost of goods completed and of ending work in process.
2. Prepare summary journal entries for the use of direct materials and conversion costs. Also prepare a journal entry for the transfer of goods completed, assuming that the goods are transferred to another department.

P7-13 FIFO COMPUTATIONS.   Refer to the preceding problem, P7-12. Using FIFO, answer the same questions.

P7-14 WEIGHTED-AVERAGE PROCESS-COSTING METHOD The Magnatto Company manufactures electric drills. Material is introduced at the beginning of the process in the assembly department. Conversion costs are applied uniformly throughout the process.

As the process is completed, goods are immediately transferred to the Finishing Department. Data for the assembly department for the month of July 2007 follow:

Work-in-process, June 30: $175,500 (consisting of $138,000 materials and $37,500 conversion costs); 100% completed for direct materials, but only 25% completed for conversion costs	10,000 units
Units started during July	80,000 units
Units completed during July	70,000 units
Work-in-process, July 31: 100% completed for direct materials, but only 50% completed for conversion costs	20,000 units
Direct materials added during July	$852,000
Conversion costs added during July	$634,500

1. Compute the total cost of goods transferred out of the Assembly Department during July.
2. Compute the total costs of the ending work-in-process. Prepare a production-cost report or a similar orderly tabulation of your work. Assume weighted-average product costing.

P7-15 FIFO METHOD. Refer to problem P7-14. Using FIFO costing, answer the same questions.

P7-16 NOT-FOR-PROFIT PROCESS COSTING. Canada Revenue Agency (CRA) must process millions of income tax returns yearly. When the taxpayer sends in a return, documents such as withholding statements and cheques are matched against the data. Then various other inspections of the data are conducted. Of course, some returns are more complicated than others, so the expected time allowed to process a return is geared to an "average" return.

Some work-measurement experts have been closely monitoring the processing at a particular branch. They are seeking ways to improve productivity.

Suppose 3 million returns were received on April 30. On May 17, the work-measurement teams discovered that all supplies (data-entry edit reports, inspection check sheets, and so on) had been affixed to the returns, but 40 percent of the returns still had to undergo a final inspection. The other returns were fully completed.

1. Suppose the final inspection represents 25 percent of the overall processing time in this process. Compute the total work done in terms of equivalent units.
2. The materials and supplies consumed were $600,000. For these calculations, materials and supplies are regarded just like direct materials. The conversion costs were $4,725,000. Compute the unit costs of materials and supplies and of conversion.
3. Compute the cost of the tax returns not yet completely processed.

P7-17 PROCESS VERSUS ACTIVITY-BASED. Consider the potato chip production process at a company such as Frito-Lay. Frito-Lay uses a continuous-flow technology that is suited for high volumes of product. At the Plano, Texas, facility, between 2,700 and 3,200 kilograms of potato chips are produced each hour. The plant operates 24 hours a day. It takes 30 minutes to completely produce a bag of potato chips from the raw potato to the packed end-product.

1. What product and process characteristics of potato chips dictate the cost accounting system used? Describe the costing system best suited to Frito-Lay.
2. What product and process characteristics dictate the use of an activity-based costing system? What implications does this have for Frito-Lay?
3. When beginning inventories are present, product costing becomes more complicated. Estimate the relative magnitude of beginning inventories at Frito-Lay compared to total production. What implication does this have on the costing system?

P7-18 PROCESS COSTING AT LATHAM AND CHRIS. Latham and Chris produces crushed limestone used in highway construction, among other products. To produce the crushed limestone, the company starts with limestone rocks from its quarry in Alberta and puts the rocks through a crushing process. Suppose that on May 1, Latham and Chris had 24 tonnes of rock (75 percent complete) in the crushing process. The cost of that beginning work-in-process inventory was $6,000. During May, the company added 288 tonnes of rock from its quarry, and at the end of the month, 15 tonnes remained in process, on average one-third complete. The cost of rocks from the quarry for the last five months had been $120 per tonne. Labour and overhead cost during May in the rock crushing process were $40,670. Latham and Chris uses weighted-average process costing.

1. Compute the cost per tonne of crushed rock for production in May.
2. Compute the cost of the work-in-process inventory at the end of May.
3. Suppose the flexible budget for labour and overhead was $16,000 plus $80 per tonne. Evaluate the control of overhead and labour costs during May.

P7-19 **TWO MATERIALS.** The following data pertain to the Blending Department at Fasten Chemicals for April:

Units:	
Work-in-process, March 31	0
Units started	60,000
Completed and transferred to finishing department	40,000
Costs:	
Materials:	
Plastic compound	$300,000
Softening compound	$ 80,000
Conversion costs	$240,000

The plastic compound is introduced at the start of the process, while the softening compound is added when the product reaches an 80 percent stage of completion. Conversion costs are incurred uniformly throughout the process.

The ending work-in-process is 40 percent completed for conversion costs.

1. Compute the equivalent units and unit costs for April.
2. Compute the total cost of units completed and transferred to finished goods. Also compute the cost of the ending work-in-process.

P7-20 **MATERIALS AND CARTONS.** A Hull, England, company manufactures and sells small portable tape recorders. Business is booming. Various materials are added at various stages in the Assembly Department. Costs are accounted for on a process-cost basis. The end of the process involves conducting a final inspection and adding a cardboard carton.

The final inspection requires 5 percent of the total processing time. All materials except the carton are added by the time the recorders reach an 80 percent stage of completion of conversion.

There were no beginning inventories. During 2006, 150,000 recorders were started in production. At the end of the year, which was not a busy time, 5,000 recorders were in various stages of completion. All the ending units in work-in-process were at the 95 percent stage. They awaited final inspection and being placed in cartons.

Total direct materials consumed in production, except for cartons, cost £2,250,000. Cartons used cost £290,000. Total conversion costs were £1,198,000.

1. Present a schedule of physical units, equivalent units, and unit costs of direct materials, cartons, and conversion costs.
2. Present a summary of the cost of goods completed and the cost of ending work-in-process.

P7-21 BACKFLUSH COSTING. Ajax Meter Company manufactures a variety of measuring instruments. One product is an altimeter used by hikers and mountain climbers. Ajax adopted a just-in-time philosophy with an automated, computer-controlled, robotic production system. Production is scheduled after an order is received, materials and parts arrive just as they are needed, the production cycle time for altimeters is less than one day, and completed units are packaged and shipped as part of the production cycle.

Ajax's backflush costing system has only three accounts related to production of altimeters: materials and parts inventory, conversion costs, and finished goods inventory. At the beginning of April (as at the beginning of every month) each of the three accounts had a balance of zero. Following are the April transactions related to the production of altimeters:

Materials and parts purchased	$287,000
Conversion costs incurred	$ 92,000
Altimeters produced	11,500 units

The budgeted (or standard) cost for one altimeter is $24 for materials and parts and $8 for conversion costs.

1. Prepare summary journal entries for the production of altimeters in April.
2. Compute the cost of goods sold for April. Explain any assumptions you make.
3. Suppose the actual conversion costs incurred during April were $94,600 instead of $92,000, and all other facts were as given. Prepare the additional journal entry that would be required at the end of April. Explain why the entry was necessary.

P7-22 BACKFLUSH COSTING. Digital Controls Inc. makes electric thermostats for homes and offices. The Westplains division makes one product, Autotherm, that has a standard cost of $37, consisting of $22 of materials and $15 of conversion costs. In January, actual purchases of materials totalled $46,000, labour payroll costs were $11,000, and manufacturing overhead was $19,000. Completed output was 2,000 units.

The Westplains division uses a backflush costing system that records costs in materials inventory and conversion costs accounts and applies costs to products at the time production is completed. There were no finished goods inventories on January 1 and 20 units on January 31.

1. Prepare journal entries (without explanations) to record January's costs for the Westplains division. Include the purchase of materials, incurrence of labour and manufacturing overhead costs, application of product costs, and recognition of cost of goods sold.
2. Suppose January's actual manufacturing overhead costs had been $21,000 instead of $19,000. Prepare the journal entry to recognize underapplied conversion costs at the end of January.

P7-23 BACKFLUSH COSTING. Audio Components Ltd. recently installed a backflush costing system. One department makes speakers with a standard cost as follows:

Materials	$10.00
Conversion costs	4.20
Total	$14.20

Speakers are scheduled for production only after orders are received, and products are shipped to customers immediately upon completion. Therefore, no finished goods inventories are kept, and product costs are applied directly to cost of goods sold.

In October, 1,500 speakers were produced and shipped to customers. Materials were purchased at a cost of $16,000, and actual conversion costs (labour plus manufacturing overhead) of $6,300 were recorded.

1. Prepare journal entries to record October's costs for the production of speakers.
2. Suppose October's actual conversion costs had been $5,900 instead of $6,300. Prepare a journal entry to recognize overapplied conversion costs.

P7-24 **BASIC OPERATION COSTING.** Study the Appendix to this chapter (page 320). Oak Furniture Co. manufactures a variety of wooden chairs. The company's manufacturing operations and costs applied to products for June were

	CUTTING	ASSEMBLY	FINISHING
Direct labour	$ 60,000	$30,000	$ 96,000
Factory overhead	115,500	37,500	156,000

Three styles of chairs were produced in June. The quantities and direct materials cost were

STYLE	QUANTITY	DIRECT MATERIALS
Standard	6,000	$108,000
Deluxe	4,500	171,000
Unfinished	3,000	66,000

Each unit, regardless of style, required the same cutting and assembly operations. The unfinished chairs, as the name implies, had no finishing operations whatsoever. Standard and deluxe styles required the same finishing operations.

1. Tabulate the total conversion costs of each operation, the total units produced, and the conversion cost per unit.
2. Tabulate the total costs, the units produced, and the cost per unit for each chair type.

P7-25 **OPERATION COSTING WITH ENDING WORK-IN-PROCESS.** Study the Appendix to this chapter. Sonor Instruments Co. uses three operations in sequence to make two models of its depth finders for sport fishing. Consider the following:

	PRODUCTION ORDERS	
	FOR 1,000 STANDARD DEPTH FINDERS	FOR 1,000 DELUXE DEPTH FINDERS
Direct materials (actual costs applied)	$57,000	$100,000
Conversion costs (predetermined costs applied on the basis of machine-hours used)		
Operation 1	19,000	19,000
Operation 2	?	?
Operation 3	–	15,000
Total manufacturing costs applied	$?	$?

1. Operation 2 is highly automated. Product costs depend on a budgeted application rate for conversion costs based on machine hours. The budgeted costs for 2006 were $220,000 direct labour and $580,000 factory overhead. Budgeted machine hours were 20,000. Each depth finder requires 6 minutes of time in Operation 2. Compute the costs of processing 1,000 depth finders in Operation 2.

2. Compute the total manufacturing costs of 1,000 depth finders and the cost per standard depth finder and per deluxe depth finder.

3. Suppose that at the end of the year, 500 standard depth finders were in process through Operation 1 only and 600 deluxe depth finders were in process through Operation 2 only. Compute the cost of the ending work-in-process inventory. Assume that no direct materials are applied in Operation 2, but that $10,000 of the $100,000 direct-materials cost of the deluxe depth finders are applied to each 1,000 depth finders processed in Operation 3.

MANAGERIAL DECISION CASE

C7-1   PROCESS/JOB PRICING.   In February 2001, Randy White, President of Arriscraft Corporation,[2] had just received two requests for a price on two of their marble products. The first request was from a nearby city for 140,000 square feet, or approximately 2,000 tonnes, of paving stones. The second request was from a construction firm in Ohio, which requested a price on 3,000 tonnes of window sills of varying sizes. While White was confident that a price of $300 a tonne for the paving stones and $500 a tonne for the window sills would result in Arriscraft receiving the orders, he was unsure that these prices would result in a reasonable profit.

COMPANY BACKGROUND

Arriscraft
www.arriscraft.com

Arriscraft was established in Cambridge, Ontario, in 1949 by E. B. Ratcliffe, a chemical engineer, to produce precast stones. In 1956, he developed a unique worldwide process that compressed sand into stone without the use of cement. The result was a stone that was more durable than the normal clay bricks or other masonry products and that could be formed into a variety of shapes, sizes, colours, and textures.

In 1962, Arriscraft added a second product line that involved the cutting of limestone blocks from a quarry near Wiarton, Ontario, and the production of marble hearth slabs and window sills in Cambridge. In 1980, additional marble products, of paving stones and building stones, were added to the line. These marble products are sold under the trade name of Adair Marble.

As of 2001, the company was the only producer of manufactured stones in the world and was Canada's largest producer of marble products, with only one smaller competitor located in Winnipeg, Manitoba. Recently Arriscraft had been successful in obtaining some significant contracts that included supplying the marble stone for the Canadian Chancery in Washington, the Ontario Court House and Registry Office in Ottawa, and the reconstruction of the Rideau Canal locks. With these and other contracts, Arriscraft had established a reputation

---

[2] For subsequent developments with respect to Arriscraft (now known as Arriscraft International Income Fund), see the Strategic Insights and Company Practices box on page 150 in Chapter 4.

among architects and contractors as a leading producer of unique and top-quality stone products.

White had been with the company for nine years, after graduating from Queen's University with a degree in commerce and obtaining his Chartered Accountant designation. During his nine years, White held the positions of controller, executive vice president, and president. With this experience, he was fully aware of both the financial and technical implications of the various alternatives that he faced. In particular, he was acutely aware that the variability of the yields and product mix significantly complicated any analyses of product-line profitability.

PRODUCTION PROCESS

As the decisions facing White concerned marble products, only the production process related to these products will be described. Exhibit 7-1A illustrates the following description of this process.

First, limestone blocks are drilled and cut from a quarry. The top surface of the quarry is the side of the block; the dimensions are 75 centimetres by 210 centimetres. The depth of the block will vary depending upon the natural bed depth of the quarry, but lengths vary from 1 to 3 metres. The net results are limestone blocks that vary in size from 4 to 12 metric tonnes, with an average size being approximately 8 tonnes. These limestone blocks are then trucked to Arriscraft's plant. The total direct cost of the limestone blocks is approximately $50 per tonne, which includes the removal and transportation costs.

At the plant, each limestone block is positioned in front of a saw, which first cuts off two sides. These cuts will remove approximately 1 tonne of waste from an average 8-tonne block, leaving 7 tonnes. Next, the saw operator must make a series of critical judgment calls as he or she cuts the limestone block into slices called product blocks. The saw operator must examine the face of the stone for cracks, pits, or other faults. If any are found, a cut approximately 20 centimetres wide will be made and the product block will be further processed into paving stones. If the limestone block is reasonably clear of faults, then a 15 centimetre cut will be made and the product block will be produced into window sills. If the stone is of highest quality, then cuts varying from 6 to 75 centimetres will be made to produce specialized products and hearth slabs. A fourth product line is referred to as large units, where the quality may be low and these sections would otherwise be used for paving stones. However, if a wider cut is made, the stone can be used in place of some top-quality large pieces for some specific applications. The skill of the saw operator is extremely important, as a limestone block will normally produce many grades of products, and thus a judgment call is required after each cut is made. The cutting of the limestone block into product blocks results in an 80 percent yield of the 7 tonnes, and the cutting costs per tonne of product block vary for each of the four product lines as follows:

Paving stones	$14 per tonne
Window sills	$15 per tonne
Hearth slabs	$10 per tonne
Large units	$12 per tonne

While a variance of 10 to 15 percent exists, it is expected that 10 percent of the product block tonnage will be in paving stones, 40 percent in window sills, 40 percent in hearth slabs, and 10 percent in large units.

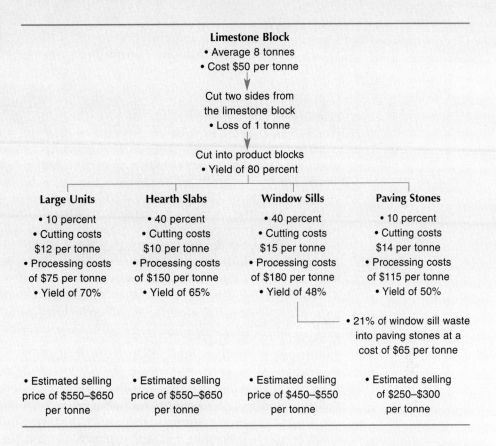

Limestone Block
- Average 8 tonnes
- Cost $50 per tonne

Cut two sides from
the limestone block
- Loss of 1 tonne

Cut into product blocks
- Yield of 80 percent

Large Units	**Hearth Slabs**	**Window Sills**	**Paving Stones**
• 10 percent	• 40 percent	• 40 percent	• 10 percent
• Cutting costs $12 per tonne	• Cutting costs $10 per tonne	• Cutting costs $15 per tonne	• Cutting costs $14 per tonne
• Processing costs of $75 per tonne	• Processing costs of $150 per tonne	• Processing costs of $180 per tonne	• Processing costs of $115 per tonne
• Yield of 70%	• Yield of 65%	• Yield of 48%	• Yield of 50%

• 21% of window sill waste into paving stones at a cost of $65 per tonne

• Estimated selling price of $550–$650 per tonne	• Estimated selling price of $550–$650 per tonne	• Estimated selling price of $450–$550 per tonne	• Estimated selling of $250–$300 per tonne

The processing of the product blocks into their designated final products first involves some additional sawing and splitting. Then, depending upon the quality of the final product, the stones are honed (smoothed) to produce the marble product. The extent of the processing varies by product line and the ultimate yield will also vary by product line. The paving stones have a 50 percent yield and the processing costs total $115 per tonne of finished product. The window sills have a yield of 48 percent with a processing cost of $180 per tonne of finished product. The waste from the window sills can be used for paving stones, and after a further processing cost of $65 per tonne of finished product, a yield of 21 percent of the waste is obtained. The hearth slabs are processed for a cost of $150 per tonne of finished product, which is a 65 percent yield of the product blocks. The large units result in a yield of 70 percent for a processing cost of $75 per finished tonne.

The above description is the typical production process; however, it is possible to produce paving stones and window sills from higher-grade material. While the cutting and processing costs for the paving stones and window sills would remain the same, the yields would increase as follows. Window sills may be cut from the material that would normally be used for hearth slabs and large units and the yields would increase by 10 percentage points to 75 percent and 80 percent respectively. Similarly, paving stones may be cut from window-sill, hearth-slab, and large-unit materials with a 15 percentage point increase in yields to 63 percent, 80 percent, and 85 percent respectively. In addition, the cutting of paving stones from window sill waste would increase to 31 percent. White was, however, concerned that this alternate production process would not yield satisfactory profit margins.

SITUATION SUMMARY

White had been faced many times with similar situations like those before him now. If 2,000 tonnes of paving stones are produced by means of the normal production process, more than the required quantities of window sills must also be produced. Furthermore, product blocks that will eventually be produced into hearth slabs and large units must also be cut even though they are not currently required. However, if the limestone blocks were cut into only paving stones, only window sills, or both paving stones and window sills, the higher-quality material would be used where lower-quality material would meet the customer requirements. The market for these marble products was somewhat unpredictable as the orders tended to be large and depended essentially upon the preferences of an architect or contractor. While Arriscraft did not have any direct competition, there was competition from companies that used less expensive alternative building products. For example, the paving stones will cost the city $4.29 a square foot, whereas interlocking brick (an alternative cement-based product) would cost $1 to $2 a square metre. The issue was essentially how much more the market was willing to pay for a marble product than for a more common alternative.

Given the common costs of the limestone block and the cutting, White also wondered whether a price of $300 per tonne of paving stones and $500 per tonne of window sills would generate sufficient profits. As a rule of thumb, the company historically attempted to attain a markup of 100 percent on the direct product costs. Typically, a markup of less than 70 percent was viewed as unprofitable. However, in a situation such as this, the measurement of the direct costs by product line was not straightforward. Furthermore, the unsold product, both finished and unfinished, had always presented a problem when costing the inventory for Arriscraft's annual financial report. Depending upon the approach adopted, the costing of the inventory could have a material effect on the net income.

Required: As Randy White, would you bid on both of the orders and, if so, at what price? Explain your reasoning.

EXCEL APPLICATION EXERCISE

E7-1 VALUE OF UNITS PRODUCED

Goal: Create an Excel spreadsheet to compute the value of units produced utilizing the weighted-average process costing method. Use the results to answer questions about your findings.

Scenario: The Magnatto Company has asked you to compute costs for the electric drills produced in their Assembly Department during the month of July. You will need to use the weighted-average process costing method to determine costs for beginning WIP, completed units and ending WIP.

The Magnatto Company manufactures electric drills. Material is introduced at the beginning of the process in the assembly department. Conversion costs are applied uniformly throughout the process. As the process is completed, goods are immediately transferred to the finishing department.

Data for the assembly department for the month of July 2006 follow:

Work-in-process, June 30: $175,500 (consisting of $138,000 materials and $37,500 conversion costs); 100% completed for direct materials, but only 25% completed for conversion costs	10,000 units
Units started during July	80,000 units
Units completed during July	70,000 units
Work-in-process, July 31, 100% completed for direct materials, but only 50% completed for conversion costs:	20,000 units
Direct materials added during July	$852,000
Conversion costs added during July	$634,500

When you have completed your spreadsheet, answer the following questions:

1. At the end of July, what is the value of the 20,000 units remaining in the WIP ending inventory?
2. What were the materials, conversion, and total cost of goods amounts for the units transferred to the finishing department during the month of July?
3. What are the materials and conversion cost per unit amounts for the accumulated units and costs in July?

Step by Step:

1. Open a new Excel spreadsheet.

2. In column A, create a bold-faced heading that contains the following:
   Row 1: Chapter 14 Decision Guideline
   Row 2: Magnatto Company
   Row 3: Weighted-Average Process Costing for July, 2006
   Row 4: Today's Date

3. Merge and centre the four heading rows across columns A through K.

4. In row 7, create the following column headings justified as indicated:
   Column B: Number   Centre-justify
   Column C: Percent Complete   Merge and centre across columns C and D
   Column E: Equivalent Units   Merge and centre across columns E and F
   Column G: Cost of Goods   Merge and centre across columns G through I
   Column J: Cost per Unit   Merge and centre across columns J and K

5. In row 8, create the following centre-justified column headings:
   Column B: of Units
   Columns C, E, G, and J: Materials
   Columns D, F, H, and K: Conversion
   Column I: Total

6. In column A, create the following row headings:
   Row 9: Beginning WIP
   Skip a row
   Row 11: Units Started
   Row 12: Less: Ending Units
   Row 13: Units Started & Completed in July

Row 14: Beginning Units Completed
Skip a row
Row 16: Accumulated Units & Costs in July
Skip a row
Row 18: Value of Transferred Units

Note: Recommended column widths:
Column A = 28
Column B = 7
Columns C, E, and J = 8
Columns D, F, G, H, and K = 9
Column I = 11

7. Format columns C and D as
Number tab: Category: Percentage
                     Decimal places: 0

8. Use data from above to enter the following amounts:
Beginning WIP: units, percent complete, cost
                                          of goods

Units Started: units
Less: Ending Units: units, percent complete
Accumulated Units & Costs in July: cost of goods for materials
                                          and conversion

Value of Transferred Units: units

9. Calculate the following amounts:
Units Started & Completed in July: units, percent complete
Beginning Units Completed: units, percent complete

10. In the sequence listed, use formulas to calculate the following amounts:
Equivalent units for: Beginning WIP
                                 Less: Ending Units
                                 Units Started & Completed in July
                                 Beginning Units Completed
                                 Accumulated Units & Costs in July
Cost per unit for: Beginning WIP
                                 Accumulated Units & Costs in July
Materials cost of goods for: Less: Ending Units
                                 Units Started & Completed in July
                                 Beginning Units Completed
                                 Value of Transferred Units
Conversion cost of goods for: Less: Ending Units
                                 Units Started & Completed in July
                                 Beginning Units Completed
                                 Value of Transferred Units
Total cost of goods for: Less: Ending Units
                                 Units Started & Completed in July
                                 Beginning Units Completed
                                 Accumulated Units & Costs in July
                                 Value of Transferred Units
Cost per unit for: Value of Transferred Units

11. Format columns B, E, F, G, H, and I as
    Number tab: Category: Number
                            Decimal places: 0
                            Use 1000 Separator (,): Checked
                            Negative numbers: Red with parentheses

12. Format columns J and K as
    Number tab: Category: Currency
                            Decimal places: 2
                            Symbol: $
                            Negative numbers: Red with parentheses

13. Format the cost of goods rows 9, 12, 16, and 18 as
    Number tab: Category: Accounting
                            Decimal places: 0
                            Symbol: $

14. Modify the format of column B, rows 13 and 18, and row 16, columns E through I to display a top border using the default Line Style.
    Border tab: Icon: Top Border

15. Modify the format of row 7, columns C, D, G, H, and I, and row 8, columns E, F, J, and K to display with a light grey fill.
    Patterns tab: Colour: Lightest Grey (above white)

16. Save your work to disk, and print a copy for your files.

    Note: Print your spreadsheet using landscape in order to ensure that all columns appear on one page.

COLLABORATIVE LEARNING EXERCISE

CL7-1 JOB, PROCESS, AND HYBRID COSTING. Form groups of three to six students. For each of the following production processes, assess whether a job-cost, process-cost, or hybrid-cost system is most likely to be used to determine the cost of the product or service. Also, explain why you think that system is most logical. (This can be done by individuals, but it is a much richer experience when done as a group, because the knowledge and judgment of several interact to produce a better analysis than can a single student.)

    a. Production of Cheerios by General Mills.
    b. Production of a sport utility vehicle by Toyota.
    c. Processing an application for life insurance by Clarica.
    d. Production of a couch by Kroehler.
    e. Building of a bridge by Kiewit Construction Co.
    f. Production of gasoline by Petro Canada.
    g. Production of 200 copies of a 140-page course packet by Kinko's.
    h. Production of a superferry by Todd Shipyards.

8

Relevant Information and Decision Making: Marketing Decisions

After studying this chapter, you will be able to

1. Discriminate between relevant and irrelevant information for making decisions.

2. Analyze data by the contribution approach to support a decision for accepting or rejecting a special sales order.

3. Explain the potential pitfalls of using a total unit-cost approach for predicting the effect of a special order on operating income.

4. Analyze data by the relevant-information approach to support a decision for adding or deleting a product line.

5. Compute product profitability when production is constrained by a scarce resource.

6. Identify the role of costs in pricing decisions in perfect and imperfect markets.

7. Discuss the factors that influence pricing decisions.

8. Identify contribution margin and absorption costing advantages and disadvantages.

9. Use target costing to decide whether to add a new product or service.

Zellers
www.hbc.com/zellers

Loblaws
www.loblaws.ca

Boeing
www.boeing.com

What price should Loblaws stores charge for a kilogram of hamburger? What should Boeing charge for a 767 airplane? Should a clothing manufacturer accept a special order from Zellers at a price lower than that generally charged? Should an appliance manufacturer add a new product to its product line? Should an existing product be dropped? Which product makes the best use of a particular limited resource? These questions relate to the marketing strategy of a firm, and accounting information can play an important role in answering each of them.

At the start of this book, we emphasized that the purpose of management accounting is to provide information that enables managers to make sound decisions. This chapter focuses primarily on marketing decisions and, more specifically, on identifying *relevant information* for particular management decisions.[1] Although the word "relevant" has been overused in recent years, the ability to separate relevant from irrelevant information is often the difference between success and failure in modern business.

THE MEANING OF RELEVANCE: THE MAJOR CONCEPTUAL LESSON

OBJECTIVE 1

Discriminate between relevant and irrelevant information for making decisions.

Relevant Information. The predicted future costs and revenues that will differ among alternative courses of action.

What information is relevant depends on the decision being made. As described in Chapter 1, decision making is choosing among several courses of action. The available actions are determined by an often time-consuming search and screening process, perhaps carried on by a company team that includes engineers, accountants, and other executives.

The decision is based on the difference in the effect of each alternative on future performance. The key question is, What difference will the choice make? **Relevant information** is the predicted future costs and revenues that will differ among the alternatives.

Note that relevant information is a prediction of the future, not a summary of the past. Historical (past) data have no *direct* bearing on a decision. Such data can have an *indirect* bearing on a decision because they may help in predicting the future, but past figures are irrelevant to the decision. Why? Because the decision cannot affect past data—decisions affect the future. Nothing can alter what has already happened.

Of the expected future data, only those that will differ from alternative to alternative are relevant to the decision. Any item that will remain the same regardless of the alternative selected is irrelevant. For instance, if a department manager's salary will be the same regardless of the products stocked, the salary is irrelevant to the selection of products kept in inventories.

Accuracy and Relevance

In the best of all possible worlds, information used for decision making would be both relevant and accurate. However, in reality, the cost of obtaining such information often exceeds its benefit. Accountants often trade off accuracy for relevance. Of course, relevant information must be reasonably accurate, but not precisely so.

Precise but irrelevant information is worthless for decision making. For example, a company president's salary may be $240,000 per year but may have no bearing on the decision of whether to buy or rent a new mainframe computer. On the other hand, imprecise but relevant information can be useful. For

---

[1] Throughout this and the next chapter, in order to concentrate on the fundamental ideas we shall ignore the time value of money and income taxes (discussed in Chapter 10).

example, sales predictions for a new product may be subject to great error, but they still are helpful in deciding whether to manufacture the product.

The degree to which information is relevant and/or precise often depends on the degree to which it is *qualitative* and/or *quantitative*. Qualitative aspects are those for which measurement in dollars and cents is difficult and imprecise; quantitative aspects are those for which measurement is easier and more precise. Accountants, statisticians, and mathematicians try to express as many decision factors as feasible in quantitative terms, since this approach reduces the number of qualitative factors to be judged. Just as we noted that relevance is more crucial than precision in decision making, so a qualitative aspect may easily carry more weight than a measurable (quantitative) financial impact in many decisions. For example, the opposition of a militant union to new labour-saving machinery may cause a manager to defer or even reject completely the contemplated installation even if it would save money. Or, to avoid a long-run dependence on a particular supplier, a company may pass up the opportunity to purchase a component from the supplier at a lower price but at larger quantities that will eliminate all other suppliers.

On the other hand, managers sometimes introduce new technology even though the expected quantitative results seem unattractive. Managers defend such decisions on the grounds that failure to keep abreast of new technology will undercut competitiveness and eventually bring unfavourable financial results.

Examples of Relevance

The following examples will help you clarify the sharp distinctions between relevant and irrelevant information.

Suppose you always buy gasoline from either of two nearby gasoline stations. Yesterday you noticed that one station was selling gasoline at $0.90 per litre; the other, at $0.85 per litre. Your automobile needs gasoline, and in making your choice of stations, you *assume* that these prices have not changed. The relevant costs are $0.90 and $0.85, the expected future costs that will differ between the alternatives. You use your past experience (i.e., what you observed yesterday) for predicting today's price. Note that the relevant cost is not what you paid in the past, or what you observed yesterday, but what you *expect to pay* when you drive in to get gasoline. This cost meets our two criteria: (1) it is the expected future cost, and (2) it differs between the alternatives.

You may also plan to have your car's oil changed. The recent price at each station was $25, and this is what you expect to pay. This expected future cost is irrelevant because it will be the same under either alternative. It does not meet our second criterion.

On a business level, consider the following decision. A manufacturer is thinking of using aluminum instead of copper in a product line. The cost of direct material will decrease from $1.00 to $0.80 The analysis in a nutshell is

	ALUMINUM	COPPER	DIFFERENCE
Direct materials	$0.80	$1.00	$0.20

The cost of copper used for this comparison probably came from historical-cost records on the amount paid most recently for copper, but the *relevant* costs in the foregoing analysis are the *expected future* costs for copper compared to the expected future cost of aluminum.

The direct labour cost, whatever it may be, will continue regardless of the material used. It is irrelevant because our second criterion—an element of difference between the alternatives—is not met.

Therefore, we can safely exclude direct labour from the comparison of the alternative. There is no harm in including irrelevant items in a formal analysis, provided that they are included properly. For example, provided that direct labour is $2.00 regardless of the material used, the total cost difference between using aluminum or copper is still $0.20 ($3.00 – $2.80).

	ALUMINUM	COPPER	DIFFERENCE
Direct materials	$0.80	$1.00	$0.20
Direct labour	$2.00	$2.00	–
Total	$2.80	$3.00	$0.20

However, confining reports to the relevant items only provides greater clarity and time savings for managers.

Exhibit 8-1 provides a more elaborate view than is necessary for this simple decision, but it serves to show the appropriate framework for more complex

The decision is whether to use aluminum instead of copper.
The objective is to minimize costs.

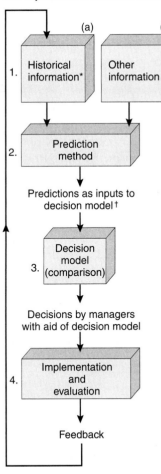

1. Historical direct material costs for copper were $1.00 per unit. Direct labour costs were $2.00 per unit and will not be affected by the switch to aluminum.

2. Use the information as a basis for predicting the future costs of direct material and direct labour. Direct material unit costs are expected to be $0.80 for aluminum and $1.00 for copper.

3. COST COMPARISON PER UNIT

	Aluminum	Copper	Difference
Direct material	$0.80	$1.00	$0.20

The outputs of the prediction method (that is, the expected future costs) together with other quantitative and qualitative information are the inputs of the decision model.

4. The chosen action (to use aluminum) is implemented. Performance evaluation and feedback is used to update historical information and improve the prediction method and the decision model in general.

* Historical data may be relevant for prediction methods.

† Historical data are never relevant *per se* for decision models. Only those expected future data that differ between alternatives are really relevant. For instance, in this example, direct material makes a difference and direct labour does not. Therefore, *under our definition here*, direct labour is irrelevant.

decisions. Box 1(a) represents historical data from the accounting system. Box 1(b) represents other data, such as price indices or industry statistics, gathered from outside the accounting system. Regardless of their source, the data in Step 1 help the formulation of *predictions* in Step 2. (Remember that while historical data may act as a guide to predicting, they are irrelevant to the decision.)

Decision Model. Any method for making a choice, sometimes requiring elaborate quantitative procedures.

In Step 3 the predictions become inputs to the *decision model*. A **decision model** is defined as any method for making a choice. Such models often require elaborate quantitative procedures. But a decision model may also be simple. It may be confined to a single comparison of costs for choosing between two materials. In this instance, our decision model is to compare the predicted unit costs and select the alternative with the lower cost. Step 4 consists of the implementation and evaluation of the chosen alternative.

Managers should focus on predictions for future outcomes, not dwell on past outcomes. The major difficulty is predicting how revenue and costs will be affected under each alternative; the key question to ask is, What difference will it make?

DECISION: ACCEPT OR REJECT A SPECIAL SALES ORDER

OBJECTIVE 2

Analyze data by the contribution approach to support a decision for accepting or rejecting a special sales order.

Exhibit 8-2 illustrates the primary data for the Samson Company. As you can see, the two income statements in absorption and contribution forms differ somewhat in format. The difference in format may be unimportant if the accompanying cost analysis leads to the same set of decisions. But these two approaches sometimes lead to different *unit* costs that must be interpreted warily.

In our illustration, suppose one million units of product were made and sold. Under the absorption-costing approach, the unit manufacturing cost would be $15,000,000 ÷ 1,000,000 units, or $15 per unit. Suppose a mail-order house near year-end offered Samson $13 per unit for a 100,000-unit special order. The special order is not expected to affect Samson's regular business in any way, or to increase total fixed costs or variable selling and administrative expenses. In addition, the special order would use some otherwise idle manufacturing capacity. Should Samson accept the order? Perhaps the question should be stated more sharply. What is the difference in the short-run financial results between not accepting and accepting the special order? What difference, if any, will it make in the contribution margin and/or operating income?

EXHIBIT 8-2

Samson Company Absorption and Contribution Forms of the Income Statement for the Year Ended December 31, 2006 (in thousands of dollars)

ABSORPTION FORM			CONTRIBUTION FORM			
Sales		$20,000	Sales			$20,000
Less: manufacturing cost of			Less: variable expenses:			
goods sold		15,000	Manufacturing		$12,000	
Gross margin or gross profit		5,000	Selling and administrative		1,100	13,100
Less: selling and			Contribution margin			$ 6,900
administrative expenses		4,000				
Operating income		$ 1,000	Less: fixed expenses:			
			Manufacturing		$ 3,000	
			Selling and			
			administrative		2,900	5,900
			Operating income			$ 1,000

Correct Analysis

The correct analysis in answering the special-order question should employ the contribution approach and concentrate on the final *overall* results. As Exhibit 8-3 shows, only variable manufacturing costs are affected by the particular order, at a rate of $12 per unit ($12,000,000 ÷ 1,000,000 units). All other variable costs and all fixed costs are unaffected so a manager may safely ignore them in making this special order decision. The contribution-approach-based income statement indicates that both contribution margin and operating income will increase by $100,000 if the order is accepted. This operating income increase occurs despite the fact that the unit selling price of $13 is less than the absorption manufacturing cost of $15.

Exhibit 8-3 includes total fixed expenses. There is no harm in including such irrelevant items in an analysis as long as they are included in a correct manner, that is, under every alternative at hand. A fixed-cost element of an identical amount that is common among all alternatives is essentially irrelevant. Whether irrelevant items should be included in an analysis is a matter of taste, not a matter of right or wrong.

MAKING MANAGERIAL DECISIONS

Suppose you are at a meeting of Samson Company managers and someone asks the following questions. Some of the answers given by your colleagues follow.

Q: What will be the change in the contribution margin if we accept this order?

A: The contribution margin will increase to $7,000,000.

Q: In your analysis (Exhibit 8-3), you show that fixed costs do not change if we accept the order. Are these costs relevant?

A: No. Fixed costs are not relevant.

Q: OK. But do fixed costs that we incur have an effect on the bottom line of our company?

A: Certainly. That is why we deduct fixed costs from the contribution margin to get operating income.

Q. Well, if fixed costs affect the bottom line, how can you say they are not relevant?

Comment on your colleague's answers, and answer the last question.

ANSWER

Your colleague's answer to the first question is technically incorrect. The question asks for change, not the new total contribution margin. The correct answer to this question is that contribution margin will increase by $100,000 (and therefore to $7,000,000). We need to be very careful when answering questions to be sure to differentiate between terms that imply totals and terms that imply changes. In this case, $7,000,000 is the answer to "What is the new total contribution margin if we accept the order?"

Your colleague's responses to the second and third questions are correct. The fixed costs of Samson are not relevant for this particular special-order situation. Nevertheless, the bottom line includes all costs or *total* costs and revenues. Do not confuse this with the *relevant costs*—a term we associated with this specific decision. In a decision situation, relevant costs include only those future costs that will differ if we accept the order. If a manager wants to know the "bottom line" after accepting the order, we would need to include the fixed costs. However, the fixed costs do not affect the *difference* between the pre-order bottom line and the bottom line after accepting the order. The difference is the same $100,000 amount by which the contribution margin increases.

EXHIBIT 8-3

Samson Company Predicted Income Statement with Special Order, Contribution Approach for the Year Ended December 31, 2006

	WITHOUT SPECIAL ORDER 1,000,000 UNITS	EFFECT OF SPECIAL ORDER 100,000 UNITS TOTAL	EFFECT OF SPECIAL ORDER 100,000 UNITS PER UNIT	WITH SPECIAL ORDER 1,100,000 UNITS
Sales	$20,000,000	$1,300,000	$13	$21,300,000
Less: variable expenses:				
Manufacturing	12,000,000	1,200,000	12	13,200,000
Selling and administrative	1,100,000	–	–	1,100,000
Total variable expenses	13,100,000	1,200,000	12	14,300,000
Contribution margin	6,900,000	100,000	1	7,000,000
Less: fixed expenses:				
Manufacturing	3,000,000	–	–	3,000,000
Selling and administrative	2,900,000	–	–	2,900,000
Total fixed expenses	5,900,000	–	–	5,900,000
Operating income	$ 1,000,000	$ 100,000	$ 1	$ 1,100,000

Incorrect Analysis

OBJECTIVE 3

Explain the potential pitfalls of using a total unit-cost approach for predicting the effect of a special order on operating income.

Faulty cost analysis sometimes occurs because of misinterpreting unit fixed costs. Managers might erroneously use the $15 absorption manufacturing cost per unit to make the prediction for the year (Exhibit 8-4).

The $1.5 million increase in manufacturing costs as a result of accepting the special order is in error. The fallacy in this approach is that it treats fixed manufacturing costs of $3,000,000 as if they were variable. The fixed manufacturing costs of $3,000,000 will not increase as a result of accepting the special order. Unit costs are useful for predicting variable costs, but often are misleading when used to predict fixed costs.

Consider the relationship between total fixed manufacturing costs and a fixed manufacturing cost per unit of product:

$$\text{fixed cost per unit of product} = \frac{\text{total fixed manufacturing costs}}{\text{some selected volume level used as the denominator}}$$

$$= \frac{\$3,000,000}{1,000,000 \text{ units}} = \$3 \text{ per unit}$$

EXHIBIT 8-4

Samson Company Predicted Income Statement with Special Order Absorption Approach for the Year Ended December 31, 2006

	WITHOUT SPECIAL ORDER 1,000,000 UNITS	INCORRECT EFFECT OF SPECIAL ORDER 100,000 UNITS	WITH SPECIAL ORDER 1,100,000 UNITS
Sales	$20,000,000	$1,300,000	$21,300,000
Less: manufacturing cost of goods sold @ $15	15,000,000	1,500,000	16,500,000
Gross margin	5,000,000	(200,000)	4,800,000
Selling and administrative expenses	4,000,000	–	4,000,000
Operating income	$ 1,000,000	$ (200,000)	$ 800,000

As noted in Chapter 2, the typical cost accounting system serves two purposes simultaneously: *planning and control* and *product costing*. The total fixed cost for *budgetary planning* and *control purposes* can be graphed as a lump sum:

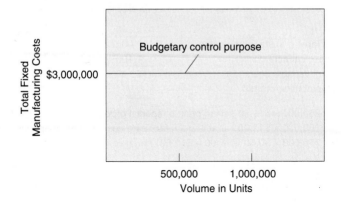

For *product-costing purposes*, however, the absorption-costing approach implies that these *fixed* costs have a *variable*-cost behaviour pattern:

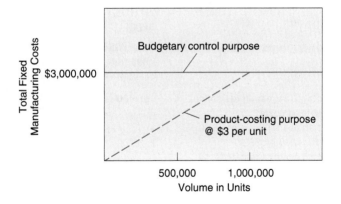

The addition of 100,000 units will *not* add any *total* fixed costs as long as total output is within the relevant range. However, incorrect analysis includes an addition of $100,000 \times \$3 = \$300,000$ of fixed cost.

In short, the increase in manufacturing costs should be computed by multiplying 100,000 units by $12, not by $15. The $15 includes a $3 component that will not affect the total manufacturing costs as volume changes.

Total Fixed Costs versus Spreading Unit Fixed Costs

As we have just seen, the unit cost–total cost distinction can become particularly troublesome when analyzing fixed-cost behaviour. Assume the same facts concerning the special order as before, except that the order was for 250,000 units at a selling price of $11.50. The analytical pitfalls of unit-cost analysis can be avoided by using the contribution approach and concentrating on totals (in thousands of dollars) instead of units:

	WITHOUT SPECIAL ORDER	EFFECT OF SPECIAL ORDER	WITH SPECIAL ORDER
	1,000,000 UNITS	250,000 UNITS	1,250,000 UNITS
Sales	$20,000	$2,875*	$22,875
Variable manufacturing costs	12,000	3,000†	15,000
Other variable costs	1,100	–	1,100
Total variable costs	13,100	3,000	16,100
Contribution margin	$ 6,900	$ (125)‡	$ 6,775

* 250,000 × $11.50 selling price of special order.
† 250,000 × $12.00 variable manufacturing cost per unit of special order.
‡ 250,000 × $0.50 ($12.00 − $11.50) negative contribution margin per unit of special order.

Short-run income will fall by $125,000 (that is, 250,000 units × $0.50) if the special order is accepted. No matter how the fixed manufacturing costs are "spread" over the units produced, at $3,000,000 ÷ 1,000,000 units = $3 or at $3,000,000 ÷ 1,250,000 units = $2.40, the total of $3 million will be *unchanged* by the special order (in thousands of dollars):

	WITHOUT SPECIAL ORDER	EFFECT OF SPECIAL ORDER	WITH SPECIAL ORDER
	1,000,000 UNITS	250,000 UNITS	1,250,000 UNITS
Contribution margin (as above)	$6,900	$ (125)	$6,775
Total fixed costs:			
At an average rate of $3.00:			
1,000,000 × $3.00	3,000		
At an average rate of $2.40:			
1,250,000 × $2.40		–	3,000
Contribution to other fixed costs			
and operating income	$3,900	$ (125)	$3,775

No matter how fixed costs are spread for *unit* product-costing purposes, *total* fixed costs are unchanged, even though fixed costs *per unit* fall from $3.00 to $2.40.

The lesson here is important. Do not be deceived. Whatever problem you are studying, start by looking at the total costs. Beware of unit costs, especially when analyzing fixed costs. When in doubt, convert all unit costs into the total costs under each alternative to get the big picture. Think in terms of totals instead.

Multiple Cost Drivers and Special Orders

To identify costs affected by a special order (or by other special decisions) more and more firms are going a step beyond simply identifying fixed and variable costs. As pointed out in Chapter 3, many different cost drivers may cause companies to incur costs. Firms that have identified all their significant cost drivers can predict the effects of special orders more accurately.

Suppose Samson Company examined its $12 million of variable costs very closely and identified two significant cost drivers: $9 million that varies directly with *units produced* at a rate of $9 per unit and $3 million that varies with the *number of production setups*. Normally, for production of 1,000,000 units, Samson has 500 setups, with an average of 2,000 units produced for each setup at a cost of $6,000 per setup. Additional sales generally require a proportional increase in the number of setups.

Now suppose the special order is for 100,000 units that vary only slightly in production specifications. Instead of the normal 50 setups (100,000 units ÷ 2,000 units per average setup), Samson will need only five setups. Therefore, to produce 100,000 units, $930,000 of additional variable costs will be required.

Additional unit-based variable cost 100,000 × $9	$900,000
Additional setup-based variable cost 5 × $6,000	30,000
Total additional variable cost	$930,000

Instead of the original estimate of 100,000 × $12 = $1,200,000 additional variable cost, the special order will cost only $930,000, or $270,000 less than the original estimate. Therefore, the special order is $270,000 more profitable than predicted from the simple, unit-based assessment of variable cost.

A special order may also be more costly than predicted by a simple fixed/variable-cost analysis. Suppose the 100,000-unit special order called for a

MAKING MANAGERIAL DECISIONS

We have presented two key lessons so far in this chapter: relevant information and misuse of unit costs. We cannot stress enough how important it is to clearly understand the definition and concept of relevant information. It is also important to understand why the use of unit fixed costs can lead to an incorrect analysis.

Suppose you are a manager in a company that makes small appliances. You are deciding whether to accept or reject a special order for 1,000 units. (Assume there is sufficient capacity available for the order.)

1. Which of the following costs are relevant: (a) parts for the order, (b) supervisor's salary, (c) hourly wages of assembly workers, (d) assembly equipment amortization, (e) power to operate the assembly equipment? (Note: These are not all of the costs that would be involved in the manufacturing operations. What other costs can you think of?)

2. Suppose the total unit manufacturing cost for the 1,000 units is $100 per unit. We determined this amount by dividing the total cost by 1,000 units. If the customer decided to double the order to 2,000 units, which costs listed in number 1 would change? Which costs *per unit* would change? Would the total cost of the order double?

ANSWERS

1. Relevant costs and revenues are predicted future costs and revenues that differ among alternative courses of action. In this case, the total cost of parts, the total wage costs of hourly paid assembly workers, and the total cost of power will increase if management accepts the order, and thus they are relevant.

2. The relevant costs are variable costs since, by definition, the *total* amount of these costs will change with production levels, even though the variable cost per unit will not change. In contrast, *total* fixed costs will not change, though fixed costs *per unit* will decrease. The total number of units to which these fixed costs are allocated is larger. For example, fixed supervisory salaries will be divided by 2,000 units instead of by 1,000 units. As a result, while variable costs per unit will stay the same, total cost per unit will decrease, since a smaller amount of fixed costs will be allocated to each unit. The *total* cost of the order won't double, even though double the number of units is ordered, because the total won't change for fixed costs.

variety of models and colours delivered at various times, so that 100 setups are required. The variable cost of the special order would be $1.5 million:

Additional unit-based variable cost, 100,000 × $9	$ 900,000
Additional setup-based variable cost, 100 × $6,000	600,000
Total additional variable cost	$1,500,000

DECISION: DELETING OR ADDING PRODUCTS OR DEPARTMENTS

OBJECTIVE 4

Analyze data by the relevant-information approach to support a decision for adding or deleting a product line.

The same principles of relevance applied to special orders are also in effect—albeit in slightly different ways—to decisions about adding or deleting products for departments. Consider a discount department store that has three major departments: groceries, general merchandise, and drugs. Management is considering dropping the grocery department, which has consistently shown a net loss. The following income statement (in thousands of dollars) reports the present annual net income.

	TOTAL	GROCERIES	DEPARTMENTS GENERAL MERCHANDISE	DRUGS
Sales	$1,900	$1,000	$ 800	$100
Variable cost of goods sold and expenses*	1,420	800	560	60
Contribution margin	$ 480 (25.3%)	$ 200 (20%)	$ 240 (30%)	$ 40 (40%)
Fixed expenses (salaries, amortization, insurance, property taxes, etc.):				
Avoidable	$ 265	$ 150	$ 100	$ 15
Unavoidable	180	60	100	20
Total fixed expenses	$ 445	$ 210	$ 200	$ 35
Operating income	$ 35	$ (10)	$ 40	$ 5

(handwritten annotations: "$50,000 Loss", "Arbitrary Allocation")

* Examples of variable expenses include paper bags and sales commissions.

Notice that the fixed expenses are divided into two categories, *avoidable* and *unavoidable*. **Avoidable costs**—costs that will *not* continue if an ongoing operation is changed or deleted—are relevant. Avoidable costs include department salaries and other costs that could be eliminated by not operating the specific department. **Unavoidable costs**—costs that continue even if an operation is halted—are not relevant because they are not affected by a decision to delete the department. Unavoidable costs include many **common costs**, which are defined as those costs of facilities and services that are shared by various users. Examples are store amortization, heating, air conditioning, and general management expenses.[2]

Avoidable Costs. Costs that will not continue if an ongoing operation is changed or deleted.

Unavoidable Costs. Costs that continue even if an operation is halted.

Common Costs. The costs of facilities and services that are shared by various users.

---

[2] The concept of avoidable cost is used by government regulators as well as business executives. For example, VIA Rail divides its costs into avoidable—costs that would "cease if the route were eliminated"—and fixed—costs that would "remain relatively constant if a single route were discontinued." The Canadian government looks at the avoidable costs that wouldn't exist if the train disappeared tomorrow—things like staff salaries, food, fuel, and upkeep of train stations—when considering approval of requests to abandon a rail route and/or determining the amount of subsidy to give to the country's passenger-rail system.

Assume first that the only alternatives to be considered are dropping or continuing the grocery department. Assume further that the total assets invested would be unaffected by the decision. The vacated space would be idle, and the unavoidable costs would continue. Which alternative would you recommend? An analysis of before and after the drop of groceries income statement (in thousands of dollars) follows:

	STORE AS A WHOLE		
	TOTAL BEFORE CHANGE (A)	DROP GROCERIES (B)	TOTAL AFTER CHANGE (A)–(B)
Sales	$1,900	$1,000	$ 900
Variable expenses	1,420	800	620
Contribution margin	$ 480	$ 200	$ 280
Avoidable fixed expenses	265	150	115
Profit contribution to common space and other unavoidable costs	$ 215	$ 50	$ 165
Common space and other unavoidable costs	180	—	180
Operating income	$ 35	$ 50	$ (15)

The preceding analysis shows that matters would be worse, rather than better, if groceries were dropped and the vacated facilities left idle. In short, as the income statement shows, groceries bring in a contribution margin of $200,000, which is $50,000 more than the $150,000 fixed expenses that would be saved by closing the grocery department.

Assume now that the space made available by the dropping of groceries could be used to expand the general merchandise department. This would increase sales by $500,000, generate a 30 percent contribution-margin percentage, and have avoidable fixed costs of $70,000. The $80,000 increase in operating income of general merchandise more than offsets the $50,000 decline from eliminating groceries and provides an overall increase in operating income of $65,000 − $35,000 = $30,000, as shown by the following analysis (in thousands of dollars):

	TOTAL BEFORE CHANGE (A)	DROP GROCERIES (B)	EXPAND GENERAL MERCHANDISE (C)	TOTAL AFTER CHANGE (A)–(B)+(C)
Sales	$1,900	$1,000	$ 500	$1,400
Variable expenses	1,420	800	350	970
Contribution margin	$ 480	$ 200	150	$ 430
Avoidable fixed expenses	265	150	70	185
Profit contribution to common space and other unavoidable costs	$ 215	$ 50	$ 80	$ 245
Common space and other unavoidable costs*	180	—	—	180
Operating income	$ 35	$ 50	$ 80	$ 65

* Includes the $60,000 of former grocery fixed costs, which were allocations of unavoidable common costs that will continue regardless of how the space is occupied.

As the following summary analysis demonstrates, the objective is to obtain, from a given amount of space or capacity, the maximum contribution to the payment of those unavoidable costs that remain unaffected by the nature of the product sold (dropping groceries and expanding general merchandise) (in thousands of dollars):

| | PROFIT CONTRIBUTION OF GIVEN SPACE | | |
	DROPPING GROCERIES	EXPANSION OF GENERAL MERCHANDISE	DIFFERENCE
Sales	$1,000	$ 500	$500 U
Variables expenses	800	350	450 F
Contribution margin	$ 200	$ 150	$ 50 U
Avoidable fixed expenses	150	70	80 F
Contribution to common space and other unavoidable costs	$ 50	$ 80	$ 30 F

F = Favourable difference resulting from replacing groceries with general merchandise.
U = Unfavourable difference.

In this case, the general merchandise will not achieve the dollar sales volume that groceries will, but the higher contribution margin percentage and the lower wage costs (mostly because of the diminished need for stocking and checkout clerks) will bring more favourable net results.

This illustration provides another lesson. The idea that relevant-cost analysis merely says, "Consider all variable costs, and ignore all fixed costs," is not absolute. In this case, fixed costs are relevant because they differ under each alternative.

MAKING MANAGERIAL DECISIONS

When managers face a decision about whether to add or delete a product, service, or department, it is useful to classify the associated fixed costs as avoidable or unavoidable. This is because avoidable fixed costs are also relevant costs for decision making, and therefore need to be considered, along with variable costs, in assessing the cost consequences of adopting or not adopting a particular course of action. Indicate whether the following fixed costs are typically avoidable or unavoidable if a company deletes a product. Assume that the company produces many products in a single plant.

1. Amortization on equipment used to produce the product. The company will sell the equipment if it discontinues the product.

2. Salary of the plant manager.

3. Amortization on the plant building.

4. Advertising costs for the product. The company places specific ads just for this product.

ANSWER
Numbers 1 and 4 are avoidable fixed costs. The company is unlikely to change the salary of the plant manager if it discontinues only one product. Thus, it is unavoidable. The plant amortization is also an unavoidable cost.

OPTIMAL USE OF LIMITED RESOURCES

OBJECTIVE 5

Compute product profitability when production is constrained by a scarce resource.

Limiting Factor (Scarce Resource). The item that restricts or constrains the production or sale of a product or service.

When a multiple-product service establishment is being operated at capacity, managers often must decide which orders to accept. Production capacity and available production time are typical limiting factors of scarce resources. Choosing to provide one service limits a firm's ability to provide another.

A **limiting factor** or **scarce resource** is that item that restricts or constrains the production or sale of a product or service. Limiting factors include labour hours and machine hours that limit production and sales, square metres of floor space or cubic metres of display space, skilled labour, and the like.

Managers sometimes mistakenly favour those products with the biggest contribution margin or gross margin per sales dollar, without regard to scarce resources.

Assume that a bank offers two credit cards to its clients: a silver credit card and a gold one with many special features.

	SILVER CARD	GOLD CARD
Fee	$60	$90
Variable costs	$48	$63
Contribution margin	$12	$27
Contribution-margin ratio	20%	30%

Which credit card is more profitable? On which card should the firm spend its resources? The correct answer is, "It depends." If sales are restricted by demand for only a limited *number* of credit cards, gold cards are more profitable. Why? Because the sale of a silver card contributes $12 to profit; the sale of a gold card contributes $27. If the limiting factor is *units* of sales, the more profitable card is the one with the higher contribution *per unit.*

But suppose annual demand for credit cards of both types is more than the company's capacity to service the next year. Now productive capacity is the limiting factor. If 10,000 hours of capacity are available, and 30 silver cards can be serviced per hour in contrast to 10 gold cards, the silver card is more profitable. Why? Because it contributes more profit per hour:

	SILVER CARD	GOLD CARD
1. Units per hour	30	10
2. Contribution margin per unit	$12	$27
Contribution margin per hour		
(1) × (2)	$360	$270
Total contribution for 10,000 hours	$3,600,000	$2,700,000

The criterion for maximizing profits when one factor limits sales is to *obtain the greatest possible contribution to profit for each unit of the limiting or scarce factor.* The product that is most profitable when one particular factor limits sales may be the least profitable if a different factor restricts sales.

When capacity is limited, the conventional contribution-margin or gross-margin-per-sales-dollar ratio provides an insufficient clue to profitability. Consider an example of two department stores. The conventional gross profit percentage (gross profit ÷ selling price) is an insufficient clue to profitability because profits also depend on the space occupied and the **inventory turnover** (number of times the average inventory is sold per year).

Inventory Turnover. The average number of times the inventory is sold per year.

Wal-Mart
www.walmartcanada.ca

Discount department stores such as Wal-Mart and Zellers have succeeded, while using lower markups than other department stores, because they have been able to increase turnover and thus increase the contribution to profit per unit of space. The following illustrates the same product, taking up the same amount of space, in each of two stores. The contribution margins per unit and per sales dollar are less in the discount store, but faster turnover makes the same product a more profitable use of space in the discount store.

	REGULAR DEPARTMENT STORE	DISCOUNT DEPARTMENT STORE
Retail price	$4.00	$3.50
Cost of merchandise and other variable costs	3.00	3.00
Contribution to profit per unit	$1.00 (25%)	$0.50 (14+%)
Units sold per year	10,000	22,000
Total contribution to profit, assuming the same space allotment in both stores	$10,000	$11,000

Notice that throughout this discussion, fixed costs have been ignored. They are irrelevant unless their total is affected by the choices.

PRICING DECISIONS IN THEORY AND PRACTICE

One of the major decisions managers face is pricing. Actually, pricing can take many forms. Among the many pricing decisions to be made are

1. Setting the price of a new product
2. Setting the price of products sold under private labels
3. Responding to a new price of a competitor
4. Pricing bids in both sealed- and open-bidding situations

The pricing decision is extensively covered in the literature of economics and marketing. Our purpose here is not to provide a comprehensive review of that literature, but simply to highlight a few important points that help define the role of costs in pricing.

Economic Theory and Pricing

OBJECTIVE 6

Identify the role of costs in pricing decisions in perfect and imperfect markets.

Perfect Competition. A market in which no firm is large enough—firms are more or less equal—to influence market price.

Pricing decisions depend on the characteristics of the market a firm faces. In **perfect competition**, a firm can sell as much of a product as it can produce, all at a single market price. If it charges more, customers will buy from competitors. If it charges less, it sacrifices profits. Therefore, every firm in such a market will charge the market price, and the only decision for managers is how much to produce.

Although costs do not directly influence prices in perfect competition, they affect the production decision. Consider the *marginal cost curve* in Exhibit 8-5. The **marginal cost** is the additional cost resulting from producing and selling one additional unit. The marginal cost often decreases as production increases up to a point because efficiencies are possible with larger production amounts. But, at some point, marginal costs begin to rise with increases in production because facilities begin to be overcrowded, resulting in inefficiencies.

Marginal Cost. The additional cost resulting from producing and selling one additional unit.

Marginal Revenue. The additional revenue resulting from the sale of an additional unit.

Exhibit 8-5 also includes a *marginal revenue curve*. The **marginal revenue** is the additional revenue resulting from the sale of an additional unit. In perfect competition, the marginal revenue curve is a horizontal line equal to the price per unit at all volumes of sales.

As long as the marginal cost is less than the price, additional production and sales are profitable. But when marginal costs exceed price, the firm loses money on each additional unit. Therefore, the profit maximizing volume is the quantity at which marginal cost equals price. In Exhibit 8-5, the firm should produce V_0 units. Producing fewer units passes up profitable opportunities; producing more units reduces profit for each additional unit.

EXHIBIT 8-5

Marginal Revenue and Cost in Perfect Competition

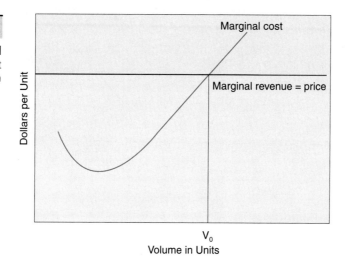

In **imperfect competition**, a firm is in a position to influence price and, therefore, the quantity it sells. At some point, price reductions are necessary to generate additional sales. Exhibit 8-6 contains a demand curve (also called the average revenue curve) that shows the volume of sales at each possible price. To sell additional units, the price of *all units sold* must be reduced. Therefore, the marginal revenue curve, also shown in Exhibit 8-6, is below the demand curve. That is, the marginal revenue for selling one additional unit is less than the price at which it is sold because the price of all other units falls as well. For example, suppose ten units can be sold for $50 per unit. The price must be dropped to $49 per unit to sell 11 units, to $48 to sell 12 units, and to $47 to sell 13 units. The fourth column of Exhibit 8-7 shows the marginal revenue for units 11 through 13. Notice that the marginal revenue decreases as volume increases.

Imperfect Competition. A market in which a firm's price will influence the quantity it sells; at some point, price reductions are necessary to generate additional sales.

Price Elasticity. The effect of price changes on sales volume.

To estimate marginal revenue, managers must predict the effect of price changes on volume, which is called **price elasticity**. If small price increases cause large volume declines, demand is *elastic*. If prices have little or no effect on volume, demand is *inelastic*.

Now suppose the marginal cost of the units is as shown in the fifth column of Exhibit 8-7. The optimal production and sales level would be 12 units. The last column illustrates that the 11th unit adds $4 to profit, the 12th adds $1, but production and sale of the 13th unit would *decrease* profit by $2. In general, firms should produce and sell units until the marginal revenue equals the marginal cost, represented by volume V_0 in Exhibit 8-6.

Notice that in economic theory the cost that is relevant for pricing decisions is the *marginal cost*. The accountant's approximation to marginal cost is *variable cost*. What is the major difference between the economist's marginal cost and the accountant's variable cost? Variable cost is assumed to be constant within a relevant range of volume, while marginal cost increases with each unit produced. However, within large ranges of production volume, increases in marginal cost are often small. Therefore, using variable cost can be a reasonable approximation to marginal cost in many situations.

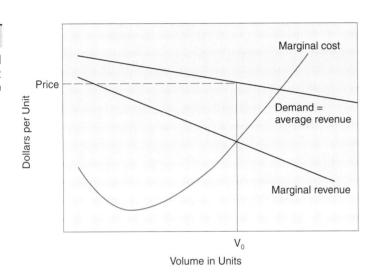

EXHIBIT 8-7

Profit Maximization in Imperfect Competition

UNITS SOLD	PRICE/ UNIT	TOTAL REVENUE	MARGINAL REVENUE	MARGINAL COST	PROFIT FROM PRODUCTION AND SALE OF ADDITIONAL UNIT
1	2	3	4	5	6
10	$50	10 × $50 = $500			
11	49	11 × 49 = 539	$539 − 500 = $39	$35	$4
12	48	12 × 48 = 576	576 − 539 = 37	36	1
13	47	13 × 47 = 611	611 − 576 = 35	37	(2)

Managers seldom compute marginal revenue curves and marginal cost curves. Instead, they use educated estimates to predict the effects of additional production and sales on profits. In addition, they examine selected volumes (within the relevant range), not the whole range of possible volumes. Such simplifications are justified because the cost of a more sophisticated analysis would exceed the benefits.

Consider a division of General Electric (GE) that makes DVDs. Suppose market researchers estimate that 700,000 DVDs can be sold if priced at $200 per unit, but 1,000,000 could be sold at $180. The variable cost of production is $130 per unit at production levels of both 700,000 and 1,000,000. Both volumes are also within the relevant range so that fixed costs are unaffected by the changes in volume. Which price should be charged?

The GE manager could compute the additional revenue and additional costs of the 300,000 additional units of sales at the $180 price:

```
Additional revenue: (1,000,000 × $180) – (700,000 × $200)    = $40,000,000
Additional costs: 300,000 × $130                             =  39,000,000
Additional profit                                              $  1,000,000
```

Alternatively, the manager could compare the total contribution for each alternative:

```
Contribution at $180: ($180 – $130) × 1,000,000  = $50,000,000
Contribution at $200: ($200 – $130) × 700,000    =  49,000,000
Difference                                          $ 1,000,000
```

Notice that comparing the total contributions is essentially the same as computing the additional revenues and costs. Further, both approaches correctly ignore fixed costs, which are unaffected by this pricing decision.

Practical Considerations in Pricing

A number of factors interact to shape the environment in which managers make pricing decisions. Legal requirements, competitors' actions, costs, and customer demands all influence pricing.

Legal Requirements

Pricing decisions must be made within constraints imposed by laws. In addition to prohibiting collusion in setting prices, laws generally prohibit prices that are *predatory* or *discriminatory*.

Predatory Pricing. Establishing prices so low that competitors are driven out of the market so that the predatory pricer has no significant competition and can raise prices dramatically.

Discriminatory Pricing. Charging different prices to different customers for the same product or service.

Dumping. Refers to the selling of goods in a foreign country at a price that is below the full cost of the product and below the selling price in the domestic market.

Predatory pricing is establishing prices so low that competitors are driven out of the market so that the predatory pricer has no significant competition and can raise prices dramatically. Courts have generally ruled that pricing is predatory only if companies set prices below average variable cost.

Discriminatory pricing is charging different prices to different customers for the same product or service. However, different pricing is not necessarily discriminatory if it reflects a cost differential incurred in providing the good or service to different customers. For example, large quantities purchased may justify charging a lower price per unit to reflect lower market and/or delivery costs.

Closely related to the issues of predatory and discriminatory pricing is the practice of *dumping*. **Dumping** refers to the selling of goods in a foreign country at a price that is below the full cost of the product and below the selling price in the domestic market. International laws prohibit this practice because it would allow large foreign competitors to force smaller domestic producers out of business.

Businesses can defend themselves against charges of predatory, discriminatory, or dumping pricing practices by citing their costs as a basis for their prices. Therefore, a good understanding of the cost of a product or service—especially the activities that cause additional costs to be incurred—is useful in avoiding legal pitfalls. Our discussion here assumes that pricing practices do not violate legal constraints.

Competitors' Actions

Competitors usually react to the price changes of their rivals. Tinkering with prices is often most heavily affected by the price-setter's expectations of competitors' reactions and of the overall effects on the total industry demand for the good or service in question. For example, an airline might cut prices even if it expects price cuts from its rivals. A justification for the price cut may be the prediction that total customer demand for the tickets of all airlines will increase sufficiently to offset the reduction in the price per ticket. On the other hand, competitors may not follow suit in reducing prices. In the summer of 2005, GM, Ford, and Chrysler lowered car prices to the level they sell to their own employees. However, Honda, Toyota, and other foreign competitors did not follow suit, claiming that their cars can sell without price incentives.

Competition is becoming increasingly international. Overcapacity in some countries causes aggressive pricing policies, particularly for a company's exported goods.

Knowledge of a competitor's costs can be useful. Therefore, many companies will gather information regarding a rival's capacity, technology, and operating policies. In this way, managers make more informed predictions of competitors' reactions to a company's prices.

Costs

The influence of costs on the setting of prices is often overstated. Frequently, the market price is regarded as a given driver. Examples include the prices of metals and agricultural commodities. Consider gold. A mining company sells at the established market prices. Whether profits or losses are forthcoming depends on how well the company controls its costs and volume, not its ability to set the price. Nevertheless, many managers say that their prices are set by cost-plus pricing. For example, consider the automobile and construction industries. Their executives describe the procedure as computing an average unit cost and then adding a "reasonable" **markup** (that is, the amount by which price exceeds cost) that will generate a target return on investment. But the key is the "plus" in cost-plus. It is rarely an unalterable markup. Its magnitude depends on the behaviour of competitors and customers.

> **Markup.** The amount by which price exceeds cost.

Prices are mostly directly related to costs in industries where revenue is based on cost reimbursement. A prime example is defence contracting. Cost-reimbursement contracts generally specify how costs should be measured and what costs are allowable.

In short, the market sets prices after all. Why? Because the price as set by a cost-plus formula is inevitably adjusted "in light of market conditions." The maximum price that may be charged is the one that does not drive the customer away. The minimum price is zero. Indeed, companies may give out free samples to gain entry into a market. A more practical guide is that, in the short run, the minimum price to be quoted, *subject to consideration of long-run effects*, should be equal to all variable costs of producing, selling, and distributing the good or service that may be avoided by not landing the order. And, in the long run, the price must be high enough to cover all costs, including fixed costs.

Target Costing/Pricing

More than ever before, managers are recognizing the needs of customers. Pricing is no exception. If customers believe a price is too high, they may turn to other sources for the product or service, substitute a different product, or decide to produce the item themselves.

Target Costing. A product strategy in which companies first determine the price at which they can sell a new product and then design a product that can be produced at a low enough cost to provide an adequate profit margin.

Most companies have traditionally started with costs and added a markup to determine prices. However, a growing number of companies are turning the equation around and developing costs based on prices. Companies that use **target costing** first determine the price at which they can sell a new product and then design a product that can be produced at a low enough cost to provide an adequate profit margin. Product designers thus become aware of the cost impacts of the design of both the product itself and the process used to produce it.

For example, market research may indicate that Toyota could sell 100,000 units of one model of a sports car annually at a list price of $35,000. The engineers who design the product might consider several different combinations of features bearing different costs. If the total product cost is sufficiently low, the product may be launched. Conversely, if the total product cost is too high, the product may be unjustified. Of course, the point here is that the customer helps determine the price. The product designers and the management accountants work together to see if an attractive product can be developed at a target cost that will provide room for an attractive profit.

Whether a company sets prices based on costs or costs based on prices, it is inevitable that prices and costs interact. If the focus is on prices that are influenced primarily by market forces, managers must make sure that all costs can be covered in the long run. If prices are based on a markup of costs, managers must examine the actions of customers and competitors to assure that products or services can be sold at the determined prices.

Cost-Plus Defined

Cost-plus is often the basis for target prices. The size of the "plus" depends on target (desired) operating incomes, which, in turn, frequently depend on the target return on investment for a division, a product line, or a product. Chapter 15 discusses return on investment. For simplicity here, we work with a target operating income.

Target prices can be based on a host of different markups based on a host of different definitions of cost. Thus, there are many ways to arrive at *the same target price*. They simply reflect different arrangements of the components of the same income statement.

Exhibit 8-8 displays the relationships of costs to target selling prices, assuming a target operating income of $1 million. The percentages there represent four popular markup formulas for pricing: (1) as a percentage of variable manufacturing costs, (2) as a percentage of total variable costs, (3) as a percentage of absorption costs, and (4) as a percentage of full costs. Of course, the percentages differ. For instance, the markup on variable manufacturing costs is 66.67 percent and on absorption costs is 33.33 percent. Regardless of the formula used, the pricing decision maker will be led toward the *same* target price. For a volume of 1 million units, assume that the target selling price is $20 per unit. If the decision maker is unable to obtain such a price consistently, the company will not achieve its $1 million operating income objective.

The history of accounting reveals that most companies' systems have gathered costs via some form of full-cost system. In recent years, variable costs and fixed costs are often identified. But many managers insist on having information regarding *both* variable costs per unit and the allocated fixed costs per unit before setting selling prices. If the accounting system routinely gathers data regarding both variable and fixed costs, such data can readily be provided. However, most absorption-costing systems do not organize their cost data collection according to

Target Costing, ABC, and the Role of Management Accounting

www.culpinc.com
www.daimlerchrysler.ca
www.philips.ca
www.kodak.com

Many companies use target costing together with an activity-based costing (ABC) system. Target costing requires a company to first determine what a customer will pay for a product and then work backward to design the product and production process that will generate a desired level of profit. ABC provides data on the costs of the various activities needed to produce the product. Knowing the costs of activities allows product and production process designers to predict the effects of their designs on the product's cost. Target costing essentially takes activity-based costs and uses them for strategic product decisions.

For example, Culp, Inc. is one of the largest producers of mattress and upholstery fabrics in North America. Based in High Point, North Carolina, Culp is active in Canada through Rayonese Textile, which was acquired by Culp in early 2005 and which operates a manufacturing facility in Saint-Jérôme, Quebec. Culp uses target costing and ABC to elevate cost management into one of the most strategically important areas of the firm. Culp found that 80 percent of its product costs are predetermined at the design stage, but earlier cost control efforts had focused only on the other 20 percent. By shifting cost management efforts to the design stage and getting accurate costs of the various activities involved in production, cost management at Culp evolved into a process of cutting costs when engineers design a product, not identifying costs that are out of line after the production is complete.

A basic goal of target costing is to reduce costs before they occur. After all, once a company has incurred costs, it cannot change them. Such a strategy is especially important when product life cycles are short. Because most product life cycles are shrinking, use of target costing is expanding. Target costing focuses on reducing costs in the product design and development stages—when costs can really be affected. For example, target costing heavily influenced DaimlerChrysler's design of the low-priced Dodge Neon between 1995 and 2005. Managers have credited target costing for helping eliminate costs that could cause managers to price products too high for the market to bear. "The design process is where you can truly leverage [reduce] your costs," according to Ron Gallaway, then CFO of Micrus Semiconductors (now part of Philips Semiconductor, a division of Netherlands-based Royal Philips Electronics).

What role does management accounting play in target costing? At Micrus, management accountants are responsible for setting final targets for all components and processes. One survey reports that 86 percent of companies using target costing take data directly from their cost systems to estimate product costs during product design. At Eastman Kodak, management accountants are a vital part of the cross-functional team that implements target costing. This team includes design and manufacturing engineers, procurement, and marketing, as well as management accounting. Peter Zampino, then director of research at the Consortium for Advanced Manufacturing—International, supported this approach: "It's like anything else; if finance doesn't bless the numbers, they won't have the credibility throughout the organization."

Sources: Adapted from R. Banham, "Off Target," *CFO*, May 2000; J. Bohn, "Chrysler Cuts Costs by Nurturing Links with Suppliers," *Automotive Age*, January 17, 1994, p. 18; G. Boer and J. Ettlie, "Target Costing Can Boost Your Bottom Line," *Strategic Finance*, July 1999, pp. 49–52; J. Brausch, "Target Costing for Profit Enhancement," *Management Accounting*, November 1994, pp. 45–49; G. Hoffman, "Future Vision," *Grocery Marketing*, March 1994, p. 6. "Culp Acquires Rayonese," *Textile World,* February 2005. See also Society of Management Accountants of Canada, Management Accounting Guideline, *Implementing Target Costing*, Mississauga, ON: Strategic Management Series, 1995, accessible at www.cma-canada.org; American Institute of Certified Public Accountants, *Target Costing Best Practices Report,* summarized in *CPA Letter* supplement, May 1999, accessible at www.aicpa.org; D. Swenson, S. Ansari, J. Bell, and I. Kim, "A Field Study of Best Practices in Target Costing," *Management Accounting Quarterly*, Winter 2003, pp. 12–17.

	ALTERNATIVE MARKUP PERCENTAGES TO ACHIEVE SAME TARGET SALES (DOLLARS IN THOUSANDS)	
Target sales	$20,000	
Variable costs:		
Manufacturing	$12,000	($20,000 − $12,000) ÷ $12,000 = 66.67%
Selling and administrative	1,100	
Total variable costs	$13,100	($20,000 − $13,100) ÷ $13,100 = 52.67%
Fixed costs:		
Manufacturing	$ 3,000	[$20,000 − ($12,000 + $3,000)] ÷ $15,000 = 33.33%
Selling and administrative	2,900	
Total fixed costs	$ 5,900	
Full costs:	$19,000	($20,000 − $19,000) ÷ $19,000 = 5.26%
Target operating income	$ 1,000	

variable and fixed costs. As a result, special analysis must be used to designate mixed costs as variable and fixed.

ADVANTAGES OF VARIOUS APPROACHES TO PRICING DECISIONS

Advantages of Contribution Approach

OBJECTIVE 8

Identify contribution margin and absorption costing advantages and disadvantages.

When it is used intelligently, the contribution approach has some advantages over the absorption-costing approach, or the full-cost approach, because the latter often fails to highlight different cost-behaviour patterns.

Obviously, the contribution approach offers more detailed information because it displays variable- and fixed-cost-behaviour patterns separately. The contribution approach emphasizes cost-volume-profit relationships. Consequently, the approach makes it easier for managers to prepare price schedules at different volume levels.

The correct analysis in Exhibit 8-9 shows how changes in volume affect operating income. The contribution approach helps managers with pricing decisions because it readily displays the interrelationships among variable costs, fixed costs, and potential changes in selling prices.

In contrast, target pricing with absorption costing or full costing presumes a given volume level. When volume changes, the unit cost used at the original planned volume may mislead managers. As indicated earlier, there have been actual cases where managers have erroneously assumed that the change in total costs may be computed by multiplying any change in volume by the full unit cost.

The incorrect analysis in Exhibit 8-9 shows how managers may be misled if the $19 full cost per unit is used to predict effects of volume changes on operating income. Suppose a manager uses the $19 figure to predict an operating income of $900,000 if the company sells 900,000 instead of 1,000,000 units. If actual operating income is $310,000 instead, as the correct analysis predicts, that manager may be stunned—and may have to look for a new job.

Besides the detailed information, the contribution approach provides two other advantages that deserve mention. First, a normal or target-pricing formula can be as easily developed by the contribution approach as by absorption-costing

EXHIBIT 8-9

Analyses of Changes in Volume on Operating Income

	CORRECT ANALYSIS			INCORRECT ANALYSIS		
Volume in units	900,000	1,000,000	1,100,000	900,000	1,000,000	1,100,000
Sales @ $20.00	$18,000,000	$20,000,000	$22,000,000	$18,000,000	$20,000,000	$22,000,000
Total variable						
costs @ $13.10	11,790,000	13,100,000	14,410,000			
Contribution						
margin	6,210,000	6,900,000	7,590,000			
Fixed costs*	5,900,000	5,900,000	5,900,000			
Full costs @ $19.00				17,100,000	19,000,000	20,900,000
Operating income	$ 310,000	$ 1,000,000	$ 1,690,000	$ 900,000	$ 1,000,000	$ 1,100,000

* Fixed manufacturing costs	$3,000,000
Fixed selling and administrative costs	2,900,000
Total fixed costs	$5,900,000

or full-costing approaches, as shown in Exhibit 8-8. Second, the contribution approach offers insight into the short-run versus long-run effects of cutting prices on special orders. For example, assume the same cost-behaviour patterns as at the Samson Company. (Exhibit 8-3). The 100,000-unit order added $100,000 to operating income at a selling price of $13, which was $7 below the target selling price of $20 and $2 below the absorption manufacturing cost of $15. Given all the stated assumptions, accepting the order appeared to be the better choice. No general answer can be given, but the relevant information was more easily generated by the contribution approach:

	CONTRIBUTION APPROACH	ABSORPTION COSTING APPROACH
Sales, 100,000 units @ $13	$1,300,000	$1,300,000
Variable manufacturing costs @ $12	1,200,000	
Absorption manufacturing costs @ $15		1,500,000
Apparent change in operating income	$ 100,000	$ (200,000)

Under the absorption approach, the decision maker has no direct knowledge of cost-volume-profit relationships. The decision maker makes the decision by hunch. On the surface, the offer is definitely unattractive because the price of $13 is $2 below absorption costs.

Under the contribution approach, the decision maker sees a short-run advantage of $100,000 from accepting the offer. Fixed costs will be unaffected by whatever decision is made and operating income will increase by $100,000. Still, there are often long-run effects to consider. Will acceptance of the offer undermine the long-run price structure? In other words, is the short-run advantage of $100,000 more than offset by highly probable long-run financial disadvantages? The decision maker may think so and may reject the offer. But—and this is important—by doing so the decision maker is, in effect, foregoing $100,000 now in order to protect long-run market advantages. Generally, the decision maker can assess problems of this sort by asking whether the probability of long-run benefits is worth an "investment" equal to the foregone contribution margin

($100,000 in this case). Under absorption approaches, the decision maker must ordinarily conduct a special study to find the immediate effects. Under the contribution approach, the manager has a system that will routinely and more surely provide such information.

Advantages of Absorption-Cost or Full-Cost Approaches

To say that either a contribution approach or an absorption-cost approach or a full-cost approach provides the "best" guide to pricing decisions is a dangerous oversimplification of one of the most perplexing problems in business. Lack of understanding and judgment can lead to unprofitable pricing regardless of the kind of cost data available or cost accounting system used.

Frequently, managers do not employ a contribution approach because they fear that variable costs will be substituted indiscriminately for full costs and will therefore lead to suicidal price cutting. This problem should *not* arise if the data are used wisely. However, if top managers perceive a pronounced danger of underpricing when variable-cost data are revealed, they may justifiably prefer an absorption-costing approach or a full-cost approach for guiding pricing decisions.

Cost-plus pricing based on absorption costs or full costs entails circular reasoning. That is, price, which influences sales volume, is often based on an average absorption cost per unit, which, in turn, is partly determined by the underlying volume of sales.

Despite these criticisms, absorption costs or full costs are far more widely used in practice than is the contribution approach. Why? In addition to the reasons already mentioned, the following may be added to the list:

1. In the long run, all costs must be recovered to stay in business. Sooner or later fixed costs do indeed fluctuate as volume changes. Therefore, it is prudent to assume that all costs are variable (even if some are fixed in the short run).
2. Computing target prices based on cost-plus formulas may indicate what competitors might charge, especially if they have approximately the same level of capacity and efficiency.
3. Absorption-cost or full-cost formula pricing meets the cost-benefit test. It is too expensive to conduct individual cost-volume-profit analysis for the many products (sometimes thousands) that a company offers.
4. Absorption-cost or full-cost pricing copes better with the correct price-demand decisions by encouraging managers not to take too much marginal business.
5. Absorption-cost or full-cost pricing tends to promote price stability. Managers prefer price stability because it eases their professional lives by making planning more dependable.
6. Absorption-cost pricing or full-cost pricing provides the most defensible basis for justifying prices to all interested parties, including government antitrust investigators.
7. Absorption-cost or full-cost pricing provides convenient reference (target) points to simplify hundreds or thousands of pricing decisions.
8. Managers are especially reluctant to focus on variable costs and ignore allocated fixed costs when their performance evaluations, and possibly their bonuses, are based on income shown in published financial statements based on absorption costing.

Target Costing and the External Value Chain

The value chain consists of functions within a company that add value to a product or service. Companies that use target costing often go beyond the internal value chain to involve both customers and suppliers during the design process.

DaimlerChrysler's target-costing team worked actively with customers when analyzing the tradeoff between cost and value of lighting for interior controls and under the hood. The value analysis resulted in adding the interior control lighting but not the under-the-hood lighting.

For many companies, a large percentage of the total cost of a product is from materials and parts that are purchased from suppliers—approximately 75% for DaimlerChrysler and Continental Teves, one of the largest manufacturers of hydraulic and electronic brake systems, electronic steering systems, and air spring systems. Both of these companies have intercompany teams to meet cost-reduction goals. At DaimlerChrysler, each supplier was asked to reduce costs by 5% annually, including improvements that reduce DaimlerChrysler's costs. For example, one supplier suggested changing the front rail system from several pieces to one unit. This improvement reduced DaimlerChrysler's costs so the supplier received credit. Continental Teves uses a cost-modelling tool to determine the target costs for components it outsources. If a supplier fails to meet its target costs, Continental might send a team to analyze the supplier's operations.

Source: Adapted from D. Swenson, S. Ansari, J. Bill, I. Kim, "A Field Study of Best Practices in Target Costing," *Management Accounting Quarterly*, Winter 2003.

Pricing Minima and Maxima, Markups for Overhead and Profits

Exhibit 8-10 is from an actual quote sheet used by the manager of a small job shop that bids on welding machinery orders in a highly competitive industry. The Exhibit 8-10 approach is a tool for informed pricing decisions. Notice that the minimum price is the total variable cost.

Of course, the manager will rarely bid the minimum price. To do so regularly would ensure eventual bankruptcy. Still, the manager wants to know the effect of a job on the company's total variable costs. Occasionally, a bid near that minimum total may be justified because of idle capacity or the desire to establish a presence in new markets or with a new customer.

EXHIBIT 8-10

Quote Sheet for Pricing

Direct materials, at cost	$25,000
Direct labour and variable manufacturing overhead, 600 direct labour hours × $30 =	18,000
Sales commission (varies with job)	2,000
Total variable costs—minimum price*	45,000
Add fixed costs allocated to job, 600 direct labour hours × $20	12,000
Total costs	57,000
Add desired markup	30,000
Selling price—maximum price that you think you can obtain*	$87,000

* This sheet shows two prices, maximum and minimum. Any amount you can get above the minimum price is a contribution margin.

One can easily conclude that no single method of pricing, variable- or full-costing, is always best. Some companies may use *both* full-cost and variable-cost information in pricing decisions because the full- versus variable-cost pricing controversy is not a case of either black or white."[3]

Note that Exhibit 8-10 classifies costs especially for the pricing task. Pricing decisions may be made by more than one person. The accountant's responsibility is to prepare an understandable format that involves a minimum of computations. Exhibit 8-10 combines direct labour and variable manufacturing overhead. All fixed costs, whether manufacturing, selling, or administrative, are lumped together and applied to the job using a single fixed-overhead rate per direct labour hour. Obviously, if more accuracy is desired, many more detailed cost items and overhead rates could be formulated.

Some managers, particularly in construction and service industries such as auto repair, compile separate categories of costs of (1) direct materials, parts, and supplies, and (2) direct labour. The managers then use different markup rates for each category. These rates are developed to provide revenue for both related overhead costs and operating profit. For example, an automobile repair shop might have the following format for each job:

	BILLED TO CUSTOMERS
Auto parts ($200 cost plus 40% markup)	$280
Direct labour (Cost is $20 per hour. Bill at 300% to recover overhead and provide for operating profit. Billing rate is $20 × 300% = $60 per hour. Total billed for 10 hours is $60 × 10 = $600)	600
Total billed to customer	$880

Another example is a consulting company that wants to price its jobs so that each one generates a margin of 28 percent of revenues—14 percent to cover selling and administrative expenses and 14 percent for profit. To achieve this, the manager uses a pricing formula of 140 percent times predicted material cost, plus $25,000 per 35-hour week of service time. The latter covers labour and overhead costs of $18,000 per week. For a product with $400,000 of materials cost and 30 weeks of billed time, the price and profit would be:

	COST		PRICE	PROFIT
Materials	$400,000	× 1.40	$560,000	$160,000
Labour and overhead (30 × $18,000)	540,000		750,000	210,000
Total	$940,000		$1,310,000	$370,000

The profit of $370,000 is approximately 40 percent of the cost of $940,000 and 28 percent of the price of $1,310,000.

Thus, there are several ways to compute selling prices. However, some general words of caution are appropriate here. Managers are better able to understand their options and the effects of their decisions on profits if they know their costs. That is, it is more informative to pinpoint costs first, before adding

---

[3] T. Bruegelmann, G. Haessly, C. Wolfangel, and M. Schiff, "How Variable Costing Is Used in Pricing Decisions," *Management Accounting*, Vol. 65, No. 10, p. 65.

markups, than to have a variety of markups already embedded in the "costs" used as guides for setting selling prices. For example, if materials cost $1,000, they should be shown on a price quotation list as $1,000, not at, say, a marked-up $1,400 because that is what the seller hopes to get.

TARGET COSTING AND NEW PRODUCT DEVELOPMENT

As we have seen, prices and costs are affected by both the actions of the company and market conditions. However, the degree to which costs and prices are affected by company actions determines the approach companies use to plan operations. For example, cost-plus pricing is used for products where company actions (for example, advertising) can influence the market.

Consider a situation in which a company is deciding whether or not to develop and market a new product. The ability to achieve a profit on this new product is determined by the difference between the market price and the cost.

But what if the market conditions are such that the company cannot influence prices? If the desired profit is to be achieved, the company must focus on the product's cost. Target costing is a tool for making cost a key throughout the life of a product. A desired, or target, cost is set before the product is created or even designed. Managers must then try to control costs so that the product's cost does not exceed its target cost. Target costing emphasizes proactive, up-front planning throughout every activity of the new product development process. However, it is most effective at reducing costs during the product design phase, when the vast majority of costs are committed. For example, the costs of resources such as new machinery, materials, parts, and even future refinements are largely determined by the design of the product and the associated production processes. These costs are not easily reduced once production begins.

Marketing might appear to have a limited role in target costing because the price is set by competitive market conditions. Actually, market research from the marketing departments at the beginning of the target-costing activity guides the whole product development process by supplying information on customer-required product functions. In fact, one of the key characteristics of successful target costing is a strong emphasis on understanding customer needs.

ITT Industries
www.itt.com

For example, consider the target costing system used by ITT Industries—one of the world's largest automotive suppliers. The company designs, develops, and manufactures a broad range of products including brake systems, electric motors, and lamps. Also, the company is the worldwide market leader in anti-lock braking systems (ABS), producing 20,000 systems a day.

What pricing approach does ITT Industries use for the ABS? The pricing process starts when one of ITT's customers sends an invitation to bid. The market for brake systems is so competitive that very little variance exists in the price companies can ask (bid). A cost targeting group is formed and charged with determining whether the price and costs allow for enough of a profit margin. This group is made up of engineers, cost accountants, and sales personnel. Factors considered in determining the feasibility of earning the desired target profit margin include competitor pricing, inflation rates, interest rates, and potential cost reductions during both the design and production stages of the ABS product life. Many of the component parts that make up the ABS are purchased from the company's suppliers. Thus, the cost targeting group works closely with suppliers during the target-costing process. After product and process design improvements are made and commitments from suppliers are received, the company has the cost information needed to decide whether or not to make a bid.

Target Costing and Cost-Plus Pricing Compared

It is important for companies to understand the market in which they operate and to use the most appropriate pricing approach. To see how target costing and cost-plus pricing can lead to different decisions, suppose that ITT Industries receives an invitation to bid from Ford on the ABS to be used in a new model car.

Assume the following data apply:

- The specifications contained in Ford's invitation lead to an estimated current manufacturing cost (component parts, direct labour, and manufacturing overhead) of $170.
- ITT Industries has a desired gross margin rate of 30 percent on sales, which means that actual costs should make up 70 percent of the price.
- Highly competitive market conditions exist and have established a sales price of $200 per unit.

- The Six Sigma effort is linked to Bombardier's business priorities and strategies and is supported by top management and full-time, well-trained resources that help to get improvement under way.
- By providing a common set of tools and techniques, Six Sigma will ensure that Bombardier has a common quality language that allows easy transfer of best practices.
- The measurable stretch goal of Six Sigma, 3.4 defects per million opportunities (DPMO), forces the search for new, innovative solutions.

The Six Sigma program requires a major training effort. Every agent is provided with four weeks of training in advanced techniques to identify and eliminate defects before they are assigned to practical and focused projects. As projects are completed, quality and costs results are carefully tracked and best practices are shared in a systematic fashion.

During the next two years, over 400 full-time Six Sigma Agents will be developed across Bombardier. Ultimately, Six Sigma methodologies will become a standard part of every manager's "tool kit" and to this end, Bombardier will offer managers an intense two-week training program.

Launched last year at Bombardier Aerospace, Six Sigma projects are already yielding concrete results. Annual savings of several million dollars will be captured by eliminating defects in manufacturing and administrative processes.

As an example, a team involved in a recent Six Sigma project at Bombardier Aerospace looked at customer and Transport Canada requirements pertaining to documentary evidence and traceability. The project objective was to reduce documentation errors by 80 percent. Actual improvements to date are in the order of 90 percent, and savings are expected to approximate $200,000 per year.

Improvements were made through standardization of criteria, better document format, training, and improved feedback.

Another Bombardier Aerospace project brought together a cross-functional project team from Toronto and Montreal facilities in an effort to reduce defects within the experimental and ground testing design process. The team identified changes that can potentially provide a tenfold reduction in defects and continues to study further possibilities to reduce defects. Potential net savings in design, manufacturing, and assembly are estimated at $1 million over four years.

In addition to improving Bombardier's performance, Six Sigma will provide many opportunities to identify and develop a large number of young future leaders within the organization.

Six Sigma is one of the most ambitious quality and productivity improvement programs undertaken by Bombardier. Six Sigma will contribute to Bombardier's success by increasing both its operating margins and the quality of its products, even in an environment of stable or declining prices.

Source: "Six Sigma" Bombardier Inc., *1998 Annual Report*, p. 3.

See also General Electric's Web section dedicated to its Six Sigma practices: www.ge.com/sixsigma, as well as a website dedicated to Six Sigma practices and research, including certification: www.isixsigma.com. There are many Canadian consultants offering Six Sigma training. See also Industry Canada, "Canadian Best Practices and Success Stories Using Lean Manufacturing, Six Sigma and Other Higher Performance Manufacturing," *Canadian Resource Guide to High Performance Manufacturing*, accessible at www.strategis.gc.ca; J. Legentil, "Le Six Sigma, Version PME," *La Presse*, October 24, 2005, p. 6; "Adventures in Six Sigma: How the Problem-Solving Technique Helped Xerox," *Financial Times of London*, September 23, 2005, p. 13; T. Belford, "Real Estate Heaven Is No Mistake: Commercial Land Firms Try to Slash Data Mistakes with Processes such as Six Sigma," *The Globe and Mail*, March 22, 2005, p. B9.

If cost-plus pricing is used to bid on the ABS, the bid price would be $243 ($170 ÷ 70 percent). This bid would most likely be rejected by Ford because the market price is only $200. ITT Industries' pricing approach would lead to a lost opportunity.

Suppose that ITT Industries recognizes that the market conditions dictate a set price of $200. If a target-costing system is used, what would the pricing decision be? The target cost is $140 (70 percent × $200), so a required cost reduction of $30 ($170 – $140) per unit is necessary. The target costing group would work with product and process engineers and suppliers to determine if the average unit cost could be reduced by $30 over the product's life. Note that it is not necessary to get costs down to the $140 target cost before production begins. The initial unit cost will likely be higher, say $150. Continuous improvement over the product's life will result in the final $10 of cost reduction. Assuming that the required commitments for cost reductions are received, the decision is to make a bid for $200 per unit. Note that if the bid is accepted, ITT Industries must carry through with its focus on cost management throughout the life of the product.

Target costing originated in Japan, but now it is used by many companies worldwide, including DaimlerChrysler, Mercedes-Benz, Procter & Gamble, Caterpillar, and ITT Industries.

What can explain the increasing popularity of target costing? With increased global competition in many industries, companies are more and more limited in influencing market prices. Cost management then becomes the key to profitability.

Mercedes-Benz
www.mercedes-benz.com

Procter & Gamble
www.pg.com

Caterpillar
www.cat.com

HIGHLIGHTS TO REMEMBER

1. **Discriminate between relevant and irrelevant information for making decisions.** To be relevant to a particular decision, a cost (or revenue) must meet two criteria: (1) it must be an expected future cost (or revenue), and (2) it must have an element of difference among the alternative courses of action.

2. **Apply the decision process to make business decisions.** All managers make business decisions based on some decision process. The best processes help decision making by focusing the manager's attention on relevant information.

3. **Decide to accept or reject a special order using the contribution margin technique.** Decisions to accept or reject a special sales order should use the contribution margin technique and focus on the additional revenues and additional costs of the order.

4. **Choose whether to add or delete a product line using relevant information.** Relevant information also plays an important role in decisions about adding or deleting products, services, or departments. Decisions on whether to delete a department or product line require analysis of the revenues foregone and the costs saved from the deletion.

5. **Compute a measure of product profitability when production is constrained by a scarce resource.** When production is constrained by a limiting resource, the key to obtaining the maximum profit from a given capacity is to obtain the greatest possible contribution to profit per unit of the limiting or scarce resource.

6. **Identify the factors that influence pricing decisions in practice.** Market conditions, the law, customers, competitors, and costs influence pricing decisions. The degree to which management actions can affect price and cost determines the most effective approach to use for pricing and cost management purposes.

7. **Compute a target sales price by various approaches, and compare the advantages and disadvantages of these approaches.** Companies use cost-plus pricing for products when management actions can influence the market price. They can add profit markups to a variety of cost bases including variable manufacturing costs, all variable costs, full manufacturing costs, or all costs. The contribution margin approach to pricing has the advantage of providing detailed cost behaviour information that is consistent with cost-volume-profit analysis.

8. **Use target costing to decide whether to add a new product.** When market conditions are such that management cannot influence prices, companies must focus on cost control and reduction. They use target costing primarily for new products, especially during the design phase of the value chain. They deduct a desired target margin from the market-established price to determine the target cost. Cost management then focuses on controlling and reducing costs over the product's life cycle to achieve that target cost.

DEMONSTRATION PROBLEMS FOR YOUR REVIEW

Problem One

1. Return to the basic illustration in Exhibit 8-3. Suppose a special order like the one described in conjunction with Exhibit 8-3 had the following terms: selling price of $13.50 instead of $13.00, but a manufacturer's agent who had obtained the potential order was paid a flat fee of $40,000 upon acceptance of the order. What would be the new special-order difference in operating income if the order were accepted?

2. Assume the original facts concerning the special order, except that the order was for 250,000 units at a selling price of $11.50. Some managers have been known to argue for acceptance of such an order as follows: "Of course, we will lose $0.50 each on the variable manufacturing costs, but we will gain $0.60 per unit by spreading our fixed manufacturing costs over 1.25 million units instead of 1 million units. Consequently, we should take the offer because it represents an advantage of $0.10 per unit."

Old fixed manufacturing cost per unit, $3,000,000 ÷ 1,000,000	$3.00
New fixed manufacturing cost per unit, $3,000,000 ÷ 1,250,000	2.40
"Saving" in fixed manufacturing cost per unit	$0.60
Loss on variable manufacturing cost per unit, $11.50 − $12.00	0.50
Net saving per unit in manufacturing cost	$0.10

Explain why this is faulty thinking.

Solution

1. Focus on the *differences* in revenues and costs. In this problem, in addition to the difference in variable costs, there is a difference in fixed costs between the two alternatives.

Additional revenue, 100,000 units @ $13.50 per unit	$1,350,000
Less additional costs:	
Variable costs, 100,000 units @ $12 per unit	1,200,000
Fixed costs, agent's fee	40,000
Increase in operating income from accepting the special order	$ 110,000

2. The faulty thinking comes from attributing a "savings" to the decrease in unit fixed costs. Regardless of how the fixed manufacturing costs are "unitized" or "spread" over the units produced, their total of $3 million will be *unchanged* by the special order. Short-run income will fall by 250,000 units × ($12.00 − $11.50) = $125,000 if the special order is accepted.

Problem Two

Custom Graphics is a printing company that bids on a wide variety of design and printing jobs. The owner of the company, Janet Solomon, prepares the bids for most jobs. She has budgeted the following costs for 2006:

Materials		$ 350,000
Labour		250,000
Overhead:		
Variable	300,000	
Fixed	150,000	450,000
Total production cost of jobs		1,050,000
Selling and administrative expenses:		
Variable	75,000	
Fixed	125,000	200,000
Total costs		$1,250,000

Solomon has a target profit of $250,000 for 2006.

Compute the average target profit percentage for setting prices as a percentage of:

1. Prime costs (materials plus labour)
2. Variable production cost of jobs
3. Total production cost of jobs
4. All variable costs
5. All costs

Solution

The purpose of this problem is to emphasize that many different approaches to pricing might be used that, if properly employed, would achieve the *same* target selling prices. To achieve $250,000 of profit, the desired revenue for 2006 is $1,250,000 + $250,000 = $1,500,000. The target markup percentages are:

1. Percent of prime cost $= \dfrac{(\$1,500,000 - \$600,000)}{(\$600,000)} = 150\%$

2. Percent of variable production cost of jobs $= \dfrac{(\$1,500,000 - \$900,000)}{(\$900,000)} = 66.7\%$

3. Percent of total production cost of jobs $= \dfrac{(\$1,500,000 - \$1,050,000)}{(\$1,050,000)} = 42.9\%$

4. Percent of all variable costs = $\dfrac{(\$1{,}500{,}000 - \$975{,}000)}{(\$975{,}000)}$ = 53.8%

5. Percent of all costs = $\dfrac{(\$1{,}500{,}000 - \$1{,}250{,}000)}{(\$1{,}250{,}000)}$ = 20%

KEY TERMS

avoidable costs *p. 350*
common costs *p. 350*
decision model *p. 344*
discriminatory pricing *p. 357*
dumping *p. 357*
imperfect competition *p. 355*
inventory turnover *p. 353*
limiting factor *p. 353*
marginal cost *p. 355*

marginal revenue *p. 355*
markup *p. 358*
perfect competition *p. 354*
predatory pricing *p. 357*
price elasticity *p. 355*
relevant information *p. 341*
scarce resource *p. 353*
target costing *p. 359*
unavoidable costs *p. 350*

ASSIGNMENT MATERIAL

QUESTIONS

Q8-1 "The distinction between precision and relevance should be kept in mind." Explain.

Q8-2 Distinguish between the quantitative and qualitative aspects of decisions.

Q8-3 Describe the accountant's role in decision making.

Q8-4 "Any future cost is relevant." Do you agree? Explain.

Q8-5 Why are historical or past data irrelevant to special decisions?

Q8-6 Describe the role of past or historical costs in the decision process. That is, how do these costs relate to the prediction method and the decision model?

Q8-7 "There is a commonality of approach to various special decisions." Explain.

Q8-8 "In relevant-cost analysis, beware of unit costs." Explain.

Q8-9 "Increasing sales will decrease fixed costs because it spreads them over more units." Do you agree? Explain.

Q8-10 "The key decision to delete a product or department is identifying avoidable costs." Do you agree? Explain.

Q8-11 "Avoidable costs are variable costs." Do you agree? Explain.

Q8-12 Give four examples of limiting factors (or scarce resources).

Q8-13 Compare and contrast *marginal cost* and *variable cost*.

Q8-14 Describe the major factors that influence pricing decisions.

Q8-15 Why are customers one of the factors influencing price decisions?

Q8-16 "In target costing, prices determine costs rather than vice versa." Explain.

Q8-17 "Basing pricing on only the variable costs of a job results in suicidal underpricing?" Do you agree? Why?

Q8-18 Provide three examples of pricing decisions other than the special order.

Q8-19 List four popular markup formulas for pricing.

Q8-20 Describe two long-run effects that may lead to managers rejecting opportunities to cut prices and obtain increases in short-run profits.

Q8-21 Give two reasons why full costs are far more widely used than variable costs for guiding pricing.

Q8-22 Why do most executives use both full-cost and variable-cost information for pricing decisions?

PROBLEMS

P8-1 **PINPOINTING OF RELEVANT COSTS.** Today you are planning to see a movie and you can attend either of two theatres. You have only a small budget for entertainment, so prices are important. You have attended both theatres recently. One charged $10 for admission; the other charged $11. You habitually buy popcorn in the theatre—each theatre charges $5. The movies now being shown are equally attractive to you, but you are virtually certain that you will never see the movie that you reject today.

Identify the relevant costs. Explain your answer.

P8-2 **INFORMATION AND DECISIONS.** Suppose the historical costs for the manufacture of a calculator were as follows: direct materials, $5 per unit; direct labour, $3 per unit. Management is trying to decide whether to replace some materials with different materials. The replacement should cut material costs by 5 percent per unit. However, direct labour time will increase by 5 percent per unit. Moreover, direct labour rates will be affected by a recent 10 percent wage increase.

Prepare an exhibit like Exhibit 8-1 (page 343), showing where and how the data about direct material and direct labour fit in the decision process.

P8-3 **IDENTIFYING RELEVANT COSTS.** Sonkar and Raji Ramaswamy were deciding whether to go to the symphony or the baseball game. They already have two nonrefundable tickets to "Pops Night at the Symphony" that cost $40 each. This is the only concert of the season they considered attending because it is the only one with the type of music they enjoy. The baseball game is the last one of the season and it will decide the league championship. They can purchase tickets for $20 each.

They will drive 50 kilometres round-trip to either event. Variable costs for operating their car are $0.14 per kilometre, and fixed costs average $0.13 per kilometre for the 20,000 kilometres they drive annually. Parking at the symphony is free, but costs $6 at the baseball game.

To attend either event, Sonkar and Raji will hire a babysitter at $4 per hour. They expect to be gone five hours to attend the baseball game but only four hours to attend the symphony.

Compare the cost of attending the baseball game to the cost of attending the symphony. Focus on relevant costs. Compute the difference in cost, and indicate which alternative is most costly to the Ramaswamys.

P8-4 **SPECIAL-ORDER DECISION.** Victory Athletic Supply (VAS) makes game jerseys for athletic teams. The F. C. Strikers soccer club has offered to buy 100 jerseys for the teams in its league for $15 per jersey. The team price for such jerseys is normally $18, an 80 percent markup over VAS's purchase price of $10 per jersey. VAS adds a name and number to each jersey at a variable cost of $2 per jersey. The annual fixed cost of equipment used in the printing process is $6,000 and other fixed costs allocated to jerseys is $2,000. VAS produces about 2,000 jerseys per year, making the fixed cost $4 per jersey. The equipment is used only for printing jerseys, and stands idle 75 percent of the usable time.

The manager of VAS turned down the offer, saying, "If we sell at $15 and our cost is $16, we lose money on each jersey we sell. We would like to help your league, but we can't afford to lose money on the sale."

1. Compute the amount by which the operating income of VAS would change if the F. C. Strikers' offer were accepted.
2. Suppose you were the manager of VAS. Would you accept the offer? In addition to considering the quantitative impact computed in requirement 1, list two qualitative considerations that would influence your decision—one qualitative factor supporting acceptance of the offer and one supporting rejection.

P8-5 **SPECIAL ORDER.** Consider the following details of the income statement of the Pocket Calculator Division (PCD) of the Kim Electronics Company for the year ended December 31, 2006:

Sales	$10,000,000
Less manufacturing cost of goods sold	6,000,000
Gross margin or gross profit	$ 4,000,000
Less selling and administrative expenses	3,300,000
Operating income	$ 700,000

PCD's fixed manufacturing costs were $2.4 million and its fixed selling and administrative costs were $2.5 million. Sales commissions of 3 percent of sales are included in selling and administrative expenses.

The company sold 2 million calculators. Near the end of the year, Pizza Hut Corporation offered to buy 150,000 calculators on a special order. To fill the order, a logo bearing the Pizza Hut emblem would have to be added to each calculator. Pizza Hut intended to use the calculators in special promotions in early 2007.

Even though PCD had some idle plant capacity, the president rejected the Pizza Hut offer of $660,000 for the 150,000 calculators. He said: "The Pizza Hut offer is too low. We'd avoid paying sales commissions, but we'd have to incur an extra cost of $0.20 per calculator to add the logo. If PCD sells below its regular selling prices, it will begin a chain reaction of competitors price-cutting and of customers wanting special deals. I believe in pricing at no lower than 8 percent above our full costs of $9,300,000 ÷ 2,000,000 units = $4.65 per unit plus the extra $0.20 less the savings in commissions."

1. Using the contribution approach, prepare an analysis similar to that in Exhibit 8-3. Use three columns: without the special order, the special order (total and per unit), and totals with the special order.
2. By what percentage would operating income increase or decrease if the order had been accepted? Do you agree with the president's decision? Why?

P8-6 **VARIETY OF COST TERMS.** Consider the following data:

Variable selling and administrative costs per unit	$ 3.00
Total fixed selling and administrative costs	$2,900,000
Total fixed manufacturing costs	$3,000,000
Variable manufacturing costs per unit	$ 10.00
Units produced and sold	500,000

1. Compute the following per unit of product: (a) total variable costs, (b) absorption cost, (c) full cost.
2. Give a synonym for full cost.

P8-7 **PROFIT PER UNIT OF SPACE.**

1. Several successful chains of warehouse stores such as Costco have merchandising policies that differ considerably from those of traditional department stores. Identify characteristics of these warehouse stores that have contributed to their success.
2. Food chains such as the Loblaw Company have regarded approximately 20 percent of selling price as an average target gross profit on canned goods and similar grocery items. What are the limitations of such an approach? Be specific.

P8-8 **CHOOSING PRODUCTS.** The Ibunez Tool Company has two products: a plain circular saw and a fancy circular saw. The plain circular saw sells for $66 and has a variable cost of $50. The fancy circular saw sells for $100 and has a variable cost of $70.

1. Compute the contribution margin and contribution-margin ratio for plain and fancy circular saws.
2. The demand is for more units than the company can produce. There are only 20,000 machine hours of manufacturing capacity available. Two plain circular saws can be produced in the same average time (one hour) needed to produce one fancy circular saw. Compute the total contribution margin for 20,000 hours for plain circular saws only and for fancy circular saws only.
3. In two or three sentences, state the major lesson of this problem.

P8-9 **FORMULAS FOR PRICING.** Greg Pino, a building contractor, constructs houses in tracts, often building as many as 20 homes simultaneously. He has budgeted costs for an expected number of houses in 2007 as follows:

Direct materials	$3,500,000
Direct labour	1,000,000
Job construction overhead	1,500,000
Cost of jobs	$6,000,000
Selling and administrative costs	1,500,000
Total costs	$7,500,000

The job construction overhead includes approximately $600,000 of fixed costs, such as the salaries of supervisors and amortization on equipment. The selling and administrative costs include $300,000 of variable costs, such as sales commissions and bonuses that depend fundamentally on overall profitability. Pino wants an operating income of $1.5 million for 2007.

Compute the average target profit percentage for setting prices as a percentage of:

1. Prime costs (direct materials plus direct labour).
2. The full "cost of jobs."
3. The variable "cost of jobs."
4. The full "cost of jobs" plus selling and administrative costs.
5. The variable "cost of jobs" plus variable selling and administrative costs.

P8-10 SPECIAL ORDER, TERMINOLOGY, AND UNIT COSTS. The following is the income statement of a manufacturer of blue jeans:

Hunter Company
Income Statement
for the Year Ended
December 31, 2006

	TOTAL	PER UNIT
Sales	$40,000,000	$20.00
Less manufacturing cost of goods sold	24,000,000	12.00
Gross margin	$16,000,000	8.00
Less selling and administrative expenses	14,000,000	7.00
Operating income	$ 2,000,000	$ 1.00

Hunter had manufactured 2 million units, which had been sold to various clothing wholesalers and department stores. In early 2007, the president, Rosemary Munoy, died of a stroke. Her son, Hector, became the new president. Hector has worked for 15 years in the marketing department of the business. He knows very little about accounting and manufacturing, which were his mother's strengths. Hector has several questions for you, including inquiries regarding the pricing of special orders.

1. To prepare better answers, you decide to recast the income statement in contribution form. Variable manufacturing cost was $19 million. Variable selling and administrative expenses, which were mostly sales commissions, shipping expenses, and advertising allowances, paid to customers based on units sold, were $9 million.
2. Hector asks, "I can't understand financial statements until I know the meaning of various terms. In scanning my mother's assorted notes, I found the following pertaining to both total and unit costs: *absorption cost, full manufacturing cost, variable cost, full cost, fully allocated cost, gross margin, contribution margin*. Using our data for 2006, please give me a list of these costs, their total amounts, and their per-unit amounts."
3. "Near the end of 2006 I brought in a special order from The Bay for 100,000 pairs of jeans at $17 each. I said I'd accept a flat $20,000 sales commission instead of the usual 6 percent of selling price, but my mother refused the order. She usually upheld a relatively rigid pricing policy, saying that it was bad business to accept orders that did not generate, at least, full manufacturing cost plus 80 percent.

   "That policy bothered me. We had idle capacity. The way I figured, our manufacturing costs would go up by 100,000 × $12 = $1,200,000, but our selling and administrative expenses would only go up by $20,000. That would mean additional operating income of 100,000 × ($17 −$12) minus 20,000, or $500,000 minus $20,000 or $480,000. That's too much money to give up just to maintain a general pricing policy. Was my analysis of the impact on operating income correct? If not, please show me the correct additional operating income."

4. After receiving the explanations offered in requirements 2 and 3, Hector said: "Forget that I had The Bay order. I had an even bigger order from Wal-Mart. It was for 500,000 units and would have filled the plant completely. I told my mother I'd settle for no commission. There would have been no selling and administrative costs whatsoever because Wal-Mart would pay for the shipping and would not get any advertising allowances.

"Wal-Mart offered $9.20 per unit. Our fixed manufacturing costs would have been spread over 2.5 million instead of 2 million units. Wouldn't it have been advantageous to accept the offer? Our old fixed manufacturing costs were $2.50 per unit. The added volume would reduce that cost more than our loss on our variable costs per unit.

"Am I correct? What would have been the impact on total operating income if we had accepted the order?"

P8-11 UNIT COSTS AND CAPACITY. Lepanto Manufacturing Company produces two industrial solvents for which the following data have been tabulated. Fixed manufacturing cost is applied to product at a rate of $1 per machine hour.

The sales manager has had a $160,000 increase in her budget allotment for advertising and wants to apply the money to the most profitable product. The solvents are not substitutes for one another in the eyes of the company's customers.

PER UNIT	XY-7	BD-4
Selling price	$6.00	$4.00
Variable manufacturing cost	3.00	1.50
Fixed manufacturing cost	0.80	0.20
Variable selling cost	2.00	2.00

1. How many machine hours does it take to produce one XY-7? To produce one BD-4? (*Hint:* Focus on applied fixed manufacturing cost.)
2. Suppose Lepanto has only 100,000 machine hours that can be made available to produce XY-7 and BD-4. If the potential increase in sales units for either product resulting from advertising is far in excess of these production capabilities, which product should be produced and advertised and what is the estimated increase in contribution margin earned?

P8-12 DROPPING A PRODUCT LINE. Hambley's Toy Store is on Regent Street in London. It has a magic department near the main door. Management is considering dropping the magic department, which has consistently shown an operating loss. The predicted income statements, in thousands of pounds (£), follow (for ease of analysis, only three product lines are shown):

	TOTAL	GENERAL MERCHANDISE	ELECTRONIC PRODUCTS	MAGIC DEPARTMENT
Sales	£6,000	£5,000	£400	£ 600
Variable expenses	4,090	3,500	200	390
Contribution margin	£1,910 (32%)	£1,500 (30%)	£200 (50%)	£ 210 (35%)
Fixed expenses (compensation, amortization, property taxes, insurance, etc.)	1,110	750	50	310
Operating income	£ 800	£ 750	£150	£(100)

The £310,000 of fixed expenses include the compensation of magic department employees of £100,000. These employees will be released if the magic department is abandoned. All equipment is fully amortized, so none of the £310,000 pertains to such items. Furthermore, disposal values of the equipment will be exactly offset by the costs of removal and remodelling.

If the magic department is dropped, the manager will use the vacated space for either more general merchandise or more electronic products. The expansion of general merchandise would not entail hiring any additional salaried help, but more electronic products would require an additional person at an annual cost of £25,000. The manager thinks that sales of general merchandise would increase by £300,000; electronic products, by £200,000. The manager's modest predictions are partially based on the fact that she thinks the magic department has helped lure customers to the store and thus improved overall sales. If the magic department is closed, that lure would be gone.

Should the magic department be closed? Explain, showing computations.

P8-13   **DELETE A PRODUCT LINE.**   Ethos Day School is a private elementary school. In addition to regular classes, after-school care is provided between 3:00 p.m. and 6:00 p.m. at SF12 per child per hour. Financial results for the after-school care for a representative month are shown, in Swiss Francs.

Revenue, 600 hours @ SF12 per hour		SF7,200
Less:		
Teacher salaries	SF5,200	
Supplies	800	
Amortization	1,300	
Sanitary engineering	100	
Other fixed costs	200	7,600
Operating income (loss)		SF (400)

The director of Ethos Day School is considering discontinuing the after-school care services because it is not fair to the other students to subsidize the after-school care program. He thinks that eliminating the program will free up SF400 a month to be used in the regular classes.

1. Compute the financial impact on Ethos Day School from discontinuing the after-school care program.
2. List three qualitative factors that would influence your decision.

P8-14   **ACCEPTING A LOW BID.**   The Velasquez Company, a maker of a variety of metal and plastic products, is in the midst of a business downturn and is saddled with many idle facilities. The National Hospital Supply Company has approached Velasquez to produce 300,000 nonslide serving trays. National will pay $1.30 each.

Velasquez predicts that its variable costs will be $1.40 each. However, its fixed costs, which had been averaging $1 per unit on a variety of other products, will now be spread over twice as much volume. The president commented, "Sure, we'll lose $0.10 each on the variable costs, but we'll gain $0.50 per unit by spreading our fixed costs. Therefore, we should take the offer, because it represents an advantage of $0.40 per unit."

Do you agree with the president? Why? Suppose the regular business had a current volume of 300,000 units, sales of $600,000, variable costs of $420,000, and fixed costs of $300,000.

P8-15 PRICING BY AUTO DEALERS. Many automobile dealers have an operating pattern similar to that of City Motors. Each month, City initially aims at a unit volume quota that approximates a break-even point. Until the break-even point is reached, City has a policy of relatively lofty pricing, whereby the "minimum deal" must contain a sufficiently high markup to ensure a contribution to profit of no less than $400. After the break-even point is attained, City tends to quote lower prices for the rest of the month.

What is your opinion of this policy? As a prospective customer, how would you react to this policy?

P8-16 TARGET SELLING PRICES. Consider the following data from Kastoria Leather Company's budgeted income statement (in thousands of dollars):

Target sales	$60,000
Variable costs:	
Manufacturing	30,000
Selling and administrative	6,000
Total variable costs	36,000
Fixed costs:	
Manufacturing	8,000
Selling and administrative	6,000
Total fixed costs	14,000
Total all costs	50,000
Operating income	$10,000

Compute the following markup formulas that would be used for obtaining the same target selling prices as a percentage of (1) total variable costs, (2) full costs, (3) variable manufacturing costs, and (4) absorption costs.

P8-17 COMPETITIVE BIDS. Griffey, Rodriguez, and Martinez, a CA firm, is preparing to bid for a consulting job. Although Alice Griffey will use her judgment about the market in finalizing the bid, she has asked you to prepare a cost analysis to help in the bidding. You have estimated the following costs for the consulting job:

Materials and supplies, at cost	$ 28,000
Hourly pay for consultants, 2,000 hours @ $36 per hour	72,000
Employee benefit costs for consultants,	
2,000 hours @ $12 per hour	24,000
Total variable costs	124,000
Fixed costs allocated to the job:	
Based on labour, 2,000 hours @ $10.30 per hour	21,600
Based on materials and supplies, 80% of $28,000	22,400
Total cost	$168,000

Of the $44,000 allocated fixed costs, $35,000 will be incurred even if the job is not undertaken.

Alice normally bids jobs at 150 percent of the estimated materials and supplies cost plus $80 per estimated labour hour.

1. Prepare a bid using the normal formula.
2. Prepare a minimum bid equal to the additional costs expected to be incurred to complete the job.
3. Prepare a bid that will cover full costs plus a markup for profit equal to 20 percent of full cost.

P8-18 **PRICING AND CONTRIBUTION APPROACH.** The Transit Transportation Company has the following operating results to date for 2006:

Operating revenues	$50,000,000
Operating costs	40,000,000
Operating income	$10,000,000

A large Toronto manufacturer has inquired about whether Transit would be interested in trucking a large order of its parts to Vancouver. Steven Minkler, operations manager, investigated the situation and estimated that the "fully allocated" costs of servicing the order would be $40,000. Using his general pricing formula, he quoted a price of $50,000. The manufacturer replied: "We'll give you $37,000, take it or leave it. If you do not want our business, we'll truck it ourselves or go elsewhere."

A cost analyst had recently been conducting studies of how Transit's operating costs tended to behave. She found that $32 million of the $40 million could be characterized as variable costs. Minkler discussed the matter with her and decided that this order would probably generate cost behaviour little different from Transit's general operations.

1. Using a contribution format, prepare an analysis for Minkler.
2. Should Transit accept the order? Explain.

P8-19 **PRICING AT THE AGAWA CANYON RAILWAY.** Suppose a tour guide approached the general manager of The Agawa Canyon Railway with a proposal to offer a special guided tour to the agent's clients. The tour would occur 20 times each summer and be part of a larger itinerary that the agent is putting together. The agent presented two options: (1) a special 65 kilometre tour with the agent's 30 clients as the only passengers on the train, or (2) adding a car to an existing train to accommodate the 30 clients on the 65 kilometre tour.

Under either option Agawa Canyon would hire a tour guide for $150 for the trip. Agawa Canyon has extra cars in its switching yard, and it would cost $40 to move a car to the main track and hook it up. The extra fuel cost to pull one extra car is $0.20 per kilometre. To run an engine and a passenger car on the trip would cost $2.20 per kilomctre, and an engineer would be paid $400 for the trip.

Amortization on passenger cars is $5,000 per year, and amortization on engines is $20,000 per year. Each passenger car and each engine travels about 50,000 kilometres a year. They are replaced every eight years.

The agent offered to pay $30 per passenger for the special tour and $15 per passenger for simply adding an extra car.

1. Which of the two options is more profitable for Agawa Canyon? Comment on which costs are irrelevant to this decision.
2. Should Agawa Canyon accept the proposal for the option you found best in requirement 1? Comment on what costs are relevant for this decision but not for the decision in requirement 1.

P8-20 **CHOICE OF PRODUCTS.** West Coast Fashions sells both designer and moderately priced women's wear in Vancouver. Profits have been volatile. Top management is trying to decide which product line to drop. Accountants have reported the following data:

	PER ITEM	
	DESIGNER	MODERATELY PRICED
Average selling price	$240	$150
Average variable expenses	120	85
Average contribution margin	$120	$ 65
Average contribution-margin percentage	50%	43%

The store has 8,000 square metres of floor space. If moderately priced goods are sold exclusively, 400 items can be displayed. If designer goods are sold exclusively, only 300 items can be displayed. Moreover, the rate of sale (turnover) of the designer items will be two-thirds the rate of moderately priced goods.

1. Prepare an analysis to show which product to drop.
2. What other considerations might affect your decision in requirement 1?

P8-21 **COST ANALYSIS AND PRICING.** The budget for the University Printing Company for 2007 follows.

Sales		$1,100,000
Direct material	$280,000	
Direct labour	320,000	
Overhead	400,000	1,000,000
Net income		$ 100,000

The company typically uses a so-called cost-plus pricing system. Direct material and direct labour are computed, overhead is added at a rate of 125 percent of direct labour, and 10 percent of the total cost is added to obtain the selling price.

The sales manager has placed a $22,000 bid on a particularly large order with a cost of $5,600 direct material and $6,400 direct labour. The customer informs him that he can have the business for $19,800, take it or leave it. If University accepted the order, total sales for 2007 will be $1,119,800.

The sales manager refuses the order, saying: "I sell on a cost-plus basis. It is bad policy to accept orders at below cost. I would lose $200 on the job." The company's annual fixed overhead is $160,000.

1. What would net income have been with the order? Without the order? Show your computations.
2. Give a short description of a contribution approach to pricing that University might follow. Include a stipulation of the pricing formula that University should routinely use if it hopes to obtain a target net income of $100,000.

P8-22 **PRICING OF EDUCATION.** You are the director of business continuing education programs for Ryerson University. Courses for executives are especially popular, and you have developed an extensive menu of one-day and two-day courses that are presented in various downtown locations. The performance of these courses for the current fiscal year, excluding the final course, which is scheduled for next Saturday, is as follows:

Tuition revenue	$2,000,000
Costs of courses	800,000
Contribution margin	1,200,000
General administrative expenses	400,000
Operating income	$ 800,000

The costs of these courses include fees for instructors, rentals of classrooms, advertising, and any other items, such as travel, that can be easily and exclusively identified as being caused by a particular course.

The general administrative expenses include your salary, your secretary's compensation, and related expenses, such as a lump-sum payment to the university's central offices as a share of university overhead.

The enrollment for your final course of the year is 30 students, who have paid $500 each. Two days before the course is to begin, a city manager phones your office. "Do you offer discounts to not-for-profit institutions?" he asks. "If so, we'll send 10 managers. But our budget will not justify spending more than $400 per person." The extra cost of including these 10 managers would entail lunches at $20 each and course materials at $40 each.

1. Prepare a tabulation of the performance for the full year, including the final course. Assume that the costs of the final course for the 40 enrollees' instruction, travel, advertising, rental of hotel classroom, lunches, and course materials would be $4,000. Show a tabulation in four columns: before final course, final course with 30 registrants, effect of 10 more registrants, and grand totals.
2. What major considerations would probably influence the pricing policies for these courses? For setting regular university tuition in private universities?

P8-23 **UTILIZATION OF PASSENGER JETS.** In a recent year, National Air Lines, Inc., filled 50 percent of the available seats on its flights, a record about 15 percentage points below the national average.

When you answer this question, suppose that National had a basic package of 3,000 flights per month that had an average of 100 seats available per flight. Also suppose that 52 percent of the seats were filled at an average ticket price of $200 per flight. Variable costs are about 70 percent of revenue.

National also had a marginal package of 120 flights per month that had an average of 100 seats available per flight. Suppose that only 20 percent of the seats were filled at an average ticket price of $100 per flight. Variable costs are about 50 percent of this revenue. Prepare a tabulation of the basic package, marginal package, and total package, showing percentage of seats filled, revenue, variable expenses, and contribution margin.

P8-24 **EFFECTS OF VOLUME ON OPERATING INCOME.** The Wittred Division of Victoria Sports Company manufactures boomerangs, which are sold to wholesalers and retailers. The division manager has set a target of 250,000 boomerangs for next month's production and sales. However, the manager has prepared an analysis of the effects on operating income of deviations from the target:

Volume in units	200,000	250,000	300,000
Sales @ $3.00	$600,000	$750,000	$900,000
Full costs @ $2.50	500,000	625,000	750,000
Operating income	$100,000	$125,000	$150,000

The costs have the following characteristics. Variable manufacturing costs are $1 per boomerang; variable selling costs are $0.20 per boomerang. Fixed manufacturing costs per month are $300,000; fixed selling and administrative costs, $50,000.

1. Prepare a correct analysis of the changes in volume on operating income. Prepare a tabulated set of income statements at levels of 200,000, 250,000, and 300,000 boomerangs. Also show percentages of operating income in relation to sales.
2. Compare your tabulation with the manager's tabulation. Why is the manager's tabulation incorrect?

P8-25 **PRICING A SPECIAL ORDER.** The Drosselmeier Corporation, which makes Christmas nut-crackers, has an annual plant capacity of 2,400 product units. Its predicted operating results (in Euros [EUR]) for the year are

Production and sales of 2,000 units, total sales	EUR92,632.54
Manufacturing costs:	
Fixed (total)	30,677.57
Variable (per unit)	13.29
Selling and administrative expenses:	
Fixed (total)	15,338.76
Variable (per unit)	5.11

Compute, ignoring income taxes:

1. If the company accepted a special order for 300 units at a selling price of EUR 20.45 each, how would the *total* predicted net income for the year be affected, assuming no effect on regular sales at regular prices?
2. Without decreasing its total net income, what is the lowest *unit price* for which the Drosselmeier Corporation could sell an additional 100 units not subject to any variable selling and administrative expenses, assuming no effect on regular sales at regular prices?
3. In solving requirement 2 above, list the numbers given in the problem that are irrelevant (not relevant).
4. Compute the expected annual net income (with no special orders) if plant capacity can be doubled by adding additional facilities at a cost of EUR 255,645.94. Assume that these facilities have an estimated life of five years with no residual value and that the current unit selling price can be maintained for all sales. Total sales are expected to equal the new plant capacity each year. No changes are expected in variable costs per unit or in total fixed costs except for amortization.

P8-26 **PRICING AND CONFUSING VARIABLE AND FIXED COSTS.**   Diaz Telecom had a fixed factory over-head budget for 2007 of $1 million. The company planned to make and sell 200,000 units of the product—a communications device. All variable manufacturing costs per unit were $10. The budgeted income statement contained the following:

Sales	$4,000,000
Manufacturing cost of goods sold	3,000,000
Gross margin	1,000,000
Selling and administrative expenses	400,000
Operating income	$ 600,000

For simplicity, assume that the actual variable costs per unit and the total fixed costs were exactly as budgeted.

1. Compute Diaz's budgeted fixed factory overhead per unit.
2. Near the end of 2007, a large computer manufacturer offered to buy 10,000 units for $120,000 on a one-time special order. The president of Diaz stated: "The offer is a bad deal. It's foolish to sell below full man-ufacturing costs per unit. I realize that this order will have only a mod-est effect on selling and administrative costs. They will increase by a $1,000 fee paid to our sales agent." Compute the effect on operating income if the offer is accepted.
3. What factors should the president of Diaz consider before finally decid-ing whether to accept the offer?
4. Suppose the original budget for fixed manufacturing costs was $1 mil-lion, but budgeted units of product were 1 million. How would your answers to requirements 1 and 2 change? Be specific.

P8-27 **DEMAND ANALYSIS.**   (SMA, adapted)   Zimmerman Manufacturing Limited produces and sells flags. During 2006, the company manufactured and sold 50,000 flags at $25 each. Existing production capacity is 60,000 flags per year.

In formulating the 2007 budget, management is faced with a number of decisions concerning product pricing and output. The following information is available:

1. A market survey shows that the sales volume depends largely on the selling price. For each $1 drop in selling price, sales volume would increase by 10,000 flags.
2. The company's expected cost structure for 2007 is as follows:
   (a) Fixed cost (regardless of production or sales activities), $360,000;
   (b) Variable costs per flag (including production, selling, and adminis-trative expenses), $16.
3. To increase annual capacity from the present 60,000 to 90,000 flags, additional investment for plant, building, equipment, and the like, of $200,000 would be necessary. The estimated average life of the addi-tional investment would be ten years, so the fixed costs would increase by an average of $20,000 per year. (Expansion of less than 30,000 addi-tional units of capacity would cost only slightly less than $200,000.)

Indicate, with reasons, what the level of production and the selling price should be for the coming year. Also, indicate whether the company should approve the plant expansion. Show your calculations. Ignore income tax considerations and the time value of money.

P8-28 **ANALYSIS OF UNIT COSTS.** The Home Appliance Company manufactures small appliances, such as electric can openers, toasters, food mixers, and irons. The peak season is at hand, and the president is trying to decide whether to produce more of the company's standard line of can openers or its premium line that includes a built-in knife sharpener, a better finish, and a higher-quality motor. The unit data follow:

	PRODUCT	
	STANDARD	PREMIUM
Selling price	$28	$38
Direct material	$ 8	$13
Direct labour	2	1
Variable factory overhead	4	6
Fixed factory overhead	6	9
Total cost of goods sold	$20	$29
Gross profit per unit	$ 8	$ 9

The sales outlook is very encouraging. The plant could operate at full capacity by producing either or both products. Both the standard and the premium products are processed through the same departments. Selling and administrative costs will not be affected by this decision, so they may be ignored.

Many of the parts are produced on automatic machinery. The factory overhead is allocated to products by developing separate rates per machine hour for variable and fixed overhead. For example, the total fixed overhead is divided by the total machine hours to determine a rate per hour. Thus the amount of overhead allocated to product depends on the number of machine hours allocated to the product. It takes one hour of machine time to produce one unit of the standard product.

Direct labour may not be proportionate with overhead because many workers operate two or more machines simultaneously. Which product should be produced? If more than one should be produced, indicate the proportions of each. Show computations. Explain your answer briefly.

P8-29 **TARGET COSTING.** Belleville Electrical Inc. makes small electric motors for a variety of home appliances. Belleville sells the motors to appliance makers, which assemble and sell the appliances to retail outlets. Although Belleville makes dozens of different motors, it does not currently make one to be used in garage door openers. The company's market research department has discovered a market for such a motor.

The market research department has indicated that a motor for garage door openers would likely sell for $25. A similar motor currently being produced has the following manufacturing costs:

Direct materials	$13.00
Direct labour	6.00
Overhead	8.00
Total	$27.00

Belleville desires a gross margin of 15 percent of the manufacturing cost.

1. Suppose Belleville used cost-plus pricing, setting the price 15 percent above the manufacturing cost. What price would be charged for the motor? Would you produce such a motor if you were a manager at Belleville? Explain.
2. Suppose Belleville uses target costing. What price would the company charge for a garage-door-opener motor? What is the highest acceptable manufacturing cost for which Belleville would be willing to produce the motor?
3. As a user of target costing, what steps would Belleville managers take to try to make production of this market feasible?

P8-30 **PRICING, ETHICS, AND THE LAW.** Great Lakes Pharmaceuticals, Inc. (GLPI) produces both prescription and over-the-counter medications. In January, GLPI introduces a new prescription drug, Capestan, to relieve the pain of arthritis. The company spent more than $50 million over the last five years developing the drug, and advertising alone during the first year of introduction will exceed $10 million. Production cost for a bottle of 100 tablets is approximately $12. Sales in the first three years are predicted to be 500,000, 750,000, and 1,000,000 bottles, respectively. To achieve these sales, GLPI plans to distribute the medicine through three sources: directly from physicians, through hospital pharmacies, and through retail pharmacies. Initially, the bottles will be given free to physicians to give to patients, hospital pharmacies will pay $25 per bottle, and retail pharmacies will pay $40 per bottle. In the second and third years, the company plans to phase out the free distributions to physicians and move all other customers toward a $50 per bottle sales price.

Comment on the pricing and promotion policies of GLPI. Pay particular attention to the legal and ethical issues involved.

P8-31 **PRICING TO MAXIMIZE CONTRIBUTION.** Frame It Company produces and sells picture frames. One particular frame for 8×10 photos was an instant success in the market, but recently competitors have come out with comparable frames. Frame It has been charging $12 wholesale for the frames, and sales have fallen from 10,000 units last year to 7,000 units this year. The product manager in charge of this frame is considering lowering the price to $10 per frame. She believes sales will rebound to 10,000 units at the lower price, but they will fall to 6,000 units at the $12 price. The unit variable cost of producing and selling the frames is $6, and $40,000 of fixed cost is assigned to the frames.

1. Assuming that the only prices under consideration are $10 and $12 per frame, which price will lead to the largest profit for Frame It? Explain why.
2. What subjective consideration might affect your pricing decision?

P8-32 **VIDEOTAPE SALES AND RENTAL MARKETS.** Is it more profitable to sell your product for $50 or $15? This is a difficult question for many movie studio executives. Consider a movie that cost $60 million to produce and required another $40 million to promote. After its theatre release, the studio must determine whether to sell videotapes directly to the public at a wholesale price of about $15 per tape or to sell to video rental store distributors for about $50 per tape. The distributors will then sell to about 14,000 video rental stores in North America.

Assume that the variable cost to produce and ship one videotape is $2.00.

1. Suppose each video rental store would purchase 10 tapes of this movie. How many tapes would need to be sold directly to customers to make direct sales a more profitable option than sales to video store distributors?
2. How does the cost of producing and promoting the movie affect this decision?
3. A production company elected to sell a new movie directly to consumers, and sold 30 million copies at an average price of $15 per tape. How many tapes would each video rental store have to purchase to provide the production company as much profit as the company received from direct sales? Assume that the production company would receive $50 per tape from the distributors. Would the production company have been better off it it had decided to sell to the distributors?

P8-33 USE OF AVAILABLE FACILITIES. The Oahu Company manufactures electronic subcomponents that can be sold directly or can be processed further into "plug-in" assemblies for a variety of intricate electronic equipment. The entire output of subcomponents can be sold at a market price of $2.20 per unit. The plug-in assemblies have been generating a sales price of $5.30 for three years, but the price has recently fallen to $5.10 on assorted orders.

Janet Oh, the vice president of marketing, has analyzed the markets and the costs. She thinks that production of plug-in assemblies should be dropped whenever the price falls below $4.70 per unit. However, at the current price of $5.10, the total available capacity should currently be devoted to producing plug-in assemblies. She has cited the data below.

OAHU AUDIO COMPANY PRODUCT PROFITABILITY DATA		
	SUBCOMPONENTS	
Selling price, after deducting relevant selling costs		$2.20
Direct material	$1.10	
Direct labour	0.30	
Manufacturing overhead	0.60	
Cost per unit		2.00
Operating profit		$0.20
	PLUG-IN ASSEMBLIES	
Selling price, after deducting relevant selling costs		$5.30
Transferred-in variable cost for subcomponents	$1.40	
Additional direct materials	1.45	
Direct labour	0.45	
Manufacturing overhead	1.20*	
Cost per unit		4.50
Operating profit		$0.80

* For additional processing to make and test plug-in assemblies.

Direct materials and direct labour costs are variable. The total overhead is fixed; it is allocated to units produced by predicting the total overhead for the coming year and dividing this total by the total hours of capacity available.

The total hours available are 600,000. It takes one hour to make 60 subcomponents and two hours of additional processing and testing to make 60 plug-in assemblies.

1. If the price of plug-in assemblies for the coming year is going to be $5.30, should sales of subcomponents be dropped and all facilities devoted to the production of plug-in assembles? Show computations.
2. Prepare a report for the vice president of marketing to show the lowest possible price for plug-in assembles that would be acceptable.
3. Suppose 40 percent of the manufacturing overhead is variable with respect to processing and testing time for the plug-in assemblies. Repeat requirements 1 and 2. Do your answers change? If so, how?

P8-34 **TARGET COSTING OVER PRODUCT LIFE CYCLE.** Mastercraft Inc. makes a variety of motor-driven products for the home and small businesses. The market research department recently identified power lawn mowers as a potentially lucrative market. As a first entry into this market Mastercraft is considering a riding lawn mower that is smaller and less expensive than those of most of the competition. Market research indicates that such a lawn mower would sell for about $995 at retail and $800 wholesale. At that price, Mastercraft expects life cycle sales as follows:

2006	1,000
2007	5,000
2008	10,000
2009	10,000
2010	8,000
2011	6,000
2012	4,000

The production department has estimated that the variable cost of production will be $475 per lawn mower, and fixed costs will be $900,000 per year for each of the seven years. Variable selling costs will be $25 per lawn mower and fixed selling costs will be $50,000 per year. In addition, the product development department estimates that $5 million of development costs will be necessary to design the lawn mower and the production process for it.

1. Compute the expected profit over the entire product life cycle of the proposed riding lawn mower. (Note: Assume that Mastercraft is selling to retailers at a cost of $800, and *not* to the consumer directly.)
2. Suppose Mastercraft expects pretax profits equal to 10 percent of sales on new products. Would the company undertake production and selling of the riding lawn mower?
3. Mastercraft uses a target costing approach to new products. What steps would management take to try to make a profitable product of the riding lawn mower?

P8-35 **REVIEW PROBLEM.** The Disposable Camera Division of Saari Optics Co. has the following cost-behaviour patterns:

Production range in units	0–5,000	5,001–10,000	10,001–15,000	15,001–20,000
Fixed costs	$15,000	$22,000	$25,000	$27,000

Maximum production capacity is 20,000 units per year. Variable costs per units are $5 at all production levels.

Each situation described below is to be considered independently.

1. Production and sales are expected to be 11,000 units for the year. The sales price is $7 per unit. How many additional units need to be sold, in an unrelated market, at $6 per unit to show a total overall net income of $900 per year?

2. The company has orders for 23,000 units at $7. If it wanted to make a minimum overall net income of $14,500 on these 23,000 units, what unit purchase price would it be willing to pay a subcontractor for 3,000 units? Assume that the subcontractor would act as Saari's agent, deliver the units to customers directly, and bear all related costs of manufacture, delivery, etc. The customers, however, would pay Saari directly as goods were delivered.

3. Production is currently expected to be 7,000 units for the year at a selling price of $7. By how much may advertising or special promotion costs be increased to bring production up to 14,500 units and still earn a total net income of 2 percent of dollar sales?

4. Net income is currently $12,500. Nonvariable costs are $25,000. However, competitive pressures are mounting. A 5 percent decrease in price will not affect sales volume but will decrease net income by $4,750. What is the present volume, in units? Refer to the original data.

P8-36   **REVIEW PROBLEM.**   The Natural Water Company is a processor of mineral water. Sales are made principally in litre bottles to grocery stores throughout the country.

The company's income statements for the past year and the coming year are being analyzed by top management.

	FOR THE YEAR 2006 JUST ENDED		FOR THE YEAR 2007 TENTATIVE BUDGET	
Sales 1,500,000 litres in 2006		$900,000		$1,000,000
Cost of goods sold:				
Direct materials	$450,000		$495,000	
Direct labour	90,000		99,000	
Factory overhead:				
Variable	18,000		19,800	
Fixed	50,000	608,000	50,000	663,800
Gross margin		$292,000		$ 336,200
Selling expenses:				
Variable:				
Sales commissions				
(based on dollar sales)	$ 45,000		$ 50,000	
Shipping and other	90,000		99,000	
Fixed:				
Salaries, advertising, etc.	110,000		138,000	
Administrative expenses:				
Variable	12,000		13,200	
Fixed	40,000	297,000	40,000	340,200
Operating income		$ (5,000)		$ (4,000)

Consider each requirement independently.

Unless otherwise stated, assume that all unit costs of inputs such as material and labour are unchanged. Also, assume that efficiency is unchanged—that is, the labour and quantity of material consumed per unit of output are unchanged. Unless otherwise stated, assume that there are no changes in fixed costs.

1. The president has just returned from a management conference at a local university, where he heard an accounting professor criticize conventional income statements. The professor had asserted that knowledge of cost-behaviour patterns was of key importance in determining managerial strategies. The president now feels that the income statement should be recast to harmonize with cost-volume-profit analysis—that is, the statement should have three major sections: sales, variable costs, and fixed costs. Using the 2006 data, prepare such a statement, showing the contribution margin as well as operating income.

2. Comment on the changes in each item in the 2007 income statement. What are the most likely causes for each increase? For example, have selling prices been changed for 2007? How do sales commissions fluctuate in relation to units sold or in relation to dollar sales?

3. The president is unimpressed with the 2007 budget: "We need to take a fresh look in order to begin moving toward profitable operations. Let's tear up the 2007 budget, concentrate on 2006 results, and prepare a new comparative 2007 budget under each of the following assumptions:

   a. A 5 percent average price cut will increase unit sales by 20 percent.

   b. A 5 percent average price increase will decrease unit sales by 10 percent.

   c. A sales commission rate of 10 percent and a 3.33 percent price increase will boost unit sales by 10 percent."

   Prepare the budgets for 2007, using a contribution-margin format and three columns. Assume that there are no changes in fixed costs.

4. The advertising manager maintains that the advertising budget should be increased by $130,000 and that prices should be increased by 10 percent. Resulting unit sales will soar by 25 percent. What would be the expected operating income under such circumstances?

5. A nearby distillery has offered to buy 300,000 litres in 2007 if the unit price is low enough. The Natural Water Company would not have to incur sales commissions or shipping costs on this special order, and regular business would be undisturbed. Assuming that 2007's regular operations will be exactly like 2006's, what unit price should be quoted in order for the Natural Water Company to earn an operating income of $10,000 in 2007?

6. The company chemist wants to add a special ingredient, an exotic flavouring that will add $0.03 per litre to the mineral water. Assuming no other changes in cost behaviour, how many units must be sold to earn an operating income of $10,000 in 2007?

MANAGERIAL DECISION CASES

C8-1 **PRICING STRATEGY.** (SMAC) Banyan Industries Limited manufactures various models of alternators, mainly for the North American automobile industry. The company, located in Canada, has grown steadily over the past 15 years and, two years ago, installed a computer automated manufacturing system that significantly increased manufacturing capacity. Sales over the past few years have not grown at the rate predicted; therefore, the plant has been operating at well below capacity. The president is very concerned about this situation and has put the objective of increasing sales volume at the top of his list of priorities.

Banyan sells alternators in three main markets: (1) North American automobile manufacturers, (2) North American automotive replacement-parts distributors, and (3) foreign automobile manufacturers and replacement-part distributors. Sales are made to automobile manufacturers through a contract bidding process and contracts are generally long term. Bids are prepared by the accounting department and are then reviewed and approved by the president before submission to the potential customer. No sales commissions are paid for sales to automobile manufacturers.

Sales to replacement-parts distributors are made by sales staff who use a standard price list for standard models of alternators. Sales staff are each paid a base salary plus a 5 percent commission on the gross value of orders received from the salesperson's designated territory. Sales staff have some discretion to deviate from listed prices; however, for orders of more than 2,000 units, any deviations from listed prices must be approved by head office.

Banyan currently has sales commitments that would utilize 60 percent of its capacity over the 2007 year. From past experience, it can expect additional short-term sales during 2007 that would require 10 percent of its capacity. Four potential contracts awaiting renewal and approval by the president are as follows:

1. Ovlov Motors is open for tenders on a contract for 50,000 alternators during 2007. The standard bid proposal prepared by the accounting department is shown in Exhibit 8A-1.
2. National Auto Parts has requested a 20 percent discount on the list price for a large order of 20,000 model Z-20 alternators for delivery at staggered times during 2007 (see Exhibit 8A-2). National Auto Parts is a retail distributor and an important customer of Banyan.
3. A Pacific Rim exporter has approached Banyan to supply 100,000 alternators to its specifications at a price well below the normal list price (see Exhibit 8A-3). The specifications are well below acceptable standards for North American automobile manufacturers. Although the alternators would not bear the Banyan logo, the president suspects that they would be packaged by the exporter to resemble brand-name products for sale in the replacement parts market both in North America and abroad.

EXHIBIT 8A-1

Ovlov Motors
Contract for 50,000
Alternators

	COST PER UNIT
Direct materials	$ 25.00
Direct labour	5.00
Factory overhead (10 machine hours @ $4/hour)	40.00
Total manufacturing cost	70.00
Target markup (20%)	14.00
Target sales price	$ 84.00
Standard bid for 50,000 units	$4,200,000
Proposed bid	$4,000,000

4. A British firm has offered to buy 5,000 modified alternators that have been in Banyan's inventory for three years (see Exhibit 8A-4). These alternators were left over from a special order from a customer who had declared bankruptcy before the alternators were delivered.

Banyan uses a standard cost system under which total overhead is charged at a standard rate based on the plant's previous year's expected activity. The standards for 2007 were based on the expected 2006 activity of 3,750,000 machine hours, which is about 75 percent of capacity. With the new automated equipment, about 80 percent of the overhead rate for 2007 represented the fixed costs.

EXHIBIT 8A-2

National Auto Parts
Order for 20,000
Model Z-20 Alternators

	COST PER UNIT
Direct materials	$24.00
Direct labour	5.00
Factory overhead (10 machine hours @ $4/hr.)	40.00
Total manufacturing cost	69.00
Target markup (30%)	20.70
Target sales price	$89.70
Standard price for 20,000 units	$1,794,000
Sales commission	$89,700
Discount requested by National Auto Parts (20%)	$358,800

Note: National Auto Parts has indicated that it could obtain the required alternators from an offshore supplier at the $71.76 per unit discounted price, but, because it has dealt with Banyan for a long time, it wanted to give Banyan a chance to match this price.

EXHIBIT 8A-3

Pacific Rim Exporter
Order for 100,000
Alternators

	COST ESTIMATE PER UNIT
Direct material	$19.00
Direct labour	3.00
Factory overhead (6 machine hours @ $4/hr.)	24.00
Total manufacturing cost	$46.00
Price offered by Pacific Rim exporter	$6,500,000
Sales commission	$325,000

EXHIBIT 8A-4

British Firm
Offer for 5,000
Alternators

	COST PER UNIT
Direct material	$21.00
Direct labour	20.00
Factory overhead (15 machine hours @ $0.80/hr.)	12.00
Total manufacturing cost	$53.00
Book carrying cost of 5,000 units	$265,000
Price offered by British firm	$200,000

Note: These units were manufactured three years ago, before the plant was fully automated. The overhead rate at that time was 50 percent fixed.

Required:

1. Assuming that Banyan has sufficient capacity to handle all four potential contracts, analyze and propose a pricing strategy for each of the four contracts. Include in your analysis a discussion of all considerations and implications involved in making a decision regarding the approval of each potential contract.

2. Assume that, for 2007, Banyan has idle capacity of only 600,000 machine hours available for the four potential contracts. Indicate how your answers to requirement 1 would change given this new assumption.

3. Evaluate Banyan's current pricing strategy.

C8-2 PRICING WITH REBATES. (Braithwaite) "I wonder if we can afford these larger rebates," commented John Wiley, president of Lakeview Beverage Products Limited (LBP) of Oshawa, Ontario. It was May 10, 2006 and John was meeting with his business partners to discuss a number of recent requests from customers for increases in the rebates they receive on dairy products. The requests were in response to higher rebates on dairy products announced recently by their major competitor, Ault Foods, a subsidiary of John Labatt Ltd. If LBP were to meet the competition in this area, they would have to increase the total rebates paid out by 15 percent.

General Background

LBP was established 11 years ago, as a partnership of three individuals: John and Marie Wiley, and Paul Lawrence. Share ownership was 50 percent, 1 percent, and 49 percent, respectively, and all three individuals were active in the management of the company. John Wiley started in the beverage business as a distributor for the Bev-a-ready line of convenience-type drinks, a "just-add-water" product suitable for offices and schools. John Wiley had expanded his business to include the distribution of snack foods and the vending of soft drinks. Paul Lawrence bought into the company, after being employed by John for one year. The partners further expanded the operation by increasing the size of the vending enterprise, and by starting to distribute office coffee services and milk to schools. LBP had evolved over the years to the point where the company was a major independent distributor of dairy products for Beatrice Foods. This activity accounted for over 80 percent of sales. The company divested itself of the vending operation in 1983, but had four other enterprises that comprised the balance of the sales.

Product Mix and Marketing

LBP distributed 810 products across five different enterprises: dairy, ice cream, coffee, soft drinks and juice, and paper products.

LBP's total trading area extended across central Ontario but was centred in the Oshawa-Pickering area. The size of the dairy trading area was restricted to a radius of 50 kilometres in each direction, by the presence of Beatrice Dairy Divisions in Barrie, Oakville, and Peterborough. Customers of the other enterprises were spread throughout the south central region of the province.

LBP was a full-line distributor for Beatrice Foods Canada since 1992 and worked in close association with Oakwood Dairy Division, a Peterborough-based profit centre of Beatrice. In 2001, LBP signed a formal written agreement stating that the company would solely distribute Beatrice dairy and ice-cream products. All products were perishable and included milk, cream, butter, eggs, and dairy by-products, such as sour cream and cheeses. This enterprise accounted for 82 percent of gross sales (see Exhibit 8B-1). Beatrice provided sales support in the Oshawa-Pickering area and promotional support to LBP in the form of point-of-purchase displays and special pricing.

EXHIBIT 8B-1

Lakeview Beverage
Products Limited
Schedule of Sales
9 Months Ended
April 30, 2001

	CURRENT MONTH	CURRENT YEAR	PRIOR YEAR
Dairy	$230,101	$2,060,418	$1,588,572
Buyback Commission	27,835	197,913	120,479
Ice Cream	27,004	180,344	142,234
Snacks	11,907	92,841	54,880
Coffee	10,870	110,150	97,985
Pop/Juice	5,444	41,133	39,375
Paper	1,623	14,307	10,904
Total	$314,784	$2,697,106	$2,054,429

LBP was a full-line distributor of Beatrice Ice Cream and Good Humour Novelties. All products required constant freezing and had a shelf life of approximately three to four months. This product line accounted for approximately 9 percent of gross sales. Beatrice provided sales and promotional support for the full product line, the same as for the dairy enterprise.

Over 50 different products were distributed including coffee, tea, and other hot drinks. The bulk of these sales were office coffee services, where LBP provided a drip coffee-maker to clients in exchange for the right to sell the coffee and complementary items at that site. The coffee enterprise accounted for 3.5 percent of gross sales. One employee was responsible for servicing all the coffee accounts, but there never had been any formal sales effort on the part of LBP to secure new accounts. Most accounts had been serviced by LBP for many years.

This enterprise had its roots in the vending operation, and had evolved over the years to a point where the juice products comprised the majority of the sales. On the whole it accounted for just under 2 percent of gross sales. In 2002, LBP entered into a distribution agreement with Dew Drop Juice Co., a full-line juice and fruit-drink manufacturer. Under the terms of the agreement, Dew Drop provided sales and promotional support.

LBP sold a variety of food items within this enterprise. The sale of products such as snack foods, soups, condiments, and candy represented just under 4 percent of the total sales revenue. Most of these sales were to schools and caterers.

This accounted for less than 1 percent of the sales and functioned mainly as a complementary enterprise to the coffee enterprise. The product line included cups, plates, plastic utensils, serviettes, etc. No sales or promotional effort existed for this product line.

Description of Clientele

More than 1,200 customers were on file across all of the enterprises. Deliveries to customers varied from six times per week to several times in a year. In 2002 there were approximately 5,400 deliveries made per month. An analysis of customer numbers revealed the following breakdown of customer types:

Restaurants	34%
Institutional Kitchens or Cafeterias	29%
Variety Stores	16%
Donut Shops	8%
Caterers/Vendors	7%
Grocery Stores	6%

The higher-volume customers tended to be institutional kitchens and cafeterias, donut shops, and grocery stores.

In addition to their own COD and credit customers, LBP serviced buyback customers. Buybacks were customers of Oakwood Dairy Division for whom LBP provided only a delivery function. The company was paid a commission on the dollar volume of product delivered.

MONTHLY DELIVERY	BUYBACK COMMISSION
> $20,000	5%
$1,400–$20,000	7%
< $1,400	10%

Billing and payment collection was the responsibility of Oakwood. Within the dairy and ice-cream enterprises (the majority of the total customers) it was an even three-way split among COD, charge, and buyback customers.

Financial Situation

Unaudited financial statements are included in Exhibit 8B-2 and cost information is included in Exhibit 8B-3 for the last three fiscal years, and for nine months of 2002.

Over the last few years, the owners had observed that the cost structure of LBP had changed considerably. The cost of goods sold to sales ratio had been reduced substantially, due to increases in the buyback commission received, but during the same time period this improvement had been almost entirely offset by increases in the rebate to sales ratio. Nevertheless, net income had tripled over the period 1998 to 2002.

EXHIBIT 8B-2

Lakeview Beverage Products Limited Unaudited Financial Statements Income Statements

	1998	1999	2000	2001*
Gross Sales	$2,144,569	$2,410,134	$2,886,757	$2,697,106
Rebates	(126,850)	(221,692)	(335,250)	(358,122)
Cost of Sales	(1,478,017)	(1,614,960)	(1,819,911)	(1,655,084)
Gross Profit	539,702	573,482	731,596	683,900
Variable Operating Expenses	(345,683)	(405,694)	(493,431)	(479,471)
Fixed Expenses	(172,905)	(167,650)	(183,439)	(124,734)
Income from Operations	21,114	138	54,726	79,695
Other Income	7,383	5,943	10,048	4,672
Provision for Income Taxes	(4,367)	–	(7,169)	–
Tax Deductible Business Loss	4,367	–	–	–
Net Income	$ 28,497	$ 6,081	$ 57,605	$ 84,367

* Figures for nine months ended April 30, 2001.

EXHIBIT 8A-2 (cont'd)

Lakeview Beverage Products Limited
Balance Sheets

	1998	1999	2000	2001*
Assets				
Current Assets				
Cash	$ 4,368	$ –	$ 5,379	$ 19,576
Accts. Receivable	102,306	122,290	140,804	168,018
Inventory	44,436	34,157	53,527	77,763
Prepaid Expenses	8,138	10,288	12,850	25,072
	159,248	166,735	212,560	290,429
Equipment	66,361	58,148	55,337	78,817
Cash Surrender Value				
of Life Insurance	14,522	18,265	22,299	24,999
Total Assets	$240,131	$243,148	$290,196	$394,245
Liabilities				
Current Liabilities				
Bank Debt	$ 48,000	$ 40,161	$ –	$ –
Accounts Payable				
and Accrued Liabilities	173,068	184,965	236,656	257,140
Current Portion of				
Long-Term Debt	9,500	6,550	812	546
Long-Term Debt	34,519	30,347	13,998	13,462
Total Liabilities	265,087	262,023	251,466	271,148
Share Capital				
Common Shares	299	299	299	299
Retained Earnings				
(Deficit)	(25,255)	(19,174)	38,431	122,798
Total Liabilities and				
Share Capital	$240,131	$243,148	$290,196	$394,245

* Balance sheet at April 30, 2001.

EXHIBIT 8B-3

Variable and Fixed Operating Expenses

	1998	1999	2000	2001*
Variable				
Bad Debt	$ 6,106	$ 7,744	$ 8,548	$ 13,734
Canada Pension Plan	3,985	4,480	5,275	5,228
Delivery	158	691	339	961
Employee Benefits	4,674	4,488	5,804	12,648
Office and Postage	7,765	9,050	8,525	6,905
Repairs – General	5,852	4,970	10,923	8,507
Sundry	2,765	5,493	6,495	6,376
Telephone	3,518	3,828	4,061	4,364
Truck Operation	64,451	72,489	89,450	65,686
Truck Lease	46,915	50,382	67,081	74,449
Employment Insurance	5,256	6,390	7,760	7,839
Uniforms	2,554	148	1,668	1,771
Wages	190,019	232,639	273,712	268,303
Workers' Compensation	1,665	2,902	3,790	2,700
Total	$345,683	$405,694	$493,431	$479,471

* Figures for nine months ended April 30, 2001.

EXHIBIT 8B-3 (cont'd)

Variable and Fixed Operating Expenses

	1998	1999	2000	2001*
Fixed				
Advertising/Promotion	$ 1,960	$ 438	$ 1,949	$ 2,962
Auto Lease	8,075	7,832	7,242	2,271
Bank Charges	1,972	2,684	2,265	1,653
Amortization	21,752	18,852	15,223	9,168
Equipment Lease	7,109	2,593	2,733	3,573
Insurance	3,852	4,282	4,698	5,793
Interest	8,544	10,534	7,585	1,566
Management Salaries	72,185	73,763	93,631	60,761
Municipal Taxes	2,565	2,842	3,697	4,025
Professional Fees	6,770	7,670	6,975	5,200
Rent	24,118	24,156	24,156	18,117
Utilities	14,003	12,004	13,285	9,645
Total	$172,905	$167,650	$183,439	$124,734

* Figures for nine months ended April 30, 2001.

Company Operations

LBP had 20 people on the payroll besides the owners. The office operations were directed by Mr. Lawrence, the company vice president, and the duties were performed by four full-time employees and one part-time employee. Marie Wiley, the secretary-treasurer, kept the books, looked after the payroll and accounts payable, and headed up the credit department. John Wiley was company president, and directed the warehouse operations. Under his authority were 12 full-time delivery people, a full-time warehouse coordinator, and two part-time utility people who could fill in in several different capacities.

A delivery fleet of 15 leased trucks was employed. Twelve of the trucks were van trucks with a refrigerated box and were equipped with an automatic transmission. This was in contrast to the large tandem trucks and tractor trailer units utilized by other distributors. There were also two standard vans, and a large straight truck with a freezer compartment. Six of the trucks had been converted to run on natural gas. The balance of the fleet was either gas-, diesel-, or propane-fuelled. Beatrice provided free decaling of their logo for the refrigerated trucks, under the distribution agreement.

The delivery process began in the office where orders were taken by phone for delivery the next working day. The orders were entered into a computer that, at the end of the day, produced a priced invoice for each delivery, a route load sheet for each of the 12 routes, and a master load sheet that listed the total amount of each product that was to be shipped the next day. The route load sheet was used by warehouse staff the next morning to build the specific route loads, while the master load sheet was used that evening in conjunction with stock figures to order dairy products from Oakwood for delivery the next morning.

Dairy products arrived daily at 4 a.m. from Oakwood in palletized loads. The product was then put into the route loads by LBP staff. The first loaded truck left LBP at approximately 4:45 a.m., the last one at approximately 8 a.m. It was common for a delivery truck to go out in the afternoon to accommodate late orders or specials. The actual process of breaking down the arriving stock into the individual route loads was labour-intensive, and did not lend itself to mechanization due to physical constraints and product variability.

More lead time was associated with the acquisition of other products handled by LBP. Ice cream had to be ordered 24 hours in advance of delivery, while products in other enterprises could have had a one-week lead time.

Description of Competition and the Industry

In the 1980s and early 1990s, the provincial dairy-processing industry was consolidated due to the acquisition of smaller regional dairies by large national companies. The market in the south of the province was primarily served by five large processors: Ault, Neilsons, Beckers, Heritage Farms, and Beatrice.

The main competitors of LBP in its dairy trading area were Ault Foods and Neilsons Dairy. Ault was a subsidiary of John Labatt Ltd. of London, and through acquisitions had gained 40 percent of the province's dairy product market. Ault Foods had purchased Runnymede Dairy, a long-time Oshawa-based company that enjoyed great loyalty among its customers. Very little processing was performed in Aults' Oshawa plant since the acquisition; it was used primarily as a distribution centre.

Two characteristics are specific to the dairy industry: buyback customers (discussed above) and price rebates. With price rebates, customers receive a check-off on their invoice, equivalent to a set percentage of their invoice total. Historically, the rebate percentage had been tied directly to volume purchased, but more recently it had become a tool used by the dairies to attract customers, and was not truly reflective of the volume purchased. Among LBP's customers, rebates ranged from zero percent to 30 percent, with little correlation to volume purchased.

Competitive Advantage

Over the years LBP had developed a reputation for excellent service. This had proven to be the main reason that the company survived and had become profitable. LBP's ability to provide fast and dependable service, and management's willingness to "bend over backward" to keep the customer happy had allowed the company to secure a market niche. Beatrice had recognized this, and decided to turn over to LBP all accounts that were not big enough to service with a tractor-trailer unit.

LBP differentiated itself from all of the competition through its policy of providing a net price to its customer by taking off the rebate directly on each sales invoice. The competition sent out month-end cheques to customers based on the monthly sales total.

The Decision

LBP's owners realized that it was only recently, after some tough times, that the business has started to show some profit. Their reputation for providing excellent service had placed them in good standing with Beatrice, and with a large core group of their clientele. The partners decided they had three alternatives:

1. They could hold at their present rebate levels and rely on their service reputation to maintain a large client base.
2. The company could give the customers 50 percent of the requested increases and attempt to compensate by reducing the level of service and cutting costs.
3. The company could give the customers the rebates requested, remain competitive, and attempt to compensate by cutting costs and service.

The company was obligated to provide the customers with a reply within the next week.

Required: | As John Wiley, what is your recommendation? Why?

C8-3 **PRICING WITH CONSTRAINTS.** (SMAC) Milt Pearson, the president of Supergrip Corporation Limited (SCL), is concerned with the results achieved by SCL for the fiscal year ended May 31, 2006, and has called a meeting of the Executive Committee. Present are the vice president of manufacturing, the vice president of sales, and Diane Crombie, CMA, who has just been hired as the corporate controller.

SCL is a large centralized manufacturer of pliers. The pliers are cast, finished and assembled in the company's plant and are distributed to wholesalers for sale to retail outlets, automotive service shops, and general manufacturing companies. Included in the product line are four different grades and sizes of locking pliers and a special chain plier that is used for many purposes, including removing oil filters from engines.

President: "I'm not very happy with our 2006 results, and the budget for next year doesn't show any improvement (see Exhibit 8C-1). The trend of declining profits that we've experienced over the past few years must be reversed. Diane, your first task was to prepare an analysis of last year's results. Please summarize the results of your analysis."

Controller: "My analysis indicated that actual manufacturing costs were equal to standard last year and that the main problems were with the selling prices and mix of sales. I'll need more information before I can identify the cause of each problem."

President: "Can either of you provide the information Diane requires?"

EXHIBIT 8C-1

Supergrip Corporation Limited Operating Budget for the Year Ending May 31, 2007

	CUSTOM PLIERS	ECONOMY PLIERS	15 CM PLIERS	20 CM PLIERS	CHAIN PLIERS
Price per unit	$9.00	$7.50	$11.25	$14.50	$35.75
Sales volume (in units)	20,000	100,000	300,000	70,000	10,000
Required machine hours per unit	1/2	1/4	1/4	1	3

		BUDGET
Revenue		$5,677,500
Manufacturing costs:		
Direct materials	$1,285,500	
Direct labour	327,500	
Overhead*	3,275,000	
		4,888,000
Gross margin		789,500
Selling and administrative:		
Variable†	299,000	
Fixed	195,000	494,000
Operating income		$ 295,500

* Manufacturing overhead is 90 percent fixed.
† Variable selling and administrative costs are composed entirely of sales commissions.

VP Sales: "Yes. Although the products with the smallest market volumes are selling well, we've been losing ground on the products with the higher-market volumes. This is mainly because we can't match the prices of our two main competitors. Halfway through last year, we had to drop our prices for both the economy and 15 centimetre pliers just to keep our largest customers. We'll have to do the same this year or risk losing 20 percent of our sales volume for these two products. For Diane's benefit, I've brought along the standard pricing and cost report that Joe, Diane's predecessor, and I had put together when planning for this year's budget (see Exhibit 8C-2). This report explains our standard pricing policy."

Controller: "From what I've seen of Joe's work, I'm sure the standard costs used in the budget and costing reports are accurate. I'll need some additional data to properly assess the situation."

President: "What can be done to achieve at least a 10 percent profit margin?"

VP Sales: "The budgeted sales volumes are the best we can expect using the budgeted sales prices. Our market research indicates that we should bring our prices more in line with our two main competitors. Here are the projected sales volumes which we can expect to achieve if we match our competitor's prices (see Exhibit 8C-3)."

President: "But we'll lose money on the 15 centimetre pliers and may only break even on the economy pliers unless we cut down the production costs."

EXHIBIT 8C-2

Supergrip Corporation Limited
Standard Pricing and Unit Cost Summary for the Year Ending May 31, 2007

	CUSTOM PLIERS	ECONOMY PLIERS	15 CM PLIERS	20 CM PLIERS	CHAIN PLIERS
Standard unit costs:					
Direct materials	$2.13	$1.10	$ 2.75	$ 3.35	$ 7.34
Direct labour	0.47	0.50	0.65	0.75	2.06
Overhead*	4.70	5.00	6.50	7.50	20.60
Total manufacturing cost	7.30	6.60	9.90	11.60	30.00
Sales commissions†	0.55	0.35	0.55	1.10	1.10
Fixed selling administrative costs††	0.17	0.26	0.40	0.46	1.20
Total cost	$8.02	$7.21	$10.85	$13.16	$32.30
Standard price§	$9.00	$7.50	$11.25	$14.50	$35.75

* Manufacturing overhead is allocated to products using the following formula:

$$\frac{\text{budgeted overhead \$}}{\text{budgeted direct labour \$}} \times \text{actual direct labour \$}$$

= $3,275,000/$327,500 × actual direct labour $
= 10 times direct labour $

Ninety percent of total overhead is composed of amortization, fixed production related salaries and other fixed manufacturing costs.

† These unit costs represent flat commission amounts per unit for each product, which were negotiated with the salespeople two years ago.

†† Fixed selling and administrative costs are allocated to products using the following formula:

$$\frac{\text{budgeted fixed selling and administrative costs}}{\text{budgeted total manufacturing costs}} \times \text{total product manufacturing cost}$$

= $195,000/$4,888,000 × total product manufacturing cost
= 0.04 times total product manufacturing cost

§ Normally, standard selling prices are determined by multiplying total cost by 1.1 and rounding up to the nearest quarter (i.e., $0.25). Due to current market conditions, the standard prices for economy and 15 cm pliers have been adjusted downward.

Date: May 31, 2006
To: Milt Pearson,
President
From:
Vice President, Sales
Subject: Product Pricing

Our competitive position in the pliers market has been steadily decreasing over the past few years. Market research indicates that the prices for all of our products should be brought into line with those of our two main competitors, which are as follows:

	CUSTOM PLIERS	ECONOMY PLIERS	15 CM PLIERS	20 CM PLIERS	CHAIN PLIERS
Competitor A	$12.25	$6.90	$9.00	$24.50	$67.00
Competitor B	$13.00	$7.40	$9.50	$23.00	$65.00

With competitive pricing, sales for the fiscal year ending May 31, 2007, are expected to be as follows:

	CUSTOM PLIERS	ECONOMY PLIERS	15 CM PLIERS	20 CM PLIERS	CHAIN PLIERS
Expected unit sales	4,000	120,000	480,000	39,000	3,000

VP Manufacturing: "I don't think there's any way that we can reduce costs further. We've about finished automating the production end of operations. We acquired a lot of computer-aided manufacturing equipment which has virtually eliminated wastage and spoiled units. Direct labour costs have been cut by 20 percent per year for the last five years. We've been working at our capacity of approximately 200,000 machine hours and costs have been right on target. Scheduling of work on machines is becoming increasingly difficult because of the uncertainty in sales volume. We've just managed to keep up with the sales orders, but, with an increase in sales, we'll end up with back orders."

VP Sales: "There is something else we may want to look at. I met with my senior salespeople and they suggested that we introduce a set of high-quality wrenches to the product line. They say the wrenches will make money, but cost and profit projections don't look very good (see Exhibit 8C-4)."

Estimated annual sales volume = 36,000 to 56,000 sets
Machine hours required per set = 1/4

Wholesale price per set		$14.00
Costs per set:		
Direct materials	$ 4.00	
Direct labour	1.00	
Overhead*	10.00	
Commission	1.10	
Fixed selling and administrative costs†	0.52	
Total costs		16.62
Profit (loss) per set		$ (2.62)

* Overhead costs = 10 × estimated direct labour costs
= 10 × $1 = $10

† The only increase in annual fixed selling and administrative costs would be $18,550 for advertising. The cost per set was calculated as follows:
Advertising/minimum sales volume
= $18,550/36,000 sets
= $0.52 per set

VP Manufacturing: "Milt, in order to help solve our capacity problems, especially if the wrench set is added to the product line, my staff has made a proposal to lease additional casting machinery. The addition of this new machinery will increase the overall production capacity by 5,000 machine hours per year and it is expected that there will be no change in variable production costs per unit. The net fixed cost to lease this machinery will be $60,000 per year."

President: "Diane, please analyze our situation and report back to me next week."

After the meeting, Diane returned to her office and determined that she would have to consider at least the following six issues:

1. Cost allocation
2. Product prices
3. The proposal to introduce a set of wrenches to the product line
4. The option to increase capacity by leasing machinery
5. Production mix planning
6. Management reporting system

Required: Assuming the role of Diane Crombie, prepare a report to Milt Pearson. Include in the report your analysis of and recommendations on the six issues above as well as any other issues you feel should be addressed. Also, include a projected income statement for the fiscal year ending May 31, 2007, which reflects the effects of your recommendations.

C8-4 **PRICING.** (CICA) Fence Company Ltd. (FC) was incorporated in March 2006, and is equally owned by Robert and Morris Wood. The company constructs residential wood fences.

FC's first year was a difficult one. It is now late March 2007, and the Wood brothers are making plans to improve FC's performance. Having decided that they need outside advice, they asked you to meet with them.

At the meeting, you asked the brothers to describe their operations and to highlight their major concerns. The following paragraphs are your notes from the meeting.

- FC lost business last year because it could not meet its promised installation dates during the peak period. The owners consider, however, that their biggest problem last year was caused by the need to repair fences. They guarantee their work, and they had to go back and change broken boards and clean up work sites, which cost them money and did nothing for their reputation.
- The owners project that FC will construct 50,000 linear metres of fence this year. To achieve this target, they think that one work team will be needed during the 12 weeks of April, October, and November, and three teams during the 20 weeks from May through September. Their projection assumes an eight-hour day and a regular five-day week. Last year they found that a good work team consisting of three people could build a 100 linear metre fence in an eight-hour day.
- The average labour cost including benefits last year was $5 per hour. Labour and material costs are expected to increase 10 percent in 2007. Last year there was little control over the amount of wood used on projects; the owners want to change this situation.
- The brothers recognize that fence building is not a year-round activity and are willing to cover any cash deficiency as long as there are prospects of profitability.

- The owners need to take out at least $15,000 each per year. In addition, they intend to hire a full-time receptionist to start on April 1, and to employ this person year-round. They expect that the salary will be about $12,000 a year but think that the cost will be worth it to ensure continuity and maintain the company's image.
- A truck will have to be rented for each work team, at $500 per month. Robert Wood thinks that they should keep two of the trucks from December to March for snow removal. He and Morris could do the work and lay off everyone except the receptionist.
- FC will also need to rent a machine for $600 a month to dig holes. In addition, it will cost approximately $120 to move the machine from one work site to another.
- The company spent $8,000 on gas and maintenance and $1,200 on telephone last year. The owners expect to hold the line on these costs this year.
- Morris Wood estimates that their costs last year were approximately $6 per linear metre for wood and $1 for nails and stain.
- The standard selling price last year was $11 per linear metre. Robert Wood thinks that they should try for $13 this year. FC's salesperson complained last year because he could not discount the price. The brothers think that it might be a good idea to allow the salesperson to go down to $12 if forced to do so in order not to lose the sale. They are considering offering a special in April—perhaps 4 percent off—to get things rolling. They may also offer a 10 percent discount on group orders for fences for four or more houses. This discount offer worked well last year.
- According to the owners, a good incentive for their salesperson is crucial to increased sales. Last year, they paid the salesperson 5 percent of gross revenue for a basic one-house order for a fence of about 100 linear metres. For a two- or three-house order, they paid 6 percent and for a four-house order, which is about 400 linear metres, they paid 8 percent. They believe that the incentive was responsible for the fact that FC had a lot of two-house orders last year.
- Starting in April, FC will pay $2,500 a month to rent a warehouse for storing wood and equipment for the year. The landlord wants a security deposit of one month's rent. The company also has to buy new tools that cost at least $3,000, since the work teams either stole or broke all the tools used last year.

Required: Draft a report to the Wood brothers that presents your analysis of the issues and your recommendations.

C8-5 **RELEVANT COSTS.** (CGAC) Shepton Specialty Products Ltd. is a manufacturer of surgical instruments. Given the changes in surgical technology, Shepton has had to invest heavily in maintaining and upgrading its state-of-the-art product line. Shepton has become noted for the high quality of its product and the reasonableness of its prices.

Shepton is currently evaluating the design and production of its neurosurgical line of products. They want to know what the current quality costs are and how much it would cost to improve quality. Currently, the company has an expected spoilage rate in the neurosurgical line of one unit for every 200 units produced. It costs $2,000 per week plus $0.10 per unit to inspect this product. With the current inspection policy and production specifications, the company experiences a return and warranty claim of one unit for every 500 units produced. Such a return normally costs the company the cost of the replacement unit and creates the potential for lost customers. Shepton estimates that every warranty claim loses five unit sales for the company.

Shepton has looked at revamping its quality control system. Using a new computer-assisted design and manufacturing system (that can be leased for $200,000 per year) the company could reduce the spoilage rate to one unit for every 350 units produced and reduce variable inspection costs to $0.065 per unit. As well, product returns are expected to drop to one unit for every 900 units produced. Average unit cost for the neurosurgical line is shown below.

SHEPTON SPECIALTY PRODUCTS LTD.
NEUROSURGICAL PRODUCT LINE
AVERAGE UNIT COST*
FOR THE YEAR 2006

Material	$5.00
Labour	6.50
Variable overhead	6.00
Fixed overhead†	5.00
	$22.50

* Excludes inspection costs.

† Based on estimated production of 5,000,000 good units of production in 2006.

The average selling price is $33 per unit and variable selling costs are 15 percent of the selling price.

Required: Given Shepton's interest in quality control, determine whether they should lease the computer system.

C8-6 **USE OF CAPACITY.** (CMA, adapted) St. Tropez manufactures several different styles of jewellery cases in southern France. Management estimates that during the second quarter of 2007 the company will be operating at 80 percent of normal capacity. Because the company desires a higher utilization of plant capacity, it will consider a special order.

St. Tropez has received special-order inquiries from two companies. The first is from Lyon, Inc., which would like to market a jewellery case similar to one of St. Tropez's cases. The Lyon jewellery case would be marketed under Lyon's own label. Lyon, Inc., has offered St. Tropez EUR10.29 per case for 20,000 cases to be shipped by July 1, 2007. The cost data for the St. Tropez case, which would be similar to the specifications of the Lyon special order, are as follows:

Regular selling price per unit	EUR15.24
Costs per unit:	
Raw materials	EUR5.33
Direct labour 0.5 hours @ EUR9.14	4.57
Overhead 0.25 machine hours @ EUR6.09	1.52
Total costs	EUR11.43

According to the specifications provided by Lyon, Inc., the special-order case requires less expensive raw materials, which will cost only EUR4.95 per case. Management has estimated that the remaining costs, labour time, and machine time will be the same as those for the St. Tropez case.

The second special order was submitted by the Avignon Co. for 7,500 cases at EUR12.95 per case. These cases would be marketed under the Avignon label and would have to be shipped by July 1, 2007. The Avignon case is different from any case in the St. Tropez line; its estimated per-unit costs are as follows:

Raw materials	EUR6.47
Direct labour 0.5 hours @ EUR 9.14	4.57
Overhead 0.5 machine hours @ EUR 6.09	3.04
Total costs	EUR14.08

In addition, St. Tropez will incur EUR2,286.74 in additional setup costs and will have to purchase a EUR3,811.23 special device to manufacture these cases; this device will be discarded once the special order is completed.

The St. Tropez manufacturing capabilities are limited by the total machine hours available. The plant capacity under normal operations is 90,000 machine hours per year, or 7,500 machine hours per month. The budgeted fixed overhead for 2007 amounts to EUR320,142.94, or EUR3.56 per hour. All manufacturing overhead costs are applied to production on the basis of machine hours at EUR6.09 per hour.

St. Tropez will have the entire second quarter to work on the special orders. Management does not expect any repeat sales to be generated from either special order. Company practice precludes St. Tropez from subcontracting any portion of an order when special orders are not expected to generate repeat sales.

Required:

Should St. Tropez accept either special order? Justify your answer and show your calculations.
(Hint: Distinguish between variable and fixed overhead.)

EXCEL APPLICATION EXERCISE

E8-1 OPTIMAL PRODUCT MIX TO MAXIMIZE TOTAL CONTRIBUTION MARGIN DOLLARS

Goal: Create an Excel spreadsheet to determine the optimal product mix for a company that wants to maximize total contribution margin dollars. Use the results to answer questions about your findings.

Scenario: The Ibunez Tool Company has two products: a plain circular saw and a professional circular saw. The plain saw sells for $66 and has a variable cost of $50. The professional circular saw sells for $100 and has a variable cost of $70.

The company has only 20,000 machine hours of manufacturing capacity available. Two plain saws can be produced in the same average time (one hour) needed to produce one professional saw.

Note: This scenario is based on data in Problem P8-8 on page 375.

When you have completed your spreadsheet, answer the following questions:

1. What is the contribution margin and contribution-margin ratio per unit for the plain circular saw? For the professional circular saw?

2. What is the potential total contribution margin for the plain circular saw if you assume that it is the only saw manufactured by Ibunez? For the professional circular saw?

3. What general conclusion can you draw from the data illustrated by the Excel problem?

Step by Step:

1. Open a new Excel spreadsheet.

2. In column A, create a bold-faced heading that contains the following:
   Row 1: Chapter 5 Decision Guideline
   Row 2: Ibunez Tool Company
   Row 3: Product Mix Analysis
   Row 4: Today's Date

3. Merge and centre the four heading rows across columns A through E.

4. Adjust column widths as follows:
   Column A: 17
   Column B: 15
   Column C: 10
   Column D: 15
   Column E: 10

5. In row 7, create the following bold-faced column heading:
   Column B: Products

6. Merge and centre the Products heading across columns B through E.

7. In row 8, create the following bold-faced column headings:
   Column B: Plain Circular Saw
   Column D: Professional Circular Saw

8. Merge and centre the Plain Circular Saw heading across columns B and C.

9. Merge and centre the Professional Circular Saw heading across columns D and E.

10. In column A, create the following row headings:
    Row 9: Selling Price
    Row 10: Variable Cost
    Row 11: Contribution Margin
    Skip 2 rows
    Row 14: Available Machine Hours
    Row 15: Saws Manufactured per Machine Hour

Row 16: Manufacturing Capacity
Skip 1 row
Row 18: Potential Total Contribution Margin

11. Merge the headings in rows 14 through 18 across columns A and B, then right-justify.
Alignment tab: Horizontal: Right

12. Enter the selling price and variable cost for plain and professional saws in columns B and D, respectively.

13. Enter the available machine hours and the number of saws manufactured per machine hour for plain and professional saws in columns C and E, respectively.

14. In row 11, create formulas to calculate the contribution margin for each type of saw in columns B and D respectively.

15. In row 11, create formulas to calculate the contribution-margin percent for each type of saw in columns C and E respectively.

16. In row 16, create formulas to calculate the manufacturing capacity for each type of saw in columns C and E, respectively.

17. In row 18, create formulas to calculate potential total contribution margin for each type of saw in columns C and E, respectively.

18. Format all amounts in columns B and D as
Number tab: Category: Accounting ($ sign is left-justified)
              Decimal places: 2
                    Symbol: $

19. Modify the format of the variable cost amounts to exclude the dollar ($) sign.
Number tab: Symbol: None

20. Modify the format of the contribution margin amounts to display a top border, using the default Line Style.
Border tab: Icon: Top Border

21. Format the contribution margin percent in columns C and E as
Number tab: Category: Percentage
              Decimal places: 0
           Alignment tab: Horizontal: Center

22. Format amounts in rows 14 through 16 as
Number tab: Category: Number
              Decimal places: 0
      Use 1000 Separator (,): Checked
    Alignment tab: Horizontal: Center

23. Format potential total contribution margin amounts as
        Number tab: Category: Accounting
              Decimal places: 0
                   Symbol: $

24. Save your work to disk, and print a copy for your files.

COLLABORATIVE LEARNING EXERCISE

CL8-1 UNDERSTANDING PRICING DECISIONS

Form teams of three to six students. Each team should contact and meet with a manager responsible for pricing in a company in your area. This might be a product manager or brand manager for a large company or a vice president of marketing or sales for a smaller company.

Explore with the manager how his or her company sets prices. Among the questions you might ask are:

- How do costs influence your prices? Do you set prices by adding a markup to costs? If so, what measure of costs do you use? How do you determine the appropriate markup?
- How do you adjust prices to meet market competition? How do you measure the effects of price on sales level?
- Do you use target costing? That is, do you find out what a product will sell for and then try to design the product and production process to make a desired profit on the product?
- What is your goal in setting prices? Do you try to maximize revenue, market penetration, contribution margin, gross margin, or some combination of these, or do you have other goals when setting prices?

After each team has conducted its interview, it would be desirable, if time permits, to get together as a class and share your findings. How many different pricing policies did the groups find? Can you explain why policies differ across companies? Are there characteristics of different industries or different management philosophies that explain the different pricing policies?

9

Relevant Information and Decision Making: Production Decisions

LEARNING OBJECTIVES

After studying this chapter, you will be able to

1. Use differential and opportunity cost to analyze the income effects of a given alternative.

2. Decide whether to make or buy certain parts or products.

3. Decide whether a joint product should be processed beyond the split-off point.

4. Decide whether to rework or scrap obsolete inventory and to keep or replace old equipment.

5. Discuss how performance measures can affect decision making.

Should Ford make the tires it mounts on its cars, or should the company buy them from suppliers? Should General Mills sell the flour it mills, or should it use the flour to make more breakfast cereal? Should Air Canada add routes to use idle airplanes, or should it sell the planes? Successful managers can discriminate between relevant and irrelevant information in making similar decisions.

In the preceding chapter we provided a framework for identifying relevant costs and applied the framework to various decisions. In this chapter we extend the analysis by introducing the concepts of opportunity cost and differential costs and by examining additional decisions: make or buy, sell or process further, and whether to replace equipment.

This chapter and the preceding one illustrate relevant costs for many types of decisions. Does this mean that each decision requires a different approach to identifying relevant costs? No. *The fundamental principle in all decision situations is that relevant costs are future costs that differ among alternatives.* The principle is simple, but its application is not always straightforward. Because it is so important to be able to apply this principle, we present multiple examples.

DIFFERENTIAL AND OPPORTUNITY COSTS

Use differential and opportunity cost to analyze the income effects of a given alternative.

Consider the following scenario. Maria Morales, a chartered accountant employed by a large accounting firm at $60,000 per year, wants to have her own practice and is thinking about quitting her job and starting her own business.

A straightforward comparison of Maria's alternatives is as follows:

	ALTERNATIVES UNDER CONSIDERATION		
	REMAIN AS AN EMPLOYEE	OPEN AN INDEPENDENT PRACTICE	DIFFERENCE
Revenues	$60,000	$200,000	$140,000
Outlay costs (operating expenses)	–	120,000	120,000
Income effects per year	$60,000	$ 80,000	$ 20,000

The annual difference of $20,000 favours Maria's choosing independent practice.

This tabulation is sometimes called a *differential analysis*. The *differential revenue* is $140,000, the *differential cost* is $120,000, and the *differential income* is $20,000. Each amount is the difference between the corresponding items under each alternative being considered. **Differential cost** and **incremental cost** are widely used synonyms. They are defined as the difference in total cost between two alternatives. For instance, the differential costs or incremental costs of increasing production from 1,000 automobiles to 1,200 automobiles per week would be the costs of producing an additional 200 automobiles each week. In the reverse situation, the decline in costs caused by reducing production from 1,200 to 1,000 automobiles per week would be called differential or incremental savings.

What is the contribution to profit of the best of the rejected alternatives available to Maria Morales? Independent practice has an opportunity cost of $60,000, the foregone annual salary.

Differential Cost (Incremental Cost). The difference in total cost between two alternatives.

These same facts may also be presented with focus on opportunity cost as follows:

	ALTERNATIVE CHOSEN: INDEPENDENT PRACTICE	
Revenue		$200,000
Expenses:		
Outlay costs (operating expenses)	$120,000	
Opportunity cost of employee salary	60,000	180,000
Income effects per year		$ 20,000

Ponder the two preceding tabulations. Each produces the correct key difference between the alternatives, $20,000. The first tabulation does not mention opportunity cost because the economic impacts (in the form of revenues and outlay costs) are individually measured for each of the alternatives (two in this case). Neither alternative has been excluded from consideration. The second tabulation mentions opportunity cost because the $60,000 annual economic impact of the *best excluded* alternative is included as a cost of the chosen alternative. The failure to recognize opportunity cost in the second tabulation will misstate the difference between alternatives.

Opportunity Cost. The maximum foregone benefit (contribution to profit) by choosing to forego an alternative opportunity cost.

So, **opportunity cost** can be defined as the maximum foregone benefit (contribution to profit) by choosing to forego an alternative opportunity cost. Unlike a cost outlay, opportunity cost does not require any cash disbursement and, as a result, is not recorded in financial accounting ledgers.

Suppose Morales prefers less risk and chooses to stay on as an employee:

	ALTERNATIVE CHOSEN: REMAIN AS EMPLOYEE	
Revenue		$ 60,000
Expenses:		
Outlay costs	$ 0	
Opportunity cost of independent practice	80,000	80,000
Decrease in income per year		$(20,000)

If the employee alternative is selected, the key difference in favour of independent practice is again $20,000. The opportunity cost is $80,000, the annual operating income foregone by rejecting the best excluded alternative. Morales is sacrificing $20,000 annually to avoid the risks of an independent practice. In sum, the opportunity cost is the contribution of the best alternative that is excluded from consideration.

Decision: Make or Buy (Idle Facilities)

Managers apply relevant cost analysis to a variety of make-or-buy decisions, including

- IBM's decision whether to produce all the components for a new computer or to buy some from reliable suppliers.
- A university's decision whether to use its own personnel or hire a consulting firm to design and implement a new computerized accounting system.

Relevant Information and Decision Making at Royco Hotels and Resorts

Royal Host Hotels and Resorts
www.royalhost.com

Royal Host Hotels and Resorts operates through the Royal Host Real Estate Investment Trust (REIT), which is a mutual fund trust for the purpose of investing in and managing hotel properties. People pool their investment funds to make real estate investments and share in the benefits or losses from such investments. Royal Host started as a single, family-owned hotel in Red Deer, Alberta, and has grown to either own, franchise, or manage hotels throughout Canada and internationally, under such well-known names as Travelodge and Super 8. Its head office is now located in Calgary, from which it owns 37 hotels, manages 123 properties, and franchises 115 locations.

During Royal Host's period of growth, Kirk Morgan, C.A., former executive vice president (finance), had occasion to comment on the accounting and related functions of predecessor Royco Hotels and Resorts, as follows.

The structure of the management is such that there is centralized accounting and associated functions. This allows uniformity and consistency in the production of financial information and analysis. Additional benefits of centralized accounting are economies of scale and the synergy from the efforts of the accounting team.

In our business environment, an ongoing analysis of the optimal pricing strategy for our hotel properties is critical. In pricing decisions, all the relevant information is taken into account without losing the focus of the pricing issue, by ensuring that costs or revenues that are not affected by the decision are not considered. An example of the analytical process used in pricing decisions is as follows:

1. **Determine the purpose of the pricing decision.** Is it a special promotion, one-time price, or is it the standard price? The relevant costs are significantly different in each of these cases.
2. **Competitive analysis.** It is important that we take into account the position of the competitors in our marketplace and our niche within the market. Pricing decisions can have competitive reactions that need to be considered.
3. **Costs.** While cost controls are a critical component to ensure long-term success of the organization, costs play a relatively small role in pricing decisions, due to our competitive environment.
4. **Profit maximization.** For the long-term success of our company and all the stakeholders (owners, suppliers, creditors, and employees), it is imperative that the company remains profitable. In this regard, the maximization of contribution is the core of the analysis. In this we must take into account the price (average room rate), variable costs, and volume (occupancy rate). Together these factors provide a yield calculation which enables us to determine the optimal price.

Sources: Kirk Morgan, C.A., chief financial officer, Genoil Inc. (former executive vice president, finance, Royal Host REIT), plus additional corporate information obtained from www.royalhost.com. For relevant information and decision making in government, see Treasury Board of Canada Secretariat, *Guide to the Costing of Outputs in the Government of Canada* (1989; revised 1994), accessible via www.tbs-sct.gc.ca.

OBJECTIVE 2

Decide whether to make or buy certain parts or products.

Consider manufacturers who must often decide whether to make or buy a product. For example, should a firm manufacture its own parts and subassemblies or buy them from vendors? Some manufacturers always make parts because they want to control quality, others because they possess special know-how—usually skilled labour or rare materials needed in production. Alternatively, some companies always purchase parts to protect long-run relationships with their suppliers. These companies may deliberately avoid the practice of making their own parts during slack times to avoid difficulties in obtaining needed parts during boom times, when there may well be shortages of material and workers but no shortage of sales orders. These qualitative considerations often dominate quantitative cost assessments so decisions are not made exclusively on numbers alone.

General Electric
www.ge.com

What factors are relevant to the decision of whether to make or buy? The answer, again, depends on the situation. A key factor is whether there are idle facilities. Many companies make parts only when their facilities cannot be used to better advantage.

Assume that the following costs are reported at General Electric Company (GE) for Part No. 900:

	TOTAL COST FOR 20,000 UNITS	COST PER UNIT
Direct material	$ 20,000	$ 1
Direct labour	80,000	4
Variable factory overhead	40,000	2
Fixed factory overhead	80,000	4
Total costs	$220,000	$11

Another manufacturer offers to sell GE the same part for $10. Should GE make or buy the part?

Although the $11 unit cost seems to indicate that the company should buy, the answer is rarely so obvious. The essential question is the difference in expected future costs between the alternatives. If the $4 fixed overhead per unit consists of costs that will continue regardless of the decision, the entire $4 becomes irrelevant. Examples of such costs include amortization, property taxes, insurance, and allocated executive salaries.

Again, are only the variable costs relevant? No. Perhaps $20,000 of the fixed costs will be eliminated if the parts are bought instead of made. For example, a worker with a $20,000 salary might be released. In other words, fixed costs that may be avoided in the future are relevant.

For the moment, suppose the capacity now used to make parts will become idle if the parts are purchased and the $20,000 worker's salary is the only fixed cost that would be saved. The relevant computations follow:

	MAKE		BUY	
	TOTAL	PER UNIT	TOTAL	PER UNIT
Direct material	$ 20,000	$1		
Direct labour	80,000	4		
Variable factory overhead	40,000	2		
Fixed factory overhead that can be avoided by not making (worker's salary)	20,000*	1*		
Total relevant costs	$160,000	$8	$200,000	$10
Difference in favour of making	$ 40,000	$2		

* Note that fixed costs of $80,000 − $20,000 = $60,000 are irrelevant. Thus, the irrelevant costs per unit are $4 − $1 = $3.

The key to make-or-buy decisions is identifying the *additional costs* for making (or the *costs avoided* by buying) a part or subcomponent. Activity analysis, described in Chapter 3, helps identify these costs. Production of a product requires a set of activities. A company with accurate measurements of the costs of its various activities can better estimate the additional costs incurred to produce an item. GE's activities for production of part number 900 were measured by two cost drivers, units of production of $8 per unit and worker's salary at a

Consider how difficult it is to estimate opportunity costs. There is no sale or purchase to establish an appropriate cost. Further, the opportunity cost depends on the alternatives that are available at a point in time. The same alternatives may not be available at a different time. For example, excess capacity in September does not mean that there will also be excess capacity in October. How might a manager at Mattel, the toy company, estimate the opportunity cost of excess warehouse space in January?

Mattel
www.mattel.com

ANSWER
The Mattel manager would know that excess warehouse space is a seasonal phenomenon. There is unlikely to be excess space late in the year as Christmas approaches. Therefore, the manager would look for temporary alternatives, ones that use the space for only a few months. After identifying alternatives, the manager would estimate the value of each. Because most of the alternatives are ones that a company never undertakes, estimating their values is a subjective process. The highest valued alternative would establish the opportunity cost of the space.

$20,000 fixed cost. Sometimes identification and measurement of additional cost drivers, especially non-volume-related cost drivers, can improve the predictions of the additional cost to produce a part or subcomponent.

Decision: Make or Buy (Utilizing Freed Facilities Elsewhere)

Make-or-buy decisions are rarely as simple as is the one in our GE example. As we said earlier, the use of facilities is a key to the make-or-buy decision. For simplicity we assumed that the GE facilities would remain idle if the company chose to buy the product. Of course, in most cases companies will not leave their facilities idle. Instead, idle facilities will often be put to some other use, and the financial outcomes of these uses must be considered when choosing to make or buy.

Suppose the released facilities can be used advantageously in some other manufacturing activity (to produce a contribution to profits of, say, $55,000) or can be rented out (say, for $35,000).

We now have four alternatives to consider (figures are in thousands):

	MAKE	BUY AND LEAVE FACILITIES IDLE	BUY AND RENT	BUY AND USE FACILITIES FOR OTHER PRODUCTS
Rent revenue	$ –	$ –	$ 35	$ –
Contribution from other products	–	–	–	55
Obtaining of parts	(160)	(200)	(200)	(200)
Net relevant costs	$(160)	$(200)	$(165)	$(145)

The final column indicates that buying the parts and using the vacated facilities for the production of other products would yield the lowest net costs in this case.

In all cases, companies should relate make-or-buy decisions to the long-run policies for the use of capacity. To illustrate, suppose a company uses its facilities, *on average*, 80 percent of the time. However, because of seasonal changes in the demand for its product, the actual demand for the facilities varies from 60 percent in the off season to over 100 percent in the peak season.

During the off season, the company may decide to perform special projects for other manufacturers (on a subcontract). There is profit on these projects but not enough to justify expanding the capacity of the facilities.

During the peak season, the company meets the high volume by purchasing parts. The cost of purchased parts is higher than the cost to make them in the company's own facilities, but the additional purchasing cost is less than the expanding capacity costs would be if new equipment were used only part of the time. In sum, the make-or-buy decision should focus on the relevant costs in each particular situation.

BEWARE OF UNIT COSTS

The pricing illustration in the preceding chapter showed that unit costs should be analyzed with care in decision making. There are two ways one can go wrong in decision making: (1) the inclusion of irrelevant costs, such as the $3 allocation of unavoidable fixed costs in the make-or-buy example (page 413), which would result in a unit cost of $11 instead of the relevant unit cost of $8, and (2) comparisons of unit costs not computed on the same volume basis, as the following example demonstrates. Generally, be wary of unit fixed costs. Use total costs rather than unit costs. Then, if desired, the totals may be unitized. Machinery sales personnel, for example, often brag about the low unit costs of using the new machines. Sometimes they neglect to point out that the unit costs are based on outputs far in excess of the volume of activity of their prospective customer.

Assume that a new machine can produce 100,000 units a year at a variable cost of $1 per unit, as opposed to a variable cost per unit of $1.50 with an old machine. The new machine can be rented for $20,000 per year. A sales representative claims that it will reduce cost by $0.30 per unit. Is the new machine a worthwhile acquisition?

The new machine is attractive at first glance. If the customer's expected volume is 100,000 units, unit-cost comparisons are valid, provided that the new rent is also considered. Assume that the disposal value of the old equipment is zero. The rent on the new machine is relevant because the new machine entails a *future* cost that can be avoided by not acquiring it:

	OLD MACHINE	NEW MACHINE
Units	100,000	100,000
Variable costs	$150,000	$100,000
Rent	–	20,000
Total relevant costs	$150,000	$120,000
Unit relevant costs	$1.50	$1.20

Apparently, the sales representative is correct. However, if the customer's expected volume is only 30,000 units per year, the unit costs change in favour of the old machine:

An Example of Make or Buy: Outsourcing

Make-or-buy decisions apply to services as well as to products. Companies are increasingly deciding to hire service firms to handle some of their internal operations, an option called *outsourcing*. The Outsourcing Institute was formed to provide "objective, independent information on the strategic use of outside resources." Outsourcing is "the strategic use of outside resources to perform activities traditionally handled by internal staff and resources."

Outsourcing Institute
www.outsourcing.com

Outsourcing Canada
www.outsourcing canada.com

Companies use outsourcing for many business processes. How do these processes compare to the value-chain functions we have discussed? Companies often outsource the following business functions:

BUSINESS FUNCTION	PERCENT OF COMPANIES OUTSOURCING	VALUE-CHAIN FUNCTION
Information technology	55%	Corporate support
Administration	47%	Corporate support
Distribution and logistics	22%	Distribution
Finance	20%	Corporate support
Human resources	19%	Corporate support
Manufacturing	18%	Production
Contact centres/call centres	15%	Marketing
Sales and marketing	13%	Marketing

The processes listed include almost all the value-chain functions, including corporate support. Research and development and design are the two value-chain functions not frequently outsourced. That makes sense because most companies perceive these functions as core business processes. Although companies can outsource many processes, the Internet has driven much of the recent growth in outsourcing. During the 1990s, many companies installed enterprise resource planning (ERP) systems to handle all their computing needs. However, by the beginning of the twenty-first century, many companies realized that the huge investments necessitated by ERP systems may be unnecessary. They could purchase the required services over the Internet without investing in the systems' purchase and development costs. The formerly expensive process of communication using service providers had become essentially free via the Internet. A new group of computing service providers—called application service providers (ASP)—arose to provide outsourcing opportunities for a variety of computing applications.

What are the key reasons for outsourcing? Over half of the companies in Outsourcing Institute's 2002 annual survey say they wanted to improve the company's focus and reduce operating costs. Other reasons include gaining access to world-class capabilities, accelerating reengineering benefits, and making capital funds available. (For a full list of the top ten reasons to outsource, go to www.outsourcing.com.) The fastest growing area of outsourcing is in the area of information technology. According to Todd Kirtley, a general manager at IBM Global Services, "Corporations increasingly want to focus on their core businesses, not technology." As the complexity of data processing and especially networking has grown, companies have found it harder and harder to keep current with the technology. Instead of investing huge sums in personnel and equipment and diverting attention from the value-added activities of their own businesses, many firms have found outsourcing financially attractive. The big stumbling block to outsourcing has been subjective factors, such as control. To make outsourcing attractive, the services must be reliable, be available when needed, and be flexible enough to adapt to changing conditions. Companies that have successful outsourcing arrangements have been careful to include the subjective factors in their decisions.

Outsourcing has become so profitable that more than 75 percent of Fortune 500 companies outsource some aspect of their business support services. The total value of outsourcing contracts in the United States is more than $10 billion.

Sources: Adapted from T. Kearney, "Why Outsourcing Is In," *Strategic Finance,* January 2000, pp. 34–38; R. E. Drtina, "The Outsourcing Decision," *Management Accounting,* March, 1994, pp. 56–62; J. Hechinger, "IBM to Take Over Operations of Auto-Parts Maker Visteon," *Wall Street Journal,* February 12, 2003; and the Outsourcing Institute (www.outsourcing.com).

	OLD MACHINE	NEW MACHINE
Units	30,000	30,000
Variable costs	$45,000	$30,000
Rent	–	20,000
Total relevant costs	$45,000	$50,000
Unit relevant costs	$1.50	$1.67

The allocation of the $20,000 rent fixed cost to a unit-cost basis leads to an analysis that distorts the actual differential costs.

Decision: Sell at the Split-off Point or Process Further

OBJECTIVE 3

Decide whether a joint product should be processed beyond the split-off point.

Joint Products. Two or more manufactured products that (1) have relatively significant sales values and (2) are not identifiable as individual products until their split-off point.

Split-off Point. The juncture in manufacturing where the joint products become individually identifiable.

Separable Costs. Any costs beyond the split-off point in a joint product production process.

Joint Costs. The costs of manufacturing joint products prior to the split-off point.

When two or more manufactured products (1) have relatively significant sales values and (2) are not separately identifiable as individual products until their split-off point, they are called **joint products**. The **split-off point** is that juncture of manufacturing where the joint products become individually identifiable. Any costs beyond that stage are called **separable costs** because they are not part of the joint process and can be exclusively identified with individual products. The costs of manufacturing joint products prior to the split-off point are called **joint costs**; a popular synonym is "common costs." Examples of joint products include chemicals, lumber, flour, and the products of petroleum-refining and meat-packing. A meat-packing company cannot kill a sirloin steak; it has to slaughter a steer, which supplies various cuts of dressed meat, hides, and trimmings.

To illustrate joint costs, suppose Dow Chemical Company produces two chemical products, X and Y, as a result of a particular joint process. The joint processing cost is $100,000. This includes raw-material costs and the cost of processing to the point where X and Y go their separate ways. Both products are sold to the petroleum industry to be used as ingredients of gasoline. The relationships follow:

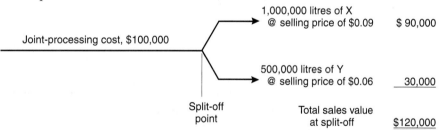

	1,000,000 litres of X @ selling price of $0.09	$ 90,000
Joint-processing cost, $100,000		
	500,000 litres of Y @ selling price of $0.06	30,000
Split-off point	Total sales value at split-off	$120,000

Management frequently faces decisions of whether to sell joint products at split-off or to process some or all products further. Suppose the 500,000 litres of Y can be processed further and sold to the plastics industry as product YA—an ingredient for plastic sheeting—the additional processing cost would be $0.08 per litre for manufacturing and distribution, a total of $40,000. The net sales price of YA would be $0.16 per litre, a total of $80,000 for 500,000 litres.

Product X cannot be processed further and will be sold at the split-off point, but management is undecided about Product Y. Should Y be sold or should it be processed into YA? To answer this question we need to find the relevant costs involved. Because the joint costs must be incurred to reach the split-off point, they might seem relevant. However, they cannot affect anything beyond the split-off point. Therefore, they do not differ between alternatives and are completely irrelevant to the question of whether to sell or process further. The only approach that will yield valid results is to concentrate on the separable costs and revenue *beyond* split-off, as shown in the following table. This analysis shows that it would be $10,000 more profitable to process Y beyond split-off than to sell Y at split-off. Briefly, it is profitable to extend processing or to incur additional distribution costs on a joint product *if* the additional revenue exceeds the additional expenses.

	SELL AT SPLIT-OFF AS Y	PROCESS FURTHER AS YA	DIFFERENCE
Revenues	$30,000	$80,000	$50,000
Separable costs beyond split-off @ $0.08	–	40,000	40,000
Income effects	$30,000	$40,000	$10,000

For decisions regarding whether to sell or process further, the most straightforward analysis is shown above. An alternative opportunity cost format is shown next.

	PROCESS FURTHER	
Revenue		$80,000
Outlay cost: separable cost beyond split-off, @ $0.08	$40,000	
Opportunity cost: sales value of Y at split-off	30,000	70,000
Income effects		$10,000

This format is merely a different way of recognizing another alternative (sell Y at split-off) when considering the decision to process further.

When decision alternatives are properly analyzed, they may be compared either (1) by excluding the idea of opportunity costs altogether, or (2) by including opportunity costs, derived from the best excluded alternative, as is shown here. The key difference, $10,000, is generated either way. Exhibit 9-1 illustrates still another way to compare the alternatives of (1) selling Y at the split-off point and (2) processing Y beyond split-off. It includes the joint costs, which are the same for each alternative and therefore do not affect the difference.

Earlier discussions have emphasized the desirability of concentrating on totals and being wary of unit costs and allocations of fixed costs. Similarly, the allocation of joint product costs to units of product is fraught with analytical perils.

The allocation of joint costs would not affect the decision, as Exhibit 9-1 demonstrates. The joint costs are not allocated in the exhibit, but no matter how they might be allocated, the total income effects would be unchanged. Additional coverage of joint costs and inventory valuation is in Chapter 13.

EXHIBIT 9-1 Firm as a Whole	(1) ALTERNATIVE ONE			(2) ALTERNATIVE TWO			(3) DIFFERENTIAL EFFECTS
	X	Y	TOTAL	X	YA	TOTAL	
Revenues	$90,000	$30,000	$120,000	$90,000	$80,000	$170,000	$50,000
Joint costs			$100,000		–	$100,000	–
Separable costs		–			$40,000	40,000	40,000
Total costs			$100,000			$140,000	$40,000
Income effects			$ 20,000			$ 30,000	$10,000

IRRELEVANCE OF PAST COSTS

The ability to recognize and thereby ignore irrelevant costs is sometimes just as important to decision makers as identifying relevant costs. How do we know that past costs are irrelevant in decision making? Obsolete inventory and the book value of old equipment are typical irrelevant past costs.

Decision: To Rework Obsolete Inventory or Scrap

General Dynamics
www.generaldynamics.com

Decide whether to rework or scrap obsolete inventory and to keep or replace old equipment.

Suppose General Dynamics has 100 obsolete aircraft parts that it is carrying in its inventory. The original manufacturing cost of these parts was $100,000. General Dynamics can (1) remachine the parts for $30,000 and then sell them for $50,000 or (2) scrap them for $5,000. Which should it do?

This is an unfortunate situation, yet the $100,000 past cost is irrelevant to the decision to remachine or scrap. The only relevant factors are the expected future revenue and costs:

	REMACHINE	SCRAP	DIFFERENCE
Expected future revenue	$ 50,000	$ 5,000	$45,000
Expected future costs	30,000	–	30,000
Relevant excess of revenue over costs	$ 20,000	$ 5,000	$15,000
Accumulated historical inventory cost*	100,000	100,000	–
Net overall loss on project	$(80,000)	$(95,000)	$15,000

* Irrelevant because it is unaffected by the decision.

We can completely ignore the $100,000 historical cost and still arrive at the $15,000 difference, the key figure in the analysis.

Decision: Keep Old Equipment or Replace It

Amortization (Depreciation). The cost of plant and equipment, which is charged periodically to the future periods over which the plant and equipment is used.

Like obsolete inventory, the book value of equipment is not a relevant consideration in deciding whether to replace such equipment. When equipment is purchased, its cost is spread over (or charged to) the future periods in which the equipment is expected to be used. This periodic cost is called **amortization** or **depreciation**. The equipment's **book value** (or **net book value**) is the original cost less **accumulated amortization**, which is the summation of amortization charged to past periods. For example, suppose a $10,000 machine with a

Book Value (Net Book Value). The original cost of equipment less accumulated amortization, which is the summation of amortization charged to past periods.

Accumulated Amortization. The summation of amortization charged to past periods.

ten-year life has amortization of $1,000 per year. At the end of six years, accumulated amortization is $6 \times \$1,000 = \$6,000$, and the book value is $\$10,000 - \$6,000 = \$4,000$.

Consider the following data for a decision whether to replace an old machine:

	OLD MACHINE	REPLACEMENT MACHINE
Original cost	$10,000	$8,000
Useful life in years	10	4
Current age in years	6	0
Useful life remaining in years	4	4
Accumulated amortization	$ 6,000	0
Book value	$ 4,000	Not acquired yet
Disposal value (in cash) now	$ 2,500	Not acquired yet
Disposal value in 4 years	0	0
Annual cash operating costs (maintenance, power, repairs, coolants, etc.)	$ 5,000	$3,000

We have been asked to prepare a comparative analysis of the two alternatives. Before proceeding, consider some important concepts. The most widely misunderstood facet of replacement decision making is the role of the book value of the old equipment in the decision. The book value, in this context, is sometimes called a **sunk cost**, which is really just another term for historical or past cost—a cost that has already been incurred and, therefore, is irrelevant to the decision. At one time or another, we all try to soothe the wounded pride arising from having made a bad purchase decision by using an item instead of replacing it. But it is a serious mistake to think that a current or future action can influence the long-run impact of a past outlay. All past costs are down the drain. Nothing can change what has already happened.

Sunk Cost. A cost that has already been incurred and, therefore, is irrelevant to making future decisions.

The irrelevance of past costs for decisions does not mean that knowledge of past costs is useless. Often managers use past costs to help predict future costs. But the past cost itself is not relevant. The only relevant cost is the predicted future cost.

In deciding whether to replace or keep using equipment, four commonly encountered items differ in relevance.[1]

- *Book value of old equipment.* Irrelevant, because it is a past (historical) cost. Therefore, amortization on old equipment is irrelevant.
- *Disposal value of old equipment.* Relevant (ordinarily), because it is an expected future inflow that usually differs among alternatives.
- *Gain or loss on disposal.* This is the algebraic difference between book value and disposal value. It is therefore a combination of book value, which is always irrelevant, and disposal value, which is relevant. The combination form, *loss* (or *gain*) *on disposal* blurs the distinction between the irrelevant book value and the relevant disposal value. Consequently, it is best to think of each item separately and not in combination.
- *Cost of new equipment.* Relevant, because it is an expected future outflow that will differ among alternatives. Therefore, amortization on new equipment is relevant.

---

[1] For simplicity, we ignore income tax considerations and the effects of the interest value of money in this chapter. Book value is irrelevant even if income taxes are considered because the relevant item is then the tax cash flow, not the book value. For elaboration, see Chapter 11.

Exhibit 9-2 deserves close study because it should clarify the foregoing assertions. Book value of old equipment is irrelevant regardless of the decision-making technique used. The "difference" column in Exhibit 9-2 shows that the $4,000 book value of the *old* equipment does not differ between alternatives. It should be completely ignored for decision-making purposes.

The $4,000 appears in the income statement either as a $4,000 deduction from the $2,500 cash proceeds received to obtain a $1,500 loss on disposal in one year or as a $1,000 amortization in each of four years. But how it appears is irrelevant to the replacement decision. In contrast, the $2,000 annual amortization on the new equipment is relevant because the total $8,000 amortization is a future cost that may be avoided by not replacing.

Exhibit 9-2 is the first example that looks beyond one year. Examining the alternatives over their entire life ensures that peculiar nonrecurring items (such as loss on disposal) will not obstruct the long-run view vital to many managerial decisions.

Exhibit 9-3 concentrates on relevant items only: the cash operating costs, the disposal value of the old equipment, and the amortization on the new equipment. To demonstrate that the amount of the book value will not affect the answer, suppose the book value of the old equipment is $500,000 rather than $4,000. Your final answer will not change. The cumulative advantage of replacement is still $2,500. (If you are in doubt, rework this example, using $500,000 as the book value.)

EXHIBIT 9-2

Cost Comparison—
Replacement of
Equipment Including
Relevant and
Irrelevant Items

	FOUR YEARS TOGETHER		
	KEEP	REPLACE	DIFFERENCE
Cash operating costs	$20,000	$12,000	$8,000
Old equipment (book value):			
Periodic write-off as amortization	4,000	–	
or			–
Lump-sum write-off		4,000*	
Disposal value	–	(2,500)*	2,500
New machine acquisition cost	–	8,000†	(8,000)
Total costs	$24,000	$21,500	$2,500

The advantage of replacement is $2,500 for the four years together.

* In a formal income statement, these two items would be combined as "loss on disposal" of $4,000 – $2,500 = $1,500.

† In a formal income statement, written off as straight-line amortization of $8,000 ÷ 4 = $2,000 for each of four years.

EXHIBIT 9-3

Cost Comparison—
Replacement of
Equipment, Relevant
Items Only

	FOUR YEARS TOGETHER		
	KEEP	REPLACE	DIFFERENCE
Cash operating costs	$20,000	$12,000	$8,000
Disposal value of old machine	–	(2,500)	2,500
New machine, acquisition cost	–	8,000	(8,000)
Total relevant costs	$20,000	$17,500	$2,500

It is sometimes difficult to accept the proposition that past or sunk costs are irrelevant to decisions. Consider the ticket you have to a major football game in December. After getting the ticket, you learn that the game will be on television, and you really prefer to watch the game in the comfort of your warm home. Does your decision about attending the game or watching it on TV depend on whether you were given the ticket for free or you paid $80 for it? What does this tell you about a manager's decision to replace a piece of equipment?

ANSWER

The amount paid, whether it be $0, $80, or $1,000, should make no difference to the decision. You have the ticket, and it was paid for. That cannot be changed. If you really prefer to watch the game on TV, it may have been a bad decision to pay $80 for a ticket. But you cannot erase that bad decision. All you can do is choose the future action that has most value to you. You should not suffer through a less pleasant experience just because you paid $80 for the ticket.

A manager must make the same analysis regarding the replacement of a piece of equipment. What the company spent for the equipment is irrelevant. Keeping equipment that is no longer economical is just like using a ticket for an event that you would rather not attend.

CONFLICTS BETWEEN DECISION MAKING AND PERFORMANCE EVALUATION

OBJECTIVE 5

Discuss how performance measures can affect decision making.

We have focused on using relevant information in decision making. To motivate people to make optimal decisions, methods of performance evaluation should be consistent with the decision making.

Consider the replacement decision shown in Exhibit 9-3, where replacing the machine had a $2,500 advantage over keeping it. To motivate managers to make the right choice, the method used to evaluate performance should be consistent with the decision model. That is, it should show better performance when managers replace the machine than when they keep it. Because performance is often measured by accounting income, consider the accounting income in the first year after replacement compared to that in Years 2, 3, and 4:

	YEAR 1		YEARS 2, 3, AND 4	
	KEEP	**REPLACE**	**KEEP**	**REPLACE**
Cash operating costs	$5,000	$3,000	$5,000	$3,000
Amortization	1,000	2,000	1,000	2,000
Loss on disposal ($4,000 – $2,500)	–	1,500	–	–
Total charges against revenue	$6,000	$6,500	$6,000	$5,000

If the machine is kept rather than replaced, first-year expenses will be $6,500 – $6,000 = $500 lower, and first-year income will be $500 higher. Because managers naturally want to make decisions that maximize the measure of their performance, they may be inclined to keep the machine. This is an example of a conflict between the analysis for decision making and the method used to evaluate performance.

The conflict is especially severe if managers jump from one position to another. Why? Because the $500 first-year advantage will be offset by a $1,000 per-year advantage of replacing in Years 2, 3, and 4. (Note that the net difference of $2,500 in favour of replacement over the four years together is the same as in Exhibit 9-3.) But a manager who moves to a new position after the first year bears the entire loss on disposal without reaping the benefits of lower operating costs in Years 2, 3, and 4.

The decision to replace a machine earlier than planned also reveals that the original decision to purchase the machine may have been flawed. The old machine was bought six years ago for $10,000; its expected life was ten years. However, if a better machine is now available, then the useful life of the old machine was really six years, not ten. This feedback on the actual life of the old machine has two possible effects: the first good and the second bad. First, managers might learn from the earlier mistake. If the useful life of the old machine was over-estimated, how believable is the prediction that the new machine will have a four-year life? Feedback can help avoid repeating past mistakes. Second, another mistake might be made to cover up the earlier one. A "loss on disposal" could alert superiors to the incorrect economic-life prediction used in the earlier decision. By avoiding replacement, the $4,000 remaining book value is spread over the future as "amortization"—a more appealing term than "loss on disposal." The superiors may never find out about the incorrect prediction of economic life. The accounting income approach to performance evaluation mixes the financial effects of various decisions, hiding both the earlier misestimation of useful life and the current failure to replace.

The conflict between decision making and performance evaluation is a widespread problem in practice. Unfortunately, there are no easy solutions. In theory, accountants could evaluate performance in a manner consistent with decision making. In our equipment example, this would mean predicting year-by-year income effects over the planning horizon for four years, noting that the first year would be poor, and evaluating actual performance against the predictions.

The trouble is that evaluating performance, decision by decision, is a costly procedure. Therefore, aggregate measures are used. For example, an income statement shows the results of many decisions, not just the single decision of buying a machine. Consequently, in many cases like our equipment example, managers may be most heavily influenced by the first-year effects on the income statement. Thus, managers refrain from taking the longer view that would benefit the company.

Conflicts between decision making and performance evaluation are commonly referred to as problems of "goal congruency." These issues will be examined in more detail in Chapters 14 and 15.

IRRELEVANCE OF FUTURE COSTS THAT WILL NOT DIFFER BETWEEN ALTERNATIVES

In addition to past costs, some *future* costs may be irrelevant because they will be the same under all feasible alternatives. These, too, may be safely ignored for a particular decision. The salaries of many members of top management are examples of expected future costs that will be unaffected by the decision to follow one alternative or another.

Other irrelevant future costs include fixed costs that will be unchanged by such considerations as whether Machine X or Machine Y is selected. However, it is not merely a case of saying that fixed costs are irrelevant and variable costs are relevant. Variable costs can be irrelevant and fixed costs can be relevant. For instance, sales commissions might be paid on an order regardless of whether the order was filled from Plant G or Plant H. Variable costs are irrelevant whenever they do not differ among the alternatives at hand. Fixed costs are relevant whenever they differ under the alternatives at hand.

The key issue again is to identify which costs will differ between alternatives and by how much.

HIGHLIGHTS TO REMEMBER

1. **Use opportunity cost to analyze the income effects of a given alternative.** One should always consider opportunity costs when deciding on the use of limited resources. The opportunity cost of a course of action is the maximum profit foregone from other alternative actions. Decision makers may fail to consider opportunity costs because accountants do not report them in the financial accounting system.

2. **Decide whether to make or to buy certain parts or products.** One of the most important production decisions is the make-or-buy decision. Should a company make its own parts or products or should it buy them from outside sources? Both qualitative and quantitative factors affect this decision. In applying relevant cost analysis to a make-or-buy situation, a key factor to consider is the use of facilities.

3. **Decide whether a joint product should be processed beyond the split-off point.** Another typical production situation is deciding whether to process further a joint product or sell it at the split-off point. The relevant information for this decision includes the costs that differ beyond the split-off point. Joint costs that occur before split-off are irrelevant.

4. **Identify irrelevant information in disposal of obsolete inventory.** In certain production decisions, it is important to recognize and identify irrelevant costs. In the decision of whether to dispose of obsolete inventory, the original cost of the inventory is irrelevant because there is no way to restore the resources used to buy or produce the inventory.

5. **Decide whether to keep or replace equipment.** In the decision to keep or replace equipment, the book value of old equipment is irrelevant. This sunk cost is a past or historical cost that a company has already incurred. Relevant costs normally include the disposal value of old equipment, the cost of new equipment, and the difference in the annual operating costs.

6. **Explain how unit costs can be misleading.** Unit fixed costs can be misleading because of the differences in the assumed level of volume on which they are based. The more units a company makes, the lower the unit fixed cost will be. If a salesperson assumes a company will produce 100,000 units and it actually produces only 30,000 units, the unit costs will be understated. You can avoid being misled by unit costs by always using total fixed costs.

7. **Discuss how performance measures can affect decision making.** If companies evaluate managers using performance measures that are not in line with relevant decision criteria, there could be a conflict of interest. Managers often make decisions based on how the decision affects their performance measures. Thus, performance measures work best when they are consistent with the long-term good of the company.

8. **Construct absorption and contribution format income statements and identify which is better for decision making.** The major difference between the absorption and contribution formats for the income statement is that the contribution format focuses on cost behavior (fixed and variable), whereas the absorption format reports costs by business functions. The contribution approach makes it easier for managers to evaluate the effects of changes in volume on income and thus it is better for decision making.

DEMONSTRATION PROBLEM FOR YOUR REVIEW

Problem

Block Company makes industrial power drills. The data on the following page show the costs of the plastic housing separately from the costs of the electrical and mechanical components.

1. During the year, a prospective customer in an unrelated market offered $82,000 for 1,000 finished units. The latter would be in addition to the 100,000 units sold. The regular sales commission rate would have been paid. The president rejected the order because "it was below our costs of $97 per unit." What would operating income have been if the order had been accepted?

2. A supplier offered to manufacture the year's supply of 100,000 plastic housings for $13.50 each. What would be the effect on operating income if the Block Company purchased rather than made the plastic housings? Assume that $350,000 of the separable fixed costs assigned to plastic housings would have been avoided if the parts were purchased.

3. The company could have purchased their entire supply of the plastic housings for $13.50 each and used the vacated space for the manufacture of a deluxe version of its drill. Assume that 20,000 deluxe units could have been made (and sold in addition to the 100,000 regular units) at a unit variable cost of $90, exclusive of plastic housings and exclusive of the 10 percent sales commission. The 20,000 extra plastic housings could also be purchased for $13.50 each. The sales price would have been $130. All the fixed costs pertaining to the plastic housings would have continued, because these costs related primarily to the manufacturing facilities used. What would operating income have been if Block had bought the necessary plastic housings and made and sold the deluxe units?

	A ELECTRICAL & MECHANICAL COMPONENTS*	B PLASTIC HOUSING	A + B INDUSTRIAL DRILLS
Sales: 100,000 units, @ $100			$10,000,000
Variable costs:			
Direct materials	$4,400,000	$ 500,000	$4,900,000
Direct labour	400,000	300,000	700,000
Variable factory overhead	100,000	200,000	300,000
Other variable costs	100,000	–	100,000
Sales commissions, @ 10% of sales	1,000,000	–	1,000,000
Total variable costs	$6,000,000	$1,000,000	$7,000,000
Contribution margin			$3,000,000
Separable fixed costs	$1,900,000	$ 400,000	$2,300,000
Common fixed costs	320,000	80,000	400,000
Total fixed costs	$2,220,000	$ 480,000	$2,700,000
Operating income			$ 300,000

* Not including the costs of parts (column B).

Solution

1. Costs of filling the special order:

Direct materials	$49,000
Direct labour	7,000
Variable factory overhead	3,000
Other variable costs	1,000
Sales commission @ 10% of $82,000	8,200
Total variable costs	$68,200
Selling price	82,000
Contribution margin	$13,800

Operating income would have been $300,000 + $13,800, or $313,800, if the order had been accepted. In a sense, the decision to reject the offer implies that the Block Company is willing to invest $13,800 in immediate gains foregone (an opportunity cost) in order to preserve the long-run selling-price structure.

2. Assuming that $350,000 of the fixed costs could have been avoided by not making the plastic housings and that the other fixed costs would have been continued, the alternatives can be summarized as follows:

	MAKE	BUY
Purchase cost		$1,350,000
Variable costs	$1,000,000	
Avoidable fixed costs	350,000	
Total relevant costs	$1,350,000	$1,350,000

If the facilities used for plastic housings became idle, the Block Company would be indifferent as to whether to make or buy. Operating income would be unaffected.

3. The effect of purchasing the plastic housings and using the vacated facilities for the manufacture of a deluxe version of its main product is

Sales would increase by 20,000 units @ $130		$2,600,000
Variable costs exclusive of housing would increase		
by 20,000 units @ $90	$1,800,000	
Plus: sales commission, 10% of		
$2,600,000	260,000	2,060,000
Contribution margin on 200,000 units		$ 540,000
Plastic housings: 120,000 rather than 100,000 would		
be needed		
Buy 120,000 @ $13.50	$1,620,000	
Make 100,000 @ $10 (only the variable costs		
are relevant)	1,000,000	
Excess cost of outside purchase		620,000
Fixed costs, unchanged		–
Disadvantage of making deluxe units		$ (80,000)

Operating income would decline to $220,000 ($300,000 – $80,000, the disadvantage of selling the deluxe units). The deluxe units bring in a contribution margin of $540,000, but the additional costs of buying rather than making plastic housings is $620,000, leading to a net disadvantage of $80,000.

It is also necessary to consider other more qualitative considerations in addition to the above analysis. For example, what are the implications of the above decisions in terms of developing and maintaining a long-term relationship with your existing customers? Further, could one argue that there may be ethical concerns, for example, in the first scenario, of accepting a lower-than-normal price?

KEY TERMS

accumulated amortization *p. 419*

amortization *p. 419*

book value *p. 419*

depreciation *p. 419*

differential cost (incremental cost) *p. 410*

joint costs *p. 417*

joint products *p. 417*

net book value *p. 419*

opportunity cost *p. 411*

separable costs *p. 417*

split-off point *p. 417*

sunk cost *p. 420*

ASSIGNMENT MATERIAL

QUESTIONS

Q9-1 Distinguish between an opportunity cost and an outlay cost.

Q9-2 "I had a chance to rent my summer home for two weeks for $800. But I chose to leave it empty. I didn't want strangers living in my summer house." What term in this chapter describes the $800? Why?

Q9-3 "Accountants do not ordinarily record opportunity costs in the formal accounting records." Why?

Q9-4 Distinguish between an incremental cost and a differential cost.

Q9-5 "Incremental cost is the addition to costs from the manufacture of one unit." Do you agree? Explain.

Q9-6 "The differential costs or incremental costs of increasing production from 1,000 automobiles to 1,200 automobiles per week would be the additional costs of producing the additional 200 automobiles." If production were reduced from 1,200 to 1,000 automobiles per week, what would the decline in costs be called?

Q9-7 "Qualitative factors generally favour making over buying a component." Do you agree? Explain.

Q9-8 "Choices are often mislabelled as simply *make or buy*." Do you agree? Explain.

Q9-9 What is the split-off point and why is it important in analyzing joint costs?

Q9-10 "No technique used to assign the joint cost to individual products should be used for management decisions regarding whether a product should be sold at the split-off point or processed further." Do you agree? Explain.

Q9-11 "Inventory that was purchased for $5,000 should not be sold for less than $5,000 because such a sale would result in a loss." Do you agree? Explain.

Q9-12 "Recovering sunk costs is a major objective when replacing equipment." Do you agree? Explain.

Q9-13 "Past costs are indeed relevant in most instances because they provide the point of departure for the entire decision process." Do you agree? Why?

Q9-14 Which of the following items are relevant to replacement decisions? Explain.

a. Book value of old equipment

b. Disposal value of old equipment

c. Cost of new equipment

Q9-15 "Some expected future costs may be irrelevant." Do you agree? Explain.

Q9-16 "Variable costs are irrelevant whenever they do not differ among the alternatives at hand." Do you agree? Explain.

Q9-17 There are two major reasons why unit costs should be analyzed with care in decision making. What are they?

Q9-18 "Machinery sales personnel sometimes erroneously brag about the low unit costs of using their machines." Identify one source of an error concerning the estimation of unit costs.

Q9-19 Give an example of a situation where the performance evaluation model is not consistent with the decision model.

Q9-20 "Evaluating performance, decision by decision, is costly. Aggregate measures, like the income statement, are frequently used." How might the wide use of income statements affect managers' decisions about buying equipment?

PROBLEMS

P9-1 UNIT COSTS. Brandon Company produces and sells a product that has variable costs of $9 per unit and fixed costs of $110,000 per year.

1. Compute the unit cost at a production and sales level of 10,000 units per year.
2. Compute the unit cost at a production and sales level of 20,000 units per year.
3. Which of these unit costs is more accurate? Explain.

P9-2 WEAK DIVISION. Lake Superior Electronics Company paid $7 million in cash four years ago to acquire a company that manufactures CD-ROMs. This company operates as a division of Lake Superior and has lost $500,000 each year since its acquisition.

The minimum desired return for this division is that, when a new product is fully developed, it should return a net profit of $500,000 per year for the foreseeable future.

Recently the IBM Corporation offered to purchase the division from Lake Superior for $4 million. The president of Lake Superior commented, "I've got an investment of $9 million to recoup ($7 million plus losses of $500,000 for each of four years). I have finally got this situation turned around, so I oppose selling the division now."

Prepare a response to the president's remarks. Indicate how to make this decision. Be as specific as possible.

P9-3 MAKE OR BUY.   A BMW executive in Germany is trying to decide whether the company should continue to manufacture an engine component or purchase it from Hanover Corporation for 25.56 Euros (EUR) each. Demand for the coming year is expected to be the same as for the current year, 200,000 units. Data for the current year follow:

Direct material	EUR2,556,459.41
Direct labour	971,454.57
Factory overhead, variable	562,421.07
Factory overhead, fixed	1,278,229.70
Total costs	EUR5,368,564.75

If BMW makes the components, the unit costs of direct material will increase 10 percent. If BMW buys the components, 40 percent of the fixed costs will be avoided. The other 60 percent will continue regardless of whether the components are manufactured or purchased. Assume that variable overhead varies with output volume.

1. Tabulate a comparison of the make-and-buy alternatives. Show totals and amounts per unit. Compute the numerical difference between making and buying. Assume that the capacity now used to

make the components will become idle if the components are purchased.

2. Assume also that the BMW capacity in question can be rented to a local electronics firm for EUR127,822.97 for the coming year. Tabulate a comparison of the net relevant costs of the three alternatives: make, buy and leave capacity idle, buy and rent. Which is the most favourable alternative? By how much in total?

P9-4 **HOSPITAL OPPORTUNITY COST.** An administrator at Riverview Hospital is considering how to use some space made available when the outpatient clinic moved to a new building. She has narrowed her choices as follows:

a. Use the space to expand laboratory testing. Expected future annual revenue would be $320,000; future costs, $290,000.

b. Use the space to expand the eye clinic. Expected future annual revenue would be $500,000; future costs, $480,000.

c. The gift shop is rented by an independent retailer who wants to expand into the vacated space. The retailer has offered an $11,000 early rental for the space. All operating expenses will be borne by the retailer.

The administrator's planning horizon is unsettled. However, she has decided that the yearly data given will suffice for guiding her decision.

Tabulate the total relevant data regarding the decision alternatives. Omit the concept of opportunity cost in one tabulation, but use the concept in a second tabulation. As the administrator, which tabulation would you prefer if you could receive only one?

P9-5 **JOINT PRODUCTS: SELL OR PROCESS FURTHER.** Mussina Chemical Company produced three joint products at a joint cost of $117,000. These products were processed further and sold as follows:

CHEMICAL PRODUCT	SALES	ADDITIONAL PROCESSING COSTS
A	$230,000	$190,000
B	330,000	300,000
C	175,000	100,000

The company has had an opportunity to sell at split-off directly to other processors. If that alternative had been selected, sales would have been: A, $56,000; B, $28,000; and C, $54,000.

The company expects to operate at the same level of production and sales in the forthcoming year.

Consider all the available information, and assume that all costs incurred after split-offs are variable.

1. Could the company increase operating income by altering its processing decisions? If so, what would be the expected overall operating income?

2. Which products should be processed further and which should be sold at split-off?

P9-6 MAKE OR BUY. Assume that a division of Sony, Inc. makes an electronic component for its speakers. Its manufacturing process for the component is a highly automated part of a just-in-time production system. All labour is considered to be an overhead cost, and all overhead is regarded as fixed with respect to output volume. Production costs for 100,000 units of the component are

Direct materials		$300,000
Factory overhead:		
Indirect labour	$80,000	
Supplies	30,000	
Allocated occupancy cost	40,000	150,000
Total cost		$450,000

A small, local company has offered to supply the components at a price of $3.45 each. If the division discontinued its production of the component, it would save two-thirds of the supplies cost and $30,000 of indirect labour cost. All other overhead costs would continue.

The division manager recently attended a seminar on cost behaviour and learned about fixed and variable costs. He wants to continue to make the component because the variable cost of $3.00 is below the $3.45 bid.

1. Compute the relevant costs of (a) making, and (b) purchasing the component. Which alternative is less costly and by how much?
2. What qualitative factors might influence the decision about whether to make or buy the component?

P9-7 REPLACING OLD EQUIPMENT. Consider these data regarding Muskoka County's photocopying equipment:

	OLD EQUIPMENT	PROPOSED REPLACEMENT EQUIPMENT
Useful life, in years	5	3
Current age, in years	2	0
Useful life remaining, in year	3	3
Original cost	$32,000	$15,000
Accumulated amortization	12,000	0
Book value	18,000	Not acquired yet
Disposal value (in cash) now	3,000	Not acquired yet
Disposal value in two years	0	0
Annual cash operating costs for power maintenance, toner, and supplies	14,000	7,500

The county administrator is trying to decide whether to replace the old equipment. Because of rapid changes in technology, she expects the replacement equipment to have only a three-year useful life. Ignore the effects of taxes.

1. Tabulate a cost comparison that includes both relevant and irrelevant items for the next three years together.

2. Tabulate a cost comparison of all relevant items for the next three years together. Which tabulation is clearer, this one or the one in requirement 1?

3. Prepare a simple "shortcut"or direct analysis to support your choice of alternatives.

P9-8 **DECISIONS AND PERFORMANCE MODELS.**   Refer to the preceding problem (9-7).

1. Suppose the "decision model" favoured by top management consisted of a comparison of a three-year accumulation of cash under each alternative. As the manager of office operations, which alternative would you choose? Why?

2. Suppose the "performance evaluation model" emphasized the minimization of overall costs of photocopying operations for the first year. Which alternative would you choose?

P9-9 **OPPORTUNITY COSTS.**   Martina Bridgeman is a lawyer employed by a large law firm at $90,000 per year. She is considering whether to become a sole practitioner, which would probably generate annually $320,000 in operating revenues and $220,000 in operating expenses.

1. Present two tabulations of the annual income effects of these alternatives. The second tabulation should include the opportunity cost of Bridgeman's compensation as an employee.

2. Suppose Bridgeman prefers less risk and chooses to remain at the law firm. Show a tabulation of the income effects of rejecting the opportunity of independent practice.

P9-10 **OPPORTUNITY COST OF HOME OWNERSHIP.**   Oliver Scott has just made the final payment on his mortgage. He could continue to live in the home; cash expenses for repairs and maintenance (after any tax effects) would be $500 monthly. Alternatively, he could sell the home for $200,000, invest the proceeds in 8 percent bonds, and rent an apartment for $18,000 annually. The landlord would then pay for repairs and maintenance.

Prepare two analyses of alternatives, one showing no explicit opportunity cost and the second showing the explicit opportunity cost of the decision to hold the present home.

P9-11 **MAKE OR BUY.**   Sunshine State Fruit Company sells premium-quality oranges and other citrus fruits by mail-order. Protecting the fruit during shipping is important, so the company has designed and produces special shipping boxes. The annual cost of 80,000 boxes is

Materials	$120,000
Labour	20,000
Overhead	
Variable	16,000
Fixed	60,000
Total	$216,000

Therefore, the cost per box averages $2.70.

Suppose National Boxes Inc. submits a bid to supply Sunshine State with boxes for $2.40 per box. Sunshine State must give National Boxes Inc. the box design specifications, and the boxes will be made according to those specifications.

1. How much, if any, would Sunshine State save by buying the boxes from National Boxes Inc.?
2. What subjective factors should affect Sunshine State's decision whether to make or buy the boxes?
3. Suppose all the fixed costs represent amortization on equipment that was purchased for $600,000 and is just about at the end of its ten-year life. New replacement equipment will cost $1 million and is also expected to last ten years. In this case, how much, if any, would Sunshine State save by buying from National Boxes Inc.?

P9-12 **OPPORTUNITY COST.** Renee Minelli, MD, is a psychiatrist who is in heavy demand. Even though she has raised her fees considerably during the past five years, Dr. Minelli still cannot accommodate all the patients who wish to see her.

Minelli has conducted six hours of appointments a day, six days a week, for 48 weeks a year. Her fee averages $140 per hour.

Her variable costs are negligible and may be ignored for decision purposes. Ignore income taxes.

1. Dr. Minelli is weary from working a six-day week. She is considering taking every other Saturday off. What would be her annual income (a) if she worked every Saturday, and (b) if she worked every other Saturday?
2. What would be her opportunity cost for the year of not working every other Saturday?
3. Assume that Dr. Minelli has definitely decided to take every other Saturday off. She loves to repair her sports car by doing the work herself. If she works on her car during half a Saturday when she otherwise would not see patients, what is her opportunity cost?

P9-13 **SELL OR PROCESS FURTHER.** A petrochemical factory produces two products, L and M, as a result of a joint process. Both products are sold to manufacturers as ingredients for assorted chemical products.

Product L sells at split-off for $0.25 per litre; M, for $0.30 per litre. Data for April follow:

Joint processing cost	$1,600,000
Litres produced and sold:	
L	4,000,000
M	2,500,000

Suppose that in April the 2,500,000 litres of M could have been processed further into Super M at an additional cost of $225,000. The Super M output would be sold for $0.38 per litre. Product L would be sold at split-off in any event.

Should M have been processed further in April and sold as Super M? Show computations.

P9-14 OBSOLETE INVENTORY. The local book store bought more calendars than it could sell. It was nearly June and 200 calendars remained in stock. The store paid $4.50 each for the calendars and normally sold them for $8.95. Since February, they had been on sale for $6, and two weeks ago the price was dropped to $5. Still, few calendars were being sold. The book store manager felt it was no longer worthwhile using shelf space for the calendars.

The proprietor of Mac's Collectibles offered to buy all 200 calendars for $250. He intended to store them a few years, then sell them as novelty items.

The book store manager was not sure he wanted to sell for $1.25 calendars that cost $4.50. But the only alternative was to scrap them because the publisher would not take them back.

1. Compute the difference in profit between accepting the $250 offer and scrapping the calendars.
2. Describe how the $4.50 × 200 = $900 paid for the calendars affects your decision.

P9-15 REPLACE OLD EQUIPMENT. Three years ago the TCBY at the local mall bought a frozen-yogurt machine for $8,000. A salesperson has just suggested to the manager that she replace the machine with a new $12,500 machine. The manager has gathered the following data:

	OLD MACHINE	NEW MACHINE
Original cost	$8,000	$12,500
Useful life in years	8	5
Current age in years	3	0
Useful life remaining in years	5	5
Accumulated amortization	$3,000	Not acquired yet
Book value	$5,000	Not acquired yet
Disposal value (in cash) now	$2,000	Not acquired yet
Disposal value in 5 years	0	0
Annual cash operating cost	$4,500	$2,000

1. Compute the difference in total costs over the next five years under both alternatives, that is, keeping the original machine or replacing it with the new machine. Ignore taxes.
2. The manager replaces the original machine. Compute the "loss on disposal" of the original machine. How does this amount affect your computation in requirement 1? Explain.

P9-16 HOTEL ROOMS AND OPPORTUNITY COSTS. International Hotels operates many hotels throughout the world. One of its hotels is facing difficult times because several new competing hotels are opening.

To accommodate its flight personnel, Air Canada has offered International a contract for the coming year that provides a rate of $50 per night per room for a minimum of 50 rooms for 365 nights. This contract would assure International of selling 50 rooms of space nightly, even if some of the rooms are vacant on some nights.

The International manager has mixed feelings about the contract. On several peak nights during the year, the hotel could sell the same space for $100 per room.

1. Suppose the contract is signed. What is the opportunity cost of the 50 rooms on October 20, the night of a big convention of retailers when every midtown hotel room is occupied? What is the opportunity cost on December 28, when only 10 of these rooms would be expected to be rented at an average rate of $80?
2. If the year-round rate per room averaged $90, what percentage of occupancy of the 50 rooms in question would have to be rented to make International indifferent about accepting the offer?

P9-17 **EXTENSION OF PRECEDING PROBLEM.** Assume the same facts as in the preceding problem. However, also assume that the variable costs per room per day are $10.

1. Suppose the best estimate is a 53 percent general occupancy rate at an average $90 room rate for the next year. Should International accept the contract?
2. What percentage of occupancy of the 50 rooms in question would have to make International indifferent about accepting the offer?

P9-18 **IRRELEVANCE OF PAST COSTS AT TIM HORTON'S.** Tim Horton's purchases and roasts high-quality whole bean coffees and sells them, along with other coffee-related products, primarily through its company-operated retail stores. The company is known for its high-quality coffees.

Suppose that the quality control manager at Tim Horton's discovered a 1,000 kilogram batch of roasted beans that did not meet the company's quality standards. Company policy would not allow such beans to be sold with the Tim Horton's name on it. However, it could be reprocessed, at which time it could be sold by Tim Horton's retail stores, or it could be sold as-is on the wholesale coffee-bean market.

Assume that the beans were initially purchased for $2,000, and the total cost of roasting the batch was $1,500, including $500 of variable cost and $1,000 of fixed costs (primarily amortization on the equipment).

The wholesale price at which Tim Horton's could sell the beans was $2.75 per kilogram. Purchasers would pay the shipping costs from the Tim Horton's plant to their warehouses.

If the beans were reprocessed, the processing cost would be $600 because roasted beans would not require as much processing as new beans. All $600 would be additional costs, that is, costs that would not be incurred without the reprocessing. The beans would be sold to the retail stores for $3.70 per kilogram, and Tim Horton's would have to pay an average of $0.20 per kilogram to ship the beans to the stores.

1. Should Tim Horton's sell the beans on the market as-is for $2.75 per kilogram, or should the company reprocess the beans and sell them through its own retail stores? Why?
2. Compute the amount of extra profit Tim Horton's earns from the alternative you selected in requirement 1 compared to what it would earn from the other alternative.
3. What cost numbers in the problem were irrelevant to your analysis? Explain why they were irrelevant.

P9-19 **HOTEL PRICING AND DISCOUNTS.**   A growing corporation in a large city has offered a 200-

room hotel a one-year contract to rent 40 rooms at reduced rates of $50 per room instead of the regular rate of $85 per room. The corporation will sign the contract for 365-day occupancy because its visiting manufacturing and marketing personnel are virtually certain to use all the space each night.

Each room occupied has a variable cost of $10 per night (for cleaning, laundry, lost linens, and extra electricity).

The hotel manager expects an 85 percent occupancy rate for the year, so she is reluctant to sign the contract. If the contract is signed, the occupancy rate on the remaining 160 rooms will be 95 percent.

1. Compute the total contribution margin for the year with and without the contract.
2. Compute the lowest room rate that the hotel should accept on the contract so that the total contribution margin would be the same with or without the contract.

P9-20 **SPECIAL AIR FARES.**   The manager of operations of Air Canada is trying to decide whether to adopt a new discount fare. Focus on one 134-seat airplane now operating at a 56 percent load factor. That is, on the average the airplane has $0.56 \times 134 = 75$ passengers. The regular fares produce an average revenue of $0.12 per passenger-kilometre.

Suppose an average 40 percent fare discount (which is subject to restrictions regarding time of departure) will produce three new additional passengers. Also suppose that three of the previously committed passengers accept the restrictions and switch to the discount fare from the regular fare.

1. Compute the total revenue per airplane-kilometre with and without the discount fares.
2. Suppose the maximum allowed allocation to new discount fares is 50 seats. These will be filled. As before, some previously committed passengers will accept the restrictions and switch to the discount fare from the regular fare. How many will have to switch so that the total revenue per mile will be the same either with or without the discount plan?

P9-21 **JOINT COSTS AND INCREMENTAL ANALYSIS.**   (CMA)   Jacques de Paris, a high-fashion

women's dress manufacturer, is planning to market a new cocktail dress for the coming season. Jacques de Paris supplies retailers in Europe.

Four metres of material are required to lay out the dress pattern. Some material remains after cutting, which can be sold as remnants.

The leftover material could also be used to manufacture a matching scarf and handbag. However, if the leftover material is to be used for the scarf and handbag, more care will be required in the cutting, which will increase the cutting costs.

The company expected to sell 1,250 dresses if no matching scarf or handbag were available. Market research reveals that dress sales will be 20 percent higher if a matching scarf and handbag are available. The market research indicates that the scarf and/or handbag will not be sold individually but only as accessories with the dress. The various combinations of dresses, scarves, and handbags that are expected to be sold by retailers are as follows:

	PERCENT OF TOTAL
Complete sets of dress, scarf, and handbag	70%
Dress and scarf	6
Dress and handbag	15
Dress only	9
Total	100%

The material used in the dress costs EUR75 per metre, or EUR300 for each dress. The cost of cutting the dress if the scarf and handbag are not manufactured is estimated at EUR100 a dress, and the resulting remnants can be sold for EUR25 for each dress cut out. If the scarf and handbag are to be manufactured, the cutting costs will be increased by EUR36 per dress. There will be no saleable remnants if the scarves and handbags are manufactured in the quantities estimated.

The selling prices and the costs to complete the three items once they are cut are

	SELLING PRICE PER UNIT	UNIT COST TO COMPLETE (EXCLUDES COST OF MATERIAL AND CUTTING OPERATION)
Dress	EUR1,050	EUR400
Scarf	140	100
Handbag	50	30

1. Calculate the incremental profit or loss to Jacques de Paris from manufacturing the scarves and handbags in conjunction with the dresses.
2. Identify any nonquantitative factors that could influence the company's management in its decision to manufacture the scarves and handbags that match the dress.

P9-22 **MAKE OR BUY.** Magna Corporation manufactures automobile parts. It frequently subcontracts work to other manufacturers, depending on whether Magna's facilities are fully occupied. Magna is about to make some final decisions regarding the use of its manufacturing facilities for the coming year.

The following are the costs of making part EC113, a key component of an emission-control system:

	TOTAL COST FOR 50,000 UNITS	COST PER UNIT
Direct materials	$ 400,000	$ 8
Direct labour	300,000	6
Variable factory overhead	150,000	3
Fixed factory overhead	300,000	6
Total manufacturing costs	$1,150,000	$23

Another manufacturer has offered to sell the same part to Magna for $21 each. The fixed overhead consists of amortization, property taxes, insurance, and supervisory salaries.

All the fixed overhead would continue if Magna bought the component except that the costs of $100,000 pertaining to some supervisory and custodial personnel could be avoided.

1. Assume that the capacity now used to make parts will become idle if the parts are purchased. Should the parts be made or bought? Show computations.
2. Assume that the capacity now used to make parts will either (a) be rented to a nearby manufacturer for $65,000 for the year or (b) be used to make oil filters that will yield a profit contribution of $200,000. Should part EC113 be made or bought? Show computations.

P9-23 **RELEVANT COST AND SPECIAL ORDER.** Antonio Company's *unit* costs of manufacturing and selling a given item at a planned activity level of 10,000 units per *month* are as follows:

Manufacturing costs:	
Direct materials	$4.10
Direct labour	0.60
Variable overhead	0.70
Fixed overhead	0.80
Selling expenses:	
Variable	3.00
Fixed	1.10

Ignore income taxes in all requirements. These four parts have no connection with each other.

1. Compute the planned *annual* operating income at a selling price of $12 per unit.
2. Compute the expected *annual* operating income if the volume can be increased by 20 percent when the selling price is reduced to $11. Assume the implied cost-behaviour patterns are correct.
3. The company desires to seek an order for 5,000 units from a foreign customer. The variable selling expenses for the order will be 40 percent less than usual, but the fixed costs for obtaining the order will be $6,000. Domestic sales will not be affected. Compute the minimum break-even price per unit to be considered.
4. The company has an inventory of 2,000 units of this item left over from last year's model. These must be sold through *regular channels* at reduced prices. The inventory will be valueless unless sold this way. What unit cost is relevant for establishing the minimum selling price of these 2,000 units?

P9-24 **NEW MACHINE.** A new $300,000 machine is expected to have a five-year life and terminal value of zero. It can produce 40,000 units a year at a variable cost of $4 per unit. The variable cost is $6 per unit with an old machine, which has a book value of $100,000. It is being amortized on a straight-line basis at $20,000 per year. It too is expected to have a terminal value of zero. Its current disposal value is also zero because it is highly specialized equipment.

The salesperson of the new machine prepared the following comparison:

	NEW MACHINE	OLD MACHINE
Units	40,000	40,000
Variable costs	$160,000	$240,000
Straight-line amortization	60,000	20,000
Total cost	$220,000	$260,000
Unit cost	$5.50	$6.50

He said, "The new machine is obviously a worthwhile acquisition. You will save $1 for every unit you produce."

1. Do you agree with the salesperson's analysis? If not, how would you change it? Be specific. Ignore taxes.
2. Prepare an analysis of total and unit costs if the annual volume is 20,000 units.
3. At what annual volume would both the old and new machines have the same total relevant costs?

P9-25 ROLE OF OLD EQUIPMENT REPLACEMENT. On January 2, 2006, the S. H. Park company installed a brand new $87,000 special moulding machine for producing a new product. The product and the machine have an expected life of three years. The machine's expected disposal value at the end of three years is zero.

On January 3, 2006, Kimiyo Lee, a star salesperson for a machine tool manufacturer, tells Mr. Park: "I wish I had known earlier of your purchase plans. I can supply you with a technically superior machine for $99,000. The machine you just purchased can be sold for $16,000. I guarantee that our machine will save $35,000 per year in cash operating costs, although it too will have no disposal value at the end of three years."

Park examines some technical data. Although he has confidence in Lee's claims, Park contends: "I'm locked in now. My alternatives are clear: (a) disposal will result in a loss, (b) keeping and using the 'old' equipment avoids such a loss, I have brains enough to avoid a loss when my other alternative is recognizing a loss. We've got to use that equipment until we get our money out of it."

The annual operating costs of the old machine are expected to be $60,000, exclusive of amortization. Sales, all in cash, will be $910,000 per year. Other annual cash expenses will be $810,000 regardless of this decision. Assume that the equipment in question is the company's only fixed asset.

Ignore income taxes and the time value of money.

1. Prepare statements of cash receipts and disbursements as they would appear in each of the next three years under both alternatives. What is the total cumulative increase or decrease in cash for the three years?
2. Prepare income statements as they would appear in each of the next three years under both alternatives. Assume straight-line amortization. What is the cumulative increase or decrease in net income for the three years?
3. Assume that the cost of the "old" equipment was $1 million rather than $87,000. Would the net difference computed in requirements 1 and 2 change? Explain.
4. As Kimiyo Lee, reply to Mr. Park's contentions.
5. What are the irrelevant items in each of your presentations for requirements 1 and 2? Why are they irrelevant?

P9-26 DECISION AND PERFORMANCE MODELS.   Refer to the preceding problem P9-25.

1. Suppose the "decision model" favoured by top management consisted of a comparison of a three-year accumulation of wealth under each alternative. Which alternative would you choose? Why? (Accumulation of wealth means cumulative increase in cash.)
2. Suppose the "performance evaluation model" emphasized the net income of a subunit (such as a division) each year rather than considering each project, one by one. Which alternative would you expect a manager to choose? Why?
3. Suppose the same quantitative data existed, but the "enterprise" was a city and the "machine" was a computer in the treasurer's department. Would your answers to the first two parts change? Why?

P9-27 BOOK VALUE OF OLD EQUIPMENT.   Consider the following data:

	OLD EQUIPMENT	PROPOSED NEW EQUIPMENT
Original cost	$24,000	$12,000
Useful life, in years	8	3
Current age, in years	5	0
Useful life remaining, in years	3	3
Accumulated amortization	15,000	0
Book value	9,000	Not acquired yet
Disposal value (in cash) now	3,000	Not acquired yet
Annual cash operating costs (maintenance, power, repairs, lubricants, etc.)	$10,000	$ 6,000

1. Prepare a cost comparison of all relevant items for the next three years together. Ignore taxes.
2. Prepare a cost comparison that includes both relevant and irrelevant items.
3. Prepare a comparative statement of the total charges against revenue for the first year. Would the manager be inclined to buy the new equipment? Explain.

P9-28 CONCEPTUAL APPROACH.   A large automobile-parts plant was constructed four years ago in an Ontario city served by two railroads. The PC Railroad purchased 40 specialized 20 metre freight cars as a direct result of the additional traffic generated by the new plant. The investment was based on an estimated useful life of 20 years.

Now the competing railroad has offered to service the plant with new 29 metre freight cars, which would enable more efficient shipping operations at the plant. The automobile company has threatened to switch carriers unless PC Railroad buys 10 new 29 metre freight cars.

The PC marketing management wants to buy the new cars, but PC operating management says, "The new investment is undesirable. It really consists of the new outlay plus the loss on the old freight cars. The old cars must be written down to a low salvage value if they cannot be used as originally intended."

Evaluate the comments. What is the correct conceptual approach to the quantitative analysis in this decision?

P9-29 **RELEVANT-COST ANALYSIS.**   Following are the unit costs of making and selling a single product at a normal level of 5,000 units per month and a current unit selling price of $90:

Manufacturing costs:	
Direct materials	$35
Direct labour	12
Variable overhead	8
Fixed overhead (total for the year, $300,000)	5
Selling and administrative expenses:	
Variable	15
Fixed (total for the year, $480,000)	8

Consider each requirement separately. Label all computations, and present your solutions in a form that will be comprehensible to the company president.

1. This product is usually sold at a rate of 60,000 units per year. It is predicted that a rise in price to $98 will decrease volume by 10 percent. How much may advertising be increased under this plan without having annual operating income fall below the current level?

2. The company has received a proposal from an outside supplier to make and ship this item directly to the company's customers as sales orders are forwarded. Variable selling and administrative costs would fall 40 percent. If the supplier's proposal is accepted, the company will use its own plant to produce a new product. The new product would be sold through the manufacturer's agents at a 10 percent commission based on a selling price of $40 each. The cost characteristics per unit of this product, based on predicted yearly normal volume, are as follows:

Direct materials	$ 6
Direct labour	12
Variable overhead	8
Fixed overhead	6
Manufacturing costs	$32
Selling and administrative expenses:	
Variable	10% of selling price
Fixed	$2

What is the maximum price per unit that the company can afford to pay to the supplier for subcontracting the entire old product? This is not easy. Assume the following:

- Total fixed factory overhead and total fixed selling expenses will not change if the new product line is added.

- The supplier's proposal will not be considered unless the present annual net income can be maintained.
- Selling price of the old product will remain unchanged.
- All $300,000 of fixed overhead will be assigned to the new product.

P9-30 **SELL OR PROCESS FURTHER.** Alpha-Alpha Inc. produces meat products. Suppose one of the company's plants processes beef cattle into various products. For simplicity, assume that there are only three products—steak, hamburger, and hides—and that the average steer costs $700. The three products emerge from a process that costs $100 per cow to run, and output can be sold for the following net amounts:

Steak (100 kilograms)	$400
Hamburger (500 kilograms)	600
Hides (120 kilograms)	100
Total	$1,100

Assume that each of these three products can be sold immediately or processed further in another plant. The steak can be the main course in frozen dinners sold under one label. The vegetables and desserts in the 400 dinners produced from the 100 kilograms of steak would cost $120, and production, sales, and other costs for the 400 meals would total $350. Each meal would be sold wholesale for $2.15.

The hamburger could be made into frozen Salisbury steak patties sold under a different label. The only additional cost would be a $200 processing cost for the 500 kilograms of hamburger. Frozen Salisbury steaks sell wholesale for $1.70 per kilogram.

The hides can be sold before or after tanning. The cost of tanning one hide is $80, and a tanned hide can be sold for $175.

1. Compute the total profit if all three products are sold at the split-off point.
2. Compute the total profit if all three products are processed further before being sold.
3. Which products should be sold at the split-off point? Which should be processed further?
4. Compute the total profit if your plan in requirement 3 is followed.

P9-31 **RELEVANT COSTS.** A cable television network is considering cancelling the program "Law and Order" because it is watched by only 2.3 percent of the audience in its Monday evening time slot. It would be replaced by "Desperately Seeking Mr. Right," a new show being created from the same formula as the popular "Friends." Market research indicates that "Desperately Seeking Mr. Right" would be watched by 4 percent of the audience in the same time slot. For audiences between 1.5 percent and 5 percent, the network believes each 1 percent of the audience in this time slot results in additional advertising revenue of $40,000 per week (including beneficial effects on other programs, both present and future). Replacement would come halfway through the 30-week season.

The network's accounting staff has prepared the following financial information to be used in making the decision:

- Developmental expenses for "Law and Order" were $600,000, and these are being amortized over the originally projected complete season (30 programs).
- Developmental expenses for "Desperately Seeking Mr. Right" were $900,000. If "Desperately Seeking Mr. Right" is shown for the second half of this season, the entire development cost must be amortized over those 15 programs. If it is not aired until next season, amortization will take place over 30 programs.
- The cost of a script for one program of "Law and Order" is $20,000 and for "Desperately Seeking Mr. Right" is $24,000. No contract for scripts for "Desperately Seeking Mr. Right" has yet been signed, but a contract for 20 programs of "Law and Order" was signed and the $400,000 was already paid.
- The star of "Law and Order" is under contract to the network for the entire season at $240,000. If "Law and Order" is cancelled, the star will do one special in the spring; if "Law and Order" continues, he will not do the special. If the star does not do the special, another person (with completely equivalent audience appeal) will be hired for $40,000 to do the special.
- The star of "Desperately Seeking Mr. Right" has been hired for the next season for $180,000. If she does 15 shows this season, she will have to forego a part in a movie. Consequently, she must be paid $120,000 for 15 shows this season.
- Investment in the set for "Law and Order" was $100,000, which was immediately expensed. Additional expense for the set averages $10,000 per show. If "Law and Order" is cancelled, the set can be sold for $20,000. Another alternative use of the set is for a TV movie that the network is planning. Additional set expenses for the movie would be $50,000, but building a completely new set would cost $80,000.
- "Desperately Seeking Mr. Right" is filmed on location; thus, there is no investment required for a set. However, $20,000 per show is required to make the location suitable for filming.
- The production crew of "Law and Order" (including actors other than the star) receives $50,000 per show. Most of these people could be used profitably in other operations at the network. However, two actors must be fired if the show is cancelled, and the actors' union requires severance pay of $4,000 each.
- There will be a large startup cost of production for "Desperately Seeking Mr. Right" because of suddenly needing it six months ahead of schedule. This will amount to $150,000, only $60,000 of which would be necessary if it were not aired until next season. The production crew is very important to "Desperately Seeking Mr. Right," and they receive $80,000 per show.
- The network allocates corporate overhead to each show by a complex formula. Each program of "Law and Order" was allocated $20,000 of overhead; each program of "Desperately Seeking Mr. Right" will be allocated $30,000 of overhead. The only corporate

overhead expense that would change if "Desperately Seeking Mr. Right" replaced "Law and Order" is the consultation time that corporate management spends with the production staff. This averages 10 percent of the total production crew expense.

- This decision is to be made by top management, who will invest about $20,000 of their time and effort in it. In addition, a consultant will be paid $4,000 to review the decision.

Should the network cancel "Law and Order" and replace it with "Desperately Seeking Mr. Right" immediately? Explain. Be sure to describe the information that was relevant to this decision and compute the monetary advantage or disadvantage to switching from "Law and Order" to "Desperately Seeking Mr. Right."

P9-32 **RELEVANT COSTS ON BROADWAY.** The *New York Times* reported that Neil Simon planned to open his play "London Suite" off Broadway. Why? For financial reasons. Producer Emanuel Azenberg predicted the following costs before the play even opens:

	ON BROADWAY	OFF BROADWAY
Sets, costumes, lights	$ 357,000	$ 87,000
Loading in (building set, etc.)	175,000	8,000
Rehearsal salaries	102,000	63,000
Director and designer fees	126,000	61,000
Advertising	300,000	121,000
Administration	235,000	100,000
Total	$1,295,000	$440,000

Broadway ticket prices average $55, and theatres can seat about 1,000 persons per show. Off-Broadway prices average $40, and the theatres seat only 500. Normally, plays run eight times a week, both on and off Broadway. Weekly operating expenses off Broadway average $82,000; they average a weekly $206,000 on Broadway.

1. Suppose 400 persons attended each show, whether on or off Broadway. Compare the weekly financial results from a Broadway production to one produced off Broadway.
2. Suppose attendance averaged 75 percent of capacity, whether on or off Broadway. Compare the weekly financial results from a Broadway production to one produced off Broadway.
3. Compute the attendance per show required to just cover weekly expenses (a) on Broadway, and (b) off Broadway.
4. Suppose average attendance on Broadway was 600 per show and off Broadway was 400. Compute the total net profit for a 26-week run (a) on Broadway, and (b) off Broadway.
5. Repeat requirement 4 for a 100-week run.
6. Using attendance figures from requirements 4 and 5, compute (a) the number of weeks a Broadway production must run before it breaks even, and (b) the number of weeks an off-Broadway production must run before it breaks even.

7. Using attendance figures from requirements 4 and 5, determine how long a play must run before the profit from a Broadway production exceeds that of an off-Broadway production.

8. If you were Neil Simon, would you prefer "London Suite" to play on Broadway or off Broadway? Explain.

P9-33 **MAKE OR BUY, OPPORTUNITY COSTS, AND ETHICS.** Agribiz Food Products, Inc. produces a wide variety of food and related products. The company's tomato canning operation relies partly on tomatoes grown on Agribiz's own farms and partly on tomatoes bought from other growers.

Agribiz's tomato farm is on the edge of Sharpestown, a fast-growing and medium-sized city. The farm produces 8 million kilograms of tomatoes a year and employs 55 persons. The annual costs of tomatoes grown on this farm are:

Variable production costs	$ 550,000
Fixed production costs	1,200,000
Shipping costs (all variable)	200,000
Total costs	$1,950,000

Fixed production costs include amortization on machinery and equipment, but not on land, because land cannot be amortized. Agribiz owns the land, which was purchased for $600,000 many years ago. A recent appraisal placed the value of the land at $15 million because it is prime land for development of an industrial park and shopping centre.

Agribiz could purchase all the tomatoes it needs on the market for $0.25 per kilogram delivered to its factory. If it did this, it would sell the farmland and shut down the operations in Sharpestown. If the farm were sold, $300,000 of the annual fixed costs would be saved. Agribiz can invest excess cash and earn an annual rate of 10 percent.

1. How much does it cost Agribiz annually for the land used by the tomato farm?

2. How much would Agribiz save annually if it closed the tomato farm? Is this more or less than would be paid to purchase the tomatoes on the market?

3. What ethical issues are involved with the decision of whether to shut down the tomato farm?

MANAGERIAL DECISION CASES

C9-1 **MAKE OR BUY.** The Minnetonka Corporation, which produces and sells a highly successful line of water skis, has decided to diversify to stabilize sales throughout the year. The company is considering the production of cross-country skis.

After considerable research, a cross-country ski line has been developed. However, because of the conservative nature of the company management, Minnetonka's president has decided to introduce only one model of the new skis for this coming winter. If the product is a success, further expansion in future years will be initiated.

The cross-country skis will be sold to wholesalers for $80 per pair. Because of available capacity, no additional fixed charges will be incurred to produce the skis. However, a $100,000 fixed charge will be absorbed to allocate a fair share of the company's present fixed costs to the new product.

Using the estimated sales and production of 10,000 pairs of skis as the expected volume, the accounting department has developed the following costs per pair:

Direct labour	$35
Direct material	30
Total overhead	15
Total	$80

Minnetonka has approached a subcontractor to discuss the possibility of purchasing the bindings. The purchase price of the bindings would be $5.25 per binding or $10.50 per pair. If the Minnetonka Corporation accepts the purchase proposal, it is predicted that direct labour and variable overhead costs would be reduced by 10 percent and direct material costs would be reduced by 20 percent.

Required:

1. Should the Minnetonka Corporation make or buy the bindings? Show calculations to support your answer.
2. What would be the maximum purchase price acceptable to Minnetonka for the bindings? Support your answer with an appropriate explanation.
3. Instead of sales of 10,000 pairs of skis, revised estimates show sales volume at 12,500 pairs. At this new volume, additional equipment, at an annual rental of $10,000, must be acquired to manufacture the bindings. However, this incremental cost would be the only additional fixed cost required even if sales increased to 30,000 pairs. (The 30,000 level is the goal for the third year of production.) Under these circumstances, should the Minnetonka Corporation make or buy the bindings? Show calculations to support your answer.
4. The company has the option of making and buying at the same time. What would be your answer to requirement 3 if this alternative were considered? Show calculations to support your answer.
5. What nonquantifiable factors should the Minnetonka Corporation consider in determining whether they should make or buy the bindings?

C9-2 MAKE OR BUY. The Rohr Company's old equipment for making subassemblies is worn out. The company is considering two courses of action: (a) completely replacing the old equipment with new equipment, or (b) buying subassemblies from a reliable outside supplier, who has quoted a unit price of $1 on a seven-year contract for a minimum of 50,000 units per year.

Production was 60,000 units in each of the past two years. Future needs for the next seven years are not expected to fluctuate beyond 50,000 to 70,000 units per year. Cost records for the past two years reveal the following unit costs of manufacturing the subassembly:

Direct materials	$0.30
Direct labour	0.35
Variable overhead	0.10
Fixed overhead (including $0.10 amortization and $0.10 for direct departmental fixed overhead)	0.25
	$1.00

The new equipment will cost $188,000 cash, will last seven years, and will have a disposal value of $20,000. The current disposal value of the old equipment is $10,000.

The salesperson for the new equipment has summarized her position as follows: the increase in machine speeds will reduce direct labour and variable overhead by $0.35 per unit. Consider last year's experience of one of your major competitors with identical equipment. They produced 100,000 units under operating conditions very comparable to yours and showed the following unit costs:

Direct materials	$0.30
Direct labour	0.05
Variable overhead	0.05
Fixed overhead (including amortization of $0.24)	0.40
	$0.80

For purposes of this case, assume that any idle facilities cannot be put to alternative use. Also assume that $0.05 of the old Rohr unit cost is allocated to fixed overhead that will be unaffected by the decision.

Required:

1. The president asks you to compare the alternatives on a total-annual-cost basis and on a per-unit basis for annual needs of 60,000 units. Which alternative seems more attractive?
2. Would your answer to requirement 1 change if the needs were 50,000 units? 70,000 units? At what volume level would Rohr be indifferent between make and buy? Show your computations.
3. What factors, other than those above, should the accountant bring to the attention of management to assist them in making their decision? Include the considerations that might be applied to the outside supplier.

C9-3 **HOTEL PRICING.** (Braithwaite) "I will give you my decision in about a week," said Georges Villedary, directeur general of Le Centre Sheraton, Montreal, as he put down the phone and looked pensively at the letter before him. The letter was from Alitalia requesting a one-year contract for 40 rooms at $42 per night. In addition, the hotel would have to provide a crew allowance of $25,000 per day. Bills are to be paid within seven days of receipt of statement on a weekly basis. The problem facing Villedary was a simple one: does he take Alitalia and fill the 40 rooms for 365 days at $42 or does he refuse the business and hope that he can sell the rooms at the full rack rate of $105.00? Last year he had 115 nights sold out.

General Background of the Hotel

Le Centre Sheraton was located in the downtown area of Montreal. It was viewed as a corporate/convention hotel. In 1987 the hotel was named winner of the Canadian Automobile Association "Four Diamond Award" and the "Four Star Award" from the *Mobil Travel Guide*. The hotel had 824 rooms including the Sheraton Towers—a prestigious five-storey hotel within a hotel. The Towers had its own check-in facilities, lounge, and special amenities. It contained 131 rooms, including 16 suites. The balance of the hotel offered a choice of king, queen, and double beds with an additional 24 suites and six rooms specially equipped for people with disabilities. All rooms were equipped with a pay-TV system.

The hotel operated three restaurants. Le Point de Vue on the 37th floor offered gourmet French cuisine and an exceptional wine list. It had a seating capacity of 84. Le Boulevard on the third floor was open for breakfast, lunch, and dinner and had a seating capacity of 259. La Musette was a European-style "express" restaurant on the promenade level for people in a hurry. It had a seating capacity of 60. In addition to the restaurants, the hotel had five lounges and 14 function rooms, including a ballroom that would accommodate 1,100 people for banquets and 2,600 people for receptions. Other features of the hotel included a five-storey glassed-in atrium, a glass-enclosed year-round pool and a health club with gymnasium, sauna, whirlpool, and masseuse. There was indoor parking for 500 cars and boutiques and specialty shops on the promenade level. Other services included multilingual staff and audio-visual services. All meeting rooms had cable-TV outlets, audio-visual facilities, and telephone jacks.

Competition

For airline crews, all hotels in the Montreal area were Sheraton's competitors because airlines choose hotels based on price. Nevertheless, for Alitalia, the criteria for selecting a hotel were slightly different. They preferred four-star hotels located near shopping and entertainment facilities. Hence, the competition was limited to about ten hotels located in the downtown area. Since all ten hotels met the Alitalia criteria, the decision would be made on the basis of price and service. Georges was well aware that a number of his competitors had expressed interest in the Alitalia business. He was also aware that if he took the contract and satisfied the Alitalia crew, then he would have more negotiating power when the contract came up for renewal next year (i.e., the room rate could be increased). In the hotel business, it was always easier to renew existing room contracts than to solicit new ones.

The Proposal

Sheraton's target market included all forms of corporate groups, professional associations, and conventions. The Alitalia proposal appeared to be a good opportunity for Le Centre Sheraton because it guaranteed 40 rooms per night for the entire year plus potential clients from their flights. The contract, if accepted, would require the hotel to have clean rooms immediately upon check-in; to have on hand $25,000 every day as an allowance for crews and to distribute the allowance as instructed; and to control the crew's wake-up calls. These services were standard tasks for the Sheraton Centre; however, because of the late departure of aircraft to Europe, check-out time for Alitalia would be between 4:00 p.m. and 6:00 p.m., while the other crews would be arriving sometime between 9:00 p.m. and 10:00 p.m. the same night. This meant the hotel had to keep extra maids on duty to have these rooms ready within two to four hours. In addition, when flight schedules were changed, there would be changes in wake-up calls and in the distribution of the allowances. This extra service to the crews would be at the expense of the other guests who were paying the full rack rate.

Experience with other airlines had shown that airline crews spend less during their stay at a hotel than a regular guest. This was because their usual stay was only one night. If they were grounded for several days, they preferred to explore the city of Montreal, hence food and beverage purchases were often made outside the hotel.

Sales and Cost Data

Georges knew he would have to work fast on this proposal so he called in his assistant, Marie Alfieri, and asked her to collect all the data required to estimate the additional revenue and costs that would be involved if the hotel decided to accept the Alitalia offer.

She began with an analysis of room statistics for the previous year, which showed that if the proposal had been in place, then the number of regular guest rooms lost was equivalent to 115 sold-out nights. An analysis of food and beverage statistics for the previous year showed average food revenue (not including banquets) of $17 per occupied room and average beverage revenue (not including banquets) of $13 per occupied room. The hotel's standard cost percentage was 36 percent for food and 32 percent for beverage.

In analyzing the probable effect on operating costs, Marie found that during the period when the hotel was not full they would require the equivalent of one additional front-desk clerk to handle the Alitalia crew. The average hourly wage for this job was $9.20 per hour. Employee benefits were calculated at 35 percent of wage cost. In addition to this cost, Marie estimated the following variable costs per occupied room:

1. Housekeeping—one half-hour per room. Housekeepers were paid $8.60 per hour.
2. Laundry and linen—$0.75 per occupied room
3. Utilities—$1.00 per occupied room
4. Amenities—$2.25 per occupied room

With this information in hand, she turned it over to Georges for final analysis and a decision. As he sat in his office with the new information supplied by Marie, he remembered a discussion at the recent meeting of general managers of all Sheraton hotels where they were told that one of the Company's objectives for the coming fiscal year was a 12 percent return on investment. He was also very aware of the serious cash-flow problem facing the hotel at that time. Cash flow for the last fiscal year was negative by over $2 million and with a $50 million long-term mortgage at a floating interest rate and $4.2 million in annual municipal taxes to pay, the Alitalia business promised a steady and certain cash flow every week.

Required: | As Georges Villedary, what is your decision? Why?

C9-4 **MAKE OR BUY.** (ICAO)   Maxim Auto Parts Ltd. has operated three automobile parts manufacturing plants in Ontario for many years. Two produce engine parts, and the third makes seats ("the seat division"). In recent years, the seat division's plant has been operating at well below capacity as a result of the loss of a major contract. The operating results of the seat division for the past three years are as follows:

	YEARS ENDED APRIL 30		
	2006	2005	2004
Revenue	$9,000,000	$9,000,000	$9,000,000
Variable cost of goods sold	7,580,000	7,490,000	7,380,000
Gross margin	1,420,000	1,510,000	1,620,000
Expenses:			
Amortization	130,000	130,000	130,000
Interest on bank loan (10% rate)	520,000	500,000	475,000
Sales commissions	900,000	900,000	900,000
Other selling expenses	115,000	110,000	105,000
Head office allocation	280,000	270,000	270,000
Factory overhead	200,000	200,000	200,000
Capital investment charge	220,000	210,000	205,000
Total expenses	2,365,000	2,320,000	2,285,000
Net	$ (945,000)	$ (810,000)	$ (665,000)

All revenue is from one sales contract with a large automobile manufacturer. Amortization is calculated on a straight-line basis on each of the division's assets: building, machinery and equipment, and vehicles. Interest is based on a $5.2 million bank loan made directly to the seat division. Sales commissions are based on revenue and are payable to the agent who negotiated the sales contract several years ago. Other selling expenses consist primarily of transportation expenses (approximately one percent of revenue) plus other non-transportation costs to service the automobile manufacturer's needs. The head office allocation is a charge for the use of the head office staff and is based on relative sales revenue of the three divisions. Factory overhead is for non-variable costs of manufacturing the seats. The capital investment charge is for imputed interest on the current replacement cost of the division's land, building, inventories, and other assets (net of divisional debt).

The seat division has received an offer to lease its land and building for five years at $1,000,000 per annum, receivable at the beginning of each year with an agreement to sell the building and land at the end of the five years for $5,000,000. The prospective lessee has agreed to pay for all operating expenses of the building, such as property taxes, insurance, heating, and water. If Maxim does not enter into the lease and sale agreement, the net realizable value of the land is expected to increase at least enough to offset any decline in the value of the building over the next five years.

The machinery and equipment has a replacement cost of $3 million. Management estimates that it could be sold now for about $500,000. The machinery and equipment will be worth only about $100,000 in scrap value in another five years.

Seat-division management has determined that another auto parts manufacturer would be willing to produce the seats for the five years that remain on the contract with the automobile manufacturer. The contract cannot be cancelled without incurring heavy penalties. The seat division is required to manufacture exactly 100,000 seats. The other manufacturer will charge $95 per seat for the entire five-year period, and will deliver them at no cost to Maxim.

If the seat division is closed, sales commissions would still have to be paid by Maxim, as would $150,000 of head office allocation that is currently being charged to the seat division. In addition, 25 percent of the "factory overhead" would still have to be paid if the seat division were closed or if the land and building were leased. The non-transportation portion of "other selling expenses" would not be incurred if the division is sold.

No other long-term liabilities exist in the seat division, other than the bank loan at 10 percent interest per annum.

You have been requested by Maxim's management to prepare a report on the course of action they should follow. Management wants you to include in your report the analysis supporting your recommendations.

Required: | Write the report requested by Maxim's management. (Ignore income taxes and the time value of money.)

C9-5 **MAKE OR BUY.** (ICAO) Pandagan Vacuums Limited (PVL) is a worldwide leader in the manufacturing of industrial vacuums. The company is located in Thorold, Ontario. PVL sells vacuums to distributors in North America, Europe, and Asia. Over the last ten years, PVL has seen its sales and market share deteriorate due to foreign competition. While PVL is considered a leader in product development and quality, the company has been unable to secure large contracts due to its higher-than-average selling prices. Management attributes this to the high cost of labour in Canada.

PVL has two divisions—the vacuum assembly division and the components production division. Currently, PVL manufactures seven standard industrial vacuum models in its vacuum assembly division (see Exhibit 9A-1). This division also manufactures special order models for its customers when its standard models are unsuitable. The vacuum assembly division also has a service department that repairs vacuums under warranty or, when the warranty has expired, for a service fee. PVL's distributors also provide warranty service on PVL's behalf. PVL's components production division currently produces about 60 percent of the components used in the manufacturing of its vacuums. The other 40 percent is purchased from external suppliers by the vacuum assembly division. Components are sold from the components production division to the vacuum assembly division using a negotiated transfer price, which approximates market value.

Recently, PVL was approached by a Korean manufacturing company, Engine Tech Limited (ETL). ETL specializes in manufacturing small engines. ETL has proposed an arrangement whereby it would produce engine model P12, which PVL currently uses in two of its standard vacuum models. PVL currently produces these engines in its components division. ETL has agreed to provide P12 engines for a five-year period at a cost of 130,000 Korean won per unit. At current exchange rates, this would amount to $2,200 Canadian per

MODEL	SELLING PRICE	ESTIMATED (1) ANNUAL SALES VOLUME (UNITS)	ENGINE MODEL USED	ENGINE SOURCE
3	$20,000	4,000	P10	External vendor
3A	$25,000	2,000	P12	Components division
4	$40,000	2,000	P12	Components division
4A	$50,000	1,500	P14	External vendor
5	$70,000	500	P16	External vendor
6	$80,000	500	S4	Components division
7	$95,000	200	S8	Components division

Note 1: Estimated sales amounts were prepared by the marketing department of PVL. Historically, the marketing department's estimates have been reasonably accurate.

	CURRENT PRODUCTION COSTS (IN DOLLARS)						
MODEL	3	3A	4	4A	5	6	7
LABOUR	$ 5,000	$ 7,000	$11,000	$15,000	$20,000	$25,000	$30,000
DIVISIONAL OVERHEAD (1)	1,000	1,400	2,200	3,000	4,000	5,000	6,000
COMPONENTS							
ENGINE	3,000	4,000	4,000	5,000	7,000	10,000	15,000
HOUSING	2,000	2,500	3,000	3,500	4,000	6,000	7,000
OTHER	6,000	6,100	9,000	18,400	20,200	20,200	28,000
TOTAL COST	$17,000	$21,000	$29,200	$44,900	$55,200	$66,200	$86,000

Note 1: Divisional overhead has been applied at a rate of 20 percent of direct labour. Divisional overhead includes purchasing costs, management salaries, rent, utilities, warranty service costs, and administrative costs.

unit. Duty and freight would cost approximately $300 per unit for a total of $2,500 Canadian per unit. PVL would agree to purchase a minimum of 5,000 units per year during the five-year term of the contract. If PVL failed to purchase the minimum amount, it would be required to pay a penalty of 30,000 won (currently $500 Canadian) per unit of shortfall from the minimum. This penalty payment would be due at the end of the year in which the shortfall occurs.

PVL is considering modifying two of its existing models so that they use the P12 engine. The model 3 unit could be modified to use the P12 engine instead of its existing engine, the P10, which is a less powerful engine than the P12. If this occurred, the cost of the engine to the vacuum assembly division would increase by $1,000 per unit. All other costs would remain the same. Annual sales of the Model 3 would be expected to rise by 20 percent if this modification was made. PVL is also considering modifying the model 4A to use the P12 engine instead of its existing engine, the P14, which is more powerful engine than the P12. If this occurs, the cost of the engine to the vacuum assembly division would decrease by $1,000 per unit. All other costs would remain the same. Annual sales of the model 4A would be expected to decrease by 20 percent if this modification was made.

You are the assistant controller of PVL. The controller of PVL has asked you to prepare a report on whether the offer from ETL should be accepted. She would also like you to discuss whether the P12 engine should be used in models 3 and 4A. In order to assist you in your analysis, she has asked the accounting and marketing departments of the vacuum assembly division to prepare information on expected sales and costs for the seven standard models that PVL produces (Exhibit 9A-1). This information represents management's best estimate of average selling prices and costs for the five-year term of the contract proposed by ETL. Costs and selling prices are not expected to change substantially over the five-year term of the contract. The controller has also had the accounting department of the component production division provide you with the current costs of producing the P12 engine (Exhibit 9A-2). These costs are not expected to change substantially over the five-year term of the proposed contract with ETL either. The controller has instructed you to provide a quantitative analysis of the decisions in your report. She would also like your report to address the qualitative aspects of these decisions.

Required: | Prepare the report requested by the controller.

EXHIBIT 9A-2

Pandagan Vacuums
Limited
Information on Current
Cost of Producing P12
Engine

Process Description

The division's purchasing department purchases all of the subcomponents needed to produce the engine. These subcomponents are then inspected. The engine is then assembled and inspected before being transferred to the vacuum assembly division.

PRODUCTION COSTS PER UNIT

Materials and subcomponents	$1,200.00
Direct Labour (including employee benefits):	
Subcomponent inspection	100.00 (1)
Assembly	500.00 (2)
Testing	150.00 (3)
Identifiable overhead:	
Amortization of equipment	300.00 (4)
Management salaries	240.00 (5)
Rent	200.00 (6)
Repairs and maintenance of equipment	200.00 (7)
Other	300.00 (8)
Allocated divisional overhead	300.00 (9)
	$3,490.00

Note 1: Costs consist of a supervisor and a team of inspection workers. One inspection worker can, in one year, inspect the components needed to assemble 500 engines. Each inspector's yearly salary and benefits cost $40,000. One supervisor is needed who can supervise up to 20 inspection workers.

Based on annual production of 4,000 units, expected costs are
Inspection workers

4,000 units/500 units per worker × $40,000	$320,000
Supervisor's salary and benefits	80,000
	$400,000
Annual production	4,000
Cost per unit	$ 100.00

Note 2: Assembly is conducted by production teams. Each team can assemble up to 500 units per year. Each team consists of ten workers and a supervisor. Total salaries and benefits per team average $250,000 per year.

Cost per team	$250,000
Production per team	500
Cost per unit	$ 500.00

Note 3: Costs consist of quality control inspectors, who each receive an annual salary and benefits of $75,000 per year. Each can inspect a maximum of 500 units per year.

Cost per inspector	$ 75,000
Units inspected	500
Cost per unit	$ 150.00

Note 4: Amortization is calculated based on the percentage of use of the component production division's machines. Currently, these machines are being used at 70 percent of their full capacity. All of these machines are required for the production of components other than the P12. Cost is determined as follows:

Cost per hour of machine usage	$ 9,000
Units produced per hour	30
Cost per unit	$300.00

Note 5: Management salaries are for 14 managers who work exclusively on the P12. These costs are not expected to increase if the volume of P12 engines produced changes.

Annual costs	$960,000
Units produced	4,000
Cost per unit	$240.00

Note 6: Rent relates to space used exclusively in the plant for the production of the P12 engine. The space currently being used would allow the component production division to produce up to 90,000 units per year without any increase in costs. If the P12 engine was no longer manufactured, PVL could sublease the space currently used for manufacturing this component. However, it would only be able to recover 50 percent of the cost it is currently incurring.

Annual cost	$800,000
Units produced	4,000
Cost per unit	$ 200.00

Note 7: Repairs and maintenance costs (like amortization) are also allocated based on machine usage. The actual amount of repairs and maintenance costs incurred during a year has been found to be directly related to the number of machine hours used.

Rate per hour of usage	$ 6,000
Units produced per hour	30
Costs per unit	$200.00

Note 8: Other overhead consists of utilities, training and other administrative costs. Approximately 50 percent of these costs are dependent upon the volume of units produced. The other 50 percent of these costs are not dependent on the volume of units produced.

Expected annual cost based on 4,000 units produced	$1,200,000
Annual volume	4,000
Cost per unit	$ 300.00

Note 9: Divisional overhead costs consist of costs that cannot be specifically attributed to a particular component. Divisional overhead costs are allocated based on the direct labour costs attributable to each component. Based on past results, a rate of 40 percent of direct labour is used to allocate divisional overhead. These costs are expected to remain the same regardless of the volume of P12 engines produced.

E9-1 IDENTIFYING RELEVANT REVENUE, COSTS, AND INCOME EFFECTS

Goal: Create an Excel spreadsheet to assist with sell-or-process-further decisions by identifying the relevant revenue, costs, and income effects. Use the results to answer questions about your findings.

Scenario: Mussina Chemical Company has asked you to prepare an analysis to help them make decisions about whether to sell joint products at the split-off point or process them further. Prepare the report of your analysis using a format similar to the one on page 418.

JOINT PRODUCTS: SELL OR PROCESS FURTHER

The Mussina Chemical Company produced three joint products at a joint cost of $117,000. These products were processed further and sold as follows.

CHEMICAL PRODUCT	SALES	ADDITIONAL PROCESSING COSTS
A	$230,000	$190,000
B	330,000	300,000
C	175,000	100,000

The company has had an opportunity to sell at split-off directly to other processors. If that alternative had been selected, sales would have been A, $54,000; B, $28,000; and C, $54,000.

The company expects to operate at the same level of production and sales in the forthcoming year.

Consider all the available information, and assume that all costs incurred after split off are variable.

When you have completed your spreadsheet, answer the following questions:

1. How should the $117,000 be allocated to the three products?

2. Is the company currently making the right processing decisions? Explain.

3. If the company alters its processing decisions, what would be the expected combined operating income from the three products?

Step by Step:

1. Open a new Excel spreadsheet.

2. In column A, create a bold-faced heading that contains the following:
   Row 1: Chapter 6 Decision Guideline
   Row 2: Mussina Chemical Company
   Row 3: Sell-or-Process-Further Analysis
   Row 4: Today's Date

3. Merge and centre the four heading rows across columns A through J.

4. In row 7, create the following bold-faced column headings:
Column B: Chemical Product A
Skip two columns
Column E: Chemical Product B
Skip two columns
Column H: Chemical Product C

5. Merge and centre the heading in row 7, column B across columns B through D.
Merge and centre the heading in row 7, column E across columns E through G.
Merge and centre the heading in row 7, column H across columns H through J.

6. In row 8, create the following centre-justified column headings:
Column B: Sell at Split-Off
Column C: Process Further
Column D: Difference
Column E: Sell at Split-Off
Column F: Process Further
Column G: Difference
Column H: Sell at Split-Off
Column I: Process Further
Column J: Difference

7. Change the format of the column headings in row 8 to permit the titles to be displayed on multiple lines within a single cell.
Alignment tab: Wrap Text: Checked

8. In column A, create the following bold-faced row headings:
Row 9: Revenues
Row 10: Costs beyond Split-Off
Skip a row
Row 11: Income Effects

   Note: Adjust width of column A to accommodate row headings.

9. Use the scenario data to fill in revenues and costs beyond split-off amounts for each of the products.

10. Use appropriate formulas to calculate the difference and income effects columns for each product as absolute values.
=ABS(formula)

11. Format all amounts as
Number: Category: Accounting
                  Decimal places: 0
                      Symbol: $

12. Change the format of the costs beyond split-off amounts to not display a dollar symbol.

13. Change the format of the income effects amounts to display as bold.

14. Change the format of the revenues amounts to display a top border, using the default line style.
Border tab: Icon: Top Border

15. Change the format of the costs beyond split-off amounts to display a bottom border, using the default line style.

Border tab: Icon: Bottom Border

16. Change the format of row 7, column B to display an outline border, using the default line style.

Border tab: Presets: Outline

Repeat this step for column E.
Repeat this step for column H.

17. Save your work to disk, and print a copy for your files.

Note: Print your spreadsheet using landscape in order to ensure that all columns appear on one page.

COLLABORATIVE LEARNING EXERCISE

CL9-1 OUTSOURCING A popular term for make-or-buy decisions is *outsourcing decisions.* There are many examples of outsourcing, from Nike's outsourcing of nearly all its production activities to small firms' outsourcing of their payroll activities. Especially popular outsourcing activities are warehousing and computer systems.

The purpose of this exercise is to share information on different types of outsourcing decisions. It can be done in small groups or as an entire class. Each student should pick an article from the literature that tells about a particular company's outsourcing decision. There are many such articles: a recent electronic search of the business literature turned up more than 4,000 articles. An easy way to find such an article is to search an electronic database of business literature. Magazines that have published outsourcing articles include *Fortune, Forbes, Business Week, Strategic Finance, CA* and *CMA Management* magazines. Many business sections of newspapers also include such articles.

1. List as many details about the outsourcing decision as you can. Include the type of activity that is being outsourced, the size of the outsourcing, and the type of company providing the outsourcing service.
2. Explain why the company decided to outsource the activity. If reasons are not given in the article, prepare a list of reasons that you think influenced the decision.
3. What disadvantages are there to outsourcing the activity?
4. Be prepared to make a three-to-five-minute presentation to the rest of the group or to the class covering your answers to numbers 1, 2, and 3.

Capital Budgeting Decisions

Should the Waterloo County Board of Education purchase new photocopy equipment? Should the law partners of Stone, Goldberg, and Gomez buy new personal computers for the staff? Should Boeing begin production of a proposed new airplane? Should Procter & Gamble introduce a new mouthwash?

Such decisions, which have significant financial effects beyond the current year, are called capital-budgeting decisions. **Capital-budgeting decisions** are faced by managers in all types of organizations, including religious, medical, and government enterprises.

Capital budgeting has three phases: (1) identifying potential investments, (2) selecting the investments to undertake (including the gathering of data to aid in the decision), and (3) follow-up monitoring or "postaudit" of investments.

Managers use many different capital-budgeting models in *selecting* investments. Each model provides unique information for a decision maker to choose among different investment proposals. Accountants contribute to this choice process in their problem-solving role. In this chapter we compare the uses and limitations of various capital-budgeting models, with particular attention to relevant-cost analysis.

> **Capital-Budgeting Decisions.** Refer to the process of evaluating and choosing among long-term capital projects.

CAPITAL INVESTMENT DECISIONS

In planning and controlling, operations managers typically focus on a particular *time period*. For example, the chief administrator of a university will be concerned with all activities for a given academic year. But the administrator will also be concerned with individual *programs* or *projects* that have a longer-range focus. Examples are new programs in educational administration or health-care education, joint law-management programs, new athletic facilities, new buildings, or new parking lots.

> **Capital Assets.** Assets used to generate revenues or cost savings that affect more than one year's financial results.

This chapter concentrates on the planning and controlling of those **capital assets** that affect more than one year's financial results. Such decisions require investments of resources that are often called capital outlays. Hence, the term *capital budgeting* has arisen to describe the long-term planning for making and financing such outlays.

All capital outlays involve risk. The organization must commit funds to the project or program but cannot be sure what—if any—returns this investment will yield later on. Many factors affecting future returns are unknown, but well-managed organizations try to gather and quantify as many known or predictable factors as possible before making a decision. Capital-budgeting models facilitate this process.

Most large organizations use more than one capital-budgeting model. Why? Because each model summarizes information in a different way and reveals various useful perspectives on investments. There are three general types of capital-budgeting models:

- discounted-cash-flow models,
- payback models, and
- rate-of-return models.

We will look at each of these model types in turn in this chapter.

DISCOUNTED-CASH-FLOW MODELS

Discounted-Cash-Flow (DCF) Model. A capital-budgeting model that focuses on cash inflows and outflows, the time value of money, and identifying criteria for accepting or rejecting capital projects.

Financial Post
www.financialpost.com

According to a list of *Financial Post* 500 industries, **discounted-cash-flow (DCF) models**, conceptually the most attractive models, are used by over 65 percent of industries and are the best measures of the financial effects of an investment. They are based on the old adage that a bird in the hand is worth two in the bush—that a dollar in the hand today is worth more than a dollar to be received (or spent) five years from today. This adage applies because the use of money has a cost, and we call that cost interest. Because the discounted-cash-flow model focuses on a project's cash inflows and outflows and explicitly and systematically incorporates the time value of money, it is the best method to use for capital-budgeting decisions.

Major Aspects of DCF

OBJECTIVE 1

Compute a project's net present value (NPV).

DCF models focus on expected *cash* inflows and outflows rather than on *net income*. Companies invest cash today (cash outflow) to receive cash returns in future periods (cash inflow). DCF compares the value of the cash outflows with the cash inflows.

There are two main variations of DCF: (a) net present value (NPV) and (b) internal rate of return (IRR). Both variations are based on the theory of compound interest. A brief summary of the tables and formulas used is included in Appendix B at the end of this book. Before reading on, examine Appendix B to be sure you understand the concept of compound interest and how to use Table 1 on page 825 and Table 2 on page 826. The mechanics of compound interest may appear formidable to those readers who are encountering them for the first time. However, a little practice with the interest tables may easily clarify their use.

Example

Throughout the rest of this section, we will use the following example to illustrate how capital budgeting decisions are made: A buildings and grounds manager of a university is contemplating the purchase of some lawn-maintenance equipment that is expected to increase efficiency and produce cash operating savings of $2,000 per year. The useful life of the equipment is four years, after which it will have a net disposal value of zero. The equipment will cost $6,075 now and the minimum desired rate of return is 10 percent per year.

Net Present Value (NPV)

Net-Present-Value (NPV) Method. An investment evaluation technique that discounts all expected future cash flows to the present using a minimum desired rate of return.

The **net-present-value (NPV) method** is an investment evaluation technique that discounts all expected future cash flows to the present using a minimum desired rate of return. To apply the net present value (NPV) method to a proposed investment project, a manager first determines some minimum desired rate of return. The rate depends on the risk of a proposed project—the higher the risk, the higher the minimum desired rate of return. The minimum rate is often called the **required rate of return, hurdle rate, or discount rate**. Managers then determine the present values of all expected cash flows from the project, using this minimum desired rate. If the sum of the present values of the cash flow is positive, the project is desirable. If the sum is negative, the project is undesirable. Why? A positive NPV means that accepting the project will increase the value of the firm because the present value of the project's cash inflows exceeds the present value of its cash outflows. (If by some chance, the NPV were exactly zero, a decision maker would be indifferent between accepting and rejecting the project.) When choosing among several investments, the one with the greatest net present value, notwithstanding qualitative non-financial considerations, is the most desirable.

The NPV method is applied in three steps, outlined below:

1. Prepare a list of all expected cash inflows and outflows preferably in chronological order starting with the initial investment at the time of the acquisition of the capital asset at time zero. Cash outflows are set in parentheses; cash inflows are not.

2. Find the present value of each expected cash inflow and outflow. This can be done by using a financial calculator or using the Tables 1 and 2 in Appendix B. Simply find the discount factor from the correct row and column of the tables and multiply each cash flow by the relevant discount factor.

3. Total up the individual present values calculated in step 2. If the total is negative (in parentheses) reject the project; if it is positive, accept the project.

Exhibit 10-1 illustrates how these steps can be sketched. Although a sketch is not necessary to calculate the NPV, it may be helpful to some students in clarifying the process of calculating the NPV of a capital project.

Exhibit 10-1 shows that the value today (that is, at time zero) of the four $2,000 cash inflows is $6,340. The manager pays only $6,075 to obtain these cash inflows. Thus a favourable difference can be achieved at time zero of $265 ($6,340 − $6,075). The NPV of $265 is positive, and, therefore, the investment proposal is acceptable.

The minimum desired rate of return could have a large effect on net present values. The higher the minimum desired rate of return, the lower the present value of each future cash inflow and thus the lower the net present value of the project. At a rate of 16 percent, the net present value of the project in Exhibit 10-1 would be a negative of $479 (i.e., $2,000 × 2.7982 = $5,596, which is $479 less than the required investment of $6,075), instead of the +$265 computed with a 10 percent rate. (Present-value factor 2.7982 is taken from Table 2 in Appendix B.) When the desired rate of return is 16 percent rather than 10 percent, the project is undesirable at a price of $6,075.

Choosing the Correct Table

Exhibit 10-1 also shows another way to calculate NVP, shown here as Approach 2. The basic steps are the same as for Approach 1. The only difference is that Approach 2 uses Table 2 in Appendix B instead of Table 1. Table 2 is an annuity table that provides a shortcut to reduce the number of calculations. That is, it gives discount factors for computing the present value of a *series* of *equal* cash flows at

EXHIBIT 10-1

Net-Present-Value Method

Original investment, $6,075. Useful life, four years. Annual cash inflow from operations, $2,000. Minimum desired rate of return, 10 percent. Cash outflows are in parentheses; cash inflows are not. Total present values are rounded to the nearest dollar.

	PRESENT VALUE OF $1, DISCOUNTED AT 10%	TOTAL PRESENT VALUE	SKETCH OF CASH FLOWS AT END OF YEAR				
			0	1	2	3	4
APPROACH 1: DISCOUNTING EACH YEAR'S CASH INFLOW SEPARATELY*							
Cash flows:							
Annual savings	0.9091	$1,818	← ---------------------- $2,000				
	0.8264	1,653	← ------------------------------------ $2,000				
	0.7513	1,503	← -- $2,000				
	0.6830	1,366	← --- $2,000				
Present value of future inflows		$6,340					
Initial outlay	1.0000	(6,075)	$(6,075)				
Net present value		$ 265					
APPROACH 2: USING ANNUITY TABLE†							
Annual savings	3.1699	$6,340	← ---------------------- $2,000	$2,000	$2,000	$2,000	
Initial outlay	1.0000	(6,075)	$(6,075)				
Net present value		$ 265					

* Present values from Table 1, Appendix B, page 825. (You may wish to put a paper clip on this page).

† Present values of annuity from Table 2, Appendix B, page 826. (Incidently, hand-held programmable calculators may give slightly different answers than tables due to rounding differences.)

equal intervals at the same desired rate of return. Because the series of four cash flows in our example are all equal, you can use Table 2 to make one present value computation instead of four individual computations. Table 2 is merely a summation of the pertinent present-value factors of Table 1.[1]

$$0.9091 + 0.8264 + 0.7513 + 0.6830 = 3.1698$$

In this example, Table 2 accomplishes in one computation what Table 1 accomplishes in four multiplications and one summation.

Beware of using the wrong table. Table 1 should be used for discounting *individual* amounts; Table 2 for a *series* of equal amounts.

The use of Tables 1 and 2 can be avoided entirely by those with a present-value function on their hand-held calculator or those who use the present-value function on a spreadsheet program on their personal computer. However, using the tables leads to an understanding of the process that does not come if calculators or computers are used exclusively. Once you are comfortable with the method, you can take advantage of the speed and convenience of calculators and computers.

---

[1] Rounding error causes a 0.0001 difference between the Table 2 factor and the summation of Table 1 factors.

Managers often find it useful to develop an intuitive feel for the effect of the time value of money. For each of the following three items, first estimate the amount and then compute the amount using a discount rate of 8 percent. Use Tables 1 and 2 from Appendix B.

1. Present value of $1,000 to be received in 5 years.

2. Present value of $1,000 to be received at the end of each year for 5 years.

3. Present value of $1,000 to be received at the end of years 3, 4, and 5.

ANSWERS

Estimates will vary depending on your skill and experience with present-value computations. The computed solutions follow.

The solution to number 1 requires the factor from row 5, 8 percent column of Table 1:

$1,000 × 0.6806 = $680.60.

The solution to number 2 requires the factor from row 5, 8 percent column of Table 2:

$1,000 × 3.9927 = $3,992.70.

The solution to number 3 can be done in several ways. Two of them are

Use only Table 2: $1,000 × (3.9927 − 1.7833) = $2,209.40

Use Tables 1 and 2: $1,000 × 2.5771 × 0.8573 = $2,209.35

These two solutions differ by a $0.05 rounding error.

Internal Rate of Return (IRR)

OBJECTIVE 2

Compute a project's internal rate of return (IRR).

Internal Rate of Return (IRR). The discount rate that makes the net present value of the project equal to zero.

Another way to decide whether to make a capital outlay is to calculate a project's **internal rate of return (IRR)**, which is the discount rate that makes the net present value of the project equal zero. Expressed another way, the internal rate of return is the discount rate that makes the present value of a project's expected cash inflows equal to the present value of the expected cash outflows, including the investment in the project. If the IRR is greater than the minimum desired rate of return, a project is to be accepted. If the IRR is lower than the minimum desired rate of return, a project is to be rejected.

The three steps in calculating the IRR are shown in Exhibit 10-2:

1. Prepare a diagram of the expected cash inflows and outflows exactly as you did in calculating the NPV (see Exhibit 10-1).

2. Find an interest rate that equates the present value of the cash inflows to the present value of the cash outflows, that is, produces an NPV of zero.

3. Compare the IRR with the minimum desired rate of return. If the IRR is equal to or greater than the minimum desired rate, the project should be accepted. Otherwise it should be rejected. In Exhibit 10-2, Approach 1 uses Table 1 in Appendix B and can be used with any set of cash flows. If one outflow is followed by a series of equal inflows, you can use the following equation:

$$\text{initial investment} = \text{annual cash flow} \times \text{annuity PV factor (F)}$$
$$\$6,075 = \$2,000 \times F$$
$$F = \frac{\$6,075}{\$2,000} = 3.0375$$

EXHIBIT 10-2

Internal Rate-of-Return Method

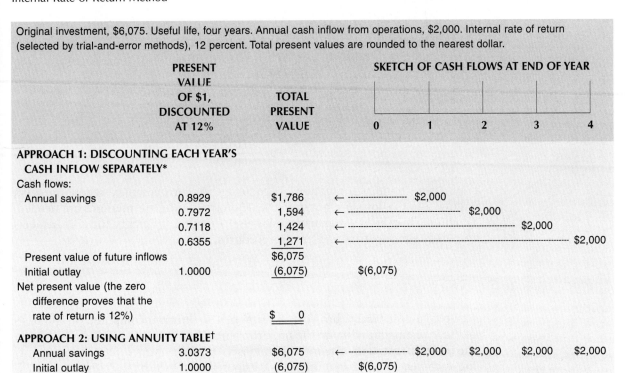

Original investment, $6,075. Useful life, four years. Annual cash inflow from operations, $2,000. Internal rate of return (selected by trial-and-error methods), 12 percent. Total present values are rounded to the nearest dollar.

	PRESENT VALUE OF $1, DISCOUNTED AT 12%	TOTAL PRESENT VALUE	SKETCH OF CASH FLOWS AT END OF YEAR				
			0	1	2	3	4
APPROACH 1: DISCOUNTING EACH YEAR'S CASH INFLOW SEPARATELY*							
Cash flows:							
Annual savings	0.8929	$1,786	← $2,000				
	0.7972	1,594	← $2,000				
	0.7118	1,424	← $2,000				
	0.6355	1,271	← $2,000				
Present value of future inflows		$6,075					
Initial outlay	1.0000	(6,075)	$(6,075)				
Net present value (the zero difference proves that the rate of return is 12%)		$ 0					
APPROACH 2: USING ANNUITY TABLE†							
Annual savings	3.0373	$6,075	← $2,000	$2,000	$2,000	$2,000	
Initial outlay	1.0000	(6,075)	$(6,075)				
Net present value		$ 0					

* Present values from Table 1, Appendix B.
† Present values of annuity from Table 2, Appendix B.

In Table 2 of Appendix B, scan the row that represents the relevant life of the project, row 4 in our example. Select the column with an entry closest to the annuity PV factor that was calculated. The factor closest to 3.0375 is 3.0373 in the 12 percent column. Because these factors are extremely close, the IRR is almost exactly 12 percent. Approach 2 shows that an interest rate of 12 percent indeed produces an NPV of zero.

Interpolation and Trial and Error

Not all IRR calculations work out exactly. Suppose the expected cash inflow in step 1 were $1,800 instead of $2,000. The equation in step 2 would produce

$$\$6,075 = \$1,800 \times F$$
$$F = \frac{\$6,075}{\$1,800} = 3.3750$$

On the period 4 line of Table 2, the column closest to 3.3750 is 7 percent, which may be close enough for most purposes. To obtain a more accurate rate, interpolation is needed: the factor 3.3750 is between the 7 percent factor (3.3872) and the 8 percent factor (3.3121).

	PRESENT-VALUE FACTORS	
7%	3.3872	3.3872
True rate		3.3750
8%	3.3121	
Difference	0.0751	0.0122

$$\text{true rate} = 7\% + \frac{0.0122}{0.0751}(1\%) = 7.16\%$$

These hand computations become even more complex when the cash inflows and outflows are not uniform. Then trial-and-error methods are needed. Of course, in practice, managers today use computer programs and spreadsheets to greatly simplify trial-and-error procedures.

Another Look at the IRR

Exhibit 10-3 highlights how the internal rate of return is computed on the basis of the investment tied up in the project from period to period instead of solely on the initial investment. The internal rate is 12 percent of the capital invested during each year. The $2,000 inflow is composed of two parts, interest and principal, as analyzed in columns 3 and 4. Consider Year 1. Column 3 shows the interest on the $6,075 invested capital as $0.12 \times \$6,075 = \$729$. Column 4 shows that the amount of investment recovered at the end of the year is $2,000 – $729 = $1,271. By the end of Year 4, the series of four cash inflows exactly recovers the initial investment plus annual interest at a rate of 12 percent on the as yet unrecovered capital.

EXHIBIT 10-3

Rationale Underlying Internal Rate-of-Return Model

Original investment, $6,075. Useful life, 4 years. Annual cash savings from operations, $2,000. Internal rate of return, 12 percent. Amounts are rounded to the nearest dollar.

YEAR	(1) UNRECOVERED INVESTMENT AT BEGINNING OF YEAR	(2) ANNUAL CASH SAVINGS	(3) INTEREST AT 12% PER YEAR (1) × 12%	(4) AMOUNT OF INVESTMENT RECOVERED AT END OF YEAR (2) – (3)	(5) UNRECOVERED INVESTMENT AT END OF YEAR (1) – (4)
1	$6,075	$2,000	$729	$1,271	$4,804
2	4,804	2,000	576	1,424	3,380
3	3,380	2,000	406	1,594	1,786
4	1,786	2,000	214	1,786	0

Assumptions: Unrecovered investment at the beginning of each year earns interest for a whole year. Annual cash inflows are received at the end of each year. For simplicity in the use of tables, all operating cash inflows are assumed to take place at the end of the years in question. This is unrealistic because such cash flows ordinarily occur uniformly throughout the given year.

If money were obtained at an effective interest rate of 12 percent, the cash inflow produced by the project would exactly repay the principal plus the interest over the four years. If money is available at less than 12 percent, the organization will have cash left over after repaying the principal and interest.

Assumptions of DCF Models

Two major assumptions underlie DCF models. First, we assume a world of certainty. That is, we act as if the predicted cash inflows and outflows are certain to occur at the times specified. Second, we assume perfect capital markets. That is, if we have extra cash at any time, we can borrow or lend money at the same interest rate. This rate is our minimum desired rate of return for the NPV model and the internal rate of return for the IRR model. If these assumptions are met, no model could possibly be better than a DCF model.

Unfortunately, our world has neither certainty nor perfect capital markets. Therefore, both the NPV and IRR, although good, are not perfect models.

Nevertheless, the DCF model is usually preferred to other models. The assumptions of most other models are even less realistic. The DCF model is not perfect, but it generally meets our cost-benefit criterion. The payoff from better decisions is greater than the cost of applying the DCF model.

USING DCF MODELS

<table>
<tr><td>

OBJECTIVE 3

Use discounted-cash-flow (DCF) models for decision making.

</td><td>

Managers must keep in mind the limitations of the two DCF models. Using such models is also complicated by the difficulties of determining a desired rate of return.

</td></tr>
</table>

Choosing the Minimum Desired Rate

There are two key aspects of capital budgeting: investment decisions and financing decisions. *Investment decisions* focus on whether to acquire an asset, a project, a company, a product line, and so on. *Financing decisions* focus on whether to raise the required funds via some form of debt or equity or both. Management accounting concentrates on the investment decision. Finance courses provide ample discussions of financing decisions.

A common mistake occurs when students do not clearly make this distinction between the investment decision and the financing decision. The faulty logic occurs when students include the interest payments as a cash outflow and then proceed to perform a DCF analysis on the cash flows. Remember that we employ DCF analysis to incorporate the time value of money—the interest—into the analysis. Thus, if interest payments are included in a DCF analysis, the interest has been incorrectly included twice. Remember, do not include the financing costs in the DCF analysis of an investment decision. How a project is financed may affect the desired rate of return, but it should not alter the amount of the cash flows.

Depending on a project's risk (that is, the probability that the expected cash inflows will not be achieved) and what alternative investments are available,

Property Valuation and DCF

The use of discounted-cash-flow analysis (DCF) began to be widely applied in industrial firms in the 1950s. By the 1970s most large companies used DCF. In the 1980s, real estate appraisers began using DCF to estimate the value of commercial properties. By the mid-1990s, lenders of all types (including appraisers, banks, insurance companies, pension funds) routinely used DCF to value properties for purposes such as determining offering prices for properties for sale, establishing limits on loans for which property was used as collateral, and estimating market prices for portfolios that include real estate.

Telewest Communications
www.telewest.co.uk
Dresdner Kleinwort Wasserstein
www.drkw.com

In addition to using DCF to value specific properties, many corporations acquiring another firm use DCF, often in combination with other methods, to establish an appropriate bid price. For example, consider Telewest, a British cable television company. When it made plans for being listed on both U.S. and U.K. stock markets in 1995, discounted cash flow was used to estimate its market value. The securities house of Kleinwort Benson computed net present values of £1.379 billion using a 17 percent rate and £1.667 billion using a rate of 15 percent. Kleinwort Benson (now known as Dresdner Kleinwort Wasserstein) also estimated the net present value of a single cable subscriber. Using a rate of 16 percent, each cable subscriber was worth £876. Using this figure, investors could use their own estimates of population, cable penetration rates, and churn rates (rates at which current subscribers cancel their subscriptions) to predict Telewest's market value.

Despite its widespread use, not everyone is convinced that DCF is superior to other valuation methods. A well-known controversy in Britain was prompted by the 1993 failure of the Queens Moat chain of hotels. Two different appraisers came up with estimates of the value of the chain's assets that diverged by more than £1 billion. The British Association of Hospitality Accountants supported a valuation based on DCF, while the Royal Institute of Chartered Surveyors (RICS) backed a method based on applying a multiple to the company's accounting earnings. RICS believed that an earnings-based valuation was more objective due to being based on "achieved" profits, rather than on cash-flow estimates. Supporters of DCF tend to argue that estimates based on "best predictions" of cash flow are more accurate than those based on current earnings, particularly since accounting earnings are based on costs such as amortization that may have little relation to the current values of the assets being used.

Sources: R. J. Okaneski, "Present Values: A Useful Underwriting Tool?" *Appraisal Journal*, October 1994, p. 609; "Telewest Is Good Four-Way Bet, Says Kleinwort Benson," *New Media Markets*, October 27, 1994; S. London, "Facts and Forecasts: The Paucity of Credible Market Analysis," *Financial Times*, September 23, 1994, p. 12; P. Sikka, "The Institutionalisation of Audit Failures: Some Observations," Submission to Select Committee on Treasury, United Kingdom Parliament, April 16, 2002; Uncredited, "Queens Moat: No Checking Out Yet," *Shares Magazine*, February 19, 2004, accessible at www.moneyam.com. See also "Show Your Investment Potential," *Steps to Growth Capital: Self-Study Guide*, Industry Canada (updated 2005), accessible at www.strategis.gc.ca.

investors usually have some notion of a minimum rate of return that would make various projects desirable investments. The problem of choosing this required rate of return is complex and is really more a problem of finance than of accounting. In general, the higher the risk, the higher the required rate of return. In this book we shall assume that the minimum acceptable rate of return is given to the accountant by management.

Note too that the minimum desired rate is not affected by whether the *specific project* is financed by all debt, all ownership capital, or some of each. Thus the cost of capital is not "interest expense" on borrowed money as the accountant ordinarily conceives it. For example, a mortgage-free home still has a cost of capital—the maximum amount that could be earned with the proceeds if the home were sold.

It is nearsighted to think that the required rate is the interest expense on any financing associated with a specific project. Under this faulty approach, a project will be accepted as long as its expected internal rate of return exceeds the interest rate on funds that might be borrowed to finance the project. Thus, a project would be desirable if it has an expected internal rate of 11 percent and a borrowing rate of 9 percent. The trouble here is that a series of such decisions will lead to a staggering debt that will cause the borrowing rate to skyrocket or will result in an inability to borrow at all. Conceivably, during the next year, some other project might have an expected internal rate of 16 percent and will have to be rejected, even though it is the most profitable in the series, because the heavy debt permits no further borrowing.

Amortization and Discounted Cash Flow

Accounting students are sometimes mystified by the apparent exclusion of amortization from discounted-cash-flow computations. A common error is to deduct amortization from cash inflows. This is a misunderstanding of one of the basic ideas involved in the concept of DCF. Because the discounted-cash-flow approach is fundamentally based on cash inflows and cash outflows and not on the accounting concepts of revenues and expenses, no adjustments should be made to the cash flows for amortization expense. Amortization is not a cash flow.[2] In the discounted-cash-flow approach, the entire cost of an asset is typically a *lump-sum* outflow of cash at time zero. Therefore, it is wrong to also deduct amortization from operating cash inflows. To deduct periodic amortization would be a double-counting of a cost that has already been considered as a lump-sum outflow.

Use of DCF Models by Not-for-Profit Organizations

Religious, educational, health-care, governmental, and other not-for-profit organizations face a variety of capital-budgeting decisions. Examples include investments in buildings, equipment, national defence systems, and research programs. Thus, even when no profit is involved, organizations try to choose projects with the least cost for any given set of objectives.

The unsettled question of the appropriate discount rate plagues all types of organizations, both profit-seeking and not-for-profit. One thing is certain: as all cash-strapped organizations soon discover, capital is not cost-free. A discussion of the appropriate required rate of return for not-for-profit organizations is beyond the scope of this book. But typically long-term debt rates are used. They represent a crude approximation of the opportunity cost to the economy of having investments made by public agencies instead of by private organizations.

---

[2] Throughout this and the next chapter, our examples assume that revenues are in cash and that all expenses (except for amortization) are in cash. Of course, if the revenues and expenses are accounted for on the accrual basis of accounting, there will be leads and lags of cash inflows and cash outflows that a precise DCF model must recognize. For example, a $10,000 sale on credit may be recorded as revenue in one period, but the related cash inflow would not be recognized in a DCF model until collected, which may be in a second period.

Cash Flows for Investments in Technology

Many capital budgeting decisions compare a possible investment with a continuation of the status quo. One such typical decision is an investment in a more automated production system to replace an existing system.

Cash flows predicted for the automated system should be compared to those predicted for continuation of the present system into the future. The latter are not necessarily the cash flows currently being experienced. Why? Because the competitive environment is changing. If competitors invest in automated systems and we do not we may experience a decline in market share and therefore lower revenues. The future without an automated system might be a continual decline in revenues and a non-competitive cost structure.

It is not easy to deal with hard-to-predict revenue and cost flows. However, predicted cash flows can be quantified as best as possible and included in an NPV analysis. Then, they can be determined subjectively. For example, investment in an automated system may have a *negative* NPV of $500,000 without considering subjective effects. Potential losses in contribution margin from a decline in competitiveness—plus possible non-quantified cost savings may exceed $500,000. If so, the automated system could have a positive NPV, and be a desirable investment, despite its original negative NPV.

Review of DCF Model

Before proceeding, take time to review the basic ideas of discounted cash flow. The net present value model expresses all amounts in equivalent terms, that is, in today's monetary units (for example, dollars, euros, yen) at time zero. An interest rate measures the decision maker's preference for receiving money sooner rather than later.

At 12 percent, the decision maker is indifferent between having $6,075 now and having a stream of four annual inflows of $2,000 each, since the NPV is zero:

Outflow in today's dollars	$(6,075)
Inflow equivalent in today's dollars @ 12% =	
$2,000 × 3.0373 (from Table 2) =	6,075
Net present value	$ 0

At 16 percent, the NPV is negative and the decision maker would find the project unattractive:

Outflow	$(6,075)
Inflow equivalent in today's dollars @ 16% =	
$2,000 × 2.7982 (from Table 2) =	5,596
Net present value	$ (479)

At 10 percent, the NPV is positive, and the project is desirable:

Outflow	$(6,075)
Inflow equivalent in today's dollars @ 10% =	
$2,000 × 3.1699 (from Table 2) =	6,340
Net present value	$ 265

Total Project versus Differential Approach

Total Project Approach. An approach that compares two or more alternatives by computing the total NPV of cash flows of each.

Differential Approach. An approach that compares two alternatives by computing the NPV differences in cash flows.

Managers are seldom asked to perform analyses on a single investment option. More often, managers want to compare several capital investment alternatives.

Two common methods for comparing such alternatives are (1) the total project approach and (2) the differential approach.

The **total project approach** compares two or more alternatives by computing the total effect of each alternative on cash flows and then converting these total cash flows to their present values. It is the most popular approach and can be used for any number of alternatives. The alternative with the largest NPV of total cash flows is preferred.

The **differential approach** compares two alternatives by computing the differences in cash flows between alternatives and then converting these differences in cash flows to their present values. Its use is restricted to cases where only two alternatives are being examined.

To compare these approaches, suppose a company owns a packaging machine that it purchased three years ago for $56,000. The machine has a remaining useful life of five years but will require a major overhaul at the end of two more years at a cost of $10,000. Its disposal value now is $20,000. In five years its disposal value is expected to be $8,000, assuming that the $10,000 major overhaul will be done on schedule. The cash operating costs of this machine are expected to be $40,000 annually. A sales representative has offered a substitute machine for $51,000, or for $31,000 plus the old machine. The new machine will reduce annual cash operating costs by $10,000, will not require any overhauls, will have a useful life of five years, and will have a disposal value of $3,000. If the minimum desired rate of return is 14 percent, what should the company do? (Try to solve this problem yourself before examining the solution that follows.)

The following steps apply to either the total project or the differential approach, and are illustrated in Exhibit 10-4.

- **Step 1:** Arrange the relevant cash flows by project, so that a sharp distinction is made between total project flows and differential flows. The differential flows are merely algebraic differences between the two alternatives.
- **Step 2:** Total Project Approach: Determine the net present value of the cash flows for each individual project. Choose the project with the largest positive present value (i.e., largest benefit) or smallest negative present value (i.e., smallest cost).

  Differential Approach: Compute the differential cash flows; that is, subtract the cash flows for project B from the cash flows for project A for each year. Calculate the present value of the differential cash flows. If this present value is positive, choose project A; if it is negative, choose project B.

  When there are only two alternatives the differential approach may be superior to the total approach, as it focuses on the differences between the two alternatives, and we choose on the basis of the differences, not the commonalities. The total project approach is necessary when analyzing three or more alternatives simultaneously. To develop proper skills in this area, you should work with both at the start. One approach can serve as proof of the accuracy of the other. In this example, the $8,429 net difference in favour of replacement is the result under either approach.

Analysis of Typical Items under Discounted Cash Flow

When you array the relevant cash flows, be sure to consider four types of inflows and outflows: (1) initial cash inflows and outflows at time zero, (2) investments in receivables and inventories, (3) future disposal values, and (4) operating cash flows.

1. *Initial cash inflows and outflows at time zero.* These cash flows include both outflows for the purchases and installation of equipment and other items required by the new project and either inflows or outflows from disposal of any items that are replaced. In Exhibit 10-4 the $20,000 received from selling the old machine was offset against the $51,000 purchase price of the new machine; the net cash outflow of $31,000 was shown. If the old machine could not be sold, any cost incurred to dismantle and discard it would be added to the purchase price of the new machine.

2. *Investments in working capital (mostly in receivables and inventories).* Investments in working capital are basically no different from investments in plant and equipment. In the discounted-cash-flow model, the initial capital cost and working capital outlays are entered in the sketch of cash flows at time zero. At the end of the useful life of the project, the original capital investment, say for machines, may not be recouped at all or may be partially recouped in the amount of the salvage values. In contrast, the entire working capital is typically regarded as cash inflows at the end of the project's useful life.

   The difference between the initial outlay for working capital (mostly receivables and inventories) and the present value of its recovery is the present value of the cost of using working capital in the project. Working capital is constantly revolving in a cycle from cash to inventories to receivables and back to cash throughout the life of the project. But to be sustained, the project required that money be tied up in the cycle until the project ends.

3. *Future disposal values.* The disposal value at the end of a project is an increase in the cash inflow in the year of disposal. Errors in forecasting terminal disposal values are usually not crucial because the present value of disposal values is usually small.

4. *Operating cash flows.* The major purpose of most investments is to effect positive revenues or cost reductions (or both). Three points, though, deserve special mention.

   First, in relevant-cost analysis, the only pertinent overhead costs are those that will differ among alternatives. Fixed overhead under the available alternatives may be the same.

   Second, amortization and book values should be ignored. The cost of assets is recognized by the initial outlay, not by amortization as computed under accrual accounting.

   Third, a reduction in a cash outflow is treated the same as a cash inflow.

5. *Mutually exclusive projects.* When the projects are mutually exclusive, the acceptance of one automatically entails the rejection of the other (e.g., buying Toyota or Ford trucks).

6. *Unequal lives.* What if alternative projects have unequal lives? Comparisons may be made over the useful life of either the longer-

EXHIBIT 10-4

Using NPV to Compare Two Alternatives (Keep, Replace)
Total Project versus Differential Approach

	PRESENT VALUE DISCOUNT FACTOR AT 14%	TOTAL PRESENT VALUE	SKETCH OF CASH FLOWS AT END OF YEAR					
			0	1	2	3	4	5
I. TOTAL PROJECT APPROACH								
A. REPLACE								
Recurring cash operating costs, using an annuity table*	3.4331	$(102,993)		($30,000)	($30,000)	($30,000)	($30,000)	($30,000)
Disposal value, end of year 5	0.5194	1,558						3,000
Initial required investment	1.0000	(31,000)	($31,000)					
Present value of net cash outflows		$(132,435)						
B. KEEP								
Recurring cash operating costs, using an annuity table*	3.4331	$(137,324)		(40,000)	(40,000)	(40,000)	(40,000)	(40,000)
Overhaul, end of year 2	0.7695	(7,695)			(10,000)			
Disposal value, end of year 5	0.5194	4,155						8,000
Present value of net cash outflows		$(140,864)						
Difference in favour of replacement		$ 8,429						
II. DIFFERENTIAL APPROACH								
A–B. ANALYSIS CONFINED TO DIFFERENCES								
Difference in recurring cash operating savings, using an annuity table*	3.4331	$ 34,331		$10,000	$10,000	$10,000	$10,000	$10,000
Overhaul avoided, end of year 2	0.7695	7,695			$10,000			
Difference in disposal values, end of year 5	0.5194	(2,597)						(5,000)
Incremental initial investment	1.0000	(31,000)	($31,000)					
Net present value of replacement		$ 8,429						

* Table 2, Appendix B.

lived project or the shorter-lived one. For our purposes, we will use the life of the longer-lived project. To provide comparability, we assume reinvestment in the shorter-lived project at the end of its life and give it credit for any residual value at the time the longer-lived project ends. The important consideration is what would be done in the time interval between the termination dates of the shorter-lived and longer-lived projects.

7. *Income taxes.* Comparison between alternatives is best made after considering tax effects, because the tax impact may alter the picture.

8. *Inflation.* Predictions of cash flows and discount rates should incorporate consistent inflation assumptions that affect the real purchasing power of future cash flows.

OTHER MODELS FOR ANALYZING LONG-RANGE DECISIONS

Although the use of discounted-cash-flow models for business decisions has increased steadily over the past four decades, simpler models are also used. They may include the payback and the accounting rate-of-return models. Often managers use them in *addition* to DCF models.

These models, which we are about to explain, are conceptually inferior to discounted-cash-flow approaches. Then why do we bother studying them? First, because changes in business practice occur slowly. Many businesses still use the simpler models. Second, because where simpler models are in use, they should be used properly, even if better models are available. Third, the simpler models might provide some useful information to supplement the DCF analysis.

One capital budgeting technique is the emergency-persuasion method. No formal planning is used. Fixed assets are operated until they crumble, product lines are carried until they are obliterated by competition, and requests by managers for authorization of capital outlays are judged on the basis of their ability to convince top management that the investment is necessary. This approach to capital budgeting is an example of the unscientific management that often leads to bankruptcy.

In contrast, both the payback and the accounting rate-of-return models, while flawed, are attempts to approach capital budgeting systematically.

Payback Model

OBJECTIVE 5

Use the payback model and the accounting rate of return on a project, and compare them with DCF models.

Payback time or **payback period** is the measure of the time it will take to recoup, in the form of cash inflows from operations, the initial dollars of outlay. Assume that $12,000 is spent for a machine with an estimated useful life of eight years. Annual savings of $4,000 in cash outflows are expected from operations. Amortization is ignored. The payback of three years is calculated as follows:

$$\text{payback time} = \frac{\text{initial incremental amount invested}}{\substack{\text{equal annual incremental cash} \\ \text{inflow from operations}}}$$

$$P = \frac{I}{O} = \frac{\$12,000}{\$4,000} = 3 \text{ years}$$

Payback Time (Payback Period). The measure of the time it will take to recoup, in the form of cash inflows from operations, the initial dollars of outlay.

The payback model merely measures how quickly investment dollars may be recouped; it does not measure profitability. This is its major weakness. A project with a shorter payback time is not necessarily preferable to one with a longer payback time. On the other hand, the payback time might provide a rough estimate of riskiness, especially in decisions involving rapid technological change.

Assume that an alternative to the $12,000 machine is a $10,000 machine whose operation will also result in a reduction of $4,000 annually in cash outflow. Then

$$P_1 = \frac{\$12,000}{\$4,000} = 3.0 \text{ years}$$

$$P_2 = \frac{\$10,000}{\$4,000} = 2.5 \text{ years}$$

The $10,000 machine has a shorter payback time, and therefore it may appear more desirable. However, one fact about the $10,000 machine has been purposely withheld. What if its useful life is only 2.5 years? Ignoring the impact of compound interest for the moment, the $10,000 machine results in zero benefit, while the $12,000 machine (useful life eight years) generates cash inflows for five years beyond its payback period.

The main objective in investing is profit, not the recapturing of the initial outlay. If a company wants to recover its outlay fast, it need not spend in the first place, then no waiting time is necessary; the payback time is zero.

When the promoter of a risky oil venture assured a wealthy investor that he would have his money back within two years, the investor replied, "I already have my money."

Payback with Uneven Cash Flows

The formula $P = I \div O$ can be used with assurance only when there are equal annual cash inflows from operations. When annual cash inflows are not equal, the payback computation must take a cumulative form—that is, each year's net cash flows are accumulated until the initial investment is recouped:

YEAR	INITIAL INVESTMENT	NET CASH INFLOWS EACH YEAR	NET CASH INFLOWS ACCUMULATED
0	$31,000	–	–
1	–	$10,000	$10,000
2	–	20,000	30,000
2.1	–	1,000	31,000

In this situation, the payback time is slightly beyond the second year. Straight-line interpolation within the third year reveals that the final $1,000 needed to recoup the investment would be forthcoming in 2.1 years:

$$2 \text{ years} + \frac{\$1,000}{\$10,000} \times 1 \text{ year} = 2.1 \text{ years}$$

Accounting Rate-of-Return Model

Accounting Rate of Return (ARR). A non-discounted-cash-flow capital-budgeting model expressed as the increase in expected average annual operating income divided by the initial increase in required investment.

Another non-DCF capital-budgeting model is the **accounting rate-of-return (ARR)** model:

$$\text{accounting rate of return (ARR)} = \frac{\text{increase in expected average annual operating income}}{\text{initial required investment}}$$

$$\text{ARR} = \frac{O - D}{I}$$

O is the average operating income from the investment annual incremental cash inflow from operations. D is the annual amortization of the investment. I is the initial amount invested. The *accounting rate-of-return model* is also known as the *accrual accounting rate-of-return model* (a more accurate description). Its computations dovetail most closely with conventional accounting models of calculating income and required investment and show the effect of an investment in an organization's financial statements.

Assume the same facts as in Exhibit 10-1: investment is $6,075, useful life is four years, estimated disposal value is zero, and expected annual cash inflow from operations is $2,000. Annual amortization would be $6,075 ÷ 4 = $1,518.75, rounded to $1,519. Substitute these values in the accounting rate-of-return equation:

$$\text{ARR} = \frac{\$2,000 - \$1,519}{\$6,075} = 7.9\%$$

If the denominator is the "average" investment, which is often assumed for equipment as being the average book value over the useful life, or $6,075 ÷ 2 = $3,037.50, rounded to $3,038, the rate would be doubled:[3]

$$R = \frac{\$2,000 - \$1,519}{\$3,038} = 15.8\%$$

The *accounting rate-of-return* model is based on the familiar financial statements prepared under accrual accounting. The accrual accounting model has profitability as an objective. But, it has a major drawback: it ignores the time value of money. Expected future dollars are erroneously regarded as equal to present dollars. Assets are totalled up horizontally without taking into account that assets purchased, say, in the 1960s do not have the same time value of money as assets bought, say, in 2005.

The accrual accounting model uses concepts that are designed for the quite different purpose of accounting for periodic income and financial position. As a result, the *accounting* rate of return may differ greatly from the project's *internal* rate of return.

---

[3] The measure of the investment recovered in the example above is $1,519 per year, the amount of the annual amortization. Consequently, the average investment committed to the project would decline at a rate of $1,519 per year from $6,075 to zero; hence the average investment would be the beginning balance plus the ending balance ($6,075) divided by 2, or $3,038. Note that when the ending balance is not zero, the average investment will not be half the initial investment.

To illustrate, consider a petroleum company with three potential projects to choose from: an expansion of an existing gasoline station, an investment in an oil well, and the purchase of a new gasoline station. To simplify the calculations, assume a three-year life for each project. Exhibit 10-5 summarizes the comparisons. The projects differ only in the timing of the cash inflows. Note that the accounting rate of return would indicate that all three projects are equally desirable and that the internal rate of return properly discriminates in favour of earlier cash inflows.

	EXPANSION OF EXISTING GASOLINE STATION	INVESTMENT IN AN OIL WELL	PURCHASE OF NEW GASOLINE STATION
Initial investment	$ 90,000	$ 90,000	$ 90,000
Cash inflows from operations:			
Year 1	$ 40,000	$ 80,000	$ 20,000
Year 2	40,000	30,000	40,000
Year 3	40,000	10,000	60,000
Totals	$120,000	$120,000	$120,000
Average annual cash inflow	$ 40,000	$ 40,000	$ 40,000
Less: average annual amortization			
($90,000 ÷ 3)	30,000	30,000	30,000
Increase in average annual net income	$ 10,000	$ 10,000	$ 10,000
Accounting rate of return on initial			
investment	11.1%	11.1%	11.1%
Internal rate of return, using			
discounted-cash-flow techniques	16.0%*	23.2%*	13.4%*

* Computed by trial-and-error approaches using Tables 1 and 2, pages 825 and 826. See below for a detailed explanation.

Expansion of an Existing Gasoline Station

The formula from page 464 can be used to compute the IRR of the expansion of the existing gas station:

$90,000 =$ present value of annuity of $40,000 at X percent for three years, or what factor F in the table of the present values of an annuity will satisfy the following equation:

$90,000 = $40,000 F$

$F = $90,000 \div $40,000 = 2.2500$

Now, on the year 3 line of Table 2, page 826, find the column that is closest to 2.2500. You will find that 2.2500 is extremely close to a rate of return of 16 percent—so close that straight-line interpolation is unnecessary between 14 percent and 16 percent. Therefore, the internal rate of return is 16 percent.

Investment in an Oil Well

Trial-and-error methods must be used to calculate the rate of return that will equate the future cash flows with the $90,000 initial investment. As a start, note that the 16 percent rate was applicable to a uniform annual cash inflow. But now use Table 1, page 825 because the flows are not uniform, and try a higher rate, 22 percent, because you know that the cash inflows are coming in more quickly than under the uniform inflow:

		TRIAL AT 22%		TRIAL AT 24%	
YEAR	CASH INFLOWS	PRESENT-VALUE FACTOR	TOTAL PRESENT VALUE	PRESENT-VALUE FACTOR	TOTAL PRESENT VALUE
1	$80,000	0.8197	$65,576	0.8065	$64,520
2	30,000	0.6719	20,157	0.6504	19,512
3	10,000	0.5507	5,507	0.5245	5,245
			$91,240		$89,277

Because $91,240 is greater than $90,000, the true rate must be greater than 22 percent. Try 24 percent. Now $89,277 is less than $90,000 so the true rate lies somewhere between 22 percent and 24 percent. It can be approximated by interpolation:

INTERPOLATION	TOTAL PRESENT VALUES	
22%	$91,240	$91,240
True rate		90,000
24%	89,277	
Difference	$ 1,963	$ 1,240

Therefore:

$$\text{true rate} = 22\% + \frac{1,240}{1,963} \times 2\%$$
$$= 22\% + 1.3\% = 23.3\%$$

Purchase of a New Gasoline Station

In contrast to the oil-well project, this venture will have slowly increasing cash inflows. The trial rate should be much lower than the 16 percent rate applicable to the expansion project. Let us try 12 percent:

YEAR	CASH INFLOWS	TRIAL AT 12% PRESENT-VALUE FACTOR	TRIAL AT 12% TOTAL PRESENT VALUE	TRIAL AT 14% PRESENT-VALUE FACTOR	TRIAL AT 14% TOTAL PRESENT VALUE
1	$20,000	.8929	$17,858	.8772	$17,544
2	40,000	.7972	31,888	.7695	30,780
3	60,000	.7118	42,708	.6750	40,500
			$92,454		$88,824

Because $92,454 is greater than $90,000, try 14 percent, and then interpolate a rate between 12 percent and 14 percent.

INTERPOLATION	TOTAL PRESENT VALUES	
12%	$92,454	$92,454
True rate		90,000
14%	88,824	
Difference	$ 3,630	$ 2,454

$$\text{true rate} = 12\% + \frac{2,454}{3,630} \times 2\%$$
$$= 12\% + 1.4\% = 13.4\%$$

PERFORMANCE EVALUATION

OBJECTIVE 6

Identify the issues related to performance evaluation using DCF models.

Many managers are reluctant to accept DCF models as the best way to make capital-budgeting decisions. Their reluctance stems from the wide usage of the accrual accounting model for evaluating performance. That is, managers become frustrated if they are instructed to use a DCF model for making decisions that are evaluated later by a non-DCF model, such as the typical accrual accounting rate-of-return model.

To illustrate, consider the potential conflict that might arise in the example of Exhibit 10-1. Recall that the internal rate of return was 12 percent, based on an outlay of $6,075 that would generate cash savings of $2,000 for each of four years and no terminal disposal value. Under accrual accounting, using straight-line amortization, the evaluation of performance for years 1 through 4 would be

	YEAR 1	YEAR 2	YEAR 3	YEAR 4
Cash operating savings	$2,000	$2,000	$2,000	$2,000
Straight-line amortization, $6,075 ÷ 4	1,519	1,519	1,519	1,519*
Effect on operating income	481	481	481	481
Book value at beginning of year	6,075	4,556	3,037	1,518
Accounting rate of return	7.9%	10.6%	15.8%	31.7%

* Total amortization of 4 × $1,519 = $6,076 differs from $6,075 due to rounding error.

The accrual accounting model and the ARR understate the return in early years. As the book value of the investment declines, the ARR increases although the cash savings resulting from the investment ($2,000) remains the same. Many managers would be reluctant to replace equipment, despite the internal rate of

12 percent, if their performance were evaluated by accrual accounting models. They might be especially reluctant if they were likely to be transferred to new positions every year or two.

The reluctance to replace equipment is reinforced if a heavy book loss on old equipment would appear in Year 1's accrual income statement even though such a loss would be irrelevant in a properly constructed decision model.

Thus, performance evaluation based on typical accounting measures can cause rejection of major, long-term projects such as investment in technologically advanced production systems. This pattern may help explain why many North American firms seem to be excessively short-term oriented.

How can the foregoing conflict be reconciled? An obvious solution would be to use the ARR for making capital-budgeting decisions and for evaluating performance. The accrual accounting model is often dominant for evaluating all sorts of performance; that is why many organizations use it for both purposes and do not use a DCF model at all. Critics claim that not using DCF may lead to many instances of poor capital-budgeting decisions.

MAKING MANAGERIAL DECISIONS

Consider the expansion of Deer Valley's gift shop. Suppose it entails an additional investment of $10,000 in a building and fixtures that have a 20-year life and a $1,000 salvage value at the end of 20 years. It also entails an initial investment of cash of $6,000 for inventories at time zero. Deer Valley will sell the initial inventory in Year 1 for $12,000 and will replace it with a new inventory that it buys for $6,000 cash. It will do this each year through Year 19. However, it will not replace the inventory that it sells in Year 20 because no sales will occur beyond the end of the project's life. Assume that Deer Valley uses revenues and expenses as approximations to cash flows each year as shown in the table below. Complete the sketch of cash flows by adding the net cash flows for inventory (a, b, c, d, and e) in the table.

SKETCH OF CASH FLOWS					
End of year	0	1	2 . . .	19	20
Investment in building and fixtures	$(10,000)				$1,000
Investment in working capital (inventories)	a	b	c	d	e
Revenue (an approximation for cash inflow)	$0	12,000	12,000 . . .	12,000	12,000
Cost of goods sold (an approximation for cash outflow)	$0	(6,000)	(6,000) . . .	(6,000)	(6,000)

ANSWER

We pay $6,000 at time zero for inventories, so a = $(6,000). This becomes a $6,000 expense (cost of goods sold) in Year 1, when we spend another $6,000 to buy inventory, and so on through Year 19. Thus, years 1 through 19 have both an expense and a cash flow for inventory of $6,000. The expense is an acceptable measure of the cash flow each of those years. Thus, we record no additional investment in inventories, and b = c = d = $0. However, in Year 20 there is only an expense of $6,000 with no cash outflow. Since the expense overstates the cash outflow by $6,000, we must add a $6,000 cash inflow to the investment in working capital, making e = $6,000. Essentially, this represents the recoupment of the $6,000 originally spent for inventory. The investment in working capital (in this case, only inventory) recognizes this difference between accrual measures of revenue and expense and the cash flow measure used for capital budgeting. As the table shows, the residual value of the building and fixtures might be small. However, the gift shop would ordinarily recover the entire investment in inventories when the company terminates the venture.

Another obvious solution would be to use DCF for both capital-budgeting decisions and performance evaluation. A survey showed that most large companies conduct a follow-up evaluation of at least some capital-budgeting decisions, often called a **postaudit**. The purposes of postaudits include the following:

Postaudit. A follow-up evaluation of capital-budgeting decisions.

1. To see that investment expenditures are proceeding on time and within budget.
2. To compare actual cash flows with those originally predicted, in order to motivate careful and honest predictions.
3. To provide information for improving future predictions of cash flows.
4. To evaluate the continuation of the project.

By focusing the postaudit on actual versus predicted *cash flows*, the evaluation is consistent with the decision process.

However, postauditing of all capital-budgeting decisions is costly. Most accounting systems are designed to evaluate operating performances of products, departments, divisions, territories, and so on, year by year. In contrast, capital-budgeting decisions frequently deal with individual *projects*, not the collection of projects that are usually being managed simultaneously by several divisional or departmental managers. Therefore, usually only selected capital-budgeting decisions are audited.

The conflicts between the longstanding, accrual accounting model and DCF models represent one of the most serious unsolved problems in the design of management control systems. Top management cannot expect goal congruence if it favours the use of one type of model for decisions and the use of another type for performance evaluation.

INCOME TAXES AND CAPITAL BUDGETING

General Characteristics

Income taxes are in effect cash disbursements to the government. Income taxes can influence the *amount* and/or the *timing* of cash flows. The effect of taxes paid in capital budgeting is no different from that of any other cash disbursement. Taxes tend to reduce the net cash inflows and therefore narrow the cash differences between capital-budgeting projects.

The Canadian federal and provincial governments raise money through corporate income taxes. Income tax rates differ considerably and, thus, overall corporate income tax rates can vary widely.

Income tax rates depend on the amount of pretax income. Larger income is taxed at higher rates. In capital budgeting, the relevant rate is the **marginal income tax rate**, that is, the tax rate paid on additional amounts of pretax income. Suppose a Canadian Controlled Private Corporation (CCPC) pays income taxes of 20 percent on the first $300,000 of pretax income and 40 percent on pretax income over $300,000. What is the *marginal income tax rate* of a company with $400,000 of pretax income? It is 40 percent, because 40 percent of any *additional* income will be paid in taxes. In contrast, the company's *average income tax rate* is only 25 percent (i.e., 20 percent × $300,000 + 40 percent × $100,000 = $100,000 of taxes on $400,000 of pretax income). When we assess tax effects of capital-budgeting decisions, we will always use the *marginal* tax rate. Why? Because that is the rate applied to the additional cash flows generated by a proposed project.

Organizations that pay income taxes generally report two net incomes—one for reporting to the public and one for reporting to the tax authorities. This is not illegal

Marginal Income Tax Rate. The tax rate paid on additional amounts of pre-tax income.

Capital Budgeting for Information Technology

Many companies use discounted cash flow (DCF) methods for their capital budgeting decisions. DCF techniques are nonetheless criticised by some for leading to overly cautious investment decisions, such as in the area of Information Technology.[4] Critics maintain that the benefits of IT investments are difficult to quantify and such investments often lead to unforeseen opportunities. By ignoring some of the potential benefits and opportunities, companies pass up desirable IT investments.

Two ways to rectify this situation have been recently suggested. Both use the basic tenets of DCF analysis but add degrees of sophistication to help identify and value all the benefits of IT investments: (1) use of activity-based costing (ABC) to better define and qualify the benefits of IT investments, and (2) use of options pricing models to recognize the value of future options that result from IT investments.

Using ABC to better assess the benefits of an IT investment is simply a refinement to measuring the cash flows of a DCF model. Scott Gamster of Grant Thornton's Performance Management Practice suggests that the capital-budgeting analysis of IT investments often looks primarily at the direct costs and benefits and ignores many of the savings in indirect costs. Because an ABC system focuses on indirect costs, it can help identify other cost impacts of new IT systems. This attention to activities allows managers to better assess the various impacts on a new IT system. For example, an enterprise resource planning (ERP) system will transform much of the work in many company activities. Examining each activity in light of the potential implementation of an ERP will help managers assess the full impact of the new system.

The other suggestion is to use an options pricing model for valuing IT investments. This is a refinement of DCF, not an alternative to it. It explicitly recognizes the future opportunities created by a current investment decision, and it uses the complete range of possible outcomes to determine a potential investment's value. It is not our purpose to describe options pricing models; we leave that to the finance textbooks. However, the essence of the models is the impact of the possible future options on the value of a current investment decision. For example, investment today may eliminate the option of making a similar investment in six months when more information is available. Or an investment today may create an infrastructure that will allow additional investments in the future that would not be otherwise possible. Limiting or expanding future options by today's investment decision can certainly affect the desirability of the investment.

Criticisms of DCF models for IT investments should lead to refinements of DCF, not rejection of it. Of course, if refinements are not used, managers must use judgment regarding subjective impacts of the investment that are not measured in the DCF analysis.

Source: Adapted from S. Gamster, "Using Activity Based Management to Justify ERP Implementations," *Journal of Cost Management*, September/October 1999, pp. 24–33; M. Benaroch and R. J. Kauffman, "A Case for Using Real Options Pricing Analysis to Evaluate Information Technology Project Investments," *Information Systems Research*, March 1999, pp. 70–76; and G. C. Arnold and P. D. Aatzopoulos, "The Kingdom," *Journal of Business Finance and Accounting*, June/July 2000, pp. 603–626.

or immoral; in fact, it is necessary. Tax reporting must follow detailed rules designed to achieve certain social goals. These rules do not lead to financial statements that best measure an organization's financial results and position, so it is more informative to financial-statement users if a separate set of rules is used for financial reporting. In this chapter we are concerned with effects of taxes on cash flows. Therefore, we focus on the *tax reporting* rules, not those for public financial reporting.

---

[4] This is one reason that many companies, to the surprise of researchers, continue to use simple payback approaches in evaluating investments. See, for example, D. Brounen, A. de Jong, and K. Koedijk, "Corporate Finance in Europe: Confronting Theory with Practice," *Financial Management*, December 22, 2004, accessible at www.highbeam.com; J.R. Graham and C.R. Harvey, "The Theory and Practice of Corporate Finance: Evidence from the Field," *Journal of Financial Economics* 61 (2001), pp. 187–243.

Tax Impact on Operating Cash Flows

OBJECTIVE 7

Analyze the impact of income taxes on cash flows and compute the after-tax net present values of projects.

Recognizing the impact of income taxes on operating cash flows is straightforward. If a capital proposal results in annual savings of $60,000 and the company has a marginal tax rate of 40 percent, then the company's income taxes will increase by $24,000 ($60,000 × 0.40). Net annual after-tax savings of $36,000 result. This can be computed by deducting the $24,000 of extra income taxes from the pretax annual savings of $60,000. Conversely the $36,000 can be computed by multiplying the $60,000 by (1 minus the tax rate of 40 percent) or 60 percent.

If operating expenses increase by $250,000, with a 40 percent marginal tax rate, the net after-tax cost is $150,000 [$250,000 × (1 – 40%)]. The $150,000 is the net of the $100,000 in tax savings ($250,000 multiplied by 40 percent), and the $250,000.

Thus, to incorporate the impact of income taxes on operating cash flows poses no real difficulty. The difficulty occurs in the recognition of the tax effects of investment expenditures in capital equipment.

TAX IMPACT ON INVESTMENT CASH FLOWS

In financial reporting, purchases of capital equipment result in the recording of the asset at the time of purchase and the related amortization expense over the asset's useful economic life. Amortization rates and policies are determined by the company's management and vary from company to company even for the same asset.

Capital Cost Allowance (CCA). A deduction allowed for Canadian income tax purposes with regard to the acquisition of a capital asset.

To apply a consistent set of regulations and to provide a means to implement government initiatives, the federal government has implemented its own system of **capital cost allowance (CCA)**. The Income Tax Act (ITA) does not permit a company to deduct amortization expense in determining taxable income but rather a company is allowed to deduct CCA.

Capital Cost Allowance—Declining Balance Classes

The ITA assigns all capital purchases to a CCA class. (The Appendix on page 498 provides a list of some of the more commonly used CCA classes.) For example, a desk would qualify as a Class 8 asset that includes all furniture and fixtures. Class 8 has a predetermined rate of 20 percent declining balance capital cost allowance. Exhibit 10-6 depicts the calculation of CCA for a desk that costs $10,000.

A number of years ago, a company could deduct a full year's worth of CCA on any asset acquired during the year, as long as the company had been in business for the entire year. Thus companies with a December 31 year-end would buy assets on or about December 31 and claim a full year's deduction even though the asset had not really been used to generate the income. To minimize this problem, the government implemented the so-called "half-year rule."

Half-Year Rule. An income tax requirement that treats all assets as if they were purchased at the midpoint of the tax year.

The **half-year rule** assumes that all net additions are purchased in the middle of the year, and thus only one-half of the stated CCA rate is allowed in the first year. Thus in Year 1 of the example in Exhibit 10-6, the CCA is $1,000 or 1/2 times 20 percent multiplied by the $10,000 capital expenditure.

EXHIBIT 10-6

Capital Cost Allowance
Illustration

CCA – CLASS 8 RATE – 20% DECLINING BALANCE (ROUNDED TO THE NEAREST DOLLAR)			
Year 1 (Day 1) Addition	$10,000	Year 13 - UCC	$ 618
CCA - Year 1 (10%)	1,000	CCA - Year 14	124
Year (end) - UCC	9,000	Year 14 - UCC	494
CCA - Year 2 (20%)	1,800	CCA - Year 15	99
Year 2 - UCC	7,200	Year 15 - UCC	395
CCA - Year 3 (20%)	1,440	CCA - Year 16	79
Year 3 - UCC	5,760	Year 16 - UCC	316
CCA - Year 4	1,152	CCA - Year 17	63
Year 4 - UCC	4,608	Year 17 - UCC	253
CCA - Year 5	922	CCA - Year 18	51
Year 5 - UCC	3,686	Year 18 - UCC	202
CCA - Year 6	737	CCA - Year 19	40
Year 6 - UCC	2,949	Year 19 - UCC	162
CCA - Year 7	590	CCA - Year 20	32
Year 7 - UCC	2,359	Year 20 - UCC	130
CCA - Year 8	472	CCA - Year 21	26
Year 8 - UCC	1,887	Year 21 - UCC	104
CCA - Year 9	377	CCA - Year 22	21
Year 9 - UCC	1,510	Year 22 - UCC	83
CCA - Year 10	302	CCA - Year 23	17
Year 10 - UCC	1,208	Year 23 - UCC	66
CCA - Year 11	242	CCA - Year 24	13
Year 11 - UCC	966	Year 24 - UCC	53
CCA - Year 12	193	CCA - Year 25	11
Year 12 - UCC	773	Year 25 - UCC	42
CCA - Year 13	155		

Undepreciated Capital Cost (UCC). The balance in the pool of assets after deducting capital cost allowance.

This leaves a balance of $9,000 ($10,000 – $1,000), which is known as the **undepreciated capital cost (UCC)**.

In Year 2 and all succeeding years, the rate of 20 percent is applied to the UCC of the previous year. This results in a declining amount of capital cost allowance for each year. Even after the 25 years shown in Exhibit 10-6, a UCC of $42 remains and will require 15 more years to get to a zero balance (which in practice can only be obtained by rounding to the nearest dollar).

The CCA of each year is deducted in the calculation of a company's taxable income. Thus the CCA is not a cash flow. Rather we must multiply the CCA of each year by the company's marginal tax rate to calculate the actual tax savings in each year. To determine the present value of the tax savings, we would need to multiply the tax savings of each year by the present value factor from Table 1, p. 825, for each year at the company's required rate of return (say, 10 percent).

Tax Shield Formula. Formula used to efficiently calculate the present value of the tax savings generated by tax shields.

This, as you could well imagine, would be a long and laborious task to perform for each capital proposal. An efficient way to calculate the present value of the tax savings is to use the following **tax shield formula**:

$$\frac{\text{present value}}{\text{of tax savings}} = \left(\begin{array}{c} \text{investment} \times \\ \text{marginal} \\ \text{tax rate} \end{array} \right) \left(\frac{\text{CCA rate}}{\text{CCA rate} + \text{required rate}} \right) \left(\frac{2 + \frac{\text{required}}{\text{rate of return}}}{2 \left(\frac{1 + \text{required}}{\text{rate of return}} \right)} \right)$$

In the case of the $10,000 desk, the present value of the tax savings from deducting CCA, commonly referred to as the tax shield, is $2,548, computed as follows assuming a 10 percent required rate of return.

$$\text{tax shield} = (\$10,000 \times 40\%)\left(\frac{20\%}{20\% + 10\%}\right)\left(\frac{2 + 10\%}{2(1 + 10\%)}\right)$$
$$= \$4,000 \times 0.667 \times 0.955$$
$$= \$2,668 \times 0.955$$
$$= \$2,548$$

Therefore, the net after-tax cost of the desk is $7,452, or $10,000 less $2,548.

A detailed proof of the tax shield formula is not necessary for our purposes, but some explanation will be useful.

The first component of the formula, investment times the marginal tax rate ($4,000), computes the total tax savings over the life of the asset resulting from the CCA deduction.

The second component, namely the CCA rate divided by the sum of the CCA rate plus the required rate of return, calculates the present values of all the annual tax savings assuming the half-year rule did not exist.

The third component incorporates an adjustment for the half-year rule. For example, in the above scenario, the tax shield was reduced to 95.5 percent of the benefit that exists without consideration of the half-year rule.

Capital Cost Allowance—Other Classes

Most CCA classes use the declining-balance method. However, occasionally the straight-line method is used in which the CCA is the same for each year, except for the first and last years where the half-year rule applies. For example, for patents, the CCA is computed on a straight-line basis over the legal life of the patent.

Another exception occurs where the CCA rate is varied year by year. For example, Class 39 upon its introduction in 1988 allowed 40 percent in Year 1 (subject to the half-year rule), 35 percent in Year 2, and 30 percent in the remaining years. Thus the first two years needed to be computed separately and then the tax shield formula could be applied to the UCC at the end of Year 2.

Trade-Ins and Disposals of Capital Assets

In the case when a capital asset is traded in on another asset or is sold, we do not need to concern ourselves with the net tax book value of the asset.

Assume that a company's Class 8 UCC for all of its furniture and fixtures is $50,000 at the end of Year 3. Let us also assume that included in the $50,000 is the remaining UCC on the desk of $5,760. (See Exhibit 10-7.)

If in Year 3 the desk was traded in on a new desk, where the price of the new desk is $12,000 and $4,000 was allowed as a trade-in for the old desk, the CCA Class 8 would increase by $8,000 to $58,000. Note that the CCA system works on a pool basis, in that we are not concerned with the UCC of the specific desk being sold. The actual amount of the UCC of the specific asset is irrelevant to the decision.

The CCA for Year 4 is $10,800. This is a combination of the CCA at the rate of 20 percent on the opening UCC of $50,000 ($10,000) and the CCA at the half-year rule rate of 10 percent on the net addition of $8,000 ($800). What is relevant with the specific desk is the net capital cash flows presented in Exhibit 10-8.

The net after-tax present value of the cost of the new desk is $5,962. This amount recognizes the fact that the tax shield of $2,038 on the net addition of $8,000 must take into consideration the half-year rule.

If, in the above scenario, a new desk had not been purchased but rather the old desk was sold for $4,000, the CCA would be 20 percent of ($50,000 UCC − $4,000) $46,000 or $9,200. Note the half-year rule does not apply to disposals where no additions have occurred during the year.

From Exhibit 10-8, we note that the sale of $4,000 reduces the future CCA and results in a lost tax shield of $1,067. Thus, the net after-tax present value of the sale is $2,933.

SIMPLIFYING INCOME TAX ASSUMPTIONS

It is useful to note that a number of simplifying assumptions have been made when using the tax shield formula.

1. We have assumed that the company's marginal tax rate will remain the same (at 40 percent in our examples). Further, the examples also assume that the company will have a taxable income each year.

EXHIBIT 10-7	**CCA CLASS 8**	
UCC of a Capital Asset Trade-In	UCC - Year 3	$50,000
	Purchase	12,000
	Less trade-in	(4,000)
		8,000
	Revised UCC	58,000
	Year 4 - CCA	
	20% × 50,000	10,000
	10% × 8,000	800
		10,800
	UCC - Year 4	$47,200

EXHIBIT 10-8		
Net Capital Cash Flow of Trade-Ins and Disposals	A: Trade-in: purchase price	$12,000
	Trade-in	(4,000)
	Net cash payment	8,000
	Tax shield*	(2,038)
	NPV cash outflow	$5,962
	B: Sale: selling price	$4,000
	Lost tax shield†	(1,067)
	NPV cash inflow	$2,933

* Includes the half-year adjustment.

$$\left(\$8,000 \times 40\%\right) \times \left(\frac{20\%}{20\% + 10\%}\right) \times \left(\frac{2 + 10\%}{2(1 + 10\%)}\right) = \$2,038$$

† Excludes the half-year adjustment.

$$(\$4,000 \times 40\%) \times \left(\frac{20\%}{20\% + 10\%}\right) = \$1,067$$

2. While it is uncommon, governments can change the CCA rates that we have assumed to be constant.
3. We have also assumed that all CCA tax savings occur at the year-end. In reality, companies make monthly instalments. However, the additional cost of attempting to be more precise is not warranted, given the degree of uncertainty that already exists in the estimation of the cash flows.

In the foregoing illustrations, we deliberately avoided many possible income tax complications. As all taxpaying citizens know, income taxes are affected by many intricacies, including progressive tax rates, loss carrybacks and carryforwards, varying provincial income taxes, capital gains, distinctions between capital assets and other assets, offsets of losses against related gains, exchanges of property of like kind, exempt income, and so forth.

Keep in mind that changes in the tax law occur each year. Always check the current tax law before calculating the tax consequences of a decision.

AMORTIZATION AND REPLACEMENT OF EQUIPMENT

The following points summarize the role of amortization regarding the replacement of equipment:

1. *Initial investment.* The amount paid for (and, hence, amortization on) old equipment is irrelevant except for its effect on tax cash flows. In contrast, the amount paid for new equipment is relevant because it is an expected future cost that will not be incurred if replacement is rejected. The investment in equipment is a one-time outlay at time zero.
2. *Amortization.* Amortization by itself is irrelevant; it is not a cash outlay.
3. *Relation to income tax cash flows.* Book values and past amortization are irrelevant in all capital-budgeting decision models. The relevant item is the *income tax cash effect*, not the book value or the amortization. The book value and amortization are essential data in anticipating and making predictions, but the expected future income tax cash disbursements are the relevant data for the capital-budgeting decision model.

CAPITAL BUDGETING AND INFLATION

OBJECTIVE 8

Compute the impact of inflation on a capital-budgeting project.

Inflation. The decline in the general purchasing power of the monetary unit.

Nominal Rates. Quoted market interest rates that include an inflation element.

Inflation is the decline in the general purchasing power of the monetary unit. For example, a dollar today will buy about half as much as it did in the early 1980s. If significant inflation is expected over the life of a project, it should be specifically and consistently analyzed in a capital-budgeting model. Indeed, even a relatively small inflation rate, say, 3 percent, can have sizable cumulative effects over a number of years.

The key to appropriate consideration of inflation in capital budgeting is to consistently include an element for inflation in both the minimum desired rate of return and in the anticipated cash inflows and outflows.

1. Many firms base their minimum desired rate of return on market interest rates, also called **nominal rates**, which include an inflation element. For example, consider the three components of a 15 percent nominal rate (using assumed percentages):

(a)	Risk-free element—the "pure" rate of interest that is paid on long-term government bonds	5%
(b)	Business-risk element—the "risk" premium that is demanded for taking larger risks	7
(a) + (b)	Often called the "real rate"	12%
(c)	Inflation element—the premium demanded because of expected deterioration of the general purchasing power of the monetary unit	3
(a) + (b) + (c)	Often called the "nominal rate"	15%

Three percentage points out of the 15 percent return compensate an investor for receiving future payments in inflated dollars, that is, dollars with less purchasing power than those invested. Therefore, basing the minimum desired rate of return on quoted market rates automatically includes an inflation element in the rate.

2. The predictions used in capital budgeting should include those inflation effects. For example, suppose 1,000 units of a product are expected to be sold in each of the next two years. Assume this year's price is \$50 and inflation causes next year's price to be \$52.50. This year's predicted cash inflow is 1,000 × \$50 = \$50,000 and next year's *inflation adjusted* cash inflow is 1,000 × \$52.50 = \$52,500.

Consider an illustration: the purchase of equipment with a useful life of five years; a pretax operating cash savings per year of \$83,333 (in Year 0 dollars); and an income tax rate of 40 percent. The after-tax minimum desired rate, based on quoted market rates, is 15 percent. It includes an inflation factor of 3 percent.

Exhibit 10-9 displays correct and incorrect ways to analyze the effects of inflation. The key words are *internal consistency*. The correct analysis (1) uses a

EXHIBIT 10-9

Inflation and Capital Budgeting

DESCRIPTION END OF YEAR		AT 15% PV FACTOR	AT 15% PRESENT VALUE
Correct Analysis (Be sure the discount rate includes an element attributable to inflation and adjust the predicted cash flows for inflationary effects.)			
Cash operating inflows:			
Pretax inflow in Year 0 dollars	\$83,333		
Income tax effect at 40%	33,333		
After-tax effect on cash	\$50,000		
		Year 1: \$51,500* × 0.8696	\$ 44,784
		2: \$53,045 × 0.7561	40,107
		3: \$54,636 × 0.6575	35,923
		4: \$56,275 × 0.5718	32,178
		5: \$57,964 × 0.4972	28,820
			\$181,812

* Each year is adjusted for anticipated inflation: \$50,000 × 1.03, \$50,000 × 1.03^2, \$50,000 × 1.03^3, and so on.

Incorrect Analysis (A common error is to include an inflation element in the discount rate as above, but not adjust the predicted cash inflows.)

Cash operating inflows after taxes of 5 years @ \$50,000 × 3.3522 = \$167,610

The e-business hype of the late 1990s seemed to crumble in the economic woes of 2001 and 2002. But by 2003, it became clear that e-business had not gone away. The economic shakeout identified the winners and losers—and there were plenty of both. The dot-com crash did not mark the end of e-business, but it more clearly defined what it took to be a winner in that venue. Companies who made wise investments in e-business prospered, while those who made unwise investments floundered or even disappeared.

One thing that differentiated winners from losers was how they evaluated capital investment decisions. In the e-business boom, many companies forgot the basic economics of investment analysis. Instead of focusing on cash flows and DCF analysis, companies touted their revenue per dollar of investment or, even worse, Web site hits per dollar of investment. They forgot that only net cash flows generate value. Increasing revenues are worthless if related expenses grow faster. And no one has gotten rich because of the number of visits to their Web site. There must be a way to turn these Web site visits into cash inflows.

Companies that focused on using the Internet and other e-business technologies to enhance profitability thrived. Those who used them simply to generate activity, with little attention to the profitability of that activity, struggled. *Business Week* identified some of the winners and losers:

Winners	Losers
Expedia	Hewlett-Packard
Amazon.com	Barnes & Noble
eBay	AOL Time Warner
Yahoo!	drkoop.com
Dell	many start-ups

Expedia
www.expedia.com
Amazon.com
www.amazon.com

How did the winners approach capital-budgeting decisions? First, they identified ways to generate cash—either new inflows or savings of outflows—that e-business solutions could produce. Their business plans showed at what point the company's e-business would become profitable and how profitable it would be. Second, they did not try to protect current business while simultaneously pursuing e-business. If customers were migrating to the Internet, brick-and-mortar companies would lose them anyway. And finally, they used DCF analysis. They realized that dollars in the future are worth less than those today so that they needed large future profits to justify investments that would not pay off in the short term.

Why did a company such as Amazon.com survive? Because the company met timelines for profitability of its individual product lines. Each new product line had a period of investment without profitability, but one by one its product lines met the cash flow predictions needed for ultimate profitability. In fact, when Amazon announced a 28 percent sales increase in the first quarter of 2003, the press release first highlighted the positive cash flow that the company generated.

Also among the winners are many companies that the public does not see as e-business companies. The General Motors and Eli Lillys of the world have used e-business projects to great advantage. In fact, there was nearly $4 trillion worth of business-to-business e-business in 2003. Contrary to popular belief, investment in e-business projects continues to grow steadily, year after year, and predicted productivity growth was generally realized—much of that by mainstream companies that apply e-business principles to better achieve their objectives.

Investments in e-business ventures are still risky. However, companies that plan carefully for the cash flows using DCF analysis have a better chance of surviving and thriving than those who seek technology solutions for their own sake.

Sources: "The E-Business Surprise," *Business Week*, May 12, 2003, pp. 60–68; "Amazon.com Announces 28% Sales Growth Fueled by Lower Prices and Free Shipping," Business Wire Press Release, April 24, 2003.

minimum desired rate that includes an element attributable to inflation, and (2) explicitly adjusts the predicted operating cash flows for the effects of inflation. Note that the correct analysis biases in favour of purchasing the equipment, as the incorrect analysis has a lower net present value.

The incorrect analysis in Exhibit 10-9 *excludes* adjustments for inflation of the predicted cash flows. Instead, they are stated in Year 0 dollars. However, the discount rate *includes* an element attributable to inflation. Such an analytical flaw is inherently inconsistent (discount rate is adjusted for inflation and predicted cash flows are not) and may induce an unwise conclusion.

Another correct analysis of incorporating inflation considerations in capital budgeting is to use an inflation-free required rate of return and inflation-free operating cash flows. Using the numbers in Exhibit 10-9, the 15 percent minimum desired rate would be lowered to exclude the 3 percent expected inflation rate and the $50,000 operating cash savings in Year 0 would be also used in Years 1, 2, 3, 4, and 5. Thus the tax savings due to CCA would also be reduced to Year 0 dollars. Properly used, this type of analysis would lead to the same net present value as the analysis used in Exhibit 10-9. In this case, the inflation-free minimum desired rate (*real* rate) would be calculated as follows: (1 + market rate) ÷ (1 + inflation rate) = (1 + inflation-free rate), or 1.15 ÷ 1.03 = 1.11650. The inflation-free rate is 1.11650 − 1 = 11.65%.

The net present value can be calculated as follows:

(1) AFTER-TAX SAVINGS IN YEAR 0 DOLLARS	(2) PV FACTOR AT 11.65%	(3) PRESENT VALUE (1) × (2)
$50,000	0.8957	$ 44,783
50,000	0.8022	40,110
50,000	0.7185	35,925
50,000	0.6435	32,176
50,000	0.5764	28,818
	Total present value =	$181,812

This analysis yields a net present value of $181,812, the same as in Exhibit 10-9.

Improving Predictions and Feedback

The ability to forecast and cope with changing prices is a valuable management skill, especially when inflation is significant. Auditing and feedback should help evaluate management's predictive skills.

The adjustment of the operating cash flows in Exhibit 10-9 uses a *general-price-level* index of 3 percent. However, where feasible *specific* indexes or tailor-made predictions for price changes in materials, labour, and other items should be used. These predictions may have different percentage changes from year to year.

CAPITAL INVESTMENT AND RISK

Capital investments entail risk. Why? Because the actual cash inflows may differ from what was expected or predicted. When considering a capital-budgeting pro-

The Use of Risk Premiums—the Case of the Energy from Waste Plant

In 1982, an Environmental Assessment Hearing examined the feasibility of establishing an Energy from Waste Plant for use by Victoria Hospital in London, Ontario. The Energy from Waste Plant feasibility study involved a range of possible alternatives, each of which had the objective "to define a source of economic energy."

The alternatives ranged from remaining with conventional fuels such as natural gas, oil, and electricity to an Energy from Waste Plant. The Energy from Waste Plant had the potential to incinerate both solid waste garbage and sewage sludge from the city to produce a substantial portion of the energy requirements of the hospital.

A hospital requires a continuous and dependable supply of energy for its operating rooms, heart-lung machines, monitoring equipment, etc. Thus, for Victoria Hospital, the decision regarding its source of energy was critical to its effective operations.

The Environmental Assessment Hearing's objectives were to examine the potential environmental concerns that may occur as a result of the operating of the Energy from Waste Plant. But first, prior to considering these environmental issues, it was necessary to establish that the alternatives were technically and financially viable. All the alternatives were found to be technically viable. In terms of financial viability, the Energy from Waste Plant was found to be financially viable using a net present value analysis, when compared to the conventional fuels alternative under many of the scenarios. The Environmental Assessment Hearing then proceeded to examine the many potential environmental concerns that were difficult to evaluate given that the Energy from Waste Plant involved the use of new technology.

Given the subjectivity of the ability to quantify the potential costs of these environmental concerns, another approach would have been to return to the net present value financial analysis and consider altering the discount factor to adjust for the increased risk associated with the uncertainty of using the new technology in the Energy from Waste Plant. In fact, depending upon the assumption used for future inflation rates, a risk premium of only two percentage points reversed the financial viability analysis to indicate that the conventional fuels alternative represented a lower cost alternative than the Energy from Waste Plant.

Incorporating risk differences into a capital project analysis can have a significant impact on the net present values, particularly in projects where the time span and risk differences are significant.

Source: This material has been summarized and adapted from "Energy from Waste Plant: Victoria Hospital Corporation, London, Ontario. Environment Assessment July 1982" as obtained from the London Public Library.

---

ject, a manager should first determine the riskiness of the investment. Then the inputs to the capital-budgeting model should be adjusted to reflect the risk.

There are three common ways to recognize risk. They can be used alone or in combination:

1. Reduce individual expected cash inflows or increase expected cash outflows by an amount that depends on their riskiness.
2. Reduce the expected life of riskier projects.
3. Increase the minimum desired rate of return for riskier projects.

One method that helps identify the riskiness of a project is sensitivity analysis, a "what-if" technique that indicates how decisions would be affected by changes in the data. Another approach is to compare the results of different capital-budgeting models. A manager can compare the NPV and IRR results with those of simpler measures such as the payback period and accounting rate of return.

CAPITAL INVESTMENTS AND SENSITIVITY ANALYSIS

Sensitivity analysis shows the financial consequences that would occur if actual cash inflows and outflows differed from those expected. It answers the question: "How will my net present value or internal rate of return be changed if my predictions of useful life or cash flows are inaccurate?"

We examine two types of sensitivity analysis: (1) comparing the optimistic, pessimistic, and most likely predictions, and (2) determining the amount of deviation from expected values before a decision is changed.

1. Suppose the forecasts of annual cash inflows could range from the original cash outflow of $6,075 to a low of $1,700 to a high of $2,300 for four years. The pessimistic, most likely, and optimistic NPV predictions at 10 percent are

   Pessimistic: ($1,700 × 3.1699) − $6,075 = $5,389 − $6,075 = $(686)
   Most likely: ($2,000 × 3.1699) − $6,075 = $6,340 − $6,075 = $265
   Optimistic: ($2,300 × 3.1699) − $6,075 = $7,291 − $6,075 = $1,216

   Although the expected NPV is $265, the actual NPV might turn out to be as low as $(686) or as high as $1,216.

2. A manager would reject a project if its expected NPV were negative. How far below $2,000 must the annual cash inflow drop before the NPV becomes negative? The cash inflow at the point where NPV = 0 is the "break-even" cash flow:

$$NPV = 0$$
$$(3.1699 \times \text{cash flow}) - \$6,075 = 0$$
$$\text{cash flow} = \$6,075 \div 3.1699$$
$$= \$1,916$$

   If the annual cash inflow is less than $1,916, the project should be rejected. Therefore annual cash inflows can drop only $2,000 − $1,916 = $84, or 4 percent, before the manager would change the decision. He or she must decide whether this margin of error is acceptable or whether undertaking the project represents too great a risk.

Sensitivity analysis can also be applied in predicting the length of an asset's useful life. Suppose three years is a pessimistic prediction and five years is optimistic. Using present-value factors from the third, fourth, and fifth rows of the 10 percent column of Table 2, the NPVs are

   Pessimistic: (2.4869 × $2,000) − $6,075 = $(1,101)
   Most likely: (3.1699 × $2,000) − $6,075 = $265
   Optimistic: (3.7908 × $2,000) − $6,075 = $1,507

If the useful life is even one year less than predicted, the investment will be undesirable.

Sensitivity analysis provides an immediate financial measure of the consequences of possible errors in forecasting. Why is this useful? It helps to identify decisions that may be readily affected by prediction errors. It may be most worthwhile to gather additional information about cash flows or useful life for such decisions.

Adjusting the Required Rate of Return

An alternative to sensitivity analysis to assess the risk of a project is to increase the minimum desired rate of return. In the above breakdown of the three components of a 15 percent nominal rate (p. 488), a risk premium of seven percentage points was included. If a company was considering a project with varying degrees of riskiness, the riskiness could be assessed by adjusting the required rate of return.

For example, if annual cash inflows are estimated at $2,000 for four years, a risk premium could be added to the minimum required rate of return as follows, using 10 percent for normal risk and 17 percent for higher risk.

Normal risk ($2,000 × 3.1699) − $6,075 = $265
Higher risk ($2,000 × 2.7432) − $6,075 = $(589)

The NPV is reduced from a positive $265 to a negative $589 after incorporating a risk premium of seven additional percentage points.

Most Canadian companies tend to perform subjective assessments of risk to identify prediction errors and their financial consequences.

HIGHLIGHTS TO REMEMBER

1. **Describe capital-budgeting decisions and use the net-present-value (NPV) method to make such decisions.** Capital budgeting is long-term planning for proposed capital outlays and their financing. The net-present-value (NPV) model aids this process by computing the present value of all expected future cash flows using a minimum desired rate of return. A company should accept projects with an NPV greater than zero.

2. **Evaluate projects using sensitivity analysis.** Managers use sensitivity analysis to aid risk assessment by examining the effects if actual cash flows differ from those expected.

3. **Calculate the NPV difference between two projects using both the total project and differential approaches.** The total project approach compares the NPVs of the cash flows from each project, while the differential approach computes the NPV of the difference in cash flows between two projects. Both produce the same results if there are two alternatives. You have to use the total project approach if you have more than two alternatives.

4. **Identify relevant cash flows for NPV analyses.** Predicting cash flows is the hardest part of capital budgeting. Managers should consider four categories of cash flows: initial cash inflows and outflows at time zero, investments in working capital, future disposal values, and operating cash flows.

5. **Compute the after-tax net present values of projects.** Income taxes can have a significant effect on the desirability of an investment. Additional taxes are cash outflows, and tax savings are cash inflows. Capital cost allowance (CCA) speeds up a company's tax savings. The present value of the tax savings generated by the CCA is calculated with the tax shield formula.

6. **Explain the effect of taxes on residual values.** The sale of assets results in reduced CCA and, consequently, in lost tax shields.

7. **Use the payback model and the accounting rate-of-return model and compare them with the NPV model.** The payback model is simple to apply, but it does not measure profitability. The accounting rate-of-return model uses accounting measures of income and investment, but it ignores the time value of money. Both models are inferior to the NPV model.

8. **Reconcile the conflict between using an NPV model for making a decision and using accounting income for evaluating the related performance.** NPV is a summary measure of all the cash flows from a project. Accounting income is a one-period measure. A positive NPV project can have low (or even negative) accounting income in the first year. Managers may be reluctant to invest in such a project, despite its positive value to the company, especially if they expect to be transferred to a new position before they can benefit from the positive returns that come later.

9. **Compute the impact of inflation on a capital-budgeting project.** Consistency is the key in adjusting capital-budgeting analyses for inflation. The required rate of return should include an element attributable to anticipated inflation, and cash-flow predictions should be adjusted for the effects of anticipated inflation.

DEMONSTRATION PROBLEMS FOR YOUR REVIEW

Problem One

Consider the following investment opportunity: original cost of computer system, $125,000; five-year economic life; zero terminal salvage value; pretax annual cash inflow from operations, $60,000; income tax rate, 40 percent; required after-tax rate of return, 12 percent. Assume that the computer qualifies for CCA Class 10, which has a rate of 30 percent declining balance.

Calculate the net present value (NPV) of the investment.

Further, suppose the equipment was expected to be sold for $20,000 cash immediately after the end of Year 5. Compute the net present value of the investment.

Solution

Cash effects of operations		
$60,000 × (1 − 0.4) × 3.6048		$129,773
Cash effects of investment		
Initial outlay	$125,000	
Less tax shield	(33,725)*	91,275
Net present value		$ 38,498

$$^*(\$125{,}000 \times 40\%)\left(\frac{30\%}{30\% + 12\%}\right)\left(\frac{2 + 12\%}{2(1 + 12\%)}\right)$$
$$= \$50{,}000 \times 0.71 \times 0.95 = \$33{,}725$$

			$ 38,498
Net present value (above)			$ 38,498
Cash proceeds of sale	$ 20,000		
Less lost tax shield	(5,680)*	14,320 × 0.5674 = $ 8,125	
Net present value			$ 46,623

* ($20,000 × 40%) × 0.71 = $5,680

Problem Two

Use the appropriate interest table to compute the following:

1. It is your 65th birthday. You plan to work five more years before retiring. Then you want to take $10,000 for a round-the-world tour. What lump sum do you have to invest now in order to accumulate the $10,000? Assume that your minimum desired rate of return is
   (a) 4 percent, compounded annually
   (b) 10 percent, compounded annually
   (c) 20 percent, compounded annually

2. You want to spend $2,000 on a vacation at the end of each of the next five years. What lump sum do you have to invest now in order to take the five vacations? Assume that your minimum desired rate of return is
   (a) 4 percent, compounded annually
   (b) 10 percent, compounded annually
   (c) 20 percent, compounded annually

3. At age 60, you find that your employer is moving to another location. You receive termination pay of $50,000. You have some savings and wonder whether to retire now.
   (a) If you invest the $50,000 now at 4 percent, compounded annually, how much money can you withdraw from your account each year so that at the end of five years there will be a zero balance?
   (b) If you invest it at 10 percent?

4. At 16 percent, compounded annually, which of the following plans is more desirable in terms of present values? Show computations to support your answer.

	ANNUAL CASH INFLOWS	
YEAR	MINING	FARMING
1	$10,000	$ 2,000
2	8,000	4,000
3	6,000	6,000
4	4,000	8,000
5	2,000	10,000
	$30,000	$30,000

Solution

The general approach to these exercises centres on one fundamental question: Which of the two basic tables am I dealing with? No calculations should be made until after this question is answered with assurance. If you made any errors, it is possible that you used the wrong table.

1. From Table 1, page 825:
   (a) $8,219
   (b) $6,209
   (c) $4,019

   The $10,000 is an *amount of future worth*. You want the present value of that amount:

   $$PV = \frac{S}{(1 + i)^n}$$

   The conversion factor, $1/(1 + i)^n$, is on line 5 of Table 1. Substituting:

   $$PV = \$10,000 \ (0.8219) = \$8,219 \ (a)$$
   $$PV = \$10,000 \ (0.6209) = \$6,209 \ (b)$$
   $$PV = \$10,000 \ (0.4019) = \$4,019 \ (c)$$

   Note that the higher the interest rate, the lower the present value.

2. From Table 2, page 826:
   (a) $8,903.60
   (b) $7,581.60
   (c) $5,981.20

   The $2,000 withdrawal is a uniform annual amount, an annuity. You need to find the present value of an annuity for five years:

   PV_A = annual withdrawal $\times$ F, where F is the conversion factor.

   Substituting:

   $$PV_A = \$2,000 \ (4.4518) = \$8,903.60 \ (a)$$
   $$PV_A = \$2,000 \ (3.7908) = \$7,581.60 \ (b)$$
   $$PV_A = \$2,000 \ (2.9906) = \$5,981.20 \ (c)$$

3. From Table 2:
   (a) $11,231.41
   (b) $13,189.83

   You have $50,000, the present value of your contemplated annuity. You must find the annuity that will just exhaust the invested principal in five years:

   $$PV_A = \text{annual withdrawal} \times F(1)$$
   $$\$50,000 = \text{annual withdrawal} \ (4.4518)$$
   $$\text{annual withdrawal} = \$50,000 \div 4.4518$$
   $$= \$11,231.41$$

   $$\$50,000 = \text{annual withdrawal} \ (3.7908)$$
   $$\text{annual withdrawal} = \$50,000 \div 3.7908$$
   $$= \$13,189.83$$

4. From Table 1: Mining is preferable; its present value exceeds that of farming by $21,572 − $17,720 = $3,852. Note that the nearer dollars are more valuable than the distant dollars.

YEAR	PRESENT VALUE @ 16% FROM TABLE 1	PRESENT VALUE OF MINING	PRESENT VALUE OF FARMING
1	0.8621	$ 8,621	$ 1,724
2	0.7432	5,946	2,973
3	0.6407	3,844	3,844
4	0.5523	2,209	4,418
5	0.4761	952	4,761
		$21,572	$17,720

Problem Three

Review the problem and solution shown in Exhibit 10-4 on page 473. Conduct a sensitivity analysis as indicated below. Consider each requirement as independent of other requirements.

1. Compute the net present value if the minimum desired rate of return was 20 percent.
2. Compute the net present value if predicted cash operating costs was $35,000 instead of $30,000, using the 14 percent discount rate.
3. By how much may the cash operating savings fall before reaching the point of indifference, the point where the net present value of the project is zero, using the original discount rate of 14 percent?

Solution

1. Either the total project approach or the differential approach could be used. The differential approach would show:

	TOTAL PRESENT VALUE
Recurring cash operating savings, using an annuity table (Table 2):	
2.9906 × $10,000 =	$29,906
Overhaul avoided: 0.6944 × $10,000 =	6,944
Difference in disposal values:	
0.4019 × $5,000 =	(2,010)
Incremental initial investment	(31,000)
Net present value of replacement	$ 3,840
2. Net present value in Exhibit 10-4	$ 8,429
Present value of additional $5,000 annual operating costs,	
3.4331 × $5,000	17,166
New net present value	$ (8,737)

3. Let X = annual cash operating savings and find the value of X such that NPV = 0. Then

$$0 = 3.4331(X) + \$7,695 - \$2,597 - \$31,000$$
$$3.4331X = \$25,902$$
$$X = \$7,545$$

(Note that $7,695, $2,597, and $31,000 are at the bottom of Exhibit 10-4.)

If the annual savings fall from $10,000 to $7,545, a decrease of $2,455 or almost 25 percent, the point of indifference will be reached.

An alternative way to obtain the same answer would be to divide the net present value of $8,429 (see bottom of Exhibit 10.4) by 3.4331, obtaining $2,455, the amount of the annual difference in savings that will eliminate the $8,429 of net present value.

APPENDIX: SELECTED CCA CLASSES AND RATES

Class 1	(4%)	Buildings or other structures, including component parts acquired after 1987;
Class 3	(5%)	Buildings or other structures, including component parts acquired before 1988;
Class 8	(20%)	Miscellaneous tangible capital property and machinery or equipment not included in another class;
Class 10	(30%)	Automobiles and automotive equipment; computer equipment and systems software acquired before March 23, 2004.
Class 12	(100%)	Tools or utensils costing less than $200, video tape, certified feature films, computer software;
Class 13		Leasehold interest in property (straight-line over lease life);
Class 14		Patent, franchise, concession or licence for a limited period (straight-line over legal life);
Class 40	(25%)	Property used in manufacturing or processing;
Class 45	(45%)	Computer equipment and systems software acquired after March 22, 2004.

KEY TERMS

accounting rate of return (ARR) *p. 476*
capital assets *p. 460*
capital-budgeting decisions *p. 460*
capital cost allowance (CCA) *p. 483*
differential approach *p. 471*
discount rate *p. 462*
discounted-cash-flow (DCF) model *p. 461*
half-year rule *p. 483*
hurdle rate *p. 462*
inflation *p. 487*

internal rate of return (IRR) *p. 464*
marginal income tax rate *p. 481*
net-present-value (NPV) method *p. 461*
nominal rates *p. 487*
payback period *p. 474*
payback time *p. 474*
postaudit *p. 481*
required rate of return *p. 462*
tax shield formula *p. 484*
total project approach *p. 471*
undepreciated capital cost (UCC) *p. 484*

ASSIGNMENT MATERIAL

QUESTIONS

Q10-1   Capital budgeting has three phases: (1) identification of potential investments, (2) selection of investments, and (3) postaudit of investments. What is the accountant's role in each phase?

Q10-2	Why is discounted cash flow a superior method for capital budgeting?
Q10-3	Can net present value ever be negative? Why?
Q10-4	"The higher the minimum rate of return desired, the higher the price that a company will be willing to pay for cost-saving equipment." Do you agree? Explain.
Q10-5	"Not-for-profit organizations do not use DCF because their cost of capital is zero." Do you agree? Explain.
Q10-6	Why should the differential approach to alternatives always lead to the same decision as the total project approach?
Q10-7	"The higher the interest rate, the less I worry about errors in predicting terminal values." Do you agree? Explain.
Q10-8	What is the basic flaw in the payback model?
Q10-9	Explain how a conflict can arise between capital-budgeting decision models and performance-evaluation methods.
Q10-10	Distinguish between average and marginal tax rates.
Q10-11	What are the major influences on the present value of a tax deduction?
Q10-12	How much CCA is taken in the first year if a $10,000 asset is amortized on a 20 percent declining-balance schedule? How much in the second year?
Q10-13	Describe how internal consistency is achieved when considering inflation in a capital-budgeting model.
Q10-14	"Capital investments are always more profitable in inflationary times because the cash inflows from operations generally increase with inflation." Comment on this statement.
Q10-15	"We can't use sensitivity analysis because our cash-flow predictions are too inaccurate." Comment.
Q10-16	Name three ways to recognize risk in capital budgeting.

PROBLEMS

P10-1 **EXERCISES IN COMPOUND INTEREST.** Use the appropriate table to compute the following:

1. You have always dreamed of taking a trip to the Great Barrier Reef. What lump sum do you have to invest today to have the $12,000 needed for the trip in three years? Assume that you can invest the money at
   (a) 5 percent, compounded annually
   (b) 10 percent, compounded annually
   (c) 18 percent, compounded annually

2. You are considering partial retirement. To do so you need to use part of your savings to supplement your income for the next five years. Suppose you need an extra $15,000 per year. What lump sum do you have to invest now in order to supplement your income for five years? Assume that your minimum desired rate of return is
   (a) 5 percent, compounded annually
   (b) 10 percent, compounded annually
   (c) 18 percent, compounded annually

3. You just won a lump sum of $400,000 in a local lottery. You have decided to invest the winnings and withdraw an equal amount each

year for 10 years. How much can you withdraw each year and have a zero balance left at the end of 10 years if you invest at

(a) 6 percent, compounded annually

(b) 10 percent, compounded annually

4. A professional athlete is offered the choice of two four-year salary contracts: contract A for $1.4 million and contract B for $1.3 million:

	CONTRACT A	CONTRACT B
End of Year 1	$ 200,000	$ 450,000
End of Year 2	300,000	350,000
End of Year 3	400,000	300,000
End of Year 4	500,000	200,000
	$1,400,000	$1,300,000

Which contract has the highest present value at 14 percent compounded annually? Show computations to support your answer.

P10-2 **NPV, IRR, ARR, AND PAYBACK.** Sally's Subs is considering a proposal to invest in a speaker system that would allow its employees to service drive-through customers. The cost of the system (including installation of special windows and driveway modifications) is $60,000. Sally Holding, manager of Sally's Subs, expects the drive-through operations to increase annual sales by $50,000, with a 40 percent contribution-margin ratio. Assume that the system has an economic life of six years, at which time it will have no disposal value. The required rate of return is 14 percent.

1. Compute the payback period. Is this a good measure of profitability?
2. Compute the net present value (NPV). Should Holding accept the proposal? Why or why not?
3. Compute the internal rate of return (IRR). How should the IRR be used to decide whether to accept or reject the proposal?
4. Using the accounting rate of return model, compute the rate of return on the initial investment.

P10-3 **EXERCISE IN COMPOUND INTEREST.** Suppose General Electric (GE) wishes to borrow money from The Canadian Bank. An annual rate of 12 percent is agreed upon.

1. Suppose GE agrees to repay $400 million at the end of five years. How much will The Canadian Bank lend GE?
2. Suppose GE agrees to repay a total of $400 million at a rate of $100 million at the end of each of the next four years. How much will The Canadian Bank lend GE?

P10-4 **DEFERRED ANNUITY EXERCISE.** It is your 20th birthday. On your 25th birthday, and on three successive birthdays thereafter, you intend to spend exactly $1,000 for a birthday celebration. What lump sum do you have to invest now in order to have the four celebrations? Assume that the money will earn interest, compounded annually, of 12 percent.

P10-5 **PRESENT VALUE AND SPORTS SALARIES.** Because of a salary cap, National Basketball Association teams are not allowed to exceed a certain annual limit in total player salaries. Suppose the Toronto Raptors had scheduled salaries exactly equal to their cap of $16 million for 2006. A star player was scheduled to receive $3 million in 2006. To free up money to pay a prize rookie, the star player agreed to defer $1 million of his salary for two years, by which time the salary cap will have been increased. His contract called for salary payments of $3 million in 2006, $3.5 million in 2007, and $4 million in 2008. Now he will receive $2 million in 2006, still $3.5 million in 2007, and $5 million in 2008. For simplicity, assume that all salaries are paid on July 1 of the year they are scheduled. The star's minimum desired rate of return is 12 percent.

Did the deferral of salary cost the star anything? If so, how much? Compute the present value of the sacrifice on July 1, 2006. Explain your findings.

P10-6 INTERNAL RATE AND NPV. Fill in the blanks:

	NUMBER OF YEARS		
	8	18	28
Amount of annual cash inflow*	$10,000	$_____	$ 7,000
Required initial investment	$_____	$80,000	$29,099
Internal rate of return	18%	16%	____%
Minimum desired rate of return	14%	____%	26%
Net present value	$_____	$(13,835)	$_____

* To be received at the end of each year.

P10-7 ILLUSTRATION OF TRIAL-AND-ERROR METHOD OF COMPUTING RATE OF RETURN. Study Exhibit 10-2. Suppose the annual cash inflow will be $2,500 rather than $2,000. What is the internal rate of return?

P10-8 CAPITAL BUDGETING WITH UNEVEN CASH FLOWS. The University of Toronto Faculty of Applied Science and Engineering is considering the purchase of a special-purpose machine for $60,000. It is expected to have a useful life of three years with no terminal salvage value. The university's controller estimates the following savings in cash operating costs:

YEAR	AMOUNT
1	$28,000
2	26,000
3	24,000

Compute

1. Payback period.
2. Net present value if the required rate of return is 12 percent.
3. Internal rate of return.
4. Accounting rate of return (a) on the initial investment, and (b) on the "average" investment.

P10-9 RATIONALE OF NPV MODEL. Evergreen Outdoor School (EOS) has a chance to invest $10,000 in a project that is certain to pay $4,500 at the end of each of the next three years. The minimum desired rate of return is 10 percent.

1. What is the project's net present value?
2. Show that EOS would be equally well off undertaking the project as having its present value in cash. Do this by calculating the cash available at the end of three years if (a) $10,000 is borrowed at 10 percent, with interest paid at the end of each year, and the investment is made,

or (b) cash equal to the project's NPV is invested at 10 percent compounded annually for three years. Use the following formats. Year 1 for the first alternative is completed for you.

		ALTERNATIVE (A)—INVEST IN PROJECT			
	(1)	(2)	(3)	(4)	(5)
					(3) – (4)
	LOAN		(1) + (2)		LOAN
	BALANCE AT	INTEREST	ACCUMULATED	CASH FOR	BALANCE
	BEGINNING	AT 10%	AMOUNT AT	REPAYMENT	AT END
YEAR	OF YEAR	PER YEAR	END OF YEAR	OF LOAN	OF YEAR
1	$10,000	$1,000	$11,000	$4,500	$6,500
2					
3					

		ALTERNATIVE (B)—KEEP CASH	
	(1)	(2)	(3)
	INVESTMENT		(1) + (2)
	BALANCE	INTEREST	ACCUMULATED
	AT BEGINNING	AT 10%	AMOUNT AT
YEAR	OF YEAR	PER YEAR	END OF YEAR
1			
2			
3			

P10-10 **REPLACEMENT OF EQUIPMENT.** Assume that new equipment will cost $100,000 in cash and that the old machine cost $84,000 and can be sold now for $16,000 cash. Annual cash savings of $15,000 are expected for ten years.

1. Compute the net present value of the replacement alternative, assuming that the minimum desired rate of return is 10 percent.
2. What will be the internal rate of return?
3. How long is the payback period on the incremental investment?

P10-11 **REPLACING OFFICE EQUIPMENT.** Simon Fraser University is considering replacing some Xerox copies with faster copiers purchased from Kodak. The administration is very concerned about the rising costs of operations during the last decade.

In order to convert to Kodak, two operators would have to be retrained. Required training and remodelling would cost $2,000.

Simon Fraser's three Xerox machines were purchased for $10,000 each, five years ago. Their expected life was ten years. Their resale value is now $1,000 each and will be zero in five more years. The total cost of the new Kodak equipment will be $49,000; it will have zero disposal value in five years.

The three Xerox operators are paid $8 an hour each. They usually work a 40-hour week. Machine breakdowns occur monthly on each machine, resulting in repair costs of $50 per month and overtime of four hours, at time-and-one-half, per machine per month, to complete the normal monthly workload. Toner, supplies, etc., cost $100 a month for each Xerox copier.

The Kodak system will require only two regular operators, on a regular workweek of 40 hours each, to do the same work. Rates are $10 an hour, and no overtime is expected. Toner, supplies, etc., will cost $3,300 annually. Maintenance and repairs are fully serviced by Kodak for $1,050 annually. (Assume a 52-week year.)

1. Using discounted-cash-flow techniques, compute the present value of all relevant cash flows, under both alternatives, for the five-year period discounted at 12 percent. As a not-for-profit organization, Simon Fraser University does not pay income taxes.
2. Should Simon Fraser keep the Xerox copiers or replace them if the decision is based solely on the given data?
3. What other considerations might affect the decision?

P10-12 REPLACEMENT DECISION FOR RAILWAY EQUIPMENT. The CN Railroad is considering replacement of a Montreal Power Jack Tamper, used for maintenance of track, with a new automatic raising device that can be attached to a production tamper.

The present power jack tamper cost $18,000 five years ago and has an estimated life of 12 years. A year from now the machine will require a major overhaul estimated to cost $5,000. It can be disposed of now via an outright cash sale for $3,500. There will be no value at the end of 12 years.

The automatic raising attachment has a delivered selling price of $72,000 and an estimated life of 12 years. Because of anticipated future developments in combined maintenance machines, it is felt that the machine should be disposed of at the end of the seventh year to take advantage of newly developed machines. Estimated sales value at the end of seven years is $5,000.

Tests have shown that the automatic raising machine will produce a more uniform surface on the track than the power jack tamper now in use. The new equipment will eliminate one labourer whose annual compensation, including fringe benefits, is $30,000.

Track maintenance work is seasonal, and the equipment normally works from May 1 to October 31 each year. Machine operators and labourers are transferred to other work after October 31, at the same rate of pay.

The salesperson claims that the annual normal maintenance of the new machine will run about $1,000 per year. Because the automatic raising machine is more complicated than the manually operated machine, it is felt that it will require a thorough overhaul at the end of the fourth year at an estimated cost of $7,000.

Records show the annual normal maintenance of the Montreal machine to be $1,200. Fuel consumption of the two machines is equal. Should CN keep or replace the Montreal Power Jack Tamper? A 10 percent rate of return is desired. Compute present values. Ignore income taxes.

P10-13 DISCOUNTED CASH FLOW, UNEVEN REVENUE STREAM, RELEVANT COSTS. Anika Paar, the owner of a nine-hole golf course on the outskirts of Hamilton, Ontario, is considering the proposal that the course be illuminated and operated at night. Ms. Paar purchased the course early last year for $90,000. Her receipts from operations during the 28-week season were $24,000. Total disbursements for the year, for all purposes, were $16,500.

The required investment in lighting this course is estimated at $20,000. The system will require 150 lamps of 1,000 watts each. Electricity costs $0.032 per kilowatt-hour. The expected average hours of operation per night are five. Because of occasional bad weather and the probable curtailment of night operation at the beginning and end of the season, it is estimated that there will be only

130 nights of operation per year. Labour for keeping the course open at night will cost $15 per night. Lamp renewals are estimated at $300 per year; other maintenance and repairs, per year, will amount to 4 percent of the initial cost of the lighting system. Property taxes on this equipment will be about 2 percent of its initial cost. It is estimated that the average revenue, per night of operation, will be $90 for the first two years.

Considering the probability of competition from the illumination of other golf courses, Ms. Paar decides that she will not make the investment unless she can make at least 10 percent per annum on her investment. Because of anticipated competition, revenue is expected to drop to $60 per night for years 3 through 5. It is estimated that the lighting equipment will have a salvage value of $7,000 at the end of the five-year period.

Using discounted-cash-flow techniques, determine whether Ms. Paar should install the lighting system.

P10-14 **MINIMIZING TRANSPORTATION COSTS.** The Luxon Company produces industrial and residential lighting fixtures at its manufacturing facility located in Calgary. Shipment of company products to an eastern warehouse is presently handled by common carriers at a rate of $0.25 per kilogram of fixtures. The warehouse is located 2,500 kilometres from Calgary.

The treasurer of Luxon Company is presently considering whether to purchase a truck for transporting products to the eastern warehouse. The following data on the truck are available:

Purchase price	$35,000
Useful life	5 years
Salvage value after 5 years	zero
Capacity of truck	10,000 kilograms
Cash costs of operating truck	$0.90 per kilometre

Luxon feels that an investment in this truck is particularly attractive because of their successful negotiation with Retro Company to back-haul Retro's products from the warehouses to Calgary on every return trip from the warehouse. Retro has agreed to pay Luxon $2,400 per load of Retro's products hauled from the warehouse to Calgary up to and including 100 loads per year.

Luxon's marketing manager has estimated that 500,000 kilograms of fixtures will have to be shipped to the eastern warehouse each year for the next five years. The truck will be fully loaded on each round trip.

Ignore income taxes.

1. Assume that Luxon requires a minimum rate of return of 20 percent. Should the truck be purchased? Show computations to support your answer.
2. What is the minimum number of trips that must be guaranteed by the Retro Company to make the deal acceptable to Luxon, based on the foregoing numbers alone?
3. What qualitative factors might influence your decision? Be specific.

P10-15 **COMPARISON OF INVESTMENT MODELS.** Dominique's Frozen Food Company makes frozen dinners and sells them to retail outlets near London. Dominique has just inherited £10,000 and has decided to invest it in the business. She is trying to decide between the following alternatives:

Alternative A: Buy a £10,000 contract, payable immediately, from a local reputable sales promotion agency. The agency would provide various advertising services, as specified in the contract, over the next ten years. Dominique is convinced that the sales promotion would increase net cash inflow from operations, through increased volume, by £2,000 per year for the first five years, and by £1,000 per year thereafter. There would be no effect after the ten years had elapsed.

Alternative B: Buy new mixing and packaging equipment, at a cost of £10,000, which would reduce operating cash outflows by £1,500 per year for the next ten years. The equipment would have zero salvage value at the end of the ten years.

Ignore any tax effect.

1. Compute the rates of return on initial investment by the accounting model for both alternatives.
2. Compute the rates of return by the discounted-cash-flow model for both alternatives.
3. Are the rates of return different under the discounted-cash-flow model? Explain.

P10-16 **FIXED AND CURRENT ASSETS; EVALUATION OF PERFORMANCE.** Metro Hospital has been under pressure to keep costs down. Indeed, the hospital administrator has been managing various revenue-producing centres to maximize contributions to the recovery of the operating costs of the hospital as a whole. The administrator has been considering whether to buy a special-purpose X-ray machine for $193,000. Its unique characteristics would generate additional cash operating income of $50,000 per year for the hospital as a whole.

The machine is expected to have a useful life of six years and a terminal salvage value of $22,000.

The machine is delicate. It requires a constant inventory of various supplies and spare parts. When these items can no longer be used, they are instantly replaced, so an investment of $15,000 must be maintained at all times. However, this investment is fully recoverable at the end of the useful life of the machine.

1. Compute the net present value if the required rate of return is 14 percent.
2. Compute the internal rate of return (to the nearest whole percentage).
3. Compute the accounting rate of return on (a) the initial investment, and (b) the "average" investment.
4. Why might the administrator be reluctant to base her decision on the DCF model?

P10-17 **CAFETERIA FACILITIES.** The cafeteria in Haekon Towers, an office building in downtown Oslo, is open 250 days a year. It offers typical cafeteria-line service. At the noon meal (open to the public), serving-line facilities can accommodate 200 people per hour for the two-hour serving period. The average customer has a 30-minute lunch period. Serving facilities are unable to handle the overflow of noon-hour customers with the result that, each day, 20 dissatisfied customers who do not wish to stand in line choose to eat elsewhere. Projected over a year, this results in a considerable loss to the cafeteria.

To tap this excess demand, the cafeteria is considering two alternatives: (a) installing two vending machines, at a cost of NK25,000 apiece (NK means Norwegian kroner), or (b) completely revamping present serving-line facilities with new equipment, at a cost of NK150,000. The vending machines and serving-line equipment have a useful life of ten years and will be amortized on a straight-line basis. The minimum desired rate of return for the cafeteria is 10 percent. The average sale is NK15, with a contribution margin of 30 percent. This will remain the same if new serving-line facilities are installed.

Data for alternative (a) vending machines are as follows:

- Service cost per year is NK2,000; salvage value of each machine at the end of ten years is NK5,000.
- Contribution margin is 20 percent. It is estimated that 60 percent of the dissatisfied customers will use the vending machines and spend an average of NK15. The estimated salvage value of the present equipment will net NK20,000 at the end of the ten-year period.

Data for alternative (b) new serving-line facilities are as follows:

- Yearly salary for an extra part-time cashier is NK8,000; salvage value of old equipment is NK50,000; salvage value of new equipment, at the end of ten years, is NK50,000; cost of dismantling old equipment is NK5,000. It is estimated that all the previously dissatisfied customers will use the new facilities.

All other costs are the same under both alternatives and need not be considered.

Using the net-present-value model, which is the better alternative?

P10-18 **CAPITAL COST ALLOWANCE AND PRESENT VALUES.** The president of a software company is contemplating acquiring some computers used for designing software. The computers will cost $150,000 cash and will have zero terminal salvage value. The recovery period and useful life are both three years. Annual pretax cash savings from operations will be $75,000. The income tax rate is 40 percent, and the required after-tax rate of return is 16 percent.

1. Compute the net present value, assuming Class 10, 30 percent declining balance for tax purposes.
2. Suppose the required after-tax rate of return is 12 percent instead of 16 percent. Should the computers be acquired? Show computations.

P10-19 **GAINS OR LOSSES ON DISPOSAL.** An asset with an accounting book value of $50,000 was sold for cash on January 1, 2006.

Assume two selling prices: $65,000 and $30,000. For each selling price, prepare a tabulation of the accounting gain or loss, the effect on income taxes, and the total after-tax effect on cash. Assume the asset qualifies for Class 8, 20 percent declining balance and assume a required rate of return of 10 percent. The applicable income tax rate is 30 percent.

P10-20 **TAX INCENTIVES FOR CAPITAL INVESTMENT.** Goladen Vineyards is a successful small winery. The owner, Gino Colucchio, is considering an additional line of business: selling wind-generated electricity to the local utility. Tax law requires power utilities to purchase windmill electricity. Gino could put windmills on his current land without disturbing the grape crop. A windmill generates 200,000 kilowatt-hours annually, and the utility would pay $0.07 per kilowatt-hour. There are essentially no operating costs.

At the time Gino considered purchasing his first windmill, the cost was $100,000 per windmill. Initially he was discouraged and almost abandoned the idea. But then he learned about two government tax-credit programs that applied to investments in windmills. First, a general investment tax credit of 8 percent could be taken. That is, Goladen's federal income taxes could be immediately reduced by 8 percent of the cost of the windmill. In addition, windmills qualified for a "business energy credit" of 15 percent, reducing federal income taxes by another 15 percent of the cost.

Assume that a windmill's economic life is 20 years. Goladen's required rate of return is 14 percent after taxes, and the marginal income tax rate is 45 percent. Assume windmills qualify for a CCA rate of 25 percent declining balance.

1. Would Gino purchase a windmill without the tax credits? Calculate the net present value.
2. Would Gino purchase a windmill with the tax credits? Calculate the net present value.
3. What is the most that Gino would pay for a windmill, provided the tax credits are available?

P10-21 INCOME TAXES AND INCREMENTAL COSTS. Yvette Thirdgill has a small sewing and tailoring shop in the basement of her home. She uses the single telephone line into the home for both business and personal calls. She estimates that 50 percent of the phone use is for business. Until 2006 she allocated the basic cost of the telephone line, $20 per month, between business and personal use and charged $10 per month for telephone services on her income statement submitted to the tax authorities.

Assume that beginning in 2006, Canada Revenue Agency rules that no portion of the first phone line into a residence is allowed as an expense for tax purposes. However, if a second line is installed and used strictly for business purposes, its total cost is allowed as an expense. The phone company charges $20 per month for a second line.

Thirdgill's marginal income tax rate is 40 percent.

1. Under the old tax law (in effect before 2006), how much extra per month (after tax effects) would Thirdgill have paid for a second phone line?
2. Under the new tax law (in effect beginning in 2006), how much extra per month (after tax effects) would Thirdgill pay for a second phone line?
3. How might the new tax law affect the demand for second phone lines?

P10-22 PRODUCT VERSUS PERIOD COSTS AND MINIMIZING TAXES. South Chemicals Corporation was adversely affected by a tax ruling that certain selling and administrative expenses must be treated as product costs instead of period costs for reporting to the tax authorities. (Recall that period costs are charged as expenses in the period they are incurred. Product costs are added to the inventory value of the products and are charged as expenses when the products are sold.)

South is a maker of wax compounds with annual sales of more than $15 million. The company keeps large inventories to be able to respond quickly to customer demands. Suppose in 2007 South's financial reporting system measured the revenue at $15 million, cost of goods sold (a product cost) at $10 million, and selling and administrative expenses (all period costs) at $3 million. Now suppose the tax ruling required $2 million of the $3 million selling and administrative costs to be product, not period, costs. (The remaining $1 million is still a period cost for tax reporting as well as financial reporting.) Of the $2 million additional product cost, $1.5 million was allocated to products that were sold and $0.5 million to products remaining in inventory.

1. Compute 2007 income before taxes as reported in the financial statements issued to the public.
2. Compute 2007 income before taxes as reported in the statements prepared for the tax authorities.

P10-23 **PRESENT VALUE OF AFTER-TAX CASH FLOWS.** Tsumagari Company, an electronics company in Kobe, Japan, is planning to buy new equipment to produce a new product. Estimated data (monetary amounts are in thousands of Japanese yen) are:

Cash cost of new equipment now	¥400,000
Estimated life in years	10
Terminal salvage value	¥50,000
Incremental revenues per year	¥320,000
Incremental expenses per year other than amortization	¥165,000

Assume a 60 percent flat rate for income taxes. All revenues and expenses other than amortization will be received or paid in cash. Use a 14 percent discount rate. Assume a ten-year straight-line amortization for tax purposes. Also assume that the terminal salvage value will affect the amortization per year.

Compute

1. Amortization expenses per year.
2. Anticipated net income per year.
3. Annual net cash flow.
4. Payback period.
5. Accounting rate of return on initial investment.
6. Net present value.

P10-24 **INCOME TAXES AND DISPOSAL OF ASSETS.** Assume that income tax rates are 30 percent and that the asset qualifies for a 25 percent declining balance, and the required rate of return is 10 percent.

1. The book value of an old machine is $20,000. It is to be sold for $8,000 cash. What is the effect of this decision on cash flows, after taxes?
2. The book value of an old machine is $20,000. It is to be sold for $30,000 cash. What is the effect on cash flows, after taxes, of this decision?

P10-25 **PURCHASE OF EQUIPMENT.** The Sea Pines Company is planning to spend $45,000 for modernized production equipment. It will replace equipment that has zero book value and no salvage value, although the old equipment would last another seven years.

The new equipment will save $13,500 in cash operating costs for each of the next seven years, at which time it will be sold for $4,000. A major overhaul costing $5,000 will occur at the end of the fourth year; the old equipment would require no such overhaul. The entire cost of the overhaul is deductible for tax purposes in the fourth year. The equipment is in Class 39 at a rate of 30 percent declining balance for tax purposes.

The minimum desired rate of return after taxes is 12 percent. The applicable income tax rate is 40 percent.

Compute the after-tax net present value. Is the new equipment a desirable investment?

P10-26 MINIMIZING TRANSPORTATION COSTS. The Luxon Company produces industrial and residential lighting fixtures at its manufacturing facility in Calgary. Shipment of company products to an eastern warehouse is presently handled by common carriers at a rate of $0.25 per kilogram of fixtures (expressed in year-zero dollars). The warehouse is located 2,500 kilometres from Calgary.

The treasurer of Luxon Company is presently considering whether to purchase a truck for transporting products to the eastern warehouse. The following data on the truck are available:

Purchase price	$40,000
Useful life	5 years
Terminal residual value	zero
Capacity of truck	10,000 kilogram
Cash costs of operating truck	$0.90 per kilometre
	(expressed in year-1 dollars)

Luxon believes that an investment in this truck is particularly attractive because of their successful negotiation with Retro Company to back-haul Retro's products from the warehouse to Calgary on every return trip from the warehouse. Retro has agreed to pay Luxon $2,400 per load of Retro's products hauled from the warehouse to Calgary for as many loads as Luxon can accommodate, up to and including 100 loads per year over the next five years.

The Luxon marketing manager has estimated that 500,000 kilograms of fixtures will have to be shipped to the eastern warehouse each year for the next five years. The truck will be fully loaded on each round trip.

Make the following assumptions:

a. Luxon requires a minimum 20 percent after-tax rate of return, which includes a 10 percent element attributable to inflation.
b. A 40 percent tax rate.
c. The truck qualifies for Class 10, 30 percent declining balance.
d. An inflation rate of 10 percent.

1. Should the truck be purchased? Show computations to support your answer.
2. What qualitative factors might influence your decision? Be specific.

P10-27 INFLATION AND NOT-FOR-PROFIT INSTITUTIONS. The city of Bremerton is considering the purchase of a photocopying machine for $7,300 on December 31, 2007, useful life five years, and no residual value. The cash operating savings are expected to be $2,000 annually, measured in 2007 dollars.

The minimum desired rate is 14 percent, which includes an element attributable to anticipated inflation of 6 percent. (Remember that the city pays no income taxes.)

Use the 14 percent minimum desired rate for requirements 1 and 2:

1. Compute the net present value of the project without adjusting the cash operating savings for inflation.
2. Repeat requirement 1, adjusting the cash operating savings upward in accordance with the 6 percent inflation rate.

3. Compare your results in requirements 1 and 2. What generalization seems applicable about the analysis of inflation in capital budgeting?

P10-28 **SENSITIVITY OF CAPITAL BUDGETING TO INFLATION.** G. Esteban, the president of a Toronto trucking company, is considering whether to invest $410,000 in new semiautomatic loading equipment that will last five years, have zero scrap value, and generate cash operating savings in labour usage of $160,000 annually, using 2006 prices and wage rates. It is December 31, 2006.

The minimum desired rate of return is 18 percent per year after taxes.

1. Compute the net present value of the project. Assume a 40 percent tax rate and that the truck qualifies for Class 10, 30 percent declining balance for tax purposes.
2. Esteban is wondering if the model in requirement 1 provides a correct analysis of the effects of inflation. She maintains that the 18 percent rate embodies an element attributable to anticipated inflation. For purposes of this analysis, she assumes that the existing rate of inflation, 10 percent annually, will persist over the next five years. Repeat requirement 1, adjusting the cash operating savings upward by using the 10 percent inflation rate.
3. Which analysis, the one in requirement 1 or 2, is correct? Why?

P10-29 **INFLATION AND CAPITAL BUDGETING.** The head of the consulting division of a major firm has proposed investing $300,000 in personal computers for the staff. The useful life of the computers is five years. Computers qualify for Class 10, 30 percent declining balance. There is no terminal salvage value. Labour savings of $125,000 per year (in year-zero dollars) are expected from the purchase. The income tax rate is 45 percent, the after-tax required rate of return is 20 percent, which includes a 4 percent element attributable to inflation.

1. Compute the net present value of the computers. Use the nominal required rate of return and adjust the cash flows for inflation. (For example, year-1 cash flow = 1.04 × year-zero cash flow.)
2. Compute the net present value of the computers using the nominal required rate of return without adjusting the cash flows for inflation.
3. Compare your answers in requirements 1 and 2. Which is correct? Would using the incorrect analysis generally lead to overinvestment or underinvestment? Explain.

P10-30 **MAKE OR BUY AND REPLACEMENT OF EQUIPMENT.** Toyland Company was one of the original producers of "Transformers." An especially complex part of "Sect-a-con" needs special tools that are not useful for other products. These tools were purchased on November 16, 2003 for $200,000.

It is now July 1, 2007. The manager of the Transformer Division, Ramona Ruiz, is contemplating three alternatives. First, she could continue to produce "Sect-a-con" using the current tools; they will last another five years, at which time they would have zero terminal value. Second, she could sell the tools for $30,000 and purchase the parts from an outside supplier for $1.10 each. Third, she could replace the tools with new, more efficient tools costing $180,000.

Ruiz expects to produce 80,000 units of "Sect-a-con" in each of the next five years. Manufacturing costs for the part have been as follows, and no change in costs is expected:

Direct material	$0.38
Direct labour	0.37
Variable overhead	0.17
Fixed overhead*	0.45
Total unit cost	$1.37

* Amortization accounts for two-thirds of the fixed overhead.
The balance is for other fixed overhead costs of the factory
that require cash outlays, 60 percent of which would be
saved if production of the parts were eliminated.

The outside supplier offered the $1.10 price as a once-only offer. It is unlikely such a low price would be available later. Toyland would also have to guarantee to purchase at least 70,000 parts for each of the next five years.

The new tools that are available would last for five years with a disposal value of $40,000 at the end of five years. Tools qualify for CCA at 30 percent declining balance for tax purposes. Straight-line amortization is used for book purposes. The sales representative selling the new tools stated, "The new tools will allow direct labour and variable overhead to be reduced by $0.21 per unit." Ruiz thinks this estimate is accurate. However, she also knows that a higher quality of materials would be necessary with the new tools. She predicts the following costs with the new tools:

Direct material	$0.40
Direct labour	0.25
Variable overhead	0.08
Fixed overhead*	0.60*
Total unit cost	$1.33

* The increase in fixed overhead is caused by amortization
on the new tools.

The company has a 40 percent marginal tax rate and requires a 12 percent after-tax rate of return.

1. Calculate the net present value of each of the three alternatives. Recognize all applicable tax implications. Which alternative should Ruiz select?
2. What are some factors besides the net present value that should influence Ruiz's selection?

P10-31 **SENSITIVITY ANALYSIS.** Western Power is considering the replacement of an old billing system with new software that should save $5,000 per year in net cash operating costs. The old system has zero disposal value, but it could be used for the next 12 years. The estimated useful life of the new software is 12 years and it will cost $25,000.

1. What is the payback time?
2. Compute the internal rate of return.
3. Management is unsure about the useful life. What would be the internal rate of return if the useful life were (a) six years instead of 12, and (b) 20 years instead of 12?
4. Suppose the life will be 12 years, but the savings will be $3,000 per year instead of $5,000. What would be the rate of return?

5. Suppose the annual savings will be $4,000 for eight years. What would be the rate of return?

MANAGERIAL DECISION CASES

C10-1 **INVESTMENT IN QUALITY.** The Woolongong Manufacturing Company produces a single model of a CD player that is sold to Australian manufacturers of sound systems. Each CD player is sold for $210, resulting in a contribution margin of $70 before considering any costs of inspection, correction of product defects, or refunds to customers.

In 2006, top management at Woolongong is contemplating a change in its quality control system. Currently, $40,000 is spent annually on quality control inspections. Woolongong produces and ships 50,000 CD players a year. In producing those CD players, an average of 2,000 defective units are produced. Of these, 1,500 are identified by the inspection process, and an average of $85 is spent on each to correct the defects. The other 500 players are shipped to customers. When a customer discovers a defective CD player, Woolongong refunds the $210 purchase price.

As more and more customers change to JIT inventory systems and automated production processes, the receipt of defective goods poses greater and greater problems for them. Sometimes a defective CD player causes them to delay their whole production line while the CD player is being replaced. Companies competing with Woolongong recognize this situation, and most have already begun extensive quality control programs. If Woolongong does not improve quality, sales volume is expected to fall by 5,000 CD players a year beginning in 2008.

	PREDICTED SALES VOLUME IN UNITS WITHOUT QUALITY CONTROL PROGRAM	PREDICTED SALES VOLUME IN UNITS WITH QUALITY CONTOL PROGRAM
2007	50,000	50,000
2008	45,000	50,000
2009	40,000	50,000
2010	35,000	50,000

The proposed quality control program has two elements. First, Woolongong would spend $900,000 immediately to train workers to recognize and correct defects at the time they occur. This is expected to cut the number of defective CD players produced from 2,000 to 500 without incurring additional manufacturing costs. Second, an earlier inspection point would replace the current inspection. This would require purchase of an x-ray machine at a cost of $250,000 plus additional annual operating costs of $50,000 more than the current inspection costs. Early detection of defects would reduce the average amount spent to correct defects from $85 to $50, and only 50 defective CD players would be shipped to customers. To compete, Woolongong would refund one-and-one-half times the purchase price ($315) for defective CD players delivered to customers.

Top management at Woolongong has decided that a four-year planning period is sufficient for analyzing this decision. The minimum required rate of return is 20 percent. For simplicity, assume that under the current quality control system, if the volume of production decreases, the number of defective CD players produced remains at 2,000. Also assume that all annual cash flows occur at the end of the relevant year.

Required: Should Woolongong Manufacturing Company undertake the new quality control program? Explain, using the NPV model. Ignore income taxes.

C10-2 **FEASIBILITY ANALYSIS.** (ICAO) Ydeeps Limited was incorporated under the Ontario Business Corporations Act four months ago. The owner of Ydeeps, Mr. M. Sadim, incorporated the company because he believed that he would be investing in an automobile repair franchise. After a delay, Sadim has been able to assemble the following information about the franchise opportunity:

1. For a payment of $32,000 per year, payable at the beginning of each year, the franchisee would be entitled to exclusive rights in a territory. The franchise rights are non-transferable. Except in unusual circumstances, the payments would be made for five years, and entitle the franchisee to one repair location. In addition to the annual franchise fee, the franchisee would be required to pay an annual royalty of 3 percent of gross revenue.

2. A site is available to construct a repair facility. The land would cost $250,000 and a suitable building would cost $400,000. The building would be capable of handling about $1,500,000 of revenue per year and would have a life of 40 years. A mortgage for about $500,000 could be placed on the property at an interest rate of 12 percent per annum.

3. At the end of ten years, the repair building and land probably could be sold for $1,300,000 to $1,500,000.

4. The site that Sadim has an opportunity to invest in is in the middle of a busy region in which two taxi companies compete. Sadim believes that he would have little difficulty obtaining all of the repair work for one of the taxi companies that has 210 automobiles. He believes that a two-year contract could be signed to generate revenue of $400,000 to $450,000 per year. In addition, Sadim believes that he has a good probability of obtaining the following repair revenue from different sources:

First year	$200,000–$300,000
Thereafter, each year	$450,000–$550,000

5. In order to generate repair revenue of $900,000 per year, Sadim believes that Ydeeps' annual expenses probably would be:

Repair parts and supplies	$420,000
Labour and benefits	225,000
Salary to Sadim (owner-manager)	60,000
Heat, light, water and similar expenses	25,000
Office supplies and other expenses	5,000
Amortization on building	10,000
Amortization on tools and equipment	20,000
Interest on bank loan of $200,000	28,000
Repair shop overhead (variable)	18,000
Mortgage payments	70,000
Royalty – 3% of revenue paid to franchiser	27,000
Advertising	10,000
Franchise payment	32,000

Most of the operating costs would be variable except for Sadim's salary, advertising, and the franchise fee.

6. The franchiser has provided the following estimates of the investment (except for land and building) that would be required to support a franchisee having repair revenue of roughly $1,000,000 per year:

Equipment and tools	$200,000
Receivables due from customers	150,000
Inventory on hand	60,000
Accounts payable	10,000

7. Sadim believes that he can obtain repair work of about $300,000 per year from a car rental company, if he gives them a 20 percent discount (from the $375,000 regular price). Variable costs of repairing these cars would be similar to the costs that would be encountered to earn the $900,000 of revenue. Sadim believes that other contracts are possible if discounts are given.

Sadim would like a return on investment of 40 percent on any of the dollar investments that he personally makes. However, an overall required rate of return is estimated to be 22 percent.

Required:

Sadim has asked you to prepare a report on the feasibility of operating a repair franchise. If the franchise would not be feasible under the above conditions, explain if and how feasibility could be attained. Recommend what decisions he should make with respect to signing a contract to be a franchisee and to any other alternatives that exist. Income tax effects should be ignored.

C10-3 **CAPITAL PROJECT ANALYSIS.** (ICAO) Joan Staines is the controller of the Tage division of Canam Enterprises Ltd. William Chu, head of plant engineering, has just left Staines' office after presenting to her three alternatives for submission in the capital expenditure budget for the fiscal year 2008. The budget is due in Windsor in two days and therefore Staines realizes that time is of the essence.

Chu has outlined the following alternatives to replace an outdated milling machine: (1) build a general-purpose milling machine; (2) buy a special-purpose numerically controlled milling machine; (3) buy a general-purpose milling machine. Chu has stated that Tage does not have the expertise to build a numerically controlled milling machine.

Background

Canam Enterprises Ltd. is a well-established company. The company was set up about 25 years ago by brothers Al and Steve Jablonski, in Windsor, Ontario, to produce accessories for the automobile industry. The Alpha division continues to serve the auto industry, and is the largest division in the company with sales of $35 million annually. Al's son now heads this division. Steve is still active in the company and is the chief executive officer (CEO). His office is located in the Alpha division's Windsor factory.

The Monte division supplies seals to the mining and petrochemical industry from a plant in Toronto. This division is only ten years old and until 2004 was highly profitable. As a result of the downturn in this sector of the economy, sales in 2006 were only $12 million.

The Tage division, located in Scarborough, is the engineering division. Regular product lines include industrial fans, industrial cooling units, and refrigeration units for industrial uses. The division is highly capital-intensive and sales tend to be directly related to general economic conditions.

Each division is run independently and performance is based upon budgeted return on investment. Bonuses are paid if the budget target is achieved. Annually, each division prepares a detailed budget submission to Steve, outlining expected profit performance and capital expenditure requests. The milling machine proposal is part of the capital expenditure request.

The 2007 pro forma income statement for Tage division is set out below:

Sales		$22,364,000
Cost of goods sold		14,760,240
Gross profit		7,603,760
Selling and general administrative costs		3,578,240
Allocated costs (based on sales)		1,677,300
		5,255,540
Income before income taxes		$ 2,348,220
Return on sales	10.5%	
Return on investment	8.5%	
Investment (historical cost)		$27,626,118

The Proposed Purchase

Chu has pointed out to Staines that the existing machine is not only outdated but maintenance costs are becoming prohibitive. The machine has no market or salvage value and he is sure that its book value is now zero. The trouble is that he doesn't know which proposal is best for the company. In addition to the cost and revenue data provided in Exhibit 10A-1, Chu provided comments on each alternative.

1. Build a general-purpose machine.

This machine can be built by the Tage division. The division is below capacity at present as a major contract has just been completed. The division could thus produce the machine without affecting revenue-producing activity, but it will take six months to complete. The machine is expected to last five years and have no salvage value because removal costs will probably equal selling price.

Chu believes that the division has the technical expertise to undertake the work. In 2006, the division produced a specialized drilling machine that has proven very successful. Chu pointed out that David Williams, chief engineer, loves the design challenge of new machines.

Staines sat down with Chu and produced the following cost estimates:

Material and parts	$ 55,000
Direct labour (DL$)	90,000
Variable overhead (50% of DL$)	45,000
Fixed overhead (25% of DL$)	22,500
	$212,500

Staines argues that this job should also bear a proportion of administrative costs; she suggests $12,000.

2. Buy a special-purpose machine.

The advantage of the special-purpose machine is that only one operator is required and output per hour could increase by 25 percent. In addition, maintenance costs are significantly reduced because microchip circuitry is employed.

Chu points out that this machine is state-of-the-art and would probably mean that new work could be taken on. A numerically controlled machine requires extensive training of operators. In total, 26 weeks are spent in the supplier's factory located in Minneapolis. While the training is going on, the supplier provides an operator to work the machine without charge. Expected costs of this training period including hotel, per diem, and travel will cost $3,000 per week, excluding the operator's labour.

The machine costs $625,000, and the supplier guarantees the salvage value of $25,000 at the end of five years. It is available immediately.

3. Buy a general-purpose machine.

The purchase price of this machine is $295,000 and cost levels associated with the machine are expected to be the same as the general-purpose machine built by the company because the technology is similar. The salvage value of the machine net of removal costs, is estimated to be $5,000 in five years. It can be delivered immediately.

General Comments

The required rate of return for this investment class has been set at 8 percent by Steve Jablonski.

Required:

Prepare a budget submission to Jablonski outlining the qualitative and quantitative analysis required. Ignore income taxes. Outline the assumptions you have employed and your recommended course of actions.

EXHIBIT 10A-1

Cost and Revenue Data on an Annual Basis*

	GENERAL PURPOSE EQUIPMENT	SPECIAL PURPOSE
Supervisor	$20,000	$20,000
Operators – required	2	1
– wages and benefits	$15.00/hour	$15.00/hour
Insurance	$3,000	$5,000
Maintenance	$26,000	$12,000
Capacity (sales)	$195,000	$243,750
Direct materials	$19,500	$19,500
Variable overhead	50% of DL$	50% of DL$
Fixed overhead (including amortization)	25% of DL$	25% of DL$
Amortization method	5 years straight line	5 years straight line

* Assumes single-shift operation will continue.

C10-4 CAPITAL BUDGETING. (CICA) Steve Hammer started his contracting business, Hammer Contractors (HC), six years ago and now owns three machines: a bulldozer, an excavator, and a front-end loader. His business is primarily excavating, landscaping, and moving earth. His sole proprietorship has a year-end of December 31. He employs three full-time people, and his wife, Judy, does all the bookkeeping and office work on a part-time basis. HC has been quite successful. According to Judy's figures, the business earned $86,000 before amortization in 2006 after deducting $26,000 of "salary" paid to Steve.

Steve and Judy have no training in accounting or financial matters and have approached you, early in 2007, for assistance in deciding whether a new grader should be purchased.

Some of HC's jobs are obtained by sealed tender but others are from repeat customers who like Steve's reliability and ability to offer full service. Steve wants to extend this service by purchasing a grader in time for the spring construction season. He has made the following estimates about the new grader:

Cost of machine	$110,000
Useful life	10 years
Value at the end of 10 years	$ 20,000
Operating costs per hour:	
Operator's wage	$14.00
Fuel	16.00
On-job maintenance	8.00
	$38.00

Major repair expenses were predicted by his dealer to be $6,000 in Year 4, $20,000 in Year 6 and $28,000 in Year 9. Insurance on the machine is expected to amount to $2,400 a year.

Steve estimates that on some jobs he can charge $60 per hour for use of this machine. However, other jobs are very competitive and he would like to know how low he could drop his price on the grader before he starts losing money.

Steve estimates about 2,000 hours use from the grader yearly.

Required: Draft a report to Steve Hammer that analyzes the issue and provides your recommendation. Assume a required rate of return of 10 percent, an income tax rate of 35 percent, and a capital cost allowance of 25 percent.

C10-5 CAPITAL BUDGETING. (CICA) Tube and Pipe Ltd. (T & P) was founded in the early seventies and its sales grew very rapidly until the beginning of the eighties. At that time, several competitors expanded their operations, and sales by T & P stabilized.

T & P uses substantial amounts of electricity in its manufacturing process. Therefore, the company had built a power plant that supplies all its electricity needs.

Annual consumption of electricity over the last two years has reached 9,300,000 kilowatt-hours (kWh). The annual production cost of electricity was $492,000 as follows:

Fuel	$201,000
Other variable costs	195,000
Property tax	15,000
Manager of the power plant	51,000
Amortization	30,000
Total	$492,000

In June 2006, Regional Hydro Ltd. approached T & P with an offer to supply all of its electricity needs. Regional Hydro will guarantee the supply for the next 20 years, but each party has the option of cancelling the agreement after ten years.

If T & P signs the contract, it can sell its own power plant for $180,000. The book value of the plant is currently $300,000. In June 2006, the remaining life of the generators in the plant is 20 years. At the end of the tenth year, the generators must be given a major overhaul that would cost $450,000.

According to the proposed agreement, Regional Hydro will transfer the necessary power from its main plant to a secondary station that T & P will build. The secondary station will cost $1,200,000, its estimated life is 20 years, and it will have no salvage value. The firm will receive a 5 percent rebate on the cost of the secondary station from the government. The secondary station will convert the electricity from alternating current into direct current that T & P requires. The cost of electricity will be 1.5 cents per kWh and T & P is required to purchase at least 8,000,000 kWh annually. The maximum amount of electricity it can purchase is 10,000,000 kWh per year. T & P will pay the secondary station operation expenses (excluding amortization) of $30,000 annually.

Management of T & P decided that if it sells its power plant, the manager would be transferred to another department in need of a manager. It estimated that a new manager for the department would cost the company $45,000 a year, but the salary of the manager of the power plant will not change if he is transferred to the other department. Other employees of the power plant will be dismissed (their salaries are included in the "other variable costs" figure above).

Required:

For simplification, assume that the CCA rate is 6 percent (Class 2), and all capital assets are in the same class for income tax purposes. Also assume that the corporate tax rate is 40 percent.

Assume that the after-tax cost of capital is 12 percent. Prepare a report to the management of T & P advising them whether they should enter into the agreement with Regional Hydro.

C10-6 **RELEVANT COST INVESTMENT ANALYSIS.** (ICAO) Desteur Plastics Limited (DPL) manufactures a wide range of household plastic products for kitchens and bathrooms. The company's products are sold primarily to large retailers, including department stores, discount chains, and grocery chains. One of DPL's products is a line of plastic dishware that is sold prepackaged as four-piece place settings. DPL sells the dishes to the retailers at $8 per set, and has in recent years been operating at or near the limited capacity of the equipment, which is approximately 500,000 sets per year.

The costs of producing the dishes have been determined by DPL's bookkeeper as follows:

Material	$2.00 per set
Direct labour	1.60
Factor overheads:	
Assignable variable	0.60
Allocated fixed	0.40
Equipment amortization	0.15
Selling, delivery, and administration	0.20
Total cost per set	$4.95

The selling, delivery, and administration costs are those that are identifiable with the product, and are essentially variable.

The equipment used for the dishes is old and substantially amortized, and will have to be retired or replaced within the next two years. Its present book value is $130,000, although it would probably fetch only about $15,000 scrap value (or twice that on a trade-in). The equipment has no other uses within DPL.

A major grocery chain that is not a regular customer of DPL approached the company in late 2007 and offered to buy 700,000 sets per year for at least four years to use in special promotions commencing the following June 2008. The additional sets would be identical to DPL's regular line, except that the packaging would bear the grocery chain's name and teddy bear logo. The chain proposes to buy the special sets for $5 per set. They would be priced in the stores at two-thirds the price of the regular line.

Since DPL does not presently have the capacity to produce the additional sets, they would have to buy additional dish-making capacity if the company decides to accept the order. Rather than supplement the current capacity, DPL proposes to retire the old equipment and to buy new equipment that has triple the capacity of the old. This would allow for possible expansion of the regular line as well as provide the capacity for both the regular and the special dishes.

The DPL plant manager estimates that if the new equipment were purchased, the greater efficiency of the machine would permit a 10 percent savings in material cost and 25 percent savings in labour cost. Amortization, however, would go from $0.15 per set to $0.40 per set, and there would also be the added cost of the interest on the loan to buy the new equipment. The bookkeeper has also pointed out that the fixed overhead allocation would increase because the allocation is based partially on the cost of the equipment in use. The estimated cost per set to produce the additional 700,000 sets is estimated as follows:

Material	$1.80
Direct labour	1.20
Factor overheads:	
Assignable variable	0.50
Allocated fixed	0.64
Equipment amortization	0.40
Selling, delivery, and administration	0.10
Interest on loan	0.41
Total per set	$5.05

The selling, delivery and administration cost is less per set on the special 700,000 set order, but the cost of servicing the regular line would not change. The interest cost is 12 percent per annum on the $2,400,000 loan that would be required to purchase the new equipment, divided by the 700,000 additional sets. The total cost of the new equipment is $3,000,000.

DPL's cost of capital is 14 percent after income tax. The new equipment would probably be purchased by means of a bank term loan with a five-year term, although DPL would also be willing to consider a long-term lease arrangement through its bank's leasing subsidiary. DPL's fiscal year ends on December 31.

Required: Perform the necessary calculations to determine whether DPL should accept the offer for the 700,000 additional sets of dishes per year. Indicate what uncertainties exist and what qualitative factors are important in this decision.

Assume a 40 percent tax rate. The new equipment is in Class 39 for CCA. The CCA rate in Class 39 is 30 percent for 2008, dropping to 25 percent for 2009 and later years. The half-year rule applies.

C10-7 **CAPITAL BUDGETING AND INFLATION.** (Braithwaite) In November 2006, Charles Bird, President of Bird Packaging Co., Guelph, Ontario, was trying to decide whether the company should purchase a new scoring-printing machine. The attraction of the new machine was that it would double capacity and also reduce labour costs. However, the relatively large capital outlay and the uncertainty of projected sales concerned Bird so he was anxious for a thorough and careful analysis of future cash flows.

Bird Packaging is a small firm, which caters to the packaging needs of small and medium-sized firms within an 80-kilometre radius of Guelph, including the cities of Hamilton, Kitchener-Waterloo, and Mississauga. Bird Packaging was established about ten years ago with first-year sales of $120,000. Sales in 2006 were projected to reach $1,900,000. The present workforce comprises 24 employees. Its operations include cutting, folding, and printing boxes. Bird Packaging stresses service as its main selling point; this includes custom box sizes, printing, and fast delivery. According to Charles Bird, "If a prospective customer just wants boxes, we send him to Domtar or MacMillan-Bloedel." In effect, Bird Packaging has carved out a niche for itself, dealing with customers who require different types of services, along with the actual box.

Although Bird Packaging expected sales of $1.9 million in 2006, Bird estimated that the sales attributable to the present machine were only $400,000, since this represents its production capacity on a one-shift basis. If the new investment were not undertaken, this sales level would remain constant in real dollar terms, but would grow by the full inflation rate in nominal terms. If the new machine was purchased, Bird expected sales to increase by $400,000 in real terms over the next five years, but even he admitted that this outcome was far from certain.

Materials were approximately 55 percent of sales, and were expected to remain at the same percentage regardless of sales volume. Bird estimated that manufacturing overhead was presently 10.7 percent of sales, 80 percent of this overhead (0.086 of sales) was fixed, and 20 percent (0.021 of sales) was variable. Labour costs were considered 100 percent variable, and were expected to fall from 12 percent of sales to 10 percent of sales. This labour savings results from a decrease in time required for setup and an increase in speed of production runs. Fewer people would be needed to run the new machine at higher production rates.

Selling expenses were presently 10.7 percent of sales, of which 80 percent is fixed and 20 percent is variable (similar to manufacturing overhead). Administrative overhead was budgeted at $33,200 for 2006 and was considered by Bird to be totally fixed.

Bird Packaging was subject to the small business tax rate of 20 percent and was expected to qualify for this reduced rate over the life of the investment.

The new machine would cost $120,000 plus installation costs of $10,000. The company used five years as the expected life for all equipment purchases. Bird estimated that the new machine could be sold for $120,000 at the end of the five-year period. The salvage value was expected to remain the same as the purchase price because there are few technological advances in this type of machinery and any amortization on the machine would be offset by price increases due to inflation. The salvage value of the old machine was $17,000. Assume a capital cost allowance rate of 30 percent.

The minimum required rate of return for the firm was estimated between 15 and 20 percent, depending upon the expected future rate of inflation and interest costs selected.

The last federal budget predicted that inflation would peak at 6 percent in 2006 and would then fall continuously to between 3 and 5 percent in 2007.

Bird prided himself on the company's ability to fill orders much more quickly than competitors. The new machine would enable the company to improve its service in this area. The new machine would also provide a boost to the morale of Bird Packaging's employees, who would benefit from both the change and the increased ease of operation. Workers tended to identify with the company, so when production ran smoothly, job satisfaction was increased.

Required: | Should Bird buy the new machine?

C10-8 **CAPITAL BUDGETING AND SENSITIVITY ANALYSIS.** (SMAC) Lemont Electronics Limited is a Canadian public corporation that manufactures special electronic steering systems for various types of vehicles. Lemont's sales have grown steadily since it was incorporated. The draft financial statements for 2007, however, show a net income of $1,685,600, which is a decrease in profits for the first time (see Exhibit 10A-2).

Recently, Lemont was awarded a large contract with DOF Motor Company, a large North American automobile manufacturer. The contract is for 100,000 electronic steering systems, 40 percent to be delivered to DOF uniformly throughout 2008 and 60 percent to be delivered uniformly throughout 2009. In order to accommodate this contract, Lemont is required to make a capital investment of $5,000,000 for specialized manufacturing equipment. After two years, this equipment can be adapted to the regular production process. Net-present-value analysis indicates that investment in this equipment is worthwhile. However, Lemont has insufficient cash to pay for the equipment and, since it cannot lease the equipment and DOF is not prepared to advance any funds, Lemont's president decided to meet with the bank manager to arrange the necessary financing.

President: As you know, four years ago you helped to finance a replacement of all of Lemont's manufacturing equipment. Now, we've won a large contract with DOF, a large automobile manufacturer, but, to fill the order, we need to buy some special equipment. Will the bank finance the $5,000,000 we need for the special equipment?

Bank manager: I've seen your 2007 draft financial statements, which indicate that profits are down. Also, your cash position could be better. What are your total sales expectations for 2008?

President: The DOF contract is for $25,000,000 over two years, which is a good start. Other than that, I'm not sure since sales depend on what other contracts we win. Some new foreign competition has invaded the market by undercutting domestic manufacturers. We've had to cut our bids to a minimum in order to compete. That's why our profits dropped for 2007. This new competition is making it increasingly difficult to predict sales. There's simply no way to anticipate which contracts we'll win. All we can do is adjust our bidding policy to try to maximize capacity utilization.

EXHIBIT 10A-2

Draft (Summarized)
2007 Financial
Statements
Lemont Electronics
Limited
Balance Sheet as at
December 31, 2007

ASSETS

Current assets:		
Cash	$ 200,000	
Accounts receivable	10,000,000	
Inventory	10,000,000	$20,200,000
Fixed assets:		
Machinery and equipment	70,000,000	
Less accumulated amortization	(28,000,000)	42,000,000
Total assets		$62,200,000

LIABILITIES AND SHAREHOLDERS' EQUITY

Current liabilities:			
Accounts payable			$ 2,736,000
Long-term liabilities:			
Bank loan payable (Note 1)			30,000,000
Shareholders' equity:			
Common shares		$12,500,000	
Retained earnings			
Opening balance	$15,778,400		
2007 net income	1,685,600		
2007 dividends	(500,000)	16,964,000	29,464,000
Total liabilities and shareholders' equity			$62,200,000

Lemont Electronics
Limited
Operating Statement
for the Year Ended
December 31, 2007

Sales:		$60,000,000
Manufacturing cost of goods sold:		
Variable manufacturing cost	$30,000,000	
Machinery and equipment amortization	7,000,000	
Fixed manufacturing overhead	8,000,000	45,000,000
Gross margin		15,000,000
Expenses:		
Variable selling and administration expenses	4,200,000	
Interest expense (Note 1)	4,200,000	
Fixed selling and administration expenses	4,500,000	12,900,000
Income before taxes		2,100,000
Income taxes (Note 2)		414,400
Net income		$ 1,685,600

1. In January 2003, the bank loaned Lemont $50,000,000 to help finance replacement of its equipment. The terms of the loan stipulated that a payment of $5,000,000 plus interest be made at the end of each year for ten years. The annual interest rate was set at 12 percent.
2. Income taxes were calculated as 40 percent times taxable income as follows:

Income before taxes	$2,100,000
Plus amortization	7,000,000
Less CCA (UCC of 40,320,000 × 20%)	8,064,000
Taxable income	1,036,000
Times tax rate	× 0.40
Income taxes	$ 414,400

Bank manager: Well, the bank will need a cash budget for at least 2008 before it will consider lending Lemont any more money.

President: The last time we prepared any kind of budget was for you four years ago. You saw how useless that was. Sales turned out to be lower and expenses higher than the budget. That's why we don't have any cash now to finance the new equipment. We even had to reduce dividends to $500,000 in 2007 in order to maintain our $200,000 minimum cash balance.

Bank manager: You'll just have to do your best to estimate sales. Are there any other major factors that would affect cash flow over the next few years?

President: Only a reasonable increase in fixed costs. Under the circumstances, we will continue to pay dividends of $500,000 annually until cash flow has improved. It is doubtful that sales will increase sufficiently to necessitate further capital expenditure other than the $5,000,000 that we need now.

Bank manager: If the loan is approved, the bank would prefer that it be repaid within two years at an interest rate of 12 percent per year payable at the end of each year. Next Monday, I'll expect to see a cash budget to support your loan request.

The next day, the president asked Lemont's newly appointed controller for his advice on how best to finance the required equipment purchase. After being briefed on the president's meeting with the bank manager, the controller indicated that he would conduct a quick initial analysis and present his preliminary findings within 24 hours.

Back in his office, the controller decided that his initial analysis should consist of the following:

1. Preparation of a draft cash budget for 2008.
2. Analysis of Lemont's general financial planning and control system, and identification of alternatives for improvement.

The controller then gathered some data on which to base his cash budget (see Exhibit 10A-3 on the next page).

Required: | As Lemont's newly appointed controller, what would you recommend?

C10-9 **CAPITAL BUDGETING.** (CGAC) Calgary Pipefitters Ltd. (CPL) is considering the purchase of a new fabricating machine for $40,000. The new machine will replace an old machine that has a book value of $10,000 but can be sold for $7,500. The new machine has an estimated life of five years, after which it would have a salvage value of $5,000. The operating cost of the new machine is estimated at $12,500 per annum. This machine will be in Class 8 (with a 20 percent CCA rate), the firm's marginal tax rate is 30 percent, and the cost of capital is 15 percent.

As an alternative to the new machine, CPL could overhaul the existing machine at a cost of $25,000. With this overhaul, the machine will cost $15,000 per year to operate, will last for five years, and will have zero salvage value at the end of its life. The existing machine is in Class 8 and the firm expects to always have assets in this class.

The new machine may be leased at a cost of $12,000 per year payable in advance. The leasing company will not be responsible for any operating or maintenance costs. Alternatively, CPL can obtain a five-year loan at 10 percent from its bank to finance the new machine.

Should the new machine be acquired? Why?

EXHIBIT 10A-3

Underlying Data for 2008 Cash Budget

Sales:

DOF contract, 2008, 40,000 units @ $250/unit = $10,000,000

Other sales—The president estimated that sales for 2008, other than the DOF contract, would be as follows:

Low	$40,000,000
Most likely	$50,000,000
High	$60,000,000

Manufacturing cost of goods sold:

For all sales, including the DOF contract, the relationship of variable manufacturing cost of goods-sold dollars to sales dollars is expected to be the same as for 2007.

If the new equipment is purchased, related fixed manufacturing overhead of $750,000 will be required in 2008. Fixed manufacturing overhead related to current operations for 2008 is expected to be 5 percent greater than for 2007.

Both the existing machinery and equipment and the new special equipment have useful lives of ten years and are amortized on a straight-line basis. The net disposal costs are expected to be zero. The CCA rate for all machinery and equipment owned by Lemont, including the new special equipment, is 20 percent declining balance.

Selling and administration expenses:

For all sales, including the DOF contract, the relationship of variable selling and administration expenses dollars to sales dollars is expected to be the same as for 2007.

If the DOF contract is accepted, related fixed selling and administration expenses of $300,000 will be required in 2008. Fixed selling and administrative expenses related to current operations for 2008 are expected to be 5 percent greater than for 2007.

Working capital:

Sales are made uniformly over the year and all customers, including DOF, pay 60 days after delivery. Lemont's policy is to maintain a minimum cash balance of $200,000 and inventory levels are expected to be maintained at the $10,000,000 level.

The average accounts payable balance will be maintained at 8 percent of the total variable costs (i.e., variable manufacturing, selling and administration costs) incurred during the year. All fixed costs are paid in the year they are incurred.

EXCEL APPLICATION EXERCISE

E10-1 **NET PRESENT VALUE AND PAYBACK PERIOD FOR A PURCHASE DECISION.**

Goal: Create a spreadsheet to compute the net present value and payback period to assist with a purchase decision. Ignore taxes and capital cost allowance issues. Use the results to answer questions about your findings.

Scenario: Amazon is considering the purchase a new bar-coding machine for one of its warehouses. You have been asked to prepare a simple analysis to determine whether the machine should be purchased. The bar-coding machine costs $60,000. It has a five-year economic life and an estimated residual value of $10,000. The estimated annual net cash flow from the machine is $16,000. Amazon's required rate of return is 16 percent.

When you have completed your spreadsheet, answer the following questions:

1. What is the machine's net present value (NPV)?

2. What is the machine's payback period?

3. Should Amazon purchase the machine? Why or why not?

Step by Step:

1. Open a new Excel spreadsheet.

2. In column A, create a bold-faced heading that contains the following:
   Row 1: Chapter 10 Decision Guideline
   Row 2: Amazon
   Row 3: Analysis for Purchase of Bar-Coding Machine
   Row 4: Today's Date

3. Merge and centre the four heading rows across columns A through H.

4. In row 7, create the following bold-faced headings:
   Column A: Cash Outflow
   Column B: Calculations
   Column D: Annualized Cash Flows

5. Centre the heading in column A, row 7 and then shade the heading as follows:
   Patterns tab: Colour: Lightest grey (above white)

   Note: Adjust column width as necessary.

6. Merge and centre the heading in column B, row 7 across columns B through C.

7. Merge and centre the heading in column D, row 7 across columns D through H and shade the heading as follows:
   Patterns tab: Colour: Lightest grey (above white)

8. In row 8, create the following bold-faced, centre-justified column headings:
   Column A: Investment
   Column B: Net Present Value
   Column C: Payback Period
   Column D: Year 1
   Column E: Year 2
   Column F: Year 3
   Column G: Year 4
   Column H: Year 5

   Note: Adjust the width of columns B and C as necessary.

9. Use the scenario data to fill in the investment and annualized cash flows for each of the five years.

   Note: The amount in the Investment column should be entered as a negative amount because it represents cash outflow. Be sure to include the machine's residual value in the appropriate column when entering the Annualized Cash Flows data.

10. Use the NPV function to calculate the net present value of the machine in column B, row 9. Click Insert on the tool bar and select Function. Then do the following:

Function category: Financial
Function name: NPV

Complete the fill-in form that appears with the appropriate data from the scenario.

Hint: Go to "Help" and search the topic "NPV." Review the help text that appears. Carefully read the examples given and their associated formulas. Use the formula that matches the scenario data for the problem.

11. Enter a formula to calculate the payback period in column C, row 9. Ensure a positive result by using the absolute value function in your payback formula. (The formula can be found in the chapter.)

12. Modify the format of the payback period result by clicking in the cell containing the results. At the end of the formula that appears in the formula bar, type the following: & " years"

Right justify the result.

13. Format row 9, columns A through B and columns D through H as Number tab:

Category: Currency
Decimal places: 2
Symbol: $
Negative numbers: Red with parentheses

14. Save your work to disk, and print a copy for your files.

Note: Print your spreadsheet using landscape to ensure that all columns appear on one page.

COLLABORATIVE LEARNING EXERCISE

CL10-1   **CAPITAL BUDGETING, SENSITIVITY ANALYSIS, AND ETHICS.** Muriel Santelli had recently been appointed controller of the breakfast cereals division of a major food company. The division manager, Ram Krishnamurthi, was known as a hard-driving, intelligent, uncompromising manager. He had been very successful and was rumoured to be on the fast track to corporate top management, maybe even in line for the company presidency. One of Santelli's first assignments was to prepare the financial analysis for a new cold cereal, Krispie Krinkles. This product was especially important to Krishnamurthi because he was convinced that it would be a success and thereby a springboard for his ascent to top management.

Santelli discussed the product with the food lab that had designed it, with the market research department that had tested it, and with the finance people who would have to fund its introduction. After putting together all the information, she developed the following optimistic and pessimistic sales projections:

	Optimistic	Pessimistic
Year 1	$ 1,600,000	$ 800,000
Year 2	3,600,000	1,200,000
Year 3	5,000,000	1,000,000
Year 4	8,000,000	800,000
Year 5	10,000,000	400,000

The optimistic predictions assume a successful introduction of a popular product. The pessimistic predictions assume that the product is introduced but does not gain wide acceptance and is terminated after five years. Santelli thinks the most likely results are halfway between the optimistic and pessimistic predictions.

Santelli learned from finance that this type of product introduction requires a predicted rate of return of 16 percent before top management will authorize funds for its introduction. She also determined that the contribution margin should be about 50 percent on the product, but could be as low as 42 percent or as high as 58 percent. Initial investment would include $3 million for production facilities, $2.5 million for advertising and other product introduction expenses, and $500,000 for working capital (inventory, etc.). The production facilities would have a value of $800,000 after five years.

Based on her preliminary analysis, Santelli recommended to Krishnamurthi that the product not be launched. Krishnamurthi was not pleased with the recommendation. He claimed that Santelli was much too pessimistic and asked her to redo her numbers so that he could justify the product to top management.

Santelli carried out further analysis, but her predictions came out no different. In fact, she became even more convinced that her projections were accurate. Yet, she was certain that if she returned to Krishnamurthi with numbers that did not support introduction of the product, she would incur his wrath. And, in fact, he could be right—that is, there is so much uncertainty in the forecasts that she could easily come up with believable numbers that would support going forward with the product. She would not believe them, but she believed she could convince top management that they were accurate.

The entire class could role-play this scenario, or it could be done in teams of three to six persons. Here, it is acted out by a team.

Choose one member of the team to be Muriel Santelli and one to be Ram Krishnamurthi.

1. With the help of the entire team except the person chosen to be Krishnamurthi, Santelli should prepare the capital-budgeting analysis used for her first meeting with Krishnamurthi.
2. Next, Santelli should meet again with Krishnamurthi. They should try to agree on the analysis to take forward to top management. As they discuss the issues and try to come to an agreement, the remaining team members should record all the ethical judgments each discussant makes.
3. After Santelli and Krishnamurthi have completed their role-playing assignment, the entire team should assess the ethical judgments made by each and recommend an appropriate position for Santelli to take in this situation.

The Master Budget

LEARNING OBJECTIVES

After studying this chapter, you will be able to

1. Explain the major features and advantages of a master budget.

2. Distinguish between operating and financial budgets.

3. Follow the principal steps in preparing a master budget.

4. Prepare the operating budget, the financial budget, and the supporting schedules.

5. Understand the difficulties of sales forecasting and human behaviour problems in formulating and implementing budgets.

6. Identify the uses of a financial planning model.

7. Use a spreadsheet to develop a budget (Appendix).

Planning is the key to good management. This is true for all organizations: small family-owned companies, new high-technology companies, large corporations, government agencies, not-for-profit companies, as well as individuals. For example, most successful students, who earn good grades, finance their education, and finish their degrees in a reasonable amount of time, do so in part because they are able to plan their time, work, recreation, and social activities. These students are *budgeting* their scarce resources in order to make the best use of their time, money, and energy. Likewise, owners of successful small companies who survive and grow even in difficult economic times carefully plan or budget their inventory purchases and their expansion of facilities so that they do not overextend themselves financially but can still meet customers' needs.

Firms are often started by highly intelligent and motivated people who have valuable product ideas, but the firms that thrive are those whose managers also have superior planning and budgeting skills. Coordinating the use of scarce resources in a large, diverse corporation is an extremely complex and vital activity. Budgeting in large corporations takes place throughout the year. Taxpayers demand that governments plan for the effective use of their hard-earned dollars, so government budgeting is especially important in difficult economic times, when tax dollars could otherwise have been spent for private purposes. Not-for-profit organizations must develop more effective plans to achieve their objectives as they compete for scarce donations or grant monies. Not only are budgets critical to good planning in any endeavour, they are necessary for evaluation of performance. A **budget**—a formal, quantitative expression of plans (whether for an individual, business, or other organization)—provides a benchmark against which to measure actual performance.

As you will see in this chapter, a budget can be much more than a limit on expenditures. While government agencies too often use a budget merely as a limit on their spending, businesses and other organizations generally use budgets to focus on operating or financial problems early, so that managers can take steps to avoid or remedy the problems. Thus a budget is a tool that helps managers both *plan* and *control* operations. Advocates of budgeting maintain that the process of budgeting *forces a manager to become a better administrator and puts planning in the forefront of the manager's mind.* Indeed, failure to draw up, monitor, and adjust budgets to changing conditions is one of the primary reasons behind the collapse of many businesses.

In this chapter we will look at all major aspects of budgeting and how to construct a master budget.

Budget. A quantitative expression of a plan of action, aids in coordinating and implementing the plan.

BUDGETS: WHAT THEY ARE AND HOW THEY BENEFIT THE ORGANIZATION

OBJECTIVE 1

Explain the major features and advantages of a master budget.

A budget may be described as a condensed business plan for the forthcoming year. Few investors or bank loan officers today will provide funds for the would-be entrepreneur without a credible business plan including a cash-flow budget. Similarly, within a firm, managers need budgets to guide them in allocating resources and maintaining control and to enable them to measure and reward progress.

Types of Budgets

Strategic Plan. A plan that sets the overall goals and objectives of the organization.

Long-Range Planning. Producing forecasted economic targets and/or financial statements for five- or ten-year periods.

Capital Budgets. Budgets that detail the planned expenditures for facilities, equipment, new products, and other long-term investments.

Master Budget. A budget that summarizes the planned activities of all subunits of an organization from the very first stage of production to the delivery of goods to the consumer.

Pro Forma Financial Statements. The planned financial statements based upon the planned activities in the master budget.

Continuous Budget (Rolling Budget). A common form of master budget that adds a month at the end of the budget period as a month ends.

There are several different types of budgets used by organizations. The most forward-looking budget is the **strategic plan**, which sets the overall goals and objectives of the organization.

Some business analysts won't classify the strategic plan as an actual budget, though, because it does not deal with a specific time frame, and it does not produce forecasted financial statements. In any case, the strategic plan leads to **long-range planning**, which produces forecasted financial targets for five-to-ten-year periods. The financial statements are estimates of what management would like to see in the company's future financial statements.

Decisions made during long-range planning include addition or deletion of product lines, design and location of new plants, acquisitions of buildings and equipment, and other long-term commitments. Long-range plans are coordinated with **capital budgets**, which detail the planned expenditures for facilities, equipment, new products, and other long-term investments. Capital budgeting was covered in Chapter 10.

Long-range plans and budgets give the organization direction and goals for the future, while short-term plans and budgets guide day-to-day operations. Managers who pay attention only to short-term budgets will quickly lose sight of long-term goals. Similarly, managers who pay attention only to the long-term budget could wind up mismanaging day-to-day operations. There has to be a happy medium that allows managers to pay attention to their short-term budgets while still keeping an eye on long-term plans.

A **master budget** summarizes the planned activities of all subunits of an organization—sales, production, distribution, and finance—starting with the very first stage of production to the delivery of goods to the consumer. The master budget quantifies targets for sales, cost-driver activity, purchases, production, net income, and cash position, and any other objective that management specifies. It ends up expressing these amounts in the form of forecasted financial statements. These supporting schedules provide the information that is too highly detailed to appear in the actual financial statements. *Thus, the master budget is a periodic business plan that includes a coordinated set of detailed operating schedules and financial statements, including cash receipts and disbursements.* Sometimes master budgets are also called **pro forma financial statements**, another term for forecasted financial statements. Management might prepare monthly budgets for the year or, perhaps, only the first quarter and quarterly budgets for the three remaining quarters. Individual managers also may prepare daily or weekly *task-oriented* budgets to help them carry out their particular functions and meet operating and financial goals.

Continuous budgets (rolling budgets) are a very common form of master budget that adds a month at the end of the budget period. Continuous annual budgets compel managers to think specifically about the forthcoming 12 months and thus maintain a stable planning horizon. As they add a new 12th month to a continuous budget, managers may update the other 11 months as well. Then they can compare actual monthly results with both the original plan and the most recently revised plan.

Level 3 Communications, based in Broomfield, Colorado,[1] is one of the largest providers of whole-sale dial-up service to ISPs in North America and is the primary provider of Internet connectivity for millions of broadband subscribers through its cable and DSL partners. The company has incurred losses for several years. Over the past few years, its annual losses from continuing operations are as follows:

(millions of dollars)

2004	$458
2003	$721
2002	$860
2001	$4,373

Suppose company management budgeted that continuing operations would break even in 2004. Evaluate performance in 2004.

ANSWER

Comparing Level 3's performance in 2004 to 2003 and prior years makes it appear that there is a continuous pattern of improvement. However, the results in 2004 were in fact $458 million worse than budgeted. Furthermore, given the pattern of losses, a question arises as to whether it was at all reasonable to budget for anything other than a smaller loss in 2004, as compared to 2003. Further investigation is required; for example, how did management of Level 3 explain the losses in each of the four years? Why did the losses decrease so dramatically between 2001 and 2002?

Advantages of Budgets

Sometimes plans and budgets are unwritten, especially in small organizations. As an organization grows, however, informal, seat-of-the-pants planning is not enough. A more formal budgetary system becomes a necessity.

Sceptical managers have claimed, "I face too many uncertainties and complications to make budgeting worthwhile for me." Be wary of such claims. Planning and budgeting are especially important in uncertain environments. A budget allows *systematic rather than chaotic reaction to change*. For example, an oil company may increase a planned expansion in reaction to a worldwide shortage of oil and gas. Management may use the business planning process to adjust to changes in environmental conditions.

There are three major benefits of budgeting.

1. It compels management to formalize responsibilities for planning.
2. It provides definite expectations that are the best framework for judging subsequent performance.
3. It aids managers in coordinating their efforts, so that the objectives of the organization as a whole match the objectives of its parts.

Let's look more closely at each of these benefits.

---

[1] Canadian companies providing comparable services are often privately or cooperatively run, and include Montreal-based Inter.net Canada (www.ca.inter.net), Victoria, B.C.-based Islandnet.com (www.islandnet.com), and Saskatchewan-based Access Communications Cooperative (www.access comm.ca).

Formalization of Planning

Budgeting forces managers to think ahead—to anticipate and prepare for changing conditions. The budgeting process makes planning an *explicit* management responsibility. Too often, managers operate from day to day, extinguishing one business brush fire after another. They simply have "no time" for any tough-minded thinking beyond the next day's problems. Planning takes a back seat to, or is actually obliterated by, daily pressures.

The trouble with the day-to-day approach to managing an organization is that objectives are never crystallized. Managers react to current events rather than plan for the future. To prepare a budget, a manager should set goals and objectives and establish policies to aid their achievement. The objectives are the destination points, and budgets are the roadmaps guiding us to those destinations. Without goals and objectives, company operations lack direction; problems are not foreseen; and results are hard to interpret afterward.

Framework for Judging Performance

Budgeted goals and performance are generally a better basis for judging actual results than is past performance. The news that a company had sales of $100 million this year, compared with $80 million the previous year, may or may not indicate that the company has been effective and has met objectives. Perhaps sales should have been $110 million this year. Recognize as well that without the budget, the $110 million of potential sales would not even be assumed. The major drawback of using historical results for judging current performance is that inefficiencies may be concealed in the past performance. Intervening changes in economic conditions, technology, manoeuvres by competitors, personnel, and so forth also limit the usefulness of comparisons with the past.

Communication and Coordination

Budgets tell employees what is expected of them. Nobody likes to drift along, not knowing what "the boss" expects or hopes to achieve. A good budget process communicates from the top down and from the bottom up. Top management clarifies the goals and objectives of the organization in its budgetary directives to middle- and lower-level managers, and increasingly to all employees. Employees and lower-level managers inform higher-level managers how they plan to achieve the goals and objectives.

Budgets also help managers coordinate objectives. For example, a budget forces purchasing personnel to integrate their plans with production requirements, while production managers use the sales budget and delivery schedule to help them anticipate and plan for the employees and physical facilities they will require. Similarly, financial officers use the sales budget, purchasing requirements, and so forth to anticipate the company's need for cash. Thus the budgetary process obliges managers to visualize the relationship of their department's activities to other departments, and to the company as a whole.

Components of the Master Budget

The terms used to describe specific budget schedules vary from organization to organization. However, most master budgets have common elements. The usual master budget for a nonmanufacturing company has the following components:

A. Operating budget
   1. Sales budget (and other cost driver budgets as necessary)
   2. Purchases budget
   3. Cost of goods sold budget
   4. Operating expenses budget
   5. Budgeted income statement
B. Financial budget
   1. Capital budget
   2. Cash budgets (cash collection and cash disbursements)
   3. Budgeted (pro forma) balance sheet

Exhibit 11-1 presents a condensed diagram of the relationships among the various parts of a master budget for a nonmanufacturing company. In addition to these categories, manufacturing companies that maintain physical product inventories prepare ending inventory budgets and additional budgets such as labour, materials, and factory overhead.

EXHIBIT 11-1

Preparation of Master Budget for a Nonmanufacturing Company

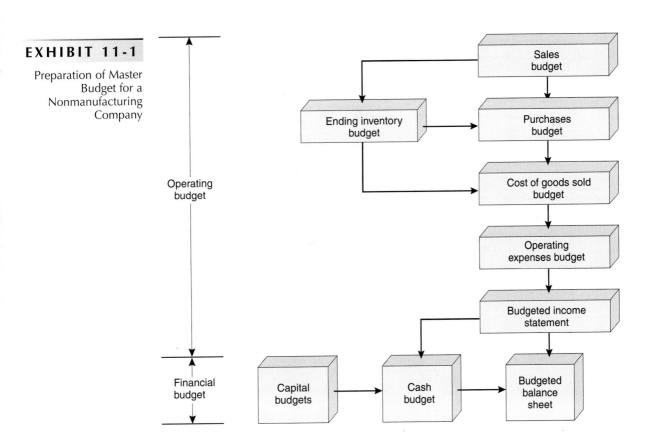

Operating Budget (Profit Plan). A major part of a master budget that focuses on the income statement and its supporting schedules.

Financial Budget. The part of the master budget that focuses on the effects that the operating budget and other plans (such as capital budgets and repayments of debt) will have on cash flow and the balance sheet.

The two major parts of a master budget are the **operating budget** and the financial budget. The operating budget focuses on the income statement and its supporting schedules. Though sometimes called the **profit plan**, an operating budget may show a budgeted *loss*, or even be used to budget expenses in an organization or agency with no sales revenues. In contrast, the **financial budget** focuses on the effects that the operating budget, capital budgets, cash receipts, and repayments will have on cash on hand and the balance sheet.

In addition to the master budget, there are countless forms of special budgets and related reports. For example, a report might detail goals and objectives for special projects, improvements in quality, or customer satisfaction during the budget period.

PREPARING THE MASTER BUDGET

Although the budgetary process may seem largely mechanical, remember that the master-budgeting process of Exhibit 11-1 generates key decisions regarding pricing, product lines, capital expenditures, research and development, and personnel assignments. Therefore, the first draft of the budget leads to decisions that prompt subsequent drafts before a final budget is chosen. Because budget preparation is somewhat mechanical, many organizations use spreadsheet or modelling software to prepare and modify budget drafts. Appendix 11 discusses using personal computer spreadsheets for budgeting.

Description of Problem

To illustrate the budgeting process, we will use, as an example, the Kitchen Plus Company (KPC), a local retailer of a wide variety of kitchen and dining-room items. The company rents a retail store in a mid-sized community near a large metropolitan area. KPC's management prepares a continuous budget to aid financial and operating decisions. For simplicity in this illustration, the planning horizon is four months, April through July. In the past, sales have increased during this season. However, the company's collections have always lagged well behind its sales. As a result, the company has often found itself pressed to come up with the cash for purchases, employees wages, and other operating outlays. To help meet this cash squeeze, KPC has used short-term loans from local banks, paying them back when cash comes in. KPC plans to keep on using this system.

Exhibit 11-2 is the closing balance sheet for the fiscal year ending March 31, 2006. Sales in March were $40,000. Monthly sales are forecasted as follows:

April	$50,000
May	$80,000
June	$60,000
July	$50,000
August	$40,000

EXHIBIT 11-2

The Kitchen Plus
Company
Balance Sheet
March 31, 2006

ASSETS		
Current assets:		
Cash	$10,000	
Accounts receivable, net (0.4 × March sales of $40,000)	16,000	
Merchandise inventory, $20,000 + 0.7 (0.8 × April sales of $50,000)	48,000	
Unexpired insurance	1,800	$ 75,800
Plant assets:		
Equipment, fixtures, and other	$37,000	
Accumulated amortization	12,800	24,200
Total assets		$100,000

LIABILITIES AND OWNERS' EQUITY		
Current liabilities:		
Accounts payable (0.5 × March purchases of $33,600)	$16,800	
Accrued wages and commissions payable ($1,250 + $3,000)	4,250	$ 21,050
Owners' equity		78,950
Total liabilities and owners' equity		$100,000

Management expects future sales collections to follow past experience: 60 percent of the sales should be in cash, and 40 percent on credit. All credit accounts are collected in the month following the sales. The $16,000 of accounts receivable on March 31 represents credit sales made in March (40 percent of $40,000). Uncollectible accounts are negligible and are to be ignored. Also ignore taxes for this illustration.

Because deliveries from suppliers and customer demands are uncertain, at the end of each month, KPC wants to have on hand a basic inventory of items valued at $20,000 plus 80 percent of the expected cost of goods sold for the following month. The cost of merchandise sold averages 70 percent of sales. Therefore, the inventory on March 31 is $20,000 + 0.7(0.8 × April sales of $50,000) = $20,000 + $28,000 = $48,000. The purchase terms available to KPC are net, 30 days. It pays for each month's purchases as follows: 50 percent during that month and 50 percent during the next month. Therefore, the accounts payable balance on March 31 is 50 percent of March's purchases, or $33,600 (as explained in Step 1c, page 538) × 0.5 = $16,800.

KPC pays wages and commissions semi-monthly, half a month after they are earned. They are divided into two portions: monthly fixed wages of $2,500 and commissions, equal to 15 percent of sales, which we will assume are uniform throughout each month. Therefore, the March 31 balance of accrued wages and commissions payable is (0.5 × $2,500) + 0.5(0.15 × $40,000) = $1,250 + $3,000 = $4,250. KPC will pay this amount on April 15.

In addition to buying new fixtures for $3,000 cash in April, KPC's other monthly expenses are

Miscellaneous expenses	5% of sales, paid as incurred
Rent	$2,000, paid as incurred
Insurance	$200 expiration per month
Amortization, including new fixtures	$500 per month

The company wants a minimum of $10,000 as a cash balance at the end of each month. To keep this simple, we will assume that KPC can borrow or repay loans in multiples of $1,000. Management plans to borrow no more cash than necessary and to repay any loans as promptly as possible. Assume that borrowing takes place at the beginning and repayment at the end of the months in question. Interest is paid, under the terms of this credit arrangement, when the related loan is repaid. The interest rate is 18 percent per year.

Steps in Preparing the Master Budget

OBJECTIVE 3

Follow the principal steps in preparing a master budget.

The principal steps in preparing the master budget are listed on page 533.

You will need all preceding schedules to prepare the budgeted income statement (Exhibit 11-3), and schedules b, d, and f to prepare the cash budget (Exhibit 11-4).

Organizations with effective budget systems have specific guidelines for the steps and timing of budget preparation. Although the details differ, the guidelines invariably include the above-mentioned master budget steps. As we follow these steps to examine the schedules of this illustrative problem, *be sure that you understand the source of each figure in each schedule and budget.*

EXHIBIT 11-3

The Kitchen Plus Company Budgeted Income Statement for the Four Months Ended July 31, 2006

		DATA	SOURCE OF DATA
Sales		$240,000	Schedule a
Costs of goods sold		168,000	Schedule c
Gross margin		$ 72,000	
Operating expenses:			
Wages and commissions	$46,000		Schedule e
Miscellaneous expenses	12,000		Schedule e
Rent	8,000		Schedule e
Insurance	800		Schedule e
Amortization	2,000	68,800	Schedule e
Income from operations		$ 3,200	
Interest expense		675	Exhibit 11-4*
Net income		$ 2,525	

* For May, June, and July: $30 + $405 + $240 = $675.

	MARCH	APRIL	MAY	JUNE	JULY	TOTAL APRIL–JULY
Schedule a: Sales budget						
Credit sales, 40 percent	$16,000	$20,000	$32,000	$24,000	$20,000	
Plus cash sales, 60 percent	24,000	30,000	48,000	36,000	30,000	
Total sales	$40,000	$50,000	$80,000	$60,000	$50,000	$240,000
Schedule b: Cash collections						
Cash sales this month		$30,000	$48,000	$36,000	$30,000	
Plus 100 percent of last month's credit sales		16,000	20,000	32,000	24,000	
Total collections		$46,000	$68,000	$68,000	$54,000	

EXHIBIT 11-4

The Kitchen Plus Company
Cash Budget for the Four Months Ending July 31, 2006

	APRIL	MAY	JUNE	JULY
Cash balance, beginning	$10,000	$10,550	$10,970	$10,965
Cash receipts:				
Collections from customers (Schedule b)	46,000	68,000	68,000	54,000
w.* Total cash available for needs, before financing	56,000	78,550	78,970	64,965
Cash disbursements:				
Merchandise (Schedule d)	42,700	48,300	40,600	32,900
Operating expenses (Schedule f)	13,750	18,250	18,000	15,250
Fixtures purchase (given)	3,000	–	–	–
x. Total disbursements	59,450	66,550	58,600	48,150
y. Minimum cash balance desired	10,000	10,000	10,000	10,000
Total cash needed	69,450	76,550	68,600	58,150
Excess (deficiency) of total cash available over total cash needed before current financing (w − x − y)	(13,450)	2,000	10,370	6,815
Financing:				
Borrowings (at beginning)	14,000†			
Repayments (at ends)	–	(1,000)	(9,000)	(4,000)
Interest (at 18% per annum)‡	–	(30)	(405)	(240)
z. Total cash increase (decrease) from financing	14,000	(1,030)	(9,405)	(4,240)
Cash balance, ending (w − x + z)	$10,550	$10,970	$10,965	$12,575

Note: Expired insurance and amortization do not entail cash outlays.

* Letters are keyed to the explanation in the table and in step 3b on page 540.

† Borrowings and repayments of principal are made in multiples of $1,000, at an interest rate of 18% per annum.

‡ Interest computations: $0.18 \times \$1,000 \times 2/12 = \$30$; $0.18 \times \$9,000 \times 3/12 = \$405$; $0.18 \times \$4,000 \times 4/12 = \$240$.

Step 1: Preparing the Operating Budget

Step 1a: Sales budget

The sales budget (Schedule a on page 536) is the starting point for budgeting because inventory levels, purchases, and operating expenses are geared to the rate of sales activities (sales volume is a major cost driver in this example). Accurate sales and cost-driver activity forecasting is essential to effective budgeting; sales forecasting is considered in a later section of this chapter. March sales are included in Schedule a because they affect cash collections in April. Trace the final column in Schedule a to the first row of Exhibit 11-3. In not-for-profit organizations, forecasts of revenue or some level of services are also the focal points for budgeting. Examples are patient revenues and government reimbursement expected by hospitals and donations expected by churches. If no revenues are generated, as in the case of municipal fire protection, a desired level of service is predetermined.

Step 1b: Cash collections

It is easiest to prepare Schedule b, cash collections, at the same time as preparing the sales budget. Cash collections include the current month's cash sales plus the previous month's credit sales. We will use total collections in preparing the cash budget—see Exhibit 11-4.

Step 1c: Purchases budget

OBJECTIVE 4

Prepare the operating budget, the financial budget, and the supporting schedules.

After sales are budgeted, prepare the purchases budget (Schedule c). The total merchandise needed will be the sum of the desired ending inventory plus the amount needed to fulfill budgeted sales demand. The total need will be partially met by the beginning inventory but the remainder must come from planned purchases. These purchases are computed as follows:

budgeted purchases = desired ending inventory + cost of goods sold – beginning inventory

Trace the total cost of goods sold figure in the final column of Schedule c to the second row of Exhibit 11-3. (In many organizations, additional budgets would be prepared for other appropriate cost drivers as well.)

	MARCH	APRIL	MAY	JUNE	JULY	TOTAL APRIL–JULY
Schedule c: Purchases budget						
Desired ending inventory	$48,000*	$64,800	$ 53,600	$48,000	$42,400	
Plus cost of goods sold	28,000†	35,000	56,000	42,000	35,000	$168,000
Total needed	$76,000	$99,800	$109,600	$90,000	$77,400	
Less beginning inventory	42,400‡	48,000	64,800	53,600	48,000	
Purchases	$33,600	$51,800	$ 44,800	$36,400	$29,400	
Schedule d: Disbursements for purchases						
50 percent of last month's purchases		$16,800	$ 25,900	$22,400	$18,200	
Plus 50 percent of this month's purchases		25,900	22,400	18,200	14,700	
		$42,700	$ 48,300	$40,600	$32,900	

* $20,000 + 0.8 × April cost of goods sold = $20,000 + 0.8($35,000) = $48,000.
† 0.7 × March sales of $40,000 = $28,000; 0.7 × April sales of $50,000 = $35,000, and so on.
‡ $20,000 + 0.8 × March cost of goods sold of $28,000 = $20,000 + $22,400 = $42,400.

Step 1d: Disbursements for purchases

Schedule d, disbursements for purchases, is based on the purchases budget. Disbursements include 50 percent of the current month's purchases and 50 percent of the previous month's purchases. We will use total disbursements in preparing the cash budget, Exhibit 11-4, for the financial budget.

Step 1e: Operating expense budget

The budgeting of operating expenses depends on several factors. Month-to-month fluctuations in sales volume and other cost-driver activities directly influence many operating expenses. Examples of expenses driven by sales volume include sales commissions and many delivery expenses. Other expenses are not influenced by sales or other cost-driver activity (such as rent, insurance, amortization, and salaries) within appropriate relevant ranges and are regarded as fixed. Trace the total operating expenses in the final column of Schedule e, which summarizes these expenses, to the budgeted income statement, Exhibit 11-3.

Step 1f: Disbursements for operating expenses

Disbursements for operating expenses are based on the operating expense budget. Disbursements include 50 percent of last month's and this month's wages and commissions, miscellaneous, and rent expenses. We will use the total of these disbursements in preparing the cash budget, Exhibit 11-4.

	MARCH	APRIL	MAY	JUNE	JULY	TOTAL APRIL–JULY
Schedule e: Operating expense budget						
Wages (fixed)	$2,500	$ 2,500	$ 2,500	$ 2,500	$ 2,500	
Commissions (15 percent						
of current month's sales)	6,000	7,500	12,000	9,000	7,500	
Total wages and commissions	$8,500	$10,000	$14,500	$11,500	$10,000	$46,000
Miscellaneous expenses						
(5 percent of current sales)		$ 2,500	$ 4,000	$ 3,000	$ 2,500	$12,000
Rent (fixed)		2,000	2,000	2,000	2,000	8,000
Insurance (fixed)		200	200	200	200	800
Amortization (fixed)		500	500	500	500	2,000
Total operating expenses		$15,200	$21,200	$17,200	$15,200	$68,800
Schedule f: Disbursements for operating expenses						
Wages and commissions:						
50 percent of last month's expenses		$ 4,250	$ 5,000	$ 7,250	$ 5,750	
50 percent of this month's expenses		5,000	7,250	5,750	5,000	
Total wages and commissions		$ 9,250	$12,250	$13,000	$10,750	
Miscellaneous expenses		2,500	4,000	3,000	2,500	
Rent		2,000	2,000	2,000	2,000	
Total disbursements		$13,750	$18,250	$18,000	$15,250	

Step 2: Preparing the Budgeted Income Statement

Steps 1a through 1f provide enough information to construct a budgeted income statement *from operations* (Exhibit 11-3). The income statement will be complete after addition of the interest expense, which is computed after the cash budget has been prepared. Budgeted income from operations is often a benchmark for judging management performance.

The second major part of the master budget is the financial budget, which consists of the capital budget, cash budget, and ending balance sheet. In our illustration, the $3,000 purchase of new fixtures would be included in the capital budget.

Step 3a: Capital budget

Capital budget was dealt with in Chapter 10. In this example, it is ignored.

Step 3b: Cash budget

Cash Budget. A statement of planned cash receipts and disbursements.

The **cash budget** is a statement of planned cash receipts and disbursements. The cash budget is heavily affected by the level of operations summarized in the budgeted income statement. The cash budget has the following major sections, where the letters w, x, y, and z refer to the lines in Exhibit 11-4 that summarize the effects of that section:

w. The *total cash available before financing* equals the beginning cash balance plus cash receipts. Cash receipts depend on collections from customers' accounts receivable and cash sales and on other operating income sources. Trace total collections from Schedule b to Exhibit 11-4.

x. *Cash disbursements for:*
1. purchases depend on the credit terms extended by suppliers and the bill-paying habits of the buyer (disbursements for merchandise from Schedule d should be traced to Exhibit 11-4)
2. payroll depends on wage, salary, and commission terms and on payroll dates (wages and commissions from Schedule f should be traced as part of operating expenses to Exhibit 11-4)
3. some costs and expenses depend on contractual terms for installment payments, mortgage payments, rents, leases, and miscellaneous items (miscellaneous and rent from Schedule f should be traced as part of operating expenses to Exhibit 11-4)
4. other disbursements include outlays for fixed assets, long-term investments, dividends, and the like (the $3,000 expenditure for new fixtures).

y. Management determines the *minimum cash balance desired* depending on the nature of the business and credit arrangements.

z. *Financing requirements* depend on how the *total cash available*, w in Exhibit 11-4, compares with the *total cash needed*. Needs include the disbursements, x, plus the minimum desired ending cash balance, y. If the total cash available is less than the cash needed, borrowing is necessary (Exhibit 11-4 shows that KPC will borrow $14,000 in April to cover the planned *deficiency*). If there is an *excess*, loans may be repaid—$1,000, $9,000, and $4,000 are repaid in May, June, and July, respectively. The pertinent outlays for interest expenses are usually contained in this section of the cash budget. Trace the calculated interest expense to Exhibit 11-3.

The *ending cash balance* is w − x + z. Financing, z, has either a positive (borrowing) or a negative (repayment) effect on the cash balance. The illustrative cash budget shows the pattern of short-term, "self-liquidating" financing. Seasonal peaks often result in heavy drains on cash—for merchandise purchases and operating expenses—before the sales are made and cash is collected from customers. The resulting loan is self-liquidating—that is, the borrowed money is used to acquire merchandise for sale, and the proceeds from sales are used to repay the loan. This "working capital cycle" moves from cash to inventory to receivables and back to cash.

Cash budgets help management to avoid having unnecessary idle cash, on the one hand, and unnecessary cash deficiencies on the other. An astutely mapped financing program keeps cash balances from becoming too large or too small.

Step 3c: Preparing the budgeted balance sheet

The final step in preparing the master budget is to construct the budgeted balance sheet (Exhibit 11-5) that projects each balance-sheet item in accordance with the business plan as expressed in the previous schedules. Specifically, the beginning balances at March 31 would be increased or decreased in light of the expected cash receipts and cash disbursements in Exhibit 11-4 and in light of the effects of noncash items appearing on the income statement in Exhibit 11-3. For example, unexpired insurance would decrease from its balance of $1,800 on March 31 to $1,000 on July 31, even though it is a noncash item.

When the complete master budget is formulated, management can consider all the major financial statements as a basis for changing the course of events. For example, the initial formulation of the financial statements may prompt management to try new sales strategies to generate more sales. Or management may explore the effects of various adjustments in the timing of receipts and disbursements. The large cash deficiency in April, for example, may lead to an emphasis

EXHIBIT 11-5

The Kitchen Plus
Company
Budgeted Balance Sheet
July 31, 2006

ASSETS		
Current assets:		
Cash (Exhibit 11-4)	$12,575	
Accounts receivable (0.40 × July sales of $50,000) (Schedule a)	20,000	
Merchandise inventory (Schedule c)	42,400	
Unexpired insurance ($1,800 old balance − $800 expired)	1,000	$ 75,975
Plant:		
Equipment, fixtures, and other ($37,000 + $3,000)	$40,000	
Accumulated amortization ($12,800 + $2,000 amortization)	14,800	25,200
Total assets		$101,175

LIABILITIES AND OWNERS' EQUITY		
Current liabilities:		
Accounts payable (0.5 × July purchases of $29,400) (Schedule d)	$14,700	
Accrued wages and commissions payable (0.5 × $10,000)		
(Schedule e)	5,000	$ 19,700
Owners' equity ($78,950 + $2,525 net income)		81,475
Total liabilities and owners' equity		$101,175

Note: Beginning balances were used as a start for the computations of unexpired insurance, plant, and owners' equity.

Budgeting: Value Driver or Value Buster?

Ford Motor Company
www.ford.com

Recently, some controversy has developed over the value of budgeting. Some critics claim that the budgeting process is not an effective cost-management tool. Critics focus on three problems with the budgeting process: (1) The process is too time-consuming and expensive; (2) the resulting annual budgets, operating and financial, are not accurate and hence not relevant—especially in industries where marketplace change is frequent and unpredictable; and (3) evaluating performance against a budget causes managers to bias their budgets, resulting in inaccurate planning.

Some studies suggest that the annual budgeting process can take up to 30 percent of management's time. Estimates place Ford Motor Company's cost of budgeting at $1.2 billion a year. Even after spending these resources, some companies react to changing economic conditions by ignoring the budget rather than changing it. In contrast, successful budget processes use the budget as the basis for making systematic adjustments in response to changing economic conditions.

Performance evaluation using budgets creates special problems if not done carefully. For a few companies, once they set the budget, managers attempt to manipulate performance measures to meet budget targets. This can lead to unethical behaviour such as "cooking the books" (reporting false accounting numbers) or putting undue pressure on employees to meet budgeting numbers using whatever means possible. WorldCom and Enron used budgets inappropriately, motivating managers to do whatever was necessary to meet targeted goals. In other cases, managers anticipate the effect of performance evaluations when setting their budgets. Consequently, they present biased planning information to make sure that the budget targets are reachable.

Are companies that have experienced problems with their budgeting process abandoning traditional budgeting? No. Instead, they are modifying their approach to budgeting. Some companies are tying their budgets to benchmarks based on actual performance of peers and best-in-class operations. Some are separating planning budgets from control budgets. Most are tying their budgeting process more closely to their overall strategy. They then measure performance both in financial terms, such as cost to income, and in nonfinancial terms, such as time to market for new products or services, and compare actual performance to industry benchmarks in addition to budgeted performance.

Most managers still agree that budgeting, correctly used, has significant value to management. A recent survey of more than 150 North American organizations reported that budgeting was used by over 92 percent of the companies and was ranked among the top three cost-management tools.

Companies such as Allstate, Owens Corning, Sprint, Battelle, and Texaco are modifying their approach to budgeting by implementing new technologies. For example, at Battelle's Pacific Northwest National Laboratory, an intranet is used to reduce the time and expense of developing the annual budget. The new system enables support staff and managers to input their budget data and plans using this corporate intranet, eliminating the need for central business planning staff to upload data and the numerous changes made during the budgeting process. According to managers at Battelle, "This results in higher quality and more accurate budgeting, reporting, and analysis."

Sources: Adapted from R. Banham, "Better Budgets" *Journal of Accountancy,* February 2000, pp. 37–40; J. Hope and R. Fraser, "Who Needs Budgets?" *Harvard Business Review,* February 2003, pp. 108–115; P. Smith, C. Goranson, M. Astley, "Intranet Budgeting," *Strategic Finance,* May 2003, pp. 30–33; T. Hatch and W. Stratton, "Scorecarding in North America: Who Is Doing What?" Paper presented at the CAM–I/CMS 3rd quarter meeting, Portland, Oregon, September 10, 2002; and M. Jensen, "Corporate Budgeting Is Broken, Let's Fix It," *Harvard Business Review,* November 2001, pp. 94–101.

Some managers may focus on the operating budget, while others may be more concerned with the financial budget. How does the operating budget differ from the financial budget?

ANSWER

The operating budget focuses on the income statement, which is prepared using accrual accounting. It measures revenues and expenses. Line operating managers usually prepare and use the operating bud-

get. In contrast, the financial budget focuses primarily on cash flow. It measures the receipts and disbursements of cash. Financial managers such as controllers and treasurers use the financial budget. The operating budget is a better measure of overall performance, but the financial budget is essential to plan for cash needs. A lack of cash rather than poor operating performance often gets companies into trouble. Thus, both operating and financial budgets are important to an organization.

on cash sales or an attempt to speed up collection of accounts receivable. In any event, the first draft of the master budget is rarely the final draft. As it is reworked, the budgeting process becomes an integral part of the management process itself—budgeting is planning and communicating.

DIFFICULTIES OF SALES FORECASTING

OBJECTIVE 5

Understand the difficulties of sales forecasting and human behaviour problems in formulating and implementing budgets.

Sales Forecast. A prediction of sales under a given set of conditions.

Sales Budget. The result of choosing one of the sales forecasts and implementing it.

As you have seen in the foregoing illustration, the sales budget is the foundation of the entire master budget. The accuracy of estimated purchases budgets, production schedules, and costs depends on the detail and accuracy (in dollars, units, and mix) of the budgeted sales.

Sales forecasting is a key to preparing the sales budget, but a forecast and a budget are not necessarily identical. A **sales forecast** is a *prediction* of sales under a given set of conditions. A **sales budget** is the result of choosing one of the sales forecasts and implementing it.

Sales forecasts are usually prepared under the direction of the top sales executive. Important factors considered by sales forecasters include

1. *Past patterns of sales.* Past experience combined with detailed past sales by product line, geographic region, and type of customer can help predict future sales.
2. *Estimates made by the sales force.* A company's sales force is often the best source of information about the desires and plans of customers.
3. *General economic conditions.* Predictions for many economic indicators, such as gross domestic product and industrial production indexes (local and foreign), are published regularly. Knowledge of how sales relate to these indicators can aid sales forecasting.
4. *Competitors' actions.* Sales depend on the strength and actions of competitors. To forecast sales, a company should consider the likely strategies and reactions of competitors, such as changes in their prices, product quality, or services.
5. *Changes in the firm's prices.* Sales can be increased by decreasing prices, and vice versa. A company should consider the effects of price changes in customer demand.

6. *Changes in product mix.* Changing the mix of products can affect not only sales levels but also overall contribution margin. Identifying the most profitable products and devising methods to increase their sales is a key part of successful management.

7. *Market research studies.* Some companies hire market research experts to gather information about market conditions and customer preferences. Such information is useful to managers making sales forecasts and product mix decisions.

8. *Advertising and sales promotion plans.* Advertising and other promotional costs affect sales levels. A sales forecast should be based on anticipated effects of promotional activities.

Sales forecasting usually combines various techniques. In addition to the opinions of the sales staff, statistical analyses of correlations between sales and economic indicators (prepared by economists and members of the market research staff) provide valuable help. The opinions of line management also heavily influence the final sales forecasts. Ultimately, no matter how many technical experts are used in forecasting, the *sales budget* is the responsibility of line management.

Sales forecasting is still somewhat mystical, but its procedures are becoming more formalized and are being reviewed more seriously because of the intensity of global competitive pressures. Although this book does not include a detailed discussion of the preparation of the sales budget, the importance of an accurate sales forecast cannot be overstressed.

Governments and other not-for-profit organizations also face a problem similar to sales forecasting. For example, the budget for city revenues may depend on a variety of factors, such as predicted property taxes, traffic fines, parking fees, and licence fees. In turn, property taxes depend on the extent of new construction and, in most localities, general increases in real estate values. Thus, a municipal budget may require forecasting that is just as sophisticated as that required by a private firm.

MAKING A BUDGET WORK: ANTICIPATING HUMAN BEHAVIOUR

No matter how accurate sales forecasts are, if budgets are to benefit an organization, they need the support of all the organization's employees. Lower-level workers' and managers' attitudes toward budgets will be heavily influenced by the attitude of top management. But even with the support of top management, budgets—and the managers who implement them—can run into opposition.

Managers often compare actual results with budgets in evaluating subordinates. Few individuals are immediately ecstatic about techniques used to check their performance. Lower-level managers sometimes regard budgets as embodiments of restrictive, negative top-management attitudes. Accountants reinforce this view if they use a budget only to point out managers' failings. Such negative attitudes are even greater when the budget's primary purpose is to limit spending. For example, budgets are generally unpopular in government agencies where usually their only use is to request and authorize funding. To avoid negative attitudes toward budgets, accountants and top management must demonstrate how budgets can *help each manager and employee* achieve better results. Only then will the budget become a positive aid in motivating employees at all levels to work toward goals, set objectives, measure results accurately, and direct attention to the areas that need investigation.

Another serious human relations problem, which may preclude some of these benefits of budgeting, can result if budgets stress one set of performance goals, but employees and managers are rewarded for performance on other dimensions. For example, a budget may concentrate on keeping current costs of production within the budget, but managers and employees may be rewarded based on quality of production and on timely delivery of products to customers. These dimensions of performance could be in direct conflict.

The overriding importance of the human aspects of budgeting cannot be overemphasized. Too often, top management and accountants are overly concerned with the mechanics of budgets, ignoring the fact that the effectiveness of any budgeting system depends directly on whether the affected managers and employees understand and accept the budget. Budgets formulated with the active participation of all affected employees are generally more effective than budgets imposed on subordinates. This involvement is usually called **participative budgeting**.

Participative Budgeting. Budgets formulated with the active participation of all affected employees.

FINANCIAL PLANNING MODELS

Financial Planning Models. Mathematical models of the master budget that can react to any set of assumptions about sales levels, sales prices, product mix, or cost fluctuations.

Because a well-made master budget considers all aspects of the company (the entire value chain), it serves as an effective model for decision making. For example, managers can use the master budget to predict how various decisions might affect the company by changing some of the budgetary assumptions. Using the master budget in this way is a step-by-step process whereby tentative plans are revised as managers exchange views on various possibilities of expected activities.

Today, most companies have developed **financial planning models**, master-budget-based mathematical models that can react to any set of assumptions about sales, costs, product mix, and so on. For instance, Dow Chemical's model uses 140 separate, constantly revised cost inputs that are based on a number of different cost drivers.

By mathematically describing the relationships among all the operating and financial activities, and among the other major internal and external factors that can affect the results of management decisions, financial planning models allow managers to assess the predicted impacts of various alternatives before final decisions are selected. For example, a manager might want to predict the consequences of changing the mix of products offered for sale to emphasize several products with the highest prospects for growth. A financial planning model would provide budgeted operational and financial budgets well into the future under alternative assumptions about the product mix, sales levels, production constraints, quality levels, scheduling, and so on. Most importantly, managers can get answers to "what if" questions, such as "What if sales are 10 percent below forecasts? What if material prices increase 8 percent instead of 4 percent, as expected? What if the new union contract grants a 6 percent raise in consideration for productivity improvements?" Building models that can help answer "what if" questions is the subject of the appendix to this chapter.

Financial planning models have shortened managers' reaction times dramatically. A revised plan for a large company that took many accountants many days to prepare by hand can be prepared with computers and spreadsheets in minutes.

The use of spreadsheet software on personal computers has put financial planning models within reach of even the smallest organizations. But the ready access to powerful modelling does not guarantee plausible or reliable results. Financial planning models are only as good as the assumptions and the inputs used to build and manipulate them—what computer specialists call GIGO (garbage in, garbage out).

HIGHLIGHTS TO REMEMBER

1. **Explain the major features and advantages of a master budget.** A budget expresses, in quantitative terms, an organization's objectives and possible steps for achieving them. Thus, a budget is a tool that helps managers in both their planning and control functions. The two major parts of a master budget are the operating budget and the financial budget. Advantages of budgets include formalization of planning, providing a framework for judging performance, and aiding managers in coordinating their efforts.

2. **Follow the principal steps in preparing a master budget.** Master budgets typically cover relatively short periods—usually one month to one year. The steps involved in preparing the master budget vary across organizations but follow the general outline given on page 533. Invariably, the first step is to forecast sales or service levels. The next step should be to forecast cost-driver activity levels, given expected sales and service. Using these forecasts and knowledge of cost behaviour, collection patterns, and so on, managers can prepare the operating and financing budgets.

3. **Prepare the operating budget and the supporting schedules.** The operating budget is the income statement for the budget period. Managers prepare it using the following supporting schedules: sales budget, purchases budget, and operating expenses budget.

4. **Prepare the financial budget.** The second major part of the master budget is the financial budget. The financial budget consists of a cash budget, capital budget, and a budgeted balance sheet. Managers prepare the cash budget from the following supporting schedules: cash collections, disbursements for purchases, and disbursements for operating expenses.

5. **Explain the difficulties of sales forecasting.** Sales forecasting combines various techniques as well as opinions of sales staff and management. Sales forecasters must consider many factors such as past patterns of sales, economic conditions, and competitors' actions. Sales forecasting is difficult because of its complexity and the rapid changes in the business environment in which most companies operate.

6. **Anticipate possible human relations problems caused by budgets.** The success of a budget depends heavily on employee reaction to it. Negative attitudes toward budgets often prevent realization of many of the potential benefits. Such attitudes are usually caused by managers who use budgets to force behaviour or to punish employees or who use budgets only to limit spending. Budgets generally are more useful when all affected parties participate in their preparation.

Activity-Based Budgeting (ABB)

BorgWarner Inc.
www.bwauto.com
Dow Chemical
www.dow.com

Activity-based costing (ABC) is growing in popularity. However, companies do not realize the real benefits of ABC until they totally integrate it into their budgeting system. Often accountants "own" the costing system of a company, but the budgeting system "belongs" to managers. To use an activity-based framework for budgeting means that all managers must focus on managing activities. They must prepare their budgets using the same framework used by the ABC system. For example, in 1997 and 1998, Dow Chemical integrated its new ABC system with its budgeting process. To be successful, this required a massive training effort attended by "controllers, accountants, work process subject matter experts, cost centre owners, business manufacturing leaders, and site general managers." With budgets consistent with cost reports, Dow gained much greater benefit from its activity-based budgeting system.

To see how activity-based budgeting helps a company, let's compare methods using a company's purchasing department as an example. The purchasing department's previous-year results might appear as follows, based on a traditional view of costs:

PURCHASING DEPARTMENT

Salaries	$200,000
Benefits	75,000
Supplies	30,000
Travel	10,000
Total	$315,000

If management wants to reduce costs by 10 percent overall ($31,500) using the traditional view of costs, purchasing may simply reduce each cost category by 10 percent. Some critics refer to this method of cost reduction as "slash and burn." However, it is the managers who often wind up getting burned by this technique. For example, at BorgWarner Automotive, virtually all managers expressed dissatisfaction with the budgeting process. Each year managers made cost estimates as part of the annual budgeting procedure. But, because the company used a slash-and-burn cost-cutting technique, top management almost always returned these budgets with a directive to cut costs across the board. Managers got so frustrated that they started overestimating costs to compensate for the cuts they knew were coming.

Using activity-based cost information, the purchasing department's budget might appear as follows:

PURCHASING DEPARTMENT

Activity	
Certify 10 new vendors	$ 65,450
Issue 450 purchase orders	184,640
Issue 275 releases	64,910
Total	$315,000

ABB links financial data with the activity that consumes the related resource. Instead of using the slash-and-burn method, the department now targets specific activities that it can reduce without hurting its overall effectiveness. For example, the department may be able to reduce the number of vendor certifications to five. Assuming that vendor certification costs are variable with respect to the number of vendors, this would reduce certification costs by $5 \times (\$65,450 \div 10)$ or $32,725, enabling the department to meet or exceed its budget target.

Government organizations are also using ABC. For example, the Treasury Board of Canada has a section about activity-based costing on its website (www.tbs-sct.gc.ca/fin/sigs/ABC/index_e.asp).

Sources: Adapted from G. Hanks, M. Fried, and J. Huber, "Shifting Gears at Borg Warner Automotive," *Management Accounting,* February 1994, pp. 25–29; J. Damitio, G. Hayes, and P. Kintzele, "Integrating ANC and ABM at Dow Chemical," *Management Accounting Quarterly,* Winter 2000, pp. 22–26. See also the Society of Management Accountants of Canada, Management Accounting Guideline, *Implementing Activity-Based Costing,* 1993; M. Gosselin, "The Effect of Strategy and Organizational Structure on the Adoption and Implementation of Activity-Based Costing," *Accounting, Organizations and Society* 22:2, 1997, pp. 105–122; P. L. Bescos, E. Cauvin, and M. Gosselin, "Activity-Based Costing and Activity-Based Management: A Comparison of the Practices in Canada and France," *Comptabilité, contrôle et audit,* Special Edition, May 2002, pp. 209–244.

DEMONSTRATION PROBLEM FOR YOUR REVIEW

Do not attempt to solve this problem until you understand the *step-by-step* illustration in this chapter.

The Country Store is a retail outlet for a variety of hardware and homewares. The owner of the Country Store is anxious to prepare a budget for the next quarter, which is typically quite busy. She is most concerned with her cash position because she expects that she will have to borrow to finance purchases in anticipation of sales. She has gathered all the data necessary to prepare a simplified budget. Exhibit 11-6 shows these data in tabular form. Review the structure

EXHIBIT 11-6

The Country Store Budget Data Balance Sheet as of March 31, 2006

Assets:			Budgeted sales:	
Cash	$	9,000	March (actual)	$60,000
Accounts receivable		48,000	April	70,000
Inventory		12,600	May	85,000
Plant and equipment (net)		200,000	June	90,000
Total assets		$269,600	July	50,000
Liabilities and equities:				
Interest payable		0		
Note payable		0	Required cash balance:	$ 8,000
Accounts payable		18,300		
Share capital		180,000		
Retained earnings		71,300		
Total liabilities and equities		$269,600		
Budgeted expenses (per month):			Sales mix, cash/credit:	
Wages and salaries		$ 7,500	Cash sales	20%
Freight out as a % of sales		6%	Credit sales (collected the following	
Advertising		$ 6,000	month)	80%
Amortization		$ 2,000	Gross margin rate	40%
Other expense as a % of sales		4%	Loan interest rate (interest paid	
Minimum inventory policy as a %			in cash monthly on the loan amount	
of next month's cost of goods			outstanding during the previous	
sold		30%	month)	12%
Equipment purchases:			Inventory paid for in:	
April		$19,750	Month purchased	50%
May		0	Month after purchase	50%
June		0	Dividends to be paid:	
			April	$0
			May	0
			June	4,000

EXHIBIT 11-6 (cont'd)

SCHEDULE A: SALES BUDGET

	APRIL	MAY	JUNE	TOTAL
Credit sales, 80%	$56,000	$68,000	$72,000	$196,000
Cash sales, 20%	14,000	17,000	18,000	49,000
Total sales	$70,000	$85,000	$90,000	$245,000

SCHEDULE B: CASH COLLECTIONS

	APRIL	MAY	JUNE	TOTAL
Cash sales	$14,000	$17,000	$18,000	$ 49,000
Collection from prior month	48,000	56,000	68,000	172,000
Total collections	$62,000	$73,000	$86,000	$221,000

SCHEDULE C: PURCHASES BUDGET

	APRIL	MAY	JUNE	TOTAL
Desired ending inventory	$15,300	$16,200	$ 9,000	$ 9,000
Plus COGS	42,000	51,000	54,000	147,000
Total needed	$57,300	$67,200	$63,000	$156,000
Less beginning inventory	12,600	15,300	16,200	12,000
Total purchases	$44,700	$51,900	$46,800	$143,400

SCHEDULE D: CASH DISBURSEMENTS FOR PURCHASES

	APRIL	MAY	JUNE	TOTAL
For March*	$18,300			$ 18,300
For April	22,350	$22,350		44,700
For May		25,950	$25,950	51,900
For June			23,400	23,400
Total disbursements	$40,650	$48,300	$49,350	$138,300

* The amount payable from the previous month.

SCHEDULES E AND F: OPERATING EXPENSES AND DISBURSEMENTS FOR EXPENSES (EXCEPT INTEREST)

	APRIL	MAY	JUNE	TOTAL
Cash expenses:				
Salaries and wages	$ 7,500	$ 7,500	$ 7,500	$22,500
Freight out	4,200	5,100	5,400	14,700
Advertising	6,000	6,000	6,000	18,000
Other expenses	2,800	3,400	3,600	9,800
Total disbursements for expenses	$20,500	$22,000	$22,500	$65,000
Noncash expenses:				
Amortization	2,000	2,000	2,000	6,000
Total expenses	$22,500	$24,000	$24,500	$71,000

The Country Store Cash Budget April–June, 2006	APRIL	MAY	JUNE
Beginning cash balance	$ 9,000	$ 8,000	$ 8,000
Cash collections	62,000	73,000	86,000
Total cash available	71,000	81,000	94,000
Cash disbursements:			
Inventory purchases	40,650	48,300	49,350
Operating expenses	20,500	22,000	22,500
Equipment purchases	19,750	0	0
Dividends	0	0	4,000
Interest*	0	179	179
Total disbursements	80,900	70,479	76,029
Minimum cash balance	8,000	8,000	8,000
Total cash needed	$88,900	$78,479	$84,029
Cash excess (deficit)	$(17,900)	$ 2,521	$ 9,971
Financing:			
Borrowing†	17,900	0	0
Repayments	0	(2,521)	(9,971)
Total cash from financing	17,900	(2,521)	(9,971)
Ending cash balance	$ 8,000	$ 8,000	$ 8,000

* In this example interest is paid on the loan amounts outstanding during the previous month: May and June: (0.12/12) × $17,900 = $179.

† In this example, borrowings are at the beginning of the month in the amounts needed. Repayments are made at the end of the month as excess cash permits.

The Country Store Budgeted Income Statement April–June, 2006	APRIL	MAY	JUNE	APRIL–JUNE TOTAL
Sales	$70,000	$85,000	$90,000	$245,000
Cost of goods sold	42,000	51,000	54,000	147,000
Gross margin	28,000	34,000	36,000	98,000
Operating expenses:				
Salaries and wages	7,500	7,500	7,500	22,500
Freight-out	4,200	5,100	5,400	14,700
Advertising	6,000	6,000	6,000	18,000
Other	2,800	3,400	3,600	9,800
Interest*	179	179	154	512
Amortization	2,000	2,000	2,000	6,000
Total expense	$22,679	$24,179	$24,654	$ 71,512
Net operating income	$ 5,321	$ 9,821	$11,346	$ 26,488

* Note that interest expense is the monthly interest rate times the borrowed amount held for the month; April: (0.12/12) × $17,900 = $179. Amount is accrued in the month incurred but paid in the following month.

ASSETS	APRIL	MAY	JUNE*
Current: assets			
Cash	$ 8,000	$ 8,000	$ 8,000
Accounts receivable	56,000	68,000	72,000
Inventory	15,300	16,200	9,000
Total current assets	79,300	92,200	89,000
Plant, less accum. amort.†	217,750	215,750	213,750
Total assets	$297,050	$307,950	$302,750

LIABILITIES AND EQUITIES			
Liabilities:			
Accounts payable	$ 22,350	$ 25,950	$ 23,400
Interest payable	179	179	154
Notes payable	17,900	15,379	5,408
Total liabilities	40,429	41,508	28,962
Shareholders' equity:			
Capital stock	180,000	180,000	180,000
Retained earnings	76,621	86,442	93,788
Total equities	256,621	266,442	273,788
Total liabilities & equities	$297,050	$307,950	$302,750

* The June 30, 2006 balance sheet is the ending balance sheet for the entire three-month period.

† $200,000 + $19,750 − $2,000 = $217,750.

of the example in the chapter and then prepare the Country Store's master budget for the months of April, May, and June. The solution follows after the budget data. Note that there are a few minor differences between this example and the one in the chapter. These are identified in Exhibit 11-6 and in the solution. The primary difference is in the payment of interest on borrowing. Borrowing occurs at the beginning of a month when cash is needed. Repayments (if appropriate) occur at the end of a month when cash is available. Interest also is paid in cash at the beginning of the month at an annual rate of 12 percent on the amount of note payable outstanding during the previous month.

APPENDIX: USING SPREADSHEETS FOR BUDGETING

OBJECTIVE 7

Use a spreadsheet to develop a budget.

Spreadsheet software for personal computers is an extremely powerful and flexible tool for budgeting. An obvious advantage of the spreadsheet is that arithmetic errors are virtually non-existent. The real value of spreadsheets, however, is that they can be used to make a mathematical model (a financial planning model) of the organization. This model can be used repeatedly at very low cost and can be altered to reflect possible changes in expected sales, cost drivers, cost functions, and so on. The objective of this appendix is to illustrate *sensitivity analysis*—one aspect of the power and flexibility of spreadsheet software that has made this software an indispensable budgeting tool. It is necessary to emphasize that the assumptions underlying the spreadsheet first need a careful examination.

Recall the chapter's master budgeting example. Suppose KPC has prepared its master budget using spreadsheet software. In order to simplify making changes to the budget, the relevant forecasts and other budgeting details have been placed in Exhibit 11-7. Note that for simplification, only the data necessary for the purchases budget have been shown here. The full master budget would require a larger table with all the data given in the chapter. Each part of the table can be identified by its column and row intersection or "cell address." For example, the beginning inventory for the budget period can be located with the cell address "D4," which is shown as $48,000.

By referencing the budget data's cell addresses, you can generate the purchases budget (Exhibit 11-9) within the same spreadsheet by entering *formulas* instead of numbers into the schedule. Consider Exhibit 11-8. Instead of typing $48,000 as April's beginning inventory in the purchases budget at cell D17, type a "formula" with the cell address for the beginning inventory from the preceding *table*, =D4 (Excel spreadsheets use "=" to indicate a formula). Likewise, all the cells of the purchases budget will be composed of formulas containing cell addresses instead of numbers. The *total needed* in April (D16) is =D13+D14, and purchases in April (D19) are budgeted to be =D16–D17. The figures for May, June, and July are computed similarly within the respective columns. This approach gives the spreadsheet the most flexibility, because you could change any number in the budget data in Exhibit 11-7 (e.g., a sales forecast), and the software automatically recalculates the formulas in the entire purchases budget. Exhibit 11-8 shows the formulas used for the purchases budget. Exhibit 11-9 is the purchases budget displaying the numbers generated by the formulas in Exhibit 11-8.

Now, what if sales could be 10 percent higher than initially forecasted during April through August? What effect will this alternative forecast have on budgeted purchases? Even to revise this simple purchases budget would require a

EXHIBIT 11-7

The Kitchen Plus Company Budget Data

	A	B	C	D	E	F	G
1	BUDGET DATA						
2	Sales Forecasts		Other information				
3							
4	March (actual)	$40,000	Beginning inventory	$48,000			
5	April	50,000	Desired ending inventory: Base amount	$20,000			
6	May	80,000	plus percent of next				
7	June	60,000	month's cost of				
8	July	50,000	goods sold	80%			
9	August	40,000	Cost of goods sold				
10			as percent of sales	70%			

Column and row labels are given by the spreadsheet.

EXHIBIT 11-8

The Kitchen Plus Company
Purchases Budget Formulas

	A	B	C	D	E	F	G
11	SCHEDULE C						
12	Purchases budget			April	May	June	July
13	Desired ending inventory			=D5+D8* D10*B6	=D5+D8* D10*B7	=D5+D8* D10*B8	=D5+D8* D10*B9
14	Plus cost of goods sold			=D10*B5	=D10*B6	=D10*B7	=D10*B8
15							
16	Total needed			=D13+D14	=E13+E14	=F13+F14	=G13+G14
17	Less beginning inventory			=D4	=D13	=E13	=F13
18							
19	Purchases			=D16–D17	=E16–E17	=F16–F17	=G16–G17
20							

EXHIBIT 11-9

The Kitchen Plus Company
Purchases Budget

	A	B	C	D	E	F	G
11	Schedule C						
12	Purchases budget			April	May	June	July
13	Desired ending inventory			$64,800	$53,600	$48,000	$42,400
14	Plus cost of goods sold			35,000	56,000	42,000	35,000
15							
16	Total needed			99,800	109,600	90,000	77,400
17	Less beginning inventory			48,000	64,800	53,600	48,000
18							
19	Purchases			$51,800	$44,800	$36,400	$29,400
20							

considerable number of manual recalculations. Merely changing the sales fore-casts in spreadsheet Exhibit 11-7, however, results in a nearly instantaneous revision of the purchases budget. Exhibit 11-10 shows the alternative sales fore-casts (in boldface type) and other, unchanged data along with the revised pur-chases budget. We could alter every piece of budget data in the table, and easily view or print out the effects on purchases.

Sensitivity Analysis. The systematic varying of budget assumptions in order to determine the effects of each change on the budget.

This sort of analysis, assessing the effects of varying one of the budget inputs, up or down, is called *sensitivity analysis*. **Sensitivity analysis** for budget-ing is the systematic varying of budget data input in order to determine the effects of each change on the budget. Such "what if" analysis is one of the most powerful uses of spreadsheets for financial planning models. Note, though, that it is generally not a good idea to vary more than one of the types of budget inputs at a time, unless they are obviously related, because doing so makes it difficult to isolate the effect of each change.

EXHIBIT 11-10

The Kitchen Plus Company
Purchases Budget

	A	B	C	D	E	F	G
1	BUDGET DATA						
2	Sales Forecasts		Other information				
3							
4	March (actual)	$40,000	Beginning inventory	$48,000			
5	April	**55,000**	Desired ending inven-tory: Base amount	$20,000			
6	May	**88,000**	plus percent of next				
7	June	**66,000**	month's cost of				
8	July	**55,000**	goods sold	80%			
9	August	**44,000**	Cost of goods sold as				
10			a percent of sales	70%			
11	SCHEDULE C						
12	Purchases Budget			APRIL	MAY	JUNE	JULY
13	Desired ending inventory			$ 69,280	$ 56,960	$50,800	$44,640
14	Cost of goods sold			38,500	61,600	46,200	38,500
15							
16	Total needed			107,780	118,560	97,000	83,140
17	Beginning inv.			48,000	69,280	56,960	50,800
18							
19	Purchases			$ 59,780	$ 49,280	$40,040	$32,340

Every schedule, operating budget, and financial budget of the master budget can be prepared on the spreadsheet. Each schedule would be linked by the appropriate cell addresses just as the budget input data (Exhibit 11-7) are linked to the purchases budget (Exhibits 11-8 and 11-9). As in the purchases budget, ideally all cells in the master budget are formulas, not numbers. That way, every budget input can be the subject of sensitivity analysis, if desired, by simply changing the budget data in Exhibit 11-7.

Preparing the master budget on a spreadsheet the first time is time-consuming. After that, the time savings and planning capabilities through sensitivity analysis are enormous compared to a manual approach. However, a problem can occur if the master budget model is not well-documented when a person other than the author attempts to modify the spreadsheet model. Any assumptions that are made should be described either within the spreadsheet or in a separate budget preparation document.

KEY TERMS

budget *p. 529*	participative budgeting *p. 545*
capital budgets *p. 530*	profit plan *p. 534*
cash budget *p. 540*	pro forma financial statements *p. 530*
continuous budget *p. 530*	rolling budget *p. 530*
financial budget *p. 534*	sales budget *p. 543*
financial planning models *p. 545*	sales forecast *p. 543*
long-range planning *p. 530*	sensitivity analysis *p. 554*
master budget *p. 530*	strategic plan *p. 530*
operating budget *p. 534*	

ASSIGNMENT MATERIAL

QUESTIONS

Q11-1 Is budgeting used primarily for scorekeeping, attention directing, or problem solving?

Q11-2 "Budgets are primarily a tool used to limit expenditures." Do you agree? Explain.

Q11-3 How do strategic planning, long-range planning, and budgeting differ?

Q11-4 "Capital budgets are plans for managing long-term debt and common shares." Do you agree? Explain.

Q11-5 "I oppose continuous budgets because they provide a moving target. Managers never know what to aim at." Discuss.

Q11-6 "Pro forma statements are those statements prepared in conjunction with continuous budgets." Do you agree? Explain.

Q11-7 Differentiate between an operating budget and a financial budget.

Q11-8 "Budgets are okay in relatively certain environments. But everything changes so quickly in the electronics industry that budgeting is a waste of time." Comment on this statement.

Q11-9 What are the major benefits of budgeting?

Q11-10 "Budgeting is an unnecessary burden on many managers. It takes time away from important day-to-day problems." Do you agree? Explain.

Q11-11 Why is budgeted performance better than past performance, as a basis for judging actual results?

Q11-12 Why is the sales forecast the starting point for budgeting?

Q11-13 Explain the relationship between the sales (or service) forecast and cost-driver activity.

Q11-14 Distinguish between operating expenses and disbursements for operating expenses.

Q11-15 What is the principal objective of a cash budget?

Q11-16 Differentiate between a sales forecast and a sales budget.

Q11-17 What factors influence the sales forecast?

Q11-18 "Education and salesmanship are key features of budgeting." Explain.

Q11-19 What are financial planning models?

Q11-20 "Financial planning models guide managers through the budget process so that managers do not need to really understand budgeting." Do you agree? Explain.

Q11-21 "I cannot be bothered with setting up my monthly budget on a spreadsheet. It just takes too long to be worth the effort." Comment.

Q11-22 How do spreadsheets aid the application of sensitivity analysis?

PROBLEMS

P11-1 SALES BUDGET. Eckart's Runners Inc. has the following data:

- Accounts receivable, May 31: (0.3 × May sales of $400,000) = $120,000.
- Monthly forecasted sales: June, $400,000; July, $440,000; August, $500,000; September, $530,000.

Sales consist of 70 percent cash and 30 percent credit. All credit accounts are collected in the month following the sales. Uncollectible accounts are negligible and may be ignored.

Prepare a sales budget schedule and a cash collections budget schedule for June, July, and August.

P11-2 SALES BUDGET. A Tokyo wholesaler was preparing its sales budget for the first quarter of 2007. Forecast sales are (in thousands of yen)

January	¥180,000
February	¥210,000
March	¥240,000

Sales are 20 percent cash and 80 percent on credit. Fifty percent of the credit accounts are collected in the month of sale, 40 percent in the month following the sale, and 10 percent in the following month. No uncollectible accounts are anticipated. Accounts receivable at the beginning of 2007 are

¥96 million (10 percent × November credit sales of ¥180 million and 50 percent of December credit sales of ¥156 million).

Prepare a schedule showing sales and cash collections for January, February, and March, 2007.

P11-3 **CASH COLLECTION BUDGET.**   Pioneer Carpets has found that cash collections from customers tend to occur in the following pattern:

Collected within cash discount period in month of sale	50%
Collected within cash discount period in first month after month of sale	10
Collected after cash discount period in first month after month of sale	25
Collected after cash discount period in second month after month of sale	12
Never collected	3
Total sales in any month (before cash discounts)	100%
Cash discount allowable as a percentage of invoice price	1%

Compute the total cash budgeted to be collected in March if sales are predicted as $300,000 for January, $400,000 for February, and $450,000 for March.

P11-4 **PURCHASE BUDGET.**   Fernandez Furniture Mart plans inventory levels (at cost) at the end of each month as follows: May, $250,000; June, $220,000; July, $270,000; August, $250,000.

Sales are expected to be: June, $440,000; July, $350,000; August, $400,000. Cost of goods sold is 60 percent of sales.

Purchases in April were $250,000; in May, $180,000. A given month's purchases are paid as follows: 10 percent during that month; 80 percent the next month; and the final 10 percent the next month.

Prepare budget schedules for June, July, and August for purchases and for disbursements for purchases.

P11-5 **PURCHASE BUDGET.**   The inventory of the Manchester Appliance Company was £200,000 on May 31. The manager was upset because the inventory was too high. She has adopted the following policies regarding merchandise purchases and inventory. At the end of any month, the inventory should be £15,000 plus 90 percent of the cost of goods to be sold during the following month. The cost of merchandise sold averages 60 percent of sales. Purchase terms are generally net, 30 days. A given month's purchases are paid as follows: 20 percent during that month and 80 percent during the following month.

Purchases in May had been £150,000. Sales are expected to be: June, £300,000; July, £280,000; August, £340,000; and September, £400,000.

1. Compute the amount by which the inventory on May 31 exceeded the manager's policies.
2. Prepare budget schedules for June, July, and August for purchases and for disbursements for purchases.

P11-6 PURCHASES AND COST OF GOODS SOLD. The Astro Co., a wholesaler of food products, budgeted the following sales for the months shown below:

	JUNE 2007	JULY 2007	AUGUST 2007
Sales on account	$1,800,000	$1,920,000	$2,040,000
Cash sales	240,000	250,000	260,000
Total sales	$2,040,000	$2,170,000	$2,300,000

All merchandise is marked up to sell at its invoice cost plus 25 percent. Merchandise inventories at the beginning of each month are at 30 percent of that month's projected cost of goods sold.

1. Compute the budgeted cost of goods sold for the month of June 2007.
2. Compute the budgeted merchandise purchases for July 2007.

P11-7 PURCHASES AND SALES BUDGETS. All sales of Dunn's Building Supplies (DBS) are made on credit. Sales are billed twice monthly, on the tenth of the month for the last half of the prior month's sales and on the 20th of the month for the first half of the current month's sales. The terms of all sales are 2/10, net 30. Based on past experience, the collection experience of accounts receivable is as follows:

Within the discount period	80%
On the 30th day	18%
Uncollectible	2%

The sales value of shipments for May 2007 was $750,000. The forecast sales for the next four months are

June	$800,000
July	900,000
August	900,000
September	600,000

DBS's average markup on its products is 20 percent of the sales price.

DBS purchases merchandise for resale to meet the current month's sales demand and to maintain a desired monthly ending inventory of 25 percent of the next month's sales. All purchases are on credit with terms of net 30. DBS pays for one-half of a month's purchases in the month of purchase and the other half in the month following the purchase.

All sales and purchases occur uniformly throughout the month.

1. How much cash can DBS plan to collect from accounts receivable collections during July 2007?
2. How much can DBS plan to collect in September from sales made in August 2007?
3. Compute the budgeted dollar value of DBS's inventory on August 31, 2007.
4. How much merchandise should DBS plan to purchase during June 2007?
5. How much should DBS budget in August 2007 for the payment of merchandise?

P11-8 CASH BUDGET. Consider the following information for the month ending June 30, 2007 for the Johnson Company:

The cash balance, May 31, 2007, is $15,000. Sales proceeds are collected as follows: 80 percent month of sale, 10 percent second month, 10 percent third month.

Accounts receivable are $40,000 on May 31, 2007, consisting of $16,000 from April sales and $24,000 from May sales.

Accounts payable on May 31, 2007, are $145,000. Johnson Company pays 25 percent of purchases during the month of purchase and the remainder during the following month. All operating expenses requiring cash are paid during the month of recognition. However, insurance and property taxes are paid annually in December.

Johnson Company Budgeted Income Statement for the Month Ended June 30, 2007 (in thousands)		
Sales		$290
Inventory, May 31	$ 50	
Purchases	192	
Available for sale	$242	
Inventory, June 30	40	
Cost of goods sold		202
Gross margin		$ 88
Operating expenses:		
Wages	$ 36	
Utilities	5	
Advertising	10	
Amortization	1	
Office expenses	4	
Insurance and property taxes	3	59
Operating income		$ 29

Prepare a cash budget for June. Confine your analysis to the given data. Ignore income taxes and other possible items that might affect cash.

P11-9 CASH BUDGET. Jane Myers is the manager of an extremely successful gift shop, Jane's Gifts, which is operated for the benefit of local charities. From the data below, she wants a cash budget showing expected cash receipts and disbursements for the month of April, and the cash balance expected as of April 30, 2008:

- Bank note due April 10: $90,000 plus $4,500 interest
- Amortization for April: $2,100
- Two-year insurance policy due April 14 for renewal: $1,500, to be paid in cash
- Planned cash balance, March 31, 2008: $80,000
- Merchandise purchases for April: $500,000, 40 percent paid in month of purchase, 60 percent paid in next month
- Customer receivables as of March 31: $60,000 from February sales, $450,000 from March sales
- Payrolls due in April: $90,000
- Other expenses for April, payable in April: $45,000
- Accrued taxes for April, payable in June: $7,500
- Sales for April: $1,000,000, half collected in month of sale, 40 percent in next month, 10 percent in third month
- Accounts payable, March 31, 2008: $460,000

Prepare the cash budget.

P11-10   **CASH BUDGET.**   Prepare a statement of estimated cash receipts and disbursements for October 2007 for the Aquarius Company, which sells one product, herbal soap, by the case. On October 1, 2007, part of the trial balance showed:

Cash	$ 4,800
Accounts receivable	15,600
Allowance for bad debts	1,900
Merchandise inventory	9,000
Accounts payable, merchandise	7,200

The company pays for its purchases within 10 days. Assume that one-third of the purchases of any month are due and paid for in the following month.

The cost of the merchandise purchased is $12 per case. At the end of each month it is desired to have an inventory equal in units to 50 percent of the following month's sales in units.

Sales terms include a 1 percent discount if payment is made by the end of the calendar month. Past experience indicates that 60 percent of the billings will be collected during the month of the sale, 30 percent in the following calendar month, and six percent in the next following calendar month. Four percent will be uncollectible. The company's fiscal year begins August 1.

Unit selling price	$ 20
August actual sales	12,000
September actual sales	36,000
October estimated sales	30,000
November estimated sales	22,000
Total sales expected in the fiscal year	360,000

Exclusive of bad debts, total budgeted selling and general administrative expenses for the fiscal year are estimated at $55,500, of which $18,000 is fixed expense, which includes a $7,200 annual amortization charge. Aquarius incurs these fixed expenses uniformly throughout the year. The balance of the selling and general administrative expenses varies with sales. Expenses are paid as incurred.

P11-11   **MASTER BUDGET.**   Computer Superstores Inc. has a strong belief in using highly decentralized management. You are the new manager of one of its small "computer boutiques." You know a great deal about how to buy, how to display, how to sell, and how to reduce shoplifting. However, you know little about accounting and finance.

Top management is convinced that training for higher management should include the active participation of store managers in the budgeting process. You have been asked to prepare a complete master budget for your store for June, July, and August. You are responsible for its preparation. All accounting is done centrally, so you have no expert help on the premises. In addition, the branch manager and the assistant controller will arrive tomorrow to examine your work; at that time they will assist you in formulating the final budget document. The idea is to have you prepare the budget a few times so that you gain more confidence about accounting matters. You want to make a favourable impression on your superiors, so you gather the following data as of May 31, 2007:

Cash	$ 29,000	Recent and	
Inventory	420,000	Projected Sales	
Accounts receivable	369,000		
Net furniture and fixtures	168,000	April	$300,000
Total assets	$986,000	May	350,000
		June	700,000
Accounts payable	$475,000	July	400,000
Owners' equity	511,000	August	400,000
Total liabilities and owners'		September	300,000
equities	$986,000		

Credit sales are 90 percent of total sales. Credit accounts are collected 80 percent in the month following the sale and 20 percent in the next following month. Assume that bad debts are negligible and can be ignored. The accounts receivable on May 31 are the result of the credit sales for April and May: (0.20 × 0.90 × $300,000 = $54,000) + (1.00 × 0.90 × $350,000 = $315,000) = $369,000. The average gross profit on sales is 40 percent.

The policy is to acquire enough inventory each month to equal the following month's projected sales. All purchases are paid for in the month following purchase.

Salaries, wages, and commissions average 20 percent of sales; all other expenses, excluding amortization, are 4 percent of sales. Fixed expenses for rent, property taxes, and miscellaneous payroll and other items are $55,000 monthly. Assume that these expenses require cash disbursements each month. Amortization is $2,500 monthly.

In June, $55,000 is going to be disbursed for fixtures acquired in May. The May 31 balance of accounts payable includes this amount.

Assume that a minimum cash balance of $25,000 is to be maintained. Also assume that all borrowings are effective at the beginning of the month and all repayments are made at the end of the month of repayment. Interest is paid only at the time principal is repaid. Interest rate is 10 percent per annum; round interest computations to the nearest 10 dollars. All loans and repayments of principal must be made in multiples of $1,000.

1. Prepare a budgeted income statement for the coming quarter, a budgeted statement of monthly cash receipts and disbursements (for the next three months), and a budgeted balance sheet for August 30, 2007. All operations are evaluated on a before-income-tax basis, so income taxes may be ignored here.
2. Explain why there is a need for a bank loan and what operating sources supply cash for repaying the bank loan.

P11-12 **MASTER BUDGET.** Daphne Kite Company wants a master budget for the next three months, beginning January 1, 2008. It desires an ending minimum cash balance of $5,000 each month. Sales are forecasted at an average selling price of $8 per kite. In January, Daphne Kite is beginning just-in-time deliveries from suppliers, which means that purchases equal expected sales. The December 31 inventory balance will be drawn down to $6,000, which will be the desired ending inventory thereafter. Merchandise costs are $4 per kite. Purchases during any given month are paid in full during the following month. All sales are on credit, payable within 30 days, but experience has shown that 60 percent of current sales is collected in the current month, 30 percent in the next month, and 10 percent in the month thereafter. Bad debts are negligible.

Wages and salaries	$15,000
Insurance expired	125
Amortization	250
Miscellaneous	2,500/month
Rent	250/month + 10% of quarterly sales over $10,000

Cash dividends of $1,500 are to be paid quarterly, beginning January 15, and are declared on the fifteenth of the previous month. All operating expenses are paid as incurred, except insurance, amortization, and rent. Rent of $250 is paid at the beginning of each month and the additional 10 percent of sales is paid quarterly on the tenth of the month following the quarter. The next settlement is due January 10.

The company plans to buy some new fixtures for $3,000 cash in March.

Money can be borrowed and repaid in multiples of $500, at an interest rate of 10 percent per annum. Management wants to minimize borrowing and repay rapidly. Interest is computed and paid when the principal is repaid. Assume that borrowing takes place at the beginning, and repayments at the end, of the months in question. Money is never borrowed at the beginning and repaid at the end of the same month. Compute interest to the nearest dollar.

ASSETS AS OF DECEMBER 31, 2007		LIABILITIES AS OF DECEMBER 31, 2007	
Cash	$ 5,000	Accounts payable (merchandise)	$35,550
Accounts receivable	12,500	Dividends payable	1,500
Inventory*	39,050	Rent payable	7,800
Unexpired insurance	1,500		$44,850
Fixed assets, net	12,500		
	$70,550		

* November 30 inventory balance = $16,000.

Recent and forecasted sales:

October	$38,000	December	$25,000	February	$75,000	April	$45,000
November	$25,000	January	$62,000	March	$38,000		

1. Prepare a master budget including a budgeted income statement, balance sheet, statement of cash receipts and disbursements, and supporting schedules for the months January through March 2008.
2. Explain why there is a need for a bank loan and what operating sources provide the cash for the repayment of the bank loan.

P11 13 **BUDGETING AT RITZ-CARLTON.** Suppose Ritz-Carlton has a 300-room hotel in a tropical climate. Management expects occupancy rates to be 95 percent in December, January, and February, 85 percent in November, March, and April, and 70 percent the rest of the year. The average room rental is $250 per night. Of this, on average 10 percent is received as a deposit the month before the stay, 60 percent is received in the month of the stay, and 28 percent is collected the month after. The remaining 2 percent is never collected.

Most of the costs of running the hotel are fixed. The variable costs are only $30 per occupied room per night. Fixed salaries (including benefits) run $400,000 per month, amortization is $350,00 a month, other fixed operating costs are $120,000 per month, and interest expense is $500,000 per month. Variable costs and salaries are paid in the month they are incurred, amortization is recorded at the end of each quarter, other fixed operating costs are paid as incurred, and interest is paid each June and December.

1. Prepare a monthly cash budget for this Ritz-Carlton hotel. For simplicity, assume that there are 30 days in each month.
2. How much would the hotel's annual profit increase if occupancy rates increased by 5 percentage points each month in the off-season (that is, from 70 percent to 75 percent in May through October)?

P11-14 **CASH BUDGETING FOR A HOSPITAL.**   (CMA, adapted)   Grace Hospital provides a wide range of health services in its community. The board of directors has authorized the following capital expenditures:

Interaortic balloon pump	$1,300,000
CT scanner	850,000
X-ray equipment	550,000
Laboratory equipment	1,200,000
	$3,900,000

The expenditures are planned for October 1, 2008, and the board wants to know how much, if anything, the hospital has to borrow. Jill Todd, hospital controller, has gathered the following information to be used to prepare an analysis of future cash flows.

a. Billings, made in the month of service, for the first half of 2008 are

MONTH	ACTUAL AMOUNT
January	$5,300,000
February	5,300,000
March	5,400,000
April	5,400,000
May	6,000,000
June	6,000,000

Ninety percent of the billings are made to third parties such as Blue Cross, provincial governments, and private insurance companies. The remaining 10 percent of the billings are made directly to patients. Historical patterns of billing collections are

	THIRD-PARTY BILLINGS	DIRECT PATIENT BILLINGS
Month of service	20%	10%
Month following service	50	40
Second month following service	20	40
Uncollectible	10	10

Estimated billings for the last six months of 2008 are listed next. Todd expects the same billing and collection patterns that have been experienced during the first six months of 2008 to continue during the last six months of the year.

MONTH	ESTIMATED AMOUNT
July	$5,400,000
August	6,000,000
September	6,600,000
October	6,800,000
November	7,000,000
December	6,600,000

b. The following schedule presents the purchases that have been made during the past three months and the planned purchases for the last six months of 2008.

MONTH	AMOUNT
April	$1,300,000
May	1,450,000
June	1,450,000
July	1,500,000
August	1,800,000
September	2,200,000
October	2,350,000
November	2,700,000
December	2,100,000

All purchases are made on account, and accounts payable are remitted in the month following the purchase.

c. Salaries for each month during the remainder of 2008 are expected to be $1,800,000 per month plus 20 percent of that month's billings. Salaries are paid in the month of service.

d. Grace's monthly amortization charges are $150,000.

e. Grace incurs interest expense of $180,000 per month and makes interest payments of $540,000 on the last day of each calendar quarter.

f. Endowment fund income is expected to continue to total $210,000 per month.

g. Grace has a cash balance of $350,000 on July 1, 2008, and has a policy of maintaining a minimum end-of-month cash balance of 10 percent of the current month's purchases.

h. Grace Hospital employs a calendar-year reporting period.

1. Prepare a schedule of budgeted cash receipts by month for the third quarter of 2008.

2. Prepare a schedule of budgeted cash disbursements by month for the third quarter of 2008.

3. Determine the amount of borrowing, if any, necessary on October 1, 2008, to acquire the capital items totalling $3,900,000.

P11-15 **COMPREHENSIVE BUDGETING FOR A UNIVERSITY.** (CPA, adapted) Suppose you are the controller of Ryerson University. The university president is preparing for her annual fundraising campaign for 2008–09. To set an appropriate target, she has asked you to prepare a budget for the academic year. You have collected the following data for the current year (2007–08).

a. For 2008–09, all faculty and staff will receive a 6 percent salary increase. Undergraduate enrolment is expected to decline by 2 percent, but graduate enrolment is expected to increase by 5 percent.

	UNDERGRADUATE DIVISION	GRADUATE DIVISION
Average salary of faculty member	$48,760	$48,760
Average faculty teaching load in semester credit hours per year (eight undergraduate or six graduate courses)	24	18
Average number of students per class	30	20
Total enrolment (full-time and part-time students)	3,600	1,800
Average number of semester credit hours carried each year per student	25	20
Full-time load, semester hours per year	30	24

b. The 2007–08 budget for operation and maintenance of facilities is $500,000, which includes $240,000 for salaries and wages. Experience so far this year indicates that the budget is accurate. Salaries and wages will increase by 6 percent and other operating costs by $12,000 in 2008–09.

c. The 2007–08 and 2008–09 budgets for the remaining expenditures are

	2007–08	2008–09
General administrative	$500,000	$525,000
Library:		
Acquisitions	150,000	155,000
Operations	190,000	200,000
Health services	48,000	50,000
Intramural athletics	56,000	60,000
Intercollegiate athletics	240,000	245,000
Insurance and retirement	520,000	560,000
Interest	75,000	75,000

d. Tuition is $70 per credit hour. In addition, the provincial government provides $780 per full-time-equivalent student. (A full-time equivalent is 30 undergraduate semester credit-hours or 24 graduate semester credit-hours.) Tuition scholarships are given to 30 *full-time* undergraduates and 50 *full-time* graduate students.

e. Revenues other than tuition and the government apportionment are

	2007–08	2008–09
Endowment income	$200,000	$210,000
Net income from auxiliary services	325,000	335,000
Intercollegiate athletic receipts	290,000	300,000

f. The chemistry/physics classroom building needs remodelling during the 2008–09 period. Projected cost is $550,000.

1. Prepare a schedule for 2008–09 that shows, by division, (a) expected enrolment, (b) total credit hours, (c) full-time-equivalent enrolment, and (d) number of faculty members needed.
2. Calculate the budget for faculty salaries for 2008–09 by division.
3. Calculate the budget for tuition revenue and government apportionment for 2008–09 by division.
4. Prepare a schedule for the president showing the amount that must be raised by the annual fundraising campaign.

P11-16 **ACTIVITY-BASED BUDGETING.** A recent directive from Eugenia Yu, CEO of Comtel, had instructed each department to cut its cost by 10 percent. The traditional budget for the warehousing department was as follows:

Salaries, 4 employees @ $42,000	$168,000
Benefits @ 20%	33,600
Amortization, straight-line basis	76,000
Parts and supplies	42,400
Overhead @ 35% of direct costs	112,000
Total	$432,000

Therefore, the warehousing division needed to find $43,200 to cut.

Athan Viris, a recent MBA graduate, was asked to pare $43,200 from the warehousing department's budget. As a first step, he recast the traditional budget into an activity-based budget:

Receiving, 620,000 kilograms	$ 93,000
Shipping, 402,000 boxes	201,000
Handling, 11,200 moves	112,000
Record-keeping, 65,000 transactions	26,000
Total	$432,000

1. What actions might Viris suggest to attain a $43,200 budget cut? Why would these be the best actions to pursue?
2. Which budget helped you most in answering requirement 1? Explain.

P11-17 **SPREADSHEETS AND SENSITIVITY ANALYSIS OF THE INCOME STATEMENT.** Study the appendix beginning on page 551. The Speedy-Mart Store has the following budgeted sales, which are uniform throughout the month:

May	$450,000
June	375,000
July	330,000
August	420,000

Cost of goods sold averages 70 percent of sales and is purchased as it is needed. Employees earn fixed salaries of $22,000 (total) monthly and commissions of 10 percent of the current month's sales. Other expenses are rent, $6,000, paid on the first of each month; miscellaneous expenses, 6 percent of sales, paid as incurred; insurance, $450 per month, from a one-year policy that was paid for on January 2; and amortization, $2,850 per month.

1. Using spreadsheet software, prepare a table of budget data for the Speedy-Mart Store.
2. Continue the spreadsheet in requirement 1 to prepare budget schedules for (a) disbursements for operating expenses and (b) operating income for June, July, and August.
3. Adjust the budget data appropriately for each of the following scenarios independently and recompute operating income using the spreadsheet.
   a. A sales promotion that will cost $30,000 in May could increase sales in each of the following three months by 5 percent.
   b. Eliminating the sales commissions and increasing employees' salaries to $52,500 per month could decrease sales thereafter by a net of 2 percent.

P11-18 **SPREADSHEETS AND SENSITIVITY ANALYSIS OF OPERATING EXPENSES.** Study the appendix beginning on page 551. The CD-ROM division (CDRD) of Micro Storage, Inc. produces CD-ROM drives for personal computers. The drives are assembled from purchased components. The costs (value) added by CDRD are indirect costs (which include assembly labour), packaging, and shipping. Cost behaviour is as follows:

	FIXED	VARIABLE
Purchased components		
10X drives		$100 per component
5X drives		$40 per component
Indirect costs	$40,000	$16 per component
Packaging	$8,000	$4 per drive
Shipping	$8,000	$2 per drive

Both CD-ROM drives require five components. Therefore, the total cost of components for A100 drives is $500 and for A50 drives is $200. CDRD uses a six-month continuous budget that is revised monthly. Sales forecasts for the next eight months are as follows:

	A100 DRIVES	A50 DRIVES
October	3,200 units	4,000 units
November	2,400	3,000
December	5,600	7,000
January	3,200	4,000
February	3,200	4,000
March	2,400	3,000
April	2,400	3,000
May	2,800	3,500

Treat each event in succession.

1. Use spreadsheet software to prepare a table of budgeting information and an operating expense budget for the CD-ROM division for October through March. Incorporate the expectation that sales of A50 drives

will be 125 percent of A100 drives. Prepare a spreadsheet that can be revised easily for succeeding months.

2. October's actual sales were 2,800 A100 drives and 3,600 A50 drives. This outcome has caused CDRD to revise its sales forecasts downward by 10 percent. Revise the operating expense budget for November through April.

3. At the end of November, CDRD decides that the proportion of A100 drives to A50 drives is changing. Sales of A50 drives are expected to be 150 percent of A100 drive sales. Expected sales of A100 drives are unchanged from requirement 2. Revise the operating expense budget for December through May.

P11-19 **BUDGETING, BEHAVIOUR, AND ETHICS.**   Since Mitch Banks had become president of Alberta Mining, Ltd., budgets had become a major focus for managers. In fact, making budget was such an important goal that the two managers who had missed their budgets in 2007 (by 2 percent and 4 percent, respectively) were fired. This caused all managers to be wary when setting their 2008 budgets.

The GSL copper division of Alberta Mining had the following results for 2007:

Sales, 1.6 million kilograms @ $0.95/kilogram	$1,520,000
Variable costs	880,000
Fixed costs, primarily amortization	450,000
Pretax profit	$ 190,000

Sheila Masur, general manager of GSL, received a memo from Banks that stated:

"We expect your profit for 2008 to be at least $209,000. Prepare a budget showing how you plan to accomplish this."

Masur was concerned that the market for copper had recently softened. Her market-research staff forecast that sales would be at or below the 2007 level and prices would likely be between $0.92 and $0.94 per kilogram. Her manufacturing manager reported that most of the fixed costs were committed and there were few efficiencies to be gained in the variable costs. He indicated that a 2 percent savings might be achievable, but certainly no more.

1. Prepare a budget for Masur to submit to headquarters. What dilemmas does Masur face in preparing this budget?
2. What problems do you see in the budgeting process at Alberta Mining?
3. Suppose Masur submitted a budget showing a $209,000 profit. It is now late in 2008, and she has had a good year. Despite an industry-wide decline in sales, GSL's sales matched last year's 1.6 million kilograms, and the average price per kilogram was $0.945, nearly at last year's level and well above that forecast. Variable costs were cut by 2 percent through extensive efforts. Still, profit projections were $9,000 below budget. Masur was concerned for her job, so she approached the controller and requested that amortization schedules be changed. By extending the lives of some equipment by two years, $15,000 of amortization could be saved in 2008. Estimating the economic lives of equipment is difficult, and it would be hard to prove that the old lives were better than the new proposed lives. What should the controller do? What ethical issues does this raise?

C11-1 BUDGETING FOR EXPANSION. (ICAO) Tom's Outdoor Experience (TOE) is a sporting goods

store owned by Tom Dennison. Tom handles limited product lines. Summer sales centre on bicycles, camping gear, and clothing for both activities. Cross-country skis and related equipment and clothing are the major winter lines. The store is a year-round centre for running enthusiasts because better footwear and clothing for this sporting activity are featured. The store is situated in a small city in Ontario.

Operations began 14 years ago when Tom purchased the building that houses the store. The business provided adequate cash flow to raise a family of three children. Now that the children are grown, Tom's wife has resumed her career. Tom has decided to open a new store in a nearby city as he is certain there is an available market.

Tom has been a close friend of your family for many years. In April 2007, he telephoned to ask your advice about preparing a presentation to his banker so that he could proceed with his expansion plans.

The conversation proceeded as follows:

Tom: I spoke to the bank manager about borrowing $200,000 to buy that building, clean it up a little, and install some equipment. The building, at $175,000, is a good buy according to the real estate agent. I got a $15,000 quote from a contractor to do the renovations it requires. I think that $10,000 is enough to buy a cash register, display racks, and the little pieces of equipment needed to repair bikes and skis.

You: I guess the banker needs some collateral and some indication that you'll be able to repay the loan.

Tom: That's right. And that's where I thought you might be able to help. Tell me what you think he wants and how to put it together.

You: He probably wants to see cash-flow statements and anticipated results for the new location. Do you have financial statements prepared?

Tom: Yes, the January 31, 2007 year-end balance sheet and income statements are done (Exhibits 11A-1 and 11A-2). I also have written a list of things that I expect will happen with the new store (Exhibit 11A-3).

You: Good. Have you borrowed money from this bank before?

Tom: Yes, I have a line of credit with them, and I'm still paying the $386 per month on the mortgage of the old store. The banker says my credit rating is good, and that I could probably get both long- and short-term money at 12 percent. I asked him if a working capital loan of $20,000 for the new store would be possible. He said that he would consider it at the same time as the new building package.

You: You seem to have thought this out thoroughly.

Tom: If I brought over the documentation, could we put something together tonight? I'm seeing the banker tomorrow morning. If you can do the numbers, I can justify the marketing aspects. I'd really like to know what you think about this new venture.

You: Sure, Tom. I'll see you about 7:30.

Tom arrived with his documentation and financial statements. He assured you that he could have the presentation typed in the morning before his meeting with the banker.

Prepare the necessary quantitative and qualitative analysis that would help Tom present his request to his banker. State any assumptions you make.

EXHIBIT 11A-1

Tom's Outdoor Experience
Tom Dennison, Proprietor
Balance Sheet as at January 31, 2007

ASSETS	2007	2006	2005
Current assets			
Cash	$ 2,570	$ 2,400	$ 1,500
Accounts receivable	840	1,160	950
Inventory	49,130	44,760	38,950
Prepaids	2,010	1,860	1,400
	54,550	50,180	42,800
Fixed assets			
Equipment	8,500	8,500	6,000
Building	40,000	40,000	40,000
Land	6,000	6,000	6,000
	54,500	54,500	52,000
Less: Accumulated amortization	24,700	21,450	18,200
	29,800	33,050	33,800
Total assets	$84,350	$83,230	$76,600

LIABILITIES AND OWNER'S EQUITY			
Current liabilities			
Bank indebtedness	$ 7,000	$ 9,300	$ 4,700
Accounts payable	24,410	28,580	27,700
Accrued liabilities	1,450	1,950	1,700
	32,860	39,830	34,100
Mortgage payable	30,830	32,300	33,600
Owner's equity			
Tom Dennison, capital	20,660	11,100	8,900
Total liabilities and owner's equity	$84,350	$83,230	$76,600

EXHIBIT 11A-2

Tom's Outdoor Experience
Tom Dennison, Proprietor
Statement of Income and Owner's Equity for the Year Ended January 31, 2007

	2007	2006	2005
Sales	$265,360	$233,800	$203,100
Cost of goods sold	171,690	147,360	125,860
Gross profit	93,670	86,440	77,240
Expenses			
Selling and administration	43,120	44,580	35,130
Amortization	3,250	3,250	3,000
Interest on long-term debt	3,160	3,330	3,400
Interest on short-term debt	1,180	980	1,360
	50,710	52,140	42,890
Net income for the year	42,960	34,300	34,350
Owner's equity beginning of year	11,100	8,900	6,400
Drawings	(33,400)	(32,100)	(31,850)
Owner's equity, end of year	$ 20,660	$ 11,100	$ 8,900

1. The deal for the store will close May 31 if financing is secured. This will allow time for renovations and inventory stocking. Projected opening date: August 1, 2007.
2. Sales in the old store are expected to increase by a minimum of 15 percent per year during the next few years since fitness is becoming an essential part of many lifestyles.

    Sales in the new store in the first six months will be about 80 percent of the projected results in the old store, then will equal or better the level of the old store. I expect better sales because the new store is in a larger community and the store area is larger.
3. Profit margins in the old store have slipped slightly in past years because of pressure from the chain stores. With two stores, purchasing economies will ensure that my profit margin won't slip more than one percent per year. I am even expecting a slight recovery because we provide excellent service on all equipment. Customers appreciate that and are willing to pay for it.
4. Selling and administration expenses have levelled off because we are using more part-time staff. I expect that in addition to the regular costs, I'll have to pay about $5,000 per year more for one of the staff to act as a manager.
5. Drawings can be reduced to $15,000 per year. My wife's income is more than sufficient for living expenses, since our house mortgage has been paid.

C11-2 **CASH BUDGETING.** (SMAC) George Brown, a self-employed management consultant, had just settled down to work when he received a call from Ray Sharma, vice president of Software Corporation (SC), a software distributing and consulting firm.

Sharma had been through a hectic holiday period and, to some extent, he had let the financial controls slip away. Preoccupied with devoting much of his attention to the customer service side, Sharma had suddenly become aware that cash flow was devastated. In December, three suppliers put him on a C.O.D. basis and three more threatened to stop supplying. At the end of November, the bank line of credit was $260,000 over limit and the bank had refused to honour any cheques except payroll until SC either reduced the outstanding balance to the limit or renegotiated its bank loan. As a condition of refinancing the bank loan, the bank wanted audited financial statements as support for Sharma's claim that business was great.

"Business is great," Sharma had said to Brown. "We just don't have any cash! George, I was wondering if you could come over here and help me out. I need you to analyze our cash-flow problem. Specifically, I would like you to prepare a statement of cash flow for each of the last four months of 2007 for me so that I can answer any questions that the bank manager may have when I meet with her."

Brown visited SC two days later to analyze the cash-flow problem. Exhibit 11A-4 presents information gathered by Brown in support of his analysis. Exhibit 11A-5 contains a condensed balance sheet of SC as at August 31, 2007, and December 31, 2007.

Required: | Analyze the cash-flow problem at SC and make recommendations for improvement.

EXHIBIT 11A-4

Schedules Prepared
by George Brown
Regarding the
Cash-Flow Problem

2007 SALES (000s)

April	$150
May	200
June	275
July	300
August	400
September	450
October	535
November	580
December	690

AGED ACCOUNTS RECEIVABLE TOTALS AT MONTH END (000s)
SEPTEMBER TO DECEMBER, 2007

	AGE IN DAYS						
	CURRENT	30	60	90	120	OVER 120	TOTAL
September	$540	$480	$405	$380	$350	$ 315	$2,470
October	600	515	460	400	370	520	2,865
November	670	585	475	450	360	825	3,365
December	750	660	555	465	410	1,050	3,890

ANALYSIS OF WORK-IN-PROCESS (000s)
AUGUST TO DECEMBER, 2007

	MONTH				
	AUG.	SEPT.	OCT.	NOV.	DEC.
Consulting work-in-process at month end	$310	$375	$460	$575	$675
Consulting fees invoiced		240	225	225	100

AGED ACCOUNTS PAYABLE TOTALS AT MONTH END (000s)
SEPTEMBER TO DECEMBER, 2007

	AGE IN DAYS					
	CURRENT	30	60	90	OVER 90	TOTAL
September	$615	$640	$450	$360	–	$2,065
October	750	615	640	450	150	2,605
November	510	750	615	640	200	2,715
December	400	510	750	615	645	2,920

EXHIBIT 11A-5		AUGUST	DECEMBER
Information Collected by George Brown Software Corporation Condensed Balance Sheet as at August 31 and December 31, 2007 (Before December Adjustments) (000s)	Accounts receivable	$2,055	$3,890
	Work-in-process—consulting*	310	675
	Fixed assets—net	695	815
		$3,060	$5,380
	Bank loan payable	$ 350	$ 615
	Accounts payable	1,750	2,920
	Shareholders' equity	960	1,845
		$3,060	$5,380

* Obtained from time sheet summaries costed at a regular billing rate.

Other information with respect to SC's cash flows:

1. Bank advances of $80,000 were received in September.
2. Regular operating cash outflows per month are $75,000.
3. Fixed assets of $150,000 were acquired in September for cash.
4. No purchases are paid for in the month in which they are bought.

C11-3 PRODUCTION AND CASH BUDGETING. (ICAO)

Part A

Millie Bandes, a successful entrepreneur, is setting up a new division for the manufacture of three new products that will complement her current line of business. Millie is currently involved in the manufacture of motorboats. She believes that overall corporate profits can be enhanced by manufacturing custom boat covers (CBC), waterskis (WS), and boat ladders (BL) in her new division and has asked you to assist her in planning a production schedule for the next month.

The three products will be manufactured in a plant with three departments. As the products proceed through each department, applicable labour and machine time are applied. Each department is composed of specialized machinery and specialized labour skills and, accordingly, neither machine time nor labour time can be switched between departments.

The following data have been accumulated by Millie:

	DEPARTMENT		
	1	2	3
Available machine capacity in machine hours per month	10,000	10,000	10,000
Available direct labour hours per month	15,000	15,000	15,000
UNIT SPECIFICATIONS:			
Product			
CBC — machine hours	3	1	2
CBC — direct labour hours	5	2	3
WS — machine hours	2	2	1
WS — direct labour hours	4	3	1
BL — machine hours	1	2	3
BL — direct labour hours	3	4	5

MONTHLY DEMAND

CBC	1,000 units
WS	1,500 units
BL	2,000 units

UNIT COSTS

	PRODUCT		
	CBC	WS	BL
	$	$	$
Direct materials	20	30	40
Direct labour:			
Department 1	25	20	15
Department 2	20	30	40
Department 3	15	5	25
Variable overhead	60	95	150
Fixed overhead	40	50	40
Variable selling and administrative	10	20	15
Fixed selling and administrative	10	30	10
Unit selling prices	240	300	360

Other information:

Since the business is seasonal and space is limited, Millie has asked you to assume zero inventory and work-in-process at the end of each month. Unit fixed costs are based on sufficient monthly production to meet sales demand. Fixed overhead costs for a given product are incurred only if that product is produced.

Required:

1. Prepare a monthly production schedule for one month only that will maximize the division's profit given the above information, and prepare a schedule of estimated divisional profit.
2. What steps would you advise Millie to consider for next year in order to further enhance her divisional profit?

Part B

Millie's banker is convinced that only the custom boat covers (CBC) should be manufactured. In order to authorize a long-term bank loan for equipment and an operating line of credit for day-to-day operations, the banker requires a three-month schedule of cash flows that will identify the amount of operating line of credit required and illustrate the division's ability to adhere to the long-term loan repayment schedule and maintain adequate collateral for the operating line of credit.

Millie has provided the following *additional* information in this regard:

a. All of the data described in Part A will be valid for the entire three-month period.

b. Millie will deposit $100,000 into the division's bank account as startup funds.

c. Direct material for one month's production is ordered in the month prior to production, is delivered on the first day of the month of production, and is paid for in the month of production.

d. Fixed costs are paid for in the month of production.

e. Variable selling expenses are paid for in the month of production.

f. Anticipated cash flows from sales are as follows:
20 percent of monthly sales will be cash sales; 80 percent of monthly sales will be credit sales with 30 day net terms; and 10 percent of credit sales are expected to be uncollectible.

g. The division will require a term loan of $120,000 in order to purchase equipment for the production of custom boat covers. The bank has agreed to a 12 percent annual interest rate for 60 months with payments at the end of each month of $2,000 principal plus interest. The term loan proceeds will be advanced and the equipment will be purchased at the beginning of the first month.

h. The required operating funds (as per the cash-flow statement) will be advanced at the beginning of each month to a maximum of 75 percent of the anticipated collectible receivables, as at the end of the month the operating line of credit funds are advanced. Operating line of credit funds are advanced in multiples of $20,000.

i. Interest expense on the operating line of credit funds, charged at an annual rate of 18 percent, is to be minimized subject to a desired minimum cash-on-hand balance of $15,000. Any repayments of operating line of credit funds will be made at the end of the month and can be made only in multiples of $10,000.

Required:
Prepare the three-month schedule of cash flows required by the banker. (Your schedule should include four numeric columns: one column for each of the three months and one column containing the totals for the three months. The columns should only include cash flows pertaining to custom boat covers (CBC). *All* information available relating to custom boat covers (CBC) should be utilized.

C11-4 CASH BUDGETING. (CGAC) Ivan Sharpova is trying to decide whether he is going to need to take a loan in January to buy a new microcomputer system for his business. The microcomputer will cost $10,800.

Sharpova has collected the following information about his operations as of December 31:

1. Balances of selected ledger accounts:

Cash	$2,120
Accounts payable	6,667

2. Sales history and forecast (unit selling price $10):

(Actual)	October	$43,000
(Actual)	November	35,000
(Actual)	December	40,000
(Forecast)	January	50,000

3. All sales are on credit and are due (required to be paid) 30 days after the sale.

4. Fifty percent of a given month's sales are collected one month after the sale (that is, 30 days), 45 percent are collected two months after sales and 5 percent are uncollectible.

5. Inventory is purchased under terms of 2/10 net 30. Sharpova always takes the 2 percent discount, but records purchases at gross cost. Accounts payable (shown above) related solely to inventory purchases. Inventory costs $5 per unit, gross.

6. Other expenses, all paid in cash as required, average about 30 percent of sales dollars. Amortization is part of these expenses and costs $3,000 per month.

7. Sharpova keeps a minimum cash balance of $1,000.

Required: Prepare a cash budget for January, indicating whether Sharpova will need a loan to finance his computer acquisition.

EXCEL APPLICATION EXERCISE

E11-1 PREPARING A CASH BUDGET TO ASSIST LONG-RANGE PLANNING

Goal: Create an Excel spreadsheet to prepare a cash budget to assist with long-range planning. Use the results to answer questions about your findings.

Scenario: Brenda Peterson and Molly Chan are preparing a plan to submit to venture capitalists to fund their business, Peterson Chan Inc. The company plans to spend $300,000 on equipment in the first quarter of 2007. Salaries and other operating expenses (paid as incurred) will be $30,000 per month beginning in January 2007 and will continue at that level thereafter. The company will receive its first revenues in January 2008, with cash collections averaging $25,000 per month for all of 2008. In January 2009 cash collections are expected to increase to $100,000 per month and continue at that level thereafter. Peterson Chan Inc. has asked you to prepare an analysis of their cash requirements until such time as their forecasted cash receipts begin to exceed their forecasted cash disbursements. The company will use your analysis to determine venture capital funding levels requests.

How much venture capital funding should Peterson Chan Inc. seek? Assume that the company needs enough funding to cover all of its cash needs until cash receipts start exceeding cash disbursements.

When you have completed your spreadsheet, answer the following questions:

1. Based on their stated objective of stopping venture capital funding when cash receipts begin to exceed cash disbursements, in what month/year should Peterson Chan Inc. no longer require venture capital funding? Why?

2. What is the total amount of expenditures Peterson Chan Inc. will incur before their cash receipts begin to exceed their cash disbursements? What is the total amount of venture capital funding that Peterson Chan Inc. should request?

3. Is the amount of venture capital funding that Peterson Chan Inc. should request equal to their total expenditures? If not, why are the amounts different?

Step by Step:

1. Open a new Excel spreadsheet.

2. In column A, create a bold-faced heading that contains the following:
   Row 1: Chapter 11 Decision Guideline
   Row 2: Peterson Chan Inc.
   Row 3: Cash Budget for Venture Capital Requirements
   Row 4: Today's Date

3. Merge and centre the four heading rows across columns A through F.

4. In row 7, create the following bold-faced, centre-justified column headings with a column width of 10.57:
   Column B: 2007
   Column C: 2008
   Column D: 2009
   Column E: 2010
   Column F: Total

5. In column A, create the following row headings:
   Row 8: Equipment Purchase
   Row 9: Salaries and Other Operating Expenses
   Row 10: Revenues
   Row 11: Net Cash Requirements

   Note: Adjust column width as necessary.

6. Use data from the scenario to enter the amounts for the yearly cash requirements for the three income/expense categories. Use formulas to calculate the appropriate yearly amounts within each category when necessary.

   Hint: Use different signs for the cash receipt (revenue) and cash disbursement (expense) amounts.

7. Use the SUM function to calculate totals for each column in row 11 and for each row in column F.

8. Format amounts in rows 8 and 11 as
   Number tab: Category: Accounting
                   Decimal: 0
                   Symbol: $

9. Format amounts in rows 9 and 10 as
   Number tab: Category: Accounting
                   Decimal: 0
                   Symbol: None

10. Apply top and bottom borders to the amounts in row 11 by clicking the drop down indicator on the Borders icon from the toolbar. Select the "Top and Double Bottom Border."

11. Save your work to disk, and print a copy for your files.

COLLABORATIVE LEARNING EXERCISE

CL11-1 **PERSONAL BUDGETING** Budgeting is useful to many different types of entities, including the individual. Consider the entity that you know best, the college or university student. Form groups of two to six students, and pool the information that you have about what it costs to spend a year as a full-time student.

Prepare a revenue and expense budget for an average prospective full-time student at your college or university. Identify possible sources of revenue and the amount to be received from each. Identify the costs a student is likely to incur during the year. You can assume that cash disbursements are made immediately for all expenses, so the budgeted income statement and cash budget are identical.

When all groups have completed their budgets, compare those budgets. What are the differences? What assumptions led to the differences?

Flexible Budgets and Variance Analysis

LEARNING OBJECTIVES

After studying this chapter, you will be able to

1. Distinguish between flexible budgets and master (static) budgets.

2. Use flexible-budget formulas to construct a flexible budget based on the volume of sales.

3. Understand the performance evaluation relationship between master (static) budgets and flexible budgets.

4. Compute flexible-budget variances and sales-volume variances.

5. Distinguish between standard costs and standard cost systems.

6. Compute and interpret price and usage variances for material, labour, and overhead inputs.

7. Compute the production-volume variance.

8. Identify the differences between the three alternative cost bases of an absorption-costing system: actual, normal, and standard.

9. Identify the two methods for disposing of the standard cost variances at the end of a year and give the rationale for each.

As we saw in Chapter 11, formal budgeting procedures result in comprehensive operational and financial plans for future periods. These budgets guide managers and employees as they make their daily decisions and as they try to anticipate future problems and opportunities. As the budget period unfolds, it is only natural that employees and managers want to know, "How did we do so far?" For example, employees and their supervisors may want to know how they are doing in meeting their non-financial objectives. Similarly, upper-level managers may want to know how the organization is meeting its financial targets as spelled out in the master budget. Managers obtain feedback on how accurately economic conditions were forecast and how well plans were executed by comparing budgets to actual results. Knowing what went right and what went wrong helps managers plan and manage more effectively in future periods. The accounting system in most organizations is designed to record transactions continuously and report actual financial results at designated intervals, usually monthly, quarterly, or annually. The actual financial results contained in the financial statements are of limited feedback value on their own. However, when these actual results are compared to the targets set by the budgets, the value of their feedback becomes significant.

This chapter introduces the concept of flexible budgets. Flexible budgets are designed to direct management to areas where actual financial performance significantly differs from budgets and therefore deserves attention. Managers can apply this same basic process of control (comparison of actual and budgetary data) to other important areas of performance, such as quality or customer services. After discussing flexible budgets and basic budget variances, we will take a detailed look at variances for traditional manufacturing inputs such as material, labour, and overhead.

FLEXIBLE BUDGETS: THE BRIDGE BETWEEN STATIC BUDGETS AND ACTUAL RESULTS

Static Budgets

OBJECTIVE 1

Distinguish between flexible budgets and master (static) budgets.

Static budget is another name for *master budget.* All the master budgets discussed in Chapter 11 are *static* or inflexible, because even though they may be easily revised, the budgets assume fixed levels of activity. In other words, a master budget is prepared for only one level of a given type of activity. For example, consider the Dominion Company, a one-department firm in Toronto that manufactures and sells a wheeled, collapsible suitcase carrier. Manufacture of this suitcase carrier requires several manual and machine operations. The product has some variations, but may be viewed, for our purposes, as a single product bearing one selling price. Assume that the cost driver is sales volume (units sold), and the projected level of activity (sales volume) is 9,000 units. All of the budget figures are then based on projected sales of 9,000 units.

All *actual* results would be compared with the original budgeted amounts, even though, for example, sales volume turned out to be only 7,000 units instead of the originally planned 9,000 units.

The master (static) budget for June 2006 included the condensed income statement shown in Exhibit 12-1, column 2. The actual results for June 2006 are in column 1. Differences or variances between actual results and the master budget are in column 3. The master budget called for production and sales of 9,000 units, but only 7,000 units were actually produced and sold. There were no beginning or ending inventories, so the units made in June were sold in June.

The performance report in Exhibit 12-1 compares the actual results with the master budget. *Performance report* is a generic term that usually means a comparison of actual results with a budget. A helpful performance report will include *variances* that direct upper management's attention to significant deviations from expected results, allowing management by exception. Recall that a *variance* is a deviation of an actual amount from the expected or budgeted amount. Each significant variance should cause a manager to ask "Why?" By explaining why a variance occurs, managers are forced to recognize changes that have affected costs and that might affect future decisions. Exhibit 12-1 shows variances of actual results from the master budget; these are called **master (static) budget variances**. Actual *revenues* that *exceed* expected revenues result in *favourable* variances, while budgeted revenues that exceed actual revenues result in unfavourable variances. Similarly, actual *expenses* that *exceed* expected expenses result in *unfavourable* variances, and vice versa.

Suppose the president of Dominion Company asks you to explain *why* there was an operating loss of $11,570 when a profit of $12,800 was predicted. Clearly, sales of 7,000 units were below expectations of 9,000 units. However, the favourable variances for the variable costs are misleading considering the lower-than-projected volume of sales. Should the variable cost variances have been higher because of the lower sales volume? The comparison of actual results with a master budget is not much help in answering that question. Master budget variances are not very useful for management by exception.

Master (Static) Budget Variances. The variances of actual results from the master budget.

Flexible Budgets

Flexible Budget. A budget that adjusts for changes in sales volume and other cost-driver activities.

A more helpful benchmark for analysis is the *flexible budget*. A **flexible budget** is a budget that adjusts for changes in sales volume or any other cost driver. The flexible budget is identical to the master budget in format. Managers may prepare

EXHIBIT 12-1

Dominion Company Performance Report Using Master Budget for the Month Ended June 30, 2006

	ACTUAL	MASTER BUDGET	MASTER BUDGET VARIANCES
Units	7,000	9,000	2,000 U
Sales	$217,000	$279,000	$62,000 U
Variable expenses:			
Variable manufacturing expenses	$151,270	$189,000	$37,730 F
Shipping expenses (selling)	5,000	5,400	400 F
Administrative expenses	2,000	1,800	200 U
Total variable expenses	$158,270	$196,200	$37,930 F
Contribution margin	$ 58,730	$ 82,800	$24,070 U
Fixed expenses:			
Fixed manufacturing expenses	$ 37,300	$ 37,000	$ 300 U
Fixed selling and administrative expenses	33,000	33,000	–
Total fixed expenses	$ 70,300	$ 70,000	$ 300 U
Operating income (loss)	$ (11,570)	$ 12,800	$24,370 U

U = Unfavourable expense variances occur when actual expenses are more than budgeted expenses.
F = Favourable expense variances occur when actual expenses are less than budgeted expenses.

it for any level of activity after the actual level of activity is known. So, when at month end, sales turn out to be 7,000 units instead of 9,000, managers can prepare a new flexible budget *based on this new cost-driver level.* We can then see what the total variable expenses should be based on a sales level of 7,000 and compare this amount to the actual result. For performance evaluation, the flexible budget would be prepared at the actual levels of activity. In contrast, the master budget is kept fixed or static to serve as the primary benchmark showing revenues and costs or expenses at the *planned* levels of activity.

The flexible budget approach says, "Give me any activity level you choose, and I'll provide a budget tailored to that particular level." Many companies routinely "flex" their budgets to help evaluate recent financial performance. For example, Procter & Gamble evaluates monthly financial performance of all its business units by comparing actual results to new results using flexible budgets that are prepared for actual levels of activity.

Procter & Gamble
www.pg.com

Flexible-Budget Formulas

OBJECTIVE 2

Use flexible-budget formulas to construct a flexible budget based on the volume of sales.

The flexible budget is based on the same assumptions of revenue and cost behaviour (within the relevant range) as is the master budget. Cost behaviour is illustrated by *cost functions* or *flexible-budget formulas.* The cost functions that you used in Chapters 2 and 3 can be used as flexible-budget formulas. The flexible budget incorporates how each cost and revenue is affected by changes in a single cost driver's activity. Exhibits 12-2 and 12-3 show Dominion Company's simple flexible budget, which has units of output as a single cost driver. Dominion Company's cost functions or flexible-budget formulas are believed to be valid within the relevant range of 7,000 to 9,000 units. Each column of Exhibit 12-2 (7,000 units, 8,000 units, and 9,000 units) is prepared using the same flexible-budget formulas, and any activity within this range could be used, as shown in the graph in Exhibit 12-3. Note that fixed costs are expected to be constant across this range of activity.

EXHIBIT 12-2

Dominion Company
Flexible Budgets

BUDGET FORMULA PER UNIT		FLEXIBLE BUDGETS FOR VARIOUS LEVELS OF SALES/PRODUCTION ACTIVITY		
Units		7,000	8,000	9,000
Sales	$ 31.00	$217,000	$248,000	$279,000
Variable costs/expenses:				
Variable manufacturing costs	$ 21.00	$147,000	$168,000	$189,000
Shipping expenses (selling)	0.60	4,200	4,800	5,400
Administrative	0.20	1,400	1,600	1,800
Total variable costs/expenses	$ 21.80	$152,600	$174,400	$196,200
Contribution margin	$ 9.20	$ 64,400	$ 73,600	$ 82,800

BUDGET FORMULA PER MONTH				
Fixed costs/expenses:				
Fixed manufacturing costs	$37,000	$ 37,000	$ 37,000	$ 37,000
Fixed selling and administrative				
costs	33,000	33,000	33,000	33,000
Total fixed costs/expenses	$70,000	$ 70,000	$ 70,000	$ 70,000
Operating income (loss)		$ (5,600)	$ 3,600	$ 12,800

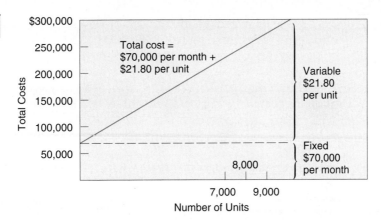

EXHIBIT 12-3

Dominion Company
Graph of Flexible
Budget of Costs

Activity-Based Flexible Budgets

Activity-Based Flexible Budget. A budget based on costs for each activity centre and cost driver at varying volumes of activity.

The flexible budget for Dominion Company shown in Exhibit 12-2 is based on a single cost driver—units of product. For companies that use a traditional, volume-based costing system, this is an appropriate approach to flexible budgeting.

Companies that use an activity-based costing system use a more detailed **activity-based flexible budget.** The activity-based flexible budget is based on budgeted costs for each activity centre and related cost driver at varying volumes of activity. Exhibit 12-4 shows an activity-based flexible budget for the Dominion Company. There are four activity centres: processing, setup, marketing, and administration. Within each activity centre, costs depend on an appropriate cost driver.

Compare the traditional flexible budget (Exhibit 12-2) and the activity-based flexible budget (Exhibit 12-4). The key difference is that some manufacturing costs that are fixed with respect to *units* are variable with respect to the more appropriate cost driver *setups*. The fixed manufacturing costs ($37,000) in Exhibit 12-2 include setup costs that are largely fixed with respect to "units produced" but that vary with respect to the "number of setups." An example is the cost of supplies used to set up the production run. Each time a setup is done, supplies are used. Therefore, the cost of supplies varies directly with the number of setups. However, no setup supplies are used during production, so there is little change in the cost of supplies over wide ranges of units produced. This basic difference explains why the total costs differ using the two approaches—activity-based flexible budgets provide more detailed measures of cost behaviour.

When should a company use activity-based flexible budgets? When a significant portion of its costs varies with cost drivers other than units of production. In our Dominion Company example, the $500 per setup is the only such cost. For the rest of this chapter we will ignore the fact that this cost varies with the number of setups, and go back to assuming that Dominion's operations are simple enough that a traditional flexible budget with a single cost driver is appropriate.

EXHIBIT 12-4

	BUDGET FORMULA	UNITS		
		7,000	8,000	9,000
Sales	$31.00	$217,000	$248,000	$279,000

ACTIVITY CENTRE

Processing

Cost Driver: Number of Machine Hours

	BUDGET FORMULA			
Cost-driver level		14,000	16,000	18,000
Variable costs	$10.50	$147,000	$168,000	$189,000
Fixed costs	$13,000	13,000	13,000	13,000
Total costs of processing activity		$160,000	$181,000	$202,000

Setup

Cost Driver: Number of Setups

	BUDGET FORMULA			
Cost-driver level		21	24	27
Variable costs	$500	$10,500	$12,000	13,500
Fixed costs	$12,000	12,000	12,000	12,000
Total costs of setup activity		$22,500	$24,000	$25,500

Marketing

Cost Driver: Number of Orders

	BUDGET FORMULA			
Cost-driver level		350	400	450
Variable costs	$12.00	$4,200	$4,800	$5,400
Fixed costs	$15,000	15,000	15,000	15,000
Total costs of marketing activity		$19,200	$19,800	$20,400

Administration

Cost Driver: Number of Units

	BUDGET FORMULA			
Cost-driver level		7,000	8,000	9,000
Variable costs	$0.20	$1,400	$1,600	$1,800
Fixed costs	$18,000	18,000	18,000	18,000
Total costs of administration activity		$19,400	$19,600	$19,800
Total costs		$221,100	$244,400	$267,700
Operating Income (loss)		$(4,100)	$3,600	$11,300

Evaluation of Financial Performance Using the Flexible Budget

OBJECTIVE 3

Understand the performance evaluation relationship between master (static) budgets and flexible budgets.

Comparing the flexible budget to actual results accomplishes an important performance evaluation purpose. There are basically two reasons why actual results might differ from the master budget. One is that sales and cost-driver activities were not the same as originally forecasted. The second is that revenues or variable costs per unit of activity and fixed costs per period were not as expected. Though these reasons may not be completely independent (e.g., higher sales prices may have caused lower sales levels), it is useful to separate these effects because different people may be responsible for them, and different management actions may be indicated. The intent of using the flexible budget for performance evaluation is to isolate varied, significant effects on actual results that can be corrected if adverse, or enhanced if beneficial. Because the flexible budget is prepared at the actual levels of activity (in our example, sales volume), any variances between the flexible budget and actual results cannot be due to activity levels. These *variances between the flexible budget and actual results are called* **flexible-budget** or **efficiency variances** *and must be due to departures of actual costs or revenues from flexible-budget formula amounts.* In contrast, any differences or *variances between the master budget and the flexible budget are due to activity levels,* not cost control. These differences between the master budget amounts and the amounts in the flexible budget are called **activity-level** or **sales-volume variances**.

Flexible-Budget (Efficiency) Variances. Variances between the flexible budget and the actual results.

Activity-Level (Sales-Volume) Variances. Variances between the flexible budget and the master budget.

Consider Exhibit 12-5. The flexible budget (column 3) from Exhibit 12-2 (and simplified) provides an explanatory bridge between the master budget (column 5) and the actual results (column 1). The variances for operating income are summarized at the bottom of columns 2 and 4, and are the sum of the sales volume variances and the flexible-budget variances. The difference between actual results and the original master budget can also be divided into two components: the sales-volume variances and the flexible-budget (efficiency) variances.

BUDGET VARIANCES AND THEIR CAUSES

Effectiveness. The degree to which a goal, objective, or target is met (doing the right things).

Managers use comparisons between actual results, master budgets, and flexible budgets to evaluate organizational performance. When evaluating performance, it is useful to distinguish between **effectiveness**—the degree to which a goal,

EXHIBIT 12-5

Dominion Company
Summary of Performance for the Month Ended June 30, 2006

	(1) ACTUAL RESULTS AT ACTUAL ACTIVITY LEVEL*	(2) (1) – (3) FLEXIBLE-BUDGET VARIANCES†	(3) FLEXIBLE BUDGET FOR ACTUAL SALES ACTIVITY‡	(4) (3) – (5) SALES ACTIVITY VARIANCES	(5) MASTER BUDGET*
Units	7,000	–	7,000	2,000 U	9,000
Sales	$217,000	–	$217,000	$62,000 U	$279,000
Variable costs	158,270	5,670 U	152,600	43,600 F	196,200
Contribution margin	$ 58,730	$5,670 U	$ 64,400	$18,400 U	$ 82,800
Fixed costs	70,300	300 U	70,000	–	70,000
Operating income	$ (11,570)	$5,970 U	$ (5,600)	$18,400 U	$ 12,800

Total flexible-budget variances
$5,970 Unfavourable

Total sales-volume variances
$18,400 Unfavourable

Total master budget variances, $24,370 Unfavourable

U = Unfavourable   F = Favourable
* Figures are from Exhibit 12-1.
† Figures are shown in more detail in Exhibit 12-6.
‡ Figures are from the 7,000-unit column in Exhibit 12-2.

Efficiency. The degree to which minimum inputs are used to produce a given level of outputs (doing the right things right).

objective, or target is met (doing the right things)—and **efficiency**—the degree to which minimum inputs are used to produce a given level of output (doing the right things right).

Performance may be effective, efficient, both, or neither. Was Dominion's performance effective? Dominion Company set a master budget objective of manufacturing and selling 9,000 units. However, only 7,000 units were actually made and sold. Performance, as measured by sales activity variances, was ineffective because the sales objective was not met.

Managers judge the degree of efficiency by comparing actual outputs achieved (7,000 units) with actual inputs allowed for the level of output achieved. *The less input used to produce a given output, the more efficient the operation.* As indicated by the flexible-budget variances, Dominion was inefficient in its use of a number of inputs by $5,970. Later in this chapter we consider in detail direct material, direct labour, and variable overhead flexible-budget variances.

Flexible-Budget Variances

OBJECTIVE 4

Compute flexible-budget variances and sales-volume variances.

Flexible-budget variances measure the efficiency of operations at the actual level of activity. The first three columns of Exhibit 12-5 compare the actual results with the flexible-budget amounts. The flexible-budget variances are the differences between columns 1 and 3, which total $5,970. The results are unfavourable because

$$\text{total flexible-budget variance} = \text{total actual results} - \text{total flexible budget}$$
$$= \$(11{,}570) - \$(5{,}600)$$
$$= \$(5{,}970) \text{ or } \$5{,}970 \text{ unfavourable}[1]$$

The total flexible-budget variance arises from sales price differences incurred and budgeted and variable and fixed costs differences incurred and budgeted. Dominion Company had no difference between actual sales price and the flexible-budgeted sales price, so the focus is on the differences between actual costs and flexible-budgeted costs at the actual 7,000-unit level of activity. Without the flexible budget in column 3, we cannot separate these variances from the effects of changes in sales activity. The flexible budget variances indicate whether operations were efficient or not, and may form the basis for periodic performance evaluation. Operations managers are in the best position to explain flexible-budget variances and in many organizations are held accountable for meeting quality and cost targets as expressed in the budget.

Companies that use variances primarily to fix blame often find that managers resort to cheating and subversion to beat the system. Managers of operations usually have more information about those operations than higher-level managers. If that information is used against them, lower-level managers may withhold or misstate valuable information for their own self-protection. For example, one manufacturing firm actually *reduced* the next period's departmental budget by the amount of the department's unfavourable variances in the current period. If a division had a $50,000 budget and experienced a $2,000 unfavourable variance, the following period's budget would be set at $48,000. This system led managers to cheat and to falsify reports to avoid unfavourable variances. We can criticize departmental managers' ethics, but the system was as much at fault.

---

[1] What if the total flexible-budget results were positive, say, a profit of $4,000? The total flexible-budget variance would be $(11,570) + $(4,000) = $(15,570) or $15,570 unfavourable.

Exhibit 12-6 gives an expanded, line-by-line computation of variances for all master budget items at Dominion Company. Note how most of the costs that had seemingly favourable variances when a master budget was used as a basis for comparison have, in reality, unfavourable variances. Do not conclude automatically that favourable flexible-budget variances are good and unfavourable flexible-budget variances are bad. Instead, *interpret all variances as signals that actual operations have not occurred exactly as anticipated* when the flexible-budget formulas were set. Any cost that differs significantly from the flexible budget deserves an explanation. The last column of Exhibit 12-6 gives possible explanations for Dominion Company's variances.

Sales-Volume Variances

Sales-volume variances measure how *effective* managers have been in meeting the planned sales volume. In Dominion Company, sales activity fell 2,000 units short of the planned level. The final three columns of Exhibit 12-5 clearly show how the sales-volume variances (totalling $18,400 U) are unaffected by any changes in unit prices or variable costs. Why? Because the same budgeted unit prices and variable

EXHIBIT 12-6

Dominion Company
Cost-Control Performance Report for the Month Ended June 30, 2006

	ACTUAL COSTS INCURRED	FLEXIBLE BUDGET*	FLEXIBLE-BUDGET VARIANCES[†]	EXPLANATION
Units	7,000	7,000	–	
Variable costs:				
Direct material	$ 69,920	$ 70,000	$ 80 F	Lower prices but higher usage
Direct labour	61,500	56,000	5,500 U	Higher wage rates and higher usage
Indirect labour	9,100	11,900	2,800 F	Decreased setup time
Idle time	3,550	2,800	750 U	Excessive machine breakdowns
Cleanup time	2,500	2,100	400 U	Cleanup of spilled solvent
Supplies	4,700	4,200	500 U	Higher prices and higher usage
Variable manufacturing costs	$151,270	$147,000	$4,270 U	
Shipping	5,000	4,200	800 U	Use of air freight to meet delivery
Administration	2,000	1,400	600 U	Excessive copying and long-distance calls
Total variable costs	$158,270	$152,600	$5,670 U	
Fixed costs:				
Factory supervision	$ 14,700	$ 14,400	$ 300 U	Salary increase
Factory rent	5,000	5,000	–	
Equipment amortization	15,000	15,000	–	
Other fixed factory costs	2,600	2,600	–	
Fixed manufacturing costs	$ 37,300	$ 37,000	$ 300 U	
Fixed selling and administrative costs	33,000	33,000	–	
Total fixed costs	$ 70,300	$ 70,000	$ 300 U	
Total variable and fixed costs	$228,570	$222,600	$5,970 U	

* From 7,000-unit column of Exhibit 12-2.
[†] This is a line-by-line breakout of the variances in column 2 of Exhibit 12-5.

Sales-Volume Variances. Variances that measure how effective managers have been in meeting the planned sales objective, calculated as actual unit sales less master-budget unit sales times the budgeted unit-contribution margin.

costs are used in constructing both the flexible budget and master budget. Therefore, all unit prices and variable costs are held constant in columns 3, 4, and 5.

The total of the sales-volume variances informs the manager that falling short of the sales target by 2,000 units caused operating income to be $18,400 lower than initially budgeted (a $5,600 loss instead of a $12,800 profit). In summary, the shortfall of sales by 2,000 units caused Dominion Company to incur a total sales-volume variance of 2,000 units at a contribution margin of $9.20 per unit (from the first column of Exhibit 12-2).

$$\begin{aligned} \text{total sales volume variance} &= \left(\begin{array}{c} \text{flexible-budget units} - \\ \text{master budget units} \end{array} \right) \times \left(\begin{array}{c} \text{budgeted contribution} \\ \text{margin per unit} \end{array} \right) \\ &= (9{,}000 - 7{,}000) \times \$9.20 \\ &= \$18{,}400 \text{ unfavourable} \end{aligned}$$

Who has responsibility for the sales-activity variance? Marketing managers usually have the primary responsibility for reaching the sales level specified in the static budget. Of course, variations in sales may be attributable to many factors. For example, it is common to analyze the change in sales-volume variances due to changes in market share and market size. A *market share* variance assumes the market or industry sales volume is on budget, but that the volume variance was due to a change in the company's share of the total industry sales. A *market size* variance assumes that the company's share as a percentage of the total market is on target, and then attributes the sales-volume variance to the change in market sales volume.

Assume that Dominion's planned sales objective of 9,000 units was based on a 40 percent market share of a budget industry sales volume of 22,500 units. If the total market for Dominion's product was 21,000 units, then the actual volume of 7,000 units would represent 33.33 percent of the market. Given these facts the following variances can be computed:

$$\begin{aligned} \text{market share variance} &= \left(\begin{array}{c} \text{actual} \\ \text{market share} \\ \text{percentage} \end{array} - \begin{array}{c} \text{budgeted} \\ \text{market share} \\ \text{percentage} \end{array} \right) \times \left(\begin{array}{c} \text{actual} \\ \text{industry sales} \\ \text{volume in units} \end{array} \right) \times \left(\begin{array}{c} \text{budgeted} \\ \text{contribution} \\ \text{margin per unit} \end{array} \right) \\ &= (33.33\% - 40\%) \times 21{,}000 \text{ units} \times \$9.20 \\ &= (6.67\%) \times 21{,}000 \times \$9.20 \\ &= 1{,}400* \text{ units} \times \$9.20 \\ &= \$12{,}880 \text{ unfavourable} \end{aligned}$$

* Rounded to the nearest 100 units.

$$\begin{aligned} \text{market size variance} &= \begin{array}{c} \text{budgeted} \\ \text{market share} \\ \text{percentage} \end{array} \times \left(\begin{array}{c} \text{actual} \\ \text{industry sales} \\ \text{volume in units} \end{array} - \begin{array}{c} \text{budgeted} \\ \text{industry sales} \\ \text{volume in units} \end{array} \right) \times \left(\begin{array}{c} \text{budgeted} \\ \text{contribution} \\ \text{margin per unit} \end{array} \right) \\ &= 40\% \times (21{,}000 - 22{,}500 \text{ units}) \times \$9.20 \\ &= 40\% \times (-1{,}500) \times \$9.20 \\ &= 600 \text{ units} \times \$9.20 \\ &= \$5{,}520 \text{ unfavourable} \end{aligned}$$

Thus, of the $18,400 unfavourable sales-volume variance, $12,880 is due to a 6.67 percent reduction in market share and $5,520 is the result of a decreased market of 1,500 units. These sales-volume variances might result from changes in the product, changes in customer demand, effective advertising, and so on.

Standard Costs and Standard Cost Systems

A **standard cost** is a carefully designed cost per unit that *should* or is most likely to be attained. **Standard cost systems** value products according to standard costs only. These inventory valuation systems simplify financial reporting, but they are usually expensive to install and to maintain. Standard costs may not be revised often enough to be useful for management decision making regarding specific products or services. (Ideally, only one cost system should be necessary in any organization, but in practice many organizations have developed multiple cost systems.) Budgeting may use standard cost systems: standard costs as benchmarks of objectives to be attained are expected costs. Future costs are expected to be on or close to standard costs. Standard costs do not imply that one also must have a standard cost system for inventory valuation or that one must use the standard cost system for planning and control.

Current Attainability: The Most Widely Used Standard

What standard of expected performance should be used? Should it be so strict that it is rarely, if ever, attained? Should it be attainable 50 percent of the time? Ninety percent? Twenty percent? Individuals who have worked a lifetime setting and evaluating standards for performance disagree, so there is no one single answer to this question.

Ideal standards are expressions of the most efficient performance possible under the best conceivable conditions, using existing specifications, production processes, and equipment. No provision is made for waste, spoilage, machine breakdowns, and the like. Those who favour using ideal standards maintain that the resulting unfavourable variances will constantly remind personnel of the continuous need for improvement in all phases of operations. Though concern for continuous improvement is widespread, these standards are not widely used because they have an adverse effect on employee motivation. Employees tend to ignore unreasonable goals, especially if they would not share the gains from meeting imposed perfection standards. Organizations that apply the just-in-time philosophy attempt to achieve continuous improvement from "the bottom up," not by prescribing what should be achieved via perfection standards.

(Currently) attainable standards are levels of performance that can be achieved by realistic levels of effort. Allowances are made at normal rates for defects, spoilage, waste, and non-productive time. There are at least two popular interpretations of the meaning of currently attainable standards. The first interpretation has standards set just tightly enough that employees regard their attainment as highly probable if normal effort and diligence are exercised. That is, variances should be random and negligible. Hence, the standards are predictions of what will indeed occur, anticipating some inefficiencies. Managers accept the standards as being reasonable goals. The reasons for setting "reasonable" standards, then, are:

1. The attainable standards serve multiple purposes. For example, the same cost can be used for financial budgeting, inventory valuation, and budgeting departmental performance. In contrast, ideal standards cannot be used for inventory valuation or financial budgeting, because the costs are known to be inaccurate.

2. Attainable standards have a desirable motivational impact on employees, especially when combined with incentives for continuous improvement. The standard represents reasonable future performance, not fanciful goals. Therefore, unfavourable variances direct attention to performance that is not meeting reasonable expectations.

A second interpretation of (currently) attainable standards is that standards are set tightly. That is, employees regard their fulfilment as possible, though unlikely. Standards can only be achieved by very efficient operations. Variances tend to be unfavourable; nevertheless, employees accept the standards as being tough, but not unreasonable, goals. Is it possible to achieve continuous improvement using currently attainable standards? Yes, but expectations must reflect improved productivity and must be tied to incentive systems that reward continuous improvement.

Tradeoffs among Variances

Because the operations of organizations are linked, the level of performance in one area of operations will affect performance in other areas. Nearly any combination of effects is possible: improvements in one area could lead to improvements in others, and vice versa. Also, substandard performance in one area may be balanced by superior performance in others. For example, a service organization may generate favourable labour variances by hiring less-skilled and thus lower-paid customer representatives, but this favourable variance may lead to unfavourable customer satisfaction and future unfavourable sales volume variances. In another situation, a manufacturer may experience unfavourable materials variances by purchasing higher-quality materials, but this variance will be more than offset by the favourable variances caused by lower inventory handling costs (e.g., inspections) and higher-quality products (e.g., favourable scrap and rework variances).

Because of the many interdependencies among activities, an "unfavourable" or "favourable" label should not lead the manager to jump to conclusions. By themselves, such labels merely raise questions and provide clues to the causes of performance. Variances on their own are not problem solvers, but they attract management's attention. Furthermore, the cause of variances might be faulty expectations rather than the execution of plans by managers. One of the first questions a manager should consider when explaining a large variance is whether expectations, targets, and budgets were valid.

When to Investigate Variances

When should variances be investigated? Frequently the answer is based on subjective judgments, hunches, guesses, and rules of thumb that have proven to be useful. The most troublesome aspect of using the feedback from flexible budgeting is deciding when a variance is large enough to warrant management's attention. The master and flexible budgets imply that the standard cost is the only permissible outcome. Practically speaking, the accountant (and everybody else) realizes that the standard is one of many possible acceptable cost outcomes. Consequently, the accountant expects variances to fluctuate randomly within some normal limits. Of course, an activity that allows wildly fluctuating variances as "normal" may be poorly designed.

The Need to Adapt Standard Cost Approaches

The use of standard costs and variance analysis came under attack during the last two decades of the 20th century. Critics maintained that comparing actual costs to predetermined standards is a static approach that does not work well in today's dynamic, fast-paced, just-in-time environment. However, companies continue to use standards and to measure performance against them. Surveys in five different countries have shown that between 65 percent and 86 percent of manufacturing companies use standard costs. Companies have apparently adapted the approach to fit their modern environments.

Parker Hannifin Corporation
www.parker.com

To apply standards in a dynamic environment, how should managers measure and report variances? First, standards should be regularly evaluated. If a company is in a continuous-improvement environment, standards must be constantly revised. Second, standards and variances should measure key strategic variables. The concept of setting a benchmark, comparing actual results to the benchmark, and identifying causes for any differences is universal. It can be applied to many types of measures, such as production quantity or quality, as well as to costs. Finally, variances should not lead to affixing blame. Standards are plans, and things do not always go according to plan—often with no one being at fault.

One company that has adapted standard costs to meet its particular needs is the brass products division (BPD) at Parker Hannifin Corporation. The BPD uses standard costs and variances to pinpoint problem areas that need attention if the division is to meet its goal of continuous improvement. Among the changes that have increased the value of the standard cost information are more timely product cost information, variances computed at more detailed levels, and holding regular meetings to help employees understand their impact on the variances.

The BPD also created three new variances: (1) standard-run quantity variance—examines the effect of actual compared to optimal batch size for production runs, (2) material-substitution variance—compares material costs to the costs of alternative materials, and (3) method variance—measures costs using actual machines compared to costs using alternative machines. All three variances use the concept of setting a standard and comparing actual results to the standard, but they do not apply the traditional standard cost variance formulas.

It was premature to declare standard costs dead. They are alive and well in many companies. However, there are fewer and fewer environments where traditional variance analysis is useful, and more and more environments where managers and accountants must adapt the standard cost concept to fit the particular needs of a company.

Sources: Adapted from D. Johnsen and P. Sopariwala, "Standard Costing Is Alive and Well at Parker Brass," *Management Accounting Quarterly*, Winter 2000, pp. 12–20; C. B. Cheatham and L. R. Cheatham, "Redesigning Cost Systems: Is Standard Costing Obsolete?" *Accounting Horizons*, December 1996, pp. 23–31; and C. Horngren, G. Foster, and S. Datar, *Cost Accounting: A Managerial Emphasis*, Prentice Hall, 2000, p. 226. See also the Society of Management Accountants of Canada, Management Accounting Guideline, *Post Appraisal of Capital Expenditures*, 1999.

A random variance from a well-designed activity, by definition, is not caused by controllable actions and calls for no corrective action. In short, a random variance is attributable to chance rather than to management's implementation of plans. Consequently, the more a variance randomly fluctuates, the larger the variance that is required to make investigation worthwhile. There are two questions: First, what is a large versus a small variance? Second, is a large variance random or controllable? Usually, the second question is answered only after an investigation, so answering the first question is critical.

Managers recognize that, even if everything operates as planned, variances are unlikely to be exactly zero. They predict a range of "normal" variances; this variance range may be based on economic criteria (i.e., how big a variance must be before investigation could be worth the effort) or on statistical criteria (e.g., whether a variance is more than one *standard deviation* away from the expected or historical *mean* level of cost). For some critical items, any deviation may prompt an investigation and follow-up. For most items, firms set a minimum dollar or percentage deviation from budget before investigations are expected to be worthwhile. For example, a 4 percent variance in a $1 million material cost may deserve more attention than a 20 percent variance in a $10,000 repair cost. Because knowing exactly when to investigate is difficult, many organizations have developed such rules of thumb as, "Investigate all variances exceeding $5,000 or 25 percent of expected cost, whichever is lower."

Comparisons with Prior Period's Results

Some organizations compare the most recent budget period's actual results with last year's results for the same period rather than using flexible budget benchmarks. For example, an organization might compare June 2007's actual results to June 2006's actual results. In general these comparisons are not as useful for evaluating the performance of an organization as comparisons of actual outcomes with planned results for the same period. Why? Because many changes have probably occurred in the environment and in the organization that make a comparison to a prior period invalid. Very few organizations and environments are so stable that the only difference between now and a year ago is merely the passage of time. Even comparisons with last month's actual results may not be as useful as comparisons with flexible budgets. Comparisons over time may be useful for analyzing *trends* in such key variables as sales volume, market share, and product mix, but they do not help answer questions such as "Why did we have a loss of $11,570 in June, when we expected a profit of $12,800?"

FLEXIBLE-BUDGET VARIANCES IN DETAIL

OBJECTIVE 6

Compute and interpret price and usage variances for material, labour, and overhead inputs.

The rest of this chapter probes the variance analysis in detail. The emphasis is on subdividing budget variances into labour, material, and overhead cost variances. These variances are further broken down into usage and price or spending variances. Note that in companies where direct labour costs are small in relation to total costs (that is, in highly automated companies), direct labour costs may be treated as an overhead cost item, so separate labour variances need not be analyzed.

Material and Labour Variances

Consider Dominion Company's $10 standard cost of direct materials and $8 standard cost of direct labour. As shown below, these standards per unit are derived from two components, a standard quantity and a standard price:

	STANDARDS		
	STANDARD INPUTS EXPECTED PER UNIT OF OUTPUT	STANDARD PRICE EXPECTED PER UNIT OF INPUT	STANDARD COST EXPECTED PER UNIT OF OUTPUT
Direct materials	5 kilograms	$ 2.00	$10.00
Direct labour	1/2 hour	$16.00	$ 8.00

Consider a simple example of a company that plans to sell 1,000 units of a product for $2 per unit. Budgeted variable costs are $1 per unit, and the master-budget operating income is $400. Suppose the company actually sells 800 units and makes an operating income of $200. Compute and interpret the master-budget variance, the sales-activity variance, and the flexible-budget variance.

ANSWER

The key to understanding this problem is to distinguish between *contribution margin* (sales − variable costs) and *operating income* (sales − variable costs − fixed costs). Therefore, if the master budget projects an *operating income* of $400, what must the budgeted fixed costs be?

Budgeted sales revenue: 1,000 × $2 = $2,000
Budgeted variable costs: 1,000 × $1 = $1,000

So, the budgeted contribution margin = $2,000 − $1,000 (or $1,000).

If the budgeted contribution margin is $1,000 and the budgeted operating income is $400, budgeted *fixed costs* must be $600. The result is:

Budgeted sales	$2,000
Budgeted variable costs	1,000
Budgeted contribution margin	1,000

Budgeted fixed costs	600
Budgeted operating income	$400

What were the actual results?

Only 800 units were sold, so a variation from the budgeted amounts is to be expected. How much of that variance is simply due to changes in volume? How much of it is due to changes in unit prices, costs, or usage? Since we have no information as to changes in unit prices, costs, or usage, we can conclude that the entire master budget variance is due to changes in the volume of sales, compared to what was budgeted. Here's the proof:

Actual operating income:	$200
Fixed costs haven't changed:	$600

Therefore, working backwards, the actual contribution margin must be $200 + $600 = $800.

If 800 units were sold and prices and costs haven't changed:

Sales: 800 × $2	$1,600
Variable costs: 800 × $1	800
Contribution margin	$ 800

(the same number we arrived at through "working backward" from actual operating income)

Once standards are set and actual results are observed, we can measure variances from the flexible budget. To show how the analysis of inputs variances can be pursued in detail, we will reconsider Dominion's direct material and direct labour costs, as shown in Exhibit 12-6. We also assume that the following actually occurred for the production of 7,000 units of output:

- *Direct material*: 36,800 kilograms of material were purchased and *used* at an actual unit *price* of $1.90 for a total actual cost of $69,920.
- *Direct labour*: 3,750 hours of labour were used at an actual hourly *price* (rate) of $16.40, for a total cost of $61,500.

Note that the flexible-budget variances for direct material and direct labour can be attributed to (1) using more or less of the resource (quantity of raw materials and/or labour hours) than planned, and (2) spending more or less for the resource (higher material prices and/or higher labour rates) than planned at the actual level of output achieved. These additional data enable us to subdivide the direct material and direct labour flexible-budget variances (first two lines of variable costs) from Exhibit 12-6 into the separate *usage* and *price* components.

The flexible-budget totals for direct materials and direct labour (column 3 from Exhibit 12-6) are the amounts that would have been spent with expected efficiency. They are often labelled total *standard costs allowed*, computed as follows:

$$\begin{array}{c} \text{flexible} \\ \text{budget or} \\ \text{total standard} \\ \text{cost allowed} \end{array} = \begin{array}{c} \text{units of good} \\ \text{output} \\ \text{achieved} \end{array} \times \begin{array}{c} \text{input allowed} \\ \text{per unit of} \\ \text{output} \end{array} \times \begin{array}{c} \text{standard unit} \\ \text{price of input} \end{array}$$

$$\begin{array}{l} \text{standard direct} \\ \text{materials cost} \\ \text{allowed} \end{array} = 7{,}000 \text{ units} \times 5 \text{ kilograms} \times \$2.00 \text{ per kilogram} = \$70{,}000$$

$$\begin{array}{l} \text{standard direct} \\ \text{labour cost} \\ \text{allowed} \end{array} = 7{,}000 \text{ units} \times \tfrac{1}{2} \text{ hour} \times \$16.00 \text{ per hour} = \$56{,}000$$

Always ask yourself: What was the good output? Then proceed with your computations of the total standard cost allowed for the good output achieved.

Price and Efficiency Variances

As noted earlier, we computed the flexible-budget amounts using the flexible-budget formulas, or currently attainable standards. Flexible-budget variances measure the relative efficiency of achieving the actual output. Price and usage variances subdivide each flexible-budget variance into two parts:

Price Variance. The difference between actual input prices and expected input prices multiplied by the actual quantity of inputs used.

1. **Price variance**—difference between actual input prices and standard input prices multiplied by the actual quantity of inputs used; and
2. **Efficiency variance** (also called **quantity or usage variance**)—difference between the quantity of inputs actually used and the quantity of inputs that should have been used to achieve the actual quantity of output multiplied by the standard price.

Efficiency Variance (Quantity Variance or Usage Variance). The difference between the quantity of inputs actually used and the quantity of inputs that should have been used to achieve the actual quantity of output multiplied by the expected price of input.

When feasible, you should separate the variances that are subject to separate price factors from quantity factors. Price factors are less subject to immediate managerial control than are quantity factors, principally because of external forces, such as general economic conditions and competitive forces that can influence prices. Even when price factors are regarded as being outside management control, isolating them helps to focus on the efficient use of inputs. For example, the commodity prices of wheat, oats, corn, and rice are outside the control of General Mills management. By separating price variances from efficiency variances, the breakfast-cereal maker can focus on whether grain was used efficiently.

General Mills
www.generalmills.com

Calculation of price and usage variances is a good idea because the system provides control feedback to those responsible for inputs. But these variances should not be the only information used for decision making, control, or evaluation. Exclusive focus on material price variances by purchasing agents or buyers, for example, can work against an organization's just-in-time and total quality management goals. A buyer may be motivated to earn favourable material price variances by buying low-quality material in large quantities. The result could be excessive inventory-handling and opportunity costs, and increased manufacturing defects due to faulty material. Similarly, exclusive focus on labour price and usage variances could motivate supervisors to use lower-skilled workers or to rush workers through critical tasks, both of which could impair the quality of products and services.

Calculating price and usage variances is not difficult. The objective of these variance calculations is to hold either price or usage constant so that the effect of the other can be isolated. When calculating the price variance, you hold use of inputs constant at the actual level of usage. When calculating the quantity of variance, you hold price constant at the standard price. For Dominion Company the price and quantity variances are computed as follows:

direct material price variance = difference in prices × actual quantity
(actual price − standard price) × actual quantity
(AP − SP) × AQ
= ($1.90 − $2.00) per kilogram × 36,800 kilograms (actual)
= $3,680 favourable

direct labour price variance = (difference in prices) × actual quantity
(actual price − standard price) × actual quantity
(AP − SP) × AQ
= ($16.40 − $16.00) per hour × 3,750 hours (actual)
= $1,500 unfavourable

The usage variances are computed as:

direct material usage variance = (difference in quantities) × standard prices
(actual quantity used − standard quantity allowed) × standard price
(AQ − SQ) × SP
= [36,800 − (7,000 × 5)] kilograms × $2.00 per kilogram (standard)
= $3,600 unfavourable

direct labour usage variance = (difference in quantities) × standard prices
(actual quantity used − standard quantity allowed) × standard price
(AQ − SQ) × SP
= [3,750 − (7,000 × ½)] hours × $16.00 per hour (standard)
= (3,750 − 3,500) × $16.00
= $4,000 unfavourable

Note that the sum of the direct labour price and usage variances equals the direct labour flexible-budget variance. Furthermore, the sum of the direct material price and usage variances equals the total direct material flexible-budget variance.

$$\text{direct materials flexible-budget variance} = \$80 \text{ favourable}$$
$$= \$3,680 \text{ favourable} + \$3,600 \text{ unfavourable}$$

$$\text{direct labour flexible-budget variance} = \$5,500 \text{ unfavourable}$$
$$= \$1,500 \text{ unfavourable} + \$4,000 \text{ unfavourable}$$

EXHIBIT 12-7

Dominion Company Price and Usage Variances for Direct Materials and Direct Labour

	(1) ACTUAL COSTS	(2) FLEXIBLE BUDGET	(3) FLEXIBLE-BUDGET VARIANCE	(4) PRICE VARIANCE*	(5) USAGE VARIANCE
Direct materials	$69,920	$70,000	$ 80 F	$3,680 F	$3,600 U
Direct labour	61,500	56,000	5,500 U	1,500 U	4,000 U

* Computations to be explained shortly.

So, the flexible budget variances for direct material and labour of Exhibit 12-6 are broken down into the price and usage variances of Exhibit 12-7. To determine whether a variance is favourable or unfavourable, use logic rather than memorizing a formula. A price variance is favourable if the actual price is less than the standard. A usage variance is favourable if the actual quantity used is less than the standard quantity allowed. The opposite relationships imply unfavourable variances.

Variances themselves do not show why the budgeted operating income was not achieved. But they raise questions, provide clues, and direct attention to what may have happened. For instance, one possible explanation for this set of variances is that a manager might have made a tradeoff—the manager might have purchased at a favourable price some materials that were of sub-standard quality, saving $3,680 (the materials price variance). Excessive waste might have nearly offset this saving, as indicated by the $3,600 unfavourable material usage variance and net flexible-budget variance of $80 favourable. The material waste also might have caused at least part of the excess use of direct labour. Suppose that more than $80 of the $4,000 unfavourable direct labour usage variance was caused by reworking units with defective materials. Then the manager's tradeoff was not successful. The cost inefficiencies caused by using substandard materials exceeded the savings from the favourable price.

Exhibit 12-8 shows the price and usage variance computations graphically. The standard cost (or flexible budget) is the standard quantity multiplied by the standard price—the unshaded rectangle. The price variance is the difference between the unit prices (actual and standard) multiplied by actual quantity

EXHIBIT 12-8

Dominion Company Graph of Flexible Budget of Costs

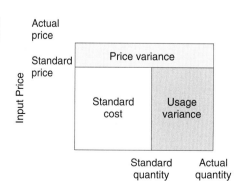

used—the area of the shaded rectangle on top. The usage variance is the standard price multiplied by the difference between the actual quantity used and the standard quantity allowed for the goods output achieved—the area of the shaded rectangle on the lower right. (Note that for clarity the graph portrays only unfavourable variances.)

Material and Finished Goods Inventories' Effect on Variances

The analysis of Dominion Company was simplified because: (1) there were no finished goods inventories—any units produced were sold in the same period—and (2) there was no direct material inventory—the materials were purchased and used in the same period.

What if production does not equal sales? Generally, managers want quick feedback and want variances to be identified as early as is practical. In the case of direct materials, that time is when the materials are purchased rather than when they are used, which may be much later. Therefore, the material price variance is usually based on the quantity purchased, measured at the time of purchase. The material usage variance remains based on the quantity used. Suppose Dominion Company purchased 40,000 kilograms of material (rather than the 36,800 kilograms used) at $1.90 per kilogram.

The material price variance would be (actual price – standard price) × material purchased = ($1.90 – $2.00) per kilogram × 40,000 kilograms = $4,000 favourable. The material usage variance would remain at $3,600 unfavourable because it is based on the material used. That is, (1) sales volume variance is based on units sold (not units produced) and (2) material price variance is based on units purchased while material quantity variance is based on material used.

Three-Column Approach to Variance Analysis

Exhibit 12-9 presents the previous analysis in a format that deserves close study. The three columns appear at the top of the exhibit. The specific applications then follow. Even though the exhibit may seem unnecessarily complex at first, its repeated use will solidify your understanding of variance analysis. Of course, the other flexible-budget variances in Exhibit 12-6 could be further analyzed in the same manner in which direct labour and direct material are analyzed in Exhibit 12-9. Such a detailed investigation depends on the manager's perception of whether the extra benefits will exceed the extra costs of the analysis.

Column A of Exhibit 12-9 contains the actual costs incurred using both actual prices and actual quantities incurred for the inputs during the budget period being evaluated. Column C is the flexible budget amount using both expected prices and expected usage for the outputs actually achieved. (This is the flexible-budget amount from Exhibit 12-6 for 7,000 units.) Column B is inserted between A and C by using expected prices and actual usage. Column B is the flexible-budgeted costs for the inputs given the actual inputs used, using expected prices but actual usage.

The difference between columns A and B is attributed to changing prices since usage is held constant between A and B at actual levels. The difference between columns B and C is attributed to changing usage since price is held constant between B and C at expected levels.

EXHIBIT 12-9

Three-Column Approach to Variance Analysis

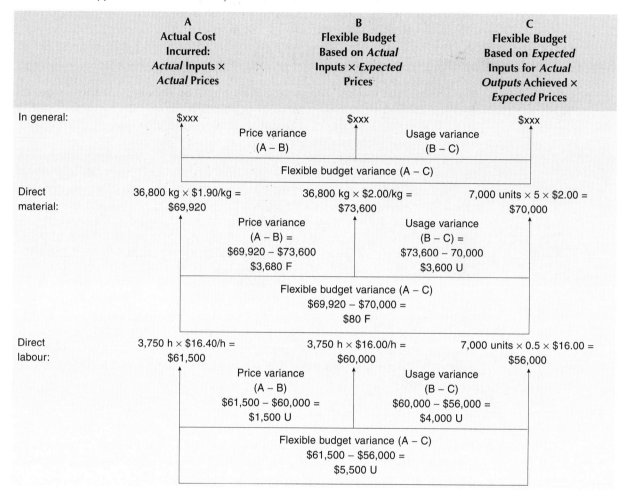

Note that we can express output activity levels in units of inputs. For example, in Exhibit 12-9 we could use labour hours or kilograms of material as activity levels. This is a common practice. Most organizations manufacture a variety of products. When the variety of units are added together, the sum is frequently a nonsensical number (such as apples and oranges). Therefore, all units of output are expressed in terms of the standard inputs allowed for their production (such as kilograms of fruit). Labour hours may also become the common denominator for measuring total output volume. Thus production, instead of being expressed as 12,000 chairs and 3,000 sofas, could be expressed as 20,000 *standard hours allowed* (or more accurately as *standard hours of input allowed for output achieved*). Remember that *standard hours allowed* is a measure of actual *output* achieved. A key idea illustrated in Exhibit 12-9 is the versatility of the flexible budget. A flexible budget is geared to activity volume, and Exhibit 12-9 shows that activity volume can be measured in terms of either *actual inputs allowed* or *actual outputs achieved*.

The concept of variance analysis is not restricted to financial budgets. Consider a production plant that is supposed to produce 50 units per hour and work 8 hours each day. On March 23 the plant produced 325 units. Because of machine breakdowns, the plant operated for only 7.5 hours that day. Using the same conceptual framework as used for separating usage and price variances, determine how much of the 75-unit shortfall in production was caused by working only 7.5 hours and how much was caused by inefficiencies during the hours of actual operation.

ANSWER

Normal production would be 8 × 50 = 400 units per day. If the only difference was the loss of 1/2 hour of productive time, production would have been 7.5 × 50 = 375 units. Therefore, 25 units of shortfall were caused by the machine breakdowns. The other 375 − 325 = 50 units of shortfall were caused by producing fewer than 50 units per hour. The actual rate of production was 325 ÷ 7.5 = 43.3 units per hour, 6.7 units fewer than budgeted.

VARIABLE OVERHEAD VARIANCES

We have just seen that direct material and direct labour variances are often subdivided into price and usage components. In contrast, many organizations believe that it is not worthwhile to monitor individual overhead items to the same extent. Therefore, overhead variances often are not subdivided beyond the flexible-budget variances—the complexity of the analysis may not be worth the effort.

In some cases, however, it may be worthwhile to subdivide variable overhead flexible-budget variances. Part of the variable overhead flexible-budget variance is related to the control of overhead spending itself and part to the quantity variations of the cost driver. When the actual cost driver varies from the standard amount allowed for the actual output achieved, a **variable overhead efficiency variance** will occur. The variable overhead efficiency variance is the difference between the cost of variable overhead for the actual hours worked and the cost of variable overhead for the number of hours that should have been worked. Suppose that Dominion Company's supplies cost (a variable overhead cost) was driven by direct labour hours. A variable overhead cost rate of $0.60 per unit at Dominion would be equal to $1.20 per hour (because one half-hour is allowed to produce a unit of output). Of the $500 unfavourable variance, $300 is due to using 3,750 direct labour hours rather than the 3,500 expected direct labour hours, as calculated below:

Variable Overhead Efficiency Variance. Measures the difference in variable overhead cost that results from using more or fewer factors (hours) than planned for overhead.

variable overhead
efficiency variance = [3,750(actual) − 3,500(expected)] × $1.20 per hour
  for supplies   = $300 unfavourable

This $300 excess usage of supplies is attributable to inefficient use of the cost-driver activity: direct labour hours. Whenever actual cost-driver activity exceeds that allowed for the actual output achieved, overhead efficiency variances will be unfavourable, and vice versa. In essence, this efficiency variance tells management the cost of *not* controlling the use of cost-driver activity.

The remainder of the flexible-budget variance measures control of overhead spending itself, given actual cost-driver activity as

variable overhead
spending variance = $500 U − $300 U
  for supplies   = $200 U

That is, the **variable overhead spending variance** can be calculated as the difference between the actual variable overhead and the amount of variable overhead that should have been incurred for the actual level of cost-driver activity (actual hours worked at the standard rate).

As with other variances, the overhead variances alone cannot identify causes for results that differ from the static and flexible budgets. The only way for management to discover why overhead performance did not agree with the budget is to investigate possible causes. However, the distinction between spending and usage variances provides a springboard for more investigation.

Exhibit 12-10 summarizes the three-column approach for overhead variance analysis. Fixed overhead flexible-budget variances only arise in absorption cost systems. Note that the sales activity variance for fixed overhead is zero, because as long as activities remain within relevant ranges, the fixed overhead budget is the same at both planned and actual levels of activity.

Fixed Overhead Variance

OBJECTIVE 7

Compute the production-volume variance.

In Chapter 4, the *production-volume variance* was introduced and calculated as follows:

production-volume
variance = applied fixed overhead − budgeted fixed overhead
= actual production volume × fixed predetermined overhead rate
   − budgeted production volume × fixed predetermined overhead rate
= (actual production volume − budgeted production volume) × fixed
   predetermined overhead rate

EXHIBIT 12-10

Three-Column Approach to Analysis of Overhead Variances

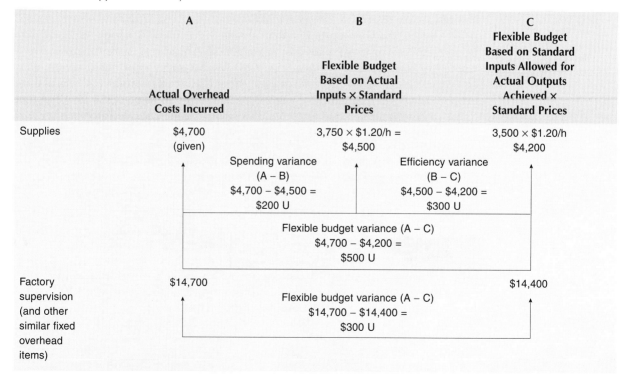

In practice, the **production-volume variance** is usually called simply the *volume variance*. We use the term production-volume variance because it is a more precise description of the fundamental nature of the variance. Production-volume variance is the difference between budgeted fixed overhead and the amount of fixed overhead applied to the work-in-process inventory account. It is caused solely by a difference between actual and budgeted activity. Do not confuse the production-volume variance with the sales volume variance described earlier in this chapter. Despite similar names they are two completely different concepts.

A production-volume variance arises when the actual production volume achieved does not coincide with the expected volume of production used as a denominator for computing the fixed-overhead rate for product-costing purposes:

1. When expected production volume and actual production volume are identical, there is no production-volume variance.
2. When actual volume is less than expected volume, the production-volume variance is unfavourable because usage of facilities is less than expected and fixed overhead is underapplied.
3. Where actual volume exceeds expected volume, the production-volume variance is favourable because the use of facilities is better than expected and fixed overhead is overapplied.

Production-volume variance is also known as capacity variance because the fixed predetermined overhead rate per unit is calculated at what is considered normal capacity. If the firm is operating above or below normal capacity the over- or underapplied overhead in product costing is known as capacity or volume variance. Here is an example:

Analysis:
1. The 280,000 product units should have taken 280,000 units ÷ 4 per hour = 70,000 machine hours.
2. Normal production capacity: 100,000 machine hours × 4 units per hour = 400,000 units
3. Fixed predetermined overhead rate:

Annual fixed budgeted overhead	$600,000
Annual normal operational capacity	100,000 machine hours
Annual production	280,000 units
Budgeted production time per unit	15 minutes
Actual fixed overhead costs	$700,000

4. Budgeted fixed overhead per product unit:
   $6 ÷ 4 units per hour = $1.50
5. Applied fixed overhead: 70,000 machine hours × $6 per machine hour = $420,000
   or 280,000 product units × $1.50 = $420,000
6. Production volume variance:

Budgeted fixed overhead $600,000/Normal capacity 100,000 machine hours = $6 per machine hour

Applied fixed overhead: $420,000 less
Budgeted fixed overhead $600,000 = $180,000 underapplied overhead or unfavourable capacity (400,000 units – 280,000 units × $1.50 = $180,000) or production volume variance

Cautions in Fixed Overhead Analysis

In conclusion, volume variance is a measure of available planned facilities utilization. An unfavourable variance means that the company operated at an activity level below that planned for the period. A favourable variance would mean that the company operated at an activity level greater than that planned for the period. Please note that a company normally would spend the same dollar amount on fixed overhead regardless of whether the period's activity is above or below the planned denominator level of activity. In short, the production volume variance is caused by variations in the activity level, and it is controllable only by adjusting the activity level.

Total fixed costs are fixed within the relevant range and do not depend on activity level. Yet, when we apply fixed costs on a per unit basis for product costing purposes to work-in-process, we treat fixed costs as if they were variable and the danger is for a manager to start thinking of fixed costs as variable.

Even though fixed costs are expressed on a per unit or per hour basis ($1.50 and $6.00 in our example), they are not proportional to activity. In a sense, the volume variance is the error that occurs as a result of treating fixed costs as variable costs per unit in the costing system. Because of the potential confusion in interpreting the production volume variance, some companies present it only in physical units or hours (400,000 − 280,000 = 120,000 units or 100,000 machine hours − 70,000 machine hours = 30,000). In our example, 120,000 units × $1.50 = $180,000 or 30,000 hours × $6.00 = $180,000.

The production-volume variance is the conventional measure of the cost of departing from the level of activity originally used to set the fixed-overhead rate. Most companies consider production-volume variances to be beyond immediate control, although on occasion a manager responsible for volume has to do some explaining or investigating. Sometimes failure to reach the expected volume is caused by idleness due to disappointing total sales, poor production scheduling, unusual machine breakdowns, shortages of skilled workers, strikes, storms, and the like.

There is no production-volume variance for variable overhead. The concept of production-volume variance arises for fixed overhead because of the conflict between accounting for control (by flexible budgets) and accounting for product costing (by application rates). Note again that the fixed-overhead budget serves the control purpose, whereas the development of a product-costing rate results in the treatment of fixed overhead as if it were a variable cost.

Above all, bear in mind that fixed costs are simply not as divisible as variable costs are. Rather, they come in big chunks and are related to the provision of big chunks of production or sales capability, not to the production or sale of a single unit of product.

The selection of an appropriate volume for the denominator is a matter of judgment. Management usually wants to apply a single representative standard fixed cost for a unit of product over a period of at least one year, despite month-to-month changes in production volume. Therefore, the predicted total fixed cost and the expected volume used in calculating the fixed-overhead rate should cover at least a one-year period. Most managers favour using the budgeted annual volume as the expected volume in the denominator. Others favour using some longer-run (three- to five-year) approximation of "normal" activity to adjust for annual fluctuations in volume. Still others favour using maximum or full capacity.

Although fixed-overhead rates are often important for product costing and long-run pricing, such rates have limited significance for control purposes. At the lower levels of supervision, almost no fixed costs are under direct control. Even at higher levels of supervision, many fixed costs are uncontrollable in the short run within wide ranges of anticipated activity.

Actual, Normal, and Standard Costing

Overhead variances are not restricted to standard-costing systems. Many companies apply *actual* direct materials and *actual* direct labour costs to products or services but use *standards* for applying overhead. Such a procedure is called **normal costing**. The following chart compares normal costing with two other basic ways for applying costs by the absorption-costing method:

	ACTUAL COSTING	NORMAL COSTING	STANDARD COSTING
Direct materials	Actual costs	Actual costs	Budgeted prices or rates × standard inputs allowed for actual output achieved
Direct labour	Actual costs	Actual costs	
Variable factory overhead	Actual costs	Budgeted rates × actual inputs	
Fixed factory overhead			

Dropping fixed factory overhead from this chart produces a comparison of the same three basic ways of applying costs by the variable-costing method.

Both normal absorption costing and standard absorption costing generate production-volume variances. In addition, normal- and standard-costing systems produce all other overhead variances under both variable and absorption formats.

Budget Variances

The budget variance is the difference between budgeted fixed overhead costs and actual fixed overhead costs incurred during the period. The formula that can be used is

Budget variance = actual fixed overhead costs – flexible budget fixed overhead costs

The budget variance for our example is

Actual fixed overhead $700,000 less budgeted fixed overhead $600,000 = $100,000

This budget variance is similar to the spending variance for variable overhead. It is the difference between the amount that was actually spent and the amount that should have been spent. Exhibit 12-11 summarizes the computation of fixed overhead variances.

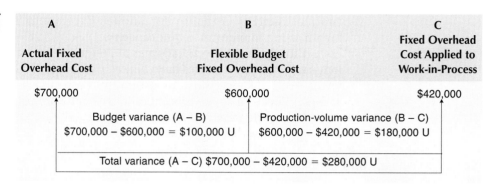

EXHIBIT 12-11

Computation of the Fixed Overhead Variances

A	B	C
Actual Fixed Overhead Cost	**Flexible Budget Fixed Overhead Cost**	**Fixed Overhead Cost Applied to Work-in-Process**
$700,000	$600,000	$420,000

Budget variance (A – B)	Production-volume variance (B – C)
$700,000 – $600,000 = $100,000 U	$600,000 – $420,000 = $180,000 U

Total variance (A – C) $700,000 – $420,000 = $280,000 U

Disposition of Standard Cost Variances

OBJECTIVE 9

Identify the two methods for disposing of the standard cost variances at the end of a year and give the rationale for each.

Prorating the Variances. Assigning the variances to the inventories and cost of goods sold related to the production during the period in which the variances arose.

Advocates of standard costing contend that variances are generally subject to current control, especially when the standards are viewed as being currently attainable. Therefore, variances are not inventoriable and should be considered as adjustments to the income of the period instead of being added to inventories. In this way, inventory valuations will be more representative of desirable and attainable costs.

Others favour assigning the variances to the inventories and cost of goods sold related to the production during the period that the variances arose. This is often called **prorating the variances**. Prorating makes inventory valuations more representative of the "*actual*" costs incurred to obtain the products. In practice, unless variances and inventory levels are significant, the variances are usually not prorated.

Therefore, in practice, all cost variances are typically regarded as adjustments to current income. Where variances appear on the income statement is generally unimportant. Variances could appear as adjustments to the gross profit figure in the income statement or in a completely separate section elsewhere in the income statement. Placing them in a separate section helps to distinguish between product costing (that is, the cost of goods sold, at standard) and loss recognition (unfavourable variances are "lost" or "expired" costs because they represent waste and inefficiency thereby not qualifying as inventoriable costs; that is, waste is not an asset). The *placement* of the variance does not affect operating income.

SUMMARY

Let us examine the variances in perspective by using the approach originally demonstrated in Exhibit 12-9. The results of the approach appear in Exhibit 12-12, which deserves your careful study, particularly the two notes. Please examine the exhibit before reading on.

Exhibit 12-13 graphically compares the variable- and fixed-overhead costs analyzed in Exhibit 12-12. Note how the control-budget line and the product-costing line (the applied line) are superimposed in the graph for variable overhead but differ in the graph for fixed overhead.

Underapplied or overapplied overhead is always the difference between the actual overhead incurred and the overhead applied. An analysis may then be made:

$$\text{underapplied overhead} = \binom{\text{flexible-budget}}{\text{variance}} + \binom{\text{production-volume}}{\text{variance}}$$

$$\text{for variable overhead} = \$3,000 + 0 = \$3,000$$
$$\text{for fixed overhead} = \$7,000 + \$10,000 = \$17,000$$

EXHIBIT 12-11

Analysis of Variances

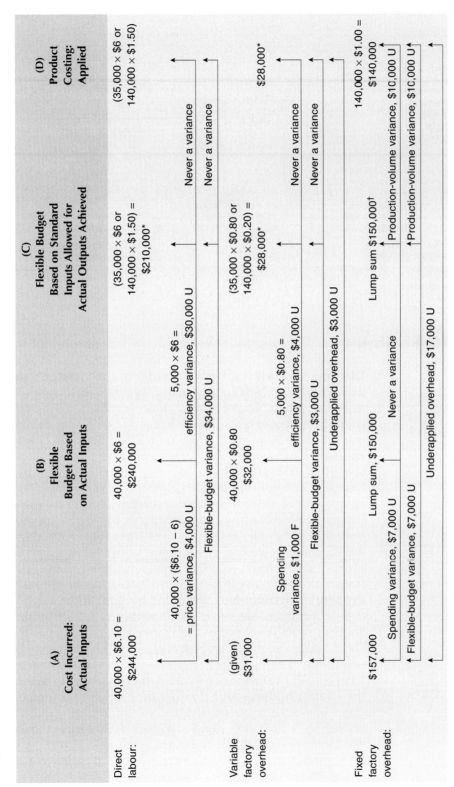

U = Unfavourable   F = Favourable

* Note especially that the flexible budget for variable costs rises and falls in direct proportion to production. Note also that the control-budget purpose and the product-costing purpose harmonize completely; the total costs in the flexible budget will always agree with the standard variable costs applied to the product, because they are based on standard costs per unit multiplied by units produced.

† In contrast to variable costs, the flexible-budget total for fixed costs will always be the same regardless of the units produced. However, the control-budget purpose and the product-costing purpose conflict; whenever actual production differs from denominator production, the standard costs applied to the product will differ from the flexible budget. This difference is the production-volume variance. In this case, the production-volume variance may be computed by multiplying the $1 rate by the difference between the 150,000 denominator volume and the 140,000 units of output achieved.

605

EXHIBIT 12-13

Comparison of Control and Product-Costing Purposes
Variable Overhead and Fixed Overhead (not to scale)

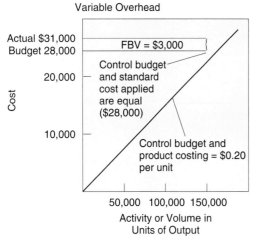

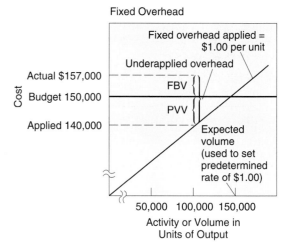

FBV = Flexible-budget variance.
PVV = Production-volume variance.

HIGHLIGHTS TO REMEMBER

1. **Distinguish between flexible budgets and master (static) budgets.** Flexible budgets are geared to changing levels of cost-driver activity rather than to the single static level of the master budget. Organizations may tailor flexible budgets to particular levels of sales or cost-driver activity—before or after the fact. They tell how much revenue and cost to expect for any level of activity.

2. **Use flexible-budget formulas to construct a flexible budget based on the volume of sales.** Cost functions, or flexible-budget formulas, reflect fixed- and variable-cost behaviour and allow managers to compute budgets for any desired output or cost-driver activity level. We compute the flexible-budget amounts for variable costs by multiplying the variable cost per cost-driver unit times the level of activity, as measured in cost-driver units. The flexible-budgeted fixed cost is a lump sum, independent of the level of activity (within the relevant range).

3. **Prepare an activity-based flexible budget.** When a significant portion of operating costs varies with cost drivers other than units of production, a company benefits from using activity-based flexible budgets. These budgets are based on budgeted costs for each activity and related cost driver.

4. **Explain the performance evaluation relationship between master (static) budgets and flexible budgets.** The differences or variances between the master budget and the flexible budget are due to activity levels, not cost control. We call these variances activity-level variances or sales-volume variances.

5. **Compute flexible-budget variances and sales-volume variances.** The flexible-budget variance is the difference between the total

actual results and the total flexible-budget amounts for the actual unit volume. We compute the sales-volume variances by multiplying actual unit sales less master-budget unit sales times the budgeted unit-contribution margin.

6. **Compute and interpret price and usage variances for inputs based on cost-driver activity.** Managers often want to subdivide flexible-budget variances for variable inputs into price (or spending) and usage (or efficiency) variances. Price variances reflect the effects of changing input prices, holding usage of inputs constant at actual input use. Usage variances reflect the effects of different levels of input usage, holding prices constant at expected prices.

7. **Compute variable overhead spending and efficiency variances.** The variable-overhead spending variance is the difference between the actual variable overhead and the amount of variable overhead budgeted for the actual level of cost-driver activity. The variable-overhead efficiency variance is the difference between the actual cost-driver activity and the amount allowed for the actual output achieved, costed at the standard variable-overhead rate.

DEMONSTRATION PROBLEMS FOR YOUR REVIEW

Problem One

Refer to the data contained in Exhibits 12-1 and 12-2. Suppose actual production and sales were 8,500 units instead of 7,000 units; actual variable costs were $188,800; and actual fixed costs were $71,200.

1. Compute the master budget variance. What does this tell you about the efficiency of operations? The effectiveness of operations?
2. Compute the sales-volume variance. Is the performance of the marketing function the sole explanation for this variance? Why?
3. Using a flexible budget, compute the budgeted contribution margin, budgeted operating income, and flexible-budget variance. What do you learn from this variance?

Solution

1. actual operating income = $(8,500 \times \$31) - \$188,800 - \$71,200 = \$3,500$

   master budget
   operating income = $12,800 (from Exhibit 12-1)

   master budget variance = $12,800 - $3,500 = $9,300 U

Three factors affect the master budget variance: sales activity, efficiency, and price changes. There is no way to tell from the master budget variance how much of the $9,300 U was caused by any of these factors alone.

2. sales-volume variance = budgeted unit contribution margin × difference between the master budget unit sales and the actual unit sales
   = $9.20 per unit CM × (9,000 − 8,500)
   = $4,600 U

This variance is labelled as a sales-volume variance because it quantifies the effect on operating income of the deviation from an original sales target while holding price and efficiency factors constant. This is a measure of the effectiveness of the operations—Dominion Company was ineffective in meeting its sales objective. Of course, the failure to reach target sales may be traced to a number of causes beyond the control of marketing personnel, including material shortages, factory breakdowns, reduction in market demand, and so on.

3. The budget formulas in Exhibit 12-2 are the basis for the following answers:

$$\text{flexible-budget contribution margin} = \$9.20 \times 8,500 = \$78,200$$
$$\text{flexible-budget operating income} = \$78,200 - \$70,000 = \$8,200$$
$$\text{actual operating income} = \$3,500$$
$$\text{flexible-budget variance} = \$8,200 - \$3,500 = \$4,700 \text{ U}$$

The flexible-budget variance shows that the company spent $4,700 more to produce and sell the 8,500 units than it should have if operations had been efficient and unit costs had not changed. Note that this variance plus the $4,600 U sales activity variance total the $9,300 U master budget variance.

Problem Two

The following questions are a continuation of Problem One, and are based on the data contained in the Dominion Company illustration used on page 581.

- Direct materials: standard, 5 kilograms per unit @ $2 per kilogram
- Direct labour: standard, one-half hour @ $16 per hour

Suppose the following were the actual results for production of 8,500 units:

1. Direct material: 46,000 kilograms purchased and used at an actual unit price of $1.85 per kilogram for an actual total cost of $85,100.
2. Direct labour: 4,125 hours of labour used at an actual hourly rate of $16.80, for a total actual cost of $69,300.

1. Compute the flexible-budget and the price and usage variances for direct labour and direct material.
2. Suppose the company is organized so that the purchasing manager bears the primary responsibility for purchasing materials, and the production manager is responsible for the use of materials. Assume that the purchasing manager bought 60,000 kilograms of material. This means that there is an ending inventory of 14,000 kilograms of material. Recompute the materials variances.

Solution

1. The variances are as follows:

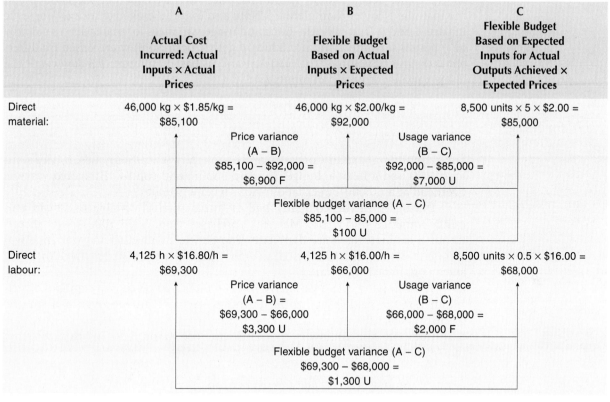

	A **Actual Cost Incurred: Actual Inputs × Actual Prices**	B **Flexible Budget Based on Actual Inputs × Expected Prices**	C **Flexible Budget Based on Expected Inputs for Actual Outputs Achieved × Expected Prices**
Direct material:	46,000 kg × $1.85/kg = $85,100	46,000 kg × $2.00/kg = $92,000	8,500 units × 5 × $2.00 = $85,000

Price variance
(A – B)
$85,100 – $92,000 =
$6,900 F

Usage variance
(B – C)
$92,000 – $85,000 =
$7,000 U

Flexible budget variance (A – C)
$85,100 – 85,000 =
$100 U

Direct labour:	4,125 h × $16.80/h = $69,300	4,125 h × $16.00/h = $66,000	8,500 units × 0.5 × $16.00 = $68,000

Price variance
(A – B) =
$69,300 – $66,000
$3,300 U

Usage variance
(B – C)
$66,000 – $68,000 =
$2,000 F

Flexible budget variance (A – C)
$69,300 – $68,000 =
$1,300 U

2. Price variances are isolated at the most logical control point—time of purchase rather than time of use. In turn, the operating departments that later use the materials are generally charged at some predetermined budget, expected, or standard price rather than actual prices. This represents a slight modification of the approach in part 1 as follows:

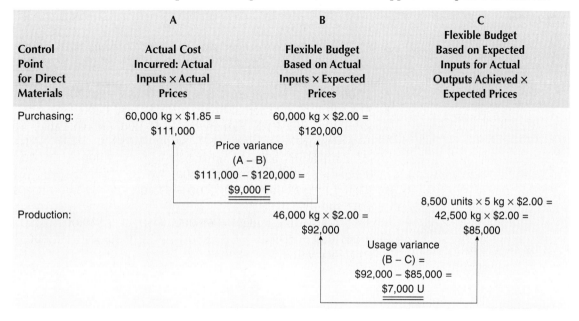

Control Point for Direct Materials	A **Actual Cost Incurred: Actual Inputs × Actual Prices**	B **Flexible Budget Based on Actual Inputs × Expected Prices**	C **Flexible Budget Based on Expected Inputs for Actual Outputs Achieved × Expected Prices**
Purchasing:	60,000 kg × $1.85 = $111,000	60,000 kg × $2.00 = $120,000	

Price variance
(A – B)
$111,000 – $120,000 =
$9,000 F

Production:		46,000 kg × $2.00 = $92,000	8,500 units × 5 kg × $2.00 = 42,500 kg × $2.00 = $85,000

Usage variance
(B – C) =
$92,000 – $85,000 =
$7,000 U

Note that this favourable price variance on balance may not be a good outcome—Dominion Company may not desire the extra inventory in excess of its immediate needs, and the favourable price variance may reflect that quality of the material is lower than planned. Note also that the usage variance is the same in parts 1 and 2. Typically, the price and usage variances for materials would now be reported separately and not added together because they are based on different measures of volume. The price variance is based on inputs *purchased*, but the usage variance is based on inputs *used*.

Problem Three

The Korenthian Leather Company makes a variety of leather goods. It uses standard costs and a flexible budget to aid planning and control. Budgeted variable overhead at a 60,000-direct-labour-hour level is $36,000.

During April the company had an unfavourable variable overhead efficiency variance of $1,200. Material purchases were $322,500. Actual direct-labour costs incurred were $187,600. The direct labour efficiency variance was $6,000 unfavourable. The actual average wage rate was $0.20 lower than the average standard wage rate.

The company uses a variable overhead rate of 20 percent of standard direct-labour *cost* for flexible-budgeting purposes. Actual variable overhead for the month was $41,000.

Compute the following amounts and use U or F to indicate whether requested variances are unfavourable or favourable.

1. Standard direct labour cost per hour.
2. Actual direct labour hours worked.
3. Total direct labour price variance.
4. Total flexible budget for direct labour costs.
5. Total direct labour variance.
6. Variable overhead spending variance in total.

Solution

1. $3. The variable overhead rate is $0.60, obtained by dividing $36,000 by 60,000 hours. Therefore, the direct labour rate must be $0.60 ÷ 0.20 = $3.
2. 67,000 hours. Actual costs, $187,600 ÷ ($3 − $0.20) = 67,000 hours.
3. $13,400 F. 67,000 actual hours × $0.20 = $13,400.
4. $195,000. Efficiency variance was $6,000 unfavourable. Therefore, excess hours must have been $6,000 ÷ $3 = 2,000. Consequently, standard hours allowed must be 67,000 − 2,000 = 65,000. Flexible budget = 65,000 × $3 = $195,000.
5. $7,400 F. $195,000 − $187,600 = $7,400 F; or $13,400 F − $6,000 U = $7,400 F.
6. $800 U. Flexible budget = 65,000 × $0.60 = $39,000. Total variance = $41,000 − $39,000 = $2,000 U. Price variance = $2,000 − $1,200 efficiency variance = $800 U.

KEY TERMS

activity-based flexible budget *p. 583*	production-volume variance *p. 601*
activity-level variances *p. 585*	prorating the variances *p. 604*
(currently) attainable standards *p. 589*	quantity variance *p. 594*
effectiveness *p. 585*	sales-volume variances *pp. 585, 587*
efficiency *p. 586*	standard cost *p. 589*
efficiency variances *pp. 585, 594*	standard cost systems *p. 589*
flexible budget *p. 581*	usage variance *p. 594*
flexible-budget variances *p. 585*	variable overhead efficiency
ideal standards *p. 589*	variance *p. 599*
master (static) budget variances *p. 581*	variable overhead spending
normal costing *p. 603*	variance *p. 600*
price variance *p. 594*	

ASSIGNMENT MATERIAL

QUESTIONS

Q12-1 Distinguish between favourable and unfavourable variances.

Q12-2 "The flex in the flexible budget relates solely to variable costs." Do you agree? Explain.

Q12-3 "We want a flexible budget because costs are hard to predict. We need the flexibility to change budgeted costs as input prices change." Does a flexible budget serve this purpose? Explain.

Q12-4 Explain the role of understanding cost behaviour and cost-driver activities for flexible budgeting.

Q12-5 "An activity-based flexible budget has a "flex" for every activity." Do you agree? Explain.

Q12-6 "Effectiveness and efficiency go hand in hand. You can't have one without the other." Do you agree? Explain.

Q12-7 Differentiate between a master budget variance and a flexible-budget variance.

Q12-8 "Managers should be rewarded for favourable variances and punished for unfavourable variances." Do you agree? Explain.

Q12-9 "A good control system places the blame for every unfavourable variance on someone in the organization. Without affixing blame, no one will take responsibility for cost control." Do you agree? Explain.

Q12-10 Who is usually responsible for sales-activity variances? Why?

Q12-11 Differentiate between ideal standards and currently attainable standards.

Q12-12 What are two possible interpretations of "currently attainable standards?"

Q12-13 "A standard is one point in a band or range of acceptable outcomes." Criticize.

Q12-14 "Price variances should be computed even if prices are regarded as being outside of company control." Do you agree? Explain.

Q12-15 What are some common causes of usage variances?

Q12-16 "Failure to meet price standards is the responsibility of the purchasing officer." Do you agree? Explain.

Q12-17 Are direct material price variances generally recognized when the materials are purchased or when they are used? Why?

Q12-18 Why do the techniques for controlling overhead differ from those for controlling direct materials?

Q12-19 How does the variable overhead spending variance differ from the direct labour price variance?

Q12-20 When should managers investigate variances?

Q12-21 "In a standard absorption-costing system, the amount of fixed manufacturing overhead applied to the products rarely equals the budgeted fixed manufacturing overhead." Do you agree? Explain.

Q12-22 "The dollar amount of the production-volume variance depends on what expected volume of production was chosen to determine the fixed-overhead rate." Explain.

Q12-23 Why is there no production-volume variance for direct labour?

Q12-24 "An unfavourable production-volume variance means that fixed manufacturing costs have not been well controlled." Do you agree? Explain.

Q12-25 "Production-volume variances arise with normal-absorption and standard-absorption costing, but not with actual costing." Explain.

Q12-26 "Overhead variances arise only with absorption-costing systems." Do you agree?

PROBLEMS

P12-1 **FLEXIBLE BUDGET.** Shakie Sports Company made 20,000 leather basketballs in a given year. Its total manufacturing costs were $170,000 variable and $70,000 fixed. Assume that no price changes will occur in the following year and that no changes in production methods are applicable. Compute the budgeted cost for producing 25,000 basketballs in the following year.

P12-2 **BASIC FLEXIBLE BUDGET.** The superintendent of police in Calgary is attempting to predict the costs of operating a fleet of police cars. Among the items of concern are fuel, $0.15 per kilometre, and amortization, $6,000 per car per year.

The superintendent is preparing a flexible budget for the coming year. Prepare the flexible-budget amounts for fuel and amortization for each car at a level of 30,000, 40,000, and 50,000 kilometres.

P12-3 **FLEXIBLE BUDGET.** Consider the following data for the Boulder Delivery Service for a given month:

	BUDGET FORMULA PER UNIT	VARIOUS LEVELS OF OUTPUT		
Units	–	6,000	7,000	8,000
Sales	$18	$?	$?	$?
Variable costs:				
Direct material	?	48,000	?	?
Fuel	2	?	?	?
Fixed costs:				
Amortization		?	15,000	?
Salaries		?	?	40,000

Fill in the unknowns.

P12-4 **BASIC FLEXIBLE BUDGET.** The budgeted prices for materials and direct labour per unit of finished product are $12 and $5, respectively. The production manager is delighted about the following data:

	STATIC (MASTER) BUDGET	ACTUAL COSTS	VARIANCE
Direct materials	$96,000	$90,000	$6,000 F
Direct labour	40,000	37,600	2,400 F

Is the manager's happiness justified? Prepare a report that might provide a more detailed explanation of why the static (master) budget was not achieved. Good output was 6,800 units.

P12-5 **MATERIAL AND LABOUR VARIANCES.** Consider the following data.

	DIRECT MATERIAL	DIRECT LABOUR
Costs incurred: actual inputs × actual prices incurred	$153,000	$79,000
Actual inputs × standard prices	165,000	74,000
Standard inputs allowed for actual	172,500	71,300

Compute the price, usage, and flexible-budget variances for direct material and direct labour. Use U or F to indicate whether the variances are unfavourable or favourable.

P12-6 **USAGE VARIANCES.** Ols Toy Company produced 9,000 stuffed bears. Suppose the standard direct material allowance is two kilograms per bear, at a cost per kilogram of $3. Actually, 17,000 kilograms of materials (input) were used to produce the 9,000 bears (output).

Similarly, assume that it is supposed to take five direct labour hours to produce one bear, and that the standard hourly labour cost is $3. But 46,500 hours (input) were used to produce the 9,000 bears in this Hong Kong factory.

Compute the usage variances for direct material and direct labour.

P12-7 **DIRECT MATERIAL VARIANCES.** Tailored Shirt Company (TSC) uses a special fabric in the production of dress shirts. During August TSC purchased 10,000 square metres of the fabric @ $6.90 per metre and used 7,900 square metres in the production of 3,800 jackets. The standard allows 2 metres @ $7.10 per metre for each jacket.

Calculate the material price variance and the material efficiency variance.

P12-8 **LABOUR VARIANCES.** The city of Sydney, Nova Scotia, has a sign shop where street signs of all kinds are manufactured and repaired. The manager of the shop uses standards to judge performance. However, because a clerk mistakenly discarded some labour records, the manager has only partial data for April. She knows that the total direct labour variance was $1,855 favourable, and that the standard labour price was $12 per hour. Moreover, a recent pay raise produced an unfavourable labour price variance for April of $945. The actual hours of input were 1,750.

1. Find the actual labour price per hour.
2. Determine the standard hours allowed for the output achieved.

P12-9   VARIABLE OVERHEAD VARIANCES. Materials support cost for the Industrial Equipment Manufacturing Company depends on the weight of material (plate steel, castings, etc.) moved. For the current budget period and based on scheduled production, Industrial expected to move 750,000 kilograms of material at a cost of $0.20 per kilogram. Several orders were cancelled by customers and Industrial moved only 650,000 kilograms of material. Total materials support costs for the period were $175,000.

Compute materials support static and flexible-budget variances.

P12-10   LABOUR AND MATERIAL VARIANCES.

1. Information on Li Company's direct labour and direct material costs is as follows:

Standard direct labour rate	$ 13.50
Actual direct labour rate	$ 12.20
Standard direct labour hours	12,000
Direct labour, efficiency variance—unfavourable	$14,500

Complete the actual hours worked, rounded to the nearest hour.

2. Information on Oseok Kwon Company's direct material costs is as follows:

Standard unit price	$ 4.50
Actual quantity purchased	1,800
Standard quantity allowed for actual production	1,650
Materials purchase price variance—favourable	$ 288

Compute the actual purchase price per unit, rounded to the nearest penny.

P12-11   PARKS CANADA. Parks Canada prepared the following budget for one of its national parks for 2006:

Revenue from fees	$5,000,000
Variable costs (miscellaneous)	500,000
Contribution margin	$4,500,000
Fixed costs (miscellaneous)	4,500,000
Operating income	$ 0

The fees were based on an average of 50,000 vehicle-admission days (vehicles multiplied by number of days in park) per week for the 20-week session, multiplied by average entry and other fees of $10 per vehicle-admission day.

The season was booming for the first four weeks. However, there were major forest fires during the fifth week. A large percentage of the park was scarred by the fires. As a result, the number of visitors dropped sharply during the remainder of the season.

Total revenue fell $1 million short of the original budget. Moreover, extra firefighters had to be hired at a cost of $360,000. The latter was regarded as a fixed cost.

Prepare a columnar summary of performance, showing the original (static) budget, sales volume variances, flexible budget, flexible-budget variances, and actual results.

P12-12 **SIMILARITY OF DIRECT LABOUR AND VARIABLE OVERHEAD VARIANCES.** The L. Ming Company has had great difficulty controlling costs in Singapore during the past three years. Last month a standard cost and flexible-budget system was installed. Results for a department follow.

	EXPECTED COST PER STANDARD DIRECT LABOUR HOUR	FLEXIBLE-BUDGET VARIANCE
Lubricants	$0.60	$300 F
Other supplies	0.30	225 U
Rework	0.60	450 U
Other indirect labour	1.50	450 U
Total variable overhead	$3.00	$825 U

F = Favourable   U = Unfavourable

The department initially planned to manufacture 9,000 audio-speaker assemblies in 6,000 standard direct labour hours allowed. However, material shortages and a heat wave resulted in the production of 8,100 units in 5,700 actual direct labour hours. The standard wage rate is $5.25 per hour, which is $0.20 higher than the actual average hourly rate.

1. Prepare a detailed performance report with two major sections: direct labour and variable overhead.
2. Prepare a summary analysis of price and efficiency variances for direct labour and spending and variances for variable overhead.
3. Explain the similarities and differences between the direct labour and variable overhead variances. What are some of the likely causes of the overhead variances?

P12-13 **ACTIVITY-BASED FLEXIBLE BUDGET.** Cost-behaviour analysis for the four activity centres in the Billing Department of Great Lakes Power Company is as follows:

	TRACEABLE COSTS		
ACTIVITY CENTRE	VARIABLE	FIXED	COST DRIVER ACTIVITY
Account inquiry	$ 79,910	$155,270	3,300 labour hours
Correspondence	9,800	25,584	2,800 letters
Account billing	156,377	81,400	2,440,000 lines
Account verification	10,797	78,050	20,000 accounts

The Billing Department constructs a flexible budget for each activity centre, based on the following ranges of cost-driver activity:

ACTIVITY CENTRE	COST DRIVER	RELEVANT RANGE	
Account inquiry	Labour hours	3,000	5,000
Correspondence	Letters	2,500	3,500
Account billing	Lines	2,000,000	3,000,000
Account verification	Accounts	15,000	25,000

1. Develop flexible budget formulas for each of the four activity centres. Use the same format illustrated in Exhibit 12-4.
2. Compute the budgeted total cost in each activity centre for each of these levels of cost-driver activity: (a) the smallest activity in the relevant range, (b) the midpoint of the relevant range, and (c) the highest activity in the relevant range.
3. Determine the total cost function for the Billing Department.
4. The following table gives the actual results for the Billing Department. Prepare a cost-control performance report comparing the flexible budget to actual results for each activity centre. Compute flexible budget variances.

ACTIVITY CENTRE	COST-DRIVER LEVEL (ACTUAL)	ACTUAL COST
Account inquiry	4,400 labour hours	$229,890
Correspondence	3,250 letters	38,020
Account billing	2,900,000 lines	285,000
Account verification	22,500 accounts	105,320

P12-14 **VARIANCE ANALYSES.** The Geneva Chocolate Company uses standard costs and a flexible budget to control its manufacture of fine chocolate. The purchasing agent is responsible for material price variances, and the production manager is responsible for all other variances. Operating data for the past week are summarized as follows:

1. Finished units produced: 4,000 boxes of chocolates.
2. Direct material: Purchases, 6,400 kilograms of chocolate @ 15.50 Swiss francs (SF) per kilogram; standard price is SF16 per kilogram. Used, 4,300 kilograms. Standard allowed of 1 kilogram per box.
3. Direct labour. Actual costs, 6,400 hours @ SF30.50, or SF195,200. Standard allowed per box produced, 1.5 hours. Standard price per direct labour hour, SF30.
4. Variable manufacturing overhead: Actual costs, SF69,500. Budget formula is SF10 per standard direct labour hour.

1. Compute the following variances
   a. Material purchase price variance
   b. Material efficiency variance
   c. Direct labour price variance
   d. Direct labour efficiency variance
   e. Variable manufacturing overhead spending variance
   f. Variable manufacturing overhead efficiency variance

Hint: For format, see the solution to the second Demonstration Problem, pages 608 to 610.

2. a. What is the budget allowance for direct labour?
   b. Would it be any different if production were 5,000 boxes?

P12-15 **SUMMARY EXPLANATION.** Wilcox Company produced 80,000 units, 8,000 more units than budgeted. Production data are as follows. Except for physical units, all quantities are in dollars:

	ACTUAL RESULTS AT ACTUAL PRICES	FLEXIBLE-BUDGET VARIANCES	FLEXIBLE BUDGET	SALES VOLUME VARIANCES	STATIC (MASTER) BUDGET
Physical units	80,000	–	?	?	72,000
Sales	?	$6,400 F	?	?	$720,000
Variable costs	$492,000	?	$480,000	?	?
Contribution margin	?	?	?	?	?
Fixed costs	?	$8,000 U	?	?	$195,000
Operating income	?	?	?	?	?

1. Fill in the unknowns.
2. Briefly explain why the original target operating income was not attained.

P12-16 **EXPLANATION OF VARIANCE IN INCOME.** Diaz Credit Services produces reports for consumers about their credit ratings. The company's standard contribution margins average 70 percent of dollar sales and average selling prices are $50 per report. Average productivity is four reports per hour. Some preparers work for sales commissions and others for an hourly rate. The master budget for 2006 had predicted sales of 800,000 reports, but only 700,000 reports were processed.

Fixed costs of rent, supervision, advertising, and other items were budgeted at $21.5 million, but the budget was exceeded by $700,000 because of extra advertising in an attempt to boost revenue.

There were no variances from the average selling prices, but the actual commissions paid to preparers and the actual productivity per hour resulted in flexible-budget variances (that is, total price and efficiency variances) for variable costs of $900,000 unfavourable.

The president was unhappy because the budgeted operating income of $6.5 million was not achieved. He said, "Sure, we had unfavourable variable cost variances, but our operating income was down far more than that. Please explain why."

Explain why the budgeted operating income was not attained. Use a presentation similar to Exhibit 12-5. Enough data have been given to permit you to construct the complete exhibit by filling in the known items and then computing the unknown. Complete your explanation by briefly summarizing what happened.

P12-17 **OVERHEAD VARIANCES.** Consider these data:

	FACTORY OVERHEAD	
	FIXED	VARIABLE
Actual incurred	$ 14,200	$13,300
Budget for standard hours allowed for output achieved	12,500	11,000
Applied	11,600	11,000
Budget for actual hours of input	12,500	11,400

From the information given, fill in the blanks below:

The flexible-budget variance is $ _____	Fixed $ _____
	Variable $ _____
The production-volume variance is $ _____	Fixed $ _____
	Variable $ _____
The spending variance is $ _____	Fixed $ _____
	Variable $ _____
The efficiency variance is $ _____	Fixed $ _____
	Variable $ _____

Mark your variances F for favourable and U for unfavourable.

P12-18 **VARIANCES.** Consider the following data regarding factory overhead:

	VARIABLE	FIXED
Budget for actual hours of input	45,000	70,000
Applied	41,000	64,800
Budget for standard hours allowed for output achieved	?	?
Actual incurred	$48,500	$68,500

Using the above data, fill in the blanks in the following table. Use F for favourable or U for unfavourable for each variance.

	TOTAL OVERHEAD	VARIABLE	FIXED
1. Spending variance	_____	_____	_____
2. Efficiency variance	_____	_____	_____
3. Production-volume variance	_____	_____	_____
4. Flexible-budget variance	_____	_____	_____
5. Underapplied overhead	_____	_____	_____

P12-19 **SUMMARY OF AIRLINE PERFORMANCE.** Consider the performance (in thousands of dollars) of Eastern Airlines for a given year in the table below.

The static (master) budget had been based on a budget of $0.20 per revenue passenger kilometre. A revenue passenger kilometre is one paying passenger who has flown one kilometre. An average airfare decrease of 8 percent helped to generate an increase in passenger kilometres flown that exceeded the static budget for the year by 10 percent.

The price per litre of jet fuel rose above the price used to formulate the static budget. The average price increase for the year was 12 percent.

	ACTUAL RESULTS AT ACTUAL PRICES	STATIC (MASTER) BUDGET	VARIANCE
Revenue	$?	$300,000	$?
Variable expenses	200,000	195,000*	5,000 U
Contribution margin	?	105,000	?
Fixed expenses	77,000	75,000	2,000 U
Operating income	$?	$ 30,000	$?

* Includes the $90,000 cost of jet fuel.

1. Prepare a summary performance report for the president that is similar to Exhibit 12-5.
2. Assume that jet fuel costs are purely variable and the use of fuel was at the same level of efficiency as predicted in the static budget. What portion of the flexible-budget variance for variable expenses is attributable to jet fuel expenses? Explain.

P12-20 **ACTIVITY AND FLEXIBLE-BUDGET VARIANCES AT McDONALD'S.** Suppose a McDonald's franchise in Bangkok had budgeted sales for 2006 of B7.5 million (where B stands for baht, the Thai unit of currency). Cost of goods sold and other variable costs were expected to be 70 percent of sales. Budgeted annual fixed costs were B1.8 million. A booming Thai economy caused actual 2006 sales to soar to B9.3 million and actual profits to increase to B600,000. Fixed costs in 2006 were as budgeted. The franchisee was pleased with the increase in profit.

1. Compute the sales activity variance and the flexible budget variance for 2006. What can the franchisee learn from these variances?
2. In 2007 the Thai economy plummeted, and the franchise's sales fell back to the B7.5 million level. Given what happened in 2006, what do you expect to happen to profits in 2007?

P12-21 **FLEXIBLE AND STATIC BUDGETS.** Beta Alpha Psi, the accounting fraternity, recently held a dinner dance. The original (static) budget and actual results were as follows:

	BUDGET	**ACTUAL**	**VARIANCE**
Attendees	75	90	
Revenue	$2,625	$3,255	$630 F
Chicken dinners: $17.60 per person	1,320	1,668	348 U
Beverages: $6 per person	450	466	16 U
Club rental, $75 plus 8% tax	81	81	0
Music, 3 hours @ $240			
per hour	720	840	120 U
Profit	$ 54	$ 200	$ 146 F

1. Subdivide each variance into a sales-volume variance portion and a flexible-budget variance portion. Use the format of Exhibit 12-5.
2. Provide possible explanations for the variances.

P12-22 **UNIVERSITY FLEXIBLE BUDGETING.** (CMA, adapted) The University of Liverpool offers an extensive continuing education program in many cities throughout Britain. For the convenience of its faculty and administrative staff and to save costs, the university operates a motor pool. The motor pool operated with 25 vehicles until February of this year, when an additional automobile was acquired. The motor pool furnishes gasoline, oil, and other supplies for the cars and hires one mechanic who does routine maintenance and minor repairs. Major repairs are done at a nearby commercial garage. A supervisor manages the operations.

Each year the supervisor prepares an operating budget, informing university management of the funds needed to operate the pool. Amortization on the automobiles is recorded in the budget in order to determine the cost per kilometre.

The schedule below presents the annual budget approved by the university. The actual costs for March are compared with one-twelfth of the annual budget.

University Motor Pool Budget Report for March	ANNUAL BUDGET	ONE-MONTH BUDGET	MARCH ACTUAL	OVER (UNDER)
Gasoline	£75,000	£6,250	£7,500	£1,250
Oil, minor repairs, parts, and supplies	15,000	1,250	1,300	50
Outside repairs	2,700	225	50	(175)
Insurance	4,800	400	416	16
Salaries and benefits	21,600	1,800	1,800	—
Amortization	22,800	1,900	1,976	76
	£141,900	£11,825	£13,042	£1,217
Total kilometres	1,500,000	125,000	140,000	
Cost per kilometre	£0.0946	£0.0946	£0.0932	
Number of automobiles	25	25	26	

The annual budget was constructed upon the following assumptions:

1. 25 automobiles in the pool
2. 60,000 kilometres per year per automobile
3. 8 kilometres per litre per automobile
4. £0.40 per litre of gas
5. £0.01 per kilometre for oil, minor repairs, parts, and supplies
6. £108 per automobile in outside repairs

The supervisor is unhappy with the monthly report comparing budget and actual costs for March; he claims it presents his performance unfairly. His previous employer used flexible budgeting to compare actual costs with budgeted amounts.

1. Employing flexible-budgeting techniques, prepare a report that shows budgeted amounts, actual costs, and monthly variation for March.
2. Briefly explain the basis of your budget figure for outside repairs.

P12-23 **STRAIGHTFORWARD VARIANCE ANALYSIS.** Algoma Metals Inc. uses a standard cost system. The month's data regarding its cast iron vats follow:

- Material purchased and used, 3,400 kilograms
- Direct labour costs incurred, 5,500 hours, $20,900
- Variable overhead costs incurred, $4,780
- Finished units produced, 1,000
- Actual material cost, $0.95 per kilogram
- Variable overhead rate, $0.80 per hour
- Standard direct labour cost, $4 per hour
- Standard material cost, $1 per kilogram
- Standard kilograms of material in a finished unit, 3
- Standard direct labour hours per finished unit, 5

Prepare schedules of all variances, using the format of Exhibit 12-9 (the general three-column analysis).

P12-24 **STANDARD MATERIAL ALLOWANCES.** Horst Company is a chemical manufacturer that supplies industrial users. The company plans to introduce a new solution and needs to develop a standard product cost for this new solution.

The new chemical solution is made by combining altium and bollium, boiling the mixture, adding a second compound (credix), and bottling the resulting solution in 20 litre containers. An initial mix of altium and bollium is put through a boiling process, which results in a 20 percent reduction in volume. After reduction, the resulting solution comprises 24 kilograms of altium and 19.2 litres of bollium, and has a total volume of 20 litres. The solution is then cooled slightly before 10 kilograms of credix are added; the addition of credix does not affect the total liquid volume.

The purchase prices of the raw materials used in the manufacture of this new chemical solution are as follows:

Altium	$1.50 per kilogram
Bollium	2.10 per litre
Credix	2.80 per kilogram

Determine the standard quantity for each of the raw materials needed to produce a 20 litre container of Horst Company's new chemical solution and the standard materials cost of a 20 litre container of the new product.

P12-25 FLEXIBLE AND STATIC BUDGETS. Kronos Shipping Company's general manager reports quarterly to the company's president on the firm's operating performance. The company has used a budget based on detailed expectations for the forthcoming quarter. For example, the condensed performance report for a recent quarter was (in dollars):

	BUDGET	ACTUAL	VARIANCE
Net revenue	$8,000,000	$7,600,000	$400,000 U
Fuel	160,000	$ 157,000	$ 3,000 F
Repairs and maintenance	80,000	78,000	2,000 F
Supplies and miscellaneous	800,000	788,000	12,000 F
Variable payroll	5,360,000	5,200,000	160,000 F
Total variable costs*	$ 6,400,000	$6,223,000	$177,000 F
Supervision	$ 160,000	$ 164,000	4,000 U
Rent	160,000	160,000	–
Amortization	480,000	480,000	–
Other fixed costs	160,000	158,000	2,000 F
Total fixed costs	$ 960,000	$ 962,000	2,000 U
Total costs charged against revenue	$7,360,000	$7,185,000	$175,000 F
Operating income	$ 640,000	$ 415,000	$225,000 U

U = Unfavourable   F = Favourable
* For purposes of this analysis, assume that these costs are totally variable with respect to sales revenue. In practice, many are mixed and have to be subdivided into variable and fixed components before a meaningful analysis can be made. Also assume that the prices and mix of services sold remain unchanged.

Although the general manager was upset about not obtaining enough revenue, she was happy that her cost performance was favourable; otherwise her net operating income would be even worse.

The president was totally unhappy and remarked: "I can see some merit in comparing actual performance with budgeted performance because we can see whether actual revenue coincided with our best guess for budget purposes. But I can't see how this performance report helps me evaluate cost-control performance."

1. Prepare a columnar flexible budget for Kronos Shipping at revenue levels of $7,000,000, $8,000,000, and $9,000,000. Use the format of the last three columns of Exhibit 12-2. Assume that the prices and mix of products sold are equal to the budgeted prices and mix.
2. Express the flexible budget for costs in formula form.
3. Prepare a condensed table showing the static (master) budget variance, the sales activity variance, and the flexible-budget variance. Use the format of Exhibit 12-5.

P12-26 **DIRECT MATERIAL AND DIRECT LABOUR VARIANCES.** Artistic Metalworks Company manufactures sculptured metal ornaments that are shaped and finished by hand. The following standards were developed for a line of lampposts:

	STANDARD INPUTS EXPECTED FOR EACH UNIT OF OUTPUT ACHIEVED	STANDARD PRICE PER UNIT OF INPUT
Direct materials	10 kilograms	$5 per kilogram
Direct labour	5 hours	$25 per hour

During April, 550 lampposts were scheduled for production. However, only 525 were actually produced.

Direct materials purchased and used amounted to 5,500 kilograms at a unit price of $4.25 per kilogram. Direct labour was actually paid $26 per hour, and 2,850 hours were used.

1. Compute the standard cost per lamppost for direct materials and direct labour.
2. Compute the price variances and usage variances for direct materials and direct labour.
3. Based on these data, what clues for investigation are provided by the variances?

P12-27 **FUNDAMENTALS OF OVERHEAD VARIANCES.** The Mendoza Company is installing an absorption standard-costing system and a flexible-overhead budget. Standard costs have recently been developed for its only product and are as follows:

Direct material, 3 kilograms @ $20	$60
Direct labour, 2 hours @ $14	28
Variable overhead, 2 hours @ $5	10
Fixed overhead	?
Standard cost per unit of finished product	$?

Expected production activity is expressed as 7,500 standard direct labour hours per month. Fixed overhead is expected to be $60,000 per month. The predetermined fixed-overhead rate for product costing is not changed from month to month.

1. Calculate the proper fixed-overhead rate per standard direct labour hour and per unit.
2. Graph the following for activity from zero to 10,000 hours:
   a. Budgeted variable overhead

b. Variable overhead applied to product

3. Graph the following for activity from zero to 10,000 hours:
   a. Budgeted fixed overhead
   b. Fixed overhead applied to product

4. Assume that 6,000 standard direct labour hours are allowed for the output achieved during a given month. Actual variable overhead of $30,600 was incurred: actual fixed overhead amounted to $62,000. Calculate the
   a. Fixed-overhead flexible-budget variance
   b. Fixed-overhead production-volume variance
   c. Variable-overhead flexible-budget variance

5. Assume that 7,800 standard direct labour hours are allowed for the output achieved during a given month. Actual overhead incurred amounted to $99,700, $62,200 of which was fixed. Calculate the
   a. Fixed-overhead flexible-budget variance
   b. Fixed-overhead production-volume variance
   c. Variable-overhead flexible-budget variance

P12-28 FIXED OVERHEAD AND PRACTICAL CAPACITY. The expected activity of the paper-making plant of Leventhal Paper Company was 45,000 machine hours per month. Practical capacity was 60,000 machine hours per month. The standard machine hours allowed for the actual output achieved in January were 54,000. The budgeted fixed-factory-overhead items were as follows:

Amortization, equipment	$340,000
Amortization, factory building	64,000
Supervision	47,000
Indirect labour	234,000
Insurance	18,000
Property taxes	17,000
Total	$720,000

Because of unanticipated scheduling difficulties and the need for more indirect labour, the actual fixed factory overhead was $751,000.

1. Using practical capacity as the denominator for applying fixed factory overhead, prepare a summary analysis of fixed-overhead variances for January.
2. Using expected activity as the denominator for applying fixed factory overhead, prepare a summary analysis of fixed-overhead variances for January.
3. Explain why some of your variances in requirements 1 and 2 are the same and why some differ.

P12-29 VARIANCE ANALYSIS. Study the format of the analysis of variances in Exhibit 12-12. Suppose production is 156,000 units. Also assume the following:

Standard direct labour hours allowed per unit produced	0.25
Standard direct labour rate per hour	$6.00
Actual direct labour hours of input	42,000
Actual direct labour rate per hour	$6.15
Variable manufacturing overhead actually incurred	$36,000
Fixed manufacturing overhead actually incurred	$154,000

Other data are as shown in Exhibit 12-12.

Prepare an analysis of variances similar to that shown in Exhibit 12-12.

P12-30 **ROLE OF DEFECTIVE UNITS AND NONPRODUCTIVE TIME IN SETTING STANDARDS.** Sung Park owns and operates Transpac Machining, a subcontractor to several aerospace-industry contractors. When Mr. Park wins a bid to produce a piece of equipment, he sets standard costs for the production of the item. He then compares actual manufacturing costs with the standards to judge the efficiency of production.

In April 2006 Transpac won a bid to produce 15,000 units of a shielded component used in a navigation device. Specifications for the components were very tight, and Mr. Park expected that 20 percent of the components would fail his final inspection, even if every care was exercised in production. There was no way to identify defective items before production was complete. Therefore, 18,750 units had to be produced to get 15,000 good components. Standards were set to include an allowance for the expected number of defective items.

Each final component contained 2.8 kilograms of direct materials, and normal scrap from production was expected to average an additional 0.4 kilograms per unit. The direct material was expected to cost $11.25 per kilogram plus $0.75 per kilogram for shipping and handling.

Machining of the components required close attention by skilled machinists. Each component required four hours of machining time. The machinists were paid $22 per hour and worked 40-hour weeks. Of the 40 hours, an average of 32 hours was spent directly on production. The other eight hours consisted of time for breaks and waiting time when machines were broken down or there was no work to be done. Nevertheless, all payments to machinists were considered direct labour, whether or not they were for time spent directly on production. In addition to the basic wage rate, Transpac paid employee benefits averaging $5 per hour and payroll taxes of 10 percent of the basic wages.

Determine the standard cost of direct materials and direct labour for each good unit of output.

P12-31 **AUTOMATION AND DIRECT LABOUR AS OVERHEAD.** Precision AutoParts Company has a highly automated manufacturing process for producing a variety of auto parts. Through the use of computer-aided manufacturing and robotics, the company has reduced its labour costs to only 5 percent of total manufacturing costs. Consequently, labour is not accounted for as a separate item but is considered part of overhead.

The static budget for producing 750 units of part Z624 in March 2006 is

Direct materials	$18,000*
Overhead:	
Supplies	1,875
Power	1,310
Rent and other building services	2,815
Factory labour	1,500
Amortization	4,500
Total manufacturing costs	$30,000

* 3 kilograms per unit × $8 per kilogram × 750 units.

Supplies and power are considered to be variable overhead. The other overhead items are fixed costs.

Actual costs in March 2006 for producing 900 units of Z624 were

Direct materials	$21,645*
Overhead:	
Supplies	2,125
Power	1,612
Rent and other building services	2,775
Factory labour	1,625
Amortization	4,500
Total manufacturing costs	$34,282

* 2,775 kilograms purchased and used at $7.80 per kilogram.

1. Compute (a) the direct-materials price and efficiency variances, and (b) the flexible-budget variance for each overhead item.
2. Comment on the way Precision AutoParts Company accounts for and controls factory labour.

P12-32 **REVIEW OF MAJOR POINTS IN CHAPTER.** The following questions are based on the data contained in Exhibit 12-9.

1. Suppose actual production and sales were 8,000 units instead of 7,000 units. (a) Compute the sales-volume variance. Is the performance of the marketing function the sole explanation for this variance? Why? (b) Using a flexible budget, compute the budgeted contribution margin, the budgeted operating income, budgeted direct material, and budgeted direct labour.
2. Suppose the following were the actual results for the production of 8,000 units:
   Direct material: 42,000 kilograms were used at an actual unit price of $1.85, for a total actual cost of $77,700.
   Direct labour: 4,125 hours were used at an actual hourly rate of $16.40, for a total actual cost of $67,650.
   Compute the flexible-budget variance and the price and usage variances for direct materials and direct labour. Present your answers in the form shown in Exhibit 12-5.
3. Suppose the company is organized so that the purchasing manager bears the primary responsibility for the acquisition prices of materials, and the production manager bears the primary responsibility for efficiency but no responsibility for unit prices. Assume the same facts as in requirement 2 except that the purchasing manager acquired 60,000 kilograms of materials at $1.85 per kilogram. This means that there is an ending inventory of 18,000 kilograms. Would your variance analysis of materials in requirement 2 change? Why? Show computations.

P12-33 **HOSPITAL COSTS AND EXPLANATION OF VARIANCES.** The emergency room at University Hospital uses a flexible budget based on patients seen as a measure of volume. An adequate staff of attending and on-call physicians must be maintained at all times, so physician scheduling is unaffected by volume. However, nurse scheduling varies as volume changes. A standard of 0.5 nurse hours per patient visit was set. Average hourly pay for nurses is $14, ranging from $8 to $17 per hour. All materials are considered to be supplies, which are a part of overhead; there are no direct materials. A statistical study showed that the cost of supplies and other variable overhead is more closely associated with nurse-hours than with patient visits. The standard for supplies and other variable overhead is $10 per nursing hour.

The head physician of the emergency room unit, Sue Cox, is responsible for control of costs. During October the emergency room unit treated 4,000 patients. The budget and actual costs were as follows:

	BUDGET	ACTUAL	VARIANCE
Patient visits	3,800	4,000	200
Nursing hours	1,900	2,075	175
Nursing cost	$ 26,600	$ 31,050	$4,450
Supplies and other			
variable overhead	19,000	21,320	2,320
Fixed costs	92,600	92,600	0
Total cost	$138,200	$144,970	$6,770

1. Calculate price and usage variances for nursing costs.
2. Calculate spending and usage variances for supplies and other variable overhead.
3. Dr. Cox has been asked to explain the variances to the chief of staff. Provide possible explanations.

P12-34 **MATERIAL, LABOUR, AND OVERHEAD VARIANCES.** Belfair Kayak Company makes molded plastic kayaks. Standards costs for an entry-level whitewater kayak are:

Direct materials, 60 kilograms @ $5.50 per kilogram	$330
Direct labour, 1.5 hours @ $16 per hour	24
Overhead, @ $12 per kayak	12
Total	$366

The overhead rate assumes production of 450 kayaks per month. The overhead cost function is $2,808 + $5.76 × number of kayaks.

During March, Belfair produced 430 kayaks and had the following actual results:

Direct materials purchased	28,000 kilograms @ $5.30/kg
Direct materials used	27,000 kilograms
Direct labour	660 hours @ $15.90/hour
Actual overhead	$5,320

1. Compute material, labour, and overhead variances.
2. Interpret the variances.
3. Suppose variable overhead was $3.84 per labour hour instead of $5.76 per kayak. Compute the variable overhead efficiency variance and the total overhead spending variance. Would these variances lead you to a different interpretation of the overhead variances from the interpretation in requirement 2? Explain.

P12-35 **ACTIVITY-BASED COSTING AND FLEXIBLE BUDGETING.** The new printing department of Shark Advertising Inc. provides printing services to the other departments. Prior to the establishment of the in-house printing department, the departments contracted with external printers for their printing work. The Shark printing policy is to charge those departments using variable printing costs on the basis of number of pages printed. Fixed costs are recovered in pricing of external jobs.

The first year's budget for the printing department was based on the department's expected total costs divided by the planned number of pages to be printed.

The annual number of pages to be printed was 420,000 and total variable costs were budgeted to be $420,000. Most government accounts and all internal jobs were expected to use only single-colour printing. Commercial accounts were primarily colour printing. Variable costs were estimated based on the average variable cost of printing a two-colour page that is one-fourth graphics and three-fourths text. The expected annual variable costs for each division were as follows:

DEPARTMENT	PLANNED PAGES PRINTED	VARIABLE COST PER PAGE	BUDGETED COSTS
Government accounts	120,000	$1.00	$120,000
Commercial accounts	250,000	$1.00	250,000
Central administration total	50,000	$1.00	50,000
	420,000		$420,000

After the first month of operation, the printing department announced that its variable cost estimate of $1 per page was too low. The first month's actual costs were $50,000 to print 40,000 pages:

Government accounts	9,000 pages
Commercial accounts	27,500 pages
Central administration	3,500 pages

Three reasons were cited for higher-than-expected costs: all departments were using more printing services than planned and government and internal jobs were using more four-colour printing and more graphics than expected. The printing department also argued that additional four-colour printing equipment would have to be purchased if demand for four-colour printing continued to grow.

1. Compare the printing department actual results, static budget, and flexible budget for the month just completed.
2. Discuss possible reasons why the printing department static budget was inaccurate.
3. An activity-based costing (ABC) study completed by a consultant indicated that printing cost is to be driven by number of pages (@ $0.30 per page) and use of colours (@ $0.25 extra per colour).
   a. Discuss the likely effects of using the ABC results for budgeting and control of printing department use.
   b. Discuss the assumptions regarding cost behaviour implied in the ABC study results.
   c. Commercial accounts during the first month (27,500 pages) used four colours per page. Compare the cost of the commercial accounts under the old and the proposed ABC system.

P12-36 **PERFORMANCE EVALUATION.** Imperial Mills is a small flour company in the West. Claude Laurent became president in 2006. He is concerned with the ability of his production manager to control costs. To aid his evaluation, Laurent set up a standard-cost system.

Standard costs were based on 2006 costs in several categories. Each 2006 cost was divided by 1,520,000 cwt (cwt means hundredweight, or 100 pounds), which was the volume of 2006 production, to determine a standard for 2007:

	2006 COST (IN THOUSANDS)	2007 STANDARD (PER HUNDREDWEIGHT)
Direct materials	$1,824	$1.20
Direct labour	836	0.55
Variable overhead	1,596	1.05
Fixed overhead	2,432	1.60
Total	$6,688	$4.40

At the end of 2007, Laurent compared actual results with the standards he established. Production was 1,360,000 cwt, and variances were as follows:

	ACTUAL	STANDARD	VARIANCE
Direct materials	$1,802	$1,632	$170 U
Direct labour	735	748	13 F
Variable overhead	1,422	1,428	6 F
Fixed overhead	2,418	2,176	242 U
Total	$6,377	$5,984	$393 U

Laurent was not surprised by the unfavourable variance in direct materials. After all, wheat prices in 2007 averaged 10 percent above those in 2006. But he was disturbed by the lack of control of fixed overhead. He called in the production manager and demanded an explanation.

1. Prepare an explanation for the large unfavourable fixed-overhead variance.
2. Discuss the appropriateness of using one year's costs as the next year's standards.

MANAGERIAL DECISION CASES

C12-1 **ANALYSIS OF OPERATING RESULTS.** Manchester Machining Company (MMC) produces and sells three main product lines. The company employs a standard cost-accounting system for record-keeping purposes.

At the beginning of 2006, the president of MMC presented the budget to the parent company and accepted a commitment to earn a profit of £16,400 in 2006. The president has been confident that the year's profit would exceed the budget target, since the monthly sales reports that he has been receiving have shown that sales for the year will exceed budget by 10 percent. The president is both disturbed and confused when the controller presents an adjusted forecast as of November 30, 2006, indicating that profit will be 14 percent under budget:

Manchester Machining Company Forecasts of Operating Results

	FORECASTS AS OF	
	1/1/06	11/30/06
Sales	£156,000	£171,600
Cost of sales at standard	108,000*	118,800
Gross margin at standard	£ 48,000	£ 52,800
Over- (Under-) absorbed fixed manufacturing overhead		(6,000)
Actual gross margin	£ 48,000	£ 46,800
Selling expenses	£ 11,200	£ 12,320
Administrative expenses	20,400	20,400
Total operating expenses	£ 31,600	£ 32,720
Earnings before tax	£ 16,400	£ 14,080

*Includes fixed manufacturing overhead of £36,000.

There have been no sales price changes or product-mix shifts since the 1/1/06 forecast. The only cost variance on the income statement is the under-absorbed manufacturing overhead. This arose because the company produced only 16,000 standard machine hours (budgeted machine hours were 20,000) during 2006 as a result of a shortage of raw materials while its principal supplier was closed by a strike. Fortunately, MMC's finished-goods inventory was large enough to fill all sales orders received.

Required:

1. Analyze and explain why the profit has declined in spite of increased sales and good control over costs. Show computations.
2. What plan, if any, could MMC adopt during December to improve its reported profit at year-end? Explain your answer.
3. Illustrate and explain how MMC could adopt an alternative internal cost-reporting procedure that would avoid the confusing effect of the present procedure. Show the revised forecasts under your alternative.
4. Would the alternative procedure described in requirement 3 be acceptable to MMC for financial-reporting purposes? Explain.

C12-2 **VARIANCE ANALYSIS MANUFACTURING.** (CICA)   Pitfall Industries manufactures an industrial detergent called SCRAM. On November 15, 2006, Donald Teague, the president of the company, met with his executive committee and stated:

I have reviewed the company's preliminary operating results for the year ended September 30, 2006. Notwithstanding that the results are subject to audit, it is evident that we failed to achieve planned profits. A shortfall in net income before taxes for the year in the amount of $63,800 is indicated.

In view of the significant accumulated losses to the end of the company's 2006 fiscal year, I have requested our controller, Cathy Collins, to prepare an analysis of the current year's results, together with her recommendations for corrective action, which, if adopted, would enhance future performance. That analysis should consider both short- and long-run considerations.

I am requesting that you cooperate fully with Cathy in the preparation of her report. In particular, John and Mark, our vice presidents of manufacturing and marketing respectively, will be expected to "open their books," so to speak.

At the conclusion of the meeting, Teague tabled the following condensed Statement of Income:

Pitfall Industries
Statement of Income
Year Ended
September 30, 2006

	ACTUAL 2005	ACTUAL 2006	BUDGET 2006	BUDGET VARIANCE*
Sales	$910,000	$880,000	$1,000,000	$(120,000)
Cost of sales	837,200	809,800	860,000	50,200
Gross profit	72,800	70,200	140,000	(69,800)
Selling and administration expenses	120,000	132,000	138,000	6,000
Net income (loss) before taxes	$ (47,200)	$ (61,800)	$ 2,000	$ (63,800)

* ( ) Denotes unfavourable variances.

With the assistance of John and Mark, Cathy extracted the additional data outlined below from various records maintained independent of the accounting department.

1. A publication dated October 2006, containing marketing statistics for industrial detergents similar to SCRAM, revealed the following, relative to the years ending September 30:

	2004	2005	2006
Industry (including Pitfall):			
Sales — Dollars	$6,100,000	$6,500,000	$6,970,000
— Units	610,000	650,000	689,000
Pitfall's comparable performance:			
Sales — Dollars	$ 820,000	$ 910,000	$ 880,000
— Units	82,000	91,000	80,000

In August 2005, the Economic Council of Canada forecast a 5 percent rate of growth in the economy for the ensuing year. At that time, the company had planned to market 100,000 units of product during fiscal 2006, at a selling price of $10 per unit.

2. Marketing instituted a selling price increase of $1 per unit in late September 2005. Severe cost pressures resulting from labour contract settlements, coupled with a deterioration in manufacturing efficiency, were cited as the reasons for the price increase. Marketing believes that the company could have maintained its increasing share of total industry sales had a price increase not been implemented.

3. Inventories of work-in-process and finished goods have remained virtually unchanged during the past four years. Inventories are costed at "standard" and all manufacturing cost variances are charged to cost of sales at the end of each year.

An analysis of cost of sales revealed the following for the years ended September 30:

	2005 ACTUAL	2006 ACTUAL	2006 PLAN
Direct materials	$445,900	$408,000	$460,000
Direct labour	191,100	201,600	200,000
Variable overhead	100,100	88,200	100,000
Fixed overhead	100,100	112,000	100,000
	$837,200	$809,800	$860,000

Included in the above analysis is a write-off of $10,100 during 2006 as a result of spring flood damage. This charge was allocated to materials ($2,100) and fixed overhead ($8,000).

4. During 2006, 82,000 kilograms of materials and 42,000 direct labour hours were consumed in the manufacturing process. Eighty thousand (80,000) units of good product were produced and sold during the year. The standard cost of SCRAM is determined to be as follows:

Direct material—1 kilogram	$4.60
Direct labour—1/2 hour	2.00
Variable overhead @ $2.00 per direct labour hour	1.00
Fixed overhead	1.00
Total standard cost per unit	$8.60

Combined variable and fixed overhead are applied to the product on the basis of $2 per unit, based on a normal activity of 100,000 units that represents 80 percent of the company's manufacturing capacity.

For the previous year, 2005, manufacturing records revealed a net unfavourable cost variance from standard of approximately 7 percent. Direct material variances are not recognized until after the manufacturing process commences.

John maintained that Pitfall's product was superior in quality to that of similar industrial detergents presently being marketed by competition.

5. Selling and administrative expenses are fixed with the exception of sales staff's commissions, which are paid on the basis of $0.70 per unit of SCRAM sold. During the year, there was an unplanned addition to the administrative clerical staff.

6. Of the $188,000 of fixed costs recorded by the organization in 2006, $90,000 are considered "sunk." Management does not attach any scrap value to plant equipment due to the unique attributes of the manufacturing process.

Upon receipt of the above information, Collins proceeded with her analysis and report. Throughout this period, a "strained" atmosphere prevailed among manufacturing, marketing, and accounting.

Required: Write Collins's report to the president presenting adequate analysis to support your recommendations.

C12-3 **VARIANCE ANALYSIS—SERVICE.** (ICAO) The Holcomb Hotel is a 200-room hotel located in a residential section of Kingston, Ontario. It is an older hotel of distinction that is very popular with those who appreciate the amenities of the older style of service.

While the Holcomb is a respected hotel, it has not always been a profitable one. Competition from newer hotels and motels in the area, plus the simple inefficiencies of running a hotel in the "old style" has placed pressure on management to improve efficiency without impairing service. As a result, the newly appointed general manager of the Holcomb is attempting to tighten cost control.

The Holcomb operates its own laundry facilities instead of contracting with a laundry service as most modern hotels do. The general manager has been examining the operating results of the laundry for June, the month just ended. The budget for the laundry called for operating expenses of $5,310 at an occupancy rate of 70 percent for all types of rooms. The actual occupancy rate for the 30-day month was 75 percent, or 4,500 room-days instead of the 4,200 room-days budgeted. The higher-than-expected occupancy rate would, of course, cause proportionately higher costs in the laundry, but the actual expenses of $6,213 were higher than expected. The budgeted and actual expenses were as follows:

	BUDGET	ACTUAL
Labour	$2,230	$2,599
Soap and supplies	1,596	1,898
Supervision	480	520
Maintenance and repairs	500	656
Space charge	504	540
Total	$5,310	$6,213

To help her understand the reasons for the deviations from budget, the general manager assembled the following information from several sources within the hotel:

1. The hotel has two types of rooms, standard and superior. Standard rooms are expected to average six kilograms of laundry (bed linen and towels) per day, while superior rooms are expected to generate an average of ten kilograms per day.
2. In June, the 120 standard rooms had 65 percent occupancy, while the 80 superior rooms had 90 percent occupancy.
3. In June, the laundry washed 38,760 kilograms of bed linen and towels. The laundry can process 70 kilograms of laundry per hour.
4. The laundry is staffed by one permanent full-time employee who is paid $5.60 per hour (including fringe benefits) for 7.5 hours a day for six days a week. On Sundays, the full-time person is replaced by a local university student who is paid the same rate for the same number of hours. In total, the full-time employee and his Sunday replacement receive $1,260 for a 30 day-month. Hourly employees are also retained, at a cost of $4.20 per hour.
5. The laundry is supervised by the assistant housekeeper. One-third of her salary is allocated to the laundry. In May, the assistant housekeeper received a raise from $1,440 per month to $1,560 per month.
6. Routine maintenance on the washers and dryers is covered by a maintenance contract. In June, a motor on one of the washing machines burned out and had to be replaced.
7. The space charge allocates the hotel's total variable costs of electricity and water to user departments. The allocation to the laundry is $0.12 per room-day of occupancy.

Required: Prepare an analysis of the difference between the budgeted and actual expenses of the laundry department that explains the reasons for the variances.

C12-4 **FLEXIBLE BUDGETS AND VARIANCES ANALYSIS.** (SMAC) Sam Leaf, the president of Ginkgo Manufacturing Limited, was very pleased but puzzled by the 2006 operating results (Exhibit 12A-1). He knew that both manufacturing and marketing had problems during the year and he had not anticipated that the actual income from operations would exceed the budget. Sam placed a lot of importance on his managers' staying within the budget to ensure that the target profit was attained.

Ginkgo manufactured two product lines—chlorine and bromine pellets—for home swimming pools. Production and sales were measured in kilograms, with the bromine being more expensive. The controller prepared a budget each December for the following year, but it was difficult to forecast sales, which were largely determined by the weather. As well, the mix of sales was difficult to forecast because of unpredictable switching of demand from one product to the other. In consultation with the sales manager, an estimate was made of total market sales in kilograms and the share each of Ginkgo's two products would achieve. From the resulting sales forecast, the budget was prepared. The fixed and variable cost elements in the budget were based on adjustments to the current year's figures to reflect the best estimates for the following year.

During 2006, the production schedule had to be changed numerous times to match sales demand. This had resulted in production problems and waste. The sales manager had attempted to stimulate sales of the higher-priced bromine and was pleased with the excess sales over budget.

EXHIBIT 12A-1

Ginkgo Manufacturing Limited
Operating Results for the Year Ended December 31, 2006

	STATIC BUDGET	ACTUAL
Sales in units (kilograms)	1,425,000	1,920,000
Sales in dollars	$17,575,000	$24,672,000
Variable costs:		
Manufacturing	10,022,500	13,440,000
Selling	4,560,000	7,968,000
Total variable costs	14,582,500	21,408,000
Contribution margin	2,992,500	3,264,000
Fixed costs:		
Manufacturing	550,000	565,000
Selling	345,000	370,000
Administration	150,000	140,000
Total fixed costs	1,045,000	1,075,000
Income from operations	$ 1,947,500	$ 2,189,000

Sam asked his controller to provide him with a detailed analysis of operating results and a recommendation for awarding bonuses to the sales and production managers. As a first step, the controller put together the original underlying budget cost and revenue estimates, and the actual 2006 data, which he obtained from the cost records and trade statistics (Exhibit 12A-2).

EXHIBIT 12A-2

Ginkgo Manufacturing Limited
2006 Sales, Cost, and Market Data

	STATIC BUDGET		ACTUAL	
	CHLORINE	BROMINE	CHLORINE	BROMINE
Variable costs per kilogram:				
Manufacturing	$ 5.75	$ 8.50	$ 6.25	$ 7.50
Selling	2.50	4.00	2.50	5.25
Selling price per kilogram	$10.00	$15.00	$10.00	$14.75

	SALES AND MARKET VOLUMES (MARKET SHARE)	
	BUDGETED KILOGRAMS	ACTUAL KILOGRAMS
Ginkgo's sales volume:		
Chlorine	760,000 (8%)	768,000 (8%)
Bromine	665,000 (7%)	1,152,000 (12%)
Total market volume	9,500,000 (100%)	9,600,000 (100%)

Required:

1. Prepare a 2006 flexible budget for Ginkgo based on the data in the two exhibits. Your flexible budget should include columns for the two product lines as well as for the company overall.
2. Prepare a profit variance analysis. Explain the causes of the variances, identifying the effect of market factors as well as responsibility for variances between marketing and production.

C12-5 **DETAILED VARIANCE ANALYSIS.** (SMAC) Ron Miron, president of Champion's Sporting Goods (CSG), was concerned about the profits earned by CSG during the fiscal year ending July 31, 2006. He had expected to sell 4,400 ski packages and earn $143,250 before taxes; actual profits earned were only $36,950.

The market for ski equipment is large and competitive. Ron had established a successful operation by specializing in low-cost mail-order ski packages. By offering only two packages, Ron was able to keep overhead costs to a minimum and negotiate favourable discounts from the ski equipment manufacturers. Both the downhill and cross-country ski packages contained skis, boots, poles, and a waxing kit.

Ron hired a consultant, Doreen Wilson, CMA, to analyze the last fiscal year's results. "I just don't understand what went wrong," said Ron. "Things just did not happen the way I thought they would. For example, I was forced to cut our prices midway through the season because one of the big chain stores cut their prices. But I bargained with our suppliers and they gave us a break, which I thought would keep us on target. Then we had to spend a bit more on advertising to let everybody know about our new prices and another clerk had to be hired to speed up the order processing. Still, these two changes account for only $40,000. To top it all off, the Ski Retailers Association magazine just reported that more Canadians bought ski packages this past season than ever before. Early estimates were that 44,000 ski packages would be sold and it ended up that 48,000 packages were sold in Canada last season. My bookkeeper, Teresa, has put together these numbers." (See Exhibits 12A-3 and 12A-4.) "Please conduct a detailed analysis of last year's results. Prepare a report that explains why we did not realize our expected profits and include a recommended strategy, detailing information required, which will bring our profits back up."

EXHIBIT 12A-3

Champion's Sporting Goods Master Budget for the Year Ended July 31, 2006

	CROSS-COUNTRY PACKAGE	DOWNHILL PACKAGE	TOTAL
Sales volume	3,100	1,300	4,400
Total sales revenue	$542,500	$455,000	$997,500
Cost of goods sold	263,500	221,000	484,500
Shipping	54,250	45,500	99,750
Total variable costs	317,750	266,500	584,250
Contribution margin	$224,750	$188,500	413,250
Fixed costs: Advertising & promotion			210,000
Administration			60,000
Net income before taxes			$143,250

BUDGETED DATA PER PACKAGE	CROSS-COUNTRY	DOWNHILL
Selling price	$175.000	$350.00
Cost of goods sold	$ 85.00	$170.00
Shipping	17.50	35.00
Total variable costs per package	$ 102.50	$205.00

EXHIBIT 12A-4

Champion's Sporting
Goods
Actual Results
for the Year Ended
July 31, 2006

	CROSS-COUNTRY PACKAGE	DOWNHILL PACKAGE	TOTAL
Sales volume	3,100	980	4,080
Total sales revenue	$511,500	$333,200	$844,700
Cost of goods sold	257,300	151,900	409,200
Shipping	54,250	34,300	88,550
Total variable costs	311,550	186,200	497,750
Contribution margin	$199,950	$147,000	346,950
Fixed costs: Advertising & promotion			230,000
Administration			80,000
Net income before taxes			$ 36,950

ACTUAL DATA PER PACKAGE	CROSS-COUNTRY	DOWNHILL
Average selling price	$165.00	$340.00
Average cost of goods sold	$83.00	$155.00
Shipping	17.50	35.00
Total average variable costs per package	$100.50	$190.00

Required: | Prepare the analysis and the report requested by Ron Miron.

C12-6 **CONTRIBUTION MARGIN AND VARIANCE ANALYSIS.** (SMAC) Mark Ferguson, the president of Ferguson Foundry Limited (FFL), sat in his office early on June 2, 2006, reviewing the financial statements of FFL for the fiscal year ended May 31, 2006. The results for the year were both a shock and a disappointment.

Ferguson called Carl Holitzner, an independent consultant, to meet him in his office. When Holitzner arrived, Ferguson described his concerns.

I don't know what went wrong last year. Everybody kept telling me that we were selling more woodstoves than we thought we would and I knew from attending the trade shows that the sale of woodstoves throughout the province was rising. When I saw the statements for last year, I couldn't believe the drop in profits.

This company began in 1905. My grandfather used to make farm implements and sled runners; my father produced mostly trailers. I've dabbled in a few product lines like sewer grates and staircase railings, but, for the last five years, we've concentrated solely on woodstoves. Sales were slow at first and there were many producers in the market. But we have a good salesforce and things have been steadily improving for the last two years. In 2005, we achieved record profits.

In addition to profits dropping, we have lost our management team. The sales manager took early retirement last month, the production manager is in the hospital for major surgery, and the accountant quit after we discussed the kind of information I felt he should be providing. He kept telling me that everything was running smoothly. Boy, was he wrong!

I called you here this morning because I need some help in understanding what went wrong last year. I want to be sure that similar mistakes are not made in the future. I'll be hiring some new people, but I need some answers quickly. Here is the statement of budgeted and actual results (Exhibit 12A-5). I was also able to dig up a statement of standard costs (Exhibit 12A-6) that was prepared last year plus some market and cost data that the accountant had prepared before he left (Exhibit 12A-7). The standard costs are an accurate reflection of what it should cost to make either of the woodstove models.

Required:

Assume the role of Carl Holitzner and provide an explanation for FFL's lower-than-budgeted profit for the fiscal year ended May 31, 2006. Support your explanation with a detailed variance analysis.

EXHIBIT 12A-5

Ferguson Foundry Limited
Static Budget and Actual Results
for the Year Ended May 31, 2006

| | STATIC BUDGET | | |
	BASIC	DELUXE	TOTAL
Sales volume (in units)	4,500	5,500	10,000
Sales revenue	$1,350,000	$4,400,000	$5,750,000
Variable costs:			
Direct materials	315,000	1,045,000	1,360,000
Direct labour	405,000	1,320,000	1,725,000
Overhead	202,500	660,000	862,500
Selling and administration	67,500	220,000	287,500
Total variable costs	990,000	3,245,000	4,235,000
Contribution margin	$ 360,000	$1,155,000	1,515,000
Fixed costs:			
Manufacturing			750,000
Selling and administration			132,500
Total fixed costs			882,500
Operating income			$ 632,500

| | ACTUAL RESULTS | | |
	BASIC	DELUXE	TOTAL
Sales volume (in units)	7,200	4,800	12,000
Sales revenue	$2,340,000	$3,360,000	$5,700,000
Variable costs:			
Direct materials	486,000	820,800	1,306,800
Direct labour	748,800	1,190,400	1,939,200
Overhead	374,400	595,200	969,600
Selling and administration	108,000	192,000	300,000
Total variable costs	1,717,200	2,798,400	4,515,600
Contribution margin	$ 622,800	$ 561,600	$1,184,400
Fixed costs:			
Manufacturing			780,000
Selling and administration			139,500
Total fixed costs			919,500
Operating income			$ 264,900

EXHIBIT 12A-6

Ferguson Foundry Limited
Unit Cost Standards
for the Year Ended May 31, 2006

	BASIC WOODSTOVE	DELUXE WOODSTOVE
Direct materials:		
Standard quantity per unit	70 kg	190 kg
Standard price per kilogram	$ 1.00	$ 1.00
Direct labour:		
Standard quantity per unit	6 hrs.	16 hrs.
Standard rate per hour	$15.00	$15.00
Variable overhead:		
Standard quantity per unit	6 hrs.	16 hrs.
Standard rate per hour	$ 7.50	$ 7.50
Variable selling and		
administration rate per unit	$15.00	$40.00

PART FOUR   MANAGEMENT ACCOUNTING FOR PLANNING AND CONTROL

EXHIBIT 12A-7

Ferguson Foundry
Limited
Market and Cost Data
for the Year Ended
May 31, 2006

Market data:

Expected total market sales of woodstoves		100,000 units
Actual total market sales of woodstoves		133,333 units

Summary of cost sheets:

	BASIC	DELUXE	TOTAL
Units of woodstoves produced	7,200	4,800	12,000
Direct materials:			
Actual quantity used in kilograms	540,000	912,000	1,452,000
Actual price per kilogram			$0.90
Direct labour:			
Actual direct labour hours worked	46,800	74,400	121,200
Actual rate per hour			$16.00
Actual variable overhead allocated			
on the basis of direct labour hours	$374,400	$595,200	$ 969,600

EXCEL APPLICATION EXERCISE

E12-1 FLEXIBLE-BUDGET AND SALES-ACTIVITY VARIANCES

Goal: Create an Excel spreadsheet to prepare a summary performance report that identifies flexible-budget and sales-volume variances. Use the results to answer questions about your findings.

Scenario: Tax Preparation Services, Inc. has asked you to prepare a summary performance report identifying their flexible-budget and sales-activity variances. The background data for the summary performance report is as follows:

	Master budget data:	Actual results at actual prices:
Sales	2,500 clients at $350 per client	3,000 clients at $360 per client
Variable costs	$250 per client	$800,000
Fixed costs	$150,000	$159,500

Prepare the summary performance report using a format similar to Exhibit 12-5. When you have completed your spreadsheet, answer the following questions:

1. What caused the flexible-budget variance for sales?

2. What was the change in actual operating income compared to the operating income calculated in the master budget?

3. Can the amount in question 2 be explained by the flexible-budget and sales-volume variances? Explain.

Step by Step:

1. Open a new Excel spreadsheet.

2. In column A, create a bold-faced heading that contains the following:
   Row 1: Chapter 12 Decision Guideline
   Row 2: Tax Preparation Services, Inc.
   Row 3: Summary Performance Report
   Row 4: Today's date

3. Merge and centre the four heading rows across columns A through H.

4. In Column A, create the following row headings:
   Row 8: Clients
   Skip a row
   Row 10: Sales

Row 11: Variable Costs
Row 12: Contribution Margin
Row 13: Fixed Costs
Skip a row
Row 15: Operating Income

5. Change the format of Contribution Margin (Row 12) and Operating Income (Row 15) to bold-faced headings.

   Note: Adjust width of row A to accommodate row headings.

6. In row 7, create the following bold-faced, centre-justified column headings:
   Column B: Actual Results at Actual Activity
   Column C: Flexible Budget Variances
   Skip a column
   Column E: Flexible Budget at Actual Activity
   Column F: Sales-Volume Variances
   Skip a column
   Column H: Master Budget

7. Change the format of the column headings in row 7 to permit the titles to be displayed on multiple lines within a single cell.

   Alignment tab: Wrap Text: Checked

   Note: Adjust column widths so that headings only use two lines.

   Adjust row height to ensure that row is the same height as adjusted headings.

8. Change the format of the column width of columns D and G to a size of 2.

9. Use the scenario data to fill in client and fixed cost amounts for Actual, Flexible Budget, and Master Budget columns as well as variable costs for the Actual column.

10. Calculate variable costs for Flexible Budget and Master Budget columns. Use appropriate formulas to calculate Sales, Contribution Margin, and Operating Income amounts for Actual, Flexible Budget, and Master Budget columns.

11. Use appropriate formulas to calculate Flexible Budget and Sales-Volume Variances and display as absolute values.
    =ABS(*variance formula*)

12. Use one of the following formula templates to indicate whether variances are favourable (F) or unfavourable (U):
    =IF(*variance formula*>0,"F",IF(*variance formula*<0,"U","–"))
    For Sales, margin and income variances only.
    =IF(*variance formula*<0,"F",IF(*variance formula*>0,"U","–"))
    For Client, variable and fixed cost variances only.

    Hint: Go to the "Help" text and type "copy formulas" in the search area to obtain instructions for copying formulas from one cell to another. If done correctly, you should have to type in each of the formula templates only once.

13. Format all amounts as:
    Number: Category: Currency

    Decimal places: 0

    Symbol: None

    Negative numbers: Red with parentheses

14. Change the format of the amounts for Sales, Contribution Margin, and Operating Income to display a dollar symbol.

15. Change the format of the operating income amounts for Actual, Flexible Budget, and Master Budget to display as bold.

16. Change the format of the row headings for Contribution Margin and Operating Income to display as indented.

    Alignment tab: Horizontal: Left (Indent)

                       Indent: 1

    Note: Adjust width of row A to accommodate row headings.

17. Save your work to disk, and print a copy for your files.

    Note: Print your spreadsheet using landscape format in order to ensure that all columns appear on one page.

COLLABORATIVE LEARNING EXERCISE

CL12-1 SETTING STANDARDS Form groups of two to six persons each. The groups should each select a simple product or service. Be creative, but do not pick a product or service that is too complex. For those having difficulty choosing a product or service, some possibilities are

- One dozen chocolate-chip cookies
- A ten-mile taxi ride
- One copy of a 100-page course syllabus
- A machine-knit wool sweater
- A hand-knit wool sweater
- One hour of lawn mowing and fertilizing
- A hammer

1. Each student should individually estimate the direct materials and direct labour inputs needed to produce the product or service. For each type of direct material and direct labour, determine the standard quantity and standard price. Also, identify the overhead support needed, and determine the standard overhead cost of the product or service. The result should be a total standard cost for the product or service.

2. Each group should compare the estimates of its members. Where estimates differ, determine why there were differences. Did assumptions differ? Did some members have more knowledge about the product or service than others? Form a group estimate of the standard cost of the product or service.

3. After the group has agreed on a standard cost, discuss the process used to arrive at the cost. What assumptions did the group make? Is the standard cost an "ideal" standard or a "currently attainable" standard? Note how widely standard costs can vary depending on assumptions and knowledge of the production process.

Management Control Systems, the Balanced Scorecard, and Responsibility Accounting

After studying this chapter, you will be able to

1. Understand a management control system and how it relates to organizational goals.

2. Use responsibility accounting to define an organizational subunit as a cost centre, expense centre, revenue centre, profit centre, or investment centre.

3. Explain how corporate performance is affected by employee motivation and goal congruence.

4. Compare financial and non-financial performance, and explain why management control systems should consider both.

5. Prepare segment income statements using the contribution margin approach for evaluating profit and investment centres.

6. Measure performance against quality, cycle time, and productivity objectives.

7. Describe the difficulties of management control in service and not-for-profit organizations.

8. Explain how management control systems must evolve with changing times.

In the previous chapters we have considered many important tools of management accounting, such as activity-based costing, relevant costing, budgeting, and variance analysis. Each of these tools is useful by itself. However, the tools are most useful when they are part of an integrated *system*. An integrated system is an orderly, logical plan to coordinate and evaluate all the activities of the organization, from the long-range planning of the chief executive officer, to the individual responses to customer or client inquiries, to the maintenance of physical assets. Managers of most organizations today realize that long-run success depends on efficiency and quality. This chapter considers how management accounting tools combined into a management control system focus resources and talents of the individuals in the organization on such goals as efficiency and quality. As you will see, no single system is inherently superior to another. The "best" system is the one that consistently leads to decisions that meet the organization's goals and objectives.

MANAGEMENT CONTROL SYSTEMS

OBJECTIVE 1

Understand a management control system and how it relates to organizational goals.

Management Control System. A logical integration of management accounting tools to gather and report data and to evaluate performance.

A **management control system** is a logical integration of management accounting tools to gather and report data and to evaluate performance. The purposes of a management control system are to

- Clearly communicate the organization's goals
- Ensure that all managers and employees understand the specific actions required of them to achieve organizational goals
- Communicate results of actions across the organization
- Ensure that the management control system adjusts to changes in the environment.

Exhibit 13-1 shows the components of a management control system. We will refer to Exhibit 13-1 often in this chapter as we consider the design and operation of management control systems.

Management Control Systems and Organizational Goals

The first and most important component in a management control system is the organization's goals. Why? Because the focus of the management control system is on internal management decision making and evaluation of performance consistent with the organization's goals. As shown in Exhibit 13-2, setting goals, objectives, and performance measures involves managers at all levels.

A well-designed management control system aids and coordinates the process of making decisions and motivates individuals throughout the organization to work toward the same goals. It also coordinates forecasting revenue- and cost-driver levels, budgeting, measuring, and evaluating performance.

Exhibit 13-2 shows that organization-wide (overall company) goals, performance measures, and targets are set by top management. Although these goals are not changed often, they are reviewed on a periodic basis, usually once a year. They are specific results that are desired in the future, and they spell out how an organization will form its comprehensive plan for positioning itself in the market. As shown in Exhibit 13-1, goals answer the question, "What do we want to achieve?"

EXHIBIT 13-1

The Management
Control System

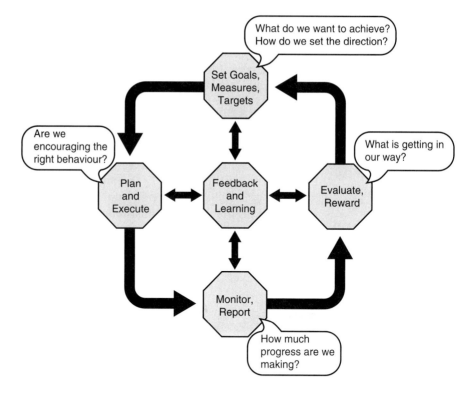

EXHIBIT 13-2

Setting Goals,
Objectives, and
Performance Measures

However, goals without performance measures do not motivate managers.

The purpose of performance measures is to motivate managers to achieve organizational goals. In other words, they give managers a more specific idea of how to achieve a better goal. For example, the goals and related performance measures of Luxury Suites, a major luxury hotel chain, are shown on the next page.

ORGANIZATIONAL GOALS	PERFORMANCE MEASURES
Exceed guest expectations	• Satisfaction index • # of repeat stays
Maximize revenue yield	• Occupancy rate • Room rate • Income before fixed costs
Focus on Innovation	• New products/services implemented per year • # of employee suggestions

Targets for goals are specific quantified levels of the measures. For example, a target for the performance measure *occupancy rate* might be "at least 70 percent."

As you can see, goals and performance measures are very broad. In fact, they are often too vague to guide managers and employees. As a result, top managers also identify critical processes and critical (key) success factors. A **critical process** is a series of related activities that directly impacts the achievement of organizational goals. For example, the organizational goal "exceed guest expectations" would have "produce and deliver services" as a critical process. The next step in goal setting is for both top managers and the managers of the critical processes to develop subgoals or critical success factors and related performance measures. **Critical success factors** are activities that must be managed well in order to drive the organization toward its goals. An example of a critical success factor for the *produce and deliver services* process is *timeliness*. Performance measures for timeliness would include *check-in time*, *check-out time*, and *response time to guest requests (number of rings before pickup)*.

Critical Process. A series of related activities that directly impacts on the achievement of organizational goals.

Critical Success Factors. Activities that must be managed well in order for an organization to meet its goals.

Although critical success factors and related performance measures give managers more focus than do overall, organization-wide goals, they still do not give lower-level managers and employees the direction they need to guide their daily actions. As shown in Exhibit 13-2, to set this direction, critical-process managers work with lower-level managers within the appropriate business unit to establish performance measures—specific tangible actions (or activities) that can be observed on a short-term basis. An example of a specific action related to timeliness for Luxury Suites is tracking travel details of arriving and departing guests.

Balancing the various objectives is a critical part of management control. Sometimes the management control system ignores critical success factors or inadvertently emphasizes the wrong factors. Managers often face tradeoff decisions. For example, a sales manager can increase the "employee satisfaction" derived from an employee survey by setting lower standards for responding to customer inquires. Although this action may improve the employee satisfaction measure of the manager, it may result in dissatisfied customers.

DESIGN, PLAN, AND EXECUTE MANAGEMENT CONTROL SYSTEMS

As shown in Exhibit 13-1, developing plans and then executing them is the second major function of a management control system. To create a management control system that meets the organization's needs, designers need to recognize existing constraints, identify responsibility centres, weigh costs and benefits, provide motivations to achieve goal congruence, and install internal controls.

Organizational Structure

Every management control system needs to fit the organization's goals. Though it is theoretically possible to persuade top management to change these goals, such alterations by designers of management control systems are very rare. One of the primary purposes of planning (budgeting) is to encourage managers throughout the organization to act in congruence with overall goals. As a result, specifying how the organization will be structured is an important part of the planning process and the control system. Some firms are organized primarily by *functions* such as production, finance, marketing, and human resources. Others are organized by *divisions* bearing profit responsibility along product or geographic lines. Still others may be organized by some hybrid arrangement, such as a matrix structure. Exhibit 13-3 depicts an example of functional, divisional, and matrix structures.

Most of the time, changes in control systems are piecemeal improvements rather than complete replacements. Occasionally, however, the management control system designer is able to persuade top management to change the orga-

EXHIBIT 13-3

Alternative Organizational Structures

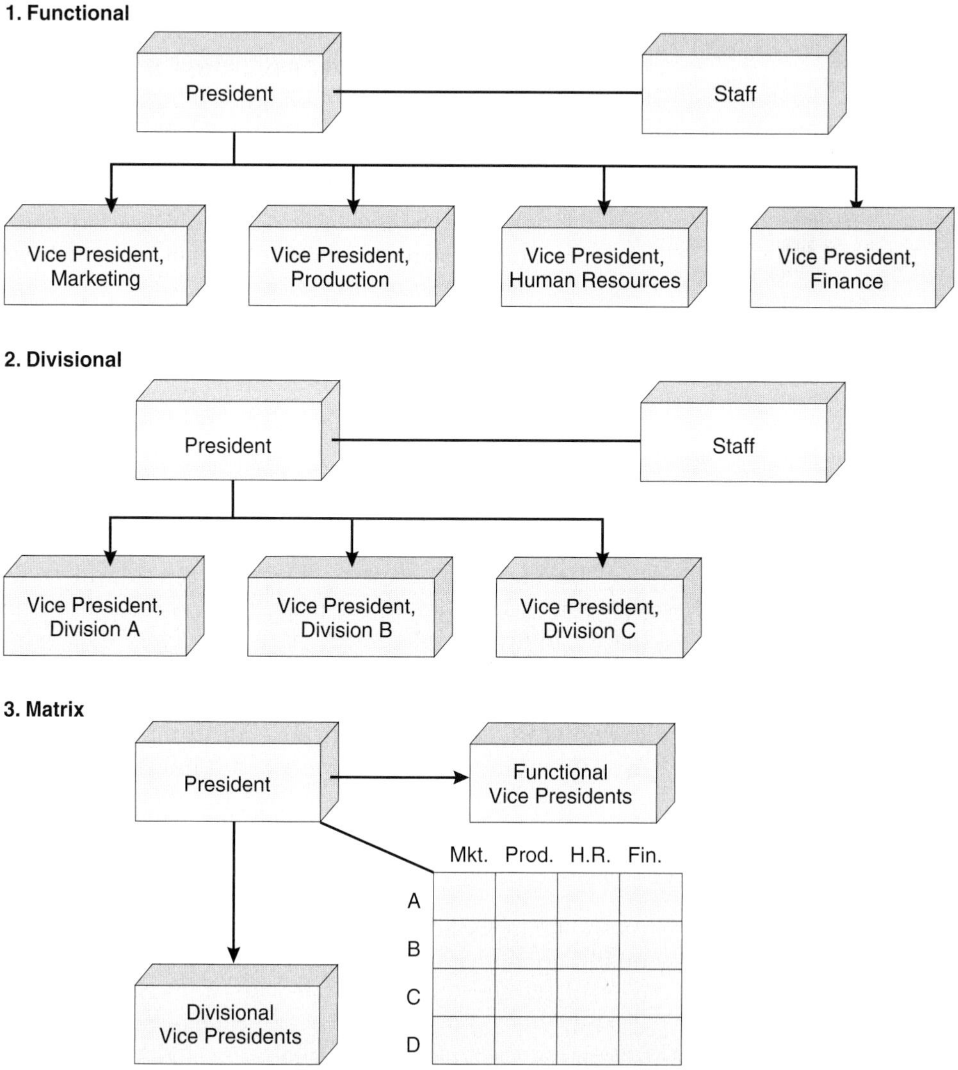

1. Functional

2. Divisional

3. Matrix

nizational structure before redesigning the system. Large companies may use an autonomous division to experiment with changes in organizational structure and/or management control systems before implementing wholesale changes throughout the organization.

Crayola
www.crayola.com
Binney & Smith
www.binney-smith.com

Binney & Smith (Canada), a manufacturer of Crayola crayons, seized the U.S. parent's interest in a leaner corporate and work team structure. The Lindsay, Ontario, plant was reorganized into ten teams, with only one layer of management—the team leaders—between the operations director and the factory workers.

By moving managers and workers closer together, and by letting each team take responsibility for the entire manufacturing process, from scheduling to customer service, substantial improvements were realized. In one year, costs were reduced 9 percent, inventory levels were reduced 75 percent, and profits were up 140 percent. As a result of these increases in efficiency and profitability, Binney & Smith International shifted production to the plant so that production doubled and a third shift became necessary.[1]

Responsibility Centres

In addition to organizational structures, designers of management control systems must consider the desired *responsibility centres* in an organization. A **responsibility centre** is defined as a set of activities assigned to a manager, a group of managers, or a group of employees in order to create "ownership of management" decisions. A set of customers, for example, may be a responsibility centre for a marketing supervisor; the full marketing department may be a responsibility centre for the department head; and the entire organization may be a responsibility centre for the president. In some organizations, management responsibility is shared by groups of employees in order to create wide "ownership" of management decisions, allow creative decision making, and prevent one person's concern (or lack of concern) for the risk of failure to dominate decisions.

Responsibility Centre. A set of activities assigned to a manager, a group of managers, or a group of employees in order to create "ownership of management" decisions.

Responsibility Accounting. Identifying what parts of the organization have primary responsibility for each objective, developing measures of achievement of the objectives, and creating reports of these measures by organization subunit or responsibility centre.

An effective management control system gives each lower-level manager responsibility for a group of activities and objectives and then reports on (1) the results of the activities, (2) the manager's influence on those results, and (3) effects of uncontrollable events. Such a system has innate appeal for most top managers because it helps them delegate decision making and gives them the freedom to plan and control. Lower-level managers appreciate the autonomy of the decision making they inherit. Thus, system designers apply **responsibility accounting** to identify what parts of the organization have primary responsibility for each objective, develop measures and targets to achieve objectives, and design reports of these measures by organization subunit or responsibility centre. Responsibility centres usually have multiple objectives that the management control system monitors. Responsibility centres are usually classified according to their *financial* responsibility, as cost centres, expense centres, revenue centres, profit centres, or investment centres.

Cost Centres

Cost Centre. A responsibility centre for which the objective is to manage (minimize) costs efficiently.

A **cost centre** is a responsibility centre in which a manager is accountable only for costs. Its financial responsibilities are to control and report costs only. An entire department may be considered a single cost centre, or a department may contain

---

[1] "Crayon Plant a Brighter Place," *The Globe and Mail*, June 18, 1992.

several cost centres. For example, although a university's registration department may be supervised by one manager, it may contain several activities (new incoming students, returning students, and full-time, part-time, and continuing education students) and management may regard each activity as a separate cost centre. Likewise, within an activity, separate faculties, projects, or equipment may be regarded as separate cost centres. The determination of the number of cost centres depends on cost-benefit considerations—do the benefits of smaller cost centres (for planning, control, and evaluation) exceed the higher costs of reporting?

Expense Centres

Expense Centre. A responsibility centre for which the objective is to spend the budget but maximize the specific service objective of the centre.

An **expense centre**, sometimes referred to as a *discretionary cost centre*, must attain its objectives and spend its budget. For example, a training and development department may have a budget of $250,000 and have as its objective to maximize the value of the training and development that can be attained for an expenditure of $250,000.

Revenue Centres

Revenue Centre. A responsibility centre for which the objective is to maximize the revenues generated.

A **revenue centre** has a responsibility to maximize the total revenues. While frequently constrained by an expense budget, the revenue centre focuses on maximizing factors such as volume, price, and market share to maximize the revenues.

Profit Centres

Profit Centre. A responsibility centre for which the objective is to control revenues as well as costs (or expenses).

A **profit centre** is responsible for controlling costs (or expenses) as well as revenues—that is, profitability. Despite the name, a profit centre can exist in not-for-profit organizations (though it may not be referred to as such) when a responsibility centre receives revenues for its services. All profit centre managers are responsible for both revenues and costs, but they may not be expected to maximize profits.

Investment Centres

Investment Centre. A responsibility centre for which the objective is to measure not only the income it generates, but also to relate that income to its invested capital, as in a ratio of income to the value of the capital employed.

An **investment centre** goes a step further than a profit centre. Its success is measured not only by the income it generates, but also by relating that income to its invested capital—as in a ratio of income to the value of the capital employed. In practice, the term investment centre is not widely used. Instead, the term profit centre is used indiscriminately to describe centres that are always assigned responsibility for revenues and expenses, but may or may not be assigned responsibility for the capital investment.

Exhibit 13-4 provides a summary of the objective of each of the five types of responsibility centres.

Weighing Costs and Benefits

The designer of the management control system must also weigh the costs and benefits of various alternatives, given the organization's needs. No system is perfect, but one system may be better than another if it can improve operating decisions at a reasonable cost.

EXHIBIT 13-4

Responsibility Centres

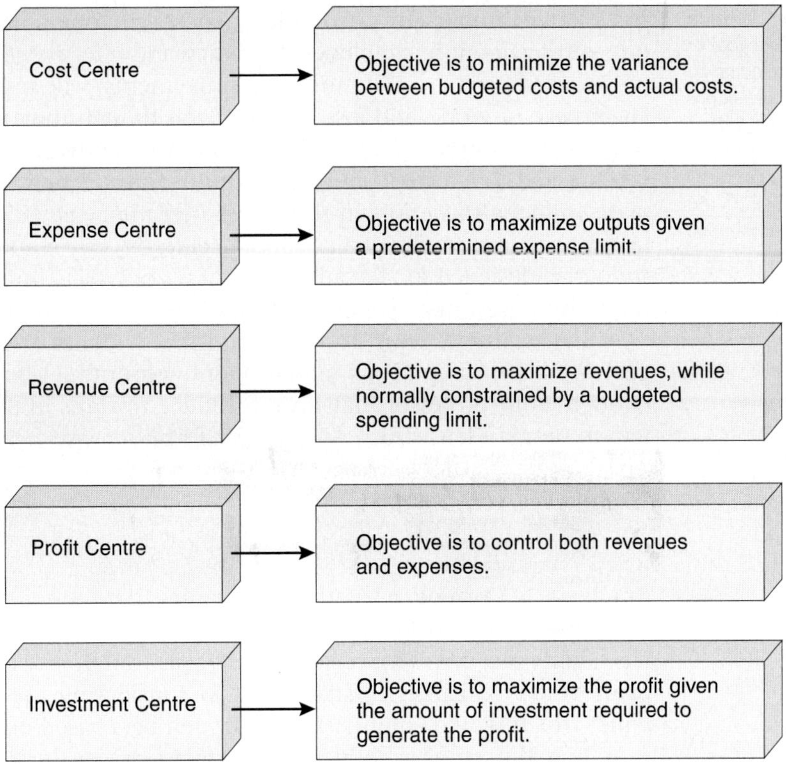
Cost Centre
Objective is to minimize the variance between budgeted costs and actual costs.
Expense Centre
Objective is to maximize outputs given a predetermined expense limit.
Revenue Centre
Objective is to maximize revenues, while normally constrained by a budgeted spending limit.
Profit Centre
Objective is to control both revenues and expenses.
Investment Centre
Objective is to maximize the profit given the amount of investment required to generate the profit.

Both benefits and costs of management control systems are often difficult to measure, and may become apparent only after experimentation or use. For example, the director of accounting policy of Citicorp has stated that, after several years of experience with a very detailed management control system, the system has proved to be too costly to administer relative to the perceived benefits. Accordingly, Citicorp plans to return to a simpler, less costly—and less precise—management control system.

MOTIVATING EMPLOYEES TO EXCEL AND ACHIEVE GOAL CONGRUENCE

OBJECTIVE 3

Explain how corporate performance is affected by employee motivation and goal congruence.

Goal Congruence. Exists when individuals and groups aim for the same organizational goals.

To achieve maximum benefits at minimum cost, a management control system must foster *goal congruence* and *managerial effort.* **Goal congruence** exists when individuals and groups aim for the same organizational goals. Goal congruence is achieved when employees, working in their own perceived best interests, make decisions that meet the overall goals of the organization. **Managerial effort** is defined as exertion toward a goal or objective. Effort here means not merely working faster, but also working *better*. Effort includes all conscious actions (such as supervising, planning, thinking) that result in more efficiency and effectiveness. Effort is a matter of degree—it is optimized when individuals and groups *strive* for their objectives.

Goal congruence can exist with little accompanying managerial effort, and vice versa, but *incentives* are necessary for both to be achieved. The challenge of a management-control-system design is to specify objectives and rewards that induce (or at least do not discourage) employee decisions that will achieve organizational

Corning
www.corning.com

Allen-Bradley Co.
www.ab.com

goals. For example, an organization may specify one of its subgoals to be continuous improvement in employee efficiency and effectiveness. Employees, however, might perceive that continuous improvements will result in tighter standards, faster pace of work, and loss of jobs. Even though they may agree with management that continuous improvements are competitively necessary, they should not be expected to exert effort for continuous improvements unless incentives are in place to make this effort in their own best interests. One may be pleasantly surprised that some individuals will act selflessly, but management control systems should be designed to take advantage of more typical human behaviour. Be aware that self-interest may be perceived differently in different cultures.

For example, your professor and the students of this class share the same goal—to learn more about management accounting—but goal congruence is not enough. Your professor may also introduce rewards in the form of a grading system to spur student effort. Grading is a form of *performance evaluation*, as is the use of management control reports for employee raises, promotions, and other employment rewards. Performance evaluation is a widely used means of improving goal congruence and effort because most individuals tend to perform better when they receive feedback that is tied to their own self-interest. Thus Allen-Bradley Co., Corning, and other companies that set quality improvements as critical subgoals put quality objectives into the bonus plans of top managers. Corning has quality incentives for factory workers as well. In the Binney & Smith (Canada) plant described earlier, management is considering the "pay-of-knowledge system," which would compensate team members based on their skills.

In addition to incentives and performance evaluation, goal congruence can only be attained if the management control system is fair. *Fairness* is achieved if the employees understand how the incentives and performance evaluation are measured and used. Employees must also understand how they may make decisions and change their behaviour to influence the performance evaluation and ultimately the incentives.

Continuing with the example of university students, if a professor desires to achieve a better learning experience in a course through class participation, a participation grade would likely be included in the grading system. However, to effectively achieve the goal of increased classroom participation and discussion, the professor should clearly explain how participation will be graded and provide some indication of the grade that could be expected with certain levels of participation.

To achieve goal congruence and managerial effort, designers of management control systems focus on motivating employees. **Employee motivation** has been defined as the drive to achieve some selected organizational goal that generates action toward that goal. Yet employees differ widely in their motivations. The system designer's task is more complex, ill-structured, and more affected by human behaviour than many people believe at first. The system designer must align individuals' self-interest with the goals of the organization. Thus the designer must focus on the different motivational impact—how each system will cause people to respond—of one management control system versus another.

To see how failure to anticipate motivational impact can cause problems, consider the following example. Some years ago in Russia, managers of the Moscow Cable Company decided to reduce copper wastage and put a new program in place. The new program worked and copper waste was slashed by 60 percent. As a result they had only $40,000 worth of scrap instead of the $100,000 originally budgeted. Top management then fined the plant $45,000 for not meeting its scrap revenue budget. What do you think this did to the cable company managers' motivation to control waste?

Responsibility accounting, budgets, variances, and the entire inventory of management control tools should constructively influence behaviour. However, they may be misused as weapons to punish, place blame, or find fault. They pose a threat to managers, who will resist and undermine the use of such techniques. Viewed positively, they assist managers to improve decisions.

Designing Internal Controls

Internal Control System.
Methods and procedures to prevent errors and irregularities, detect errors and irregularities, and promote operating efficiency.

It is common in Canadian companies to ensure that an *internal control system* is in place. Both managers and accountants are responsible for developing, maintaining, and evaluating internal control systems. An **internal control system** consists of methods and procedures to

1. Prevent errors and irregularities by a system of authorization for transactions, accurate recording of transactions, and safeguarding of assets;
2. Detect errors and irregularities by reconciling accounting records with independently kept records and physical counts and reviewing accounts for possible reductions of values; and
3. Promote operating efficiency by examining policies and procedures for possible improvements.

A management control system encompasses *administrative controls* (such as budgets for planning, controlling, and evaluating operations) and *accounting controls* (such as the common internal control procedure of separating the duties of the person who counts cash from the duties of the person who has access to the accounts receivable records). This text concentrates on the administrative control aspects of the management control system.

Develop Financial and Non-Financial Measures of Performance

OBJECTIVE 4

Compare financial and non-financial performance, and explain why management control systems should consider both.

Since most responsibility centres have multiple objectives, only some of these objectives are expressed in financial terms, such as operations budgets, profit targets, or required return on investment, depending on the financial classification of the centre. Other objectives, which are to be achieved concurrently, are non-financial in nature. For example, some companies list environmental stewardship and social responsibility as key objectives. The well-designed management control system functions alike for both financial and non-financial objectives to develop and report measures of performance. Good performance measures will

1. Relate to the goals of the organization
2. Balance long-term and short-term concerns
3. Reflect the management of key decisions and activities
4. Be affected by actions of managers and employees
5. Be readily understood by managers and employees
6. Be used in evaluating and rewarding employees
7. Be reasonably objective and easily measured
8. Be used consistently and regularly

Both financial and non-financial performance measures are important. Sometimes accountants and managers focus too much on financial measures such as profit or cost variances because they are readily available from the accounting system. However, managers can improve operational control by also considering non-financial measures of performance. Such measures may be more timely and more closely affected by employees at lower levels of the organization where the product is made or the service is rendered.

Non-financial measures are often easier to quantify then some people believe. Non-financial performance measures may be a great motivator of employee performance. For example, AT&T Universal Card Services, which was awarded the prestigious Baldrige National Quality Award (presented by the U.S. Department of Commerce), uses 18 performance measures for its customer enquiries process. Examples include average speed of answer, abandon rate, and application processing time (three days compared to the industry average of 24 days).

Often the effects of poor non-financial performance (quality, productivity, and customer satisfaction) do not show up in the financial measures until considerable ground has been lost. Financial measures are lagging indicators that may arrive too late to help prevent problems and issues that affect the organization's wealth. What is needed are leading indicators. As a result, many companies now stress management of the *activities* that drive revenues and costs rather than waiting to explain the revenues or costs themselves after the activities have taken place. Superior financial performance usually follows from superior non-financial performance.

Baldrige National
Quality Award
**www.software.org/
quagmire/descriptions/
baldrige.asp**

CONTROLLABILITY CRITERION OF MEASURING FINANCIAL PERFORMANCE

Management control systems often distinguish between controllable and uncontrollable events and between controllable and uncontrollable costs. Usually, responsibility centre managers are in the best position to explain their centre's results even if the managers had little influence over them. For example, an importer of grapes from Chile to the United States suffered a sudden loss of sales several years ago after a few grapes were found to contain cyanide. The tampering of the grapes was beyond the importer's control, and the importer's management control system compared actual profits to flexible-budgeted profits that should have been achieved for the actual sales. This comparison separated the uncontrollable effects of sales volume drop due to the grape tampering from effects of efficiency.

Uncontrollable Cost. Any cost that cannot be affected by the management of a responsibility centre within a given time span.

An **uncontrollable cost** is any cost that cannot be affected by the management of a responsibility centre within a given time span. For example, a mail-order supervisor may only be responsible for costs of labour, shipping costs, ordering errors and adjustments, and customer satisfaction. The supervisor is not responsible for costs of the supporting information system since the supervisor cannot control that cost.

Controllable Costs. Any costs that are influenced by a manager's decisions and actions.

Controllable costs should include all costs that are *influenced* by a manager's decisions and actions. For example, the costs of the mail-order information system, though uncontrollable by the mail-order supervisor, are controllable by the manager in charge of information systems.

In a sense, the term "controllable" is a misnomer because no cost is completely under the control of a manager. But the term is widely used to refer to any cost that is affected by a manager's decisions. Thus, the cost of operating the mail-order information system may be affected by equipment or software failures that are not completely—but are partially—under the control of the information systems manager, who would be held responsible for all of the costs of the information system, even the costs of downtime.

The distinction between controllable and uncontrollable costs serves an information purpose. Costs that are completely uncontrollable tell nothing about a manager's decisions and actions because, by definition, nothing the manager does will affect the costs. Such costs should be ignored in evaluating the responsibility centre manager's performance. In contrast, reporting controllable costs provides evidence about a manager's performance.

Because responsibility for costs may be widespread, systems designers must depend on understanding cost behaviour to help identify controllable costs. This understanding is increasingly gained through activity-based costing. Both Procter & Gamble and Upjohn, Inc., for example, are experimenting with activity-based costing systems in some divisions. Procter & Gamble credits its experimental activity-based management control system for identifying controllable costs in one of its detergent divisions, which led to major strategic changes.

Procter & Gamble
www.pg.com

Upjohn, Inc.
www.upjohn.com

Using Contribution Margin for Measuring Financial Performance

OBJECTIVE 5

Prepare segment income statements using the contribution margin approach for evaluating profit and investment centres.

Many organizations combine the contribution approach to measuring income with responsibility accounting—that is, they report by cost behaviour as well as by degrees of controllability.

Exhibit 13-5 displays the contribution approach to measuring the financial performance of a retail food company. Study this exhibit carefully. It provides perspective on how a management control system can be designed to stress cost behaviour, controllability, manager performance, and responsibility centre performance simultaneously.

Line (a) in Exhibit 13-5 shows the contribution margin, sales revenue less all variable expenses. The contribution margin is especially helpful for predicting the effect on income of short-run changes in activity volume. Managers may quickly calculate any expected changes in income by multiplying increases in dollar sales by the contribution-margin ratio (see Chapter 2). The contribution-margin ratio for meats in Branch B is 0.20. Thus, a $900 increase in sales of meats in Branch B should produce a $180 increase in income ($0.20 \times \$900 = \$180$) if there are no changes in selling prices, operating expenses, or mix of sales between Stores 1 and 2.

Lines (b) and (c) in Exhibit 13-5 separate the contribution that is controllable by segment managers (b) and the overall segment contribution (c). The manager of Store 1 may have influence over some local advertising, but not other advertising, some fixed salaries but not other salaries, and so forth. Moreover, the meat manager at both the branch and store levels may have no influence over store amortization or the president's salary. Therefore, Exhibit 13-5 separates costs by controllability. Managers on all levels are asked to explain the total segment contribution but are held responsible only for the controllable contribution.

Note that fixed costs controllable by the segment managers are deducted from the contribution margin to obtain the *contribution* controllable by segment managers. These controllable costs are usually discretionary fixed costs such as local advertising and some salaries, but not the manager's own salary. Other, noncontrollable, fixed costs (shown between lines [a] and [b]) are not allocated in the breakdown because they are not considered controllable this far down in the organization. That

EXHIBIT 13-5

The Contribution Approach: Model Income Statement, by Segments*
(in thousands of dollars)

	RETAIL FOOD COMPANY AS A WHOLE	COMPANY BREAKDOWN INTO TWO DIVISIONS		POSSIBLE BREAKDOWN OF BRANCH B ONLY				POSSIBLE BREAKDOWN OF BRANCH B, MEATS ONLY		
		BRANCH A	BRANCH B	NOT ALLOCATED†	GROCERIES	PRODUCE	MEATS	NOT ALLOCATED†	STORE 1	STORE 2
Net sales	$4,000	$1,500	$2,500	—	$1,300	$300	$900	—	$600	$300
Variable costs:										
Cost of merchandise sold	$3,000	$1,100	$1,900	—	$1,000	$230	$670	—	$450	$220
Variable operating expenses	260	100	160	—	100	10	50	—	35	15
Total variable costs	$3,260	$1,200	$2,060	—	$1,100	$240	$720	—	$485	$235
(a) Contribution margin	$ 740	$ 300	$ 440	—	$ 200	$ 60	$180	—	$115	$ 65
Less: fixed costs controllable by segment managers‡	260	100	160	$ 20	40	10	90	$ 30	35	25
(b) Contribution controllable by segment managers	$ 480	$ 200	$ 280	$(20)	$ 160	$ 50	$ 90	$(30)	$ 80	$ 40
Less: fixed costs controllable by others§	200	90	110	20	40	10	40	10	22	8
(c) Contribution by segments	$ 280	$ 110	$ 170	$(40)	$ 120	$ 40	$ 50	$(40)	$ 58	$ 32
Less: unallocated costs¶	100									
(d) Income before income taxes	$ 180									

* Three different types of segments are illustrated here: branches, product lines, and stores. As you read across, note that the focus becomes narrower: from Branch A and B, to Branch B only, to meats in Branch B only.

† Only those costs clearly indentifiable to a product line cr store should be allocated.

‡ Examples are certain advertising, sales promotion, salespersons' salaries, management consulting, training, and supervision costs.

§ Examples are amortization, property taxes, insurance, and perhaps the segment manager's salary.

¶ These costs are not clearly or practically allocable to any segment except by some highly questionable allocation base.

is, of the $160,000 fixed cost that is controllable by the manager of Branch B, $140,000 is also controllable by subordinates (grocery, produce, and meat managers), but $20,000 is not. The latter are controllable by the Branch B manager, but not by lower managers. Similarly, the $30,000 in that same line are costs that are attributable to the meat department of Branch B, but not to individual stores.

In many organizations, managers have latitude to trade off some variable costs for fixed costs. To save variable material and labour costs, managers might make heavier outlays for automation, quality management and employee training programs, and so on. Moreover, decisions on advertising, research, and sales promotion affect sales activity and hence contribution margins. The controllable contribution includes these expenses and attempts to capture the results of these tradeoffs.

In Exhibit 13-5, the distinctions made about which items belong in what cost classification are inevitably not clear-cut. For example, determining controllability is always a problem when service department costs are allocated to other departments. Should the store manager bear a part of the division headquarters costs? If so, how much and on what basis? How much, if any, store amortization or lease rentals should be deducted in computing the controllable contribution? There are no easy answers to these questions. Each organization chooses ways that benefit it most with the lowest relative cost.

The *contribution by segments*, line (c) in Exhibit 13-5, is an attempt to approximate the financial performance of the *segment*, as distinguished from the financial performance of its *manager*, which is measured in line (b). The "fixed costs controllable by others" typically include committed costs (such as amortization and property taxes) and discretionary costs (such as the segment manager's

MAKING MANAGERIAL DECISIONS

Managers should try to distinguish between controllable and uncontrollable events and costs when designing segment financial reports. For each of the following costs of a merchandising business (for example, a department store), indicate whether it is a variable cost, fixed cost controllable by segment managers, fixed cost controllable by someone other than the segment manager, or a cost that a company normally does not allocate.

Property taxes
Supervision of sales force
Amortization of store
Cost of goods sold
Local store advertising
Corporate-level advertising
Corporate-level public relations
Temporary sales labour

ANSWER

In this example, the segment could be viewed as an individual store. Variable costs are generally controllable by the store manager. Costs of goods sold and

temporary sales labour are examples. Even though the store manager may not control the actual cost of store inventory (due to centralized purchasing, as an example), she would generally have decision-making authority affecting inventory turnover, such as price discounting and stock reordering authorities. If so, the store manager may be held accountable for cost of goods sold.

Fixed costs controllable by the segment (store) manager include local store advertising and supervision of the local salesforce. The store manager usually decides the appropriate level for these costs. Even though local store advertising will differ from period to period, it is generally considered to have no direct relationship to sales, and therefore is not viewed as a variable cost.

Fixed costs controllable by those other than the store manager include property taxes and amortization of the store. These costs relate directly to the store, but the store manager cannot change them. Unallocated costs include corporate-level advertising and public relations. These costs have a tenuous link to the store.

salary). These costs are attributable to the segment but primarily are controllable only at higher levels of management.

Exhibit 13-5 shows "unallocated costs" immediately before line (d). These might include central corporate costs such as the costs of top management and some corporate-level services (e.g., legal and taxation). When a persuasive cause-and-effect, or activity-based justification for assigning such costs cannot be found, many organizations favour not allocating them to segments.

The contribution approach highlights the relative objectivity of various means of measuring financial performance. The contribution margin itself tends to be the most objective. As you read downward in the report, the assignments become more subjective, and the resulting measures of contributions or income become more subject to dispute. Though such disputes may not be a productive use of management time, the analysis directs managers' attention to the costs of the entire organization and lead to organizational cost control. These issues are covered in more detail in Chapter 15.

NON-FINANCIAL MEASURES OF PERFORMANCE

OBJECTIVE 6

Measure performance against quality, cycle time, and productivity objectives.

International Paper
www.internationalpaper.
com

For many years, organizations have monitored their non-financial performance. For example, sales organizations have followed up on customers to assure their satisfaction. Manufacturers have tracked manufacturing defects and product performance. Government health organizations have kept meticulous statistics on disease incidence and reduction, which indicates the effectiveness of disease control efforts such as education, sanitation, and inoculation. In recent years, most organizations have developed a new awareness of the importance of controlling such non-financial performance as quality, cycle time, and productivity.

For example, Champion International Corporation's mill in Hamilton, Ohio (which was acquired by International Paper in 2001), which produces for the premium paper market, changed its organizational structure when it implemented flexible manufacturing and just-in-time production. Newly adopted goals such as reduced cycle time and first-pass yield (the percentage of product

MAKING MANAGERIAL DECISIONS

When top managers set organizational goals, they should attempt to provide a balance between financial and non-financial goals. Using the components of a successful organization shown in Exhibit 13-1, indicate the component associated with the following goals of Whirlpool:

    People commitment
    Total quality
    Customer satisfaction
    Financial performance
    Growth and innovation

ANSWER
The components listed in Exhibit 13-1 form a causal link from organizational learning to business process

improvement, to customer satisfaction, and finally to financial strength. Using the five goals set by top managers at Whirlpool, we can make the following cause-effect statement:

If Whirlpool makes a solid commitment to its people, then growth and innovation will occur as part of the company's organizational learning. This will lead to business process improvements that increase the total quality of its products, which will then lead to increased customer satisfaction. The ultimate result of satisfied customers is improved financial performance. Sustainable financial strength should result in reinvestment in both Whirlpool's people and its internal processes.

flowing directly without rework to its intended destination) resulted in new demands on the accounting function. Accountants now include non-financial performance measures along with financial results and work with production management as "business partners."

It is not coincidental that all types of organizations are concerned about quality, cycle time, and productivity. They are key subgoals that lead to long-term profitability for companies and are increasingly important in not-for-profit and government organizations, where tighter appropriations and increasing demands for services are facts of life.

Quality Control

Quality Control. The effort to ensure that products and services perform to customer requirements.

Quality control is the effort to ensure that products and services perform to customer requirements. Organizations around the globe have adopted formal quality management programs. It has also become apparent that increasing quality can be achieved by reducing the cycle time of delivering a product or service. Improvements in quality (from inception of the product to delivery and after-sales service) lead to reduced cycle time and increased productivity.

In essence, customers or clients define quality by comparing their needs and expectations to the attributes of the product or service. For example, buyers judge the quality of an automobile based on reliability, performance, styling, safety, and image relative to their needs, budget, and the alternatives. Defining quality in terms of customer requirements is only half the battle, though. There remains the problem of reaching and maintaining the desired level of quality. There are many approaches to controlling quality. The traditional approach was to inspect products after they were completed and reject or rework those that failed the inspections. Because testing is expensive, often only a sample of products were inspected. The process was judged to be in control as long as the number of defective products did not exceed an *acceptable quality level.* This meant that some defective products could still make their way to customers.

In recent years, however, North American companies have learned that this is a very costly way to control quality. All the resources consumed to make a defective product and to detect it are wasted. Also the often considerable rework necessary to correct the defects add to the waste. In addition it is very costly to repair products in use by a customer or to win back a dissatisfied customer. IBM's CEO John Akers was quoted in *The Wall Street Journal* as saying, "I am sick and tired of visiting plants to hear nothing but great things about quality and cycle time—and then to visit customers who tell me of problems." The high costs of

Quality Cost Report. A report that displays the financial impact of quality.

achieving quality by "inspecting it in" are evident in a **quality cost report**, which displays the financial impact of quality. The quality cost report shown in Exhibit 13-6 measures four categories of quality costs:

1. Prevention—costs incurred to prevent the production of defective products or delivery of substandard services, including engineering analyses to improve product design for better manufacturing, improvements in production processes, increased quality of material inputs, and programs to train personnel.
2. Appraisal—costs incurred to identify defective products or services, including inspection and testing.

EXHIBIT 13-6

Eastside Manufacturing Company Quality Cost Report* (thousands of dollars)

ACTUAL	PLAN	VARIANCE	QUALITY COST AREA	ACTUAL	PLAN	VARIANCE
			MONTH — left group / **QUALITY COST AREA** / **YEAR-TO-DATE**			
			1. Prevention Cost			
3	2	1	A. Quality—Administration	5	4	1
16	18	(2)	B. Quality—Engineering	37	38	(1)
7	6	1	C. Quality—Planning by Others	14	12	2
5	7	(2)	D. Supplier Assurance	13	14	(1)
31	33	(2)	Total Prevention Cost	69	68	1
5.5%	6.1%		% of Total Quality Cost	6.3%	6.3%	
			2. Appraisal Cost			
31	26	5	A. Inspection	55	52	3
12	14	(2)	B. Test	24	28	(4)
7	6	1	C. Insp. & Test of Purchased Mat.	15	12	3
11	11	0	D. Product Quality Audits	23	22	1
3	2	1	E. Maint of Insp. & Test Equip.	4	4	0
2	2	0	F. Mat. Consumed in Insp. & Test	5	4	1
66	61	5	Total Appraisal Cost	126	122	4
11.8%	11.3%		% of Total Quality Cost	11.4%	11.3%	
			3. Internal Failure Cost			
144	140	4	A. Scrap & Rework—Manuf.	295	280	15
55	53	2	B. Scrap & Rework—Engineering	103	106	(3)
28	30	(2)	C. Scrap & Rework—Supplier	55	60	(5)
21	22	(1)	D. Failure Investigation	44	44	0
248	245	3	Total Internal Failure Cost	497	490	7
44.3%	45.4%		% of Total Quality Cost	44.9%	45.3%	
345	339	6	Total Internal Quality Cost (1 + 2 + 3)	692	680	12
61.6%	62.8%		% of Total Quality Cost	62.6%	62.9%	
			4. External Failure Quality Cost			
75	66	9	A. Warranty Exp.—Manuf.	141	132	9
41	40	1	B. Warranty Exp—Engineering	84	80	4
35	35	0	C. Warranty Exp.—Sales	69	70	(1)
46	40	6	D. Field Warranty Cost	83	80	3
18	20	(2)	E. Failure Investigation	37	40	(3)
215	201	14	Total External Failure Cost	414	402	12
38.4%	37.2%		% of Total Quality Cost	37.4%	37.1%	
560	540	20	Total Quality Cost	1,106	1,082	24
9,872	9,800		Total Product Cost	20,170	19,600	
5.7%	5.5%		% Tol. Qual. Cost to Tot. Prod. Cost	5.5%	5.5%	

* Adapted from Allen H. Seed III, *Adapting Management Accounting Practice to an Advanced Manufacturing Environment* (National Association of Accountants, 1988), Table 5-2, p. 76. Institute of Management Accountants.

3. Internal failure—costs of defective components and final products or services that are scrapped or reworked; also costs of delays caused by defective products or services.

4. External failure—costs caused by delivery of defective products or services to customers, such as field repairs, returns, and warranty expenses.

Performance Measures in Practice

An organization's performance measures depend on its goals and objectives. For example, a software company and an auto manufacturer will have vastly different performance measures. The measures also must span a variety of key success factors for the organization. Performance measures too focused on one aspect of performance may foster neglect of other important factors.

Southwest Airlines
www.southwest.com

Let's look at a classic management control system, the one developed by General Electric in the 1950s. The system focused on eight "key result areas," as GE called them:

Financial Key Result Areas
- Profitability
- Productivity
- Market position

Nonfinancial Key Result Areas
- Product leadership
- Personnel development
- Employee attitudes
- Public responsibility
- Balance between short-run and long-range goals

Measures in each of these eight areas would be just as relevant today as in the 1950s. These are clearly long-run strategic goals. Measures might change as an organization adapts the means of achieving the goals, but the basic framework of a management control system need not change as management fads come and go.

A more recent example is Southwest Airlines, which has been in business for 35 years (as of 2006). The mission of Southwest Airlines is "dedication to the highest quality of customer service delivered with a sense of warmth, friendliness, individual pride, and company spirit." Yet, until recently, the company focused mainly on financial measures in evaluating managers. Recently, Southwest introduced non-financial measures into the mix, including:

- Load factor (percentage of seats occupied)
- Utilization factors on aircraft and personnel
- On-time performance
- Available seat miles
- Denied boarding rate
- Lost bag reports per 10,000 passengers
- Flight cancellation rate
- Employee head count
- Customer complaints per 10,000 passengers

By including non-financial measures, Southwest could focus managers' attention on the key success factors that related most closely to Southwest's mission and goals. Southwest's customer focus is illustrated by "The 1544 Club," found on its corporate Web site.

Sources: David Solomons, *Divisional Performance: Measurement and Control* (Homewood, IL: Irwin, 1965); Southwest Airlines Web site (www.southwest.com).

This report shows that the great majority of costs spent by Eastside Manufacturing Company are due to internal or external failures. But these costs are almost certainly understated. Poor quality can result in large opportunity costs due to internal delays and lost sales. For example, quality problems in North American–built automobiles in the 1970s and 1980s probably caused foregone sales to Japanese-made cars that were significantly more costly than the tangible costs measured in any quality cost report.

In recent years, more and more North American companies have been rethinking this approach to quality control. Instead, they have adopted an approach first espoused by an American named William Deming and embraced by Japanese companies decades ago: *total quality management*. Following the old adage, "an ounce of prevention is worth a pound of cure," it focuses on *prevention* of defects and on customer satisfaction. The total quality management approach is based on the assumption that the cost of quality is minimized when a company achieves high-quality levels. **Total quality management (TQM)** is the application of quality principles to *all* of the organization's endeavours to satisfy customers. TQM has significant implications for organization goals, structure, and management control systems. A complete discussion of TQM is beyond the scope of this text, but it includes delegating responsibility for many management functions to employees. For TQM to work, though, employees must be very well trained in the process, the product or service, and the use of quality control information.

Total Quality Management (TQM). The application of quality principles to all of the organization's endeavours to satisfy customers.

To implement TQM, employees are trained to prepare, interpret, and act on quality control charts, like that shown in Exhibit 13-7. The most common form of quality control information that is used by employees is the *quality control chart*. The **quality control chart** is a statistical plot of measures of various product dimensions or attributes. This plot helps detect process deviations before the process generates defects. These plots also identify excessive variation in product dimensions or attributes that should be addressed by process or design engineers. Exhibit 13-7 shows that the Eastside Manufacturing Company generally is not meeting its defects objective of 0.5 percent defects (which is a relatively high defect rate). A manager looking at this chart would know that corrective action must be taken.

Quality Control Chart. The statistical plot of measures of various product dimensions or attributes.

Control of Cycle Time

Cycle Time. The time taken to complete a product or service, or any of the components of a product or service.

One key to improving quality is to reduce *cycle time*. **Cycle time**, or throughput time, is the time taken to complete a product or service from initiation of the order by the customer to the receipt of the product or service. It is a summary measure of manufacturing or service efficiency and effectiveness, and an important cost driver. The longer a product or service is in process, the more costs are consumed. Low cycle time means quick completion of a product or service (without defects). Lowering cycle time requires smooth-running processes and high quality, and also creates increased flexibility and quicker reactions to customer needs. As cycle time is decreased, quality problems become apparent throughout the process and must be solved if quality is to be improved. Decreasing cycle time also results in bringing products or services more quickly to customers—a service that customers value.

EXHIBIT 13-7

Eastside Manufacturing Company Quality Control Chart

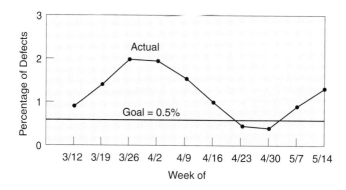

Firms measure cycle time for the important stages of a process and for the process as a whole. An effective means of measuring cycle time is to use *barcoding*, where a barcode (similar to symbols on most grocery products) is attached to each component or product and read at the end of each stage of completion. Cycle time is measured for each stage as the time between readings of barcodes. Barcoding also permits effective tracking of materials and products for inventories, scheduling, and delivery.

Exhibit 13-8 shows a sample cycle time report. (Cycle time can also be displayed on a control chart.) This report shows that Eastside Manufacturing Company is meeting its cycle time objectives at two of its five production process stages. This report is similar to the flexible budget reports of Chapter 12. Explanations of the variances indicate that poor-quality materials and poor design led to extensive rework and retesting.

Control of Productivity

Productivity. A measure of outputs divided by inputs.

Most companies in North America manage productivity as part of the effort to improve their competitiveness. **Productivity** is a measure of outputs divided by inputs. The fewer inputs needed to produce a given output, the more productive the organization. But this simple definition raises difficult measurement questions. How should outputs and inputs be measured? Specific management control problems usually determine the most appropriate measures of inputs and outputs. Labour-intensive (especially service) organizations are concerned with increasing the productivity of labour, so labour-based measures are appropriate. Highly automated companies are concerned with machine utilization and productivity of capital investments, so capacity-based measures, such as the percentage of time machines are available, may be most important to them. Manufacturing companies in general are concerned with the efficient use of materials, and so for them measures of material *yield* (a ratio of material outputs over material inputs) may be useful indicators of productivity. On the other hand, service industries that are labour intensive are more concerned with labour yield, how much is produced given labour input. In all cases of productivity ratios, a measure of the resource that management wishes to control is in the denominator (the input) and some measure of the objective of using the resource is in the numerator (the output).

EXHIBIT 13-8

Eastside Manufacturing Company Cycle Time Report for the Second Week of May

PROCESS STAGE	ACTUAL CYCLE TIME*	STANDARD CYCLE TIME	VARIANCE	EXPLANATION
Materials processing	2.1	2.5	0.4 F	
Circuit board	44.7	28.8	15.9 U	Poor quality materials caused rework
Power unit	59.6	36.2	23.4 U	Engineering change required rebuild of all power units
Assembly	14.6	14.7	0.1 F	
Functional and environmental test	53.3	32.0	21.3 U	Software failure in test procedures required retesting

* Average time per stage over the week.

Exhibit 13-9 shows ten possible productivity measures. As you can see, they vary widely according to the type of resource with which management is concerned.

EXHIBIT 13-9	**RESOURCE (DENOMINATOR)**	**POSSIBLE OUTPUTS (NUMERATOR)**		**POSSIBLE INPUTS**
Measures of Productivity	1. Labour	a.	Expected direct labour hours for good output	÷ Actual direct labour hours used
		b.	Sales revenue	÷ Number of employees
		c.	Bank deposit/loan activity (by a bank)	÷ Number of employees
		d.	Service calls	÷ Number of employees
		e.	Customer orders	÷ Number of employees
	2. Materials	a.	Weight of output	÷ Weight of input
		b.	Number of good units	÷ Total number of units
	3. Equipment, capital, physical capacity	a.	Time (e.g., hours) utilized	÷ Time available for use
		b.	Time available for use	÷ Time (e.g., 24 hours per day)
		c.	Expected machine hours for good output	÷ Actual machine hours

Choosing Productivity Measures

Which productivity measures should a company choose to manage? The choice depends on the behaviours desired. Managers generally concentrate on achieving the performance levels desired by their superiors. Thus, if top management evaluates subordinates' performance based on direct labour productivity, lower-level managers will focus on improving that specific measure.

The challenge in choosing productivity measures is that a manager may be able to improve a single measure but hurt performance elsewhere in the organization. For example, long production runs may improve machine productivity but result in excessive inventories. Or, improved labour productivity in the short run may be accompanied by a high rate of product defects.

Use of a single measure of productivity is unlikely to result in overall improvements in performance. The choice of management controls requires balancing expected tradeoffs that employees can be expected to make to improve their performance evaluations. Many organizations focus management control on more fundamental activities, such as control of quality and service, and use productivity measures to monitor the actual benefits of improvements in these activities.

It is necessary to consider the many dimensions of productivity. When assessing labour productivity, the Productivity Improvement Service of the federal department of Industry, Science, and Technology Canada uses a number of measures, such as those listed below, before making any decisions. They all add to the understanding of changes in labour productivity:

**Industry Canada (Strategis)
www.strategis.ic.gc.ca**

- Labour costs as a percentage of sales dollars
- Sales per employee
- Direct labour wage rate
- Total labour cost per hour
- Investment in machinery and equipment per production employee

Also be careful about comparing productivity measures over time. Changes in the process or in the rate of inflation can prove misleading. For example, consider labour productivity at ABC Corporation. One measure of productivity that can be tracked is *sales revenue per employee*:

	2006	2000	PERCENT CHANGE
Total revenue ($ millions) (a)	$ 49,489	$ 37,134	+33.3%
Number of employees (b)	204,530	182,610	+12.0%
Revenue per employee (a) ÷ (b) (unadjusted for inflation)	$241,965	$203,351	+18.9%

By this measure, ABC appears to have achieved an 18.9 percent increase in the productivity of labour. However, total revenue has not been adjusted for the effects of inflation. Because of inflation, say that each 2000 dollar is equivalent to 1.10 2006 dollars. Therefore, ABC's 2000 sales revenue, expressed in 2006 dollars (to be equivalent with 2006 sales revenue) is $37,134 × 1.10 = $40,847. The adjusted 2000 sales revenue per employee is as follows:

	2006	2000 (ADJUSTED)	PERCENT CHANGE
Total revenue ($ millions) (a)	$ 49,489	$ 40,847	+21.12%
Number of employees (b)	204,530	182,610	+12.0%
Revenue per employee (a) ÷ (b) (adjusted for inflation)	$241,965	$223,685	+8.17%

Adjusting for the effects of inflation reveals that ABC's labour productivity has increased only 8.17 percent, not 18.9 percent. This is a signal to management that corrective action may need to be taken to realize improvements—such as raise prices or reduce the number of employees.

Feedback and Learning

At the centre of Exhibit 13-1 there is feedback and learning because at all points in the planning and control process, it is vital that effective communications exist among all levels of management and employees. In fact, organization-wide learning is a foundation for gaining and maintaining financial strength. Rich Teerlink, former CEO of Harley Davidson said, "If you empower dummies, they make dumb decisions faster." Harley Davidson spends a large amount of money, $1,000 per year per employee, on training to facilitate learning.

It has also been said that the only sustainable competitive advantage is the rate at which a company's managers learn. However, even this powerful competitive edge can be overcome by competitors who develop or hire intellectual capital faster. Once a company has superior intellectual capital, how can it best maintain its leadership? Exhibit 13-10 shows how organizational learning leads to financial strength.

Organizational learning is monitored by measures such as training time, employee turnover, and staff satisfaction scores on employee surveys. The result of learning is continuous process improvement that is monitored by measures such as cycle time, number of defects (quality), and activity cost. Customers will

EXHIBIT 13-10

The Components of a
Successful Organization
and Measures of
Achievement

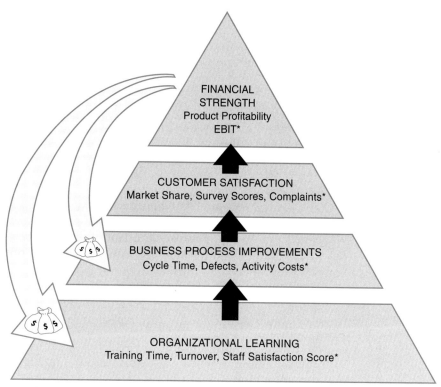

*Examples of performance measures used to monitor the achievement of the component.

value improved response (lower cycle time), higher quality, and lower prices, and thus increase their demand for products and services. Increased demand, combined with lower costs in making and delivering products and services, results in financial strength as monitored by such measures as product profitability and earnings before interest and taxes (EBIT).

It is important to note that the successful organization does not stop with one cycle of learning, process improvement, increased customer satisfaction, and improved financial strength. The benefits of improved financial strength, excess financial resources, must be reinvested within the organization by supporting both continuous learning and continuous process improvement. A key driver of enterprise performance is the culture within the company that fosters continual learning and growth at all levels of management. It is not enough to throw money at managers in order to train them if the resulting learning does not translate into improved processes, products, and services. It requires a culture of learning so that managers are motivated to translate learning into growth.

There are no guarantees that each of the components will "automatically" follow from success at the previous component. If there is no improvement in one or more core business processes, the cause-effect chain can be broken. For example, a lack of improvement in marketing and distribution techniques can lead to failure due to the inability to place the "new and improved" products or services at the location desired by the customer. E-commerce is a good example of this. The point is that improvement in business processes must take place across all parts of the value chain.

A good example of the application of an enterprise learning culture is the General Electric Company (GE). With sales of more than $100 billion, GE has demonstrated a remarkable ability to generate formidable profits in a wide range of industries, including broadcasting (NBC), transportation equipment, aircraft engines, appliances, lighting, electric distribution and control equipment, generators and turbines, nuclear reactors, medical imaging equipment, plastics, and financial services.

Former CEO John Welch claims GE's success is due to "a General Electric culture that values the contributions of every individual, thrives on learning, thirsts for the better idea, and has the flexibility and speed to put the better idea into action every day. We are a learning company, a company that studies its own successes and failures and those of others—a company that has the self-confidence and the resources to take big swings and pursue numerous opportunities based on winning ideas and insights, regardless of their source. That appetite for learning, and the ability to act quickly on that learning, will provide GE with what we believe is an insurmountable and sustainable competitive advantage."[2]

Exactly what does John Welch mean by the "ability to act quickly on that learning"? He refers to a management leadership philosophy that ignores organizational boundaries when implementing learning. According to Welch, "These new leaders are changing the very DNA of GE culture. Work-Out, in the 80s, opened our culture up to ideas from everyone, everywhere, killed NIH (Not Invented Here) thinking, decimated the bureaucracy, and made boundaryless behavior a reflexive and natural part of our culture, thereby creating the learning culture... ."[3]

Monitoring Progress

As shown in Exhibit 13-1, monitoring and reporting the results of business activities is a key component of a management control system. Managers identify actions and related performance measures that are linked to the achievement of goals and objectives. Once these performance measures and actions are identified, an organization must obtain information on the achievement of desired outcomes. This is done through the performance reporting system. Effective performance reports align results with managers' goals and objectives, provide guidance to managers, communicate goals and their level of attainment throughout the organization, and enable organizations to anticipate and respond to change in a timely manner.

Balanced Scorecard.
A performance measurement system that strikes a balance between financial and operating measures, links performance to rewards, and gives explicit recognition to the diversity of stakeholder interests.

There are several approaches to performance reporting. Each approach attempts to link organizational strategy to actions of managers and employees. One popular approach to performance reporting is the balanced scorecard. A **balanced scorecard** is a performance measurement and reporting system that strikes a balance between financial and operating measures, links performance to rewards, and gives explicit recognition to the diversity of organizational goals. Companies such as Champion International, Nova Chemical, Bank of Montreal, AT&T, Allstate, Apple Computer and many others use the balanced scorecard to

---

[2] *Source:* General Electric's 1998 Annual Report.
[3] The term Work-Out refers to a process at GE where groups of employees meet at regular intervals to think of ways to improve GE. Then leadership comes in and listens to their ideas.

Productivity Performance Is Key in Auto Industry

Productivity is an important component of profitability for auto manufacturers. In 2002, for the eighth year in a row, Nissan was rated by Harbour and Associates as the most productive auto assembly company in North America. The measure used was the number of hours per vehicle (HPV). Nissan averaged 17.92 hours to produce each vehicle. Two other foreign-owned manufacturers, Honda and Toyota, finished just behind Nissan. General Motors, Ford, and DaimlerChrysler were far behind at 26, 27, and 31 HPV, respectively.

Although Nissan's plant in Smyrna, Tennessee, continued to have high productivity, its performance declined by 3.2 percent in 2002. For the first time ever, a General Motors plant (Oshawa #1) took the top place among individual plants with a 16.79 HPV. In addition, GM surpassed Ford in average HPV for the first time in history. Finally, Mitsubishi's plant in Normal, Illinois, showed exceptional improvement—8.6 percent in 2002 and 41 percent over the last four years, moving its HPV down to 21.82.

Other productivity measures indicate performance in specific parts of the manufacturing process. Harbour and Associates measures hours per engine (HPE) in the production of engines. For example, Toyota had the best productivity in 4-cylinder engines with an HPE of 2.71, Honda led in 6-cylinder productivity with an HPE of 3.47, and GM topped V8 productivity with an HPE of 4.55. Harbour also evaluates the stamping process, where it measures hits per hour (HPH) and pieces per hour (PPH), among other metrics.

Industry analysts look closely at these productivity numbers and their trends. They are a precursor of future profitability. Further, they want to find out how the various plants achieve their productivity levels so that other companies may copy successful methods and avoid others.

Nissan has more than 40 percent of its nearly $50 billion of sales in North America. Thus, productivity in its North American operations is important to the company. How has Nissan managed to achieve consistently high productivity? The key is a "highly motivated workforce," according to Barry Watson, Nissan's Smyrna plant department manager. A number of "simple but effective" efforts are at the heart of the plant's success. These efforts include

- Social events, such as family day and picnics
- Continuous training
- Manager and employee involvement through group meetings at the start of every shift—open, two-way discussions that focus on ideas for improving productivity and reducing costs
- Impact teams of managers and employees for evaluation and implementation of ideas

For example, an idea was submitted to build a special table that would significantly reduce the time it took to change equipment between production runs. The idea was implemented and resulted in a 15 percent increase in the number of units assembled on each production run.

Sources: Harbour and Associates, Inc., *Auto Manufacturing Productivity Report*, June, 2002 (www.harbourinc.com); Harbour and Associates, Inc., *Auto Manufacturing Productivity Report*, June, 1997; "Pick Me as Your Strike Target! No, Me!" *Business Week*, April 21, 2003; Nissan, Nissan Motor Company Annual Report, Year Ended March 31, 2003.

Apple
www.apple.com

focus management's attention on items subject to action on a month-by-month and day-to-day basis.

One advantage of the balanced scorecard approach is that line managers can see the relationship between non-financial measures, which they often can relate more easily to their own actions, and the financial measures that relate to organizational goals. Another advantage of the balanced scorecard is its focus on performance measures from each of the four components of the successful organization shown in Exhibit 13-10. This enhances the learning process because managers learn the results of their actions and how these actions are linked to the organizational goals.[4]

What does a balanced scorecard look like? Exhibit 13-11 shows a balanced scorecard for the Luxury Suites hotel chain. This scorecard is for the organization as a whole. It has performance measures for all four components of organizational success. There are many scorecards within an organization. In fact, each area of responsibility will have its own scorecard. Scorecards for some lower-level responsibility centres that are focused strictly on day-to-day operations may be totally focused on only one of the four components. We should also note that not all performance measures appear on scorecards. Managers of responsibility centres include only those measures that are key performance indicators—measures that drive the organization to achieve its goals. For example, top management at Luxury Suites set "exceed guest expectations" as one organizational goal. The balanced scorecard should have at least one key performance indicator that is linked to this goal. The customer satisfaction index, brand loyalty index, number of improvements, and average cycle time for check-in and check-out measures all are linked to this goal.

MANAGEMENT CONTROL SYSTEMS IN SERVICE, GOVERNMENT, AND NOT-FOR-PROFIT ORGANIZATIONS

OBJECTIVE 7

Describe the difficulties of management control in service and not-for-profit organizations.

Most service, government, and not-for-profit organizations have more difficulty implementing management control systems than do manufacturing firms. The main problem is that the outputs of service and not-for-profit organizations are harder to measure than the cars or computers that are produced by manufacturers. As a result, it may be more difficult to know whether the service provided is, for example, of top quality until (long) after the service has already been delivered.

The key to successful management control in any organization is proper training and motivation of employees to achieve goal congruence and effort, followed by consistent monitoring of objectives set in accordance with critical

EXHIBIT 13-11

Balanced Scorecard for Luxury Suites Hotels

COMPONENT AND MEASURES	TARGET	RESULT
Financial Strength		
Revenue (millions of dollars) per new service	$50	$58
Revenue per arrival	$75	$81
Customer Satisfaction		
Customer satisfaction index	95	88
Brand loyalty index	60	40
Business Process Improvement		
Number of improvements	8	8
Average cycle time (minutes) for check-in and check-out	15	15
Organizational Learning		
Percent of staff retrained	80	85
Training hours per employee	30	25

---

[4] For a more detailed discussion, see Anthony Atkinson and Marc Epstein, "Measure for Measure: Realizing the Power of the Balanced Scorecard," *Management*, September 2000, pp. 23–28.

MBNA America
www.mbna.com

CUSO
www.cuso.org

processes and success factors. This is even more important in service-oriented organizations. For example, MBNA America, a large issuer of bank credit cards, identifies customer retention as its primary critical success factor. MBNA trains its customer representatives carefully, measures and reports performance on 14 objectives consistent with customer retention (such as answering every call by the second ring, keeping the computer up 100 percent of the time, processing credit-line requests within one hour) each day, and rewards every employee based on those 14 objectives. Employees have earned bonuses as high as 20 percent of their annual salaries by meeting those objectives.

Not-for-profit and government organizations also have additional problems designing and implementing an objective that is similar to the financial "bottom line" that so often serves as a powerful incentive in private industry. Furthermore, many people seek positions in not-for-profit organizations for other than monetary rewards. For example, volunteers in CUSO receive very little pay but derive much satisfaction from helping to improve conditions in underdeveloped countries. Thus, monetary incentives are generally less effective in not-for-profit organizations. Control systems in not-for-profit organizations probably will never be as highly developed as are those in profit-seeking firms because

1. Organizational goals and objectives are less clear. Moreover, they are often multiple, requiring difficult tradeoffs.
2. Professionals (for example, teachers, lawyers, physicians, scientists, economists) tend to dominate not-for-profit organizations. Because of their perceived professional status, they have been less receptive to the installation or improvement of formal control systems.
3. Measurements are more difficult because
    a. There is no profit measure.
    b. Heavy amounts of discretionary fixed costs make the relationship of inputs to outputs difficult to specify and to measure.
4. There is less competitive pressure from other organizations or from "owners" to improve management control systems. As a result, for example, many cities are "privatizing" some essential services such as sanitation by contracting with private firms.
5. The role of budgeting is often more a matter of playing bargaining games with sources of funding to get the largest possible authorization than it is rigorous planning.
6. Motivations and incentives of individuals may differ from those in for-profit organizations.

MAKING MANAGERIAL DECISIONS

Study Exhibit 13-1 again. Use the same four general components, but rearrange them a bit to reflect a framework that might help managers of a successful governmental or not-for-profit organization.

ANSWER

For government and not-for-profit organizations, the ultimate objective is not to focus on financial results but to deliver the maximum benefits to customers (or citizens) based on an available pool of financial resources. Thus the causal relationships might be

organizational learning → process improvements in delivering programs → fiscal or financial strength → greater program benefits for citizens or clients

Balanced Scorecard Hall of Fame

Robert Kaplan and David Norton created the balanced scorecard in 1992. In 2000, their company, Balanced Scorecard Collaborative, created a Balanced Scorecard Hall of Fame, which comprises 69 members as of early 2006, including Ottawa-based Cognos Inc. To be selected, a company must apply one or more of these five principles to create a strategy-focused organization:

Balanced Scorecard Collaborative www.bscol.com

1. Mobilize change through executive leadership
2. Translate the strategy into operational terms
3. Align the organization around its strategy
4. Make strategy everyone's job
5. Make strategy a continual process

Three Balanced Scorecard Hall of Fame honorees are AT&T Canada, Cognos Inc. and Nova Scotia Power. Their profiles are as follows:

AT&T Canada (formerly known as Unitel) offers a range of data services, including managed network services. It is particularly focused on providing reliable data services to multinational businesses, as well as local, long-distance, international, and wireless telephone services. Under the leadership of Bill Catucci from 1996 and 1999, management used the balanced scorecard to address repeated losses, with a view to becoming a perceived leader with customers, employees, shareholders, and the community. The company went from losing more than $1 million per day to an annual growth rate of 32 percent, compared to an industry average of 4 percent. This turnaround was accompanied by an 11 percent rise in revenue per employee. Catucci went on to become the executive vice-president of global operations at Equifax Corporation and later became the president and CEO of Regulatory DataCorp. Throughout his career, he has continued to extol the virtues of the balanced scorecard.

Headquartered in Ottawa, Cognos Inc. is the world leader in business intelligence and corporate performance management solutions. In 2004, Cognos was named to the Balanced Scorecard Hall of Fame for its "breakthrough performance" between 2002 and 2004, which included an average annual revenue growth of 20 percent and a fivefold increase in net income (from $19.4 million to nearly $101 million). Cognos is so impressed with the balanced scorecard that it has designed its own balanced scorecard software, certified by the Balanced Scorecard Collaborative. For Cognos, the balanced scorecard has become an integrating mechanism among strategic planning processes, financial planning, and ongoing monitoring and measurement of core initiatives.

Nova Scotia Power Services Limited adopted the balanced scorecard in 1996. Nova Scotia Power is the principal operating subsidiary of Emera Inc., and is a regulated utility. Emera also owns another regulated utility (Bangor Hydro-Electric in Maine), and it owns a minority equity interest in the Maritimes and Northeast Pipeline, which delivers Nova Scotia's offshore natural gas to Maritime Canada and New England.

In 1996, Nova Scotia Power's CEO, David Mann, wanted a measurement system to evaluate the success of his new strategic plan. He also wanted assurance that various reorganized strategic business units were moving towards the same overall goals. Given that Nova Scotia Power operated in a regulatory environment, he needed to see earnings stability without price increases. From quality perspectives, he wanted fewer power interruptions, improved customer satisfaction, reduced employee accidents, and a greater sense of employee loyalty towards the corporation. All of these objectives, to varying degrees, were achieved through the use of the balanced scorecard.

Sources: Profiles of balanced scorecard nominees at www.bscol.com; AT&T news release, "Unitel Changes Name to AT&T Long Distance Services," September 9, 1996; Cognos news release, "Cognos Named to Balanced Scorecard Hall of Fame," October 14, 2004.

THE FUTURE OF MANAGEMENT CONTROL SYSTEMS

OBJECTIVE 8

Explain how
management control
systems must evolve
with changing times.

As organizations mature and as environments change, managers cope with their responsibilities by expanding and refining their management control tools. The management control techniques that were quite satisfactory ten or 20 years ago may not be adequate for many organizations today. One often hears accounting systems criticized for being especially slow to adapt to organizational change.

A changing environment often means that organizations must set different critical success factors. Different critical success factors create different objectives to be used as targets and create different benchmarks for evaluating performance. Obviously, the management control system must evolve, too, or the organization may not manage its resources effectively or efficiently. Thus, the management control tools presented in this text may not be adequate even a short time from now.

Does this mean that the time spent studying this material has been wasted? No. Certain management control principles will always be important and can guide the redesign of systems to meet new management needs:

1. Always expect that individuals will be pulled in the direction of their own self-interest. One may be pleasantly surprised that some individuals will act selflessly, but management control systems should be designed to take advantage of more typical human behaviour. Be aware that self-interest may be perceived differently in different cultures.

2. Design incentives so that individuals who pursue their own self-interest are also achieving the organization's objectives. If there are multiple objectives (as is usually the case), then multiple incentives are appropriate. Do not underestimate the difficulty of balancing these incentives—some experimentation may be necessary to achieve multiple objectives.

3. The best benchmark for evaluating actual performance is expected or planned performance, revised, if possible, for actual output achieved. The concept of flexible budgeting can be applied to most subgoals and objectives, both financial and non-financial.

4. Non-financial performance is just as important as financial performance. In the short run, a manager may be able to generate good financial performance while neglecting non-financial performance, but it is not likely over a longer haul.

5. Establish performance measures across the entire value chain of the company. Recall that the value chain is the sequence of functions that adds value to the company's products or services. These functions include research and development, product and process design, production marketing, distribution, and customer service. This ensures that all activities that are critical to the long-run success of the company are integrated into the management control system.

6. Periodically review the success of the management control system. Are objectives being met? Does meeting the objectives mean that subgoals and goals are being met, too? Do individuals have, understand, and use the management control information effectively?

7. Learn from the management control successes (and failures) of competitors around the world. Despite cultural differences, human behaviour is

remarkably similar. Successful applications of new technology and management controls may be observed in the performance of others.

How does a manager decide if the management control system requires a change or alteration? Exhibit 13-12 provides a method to answer this question.

First, ask what the critical success factors of the organization are and what key management decisions are required by managers in order for the organization to attain its goals. Second, evaluate the management control systems and consider the actual management decisions that managers are motivated to make given the existing control systems. If the actual management decisions fit (i.e., are goal congruent) with the desired key management decisions, then no change is necessary. If, however, goal congruence does not exist, change may be necessary.

The essence of an effective management control system is the fit between four key factors that have been discussed in this chapter: the organizational goals, the organizational structure, the responsibility centres, and the selection of

EXHIBIT 13-12

Do You Have a
Management Control
System Problem?

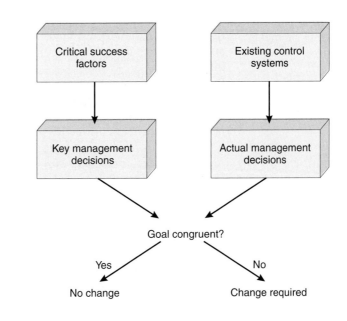

EXHIBIT 13-13

Effective Management
Control Systems

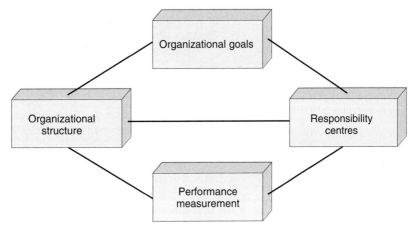

performance measures. Exhibit 13-13 illustrates the interrelationship of these factors. If a management control system is in need of change, and assuming that management has clearly defined appropriate organization goals, managers should consider alternative structures, responsibility centres, and performance measures in their decision to change to a better management control system. A better management control system will more effectively motivate employees to work toward achieving the organization's goals.

HIGHLIGHTS TO REMEMBER

1. **Describe the relationship of management control systems to organizational goals.** The starting point for designing and evaluating a management control system is the identification of organizational goals as specified by top management.

2. **Use responsibility accounting to define an organizational subunit as a cost centre, a profit centre, or an investment centre.** Responsibility accounting assigns particular revenue or cost objectives to the management of the subunit that has the greatest influence over them. Cost centres focus on costs only, profit centres on both revenues and costs, and investment centres on profits relative to the amount invested.

3. **Develop performance measures and use them to monitor the achievements of an organization.** A well-designed management control system measures both financial and non-financial performance. In fact, non-financial performance usually leads to financial performance in time. The performance measures should tell managers how well they are meeting the organization's goals.

4. **Explain the importance of evaluating performance and how it impacts motivation, goal congruence, and employee effort.** The way an organization measures and evaluates performance affects individuals' behaviour. The more it ties rewards to performance measures, the more incentive there is to improve the measures. Poorly designed measures may actually work against the organization's goals.

5. **Prepare segment income statements for evaluating profit and investment centres using the contribution margin and controllable-cost concepts.** The contribution approach to measuring a segment's income aids performance evaluation by separating a segment's costs into those controllable by the segment management and those beyond management's control. It allows separate evaluation of a segment as an economic investment and the performance of the segment's manager.

6. **Use a balanced scorecard to recognize both financial and non-financial measures of performance.** The balanced scorecard helps managers monitor actions that are designed to meet the various goals of the organization. It contains key performance indicators that measure how well the organization is meeting its goals.

7. **Measure performance against quality, cycle time, and productivity objectives.** Measuring performance in areas such as quality, cycle time, and productivity causes employees to direct attention to those areas.

Achieving goals in these non-financial measures can help meet long-run financial objectives.

8. **Describe the difficulties of management control in service and not-for-profit organizations.** Management control in service and not-for-profit organizations is difficult because of a number of factors, chief of which is a relative lack of clearly observable outcomes.

DEMONSTRATION PROBLEMS FOR YOUR REVIEW

Problem One

The Book & Game Company has bookstores in two locations: Auntie's and Merlin's. Each location has a manager who has a great deal of decision authority over the individual stores. However, advertising, market research, acquisition of books, legal services, and other staff functions are handled by a central office. The Book & Game Company's current accounting system allocates all costs to the stores. Results for 2006 were

ITEM	TOTAL COMPANY	AUNTIE'S	MERLIN'S
Sales revenue	$700,000	$350,000	$350,000
Cost of merchandise sold	450,000	225,000	225,000
Gross margin	250,000	125,000	125,000
Operating expenses:			
Salaries and wages	63,000	30,000	33,000
Supplies	45,000	22,500	22,500
Rent and utilities	60,000	40,000	20,000
Amortization	15,000	7,000	8,000
Allocated staff costs	60,000	30,000	30,000
Total operating expenses	243,000	129,500	113,500
Operating income (loss)	$ 7,000	$ (4,500)	$ 11,500

Each bookstore manager makes decisions that affect salaries and wages, supplies, and amortization. In contrast, rent and utilities are beyond the managers' control because the managers did not choose the location or the size of the store.

Supplies are variable costs. Variable salaries and wages are equal to 8 percent of the cost of merchandise sold; the remainder of salaries and wages is a fixed cost. Rent, utilities, and amortization also are fixed costs. Allocated staff costs are unaffected by any events at the bookstores, but they are allocated as a proportion of sales revenue.

1. Using the contribution approach, prepare a performance report that distinguishes the performance of each bookstore from that of the bookstore manager.
2. Evaluate the financial performance of each bookstore.
3. Evaluate the financial performance of each manager.

Solution

1.

ITEM	TOTAL COMPANY	AUNTIE'S	MERLIN'S
Sales revenue	$700,000	$350,000	$350,000
Variable costs:			
Cost of merchandise sold	450,000	225,000	225,000
Salaries and wages	36,000	18,000	18,000
Supplies	45,000	22,500	22,500
Total variable costs	531,000	265,500	265,500
Contribution margin	169,000	84,500	84,500
Less: fixed costs controllable			
by bookstore managers			
Salaries and wages	27,000	12,000	15,000
Amortization	15,000	7,000	8,000
Total controllable fixed costs	42,000	19,000	23,000
Contribution controllable by			
bookstore managers	127,000	65,500	61,500
Less: fixed costs controllable			
by others			
Rent and utilities	60,000	40,000	20,000
Contribution by bookstore	$ 67,000	$ 25,500	$ 41,500
Unallocated costs	60,000		
Operating income	$ 7,000		

2. The financial performance of the bookstores (i.e., segments of the company) are best evaluated by the line "Contribution by bookstore." Merlin's has a substantially higher contribution, despite equal levels of sales revenues in the two stores. The major reason for this advantage is the lower rent and utilities paid by Merlin's.

3. The financial performance by managers is best judged by the line "Contribution controllable by bookstore managers." By this measure, the performance of Auntie's manager is better than that of Merlin's. The contribution margin is the same for each store, but Merlin's manager paid $4,000 more in controllable fixed costs than did Auntie's manager. Of course, this decision could be beneficial in the long run. What is missing from each of these segment reports is the year's master budget and a flexible budget, which would be the best benchmark for evaluating both the bookstore and bookstore manager.

Problem Two

Consider our example, the Luxury Suites hotel chain. As we have noted, top management established *exceed guest expectations* as one organization-wide goal. The critical process for this goal is *produce and deliver services*. Critical success factors for this critical process have also been identified as *quality and timeliness of the customer service department* and *personalized service*. Susan Pierce, the vice president of sales, is the manager responsible for the *produce and deliver services* critical process. She has already identified one action—upgrade customer service department capabilities.

1. Identify several possible performance measures for the *personalized service* critical success factor.
2. Recommend several specific actions or activities associated with upgrading customer service department capabilities that would drive Luxury Suites toward its goal of exceeding customer expectations.

Solution

1. Performance measures for the personalized service critical success factor include number of changes to registration, rating on "friendly, knowledgeable staff" question on guest survey, and percent of customers with completed profile.
2. Specific actions or activities include training employees, implementing a call checklist and monitoring compliance with the list, developing a customer satisfaction survey, and reengineering the order taking process.

KEY TERMS

balanced scorecard *p. 663*
controllable costs *p. 650*
cost centre *p. 645*
critical process *p. 643*
critical success factors *p. 643*
cycle time *p. 658*
employee motivation *p. 648*
expense centre *p. 646*
goal congruence *p. 647*
internal control system *p. 649*
investment centre *p. 646*
management control system *p. 641*

managerial effort *p. 648*
productivity *p. 659*
profit centre *p. 646*
quality control *p. 655*
quality control chart *p. 658*
quality cost report *p. 655*
responsibility accounting *p. 645*
responsibility centre *p. 645*
revenue centre *p. 646*
total quality management (TQM) *p. 658*
uncontrollable cost *p. 650*

ASSIGNMENT MATERIAL

QUESTIONS

Q13-1 What is the purpose of a management control system?

Q13-2 "Goals are useless without performance measures." Do you agree? Explain.

Q13-3 "There are corporate objectives other than profit." Name four.

Q13-4 How does management determine its critical (key) success factors?

Q13-5 Give three examples of how managers may improve short-run performance to the detriment of long-run results.

Q13-6 Name five kinds of responsibility centres.

Q13-7 How do profit centres and investment centres differ?

Q13-8 "Performance evaluation seeks to achieve *goal congruence* and *managerial effort*." Describe what is meant by this statement.

Q13-9 Why do accountants need to consider behavioural factors when designing a management control system?

Q13-10 List five characteristics of a good performance measure.

Q13-11 "Managers of profit centres should be held responsible for the centre's entire profit. They are responsible for profit even if they cannot control all factors affecting it." Discuss.

Q13-12 What is a balanced scorecard and why are more and more companies using one?

Q13-13 What are four non-financial measures of performance that managers find useful?

Q13-14 "Variable costs are controllable and fixed costs are uncontrollable." Do you agree? Explain.

Q13-15 "The contribution margin is the best measure of short-run performance." Do you agree? Explain.

Q13-16 Give four examples of segments.

Q13-17 "Always try to distinguish between the performance of a segment and its manager." Why?

Q13-18 "The contribution margin approach to performance evaluation is flawed because focusing on only the contribution margin ignores important aspects of performance." Do you agree? Explain.

Q13-19 There are four categories of cost in the quality cost report. Explain them.

Q13-20 Why are companies increasing their quality control emphasis on the prevention of defects?

Q13-21 Discuss how quality, cycle time, and productivity are related.

Q13-22 "Non-financial measures of performance can be controlled just like financial measures." Do you agree? Explain.

Q13-23 Identify three measures of labour productivity, one using all physical measures, one using all financial measures, and one that mixes physical and financial measures.

Q13-24 Discuss the difficulties of comparing productivity over time.

Q13-25 "Control systems in not-for-profit organizations will never be as highly developed as in profit-seeking organizations." Do you agree? Explain.

PROBLEMS

P13-1 **MANAGEMENT CONTROL SYSTEMS AND INNOVATION.** The president of a fast-growing high-tech firm remarked, "Developing budgets and comparing performance with the budgets may be fine for some firms. But we want to encourage innovations and entrepreneurship. Budgets go with bureaucracy, not innovation." Do you agree? How can a management control system encourage innovation and entrepreneurship?

P13-2 **MULTIPLE GOALS AND PROFITABILITY.** The following multiple goals were identified by the General Electric company:

Profitability   Employee attitudes
Market position   Public responsibility
Productivity   Balance between short-range and
Product leadership   long-range goals
Personnel development

General Electric is a huge, highly decentralized corporation. It has approximately 170 responsibility centres called "departments," but that is a deceiving term. In most other companies, these departments would be called divisions. For example, some GE departments have sales of over $500 million.

Each department manager's performance is evaluated annually in relation to the specified multiple goals. A special measurements group was set up to devise ways of quantifying accomplishments in each of the areas. In this way, the evaluation of performance would become more objective as the various measures were developed and improved.

1. How would you measure performance in each of these areas? Be specific.
2. Can the other goals be encompassed as ingredients of a formal measure of profitability? In other words, can profitability *per se* be defined to include the other goals?

P13-3 **MUNICIPAL RESPONSIBILITY ACCOUNTING.** In 1975, New York City barely avoided bankruptcy. By the 1990s it had one of the most sophisticated budgeting and reporting systems of any municipality, and its budgetary problems had nearly disappeared. The Integrated Financial Management System (IFMS) "clearly identifies managers in line agencies, and correlates allocations and expenditures with organizational structure. . . . In addition, managers have more time to take corrective measures when variances between budgeted and actual expenditures start to develop."[5]

Discuss how a responsibility accounting system such as IFMS can help manage a municipality such as New York City.

P13-4 **RESPONSIBILITY FOR A STABLE EMPLOYMENT POLICY.** The Sargent Metal Fabricators has been manufacturing machine tools for a number of years and has an industry-wide reputation for high-quality work. The company has been faced with irregularity of output over the years. It has been company policy to lay off welders as soon as there was insufficient work to keep them busy and to rehire them when demand warranted. The company, however, now has poor labour relations and finds it very difficult to hire good welders because of its layoff policy. Consequently, the quality of the work has been declining steadily.

The plant manager has proposed that the welders, who earn $20 per hour, be retained during slow periods to do plant maintenance work that is normally performed by workers earning $13 per hour in the plant maintenance department.

You, as a controller, must decide the most appropriate accounting procedure to handle the wages of the welders doing plant maintenance work. What department or departments should be charged with this work, and at what rate? Discuss the implications of your plan.

P13-5 **SALES CLERK'S COMPENSATION PLAN.** You are manager of a department store in Kyoto. Sales are subject to month-to-month variations, depending on the individual salesclerk's efforts. A new salary-plus-bonus plan has been in effect for four months, and you are reviewing a sales performance report. The plan provides for a base salary of ¥50,000 per month, a ¥68,000 bonus each month if the monthly sales quota is met, and an additional commission of 5 percent of all sales over the monthly quota. The quota is set approximately 3 percent above the previous month's sales to motivate clerks toward increasing sales (in thousands):

[5] *FE: The Magazine for Financial Executives*, Vol. 1, No. 8, p. 26.

		SALESCLERK A	SALESCLERK B	SALESCLERK C
January	Quota	¥4,500	¥1,500	¥7,500
	Actual	1,500	1,500	9,000
February	Quota	1,545	1,545	9,270
	Actual	3,000	1,545	3,000
March	Quota	3,090	1,590	3,090
	Actual	5,250	750	9,000
April	Quota	5,400	775	9,270
	Actual	1,500	780	4,050

1. Compute the compensation for each sales clerk for each month.
2. Evaluate the compensation plan. Be specific. What changes would you recommend?

P13-6   RESPONSIBILITY OF PURCHASING AGENT.   GL Interiors, Inc., a privately-held enterprise, has a subcontract to produce overhead storage bins for a Boeing airplane. Although GL was a low bidder, Boeing was reluctant to award the business to GL, a newcomer to this kind of activity. Consequently, GL assured Boeing of its financial strength by submitting its audited financial statements. Moreover, GL agreed to a penalty clause of $5,000 per day to be paid by GL for each day of late delivery for whatever reason.

Leesa Martinson, the GL purchasing agent, is responsible for acquiring materials and parts in time to meet production schedules. She placed an order with a GL supplier for a critical manufactured component. The supplier, who had a reliable record for meeting schedules, gave Martinson an acceptable delivery date. Martinson checked up several times and was assured that the component would arrive at GL on schedule.

On the date specified by the supplier for shipment to GL, Martinson was informed that the component had been damaged during final inspection. It was delivered ten days late. Martinson had allowed four extra days for possible delays, but GL was six days late in delivering to Boeing and so had to pay a penalty of $30,000.

What department should bear the penalty? Why?

P13-7   PERFORMANCE EVALUATION.   Lynch, Barney, and Schwab is a stock brokerage firm that evaluates its employees on sales activity generated. Recently the firm also began evaluating its stockbrokers on the number of new accounts generated.

Discuss how these two performance measures are consistent, and how they may conflict. Do you believe that these measures are appropriate for the long-term goal of profitability?

P13-8   PRODUCTIVITY.   In early 2006, Global Telecom, a telephone communications company, purchased the controlling interest in Eurotel in an eastern European country. A key productivity measure monitored by Global Telecom is the number of customer telephone lines per employee. Consider the following data:

	2006 (without Eurotel)	2006* (with Eurotel)	2005
Customer lines	15,054,000	19,994,000	14,315,000
Employees	74,520	114,590	70,866
Lines per employee	202	174	202
Normal growth in lines and employees (prior to purchase of Eurotel)		3% per year	

* Includes customer lines and employees of Eurotel.

1. Compute Global Telecom's 2006 productivity without Eurotel.
2. Compute Eurotel's 2006 productivity.
3. What difficulties do you foresee if Global Telecom brings Eurotel's productivity in line?

P13-9 **CYCLE TIME REPORTING.** Digital Processors Ltd. monitors its cycle time closely in order to prevent schedule delays and excessive costs. The standard cycle time for the manufacture of printed circuit boards for one of its computers is 26.4 hours. Consider the following cycle time data from the past six weeks of circuit board production:

WEEK	UNITS COMPLETED	TOTAL CYCLE TIME
1	564	14,108 hours
2	544	14,592 hours
3	553	15,152 hours
4	571	16,598 hours
5	547	17,104 hours
6	552	16,673 hours

Analyze circuit-board cycle-time performance in light of the 26.4-hour objective.

P13-10 **INCENTIVES IN THE FORMER SOVIET UNION.** Officials in Russia had been rewarding managers for exceeding a five-year-plan target for production quantities. But a problem arose because managers naturally tended to predict low volumes so that the targets would be set low. This hindered planning; good information about production possibilities was lacking.

The Russians then devised a new performance evaluation measure. Suppose F is the forecast of production, A is actual production, and X, Y, and Z are positive constants set by top officials, with $X < Y < Z$.

$$performance = \begin{cases} (Y \times F) + X \times (A - F) \text{ if } F \leq A \\ (Y \times F) - Z \times (F - A) \text{ if } F > A \end{cases}$$

This performance measure was designed to motivate both high production and accurate forecasts.

Consider the Moscow Automotive Factory. During 2006, the factory manager, Nicolai Konstantin, had to predict the number of automobiles that could be produced during the next year. He was confident that at least 700,000 autos could be produced in 2007, and most likely they could produce 800,000 autos. With good luck, they might even produce 900,000. Government officials told him that the new performance evaluation measure would be used, and that $X = 0.50$, $Y = 0.80$, and $Z = 1.00$ for 2007 and 2008.

1. Suppose Konstantin predicted production of 800,000 autos and 800,000 were produced. Calculate the performance measure.
2. Suppose again that 800,000 autos were produced. Calculate the performance measure if Konstantin had been conservative and predicted only 700,000 autos. Also calculate the performance measure if he had predicted 900,000 autos.
3. Now suppose it is November 2007 and it is clear that the 800,000 target cannot be achieved. Does the performance measure motivate continued efforts to increase production? Suppose it is clear that the 800,000 target will be met easily. Will the system motivate continued effort to increase production?

P13-11 **RESPONSIBILITY ACCOUNTING, PROFIT CENTRES, AND THE CONTRIBUTION APPROACH.** Consider the following data for the year's operations of an automobile dealer:

Sales of vehicles	$ 2,600,000
Sales of parts and service	600,000
Cost of vehicle sales	2,120,000
Parts and service materials	180,000
Parts and service labour	240,000
Parts and service overhead	60,000
General dealership overhead	120,000
Advertising of vehicles	120,000
Sales commissions, vehicles	48,000
Sales salaries, vehicles	60,000

The president of the dealership has long regarded the markup on material and labour for the parts and service activity as the amount that is supposed to cover all parts and service overhead plus all general overhead of the dealership. In other words, the parts and service department is viewed as a cost-recovery operation, and the sales of vehicles as the income-producing activity.

1. Prepare a departmentalized operating statement that harmonizes with the views of the president.
2. Prepare an alternative operating statement that would reflect a different view of the dealership operations. Assume that $15,000 and $60,000 of the $120,000 general overhead can be allocated with confidence to the parts and service department and to sales of vehicles, respectively. The remaining $45,000 cannot be allocated except in some highly arbitrary manner.
3. Comment on the relative merits of requirements 1 and 2.

P13-12 **PRODUCTIVITY MEASUREMENT.** Crystal Cleaners had the following results in 2003 and 2006:

	2003	2006
Kilograms of laundry processed	680,000	762,500
Sales revenue	$360,000	$697,000
Direct labour hours worked	22,550	23,325
Direct labour cost	$158,000	$249,000

Crystal used the same facilities in 2006 as in 2003. However, over the past four years the company put more effort into training its employees. The manager of

Crystal was curious about whether the training had increased labour productivity.

1. Compute a measure of labour productivity for 2006 based entirely on physical measures. Do the same for 2003. That is, from the data given, choose measures of physical output and physical input, and use them to compare the physical productivity of labour in 2006 with that in 2003.
2. Compute a measure of labour productivity for 2006 based entirely on financial measures. Do the same for 2003. That is, from the data given, choose measures of financial output and financial input, and use them to compare the financial productivity of labour in 2006 with that in 2003.
3. Suppose the following productivity measure were used:

$$\text{productivity} = \frac{\text{sales revenue}}{\text{direct labour hours worked}}$$

Because of inflation, each 2003 dollar is equivalent to 1.4 2006 dollars. Compute appropriate productivity numbers for comparing 2006 productivity with 2003 productivity.

P13-13 TRADEOFFS AMONG OBJECTIVES. Computer Data Services (CDS) performs routine and custom information systems services for many companies in a large metropolitan area. CDS has built a reputation for high-quality customer service and job security for its employees. Quality service and customer satisfaction have been CDS's primary subgoals—retaining a skilled and motivated workforce has been an important factor in achieving those goals. In the past, temporary downturns in business did not mean layoffs of employees, though some employees were required to perform other than their usual tasks. Three months ago, a new competitor began offering the same services to CDS's customers at prices averaging 20 percent lower than CDS. Rico Estrada, the company founder and president, believes that a significant price reduction is necessary in order to maintain the company's market share and avoid financial ruin, but is puzzled about how to achieve it without compromising quality, service, and the goodwill of his workforce.

CDS has a productivity objective of 20 accounts per employee. Estrada does not believe that he can increase this productivity and still maintain both quality and flexibility to customer needs. CDS also monitors average cost per account and the number of customer satisfaction adjustments (resolutions of complaints). The average billing markup rate is 25 percent. Consider the following data from the past six months:

	JUNE	JULY	AUGUST	SEPTEMBER	OCTOBER	NOVEMBER
Number of accounts	797	803	869	784	723	680
Number of employees	40	41	44	43	43	41
Average cost per account	$153	$153	$158	$173	$187	$191
Additions to long-term lease commitments for equipment				$10,000 per month		
Average salary per employee	$3,000	$3,000	$3,000	$3,000	$3,000	$3,000

1. Discuss the tradeoffs facing Rico Estrada.
2. Can you suggest solutions to his tradeoff dilemma?

P13-14 **CONTRIBUTION APPROACH TO RESPONSIBILITY ACCOUNTING.** George McBee owns a small chain of specialty toy stores in Edmonton and Calgary. The company's organization chart follows:

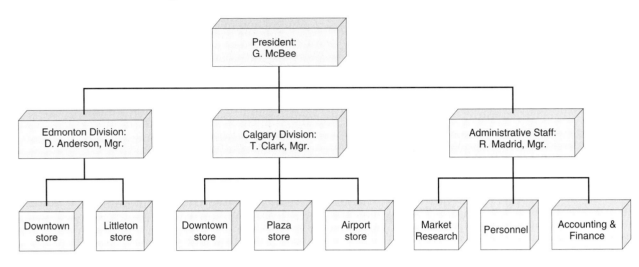

Financial results for 2006 were:

Sales revenue	$8,000,000
Cost of merchandise sold	5,000,000
Gross margin	3,000,000
Operating expenses	2,200,000
Income before income taxes	$ 800,000

The following data about 2006 operations were also available:

1. All five stores used the same pricing formula; therefore, all had the same gross margin percentage.
2. Sales were largest in the two Downtown stores, with 30 percent of the total sales volume in each. The Plaza and Airport stores each provided 15 percent of total sales volume, and the Littleton store provided 10 percent.
3. Variable operating costs at the stores were 10 percent of revenue for the Downtown stores. The other stores had lower variable and higher fixed costs. Their variable operating costs were only 5 percent of sales revenue.
4. The fixed costs over which the store managers had control were $125,000 in each of the Downtown stores, $160,000 at the Plaza and Airport stores, and $80,000 at Littleton.
5. The remaining $910,000 of operating costs consisted of
   a. $180,0000 controllable by the Calgary division manager, but not by individual stores
   b. $130,000 controllable by the Edmonton division manager, but not by individual stores
   c. $600,000 controllable by the administrative staff
6. Of the $600,000 spent by the administrative staff, $350,000 directly supported the Calgary division, with 20 percent for the Downtown store, 30 percent for each of the Plaza and Airport stores, and 20 percent for Calgary operations in general. Another $150,000 supported

the Edmonton division, 50 percent for the Downtown store, 25 percent for the Littleton store, and 25 percent supporting Edmonton operations in general. The other $100,000 was for general corporate expenses.

Prepare an income statement by segments using the contribution approach to responsibility accounting. Use the format of Exhibit 13-5. Column headings should be

COMPANY AS A WHOLE	BREAKDOWN INTO TWO DIVISIONS		BREAKDOWN OF EDMONTON DIVISION			BREAKDOWN OF CALGARY DIVISION			
	Edmonton Division	Calgary Division	Not Allocated	Down-town	Littleton	Not Allocated	Down-town	Plaza	Airport

P13-15 RESPONSIBILITY ACCOUNTING. The LaCrosse Manufacturing Company produces precision parts. LaCrosse uses a standard cost system, calculating variances for each department and reporting them to the department managers. Managers are supposed to use the information to improve their operations. Superiors use the same information to evaluate managers' performance.

Nuno Dahl was recently appointed manager of the assembly department of the company. He has complained that the system as designed is disadvantageous to his department. Included among the variances charged to the department is one for rejected units. The inspection occurs at the end of the assembly department. The inspectors attempt to identify the cause of the rejection so that the department where the error occurred can be charged with it. But not all errors can easily be identified with a department. The non-identified units are totalled and apportioned to the departments according to the number of identified errors. The variance for rejected units in each department is a combination of the errors caused by the department plus a portion of the unidentified causes of rejects.

1. Is Dahl's complaint valid? Explain the reason(s) for your answer.
2. What would you recommend that the company do to solve its problem with Dahl and his complaint?

P13-16 DIVISIONAL CONTRIBUTION, PERFORMANCE, AND SEGMENT MARGINS. The Board of Directors of Atlantic Coast Railroad wants to obtain an overview of the company's operations, particularly with respect to comparing freight and passenger business. The Board Chair has heard about some new "contribution" approaches to cost allocations that emphasize cost behaviour patterns and so-called *contribution margins, contributions controllable by segment managers,* and *contributions by segments.* The Board has hired you as a consultant and has provided you with the following information.

Total revenue in 2006 was $80 million, of which $72 million was freight traffic and $8 million was passenger traffic. Fifty percent of the latter was generated by Division 1; 40 percent by Division 2; and 10 percent by Division 3.

Total variable costs were $45 million, of which $36 million was freight traffic. Of the $9 million allocable to passenger traffic, $3.3, $2.8, and $2.9 million could be allocated to Divisions 1, 2, and 3, respectively.

Total separable discretionary fixed costs were $8 million, of which $7.6 million applied to freight traffic. Of the remainder, $80,000 could not be allocated to specific divisions, although it was clearly traceable to passenger traffic in general. Divisions 1, 2, and 3 should be allocated $240,000, $60,000, and $20,000, respectively.

Total separable committed costs, which were not regarded as being control-lable by segment managers, were $25 million, of which 90 percent was allocable to freight traffic. Of the 10 percent traceable to passenger traffic, Divisions 1, 2, and 3 should be allocated $1.5 million, $350,000, and $150,000, respectively; the balance was unallocable to a specific division.

The common fixed costs not clearly allocable to any part of the company amounted to $750,000.

1. The Board asks you to prepare statements, dividing the data for the company as a whole between the freight and passenger traffic and then subdividing the passenger traffic into three divisions.
2. Some competing railroads actively promote a series of one-day sight-seeing tours on summer weekends. Most often, these tours are timed so that the cars with the tourists are hitched to regularly scheduled pas-senger trains. What costs are relevant for making decisions to run such tours? Other railroads, facing the same general cost picture, refuse to conduct such sightseeing tours. Why?
3. For the purposes of this analysis, even though the numbers may be unrealistic, suppose that Division 2's figures represented a specific run for a train instead of a division. Suppose further that the railroad has petitioned government authorities for permission to drop Division 2. What would be the effect on overall company net income for 2007, assuming that the figures are accurate and that 2007 operations are in all other respects a duplication of 2006 operations?

P13-17 **QUALITY COST REPORT.** Red River Manufacturing Division makes a variety of home furnishings. In 2005 the company installed a system to report on quality costs. At the end of 2007 the division general manager wanted an assessment of whether quality costs in 2007 differed from those in 2005. Each month the actual costs had been compared with the plan, but at this time the manager wanted to see only total annual numbers for 2007 compared with 2005. The production supervisor prepared the following report.

Red River Manufacturing Division Quality Cost Report (in thousands of dollars)

QUALITY COST AREA	2005 COST	2007 COST
1. Prevention Cost	45	107
% of Total Quality Cost	3.3%	12.3%
2. Appraisal Cost	124	132
% of Total Quality Cost	9.1%	15.2%
3. Internal Failure Cost	503	368
% of Total Quality Cost	36.9%	42.5%
Total Internal Quality Cost (1 + 2 + 3)	672	607
% of Total Quality Cost	49.3%	70.0%
4. External Failure Cost	691	259
% of Total Quality Cost	50.7%	29.9%
Total Quality Cost	1,363	866
Total Product Cost	22,168	23,462
% Total Quality Cost to Total Product Cost	6.1%	3.7%

1. For each of the four quality cost areas, explain what types of costs are included and how those costs have changed between 2005 and 2007.
2. Assess overall quality performance in 2007 compared with 2005. What do you suppose has caused the changes observed in quality costs?

P13-18 INVENTORY MEASURES, PRODUCTION SCHEDULING, AND EVALUATING DIVISIONAL PERFORMANCE. The Paul Company stresses competition between the heads of its various divisions, and it rewards stellar performance with year-end bonuses that vary between 5 and 10 percent of division net operating income (before considering the bonus or income taxes). The divisional managers have great discretion in setting production schedules.

The Normandy Division produces and sells a product for which there is a long-standing demand but which can have marked seasonal and year-to-year fluctuations. On November 30, 2006, Byron LeDoux, the Normandy Division manager, is preparing a production schedule for December. The following data are available for January 1 through November 30 (EUR means Euro):

Beginning inventory, January 1, in units	10,000
Sales price, per unit	EUR61
Total fixed costs incurred for manufacturing	EUR1,430,000
Total fixed costs: other (not inventoriable)	EUR1,430,000
Total variable costs for manufacturing	EUR2,750,000
Total other variable costs (fluctuate with units sold)	EUR610,000
Units produced	110,000
Units sold	100,000
Variances	None

Production in October and November was 10,000 units each month. Practical capacity is 12,000 units per month. Maximum available storage space for inventory is 25,000 units. The sales outlook, for December through February, is 6,000 units monthly. To retain a core of key employees, monthly production cannot be scheduled at less than 4,000 units without special permission from the president. Inventory is never to be less than 10,000 units.

The denominator for applying fixed factory overhead is regarded as 120,000 units annually. The company uses a standard absorption-costing system. All variances are disposed of at year-end as an adjustment to standard cost of goods sold.

1. Given the restrictions as stated, and assuming that the manager wants to maximize the company's net income for 2006
   a. How many units should be scheduled for production in December?
   b. What net operating income will be reported for 2006 as a whole, assuming that the implied cost-behaviour patterns will continue in December as they did throughout the year to date? Show your computations.
   c. If December production is scheduled at 4,000 units, what would reported net income be?
2. Assume that standard variable costing is used rather than standard absorption costing:
   a. What would net income for 2006 be, assuming that the December production schedule is the one in requirement 1, part (a)?
   b. Assuming that December production was 4,000 units?
   c. Reconcile the net incomes in this requirement with those in requirement 1.
3. From the viewpoint of the long-run interests of the company as a whole, what production schedule should the division manager set? Explain fully. Include in your explanation a comparison of the motivating influence of absorption and variable costing in this situation.
4. Assume standard absorption costing. The manager wants to maximize his after-income-tax performance over the long run. Given the data at the beginning of

the problem, assume that income tax rates will be halved in 2007. Assume also that year-end write-offs of variances are acceptable for income tax purposes. How many units should be scheduled for production in December? Why?

P13-19   **COMPARISON OF PRODUCTIVITY.**   Lakehead Foods and National Food and Beverage are consumer products companies. Comparative data for 2000 and 2006 are

		LAKEHEAD FOODS	NATIONAL FOOD AND BEVERAGE
Sales revenue	2000	$5,924,000,000	$7,658,000,000
	2006	$6,764,000,000	$9,667,000,000
Number of employees	2000	56,600	75,900
	2006	54,800	76,200

Assume that each 2000 dollar is equivalent to 1.2 2006 dollars, owing to inflation.
1. Compute 2000 and 2006 productivity measures in terms of revenue per employee for Lakehead Foods and National Food and Beverage.
2. Compare the change in productivity between 2000 and 2006 for Lakehead Foods with that for National Food and Beverage.

P13-20   **QUALITY THEORIES COMPARED.**   Sketch the two graphs as they appear below. Compare the total quality management approach to the traditional theory of quality. Which theory do you believe represents the current realities of today's global competitive environment? Explain.

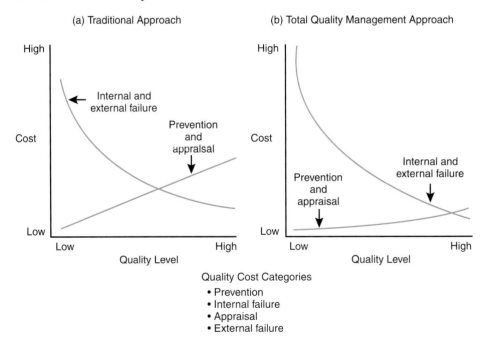

(a) Traditional Approach

(b) Total Quality Management Approach

Quality Cost Categories
• Prevention
• Internal failure
• Appraisal
• External failure

P13-21   **QUALITY CONTROL CHART.**   Baffin Manufacturing Company was concerned about a growing number of defective units being produced. At one time the company had the percentage of defective units down to less than fifty per thousand, but recently rates of defects have been near, or even above, 1 percent. The company decided to graph its defects for the last eight weeks (40 working days), beginning Monday, September 1 through Friday, October 31. The graph follows:

Baffin Manfacturing
Company
Quality Control Chart
September 1 through
October 31

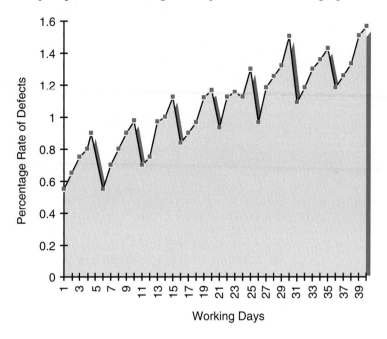

1. Identify two important trends evident in the quality control chart.
2. What might management of Baffin do to deal with each trend?

P13-22 REVIEW. As you are about to depart on a business trip, your accountant hands you the following information about your Thailand division:

1. Master budget for the fiscal year just ended on June 30, 2006

Sales	$850,000
Manufacturing cost of goods sold	670,000
Manufacturing margin	$180,000
Selling and administrative expenses	120,000
Operating income	$ 60,000

2. Budgeted sales and production mix

Product A	50,000 units
Product B	70,000 units

3. Standard variable manufacturing cost per unit

Product A	Direct materials	10 pieces	@ $0.25	$2.50
	Direct labour	1 hour	@ $3.00	3.00
	Variable overhead	1 hour	@ $2.00	2.00
				$7.50
Product B	Direct materials	5 kilograms	@ $0.10	$0.50
	Direct labour	.3 hours	@ $2.50	0.75
	Variable overhead	.3 hours	@ $2.50	0.75
				$2.00

4. All budgeted selling and administrative expenses are common, fixed expenses; 60 percent are discretionary expenses.
5. Actual income statement for the fiscal year ended June 30, 2006

Sales	$850,000
Manufacturing cost of goods sold	685,200
Manufacturing margin	$164,800
Selling and administrative expenses	116,000
Operating income	$ 48,800

6. Actual sales and production mix

Product A	53,000 units
Product B	64,000 units

7. Budgeted and actual sales prices

Product A	$10
Product B	5

8. Schedule of the actual variable manufacturing cost of goods sold by product; actual quantities in parentheses

Product A:	Material	$134,500 (538,000 pieces)
	Labour	156,350 (53,000 hours)
	Overhead	108,650 (53,000 hours)
Product B:	Material	38,400 (320,000 kilograms)
	Labour	50,000 (20,000 hours)
	Overhead	50,000 (20,000 hours)
		$537,900

9. Products A and B are manufactured in separate facilities. Of the *budgeted* fixed manufacturing cost, $130,000 is separable as follows: $45,000 to product A and $85,000 to product B. Ten percent of these separate costs is discretionary. All other budgeted fixed manufacturing expenses, separable and common, are committed.

The purpose of your business trip is a board of directors meeting. During the meeting it is quite likely that some of the information from your accountant will be discussed. In anticipation, you set out to prepare answers to possible questions. (There are no beginning or ending inventories.)

1. Determine the firm's *budgeted* break-even point in dollars, overall contribution-margin ratio, and contribution margins per unit by product.
2. Considering products A and B as segments of the firm, find the *budgeted* "contribution by segments" for each.
3. It is decided to allocate the *budgeted* selling and administrative expenses to the segments (in requirement 2) as follows: committed costs on the basis of budgeted unit sales mix and discretionary costs on the basis of actual unit sales mix. What are the final expense allocations? Briefly appraise the allocation method.
4. How would you respond to a proposal to base commissions to salespersons on the sales (revenue) value of orders received? Assume all salespersons have the opportunity to sell both products.

5. Determine the firm's *actual* "contribution margin" and "contribution controllable by segment managers" for the fiscal year ended June 30, 2006. Assume no variances in committed fixed costs.

6. Determine the "sales-volume variance" for each product for the fiscal year ended June 30, 2006.

7. Determine and identify all variances in *variable* manufacturing costs by product for the fiscal year ended June 30, 2006.

P13-23   BALANCED SCORECARD.   Zenon Medical Instruments Company (ZMIC) recently revised its performance evaluation system. The company identified four major goals and several objectives required to meet each goal. Ruth Sanchez, Controller of ZMIC, suggested that a balanced scorecard be used to report on progress toward meeting the objectives. At a recent meeting, she told the managers of ZIMC listing the objectives was only the first step in installing a new performance measurement system. Each objective has to be accomplished by one or more measures to monitor progress toward achieving the objectives. She asked the help of the managers in identifying appropriate measures.

The goals and objectives determined by the top management of ZMIC are

1. Maintain strong financial health
   a. Keep sufficient cash balances to assure financial survival
   b. Achieve consistent growth in sales and income
   c. Provide excellent returns to shareholders
2. Provide excellent service to customers
   a. Provide products that meet the needs of customers
   b. Meet customer needs on a timely basis
   c. Meet customer quality requirements
   d. Be the preferred supplier to customers
3. Be among the industry leaders in product and process innovations
   a. Bring new products to market before competition
   b. Lead competition in production process innovation
4. Develop and maintain efficient, state-of-the-art productions processes
   a. Excel in manufacturing efficiency
   b. Design products efficiently and quickly
   c. Meet or beat product introduction schedules

Propose at least one measure of performance for each of the objectives of ZMIC.

P13-24   QUALITY PROGRAMS, STRATEGIC INITIATIVES, GENERAL ELECTRIC.   One of three major strategic initiatives of General Electric Company in 1998 was Six Sigma quality. The following comments were made by John Welch, Jr., former CEO of GE in the 1998 Annual Report.

"Six Sigma quality, our third growth initiative, is, in itself, a product of learning. After observing the transformational effects this science, this way of life and work, had on the few companies that pursued it, we plunged into Six Sigma with a company-consuming vengeance just over three years ago. We have invested more than a billion dollars in the effort, and the financial returns have now entered the exponential phase—more than three quarters of a billion dollars in savings beyond our investment in 1998, with a billion and a half in sight for 1999."

"The Six Sigma–driven savings are impressive, but it is the radical change in the overall measures of operating efficiency that excite us most. For years—decades—we have been straining to improve operating margin and working capital turns. Our progress was typically measured in basis points for margins and decimal points in working capital turns. Six Sigma came along in 1995 when our margins were in the 13.6 percent range and turns at 5.8. At the end of 1998, margins hit 16.7 percent and turns hit 9.2. These numbers are an indicator of the progress and momentum in our Six Sigma journey."

"The ratio of plant and equipment expenditures to amortization is another measure of asset efficiency. This number in 1998 dropped to 1.2 and will be in the 0.7 to 0.8 range in the future, as 'hidden factory' after 'hidden factory'— literally 'free capacity'—is uncovered by Six Sigma process improvements."

"Yes, we've had some early product successes, and those customers who have been touched by them understand what this Six Sigma they've heard so much about really means. But, as we celebrate our progress and count our financial gain, we need to focus on the most powerful piece of learning we have been given in 1998, summarized perfectly in the form of what most of our customers must be thinking, which is: 'When do I get the benefits of Six Sigma?' 'When does my company get to experience the GE I read about in the GE Annual Report?'"

"Questions like these are being asked because, up to now, our Six Sigma process improvements have concentrated primarily on our own internal processes and on internal measurements such as 'order-to-delivery' or 'shop turnaround time.' And in focusing that way—inwardly on our processes—we have tended to use all our energy and Six Sigma science to 'move the mean' to, for example, reduce order-to-delivery times from an average of, say, 17 days to 12 days, as reflected in the example below. We've repeated this type of improvement over and over again in thousands of GE processes and have been rewarded for it with less 'rework' and greater cash flow."

ORDER BY ORDER DELIVER TIMES (DAYS)

Starting Point	After Project
29	11
18	24
7	10
19	6
6	12
8	8
16	15
19	10
33	4
15	20
Mean 17	Mean 12

Compute a measure of the variability in the data above. From a customer's perspective how would you view the results of Six Sigma as depicted in the example given by CEO Welch?

C13-1   **ORGANIZATION STRUCTURE.**   (SMAC)   Harold Mover has been the president of Newprod Ltd. for a little over six months. He was brought in by the Board of Directors to reverse the trend of falling profits. He had told the Board that it would take him a while to get a thorough understanding of how things worked at Newprod.

Newprod is a multi-product manufacturer (see Exhibit 13A-1) that supplies various wholesalers and distributors across Canada. Newprod services its customers from one centrally located production plant just north of Toronto. Sales offices are located across the country.

Within the operations of the plant there are some sequential interdepartmental transfers, since several products may be incorporated into the production process of other departments in addition to being sold directly to consumers.

At Newprod, there is a very clear separation among the production equipment in each production department. However, there are also significant costs related to the plant facilities, such as heat and light, that are not easily segregated. This is partly due to the fact that some product lines depend on other departments within Newprod to manufacture component parts and partly because independent facilities, by product, are not economically feasible.

During his initial months at Newprod, Mover has found that Newprod operates under a strong central management structure, with almost everything flowing to the president for decisions. He has noticed that there is little motiva-

EXHIBIT 13A-1

Newprod Ltd.
Condensed
Organization Chart

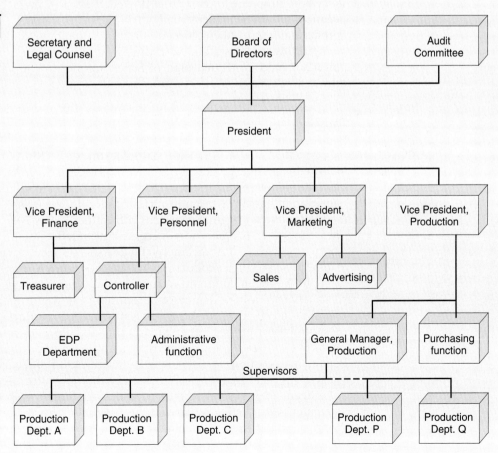

tion on the part of senior and middle managers, as they have only minimal participation in management decision making other than those decisions relating to their direct responsibilities. Furthermore, there is no system of performance measurement.

In his spare moments, Mover has been reviewing some prior correspondence and has noticed that the internal auditors have frequently suggested that some type of integrated planning structure should be put in place and that a divisional management performance system would be appropriate for Newprod.

Using this as a basis for discussion, Mover has had various meetings with his vice presidents and other supervisory personnel.

With the vision of a "light at the end of the tunnel," the managers were more than willing to contribute their ideas and their preferences. However, while some were in favour of implementing a divisional structure, others were not. One important issue that was raised for discussion was the matter of performance measurement. All managers were in favour of some form of performance measurement, but they were undecided as to what would be best. Each wanted a chance to prove that he or she was performing well but feared a measurement that would be unfair in its application.

The managers also expressed a desire to participate in corporate planning and budgeting.

As a result of these meetings, Mover has had some serious discussion with Jill Adams, the corporate controller, about how best to proceed. It was generally felt that a good planning system in conjunction with a divisional management structure may be appropriate for Newprod. However, a concern was expressed that any such changes should be implemented only if the major corporate objectives of increased profits and improved employee motivation and morale could be achieved.

Jill Adams has asked you, the assistant controller, to prepare a report and provide a recommended plan of action to address the various concerns raised throughout the consultation process.

Required: Prepare the report requested by Jill Adams. Be sure to discuss all of the issues raised above.

C13-2 **MANAGEMENT CONTROL IN A SERVICE DEPARTMENT.** (SMAC) Homestead Foods Limited is a large processor and distributor of packaged foods. Its product lines include soups, vegetables, potatoes, fruits, pasta, TV dinners, juices, and bread. In addition, it has three restaurant chains serving pizza, fish, and hamburgers.

Homestead originally started with canned soups 70 years ago. Management is proud of its past traditions. Success is attributed to the firm's good products and satisfied customers. Accordingly, the key success factors identified and upheld at Homestead are high product quality and customer research. This operating philosophy has been dominant in shaping the organization.

There is a high degree of decentralized decision making at the operating-division level. The operating divisions (called product group divisions) are responsible for production and marketing of their products and are considered to be profit centres. Performance assessment is based on profitability plus product quality and customer satisfaction. There are eight product group divisions: soups, vegetables and potatoes, fruit, pasta, TV dinners, juices, bread, and restaurants. The head office is small and its activities are limited to preparation of financial statements, marketing research, treasury and legal activities, performance monitoring, and the approval of plans and budgets. The costs of these activities are not charged to operating divisions; they are controlled through a master budget and are reported only in the overall company statements.

Management has become concerned about the increasing costs of the market research department at the head office. Three main types of work are performed by this department: gathering regular market data, testing new product markets, and handling special research requests made by the operating divisions. Because of the emphasis that management has put on customer satisfaction as a key success factor, a wide range of standard data is produced by the market research department. Management originally felt that regularly producing market research data, which are gathered in a carefully planned and controlled manner, and making them available to the divisions would result in cost efficiencies. However, the divisions frequently make special requests for data not routinely gathered.

The market research department is considered to be highly successful and the operating divisions are happy with the service provided. The professional members of the market research department are well respected by their colleagues, and a number of them have taken part-time teaching assignments at universities and have had numerous articles and studies published in reputable journals.

Until now, there has been no attempt to measure the efficiency and effectiveness of the market research department. The president suspects that costs of Homestead's market research are up to double the amount incurred by similar firms for their in-house market research or, alternatively, for contracting with professional market research firms. He wonders whether the benefits of Homestead's market research activities exceed their costs and has asked you, as assistant controller, to analyze Homestead's situation and to give recommendations.

Required: | Respond to the president's request.

C13-3 **MANAGEMENT CONTROL—SERVICE SECTOR.** (ICAO) Lynda Carson is the recently appointed general manager of Crichton General Assurance Corporation (CGAC). She has been appointed to help the company regain profitability after several years of near–break even operations.

CGAC is a general casualty insurance company, with its primary business in automobile, homeowner, and personal property insurance. The casualty insurance industry has been under severe profit pressure in recent years due to increasing claims. Political pressure has kept the industry from passing on the full cost of high damage settlements as quickly or completely as the industry would like. In addition, CGAC is a relatively small company in an industry dominated by several larger companies, some of which are controlled by major Canadian financial conglomerates. Its relatively minor position makes it more difficult to maintain a wide agent base and to advertise effectively. Therefore, there is much pressure on Lynda to make the internal operations of the company more efficient.

One of the many areas that Lynda has been exploring to increase efficiency is that of budgeting. In the past, the company has attempted to plan and control operations by means of a fixed master budget for the company as a whole. Most of the administrative responsibility centres are cost centres, and departmental managers have been evaluated on the basis of variance from budget, on a line-by-line basis.

Lynda is considering using other means and bases of budgeting, including, but not restricted to, flexible budgets, performance budgets, and zero-based budgeting. In particular, she would like to have budgets that help her to better evaluate departmental efficiency. She has engaged you as a consultant to advise her on what the most appropriate budgeting approach(es) may be, and has asked that you formulate your recommendations on the basis of the underwriting department.

The underwriting department is responsible for compiling the new initial files and drawing up the insurance contracts for new clients, including assessing the premium. It also maintains the client base by monitoring client performance and drawing up renewal policies and premiums based on the client's performance. The premiums (per $1,000 of coverage) are assessed on the basis of various factors for each client, depending on the nature of the policy. For example, fire insurance premiums on buildings are determined by factors such as type of construction, use of premises, contents of premises, quality of fire protection and detection, distance from hydrants, accessibility by firefighting equipment, and so forth. It is the responsibility of the underwriting department to assess experience factors and to recommend to the CGAC Executive Committee increases and decreases in premiums at least once every six months. The underwriting department does not have responsibility for sales; the sales department is a separate revenue centre.

The direct costs of the underwriting department are largely staff costs. There are several components or sections within the department. One such section is the investigative section, which assesses new insurance applications and recommends approval or rejection of coverage. Response time is very important both for competitive reasons and because the company is liable for coverage as soon as the insurance agent accepts the application. When surges in the volume of new policies occur, some of the policy investigation is contracted out to independent investigators in order to avoid delays.

Another section is the processing section. This group does the actual policy preparation, including the building and maintenance of the customer's computer file and the preparation of premium notices and renewals. Except for the initial inputting of the application information and sending the application to the investigation section, time constraints are not severe. In busy periods, the lag in the paper work and computer file maintenance will get larger, but without significant adverse consequences.

A third section of the underwriting department is the actuarial staff. The actuaries and their support staff are responsible for the monitoring and analysis of underwriting and claims experience in order to recommend new premium levels. Since the analysis underlying their recommendations is computerized, the level of activity in this section is not responsive to changes in underwriting volume.

The underwriting department makes extensive use of CGAC computer facilities in all aspects of its work. Many staff members work directly at computer terminals that can also function as stand-alone work stations for routine tasks such as letter-writing. The mainframe computer itself is operated and maintained by the data processing department, which is part of general administration and not a part of the underwriting department. Batch processing tasks such as premium reminder and renewal notices are performed by the data processing department and then routed through printers located in the underwriting department. In the past, there has been no charge made to user departments for the services of the data processing department.

Required:
Write a report to Lynda Carson in which you discuss the specific budget approach(es) that seems to be the most appropriate for the underwriting department and explain why it is appropriate. Also, briefly indicate the general circumstances in which the recommended approach(es) may not be appropriate for other departments in the company.

C13-4 MANAGEMENT CONTROL—GOVERNMENT SECTOR. (SMAC) The discovery of vast petroleum reserves in the country of Atlantis has led to massive expenditures on government services. Several years ago, the Minister of Communications had automated the Atlantis post office, but despite the latest equipment, the delivery of mail remained slow and unpredictable. Considerable pressure to improve the mail system was exerted on the Atlantis government by business leaders claiming that it was essential for continued economic growth. A Canadian management consulting firm was commissioned by the Atlantis Minister of Communications to recommend improvements in the mail service. Alex Peach, CMA, was sent to Atlantis to analyze the situation.

In his initial self-familiarization of Atlantis, Alex noted many similarities to Canada: size of population, large cities separated by long distances, and remote regions with poor communication systems and small populations. In recent years, since the automation of the post office, deliveries that had previously taken several weeks were now taking several days. Alex reviewed the seven organizational departments and decided to do a preliminary investigation of each.

The general manager of the post office told Alex that she wondered whether it would be feasible to use a profit-based management control system. Currently, the operating departments are organized as cost centres, except the marketing department, which is a revenue centre. The general manager's office prepares annual departmental budgets by applying a growth factor to the previous year's budgets.

Alex's investigation of the seven departments revealed the following information.

1. Transportation Department: The department manager is responsible for the domestic and international movement of bulk mail. He is evaluated on a two-part budget: fixed costs and variable operating costs. The variable portion is based on total weight moved times an average cost factor.

   The transportation manager complains that his equipment is old and always breaking down. His requests for repairs to the maintenance department are always turned down with the explanation that the equipment needs to be replaced. However, the general manager refuses equipment replacement requests from the transportation department because of a long-standing clash of personalities between the two managers.

   Another complaint of the transportation department manager is that the sorting department increases transportation costs by sorting at the source post office and shipping small bags of mail to many destinations. He also resents political interference in the awarding of international mail contracts to airlines, usually favouring Atlantis Airlines at higher rates.

2. Sorting Department: In all postal stations, sorting is performed using modern equipment. Incoming mail is first sorted into three categories: parcels, commercial, and first class. Then, the mail is sorted according to final destination. The shift supervisors tend to select commercial mail first since it includes junk mail, which is easily and quickly sorted.

The sorting department manager is evaluated on a flexible budget based on the actual number of pieces sorted in the year.

The sorting department manager is very dissatisfied with the organization system. Since the sorters are unionized, he feels that he can do very little to improve their productivity. Furthermore, the marketing department encourages high-volume junk mail, which delays the sorting of first-class mail and increases the frequency of equipment breakdowns.

3. Delivery Department: The department budget is composed of a fixed amount plus a variable cost based on the number of pieces delivered. The manager can best meet the budget in commercial areas, where whole bags are delivered to large clients. In new suburban areas, he favours central customer mail boxes, but customers and the union demand home delivery.

4. Maintenance Department: In an attempt to keep maintenance costs down, the department is on a fixed budget. There is a tendency by the department manager to recommend replacement of post office equipment rather than incurring the expense of repairing equipment, since the replacement costs are the responsibility of the administration department.

5. Marketing Department: The department is evaluated as a revenue centre, with a budget based on annual sales increases over the prior year. The manager confided that she encourages expansion in commercial junk mail and home first-class letters. The commercial market is one where promotion has produced tangible results and the home market is growing rapidly with the suburban population explosion.

6. Administration Department: The general manager is convinced that the only practical way to control administration expenses is by fixed budgets. The department manager complains that his budget is typically exceeded because, with the exception of requests from the transportation department, the general manager seldom refuses requests for capital expenditures.

7. Personnel Department: This department is also on a fixed budget that it is not allowed to exceed. The manager confided that he often had to lay off some of his own staff for a month or two at the end of each year in order to stay within the budget. Moreover, selection criteria for post office personnel are poorly defined and the manager is often pressured to hire friends and relatives of politicians.

Required: | Analyze the management control system of the Atlantis post office. Recommend, with reasons, possible improvements and discuss anticipated behavioural consequences.

C13-5 **NON-FINANCIAL PERFORMANCE MEASURES.** (McCutcheon) Current River is a medium-sized city that has experienced rapid growth in the last two decades. For several of those years the city had the highest growth rate in the country. Much of the growth has occurred in the suburbs that now have full commercial facilities that are at least equal to those in the core area. Meanwhile, the core area has stagnated with many vacant stores and an increase in the numbers of businesses such as tattoo parlours, video arcades, and second-hand stores. The core area has numerous bars and other facilities that are attractive to younger people and those of lower socioeconomic profiles. The Downtown Business Association and its members have made numerous requests that the police "clean up downtown" as they believe that customers are afraid to venture downtown. The downtown area and its problems have been the subject of many articles in the local paper. The City Council seems to be strongly supportive of the Downtown Business Association. It is noteworthy that the Mayor is an influential member of the Police Services Board.

In response to these pressures, the Police Services Board two years ago approved an experimental plan for extra policing in the core. Five officers were reassigned on a permanent basis from normal duties to the area. No particular instructions were given by the Board but there seemed to be an expectation that use would be made of foot and perhaps bicycle patrols. The Board now wishes to review the success of this project. Your role is to determine how to measure the performance of this experiment.

Required: Prepare a report to the Police Services Board with your recommendations of assessing the performance of this project.

C13-6 COMPARING THE PERFORMANCE OF TWO PLANTS. On your first day as assistant to the president of Harold Systems, Inc. (HSI), your in-box contains the following memo:

- To: Assistant to the President
- From: The President
- Subject: Mickey Mouse Watch Situation
- This note is to bring you up to date on one of our acquisition problem areas. Market research detected the current nostalgia wave almost a year ago and concluded that HSI should acquire a position in this market. Research data showed that Mickey Mouse Watches could become profitable ($5 contribution margin on $12 sales price) at a volume of 40,000 units per plant if they became popular again. Consequently, we picked up closed-down facilities on each coast, staffed them, and asked them to keep us posted on operations.
- Friday I got preliminary information from accounting that is unclear. I want you to find out why their costs of goods sold are far apart and how we should have them report in the future to avoid confusion. This is particularly important in the Mickey Mouse case, as market projections look bad and we may have to close one plant. I guess we'll close the West Coast plant unless you can show otherwise.

Preliminary Accounting Report

	EAST	WEST
Sales	$480,000	$480,000
Cost of goods sold	280,000	450,000
Gross margin	$200,000	$ 30,000
Administration costs (fixed)	30,000	30,000
Net income	$170,000	$ 0
Production	80,000 units	40,000 units
Variances (included in cost of goods sold)	$170,000 favourable	$ 85,000 unfavourable

Required: As the assistant to the president, what is your response to the president's memo?

C13-7 **ABSORPTION COSTING AND INCENTIVE TO PRODUCE.** Omar Efenti is manager of the Pacific Division of Zenna Inc. His division makes a single product that is sold to industrial customers. Demand is seasonable but is readily predictable. The division's budget for 2006 called for production and sales of 120,000 units, with production of 10,000 units each month and sales varying between 8,000 and 13,000 units a month. The division's budget for 2006 had an operating income of $780,000:

Sales (120,000 × $50)	$6,000,000
Cost of goods sold (120,000 × $40)	4,800,000
Gross margin	$1,200,000
Selling and administrative expenses (all fixed)	420,000
Operating income	$ 780,000

By the end of November, sales lagged projections, with only 105,000 units sold. Sales of 9,000 units were originally budgeted and are still expected in December. Production had remained stable at 10,000 units per month, and the cost of production had been exactly as budgeted:

Direct materials, 110,000 × $9	$ 990,000
Direct labour, 110,000 × $10	1,100,000
Variable overhead, 110 × $8	880,000
Fixed overhead	1,430,000
Total production cost	$4,400,000

The division's operating income for the first 11 months of 2006 was

Sales (105,000 × $50)	$5,250,000
Cost of goods sold (105,000 × $40)	4,200,000
Gross margin	$1,050,000
Selling and administrative expenses (all fixed)	385,000
Operating income	$ 665,000

Omar Efenti receives an annual bonus only if his division's operating income exceeds the budget. He sees no way to increase sales beyond 9,000 units in December.

Required:

1. From the budgeted and actual income statements shown, determine whether Zenna used variable or absorption costing.
2. Suppose Zenna uses a standard absorption-costing system. (a) Compute the 2006 operating income if 10,000 units are produced and 9,000 units are sold in December. (b) How could Efenti achieve his budgeted operating income for 2006?
3. Suppose Zenna uses a standard variable-costing system. (a) Compute the 2006 operating income if 10,000 units are produced and 9,000 units are sold in December. (b) How could Efenti achieve his budgeted operating income for 2006?
4. Which system motivates Efenti to make the decision that is in the best interests of Zenna? Explain.

EXCEL APPLICATION EXERCISE

E13-1 WAGES FOR NEW SALARY-PLUS-BONUS PLAN

Goal: Create an Excel spreadsheet to calculate the impact on employee wages of a new salary-plus-bonus plan established to motivate salesclerks to increase sales. Use the results to answer questions about your findings.

Scenario: You are the manager of a department store in Tokyo. As the department store manager, you must determine if the new plan is the best way to motivate salesclerks and meet the objective of increasing sales. The background data for the compensation plan appear in P13-5 on pages 675–676. Use only data for Salesclerk A and Salesclerk B to prepare your spreadsheet.

When you have completed your spreadsheet, answer the following questions:

1. Which salesclerk has the highest average total salary over the four-month period?

2. What part of the compensation plan had the most impact on the salesclerks' salaries? The least impact?

3. Do you see any problems with this compensation plan? Explain.

Step by Step:

1. Open a new Excel spreadsheet.

2. In column A, create a bold-faced heading that contains the following:
   Row 1: Chapter 13 Decision Guideline
   Row 2: Tokyo Department Store
   Row 3: Salary-Plus-Bonus Plan Analysis
   Row 4: Today's Date

3. Merge and centre the four heading rows across columns A through H.

4. In column A, create the following row headings:
   Row 7: Salesclerk A
   Row 8: Month
   Row 9: January
   Row 10: February
   Row 11: March
   Row 12: April
   Skip 3 rows
   Row 16: Salesclerk B
   Row 17: Month
   Row 18: January
   Row 19: February
   Row 20: March
   Row 21: April

5. Change the format of salesclerk names (Rows 7, 16) to bold-faced, underlined headings.

6. Change the format of Month (Rows 8, 17) to bold-faced headings.

7. In Rows 8 and 17, create the following bold-faced, right-justified column headings:
   Column B: Quota
   Column C: Sales
   Column D: Over Quota
   Column E: Base Salary
   Column F: Quota Bonus
   Column G: Commission
   Column H: Total Salary

   Note: Adjust column widths as necessary.

8. In column G, create the following right-justified cell headings:
   Row 14: Average:
   Row 23: Average:

9. Use the scenario data to fill in Quota, Sales, and Base Salary amounts from January to April for each salesclerk.

10. Use the appropriate IF statements to calculate Over Quota and Quota Bonus amounts when the clerks' sales met or exceeded their respective quotas (negative commissions should not be calculated).
    = IF(*formula*>0,*formula*,0)
    For Over Quota only.
    = IF(*formula*<0,0,68000)   OR   = IF(*formula*>=0,68000,0)
    For Quota Bonus only.

    Hint: Go to the Help text and type "copy formulas" in the search area to obtain instructions for copying formulas from one cell to another. If done correctly, you should have to type in each of the formulas only once.

11. Use appropriate formulas to calculate commission and total salary amounts for each month, as well as an average amount for the January to April period for each salesclerk.

12. Format all amounts as
    Number tab:

Category:	Currency
Decimal places:	0
Symbol:	None
Negative numbers:	Black with parentheses

13. To format specific amounts to display with a yen symbol do the following:
    a. In an empty cell, hold down the Alt key and enter "0165" from the numeric keypad. When you stop holding the Alt key down, a yen sign will be displayed.

    Note: If your keyboard does not have a numeric keypad, use the shift and NumLk keys to activate the embedded numeric keypad. Then follow the instructions in part a. Use the shift and NumLk keys to turn the feature off.

    b. Highlight the yen character you have just created, select Edit, Cut. This will paste the yen sign to the clipboard. To see the clipboard, select View, Toolbars, Clipboard.

c. Select the average amount for salesclerk A and open the Format, Cells . . . dialog box.

d. Select the custom category on the number tab. Scroll down toward the bottom of the type list and highlight the type shown below.

        Type: _($*#,##0_);_($*(#,##0);_($*"-"_);_(@_)

Change the data between the quotation marks in the third grouping from "-" to "0".

Paste the yen sign over EACH occurrence of the dollar sign.

Hint: Highlight the $ sign; press Ctrl and V. This will paste the yen sign from the clipboard over the $ sign that has been highlighted in the Type field.

e. Click the OK button.

f. Utilize the custom format, which should now be at the bottom of the type list, to print the yen sign for all January amounts for both clerks and the average amount for Salesclerk B.

14. Save your work to disk, and print a copy for your files.

Note: Print your spreadsheet using landscape in order to ensure that all columns appear on one page.

COLLABORATIVE LEARNING EXERCISE

CL13-1 GOALS, OBJECTIVES, AND PERFORMANCE MEASURES There is increasing pressure on colleges and universities to develop measures of accountability. The objective is to specify goals and objectives and to develop measures to assess the achievement of those goals and objectives.

Form groups of four to six students to be consulting teams to the accounting department at your college or university. (If you are not using this book as part of a course in an accounting department, select any department at a local college or university.) Based on your collective knowledge of the department, its mission, and its activities, formulate a statement of goals for the department. From that statement, develop several specific objectives, each of which can be measured. Then develop one or more measures of performance for each objective.

An optional second step in this exercise is to meet with a faculty member from the department, and ask him or her to critique your objectives and measures. To the department member, do the objectives make sense? Are the proposed measures feasible, and will they correctly measure attainment of the objectives? Will they provide proper incentives to the faculty? If the department has created objectives and performance measures, compare them to those your group developed.

Decentralized Organizations, Transfer Pricing, and Measures of Profitability

In 30 years, Nike has become the largest sports and fitness company in the world. With over $10 billion in revenues, Nike footwear accounts for more than half of Nike's sales; apparel sales now account for about one-third. Endorsements (promotional contracts with famous sports teams [Italian National Soccer Team] and individuals [golf star Tiger Woods]) give another perspective on the company's global presence. In fact, watch almost any sports event on television and you are likely to see the Nike "swoosh" logo.

A major reason that Nike has been successful throughout the world is that it gives much authority to managers in each country or region. To manage effectively in this decentralized environment, Nike needs information to help coordinate and evaluate widely dispersed operations. A well-designed management control system is essential to global companies such as Nike. Achieving the appropriate balance between autonomy at the local level and efficiency at the corporate level is a challenge when designing Nike's management control system.

This chapter focuses on the role of management control systems in decentralized organizations. After providing an overview of decentralization, the chapter discusses how performance measures can be used to motivate managers in a decentralized company. Measures used to assess the profitability of decentralized units are introduced and compared. Finally, we address transfer pricing, the special problems created when one segment of an organization charges another for providing goods or services.

CENTRALIZATION VERSUS DECENTRALIZATION

OBJECTIVE 1

Define decentralization and identify its expected benefits and costs.

Iberia
www.iberia.com

Air France
www.airfrance.com

Aetna
www.aetna.com

AXA Equitable
www.axa-equitable.com

Decentralization. The delegation of freedom to make decisions. The lower in the organization that this freedom exists, the greater the decentralization.

At any given time, some firms will see advantages in decentralization and some in centralization. Both centralization and decentralization have their advantages. Sometimes it seems that organizations and industries undergo cycles of decentralization followed by centralization and vice versa. Consider the international airline industry. Most airlines in the 1990s, such as Iberia Airlines and Air France, were decentralizing. At the same time Sabena, formerly Belgium's state-owned airline, was reorganizing to *reverse* its trend toward decentralization. In the insurance industry, Aetna was decentralizing at the same time Equitable was centralizing. Even the Department of National Defence, a very centralized organization, has started some decentralization in recent years.

As organizations grow and undertake more diverse and complex activities, many elect to delegate decision-making authority to managers throughout the organization. This delegation of the freedom to make decisions is called **decentralization**. The lower in the organization that this freedom exists, the greater the decentralization. Decentralization is a matter of degree along a continuum:

Costs and Benefits

Some degree of decentralization may benefit most organizations. First, lower-level managers have the best information concerning local conditions and therefore may be able to make better decisions than their superiors. Second, managers acquire decision-making ability and other management skills that help them move upward in the organization, assuring continuity of leadership. Decentralization assists in "grooming" future executives. In addition, managers enjoy higher status from being independent and thus are better motivated.

Of course, decentralization has its costs. Managers may make decisions that are not in the organization's best interests, either because they act to improve their own segment's performance at the expense of the organization's or because they are not aware of relevant facts from other segments. Managers in decentralized organizations also tend to duplicate services that might be less expensive if centralized (accounting, advertising, and personnel are examples). Furthermore, under decentralization, costs of accumulating and processing information frequently rise because responsibility accounting reports are needed for top management to learn about and evaluate decentralized units and their managers. Finally, managers in decentralized units may waste time negotiating with other units about the goods or services one unit provides to the other.

Decentralization is more popular in profit-seeking organizations (where outputs and inputs can be measured) than in not-for-profit organizations. Managers can be given freedom when their results are measurable so that they can be held accountable for them. Poor decisions in a profit-seeking firm become apparent from the inadequate profit generated. Most not-for-profit organizations lack such a reliable performance indicator, so granting managerial freedom is more risky.

Middle Ground

Philosophies of decentralization differ considerably. Cost-benefit considerations usually require that some management decisions be highly decentralized and others centralized. To illustrate, much of the controller's problem-solving and attention-directing function may be concentrated at the lower levels, whereas income tax planning and mass scorekeeping such as payroll and accounting may be highly centralized.

Decentralization is most successful when an organization's segments are relatively independent of one another—that is, the decisions of one manager will not affect the fortunes of another manager. If segments do a lot of internal buying or selling, buying from the same outside suppliers, or selling to the same outside markets, they are candidates for heavier centralization.

In Chapter 13 we stressed that cost-benefit tests, goal congruence, and managerial effort must all be considered when designing a control system. If management has decided in favour of heavy decentralization, **segment autonomy**, or the delegation of decision-making power to managers of segments of an organization, is also crucial. For decentralization to work, however, this autonomy must be real, not just lip-service. In most circumstances, top managers must be willing to abide by decisions made by segment managers.

Segment Autonomy. The delegation of decision-making power to segment managers.

Design of a management control system should consider two separate dimensions of control, (1) the responsibilities of managers and (2) the amount of autonomy they have. Some managers confuse these two dimensions, assuming that a profit centre manager must have decentralized decision-making authority, and a cost centre manager less autonomy. This need not be the case. Some profit centre managers possess vast freedom to make decisions concerning labour contracts, supplier choices, equipment purchases, personnel decisions, and so on. In contrast, other profit centre managers may need top-management approval for almost all the decisions just mentioned. Indeed, cost centres may be more heavily decentralized than profit centres if cost centre managers have more freedom to make decisions.

The fundamental question in deciding between using a cost centre or a profit centre for a given segment is not whether heavy decentralization exists. Instead, the fundamental question is, Will a profit centre better solve the problems of goal congruence and management effort than a cost centre? In other words, does one predict that a profit centre will induce managers to make a better collective set of decisions from the viewpoint of the organization as a whole?

All control systems are imperfect. The choice among systems should be based on which one will bring more of the actions top management seeks. For example, a plant may seem to be a "natural" cost centre because the plant manager has no influence over decisions concerning the marketing of its products. Nevertheless, some companies evaluate a plant manager by the plant's profitability. Why? Because they believe this broader evaluation base will positively affect the plant manager's behaviour. Instead of being concerned solely with running an efficient cost centre, the plant manager now "naturally" considers quality control more carefully and reacts to customers' special requests more sympathetically. A profit centre may thus obtain the desired plant-manager behaviour better than a cost centre does. From the viewpoint of top management, plant managers often have more influence on sales than is apparent at first glance. This is an example of how systems may evolve from cost centres to profit centres and of the importance of predicting behavioural effects when an accounting control system is designed.

PERFORMANCE MEASURES AND MANAGEMENT CONTROL

This section looks at how performance measures affect managers' incentives. A major factor in designing decentralized management control systems is how the system's performance measures affect managers' incentives. When a company gives managers decision-making autonomy, it wants to use this autonomy to meet the company's objectives, not to pursue other goals. For example, when Nike executives signed Tiger Woods to an endorsement contract, they aimed to create additional profits, not to provide Nike executives access to the inner circles of golf.

Motivation, Performance, Rewards

OBJECTIVE 2

Explain how linking rewards to responsibility centre results affects incentives and risk.

Incentives. Those formal and informal performance-based rewards that enhance employee effort toward organizational goals.

Exhibit 14-1 shows the criteria and choices faced by top management when designing a management control system. Using the criterion of cost-benefit and the motivational criteria of goal congruence and managerial effort, top management chooses responsibility centres (e.g., cost centre versus profit centre), performance measures, and rewards. As used in this context, **incentives** are defined as those informal and formal performance measures and rewards that enhance goal congruence and managerial effort. For example, how a company measures profit and attributes it to one or another division affects each manager's rewards.

Numerous performance measurement choices have been described in this book. Examples include whether to use tight or loose standards, whether to measure divisional performance by contribution margins or operating incomes, and whether to use both financial and non-financial measures of performance.

Research about rewards has generated a basic principle that is simple and important: managers tend to focus their efforts in areas where performance is measured and where their performance affects rewards. Research also shows that the more objective the measures of performance, the more likely the manager will provide effort. Thus, accounting measures, which provide relatively objective evaluations of performance, are important. Moreover, if individuals believe that there is no connection between their behaviour and their measure of performance, they will not see how to alter their performance to affect their rewards.

The choice of rewards clearly belongs with an overall system of management control. Rewards may be both monetary and nonmonetary. Examples include pay raises, bonuses, promotion, praise, self-satisfaction, elaborate offices, and private dining rooms. However, the design of a reward system is mainly the concern of top managers, who frequently get advice from many sources besides accountants.

EXHIBIT 14-1

Criteria and Choices Faced by Top Management when Designing a Management Control System

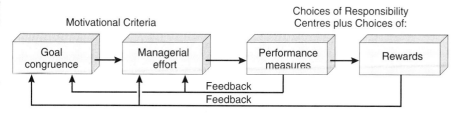

Agency Theory, Performance, Rewards, and Risk

Linking rewards to performance is desirable. But often a manager's performance cannot be measured directly. For example, responsibility centre results may be measured easily, but a manager's effect on those results (that is, managerial performance) may not. Ideally, rewards should be based on managerial performance, but in practice the rewards usually depend on the financial results in the manager's responsibility centre. Managerial performance and responsibility centre results are certainly related, but factors beyond a manager's control also affect results. The greater the influence of noncontrollable factors on responsibility centre results, the more problems there are in using the results to represent a manager's performance.

Economists describe the formal choices of performance measures and rewards as **agency theory**. For top management to hire a manager, both need to agree to an employment contract that includes specification of a performance measure and how it will affect rewards.[1] For example, a manager might receive a bonus of 15 percent of her salary if her responsibility centre achieves its budgeted profit. According to agency theory, employment contracts will trade off three factors:

1. *Incentive.* The more a manager's reward depends on a performance measure, the more incentive the manager has to take actions that maximize that measure. Top management should define the performance measure to promote *goal congruence* and base enough reward on it to achieve *managerial effort.*

2. *Risk.* The greater the influence of uncontrollable factors on a manager's reward, the more risk the manager bears. People generally avoid risk, so managers must be paid more if they are expected to bear more risk. Creating incentive by linking rewards to responsibility centre results, which is generally desirable, has the undesirable effect of imposing risk on managers.

3. *Cost of measuring performance.* The incentive versus risk tradeoff is not necessary if a manager's performance is perfectly measured. Why? Because then a manager could be paid a fixed amount if he or she performs as expected and nothing if not. Whether to perform or not is completely controllable by the manager and observation of the level of performance is all that is necessary to determine the compensation earned. But directly measuring a manager's performance is usually expensive and sometimes infeasible. Responsibility centre results are more readily available. The cost-benefit criterion usually indicates that perfect measurement of a manager's performance is not worth its cost.

Consider a concert promoter hired by a group of investors to promote and administer an outdoor rock performance. If the investors cannot directly measure the promoter's effort and judgment, they would probably pay a bonus that depended on the economic success of the concert. The bonus would motivate the promoter to put his effort toward generating a profit. On the other hand, it creates risk. Factors such as bad weather could also affect the concert's economic success. The promoter might do an outstanding job and still not receive a bonus. Suppose the investors offer a contract with part guaranteed pay and part bonus. A larger bonus portion compared with the guaranteed portion creates more incentive, but it also means a larger expected total payment to compensate the promoter for the added risk. No matter how an organization links rewards to performance measures, one pervasive performance measure is profitability. We next consider how various measures of profitability affect managers' incentives.

---

[1] Often performance measures and rewards are implicit. For example, promotion is a reward, but usually the requirements for promotion are not explicit.

Benefits and Costs of Decentralization

Many companies believe that decentralization is important to their success, including Pepsico, DuPont, Procter & Gamble, Johnson & Johnson, and Magna International. Johnson & Johnson is the maker of such products as Tylenol, Band-Aids, and Johnson's Baby Powder. Its 2004 sales totalled $47.3 billion. It has 200 independent business units operating in 57 countries and employing nearly 110,000 people. Management at Johnson & Johnson believes the company's primary competitive advantage is the fact that it empowers each of its 200 business units to operate independently.

Johnson & Johnson
www.jnj.com

Magna International
www.magnaint.com

Under the company's management structure, each of its operating companies is run autonomously. One benefit is that decisions are made by executives who are closer to the marketplace. One downfall is the expense, because many of the operating companies duplicate many overhead costs. Although ultimately accountable to executives at Johnson & Johnson headquarters in New Brunswick, New Jersey, some segment presidents see their bosses as few as four times a year. Bill Weldon, Johnson & Johnson CEO, extols the virtues of decentralization: "The magic around Johnson & Johnson is decentralization." He believes that the structure has been essential to its strategy of developing executives from within because young managers can be given responsibility for running whole companies. "This allows people to be entrepreneurial," he said, "and to grow."

Business Week summarized Weldon's approach as follows: "[Johnson & Johnson's] success has hinged on its unique culture and structure. . . . Each of its far-flung units operates pretty much as an independent enterprise. Businesses set their own strategies; they have their own finance and human resources departments, for example. While this degree of decentralization makes for relatively high overhead costs, no chief executive, Weldon included, has thought that too high a price to pay."

Markham, Ontario–based Magna International is a diversified manufacturer of automotive systems and components. It is one of the largest manufacturers of its type in the world, with annual sales of $22 billion. As of 2005, Magna employed approximately 82,000 people worldwide (including 21,600 people in Canada) at 223 manufacturing divisions and 56 product development and engineering centres throughout North and South America, Mexico, Europe, and Asia. Operations are decentralized throughout the organization, and the company is growing from its strategy of building small factories to encourage close working relationships between managers and employees. Management at Magna believes that decentralization may also be used to encourage an entrepreneurial spirit throughout the organization. At Magna, all key stakeholders—which Magna considers to be employees, management, investors, and society—share a predetermined portion of the annual profits, as guaranteed by the Corporate Constitution that was initially adopted in 1984. For example, 2 percent of pre-tax corporate profits are dedicated to social objectives, while employees share in 10 percent of pre-tax profits.

Decentralization has its benefits and costs. Some companies have vacillated between decentralization and centralization, sometimes believing that the benefits of centralizing common activities are greater than the benefits of decentralization. In contrast, both Johnson & Johnson and Magna International have continued policies of decentralization in both good and bad times.

Sources: Adapted from the 2004 annual reports of Johnson & Johnson and Magna International; M. Petersen, "From the Ranks, Unassumingly," *The New York Times*, February 4, 2002; A. Barrett, "Staying on Top," *Business Week*, May 5, 2003. Magna has recently been viewed as reconsidering some aspects of its decentralization strategy, due to a need to present a "single face" to major customers—see Dale Buss, "Out of the Frying Pan," *The Chief Executive*, May 2005, accessible via www.chiefexecutive.net.

MEASURES OF PROFITABILITY

Return on Investment (ROI)

Return on Investment (ROI). A measure of income or profit divided by the investment required to obtain that income or profit.

A favourite objective of top management is to maximize profitability. Segment managers are often evaluated based on their segment's profitability. The trouble is that profitability does not mean the same thing to all people. Is it net income? Income before taxes? Net income percentage based on revenue? Is it an absolute amount? A percentage? In this section we consider the strengths and weaknesses of several commonly used measures.

Too often, managers stress net income or income percentages without tying the measure into the investment associated with generating the income. To say that Project A has an income of $200,000 and Project B has an income of $150,000 is an insufficient statement about profitability. A better test of profitability is the rate of **return on investment (ROI)**—income or profit divided by the investment required to obtain that income or profit. Given the same risks, for any given amount of resources required, the investor wants the maximum income. If Project A requires an investment of $500,000, while Project B requires only $150,000, all other things being equal, where would you put your money?

$$ROI = \frac{income}{investment}$$

$$ROI\ Project\ A = \frac{\$200,000}{\$500,000} = 40\%$$

$$ROI\ Project\ B = \frac{\$150,000}{\$150,000} = 100\%$$

In all ROI calculations we should measure "investment" as an average for the period under review. Since income is generated over a period of time, investment should similarly measure the average investment over the same period. This average may be simply the average of the beginning and the ending investment balances, or the weighted average of investments over the period.

Return on Sales. Income divided by revenue.

Capital Turnover. Revenue divided by invested capital.

ROI is a useful basis for comparisons. It can be compared with rates inside and outside the organization and with opportunities in other projects and industries. It is affected by two major ingredients, **return on sales**—income divided by revenue—and **capital turnover**—revenue divided by invested capital.

$$\begin{aligned}
ROI &= \frac{income}{invested\ capital} \\
&= \frac{income}{revenue} \times \frac{revenue}{invested\ capital} \\
&= income\ percentage\ of\ revenue \times capital\ turnover \\
&= return\ on\ sales \times capital\ turnover
\end{aligned}$$

An improvement in either without changing the other will improve the rate of return on invested capital.

Consider an example of these relationships:

	Rate of Return on Invested Capital	=	Income / Revenue	×	Revenue / Invested Capital
Present outlook	20%	=	$\frac{16}{100}$	×	$\frac{100}{80}$
Alternatives:					
1. Increase return on sales by reducing expenses	25%	=	$\frac{20}{100}$	×	$\frac{100}{80}$
2. Increase turnover by decreasing investment in inventories	25%	=	$\frac{16}{100}$	×	$\frac{100}{64}$

Alternative 1 is a popular way to improve performance. Alert managers try to decrease expenses without reducing sales or to boost sales without increasing related expenses. Alternative 2 is less obvious, but it may be a quicker way to improve performance. Increasing the turnover of invested capital means generating higher revenue for each dollar invested in such assets as cash, receivables, inventories, or equipment, or alternatively, using fewer assets for each dollar of revenue generated.

There is an optimal level of investment in these assets. Having too much is wasteful, causing capital turnover to fall without an offsetting increase in return on sales. However, having too little investment may hurt credit standing and the ability to compete for sales. Also, it may mean passing up revenues that would generate a return on sales that more than offsets the decrease in capital turnover. Increasing capital turnover is one of the advantages of implementing the just-in-time philosophy. JIT purchasing and production systems can cause dramatic improvements on ROI because of capital turnover gains.

Residual Income (RI) and Economic Value Added (EVA)

Residual Income. Net income less capital charge.

Capital Charge. Company's cost of capital × amount of investment.

Cost of Capital. What a firm must pay to acquire more capital, whether or not it actually has to acquire more capital to take on a project.

Most managers agree that measuring return in relation to investment provides the ultimate test of profitability. ROI is one such comparison. However, some companies favour emphasizing an absolute amount of income rather than a percentage rate of return. They use **residual income (RI)**, defined as net income less "imputed" interest or capital charge. **Capital charge** refers to the **cost of capital**—what the firm must pay to acquire more capital—whether or not it actually has to acquire more capital to take on this project. In short, RI tells you how much your company's operating income exceeds what it is paying for capital. For example, suppose a division's net income was $900,000, the average invested capital in the division for the year was $10 million, and the corporate headquarters assessed an imputed interest charge of 8 percent:

Divisional net income after taxes	$900,000
Minus imputed interest on average invested capital (0.08 × $10,000,000)	800,000
Equals residual income	$100,000

There are several different ways to calculate residual income depending on how we choose to define the terms used. For example, some companies define

Economic Value Added (EVA). After-tax operating income minus the weighted-average cost of capital times the sum of the long-term liabilities and shareholders' equity.

"average invested capital" as funds provided by long-term creditors and share-holders (that is, long-term liabilities plus shareholders' equity). This variant of residual income is called economic value added (EVA), a term coined and mar-keted by Stern Stewart and Co. **Economic value added (EVA)** equals after-tax operating income minus the weighted-average cost of capital multiplied by the sum of long-term liabilities and shareholders' equity.

$$\begin{pmatrix} \text{Economic value} \\ \text{added (EVA)} \end{pmatrix} = \begin{pmatrix} \text{After-tax operating} \\ \text{income} \end{pmatrix} - \left[\begin{array}{c} \text{Weighted-average} \\ \text{cost of capital} \end{array} \times \begin{pmatrix} \text{Long-term} \\ \text{liabilities} \end{array} + \begin{array}{c} \text{Shareholders'} \\ \text{equity} \end{pmatrix} \right]$$

For example: A division has assets of $1 million, current liabilities of $200,000 and net operating income of $250,000. The weighted average cost of capital is 10 percent. What are the division's ROI and EVA?

ROI = $250,000 ÷ $1,000,000 = 25%
ROI alternatively = $250,000 ÷ 800,000 = 31.25%
EVA = $250,000 − 10% × $800,000 = $170,000

Stern Stewart makes adjustments to after-tax operating income and invested capital, converting them into a closer approximation of what may amount to cash income and cash invested on economic resources. Examples of these adjustments may include taxes paid rather than taxes expensed, capitalizing research, and development expenses, adding after-tax interest expense to after-tax operating income, adding accumulated goodwill amortization to capital goodwill amortiza-tion to after-tax operating income and so on. However, these types of adjustments are beyond the scope of this text, as Stern Stewart have identified more than 160 different adjustments. Although many companies make their own adjustments, the basic concept of EVA can be applied by all companies.

The weighted-average cost of capital is the cost of long-term liabilities and shareholders' equity weighted by their relative size for the company or division. RI and EVA have received much attention recently as scores of companies are adopting them as financial performance measures. AT&T, Coca-Cola, CSX, FMC, and Quaker Oats claim that EVA-motivated decisions have increased shareholder value. All these companies are successful. Why? Because they do a better job than their competitors at allocating, managing, and redeploying scarce capital resources (fixed assets such as heavy equipment, computers, real estate, and working capi-tal). For example, compare Company X and Y.

AT&T
www.att.com

Coca-Cola
www.cocacola.com

CSX Corporation
www.csx.com

FMC Corporation
www.fmc.com

Quaker Oats
www.quakeroats.com

	X	Y
2006 Sales revenue ($millions)	$12	$ 8
2007 Sales revenue ($millions)	$21	$19
Invested capital ($millions)	$20	$10
2007 ROI ($21/$20) ($19/$10)	105%	190%

Company X had revenue growth of 75 percent ([21 − 12]/12) compared to 138 percent ([19 − 8]/8) for Company Y. But both companies are in business to create wealth for their shareholders. So, which company created more value for its shareholders? Company X's market value was $48 million but Company Y's market value was $144 million. Thus, compared to X, Y created over three times ($48 × 3) the market value for its shareholders with half the invested capital.

ROI or Residual Income?

Why do some companies prefer net after-tax operating income of residual income (or EVA) to ROI? Assume a division with $900,000 and average invested capital of $10,000,000. The ROI approach shows

Divisional net income after taxes	$ 900,000
Average invested capital	$10,000,000
Return on investment	9%

Under ROI, the basic message is, "Go forth and maximize your rate of return, a percentage." Thus, if performance is measured by ROI, managers of divisions currently earning 20 percent may be reluctant to invest in projects at 15 percent because doing so would reduce their average ROI.

However, from the viewpoint of the company as a whole, top management may want this division manager to accept projects that earn 15 percent. Why? Suppose the company's cost of capital is 8 percent. Investing in projects earning 15 percent will increase the company's profitability ($0.15 − 0.08 = $0.07). When performance is measured by residual income, managers tend to invest in any project earning more than the cost of capital and thus raise the firm's profits. That is, the residual income approach fosters goal congruence and managerial effort. Its basic message is, "Go forth and maximize residual income, an absolute amount."

General Electric
www.ge.com

General Electric was one of the first companies to adopt a residual income approach. Consider two divisions of GE as an example. Division A has net income of $200,000; Division B has $50,000. Both have average invested capital of $1 million. Suppose a project is proposed that can be undertaken by either A or B. The project will earn 15 percent annually on a $500,000 investment, or $75,000 a year. The cost of capital for the project is 8 percent. ROI and residual income with and without the project are shown below:

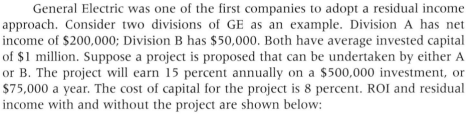

	WITHOUT PROJECT		WITH PROJECT	
	A	B	A	B
Net income	$ 200,000	$ 50,000	$ 275,000	$ 125,000
Invested capital	$1,000,000	$1,000,000	$1,500,000	$1,500,000
ROI (net income ÷ invested capital)	20%	5%	18.3%	8.3%
Capital charge (8% × invested capital)	$ 80,000	$ 80,000	$ 120,000	$ 120,000
Residual income (net income − capital charge)	$ 120,000	$ (30,000)	$ 155,000	$ 5,000

Suppose you were the manager of Division A. If your evaluation were based on ROI, would you invest in the project? No. It would decrease your ROI from 20 percent to 18.3 percent. But suppose you were in Division B. Would you invest? Yes, because ROI increases from 5 percent to 8.3 percent. In general, in companies using ROI the least profitable divisions have more incentive to invest in new projects than do the most profitable divisions.

Now suppose you are evaluated using residual income. The project would be equally attractive to either division. Residual income increases by $35,000 for each division, $155,000 − $120,000 for A and $5,000 − ($30,000) for B. Both divisions have the same incentive to invest in the project, and the incentive depends on the profitability of the project compared with the cost of the capital used by the project.

One company that improved its EVA performance dramatically during the 1990s is IBM. In 1993, its EVA was a negative $13 billion. By 2000, the company improved its EVA to $2.2 billion. Like most companies, the economic downturn in 2001 and 2002 hurt its EVA. Compute the EVA for IBM for 2002 using the following data (millions of dollars). As a manager, how would you explain this EVA to investors?

	2002
After-tax operating income	$5,706
Average stockholders' equity	23,115
Average long-term liabilities	35,444
Cost of capital (assumed)	10%

ANSWER

$$EVA = \text{After-tax operating income} - \text{cost-of-capital percentage} \times \text{capital invested}$$
$$= \$5,706 - 0.10 \times (\$23,115 + \$35,444)$$
$$= \$5,706 - 0.10 \times \$58,559$$
$$= \$5,706 - \$5,856$$
$$= \$(150)$$

The improvement from 1993 to 2000 was dramatic. The decline in EVA in 2002 is not unexpected. A majority of companies lost value in 2002, and IBM's decline was smaller than most. (*Note:* For further perspectives on EVA, see www.sternstewart.com, "About EVA"; Brian A. Schofield, "EVAluating Stocks: EVA Is a Useful Tool to Determine Value of Both Old and New Economy Companies," *Canadian Investment Review,* Spring 2000, accessible at www.investmentreview.com.)

In general, use of residual income or EVA will promote goal congruence and lead to better decisions than using ROI. Many companies are convinced that EVA has played a large role in their success. For example, Siemen Corporation, Europe's largest electronics and electrical engineering firm and Stern Stewart's first EVA client in Europe, reported in its annual report that it focuses on EVA as the yardstick by which to measure the success of efforts. The EVA performance standard encourages people to be efficient, productive, and proactive in thinking about profitable growth and higher returns. Examples of actions taken by Siemens to improve EVA include the sale of Sieccor, the fibre-optic cable business, to Corning and the sale of its retail and banking businesses. As stated by Siemens, "Divesting selected businesses has generated funds for more strategic investments." Still, many companies use ROI. Why? Probably because it is easier for managers to understand and facilitates comparison across divisions. Furthermore, combining ROI with appropriate growth and profit targets can minimize its dysfunctional motivations.

A CLOSER LOOK AT INVESTED CAPITAL

OBJECTIVE 4

Compare the advantages and disadvantages of various bases for measuring the invested capital used by organization segments.

To apply either ROI or residual income, both income and invested capital must be measured. However, there are many different interpretations of these concepts. To understand what ROI or residual income figures really mean, you must first determine how invested capital and income are being defined and measured. We discussed various definitions of income in Chapter 13, so we will not repeat them here. We will, however, explore various definitions of invested capital.

Defining Invested Capital

Consider the following balance sheet classifications:

Current assets	$ 400,000	Current liabilities	$ 200,000
Property, plant, and equipment	800,000	Long-term liabilities	400,000
Construction in progress	100,000	Shareholders' equity	700,000
Total assets	$1,300,000	Total liab. and shr. eq.	$1,300,000

Possible definitions of invested capital include

1. *Total assets.* All assets are included, $1,300,000.
2. *Total assets employed.* All assets except agreed-upon exclusions of vacant land or construction in progress, $1,300,000 – $100,000 = $1,200,000.
3. *Total assets less current liabilities.* All assets except that portion supplied by short-term creditors, $1,300,000 – $200,000 = $1,100,000. This is sometimes expressed as *long-term invested capital*; note that it can also be computed by adding the long-term liabilities and the shareholders' equity, $400,000 + $700,000 = $1,100,000, which is the definition for EVA.
4. *Shareholders' equity.* Focuses on the investment of the owners of the business, $700,000.

All the above may be computed as averages for the period under review. These averages may be based simply on the beginning and ending balances or on more complicated averages that weigh changes in investments through the months.

To measure the performance of division managers, we recommend any of the three asset definitions rather than shareholders' equity. If the division manager's mission is to put *all* assets to their best use without regard to their financing, then total assets is best. If top management directs the manager to carry extra assets that are not currently productive, then total assets employed is best. If the manager has direct control over obtaining short-term credit and bank loans, then total assets less current liabilities is best. A key behavioural factor in choosing an investment definition is that *managers will focus attention on reducing those assets and increasing those liabilities that are included in the definition.* In practice, most companies using ROI or residual income include all assets in invested capital, and about half deduct some portion of current liabilities.

A few companies allocate long-term debt to their divisions and thus have an approximation of the shareholders' equity in each division. However, this practice has doubtful merit. Division managers typically have little responsibility for the long-term *financial* management of their divisions, as distinguished from *operating* management. The investment bases of division managers from two companies could differ radically if one company has heavy long-term debt and the other is debt-free.

Asset Allocation to Divisions

Just as cost allocations affect income, asset allocations affect the invested capital of particular divisions. Companies allocate capital when a particular asset serves two or more divisions. The aim is to allocate this capital in a manner that will be goal-congruent, will spur managerial effort, and will recognize segment autonomy insofar as possible. (As long as the managers feel that they are being treated uniformly, though, they tend to be more tolerant of the imperfections of the allocation.)

A frequent criterion for asset allocation is *avoidability*. That is, the amount allowable to any given segment for the purpose of evaluating the division's performance is the amount that the corporation as a whole could avoid by not having that segment. Commonly used bases for allocation, when assets are not directly identifiable with a specific division, include the following:

ASSET CLASS	POSSIBLE ALLOCATION BASE
Corporate cash	Budgeted cash needs, as discussed shortly
Receivables	Sales weighted by payment terms
Inventories	Budgeted sales or usage
Plant and equipment	Usage of services in terms of long-run forecasts of demand or area occupied

The allocation base should be the activity that caused the asset to be acquired. Where the allocation of an asset would indeed be arbitrary (that is, no causal activity can be identified), many managers feel that it is better not to allocate.

There are two main reasons for allocating assets to divisions: (1) The divisional managers influence the amount of capital invested to benefit their divisions, and (2) Assets are an important part of the revenue-generating activities of the division. Consider for example a truck used for transportation of products by two divisions. The transportation of the products is essential to generating revenues for each division. So, the investment in the truck can possibly be allocated to the two divisions on the basis of cubic metres of products delivered for each division. In contrast, the expenses of the corporate public relations department may not be allocated in any way to the two divisions if the division managers have little influence over the PR department and public relations are not directly related to revenue-generating activities for the divisions.

Should cash be included in a division's investment if the cash balances are strictly controlled by corporate headquarters? Arguments can be made for both sides, but the manager is usually regarded as being responsible for the volume of business generated by the division. In turn, this volume is likely to have a direct effect on the overall cash needs of the corporation. A popular allocation base for cash is sales dollars. However, the allocation of cash on the basis of sales dollars seldom gets at the economic rationale of cash holdings. Cash needs are influenced by a host of factors, including payment terms of customers and creditors. Central control of cash is usually undertaken to reduce the holdings from what would be used if each division had a separate account. Fluctuations in cash needs of each division offset one another somewhat. For example, Division A might have a cash deficiency of $1 million in February, but Division B might have an offsetting cash excess of $1 million. Taken together for the year, Divisions A, B, C, D, and E might require a combined investment in cash of, say, $16 million if each were independent entities, but only $8 million if cash were controlled centrally. Hence, if Division C would ordinarily require a $4 million investment in cash as a separate entity, it would be allocated an investment of only $2 million as a segment of a company where cash was controlled centrally.

Valuation of Assets: Historical versus Current Value

Companies must measure in some way whatever assets are included in a division's invested capital. Should the assets contained in the investment base be valued at *gross book value* (original cost) or *net book value* (original cost less accumulated amortization)? Should values be based on historical cost or some version of current value? Practice is overwhelmingly in favour of using net book value based on historical cost. Very few firms use replacement cost or any other type of current value. Historical cost has been widely criticized for many years as providing a faulty basis for decision making and performance evaluation. As previously pointed out, historical costs *per se* are irrelevant for making economic decisions. Despite these criticisms, managers have been slow to depart from historical cost.

Why is historical cost so widely used? Some critics would say that sheer ignorance is the explanation. But a more persuasive answer comes from cost-benefit analysis. Accounting systems are costly. Companies must keep historical records for many legal purposes, so they are already in place. No additional money must be spent to evaluate performance based on historical costs. Furthermore, many top managers believe that a more sophisticated system will not radically improve collective operating decisions enough to warrant the additional expense. Some believe, in fact, that using current values would cause confusion unless huge sums were spent educating personnel.

Historical costs may even improve some decisions because they are more objective than current costs. Moreover, managers can better predict the historical-cost effects of their decisions, so their decisions may be more influenced by the control system. Furthermore, the uncertainty involved with current-cost measures may impose undesirable risks on the managers. In short, the historical-cost system may be superior for the *routine* evaluation of performance. In nonroutine instances, such as replacing equipment or deleting a product line, managers should conduct special studies to gather any current valuations that seem relevant.

Finally, while historical-cost systems are common, most well-managed organizations do not use historical-cost systems alone. The alternatives available to managers are not only the following:

Current-value system	versus	Historical-cost system

The alternatives are more broad and include

Historical cost: budget versus actual	versus	Current value: budget versus actual

A budget system, whether based on historical cost or current value, causes managers to worry about inflation. Most managers seem to prefer to concentrate on improving their existing historical-cost budget system.

In sum, our cost-benefit approach provides no universal answers with respect to such controversial issues as historical values versus current values or return on investment versus residual income. Instead, using a cost-benefit test, each organization must judge for itself whether an alternative control system or accounting technique will improve collective decision making. The latter is the primary criterion.

Too often, there are pro-and-con discussions about which alternative is closer to perfection or truer than another in some logical sense. The cost-benefit approach is not concerned with "truth" or "perfection" by itself. Instead it asks, "Do you think your perceived 'truer' or 'more logical' system is worth its added cost? Or will our existing system provide about the same set of decisions if it is skillfully administered?"

Plant and Equipment: Gross or Net?

Net Book Value. The original cost of an asset less any accumulated amortization.

Gross Book Value. The original cost of an asset before deducting accumulated amortization.

In valuing assets, it is important to distinguish between net and gross book values. **Net book value** is the original cost of an asset less any accumulated amortization. **Gross book value** is the original cost of an asset before deducting accumulated amortization. Most companies use net book value in calculating their investment base. However, according to a recent survey, a significant minority use gross book value. The proponents of gross book value maintain that it facilitates comparisons between years and between plants or divisions.

Consider an example of a $600,000 piece of equipment with a three-year life and no residual value.

| | OPERATING INCOME BEFORE | | | AVERAGE INVESTMENT | | | |
YEAR	AMORTIZATION	AMORTIZATION	OPERATING INCOME	NET BOOK VALUE*	RATE OF RETURN	GROSS BOOK VALUE	RATE OF RETURN
1	$260,000	$200,000	$60,000	$500,000	12%	$600,000	10%
2	260,000	200,000	60,000	300,000	20%	600,000	10%
3	260,000	200,000	60,000	100,000	60%	600,000	10%

* ($600,000 – [1/2 × 200,000]); ($400,000 – [1/2 × 200,000]); etc.

The rate of return on net book value goes up as the equipment ages. It could increase even if operating income gradually declined through the years. In contrast, the rate of return on gross book value is unchanged if operating income does not change. The rate would decrease if operating income gradually declined through the years.

Proponents of using the gross book value for performance evaluation maintain that a performance measure should not improve simply because assets are getting older. The advocates of using net book value maintain that it is consistent with the assets shown on the conventional balance sheet and with the net income computations.

Regardless of the theoretical arguments, companies should focus primarily on the effect on managers' motivation when choosing between net and gross book value. Managers evaluated using gross book value will tend to replace assets sooner than will managers in firms using net book value. Consider a four-year-old machine with an original cost of $1,000 and net book value of $200. It can be replaced by a new machine that costs $1,500. The choice of net or gross book value does not affect net income. However, the investment base increases from $200 to $1,500 in a net-book-value firm, but it increases only $500 to $1,500 in a gross-book-value firm. To maximize ROI or residual income, managers want a low investment base. Managers in firms using net book value will tend to keep old assets with their low book value. Those in firms using gross book value will have less incentive to keep old assets. Therefore, to motivate managers to use state-of-the-art production technology, gross asset value is preferred. Net asset value promotes a more conservative approach to asset replacement.

In sum, using a cost-benefit analysis and assessing the motivational effects of the alternatives, each organization must judge for itself whether a particular control system will improve decision making. There are no universal, definitive answers with respect to choices such as historical versus current asset values or gross versus net asset values.

TRANSFER PRICING

OBJECTIVE 5

Define transfer prices and state their purpose.

Transfer Prices.
The amounts charged by one segment of an organization for a product or service that it supplies to another segment of the same organization.

Now that you understand some of the issues in measuring profitability as a performance measure, we will turn our attention to transfer pricing.

Segment managers can focus only on their own segments without hurting the organization as a whole. In contrast, when segments interact greatly, there is an increased possibility that what is best for one segment hurts another segment enough to have a negative impact on the entire organization. Such a situation may occur when one segment provides products or services to another segment and charges them a transfer price. **Transfer prices** are the amounts charged by one segment of an organization for a product or service that it supplies to another segment of the same organization. Most often, the term is associated with materials, parts, or finished goods. The transfer price is revenue to the segment producing the product or service, and it is a cost to the acquiring department.

Managers' motivations that result from using profitability measures for performance evaluation are generally consistent with overall organizational goals when all the segments of a decentralized organization are independent of one another.

Purposes of Transfer Pricing

Why do transfer-pricing systems exist?

The principal reason is to communicate data that will lead to goal-congruent decisions. Assure that managers who make decisions to improve their segment's performance also increase the performance of the organization as a whole. For example, transfer prices should guide managers to make the best possible decisions regarding whether to buy or sell products and services inside or outside the total organization.

Another important reason is to evaluate segment performance and thus motivate both the selling manager and the buying manager toward goal-congruent decisions. That is, decisions that maximize a segment's profits should also maximize the profits of the entire company.

Multinational companies also use transfer pricing to minimize their worldwide taxes, duties, and tariffs. These are easy aims to describe, but they are difficult aims to achieve.

Another main goal of transfer pricing is to preserve segment autonomy. If an organization has decided that decentralization with a focus on autonomy of segment managers is desirable, then segment managers must be free to make their own decisions. In this case, top management exerts influence through segment performance measurement rather than through direct intervention in segment decision making.

Whenever there is a lull in a conversation with a manager, try asking, "Do you have any transfer-pricing problems?" The response is usually, "Let me tell

Activity-Based Costing and Transfer Pricing

Teva Pharmaceutical Industries Ltd.
www.tevapharm.com

Ivax Corporation
www.ivax.com

Teva Pharmaceutical Industries Ltd. is a global health-care company specializing in pharmaceuticals. It is headquartered in Israel, and its 2004 global sales totalled $3.06 billion. Pending regulatory approval, Teva will acquire U.S. drugmaker Ivax Corporation in 2006 at a cost of $7.3 billion. If this acquisition is completed, Teva will become the largest generic drug company in the world. Teva entered the lucrative generic drug market in the mid-1980s. As part of its strategy, the company decentralized its pharmaceutical business into cost and profit centres.

Each of the marketing divisions purchases generic drugs from the manufacturing division. Prior to decentralization, each marketing division was a revenue centre. With the new organizational structure, management had to decide how to measure marketing division costs because profits were now the key financial performance measure.

A key cost to the marketing divisions is the transfer price paid for drugs purchased from the manufacturing division. Management considered several alternative bases for the company's transfer prices. They rejected market price because there was not a ready market. They rejected negotiated prices because they believed that the resulting debates over the proper price would be lengthy and disruptive. They adopted variable cost (raw material and packaging costs) for a short time. Eventually, however, they rejected it because it did not lead to congruent decisions—managers did not differentiate products using many scarce resources from those using few. Further, when a local source for the drug did exist, the market price was always above the variable-cost transfer price. Thus, managers in Teva's manufacturing division had little incentive to keep costs low.

Management also rejected full cost because the traditional costing system did not capture the actual cost structure of the manufacturing division. Specifically, the system undercosted the low-volume products and overcosted the large-volume products. The system traced only raw materials directly to products. It divided the remaining manufacturing costs into two cost pools and allocated them based on labour hours and machine hours. One problem with the traditional system was its inability to capture and correctly allocate the non–value-added cost of setup activity. Management did not know the size of the errors in product cost, but the lack of confidence in the traditional cost system led to rejection of full cost as the transfer-pricing base.

Then Teva's management adopted an activity-based-costing (ABC) system to improve the accuracy of its product costs. The ABC system has five activity centres and related cost pools: receiving, manufacturing, packaging, quality assurance, and shipping. Because of the dramatic increase in costing accuracy, management was able to adopt full activity-based cost as the transfer price.

Teva's managers are pleased with their transfer-pricing system. The benefits include increased confidence that the costs being transferred are closely aligned with the actual short- and long-run costs being incurred, increased communication between divisions, and an increased awareness of the costs of low-volume products and the costs of capacity required to support these products. They believe that their activity-based costs are the best approximation to outlay cost plus opportunity costs because the allocation of the fixed costs is a good measure of the value (opportunity cost) of the resources being consumed.

Sources: Adapted from Robert Kaplan, Dan Weiss, and Eyal Desheh, "Transfer Pricing with ABC," *Management Accounting*, May, 1997, pp. 20–28; "EU Regulators Clear Teva's Takeover of Ivax, Creating Largest Generic Drug Firm," *Canadian Press Wire*, November 25, 2005; Teva Pharmaceutical Industries Ltd., 2004 Annual Report.

you about the peculiar transfer-pricing difficulties in my organization." A manager in a large wood-products firm called transfer pricing his firm's most troublesome management control issue.

Consider the following data concerning a subassembly that Wilamette Manufacturing Company produces in its Fabricating Division and uses in products assembled in its Assembly Division.

Fabricating Division
  Variable cost of subassembly $35
  Excess capacity (in units)   1,000
Assembly Division
  Market price for buying the
    subassembly from external sources $50
  Number of units needed   900

If you were manager of the Fabricating Division, what is the lowest transfer price you would accept for the subassembly? If you were the manager of the Assembly Division, what is the most you would be willing to pay for the subassembly? Is there a transfer price that would motivate production and transfer of the assembly? If so, what is the price?

ANSWER
The Fabricating Division has excess capacity, so its manager would be willing to accept any price above the variable cost of $35. The Assembly Division can buy the subassembly for $50 on the external market, so its manager would be willing to pay no more than $50 to buy it from the Fabricating Division. The transfer would take place at some price between $35 and $50.

A General Rule for Transfer Pricing

Although no single rule always meets the goals of transfer pricing, a general rule can provide guidance:

$$\text{transfer price} = \text{outlay cost} + \text{opportunity cost}$$

Outlay cost is the additional amount the selling division must pay to produce and transfer a product or service to another division. It is often the variable cost for producing the item transferred. Opportunity cost is the maximum contribution to profit that the selling segment foregoes by transferring the item internally. For example, if capacity constraints force a division to either transfer an item internally or sell it externally—that is, it cannot produce enough to do both—the opportunity cost for internal transfer is the contribution margin the segment could have gotten for the external sale.

Why does this rule generally work? Consider the following example, where the selling division is considering transferring a subcomponent to the buying division:

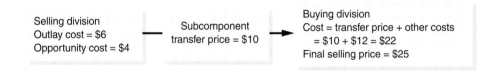

Suppose the selling division's opportunity cost arises because it can get $10 for the subcomponent on the market. Thus, the contribution from selling on the market is $10 − $6 = $4. At any transfer price less than $10, the division is better off selling the subcomponent on the market rather than transferring it. Thus, the minimum transfer price it would accept is $6 + ($10 − $6) = $6 + $4 = $10.

Now consider how much the item is worth to the buying division. For the subcomponent to be profitable to the buying division, it must be able to sell the final product for more than the transfer price plus the other costs it must incur to finish the product. Because it can sell the final product for $25 and its other costs are $12, it would be willing to pay up to $25 − $12 = $13 for it. But it will not pay more to the selling division than it would have to pay to an outside supplier. Thus, the largest transfer price acceptable to the buying division is the lesser of (1) $13, and (2) the cost charged by an outside supplier.

Now, from the company's point of view, transfer is desirable if (1) the total cost to the company for the subcomponent ($10 as determined by the selling division, including opportunity costs) is less than its value to the company ($13 as determined by the buying division), *and* (2) the selling division's costs (again including opportunity costs) are less than the price the buying division would have to pay to an outside supplier. The first criterion guarantees that the company does not pay more for the subcomponent than it is worth. The second guarantees that it does not pay more to produce the subcomponent internally than it would have to pay to buy it in the marketplace. The only transfer price that will always meet these criteria is $10, the outlay (variable) cost plus opportunity cost. Why? Any price between $10 and $13 meets the first criterion. However, only $10 meets the second if an outside supplier offers the subcomponent at a price between $10 and $13. At a $10 transfer price, we have the following result:

OUTSIDE SUPPLIER PRICE	DECISION BY DIVISION MANAGERS	DECISION BEST FOR COMPANY
<$10	Do not transfer—buying division rejects transfer because buying from outside supplier will maximize its profits	Buy from outside supplier because it is cheaper for the company as a whole
>$10	If value to buying division >$10: Transfer at $10—both divisions benefit	Transfer because internal price < external price
	If value to buying division <$10: Buying division rejects transfer	Do not transfer because the benefit of the subcomponent to the company is less than its cost

At a $10 transfer price, the division managers, acting independently, make the decision that is most profitable for the company as a whole. Any other transfer price creates a possibility of a manager making the decision that is best for his or her segment but not for the company as a whole. The selling division would reject the transfer at less than $10 regardless of how much profit it creates for the buying division. The buying division would reject the transfer whenever the transfer price is greater than the price from alternative sources. Any transfer price greater than $10 runs the risk of the buying division's purchasing outside the company even when the internal cost is lower. For example, with a transfer price of $12 and an outside bid of $11, the buying division would pay $11 to the outside supplier when the company could have spent only $10 (including opportunity cost) to produce the subcomponent in the selling division.

Because of the multiple goals of transfer-pricing systems, this general rule doesn't always produce an ideal transfer price. But it is a good benchmark by which to judge transfer-pricing systems. We will analyze the following transfer-pricing systems, the most popular systems in practice, by examining how close the transfer price comes to the outlay cost plus opportunity cost:

1. Cost-based transfer prices
   a. Variable cost
   b. Full cost (possibly plus profit)
2. Market-based transfer prices
3. Negotiated transfer prices

In addressing these transfer-pricing systems, we will assume that a company has multiple divisions that transfer items to one another and that the company wants to preserve segment autonomy in a decentralized operation.

Cost-Based Transfer Prices

OBJECTIVE 6

Identify the relative advantages and disadvantages of basing transfer prices on total costs, variable costs, and market prices.

Approximately half of the major companies in the world transfer items at cost. However, there are many possible definitions of cost. Some companies use only variable cost, others use full cost where fixed costs may be a lump sum or a per-mit charge, and still others use full cost plus a profit markup. Some use standard costs and some use actual costs.

When the transfer price is some version of cost, transfer pricing is nearly the same as cost allocation, where costs are accumulated in one segment and then assigned to (or transferred to) another segment. However, two important points deserve mention here.

First, transferring or allocating costs can disguise a cost's behaviour pattern. Consider a computer manufacturer that makes keyboards in one division and transfers them to another division for assembly into personal computers. The manager of the keyboard division may have good knowledge of the cost drivers affecting the costs of keyboards. But if a single transfer price per unit is charged when transferring the keyboards to the assembly division, the only cost driver affecting the cost to the assembly division is "units of keyboards." Cost drivers other than units produced are ignored, and distinctions between fixed and variable costs are blurred. The assembly division manager sees the entire cost of keyboards as a variable cost, regardless of what the true cost behaviour is.

Other problems arise if actual cost is used as a transfer price. Because actual cost cannot be known in advance, the buying segment will not be able to plan its costs. More important, because inefficiencies are merely passed along to the buying division, the supplying division lacks incentive to control its costs. Thus, using budgeted or standard costs instead of actual costs is recommended for both cost allocation and transfer pricing.

Transfers at Variable Costs

A variable cost based transfer pricing is most appropriate when the selling division has excess capacity, the outlay costs are about equal to variable cost, and there are no opportunity costs, meaning that the selling division foregoes no opportunities to sell to outsiders.

Transfers at Full Cost or Full Cost Plus Profit

Full-cost transfer pricing includes not only variable costs but also an allocation of fixed costs in the transfer price. In addition, some companies also add a markup for profit. This may implicitly suggest that the inclusion of fixed costs (and profit markup) is a good approximation of the opportunity cost. However, there is no guarantee that fixed costs with or without profit markup are a good approximation of the opportunity cost. In cases of constrained capacity, where the selling division cannot satisfy all internal and external demand, the opportunity cost is positive.

Market-Based Transfer Prices

If there is a competitive market for the product or service being transferred internally, using the market price as a transfer price will generally lead to the desired goal congruence and managerial effort. In such a case, the market price is equal to the variable cost plus opportunity cost. Why? Because the opportunity cost equals the market price less the variable cost:

$$\text{transfer price} = \text{variable cost} + \text{opportunity cost}$$
$$= \text{variable cost} + (\text{market price} - \text{variable cost})$$
$$= \text{market price}.$$

The market price may come from published price lists for similar products or services, or it may be the price charged by the producing division to its external customers. If the latter, the internal transfer price may be the external market price less the selling and delivery expenses that are not incurred on internal business. The major drawback to market-based prices is that market prices are not always available for items transferred internally.

To examine market-based transfer prices, consider two hypothetical divisions of Champion Inc. One makes fabrics that it sells (transfers) to other divisions for use in many final products. It also sells the fabric directly to external customers. Another division buys the fabric from the first division and uses it to make jackets. A particular jacket requires two square metres of a special waterproof fabric. Should the Jacket Division obtain the fabric from the Fabric Division of Champion or purchase it from an external supplier?

Suppose the Fabric Division can sell the fabric externally for $25 per square metre and the Jacket Division can buy it from external suppliers for $25 per metre (or 2 × $25 = $50 per jacket). Assume for the moment that the Fabric Division can sell its entire production to external customers without incurring any marketing or shipping costs. The Jacket Division manager will refuse to pay a transfer price greater than $50 for the fabric for each jacket. Why? Because if the transfer price is greater than $50, she will purchase the fabric from the external supplier in order to maximize her division's profit.

Furthermore, the manager of the Fabric Division will not sell two square metres of fabric for less than $50. Why? Because he can sell it on the market for $50, so any lower price will reduce his division's profit. The only transfer price that allows both managers to maximize their division's profit is $50, the market price. If the managers had autonomy to make decisions, one of them would decline the internally produced fabric at any transfer price other than $50.

Now suppose the Fabric Division incurs a $2.50 per square metre marketing and shipping cost that it can avoid by transferring the fabric to the Jacket Division instead of marketing it to outside customers. Most companies would then use a transfer price of $22.50 per square metre, or $45 per jacket, often called a "market-price-minus" transfer price. The Fabric Division would get the same net amount from the transfer ($45 with no marketing or shipping costs) as from an external sale ($50 less $5 marketing and shipping costs), whereas the Jacket Division saves $5 per jacket. Thus, Champion overall benefits.

Transfer Pricing When Market Prices Don't Exist

Now suppose that the Fabric Division cannot sell the fabric on the external market, either because there is no demand for the fabric or because Champion has a policy prohibiting such a sale. The prohibition may occur because Champion's strategy is to sell products only to final consumers, not to other manufacturers. Suppose the Fabric Division incurs variable production costs of $20 per square metre. On receiving two square metres of fabric, the Jacket Division spends an additional $56 to produce and sell each jacket, as shown in Exhibit 14-2. The Jacket Division manager predicts sales of 10,000 jackets, so its demand for fabric is 20,000 square metres. Whether it is best for Champion to have the Fabric Division manufacture and transfer the 20,000 square metres of fabric to the Jacket Division depends on whether the Fabric Division incurs any opportunity costs. Because there is no external market for the fabric, passing up external sales of the fabric cannot cause the opportunity cost. An opportunity cost will exist only if production of the fabric causes the Fabric Division to pass up using its production facilities for some other products that it can sell or transfer to another division.

First consider the case where there is no opportunity cost. That is, the Fabric Division passes up no opportunities because of its production of this fabric. Our rule gives a transfer price of $20 per square metre, the variable cost to the Fabric Division. This would provide a variable cost for the Jacket Division of $56 + (2 × $20) = $56 + $40 = $96 per jacket and a contribution margin of $100 − $96 = $4 per jacket. A full-cost or full-cost-plus-profit transfer price would potentially create **dysfunctional decisions**—decisions in conflict with the company's goals. Any transfer price above $44 would cause the Jacket Division manager to reject the transfer even though Champion is $4 better off with the transfer and production of the jacket—$100 of sales and a total additional cost of $40 + $56 = $96 for each jacket. In fact, any time the Jacket Division would find at least $40 of value in the transferred fabric, Champion would prefer the production and transfer of the fabric. The variable cost of $40 will motivate the two division managers to make this preferred decision. Any higher cost can cause the Jacket Division manager to buy too little fabric from the Fabric Division.

With no opportunity cost, using the market price as a transfer price can create dysfunctional decisions. This could occur when there is an external market for the fabric, thus a market price, but Champion does not allow the Fabric Division to sell to that market. The market price in this case does not represent a real opportunity for the Fabric Division. Suppose the market price is $25 per

Dysfunctional Decisions. Decisions that are in conflict with organizational goals.

EXHIBIT 14-2

Contribution Margin on Jacket

Sales price of finished jacket		$100
Variable costs:		
Transfer price (T) for 2 square metres		$2 × T*
Additional variable costs:		
Processing	$43	
Selling	13	56
Total variable cost		56 + 2 × T
Contribution margin		$44 − 2 × T

* T = transfer price per yard.

square metre. A market-based transfer price would be $50 per jacket, making the total cost to the Jacket Division $106 and causing the rejection of the transfer. But it would still be best for Champion if the transfer took place because Champion still stands to gain $4 from the transfer and $0 with no transfer (and thus no jacket production).

Now suppose the Fabric Division has a $5-per-square-metre opportunity cost. This might arise because the division passes up $5 of contribution margin on other business when it uses its capacity to produce and transfer one square metre of this fabric. In this case, Champion would prefer production and transfer of the fabric only if it is worth at least $50 to the Jacket Division. Why? Because the Fabric Division pays $40 of variable cost and passes up $10 of contribution to transfer the two square metres to the Jacket Division. At first it looks like a variable-cost transfer price might work. However, the Fabric Division manager would not produce and transfer the fabric at $20 per square metre because the division would be better off using its capacity for the other business. Champion would prefer not to transfer it because the $10 contribution to the Fabric Division from the other business is greater than the $4 contribution from production and sale of a jacket ($100 sales less $40 variable Fabric Division cost plus $56 variable Jacket Division cost). But what if the Jacket Division could sell the jacket for $110? The Fabric Division manager would still decline the business, even though Champion's contribution from the jacket would now be $110 − $96 = $14, which is greater than the $10 contribution the Fabric Division would receive. The variable-cost transfer price leads to a dysfunctional decision.

In summary, when the selling division cannot sell an item on the external market, using either a market-based or cost-based transfer for the item can lead to dysfunctional decisions. How do we resolve this dilemma? One possibility is for top management to impose a "fair" transfer price and insist that a transfer be made. But managers in a decentralized company often regard such orders as undermining their autonomy. Therefore, many companies turn to negotiated transfer prices.

Negotiated Transfer Prices

Companies heavily committed to segment autonomy often allow managers to negotiate transfer prices. The managers may consider both costs and market prices in their negotiations, but no policy requires them to do so. Supporters of negotiated transfer prices maintain that the managers involved have the best knowledge of what the company will gain or lose by producing and transferring the product or service, so open negotiation allows the managers to make optimal decisions. Critics of negotiated prices focus on the time and effort spent negotiating, an activity that adds nothing directly to the profits of the company.

Let's look at how our Fabric Division and Jacket Division managers might approach a negotiation of a transfer price. The Jacket Division manager might look at the selling price of the jacket, $100, less the additional cost the division incurs in making it, $56, and decide to purchase fabric at any transfer price less than $100 − $56 = $44. The Jacket Division will add to its profit by making the jacket if the transfer price is below $44.

Similarly, the Fabric Division manager will look at what it costs to produce and transfer the fabric. If there is no opportunity cost, any transfer price above $40 will increase the Fabric Division's profit. However, if there is a $5-per-square-metre opportunity cost, so that transferring two square metres of fabric causes the division to give up a contribution of $10 as well as paying variable costs of $40, the minimum transfer price acceptable to the Fabric Division is $50.

Negotiation will result in a transfer if the maximum transfer price the Jacket Division is willing to pay is greater than the minimum transfer price the Fabric Division is willing to accept. When the Fabric Division has no opportunity cost, a transfer will take place at a price between $40 and $44. The Fabric Division manager is willing to accept any price above $40 and the Jacket Division manager will pay up to $44. The exact transfer price may depend on the negotiating ability of the two division managers. The same result, agreeing to a transfer, will occur if the Fabric Division manager also has an opportunity cost if that cost is less than $2 per square metre. The transfer price will simply be at least equal to the $40 variable cost plus the opportunity cost for two square metres. However, if the Fabric Division has an opportunity cost of $2 or more per square metre, a transfer will not occur. This is exactly what Champion would prefer. When the Fabric Division's opportunity cost is less than $2, the jacket is more profitable than the Fabric Division's other business, and the transfer should occur. When the Fabric Division's opportunity cost is greater than $2, the additional contribution from the Fabric Division's other business will be greater than the Jacket Divison's contribution on a jacket, and the transfer should not occur. Therefore, the manager's decisions are congruent with the company's best interests.

What should top management of a decentralized organization do if it sees segment managers making dysfunctional decisions through their negotiations? As usual, the answer is, "It depends." Top management can step in and force the "correct" decision, but doing so undermines segment managers' autonomy and the overall notion of decentralization. It also assumes that top management has the information necessary to determine the correct decision. Most important, frequent intervention results in recentralization. Indeed, if more centralization is desired, the organization might want to reorganize by combining segments.

Top managers who wish to encourage decentralization will often make sure that both producing and purchasing division managers understand all the facts and then allow the managers to negotiate a transfer price. Even when top managers suspect that a dysfunctional decision might be made, they may swallow hard and accept the segment manager's judgment as a cost of decentralization. (Of course, repeated dysfunctional decision making may be a reason to change the organizational design or to change managers.)

Well-trained and informed segment managers who understand opportunity costs and fixed and variable costs will often make better decisions than will top managers. The producing division manager knows best the various uses of its capacity, and the purchasing division manager knows best what profit can be made on the items to be transferred. In addition, negotiation allows segments to respond flexibly to changing market conditions when setting transfer prices. One transfer price may be appropriate in a time of idle capacity, and another when demand increases and operations approach full capacity.

The Need for Many Transfer Prices

As you can see, there is seldom a single transfer price that will ensure the desired decisions. The "correct" transfer price depends on the economic and legal circumstances and the decision at hand. Organizations may have to make tradeoffs between pricing for congruence and pricing to spur managerial effort. Furthermore, the optimal price for either may differ from that employed for tax reporting or for other external needs.

Income taxes, property taxes, and tariffs often influence the setting of transfer prices so that the firm as a whole will benefit, even though the performance of a segment may suffer. For example, to maximize tax deductions for percentage depletion allowances, which are based on revenue, a petroleum company may want to transfer crude oil to other segments at as high a price as is legally possible.

Fair-trade laws and national antitrust acts can also influence transfer pricing in some situations. Because of the differences in national tax structures around the world, or because of the differences in the incomes of various divisions and subsidiaries, the firm may wish to shift profits and "dump" goods, if legally possible. These considerations further illustrate the limits of decentralization where there are heavy interdependencies among segments and explain why the same company may use different transfer prices for different purposes.

Multinational Transfer Prices

OBJECTIVE 7

Identify the factors affecting multinational transfer prices.

So far we have focused on how transfer pricing policies affect the motivation of managers. However, in multinational companies, other factors may dominate. For example, multinational companies use transfer prices to minimize worldwide income taxes, import duties, and tariffs. For example, Champion might prefer to make its profits in Canada, with its maximum corporate tax rate of 28 percent, rather than in the United States, where the rate is 35 percent.

Suppose a division in a high-income-tax-rate country produces a subcomponent for another division in a low-income-tax-rate country. By setting a low transfer price, the company can recognize most of the profit from the production in the low-income-tax-rate country, thereby minimizing taxes. Likewise, items produced by divisions in a low-income-tax-rate country and transferred to a division in a high-income-tax-rate country should have a high transfer price to minimize taxes.

Sometimes import duties offset income tax effects. Most countries base import duties on the price paid for an item, whether bought from an outside company or transferred from another division. Therefore, low transfer prices generally lead to low import duties.

Of course, tax authorities recognize the incentive to set transfer prices to minimize taxes and import duties. Therefore, most countries have restrictions on allowable transfer prices. Transfers should be priced at "arm's-length" market values, or at the price one division would pay another if they were independent companies. Companies in general have some latitude in deciding an appropriate "arm's-length" price.

Consider a high-end running shoe produced by a Swiss Champion division with an 8 percent income tax rate and transferred to a division in Germany with a 40 percent income tax rate. In addition, suppose Germany imposes an import duty equal to 20 percent of the price of the item and that Champion cannot deduct this import duty for tax purposes. Suppose the full unit cost of a pair of the shoes is $100, and the variable cost is $60. If tax authorities allow either variable- or full-cost transfer prices, which should Champion choose? By transferring at $100 rather than at $60, the company gains $4.80 per unit:

Effect of Transferring at $100 Instead of at $60	
Income of the Swiss division is $40 higher; therefore it pays 8% × $40 more income taxes	$(3.20)
Income of the German division is $40 lower; therefore it pays 40% × $40 less income taxes	16.00
Import duty is paid by the German division on an additional $100 − $60 = $40; therefore it pays 20% × $40 more duty	(8.00)
Net savings from transferring at $100 instead of $60	$ 4.80

Companies may also use transfer prices to avoid financial restrictions imposed by some governments. For example, a country might restrict the amount of dividends paid to foreign owners. It may be easier for a company to get cash from a foreign division as payment for items transferred than as cash dividends.

In summary, transfer pricing is more complex in a multinational company than it is in a domestic company. Multinational companies have more objectives to be achieved through transfer-pricing policies, and some of the objectives often conflict with one another. In fact, companies use a variety of transfer-price methods and may also use different methods for their domestic transfers versus international transfers. The following table provides the results of a recent survey that demonstrates this point.

TRANSFER-PRICING METHODS USED BY THE RESPONDENT FIRMS

Pricing Methods	For Domestic Transfers		For International Transfers	
	Number of Firms	Percent of Total	Number of Firms	Percent of Total
Cost-based methods:				
Actual or standard variable cost of production	8	3.6	2	1.2
Actual full production cost	20	9.0	6	3.8
Standard full production cost	34	15.2	11	7.0
Actual variable production cost plus a lump-sum subsidy	2	0.9	2	1.3
Full production cost (actual or standard) plus a markup	37	16.6	42	26.8
Other	2	0.9	2	1.3
Subtotal for cost-based transfer prices	103	46.2	65	41.4
Market-based transfer prices:				
Market price	56	25.1	41	26.1
Market price less selling expenses	17	7.6	19	12.1
Other	9	4.0	12	7.7
Subtotal for market-based methods	82	36.7	72	45.9
Negotiated price	37	16.6	20	12.7
Other methods	1	0.5	0	0
Total—all methods	223*	100.0	157*	100.0

* Many firms use more than one domestic or international transfer price.

Source: Roger W. Tong, "Transfer Pricing in the 1990s," *Management Accounting*, February 1992.

KEYS TO SUCCESSFUL PERFORMANCE MEASURES

Successful management control systems have several key factors in addition to appropriate measures of profitability and transfer-pricing policies. Like management in general, management control systems are more art than science. We next briefly explore three factors that help managers interpret and use management control information.

Focus on Controllability

As Chapter 13 explained, a distinction should be made between the performance of the division manager and the performance of the division as an investment by the corporation. Managers should be evaluated on the basis of their controllable performance (in many cases some controllable contribution in relation to controllable investment). However, decisions such as increasing or decreasing investment in a division are based on the economic viability of the *division*, not the performance of its *managers*.

This distinction helps to clarify some vexing difficulties. For example, top management may want to use an investment base to gauge the economic performance of a retail store, but the *manager* may best be judged by focusing on income and forgetting about any investment allocations. If investment is assigned to the manager, the aim should be to assign only that investment the manager can control. Controllability depends on what *decisions* managers can make regarding the size of the investment base. In a highly decentralized company, for instance, managers can influence the size of these assets and can exercise judgment regarding the appropriate amount of short-term credit and perhaps some long-term credit. Investment decisions that managers do not influence should not affect their performance evaluations.

Focus on Management by Objectives

Management by objectives (MBO) describes the joint formulation by a manager and his or her superior of a set of goals and of plans for achieving the goals for a forthcoming period. For our purposes here, the terms *goals* and *objectives* are synonyms. The plans often take the form of a responsibility accounting budget (together with supplementary goals such as levels of management training and safety that may not be incorporated into the accounting budget). The manager's performance is then evaluated in relation to these agreed-upon budgeted objectives.

A management-by-objectives approach lessens the complaints about lack of controllability because of its stress on budgeted results. That is, a budget is negotiated between a particular manager and his or her superior for a particular time period and a particular set of expected outside and inside influences. By evaluating results compared to expectations, a manager may more readily accept an assignment to a less successful segment. Why? Because a manager of an economically struggling segment can still meet agreed-upon goals. This MBO is preferable to a system that emphasizes absolute profitability for its own sake. Unless focus is placed on currently attainable results, able managers will be reluctant to accept responsibility for segments that are in economic trouble. Whether using MBO or not, skilful budgeting and intelligent performance evaluation will go a long way toward overcoming the common lament: "I'm being held responsible for items beyond my control."

Many of the troublesome motivational effects of performance evaluation systems can be minimized by the astute use of budgets. The importance of tailoring a budget to particular managers cannot be overemphasized. For example, either an ROI or a residual income system can promote goal congruence and managerial effort if top management gets everybody to focus on what is currently attainable in the forthcoming budget period. Using budgets as performance targets also has its dangers. Companies that overemphasize meeting budgetary targets can motivate unethical behaviour. At WorldCom, making the numbers became such a high priority that when it became clear that managers could not meet their goals, they fabricated the accounting reports. At Enron, the consequences of poor performance evaluations were so great that managers played bookkeeping games to make their performance look better. The lesson is that the "astute" use of budgets is good, but using budgets to put unreasonable pressure on managers for performance rating can undermine the ethics of an organization.

Accountants often focus too much on measurements by bean counters. Even good measures can lead to dysfunctional decisions when managers misuse them. Managers should also think hard about how they use measures to achieve organizational objectives. It is important to use measures that are consistent with organizational goals because "you get what you measure." A management control system is as good as the managers who use it.

HIGHLIGHTS TO REMEMBER

1. **Define decentralization and identify its expected benefits and costs.** As companies grow, the ability of managers to effectively plan and control becomes more and more difficult because top managers are further removed from day-to-day operations. One approach to effective planning and control in large companies is to decentralize decision making. This means that top management gives mid- and lower-level managers the freedom to make decisions that impact the subunit's performance. The more decision making is delegated, the greater the decentralization. Often, the subunit manager is most knowledgeable of the factors that management should consider in the decision-making process.

2. **Distinguish between responsibility centres and decentralization.** Top management must design the management control system so that it motivates managers to act in the best interests of the company. This is done through the choice of responsibility centres and the appropriate performance measures and rewards. The degree of decentralization does not depend upon the type of responsibility centre chosen. For example, a cost-centre manager in a decentralized company may have more decision-making authority than does a profit-centre manager in a highly centralized company.

3. **Explain how the linking of rewards to responsibility centre results affects incentives and risk.** It is generally a good idea to link managers' rewards to responsibility centre results. Top management should use performance measures for the responsibility centre that promote goal congruence. However, linking rewards to results creates risk

for the manager. The greater the influence of uncontrollable factors on a manager's reward, the more risk the manager bears.

4. **Compute ROI, residual income, and economic value added (EVA), and contrast them as criteria for judging the performance of organization segments.** It is typical to measure the results of investment centres using a set of performance measures that include financial measures such as return on investment (ROI), residual income (RI), or economic value added (EVA). ROI is any income measure divided by the dollar amount invested and is expressed as a percentage. Residual income, or economic value added, is after-tax operating income less a capital charge based on the capital invested (cost of capital). It is an absolute dollar amount.

5. **Compare the advantages and disadvantages of various bases for measuring the invested capital used by organization segments.** The way an organization measures invested capital determines the precise motivation provided by ROI, RI, or EVA. Managers will try to reduce assets or increase liabilities that a company includes in their division's investment base. They will adopt more conservative asset replacement policies if the company uses net book value rather than gross book value in measuring the assets.

6. **Define transfer prices and identify their purpose.** In large companies with many different segments, one segment often provides products or services to another segment. Deciding on the amount the selling division should charge the buying division for these transfers (transfer price) is difficult. Companies use various types of transfer pricing policies. The overall purpose of transfer prices is to motivate managers to act in the best interests of the company, not just the segment.

7. **State the general rule for transfer pricing and use it to assess transfer prices based on total costs, variable costs, and market prices.** As a general rule, transfer prices should approximate the outlay cost plus opportunity cost. Each type of transfer price has its own advantages and disadvantages. Each has a situation where it works best, and each can lead to dysfunctional decisions in some instances. Cost-based prices are readily available, but if a company uses actual costs, the receiving segment manager does not know the cost in advance, which makes cost planning difficult. When a competitive market exists for the product or service, using market-based transfer prices usually leads to goal congruence and optimal decisions. When idle capacity exists in the segment providing the product or service, the use of variable cost as the transfer price usually leads to goal congruence.

8. **Identify the factors affecting multinational transfer prices.** Multinational organizations often use transfer prices as a means of minimizing worldwide income taxes, import duties, and tariffs.

9. **Explain how controllability and management by objectives (MBO) aid the implementation of management control systems.** Regardless of what measures a management control system uses, when used to evaluate managers they should focus on only the controllable aspects of the measures. MBO can focus attention on performance compared to expectations, which is better than evaluations based on absolute profitability.

DEMONSTRATION PROBLEMS FOR YOUR REVIEW

Problem One

Reconsider Champion's Fabric Division and Jacket Division described on pages 721–724. In addition to the data there, suppose the Fabric Division has annual fixed manufacturing costs of $800,000 and expected annual production of 200,000 square metres. The "fully allocated cost" per square metre was computed as follows:

Variable costs per square metre	$20.00
Fixed costs, $800,000 ÷ 200,000 square metres	4.00
Fully allocated cost per square metre	$24.00

Therefore, the "fully allocated cost" of the two square metres required for one jacket is 2 × $24 = $48.

Assume that the Fabric Division has idle capacity. The Jacket Division is considering whether to buy enough fabric for 10,000 jackets. It will sell each jacket for $100. The additional costs shown in Exhibit 14-2 for the Jacket Division would prevail. If Champion bases its transfer prices on fully allocated cost, would the Jacket Division manager buy? Explain. Would the company as a whole benefit if the Jacket Division manager decided to buy? Explain.

Solution

The Jacket Division manager would not buy. The resulting transfer price of $48 would make the acquisition of the fabric unattractive to the Jacket Division:

Jacket Division			
Sales price of final product			$100
Deduct costs			
Transfer price paid to the Fabric Division			
(fully allocated cost)		$48	
Additional costs (from Exhibit 14-2)			
Processing	$43		
Selling	13	56	
Total costs to the Jacket Division			104
Contribution to profit of the Jacket Division			$ (4)
Contribution to company as a whole			
($100 − $40 − $56)			$ 4

The company as a whole would benefit by $40,000 (10,000 jackets × $4) if the Fabric Division produces and transfers the fabric.

The major lesson here is that, when there is idle capacity in the supplier division, transfer prices based on fully allocated costs may induce the wrong decisions. Working in her own best interests, the Jacket Division manager has no incentive to buy from the Fabric Division.

Problem Two

A division has assets of $200,000, current liabilities of $20,000, and net operating income of $60,000.

1. What is the division's ROI?
2. If interest is imputed at 14 percent, what is the residual income?
3. The weighted average cost of capital is 14 percent; what is the EVA?
4. What effects on management behaviour can be expected if ROI is used to gauge performance?
5. What effects on management behaviour can be expected if residual income is used to gauge performance?

Solution

1. $\$60,000 \div \$200,000 = 30$ percent.
2. $\$60,000 - 0.14 \ (\$200,000) = \$60,000 - \$28,000 = \$32,000$.
3. EVA $= \$60,000 - 0.14(\$200,000 - \$20,000)$
   $= \$60,000 - \$25,200$
   $= \$34,800$
4. If ROI is used, the manager is prone to reject projects that do not earn an ROI of at least 30 percent. From the viewpoint of the organization as a whole, this may be undesirable because its best investment opportunities may lie in that division at a rate of, say, 22 percent. If a division is enjoying a high ROI, it is less likely to expand if it is judged via ROI than if it is judged via residual income or EVA.
5. If residual income or EVA is used, the manager is inclined to accept all projects whose expected rate of return exceeds the minimum desired rate. The manager's division is more likely to expand because his or her goal is to maximize a dollar amount rather than a rate.

KEY TERMS

agency theory *p. 705*
capital charge *p. 708*
capital turnover *p. 707*
cost of capital *p. 708*
decentralization *p. 701*
dysfunctional decisions *p. 722*
economic value added (EVA) *p. 709*
gross book value *p. 715*

incentives *p. 704*
management by objectives (MBO) *p. 727*
net book value *p. 715*
residual income (RI) *p. 708*
return on investment (ROI) *p. 707*
return on sales *p. 707*
segment autonomy *p. 702*
transfer prices *p. 716*

ASSIGNMENT MATERIAL

QUESTIONS

Q14-1   "Decentralization has benefits and costs." Name three of each.

Q14-2   Sophisticated accounting and communications systems aid decentralization. Explain how they accomplish this.

Q14-3   "The essence of decentralization is the use of profit centres." Do you agree? Explain.

Q14-4   Why is decentralization more popular in profit-seeking organizations than in not-for-profit organizations?

Q14-5   What kinds of organizations find decentralization to be preferable to centralization?

Q14-6 Why are transfer-pricing systems needed?

Q14-7 Describe two problems that can arise when using actual full cost as a transfer price.

Q14-8 How does the presence or absence of idle capacity affect the optimal transfer-pricing policy?

Q14-9 "We use variable-cost transfer prices to ensure that no dysfunctional decisions are made." Discuss.

Q14-10 What is the major advantage of negotiated transfer prices? What is the major disadvantage?

Q14-11 Why does top management sometimes accept division managers' judgments, even if the division manager appears to be wrong?

Q14-12 Discuss two factors that affect multinational transfer prices but have little effect on purely domestic transfers.

Q14-13 According to agency theory, employment contracts trade off three factors. Name the three.

Q14-14 What is the major benefit of the ROI technique for measuring performance?

Q14-15 What two major items affect ROI?

Q14-16 "Both ROI and residual income use profit and invested capital to measure performance. Therefore, it really doesn't matter which we use." Do you agree? Explain.

Q14-17 Division A's ROI is 20 percent, and B's is 10 percent. Each manager is paid a bonus based on his or her division's ROI. Discuss whether each division manager would accept or reject a proposed project with a rate of return of 15 percent. Would either of them make a different decision if managers were evaluated using residual income with an imputed interest rate of 11 percent? Explain.

Q14-18 Give four possible definitions of invested capital that can be used in measuring ROI or residual income.

Q14-19 "Managers who use a historical-cost accounting system look backward at what something cost yesterday, instead of forward to what it will cost tomorrow." Do you agree? Why?

Q14-20 Company X uses net book value as a measure of invested capital when computing ROI. A division manager has suggested that the company change to using gross book value instead. What difference in motivation of division managers might result from such a change? Do you suppose most of the assets in the division of the manager proposing the change are relatively new or old? Why?

Q14-21 Describe management by objectives (MBO).

PROBLEMS

P14-1 **VARIABLE COST AS TRANSFER PRICE.** A desk calendar's variable cost is $5 and its market value is $6.25 at a transfer point from the Printing Division to the Binding Division. The Binding Division's variable cost of adding a simulated leather cover is $2.80, and the selling price of the final calendar is $8.50.

1. Prepare a tabulation of the contribution margin per unit for the Binding Division's performance and overall company performance

under the two alternatives of (a) selling to outsiders at the transfer point, and (b) adding the cover and then selling to outsiders.

2. As Binding Division manager, which alternative would you choose? Explain.

P14-2 MAXIMUM AND MINIMUM TRANSFER PRICE. Northland Company makes bicycles. Components are made in various divisions and transferred to the Western Division for assembly into final products. The Western Division can also buy components from external suppliers. The wheels are made in the Eastern Division, which also sells wheels to external customers. All divisions are profit centres and managers are free to negotiate transfer prices. Prices and costs for the Eastern and Western Divisions are

EASTERN DIVISION	
Sales price to external customers	$14
Internal transfer price	?
Costs:	
Variable costs per wheel	$9
Total fixed costs	$320,000
Budgeted production	64,000 wheels*
*Includes production for transfer to Western.	

WESTERN DIVISION	
Sales price to external customers	$175
Costs:	
Wheels, per bicycle	?
Other components, per bicycle	$90
Other variable costs, per bicycle	$20
Total fixed costs	$640,000
Budgeted production	16,000 bicycles

Fixed costs in both divisions will be unaffected by the transfer of wheels from the Eastern to the Western Division.

1. Compute the maximum transfer price per wheel the Western Division would be willing to pay to buy wheels from the Eastern Division.
2. Compute the minimum transfer price per wheel at which the Eastern Division would be willing to produce and sell wheels to the Western Division. Assume that Eastern has excess capacity. Compute the minimum transfer price per wheel if Eastern had *no* excess capacity.

P14-3 SIMPLE ROI CALCULATIONS. Given the following data, compute

1. Turnover of capital
2. Net income
3. Net income as a percentage of sales

Sales	$140,000
Invested capital	$50,000
Return on investment	10%

P14-4 SIMPLE ROI CALCULATIONS.   Fill in the blanks:

	DIVISION		
	A	B	C
Income percentage of revenue	7%	3%	%
Capital turnover	3	–	5
Rate of return on invested capital	–%	24%	20%

P14-5 SIMPLE ROI AND RESIDUAL INCOME CALCULATIONS.   Consider the following data:

	DIVISION		
	X	Y	Z
Invested capital	$2,000,000	$ –	$1,250,000
Income	$ –	$ 182,000	$ 125,000
Revenue	$4,000,000	$3,640,000	$ –
Income percentage of revenue	2.5%	–%	–%
Capital turnover	–	–	3
Rate of return on invested capital	–%	14%	–%

1. Prepare a similar tabular presentation, filling in all blanks.
2. Which division is the best performer? Explain.
3. Suppose each division is assessed an imputed interest rate of 10 percent on invested capital. Compute the residual income for each division.

P14-6 COMPARISON OF ASSET AND EQUITY BASES.   European Footwear has assets of $2 million and a long-term 10 percent debt of $800,000. Canadian Shoes has assets of $2 million and no long-term debt. The annual operating income (before interest) of both companies is $500,000.

1. Compute the rate of return on
   a. Assets available
   b. Shareholders' equity
2. Evaluate the relative merits of each base for appraising operating management.

P14-7 RATE OF RETURN AND TRANSFER PRICING.   Consider the following data regarding budgeted operations of the Regina Division of Yoshita Custom Signs:

Average available assets	
Receivables	$200,000
Inventories	250,000
Plant and equipment, net	450,000
Total	$900,000
Fixed overhead	$300,000
Variable costs	$2 per unit
Desired rate of return on average available assets	25 percent
Expected volume	75,000 units

1. **a.** What average unit sales price is needed to obtain the desired rate of return on average available assets?
   b. What would be the expected asset turnover?
   c. What would be the operating income percentage on dollar sales?
2. **a.** If the selling price is as computed above, what rate of return will be earned on available assets if sales volume is 90,000 units?
   b. If sales volume is 60,000 units?
3. Assume that 22,500 units are to be sold to another division of the same company and that only 52,500 units can be sold to outside customers. The other division manager has balked at a tentative selling price of $8. She has offered $4.50, claiming that she can manufacture the units herself for that price. The manager of the selling division has examined his own data. He has decided that he could eliminate $60,000 of inventories, $90,000 of plant and equipment, and $22,500 of fixed overhead if he did not sell to the other division and sold only 52,500 units to outside customers. Should he sell for $4.50? Show computations to support your answer.

P14-8 FINDING UNKNOWNS. Consider the following data:

	DIVISION		
	J	K	L
Income	$140,000	$ –	$ –
Revenue	$ –	$ –	$ –
Invested capital	$ –	$4,000,000	$16,000,000
Income percentage of revenue	7%	4%	–%
Capital turnover	4	–	3
Rate of return on invested capital	–%	20%	15%
Imputed interest rate on invested capital	20%	12%	–%
Residual income	$ –	$ –	$ 480,000

1. Prepare a similar tabular presentation, filling in all blanks.
2. Which division is the best performer? Explain.

P14-9 PROFIT CENTRES AND TRANSFER PRICING IN AN AUTOMOBILE DEALERSHIP. A large automobile dealership is installing a responsibility accounting system and three profit centres: parts and service; new vehicles; and used vehicles. The department managers have been told to run their shops as if they were in business for themselves. However, there are interdepartmental dealings. For example:

   a. The parts and service department prepares new cars for final delivery and repairs used cars prior to resale.
   b. The used car department's major source of inventory has been cars traded in as partial payment for new cars.

The owner of the dealership has asked you to draft a company policy statement on transfer pricing, together with specific rules to be applied to the examples cited. He has told you that clarity is of paramount importance because your statement will be relied upon for settling transfer-pricing disputes.

P14-10 ROLE OF ECONOMIC VALUE AND REPLACEMENT VALUE. "To me, economic value is the only justifiable basis for measuring plant assets for purposes of evaluating performance. By economic value, I mean the present value of expected future services. Still, we do not even do this upon acquisition of new assets—that is, we may compute a positive net present value, using discounted cash flow, but we record the asset at no more than its cost. In this way, the excess present value is not shown in the initial balance sheet. Moreover, the use of replacement costs in subsequent years is also unlikely to result in showing economic values; the replacement cost will probably be less than the economic value at any given instant of an asset's life."

"Market values are totally unappealing to me because they represent a second-best alternative value—that is, they ordinarily represent the maximum amount obtainable from an alternative that has been rejected. Obviously, if the market value exceeds the economic value of the assets in use, they should be sold. However, in most instances, the opposite is true; market values of individual assets are far below their economic value in use."

"Obtaining and recording total present values of individual assets based on discounted-cash-flow techniques is an infeasible alternative. I therefore conclude that replacement cost (less accumulated amortization) of similar assets producing similar services is the best practical approximation of the economic value of the assets in use. Of course, it is more appropriate for the evaluation of the division's performance than the division manager's performance."

Critically evaluate these comments. Please do not wander; concentrate on the issues described by the quotation.

P14-11 **TRANSFER PRICING.** The Propellers Division of Monte Carlo Sports Company produces propellers for outboard motors. It has been the sole supplier of propellers to the Outboard Motor Division and charges $32 per unit—the current market price for very large wholesale lots. The Propellers Division also sells to outside retail outlets, at $40 per unit. Normally, outside sales amount to 25 percent of a total sales volume of 1 million pumps per year. Typical combined annual data for the division follows:

Sales	$34,000,000
Variable costs, @ $26 per pump	$26,000,000
Fixed costs	3,000,000
Total costs	$29,000,000
Gross margin	$ 5,000,000

The Ocean Eleven Company, an entirely separate entity, has offered the Outboard Motor Division comparable propellers at a firm price of $30 per unit. The Propeller Division claims that it cannot possibly match this price because it could not earn any margin at $30.

1. Assume that you are the manager of the Outboard Motor Division. Comment on the Propeller Division's claim. Assume that normal outside volume cannot be increased.
2. Propeller Division believes that it can increase outside sales by 750,000 propellers per year by increasing fixed costs by $2 million and variable costs by $3 per unit while reducing the selling price to $38. Assume that maximum capacity is 1 million propellers per year. Should the division reject intracompany business and concentrate on outside sales?

P14-12 **TRANSFER PRICING CONCESSION.** The Moncton Division of Glencoe Corporation, operating at capacity, has been asked by the Antigonish Division of Glencoe to supply it with Electrical Fitting No. LX29. Moncton sells this part to its regular customers for $10 each. Antigonish, which is operating at 50 percent capacity, is willing to pay $6.90 each for the fitting. Antigonish will put the fitting into a brake unit that it is manufacturing on essentially a cost-plus basis for a commercial airplane manufacturer.

Moncton has a variable cost of producing fitting No. LX29 of $6. The cost of the brake unit being built by Antigonish is as follows:

Purchased parts—outside vendors	$28.10
Moncton fitting No. LX29	6.90
Other variable costs	17.50
Fixed overhead and administration	10.00
	$62.50

Antigonish believes the price concession is necessary to get the job.

The company uses return on investment and dollar profits in the measurement of division and division-manager performance.

1. Consider that you are the division controller of Moncton. Would you recommend that Moncton supply fitting No. LX29 to Antigonish? Why or why not? (Ignore any income-tax issues.)
2. Would it be to the short-run economic advantage of the Glencoe Corporation for the Moncton Division to supply the Antigonish Division with fitting No. LX29 at $6.90 each? (Ignore any income-tax issues.) Explain your answer.
3. Discuss the organizational and manager-behaviour difficulties, if any, inherent in this situation. As the Glencoe controller, what would you advise the Glencoe Corporation president to do in this situation?

P14-13 **TRANSFER PRICES AND IDLE CAPACITY.** The Furniture Division of Woodcraft Ltd. purchases lumber, which it uses to fabricate tables, chairs, and other wood furniture. Most of the lumber is purchased from the Southshore Mill, also a division of Woodcraft Ltd. Both the Furniture Division and Southshore Mill are profit centres.

The Furniture Division proposes to produce a new Danish-designed chair that will sell for $92. The manager is exploring the possibility of purchasing the required lumber from the Southshore Mill. Production of 800 chairs is planned, using capacity in the Furniture Division that is currently idle.

The Furniture Division can purchase the lumber from an outside supplier for $72. Woodcraft Ltd. has a policy that internal transfers are priced at *fully allocated cost*.

Assume the following costs for the production of one chair and the lumber required for the chair:

SOUTHSHORE MILL		FURNITURE DIVISION		
Variable cost	$48	Variable costs:		
Allocated fixed cost	22	Lumber from Southshore Mill		$70
Fully allocated cost	$70	Furniture Division variable costs:		
		Manufacturing	$21	
		Selling	6	27
		Total cost		$97

1. Assume that the Southshore Mill has idle capacity and therefore would incur no additional fixed costs to produce the required lumber. Would the Furniture Division manager buy the lumber for the chair from the Southshore Mill, given the existing transfer-pricing policy? Why or why not? Would the company as a whole benefit if the manager decides to buy from the Southshore Mill? Explain.

2. Assume that there is no idle capacity at the Southshore Mill and the lumber required for one chair can be sold to outside customers for $72. Would the company as a whole benefit if the manager decides to buy? Explain.

P14-14 **RATE OF RETURN AND TRANSFER PRICING.** The Seoul division of Global Toy Company manufactures chess boards and sells them in the Korean market for KRW30,000 each. (KRW is the Korean won.) The following data are from the Seoul Division's 2006 budget:

Variable cost	KRW19,000 per unit
Fixed overhead	KRW30,400,000
Total assets	KRW62,500,000

Global Toy has instructed the Seoul Division to budget a rate of return on total assets (before taxes) of 20 percent.

1. Suppose the Seoul Division expects to sell 3,400 chess boards during 2006:
   a. What rate of return will be earned on total assets?
   b. What would be the expected capital turnover?
   c. What would be the operating income percentage of sales?
2. The Seoul Division is considering adjustments in the budget to reach the desired 20 percent rate of return on total assets.
   a. How many units must be sold to obtain the desired return if no other part of the budget is changed?
   b. Suppose sales cannot be increased beyond 3,400 units. How much must total assets be reduced to obtain the desired return? Assume that for every KRW1,000 decrease in total assets, fixed costs decrease by KRW100.
3. Assume that only 2,400 units can be sold in the Korean market. However, another 1,400 units can be sold to the North American Marketing Division of Global Toy. The Seoul manager has offered to sell the 1,400 units for KRW27,500 each. The North American Marketing Division manager has countered with an offer to pay KRW25,000 per unit, claiming she can subcontract production to a North American producer at a cost equivalent to KRW25,000. The Seoul manager knows that if his production falls to 2,400 units, he could eliminate some assets, reducing total assets to KRW50 million and annual fixed overhead to KRW24.5 million. Should the Seoul manager sell for KRW25,000 per unit? Support your answer with the relevant computations. Ignore the effects of income taxes and import duties.

P14-15 **ROI OR RESIDUAL INCOME.** Keyworth Co. is a large integrated conglomerate with shipping, metals, and mining operations throughout the world. The general manager of the Shipbuilding Division plans to submit a proposed capital budget for 2006 for inclusion in the company-wide budget.

The division manager has for consideration the following projects, all of which require an outlay of capital. All projects have equal risk.

PROJECT	INVESTMENT REQUIRED	RETURN	%
1	$4,800,000	$1,200,000	25
2	1,900,000	627,000	33
3	1,400,000	182,000	13
4	950,000	152,000	16
5	650,000	136,000	21
6	300,000	90,000	30

The division manager must decide which of the projects to take. The company has a cost of capital of 15 percent. An amount of $12 million is available to the division for investment purposes.

1. What will be the total investment, total return, return on capital invested, and residual income of the rational division manager if:
   a. The company has a rule that all projects promising at least 20 percent or more should be taken?
   b. The division manager is evaluated on his ability to maximize his return on capital invested (assume that this is a new division with no invested capital)?
   c. The division manager is expected to maximize residual income as computed by using the 15 percent cost of capital?
2. Which of the three approaches will induce the most effective investment policy for the company as a whole? Explain.

P14-16 **TRANSFER-PRICING PRINCIPLES.** A consulting firm, TAC, is decentralized with 25 offices around the country. The headquarters is based in Vancouver, British Columbia. Another operating division is located in Calgary. A subsidiary printing operation, Kwik Print, is located in the headquarters building. Top management has indicated that they would like the Calgary office to use Kwik Print for printing reports. All charges are eventually billed to the client, but TAC was concerned about keeping such charges competitive.

Kwik Print charges the Calgary office the following amounts:

Photographing page for offset printing	
(a setup cost)	$0.25
Printing cost per page	0.014

At this rate, Kwik Print sales have a 60 percent contribution margin to fixed overhead.

Outside bids for 100 copies of a 120-page report needed immediately have been

Print 4V	$204.00
Jiffy Press	180.25
Kustom Print	186.00

These three printers are located within a five kilometre radius of TAC Calgary and can have the reports ready in two days. A messenger would have to be sent to drop off the original and pick up the copies. The messenger usually goes to headquarters, but in the past, special trips have been required to deliver the original or pick up the copies. It takes three to four days to get the copies from Kwik Print (because of the extra scheduling difficulties in delivery and pickup).

Quality control of Kwik Print is poor. Reports received in the past have had wrinkled pages and have occasionally been miscollated or had pages deleted. (In one circumstance an intracompany memorandum indicating TAC's economic straits was inserted in a report. Fortunately, the Calgary office detected the error before the report was distributed to the clients.) The degree of quality control in the three outside print shops is unknown.

(Although the differences in costs may seem immaterial in this case, regard the numbers as significant for purposes of focusing on the key issues.)

1. If you were the decision maker at TAC Calgary, to which print shop would you give the business? Is this an optimal economic decision from the entire corporation's point of view?
2. What would be the ideal transfer price in this case, if based only on economic considerations?
3. Time is an important factor in maintaining the goodwill of the client. There is potential return business from this client. Given this perspective, what might be the optimal decision for the company?
4. Comment on the wisdom of top management in indicating that Kwik Print should be used.

P14-17 **MULTINATIONAL TRANSFER PRICES.** Medical Instruments, Inc., produces a variety of medical products at its plant in Halifax, Nova Scotia. The company has sales divisions worldwide. One of these sales divisions is located in Oslo, Norway. Assume that the Canadian income tax rate is 34 percent, the Norwegian rate is 60 percent, and a 15 percent import duty is imposed on medical supplies brought into Norway.

One product produced in Halifax and shipped to Norway is a heart monitor. The variable cost of production is $350 per unit, and the fully allocated cost is $600 per unit.

1. Suppose the Norwegian government allows either the variable or fully allocated cost to be used as a transfer price. Which should Medical Instruments, Inc. choose to minimize the total of income taxes and import duties? Compute the amount the company saves if it uses your suggested transfer price instead of the alternative.
2. Suppose the Norwegian parliament passed a law decreasing the income tax rate to 50 percent and increasing the duty on heart monitors to 20 percent. Repeat requirement 1, using these new facts.

P14-18 **AGENCY THEORY.** The London Trading Company plans to hire a manager for its division in Kenya. London Trading's president and the vice president of personnel are trying to decide on an appropriate incentive employment contract. The manager will operate far from the London corporate headquarters, so evaluation by personal observation will be limited. The president insists that a large incentive to produce profits is necessary; he favours a salary of £12,000 and a bonus of 10 percent of the profits above £120,000. If operations proceed as expected, profits will be £480,000, and the manager will receive £48,000. But both profits and compensation might be more or less than planned.

The vice president of personnel responds that £48,000 is more than most of London Trading's division managers make. She is sure that a competent manager can be hired for a guaranteed salary of £38,000. "Why pay £48,000 when we can probably hire the same person for £38,000?" she argued.

1. What factors would affect London Trading's choice of employment contract? Include a discussion of the pros and cons of each proposed contract.
2. Why is the expected compensation more with the bonus plan than with the straight salary?

P14-19 MARGINS AND TURNOVER.   Return on investment is often expressed as the product of two components: capital turnover and margin on sales. You are considering investing in one of three companies, all in the same industry, and are given the following information:

	COMPANY		
	X	Y	Z
Sales	$9,000,000	$2,500,000	$37,500,000
Income	1,350,000	375,000	375,000
Capital	4,500,000	12,500,000	12,500,000

1. Why would you desire the breakdown of return on investment into margin on sales and turnover on capital?
2. Compute the margin on sales, turnover on capital, and return on investment for the three companies, and comment on the relative performance of the companies as thoroughly as the data permit.

P14-20 ROI BY BUSINESS SEGMENT.   Krikos Inc. does business in three different business segments: (1) Entertainment, (2) Publishing/Information, and (3) Consumer/Commercial Finance. Results for a recent year were (in millions):

	REVENUES	OPERATING INCOME	TOTAL ASSETS
Entertainment	$1,272.2	$223.0	$1,120.1
Publishing/Information	705.5	120.4	1,380.7
Consumer/Commercial Finance	1,235.0	244.6	924.4

1. Compute the following for each business segment:
   a. Income percentage of revenue
   b. Capital turnover
   c. Return on investment (ROI)
2. Comment on the differences in return on investment among the business segments. Include reasons for the differences.

P14-21 MULTINATIONAL TRANSFER PRICES.   Global Enterprises, Inc. has production and marketing divisions throughout the world. One particular product is produced in Japan, where the income tax rate is 30 percent, and transferred to a marketing division in Sweden, where the income tax rate is 60 percent. Assume that Sweden places an import tax of 10 percent on the product.

The variable cost of the product is $200 and the full cost is $400. Suppose the company can legally select a transfer price anywhere between the variable and full cost.

1. What transfer price should Global Enterprises use to minimize taxes? Explain why this is the tax-minimizing transfer price.

2. Compute the amount of taxes saved by using the transfer price in requirement 1 instead of the transfer price that would result in the highest taxes.

P14-22 **EVALUATING DIVISIONAL PERFORMANCE.** As the chief executive officer of Shoe Unlimited Company, you examined the following measures of the performance of three divisions (in thousands of dollars):

DIVISION	NET ASSETS BASED ON		OPERATING INCOME BASED ON*	
	HISTORICAL COST	REPLACEMENT COST	HISTORICAL COST	REPLACEMENT COST
Shoes	$15,000	$15,000	$2,700	$2,700
Clothing	45,000	55,000	6,750	6,150
Accessories	30,000	48,000	4,800	3,900

* The differences in operating income between historical and replacement cost are attributable to the differences in amortization expenses.

1. Calculate for each division the rate of return on net assets and the residual income based on historical cost and on replacement cost. For purposes of calculating residual income, use 10 percent as the minimum desired rate of return.

2. Rank the performance of each division under each of the four different measures computed above.

3. What do these measures indicate about the performance of the divisions? Of the division managers? Which measure do you prefer? Why?

P14-23 **USING GROSS OR NET BOOK VALUE OF FIXED ASSETS.** Assume that a particular plant acquires $800,000 of fixed assets with a useful life of four years and no residual value. Straight-line amortization will be used. The plant manager is judged on income in relation to these fixed assets. Annual net income, after deducting amortization, is $80,000.

Assume that sales and all expenses except amortization are on a cash basis. Dividends equal net income. Thus, cash in the amount of the amortization charge will accumulate each year. The plant manager's performance is judged in relation to fixed assets because all current assets, including cash, are considered under central-company control.

1. Prepare a comparative tabulation of the plant's rate of return and the company's overall rate of return based on
  a. Gross (i.e., original cost) assets
  b. Net book value of assets (assume [unrealistically] that any cash accumulated remains idle)

2. Evaluate the relative merits of gross assets and net book value of assets as investment bases.

P14-24 **NEGOTIATED TRANSFER PRICES.** The Assembly Division of Office Furniture, Inc. needs 1,200 units of a subassembly from the Fabricating Division. The company has a policy of negotiated transfer prices. The Fabricating Division has enough excess capacity to produce 2,000 units of the subassembly. Its variable cost of production is $20. The market price of the subassembly is $50.

What is the natural bargaining range for a transfer price between the two divisions? Explain why no price below your range would be acceptable. Also explain why no price above your range would be acceptable.

P14-25 **ECONOMIC VALUE ADDED.** The Coca-Cola Company uses economic value added (EVA) to evaluate top management performance. In 1996 Coca-Cola had net operating income of $3,915 million, income taxes of $1,104 million, and long-term debt plus shareholders' equity of $8,755 million. The company's capital is about 30 percent long-term debt and 70 percent equity. Assume that the after-tax cost of debt is 5 percent and the cost of equity is 12 percent.

1. Compute Coca-Cola's economic value added (EVA).
2. Explain what EVA tells you about the performance of the top management of Coca-Cola in 1996.

P14-26 **TRANSFER-PRICING DISPUTE.** A transportation equipment manufacturer, Mason Corporation, is heavily decentralized. Each division head has full authority on all decisions regarding sales to internal or external customers. The Pacific Division has always acquired a certain equipment component from the Southern Division. However, when informed that the Southern Division was increasing its unit price to $330, the Pacific Division's management decided to purchase the component from outside suppliers at a price of $300.

The Southern Division had recently acquired some specialized equipment that was used primarily to make this component. The manager cited the resulting high amortization charges as the justification for the price boost. He asked the president of the company to instruct the Pacific Division to buy from Southern at the $330 price. He supplied the following data to back his request:

Pacific's annual purchases of component	3,000 units
Southern's variable costs per unit	$285
Southern's fixed costs per unit	$30

1. Suppose there are no alternative uses of the Southern facilities. Will the company as a whole benefit if Pacific buys from the outside suppliers for $300 per unit? Show computations to support your answer.
2. Suppose internal facilities of Southern would not otherwise be idle. The equipment and other facilities would be assigned to other production operations that would otherwise require an additional annual outlay of $60,000. Should Pacific purchase from outsiders at $300 per unit?
3. Suppose there are no alternative uses for Southern's internal facilities and that the selling price of outsiders drops by $30. Should Pacific purchase from outsiders?
4. As the president, how would you respond to the request of the manager of Southern? Would your response differ, depending on the specific situations described in requirements 1 through 3 above? Why?

P14-27 **TRANSFER PRICING.** Burger-Rama Enterprises runs a chain of drive-in hamburger stands at a tourist attraction during the ten-week summer season. Managers of all stands are told to act as if they owned the stand and are judged on their profit performance. Burger-Rama Enterprises has rented an ice-cream machine for the summer to supply its stands with ice cream. Rent for the machine is $1,800.

Burger-Rama is not allowed to sell ice cream to other dealers because it cannot obtain a dairy licence. The manager of the ice-cream machine charges the stands $4 per four litres. Operating figures for the machine for the summer are as follows:

Sales to the stands (8,000 four litres at $4)		$32,000
Variable costs (@ $2.10 per four litres)	16,800	
Fixed costs		
Rental of machine	1,800	
Other fixed costs	5,000	23,600
Operating margin		$ 8,400

The manager of the Sizzling Drive-In, one of the Burger-Rama drive-ins, is seeking permission to sign a contract to buy ice cream from an outside supplier at $3.30 for four litres. The Sizzling Drive-In uses 1,500 four litres of ice cream during the summer. Linda Garton, controller of Burger-Rama, refers this request to you. You determine that the other fixed costs of operating the machine will decrease by $480 if the Sizzling Drive-In purchases from an outside supplier. Garton wants an analysis of the request in terms of overall company objectives and an explanation of your conclusion. What is the appropriate transfer price?

P14-28 **REVIEW OF MAJOR POINTS IN CHAPTER.** The Antonio Company uses the decentralized form of organizational structure and considers each of its divisions as an investment centre. Division L is currently selling 15,000 air filters annually, although it has sufficient productive capacity to produce 21,000 units per year. Variable manufacturing costs amount to $17 per unit, while the total fixed costs amount to $90,000. These 15,000 air filters are sold to outside customers at $37 per unit.

Division M, also part of the Antonio Company, has indicated that it would like to buy 1,500 air filters from Division L, but at a price of $36 per unit. This is the price that Division M is currently paying an outside supplier.

1. Compute the effect on the operating income of the company as a whole if Division M purchases 1,500 air filters from Division L.
2. What is the minimum price that Division L should be willing to accept for the air filters?
3. What is the maximum price that Division M should be willing to pay for the air filters?
4. Suppose instead that Division L is currently producing and selling 21,000 air filters annually to outside customers. What is the effect on the overall Antonio Company operating income if Division L is required by top management to sell 1,500 air filters to Division M at (a) $17 per unit, and (b) $37 per unit?
5. For this question only, assume that Division L is currently earning an annual operating income of $36,000, and the division's average invested capital is $300,000. The division manager has an opportunity to invest in a proposal that will require an additional investment of $20,000 and will increase annual operating income by $2,200. (a) Should the division manager accept this proposal if the Antonio Company uses ROI in evaluating the performance of its divisional managers? (b) If the company uses residual income? (Assume an "imputed interest" charge of 9 percent.)

P14-29 **MANAGEMENT BY OBJECTIVES.** Tom Torres is the chief executive officer of Mayberry Company. Torres has a financial management background and is known throughout the organization as a "no-nonsense" executive. When Torres became chief executive officer, he emphasized cost reduction and savings and introduced a comprehensive cost-control and budget system. The company goals and budget plans were established by Torres and given to his subordinates for implementation. Some of the company's key executives were dismissed or demoted for failing to meet projected budget plans. Under the leadership of Tom Torres, Mayberry has once again become financially stable and profitable after several years of poor performance.

Recently, Torres has become concerned with the human side of the organization and has become interested in the management technique referred to as "management by objectives (MBO)." If there are enough positive benefits of MBO, he plans to implement the system throughout the company. However, he realizes that he does not fully understand MBO because he does not understand how it differs from the current system of establishing firm objectives and budget plans.

1. Briefly explain what "management by objectives" entails and identify its advantages and disadvantages.
2. Does the management style of Tom Torres incorporate the human value premises and goals of MBO? Explain your answer.

MANAGERIAL DECISION CASES

C14-1 **PROFIT CENTRES AND CENTRAL SERVICES.** EZtronics, a manufacturer of small appliances, has an Engineering Consulting Department (ECD). The department's major task has been to help the production departments improve their operating methods and processes.

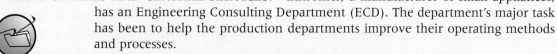

For several years the consulting services have been charged to the production departments based on a signed agreement between the managers involved. The agreement specifies the scope of the project, the predicted savings, and the number of consulting hours required. The charge to the production departments is based on the costs to ECD of the services rendered. For example, senior engineer hours cost more per hour than junior engineer hours. An overhead cost is included. The agreement is really a "fixed-price" contract. That is, the production manager knows the total cost of the project in advance. A recent survey revealed that production managers have a high level of confidence in the engineers.

The ECD manager oversees the work of about 40 senior engineers and ten junior engineers. She reports to the engineering manager, who reports to the vice president of manufacturing. The ECD manager has the freedom to increase or decrease the number of engineers under her supervision. The ECD manager's performance evaluation is based on many factors, including the annual incremental savings to the company in excess of the costs of operating ECD.

The production departments are profit centres. Their goods are transferred to subsequent departments, such as a sales department or sales division, at prices that approximate market prices for similar products.

Top management is seriously considering a "no-charge" plan. That is, engineering services would be rendered to the production departments at absolutely no cost. Proponents of the new plan maintain that it would motivate the production managers to take keener advantage of engineering talent. In all other respects, the new system would be unchanged from the present system.

Required:

1. Compare the present and proposed plans. What are their strong and weak points? In particular, will the ECD manager tend to hire the "optimal" amount of engineering talent?
2. Which plan do you favour? Why?

C14-2 **CONTRIBUTION MARGIN AND TRANSFER PRICES.** (SMAC) The Whole Company is an integrated multidivisional manufacturing firm. Two of its divisions, Rod and Champ, are profit centres and their division managers have full responsibility for production and sales (both internal and external). Both the Rod and Champ division managers are evaluated by top management on the basis of total profit.

Rod Division is the exclusive producer of a special equipment component called Q-32. The Rod Division manager used the results of a market study to set the price of Q-32 at $450 per unit. At this price, the normal sales and production volume is 21,000 units per year; however, production capacity is 26,000 units per year. Standard production costs for one unit of Q-32 based on normal production volume are as follows:

Direct materials	$175.00
Direct labour	75.00
Variable overhead	50.00
Fixed overhead	90.00
Total unit production costs	$390.00

Champ Division produces machinery for several large customers on a contractual basis. It has recently been approached by a potential customer to produce a specially designed machine that would require one unit of Q-32 as its main component. The potential customer has indicated that it would be willing to sign a long-term contract for 10,400 units of the machine per year at a maximum price of $650 per unit. Although Champ Division has sufficient idle capacity to accommodate the production of this special machine, the division manager is not willing to accept the contract unless he can negotiate a reasonable transfer price with the Rod Division manager for Q-32. He has calculated that the unit costs to produce the special machine are as follows:

Direct material other than Q-32	$100.00
Direct labour	50.00
Variable overhead	35.00
Fixed overhead	50.00
Total unit production costs before transfer of Q-32	$235.00

Required:

1. What is the maximum unit transfer price that the Champ Division manager should be willing to accept for Q-32 if he wishes to accept the contract for the special machine? Support your answer.
2. What is the minimum unit transfer price that the Rod Division manager should be willing to accept for Q-32? Support your answer.
3. Assume that Rod Division would be able to sell its capacity of 26,000 units of Q-32 per year in the outside market if the selling price was reduced by 5 percent. From top management's point of view, evaluate, considering both quantitative and qualitative factors, whether Rod Division should lower its market price or transfer the required units of Q-32 to Champ Division. What would you recommend? Why?

C14-3   **COMPENSATION PLAN.**   (CGAC)   Riverside Mining and Manufacturing is a vertically integrated company that mines, processes, and finishes various non-precious metals and minerals. Riverside has decentralized both on a geographical and on an operational basis. For example, Exploration and Development, which includes all mining operations, has been designated a strategic business unit (SBU). There are multiple divisions within this SBU, such as the North American Exploration and Development Division, the South American Exploration and Development Division, and other divisions. Similarly, Refining, which has often been located near the mines, is another SBU and is divisionalized by geographical region.

Riverside has a clearly stated management control system that includes longstanding policies on transfer pricing, performance evaluation, and management compensation. Transfers are made at full cost plus a markup to approximate net realizable value. Riverside's primary operating divisions (such as mining) are required to fill internal orders before servicing outside orders. Each division has full responsibility over setting prices and sales targets as well as monitoring costs. Also, divisional managers have decision-making authority over fixed investments (capital equipment) up to $0.5 million as long as the investments can be internally financed. For any investment exceeding $0.5 million, final approval must be given by the SBU and head office.

For performance-evaluation purposes, Riverside uses two basic measures to evaluate managers. First, it uses budgeted income and second, return on investment (ROI). Divisional managers develop their budgets in line with goals set centrally for the organization. All budgets must be approved by the SBU and central executive before their final acceptance. Net income includes headquarters' allocations based on a percentage of divisional sales. ROI is calculated as net income divided by total assets. As with the budget target, the ROI target has to be approved. Although the weighted average cost of capital for the company is 12 percent, each division negotiates its target ROI based on past performance and perceived risks and uncertainty in the environment. Progress toward the budgeted income and ROI targets are evaluated on a quarterly basis.

Riverside's bonus compensation scheme was extended to its divisional managers last year. The bonus consists of a 50/50 cash plus deferred payment scheme that is measured each quarter. For example, if a division manager exceeds budgeted income and ROI targets for the division, then the manager is awarded a bonus, 50 percent of which is paid immediately in cash and 50 percent of which is invested in "phantom shares" that can be redeemed three years hence, given continued good performance. The total value of the bonuses range from 10 percent to 100 percent of regular salary, depending on how well managers did and their level in the organization. Actual amounts of bonuses earned in any given year depend on the centrally calculated bonus pool, which is defined as a percentage of overall company income.

Some of the divisional managers have been unhappy with the bonus compensation scheme. They felt they were at a disadvantage because of their lack of control over their prices (due to the nature of the external market), and their inability to achieve the growth in the ROI required by central headquarters. The division managers believed that a shift to residual income would help, but Riverside's CEO rejected this, feeling that residual income would not allow comparison of divisional results. The results of three of these divisions are shown in Exhibit 14A-1.

	Division A	Division B	Division C
Budgeted net income	$ 185	$1,964	$895
Actual net income	148	1,968	1,020
Budgeted total assets	1,310	8,755	6,978
Actual total assets	1,109	8,811	6,955
Target ROI	14.12%	22.4%	12.8%
Actual ROI	13.3%	22.3%	14.7%

Riverside Mining and
Manufacturing
Selected Divisional Results
for the Most Recent
Quarter
(in thousands)

As well, the managers of the Primary Operating Divisions wanted the restrictions on the internal versus external sales lifted so that they could achieve better results than they were currently experiencing.

Required:

1. **a.** Calculate the residual income figure for each of the three divisions.
   b. In point form, list the advantages and disadvantages that residual income might have over the use of ROI at Riverside.
2. Evaluate the management control system currently in place at Riverside, outlining its strengths and weaknesses and make recommendations for any changes you feel are necessary.

C14-4 **TRANSFER PRICE ALTERNATIVES.** (SMAC) On your first day on the job as controller of XYZ Corporation, you, C. M. Anderson, are asked to participate in the weekly management meeting. The organizational chart (Exhibit 14A-2) represents the extent of your knowledge of the company.

After appropriate introductions and greetings, the following exchange takes place:

Mr. Rodrigues: I, for one, am glad to see someone with your qualifications as our controller, Anderson. Maybe now we can finally introduce an element of sanity to this transfer pricing problem we've been wrestling with.

Ms. Walters: Rodrigues, transfer pricing was settled two years ago. You're the only one who's wrestling with anything.

Mr. Davis: That's not entirely true. Rodrigues and I have been talking, and I'm beginning to think that our cost-based pricing formula isn't as effective as it was supposed to be when we set it up. In fact, last month's statements convinced me that my department is being taken advantage of worse than ever!

Ms. Walters: You feel that way for two reasons. First, no one has ever explained transfer pricing properly to you, and second, Rodrigues doesn't know what he's talking about.

Mr. Sharma: This is embarrassing. We're bickering like children in front of the newest member of our management team. Let's at least fill Anderson in on the issue. Perhaps we can all benefit from the infusion of new ideas. Rodrigues, you start.

Mr. Rodrigues: My division manufactures primary components for our electronics division products. Davis and his people take my parts, plus many others from various subcontractors and small, specialized manufacturers, and basically just assemble them and

EXHIBIT 14A-2

XYZ Corporation
Electronics Division

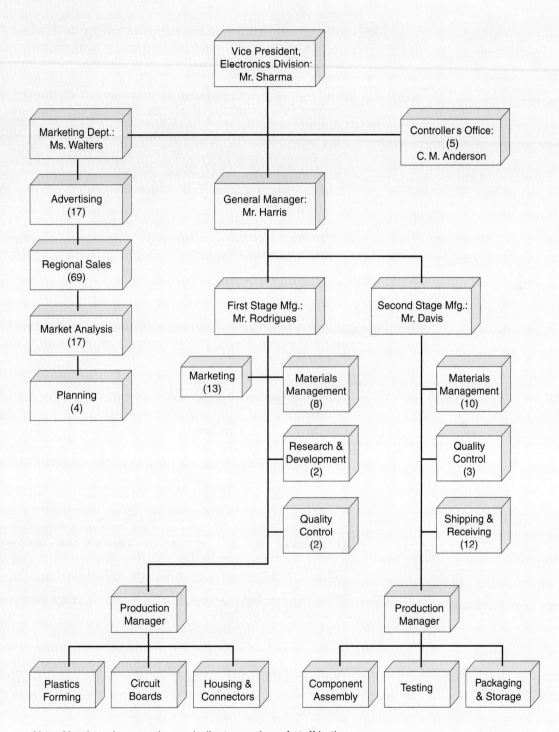

Note: Numbers in parentheses indicate number of staff in the area.

ship them out. All he has to do is perform one or two technical procedures besides assembly to get things working. That's why we call his operation "second stage" manufacturing.

Anyway, things worked fine until about two years ago. At that time, I had completed a major expansion, doubling my production facilities, in response to a forecast by Walters' marketing people. Only a fraction of the new markets materialized, however, and I was strapped with 40 percent underutilized capacity. To maximize profits, I developed a market for our circuit boards myself, and soon I had boosted production up to 90 percent of capacity. Since that time, my market has grown and I'm now running at about 110 percent of capacity with half of my product going to outside sales.

But as soon as I received one dollar in revenue, I became a profit centre. It was either that, they told me, or leave the sales end to Walters. For obvious reasons, I chose to become a profit centre.

So our controller at the time imposed what he called "a negotiated cost-based transfer price" on me. In reality, it's a dictated marginal-cost transfer price, but for appearance's sake, it has 12 percent thrown in to cover my overhead. Standard full costing would result in a markup of at least 20 percent over standard direct costs.

Ms. Walters:	You haven't much reason to complain. Regardless of how you work the percentages, you've shown a profit in each of the last two years.
Mr. Rodrigues:	How would you like your annual bonus to be based on a $5,000 profit when you produce $15 million of circuit boards a year? Of course, I'm making a profit—that's what I'm paid to do. But to do it, I've had to pare costs below the minimum in dozens of areas. My circuit boards are twice as expensive as some of our competitors'. To turn a $5,000 profit, I've delivered to Katmandu at three o'clock in the morning, worked my staff to the breaking point, and given ten-year no-fault guarantees.
	Let me warn you, no one can know what profit I've really made until two or three more years have passed. So far we've been lucky—warranty returns have been less than 0.5 percent. But if I have to honour 10 percent of my warranties, at least 20 percent of my annual production will be eaten up.
Mr. Davis:	That's where the trouble is! In the last two years, your circuit boards have gone from 1 percent defective to almost 15 percent. In fact, Anderson, the situation is so serious that I now have three people on input quality control full time, using $250,000 of testing equipment. Because of the tremendous workload in Rodrigues's department, my department reworks all of the rejects that can be salvaged. Only about 10 percent of the rejects have to be scrapped.
Mr. Rodrigues:	Our production control standards haven't fallen one bit in the past five years!

Mr. Davis: But the standards of five years ago aren't very applicable in today's markets. Walters' market research staff has raised our minimum standards three times in the last two years alone. Surely you were advised?

That brings up another problem. Although Rodrigues is working miracles flogging his boards outside at a premium price, I've been approached by two suppliers who could supply me with an identical product for even less than Rodrigues's variable cost. And they would guarantee reject rates of less than 5 percent. If I were allowed to buy outside, I could probably reduce my costs by 2 or 3 percent. That would translate into a 5 percent increase in profits. As it is, I'm constantly running over budget and not just for circuit boards. Lately our plastics, housings, and connectors have shown signs of alarmingly high variances from minimum quality standards. We all appreciate the pressures Rodrigues is under, but I can't help but wonder if anyone is benefitting from transfer pricing. That's where all these problems stem from—we didn't have any of them before this transfer pricing thing came up.

Mr. Rodrigues: Your outside suppliers are manufacturers from Hong Kong and Taiwan. They both approached my biggest client, and he ran tests on their products. The defects ranged from 1 to 20 percent consistently. Needless to say, I didn't lose my client. My defects still have a range of less than 1 percent.

Ms. Walters: You're both neglecting the corporate view of the situation. Sure, you have problems, Rodrigues. Your cost overruns are upsetting to you, Davis, but they are neither significant nor serious. Your total cost overruns are $500,000. That's about 1 percent and it's adequately covered by our margin, which is a direct result of our determination to maintain our image of high quality. During the past two years, while our competitors have had to cut their prices by as much as 20 percent, our prices have held firm, at least in most cases. Our profit may not have grown, but it certainly hasn't fallen by as much as our competitors'.

Even Rodrigues's marketing strategy should get some credit because it fits hand-in-glove with our corporate strategy. And the fact that our major competitors either use our boards or make their own to our standards prevents them from reducing their cost base.

My key marketing tool is the way XYZ sets the standard for quality in the industry. If the second stage manufacturing division were allowed to save a nickel by buying boards from other suppliers, Rodrigues would have more of his production to sell. He might even increase his profits a bit. But if word got out that the XYZ unit doesn't use XYZ circuits, I'd be the laughingstock of the industry.

Trust me, the way we're running now, the entire company makes money. And, after all, gentlemen, what else are we employed for?

Mr. Sharma: There you have it, Anderson. I don't mean to put undue pressure on you. Maybe you can just identify the key elements that we will have to take into consideration in coming up with some kind of solution.

After the meeting, Mr. Sharma expressed his personal dissatisfaction with the entire situation. He suggested that a hard-hitting, comprehensive report might be the best way to redirect his managers and solve the problems quickly.

Prepare a report addressed to the vice president of the Electronics Division, analyzing the issues brought to light at the meeting, together with a recommended plan of action.

C14-5   **TRANSFER PRICING.**   (CGAC)   Greg Soames, manager of the Pharon Division of Juneau Chemicals was studying his most recent quarterly results (shown in Exhibit 14A-3). Because of a recent economic downturn in the industry, Soames's division had not met its projected earnings, and there was no hope of meeting its annual ROI target of 18 percent.

Soames believed the problem to be compounded by the rigidity of the transfer-pricing policy imposed by Juneau Chemicals. In spite of an open market price of $85 for the major raw material, Litaline, Pharon had to pay $105 per litre to a sister division—a price set, by company policy, as full standard cost plus a 15 percent markup. Having worked in the Litaline Division before moving to Pharon, Soames knew that the variable cost of producing Litaline was considerably less than $105, probably only 70 percent of the full standard cost. With this knowledge, Soames had tried to negotiate (which is permitted under company policy) a lower price to improve Pharon's return. His suggestion had been rejected by the Litaline manager, and Soames suspected that the reason for rejecting it stemmed from the Litaline manager's desire to achieve its ROI and income targets for the period, which would not happen if it had to meet the $85 market price.

EXHIBIT 14A-3

Pharon Division Statement of Income for the Quarter Ending September 30, 2006 (in thousands)

	Budget	Actual
Sales	$3,525	$3,200
Cost of goods sold:		
Materials	900	925
Labour	600	520
Overhead	500	475
	2,000	1,920
Gross margin	1,525	1,280
Other expenses:		
Marketing	504	400
Administration[1]	751	750
Net income	$ 270	$ 130
Net assets	$1,500	$1,500
ROI	18%	8.67%

[1] Fifty percent of administration cost is allocated from central headquarters.

Soames feared that his compensation would suffer heavily in the period. Juneau paid its managers a base salary plus a bonus based on quarterly results and annual ROI targets. Bonuses were calculated on a sliding scale that ranged from 10 percent to 50 percent of salary and were paid in cash. For the past three years

Soames, as manager of Pharon, had earned a bonus equal to 40 percent of his salary. But this year he felt either he would have to take drastic action or he would lose his bonus altogether and, perhaps, face even more severe consequences.

With this in mind, Soames approached his liaison on the Juneau Executive Committee, the vice president of operations, with a proposal to purchase Litaline on the external market. Without that option he felt that there was no way Pharon could salvage its current year's projections.

Required:

1. Evaluate Soames's proposal to purchase Litaline on the external market after calculating
   a. The per-unit profit effect on the firm; and
   b. The per-unit profit effect on the Pharon Division.
2. Discuss the strengths and weaknesses of the management control system in operation at Juneau Chemicals, and make any recommendations for change that you feel are necessary.

C14-6 **INTERNATIONAL TRANSFER PRICING.** (CICA) Durst Industries Inc., a multinational company, has its head office in western Canada. Shares are listed on Canadian stock exchanges and on several foreign exchanges. For the fiscal year ended June 30, 2004, consolidated net sales amounted to $1.2 billion and net income was $45 million.

The company manufactures and markets heavy-construction and farm equipment at its 22 separate manufacturing facilities located in Canada, the United States, South America, Europe, and Asia. In this highly competitive, price-sensitive industry, Durst has maintained a reputation for high-quality, durable products. However, it recently lost several major contracts for farm tractors and combines.

While there is head office control of Durst's marketing and manufacturing strategies, the company's 22 manufacturing plants are treated as separate profit centres. Most of the subassembly and component parts are produced for internal use in the assembly of end products. There is no external market for most of these intermediate items. Those that are sold externally now generate approximately 2 percent of consolidated net sales. Selling prices to outsiders for subassembly and component parts have usually been determined at the plant level.

The following policy applies to transfers of goods between various Durst profit centres:

> Although it is necessary to have centralized control over the development and implementation of company marketing and manufacturing strategies, senior management needs to evaluate decentralized operations using a profit-centre concept. This is very important because the company's main production activity is focused on manufacturing subcomponents and subassemblies used exclusively for internal assembly of end products for consumers. Accordingly, there is a need for an appropriate pricing structure for interplant transfers.
>
> For guidance in determining transfer prices, plant managers should first refer to prices already established for outside sales. When there is no outside market, or when outside prices are not readily determinable, transfer prices are to be based on laid-down cost to the producing plant, plus a reasonable profit. This latter approach to arriving at a fair transfer price is consistent with the concept of "value-added pricing."

Thomas Smith, president and chief executive officer of Durst, received the following memorandum dated September 1, 2006 from Jim Brown, plant manager in Tulsa, Oklahoma.

I have done everything I can to negotiate a fair price for our modified X-30 carburettor used in the assembly of the DXL 1300 tractor at our plant in eastern Canada. Roger Bertrand, the manager of this plant, has been most unreasonable, given that my modified X-30 is manufactured exclusively for installation in his DXL 1300 tractors.

As you know, we still manufacture the unmodified version of the X-30, and its sales to our customers are substantial throughout the West. Unless you can convince Bertrand to be more reasonable, I shall cease production of the modified X-30 and concentrate our efforts on manufacturing the unmodified carburettor.

I expect you to let me know within ten days whether you have been able to convince Bertrand on this issue. Advise him that my last offer remains at $575 U.S., F.O.B. Tulsa.

Smith immediately called in Jean Talbot, CMA, vice president, finance, to discuss Brown's memo. Smith then asked Talbot to investigate the dispute.

Talbot obtained the following information, which she related to Smith:

1. Unmodified X-30s were currently priced at $365.00 U.S., F.O.B. Tulsa.
2. Sales volume of the unmodified X-30 had dropped significantly during the last three years, and during this time its market price had similarly declined.
3. The modified X-30 represented a significant advance in carburettor technology.
4. To date, corporate management has not permitted production of the modified version for sale on the open market.
5. Tulsa's pricing of the modified X-30 was found to be in accord with company policy. The difference in price between these models is attributed to the additional cost of production plus the recovery of related development costs, overhead, and provision for "normal profit margin."
6. Costs incurred in the manufacture of carburettors at Tulsa are considered to be 60 percent variable and 40 percent fixed. Tulsa's gross margin on the carburettors has declined in recent years and is currently 35 percent.
7. When approached by Talbot, Bertrand would not reconsider his position. He contended that the Tulsa price was unacceptable, because of the duty and excise taxes he would necessarily incur to import the modified X-30 from the United States. He mentioned the availability of a less expensive but clearly inferior carburettor manufactured by a local competitor.

In discussions with Smith, Talbot emphasized that, while this dispute must be resolved, other problems existed. The present transfer pricing policy appears to have broader, long-range implications and the system might not be properly serving Durst's overall needs. At the conclusion of their discussion, Smith asked Talbot to prepare a report on the matter.

Required: Assume the role of Jean Talbot and prepare the report to Thomas Smith. Recommend a solution to the current dispute, evaluate the present transfer pricing policy and recommend improvements. Support your recommendations.

E14-1 RETURN ON INVESTMENT AND RESIDUAL INCOME

Goal: Create an Excel spreadsheet to calculate performance of divisional segments using the return on investment (ROI) and residual income (RI) methods. Use the results to answer questions about your findings.

Scenario: The company has asked you to calculate return on investment (ROI) and residual income (RI) for three divisions. The background data for your analysis appears in the table below. Use an interest rate of 10 percent when calculating the capital charge.

	DIVISION		
	A	B	C
Average invested capital	$1,000	$ 600	$ 900
Revenue	3,600	1,800	9,000
Income	180	126	90

When you have completed your spreadsheet, answer the following questions:

1. Which division has the best performance using the return on investment method? Using the residual income method?

2. Which division has the worst performance under both methods?

3. Based on your findings, what are your recommendations to management concerning which of these three divisions should receive an increase in invested capital?

Step by Step:

1. Open a new Excel spreadsheet.

2. In column A, create a bold-faced heading that contains the following:
   Row 1: Chapter 14 Decision Guideline
   Row 2: Divisions A, B, and C
   Row 3: Measures of Profitability
   Row 4: Today's Date

3. Merge and centre the four heading rows across columns A through I.

4. In row 7, create the following centre-justified column headings:
   Column A: Division
   Column B: Invested Capital
   Column C: Revenue
   Column D: Income
   Column E: Capital Charge
   Column F: Residual Income
   Column G: Return on Investment
   Column H: Return on Sales
   Column I: Capital Turnover

5. Change the format of Residual Income and Return on Investment to bold-faced headings.

6. Change the format of the column headings in row 7 to permit the titles to be displayed on multiple lines within a single cell.

   Alignment tab: Wrap Text: Checked

   Note: Adjust column widths so the headings only use two lines. Adjust row height to insure that row is same height as adjusted headings.

7. In column A, create the following centre-justified row headings:
   Row 8: A
   Skip a row
   Row 10: B
   Skip a row
   Row 12: C

8. Use the scenario data to fill in invested capital, revenue, and income amounts for each division.

9. Use the scenario data and appropriate formulas to calculate capital charge amounts for each division.

10. Use the appropriate formulas from Chapter 14 to calculate residual income, return on investment, return on sales, and capital turnover amounts for each division.

11. Format amounts in columns B, C, D, E, and F for Division A as

Number tab:	Category:	Currency
	Decimal places:	0
	Symbol:	$
	Negative numbers:	Black with parentheses

12. Format amounts in columns B, C, D, E, and F for Divisions B and C as

Number tab:	Category:	Currency
	Decimal places:	0
	Symbol:	None
	Negative numbers:	Black with parentheses

13. Format amounts in columns G and H to display as percentages without decimal places.

Number tab:	Category:	Percentage
	Decimal places:	0

14. Format the capital turnover amounts to display two decimal places, followed by the word "times."

Number tab:	Category:	Custom

    From the Type list, highlight the type shown below:
	Type:	0.00

Change the data in the Type field from 0.00 to the following:

Type: 0.00 "times"

Click the OK button.

15. Save your work to disk, and print a copy for your files.

Note: Print your spreadsheet using landscape in order to ensure that all columns appear on one page.

COLLABORATIVE LEARNING EXERCISE

CL14-1 **RETURN ON INVESTMENT**   Form groups of three to six students. Each student should select a Canadian company. Coordinate the selection of companies so that each group has companies from a wide variety of industries. For example, a good mix of industries for a group of five students would be a retail company, a basic manufacturing company, a computer software company, a bank, and an electric utility.

1. Each student should find the latest annual report for his or her company. (The Internet is a good source. If you cannot find the company's home page, try www.sedar.com, and use the Search Database option to find the company's annual report and financial statements.) Compute
   a. Return on sales
   b. Capital turnover
   c. Return on investment (ROI)
2. As a group, compare these performance measures for the chosen companies. Why do they differ across companies? What characteristic of the company and its industry might explain the differences in the measures?

Financial Statements: Basic Concepts and Comprehensive Analysis

LEARNING OBJECTIVES

After studying this chapter, you will be able to

1. Identify the meanings and interrelationships of the principal elements of financial statements: assets, liabilities, owners' equity, revenues, expenses, dividends, and others.

2. Analyze typical business transactions to determine their effects on the principal elements of financial statements.

3. Distinguish between the accrual basis of accounting and the cash basis of accounting.

4. Perform comparisons between companies within an industry and between companies from different industries.

5. Analyze a company's financial statements to assess its liquidity, profitability, stability, and growth.

6. Evaluate the sources and uses of cash that a company has employed in its financing and investing activities.

The objective of this chapter is to provide exposure to the accounting process, fundamental accounting terminology and concepts, and the means by which a company's financial statements can be analyzed. The primary purpose of financial statements is to provide users with information about the past that will improve their ability to make decisions about the future. For example, an analyst will evaluate a company's financial statements as part of an attempt to predict the future changes in a company's share price. A bank credit manager will use financial statements to assess a company's ability to first pay interest on a loan and second, if necessary, to provide sufficient security for a loan in the event of any defaults in payments. The list of potential users and the specific reasons for analyzing a company's financial statements are endless. Thus it is impossible to provide a list of techniques that is universally complete for all situations. This chapter will provide the basis for an evaluation of a company's financial statements, upon which users can develop their own specific analysis. The range of possible techniques is limited only by the creativity of the users.

THE NEED FOR FINANCIAL STATEMENTS

Managers, investors, and other interested groups usually want the answers to two important questions about an organization: How well did the organization perform for a given period of time? and, Where does the organization stand at a given point in time? The accountant answers these questions using two major financial statements: an income statement and a balance sheet. To create these statements, accountants continually record the history of an organization. Through the *financial accounting* process, the accountant accumulates, analyzes, quantifies, classifies, summarizes, and reports the seemingly countless events that take place in an organization and their effects on the entity. An *entity* is important because accounting usually focuses on the financial impact of events as they affect a particular entity. An example of an entity is a university, which encompasses many smaller entities such as the School of Business and the School of Engineering.

Transaction. Any event that affects the financial position of an organization and requires recording.

The accounting process focuses on transactions. A **transaction** is any event that affects the financial position of an entity and requires recording. Through the years, many concepts, conventions, and rules have been developed regarding what events are to be recorded as *accounting transactions* and how their financial impact is measured. To understand financial statements fully you must recognize the decisions that go into their construction. Controversial accounting decisions by Enron, WorldCom, Tyco, and others in the last few years have illustrated how important accounting decisions are to the users of financial statements.

PRINCIPAL ELEMENTS OF FINANCIAL STATEMENTS

OBJECTIVE 1

Identify the meanings and interrelationships of the principal elements of financial statements: assets, liabilities, owners' equity, revenues, expenses, dividends, and others.

Financial statements, income statements, balance sheets, and cash flow statements are summarized reports of accounting transactions. They can apply to any point in time and to any span of time.

An efficient way to learn about accounting is to study a specific illustration. Suppose Retailer No. 1 began business as a corporation on March 1, 2006. An opening balance sheet (more accurately called statement of financial position or statement of financial condition) follows:

Retailer No. 1 Balance Sheet (Statement of Financial Position) as of March 1, 2006	ASSETS		EQUITIES	
	Cash	$100,000	Share capital	$100,000

The balance sheet is a photograph of financial status at an instant of time. It has two counterbalancing sections: assets and equities. **Assets** are economic resources that are expected to benefit future activities. **Equities** are the claims against, or interests in, the assets.

The accountant sees the balance sheet as an equation:

$$assets = equities$$

The equities side of this fundamental equation is often divided as follows:

$$assets = liabilities + owners'\ equity$$

The **liabilities** are the entity's economic obligations to non-owners. The **owners' equity** is the excess of the assets over the liabilities. For a corporation, the owners' equity is called **shareholders' equity**. In turn, the shareholders' equity is composed of the ownership claim against, or interest in, the total assets arising from any investments received, plus the ownership claim arising as a result of profitable operations (**retained earnings** or **retained income**).

Consider a summary of the *transactions* that occurred in March:

1. Initial investment by owners, $100,000 cash.
2. Acquisition of inventory for $75,000 cash.
3. Acquisition of inventory for $35,000 on open account. A purchase (or a sale) on open account is an agreement whereby the buyer pays cash some time after the date of sale, often in 30 days. Amounts owed on open accounts are usually called **accounts payable**, which are liabilities of the purchasing entity.
4. Merchandise carried in inventory at a cost of $100,000 was sold on open account for $120,000. These open customer accounts are called **accounts receivable**, which are assets of the selling entity.
5. Cash collections of accounts receivable, $30,000.
6. Cash payments of accounts payable, $10,000.
7. On March 1, $3,000 cash was disbursed for store rent for March, April, and May. Rent is $1,000 per month, payable quarterly in advance, beginning in March.

Note that these are summarized transactions. For example, all the sales will not take place at once, nor will purchases of inventory, collections from customers, or disbursements to suppliers. A vast number of repetitive transactions occur in practice, and specialized data collection techniques are used to measure their effects on the entity.

The foregoing transactions can be analyzed using the balance sheet equation, as shown in Exhibit 15-1. Explanations of Exhibit 15-1 follow:

Transaction 1, the initial investment by owners, increases assets and equities. That is, cash increases and share capital increases. Note, in this illustration, that share capital represents the claim arising from the owners' total initial investment in the corporation.

Assets. Economic resources that are expected to benefit future activities.

Equities. The claims against, or interests in, the assets.

Liabilities. The entity's economic obligations to non-owners.

Owners' Equity. The excess of the assets over the liabilities.

Shareholders' Equity. The excess of assets over liabilities of a corporation.

Retained Earnings (Retained Income). Increases in equities due to profitable operations.

Accounts Payable. Amounts owed on open accounts whereby the buyer pays cash some time after the date of sale.

Accounts Receivable. Amounts owed to a company by customers who buy on open account.

OBJECTIVE 2

Analyze typical business transactions to determine their effects on the principal elements of financial statements.

EXHIBIT 15-1

Retailer No. 1
Analysis of Transactions (in dollars) for March 2006

	ASSETS							=	EQUITIES				
TRANSACTIONS	CASH	+	ACCOUNTS RECEIVABLE	+	INVENTORY	+	PREPAID RENT	=	LIABILITIES: ACCOUNTS PAYABLE	+	SHAREHOLDERS' EQUITY: SHARE CAPITAL	+	SHAREHOLDERS' EQUITY: RETAINED EARNINGS
1. Initial investment	+100,000							=			+100,000		
2. Acquire inventory for cash	−75,000				+75,000			=					
3. Acquire inventory for credit					+35,000			=	+35,000				
4a. Sales on credit			+120,000					=					+120,000 (revenue)
4b. Cost of inventory sold					−100,000			=					−100,000 (expense)
5. Collect from customers	+30,000		−30,000					=					
6. Pay accounts of suppliers	−10,000							=	−10,000				
7a. Pay rent in advance	−3,000						+3,000	=					
7b. Recognize expiration of rental services							−1,000						−1,000 (expense)
Balance, 3/31/06	+42,000		+90,000		+10,000		+2,000		+25,000		+100,000		+19,000
				144,000							144,000		

Transactions 2 and 3, the purchases of inventory, are steps toward the ultimate goal—earning a profit. But shareholders' equity is unaffected. That is, no profit is recorded until a sale is made.

Transaction 4 is the sale of $100,000 of inventory for $120,000. Two things happen simultaneously: a new asset, accounts receivable, is acquired (4a) in exchange for giving up inventory (4b), and shareholders' equity is increased by the amount of the asset received ($120,000) and decreased by the amount of the asset given up ($100,000).

Transaction 5, cash collections of accounts receivable, are examples of events that have no impact on shareholders' equity. Collections are merely the transformation of one asset (accounts receivable) into another (cash).

Transaction 6, cash payments of accounts payable, affect assets and liabilities only; they do not affect shareholders' equity. In general, collections from customers and payments to suppliers of the *principal* amounts of debt have no direct impact on shareholders' equity. Of course, as we will learn in a subsequent section, *interest* on debt does affect shareholders' equity as an item of expense.

Transaction 7, the cash disbursement for rent, is made to acquire the right to use store facilities for the next three months. At March 1, the $3,000 measures the future benefit from these services, so the asset *prepaid rent* is created (7a). Assets are defined as economic resources. They are not confined to items that you can see or touch, such as cash or inventory. Assets also include legal rights to future services such as the use of facilities.

Transaction 7b recognizes that one-third of the rental services expired during March, so the asset is reduced and shareholders' equity is also reduced by $1,000 as rent expense for March. This recognition of rent expense means that $1,000 of the asset prepaid rent has been "used up" (or has flowed out of the entity) in the conduct of operations during March.

For simplicity, we have assumed no expenses other than *costs of goods sold* and *rent*. The accountant would ordinarily prepare at least two financial statements: the balance sheet and the income statement.

Retailer No. 1 Income Statement for the Month Ended March 31, 2006		

Sales (revenue)		$120,000
Expenses:		
Cost of goods sold	$100,000	
Rent	1,000	
Total expenses		101,000
Net income		$ 19,000

Retailer No. 1
Balance Sheet
as of March 31, 2006

ASSETS		LIABILITIES AND SHAREHOLDERS' EQUITY		
Cash	$ 42,000	Liabilities:		
Accounts receivable	90,000	Accounts payable		$ 25,000
Inventory	10,000	Shareholders' equity:		
Prepaid rent	2,000	Share capital	$100,000	
		Retained income	19,000	119,000
Total	$144,000	Total		$144,000

RELATIONSHIP OF BALANCE SHEET AND INCOME STATEMENT

Income Statement. A statement that measures the operating performance of the corporation by matching its accomplishments (revenue from customers, usually called sales) and its efforts (cost of goods sold and other expenses).

Balance Sheet. A statement of assets, liabilities, and equities.

The **income statement** measures the operating performance of the corporation by matching its accomplishments (revenue from customers, which is usually called *sales*) and its efforts (*cost of goods sold* and other expenses). The **balance sheet** shows the financial position at a specific time, but the income statement measures performance for a span of time, whether it be a month, a quarter, or longer. The income statement is the major link between balance sheets as shown below.

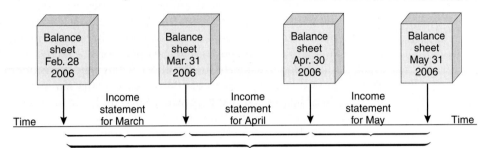

Income statement for quarter ended May 31, 2006

Examine the changes in shareholders' equity in Exhibit 15-1. The accountant records revenue and expense so that they represent increases (revenues) and decreases (expenses) in the owners' claims. At the end of a given period, these items are summarized in the form of an income statement. The heading of a balance sheet indicates a single date. The heading of an income statement indicates a specific period of time. The balance sheet is a photograph; the income statement is a motion picture.

Each item in a financial statement is frequently called an account, so that term will be used in the remaining sections of this book. In the example income statement and balance sheet above, the outflows of assets are represented by decreases in the inventory and prepaid rent accounts and corresponding decreases in shareholders' equity in the form of cost of goods sold and rent expense. Expense accounts are basically negative elements of shareholders' equity. Similarly, the sales (revenue) account is a positive element of shareholders' equity.

ACCRUAL BASIS AND CASH BASIS

OBJECTIVE 3

Distinguish between the accrual basis of accounting and the cash basis of accounting.

Measuring income and financial position is anchored to the accrual basis of accounting, as distinguished from the cash basis. The **accrual basis** is the process whereby the impact of transactions on the income statement and balance sheet is recognized as it is earned. Expenses are recognized as they are incurred—not when cash changes hands.

Transaction 4a in Exhibit 15-1 shows an example of the accrual basis. Revenue is recognized when sales are made on credit, not when cash is received. Similarly, Transactions 4b and 7b (for cost of goods sold and rent) show that expenses are recognized as efforts are expended or services are used to obtain the revenue (regardless of when cash is disbursed). Therefore, income is often affected by measurements of noncash resources and obligations. The accrual basis is the principal conceptual framework for relating accomplishments (revenues) with efforts (expenses).

Accrual Basis. A process of accounting that recognizes the impact of transactions on the financial statements in the time periods when revenues and expenses occur instead of when cash is received or disbursed.

Cash Basis. A process of accounting where revenue and expense recognition would depend solely on the timing of various cash receipts and disbursements.

If the **cash basis** of accounting were used instead of the accrual basis, revenue and expense recognition would depend solely on the timing of various cash receipts and disbursements. Our retailer example for March would show $30,000 of revenue, the amount of cash collected from customers. Similarly, rent expense would be $3,000 (the cash disbursed for rent) rather than the $1,000 rent applicable to March. A cash measurement of net income or net loss is not used in this case because it could mislead those unacquainted with the fundamentals of accounting.

Consider the rent example. Under the cash basis, March must bear expenses for the entire quarter's rent of $3,000 merely because cash outflows occurred then. In contrast, the accrual basis measures performance more sharply by allocating the rental expenses to the operations of each of the three months that benefited from the use of the facilities. In this way, the economic performance of each month will be comparable. Most accountants maintain that it is nonsense to say that March's rent expense was $3,000 and April's and May's was zero.

The biggest problem with the cash basis of accounting is that it is incomplete. It fails to *match* efforts and accomplishments (expenses and revenues) in a manner that properly measures economic performance and financial position. Moreover, it omits key assets (such as accounts receivable and prepaid rent) and key liabilities (such as accounts payable) from balance sheets.

Despite the incompleteness of the cash basis of accounting, it is used widely by individuals when they measure their income for personal income-tax purposes. Also, many government and not-for-profit organizations also use the cash basis of accounting. For these purposes, the cash basis often provides a good approximation of the net financial impact of their activities. However, accountants and managers found cash-basis financial statements to be unsatisfactory as a measure of both performance and position. Today, more than 95 percent of all business is conducted on a credit basis; cash receipts and disbursements are not the critical transactions as far as the recognition of revenue and expense is concerned. Thus, the accrual basis evolved in response to the desire for a more complete and, therefore, more accurate report of the financial impact of various events.

CLASSIFIED BALANCE SHEET

Nike, Inc.
www.nike.com

Exhibit 15-2 shows the 2002 and 2003 classified balance sheets for Nike, Inc. We will examine the five main sections of Nike's balance sheet: current assets, noncurrent assets, current liabilities, noncurrent liabilities, and shareholders' equity. By understanding what items Nike and other companies include in each of these categories you will be able to better interpret their financial position and performance. Be sure to locate each of these items in the exhibit as you read the description of the item in the following pages.

Current Assets

Current Assets. Cash and all other assets that a company reasonably expects to convert to cash or sell or consume within one year or during the normal operating cycle, if longer than a year.

Current assets include cash and all other assets that a company reasonably expects to convert to cash or sell or consume within one year or during the normal operating cycle, if longer than a year. An **operating cycle** is the time span during which a company spends cash to acquire goods and services that it uses to produce the organization's output, which it, in turn, sells to customers, who

Operating Cycle.
The time span during which a company spends cash to acquire goods and services that it uses to produce the organization's output, which it in turn sells to customers, who in turn pay for their purchases with cash.

pay for their purchases with cash. The following diagram illustrates what Nike's operating cycle might look like (figures are hypothetical):

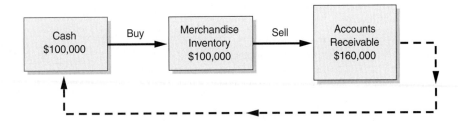

The box for accounts receivable (amounts owed to the business by customers) is larger than the other two boxes because the objective of a business is to sell goods at a price higher than their acquisition cost. The total amount of profit a firm earns during a particular period depends on how much its selling prices exceed its costs of producing or purchasing the products and additional expenses incurred during the period. The time span represented by the cycle might be as short as a few days—for a grocery store chain such as Dominion—or many years—for a timber company such as Abitibi.

As Exhibit 15-2 shows, Nike's current assets include cash and cash equivalents, accounts receivable, inventories, prepaid expenses, and other current assets. *Cash* consists of bank deposits in chequing accounts plus money on hand. **Cash equivalents** are short-term investments that a company can easily convert into cash with little delay, such as money market funds and Treasury bills. They represent an investment of excess cash that a company does not immediately need. The balance sheet usually shows these securities at their market price. At May 31, 2003, Nike had $634.0 million in cash and cash equivalents.

Cash Equivalents.
Short-term investments that a company can easily convert into cash with little delay.

Accounts receivable is the total amount owed to the company by its customers. Accountants classify all accounts receivable as current assets, even though they may not fully collect them within one year. Because some customers ultimately will not pay their bill, we reduce the total by an allowance or provision for "doubtful accounts" or "bad debts." The result represents the net amount the company will probably collect. At the end of the 2003 fiscal year,[1] Nike had gross accounts receivable of $2,189.0 million, but after deducting $87.9 million for doubtful accounts, the company expects to collect $2,101.1 million from its accounts receivable.

Inventories consist of merchandise, finished products of manufacturers, goods in the process of being manufactured, and raw materials. Accountants assume that companies do not hold inventories longer than one operating cycle. Thus, they regard all inventories as current assets. Companies state inventories at their cost or market price (defined as replacement cost), whichever is lower. Cost of manufactured products normally includes raw material cost plus the costs of converting it into a finished product (direct labour and manufacturing overhead). Companies may use FIFO (first-in, first-out), LIFO (last-in, first-out), weighted average cost, or specific identification for every item in inventory. For Nike, inventories amounted to $1,514.9 million at the end of the 2003 fiscal year.

Prepaid expenses are advance payments to suppliers. They are usually unimportant in relation to other assets. Examples are prepayment of rent and insurance premiums for coverage over the coming operating cycle. They belong in

---

[1] A fiscal year is defined as the year established for accounting purposes for the preparation of annual reports. Nike's fiscal year is June 1 through May 31.

EXHIBIT 15-2

Nike, Inc.
Balance Sheet
(in millions)

	MAY 31	
	2003	2002
ASSETS		
Current assets		
Cash and equivalents	$ 634.0	$ 575.5
Accounts receivable, less allowance for doubtful accounts of $87.9 and $80.4	2,101.1	1,804.1
Inventories	1,514.9	1,373.8
Prepaid expenses	266.2	260.5
Other current assets	163.7	140.8
Total current assets	4,679.9	4,154.7
Noncurrent assets		
Property, plant, and equipment		
At cost	2,988.8	2,741.7
Less: accumulated amortization	1,368.0	1,127.2
Net property, plant, and equipment	1,620.8	1,614.5
Identifiable intangible assets	118.2	206.0
Goodwill	65.6	232.7
Other assets	229.4	232.1
Total noncurrent assets	2,034.0	2,285.3
Total assets	$6,713.9	$6,440.0
LIABILITIES AND SHAREHOLDERS' EQUITY		
Current liabilities		
Notes payable	$ 75.4	$ 425.2
Accounts payable	572.7	504.4
Accrued liabilities	1,054.2	765.3
Income taxes payable	107.2	83.0
Current portion of long-term debt	205.7	55.3
Total current liabilities	2,015.2	1,833.2
Noncurrent liabilities		
Long-term debt	551.6	625.9
Deferred income taxes and other liabilities	156.1	141.6
Total noncurrent liabilities	707.7	767.5
Total liabilities	2,722.9	2,600.7
Shareholders' equity		
Redeemable preferred stock	0.3	0.3
Common stock at stated value	2.8	2.8
Capital in excess of stated value	589.0	538.7
Retained earnings	3,639.2	3,495.0
Other	(240.3)	(197.5)
Total shareholders' equity	3,991.0	3,839.3
Total liabilities and shareholders' equity	$6,713.9	$6,440.0

current assets because, if they were not present, the company would need more cash to conduct current operations. At May 31, 2003, Nike showed $266.2 million of prepaid expenses, which is less than 6 percent of total current assets.

Other current assets are miscellaneous current assets that do not fit into the listed categories. They might include notes receivable and short-term investments that are not cash equivalents. For Nike, such assets amounted to $163.7 million at the end of fiscal 2003.

Noncurrent Assets: Property, Plant, and Equipment

Fixed Assets (Tangible Assets). Physical items that a person can see and touch, such as property, plant, and equipment.

Property, plant, and equipment are examples of **fixed assets** or **tangible assets**— physical items that a person can see and touch. Companies usually provide details about property, plant, and equipment in a footnote to the financial statements, such as the one for Nike shown in Exhibit 15-3. Footnotes are an integral part of financial statements. They contain explanations for the summary figures that appear in the statements.

Companies typically show *land* as a separate asset and carry it indefinitely at its original cost. They also initially record *buildings* and *machinery and equipment* at cost: the invoice amount, plus freight and installation, less cash discounts. However, unlike land, buildings, machinery, and equipment gradually decline in value through amortization. The major challenge to firms is choosing an amortization method—that is, deciding how to allocate the original cost to the particular periods or products that benefit from the use of the assets. Remember that amortization only means allocating the original cost of plant and equipment, not valuing them in the ordinary sense of the term. Balance sheets typically do not show replacement cost, resale value, or the price changes since acquisition. The balance sheet amount is simply the original cost less the accumulated amortization, which is the sum of all amortization taken to date on the asset.

The amount of amortization charged as expense each year depends on three factors:

1. The amortizable amount, which is the difference between the total acquisition cost and the estimated residual value. The residual value is the amount a company expects to receive when selling the asset at the end of its economic life.
2. The estimate of the asset's useful life or economic life. This estimate often depends more on technological changes and economic obsolescence than on physical wear and tear. Thus, the useful life is usually less than the physical life.
3. The amortization method. There are three general methods of amortization: straight line, accelerated, and units of production. The straight-line method allocates the same cost to each year of an asset's useful life. Accelerated methods allocate more of the cost to the early years and less to the later years.[2] The units-of-production method allocates cost based on the amount of production rather than the passage of time.

EXHIBIT 15-3

Nike, Inc.
Footnote 3 to the 2003
Financial Statements

Note 3. Property, Plant, and Equipment (millions)	2003	2002
Land	$ 191.1	$ 178.3
Buildings	785.0	739.9
Machinery and equipment	1,538.7	1,356.9
Leasehold improvements	433.4	394.2
Construction-in-progress	40.6	72.4
	2,988.8	2,741.7
Less: accumulated amortization	1,368.0	1,127.2
Net property, plant, and equipment	$1,620.8	$1,614.5

[2] Accelerated amortization is described elsewhere in this text. However, knowledge of accelerated amortization methods is not necessary for understanding this chapter.

Which method is best? It depends on the firm's goals, the asset involved, and the type of financial statement being prepared. The straight-line method is most popular. More than 90 percent of all firms use it for at least some assets when preparing financial statements for reporting to the public. They believe that it best matches the cost of an asset with the benefits from its use. In contrast, most firms would like to use accelerated amortization when preparing financial statements for tax reporting to the CRA. Why? Because it is the most beneficial method.

Suppose a business spends $42,000 to buy equipment with an estimated useful life of four years and an estimated residual value of $2,000. If we use the straight-line method of amortization, the annual amortization expense in each of the four years would be as follows:

$$\frac{\text{original cost} - \text{estimated residual value}}{\text{years of useful life}}$$

$$= \frac{(\$42,000 - \$2,000)}{4}$$

$$= \$10,000 \text{ per year}$$

Exhibit 15-4 shows how we would display the asset in the balance sheet. In Exhibits 15-2 and 15-3, the original cost of fixed assets on Nike's 2003 balance sheet is $2,988.8 million. There is accumulated amortization of $1,368.0 million, the portion of the original cost of the asset that Nike previously charged as amortization expense, so the net property, plant, and equipment at May 31, 2003 is $2,988.8 million − $1,368.0 million = $1,620.8 million.

Amortization represents the part of an asset that a company has already used. It is gone. It is not a pool of cash set aside to replace the asset. If a company decides to accumulate specific cash to replace assets, we would label such cash a "fund," such as a "cash fund for replacement and expansion."

Leasehold improvements are investments made by a lessee (tenant) in items such as painting, decorating, fixtures, and air-conditioning equipment that it cannot remove from the premises when a lease expires. Companies write off the costs of leasehold improvements in the same manner as amortization, and also call their periodic write-off amortization. Nike's leasehold improvements of $433.4 million are 15 percent of its property, plant, and equipment.

Nike shows *construction in progress* separately from other assets because the assets are not yet ready for use. It represents assets that will be part of buildings or machinery and equipment when completed.

	BALANCES AT END OF YEAR			
	1	2	3	4
Plant and equipment (at original acquisition cost)	$42,000	$42,000	$42,000	$42,000
Less: accumulated amortization (the portion of original cost that has already been charged to operations as amortization expense)	10,000	20,000	30,000	40,000
Net book value (the portion of original cost not yet charged as expense)	$32,000	$22,000	$12,000	$ 2,000

EXHIBIT 15-4

Straight-Line Amortization (figures assumed)

Nike does not have natural resource assets, such as mineral deposits, but if it did it would group them with plant assets. Companies write off the original cost of natural resources in the form of depletion as they use the resources. For example, if a coal mine originally cost $10 million and contained an estimated 5 million tonnes, the depletion rate would be $10,000,000 ÷ 5,000,000 tonnes = $2 per tonne. If the company mined 500,000 tonnes during the first year, depletion would be $2 × 500,000 = $1,000,000 for that year. If it mined 300,000 tonnes the second year, depletion would be $2 × 300,000 = $600,000. Such depletion charges would continue until the company had charged the entire $10 million as a depletion expense.

Long-term investments are also noncurrent assets. They include long-term holdings of securities of other firms. Nike does not have any long-term investments, unless they are combined with other small, miscellaneous noncurrent assets in the $229.4 million of other assets shown in Exhibit 15-2.

Intangible Assets

Intangible Assets.
Long-lived assets that are not physical in nature. Examples are goodwill, franchises, patents, trademarks, and copyrights.

Goodwill.
The excess of the cost of an acquired company over the sum of the fair market values of its identifiable individual assets less its liabilities.

We can physically observe tangible assets such as cash or equipment. In contrast, **intangible assets** are a class of long-lived assets that are not physical in nature. They are rights to expected future benefits deriving from their acquisition and continued possession. Examples are goodwill, franchises, patents, trademarks, and copyrights. In Exhibit 15-2, Nike shows intangible assets and goodwill of $118.2 million + $65.6 million = $183.8 million at May 31, 2003.

Goodwill is the excess of the cost of an acquired company over the sum of the fair market values of its identifiable individual assets less its liabilities. For example, Nike acquired Cole Haan for $95 million. It could assign only $13 million to various identifiable assets such as receivables, plant, and patents less liabilities assumed by Nike. It recorded the remainder, $82 million, as goodwill. This $82 million represents a value that Nike saw in Cole Haan beyond its recorded assets less liabilities. Accountants record it as an asset only because Nike was willing to pay $82 million more than the identifiable value of the assets less liabilities it acquired. The same value may have existed when Cole Haan was an independent company, but it would not appear on its balance sheet. This illustrates how an exchange transaction is a basic concept of accounting. After all, many owners, like those of Cole Haan, could obtain a premium price if they sold their companies. But we never record such goodwill. The only goodwill you will find on a balance sheet arises from an actual acquisition when a purchaser pays more than the amount assigned to individual assets.

Goodwill remains on a company's books until management determines that its value is impaired. Companies do not amortize goodwill. However, they must annually apply an impairment test to assure that the goodwill has kept its value. If the goodwill has lost value, a company must reduce goodwill by the amount of the value decrease and charge that same amount as an impairment expense on the income statement. The accounting rule requiring an impairment test for goodwill is new, and Nike applied it for the first time in 2003. It found that goodwill from its Cole Haan acquisition as well as that from other acquisitions was impaired, and Nike reduced its goodwill by $266.1 million and charged an expense of the same amount on its 2003 income statement. (Note that Nike also added $99 million of goodwill in 2003.)

Liabilities

Assets are, of course, only part of the picture of any organization's financial health. Its liabilities, both current and noncurrent, are equally important.

Current liabilities are an organization's debts that fall due within the coming year or within the normal operating cycle if longer than a year. Turn again to Exhibit 15-2. *Notes payable* are short-term debts backed by formal promissory notes held by a bank or business creditors. *Accounts payable* are amounts owed to suppliers who extended credit for purchases on open account. *Accrued liabilities* (also called accrued expenses payable) are amounts owed for wages, salaries, interest, and similar items. The accountant recognizes expenses as they occur—regardless of when a company pays for them in cash. *Income taxes payable* is a special accrued expense of enough magnitude to warrant a separate classification. The *current portion of long-term debt* shows the payments due within the next year on bonds and other long-term debt. This concludes Nike's current liabilities, which total $2,015.2 million.

In addition to the current liabilities that Nike lists, some companies also list unearned revenue, also called deferred revenue. Such revenue occurs when a company receives cash before delivering the related goods or services. Nike had no unearned revenue at May 31, 2003. Now that you understand both current assets and current liabilities, we can introduce a commonly used term, **working capital,** which is current assets less current liabilities. Investors watch working capital carefully to assess whether a company has enough current assets to pay current liabilities as they come due.

Noncurrent liabilities, also called **long-term liabilities,** are an organization's debts that fall due beyond one year. Exhibit 15-2 shows Nike's noncurrent liabilities at May 31, 2003 as $707.7 million, making its total liabilities $2,722.9 million. Nike has two noncurrent liabilities, long-term debt (which we will discuss in more depth in a moment) and deferred income taxes. The latter rather technical and controversial item arises because the financial statements used for reporting to shareholders differ legitimately from those used for reporting to the income tax authorities.

Exhibit 15-5 is a footnote from Nike's financial statements that provides details about its long-term debt. Note especially the next-to-last line in this exhibit, "less: current maturities." This item refers to payments due in the next year. Nike subtracts the $205.7 million noted on this line from long-term debt because the company has already included it in current liabilities. Nike shows the remaining $551.6 million as "long-term debt," as shown in Exhibit 15-2.

Long-term debt may be secured or unsecured. Secured debt provides debt holders with first claim on specified assets. Mortgage bonds are an example of secured debt. If the company is unable to meet its regular obligations on the bonds, it may sell the specified assets and use the proceeds to pay off the firm's obligations to its bondholders, in which case secured debt holders have first claim.

Unsecured debt consists of **debentures** (bonds, notes, or loans), which are formal certificates of indebtedness accompanied by a promise to pay interest at a specified annual rate. Unsecured debt holders are general creditors who have a general claim against total assets rather than a specific claim against particular assets. Most of Nike's long-term debt is unsecured. Holders of **subordinated** bonds or debentures are junior to the other creditors in exercising claims against assets.

EXHIBIT 15-5

Nike, Inc.
Footnote 7 to the 2003
Financial Statements

Note 7. Long-Term Debt (millions)	MAY 31	
	2003	2002
6.69% Corporate bond, payable June 17, 2002	$ –	$ 50.0
6.375% Corporate bond, payable December 1, 2003	200.0	199.8
5.5% Corporate bond, payable August 15, 2006	266.3	248.2
4.8% Corporate bond, payable July 9, 2007	27.1	–
5.375% Corporate bond, payable July 8, 2009	27.6	–
5.66% Corporate bond, payable July 23, 2012	28.1	–
5.4% Corporate bond, payable August 7, 2012	16.4	–
4.3% Japanese yen note, payable June 26, 2011	90.1	83.4
2.6% Japanese yen note, maturing August 20, 2001 through November 20, 2020	69.2	67.8
2.0% Japanese yen note, maturing August 20, 2001 through November 20, 2020	30.8	30.2
Other	1.7	1.8
Subtotal	757.3	681.2
Less: current maturities	205.7	55.3
Total	$551.6	$625.9

Liquidation.
Converting assets to cash and using the cash to pay off outside claims.

Consider the following simplified example. Suppose a corporation is liquidated. **Liquidation** means converting assets to cash and using the cash to pay off outside claims. The company had a single asset, a building, that it sold for $120,000 cash:

Assets		Liabilities and Shareholders' Equity	
Cash	$120,000	Accounts payable	$ 60,000
		First-mortgage bonds payable	80,000
		Subordinated debentures payable	40,000
		Total liabilities	$180,000
		Shareholders' equity (negative)	(60,000)
Total assets	$120,000	Total liabilities and stockholders' equity	$120,000

The company would pay the mortgage (secured) bondholders in full ($80,000). It would pay trade creditors, such as suppliers, the remaining $40,000 for their $60,000 claim ($0.67 on the dollar). Other claimants would get nothing. If the debentures were unsubordinated, the company would use the $40,000 of cash remaining after paying $80,000 to the mortgage holders to settle the $100,000 claims of the unsecured creditors proportionately as follows:

To trade creditors	6/10 × $40,000 = $24,000
To debenture holders	4/10 × $40,000 = 16,000
Total cash distributed	$40,000

To increase the appeal of their bonds, many companies issue debt that is convertible into common shares. Convertibility allows bondholders to participate in a company's success without the risk of holding common shares. Suppose Nike issued convertible bonds for $1,000 when its share price was $22, with a provision that investors can convert each bond into 40 common shares. If the share price increases by 50 percent to $33 a share, the bondholder could exchange the $1,000 bond for 40 shares worth 40 × $33 = $1,320. If the share price falls (or does not increase beyond $25 a share), the bondholder can keep the bond and receive $1,000 at maturity.

Shareholders' Equity

Common Shares.
Shares that have no predetermined rate of dividends and are the last to obtain a share in the assets when the corporation liquidates. They usually confer voting power to elect the board of directors of the corporation.

The final element of a balance sheet is shareholders' equity (also called stockholders' equity or owners' equity or net worth), the total residual interest in the business. Equity is the excess of total assets over total liabilities. The main elements of shareholders' equity arise from two sources: (1) contributed or share capital, and (2) retained income.

Share capital typically comes from owners who invest in the business in exchange for share certificates that specify their ownership interest. Holders of share certificates are shareholders or stockholders. There are two major classes of capital shares: common shares and preferred shares. Some companies have several categories of each, all with a variety of different attributes.

Limited Liability.
A provision that a company's creditors cannot seek payment from shareholders as individuals if the corporation itself cannot pay its debts.

All corporations have **common shares**. Such stock has no predetermined rate of dividends and is the last to obtain a share in the assets when the corporation liquidates. It usually confers voting power to elect the board of directors of the corporation. Common shares are generally the riskiest investment in a corporation, being unattractive in dire times but attractive in prosperous times because, unlike other shares, there is no limit to the shareholder's potential participation in earnings. The corporate form of ownership provides one additional benefit to shareholders—**limited liability**. This means that a company's creditors cannot seek payment from shareholders as individuals if the corporation itself cannot pay its debts.

Preferred Shares.
Shares that typically have some priority over other shares in the payment of dividends or the distribution of assets upon liquidation.

Exhibit 15-2 shows that Nike has a small amount of preferred shares, in addition to common shares. About 40 percent of the major companies in the United States issue **preferred shares**. They typically have some priority over other shares in the payment of dividends or the distribution of assets on liquidation. For example, Nike pays an annual preferred share dividend of $0.10 per share, or $30,000 in total. Nike must pay these dividends in full before it pays dividends to any other classes of shares. Preferred shareholders in Nike, like preferred shareholders in other corporations, have no voting privileges.

Retained Earnings (Retained Income).
Increases in equities due to profitable operations.

Retained earnings, also called **retained income**, is the increase in shareholders' equity caused by profitable operations. Retained earnings is the dominant item of shareholders' equity for most companies. For instance, as of May 31, 2003, Nike had common shareholders' equity of $3,991.0 million of which $3,639.2 million or 91% was retained earnings.

INCOME STATEMENT

Most investors are vitally concerned about a company's ability to produce long-run earnings and dividends. In this regard, income statements are more important than balance sheets. Income statements show revenue first; this represents the total sales value of products delivered and services rendered to customers. Then they list expenses, which we deduct to get net income. We next examine how the format of the income statement can help users judge a company's performance.

Operating Performance

An income statement can take one of two major forms: single step or multiple step. A single-step statement merely lists all expenses without drawing subtotals. It provides an overall measure of performance, but it does not allow direct assessment of performance in specific areas. In contrast, a multiple-step statement contains one or more subtotals. By dividing expenses into categories, we can monitor a company's performance in different dimensions—primarily assessing operating management separately from financial management.

Exhibit 15-6 illustrates the two most common subtotals used to assess operating performance: *gross profit* and *income from operations* (also called operating income or operating profit). Gross profit or gross margin is sales less cost of goods sold. It measures the size of the margin above merchandise costs and is an important statistic for many managers and analysts. A shrinking gross profit can indicate increasing competition in the market for the company's goods or services. If you try to compare gross margins for two companies, you should be aware that a company's inventory method affects its gross profit. Why? Because the cost of goods sold is the inventory value for the items sold.

Operating income (or loss) summarizes the results of the basic operating activities of the company—the day-to-day activities that generate sales revenue. Income statements often group amortization expense, selling expenses, and administrative expenses as "operating expenses" and deduct them from the gross profit to obtain operating income. (Of course, cost of goods sold is also an operating expense. Why? Because we also deduct it from sales revenue to obtain "operating income.") In 2003, Nike had a gross profit of $4,383.4 million and operating income of $1,245.8 million. This summarizes Nike's success in producing and selling its products.

EXHIBIT 15-6

Nike, Inc.
Statement of Income
(millions except per
share data)

| | YEAR ENDED MAY 31 | |
	2003	**2002**
Revenues	$10,697.0	$ 9,893.0
Cost of sales	6,313.6	6,004.7
Gross profit	$ 4,383.4	$ 3,888.3
Selling and administrative expenses	3,137.6	2,820.4
Income from operations	$ 1,245.8	$ 1,067.9
Other expense (income)		
Interest expense	$ 42.9	$ 47.6
Other income/expense, net	79.9	3.0
Total other expense	$ 122.8	$ 50.6
Income before income taxes	$ 1,123.0	$ 1,017.3
Income taxes	382.9	349.0
Income before cumulative effect of accounting change	740.1	668.3
Cumulative effect of accounting change	266.1	5.0
Net income	$ 474.0	$ 663.3
Earnings per share*	$ 1.79	$ 2.48

* Computation of earnings per share:

	2003	**2002**
Net income	$474,000,000	$663,300,000
Divided by average common shares outstanding	264,500,000	267,700,000
Earnings per share	$1.79	$2.48

Financial Management

Management of a company is responsible for financial management as well as operating management. Financial management focuses on where to get cash and how to use cash for the benefit of the organization. That is, financial management attempts to answer such questions as: How much cash should we hold in our chequing accounts? Should we pay a dividend? Should we borrow money or issue common shares? The best managers are superb at both operating management and financial management. However, many managers are better operating managers than financial managers, or vice versa.

Because financial decisions and operating decisions each have their own effect on income, it is useful to separate the two effects in the income statement. Financing decisions affect primarily interest income and expense, so we present them as separate items after operating income. This approach facilitates comparisons of operating income between years and between companies. Some companies make heavy use of debt, which causes high interest expense, whereas other companies incur little debt and interest expense. Other non-operating items might also include income or loss on investments and gains or losses from foreign exchange transactions or from disposals of fixed assets.

Income, Earnings, and Profits

Although this book tends to use the term *income* most often, you will also see the terms *earnings* and *profit* used as synonyms. Other names for the income statement include statement of earnings, statement of profit and loss, and P&L statement. Most companies still use *net income* on their income statements, but the term *earnings* is becoming increasingly popular. Nike's 2003 net income was $474.0 million.

Net Income.
The "bottom line"—the residual amount after we deduct from revenues all expenses, including income taxes.

The term **net income** is the popular "bottom line"—the residual amount after we deduct all expenses including income taxes. Income taxes are often a prominent expense that companies do not merely list with operating expenses. Instead, income statements usually deduct income taxes as a separate item placed immediately before net income. Nike's 2003 income statement in Exhibit 15-6 shows income taxes followed by a subtotal labelled "income before effect of accounting change." If Nike had no changes in accounting method, which is usually the case, the line after income taxes would have been net income.

Why does Nike deduct the effect of a change in accounting methods on a separate line? In 2003, the company implemented the impairment test for goodwill for the first time, and as a result it charged $266.1 million to income for reductions in goodwill. Because this represents a cumulative effect of impairments over several years, Nike elected to show it separately so that investors did not think that the entire charge was a result of 2003's activities. The line "income before effect of accounting change" is a better summary of 2003's performance than is net income.

Earnings per Share.
Net income divided by the average number of common shares outstanding during the year.

Income statements conclude with the disclosure of **earnings per share**. Exhibit 15-6 illustrates this as the net income divided by the average number of common shares outstanding during the year. Nike earned $1.79 per share in 2003.

STATEMENT OF RETAINED EARNINGS

Statement of Retained Earnings (Statement of Retained Income).
A financial statement that explains changes in the retained earnings or retained income account for a given period.

To explain the changes in retained earnings, companies frequently include a separate financial statement, the **statement of retained earnings** (also called **statement of retained income**). This may also be one part of a larger statement, the statement of changes in shareholders' equity. As Exhibit 15-7 demonstrates, the major reasons for changes in retained earnings are dividends and net income. Net income increases retained earnings, and losses and dividends reduce retained earnings. Note especially that dividends are not expenses; companies do not deduct them in computing net income. Nike also reduced retained earnings by buying back some of its common shares, essentially giving some shareholders cash in exchange for their equity claims.

EXHIBIT 15-7

Nike, Inc.
Statement of Retained Earnings for the Year Ended May 31, 2003 (millions of dollars)

Retained earnings, May 31, 2002	$3,495.0
Net income (Exhibit 15-6)	474.0
Total	3,969.0
Deduct: Dividends on common shares	142.7
Repurchase of common shares	186.2
Other	0.9
Retained earnings, May 31, 2003	$3,639.2

STATEMENT OF CASH FLOWS

Statement of Cash Flows.
A statement that reports the cash receipts and cash payments of an organization during a particular period.

Until recently, many decision makers focused primarily on the income statement and the balance sheet. However, an increasing number of decision makers are now carefully examining another required statement, the statement of cash flows. A **statement of cash flows** reports the cash receipts and cash payments of an organization during a particular period. The statement has the following purposes:

1. It shows the relationship of net income to changes in cash balances. Cash balances can decline despite positive net income and vice versa.
2. It reports past cash flows as an aid to
   a. Predicting future cash flows
   b. Evaluating management's generation and use of cash
   c. Determining a company's ability to pay interest and dividends, and to pay debts when they are due
3. It reveals commitments to assets that may restrict or expand future courses of action.

Basic Concepts

Recall that balance sheets show the status of an entity at a point in time. In contrast, statements of cash flows, income statements, and statements of retained earnings cover periods of time. They explain why the balance sheet items have changed. The accompanying diagram depicts this linkage, where the arrows represent the flow of events that affect a company's balance sheet during the year:

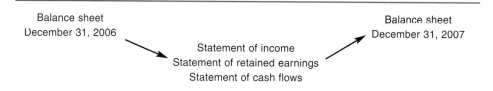

Balance sheet
December 31, 2006

Statement of income
Statement of retained earnings
Statement of cash flows

Balance sheet
December 31, 2007

The income and retained earnings statements summarize events that explain the change in retained earnings. The statement of cash flows summarizes events that explain the change in cash—where cash came from during a period and where it was spent.

The statement of cash flows explains changes in cash and cash equivalents, both of which a company can use almost immediately to meet obligations. Recall that cash equivalents are highly liquid short-term investments that a company can easily convert into cash with little delay. Hereafter, when we refer to cash, we mean both cash and cash equivalents.

Typical Activities Affecting Cash

The fundamental approach to the statement of cash flows is simple: (1) List the activities that increased cash (cash inflows) and those that decreased cash (cash outflows), and (2) place each cash inflow and outflow into one of three categories according to the type of activity that caused it: operating activities, investing activities, and financing activities.

The following activities are those found most often in statements of cash flows:

Operating Activities

Cash Inflows:
Collections from customers
Interest and dividends collected
Other operating receipts

Cash Outflows:
Cash payments to suppliers
Cash payments to employees
Interest paid
Taxes paid
Other operating cash payments

Investing Activities

Cash Inflows:
Sale of property, plant, and equipment
Sale of securities that are not cash equivalents
Receipt of loan repayments

Cash Outflows:
Purchase of property, plant, and equipment
Purchase of securities that are not cash equivalents
Making loans

Financing Activities

Cash Flows from Operating Activities. The section in the statement of cash flows that lists the cash-flow effects of transactions that affect the income statement.

Cash Inflows:
Borrowing cash from creditors
Issuing equity securities

Cash Outflows:
Repayment of amounts borrowed
Repurchase of equity shares
Payment of dividends

Cash Flows from Investing Activities.
The section in the statement of cash flows that lists the cash-flow effects of (1) lending and collecting on loans, and (2) acquiring and selling long-term assets.

Cash Flows from Financing Activities.
The section in the statement of cash flows that lists the cash-flow effects of obtaining cash from creditors and owners, repaying creditors or buying back shares from owners, and paying cash dividends.

Let's look briefly at each of the three categories. As the lists of activities indicate, **cash flows from operating activities** are generally the effects of transactions that affect the income statement. **Cash flows from investing activities** include (1) lending and collecting on loans, and (2) acquiring and selling long-term assets. **Cash flows from financing** activities include obtaining cash from creditors and owners, repaying creditors or buying back shares from owners, and paying cash dividends.

Perhaps the most troublesome classifications are the receipts and payments of interest and the receipts of dividends. After all, these items are a result of investment and financing activities. After much debate, the Financial Accounting Standards Board (FASB) decided to include these items with cash flows from operating activities. Why? Mainly because they affect the computation of income. In contrast, payments of cash dividends are financing activities because they do not affect income.

Focus of a Statement of Cash Flows

Financial Accounting Standards Board
www.fasb.org

To see the basic ideas underlying the statement of cash flows, we will first consider a simple hypothetical company, the Balmer Company, and later we will look at the real statement of cash flows for Nike. Exhibit 15-8 shows Balmer Company's summary transactions for 2007, Exhibit 15-9 shows its 2007 income statement, and Exhibit 15-10 shows condensed balance sheets for 2006 and 2007.

Because the statement of cash flows explains the causes for the change in cash, our first step is to compute the amount of the change (which represents the net effect we need to explain):

Cash, December 31, 2006	$25,000
Cash, December 31, 2007	16,000
Net decrease in cash	$ 9,000

Exhibit 15-11 illustrates a statement of cash flows that explains this $9,000 decrease in cash. Let's look at each of the three sections of this cash flow statement.

Cash Flows from Financing Activities

Although most companies list operating activities as the first section of the cash flow statement, it is better to begin our discussion with the more easily described and understood section of the cash flow statement, cash flows from financing activities. This section shows cash flows to and from providers of capital. The easiest way to determine cash flows from financing activities is to examine changes in the cash account in the balance sheet equation and identify those associated with financing activities. Balmer Company had three such transactions in 2007, as shown in Exhibit 15-8:

Transaction 9, issue long-term debt, $120,000
Transaction 10, issue common shares, $98,000
Transaction 11, pay dividends, $19,000

The first two of these transactions are cash inflows, and the last is a cash outflow. Therefore, Balmer's net cash inflow from financing activities totals $199,000:

EXHIBIT 15-8

Balmer Company Summarized Transactions, 2007 (in thousands of dollars)

	Assets					=	Liabilities and Shareholders' Equity				
							Liabilities			Shareholders' Equity	
Transaction	Cash	Accounts Receivable	Inventories	Fixed Assets, Gross	Accumulated Amortization	=	Accounts Payable	Wages & Salaries Payable	Long-Term Debt	Share Capital	Retained Earnings
Balance, 12/31/06	+25	+25	+60	+330	−110	=	+6	+4	+5	+210	+105
1a. Purchase inventory on account			+140			=	+140				
1b. Payments to suppliers	−72					=	−72				
2a. Sales on credit		+200				=					+200
2b. Cash collections from customers	+180	−180				=					
2c. Cost of goods sold			−100			=					−100
3a. Wages and salaries expense						=		+36			−36
3b. Payments to employees	−15					=		−15			
4. Amortization expense					−17	=					−17
5. Interest expense—paid in cash	−4					=					−4
6. Income tax expense—paid in cash	−20					=					−20
7. Purchase of fixed assets for cash	−287			+287		=					
8. Sales of fixed assets*	+10			−36	+26	=					
9. Issue long-term debt for cash	+120					=			+120		
10. Issue common stock for cash	+98					=				+98	
11. Pay cash dividends	−19					=					−19
Balance, 12/31/07	+16	+45	+100	+581	−101	=	+74	+25	+125	+308	+109

* Balmer Company sold assets with a gross book value of $36,000 and accumulated amortization of $26,000, receiving cash of $10,000.

EXHIBIT 15-9

Balmer Company
Statement of Income
for the Year Ended
December 31, 2007
(in thousands)

Sales		$200
Costs and expenses		
Cost of goods sold	$100	
Wages and salaries	36	
Amortization	17	
Interest	4	
Total costs and expenses		157
Income before income taxes		43
Income taxes		20
Net income		$ 23

EXHIBIT 15-10

Balmer Company
Balance Sheet as of December 31 (in thousands)

Assets	2007	2006	Increase (Decrease)	Liabilities and Shareholders' Equity	2007	2006	Increase (Decrease)
Current assets				Current liabilities			
Cash	$ 16	$ 25	$ (9)	Accounts payable	$ 74	$ 6	$ 68
Accounts receivable	45	25	20	Wages and salaries			
Inventory	100	60	40	payable	25	4	21
Total current assets	161	110	51	Total current liabilities	99	10	89
Fixed assets, gross	581	330	251	Long-term debt	125	5	120
Less accum. amortization	(101)	(110)	9	Shareholders' equity	417	315	102
Net fixed assets	480	220	260	Total liabilities and			
Total assets	$641	$330	$311	shareholders' equity	$641	$330	$311

EXHIBIT 15-11

Balmer Company
Statement of Cash
Flows for the Year
Ended December 31,
2007 (in thousands)

Cash Flows from Operating Activities

Cash collections from customers		$180
Cash payments		
To suppliers	$72	
To employees	15	
For interest	4	
For taxes	20	
Total cash payments		(111)
Net cash provided by operating activities		$ 69

Cash Flows from Investing Activities

Purchases of fixed assets	$(287)	
Proceeds from sale of fixed assets	10	
Net cash used by investing activities		(277)

Cash Flows from Financing Activities

Proceeds from issuance of long-term debt	$120	
Proceeds from issuance of common shares	98	
Payment of dividends	(19)	
Net cash provided by financing activities		199
Net decrease in cash		$ (9)
Cash, December 31, 2006		25
Cash, December 31, 2007		$ 16

Balmer Company
Cash Flows from Financing Activities, 2007

Proceeds from issuance of long-term debt	$120,000
Proceeds from issuance of common shares	98,000
Payment of dividends	(19,000)
Net cash provided by financing activities	$199,000

If you did not have access to the balance sheet equation entries, you could also look at the changes in Balmer's balance sheet during 2007. As a general rule for financing activities,

- Increases in cash (cash inflows) stem from increases in liabilities or share capital

- Decreases in cash (cash outflows) stem from decreases in liabilities or share capital or payment of dividends

Following is a list of some financing activities and their effect on cash:

Type of Transaction	Increase (+) or Decrease (−) in Cash
Increase long-term or short-term debt	+
Reduce long-term or short-term debt	−
Sell common or preferred shares	+
Repurchase common shares	−
Pay dividends	−
Convert debt to common shares	No effect

Cash Flows from Investing Activities

The section of the cash flow statement called cash flows from investing activities lists cash flows from the purchase or sale of plant, property, equipment, and other long-lived assets. It is usually the second section in the statement. To determine the cash flows from investing activities, you need to look at transactions that increase or decrease long-lived assets, loans made by the company, or securities it owns that are not cash equivalents. Balmer Company has only one such asset, fixed assets, and its related accumulated amortization account. There were two cash transactions relating to fixed assets during 2007:

Transaction 7, purchase fixed assets for cash, $287,000

Transaction 8, sale of fixed assets for cash, $10,000

The first of these transactions is a cash outflow, and the second is a cash inflow. The investing activities section of Balmer's cash flow statement is

Balmer Company
Cash Flows from Investing Activities, 2007

Purchases of fixed assets	$(287,000)
Proceeds from sale of fixed assets	10,000
Net cash used by investing activities	$(277,000)

Notice that we place cash outflows in parentheses. Because there is a net cash outflow, investing activities used cash during 2007. This contrasts with financing activities, which provided cash.

The general rule for investing activities is that

- Increases in cash (cash inflows) stem from decreases in long-lived assets, loans, and investments
- Decreases in cash (cash outflows) stem from increases in long-lived assets, loans, and investments

Following is a list of investing activities and their effects on cash:

Type of Transaction	Increase (+) or Decrease (−) in Cash
Purchase fixed assets for cash	−
Purchase fixed assets by issuing debt	No effect
Sell fixed assets for cash	+
Purchase securities that are not cash equivalents	−
Sell securities that are not cash equivalents	+
Make a loan	−
Collect a loan	+

Noncash Investing and Financing Activities

Sometimes financing or investing activities do not affect cash but are very similar to transactions that have a cash flow effect. Companies must list such activities in a separate schedule accompanying the statement of cash flows. In our example, Balmer Company did not have any noncash investing or financing activities. However, suppose Balmer's purchase of fixed assets was not for cash but was financed as follows:

a. Balmer acquired $150,000 of the fixed assets by issuing common shares, and
b. Balmer acquired the other $137,000 of fixed assets by signing a note payable for $137,000.

Balmer could have taken the $150,000 and $137,000 in cash and then used that cash to buy fixed assets, but it never actually received the cash. Thus, there is no entry to the statement of cash flows. However, because of the similarities between this noncash transaction and the purchase for cash, readers of statements of cash flows want to be informed of such noncash activities. We must report such items in a schedule of noncash investing and financing activities. Balmer Company's schedule for these hypothetical transactions would be

Balmer Company
Schedule of Noncash Investing and Financing Activities, 2007

Common shares issued to acquire store equipment	$150,000
Mortgage payable for acquisition of store equipment	$137,000

CASH FLOW FROM OPERATING ACTIVITIES

Analyzing the results of financing and investing activities informs investors about management's ability to make financial and investment decisions. However, users of financial statements are even more concerned with assessing management's operating decisions. They focus on the first major section of cash flow statements, cash flows from operating activities (or cash flows from operations). This section shows the cash effects of transactions that affect the income statement.

Approaches to Calculating the Cash Flow from Operating Activities

Direct Method.
A method for computing cash flows from operating activities that subtracts operating cash disbursements from cash collections to arrive at cash flows from operations.

Indirect Method.
A method for computing cash flows from operating activities that adjusts the previously calculated accrual net income from the income statement to reflect only cash receipts and cash disbursements.

We can use either of two approaches to compute cash flows from operating activities (or cash flow from operations). The **direct method** subtracts operating cash disbursements from cash collections to arrive at cash flows from operations. The **indirect method** adjusts the previously calculated accrual net income from the income statement to reflect only cash receipts and cash disbursements. Both methods show the same amount of cash provided by (or used for) operating activities. The only difference is the format of the statement.

The direct method is a straightforward listing of cash inflows and cash outflows and is easier for investors to understand. However, 99 percent of all companies use the indirect method. Why? Because it links cash flows directly with net income, emphasizing how income and cash flows differ. We will discuss the direct method first because, as a newcomer to accounting, you will probably find it easier to understand. However, to understand cash flow statements for real companies, it is essential to also understand the indirect method that most companies use.

Consider first the types of cash flows that accountants classify as operating activities. Exhibit 15-12 lists many such activities. These cash flows are associated with revenues and expenses on the income statement. Notice that recording revenues from the sales of goods or services does not necessarily increase cash immediately. Only sales for cash immediately increase cash. There is no cash

EXHIBIT 15-12	Type of Transaction	Increase (+) or Decrease (−) in Cash
Analysis of Effects of Transactions on Cash Flows from Operating Activities	**Operating activities**	
	Sales of goods and services for cash	+
	Sales of goods and services on credit	No effect
	Collection of accounts receivable	+
	Receive dividends or interest	+
	Recognize cost of goods sold	No effect
	Purchase inventory for cash	−
	Purchase inventory on credit	No effect
	Pay accounts payable	−
	Accrue operating expenses	No effect
	Pay operating expenses	−
	Accrue taxes	No effect
	Pay taxes	−
	Accrue interest	No effect
	Pay interest	−
	Prepay expenses for cash	−
	Record the using up of prepaid expenses	No effect
	Charge amortization	No effect

effect of credit sales until the customer actually pays. Balmer Company must collect its accounts receivable to generate any cash.

The cash effects of expenses are similar. Sometimes—amortization is an example—the cash outflow precedes the recording of the expense on the income statement. For example, Balmer Company paid $287,000 in cash for its fixed assets and recorded the purchase as an investing cash outflow. The company then records amortization expenses as it uses the equipment, long after the cash payment. Thus, amortization is not a cash flow.

In contrast, sometimes the cash outflow follows the recording of the expense. For example, most companies pay salaries and wages after employees have earned them. Suppose that Balmer Company pays salaries and wages on the tenth day of each month for the amount earned the previous month. Then the accrual of the expense would occur one month and the related cash outflow would come the following month. The expense appears in the first month's income statement, but the cash outflow appears in the second month's statement of cash flows.

Now that you know some of the operating transactions that affect cash and how the cash inflow or outflow can occur at a different time than the recording of the related revenue or expense, let's examine the two formats used for showing the cash flow effects of operations.

Cash Flow from Operations—The Direct Method

The direct method consists of a listing of cash receipts (inflows) and cash disbursements (outflows). The easiest way to construct the statement of cash flows from operations using the direct method is to examine the cash column of the balance sheet equation. The following entries from Exhibit 15-8 affect cash and were not financing and investing activities:

Transaction	Cash Effect
(1b) Payments to suppliers	−72,000
(2c) Collections from customers	+180,000
(3b) Payments to employees	−15,000
(5) Interest expense and payment	−4,000
(6) Income tax expense and payment	−20,000

From these transactions we can construct the cash flows from operating activities section of the cash flow statement:

Balmer Company
Cash Flows from Operating Activities, 2007

Cash collections from customers	$180,000
Cash payments:	
To suppliers	(72,000)
To employees	(15,000)
For interest	(4,000)
For taxes	(20,000)
Net cash provided by operating activities	$ 69,000

This completes the statement of cash flows in Exhibit 15-11. We can see that operations generated $69,000 of cash, but Balmer Company needed an additional $199,000 from financing activities to cover the $277,000 needed for investing. Even after raising those funds, cash still declined $9,000 over the year.

Cash Flow from Operations—The Indirect Method

The direct method gives a straightforward picture of where cash came from and how it was spent. However, it does not address the issue of how the cash flows from operating activities differ from net income. To do this, we use the indirect method. We can construct the indirect method cash flow statement for Balmer Company from 2007's income statement and the beginning and ending balance sheets in Exhibits 15-9 and 15-10. Each income statement item has a parallel item or items in the statement of cash flows. Each sale eventually results in cash inflows; each expense entails cash outflows at some time. When the cash inflow from a sale or the cash outflow for an expense occurs in one accounting period and we record the sales revenue or expense in another, net income can differ from the cash flows from operations. The indirect method highlights such differences by beginning with net income and then listing all the adjustments necessary to compute cash flows from operating activities. Exhibit 15-13 illustrates the indirect method, and we will next explain the entries in this exhibit.

If Balmer's sales were all for cash and it paid all expenses in cash as incurred, the cash flows from operating activities would be identical to the net income. Thus, you can think of the first line of Exhibit 15-13, net income, as the cash flow from operating activities when revenues equal cash inflows and expenses equal cash outflows. The subsequent adjustments recognize the differences between revenues and cash inflows and between expenses and cash outflows.

The first adjustment is to add the amortization expense to net income. We do this because we deducted amortization of $17,000 when computing the net income of $23,000, but it does not cause an operating cash outflow in 2007. Amortization is an expense, but the related cash flow occurred as an investing activity when Balmer purchased the equipment. Because we deducted $17,000 of amortization in computing 2007's net income, adding it back simply cancels the deduction. There is no cash flow effect of amortization.

Amortization represents an expense for which there is never an operating cash flow. The related cash flow was an investing outflow. The remaining adjustments represent situations where only timing creates differences between net income and cash flows from operations. That is, the timing of revenues or expenses differs from that of the related operating cash inflow or outflow.

The sales revenues of $200,000 shown on the income statement immediately affects the accounts receivable account on the balance sheet and eventually will affect cash. If all sales were for cash, sales would not affect accounts receivable, the associated cash flows would occur at the time of sale, and the cash inflow would equal the sales. However, Balmer's sales are all on open account. Thus, the sale initially increases accounts receivable, and the cash inflow occurs when Balmer collects the receivables. You can compute the amount of cash col-

EXHIBIT 15-13

Balmer Company
Cash Flows from
Operating Activities—
Indirect Method

Net income	$23,000
Adjustments to reconcile net income to net cash provided (used) by operating activities:	
Amortization	17,000
Net increase in accounts receivable	(20,000)
Net increase in inventories	(40,000)
Net increase in accounts payable	68,000
Net increase in wages and salaries payable	21,000
Net cash provided by operating activities	$69,000

lections from income statement and balance sheet data in one of two ways. First, you can compute the total collections Balmer could possibly collect during the year, which is the accounts receivable balance at the beginning of the year plus the sales during the year. From this, you subtract the amount that Balmer has not yet collected, the accounts receivable at the end of the year. This gives collections in 2007 of $180,000:

Beginning accounts receivable	$ 25,000
+ Sales	200,000
Potential collections	$225,000
– Ending accounts receivable	(45,000)
Cash collections from customers	$180,000

Alternatively, you can start with the sales for the year. If accounts receivable had remained unchanged, cash collections would equal sales. If accounts receivable increased, collections fell short of the sales, causing net income to be higher than cash flows from operations. If accounts receivable decreased, collections exceeded sales, causing net income to be lower than cash flows from operations. In 2007, Balmer's accounts receivables increased from $25,000 to $45,000, so cash collections were only $180,000:

Sales	$200,000
Decrease (increase) in accounts receivable*	(20,000)
Cash collections from customers	$180,000

* The format "decrease (increase)" means that decreases are positive amounts and increases are negative amounts.

Because Balmer's accounts receivable increased in 2007, we need to deduct the $20,000 from net income to get cash provided by operating activities. Entry 1 in Exhibit 15-14 shows this adjustment.

EXHIBIT 15-14

Balmer Company
Comparison of Net Income and Cash Provided by Operating Activities

Net Income		Adjustments		Cash Provided by Operating Activities	
1) Sales revenues	$200,000	Increase in accounts receivable	$(20,000)	Cash collections from customers	$180,000
		Increase in inventories	(40,000)		
2) Cost of goods sold	(100,000)	Increase in accounts payable	68,000	Cash payments to suppliers	(72,000)
3) Wages and salaries expense	(36,000)	Increase in wages and salaries payable	21,000	Cash payments to employees	(15,000)
4) Interest	(4,000)	None		Cash payments for interest	(4,000)
5) Income taxes	(20,000)	None		Cash payments for income taxes	(20,000)
6) Amortization	(17,000)	Amortization	17,000		
Net income	$ 23,000	Total adjustments ·	$ 46,000	Net cash provided by (used for) operating activities	$ 69,000

Just as we adjusted sales to compute cash collections from customers, we can adjust the cost of goods sold from the income statement to compute cash outflow for payments to suppliers. To do this, we look at one income statement account, cost of goods sold, and two balance sheet accounts, inventory and accounts payable. We adjust cost of goods sold to get cash payments to suppliers in two steps:

cost of goods → sold purchases → payments to suppliers

These two steps yield the following:

Step 1:	
Ending inventory, December 31, 2007	$100,000
+ Cost of goods sold in 2007	100,000
Inventory to account for	$200,000
− Beginning inventory, December, 31, 2006	(60,000)
Inventory purchased in 2007	$140,000
Step 2:	
Inventory purchased in 2007	$140,000
+ Beginning accounts payable, December 31, 2006	6,000
Total amount to be paid	$146,000
− Ending accounts payable, December 31, 2007	(74,000)
Amount paid in cash during 2007	$ 72,000

In step 1, we compute the amount of inventory purchased in 2007, independent of whether we purchase the inventory for cash or credit. The calculation requires taking the amount of inventory used in 2007 (that is, the cost of goods sold), plus the amount of inventory left at the end of the year, less the amount that was already in inventory at the beginning of the year. If Balmer had bought all its inventory for cash, we could stop at this point. Its cash outflow to suppliers would be equal to the amount purchased, $140,000. However, because Balmer purchased some inventory on credit, we must take step 2. If Balmer had paid off all its accounts payable by the end of the year, it would have paid an amount equal to the beginning accounts payable plus the purchases in 2007, a total of $146,000. But $74,000 remained payable at the end of 2007, meaning that of the $146,000 of potential payments, Balmer paid only $146,000 − $74,000 = $72,000 in 2007.

From these two steps we can determine the two adjustments to net income needed to adjust it to a cash outflow number:

Cost of goods sold in 2007	$100,000
Increase (decrease) in inventory during 2007	40,000
Decrease (increase) in trade accounts payable during 2007	(68,000)
Payments to suppliers during 2007	$ 72,000

Now consider the adjustment to net income required to compute cash provided by operating activities. Exhibit 15-14 shows this in entry 2. First, remember that we subtract cost of goods sold in computing net income just as we subtract the cash payments to suppliers in determining cash provided by operating activities. Any adjustment showing a cash outflow greater than the cost of goods sold will lead to cash provided by operations that is less than net income. Because the increase in inventory caused the cash outflow to exceed the cost of goods sold by $40,000, net income will be $40,000 more than cash provided by operations. In contrast, the increase in accounts payable caused the cash outflow to fall short of cost of goods sold by $68,000, which results in net income that is $68,000 less than cash provided by operations.

Before considering the other adjustments in Exhibit 15-14, let's create a general approach to adjustments. Then we can apply the approach to wages and salaries.

- Adjust for revenues and expenses not requiring cash
  Add back amortization
  (Other adjustments are beyond the scope of this chapter)
- Adjust for changes in noncash assets and liabilities relating to operating activities
  Add decreases in assets
  Deduct increases in assets
  Add increases in liabilities
  Deduct decreases in liabilities

Adjustments discussed so far have included adding back the $17,000 of amortization (entry 6 in Exhibit 15-14), deducting the $20,000 increase in accounts receivable (an asset), deducting the $40,000 increase in inventory (an asset), and adding the $68,000 increase in accounts payable (a liability). Take time now to verify that each of these adjustments is consistent with the rules in the general approach.

Now let's consider the wages and salaries expense. Notice that wages and salaries payable, a liability account, increased from $4,000 at the beginning of the year to $25,000 at the end of the year. Thus, we need to add a $21,000 adjustment for wages and salaries, as shown in entry 3 of Exhibit 15-14. This $21,000 balance is the result of charging $36,000 for wages and salaries in the income statement but paying only $15,000 in cash. This means that Balmer's expense exceeded the cash outflow by $21,000, as shown in the adjustment we made.

Finally, Balmer pays both interest expense and taxes in cash when incurred. Thus, they require no adjustment—the cash flow equals the expense, as shown in entries 4 and 5.

To summarize, look again at Exhibit 15-14. The comparison of net income to cash flows from operating activities in Exhibit 15-14 begins with the net income of $23,000 from the first column of Exhibit 15-14, adds the adjustments of $46,000 in the middle column, and ends with the $69,000 net cash provided by operating activities in the right-hand column. Exhibit 15-13 shows this same information in the proper indirect-method format.

Reconciliation Statement

When a company uses the direct method for reporting cash flows from operating activities, users of the financial statements would miss information that relates net income to operating cash flows. Thus, the FASB requires direct-method statements to include a supplementary schedule reconciling net income to net cash provided by operations. Such a supplementary statement is essentially an indirect-method cash flow statement. In essence, companies that choose to use the direct method must also report using the indirect method. In contrast, those using the indirect method never explicitly report the information on a direct-method statement. The supplementary statement included with direct-method cash flow statements would be identical to the body of Exhibit 15-13, but we would label it "Reconciliation of Net Income to Net Cash Provided by Operating Activities." No wonder 99 percent of firms use the indirect method!

INTERPRETING THE CASH FLOW STATEMENT

Let's look back on what we learned from Balmer Company's cash flow statement. For growing companies that have a strong cash position at the outset, cash often declines. Why? Because growing companies usually need cash for investment in various business assets required for expansion, including investment in accounts receivable and inventories. Notice that Balmer Company's total assets nearly doubled between 2006 and 2007, so we should not be surprised at the decrease in cash.

The statement in Exhibit 15-11 gives a direct picture of where Balmer's cash came from and where it went. Operations generated $69,000 of cash, investing activities used $277,000, and the company raised a net of $199,000 from financing activities. The excess of cash outflows over cash inflows reduced cash in total by $9,000. Without the statement of cash flows, the readers of the annual report would have to conduct their own analyses of the beginning and ending balance sheets, the income statement, and the statement of retained earnings to get a grasp of the impact of financial management decisions.

Free Cash Flow.
Cash flows from operations less capital expenditures.

A concept that has received notice recently is **free cash flow**—cash flows from operations less capital expenditures. This is the cash flow left over after undertaking the firm's operations and making the investments necessary to ensure its continued operation. Some also subtract dividends, assuming that they are necessary to keep the shareholders happy. Companies that cannot generate enough cash from operations to cover their investments need to raise more capital, either by selling assets or by issuing debt or equity. If investment is for growth, this situation may be acceptable. If the investment is merely to maintain the status quo, the company is probably in trouble. In recent years, many utilities have resorted to selling off assets because they could not generate enough free cash flow to meet their needs. Balmer Company has a large negative free cash flow, $69,000 − $287,000 = −$218,000, meaning that it cannot maintain its current plans without raising substantial capital, which it did during 2007.

The Balmer Company illustration demonstrates how a firm may simultaneously (1) have a significant amount of net income, as computed by accountants on the accrual basis, and yet (2) have a decline in cash that could become severe. Indeed, many growing businesses are desperate for cash even though reported net income zooms upward. For example, in the years leading up to Enron's bankruptcy, it had annual net income between $500,000 million and $1 billion, but it used much more cash for investment activities than it generated from operations—an average of about $2 billion a year more. Examining its free cash flow might have provided a warning to investors of bad things to come.

Role of Amortization

Readers of statements of cash flows sometimes misunderstand the reason for adding amortization to net income when computing cash flows from operating activities. Amortization is an allocation of historical cost to expense. Therefore, amortization expense does not entail a current outflow of cash. Consider again the comparison of Balmer Company's net income and cash flows in Exhibit

15-14. Why do we add the $17,000 of amortization to net income to compute cash flow? We do so simply to cancel its deduction in calculating net income. Unfortunately, use of the indirect method may at first glance create an erroneous impression that we add amortization because it, by itself, is a source of cash. If that were really true, a corporation could merely double or triple its bookkeeping entry for amortization expense when it needs cash! What would happen? Income would decline, but cash provided by operations would not change. Suppose we doubled Balmer Company's amortization:

	With Amortization of $17,000	With Amortization of $34,000
Sales	$200,000	$200,000
All expenses except amortization (including income taxes)*	(160,000)	(160,000)
Amortization	(17,000)	(34,000)
Net income	$ 23,000	$ 6,000
Nonamortization adjustments†	29,000	29,000
Add amortization	17,000	34,000
Net cash provided by operating activities	$ 69,000	$ 69,000

* $100,000 + $36,000 + $4,000 + $20,000 = $160,000
† $(20,000) + $(40,000) + $68,000 + $21,000 = $29,000

The doubling would affect amortization and net income, but it would have no direct influence on cash provided by operations, which would still amount to $69,000.

Statement of Cash Flows for Nike, Inc.

Nike's statement of cash flows for the year ended May 31, 2003, appears in Exhibit 15-15. Most publicly held corporations use the same general format for their statement of cash flows. Like Nike, they use the indirect method in the body of the statement of cash flows to report the cash flows from operating activities.

Three items deserve mention here. First, Nike adds deferred income taxes back to net income. These taxes are charged as expense but are not currently payable. Therefore, they are a noncash expense, similar to amortization. Second, the cumulative effect of the accounting change is essentially a noncash charge. It reduces goodwill by a charge to income, but it entails no cash effect. Third, proceeds from the exercise of options are cash received from issuance of shares to executives as part of a stock option compensation plan. You might also notice that we cannot compute changes in account balances directly from the balance sheets in Exhibit 15-2. This is a result of factors beyond the scope of this text, primarily the incorporation of the accounts of companies that Nike acquired during fiscal 2003.

EXHIBIT 15-15

Nike, Inc.
Statement of Cash
Flows for the Year
Ended May 31, 2003
(in millions)

Cash provided (used) by operations:	
Net income	$474.0
Income charges (credits) not affecting cash	
Depreciation	239.3
Deferred income taxes	50.4
Amortization and other	23.2
Cumulative effect of accounting change	266.1
Changes in certain working capital components:	
Increase in inventories	(102.8)
Increase in accounts receivable	(136.3)
Decrease in other current assets	60.9
Increase in accounts payable, accrued liabilities, and income taxes payable	30.1
Other	12.5
Cash provided by operations	917.4
Cash provided (used) by investing activities:	
Additions to property, plant, and equipment	(185.9)
Disposals of property, plant, and equipment	14.8
Increase in other assets	(46.3)
Increase in other liabilities	1.8
Cash used by investing activities	(215.6)
Cash provided (used) by financing activities:	
Proceeds from long-term debt issuance	90.4
Reductions in long-term debt including current portion	(55.9)
Decrease in notes payable	(349.8)
Proceeds from exercise of stock options and other stock issuances	44.2
Repurchase of stock	(196.3)
Dividends—common and preferred	(137.8)
Cash used by financing activities	(605.2)
Other	(38.1)
Net increase in cash and equivalents	58.5
Cash and equivalents, beginning of year	575.5
Cash and equivalents, end of year	$634.0

RATIO ANALYSIS

OBJECTIVE 4

Perform comparisons
between companies
within an industry and
between companies
from different
industries.

Time-Series Analysis.
Comparison of a com-
pany's financial ratios
with its own historical
ratios.

Ratios form the basis of most financial statement analysis, which fundamentally involves the comparison of a ratio. Ratios for a company can be compared in three ways: (1) with its own ratios of a previous time period (called time-series analysis), (2) with other companies' ratios (called cross-sectional analysis), and (3) with rules of thumb or objectives (sometimes referred to as benchmarks).

Time-series analysis attempts to indicate changes in certain characteristics of a particular company. For example, a company may have tried to improve its cost efficiency in an effort to improve its overall returns. A time-series analysis will provide indications as to whether the company has been successful in this strategy. It is important though in analyzing a ratio over time, to also consider any other changes that may have also occurred over the same time period. While the ratios may indicate the extent that a cost efficiency strategy is working, other factors may also produce a change in the ratios (which can be unrelated to management's efforts). For example, increased competition among suppliers may reduce costs, which in turn would indicate improved efficiency. However, the improvements may not be the result of specific decisions taken within the company. Other changes such as changes in accounting policies, changes in the company's operations, etc. may also limit the ability of an analyst to accept a ratio at face value.

Cross-sectional analysis provides a comparison of a company to other companies either in the same industry or in another industry. While cross-sectional analysis can be performed at different times, each comparison is generally performed at about the same time in order to be as comparable as possible. However, an analyst must be aware that certain limitations do exist in order to draw comparisons between companies. For example, it is rare to find two companies in exactly the same industry producing exactly the same products. In fact, in Canada, limitations in the market tend to require each company to specialize in a specific niche. As a result, many Canadian managers will say that "there is no other company exactly like us." Furthermore, there are differences in terms of year-ends, the classification of accounts, and accounting policies. All of these potential differences require the analyst to consider the possible effects of the difference on the cross-sectional comparison.

Benchmarks provide useful objectives or rules of thumb by which an analyst can assess the relative merits of a particular ratio. For example, a company may have improved its overall return over the previous five years to the point where it now has the highest return of any company in the industry. Thus both the time-series and the cross-sectional analysis are very positive. However, if the company's return of 5 percent is compared to a benchmark of 8 percent for a relatively low-risk investment, it would indicate that both the company and its industry are performing at a level of low returns. It is sometimes difficult to obtain benchmarks and thus many analysts use rules of thumb based upon their experience. Some industry associations attempt to provide industry means, which are computed from information obtained from their members. Industry ratios are also provided by sources such as *Dun and Bradstreet Key Business Ratios, Financial Post Industry Reports, Investors Digest of Canada,* and *Polymetric Report.*

Benchmarks can also be obtained by examining the ratios of specific companies. Annual reports of public companies can be obtained by contacting the company directly, through *The Globe and Mail*'s annual report service, and through the Canadian Securities Administrators' service called SEDAR.

We will next discuss specific ratios that can be analyzed for most companies. The ratios will be organized into the four categories: (1) profitability ratios, (2) liquidity ratios, (3) debt ratios, and (4) growth ratios. It is important to remember that any one ratio only provides a piece of the picture. To build a total picture of the financial strengths and weaknesses of a company, the analysis of each ratio should be considered with each other. Furthermore, it is common for an analyst to produce additional ratios beyond those listed in this chapter to examine a specific issue that may be unique to the company or its industry.

Exhibit 15-16 provides a summary of the ratios that will now be discussed. To assist in the discussion of the ratios, the 2005 and 2006 balance sheets and income statements of MartPro Corporation are provided in Exhibit 15-17 and Exhibit 15-18 respectively.

Profitability Ratios

Profitability ratios examine the company's profit from different perspectives, in order to explain the reasons underlying the level of profit. *Return on assets* measures the overall profit on the assets that the company has used to generate the profit. For MartPro, the return on assets of 7.9 percent ($65,647/$827,063) means that

EXHIBIT 15-16

Ratio Formulas

PROFITABILITY RATIOS:

Return on assets	=	Net income/total assets
Net income margin	=	Net income/sales
Asset turnover	=	Sales/assets
Return on shareholders' equity	=	Net income/shareholders' equity

LIQUIDITY RATIOS:

Current ratio	=	Current assets/current liabilities
Quick ratio	=	(Cash + short-term investments + accounts receivable)/current liabilities
Working capital	=	Current assets – current liabilities
Age of receivables	=	Accounts receivable/(sales ÷ no. of days)
Age of inventory	=	Inventory/(cost of goods sold ÷ no. of days)
Age of payables	=	Accounts payable/(purchases* ÷ no. of days)
Inventory turnover	=	Costs of goods sold/inventory

DEBT RATIOS:

Debt to assets	=	Debt/assets
Equity to assets	=	Equity/assets
Times interest earned	=	(Net income before taxes + interest)/interest

GROWTH RATIOS:

Sales	=	(Current year's sales – last year's sales)/Last year's sales
Profit	=	(Current year's profit – Last year's profit)/Last year's profit
Assets	=	(Current year's assets – Last year's assets)/Last year's assets
Equity	=	(Current year's equity – Last year's equity)/Last year's equity

* When purchases are not reported, cost of goods sold may be used.

the company earned 7.9 cents on every dollar of assets. The return on assets can be further segregated into the ratios of net income margin and asset turnover. Net income margin indicates the amount of income that remains from each dollar of sales after all expenses have been covered. The asset turnover ratio computes the number of sales dollars generated for each dollar of assets employed in the company. In 2006, MartPro's net income margin was 5.2 percent ($65,647/$1,252,115) and its asset turnover was 1.5 times ($1,252,115/$827,063). It is useful to note that the product of the *net income margin* and the *asset turnover* is the return of assets, i.e., 7.9 percent = 5.2 percent times 1.5 (with rounding). In other words, a company can improve its return on assets by maximizing its net income margin or its asset turnover or a combination of the two.

For a more detailed analysis of the return on assets ratio and thus a closer look at a company's profitability, it is possible to analyze the components of the net income margin further. For example, it is common to compute an operating earnings margin, which in MartPro's case was 8.5 percent ($106,802/$1,252,115). Likewise, any line on the income statement could be analyzed as a percentage of sales. Further it is also common to examine the *return on shareholders' equity,* which for MartPro was 14.0 percent in 2006 ($65,647/$469,545). The return on equity or any other component of the balance sheet merely provides another measure of returns that is more focused on a portion of the total assets.

EXHIBIT 15-17

MartPro Corporation
Consolidated Balance
Sheet December 31,
2006 and 2005
(millions of dollars)

	December 31 2006	December 31 2005
Assets		
Current assets		
Cash and short-term investments	$14,451	$25,199
Accounts receivable	222,281	163,102
Inventories	101,082	91,998
Prepaid expenses	15,620	1,155
Other assets	–	862
Income taxes recoverable	519	3,194
	353,953	285,510
Investment in preferred shares, at cost	686	914
Capital assets	472,424	400,155
	$827,063	$686,579
Liabilities		
Current liabilities		
Short-term bank borrowings	$129,897	$46,152
Accounts payable and accrued liabilities	182,458	161,485
Current portion of long-term debt	1,539	2,761
Advance payment from customers	5,054	3,840
	318,948	214,238
Accounts payable not due in current year	–	5,840
Long-term debt	2,508	3,024
Future income taxes	14,515	16,080
Non-controlling interests	21,547	24,107
	357,518	263,289
Shareholders' equity		
Share capital	83,381	81,669
Retained earnings	386,164	341,621
	469,545	423,290
	$827,063	$686,579

Liquidity Ratios

Liquidity Ratios.
Ratios that examine an
organization's ability
to meet its short-term
financial obligations.

Current Assets. Cash and
all other assets that are
reasonably expected to be
converted to cash or sold
or consumed during the
coming year.

Current Liabilities. An
organization's debts that
fall due within the
coming year.

Liquidity ratios tell whether a company is able to meet its short-term financial obligations. Generally, short term means any financial obligations due within one year. Normally assets and liabilities are segregated to distinguish the current assets and liabilities from other capital assets and liabilities. **Current assets** are those that are expected to be realized in the form of cash or could be turned into a cash receipt within one year. Similarly, **current liabilities** are debts that are due within one year.

The *current ratio* is computed by dividing the current assets by the current liabilities. In 2006, MartPro's current ratio was 1.1 ($353,953/$318,948). This result would indicate that MartPro would be able to cover its current liabilities 1.1 times. However, for some companies there may be sufficient uncertainty concerning the company's ability to sell its inventories or to convert its prepaid expenses into cash. Thus a more conservative test of its liquidity is warranted. The *quick ratio* or *acid test ratio* refines the current ratio by including only cash, short-term investments, and accounts receivable in the numerator. For MartPro, the quick ratio is 0.74 ([$14,451 + $222,281]/$318,948) which indicates that 74 percent of the

EXHIBIT 15-18

MartPro Corporation
Consolidated Statement
of Income Years Ended
December 31, 2006
and 2005
(thousands of dollars)

	December 31 2006	December 31 2005
Sales	$1,252,115	$ 998,312
Cost of sales and operating expenses		
before the following	1,000,261	766,034
Amortization	84,771	58,465
Selling, general, and administrative	60,281	46,093
	1,145,313	870,592
Operating earnings	106,802	127,720
Other income (expense)		
Interest earned	1,882	4,585
Other income	36	882
Interest on long-term debt	(63)	(169)
Other interest expense	(5,164)	(1,407)
	(3,309)	3,891
	103,493	131,611
Provision for (recovery of) income taxes		
Current	41,871	38,568
Future	(1,565)	4,758
	40,306	43,326
	63,187	88,285
Non-controlling interests	2,460	(3,900)
Net earnings for the year	$ 65,647	$ 84,385

current liabilities can be covered with cash and term deposits and the collection of the accounts receivable. Both of these ratios provide a comparison of the relative size of the liquid assets and liabilities while the working capital provides in dollars the amount of the current assets that is available to a company after covering its current liabilities. In the case of MartPro, the *working capital* for 2006 was $35,005 thousands ($353,953 – $318,948).

For the above liquidity analysis, it is recognized that the current assets and liabilities will be converted into cash receipts or payments within one year. It would, however, be useful to know how long it actually takes within a company for these events to occur. The next three ratios are commonly used to evaluate this issue. The *age of receivables ratio* measures the average length of time that is required from the recording of the sale until the cash is collected. By dividing the accounts receivable balance by the average day's sales, it can be determined that MartPro's customers paid their invoices on average in about 65 days ($222,281/[$1,252,115/365]). The *age of inventory* of 37 days ($101,082/[$1,000,261/365]) indicates that from the time of the purchase of materials through to the production of its products and then to the point of sale of the finished product required 37 days for MartPro in 2006. By dividing the 37 days into 365 days in a year, an inventory turnover ratio of 9.9 provides the same information. The *age of payables* measures the average length of time that a company takes to pay its suppliers of goods and services. In 2006, MartPro paid their bills in about 67 days ($182,458/[$1,000,261/365]), using cost of sales and operating expenses of $1,000,261 thousands in place of purchases.

Debt Ratios

Debt ratios provide a measure of the long-term financial strength of the company, particularly in terms of its ability to carry its debt load. For most companies it is financially advisable to finance a portion of its assets with debt financing as opposed to a form of equity financing. However, given the requirement to pay interest on debts, it is a company's inability to meet its interest obligations that can result in its bankruptcy. For this reason it is important to assess the reasonableness of a company's debt load and its ability to cover its interest expenses. The *debt to assets ratio* is a measure of the extent to which a company has financed its assets with liabilities. For MartPro, its debt to assets of 43 percent ($357,518/$827,063) means that on average 43 cents of each dollar of assets is financed with debt. The *times interest earned ratio or interest coverage ratio* indicates the number of times that the company's interest expense could have been increased before a net loss would have been reported. MartPro's interest coverage was 20.4 times ($106,802/[$5,164 + $63]) in 2006.

Growth Ratios

Growth ratios provide a means of showing the areas in which a company has increased or decreased in size over the previous year. The areas of sales, income or profit, assets, and equity are commonly used growth ratios. However, an analyst would not limit the analysis to these areas if other segments of the company such as inventory were of greater concern. For MartPro, its sales grew by 25.4 percent from the 2005 sales of $998,312, to $1,252,115 in 2006. However, over the same period, the profits declined by 22.2 percent and assets and shareholders' equity grew by 20.5 percent and 10.9 percent.

MAKING MANAGERIAL DECISIONS

Consider the concept of a holding gain on inventory. Holding gains arise only when using current rather than historical costs. They measure the specific price increases of inventory held by a company compared to some benchmark. Under the current-cost/nominal-dollars method, the benchmark is the original cost of the inventory. Under the current-cost/constant-dollars method, the benchmark is the price-level adjusted historical cost of the inventory. Suppose a company purchased $5,000 of inventory at the beginning of the year and held it until the end of the year, when its replacement cost was $6,000. The price-level index was 100 at the beginning of the year and 112 at the end of the year. Compute the holding gain under (1) the current-cost/nominal-dollars method, and (2) the current-cost/constant-dollars method. How would a manager explain each holding gain?

ANSWER

Under the current-cost/nominal-dollars method, the entire $1,000 price increase is a holding gain. It reflects the fact that inventory purchased for $5,000 is now worth $6,000. Under the current-cost/constant-dollar method, only $400 of the price increase is a holding gain. The original $5,000 of inventory is worth $5,000 × (112 ÷ 100) = $5,600 in end-of-year dollars. The only real gain is $6,000 − $5,600 = $400; the other $600 increase in value merely offsets the decline in the value of the dollar.

CASH-FLOW ANALYSIS

A critical dimension to analyzing the financial aspects of a company is to understand the *sources and uses* of its cash. Much of the ratio analysis, and in particular the profitability analysis, focuses on the operating success of the company. However, a company without sufficient cash to fund its activities will eventually go bankrupt.

The objective of the **statement of cash flows** is to provide information on the sources of cash generated by the company and on the activities that required use of its cash. Exhibit 15-19 provides the statement of changes in financial

EXHIBIT 15-19

MartPro Corporation
Consolidated Statement
of Cash Flows
Years Ended December
31, 2006 and 2005
(thousands of dollars)

Statement of Cash Flows. A
statement that reports the
cash receipts and cash
payments of an organization during a particular
period.

	December 31 2006	December 31 2005
Cash provided by (used in)		
Operating activities		
Net earnings for the year	$65,647	$84,385
Charges (credits) to earnings not involving cash:		
Amortization	84,771	58,465
Future income taxes	(1,565)	4,758
Non-controlling interests	(2,460)	3,900
Loss (gain) on disposal of capital assets	282	(75)
Government subsidy	–	(579)
	146,675	150,854
Changes in non-cash working capital (net of effects of acquisitions):		
Increase in accounts receivable	(59,179)	(45,248)
Increase in inventories	(9,084)	(18,942)
Decrease (increase) in prepaid expenses	(14,465)	139
Decrease (increase) in other assets	862	(862)
Decrease (increase) in income taxes recoverable	2,675	(3,194)
Increase (decrease) in accounts payable and accrued liabilities	23,203	(1,514)
Decrease in income taxes payable	–	(14,967)
Increase in advanced payments from customers	1,214	1,370
	91,901	67,636
Financing activities		
Proceeds from short-term bank borrowings	83,745	46,152
Proceeds from long-term debt	1,209	–
Repayment of long-term debt	(2,947)	(2,023)
Proceeds from common share issuance	2,873	11,064
Repurchase of shares	(11,000)	(9,107)
Dividends to shareholders	(11,265)	(9,639)
Dividends by subsidaries to non-controlling interests	–	(288)
	62,615	36,159
Investing activities		
Purchase of capital assets	(168,460)	(171,247)
Proceeds from disposal of capital assets	3,068	6,803
Proceeds on redemption of preferred shares	228	229
Increase (decrease) in investment by a non-controlling interest	(100)	850
Business acquisitions	–	(24,981)
	(165,264)	(188,346)
Decrease in cash and short-term investments	(10,748)	(84,551)
Cash and short-term investments—beginning of year	25,199	109,750
Cash and short-term investments—end of year	$14,451	$25,199

Technology Changes Financial Statement Analysis

The key to financial analysis is the availability of data. Companies can accumulate, categorize, and summarize basic financial data in many ways. In the past, investors and analysts had access only to the published summary data in quarterly and annual financial statements. Analysts then used the methods discussed in this chapter, along with many others, to try to predict the future financial performance of a company. Enter technology. By making more data available on a more timely basis and making mathematical analysis easier and faster, technology is enabling investors and analysts to obtain and analyze more information about a company than ever before.

Microsoft
www.microsoft.com/
msft/history.mspx

XBRL International
www.xbrl.org

Some companies are providing tools to help investors and analysts. For example, in the "Financial History" section of its investor relations Web page, Microsoft provides access to a "Financial History PivotTable." The Pivot Table is an Excel tool that provides line item financial information as far back as 1985 and sophisticated analytical tools to help examine historical trends in many categories. In the same section, Microsoft provides access to another analytical tool, the FY 2006 Microsoft "What-if?". This tool enables an investor to do Excel-based projections, based on Microsoft's 2006 fiscal year income statements and on various assumptions that the investor chooses to make. Tools such as these allow individual investors easy access to some of the analytical tools that are used by professional analysts.

Another innovation that is sure to make a big impact is XBRL (eXtensible Business Reporting Language). A group of technology firms and consultants formed XBRL International to create a common XML-based computer language for the reporting of business information. Today, a consortium of over 170 companies and agencies supports the efforts. XBRL provides "an XML-based framework that the global business information supply chain will use to create, exchange, and analyze financial reporting information including, but not limited to, regulatory filings such as annual and quarterly financial statements, general ledger information, and audit schedules." XBRL will make it easier to share information. As Robert Elliott, former chair of the AICPA and a partner at the accounting firm KPMG said, "While sharing business information has always been necessary, it has been a significant challenge. [XBRL] will revolutionize the way financial information is communicated, accessed and used." XBRL is the language of the future for exchanging financial information. It has the potential to make vast sums of data available in an easily accessible format.

Bryant University, of Smithfield, Rhode Island, has established a Resource Centre dedicated to XBRL. In February of 2005, the U.S. Securities and Exchange Commission formally established a program whereby registrants were permitted to voluntarily finish XBRL data as an exhibit to specified filings. This proposal has met with the strong approval of the Information Systems Section of the American Accounting Association, as well as the Artificial Intelligence/Emerging Technologies Section of the American Accounting Association. The sections made a joint submission, strongly in support of the proposal. Membership of the working group making the American Accounting Association submission included Canadians professors Samir Trabelsi of Brock University and Gerald Trites of St. Francis Xavier University.

With improved communication of detailed financial information and enhanced modelling and analysis tools, the future for financial analysis holds great promise.

Sources: Microsoft Web site (www.microsoft.com); XBRL International Web site (www.xbrl.org); L. Watson, B. McGuire, and E. Cohen, "Looking at Business Reports through XBRL-Tinted Glasses," *Strategic Finance,* September 2000, pp. 40–45; "Pilot Program Uses XBRL for Reports," *Financial Executive,* October 2002, p. 8. U.S. Securities and Exchange Commission News Release, "SEC Adopts Rule Establishing a Voluntary Program for Reporting Financial Information on EDGAR Using XBRL," February 3, 2005, accessed at www.sec.gov; American Accounting Association, "Comments on SEC Proposed Rule 33-8496—XBRL Voluntary Financial Reporting on the EDGAR System," joint submission to the SEC by the Information Systems Section and the Artificial Intelligence/Emerging Technologies Section, accessed at http://web.bryant.edu/~xbrl/.

position for MartPro Corporation for the years 2005 and 2006. While much of the detailed terminology in this statement requires more than an introductory knowledge of financial accounting, the essence of the statement can be quickly appreciated.

The statement of cash flows is normally divided into three parts. The first part adjusts net income for any noncash expenses and for changes in working capital to generate cash provided from operating activities. In 2006, MartPro experienced a net source of cash of $91,901 thousands within its operating activities. The second part identifies the cash provided by financing activities that, in MartPro's case, raised $62,615 thousand during the year. The third part lists the investment activities in which MartPro used $165,264 thousand, primarily in the acquisition of capital assets. The net effect of these three components of operating activities, investing activities and financing activities will indicate the net change in cash or near-cash assets. For MartPro, the sum of these three areas of activities resulted in a decrease of $10,748 thousands of its available cash that left the company in a cash position of $14,451 thousands by year-end.

In management accounting, we recognize the importance of distinguishing accounting expenses from cash expenditures. This distinction is equally relevant in analyzing the financial strengths and weaknesses of a company from its published financial statements.

SUMMARY

This chapter provides an introduction to financial statement analysis by focusing on ratios and the statement of changes in financial position that are commonly examined by analysts. While a more thorough study of this subject does not necessarily require a detailed understanding of financial accounting, an analyst's ability to understand the intricacies of interpreting certain ratios would definitely be improved with a thorough grounding in financial accounting. For our purposes, these ratios provide a useful complement to an understanding of the possible impacts of management accounting decisions on the financial statements of a company.

HIGHLIGHTS TO REMEMBER

1. **Read and interpret basic financial statements.** An underlying structure of concepts, techniques, and conventions provides a basis for accounting practice. We present two basic financial statements, the balance sheet (or statement of financial position) and income statement, in this chapter. Their main elements are assets, liabilities, owners' equity, revenues, and expenses. Income statements and balance sheets are linked because the revenues and expenses appearing on income statements are components of shareholders' equity. Revenues increase shareholders' equity; expenses decrease shareholders' equity. We also present the statement of retained earnings and the statement of cash flows.

2. **Distinguish between the accrual basis of accounting and the cash basis of accounting.** The accrual basis is the heart of accounting. Under accrual accounting, companies recognize revenues as they earn and realize them, and they record expenses as they use resources, not

necessarily when they receive or disburse cash. Do not confuse expense with the term *cash disbursement,* or revenue with the term *cash receipt.*

3. **Relate the measurement of expenses to the expiration of assets.** At the end of each accounting period, companies must make adjustments so that they can present financial statements on a full-fledged accrual basis. The major adjustments are for (a) expiration of unexpired costs, (b) recognition (earning) of unearned revenues, (c) accrual of unrecorded expenses, and (d) accrual of unrecorded revenues.

4. **Explain the nature of dividends and retained earnings.** Dividends are not expenses; they are distributions of assets that reduce ownership claims. Similarly, retained earnings is not cash; it is a claim against total assets.

5. **Recognize and define the main types of assets in the balance sheet of a corporation.** Assets are divided into current and noncurrent categories. Common current assets are cash, accounts receivable, inventories, and prepaid expenses. The largest noncurrent (or fixed) asset is generally property, plant, and equipment, which accountants list at acquisition cost less accumulated amortization.

6. **Recognize and define the main types of liabilities in the balance sheet of a corporation.** Liabilities are divided into current liabilities and long-term liabilities. Current liabilities include notes payable and accounts payable. Long-term debt in the form of debentures or mortgages is the most common noncurrent liability.

7. **Recognize and define the main elements of the shareholders' equity section of the balance sheet of a corporation.** Shareholders' equity contains capital and retained earnings.

8. **Recognize and define the principal elements in the income statement of a corporation.** Income statements contain revenues and expenses. Multistep income statements have some of the following subtotals: gross profit (gross margin), operating income, and income before income taxes.

9. **Recognize and define the elements in the statement of retained earnings.** Net income increases retained earnings and losses and dividends decrease them. For large profitable companies, retained earnings may be by far the largest component of shareholders' equity.

10. **Identify activities that affect cash and classify them as operating, investing, or financing activities.** The statement of cash flows lists cash inflows and cash outflows in one of three categories. Operating cash flows include collections from customers and payments to suppliers. Investing cash flows include purchases and sales of fixed assets. Financing cash flows include borrowings and repayment of borrowings, sales of shares, and payment of dividends.

11. **Describe how goodwill arises and how to account for it.** If a parent pays more than the fair market value of the net assets when acquiring a subsidiary, it must record the difference as goodwill. Goodwill is an intangible asset that remains on the company's books at its original amount until its value is impaired.

12. **Explain and use a variety of popular financial ratios.** Financial ratios aid the intelligent analysis of financial statements. To compare companies that differ in size, analysts use component percentages. They also prepare a variety of ratios and compare them with the

company's own historical ratios, with general benchmarks, and with ratios of other companies or industry averages. They use growth ratios, debt ratios, profitability ratios, and liquidity ratios. An especially important ratio for assessing operating performance is the rate of return on invested capital.

DEMONSTRATION PROBLEMS FOR YOUR REVIEW

Problem One

"The book value of plant assets is the amount that a company would have to spend today for their replacement." Do you agree? Explain.

Solution

Net book value of the plant assets is the result of deducting accumulated amortization from original cost. This process does not attempt to capture all the technological and economic events that may affect replacement value. Consequently, there is little likelihood that net book value will approximate replacement cost.

Problem Two

On December 31, 2006, a magazine publishing company receives $150,000 in cash for three-year subscriptions. It regards this sum as unearned revenue. Show the balances in that account at December 31, 2007, 2008, and 2009. How much revenue would the company earn in each of those three years?

Solution

The balance in unearned revenue would decline at the rate of $50,000 yearly. The company would recognize $50,000 as earned revenue in each of the three years.

	December 31			
	2006	2007	2008	2009
Unearned revenue	$150,000	$100,000	$50,000	$0

Problem Three

Companies sometimes combine the income statement and statement of retained earnings into a single statement. Prepare a combined income statement and statement of retained earnings from the following data. Use a multiple-step format for the income statement.

Cost of goods sold	$420,000
Net sales	750,000
Income taxes	80,000
Beginning retained earnings	440,000
Dividends	30,000
Interest expense	20,000
Selling and administrative expenses	110,000

Solution

Statement of Income and Retained Earnings

Net sales	$750,000
Cost of goods sold	420,000
Gross margin	330,000
Selling and administrative expenses	110,000
Operating income	220,000
Interest expense	20,000
Income before income taxes	200,000
Income taxes	80,000
Net income	120,000
Beginning retained earnings	440,000
Dividends	(30,000)
Ending retained earnings	$530,000

Problem Four

	2006	2005	2004
Annual amounts:			
Net income	NKR100*	NKR60	NKR25
Gross profit on sales	525	380	200
Cost of goods sold	975	620	300
Operating expenses	380	295	165
Income tax expense	45	25	10
End-of-year amounts:			
Capital assets	NKR250	NKR220	NKR180
Long-term debt	80	65	40
Current liabilities	70	55	35
Cash	10	5	10
Accounts receivable	95	70	40
Merchandise inventory	125	85	60
Share capital	205	205	205
Retained earnings	125	55	10
Dividends	30	15	15

* NKR is Norwegian kroner.

1. Compute the following for each of the last two years, 2006 and 2005:
   a. Net income margin
   b. Return on shareholders' equity
   c. Inventory turnover
   d. Current ratio
   e. Ratio of debt to assets
   f. Ratio of current debt to assets
   g. Gross profit margin
   h. Average collection period for accounts receivable
   i. Sales growth
2. Answer yes or no to each of these questions and indicate which of the computations in requirement 1 support your answer:
   a. Has the merchandise become more saleable?
   b. Is there a decrease in the effectiveness of accounts receivable collection efforts?

c. Has gross income margin improved?

d. Has the net income margin improved?

e. Has the rate of return on owners' investment increased?

f. Have the risks of insolvency changed significantly?

g. Have business operations margins improved?

h. Has there been a worsening of the company's ability to pay current debts on time?

3. Basing your observations on only the available data and the ratios you computed, prepare some brief comments on the company's operations and financial changes during the two years.

Solution

1. (a) Net income margin:
   (Sales: 2005: 380 + 620 = 1,000; 2006: 525 + 975 = 1,500)
   2005: 60 ÷ 1,000 = 6.0%
   2006: 100 ÷ 1,500 = 6.7%

   (b) Return on shareholders' equity:
   2005: 60 ÷ (205 + 55) = 23.1%
   2006: 100 ÷ (205 + 125) = 30.3%

   (c) Inventory turnover:
   2005: 620 ÷ 85 = 7.3 times
   2006: 975 ÷ 125 = 7.8 times

   (d) Current ratio:
   2005: (5 + 70 + 85) ÷ 55 = 2.9 to 1
   2006: (10 + 95 + 125) ÷ 70 = 3.3 to 1

   (e) Ratio of debt to assets:
   2005: (65 + 55) ÷ (220 + 5 + 70 + 85) = 31.6%
   2006: (80 + 70) ÷ (250 + 10 + 95 + 125) = 31.3%

   (f) Ratio of current debt to assets:
   2005: 55 ÷ (220 + 5 + 70 + 85) = 14.5%
   2006: 70 ÷ (250 + 10 + 95 + 125) = 14.6%

   (g) Gross profit margin:
   2005: 380 ÷ 1,000 = 38%
   2006: 525 ÷ 1,500 = 35%

   (h) Average collection period for accounts receivable:
   2005: 70 ÷ (1000 ÷ 365) = 25.6 days
   2006: 95 ÷ (1500 ÷ 365) = 23.1 days

   (i) Sales growth:
   2005: (1000 − 500) ÷ 500 = 100%
   2006: (1500 − 1000) ÷ 1000 = 50%

2. (a) Yes, c   (c) No, g   (e) Yes, b   (g) No, g
   (b) No, h   (d) Yes, a   (f) No, e, f   (h) No, d

3. The company has grown rapidly and profitably (ratios a, b, and i). Moreover, the large increase in retained earnings indicates that the expansion has been financed largely by internally generated funds. The expansion has been accompanied by increased liquidity of current assets (ratios c and d).

Problem Five

The Buretta Company has prepared the following data. In December 2006, Buretta paid $54 million cash for a new building acquired to accommodate an expansion of operations. This was financed partly by a new issue of long-term debt for $40 million cash. During 2006 the company also sold fixed assets for $5 million cash that was equal to their book value. All sales and purchases of merchandise were on credit.

Buretta Company
Statement of Cash Flows
for the Year Ended
December 31, 2006
(in millions)

CASH FLOWS FROM OPERATING ACTIVITIES		
Cash collection from customers		$ 85
Cash payments:		
Cash paid to suppliers	$(79)	
General expenses	(10)	
Interest paid	(3)	
Property taxes	(2)	(94)
Net cash used by operating activities		$ (9)
CASH FLOWS FROM INVESTING ACTIVITIES		
Purchase of capital assets (building)	$(54)	
Proceeds from sale of capital assets	5	
Net cash used by investing activities		(49)
CASH FLOWS FROM FINANCING ACTIVITIES		
Long-term debt issued	$ 40	
Dividends paid	(1)	
Net cash provided by financial activities		39
Net decrease in cash		$(19)
Cash balance, December 31, 2005		20
Cash balance, December 31, 2006		$ 1

Buretta Company
Supporting Schedule to
Statement of Cash Flows
Reconciliation of Net
Income to Net Cash
Provided by Operating
Activities
for the Year Ended
December 31, 2006
(in millions)

Net income (from income statement)	$ 4
Adjustments to reconcile net income to net cash provided by operating activities:	
Add: Amortization which was deducted in the computation of net income but does not decrease cash	8
Deduct: Increase in accounts receivable	(15)
Deduct: Increase in inventory	(31)
Deduct: Increase in prepaid general expenses	(2)
Add: Increase in accounts payable	25
Add: Increase in accrued property tax payable	2
Net cash provided by operating activities	$(9)

Because the net income of $4 million was the highest in the company's history, Mr. Buretta, the chairman of the board, was perplexed by the company's extremely low cash balance.

What is revealed by the statement of cash flows? Does it help you reduce Buretta's puzzlement? Why?

Solution

The statement of cash flows shows where cash has come from and where it has gone. Operations used $9 million of cash. Why? The statement shows that large increases in accounts receivable ($15 million) and inventory ($31 million), plus a $2 million increase in prepaid expenses, used $48 million of cash. In contrast, only $39 million (that is, $4 + $8 + $25 + $2 million) was generated. It also shows the $9 million use of cash slightly differently; the $85 million of cash receipts and $94 million in disbursements are shown directly. Investing activities also consumed cash because $54 million was invested in building, and only $5 million was received from sales of fixed assets. Financing activities generated $39 million cash, which was $19 million less than the $58 million used by operating and investing activities.

Buretta should no longer be puzzled. The statement of cash flows shows where cash has come from and where it has gone. Either operations must be changed so that they do not require so much cash, or investment must be curtailed, or more long-term debt or ownership equity must be raised. Otherwise Buretta Company will soon run out of cash.

KEY TERMS

accounts payable p. 760
accounts receivable p. 760
accrual basis p. 763
assets p. 760
balance sheet p. 763
benchmarks p. 791
cash basis p. 764
cash equivalents p. 765
cash flows from financing
  activities p. 777
cash flows from investing
  activities p. 777
cash flows from operating
  activities p. 776
common shares p. 772
cross-sectional analysis p. 791
current assets pp. 764, 793
current liabilities pp. 770, 793
debentures p. 770
debt ratios p. 795
direct method p. 782
earnings per share p. 774
equities p. 760
fixed assets p. 767
free cash flow p. 788
goodwill p. 769

growth ratios p. 795
income statement p. 763
indirect method p. 782
intangible assets p. 769
liabilities p. 760
limited liability p. 772
liquidation p. 771
liquidity ratios p. 793
long-term liabilities p. 770
net income p. 774
noncurrent liabilities p. 770
operating cycle p. 764
owners' equity p. 760
preferred shares p. 772
profitability ratios p. 791
retained earnings p. 760
retained income p. 760
shareholders' equity p. 760
statement of cash flows pp. 775, 796
statement of retained earnings p. 775
statement of retained income p. 775
subordinated p. 770
tangible assets p. 767
time-series analysis p. 790
transaction p. 759
working capital p. 770

ASSIGNMENT MATERIAL

QUESTIONS

Q15-1 Criticize: "Assets are things of value owned by the entity."

Q15-2 Criticize: "Net income is the difference in the ownership capital account balances at two points in time."

Q15-3 Distinguish between the accrual basis and the cash basis.

Q15-4 Name the three types of comparisons made with ratios.

Q15-5 Why is it useful to analyze income statements and balance sheets by component percentages?

Q15-6 What two ratios are multiplied to give the return on assets?

Q15-7 "The statement of cash flows is an optional statement included by most companies in their annual reports." Do you agree? Explain.

Q15-8 What are the purposes of a statement of cash flows?

Q15-9 What three types of activities are summarized in the statement of cash flows?

PROBLEMS

P15-1 **ANALYSIS OF TRANSACTIONS, PREPARATION OF STATEMENTS.** The Ekern Company was incorporated on April 1, 2007. Ekern had ten holders of common shares. Elke Ekern, who was the president and chief executive officer, held 51 percent of the shares. The company rented space in chain discount stores and specialized in selling women's shoes. Ekern's first location was in a store owned by Nordic Market Centres, Inc.

The following events occurred in April:

a. The company was incorporated. Common shareholders invested $90,000 cash.

b. Purchased merchandise inventory for cash, $35,000.

c. Purchased merchandise inventory on open account, $25,000.

d. Merchandise carried in inventory at a cost of $37,000 was sold for cash for $25,000 and on open account for $65,000, a grand total of $90,000. Ekern (not Nordic) carries and collects these accounts receivable.

e. Collection of the above accounts receivable, $15,000.

f. Payments of accounts payable, $18,000. See transaction (c).

g. Special display equipment and fixtures were acquired on April 1 for $36,000. Their expected useful life was 36 months with no terminal scrap value. Straight-line amortization was adopted. This equipment was removable. Ekern paid $12,000 as a down payment and signed a promissory note for $24,000.

h. On April 1, Ekern signed a rental agreement with Nordic. The agreement called for a flat $2,000 per month, payable quarterly in advance. Therefore Ekern paid $6,000 cash on April 1.

i. The rental agreement also called for a payment of 10 percent of all sales. This payment was in addition to the flat $2,000 per month. In this way, Nordic would share in any success of the venture and be compensated for general services such as cleaning and utilities. This payment was to be made in cash on the last day of each month as soon as the sales for the month were tabulated. Ekern made the payment on April 30.

j. Wages, salaries, and sales commissions were paid in cash for all earnings by employees. The amount was $38,000.

k. Amortization expense was recognized. See transaction (g).

l. The expiration of an appropriate amount of prepaid rental services was recognized. See transaction (h).

1. Prepare an analysis of Ekern Company's transactions, employing the equation approach demonstrated in Exhibit 15-1. Two additional columns will be needed: Equipment and Fixtures, and Note Payable. Show all amounts in thousands.

2. Prepare a balance sheet as of April 30, 2007, and an income statement for the month of April. Ignore income taxes.

3. Given these sparse facts, analyze Ekern's performance for April and its financial position as of April 30, 2007.

P15-2 **CASH BASIS VERSUS ACCRUAL BASIS.** Refer to the preceding problem. If Ekern company measured income on the cash basis, what revenue would be reported for April? Which basis (accrual or cash) provides a better measure of revenue? Why?

P15-3 **BALANCE SHEET EFFECTS.** A bank showed the following items (among others) on its balance sheet at January 1, 2007:

Cash	$ 2,644,000,000
Total deposits	$41,644,000,000

1. Suppose you made a bank deposit of $1,000. How would each of the bank assets and equities be affected? How much would each of your personal assets and equities be affected? Be specific.

2. Suppose a branch makes a $900,000 loan to a local hospital for remodelling. What would be the effect on each of the branch's assets and equities immediately after the loan is made? Be specific.

3. Suppose you borrowed $10,000 from a trust company on a personal loan. How would such a transaction affect your personal assets and equities?

P15-4 **BALANCE SHEET EQUATION.** Micra Technology is one of the leading producers of semiconductor components. Its revenue grew from $506 million in 2000 to more than $3.8 billion in 2007. The company's actual data (in millions of dollars) follow for its fiscal year ended September 2, 2007.

Assets, beginning of period	$4,551.4
Assets, end of period	E
Liabilities, beginning of period	A
Liabilities, end of period	2,832.8
Share capital, beginning of period	587.0
Share capital, end of period	D
Retained earnings, beginning of period	2,114.3
Retained earnings, end of period	C
Revenues	3,764.0
Costs and expenses	B
Net income (loss)	(68.9)
Dividends	0.0
Additional investments by shareholders	1,331.7

Find the unknowns (in millions), showing computations to support your answers.

P15-5   ANALYSIS OF TRANSACTIONS, PREPARATION OF STATEMENTS.   PACCAR has maintained its top position in the sales of medium- and heavy-duty diesel trucks in the U.S. since 1993. The company's actual condensed balance sheet data for January 1, 2007 follows (in millions):

ASSETS		EQUITIES	
Cash	$1,042	Accounts payable	$1,734
Accounts receivable	570	Other liabilities	4,088
Inventory	385		
Property, plant, and equipment	875	Shareholders' equity	2,111
Prepaid expenses and other assets	5,061		
Total	$7,933	Total	$7,933

Suppose the following summarizes some major transactions during January (in millions):

   a. Acquired inventory on account, $500.
   b. Trucks carried in inventory at a cost of $400, were sold for cash of $150 and on open account of $500, a grand total of $650.
   c. Collected receivables, $300.
   d. On April 2, used $250 cash to prepay some rent and insurance for 2007.
   e. Payments on accounts payable (for inventories), $450.
   f. Paid selling and administrative expenses in cash, $100.
   g. A total of $90 of prepaid expenses for rent and insurance expired in January 2007.
   h. Amortization expense of $20 was recognized for January.

   1. Prepare an analysis of the PACCAR transactions, employing the equation approach demonstrated in Exhibit 15-1. Show all amounts in millions of dollars (for simplicity, only a few major transactions are illustrated here).
   2. Prepare an income statement for the month ended January 31 and a balance sheet as of January 31. Ignore income taxes.

P15-6   CASH BASIS VERSUS ACCRUAL BASIS.   Refer to the preceding problem. If PACCAR measured income on the cash basis, what revenue would be exported for April? Which basis (accrual or cash) provides a better measure of revenue? Why?

MANAGERIAL DECISION CASES

C15-1   FINANCIAL RATIOS.   Honda Motor Company is a Japanese automobile company with sales equivalent to $80 billion. The company's income statement and balance sheet for the year ended March 31, 2006, are shown in Exhibits 15A-1 and 15A-2. Monetary amounts are in Japanese yen (¥).

Required:
   1. Prepare a common-sized income statement, that is, one showing component percentages.
   2. Compute the following ratios:
   a. Current ratio
   b. Total debt to equity
   c. Gross profit margin
   d. Return on shareholders' equity (2005 shareholders' equity was ¥1,764 billion) —use average shareholders' equity

EXHIBIT 15A-1

Honda Motor Company Income Statement for the Year Ended March 31, 2006 (billions except per share information)

Net sales	¥6,099
Cost of sales	4,206
Gross profit	¥1,893
Selling and administrative	1,133
Research and development	334
Operating income	¥ 426
Other income (expenses)	
Interest income	¥ 11
Interest expense	(19)
Other	14
Total	6
Income before income taxes	¥ 432
Income taxes	(170)
Net income	¥ 262
Amounts per share	
Net income	¥ 269
Cash dividends	¥ 21

EXHIBIT 15A-2

Honda Motor Company Balance Sheet March 31, 2006 (billions)

Assets	
Current assets	
Cash and marketable securities	¥ 431
Receivables	1,122
Inventories	568
Other	335
Total current assets	¥2,456
Property, plant, and equipment, net	1,121
Investments	389
Other assets	932
Total assets	¥4,898
Liabilities and Shareholders' Equity	
Current liabilities	
Bank loans	¥ 496
Payables	697
Accrued expenses	484
Current portion of long-term debt	343
Other	182
Total current liabilities	¥2,202
Long-term liabilities	
Long-term debt	¥ 575
Other	191
Total long-term liabilities	¥ 766
Shareholders' equity	
Common shares (974,414,215 shares outstanding)	¥ 86
Additional share capital	172
Retained earnings	2,219
Other	(547)
Total shareholders' equity	¥1,930
Total liabilities and shareholders' equity	¥4,898

Required:

3. What additional information would help you interpret the percentages and ratios you calculated?

C15-2   UNIDENTIFIED CANADIAN INDUSTRIES.   Within an industry, operating policies and practices may vary between companies. However, the underlying nature of that industry greatly affects the firms' needs for funds, how the firms meet these needs, and also the firms' financial results.

Presented in Exhibit 15A-3 are balance sheets, given in percentage form; and selected ratios, categorized as profitability, liquidity and stability ratios.

These percentages and ratios are derived from the balance sheets and income statements of eight firms from different industries. Although it is known

EXHIBIT 15A-3

Canadian Company Percentages

BALANCE SHEET PERCENTAGES	A	B	C	D	E	F	G	H
Cash and equivalents	4.8	9.5	2.5	1.5	3.3	1.1	2.4	8.9
Receivables	11.9	4.9	10.3	7.9	4.4	3.5	3.7	0.0
Inventories	10.5	16.1	1.9	2.3	0.0	6.4	1.2	0.0
Investments	47.7	1.9	0.0	0.0	0.0	0.0	35.0	78.3
Property, plant, and equipment	22.0	45.0	11.8	85.7	90.5	85.0	50.1	1.0
Other assets	3.1	22.6	73.5	2.6	1.8	4.0	7.6	11.8
TOTAL ASSETS	100.0	100.0	100.0	100.0	100.0	100.0	100.0	100.0
Current liabilities	14.1	41.6	16.7	8.3	7.1	7.6	10.8	64.7
Long-term debt	0.0	19.2	19.3	33.3	12.6	19.8	36.9	30.5
Other liabilities	0.2	2.7	9.8	28.3	6.6	13.2	12.8	0.0
Shareholders' equity	85.8	36.5	54.2	30.1	73.7	59.4	39.5	4.8
TOTAL LIABILITY & SHAREHOLDERS' EQUITY	100.0	100.0	100.0	100.0	100.0	100.0	100.0	100.0
RATIO ANALYSIS								
PROFITABILITY								
Return on investment (%)	0.13	0.10	0.07	0.15	−0.04	−0.02	0.03	0.13
Return on assets (%)	0.11	0.04	0.04	0.05	−0.03	−0.01	0.01	0.01
Operating income margin (%)	0.19	0.04	0.13	0.21	0.08	0.14	-0.03	0.23
Net profit margin (%)	0.14	0.02	0.08	0.10	−0.15	−0.04	0.03	0.08
LIQUIDITY								
Current ratio (x:1)	5.47	0.76	1.01	1.47	1.11	1.56	0.89	0.30
Quick ratio (x:1)	3.73	0.23	0.24	0.18	0.47	0.15	0.22	0.44
Age of receivables (days)	53.73	9.94	73.27	65.15	81.97	52.19	35.10	n/a
Age of inventory (days)	122.03	28.23	19.29	58.86	n/a	131.65	14.44	n/a
Age of payables (days)	124.58	53.21	97.57	155.55	88.71	35.69	120.86	n/a
Inventory turnover (times)	2.95	12.75	18.67	6.12	n/a	2.73	24.93	n/a
Fixed asset turnover (times)	3.61	3.91	4.28	0.51	0.21	0.28	0.76	7.46
Asset turnover (times)	0.80	1.76	0.50	0.44	0.19	0.24	0.38	0.08
STABILITY								
Debt to assets	0.00	0.19	0.19	0.33	0.13	0.20	0.37	0.31
Equity to assets	0.86	0.37	0.54	0.30	0.74	0.59	0.39	0.05
Times interest earned	n/a	4.84	2.99	8.51	−19.72	0.12	1.45	1.13

n/a: not applicable, or immaterial.

that certain differences between firms in the same industry exist, each firm whose figures are summarized is typical of those in its industry.

Required: Identify each of the eight industries listed below from the data given in Exhibit 15A-3. Be prepared to explain the distinctive asset structures and ratios for each:

1. Grocery chain
2. Mining
3. Utility
4. Bank
5. Oil and gas
6. Newspaper
7. Railway
8. High technology

C15-3 **STRATEGIC ANALYSIS.** (SMAC) You have been recently recruited to the newly created position of financial analyst with a large firm. Two years ago, this firm completed its fourth consecutive year of record profits and was among the top ten firms traded on the Toronto Stock Exchange in terms of return on equity. Although the shares were widely held, the directors at that time became increasingly concerned about the possibility of an unfriendly takeover bid by larger firms seeking access to the firm's growing cash surplus. In response to this situation, the board of directors authorized an expansion strategy for the firm to diversify and grow by acquiring other businesses. The relevant guidelines for this strategy are as follows:

- The cost of a single acquisition is not to exceed $10 million.
- Target firms must be in the top quartile in their own industries as demonstrated by "key" financial ratios. In other words, no "sick-company turnarounds."
- Target firms must be sufficiently well organized, staffed, and managed to continue operations independently after the acquisition, so as not to place a burden on your firm's already lean, but efficient, management team that includes its engineers.

In the two years since its inception, this program has been a remarkably effective method of reducing cash surpluses. Three of the four firms acquired have been severely affected by the recent recession and have required massive infusions of cash to continue operations. Despite these setbacks, the program continues. Your position was created because of a need for a skilled financial professional to evaluate and monitor such acquisitions.

On your first day on the job, the financial statements for Great White North Co. Ltd. (GWNCL), a potential acquisition, have been given to you by the vice president in charge of the program. (See Exhibit 15A-4.) Also provided were the industry statistics in Exhibit 15A-5.

The engineering department at your firm has analyzed GWNCL's operations and estimates that with an investment of $2,000,000 by GWNCL in robotic fabricating equipment (with a useful life of ten years), production costs would be changed as follows:

- materials would be reduced by 8 percent due to reduced scrap and rework
- direct labour would be reduced by 10 percent due to increased automation
- overhead would be increased by 20 percent due to increased maintenance and greater levels of expertise in supervisory staff

EXHIBIT 15A-4		
Great White North Company Limited Statement of Income and Retained Earnings for the Year Ended June 30, 2006 (000s)		

Sales		$10,000
Cost of goods sold:		
Materials	$4,500	
Labour	1,300	
Plant overhead	300	6,100
Gross margin		3,900
Expenses:		
Marketing	1,400	
Administration and amortization	1,400	
Interest	150	2,950
Income before taxes and extraordinary item		950
Income taxes		380
Income before extraordinary item		570
Extraordinary item		380
Net income		950
Retained earnings, beginning of year		3,100
Total		4,050
Less: Dividends paid		500
Retained earnings, end of year		$ 3,550

Great White North Company Limited Balance Sheet as at June 30, 2006 (000s)

Assets	
Current assets:	
Cash	$ 400
Accounts receivable	1,500
Inventories	1,900
Total current assets	3,800
Fixed assets (net)	2,200
Total assets	$6,000
Liabilities and Shareholders' Equity	
Current liabilities:	
Accounts payable	$1,250
Long-term debt	1,000
Total liabilities	2,250
Common shares (2,000,000 shares issued and outstanding)	200
Retained earnings	3,550
Total liabilities and shareholders' equity	$6,000

EXHIBIT 15A-5

Industry Statistics

The following statistics have been compiled from a survey of the financial statements of the top quartile of the firms in GWNCL's industry, as determined by profitability. Projected sales in this industry will remain constant in real terms for the foreseeable future. The following ratios represent the mean levels of the financial statistics of these profitable firms.

Industry statistics:

Current ratio	1.5:1	Return on total assets	12.5%
Debt equity ratio	1.7:1	Net return on sales	6.0%
Price earnings ratio	14.0:1	Return on equity	20.0%
Inventory turnover	4 times	Equity to total assets	23.0%
Receivables turnover	45 days		

The new robotic equipment could be installed and would be operational almost immediately. Your firm's engineering department has developed considerable expertise in this field and is one of the few groups in the country capable of successfully implementing such changes. Although the cost reductions could make GWNCL more price competitive, price competition is not a primary characteristic of the custom manufacturing industry. (Assume capital cost allowance rates of 30 percent declining balance for robotic equipment.)

The purchase price for the 2,000,000 outstanding shares of GWNCL has been estimated at $8,000,000, which is a premium over its current net worth. However, the market value of GWNCL is expected to be equal to its net worth at the end of the tenth year.

The question was also raised as to how the additional $2,000,000 capital expenditure will affect the ROI calculation.

Current market borrowing costs range from 12 percent to 15 percent depending on the risk.

Required: Identify and evaluate the issues associated with the proposed acquisition and make appropriate recommendations.

EXCEL APPLICATION EXERCISE

E15-1 CALCULATING FINANCIAL RATIOS

Goal: Create an Excel spreadsheet to calculate financial ratios. Use the results to answer questions about your findings.

Scenario: Albertson's, Inc., has asked you to calculate financial ratios for their company based on income statement and balance sheet data presented below:

Income statement for the year ended January 30, 2006 (in millions)

Sales	$35,626
Cost of sales	25,242
Gross profit	$10,384
Other expenses (summarized)	9,359
Earnings before income taxes	$ 1,025
Income taxes	540
Net earnings	$ 485

Balance sheet	January 30, 2006	January 31, 2005
Assets		
Inventories	$ 2,973	$ 3,196
Other current assets (summarized)	1,295	1,427
Total current assets	$ 4,268	$ 4,623
Land, buildings, and equipment (net)	9,029	9,282
Other assets	1,914	2,076
Total assets	$15,211	$15,981
Liabilities and shareholders' equity		
Current liabilities (summarized)	$ 3,448	$ 3,596
Long-term liabilities (summarized)	6,566	6,470
Total liabilities	$10,014	$10,066
Shareholders' equity (summarized)	5,197	5,915
Total liabilities and shareholders' equity	$15,211	$15,981

Other Information: Albertson's is a large retail food and drug chain, with 2,300 stores in various locations. Albertson's paid cash dividends of $0.76 per common share in fiscal 2006, and an average of 397 million shares were outstanding during the year. Assume that Albertson's has no stock options or convertible securities. The company's market price on January 30, 2006, was $21 per share.

When you have completed your spreadsheet, answer the following questions:

1. Discuss Albertson's current ratio calculations and their meaning. Compare the results to the benchmark data presented in the chapter for this calculation.

2. Discuss Albertson's total debt to equity calculations and their meaning. Compare the results to the benchmark data presented in the chapter for this calculation.

3. Discuss the results of the dividend payout calculation and your opinion regarding its percentage.

Step by Step:

1. Open a new Excel spreadsheet.

2. In column A, create a bold-faced heading that contains the following:
   Row 1: Chapter 15 Decision Guideline
   Row 2: Albertson's, Inc.
   Row 3: Financial Ratio Analysis
   Row 4: Today's Date

3. Merge and centre the four heading rows across columns A through C.

4. In row 7, create the following bold-faced column headings:
   Column A: Financial Data (in millions):
   Column B: January 30, 2006
   Column C: January 31, 2005

   Note: Adjust column widths as necessary.

5. Modify the format of the date headings in columns B and C as follows:
   Number tab: Category: Date
                 Type: March 14, 2000

6. In column A, create the following row headings:
   Row 8: Current Assets
   Row 9: Current Liabilities
   Row 10: Total Liabilities
   Row 11: Shareholders' Equity
   Row 12: Sales
   Row 13: Gross Profit
   Row 14: Net Income
   Row 15: Market Price of Stock
   Row 16: Dividends Paid
   Row 17: Avg. Common Shares Outstanding

   Note: Adjust the column width as necessary.

7. Using the financial and other information provided, enter the amounts for rows 8 through 17 in columns B and C.

8. Skip a row.

9. In row 19, create the following bold-faced column heading:
Column A: Financial Ratios:

10. In column A, create the following row headings:
Row 20: Current Ratio
Row 21: Total Debt to Equity
Row 22: Gross Profit Percentage
Row 23: Return on Sales
Row 24: Return on Shareholders' Equity
Row 25: Earnings per Share
Row 26: Price Earnings
Row 27: Dividend Yield
Row 28: Dividend Payout

11. Use cell-referenced formulas to calculate the amounts in columns B and C for rows 20 through 28.

Hint: By using cell-referenced formulas, the data in rows 8 through 17 can be changed without invalidating the Excel formulas coded in rows 20 through 28.

Example: The Excel formula for the Current Ratio in cell B20 would be 5B8/B9.

Note: The ratio formulas can be found in Exhibit 15-15.

12. Format amounts in column B, rows 8 through 15 and column C, rows 8 through 11 as

Number tab:	Category:	Accounting
	Decimal:	0
	Symbol:	$

13. Format the amount in column B, row 16 as

Number tab:	Category:	Accounting
	Decimal:	2
	Symbol:	$

14. Format the amount in column B, row 25 as

Number tab:	Category:	Currency
	Decimal:	2
	Symbol:	$
	Negative numbers:	Black with parentheses

15. Format amounts in columns B and C, row 20 and column B, row 26 as

Number tab:	Category:	Number
	Decimal:	2
	Negative numbers:	Black with parentheses

16. Format amounts in column B, rows 21 through 24 and 27 through 28, and column C, row 21 as

| Number tab: | Category: | Percentage |
| | Decimal: | 2 |

17. Save your work to disk, and print a copy for your files.

COLLABORATIVE LEARNING EXERCISE

CL15-1 INCOME STATEMENT AND BALANCE SHEET ACCOUNTS   Form teams of two persons each. Each person should make a list of ten account names, with approximately half being income statement accounts and half being balance sheet accounts. Give the list to the other member of the team, who is to write beside each account name the financial statement (I for income statement or B for balance sheet) on which it belongs. If there are errors or disagreements in classification, discuss the account and come to an agreement about which financial statement it belongs to.

Recommended Readings

The following resources will aid readers who want to pursue some topics with more depth than is possible in this book. There is a hazard in compiling a group of recommended readings. Inevitably, some worthwhile books or periodicals are omitted. Moreover, such a list cannot include books published subsequent to the compilation date. This list is not comprehensive, but it suggests many excellent readings.

PERIODICALS

Professional Journals

The following professional journals are typically available in university libraries and include articles on the application of management accounting:

- *Accounting Horizons*. Published by the American Accounting Association; stresses current practice-oriented articles in all areas of accounting.
- *CMA Management* (formerly the *CMA Magazine*). Published by the Society of Management Accountants of Canada; includes much practice-oriented research in management accounting.
- *Financial Executive*. Published by the Financial Executives Institute; emphasizes general policy issues for accounting and finance executives.
- *Harvard Business Review*. Published by Harvard Business School; directed to general managers, but contains excellent articles on applications of management accounting.
- *Journal of Accountancy*. Published by the American Institute of CPAs; emphasizes financial accounting and is directed at the practicing CPA.
- *Management Accounting*. Published by the Institute of Management Accountants; many articles on actual applications by individual organizations.
- *Planning Review*. Published by the Planning Executives Institute; a journal designed for business planners.

- *Canadian Business, Report on Business Magazine, Business Week, Forbes, Fortune, The Economist, The Wall Street Journal.* Popular publications that cover a variety of business and economics topics; often their articles relate to management accounting.

Academic Journals

The academic journal that focuses most directly on current management and cost accounting research is the *Journal of Management Accounting Research*, published by the Management Accounting section of the American Accounting Association. *The Accounting Review*, the general research publication of the American Accounting Association, *Journal of Accounting Research*, published at the University of Chicago, and *Contemporary Accounting Research*, published by the Canadian Academic Accounting Association, cover all accounting topics at a more theoretical level. *Accounting, Organizations and Society*, a British journal, publishes much research on behavioural aspects of management accounting. The *Journal of Accounting and Economics* covers economics-based accounting research.

BOOKS IN MANAGEMENT ACCOUNTING

Most of the topics in this text are covered in more detail in the many books entitled *Cost Accounting* including *Cost Accounting: A Managerial Emphasis*, 4th Canadian ed., by Charles T. Horngren, George Foster, Srikant M. Datar, and Howard D. Teall (Pearson Education Canada, 2002). You can find more advanced coverage in *Advanced Managerial Accounting*, 3rd ed., by R. S. Kaplan and Anthony A. Atkinson (Pearson Education, 1998), and in *Management Accounting*, 4th ed., by Anthony A. Atkinson, Robert S. Kaplan and S. Mark Young (Pearson Education, 2004).

Handbooks and General Texts, Readings, and Case Books

The books in this list have wide application to management accounting issues. The handbooks are basic references. The textbooks are designed for classroom use but may be useful for self-study. Readings books are collections of some of the better periodical articles. The case books present applications from real companies.

- BIERMAN, H., JR., AND S. SMIDT, *The Capital Budgeting Decision*, 7th ed. New York: Macmillan, 1992. Expands the capital budgeting discussion in Chapters 11–12.
- BINKER, B., ed., *Handbook of Cost Management*. New York: Warren, Gorham and Lamont, 1994.
- COOPER, D., R. SCAPENS, AND J. ARNOLD, eds., *Management Accounting Research and Practice*. London: Institute of Cost and Management Accountants, 1983.
- COOPER, R., AND R. KAPLAN, *The Design of Cost Management Systems: Text, Cases and Readings*. Englewood Cliffs, NJ: Prentice Hall, 1991.
- DAVIDSON, S., AND R. WEIL, eds., *Handbook of Modern Accounting*. New York: McGraw-Hill, 1989.
- KAPLAN, R., AND W. BRUNS, eds., *Accounting and Management: Field Study Perspectives*. Boston, MA: Harvard Business School Press, 1987.

- PRYOR, T., et al., *Activity Dictionary: A Comprehensive Reference Tool for ABM and ABC,* ICMS, Inc., 1992.
- ROSEN, L., ed., *Topics in Management Accounting.* Toronto: McGraw-Hill, 1984.
- ROTCH, W., B. ALLEN, AND C. SMITH, *Cases in Management Accounting and Control Systems,* 3rd ed. Upper Saddle River, NJ: Prentice Hall, 1995.
- SHANK, J., *Cases in Cost Management: A Strategic Emphasis.* Cincinnati, South-Western, 1995.

Strategic Nature of Management Accounting

Management accountants realize that cost and performance information is most useful to organizations when it helps define strategic alternatives and helps in the management of resources to achieve strategic objectives. The books in this list, though not necessarily accounting books, provide a valuable foundation to the interaction of strategy and accounting information.

- KAPLAN, R., AND H. T. JOHNSON, *Relevance Lost: The Rise and Fall of Management Accounting.* Boston, MA: Harvard Business School Press, 1987.
- PORTER, M., *Competitive Strategy.* New York: Free Press, 1980.
- PORTER, M., *Competitive Advantage.* New York: Free Press, 1985.
- RAPPAPORT, A., *Creating Shareholder Value: The New Standard for Business Performance.* New York: Free Press, 1986.
- SHANK, J., AND V. GOVIDARAJAN, *Strategic Cost Analysis: The Evolution from Managerial to Strategic Accounting.* Homewood, IL: Irwin, 1989.

Modern Manufacturing

The following books provide background on the nature of modern manufacturing.

- CHASE, R., AND N. AQUILANO, *Production and Operation Management.* Homewood, IL: Irwin, 1989.
- HAYES, R., S. WHEELRIGHT, AND K. CLARK, *Dynamic Manufacturing.* New York, Free Press, 1988.
- SCHONBERGER, R., *World Class Manufacturing.* New York, Free Press, 1986.
- TEECE, P., *The Competitive Challenge: Strategies for Industrial Innovation and Renewal.* Cambridge, MA: Ballinger, 1987.
- ZUBOFF, S., *In the Age of the Smart Machine.* New York: Basic Books, 1984.

Management Accounting in Modern Manufacturing Settings

These books present relatively recent responses of management accountants to changes in manufacturing methods and practices.

- BENNETT, E., B. FOSSUM, R. HARRIS, D. ROBERTSON, AND F. SKIPPER, *Financial Practices in a Computer Integrated System (CIS) Environment.* Morristown, NJ: Financial Executives Research Foundation, 1987.
- BENNETT, R., J. HENDRICKS, D. KEYS, AND E. RUDNICKI, *Cost Accounting for Factory Automation.* Montvale, NJ: National Association of Accountants, 1987.

- GOLDRATT, E., AND J. COX, *The Goal*. Croton-on-Hudson, NY: North River Press, Inc., 1992. A novel illustrating the new manufacturing environment.
- HOWELL, R., J. BROWN, S. SOUCY, AND A. SEED, *Management Accounting in the New Manufacturing Environment*. Montvale, NJ: National Association of Accountants, 1987.
- HOWELL, R., AND S. SOUCY, *FACTORY 2000+*. Montvale, NJ: National Association of Accountants, 1988. A collection of five articles by the authors, originally published in *Management Accounting*.
- KAPLAN, R., ed., *Measuring Manufacturing Performance*: Boston, MA: Harvard University Press, 1990.
- LEE, J., *Managerial Accounting Changes for the 1990s*. Artesia, CA: McKay Business Systems, 1987.

Management Control Systems

The topics covered in Chapters 12 to 15 can be explored further in several books, including:

- ANTHONY, R. N., J. DEARDEN, AND V. GOVINDARAJAN, *Management Control Systems*. Homewood IL: Irwin, 1994. A popular textbook that includes many cases.
- ARROW, K. J., *The Limits of Organization*. New York: Norton, 1974. A readable classic by the Nobel laureate.
- EMMANUEL, C., AND D. OTLEY, *Accounting for Management Control*. Berkshire, England: Van Nostrand Reinhold (UK), 1990.
- KAPLAN, R., AND D. NORTON, *The Balanced Scorecard*. Boston: Harvard Business School Press, 1996.
- MACIARIELLO, J. A., *Management Control Systems*. Englewood Cliffs, NJ: Prentice Hall, 1984.
- MERCHANT, K., *Control in Business Organizations*. Boston: Pitman, 1984.
- SOLOMONS, D., *Divisional Performance: Measurement and Control*. New York: Markus Wiener, 1983. A reprint of a 1965 classic that is still relevant.
- VANCIL, R. R., *Decentralization: Managerial Ambiguity by Design*. Homewood, IL: Dow Jones-Irwin, 1979.

Management Accounting in Not-for-Profit Organizations

Many books discuss management accounting in not-for-profit organizations. Four examples are

- ANTHONY, R. N., AND D. YOUNG, *Management Control in Nonprofit Organizations*, 5th ed. Homewood, IL: Irwin, 1994.
- BRIMSON, J., AND J. ANTOS, *Activity Based Management for Service Industries, Government Entities, and Non-Profit Organizations*. New York: Wiley, 1994.
- HERZLINGER, R., AND D. NITTERHOUSE, *Financial Accounting and Managerial Control for Non-Profit Organizations*. Cincinnati, OH: South-Western Publishing Co., 1994.
- NEUMAN, B., AND K. BOLES, *Management Accounting for Healthcare Organizations*, 5th ed. Bonus Books, 1998.

B

Fundamentals of Compound Interest and the Use of Present-Value Tables

NATURE OF INTEREST

Interest is the cost of using money. It is the rental charge for cash, just as rental charges are often made for the use of automobiles or boats.

Interest does not always entail an outlay of cash. The concept of interest applies to ownership funds as well as to borrowed funds. The reason why interest must be considered on *all* funds in use, regardless of their source, is that the selection of one alternative necessarily commits funds that could otherwise be invested in some other opportunity. The measure of the interest in such cases is the return foregone by rejecting the alternative use. For instance, a wholly owned home or business asset is not cost free. The funds so invested could alternatively be invested in government bonds or in some other venture. The measure of this opportunity cost depends on what alternative incomes are available.

Newspapers often contain advertisements of financial institutions citing interest rates that are "compounded." This appendix explains compound interest, including the use of present-value tables.

Simple interest is calculated by multiplying an interest rate by an unchanging principal amount. In contrast, *compound interest* is calculated by multiplying an interest rate by a principal amount that is increased each interest period by the previously accumulated (unpaid) interest. The accumulated interest is added to the principal to become the principal for the new period. For example, suppose you deposited $10,000 in a financial institution that promised to pay 10 percent interest per annum. You then let the amount accumulate for three years before withdrawing the full balance of the deposit. The *simple-interest* deposit would accumulate to $13,000 at the end of three years:

	PRINCIPAL	SIMPLE INTEREST	BALANCE, END OF YEAR
Year 1	$10,000	$10,000 × 0.10 = $1,000	$11,000
Year 2	10,000	10,000 × 0.10 = 1,000	12,000
Year 3	10,000	10,000 × 0.10 = 1,000	13,000

Compound interest provides interest on interest. That is, the principal changes from period to period. The deposit would accumulate to $10,000 \times (1.10)^3 = \$10,000 \times 1.331 = \$13,310$:

	PRINCIPAL	COMPOUND INTEREST	BALANCE, END OF YEAR
Year 1	$10,000	$10,000 × 0.10 = $1,000	$11,000
Year 2	11,000	11,000 × 0.10 = 1,100	12,100
Year 3	12,100	12,100 × 0.10 = 1,210	13,310

The "force" of compound interest can be staggering. For example, the same deposit would accumulate as follows:

	AT END OF		
	10 Years	20 Years	40 Years
Simple interest			
$10,000 + 10 ($1,000) =	$20,000		
10,000 + 20 ($1,000) =		$30,000	
10,000 + 40 ($1,000) =			$ 50,000
Compound interest			
$10,000 \times (1.10)^{10} = \$10,000 \times 2.5937 =	$25,937		
$10,000 \times (1.10)^{20} = \$10,000 \times 6.7275 =		$67,275	
$10,000 \times (1.10)^{40} = \$10,000 \times 45.2593 =			$452,593

Hand calculations of compound interest quickly become burdensome. Therefore, compound interest tables have been constructed to ease computations. (Indeed, many hand-held calculators contain programs that provide speedy answers.) Hundreds of tables are available, but we will use only the two most useful for capital budgeting.[1]

TABLE 1: PRESENT VALUE OF $1

How shall we express a future cash inflow or outflow in terms of its equivalent today (at time zero)? Table 1, page 825, provides factors that give the *present value* of a single, lump-sum cash flow to be received or paid at the *end* of a future period.[2]

---

[1] For additional tables, see R. Vichas, *Handbook of Financial Mathematics, Formulas and Tables.* Englewood Cliffs, NJ: Prentice Hall, 1979.

[2] The factors are rounded to four decimal places. The examples in this text use these rounded factors. If you use tables with different rounding, or if you use a calculator or personal computer, your answers may differ from those given because of a small rounding error.

Suppose you invest $1 today. It will grow to $1.06 in one year at 6 percent interest; that is, $1 × 1.06 = $1.06. At the end of the second year its value is ($1 × 1.06) × 1.06 = $1 × (1.06)^2 = $1.124, and at the end of the third year it is $1 × (1.06)^3 = $1.191. In general, $1 grows to $(1 + i)^n$ in n years at i percent interest.

To determine the *present value*, you reverse this accumulation process. If $1.00 is to be received in one year, it is worth $1 ÷ 1.06 = $0.9434 today at an interest rate of 6 percent. Suppose you invest $0.9434 today. In one year you will have $0.9434 × 1.06 = $1. Thus, $0.9434 is the *present value* of $1 in a year, invested at 6 percent. If the dollar will be received in two years, its present value is $1 ÷ (1.06)^2 = $0.8900. The general formula for the present value (*PV*) of an amount *S* to be received or paid in n periods at an interest rate of i percent per period is

$$PV + \frac{S}{(1 + i)^n}$$

Table 1 gives factors for the present value of $1 at various interest rates over several different periods. Present values are also called *discounted* values, and the process of finding the present value is *discounting*. You can think of this as discounting (decreasing) the value of a future cash inflow or outflow. Why is the value discounted? Because the cash is to be received or paid in the future, not today.

Assume that a prominent city is issuing a three-year non-interest-bearing note that promises to pay a lump sum of $1,000 exactly three years from now. You desire a rate of return of exactly 6 percent, compounded annually. How much would you be willing to pay now for the three-year note? The situation is sketched as follows:

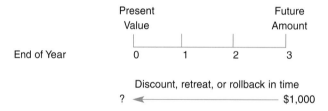

The factor in the period 3 row and 6 percent column of Table 1 is 0.8396. The present value of the $1,000 payment is $1,000 × 0.8396 = $839.60. You would be willing to pay $839.60 for the $1,000 to be received in three years.

Suppose interest is compounded semi-annually rather than annually. How much would you be willing to pay? The three years become six interest payment periods. The rate per period is half the annual rate, or 6% ÷ 2 = 3%. The factor in the period 6 row and 3 percent column of Table 1 is 0.8375. You would be willing to pay $1,000 × 0.8375, or only $837.50 rather than $839.60.

As a further check on your understanding, review the earlier example of compound interest. Suppose the financial institution promised to pay $13,310 at the end of three years. How much would you be willing to deposit at time zero if you desired a 10 percent rate of return compounded annually? Using Table 1, the period 3 row and the 10% column show a factor of 0.7513. Multiply this factor by the future amount:

$$PV = 0.7513 × \$13,310 = \$10,000$$

A diagram of this computation follows:

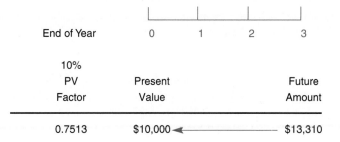

End of Year	0	1	2	3
10% PV Factor	Present Value			Future Amount
0.7513	$10,000 ◄—————————			$13,310

Pause for a moment. Use Table 1 to obtain the present values of

1. $1,600, at 20%, at the end of 20 years
2. $8,300, at 10%, at the end of 12 years
3. $8,000, at 4%, at the end of 4 years

Answers:

1. $1,600 (0.0261) = $41.76
2. $8,300 (0.3186) = $2,644.38
3. $8,000 (0.8548) = $6,838.40

TABLE 2: PRESENT VALUE OF AN ORDINARY ANNUITY OF $1

An *ordinary annuity* is a series of equal cash flows to take place at the *end* of successive periods of equal length. Its present value is denoted PV_A. Assume that you buy a note from a municipality that promises to pay $1,000 at the end of *each* of three years. How much should you be willing to pay if you desire a rate of return of 6 percent, compounded annually?

You could solve this problem using Table 1. First, find the present value of each payment, and then add the present values as in Exhibit B-1. You would be willing to pay $943.40 for the first payment, $890.00 for the second, and $839.60 for the third, a total of $2,673.00.

Since each cash payment is $1,000 with equal one-year periods between them, the note is an *ordinary annuity*. Table 2, page 826, provides a shortcut method. The present value in Exhibit B-1 can be expressed as

$$PV_A = \$1,000 \times \frac{1}{1.06} + \$1,000 \times \frac{1}{(1.06)^2} + \$1,000 \times \frac{1}{(1.06)^3}$$

$$= \$1,000 \left[\frac{1}{1.06} + \frac{1}{(1.06)^2} + \frac{1}{(1.06)^3} \right]$$

The three terms in brackets are the first three numbers from the 6% column of Table 1, and their sum is in the third row of the 6 percent column of Table 2: 0.9434 + 0.8900 + 0.8396 = 2.6730. Instead of calculating three present values and adding them, you can simply multiply the PV factor from Table 2 by the cash payment: 2.6730 × $1,000 = $2,673.

	END OF YEAR		0	1	2	3
PAYMENT	TABLE 1 FACTOR		PRESENT VALUE			
1	$\dfrac{1}{1.06} = 0.9434$		\$ 943.40	\$1,000		
2	$\dfrac{1}{(1.06)^2} = 0.8900$		890.00		\$1,000	
3	$\dfrac{1}{(1.06)^3} = 0.8396$		839.60			\$1,000
Total			$\underline{\underline{\$2,673.00}}$			

EXHIBIT B-1

This shortcut is especially valuable if the cash payments or receipts extend over many periods. Consider an annual cash payment of \$1,000 for 20 years at 6 percent. The present value, calculated from Table 2, is \$1,000 × 11.4699 = \$11,469.90.

To use Table 1 for this calculation, you would perform 20 multiplications and then add the 20 products.

The factors in Table 2 can be calculated using the following general formula:

$$PV_A = \frac{1}{i}\left[1 - \frac{1}{(1+i)^n}\right]$$

Applied to our illustration:

$$PV_A = \frac{1}{0.06}\left[1 - \frac{1}{(1.06)^3}\right] = \frac{1}{0.06}(1 - 0.8396) = \frac{0.1604}{0.06} = 2.6730$$

Use Table 2 to obtain the present values of the following ordinary annuities:

1. \$1,600 at 20% for 20 years
2. \$8,300 at 10% for 12 years
3. \$8,000 at 4% for 4 years

Answers:

1. \$1,600 (4.8696) = \$7,791.36
2. \$8,300 (6.8137) = \$56,553.71
3. \$8,000 (3.6299) = \$29,039.20

In particular, note that the higher the interest rate, the lower the present value.

TABLE 1

(Put a clip on this page for easy reference.)

Present Value of $1

$$PV = \frac{1}{(1+i)^n}$$

PERIODS	3%	4%	5%	6%	7%	8%	10%	12%	14%	16%	18%	20%	22%	24%	25%	26%	28%	30%	40%
1	.9709	.9615	.9524	.9434	.9346	.9259	.9091	.8929	.8772	.8621	.8475	.8333	.8197	.8065	.8000	.7937	.7813	.7692	.7143
2	.9426	.9246	.9070	.8900	.8734	.8573	.8264	.7972	.7695	.7432	.7182	.6944	.6719	.6504	.6400	.6299	.6104	.5917	.5102
3	.9151	.8890	.8638	.8396	.8163	.7938	.7513	.7118	.6750	.6407	.6086	.5787	.5507	.5245	.5120	.4999	.4768	.4552	.3644
4	.8885	.8548	.8227	.7921	.7629	.7350	.6830	.6355	.5921	.5523	.5158	.4823	.4514	.4230	.4096	.3968	.3725	.3501	.2603
5	.8626	.8219	.7835	.7473	.7130	.6806	.6209	.5674	.5194	.4761	.4371	.4019	.3700	.3411	.3277	.3149	.2910	.2693	.1859
6	.8375	.7903	.7462	.7050	.6663	.6302	.5645	.5066	.4556	.4104	.3704	.3349	.3033	.2751	.2621	.2499	.2274	.2072	.1328
7	.8131	.7599	.7107	.6651	.6227	.5835	.5132	.4523	.3996	.3538	.3139	.2791	.2486	.2218	.2097	.1983	.1776	.1594	.0949
8	.7894	.7307	.6768	.6274	.5820	.5403	.4665	.4039	.3506	.3050	.2660	.2326	.2038	.1789	.1678	.1574	.1388	.1226	.0678
9	.7664	.7026	.6446	.5919	.5439	.5002	.4241	.3606	.3075	.2630	.2255	.1938	.1670	.1443	.1342	.1249	.1084	.0943	.0484
10	.7441	.6756	.6139	.5584	.5083	.4632	.3855	.3220	.2697	.2267	.1911	.1615	.1369	.1164	.1074	.0992	.0847	.0725	.0346
11	.7224	.6496	.5847	.5268	.4751	.4289	.3505	.2875	.2366	.1954	.1619	.1346	.1122	.0938	.0859	.0787	.0662	.0558	.0247
12	.7014	.6246	.5568	.4970	.4440	.3971	.3186	.2567	.2076	.1685	.1372	.1122	.0920	.0757	.0687	.0625	.0517	.0429	.0176
13	.6810	.6006	.5303	.4688	.4150	.3677	.2897	.2292	.1821	.1452	.1163	.0935	.0754	.0610	.0550	.0496	.0404	.0330	.0126
14	.6611	.5775	.5051	.4423	.3878	.3405	.2633	.2046	.1597	.1252	.0985	.0779	.0618	.0492	.0440	.0393	.0316	.0254	.0090
15	.6419	.5553	.4810	.4173	.3624	.3152	.2394	.1827	.1401	.1079	.0835	.0649	.0507	.0397	.0352	.0312	.0247	.0195	.0064
16	.6232	.5339	.4581	.3936	.3387	.2919	.2176	.1631	.1229	.0930	.0708	.0541	.0415	.0320	.0281	.0248	.0193	.0150	.0046
17	.6050	.5134	.4363	.3714	.3166	.2703	.1978	.1456	.1078	.0802	.0600	.0451	.0340	.0258	.0225	.0197	.0150	.0116	.0033
18	.5874	.4936	.4155	.3503	.2959	.2502	.1799	.1300	.0946	.0691	.0508	.0376	.0279	.0208	.0180	.0156	.0118	.0089	.0023
19	.5703	.4746	.3957	.3305	.2765	.2317	.1635	.1161	.0829	.0596	.0431	.0313	.0229	.0168	.0144	.0124	.0092	.0068	.0017
20	.5537	.4564	.3769	.3118	.2584	.2145	.1486	.1037	.0728	.0514	.0365	.0261	.0187	.0135	.0115	.0098	.0072	.0053	.0012
21	.5375	.4388	.3589	.2942	.2415	.1987	.1351	.0926	.0638	.0443	.0309	.0217	.0154	.0109	.0092	.0078	.0056	.0040	.0009
22	.5219	.4220	.3418	.2775	.2257	.1839	.1228	.0826	.0560	.0382	.0262	.0181	.0126	.0088	.0074	.0062	.0044	.0031	.0006
23	.5067	.4057	.3256	.2618	.2109	.1703	.1117	.0738	.0491	.0329	.0222	.0151	.0103	.0071	.0059	.0049	.0034	.0024	.0004
24	.4919	.3901	.3101	.2470	.1971	.1577	.1015	.0659	.0431	.0284	.0188	.0126	.0085	.0057	.0047	.0039	.0027	.0018	.0003
25	.4776	.3751	.2953	.2330	.1842	.1460	.0923	.0588	.0378	.0245	.0160	.0105	.0069	.0046	.0038	.0031	.0021	.0014	.0002
26	.4637	.3607	.2812	.2198	.1722	.1352	.0839	.0525	.0331	.0211	.0135	.0087	.0057	.0037	.0030	.0025	.0016	.0011	.0002
27	.4502	.3468	.2678	.2074	.1609	.1252	.0763	.0469	.0291	.0182	.0115	.0073	.0047	.0030	.0024	.0019	.0013	.0008	.0001
28	.4371	.3335	.2551	.1956	.1504	.1159	.0693	.0419	.0255	.0157	.0097	.0061	.0038	.0024	.0019	.0015	.0010	.0006	.0001
29	.4243	.3207	.2429	.1846	.1406	.1073	.0630	.0374	.0224	.0135	.0082	.0051	.0031	.0020	.0015	.0012	.0008	.0005	.0001
30	.4120	.3083	.2314	.1741	.1314	.0994	.0573	.0334	.0196	.0116	.0070	.0042	.0026	.0016	.0012	.0010	.0006	.0004	.0000
40	.3066	.2083	.1420	.0972	.0668	.0460	.0221	.0107	.0053	.0026	.0013	.0007	.0004	.0002	.0001	.0001	.0001	.0000	.0000

TABLE 2

Present Value of Ordinary Annuity of $1

$$PV_A = \frac{1}{i}\left[1 - \frac{1}{(1+i)^n}\right]$$

PERIODS	3%	4%	5%	6%	7%	8%	10%	12%	14%	16%	18%	20%	22%	24%	25%	26%	28%	30%	40%
1	.9709	.9615	.9524	.9434	.9346	.9259	.9091	.8929	.8772	.8621	.8475	.8333	.8197	.8065	.8000	.7937	.7813	.7692	.7143
2	1.9135	1.8861	1.8594	1.8334	1.8080	1.7833	1.7355	1.6901	1.6467	1.6052	1.5656	1.5278	1.4915	1.4568	1.4400	1.4235	1.3916	1.3609	1.2245
3	2.8286	2.7751	2.7232	2.6730	2.6243	2.5771	2.4869	2.4018	2.3216	2.2459	2.1743	2.1065	2.0422	1.9813	1.9520	1.9234	1.8684	1.8161	1.5889
4	3.7171	3.6299	3.5460	3.4651	3.3872	3.3121	3.1699	3.0373	2.9137	2.7982	2.6901	2.5887	2.4936	2.4043	2.3616	2.3202	2.2410	2.1662	1.8492
5	4.5797	4.4518	4.3295	4.2124	4.1002	3.9927	3.7908	3.6048	3.4331	3.2743	3.1272	2.9906	2.8636	2.7454	2.6893	2.6351	2.5320	2.4356	2.0352
6	5.4172	5.2421	5.0757	4.9173	4.7665	4.6229	4.3553	4.1114	3.8887	3.6847	3.4976	3.3255	3.1669	3.0205	2.9514	2.8850	2.7594	2.6427	2.1680
7	6.2303	6.0021	5.7864	5.5824	5.3893	5.2064	4.8684	4.5638	4.2883	4.0386	3.8115	3.6046	3.4155	3.2423	3.1611	3.0833	2.9370	2.8021	2.2628
8	7.0197	6.7327	6.4632	6.2098	5.9713	5.7466	5.3349	4.9676	4.6389	4.3436	4.0776	3.8372	3.6193	3.4212	3.3289	3.2407	3.0758	2.9247	2.3306
9	7.7861	7.4353	7.1078	6.8017	6.5152	6.2469	5.7590	5.3282	4.9464	4.6065	4.3030	4.0310	3.7863	3.5655	3.4631	3.3657	3.1842	3.0190	2.3790
10	8.5302	8.1109	7.7217	7.3601	7.0236	6.7101	6.1446	5.6502	5.2161	4.8332	4.4941	4.1925	3.9232	3.6819	3.5705	3.4648	3.2689	3.0915	2.4136
11	9.2526	8.7605	8.3064	7.8869	7.4987	7.1390	6.4951	5.9377	5.4527	5.0286	4.6560	4.3271	4.0354	3.7757	3.6564	3.5435	3.3351	3.1473	2.4383
12	9.9540	9.3851	8.8633	8.3838	7.9427	7.5361	6.8137	6.1944	5.6603	5.1971	4.7932	4.4392	4.1274	3.8514	3.7251	3.6059	3.3868	3.1903	2.4559
13	10.6350	9.9856	9.3936	8.8527	8.3577	7.9038	7.1034	6.4235	5.8424	5.3423	4.9095	4.5327	4.2028	3.9124	3.7801	3.6555	3.4272	3.2233	2.4685
14	11.2961	10.5631	9.8986	9.2950	8.7455	8.2442	7.3667	6.6282	6.0021	5.4675	5.0081	4.6016	4.2646	3.9616	3.8241	3.6949	3.4587	3.2487	2.4775
15	11.9379	11.1184	10.3797	9.7122	9.1079	8.5595	7.6061	6.8019	6.1422	5.5755	5.0916	4.6755	4.3152	4.0013	3.8593	3.7261	3.4834	3.2682	2.4839
16	12.5611	11.6523	10.8378	10.1059	9.4466	8.8514	7.8237	6.9740	6.2651	5.6685	5.1624	4.7296	4.3567	4.0333	3.8874	3.7509	3.5026	3.2832	2.4885
17	13.1661	12.1657	11.2741	10.4773	9.7632	9.1216	8.0216	7.1196	6.3729	5.7487	5.2223	4.7746	4.3908	4.0591	3.9099	3.7705	3.5177	3.2948	2.4918
18	13.7535	12.6593	11.6896	10.8276	10.0591	9.3719	8.2014	7.2497	6.4674	5.8178	5.2732	4.8122	4.4187	4.0799	3.9279	3.7861	3.5294	3.3037	2.4941
19	14.3238	13.1339	12.0853	11.1581	10.3356	9.6036	8.3649	7.3658	6.5504	5.8775	5.3162	4.8435	4.4415	4.0967	3.9424	3.7985	3.5386	3.3105	2.4958
20	14.8775	13.5903	12.4622	11.4699	10.5940	9.8181	8.5136	7.4694	6.6231	5.9288	5.3527	4.8696	4.4603	4.1103	3.9539	3.8083	3.5458	3.3158	2.4970
21	15.4150	14.0292	12.8212	11.7641	10.8355	10.0168	8.6487	7.5620	6.6870	5.9731	5.3837	4.8913	4.4756	4.1212	3.9631	3.8161	3.5514	3.3198	2.4979
22	15.9369	14.4511	13.1630	12.0416	11.0612	10.2007	8.7715	7.6446	6.7429	6.0113	5.4099	4.9094	4.4882	4.1300	3.9705	3.8223	3.5558	3.3230	2.4985
23	16.4436	14.8568	13.4886	12.3034	11.2722	10.3711	8.8832	7.7184	6.7921	6.0442	5.4321	4.9245	4.4985	4.1371	3.9764	3.8273	3.5592	3.3254	2.4989
24	16.9355	15.2470	13.7986	12.5504	11.4693	10.5288	8.9847	7.7843	6.8351	6.0726	5.4509	4.9371	4.5070	4.1428	3.9811	3.8312	3.5619	3.3272	2.4992
25	17.4131	15.6221	14.0939	12.7834	11.6536	10.6748	9.0770	7.8431	6.8729	6.0971	5.4669	4.9476	4.5139	4.1474	3.9849	3.8342	3.5640	3.3286	2.4994
26	17.8768	15.9828	14.3752	13.0032	11.8258	10.8100	9.1609	7.8957	6.9061	6.1182	5.4804	4.9563	4.5196	4.1511	3.9879	3.8367	3.5656	3.3297	2.4996
27	18.3270	16.3296	14.6430	13.2105	11.9867	10.9352	9.2372	7.9426	6.9352	6.1364	5.4919	4.9636	4.5243	4.1542	3.9903	3.8387	3.5669	3.3305	2.4997
28	18.7641	16.6631	14.8981	13.4062	12.1371	11.0511	9.3066	7.9844	6.9607	6.1520	5.5016	4.9697	4.5281	4.1566	3.9923	3.8402	3.5679	3.3312	2.4998
29	19.1885	16.9837	15.1411	13.5907	12.2777	11.1584	9.3696	8.0218	6.9830	6.1656	5.5098	4.9747	4.5312	4.1585	3.9938	3.8414	3.5687	3.3317	2.4999
30	19.6004	17.2920	15.3725	13.7648	12.4090	11.2578	9.4269	8.0552	7.0027	6.1772	5.5168	4.9789	4.5338	4.1601	3.9950	3.8424	3.5693	3.3321	2.4999
40	23.1148	19.7928	17.1591	15.0463	13.3317	11.9246	9.7791	8.2438	7.1050	6.2335	5.5482	4.9966	4.5439	4.1659	3.9995	3.8458	3.5712	3.3332	2.5000

GLOSSARY

Absorption Approach. A costing approach that considers all factory overhead (both variable and fixed) to be product (inventoriable) costs that become an expense in the form of manufacturing cost of goods sold only as sales occur.

Account Analysis. Selecting a volume-related cost driver and classifying each account as a variable cost or as a fixed cost.

Accounting Rate of Return (ARR). A non-discounted-cash-flow capital-budgeting model expressed as the increase in expected average annual operating income divided by the initial increase in required investment.

Accounting System. A formal mechanism for gathering, organizing, and communicating information about an organization's activities.

Accounts Payable. Amounts owed on open accounts whereby the buyer pays cash some time after the date of sale.

Accounts Receivable. Amounts owed to a company by customers who buy on open account.

Accrual Basis. A process of accounting that recognizes the impact of transactions on the financial statements in the time periods when revenues and expenses occur instead of when cash is received or disbursed.

Accumulated Amortization. The summation of amortization charged to past periods.

Activity Analysis. The process of identifying appropriate cost drivers for each individual activity and their effects on the costs of making a product or providing a service.

Activity-Based Costing (ABC). A system that first accumulates overhead costs for each of the activities of an organization, and then assigns the costs of activities to the products, services, or other cost objects that caused that activity.

Activity-Based Flexible Budget. A budget based on costs for each activity centre and cost driver at varying volumes of activity.

Activity-Based Management (ABM). The use of an activity-based costing system to improve the operations of an organization.

Activity-Level (Sales-Volume) Variances. Variances between the flexible budget and the master budget.

Agency Theory. A theory used to describe the formal choices of performance measures and rewards.

Amortization (Depreciation). The cost of plant and equipment, which is charged periodically to the future periods over which the plant and equipment is used.

Assets. Economic resources that are expected to benefit future activities.

Attention-directing. Reporting and interpreting of information that helps managers focus on operating problems, imperfections, inefficiencies, and opportunities.

Avoidable Costs. Costs that will not continue if an ongoing operation is changed or deleted.

Backflush Costing. An accounting system that applies costs to products only when the production is complete.

Balance Sheet. A statement of assets, liabilities, and equities.

Balanced Scorecard. A performance measurement system that strikes a balance between financial and operating measures, links performance to rewards, and gives explicit recognition to the diversity of stakeholder interests.

Benchmarks. General rules specifying appropriate levels for financial ratios.

Book Value (Net Book Value). The original cost of equipment less accumulated amortization, which is the summation of amortization charged to past periods.

Break-Even Analysis. The study of cost-volume-profit relationships.

Break-Even Point. The level of sales at which revenue equals expenses, and income is zero.

Budget. A quantitative expression of a plan of action as an aid to coordinating and implementing the plan.

Budgeted Factory Overhead Rate. The budgeted total overhead divided by the budgeted cost-driver activity.

By-Product. A product that, like a joint product, is not individually identifiable until manufacturing reaches a split-off point, but has a relatively insignificant total sales value.

Canadian Institute of Chartered Accountants (CICA). An organization of professional accountants, Chartered Accountants.

Capacity Costs. The fixed costs associated with a desired level of production or a desired level of service, while maintaining the chosen product or service attributes.

Capital Assets. Assets used to generate revenues or cost savings that affect more than one year's financial results.

Capital Budgets. Budgets that detail the planned expenditures for facilities, equipment, new products, and other long-term investments.

Capital Charge. Company's cost of capital × amount of investment.

Capital Cost Allowance (CCA). A deduction allowed for Canadian income tax purposes with regard to the acquisition of a capital asset.

Capital Turnover. Revenue divided by invested capital.

Capital-Budgeting Decisions. Refer to the process of evaluating and choosing among long-term capital projects.

Cash Basis. A process of accounting where revenue and expense recognition would depend solely on the timing of various cash receipts and disbursements.

Cash Budget. A statement of planned cash receipts and disbursements.

Cash Equivalents. Short-term investments that a company can easily convert into cash with little delay.

Cash Flows from Financing Activities. The section in the statement of cash flows that lists the cash-flow effects of obtaining cash from creditors and owners, repaying creditors or buying back shares from owners, and paying cash dividends.

Cash Flows from Investing Activities. The section in the statement of cash flows that lists the cash-flow effects of (1) lending and collecting on loans, and (2) acquiring and selling long-term assets.

Cash Flows from Operating Activities. The section in the statement of cash flows that lists the cash-flow effects of transactions that affect the income statement.

Cellular Manufacturing. In a JIT production system, the process of organizing machines into cells according to the specific requirements of the product family.

Certified General Accountant (CGA). A professional accountant who is a member of the CGAAC.

Certified General Accountants Association of Canada (CGAAC). An organization of professional accountants, Certified General Accountants.

Certified Management Accountant (CMA). A professional accountant who is a member of the Society of Management Accountants of Canada.

Chartered Accountant (CA). A professional accountant who is a member of the CICA.

Coefficient of Determination. A measurement of how much of the fluctuation of a cost is explained by changes in the cost driver.

Committed Fixed Costs. Costs arising from the possession of facilities, equipment, and a basic organization; large, indivisible chunks of costs that are largely unavoidable.

Common Costs. The costs of facilities and services that are shared by various users.

Common Shares. Shares that have no predetermined rate of dividends and are the last to obtain a share in the assets when the corporation liquidates. They usually confer voting power to elect the board of directors of the corporation.

Computer-Integrated Manufacturing (CIM) Systems. Systems that use computer-aided design and computer-aided manufacturing together with robots and computer-controlled machines.

Continuous Budget (Rolling Budget). A common form of master budget that adds a month at the end of the budget period as a month ends.

Contribution Approach. A method of internal (management accounting) reporting that emphasizes the distinction between variable and fixed costs for the purpose of better decision making.

Contribution Margin. The sales price minus all the variable expenses.

Controllable Costs. Any costs that are influenced by a manager's decisions and actions.

Controller (Comptroller). The top accounting officer of an organization.

Conversion Costs. Direct-labour costs plus factory-overhead costs.

Cost. The monetary value of what is given up to acquire a current or future benefit (product or service) for the organization.

Cost Accounting. That part of the accounting system that determines the costs of making a product or performing a service.

Cost Accounting System. The techniques used to determine the cost of a product or service by collecting and classifying costs and assigning them to cost objects.

Cost Application. The allocation of total departmental costs to the revenue-producing products or services.

Cost Behaviour. How the activities of an organization affect its costs.

Cost Centre. A responsibility centre for which the objective is to manage (minimize) costs efficiently.

Cost Drivers. Activities that affect (drive) costs.

Cost Function. An algebraic equation used by managers to describe the relationship between a cost and its cost driver(s).

Cost Management System. Identifies how management's decisions affect costs, by first measuring the resources used in performing the organization's activities and then assessing the effects on costs of changes in those activities.

Cost Object. Any activity for which a separate measurement of costs is desired.

Cost of Capital. What a firm must pay to acquire more capital, whether or not it actually has to acquire more capital to take on a project.

Cost of Goods Sold. The cost of the merchandise that is acquired or manufactured and resold.

Cost Pool. A group of individual costs that is allocated to cost objects using a single cost driver.

Cost-Allocation Base. A cost driver when it is used for allocating costs.

Cost-Benefit Philosophy. The primary consideration in choosing among accounting systems and methods: how well they achieve management goals in relation to their costs.

Cost-Volume-Profit (CVP) Analysis. The study of the effects of output volume on revenue (sales), expenses (costs), and net profit.

Critical Process. A series of related activities that directly impact on the achievement of organizational goals.

Critical Success Factors. Activities that must be managed well in order for an organization to meet its goals.

Cross-Sectional Analysis. Comparison of a company's financial ratios with ratios of other companies or with industry averages.

Current Assets. Cash and all other assets that a company reasonably expects to convert to cash or sell or consume within one year or during the normal operating cycle, if longer than a year.

Current Liabilities. An organization's debts that fall due within the coming year or within the normal operating cycle if longer than a year.

(Currently) Attainable Standards. Levels of performance that can be achieved by realistic levels of effort.

Cycle Time. The time taken to complete a product or service, or any of the components of a product or service.

Debentures. Formal certificates of indebtedness that are accompanied by a promise to pay interest at a specified annual rate.

Debt Ratios. Ratios that examine an organization's degree of debt financing in comparison to its equity financing.

Decentralization. The delegation of freedom to make decisions. The lower in the organization that this freedom exists, the greater the decentralization.

Decision Model. Any method for making a choice, sometimes requiring elaborate quantitative procedures.

Differential Approach. An approach that compares two alternatives by computing the NPV differences in cash flows.

Differential Cost (Incremental Cost). The difference in total cost between two alternatives.

Direct Costs. Costs that are easily, clearly, and economically identified and traced exclusively to a cost object.

Direct-Labour Costs. The wages of all labour that can be traced specifically and exclusively to manufactured goods in an economically feasible way.

Direct-Materials Costs. The acquisition costs of all materials that are physically identified as a part of manufactured goods and that may be traced to manufactured goods in an economically feasible way.

Direct Method. A method for computing cash flows from operating activities that subtracts operating cash disbursements from cash collections to arrive at cash flows from operations; ignores other service departments when any given service department's costs are allocated to the revenue-producing departments.

Discounted-Cash-Flow (DCF) Model. A capital-budgeting model that focuses on cash inflows and outflows, the time value of money, and identifying criteria for accepting or rejecting capital projects.

Discretionary Fixed Costs. Costs determined by management as part of the periodic planning process in order to meet the organization's goals.

Discriminatory Pricing. Charging different prices to different customers for the same product or service.

Dumping. Refers to the selling of goods in a foreign country at a price that is below the full cost of the product and below the selling price in the domestic market.

Dysfunctional Decisions. Decisions that are in conflict with organizational goals.

Earnings per Share. Net income divided by the average number of common shares outstanding during the year.

Economic Value Added (EVA). After-tax operating income minus the weighted-average cost of capital times the sum of the long-term liabilities and shareholders' equity.

Effectiveness. The degree to which a goal, objective, or target is met (doing the right things).

Efficiency. The degree to which minimum inputs are used to produce a given level of outputs (doing the right things right).

Efficiency Variance (Quantity Variance or Usage Variance). The difference between the quantity of inputs actually used and the quantity of inputs that should have been used to achieve the actual quantity of output multiplied by the expected price of input.

Employee Benefit Costs. Employer contributions to employee benefits such as Canada/Quebec Pension, employment insurance, life insurance, health insurance, and pensions.

Employee Motivation. The drive to achieve some selected organizational goal that generates employee effort and action toward that goal.

Engineering Analysis. The systematic review of materials, supplies, labour, support services, and facilities needed for products and services; measuring cost behaviour according to what cost should be, not by what costs have been.

Equities. The claims against, or interests in, the assets.

Equivalent Units. The number of completed units that partially completed units amount to.

Expense Centre. A responsibility centre for which the objective is to spend the budget but maximize the specific service objective of the centre.

Factory Overhead Costs (Manufacturing Overhead, Indirect Manufacturing Costs). All costs other than direct material or direct labour that are associated with the manufacturing process.

Financial Accounting. The field of accounting that serves external decision makers such as shareholders, suppliers, banks, and government regulatory agencies.

Financial Budget. The part of the master budget that focuses on the effects that the operating budget and other plans (such as capital budgets and repayments of debt) will have on cash flow and the balance sheet.

Financial Planning Models. Mathematical models of the master budget that can react to any set of assumptions about sales levels, sales prices, product mix, or cost fluctuations.

First-In, First-Out (FIFO) Process-Costing Method. A process-costing method that sharply distinguishes the current work done from the previous work done on the work-in-process beginning inventory.

Fixed Assets (Tangible Assets). Physical items that a person can see and touch, such as property, plant, and equipment.

Fixed Cost. A cost that is not immediately affected by changes in the cost driver.

Fixed Overhead Rate. The amount of fixed manufacturing overhead applied to each unit of production. It is determined by dividing the budgeted fixed overhead by the expected volume of production for the budget period.

Flexible Budget. A budget that adjusts for changes in sales volume and other cost-driver activities.

Flexible-Budget (Efficiency) Variances. Variances between the flexible budget and the actual results.

Free Cash Flow. Cash flows from operations less capital expenditures.

Goal Congruence. Exists when individuals and groups aim for the same organizational goals.

Goodwill. The excess of the cost of an acquired company over the sum of the fair market values of its identifiable individual assets less its liabilities.

Gross Book Value. The original cost of an asset before deducting accumulated amortization.

Gross Margin (Gross Profit). The excess of sales over the total cost of goods sold.

Growth Ratios. Ratios that examine the areas of growth or decline within an organization over time.

Half-Year Rule. An income tax requirement that treats all assets as if they were purchased at the midpoint of the tax year.

High-Low Method. A simple method for measuring a linear cost function from past cost data, focusing on the highest-activity and lowest-activity points and fitting a line through these two points.

Hybrid-Costing System. An accounting system that is a blend of ideas from job costing and process costing.

Ideal Standards. Expressions of the most efficient performance possible under the best conceivable conditions using existing specifications, production processes, and equipment.

Idle Time. An indirect labour cost consisting of wages paid for unproductive time caused by machine breakdowns, material shortages, and sloppy scheduling.

Imperfect Competition. A market in which a firm's price will influence the quantity it sells; at some point, price reductions are necessary to generate additional sales.

Incentives. Those formal and informal performance-based rewards that enhance employee effort toward organizational goals.

Income Statement. A statement that measures the operating performance of the corporation by matching its accomplishments (revenue from customers, usually called sales) and its efforts (cost of goods sold and other expenses).

Incremental Approach. The change in results (such as revenue, expenses, or income) given a change in one of the determinants of this result.

Indirect Costs. Costs that cannot be identified and specifically traced to a particular cost object.

Indirect Labour. All factory labour wages, other than those for direct labour and managers' salaries.

Indirect Method. A method for computing cash flows from operating activities that adjusts the previously calculated accrual net income from the income statement to reflect only cash receipts and cash disbursements.

Inflation. The decline in the general purchasing power of the monetary unit.

Intangible Assets. Long-lived assets that are not physical in nature. Examples are goodwill, franchises, patents, trademarks, and copyrights.

Internal Control System. Methods and procedures to prevent errors and irregularities, detect errors and irregularities, and promote operating efficiency.

Internal Rate of Return (IRR). The discount rate that makes the net present value of the project equal to zero.

Inventory Turnover. The average number of times the inventory is sold per year.

Investment Centre. A responsibility centre for which the objective is to measure not only the income it generates, but also to relate that income to its invested capital, as in a ratio of income to the value of the capital employed.

Job-Cost Record (Job-Cost Sheet, Job Order). A document that shows all costs for a particular product, service, or batch of products.

Joint Costs. Costs of inputs added to a process before individual products are separated; the costs of manufacturing joint products prior to the split-off point.

Job-Order Costing (Job Costing). The method of allocating costs to products that are readily identified by individual units or batches, each of which receives varying degrees of attention and skill.

Joint Products. Two or more manufactured products that (1) have relatively significant sales values and (2) are not identifiable as individual products until their split-off point.

Just-in-Time (JIT) Philosophy. A philosophy to eliminate waste by reducing the time products spend in the production process and eliminating the time that products spend in activities that do not add value.

Just-in-Time (JIT) Production System. A system in which an organization purchases materials and parts and produces components just when they are needed in the production process, the goal being to have zero or near zero inventory, because holding inventory is a non-value-added activity.

Key Success Factors. The factors that must be managed successfully to achieve organizational success.

Labour Time Tickets. The record of the time a particular direct labourer spends on each job.

Least Squares Regression (Regression Analysis). Measuring a cost function objectively by using statistics to fit a cost function to all the data.

Liabilities. The entity's economic obligations to non-owners.

Limited Liability. A provision that a company's creditors cannot seek payment from shareholders as individuals if the corporation itself cannot pay its debts.

Limiting Factor (Scarce Resource). The item that restricts or constrains the production or sale of a product or service.

Line Authority. Authority exerted downward over subordinates.

Linear-Cost Behaviour. Activity that can be graphed with a straight line when a cost changes proportionately with changes in a cost driver.

Liquidation. Converting assets to cash and using the cash to pay off outside claims.

Liquidity Ratios. Ratios that examine an organization's ability to meet its short-term financial obligations.

Long-Range Planning. Producing forecasted economic targets and/or financial statements for five- or ten-year periods.

Management Accounting. The process of identifying, measuring, accumulating, analyzing, preparing, interpreting, and communicating information that helps managers fulfill organizational objectives.

Management by Exception. Concentrating on areas that deserve attention and ignoring areas that are presumed to be running smoothly.

Management by Objectives (MBO). The joint formulation by a manager and his/her superior of a set of goals and of plans for achieving the goals for a forthcoming period.

Management Control System. A logical integration of management accounting tools to gather and report data and to evaluate performance.

Managerial Effort. Exertion toward a goal or objective, including all the conscious actions (such as supervising, planning, and thinking) that result in more efficiency and effectiveness.

Margin of Safety. Equal to the planned unit sales less the breakeven unit sales; it shows how far sales can fall below the planned level before losses occur.

Marginal Cost. The additional cost resulting from producing and selling one additional unit.

Marginal Income Tax Rate. The tax rate paid on additional amounts of pre-tax income.

Marginal Revenue. The additional revenue resulting from the sale of an additional unit.

Markup. The amount by which price exceeds cost.

Master (Static) Budget Variances. The variances of actual results from the master budget.

Master Budget. A budget that summarizes the planned activities of all subunits of an organization from the very first stage of production to the delivery of goods to the consumer.

Materials Requisitions. Records of materials issued to particular jobs.

Measuring Cost Behaviour (Cost Measurement). Understanding and quantifying how activities of an organization affects level of cost.

Mixed Costs. Costs that contain elements of both fixed and variable costs.

Net Book Value. The original cost of an asset less any accumulated amortization.

Net Income. The "bottom line"—the residual amount after we deduct from revenues all expenses, including income taxes.

Net-Present-Value (NPV) Method. An investment evaluation technique that discounts all expected future cash flows to the present using a minimum desired rate of return.

Nominal Rates. Quoted market interest rates that include an inflation element.

Noncurrent Liabilities (Long-Term Liabilities). An organization's debts that fall due beyond one year.

Non-Value-Added Costs. Costs that can be eliminated without affecting a product's value to the customer.

Normal Costing. A cost system that applies actual direct materials and actual direct labour costs to products or services but uses standards for applying overhead.

Normal Costing System. The cost system in which overhead is applied on an average or normalized basis in order to get representative or normal inventory valuations.

Normalized Overhead Rate. An annual average overhead rate used consistently throughout the year without altering it from month to month.

Operating Budget (Profit Plan). A major part of a master budget that focuses on the income statement and its supporting schedules.

Operating Cycle. The time span during which a company spends cash to acquire goods and services that it uses to produce the organization's output, which it in turn sells to customers, who in turn pay for their purchases with cash.

Operating Leverage. A firm's ratio of fixed and variable costs.

Operation Costing. A hybrid-costing system often used in the batch or group manufacturing of goods that have some common characteristics plus some individual characteristics.

Opportunity Cost. The maximum foregone benefit (contribution to profit) by choosing to forego an alternative opportunity cost.

Overapplied Overhead. The excess of overhead applied to products over actual overhead incurred.

Overtime Premium. An indirect labour cost, consisting of the wages paid to all factory workers in excess of their straight-time wage rates.

Owners' Equity. The excess of the assets over the liabilities.

Participative Budgeting. Budgets formulated with the active participation of all affected employees.

Payback Time (Payback Period). The measure of the time it will take to recoup, in the form of cash inflows from operations, the initial dollars of outlay.

Perfect Competition. A market in which no firm is large enough—firms are more or less equal—to influence market price.

Performance Reports. Feedback provided by comparing results with plans and by highlighting variances.

Period Costs. The costs of resources consumed during the current period that are deducted as expenses without going through an inventory stage.

Postaudit. A follow-up evaluation of capital-budgeting decisions.

Predatory Pricing. Establishing prices so low that competitors are driven out of the market so that the predatory pricer has no significant competition and can raise prices dramatically.

Preferred Shares. Shares that typically have some priority over other shares in the payment of dividends or the distribution of assets upon liquidation.

Price Elasticity. The effect of price changes on sales volume.

Price Variance. The difference between actual input prices and expected input prices multiplied by the actual quantity of inputs used.

Prime Costs. Direct-labour costs plus direct-materials costs.

Pro Forma Financial Statements. The planned financial statements based upon the planned activities in the master budget.

Problem-solving. Aspect of accounting that quantifies the likely results of possible courses of action and often recommends the best course of action to follow.

Process Costing. The method of allocating costs to products by averaging costs over large numbers of nearly identical products.

Product Costs. Costs identified with goods produced or purchased for resale.

Product Life Cycle. The various stages through which a product passes, from conception and development through introduction into the market through maturation and, finally, withdrawal from the market.

Production-Cost Report. The report showing the calculation of total costs and unit costs, and their application to finished goods and WIP-ending inventory as part of the process-costing method.

Production Cycle Time. The time from initiating production to delivering the goods to the customer.

Production Volume Variance. A variance that appears whenever actual production deviates from the expected volume of production used in computing the fixed-overhead rate. It is calculated as (actual volume − expected volume) × fixed-overhead rate; the difference between budgeted fixed overhead and the amount of fixed overhead applied to the work-in-process inventory account. It is caused solely by a difference between actual and budgeted activity.

Productivity. A measure of outputs divided by inputs.

Profit Centre. A responsibility centre for which the objective is to control revenues as well as costs (or expenses).

Profitability Ratios. Ratios that examine an organization's degree of profitability.

Prorating the Variances. Assigning the variances to the inventories and cost of goods sold related to the production during the period in which the variances arose.

Quality Control. The effort to ensure that products and services perform to customer requirements.

Quality Control Chart. The statistical plot of measures of various product dimensions or attributes.

Quality Cost Report. A report that displays the financial impact of quality.

Reciprocal Allocation Method. Allocates costs by recognizing that the service departments provide services to each other as well as to the production departments.

Relevant Information. The predicted future costs and revenues that will differ among alternative courses of action.

Relevant Range. The limits of cost-driver activity within which a specific relationship between costs and the cost driver is valid.

Required Rate of Return (**Hurdle Rate**, **Discount Rate**). The minimum desired rate of return.

Residual Income. Net income less capital charge.

Responsibility Accounting. Identifying what parts of the organization have primary responsibility for each objective, developing measures of achievement of the objectives, and creating reports of these measures by organization subunit or responsibility centre.

Responsibility Centre. A set of activities assigned to a manager, a group of managers, or a group of employees in order to create "ownership of management" decisions.

Retained Earnings (Retained Income). Increases in equities due to profitable operations.

Return on Investment (ROI). A measure of income or profit divided by the investment required to obtain that income or profit.

Return on Sales. Income divided by revenue.

Revenue Centre. A responsibility centre for which the objective is to maximize the revenues generated.

Revenue-Producing Departments. Organizational units that are profit centres.

Sales Budget. The result of choosing one of the sales forecasts and implementing it.

Sales Forecast. A prediction of sales under a given set of conditions.

Sales Mix. The relative proportions or combinations of quantities of products that comprise total sales.

Sales-Volume Variances. Variances that measure how effective managers have been in meeting the planned sales objective, calculated as actual unit sales less master-budget unit sales times the budgeted unit-contribution margin.

Scorekeeping. The accumulation and classification of data.

Segment Autonomy. The delegation of decision-making power to segment managers.

Sensitivity Analysis. The systematic varying of budget assumptions in order to determine the effects of each change on the budget.

Separable Costs. Any costs beyond the split-off point in a joint product production process.

Service Departments. Units that exist only to serve other departments.

Shareholders' Equity. The excess of assets over liabilities of a corporation.

Society of Management Accountants of Canada (SMAC). An organization of professional accountants, Certified Management Accountants whose primary interest is in management accounting.

Split-off Point. The juncture in manufacturing where the joint products become individually identifiable.

Staff Authority. Authority to advise but not command. It may be exerted downward, laterally, or upward.

Standard Cost. A carefully determined cost per unit that should or is most likely to be attained.

Standard Cost Systems. Accounting systems that value products according to standard cost only.

Statement of Cash Flows. A statement that reports the cash receipts and cash payments of an organization during a particular period.

Statement of Retained Earnings (Statement of Retained Income). A financial statement that explains changes in the retained earnings or retained income account for a given period.

Step Costs. Costs that change at intervals or steps of activity because their costs come in indivisible bunches or chunks.

Step-Down Method. Recognizes that some service departments support the activities in other service departments as well as those in production departments.

Strategic Plan. A plan that sets the overall goals and objectives of the organization.

Subordinated. A creditor claim that is junior to the other creditors in exercising claims against assets.

Sunk Cost. A cost that has already been incurred and, therefore, is irrelevant to making future decisions.

Target Costing. A product strategy in which companies first determine the price at which they can sell a new product and then design a product that can be produced at a low enough cost to provide an adequate profit margin.

Tax Shield Formula. Formula used to efficiently calculate the present value of the tax savings generated by tax shields.

Time-Series Analysis. Comparison of a company's financial ratios with its own historical ratios.

Total Project Approach. An approach that compares two or more alternatives by computing the total NPV on cash flows of each.

Total Quality Management (TQM). The application of quality principles to all of the organization's endeavours to satisfy customers.

Transaction. Any event that affects the financial position of an organization and requires recording.

Transfer Prices. The amounts charged by one segment of an organization for a product or service that it supplies to another segment of the same organization.

Transferred-In Costs. The costs of the items a department receives from another department.

Unavoidable Costs. Costs that continue even if an operation is halted.

Uncontrollable Cost. Any cost that cannot be affected by the management of a responsibility centre within a given time span.

Undepreciated Capital Cost (UCC). The balance in the pool of assets after deducting capital cost allowance.

Underapplied Overhead. The excess of actual overhead over the overhead applied to products.

Value-Added Costs. The necessary cost of an activity that cannot be eliminated without affecting a product's value to the customer.

Value Chain. A set of business functions that add value to the product or service of an organization.

Variable Cost. A cost that changes in direct proportion to changes in the level (volume) of economic activity.

Variable-Cost Ratio (Variable-Cost Percentage). All variable costs divided by sales.

Variable Overhead Efficiency Variance. Measures the difference in variable overhead cost that results from using more or fewer factors (hours) than planned for overhead.

Variable Overhead Spending Variance. Indicates that the company either paid higher or lower prices for overhead items or used more or fewer overhead materials or services.

Variance. Deviations from plans.

Visual Fit Method. A method in which the cost analysis visually fits a straight line through a plot for all the available data, not just between the high and low points, making it more reliable than the high-low method.

Weighted-Average (WA) Process-Costing Method. A process-costing method that adds the cost of (1) all work done in the current period to (2) the work done in the preceding period on the current period's work-in-process beginning inventory and divides the total by the equivalent units of work done to date.

Working Capital. Current assets less current liabilities.

COMPANY AND ORGANIZATION INDEX

Note: *f* denotes a figure, *t* denotes a table, *n* denotes a footnote.

SUBJECT INDEX

Note: *f* denotes a figure, *t* denotes a table, *n* denotes a footnote. Key terms and the pages on which they are defined are in boldface.

sunk cost, 420
supplies, 142
systematic reaction to change, 531

tangible assets, **767**
target costing, 359
  and activity-based costing (ABC), 360
  company practices, 360, 364
  versus cost-plus pricing, 367–369
  and external value chain, 364
  and new product development, 366–369
  origins of, 369
target net profit, 55–56
tax reporting rules, 482
tax shield formula, 484–485
tech companies, and break-even points, 63
technological change, 21
technology decisions, 96, 482
technology investments, 470
three-column approach to variance analysis, 597–598, 598*f*
time cards, 259
time-series analysis, 790–791
times interest earned ratio, 792*f*, 795
total fixed costs, 347–348
total project approach, 471, 473*f*
total quality control (TQC), 214
total quality management (TQM), 658
trade-in of capital assets, 485–486, 486*f*
traditional cost system, 201*f*
transaction, 759
transfer price, 716
  see also transfer pricing
transfer pricing
  and activity-based costing (ABC), 717
  cost-based transfer pricing, 720
  and dysfunctional decisions, 722
  full-cost plus profit transfer pricing, 720–721
  full-cost transfer pricing, 720–721
  general rule, 718–720
  market-based transfer pricing, 721–722
  market prices, nonexistence of, 722–723
  multinational transfer prices, 725–726
  multiple transfer prices, need for, 724–725
  negotiated transfer prices, 723–724
  purposes of, 716–717
  regulations, 725
  variable-cost based transfer pricing, 720
  various methods, 726*f*

transferred-in costs, **312**–313
treasurer, 16
trends, 20–21

unavoidable costs, 350
uncontrollable cost, 650–651
undepreciated capital cost (UCC), 484
underapplied overhead, 268–269
unequal lives, 472
uneven cash flows, 475
unit costs
  careful analysis of, 415–418
  process costing, 305–306
  for product costing, 145
usage variance, 594–597

valuation of assets, 714–715
value-added cost, 212, **213**
value chain, 11
  of business functions, 11–12, 12*f*
  functions, and example costs, 42*f*
  target costing, and external value chain, 364
variable application rate, 269–270
variable-cost based transfer pricing, 720
variable-cost percentage, 64
variable-cost pool, 188–189
variable-cost ratio, 64
variable costing
  company practice, illustration of, 150–151
  comparison of flow of costs, 152*f*
  described, 152
  expense of, 153
  fixed manufacturing overhead, 151–152
  illustration of, 153–154, 154*f*
  and performance evaluation, 159–160
  reconciliation with absorption costing, 156–157
  restrictions on, 152–153
  and segmented reporting, 159–160
  tracing fixed manufacturing costs, 158*f*
  use of, 158–159
variable costs, 43
  best combination, with fixed costs, 61–62
  changes in, 54–55
  classification difficulties, 46
  cost-volume-profit analysis, 46–58
  versus fixed costs, 43–46
  marginal cost, 356
  relevant range, 44–45
  step costs as, 90
variable overhead efficiency variance, 599
variable overhead spending variance, 600

variable overhead variances
  actual costing, 603
  fixed overhead analysis, 602–603
  fixed overhead variance, 600–603
  normal costing, 603
  production-volume variance, 600, 601
  prorating the variances, 604
  standard costing, 603
  summary, 604
  variable overhead efficiency variance, 599
  variable overhead spending variance, 600
variance, 7
  see also budget variances; variance analysis
variance analysis, 605*f*
  see also budget variances
  comparison with prior period's results, 592
  fixed overhead analysis, 602–603
  standard costs, use of, 591
  three-column approach, 597–598, 598*f*
visual fit method, 103, **105**–106, 106*f*
volume-related cost drivers, 43

weighted-average cost of capital, 709
weighted-average (WA) process-costing method, 309–310, 312
Welch, John, 663
"what-if" technique, 491
whistle-blowers, 25
work-in-process inventory, 146
working capital, 770, 792*f*, 794
working capital investments, 472

XY graph, 108